High Performance Cluster Computing:

Architectures and Systems, Volume 1

ISBN 0-13-013784-7

High Performance Cluster Computing:

Architectures and Systems, Volume 1

Edited by
Rajkumar Buyya
(rajkumar@dgs.monash.edu.au)

School of Computer Science and Software Engineering
Monash University
Melbourne, Australia

Prentice Hall PTR
Upper Saddle River, New Jersey 07458
http://www.phptr.com

Library of Congress Cataloging-in-Publication Data

High performance cluster computing / edited by Rajkumar Buyya.
p. cm.
Includes bibliographical references and index.
Contents: v. 1. Architectures and systems.
ISBN 0-13-013784-7 (v.1)
1. High performance computing. I. Buyya, Rajkumar .
QA76.88.H489 1999
004'.3--DC21 99-17906
CIP

Editorial/Production Supervision: *Joan L. McNamara*
Acquisitions Editor: *Greg Doench*
Editorial Assistant: *Mary Treacy*
Marketing Manager: *Bryan Gambrel*
Cover Design Director: *Jerry Votta*
Cover Designer: *Anthony Gemmellaro*
Cover Illustration: *Rob Colvin (The Stock Illustration Source)*
Manufacturing Manager: *Alexis R. Heydt*

Prentice-Hall, Inc.
Upper Saddle River, New Jersey 07458

Prentice Hall books are widely used by corporations and government agencies for training, marketing, and resale. The publisher offers discounts on this book when ordered in bulk quantities.
For more information, contact: Corporate Sales Department, Phone: 800-382-3419;
FAX: 201-236-7141; email: corpsales@prenhall.com
Or write: Corp. Sales Dept., Prentice Hall PTR, 1 Lake Street, Upper Saddle River, NJ 07458

Printed in the United States of America
10 9 8 7 6 5 4 3 2

ISBN 0-13-013784-7

Prentice-Hall International (UK) Limited, *London*
Prentice-Hall of Australia Pty. Limited, *Sydney*
Prentice-Hall Canada Inc., *Toronto*
Prentice-Hall Hispanoamericana, S.A., *Mexico*
Prentice-Hall of India Private Limited, *New Delhi*
Prentice-Hall of Japan, Inc., *Tokyo*
Prentice-Hall (Singapore) Pte. Ltd., *Singapore*
Editora Prentice-Hall do Brasil, Ltda., *Rio de Janeiro*

Contents at a Glance

Contents

III Process Scheduling, Load Sharing, and Balancing .. 497

Preface

The initial idea leading to cluster[1] computing was developed in the 1960s by IBM as a way of linking large mainframes to provide a cost-effective form of commercial parallelism. During those days, IBM's HASP (Houston Automatic Spooling Priority) system and its successor, JES (Job Entry System), provided a way of distributing work to a user-constructed mainframe cluster. IBM still supports clustering of mainframes through their Parallel Sysplex system, which allows the hardware, operating system, middleware, and system management software to provide dramatic performance and cost improvements while permitting large mainframe users to continue to run their existing applications.

However, cluster computing did not gain momentum until three trends converged in the 1980s: high performance microprocessors, high-speed networks, and standard tools for high performance distributed computing. A possible fourth trend is the increased need of computing power for computational science and commercial applications coupled with the high cost and low accessibility of traditional supercomputers. These building blocks are also known as killer-microprocessors, killer-networks, killer-tools, and killer-applications, respectively. The recent advances in these technologies and their availability as cheap and commodity components are making clusters or networks of computers (PCs, workstations, and SMPs) an appealing vehicle for cost-effective parallel computing. Clusters, built using commodity-off-the-shelf (COTS) hardware components as well as free, or commonly used, software, are playing a major role in redefining the concept of supercomputing.

The trend in parallel computing is to move away from specialized traditional supercomputing platforms, such as the Cray/SGI T3E, to cheaper and general purpose systems consisting of loosely coupled components built up from single or multiprocessor PCs or workstations. This approach has a number of advantages, including being able to build a platform for a given budget which is suitable for a large class of applications and workloads.

This book is motivated by the fact that parallel computing on a network of computers using commodity components has received increased attention recently, and noticeable progress towards usable systems has been made. A number of re-

[1] Cluster is a collection of interconnected computers working together as a single system.

searchers in academia and industry have been active in this field of research. Although research in this area is still in its early stage, promising results have been demonstrated by experimental systems built in academic and industrial laboratories. There is a need for better understanding of what cluster computing can offer, how cluster computers can be constructed, and what the impacts of clustering on high performance computing will be.

Though a significant number of research articles have been published in various conference proceedings and journals, the results are scattered in many places, are hard to obtain, and are difficult to understand, especially for beginners. This book, the first of its kind, gathers in one place the current and comprehensive technical coverage of the field and presents it in a tutorial form. The book's coverage reflects the state-of-the-art in high-level architecture, design, and development, and points out possible directions for further research and development.

Organization

This book is a collection of chapters written by leading scientists active in the area of parallel computing using networked computers. The primary purpose of the book is to provide an authoritative overview of this field's state-of-the-art. The emphasis is on the following aspects of cluster computing:

- Requirements, Issues, and Services
- System Area Networks, Communication Protocols, and High Performance I/O Techniques
- Resource Management, Scheduling, Load Balancing, and System Availability
- Possible Models for Cluster-based Parallel Systems
- Programming Models and Environments
- Algorithms and Applications of Clusters

The work on High Performance Cluster Computing appears in two volumes:

- Volume 1: Systems and Architectures
- Volume 2: Programming and Applications

This book, Volume 1, consists of 36 chapters, which are grouped into the following four parts:

- Part I: Requirements and General Issues
- Part II: Networking, Protocols, and I/O
- Part III: Process Scheduling, Load Sharing, and Balancing

- Part IV: Representative Cluster Systems

Part I focuses on cluster computing requirements and issues related to components, single system image, high performance, high availability, scalability, deployment, administration, and wide-area computing. Part II covers system area networks, light-weight communication protocols, and I/O. Part III discusses techniques and algorithms of process scheduling, migration, and load balancing along with representative systems. Part IV covers system architectures of some of the popular academic and commercial cluster-based systems such as Beowulf and SP/2.

Readership

The book is primarily written for graduate students and researchers interested in the area of parallel and distributed computing. However, it is also suitable for practitioners in industry and government laboratories.

The interdisciplinary nature of the book is likely to appeal to a wide audience. They will find this book to be a valuable source of information on recent advances and future directions of parallel computation using networked computers. This is the first book addressing various technological aspects of cluster computing in-depth, and we expect that the book will be an informative and useful reference in this new and fast growing research area.

The organization of this book makes it particularly useful for graduate courses. It can be used as a text for a research-oriented or seminar-based advanced graduate course. Graduate students will find the material covered by this book to be stimulating and inspiring. Using this book, they can identify interesting and important research topics for their Master's and Ph.D. work. It can also serve as a supplementary book for regular courses, taught in Computer Science, Computer Engineering, Electrical Engineering, and Computational Science and Informatics Departments, including:

- Advanced Computer Architecture
- Advances in Networking Technologies
- High Performance Distributed Computing
- Distributed and Concurrent Systems
- High Performance Computing
- Parallel Computing
- Networked Computing
- Trends in Distributed Operating Systems
- Cluster Computing and their Architecture.

Cluster Computing Resources on the Web

The various software systems discussed in this book are freely available for download through the Internet. Please visit this book's website,

- http://www.phptr.com/ptrbooks/ptr_0130137847.html

for pointers/links to further information on downloading Educational Resources, Cluster Computing Environments, and Cluster Management Systems.

Acknowledgments

First and foremost, I am grateful to all the contributing authors for their time, effort, and understanding during the preparation of the book.

I thank Albert Zomaya (University of Western Australia) for his advice and encouragement while starting this book project.

I would like to thank Kennith Birman (Cornell University), Marcin Paprzycki (University of Southern Mississippi), Hamid R. Arabnia (The University of Georgia), and Gregory F. Pfister (IBM Server Group) for their critical comments and suggestions on improving the book.

I thank Toni Cortes (Universitat Politecnica de Catalunya) for his consistent support and invaluable LaTeX expertise.

I thank Mark Baker (University of Portsmouth), Erich Schikuta (Universitaet Wien), Dror G. Feitelson (Hebrew University of Jerusalem), Daniel F. Savarese and Thomas Sterling (California Institute of Technology), Ira Pramanick (Silicon Graphics Inc), and Daniel S. Katz (Jet Propulsion Laboratory, California Institute of Technology) for writing overviews for various parts of the book.

I thank my wife, Smrithi, and my daughter, Soumya, for their love and understanding (my long absences from home) during the preparation of the book.

I acknowledge the support of the Australian Government Overseas Postgraduate Research Scholarship, the Queensland University of Technology Postgraduate Research Award (Programming Languages and Systems Research Centre Scholarship), the Monash University Graduate Scholarship, the Monash Departmental Scholarship, and the Distributed Systems and Software Engineering Centre Scholarship.

I thank Clemens Szyperski (Queensland University of Technology) and David Abramson (Monash University) for advising my Ph.D research program.

Finally, I would like to thank the staff at Prentice Hall, particularly Greg Doench, Mary Treacy, Joan L. McNamara, Barbara Cotton, Mary Loudin, Lisa Iarkowski, and Bryan Gambrel. They were wonderful to work with!

Rajkumar Buyya
Monash University, Melbourne, Australia
(rajkumar@dgs.monash.edu.au / rajkumar@ieee.org)

February, 1999

Part I

Requirements and General Issues

This part of the book covers the components, technologies, environments, and services that are generally used in LAN and WAN cluster-based systems.

Chapter 1 provides a broad introduction and overview of all the hardware and software components that are commonly used in current cluster systems. This chapter provides a comparison of four popular cluster environments as well as attempting to predict some future trends in cluster technologies,

Chapter 2 takes an administrative view of cluster-based systems. This chapter deals with the key issues involved in setting up, installing, diagnosing, and optimizing the hardware and software components needed by applications.

Chapter 3 discusses a cache-based resource sharing algorithm in relation to environment characteristics and resultant requirements. It mainly focuses on scalability in complex networked systems.

Chapter 4 reviews the hardware and software components necessary to provide a dependable cluster system that can be used for mission critical and high-availability applications.

Chapter 5 details the framework necessary to provide a high throughput computing environment using cluster-based systems. In particular, this chapter looks at the means of providing large amounts of processing capacity from existing heterogeneous resources.

Chapter 6 discusses a means of performance evaluation of cluster-based systems with the aim of trying to provide a framework to predict a cost-effective cluster given certain financial resources and a range of application workload characteristics.

Chapter 7 defines and then describes the current notion of metacomputing. In particular, this chapter discusses and then defines a review criteria based on the set of services required by applications using a metacomputer. This review criteria is then used to help assess three state-of-the-art metacomputing environments. Finally, an attempt to predict future trends for wide-area distributed environments is discussed.

Chapter 8 looks at the means of specifying the resources and services required by users in a wide-area heterogeneous distributed system. In particular, this chapter discusses a schema that can be used to request resources in a metacomputing environment.

Chapter 1

Cluster Computing at a Glance

Mark Baker[†] and Rajkumar Buyya[‡]

[†]Division of Computer Science
University of Portsmouth
Southsea, Hants, UK

[‡] School of Computer Science and Software Engineering
Monash University
Melbourne, Australia

Email: *Mark.Baker@port.ac.uk, rajkumar@dgs.monash.edu.au*

1.1 Introduction

Very often applications need more computing power than a sequential computer can provide. One way of overcoming this limitation is to improve the operating speed of processors and other components so that they can offer the power required by computationally intensive applications. Even though this is currently possible to a certain extent, future improvements are constrained by the speed of light, thermodynamic laws, and the high financial costs for processor fabrication. A viable and cost-effective alternative solution is to connect multiple processors together and coordinate their computational efforts. The resulting systems are popularly known as parallel computers, and they allow the sharing of a computational task among multiple processors.

As Pfister [1] points out, there are three ways to improve performance:

- Work harder,
- Work smarter, and
- Get help.

In terms of computing technologies, the analogy to this mantra is that working harder is like using faster hardware (high performance processors or peripheral devices). Working smarter concerns doing things more efficiently and this revolves around the algorithms and techniques used to solve computational tasks. Finally, getting help refers to using multiple computers to solve a particular task.

1.1.1 Eras of Computing

The computing industry is one of the fastest growing industries and it is fueled by the rapid technological developments in the areas of computer hardware and software. The technological advances in hardware include chip development and fabrication technologies, fast and cheap microprocessors, as well as high bandwidth and low latency interconnection networks. Among them, the recent advances in VLSI (Very Large Scale Integration) technology has played a major role in the development of powerful sequential and parallel computers. Software technology is also developing fast. Mature software, such as OSs (Operating Systems), programming languages, development methodologies, and tools, are now available. This has enabled the development and deployment of applications catering to scientific, engineering, and commercial needs. It should also be noted that grand challenge applications, such as weather forecasting and earthquake analysis, have become the main driving force behind the development of powerful parallel computers.

One way to view computing is as two prominent developments/eras:

- Sequential Computing Era
- Parallel Computing Era

A review of the changes in computing eras is shown in Figure 1.1. Each computing era started with a development in hardware architectures, followed by system software (particularly in the area of compilers and operating systems), applications, and reaching its zenith with its growth in PSEs (Problem Solving Environments). Each component of a computing system undergoes three phases: R&D (Research and Development), commercialization, and commodity. The technology behind the development of computing system components in the sequential era has matured, and similar developments are yet to happen in the parallel era. That is, parallel computing technology needs to advance, as it is not mature enough to be exploited as commodity technology.

The main reason for creating and using parallel computers is that parallelism is one of the best ways to overcome the speed bottleneck of a single processor. In addition, the price performance ratio of a small cluster-based parallel computer as opposed to a minicomputer is much smaller and consequently better value. In short, developing and producing systems of moderate speed using parallel architectures is much cheaper than the equivalent performance of a sequential system.

The remaining parts of this chapter focus on architecture alternatives for constructing parallel computers, motivations for transition to low cost parallel computing, a generic model of a cluster computer, commodity components used in building clusters, cluster middleware, resource management and scheduling, programming environments and tools, and representative cluster systems. The chapter ends with a summary of hardware and software trends, and concludes with future cluster technologies.

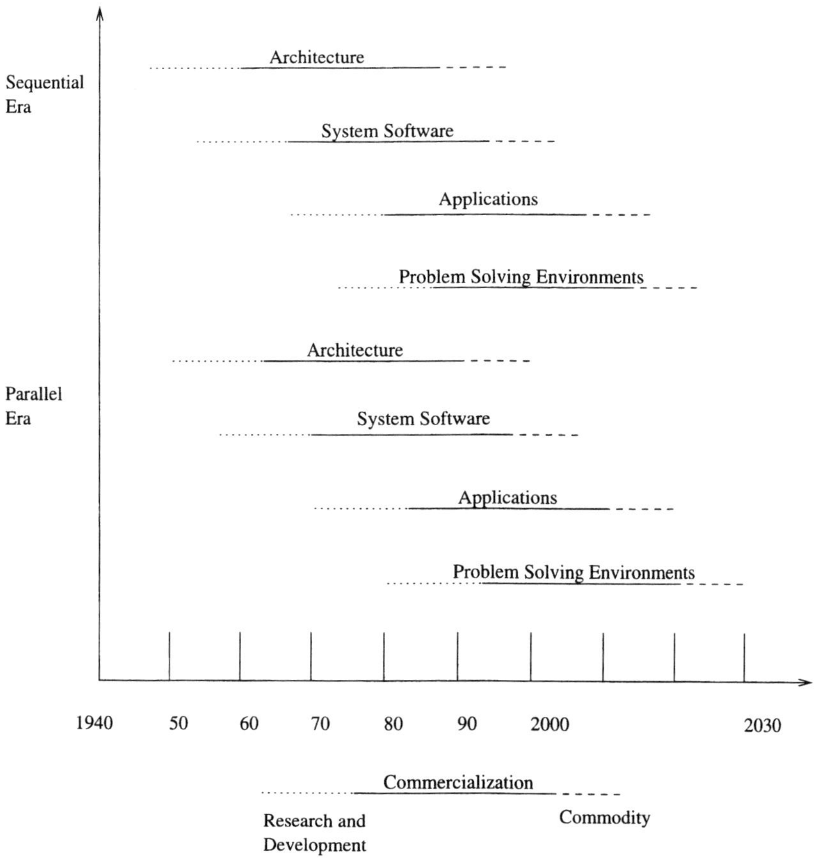

Figure 1.1 Two eras of computing.

1.2 Scalable Parallel Computer Architectures

During the past decade many different computer systems supporting high performance computing have emerged. Their taxonomy is based on how their processors, memory, and interconnect are laid out. The most common systems are:

- Massively Parallel Processors (MPP)
- Symmetric Multiprocessors (SMP)
- Cache-Coherent Nonuniform Memory Access (CC-NUMA)
- Distributed Systems
- Clusters

Table 1.1 shows a modified version comparing the architectural and functional characteristics of these machines originally given in [2] by Hwang and Xu.

An MPP is usually a large parallel processing system with a shared-nothing architecture. It typically consists of several hundred processing elements (nodes), which are interconnected through a high-speed interconnection network/switch. Each node can have a variety of hardware components, but generally consists of a main memory and one or more processors. Special nodes can, in addition, have peripherals such as disks or a backup system connected. Each node runs a separate copy of the operating system.

Table 1.1 Key Characteristics of Scalable Parallel Computers

Characteristic	**MPP**	**SMP CC-NUMA**	**Cluster**	**Distributed**
Number of Nodes	O(100)-O(1000)	O(10)-O(100)	O(100) or less	O(10)-O(1000)
Node Complexity	Fine grain or medium	Medium or coarse grained	Medium grain	Wide Range
Internode communication	Message passing/ shared variables for distributed shared memory	Centralized and Distributed Shared Memory (DSM)	Message Passing	Shared files, RPC, Message Passing and IPC
Job Scheduling	Single run queue on host	Single run queue mostly	Multiple queue but coordinated	Independent queues
SSI Support	Partially	Always in SMP and some NUMA	Desired	No
Node OS copies and type	N micro-kernels monolithic or layered OSs	One monolithic SMP and many for NUMA	N OS platform -homogeneous or micro-kernel	N OS platforms homogeneous
Address Space	Multiple - single for DSM	Single	Multiple or single	Multiple
Internode Security	Unnecessary	Unnecessary	Required if exposed	Required
Ownership	One organization	One organization	One or more organizations	Many organizations

SMP systems today have from 2 to 64 processors and can be considered to have shared-everything architecture. In these systems, all processors share all the global resources available (bus, memory, I/O system); a single copy of the operating system runs on these systems.

CC-NUMA is a scalable multiprocessor system having a cache coherent nonuniform memory access architecture. Like an SMP, every processor in a CC-NUMA system has a global view of all of the memory. This type of system gets its name (NUMA) from the nonuniform times to access the nearest and most remote parts of memory.

Distributed systems can be considered conventional networks of independent computers. They have multiple system images, as each node runs its own operating system, and the individual machines in a distributed system could be, for example, combinations of MPPs, SMPs, clusters, and individual computers.

At a basic level a cluster [1] is a collection of workstations or PCs that are interconnected via some network technology. For parallel computing purposes, a cluster will generally consist of high performance workstations or PCs interconnected by a high-speed network. A cluster works as an integrated collection of resources and can have a single system image spanning all its nodes. Refer to [1] and [2] for a detailed discussion on architectural and functional characteristics of the competing computer architectures.

1.3 Towards Low Cost Parallel Computing and Motivations

In the 1980s it was believed that computer performance was best improved by creating faster and more efficient processors. This idea was challenged by parallel processing, which in essence means linking together two or more computers to jointly solve some computational problem. Since the early 1990s there has been an increasing trend to move away from expensive and specialized proprietary parallel supercomputers towards networks of workstations. Among the driving forces that have enabled this transition has been the rapid improvement in the availability of commodity high performance components for workstations and networks. These technologies are making networks of computers (PCs or workstations) an appealing vehicle for parallel processing, and this is consequently leading to low-cost *commodity supercomputing.*

The use of parallel processing as a means of providing high performance computational facilities for large-scale and grand-challenge applications has been investigated widely. Until recently, however, the benefits of this research were confined to the individuals who had access to such systems. The trend in parallel computing is to move away from specialized traditional supercomputing platforms, such as the Cray/SGI T3E, to cheaper, general purpose systems consisting of loosely coupled components built up from single or multiprocessor PCs or workstations. This approach has a number of advantages, including being able to build a platform for a given budget which is suitable for a large class of applications and workloads.

The use of clusters to prototype, debug, and run parallel applications is becoming an increasingly popular alternative to using specialized, typically expensive, parallel computing platforms. An important factor that has made the usage of clusters a practical proposition is the standardization of many of the tools and utilities used by parallel applications. Examples of these standards are the message passing library MPI [8] and data-parallel language HPF [3]. In this context, standardization enables

[1] Clusters, Network of Workstations (NOW), Cluster of Workstations (COW), and Workstation Clusters are synonymous.

applications to be developed, tested, and even run on NOW, and then at a later stage to be ported, with little modification, onto dedicated parallel platforms where CPU-time is accounted and charged.

The following list highlights some of the reasons NOW is preferred over specialized parallel computers [5], [4]:

- Individual workstations are becoming increasingly powerful. That is, workstation performance has increased dramatically in the last few years and is doubling every 18 to 24 months. This is likely to continue for several years, with faster processors and more efficient multiprocessor machines coming into the market.
- The communications bandwidth between workstations is increasing and latency is decreasing as new networking technologies and protocols are implemented in a LAN.
- Workstation clusters are easier to integrate into existing networks than special parallel computers.
- Typical low user utilization of personal workstations.
- The development tools for workstations are more mature compared to the contrasting proprietary solutions for parallel computers, mainly due to the nonstandard nature of many parallel systems.
- Workstation clusters are a cheap and readily available alternative to specialized high performance computing platforms.
- Clusters can be easily grown; node's capability can be easily increased by adding memory or additional processors.

Clearly, the workstation environment is better suited to applications that are not communication-intensive since a LAN typically has high message start-up latencies and low bandwidths. If an application requires higher communication performance, the existing commonly deployed LAN architectures, such as Ethernet, are not capable of providing it.

Traditionally, in science and industry, a workstation referred to a UNIX platform and the dominant function of PC-based machines was for administrative work and word processing. There has been, however, a rapid convergence in processor performance and kernel-level functionality of UNIX workstations and PC-based machines in the last three years (this can be attributed to the introduction of high performance Pentium-based machines and the Linux and Windows NT operating systems). This convergence has led to an increased level of interest in utilizing PC-based systems as a cost-effective computational resource for parallel computing. This factor coupled with the comparatively low cost of PCs and their widespread availability in both academia and industry has helped initiate a number of software projects whose primary aim is to harness these resources in some collaborative way.

1.4 Windows of Opportunity

The resources available in the average NOW, such as processors, network interfaces, memory and hard disk, offer a number of research opportunities, such as:

Parallel Processing - Use the multiple processors to build MPP/DSM-like systems for parallel computing.

Network RAM - Use the memory associated with each workstation as aggregate DRAM cache; this can dramatically improve virtual memory and file system performance.

Software RAID (Redundant Array of Inexpensive Disks) - Use the arrays of workstation disks to provide cheap, highly available, and scalable file storage by using redundant arrays of workstation disks with LAN as I/O backplane. In addition, it is possible to provide parallel I/O support to applications through middleware such as MPI-IO.

Multipath Communication - Use the multiple networks for parallel data transfer between nodes.

Scalable parallel applications require good floating-point performance, low latency and high bandwidth communications, scalable network bandwidth, and fast access to files. Cluster software can meet these requirements by using resources associated with clusters. A file system supporting parallel I/O can be built using disks associated with each workstation instead of using expensive hardware-RAID. Virtual memory performance can be drastically improved by using Network RAM as a backing store instead of hard disk. In a way, parallel file systems and Network RAM reduces the widening performance gap between processors and disks.

It is very common to connect cluster nodes using the standard Ethernet and specialized high performance networks such as Myrinet. These multiple networks can be utilized for transferring data simultaneously across cluster nodes. The multipath communication software performs demultiplexing of data at the transmitting end across multiple networks and multiplexing of data at the receiving end. Thus, all available networks can be utilized for faster communication of data between cluster nodes.

1.5 A Cluster Computer and its Architecture

A cluster is a type of parallel or distributed processing system, which consists of a collection of interconnected stand-alone computers working together as a single, integrated computing resource.

A computer node can be a single or multiprocessor system (PCs, workstations, or SMPs) with memory, I/O facilities, and an operating system. A cluster generally refers to two or more computers (nodes) connected together. The nodes can exist in a single cabinet or be physically separated and connected via a LAN. An interconnected (LAN-based) cluster of computers can appear as a single system to users and applications. Such a system can provide a cost-effective way to gain features and benefits (fast and reliable services) that have historically been found only on more expensive proprietary shared memory systems. The typical architecture of a cluster is shown in Figure 1.2.

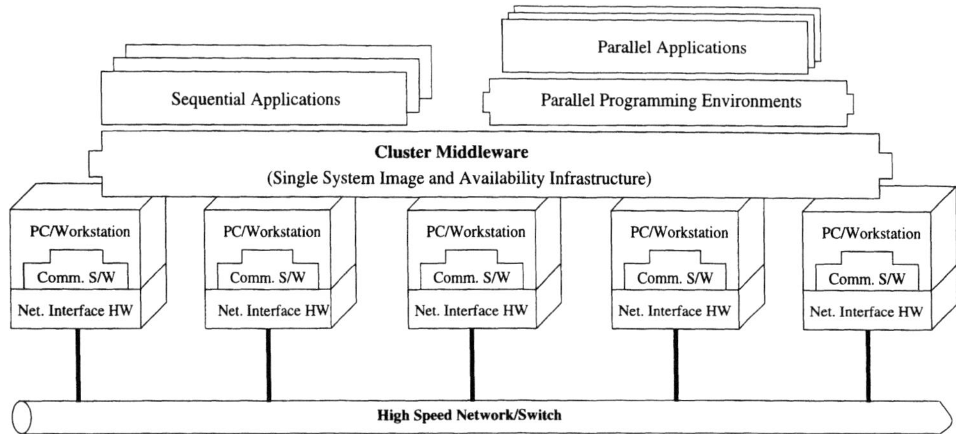

Figure 1.2 Cluster computer architecture.

The following are some prominent components of cluster computers:

- Multiple High Performance Computers (PCs, Workstations, or SMPs)
- State-of-the-art Operating Systems (Layered or Micro-kernel based)
- High Performance Networks/Switches (such as Gigabit Ethernet and Myrinet)
- Network Interface Cards (NICs)
- Fast Communication Protocols and Services (such as Active and Fast Messages)
- Cluster Middleware (Single System Image (SSI) and System Availability Infrastructure)
  - Hardware (such as Digital (DEC) Memory Channel, hardware DSM, and SMP techniques)
  - Operating System Kernel or Gluing Layer (such as Solaris MC and GLUnix)
  - Applications and Subsystems
    - Applications (such as system management tools and electronic forms)
    - Runtime Systems (such as software DSM and parallel file system)

  * Resource Management and Scheduling software (such as LSF (Load Sharing Facility) and CODINE (COmputing in DIstributed Networked Environments))

- Parallel Programming Environments and Tools (such as compilers, PVM (Parallel Virtual Machine), and MPI (Message Passing Interface))
- Applications
  - Sequential
  - Parallel or Distributed

The network interface hardware acts as a communication processor and is responsible for transmitting and receiving packets of data between cluster nodes via a network/switch. (Refer to Chapter 9 for further details on cluster interconnects and network interfaces.)

Communication software offers a means of fast and reliable data communication among cluster nodes and to the outside world. Often, clusters with a special network/switch like Myrinet use communication protocols such as active messages for fast communication among its nodes. They potentially bypass the operating system and thus remove the critical communication overheads providing direct user-level access to the network interface.

The cluster nodes can work collectively, as an integrated computing resource, or they can operate as individual computers. The cluster middleware is responsible for offering an illusion of a unified system image (single system image) and availability out of a collection on independent but interconnected computers.

Programming environments can offer portable, efficient, and easy-to-use tools for development of applications. They include message passing libraries, debuggers, and profilers. It should not be forgotten that clusters could be used for the execution of sequential or parallel applications.

1.6 Clusters Classifications

Clusters offer the following features at a relatively low cost:

- High Performance
- Expandability and Scalability
- High Throughput
- High Availability

Cluster technology permits organizations to boost their processing power using standard technology (commodity hardware and software components) that can be acquired/purchased at a relatively low cost. This provides expandability–an affordable upgrade path that lets organizations increase their computing power–while preserving their existing investment and without incurring a lot of extra expense.

The performance of applications also improves with the support of scalable software environment. Another benefit of clustering is a failover capability that allows a backup computer to take over the tasks of a failed computer located in its cluster.

Clusters are classified into many categories based on various factors as indicated below.

1. **Application Target** - Computational science or mission-critical applications.

   - High Performance (HP) Clusters
   - High Availability (HA) Clusters

   The main concentration of this book is on HP clusters and the technologies and environments required for using them in parallel computing. However, we also discuss issues involved in building HA clusters with an aim for integrating performance and availability into a single system (see Chapter 4).

2. **Node Ownership** - Owned by an individual or dedicated as a cluster node.

   - Dedicated Clusters
   - Nondedicated Clusters

   The distinction between these two cases is based on the ownership of the nodes in a cluster. In the case of dedicated clusters, a particular individual does not own a workstation; the resources are shared so that parallel computing can be performed across the entire cluster [6]. The alternative nondedicated case is where individuals own workstations and applications are executed by stealing idle CPU cycles [7]. The motivation for this scenario is based on the fact that most workstation CPU cycles are unused, even during peak hours. Parallel computing on a dynamically changing set of nondedicated workstations is called adaptive parallel computing.

   In nondedicated clusters, a tension exists between the workstation owners and remote users who need the workstations to run their application. The former expects fast interactive response from their workstation, while the latter is only concerned with fast application turnaround by utilizing any spare CPU cycles. This emphasis on sharing the processing resources erodes the concept of node ownership and introduces the need for complexities such as process migration and load balancing strategies. Such strategies allow clusters to deliver adequate interactive performance as well as to provide shared resources to demanding sequential and parallel applications.

3. **Node Hardware** - PC, Workstation, or SMP.

   - Clusters of PCs (CoPs) or Piles of PCs (PoPs)
   - Clusters of Workstations (COWs)

- Clusters of SMPs (CLUMPs)

4. **Node Operating System -** Linux, NT, Solaris, AIX, etc.
    - Linux Clusters (e.g., Beowulf)
    - Solaris Clusters (e.g., Berkeley NOW)
    - NT Clusters (e.g., HPVM)
    - AIX Clusters (e.g., IBM SP2)
    - Digital VMS Clusters
    - HP-UX clusters.
    - Microsoft Wolfpack clusters.
5. **Node Configuration -** Node architecture and type of OS it is loaded with.
    - Homogeneous Clusters: All nodes will have similar architectures and run the same OSs.
    - Heterogeneous Clusters: All nodes will have different architectures and run different OSs.
6. **Levels of Clustering -** Based on location of nodes and their count.
    - Group Clusters (#nodes: 2-99): Nodes are connected by SANs (System Area Networks) like Myrinet and they are either stacked into a frame or exist within a center.
    - Departmental Clusters (#nodes: 10s to 100s)
    - Organizational Clusters (#nodes: many 100s)
    - National Metacomputers (WAN/Internet-based): (#nodes: many departmental/organizational systems or clusters)
    - International Metacomputers (Internet-based): (#nodes: 1000s to many millions)

Individual clusters may be interconnected to form a larger system (clusters of clusters) and, in fact, the Internet itself can be used as a computing cluster. The use of wide-area networks of computer resources for high performance computing has led to the emergence of a new field called Metacomputing. (Refer to Chapter 7 for further details on Metacomputing.)

1.7 Commodity Components for Clusters

The improvements in workstation and network performance, as well as the availability of standardized programming APIs, are paving the way for the widespread usage of cluster-based parallel systems. In this section, we discuss some of the hardware and software components commonly used to build clusters and nodes. The trends in hardware and software technologies are discussed in later parts of this chapter.

1.7.1 Processors

Over the past two decades, phenomenal progress has taken place in microprocessor architecture (for example RISC, CISC, VLIW, and Vector) and this is making the single-chip CPUs almost as powerful as processors used in supercomputers. Most recently researchers have been trying to integrate processor and memory or network interface into a single chip. The Berkeley Intelligent RAM (IRAM) project [9] is exploring the entire spectrum of issues involved in designing general purpose computer systems that integrate a processor and DRAM onto a single chip – from circuits, VLSI design, and architectures to compilers and operating systems. Digital, with its Alpha 21364 processor, is trying to integrate processing, memory controller, and network interface into a single chip.

Intel processors are most commonly used in PC-based computers. The current generation Intel x86 processor family includes the Pentium Pro and II. These processors, while not in the high range of performance, match the performance of medium level workstation processors [10]. In the high performance range, the Pentium Pro shows a very strong integer performance, beating Sun's UltraSPARC at the same clock speed; however, the floating-point performance is much lower. The Pentium II Xeon, like the newer Pentium IIs, uses a 100 MHz memory bus. It is available with a choice of 512KB to 2MB of L2 cache, and the cache is clocked at the same speed as the CPU, overcoming the L2 cache size and performance issues of the plain Pentium II. The accompanying 450NX chipset for the Xeon supports 64-bit PCI busses that can support Gigabit interconnects.

Other popular processors include x86 variants (AMD x86, Cyrix x86), Digital Alpha, IBM PowerPC, Sun SPARC, SGI MIPS, and HP PA. Computer systems based on these processors have also been used as clusters; for example, Berkeley NOW uses Sun's SPARC family of processors in their cluster nodes. (For further information on industrial high performance microprocessors refer to web-based VLSI Microprocessors Guide [11].)

1.7.2 Memory and Cache

Originally, the memory present within a PC was 640 KBytes, usually 'hardwired' onto the motherboard. Typically, a PC today is delivered with between 32 and 64 MBytes installed in slots with each slot holding a Standard Industry Memory Module (SIMM); the potential capacity of a PC is now many hundreds of MBytes.

Computer systems can use various types of memory and they include Extended Data Out (EDO) and fast page. EDO allows the next access to begin while the previous data is still being read, and fast page allows multiple adjacent accesses to be made more efficiently.

The amount of memory needed for the cluster is likely to be determined by the cluster target applications. Programs that are parallelized should be distributed such that the memory, as well as the processing, is distributed between processors for scalability. Thus, it is not necessary to have a RAM that can hold the entire problem in memory on each system, but it should be enough to avoid the occurrence of too much swapping of memory blocks (page-misses) to disk, since disk access has a large impact on performance.

Access to DRAM is extremely slow compared to the speed of the processor, taking up to orders of magnitude more time than a CPU clock cycle. Caches are used to keep recently used blocks of memory for very fast access if the CPU references a word from that block again. However, the very fast memory used for cache is expensive and cache control circuitry becomes more complex as the size of the cache grows. Because of these limitations, the total size of a cache is usually in the range of 8KB to 2MB.

Within Pentium-based machines it is not uncommon to have a 64-bit wide memory bus as well as a chip set that supports 2 MBytes of external cache. These improvements were necessary to exploit the full power of the Pentium and to make the memory architecture very similar to that of UNIX workstations.

1.7.3 Disk and I/O

Improvements in disk access time have not kept pace with microprocessor performance, which has been improving by 50 percent or more per year. Although magnetic media densities have increased, reducing disk transfer times by approximately 60 to 80 percent per year, overall improvement in disk access times, which rely upon advances in mechanical systems, has been less than 10 percent per year.

Grand challenge applications often need to process large amounts of data and data sets. Amdahl's law implies that the speed-up obtained from faster processors is limited by the slowest system component; therefore, it is necessary to improve I/O performance such that it balances with CPU performance. One way of improving I/O performance is to carry out I/O operations in parallel, which is supported by parallel file systems based on hardware or software RAID. Since hardware RAIDs can be expensive, software RAIDs can be constructed by using disks associated with each workstation in the cluster.

1.7.4 System Bus

The initial PC bus (AT, or now known as ISA bus) used was clocked at 5 MHz and was 8 bits wide. When first introduced, its abilities were well matched to the rest of the system. PCs are modular systems and until fairly recently only the processor and memory were located on the motherboard, other components were typically found on daughter cards connected via a system bus. The performance of PCs has increased by orders of magnitude since the ISA bus was first used, and it has consequently become a bottleneck, which has limited the machine throughput. The ISA bus was extended to be 16 bits wide and was clocked in excess of 13 MHz. This, however, is still not sufficient to meet the demands of the latest CPUs, disk interfaces, and other peripherals.

A group of PC manufacturers introduced the VESA local bus, a 32-bit bus that matched the system's clock speed. The VESA bus has largely been superseded by the Intel-created PCI bus, which allows 133 Mbytes/s transfers and is used inside

Pentium-based PCs. PCI has also been adopted for use in non-Intel based platforms such as the Digital AlphaServer range. This has further blurred the distinction between PCs and workstations, as the I/O subsystem of a workstation may be built from commodity interface and interconnect cards.

1.7.5 Cluster Interconnects

The nodes in a cluster communicate over high-speed networks using a standard networking protocol such as TCP/IP or a low-level protocol such as Active Messages. In most facilities it is likely that the interconnection will be via standard Ethernet. In terms of performance (latency and bandwidth), this technology is showing its age. However, Ethernet is a cheap and easy way to provide file and printer sharing. A single Ethernet connection cannot be used seriously as the basis for cluster-based computing; its bandwidth and latency are not balanced compared to the computational power of the workstations now available. Typically, one would expect the cluster interconnect bandwidth to exceed 10 MBytes/s and have message latencies of less than 100 μs. A number of high performance network technologies are available in the marketplace; in this section we discuss a few of them.

Ethernet, Fast Ethernet, and Gigabit Ethernet

Standard Ethernet has become almost synonymous with workstation networking. This technology is in widespread usage, both in the academic and commercial sectors. However, its 10 Mbps bandwidth is no longer sufficient for use in environments where users are transferring large data quantities or there are high traffic densities. An improved version, commonly known as Fast Ethernet, provides 100 Mbps bandwidth and has been designed to provide an upgrade path for existing Ethernet installations. Standard and Fast Ethernet cannot coexist on a particular cable, but each uses the same cable type. When an installation is hub-based and uses twisted-pair it is possible to upgrade the hub to one, which supports both standards, and replace the Ethernet cards in only those machines where it is believed to be necessary.

Now, the state-of-the-art Ethernet is the Gigabit Ethernet[2] and its attraction is largely due to two key characteristics. First, it preserves Ethernet's simplicity while enabling a smooth migration to Gigabit-per-second (Gbps) speeds. Second, it delivers a very high bandwidth to aggregate multiple Fast Ethernet segments and to support high-speed server connections, switched intrabuilding backbones, interswitch links, and high-speed workgroup networks.

Asynchronous Transfer Mode (ATM)

ATM is a switched virtual-circuit technology and was originally developed for the telecommunications industry [12]. It is embodied within a set of protocols and standards defined by the International Telecommunications Union. The international

[2] Gigabit Ethernet is Ethernet, only faster!

ATM Forum, a non-profit organization, continues this work. Unlike some other networking technologies, ATM is intended to be used for both LAN and WAN, presenting a unified approach to both. ATM is based around small fixed-size data packets termed cells. It is designed to allow cells to be transferred using a number of different media such as both copper wire and fiber optic cables. This hardware variety also results in a number of different interconnect performance levels.

When first introduced, ATM used optical fiber as the link technology. However, this is undesirable in desktop environments; for example, twisted pair cables may have been used to interconnect a networked environment and moving to fiber-based ATM would mean an expensive upgrade. The two most common cabling technologies found in a desktop environment are telephone style cables (CAT-3) and a better quality cable (CAT-5). CAT-5 can be used with ATM allowing upgrades of existing networks without replacing cabling.

Scalable Coherent Interface (SCI)

SCI is an IEEE 1596-1992 standard aimed at providing a low-latency distributed shared memory across a cluster [13]. SCI is the modern equivalent of a Processor-Memory-I/O bus and LAN combined. It is designed to support distributed multiprocessing with high bandwidth and low latency. It provides a scalable architecture that allows large systems to be built out of many inexpensive mass-produced components.

SCI is a point-to-point architecture with directory-based cache coherence. It can reduce the delay of interprocessor communications even when compared to the newest and best technologies currently available, such as Fiber Channel and ATM. SCI achieves this by eliminating the need for runtime layers of software protocol-paradigm translation. A remote communication in SCI takes place as just part of a simple load or store process in a processor. Typically, a remote address results in a cache miss. This in turn causes the cache controller to address remote memory via SCI to get the data. The data is fetched to the cache with a delay in the order of a few μss and then the processor continues execution.

Dolphin currently produces SCI cards for SPARC's SBus; however, they have also announced availability of PCI-based SCI cards. They have produced an SCI MPI which offers less than 12 μs zero message-length latency on the Sun SPARC platform and they intend to provide MPI for Windows NT. A SCI version of High Performance Fortran (HPF) is available from Portland Group Inc.

Although SCI is favored in terms of fast distributed shared memory support, it has not been taken up widely because its scalability is constrained by the current generation of switches and its components are relatively expensive.

Myrinet

Myrinet is a 1.28 Gbps full duplex interconnection network supplied by Myricom [15]. It is a proprietary, high performance interconnect. Myrinet uses low latency cut-through routing switches, which is able to offer fault tolerance by automatic mapping of the network configuration. This also simplifies setting up the network. Myrinet supports both Linux and NT. In addition to TCP/IP support, the MPICH implementation of MPI is also available on a number of custom-developed packages such as Berkeley active messages, which provide sub-10 μs latencies.

Myrinet is relatively expensive when compared to Fast Ethernet, but has real advantages over it: very low-latency (5 μs, one-way point-to-point), very high throughput, and a programmable on-board processor allowing for greater flexibility. It can saturate the effective bandwidth of a PCI bus at almost 120 Mbytes/s with 4Kbytes packets.

One of the main disadvantages of Myrinet is, as mentioned, its price compared to Fast Ethernet. The cost of Myrinet-LAN components, including the cables and switches, is in the range of $1,500 per host. Also, switches with more than 16 ports are unavailable, so scaling can be complicated, although switch chaining is used to construct larger Myrinet clusters.

1.7.6 Operating Systems

A modern operating system provides two fundamental services for users. First, it makes the computer hardware easier to use. It creates a virtual machine that differs markedly from the real machine. Indeed, the computer revolution of the last two decades is due, in part, to the success that operating systems have achieved in shielding users from the obscurities of computer hardware. Second, an operating system shares hardware resources among users. One of the most important resources is the processor. A multitasking operating system, such as UNIX or Windows NT, divides the work that needs to be executed among processes, giving each process memory, system resources, at least one thread of execution, and an executable unit within a process. The operating system runs one thread for a short time and then switches to another, running each thread in turn. Even on a single-user system, multitasking is extremely helpful because it enables the computer to perform multiple tasks at once. For example, a user can edit a document while another document is printing in the background or while a compiler compiles a large program. Each process gets its work done, and to the user all the programs appear to run simultaneously.

Apart from the benefits mentioned above, the new concept in operating system services is supporting multiple threads of control in a process itself. This concept has added a new dimension to parallel processing, the parallelism within a process, instead of across the programs. In the next-generation operating system kernels, address space and threads are decoupled so that a single address space can have multiple execution threads. Programming a process having multiple threads of control is known as multithreading. POSIX threads interface is a standard programming environment for creating concurrency/parallelism within a process.

A number of trends affecting operating system design have been witnessed over the past few years, foremost of these is the move towards modularity. Operating systems such as Microsoft's Windows, IBM's OS/2, and others, are splintered into discrete components, each having a small, well defined interface, and each communicating with others via an intertask messaging interface. The lowest level is the micro-kernel, which provides only essential OS services, such as context switching. Windows NT, for example, also includes a hardware abstraction layer (HAL) beneath its micro-kernel, which enables the rest of the OS to perform irrespective of the underlying processor. This high level abstraction of OS portability is a driving force behind the modular, micro-kernel-based push. Other services are offered by subsystems built on top of the micro-kernel. For example, file services can be offered by the file-server, which is built as a subsystem on top of the microkernel. (Refer to Chapter 29 for details on a micro-kernel based cluster operating system offering single system image.)

This section focuses on the various operating systems available for workstations and PCs. Operating system technology is maturing and can easily be extended and new subsystems can be added without modifying the underlying OS structure. Modern operating systems support multithreading at the kernel level and high performance user level multithreading systems can be built without their kernel intervention. Most PC operating systems have become stable and support multitasking, multithreading, and networking.

UNIX and its variants (such as Sun Solaris and IBM's AIX, HP UX) are popularly used on workstations. In this section, we discuss three popular operating systems that are used on nodes of clusters of PCs or Workstations.

LINUX

Linux [16] is a UNIX-like OS which was initially developed by Linus Torvalds, a Finnish undergraduate student in 1991-92. The original releases of Linux relied heavily on the Minix OS; however, the efforts of a number of collaborating programmers have resulted in the development and implementation of a robust and reliable, POSIX compliant, OS.

Although Linux was developed by a single author initially, a large number of authors are now involved in its development. One major advantage of this distributed development has been that there is a wide range of software tools, libraries, and utilities available. This is due to the fact that any capable programmer has access to the OS source and can implement the feature that they wish. Linux quality control is maintained by only allowing kernel releases from a single point, and its availability via the Internet helps in getting fast feedback about bugs and other problems. The following are some advantages of using Linux:

- Linux runs on cheap x86 platforms, yet offers the power and flexibility of UNIX.

- Linux is readily available on the Internet and can be downloaded without cost.

- It is easy to fix bugs and improve system performance.

- Users can develop or fine-tune hardware drivers which can easily be made available to other users.

Linux provides the features typically found in UNIX implementations such as: preemptive multitasking, demand-paged virtual memory, multiuser, and multiprocessor support [17]. Most applications written for UNIX will require little more than a recompilation. In addition to the Linux kernel, a large amount of application/systems software is also freely available, including GNU software and XFree86, a public domain X-server.

Solaris

The Solaris operating system from SunSoft is a UNIX-based multithreaded and multiuser operating system. It supports Intel x86 and SPARC-based platforms. Its networking support includes a TCP/IP protocol stack and layered features such as Remote Procedure Calls (RPC), and the Network File System (NFS). The Solaris programming environment includes ANSI-compliant C and C++ compilers, as well as tools to profile and debug multithreaded programs.

The Solaris kernel supports multithreading, multiprocessing, and has real-time scheduling features that are critical for multimedia applications. Solaris supports two kinds of threads: Light Weight Processes (LWPs) and user level threads. The threads are intended to be sufficiently lightweight so that there can be thousands present and that synchronization and context switching can be accomplished rapidly without entering the kernel.

Solaris, in addition to the BSD file system, also supports several types of non-BSD file systems to increase performance and ease of use. For performance there are three new file system types: CacheFS, AutoClient, and TmpFS. The CacheFS caching file system allows a local disk to be used as an operating system managed cache of either remote NFS disk or CD-ROM file systems. With AutoClient and CacheFS, an entire local disk can be used as cache. The TmpFS temporary file system uses main memory to contain a file system. In addition, there are other file systems like the *Proc* file system and *Volume* file system to improve system usability.

Solaris supports distributed computing and is able to store and retrieve distributed information to describe the system and users through the Network Information Service (NIS) and database. The Solaris GUI, OpenWindows, is a combination of X11R5 and the Adobe Postscript system, which allows applications to be run on remote systems with the display shown along with local applications.

Microsoft Windows NT

Microsoft Windows NT (New Technology) is a dominant operating system in the personal computing marketplace [18]. It is a preemptive, multitasking, multiuser, 32-bit operating system. NT supports multiple CPUs and provides multi-tasking, using symmetrical multiprocessing. Each 32-bit NT-application operates in its own virtual memory address space. Unlike earlier versions (such as Windows for Workgroups and Windows 95/98), NT is a complete operating system, and not an addition to DOS. NT supports different CPUs and multiprocessor machines with threads. NT has an object-based security model and its own special file system (NTFS) that allows permissions to be set on a file and directory basis.

A schematic diagram of the NT architecture is shown in Figure 1.3. NT has the network protocols and services integrated with the base operating system.

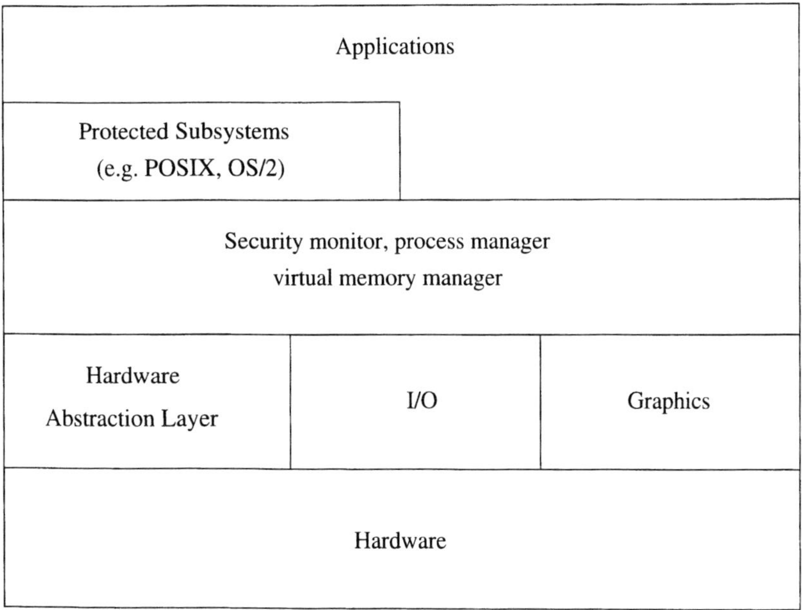

Figure 1.3 Windows NT 4.0 architecture.

Packaged with Windows NT are several built-in networking protocols, such as IPX/SPX, TCP/IP, and NetBEUI and APIs, such as NetBIOS, DCE RPC, and Windows Sockets (WinSock). TCP/IP applications use WinSock to communicate over a TCP/IP network.

1.8 Network Services/Communication SW

The communication needs of distributed applications are diverse and varied and range from reliable point-to-point to unreliable multicast communications. The communications infrastructure needs to support protocols that are used for bulk-data transport, streaming data, group communications, and those used by distributed objects.

The communication services employed provide the basic mechanisms needed by a cluster to transport administrative and user data. These services will also provide the cluster with important quality of service parameters, such as latency, bandwidth, reliability, fault-tolerance, and jitter control. Typically, the network services are designed as a hierarchical stack of protocols. In such a layered system each protocol layer in the stack exploits the services provided by the protocols below it in the stack. The classic example of such a network architecture is the ISO OSI 7-layer system.

Traditionally, the operating system services (pipes/sockets) have been used for communication between processes in message passing systems. As a result, communication between source and destination involves expensive operations, such as the passing of messages between many layers, data copying, protection checking, and reliable communication measures. Often, clusters with a special network/switch like Myrinet use lightweight communication protocols such as active messages for fast communication among its nodes. They potentially bypass the operating system and thus remove the critical communication overheads and provide direct, user-level access to the network interface.

Often in clusters, the network services will be built from a relatively low-level communication API (Application Programming Interface) that can be used to support a wide range of high-level communication libraries and protocols. These mechanisms provide the means to implement a wide range of communications methodologies, including RPC, DSM, and stream-based and message passing interfaces such as MPI and PVM. (A further discussion of communications and network protocols can be found in Chapter 10.)

1.9 Cluster Middleware and Single System Image (SSI)

If a collection of interconnected computers is designed to appear as a unified resource, we say it possesses a Single System Image (SSI). The SSI is supported by a middleware layer that resides between the operating system and user-level environment. This middleware consists of essentially two sublayers of software infrastructure [19]:

- SSI Infrastructure.
- System Availability Infrastructure.

The SSI infrastructure glues together operating systems on all nodes to offer unified access to system resources. The system availability infrastructure enables cluster services such as checkpointing, automatic failover, recovery from failure, and fault-tolerant support among all nodes of the cluster.

1.9.1 Single System Image Levels/Layers

A SSI is defined as the illusion, created by hardware or software, that presents a collection of resources as one, more powerful resource. The SSI concept can be applied to applications, specific subsystems, or the entire cluster. Single system image and system availability services can be offered by one or more of the following levels/layers:

- Hardware (such as Digital (DEC) Memory Channel, hardware DSM, and SMP techniques)
- Operating System Kernel—Underware[3] or Gluing Layer (such as Solaris MC and GLUnix)
- Applications and Subsystems—Middleware
  - Applications (such as system management tools and electronic forms)
  - Runtime Systems (such as software DSM and parallel file system)
  - Resource Management and Scheduling software (such as LSF and CODINE)

It should also be noted that programming and runtime systems like PVM can also serve as cluster middleware.

The SSI layers support both cluster-aware (such as parallel applications developed using MPI) and non-aware applications (typically sequential programs). These applications (cluster-aware, in particular) demand operational transparency and scalable performance (i.e., when a cluster capability is enhanced, applications need to run faster). Clusters, at one operational extreme, act like an SMP or MPP system with a high degree of SSI, and at another they can function as a distributed system with multiple system images.

The SSI and system availability services play a major role in the success of clusters. In the following section, we briefly discuss the layers supporting this infrastructure. A detailed discussion on cluster infrastructure can be found in the rest of the chapter with suitable pointers for further information.

Hardware Layer

Systems such as Digital (DEC's) Memory Channel and hardware DSM offer SSI at hardware level and allow the user to view cluster as a shared memory system. Digital's memory channel, a dedicated cluster interconnect, provides virtual shared memory among nodes by means of internodal address space mapping. (Refer to Chapter 9 for further discussion on DEC memory channel.)

Operating System Kernel (Underware) or Gluing Layer

Cluster operating systems support an efficient execution of parallel applications in an environment shared with sequential applications. A goal is to pool resources in a cluster to provide better performance for both sequential and parallel applications. To realize this goal, the operating system must support gang-scheduling of parallel programs, identify idle resources in the system (such as processors, memory, and networks), and offer globalized access to them. It should optimally support process migration to provide dynamic load balancing as well as fast interprocess

[3] It refers to the infrastructure hidden below the user/kernel interface.

communication for both the system and user-level applications. The OS must make sure these features are available to the user without the need for additional system calls or commands. OS kernels supporting SSI include SCO UnixWare and Sun Solaris-MC.

A full cluster-wide SSI allows all physical resources and kernel resources to be visible and accessible from all nodes within the system. Full SSI can be achieved as underware (SSI at OS level). In other words, each node's OS kernel cooperating to present the same view from all kernel interfaces on all nodes.

The full SSI at kernel level, can save time and money because existing programs and applications do not have to be rewritten to work in this new environment. In addition, these applications will run on any node without administrative setup, and processes can be migrated to load balance between the nodes and also to support fault-tolerance if necessary.

Most of the operating systems that support a SSI are built as a layer on top of the existing operating systems and perform global resource allocation. This strategy makes the system easily portable, tracks vendor software upgrades, and reduces development time. Berkeley GLUnix follows this philosophy and proves that new systems can be built quickly by mapping new services onto the functionality provided by the layer underneath.

Applications and Subsystems Layer (Middleware)

SSI can also be supported by applications and subsystems, which presents multiple, cooperating components of an application to the user/administrator as a single application. The application level SSI is the highest and in a sense most important, because this is what the end user sees. For instance, a cluster administration tool offers a single point of management and control SSI services. These can be built as GUI-based tools offering a single window for the monitoring and control of cluster as a whole, individual nodes, or specific system components.

The subsystems offer a software means for creating an easy-to-use and efficient cluster system. Run time systems, such as cluster file systems, make disks attached to cluster nodes appear as a single large storage system. SSI offered by file systems ensures that every node in the cluster has the same view of the data. Global job scheduling systems manage resources, and enables the scheduling of system activities and execution of applications while offering high availability services transparently.

1.9.2 Single System Image Boundaries

A key that provides structure to the SSI lies in noting the following points [1]:

- Every SSI has a boundary; and
- SSI support can exist at different levels within a system—one able to be built on another.

For instance, a subsystem (resource management systems like LSF and CODINE) can make a collection of interconnected machines appear as one big machine. When any operation is performed within the SSI boundary of the subsystem, it provides an illusion of a classical supercomputer. But if anything is performed outside its SSI boundary, the cluster appears to be just a bunch of connected computers. Another subsystem/application can make the same set of machines appear as a large database/storage system. For instance, a cluster file system built using local disks associated with nodes can appear as a large storage system (software RAID)/parallel file system and offer faster access to the data.

1.9.3 Single System Image Benefits

The advantages/benefits of a SSI include the following:

- It provides a simple, straightforward view of all system resources and activities, from any node of the cluster.
- It frees the end user from having to know where an application will run.
- It frees the operator from having to know where a resource (an instance of resource) is located.
- It lets the user work with familiar interface and commands and allows the administrator to manage the entire cluster as a single entity.
- It reduces the risk of operator errors, with the result that end users see improved reliability and higher availability of the system.
- It allows to centralize/decentralize system management and control to avoid the need of skilled administrators for system administration.
- It presents multiple, cooperating components of an application to the administrator as a single application.
- It greatly simplifies system management (which translates into lower cost of ownership); actions affecting multiple resources can be achieved with a single command, even where the resources are spread among multiple systems on different machines.
- It provides location-independent message communication. Because SSI provides a dynamic map of the message routing as it occurs in reality, the operator can always be sure that actions will be performed on the current system.
- It helps track the locations of all resources so that there is no longer any need for system operators to be concerned with their physical location while carrying out system management tasks.

The benefits of a SSI also apply to system programmers. It reduces the time, effort and knowledge required to perform tasks, and allows current staff to handle larger or more complex systems.

1.9.4 Middleware Design Goals

The design goals of cluster-based systems are mainly focused on complete transparency in resource management, scalable performance, and system availability in supporting user applications.

Complete Transparency

The SSI layer must allow the user to use a cluster easily and effectively without the knowledge of the underlying system architecture. The operating environment appears familiar (by providing the same look and feel of the existing system) and is convenient to use. The user is provided with the view of a globalized file system, processes, and network. For example, in a cluster with a single entry point, the user can login at any node and the system administrator can install/load software at anyone's node and have be visible across the entire cluster. Note that on distributed systems, one needs to install the same software for each node. The details of resource management and control activities such as resource allocation, de-allocation, and replication are invisible to user processes. This allows the user to access system resources such as memory, processors, and the network transparently, irrespective of whether they are available locally or remotely.

Scalable Performance

As clusters can easily be expanded, their performance should scale as well. This scalability should happen without the need for new protocols and APIs. To extract the maximum performance, the SSI service must support load balancing and parallelism by distributing workload evenly among nodes. For instance, single point entry should distribute ftp/remote exec/login requests to lightly loaded nodes. The cluster must offer these services with small overhead and also ensure that the time required to execute the same operation on a cluster should not be larger than on a single workstation (assuming cluster nodes and workstations have similar configuration).

Enhanced Availability

The middleware services must be highly available at all times. At any time, a point of failure should be recoverable without affecting a user's application. This can be achieved by employing checkpointing and fault tolerant technologies (hot standby, mirroring, failover, and failback services) to enable rollback recovery.

When SSI services are offered using the resources available on multiple nodes, failure of any node should not affect the system's operation and a particular service should support one or more of the design goals. For instance, when a file system is distributed among many nodes with a certain degree of redundancy, when a node fails, that portion of file system could be migrated to another node transparently.

1.9.5 Key Services of SSI and Availability Infrastructure

Ideally, a cluster should offer a wide range of SSI and availability services. These services offered by one or more layers, stretch along different dimensions of an application domain. The following sections discuss SSI and availability services offered by middleware infrastructures.

SSI Support Services

Single Point of Entry: A user can connect to the cluster as a single system (like telnet beowulf.myinstitute.edu), instead of connecting to individual nodes as in the case of distributed systems (like telnet node1.beowulf.myinstitute.edu).

Single File Hierarchy (SFH): On entering into the system, the user sees a file system as a single hierarchy of files and directories under the same root directory. Examples: xFS and Solaris MC Proxy.

Single Point of Management and Control: The entire cluster can be monitored or controlled from a single window using a single GUI tool, much like an NT workstation managed by the Task Manager tool or PARMON monitoring the cluster resources (discussed later).

Single Virtual Networking: This means that any node can access any network connection throughout the cluster domain even if the network is not physically connected to all nodes in the cluster.

Single Memory Space: This illusion of shared memory over memories associated with nodes of the cluster (discussed later).

Single Job Management System: A user can submit a job from any node using a transparent job submission mechanism. Jobs can be scheduled to run in either batch, interactive, or parallel modes (discussed later). Example systems include LSF and CODINE.

Single User Interface: The user should be able to use the cluster through a single GUI. The interface must have the same look and feel of an interface that is available for workstations (e.g., Solaris OpenWin or Windows NT GUI).

Availability Support Functions

Single I/O Space (SIOS): This allows any node to perform I/O operation on local or remotely located peripheral or disk devices. In this SIOS design, disks associated with cluster nodes, RAIDs, and peripheral devices form a single address space.

Single Process Space: Processes have a unique cluster-wide process id. A process on any node can create child processes on the same or different node (through a UNIX fork) or communicate with any other process (through signals and pipes) on a remote node. This cluster should support globalized process management and allow the management and control of processes as if they are running on local machines.

Checkpointing and Process Migration: Checkpointing mechanisms allow a process state and intermediate computing results to be saved periodically. When a node fails, processes on the failed node can be restarted on another working node without the loss of computation. Process migration allows for dynamic load balancing among the cluster nodes.

1.10 Resource Management and Scheduling (RMS)

Resource Management and Scheduling (RMS) is the act of distributing applications among computers to maximize their throughput. It also enables the effective and efficient utilization of the resources available. The software that performs the RMS consists of two components: a resource manager and a resource scheduler. The resource manager component is concerned with problems, such as locating and allocating computational resources, authentication, as well as tasks such as process creation and migration. The resource scheduler component is concerned with tasks such as queuing applications, as well as resource location and assignment.

RMS has come about for a number of reasons, including: load balancing, utilizing spare CPU cycles, providing fault tolerant systems, managed access to powerful systems, and so on. But the main reason for their existence is their ability to provide an increased, and reliable, throughput of user applications on the systems they manage.

The basic RMS architecture is a client-server system. In its simplest form, each computer sharing computational resources runs a server daemon. These daemons maintain up-to-date tables, which store information about the RMS environment in which it resides. A user interacts with the RMS environment via a client program, which could be a Web browser or a customized X-windows interface. Application can be run either in interactive or batch mode, the latter being the more commonly used. In batch mode, an application run becomes a job that is submitted to the RMS system to be processed. To submit a batch job, a user will need to provide job details to the system via the RMS client. These details may include information such as location of the executable and input data sets, where standard output is to be placed, system type, maximum length of run, whether the job needs sequential or parallel resources, and so on. Once a job has been submitted to the RMS environment, it uses the job details to place, schedule, and run the job in the appropriate way.

RMS environments provide middleware services to users that should enable heterogeneous environments of workstations, SMPs, and dedicated parallel platforms to be easily and efficient utilized. The services provided by a RMS environment can include:

Process Migration - This is where a process can be suspended, moved, and restarted on another computer within the RMS environment. Generally, process migration occurs due to one of two reasons: a computational resource has become too heavily loaded and there are other free resources, which can be utilized, or in conjunction with the process of minimizing the impact of users, mentioned below.

Checkpointing - This is where a snapshot of an executing program's state is saved and can be used to restart the program from the same point at a later time if necessary. Checkpointing is generally regarded as a means of providing reliability. When some part of an RMS environment fails, the programs executing on it can be restarted from some intermediate point in their run, rather than restarting them from scratch.

Scavenging Idle Cycles - It is generally recognized that between 70 percent and 90 percent of the time most workstations are idle. RMS systems can be set up to utilize idle CPU cycles. For example, jobs can be submitted to workstations during the night or at weekends. This way, interactive users are not impacted by external jobs and idle CPU cycles can be taken advantage of.

Fault Tolerance - By monitoring its jobs and resources, an RMS system can provide various levels of fault tolerance. In its simplest form, fault tolerant support can mean that a failed job can be restarted or rerun, thus guaranteeing that the job will be completed.

Minimization of Impact on Users - Running a job on public workstations can have a great impact on the usability of the workstations by interactive users. Some RMS systems attempt to minimize the impact of a running job on interactive users by either reducing a job's local scheduling priority or suspending the job. Suspended jobs can be restarted later or migrated to other resources in the systems.

Load Balancing - Jobs can be distributed among all the computational platforms available in a particular organization. This will allow for the efficient and effective usage of all the resources, rather than a few which may be the only ones that the users are aware of. Process migration can also be part of the load balancing strategy, where it may be beneficial to move processes from overloaded system to lightly loaded ones.

Multiple Application Queues - Job queues can be set up to help manage the resources at a particular organization. Each queue can be configured with certain attributes. For example, certain users have priority of short jobs run before long jobs. Job queues can also be set up to manage the usage of specialized resources, such as a parallel computing platform or a high performance graphics workstation. The queues in an RMS system can be transparent to users; jobs are allocated to them via keywords specified when the job is submitted.

There are many commercial and research packages available for RMS; a few popular ones are listed in Table 1.2. There are several in depth reviews of the available RMS systems [5], [20].

Table 1.2 Some Popular Resource Management Systems

Project	Commercial Systems - URL
LSF	http://www.platform.com/
CODINE	http://www.genias.de/products/codine/tech_desc.html
Easy-LL	http://www.tc.cornell.edu/UserDoc/SP/LL12/Easy/
NQE	http://www.cray.com/products/software/nqe/
	Public Domain Systems - URL
CONDOR	http://www.cs.wisc.edu/condor/
GNQS	http://www.gnqs.org/
DQS	http://www.scri.fsu.edu/~pasko/dqs.html
PRM	http://gost.isi.edu/gost-group/products/prm/
PBS	http://pbs.mrj.com/

1.11 Programming Environments and Tools

The availability of standard programming tools and utilities have made clusters a practical alternative as a parallel-processing platform. In this section we discuss a few of the most popular tools.

1.11.1 Threads

Threads are a popular paradigm for concurrent programming on uniprocessor as well as multiprocessors machines. On multiprocessor systems, threads are primarily used to simultaneously utilize all the available processors. In uniprocessor systems, threads are used to utilize the system resources effectively. This is achieved by exploiting the asynchronous behavior of an application for overlapping computation and communication. Multithreaded applications offer quicker response to user input and run faster. Unlike forked process, thread creation is cheaper and easier to manage. Threads communicate using shared variables as they are created within their parent process address space.

Threads are potentially portable, as there exists an IEEE standard for POSIX threads interface, popularly called pthreads. The POSIX standard multithreading interface is available on PCs, workstations, SMPs, and clusters [21]. A programming language such as Java has built-in multithreading support enabling easy development of multithreaded applications. Threads have been extensively used in developing both application and system software (including an environment used to create this chapter and the book as a whole!).

1.11.2 Message Passing Systems (MPI and PVM)

Message passing libraries allow efficient parallel programs to be written for distributed memory systems. These libraries provide routines to initiate and configure the messaging environment as well as sending and receiving packets of data. Currently, the two most popular high-level message-passing systems for scientific and engineering application are the PVM (Parallel Virtual Machine) [22] from Oak Ridge National Laboratory, and MPI (Message Passing Interface) defined by MPI Forum [8].

PVM is both an environment and a message passing library, which can be used to run parallel applications on systems ranging from high-end supercomputers through to clusters of workstations. Whereas MPI is a message passing specification, designed to be standard for distributed memory parallel computing using explicit message passing. This interface attempts to establish a practical, portable, efficient, and flexible standard for message passing. MPI is available on most of the HPC systems, including SMP machines.

The MPI standard is the amalgamation of what were considered the best aspects of the most popular message passing systems at the time of its conception. It is the result of the work undertaken by the MPI Forum, a committee composed of vendors and users formed at the SC'92 with the aim of defining a message passing standard. The goals of the MPI design were portability, efficiency and functionality. The standard only defines a message passing library and leaves, among other things, the initialization and control of processes to individual developers to define. Like PVM, MPI is available on a wide range of platforms from tightly coupled systems to metacomputers. The choice of whether to use PVM or MPI to develop a parallel application is beyond the scope of this chapter, but, generally, application developers choose MPI, as it is fast becoming the de facto standard for message passing. MPI and PVM libraries are available for Fortran 77, Fortran 90, ANSI C and C++. There also exist interfaces to other languages—one such example is `mpiJava` [23].

1.11.3 Distributed Shared Memory (DSM) Systems

The most efficient, and widely used, programming paradigm on distributed memory systems is message passing. A problem with this paradigm is that it is complex and difficult to program compared to shared memory programming systems. Shared memory systems offer a simple and general programming model, but they suffer from scalability. An alternate cost-effective solution is to build a DSM system on distributed memory system, which exhibits simple and general programming model and scalability of a distributed memory systems.

DSM enables shared-variable programming and it can be implemented by using software or hardware solutions. The characteristics of software DSM systems are: they are usually built as a separate layer on top of the communications interface; they take full advantage of the application characteristics; virtual pages, objects, and language types are units of sharing. Software DSM can be implemented either solely by run-time, compile time, or combined approaches. Two representative software DSM systems are TreadMarks [24] and Linda [25]. The characteristics of hardware DSM systems are: better performance (much faster than software DSM), no burden on user and software layers, fine granularity of sharing, extensions of the cache coherence schemes, and increased hardware complexity. Two examples of hardware DSM systems are DASH [26] and Merlin [27].

1.11.4 Parallel Debuggers and Profilers

To develop correct and efficient high performance applications it is highly desirable to have some form of easy-to-use parallel debugger and performance profiling tools. Most vendors of HPC systems provide some form of debugger and performance analyzer for their platforms. Ideally, these tools should be able to work in a heterogeneous environment, thus making it possible to develop and implement a parallel application on, say a NOW, and then actually do production runs on a dedicated HPC platform, such as the Cray T3E.

Debuggers

The number of parallel debuggers that are capable of being used in a cross-platform, heterogeneous, development environment is very limited. Therefore, in 1996 an effort was begun to define a cross-platform parallel debugging standard that defined the features and interface users wanted. The High Performance Debugging Forum (HPDF) was formed as a Parallel Tools Consortium project [28]. The forum has developed a HPD Version specification which defines the functionality, semantics, and syntax for a command-line parallel debugger. Ideally, a parallel debugger should be capable of:

- Managing multiple processes and multiple threads within a process.
- Displaying each process in its own window.
- Displaying source code, stack trace, and stack frame for one or more processes.
- Diving into objects, subroutines, and functions.
- Setting both source-level and machine-level breakpoints.
- Sharing breakpoints between groups of processes.
- Defining watch and evaluation points.
- Displaying arrays and its slices.
- Manipulating code variables and constants.

TotalView

TotalView is a commercial product from Dolphin Interconnect Solutions [29]. It is currently the only widely available GUI-based parallel debugger that supports multiple HPC platforms. TotalView supports most commonly used scientific languages (C, C++, F77/F90 and HPF), message passing libraries (MPI and PVM) and operating systems (SunOS/Solaris, IBM AIX, Digital UNIX and SGI IRIX).

Even though TotalView can run on multiple platforms, it can only be used in homogeneous environments, namely, where each process of the parallel application being debugged must be running under the same version of the OS.

1.11.5 Performance Analysis Tools

The basic purpose of performance analysis tools is to help a programmer to understand the performance characteristics of an application. In particular, it should analyze and locate parts of an application that exhibit poor performance and create program bottlenecks. Such tools are useful for understanding the behavior of normal sequential applications and can be enormously helpful when trying to analyze the performance characteristics of parallel applications.

Most performance monitoring tools consist of some or all of the following components:

- A means of inserting instrumentation calls to the performance monitoring routines into the user's application.
- A run-time performance library that consists of a set of monitoring routines that measure and record various aspects of a program performance.
- A set of tools for processing and displaying the performance data.

A particular issue with performance monitoring tools is the intrusiveness of the tracing calls and their impact on the applications performance. It is very important to note that instrumentation affects the performance characteristics of the parallel application and thus provides a false view of its performance behavior. Table 1.3 shows the most commonly used tools for performance analysis of message passing programs.

1.11.6 Cluster Administration Tools

Monitoring clusters is a challenging task that can be eased by tools that allow entire clusters to be observed at different levels using a GUI. Good management software is crucial for exploiting a cluster as a high performance computing platform.

There are many projects investigating system administration of clusters that support parallel computing, including Berkeley NOW [4], SMILE [30] (Scalable Multicomputer Implementation using Low-cost Equipment), and PARMON [31]. The Berkeley NOW system administration tool gathers and stores data in a relational database. It uses a Java applet to allow users to monitor a system from their browser. The SMILE administration tool is called K-CAP. Its environment consists of compute nodes (these execute the compute-intensive tasks), a management node (a file server and cluster manager as well as a management console), and a client that can control and monitor the cluster. K-CAP uses a Java applet to connect to the management node through a predefined URL address in the cluster. The Node Status Reporter (NSR) provides a standard mechanism for measurement and

Table 1.3 Performance Analysis and Visualization Tools

Tool	Supports	URL
AIMS	instrumentation, monitoring library, analysis	http://science.nas.nasa.gov/Software/AIMS
MPE	logging library and snapshot performance visualization	http://www.mcs.anl.gov/mpi/mpich
Pablo	monitoring library and analysis	http://www-pablo.cs.uiuc.edu/Projects/Pablo/
Paradyn	dynamic instrumentation runtime analysis	http://www.cs.wisc.edu/paradyn
SvPablo	integrated instrumentor, monitoring library and analysis	http://www-pablo.cs.uiuc.edu/Projects/Pablo/
Vampir	monitoring library performance visualization	http://www.pallas.de/pages/vampir.htm
Dimemas	performance prediction for message passing programs	http://www.pallas.com/pages/dimemas.htm
Paraver	program visualization and analysis	http://www.cepba.upc.es/paraver

access to status information of clusters [32]. Parallel applications/tools can access NSR through the NSR Interface. PARMON is a comprehensive environment for monitoring large clusters. It uses client-server techniques to provide transparent access to all nodes to be monitored. The two major components of PARMON are the parmon-server (system resource activities and utilization information provider) and the parmon-client (a Java applet or application capable of gathering and visualizing realtime cluster information).

1.12 Cluster Applications

Earlier in this chapter we have discussed the reasons why we would want to put together a high performance cluster, that of providing a computational platform for all types of parallel and distributed applications. The class of applications that a cluster can typically cope with would be considered grand challenge or supercomputing applications. GCAs (Grand Challenge Applications) are fundamental problems in science and engineering with broad economic and scientific impact [33]. They are generally considered intractable without the use of state-of-the-art parallel computers. The scale of their resource requirements, such as processing time, memory, and communication needs distinguishes GCAs.

A typical example of a grand challenge problem is the simulation of some phenomena that cannot be measured through experiments. GCAs include massive crystallographic and microtomographic structural problems, protein dynamics and biocatalysis, relativistic quantum chemistry of actinides, virtual materials design and processing, global climate modeling, and discrete event simulation.

The design and implementation of various GCAs on clusters has been discussed in Volume 2 of this book [34].

1.13 Representative Cluster Systems

There are many projects [35] investigating the development of supercomputing class machines using commodity off-the-shelf components. We briefly describe the following popular efforts:

- Network of Workstations (NOW) project at University of California, Berkeley.
- High Performance Virtual Machine (HPVM) project at University of Illinois at Urbana-Champaign.
- Beowulf Project at the Goddard Space Flight Center, NASA.
- Solaris-MC project at Sun Labs, Sun Microsystems, Inc., Palo Alto, CA.

1.13.1 The Berkeley Network Of Workstations (NOW) Project

The Berkeley NOW project [4] demonstrates building of a large-scale parallel computing system using mass produced commercial workstations and the latest commodity switch-based network components. To attain the goal of combining distributed workstations into a single system, the NOW project included research and development into network interface hardware, fast communication protocols, distributed file systems, distributed scheduling, and job control. The architecture of NOW system is shown in Figure 1.4.

Interprocess Communication

Active Messages (AM) is the basic communications primitives in Berkeley NOW. It generalizes previous AM interfaces to support a broader spectrum of applications such as client/server programs, file systems, operating systems, and provide continuous support for parallel programs. The AM communication is essentially a simplified remote procedure call that can be implemented efficiently on a wide

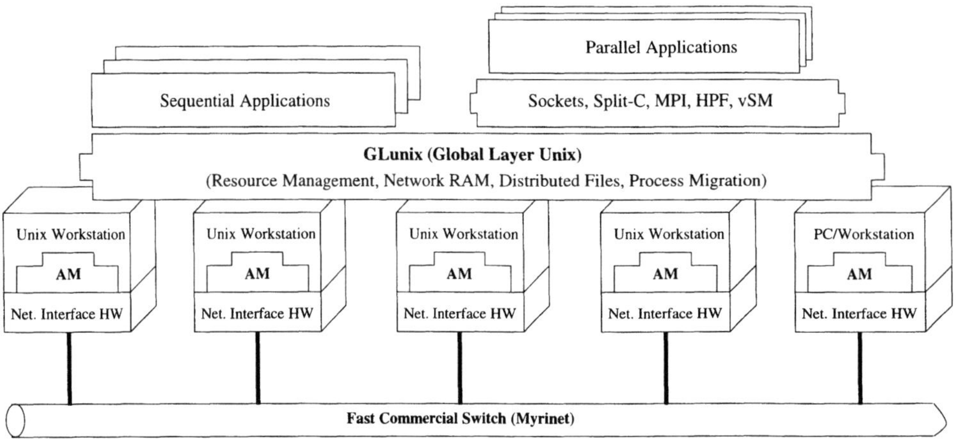

Figure 1.4 Architecture of NOW system.

range of hardware. NOW includes a collection of low-latency, parallel communication primitives: Berkeley Sockets, Fast Sockets, shared address space parallel C (Split-C), and MPI.

Global Layer Unix

(GLUnix) GLUnix is an OS layer designed to provide transparent remote execution, support for interactive parallel and sequential jobs, load balancing, and backward compatibility for existing application binaries. GLUnix is a multiuser system implemented at the userlevel so that it can be easily ported to a number of different platforms. GLUnix aims to provide a cluster-wide namespace and uses Network PIDs (NPIDs) and Virtual Node Numbers (VNNs). NPIDs are globally unique process identifiers for both sequential and parallel programs throughout the system. VNNs are used to facilitate communications among processes of a parallel program. A suite of user tools for interacting and manipulating NPIDs and VNNs, equivalent to UNIX run, kill, etc. are supported. A GLUnix API allows interaction with NPIDs and VNNs.

Network RAM

Network RAM allows us to utilize free resources on idle machines as a paging device for busy machines. The designed system is serverless, and any machine can be a server when it is idle, or a client when it needs more memory than physically available. Two prototype systems have been developed. One of these uses custom Solaris segment drivers to implement an external user-level pager, which exchanges pages with remote page daemons. The other provides similar operations on similarly mapped regions using signals.

xFS: Serverless Network File System

xFS is a serverless, distributed file system, which attempts to have low latency, high bandwidth access to file system data by distributing the functionality of the server among the clients. The typical duties of a server include maintaining cache coherence, locating data, and servicing disk requests. The function of locating data in xFS is distributed by having each client responsible for servicing requests on a subset of the files. File data is striped across multiple clients to provide high bandwidth.

1.13.2 The High Performance Virtual Machine (HPVM) Project

The goal of the HPVM project [36] is to deliver supercomputer performance on a low cost COTS (commodity-off-the-shelf) system. HPVM also aims to hide the complexities of a distributed system behind a clean interface. The HPVM project provides software that enables high performance computing on clusters of PCs and workstations. The HPVM architecture (Figure 1.5) consists of a number of software components with high-level APIs, such as MPI, SHMEM, and Global Arrays, that allows HPVM clusters to be competitive with dedicated MPP systems.

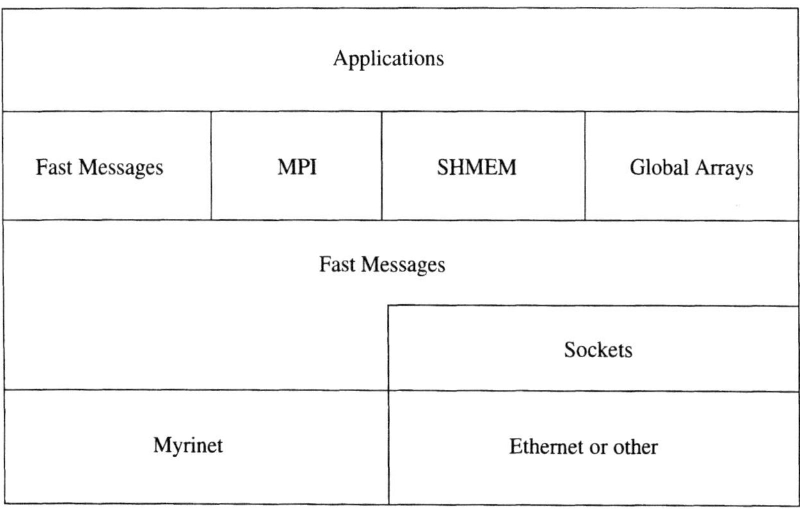

Figure 1.5 HPVM layered architecture.

The HPVM project aims to address the following challenges:

- Delivering high performance communication to standard, high-level APIs.
- Coordinating scheduling and resource management.
- Managing heterogeneity.

A critical part of HPVM is a high-bandwidth and low-latency communications protocol known as Fast Messages (FM), which is based on Berkeley AM. Unlike other messaging layers, FM is not the surface API, but the underlying semantics. FM contains functions for sending long and short messages and for extracting messages from the network. The services provided by FM guarantees and controls the memory hierarchy that FM provides to software built with FM. FM also guarantees reliable and ordered packet delivery as well as control over the scheduling of communication work.

The FM interface was originally developed on a Cray T3D and a cluster of SPARCstations connected by Myrinet hardware. Myricom's Myrinet hardware is a programmable network interface card capable of providing 160 MBytes/s links with switch latencies of under a μs. FM has a low-level software interface that delivers hardware communication performance; however, higher-level layers interface offer greater functionality, application portability, and ease of use.

1.13.3 The Beowulf Project

The Beowulf project's [6] aim was to investigate the potential of PC clusters for performing computational tasks. Beowulf refers to a Pile-of-PCs (PoPC) to describe a loose ensemble or cluster of PCs, which is similar to COW/NOW. PoPC emphasizes the use of mass-market commodity components, dedicated processors (rather than stealing cycles from idle workstations), and the use of a private communications network. An overall goal of Beowulf is to achieve the 'best' overall system cost/performance ratio for the cluster.

System Software

The collection of software tools being developed and evolving within the Beowulf project is known as *Grendel.* These tools are for resource management and to support distributed applications. The Beowulf distribution includes several programming environments and development libraries as separate packages. These include PVM, MPI, and BSP, as well as, SYS V-style IPC, and pthreads.

The communication between processors in Beowulf is through TCP/IP over the Ethernet internal to cluster. The performance of interprocessor communications is, therefore, limited by the performance characteristics of the Ethernet and the system software managing message passing. Beowulf has been used to explore the feasibility of employing multiple Ethernet networks in parallel to satisfy the internal data transfer bandwidths required. Each Beowulf workstation has user-transparent access to multiple parallel Ethernet networks. This architecture was achieved by 'channel bonding' techniques implemented as a number of enhancements to the Linux kernel. The Beowulf project has shown that up to three networks can be ganged together to obtain significant throughput, thus validating their use of the channel bonding technique. New network technologies, such as Fast Ethernet, will ensure even better interprocessor communications performance.

In the interests of presenting a uniform system image to both users and applications, Beowulf has extended the Linux kernel to allow a loose ensemble of nodes to participate in a number of global namespaces. In a distributed scheme it is often convenient for processes to have a PID that is unique across an entire cluster, spanning several kernels. Beowulf implements two Global Process ID (GPID) schemes. The first is independent of external libraries. The second, GPID-PVM, is designed to be compatible with PVM Task ID format and uses PVM as its signal transport. While the GPID extension is sufficient for cluster-wide control and signaling of processes, it is of little use without a global view of the processes. To this end, the Beowulf project is developing a mechanism that allows unmodified versions of standard UNIX utilities (e.g., ps) to work across a cluster.

1.13.4 Solaris MC: A High Performance Operating System for Clusters

Solaris MC (Multicomputer) [37] is a distributed operating system for a multicomputer, a cluster of computing nodes connected by a high-speed interconnect. It provides a single system image, making the cluster appear like a single machine to the user, to applications, and to the network. The Solaris MC is built as a globalization layer on top of the existing Solaris kernel, as shown in Figure 1.6. It extends operating system abstractions across the cluster and preserves the existing Solaris ABI/API, and hence runs existing Solaris 2.x applications and device drivers without modifications. The Solaris MC consists of several modules: C++ and object framework; and globalized process, file system, and networking.

The interesting features of Solaris MC include the following:

- Extends existing Solaris operating system
- Preserves the existing Solaris ABI/API compliance
- Provides support for high availability
- Uses C++, IDL, CORBA in the kernel
- Leverages Spring technology

The Solaris MC uses an object-oriented framework for communication between nodes. The object-oriented framework is based on CORBA and provides remote object method invocations. It looks like a standard C++ method invocation to the programmers. The framework also provides object reference counting: notification to object server when there are no more references (local/remote) to the object. Another feature of the Solaris MC object framework is that it supports multiple object handlers.

A key component in proving a single system image in Solaris MC is the global file system. It provides consistent access from multiple nodes to files and file attributes and uses caching for high performance. It uses a new distributed file system called ProXy File System (PXFS), which provides a globalized file system without the need for modifying the existing file system.

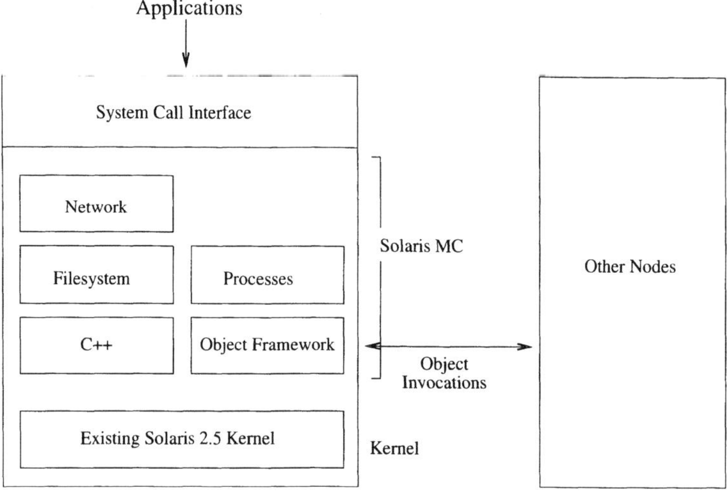

Figure 1.6 Solaris MC architecture.

The second important component of Solaris MC supporting a single system image is its globalized process management. It globalizes process operations such as signals. It also globalizes the /proc file system providing access to process state for commands such as 'ps' and for the debuggers. It supports remote execution, which allows to start up new processes on any node in the system.

Solaris MC also globalizes its support for networking and I/O. It allows more than one network connection and provides support to multiplex between arbitary the network links.

1.13.5 A Comparison of the Four Cluster Environments

The cluster projects described in this chapter share a common goal of attempting to provide a unified resource out of interconnected PCs or workstations. Each system claims that it is capable of providing supercomputing resources from COTS components. Each project provides these resources in different ways, both in terms of how the hardware is connected together and the way the system software and tools provide the services for parallel applications.

Table 1.4 shows the key hardware and software components that each system uses. Beowulf and HPVM are capable of using any PC, whereas Berkeley NOW and Solaris MC function on platforms where Solaris is available – currently PCs, Sun workstations, and various clone systems. Berkeley NOW and HPVM use Myrinet with a fast, low-level communications protocol (Active and Fast Messages). Beowulf uses multiple standard Ethernet, and Solaris MC uses NICs, which are supported by Solaris and ranges from Ethernet to ATM and SCI.

Each system consists of some middleware interfaced into the OS kernel, which

Table 1.4 Cluster Systems Comparison Matrix

Project	**Platform**	**Communications**	**OS**	**Other**
`Beowulf`	PCs	Multiple Ethernet with TCP/IP	Linux and Grendel	MPI/PVM, Sockets and HPF
`Bereley NOW`	Solaris-based PCs and workstations	Myrinet and Active Messages	Solaris + GLUunix + xFS	AM, PVM, MPI, HPF, Split-C
`HPVM`	PCs	Myrinet with Fast Messages	NT or Linux connection and global resource manager + LSF	Java-frontend, FM, Sockets, Global Arrays, SHMEM and MPI
`Solaris MC`	Solaris-based PCs and workstations	Solaris-supported	Solaris + Globalization layer	C++ and CORBA

is used to provide a globalization layer, or unified view, of the distributed cluster resources. Berkeley NOW uses the Solaris OS, whereas Beowulf uses Linux with a modified kernel and HPVM is available for both Linux and Windows NT. All four systems provide a wide variety of tools and utilities commonly used to develop, test, and run parallel applications. These include various high-level APIs for message passing and shared-memory programming.

1.14 Cluster of SMPs (CLUMPS)

The advances in hardware technologies in the area of processors, memory, and network interfaces, is enabling the availability a low cost and small configuration (2-8 multiprocessors) shared memory SMP machines. It is also observed that clusters of multiprocessors (CLUMPS) promise to be the supercomputers of the future. In CLUMPS, multiple SMPs with several network interfaces can be connected using high performance networks.

This has two advantages: It is possible to benefit from the high performance, easy-to-use-and-program SMP systems with a small number of CPUs. In addition, clusters can be set up with moderate effort (for example, a 32-CPU cluster can be constructed by using either commonly available eight 4-CPU SMPs or four 8-CPU SMPs instead of 32 single CPU machines) resulting in easier administration and better support for data locality inside a node.

This trend puts a new demand on cluster interconnects. For example, a single NIC will not be sufficient for an 8-CPU system and will necessitate the need for multiple network devices. In addition, software layers need to implement multiple mechanisms for data transfer (via shared memory inside an SMP node and the network to other nodes).

1.15 Summary and Conclusions

In this chapter we have discussed the different hardware and software components that are commonly used in the current generation of cluster-based systems. We have also described four state-of-the-art projects that are using subtly different approaches ranging from an all-COTS approach to a mixture of technologies. In this section we summarize our findings, and make a few comments about possible future trends.

1.15.1 Hardware and Software Trends

In the last five years several important advances have taken place. Prominent among them are:

- A network performance increase of tenfold using 100BaseT Ethernet with full duplex support.
- The availability of switched network circuits, including full crossbar switches for proprietary network technologies such as Myrinet.
- Workstation performance has improved significantly.
- Improvement of microprocessor performance has led to the availability of desktop PCs with performance of low-end workstations, but at significantly lower cost.
- The availability of fast, functional, and stable OSs (Linux) for PCs, with source code access.
- The performance gap between supercomputer and commodity-based clusters is closing rapidly.
- Parallel supercomputers are now equipped with COTS components, especially microprocessors (SGI-Cray T3E - DEC Alpha), whereas earlier systems had custom components.
- Increasing usage of SMP nodes with two to four processors.

A number of hardware trends have been quantified in [38]. Foremost of these is the design and manufacture of microprocessors. A basic advance is the decrease in feature size which enables circuits to work faster or consume low power. In conjunction with this is the growing die size that can be manufactured. These factors mean that:

- The average number of transistors on a chip is growing by about 40 percent per annum.

- The clock frequency growth rate is about 30 percent per annum.

It is anticipated that by the year 2000 there will be 700 MHz processors with about 100 million transistors.

There is a similar story for storage, but the divergence between memory capacity and speed is more pronounced. Memory capacity increased by three orders of magnitude between 1980 and 1995, yet its speed has only doubled. It is anticipated that Gigabit DRAM will be available in early 2000, but the gap to processor speed is getting greater all the time.

The problem is that memories are getting larger while processors are getting faster. So getting access to data in memory is becoming a bottleneck. One method of overcoming this bottleneck is to configure the DRAM in banks and then transfer data from these banks in parallel. In addition, multilevel memory hierarchies organized as caches make memory access more effective, but their design is complicated. The access bottleneck also applies to disk access, which can also take advance to parallel disks and caches.

The ratio between the cost and performance of network interconnects is falling rapidly. The use of network technologies such as ATM, SCI, and Myrinet in clustering for parallel processing appears to be promising. This has been demonstrated by many commercial and academic projects such as Berkeley NOW and Beowulf. But no single network interconnect has emerged as a clear winner. Myrinet is not a commodity product and costs a lot more than Ethernet, but it has real advantages over it: very low-latency, high bandwidth, and a programmable on-board processor allowing for greater flexibility. SCI network has been used to build distributed shared memory system, but lacks scalability. ATM is used in clusters that are mainly used for multimedia processing.

Two of the most popular operating systems of the 1990s are Linux and NT. Linux has become a popular alternative to a commercial operating system due to its free availability and superior performance compared to other desktop operating systems such as NT. Linux currently has more than 7 million users worldwide and it has become the researcher's choice of operating system.

NT has a large installed base and it has almost become a ubiquitous operating system. NT 5 will have a thinner and faster TCP/IP stack, which supports faster communication of messages, yet it will use standard communication technology. NT systems for parallel computing is in a situation similar to the UNIX workstation five to seven years ago and it is only a matter of time before NT catches up–NT developers need not invest time or money on research as they are borrowing most of the technology developed by the UNIX community!

1.15.2 Cluster Technology Trends

We have discussed a number of cluster projects within this chapter. These range from those which are commodity but proprietary components based (Berkeley NOW) to a totally commodity system (Beowulf). HPVM can be considered as a hybrid-system using commodity computers and specialized network interfaces. It should be noted that the projects detailed in this chapter are a few of the most popular and well known, rather than an exhaustive list of all those available.

All the projects discussed claim to consist of commodity components. Although this is true; one could argue, however, that true commodity technologies would be those that are pervasive at most academic or industrial sites. If this were the case, then true commodity would mean PCs running Windows 95 with standard 10 Mbps Ethernet. However, when considering parallel applications with demanding computational and network needs, this type of low-end cluster would be incapable of providing the resources needed.

Each of the projects discussed tries to overcome the bottlenecks that arise while using cluster-based systems for running demanding parallel applications in a slightly different way. Without fail, however, the main bottleneck is not the computational resource (be it a PC or UNIX workstation), rather it is the provision of a low-latency, high-bandwidth interconnect and an efficient low-level communications protocol to provide high-level APIs.

The Beowulf project explores the use of multiple standard Ethernet cards to overcome the communications bottleneck, whereas Berkeley NOW and HPVM use programmable Myrinet cards and AM/FM communications protocols. Solaris MC uses Myrinet NICs and TCP/IP. The choice of what is the best solution cannot just be based on performance; the cost per node to provide the NIC should also be considered. For example, a standard Ethernet card costs less than $100, whereas Myrinet cards cost in excess of $1000 each. Another factor that must also be considered in this equation is the availability of Fast Ethernet and the advent of GigaBit Ethernet. It seems that Ethernet technologies are likely to be more mainstream, mass produced, and consequently cheaper than specialized network interfaces. As an aside, all the projects that have been discussed are in the vanguard of the cluster computing revolution and their research is helping the following army determine which are the best techniques and technologies to adopt.

1.15.3 Future Cluster Technologies

Emerging hardware technologies along with maturing software resources mean that cluster-based systems are rapidly closing the performance gap with dedicated parallel computing platforms. Cluster systems that scavenge idle cycles from PCs and workstations will continue to use whatever hardware and software components are available on public workstations. Clusters dedicated to high performance applications will continue to evolve as new and more powerful computers and network interfaces become available in the market place.

It is likely that individual cluster nodes will be SMPs. Currently two and four processor PCs and UNIX workstations are becoming common. Software that allows SMP nodes to be efficiently and effectively used by parallel applications will be developed and added to the OS kernel in the near future. It is likely that there will be widespread usage of Gigabit Ethernet and, as such, it will become the de facto standard for clusters. To reduce message passing latencies cluster software systems will bypass the OS kernel, thus avoiding the need for expensive system calls, and exploit the usage of intelligent network cards. This can obviously be achieved using intelligent NICs, or alternatively using on-chip network interfaces such as those used by the new DEC Alpha 21364.

The ability to provide a rich set of development tools and utilities as well as the provision of robust and reliable services will determine the choice of the OS used on future clusters. UNIX-based OSs are likely to be most popular, but the steady improvement and acceptance of Windows NT will mean that it will be not far behind.

1.15.4 Final Thoughts

Our need for computational resources in all fields of science, engineering and commerce far weigh our ability to fulfill these needs. The usage of clusters of computers is, perhaps, one of most promising means by which we can bridge the gap between our needs and the available resources. The usage of COTS-based cluster systems has a number of advantages including:

- Price/performance when compared to a dedicated parallel supercomputer.
- Incremental growth that often matches yearly funding patterns.
- The provision of a multipurpose system: one that could, for example, be used for secretarial purposes during the day and as a commodity parallel supercomputing at night.

These and other advantages will fuel the evolution of cluster computing and its acceptance as a means of providing commodity supercomputing facilities.

Acknowledgments

We thank Dan Hyde, Toni Cortes, Lars Rzymianowicz, Marian Bubak, Krzysztof Sowa, Lori Pollock, Jay Fenwick, Eduardo Pinheiro, and Miguel Barreiro Paz for their comments and suggestions on this chapter.

1.16 Bibliography

[1] G. Pfister. *In Search of Clusters.* Prentice Hall PTR, NJ, 2nd Edition, NJ, 1998.

[2] K. Hwang and Z. Xu. *Scalable Parallel Computing: Technology, Architecture, Programming.* WCB/McGraw-Hill, NY, 1998.

[3] C. Koelbel et al. *The High Performance Fortran Handbook.* The MIT Press, Massachusetts, 1994.

[4] T. Anderson, D. Culler, and D. Patterson. A Case for Networks of Workstations. *IEEE Micro*, Feb. 95. http://now.cs.berkeley.edu/

[5] M.A. Baker, G.C. Fox, and H.W. Yau. *Review of Cluster Management Software.* NHSE Review, May 1996. http://www.nhse.org/NHSEreview/CMS/

[6] *The Beowulf Project.* http://www.beowulf.org

[7] *QUT Gardens Project.* http://www.fit.qut.edu.au/CompSci/PLAS/

[8] *MPI Forum.* http://www.mpi-forum.org/docs/docs.html

[9] *The Berkeley Intelligent RAM Project.* http://iram.cs.berkeley.edu/

[10] *The Standard Performance Evaluation Corporation (SPEC).* http://open.specbench.org

[11] Russian Academy of Sciences. *VLSI Microprocessors: A Guide to High Performance Microprocessors.* http://www.microprocessor.sscc.ru/

[12] ATM Forum. *ATM User Level Network Interface Specification.* Prentice Hall, NJ, June 1995.

[13] *SCI Association.* http://www.SCIzzL.com/

[14] *MPI-FM: MPI for Fast Messages.* http://www-csag.cs.uiuc.edu/projects/comm/mpi-fm.html

[15] N. Boden et. al. Myrinet - A Gigabit-per-Second Local-Area Network. *IEEE Micro*, February 1995. http://www.myri.com/

[16] *The Linux Documentation Project.* http://sunsite.unc.edu/mdw/linux.html

[17] *Parallel Processing using Linux.* http://yara.ecn.purdue.edu/~pplinux/

[18] H. Custer. *Inside Windows NT.* Microsoft Press, NY, 1993.

[19] Kai Hwang et. al. Designing SSI Clusters with Hierarchical Checkpointing and Single I/O Space. *IEEE Concurrency*, vol.7(1), Jan.- March, 1999.

[20] J. Jones and C. Bricknell. *Second Evaluation of Job Scheduling Software.* http://science.nas.nasa.gov/Pubs/TechReports/NASreports/NAS-97-013/

[21] F. Mueller. On the Design and Implementation of DSM-Threads. *In Proceedings of the PDPTA'97 Conference*, Las Vegas, USA, 1997.

[22] *The PVM project.* http://www.epm.ornl.gov/pvm/

[23] `mpiJava` *Wrapper.* http://www.npac.syr.edu/projects/prpc/mpiJava/, Aug. 1998.

[24] *TreadMarks.* http://www.cs.rice.edu/~willy/TreadMarks/overview.html

[25] N. Carriero and D. Gelernter. Linda in Context. *Communications of the ACM*, April 1989.

[26] D. Lenoski et al. The Stanford DASH Multiprocessor. *IEEE Computer*, March 1992.

[27] C. Mapples and Li Wittie. Merlin: A Superglue for Multiprocessor Systems. *In Proceedings of CAMPCON'90*, March 1990.

[28] *Parallel Tools Consortium project.* http://www.ptools.org/

[29] *Dolphin Interconnect Solutions.* http://www.dolphinics.no/

[30] P. Uthayopas et. al. Building a Resources Monitoring System for SMILE Beowulf Cluster. *In Proceedings of HPC Asia98 Conference*, Singapore, 1998.

[31] R. Buyya et. al. PARMON: A Comprehensive Cluster Monitoring System. *In Proceedings of the AUUG'98 Conference*, Sydney, Australia, 1998.

[32] C. Roder et. al. Flexible Status Measurement in Heterogeneous Environment. *In Proceedings of the PDPTA'98 Conference*, Las Vegas, 1998.

[33] *Grand Challenging Applications.* http://www.mcs.anl.gov/Projects/grand-challenges/

[34] R. Buyya. *High Performance Cluster Computing: Programming and Applications.* vol. 2, Prentice Hall PTR, NJ, 1999.

[35] *Computer Architecture Links.* http://www.cs.wisc.edu/~arch/www/

[36] *HPVM.* http://www-csag.cs.uiuc.edu/projects/clusters.html

[37] *Solaris MC.* http://www.sunlabs.com/research/solaris-mc/

[38] D. E. Culler, J. P. Singh, and A. Gupta. *Parallel Computer Architecture: A Hardware/Software Approach.* M. K. Publishers, San Francisco, CA, 1998.

Chapter 2

Cluster Setup and its Administration

MIGUEL BARREIRO PAZ AND VICTOR M. GULIAS

LFCIA – Department of Computer Science
University of A Coruña, Spain

Email: *enano@ceu.fi.udc.es, gulias@dc.fi.udc.es*

2.1 Introduction

As high speed networks and processors start becoming commodity hardware, affordable and reasonably efficient clusters seem to flourish everywhere. Also, while still expensive, more traditional clustered systems are steadily getting somewhat cheaper. The net result is that clusters are no longer too specific, too restricted access systems with completely unique requirements. However, at the same time, this brings new possibilities for researchers and opens up new questions for system administrators.

Perhaps the most significative event in cluster computing in the last few years has been the Beowulf project [1], [2]. A cheap network, some cheap nodes, and Linux underneath. Essentially, nothing new at all; however, its media coverage in the press has been impressive and many sites are pondering a similar setup as a replacement of old parallel machines with huge maintenance costs.

So far, so good. The systems are getting within reach of people with less resources, and thus developments on parallel and distributed systems appear at a growing rate. But, obviously, a pile of PCs plugged to a switch are not a system *per se*; they are just independent machines where getting some useful work done can be quite a slow and tedious task. Similarly, a group of RS/6000 is not an SP2, and several UltraSPARCs do not make an AP-3000. There is a lot to do before they become a single, workable system.

Managing a cluster means facing requirements completely different from more conventional systems. Nowadays, it also means a lot of hand tuning and custom solutions. But, at the end, it just means that the cluster gets the work done.

2.2 Setting up the Cluster

2.2.1 Starting from Scratch

With the aforementioned growing interest on Beowulf-class clusters, it is probably worthwhile to briefly discuss the setup of such a system; this is addressed to those designing a cluster like this one or thinking about doing so. Although it may be of less interest for administrators of commercial clustered systems — their vendor has already done most of this work for them — they should think about how close their systems are anyhow, conceptually, to these homebrew clusters.

Interconnection Network

One could argue whether it is better to design the interconnection network or the computing nodes first. Almost for sure neither of them: The cluster purpose is what should be defined first, with as much detail as possible. This often overlooked detail ("we all know what the system is for, don't we?") is probably the most usual cause for later implementation problems ("what, did we need such a low latency?").

Assuming this purpose is already well thought of and defined — although "general purpose" is too common in practice — the first step will be to develop a network topology and technology suitable for the cluster's communication needs. On the technology side, there are a few options available such as Fast Ethernet, Myrinet, SCI, ATM, and so on. Chapter 9 goes deeply into those technologies.

While many interconnection technologies require a certain network topology (switched, point to point, ring), others do not and there is an additional degree of freedom in choosing the most appropriate. The most obvious example is in Fast Ethernet, where you can choose between direct links, hubs, switches and endless mixes of them [3]. While hubs are obviously something to avoid (except for extremely latency-tolerant tasks as nonrealtime raytracing), some algorithms show very little performance degradation when changing from full port switching to segment switching, and the cost can be much lower. Another possibility is direct point-to-point connection with crossed cabling (MDI to MDI), conforming a hypercube or, for large networks, a torus-mesh; it is quite impractical to go over 16 or 32 nodes with a pure hypercube because of the number of interfaces in each node and the complexity of cabling and, on the software side, the routing. Even with *just* four interfaces in each node the optimal global routing tables are far from trivial if the nodes are not completely homogeneous. Using dynamic routing protocols inside the cluster to set the routes automatically introduces more traffic and complexity. Often, the lack of a switch in such a setup is considered a big gain as there is no added latency and no packets can be discarded under congestion; however, vendors are announcing switches with latencies as low as $150ns$, lowering this effect. To add even more choices, some operating systems provide support for bonding several physical interfaces into a single virtual one for higher throughput.[1]

---

[1]The Channel Bonding patches for Linux-based beowulf clusters are available from GSFC at `http://cesdis.gsfc.nasa.gov/beowulf/software`. Sun has software available for trunking multiple Fast Ethernet channels under Solaris with supported switches.

Front-end Setup

While not strictly necessary, most cluster setups include a front-end of some kind: some distinguished node where human users log in from the rest of the network, and from where they submit jobs to the rest of the cluster. On one hand, this simplified view makes things easier to users. Also, as will be discussed later, a front-end provides for ways to improve security, but makes administration much easier. It is more comfortable to see the cluster as a single system that controls a number of nodes than as just a lot of nodes, even if that is just a perception; there are no single-point dependencies and all nodes are equal.

In practice, most clusters also have one or several nodes which serve NFS to the rest. NFS is not scalable or fast, but it works; users will want an easy way for their non I/O-intensive jobs to work on the whole cluster with the same name space. Additionally, if there are external NFS user volumes, it is practical to have access to them from somewhere in the cluster for data sharing. As a result, for small to middle clusters which do not have extreme I/O demands, a common structure will be a single node serving NFS to the other nodes, connected both to the internal and external networks, and probably mounting external NFS volumes. In this context, the idea of a front-end comes on its own.

There is an additional advantage in having a front-end: users can compile there and test their software in exactly the same environment as the computing nodes. Users do not usually like the idea of leaving a long-running job just started at night only to come back the next day and find that it did not run at all because of some subtle incompatibility with their development system. For this reason, it is desirable to start installing the front-end with the same operating system – even the same release – libraries, whatever, to keep the environment as similar to the nodes as possible, with the addition of the required compilers, debuggers, and development tools for on-site testing. Any code that runs in the front-end should run in the other nodes and any exception should ideally be reflected in a use policy. Researchers want to spend their time doing something *in* the cluster, not *with* it.

Advanced IP routing capabilities are also useful in the front-end, as this will allow security improvements as well as giving selective access from outside to individual ports of nodes, load-balancing of individual services among available nodes, and intercluster connections. An additional router or intelligent switch could do this job, but it is rarely cost-effective unless very high speed networks are used.

Once the system itself is up and running, it is time to begin automating administration. Installing and removing software on a single machine is no great problem, but on dozens of nodes it can be. The same occurs when searching the logs for problems, starting or shutting down services, etc. Low-cost clusters are still a young creature for brave souls, where you are pretty much on your own; time to get some experience with *perl* or other complete scripting languages. As a reference, it is practical to start with tools like *global*[2] for running the same command on all nodes of a cluster or a selected subset, and tools for distributing commands based

[2] `http://www.vais.net/~efinch`

on the load of each machine or whatever metric you choose, such as *perfs*[3] or *dsh.*[4] Even trivial things like adding or deleting a user will require at least a small script. Low-cost clusters come at a price.

Node Setup

Once there is a clear view of the cluster purpose and topology, setting up the individual nodes should not pose any significative problem. However, commodity systems are not designed to be used as compute nodes and this will show up. How to install all of the nodes at a time? Getting them to network boot and do an automated remote installation would be well worth the while if it were at all possible, but often it is not. Provided that all of them will have the same configuration, the fastest way is usually to install a single node and then *clone* its hard disk by either copying its partition tables,[5] formatting and then copying the files, or directly low-level copying from device to device.

The same problems found during installation tend to appear later; instead of keeping a (potentially large) number of nodes, each with their own disk and configuration files, it would be easier to have them mount a single remote source of configuration files at boot. Also, how can one have access to the console of all nodes? In an environment of Sun, DEC or similar workstations, their serial console ports can be accessed through a terminal server if needed; but with commodity PCs there is no such possibility. There are keyboard/monitor selectors, some allowing for even 16 input sources, but this is obviously a hack and not a real solution, and does not scale even for a middle size cluster. The poor man's solution will still be hoping that the boot runs fine and then relying on the software console provided by the OS.

2.2.2 Directory Services inside the Cluster

A cluster is supposed to keep a consistent image across all its nodes. This means the same software or at least compatible software; it also means the same configuration – user information, network routes, etc. Unfortunately for us, there is not a single unified way to distribute such information across the cluster. Traditional approaches are NIS, which has little utility in a cluster apart from keeping a common user database, and NIS+, which is basically a nightmare unless all of the machines are running Solaris. NIS has no way of dynamically updating network routing information or any configuration changes to user-defined applications. It also has many other problems for general use which are, fortunately, not a problem in a restricted environment as a cluster. NIS+, a substantial improvement over NIS, is not so widely available, is a mess to administer, and still leaves much to be desired. There is currently a lot of work being done on LDAP, which is an interoperable

[3]`http://www.idiap.ch/%7egobry/perfs.html`

[4]`http://www.tu-chemnitz.de/~fachat/comp/dsh/index.html`

[5]While on systems using BSD-style disklabels it is enough to copy the first disk sectors, those using DOS-style partition tables can have extended partitions anywhere.

standard, has a reasonable performance, and is open enough to allow a lot of custom uses. However, there is still very little software available and it is not well tested. In the end, most clusters end up with either plain NIS for user authentication or the stone age but foolproof solution of copying the password file to each node. As for other configuration tables, there are different solutions. Network routes are not, in fact, good candidates for a directory for performance reasons; a possibility is to deploy dynamic routing daemons all across the cluster, but it is probably overkill; some SNMP management can help.[6]

2.2.3 DCE Integration

The OSF[7] Distributed Computing provides highly scalable directory services, security services, a distributed file system (DFS), clock synchronization (DTS), threads, and RPC. It is an open standard and there is even a sample implementation of the core services. The darker side of DCE is that it has never really become as mainstream as intended; it is not available on certain platforms and some of its services have already been surpassed by further developments. DCE threads are based on an early POSIX draft and there have been significant changes since then. Finally, DCE servers tend to be rather expensive and complex. Anyway, if DCE is available for the chosen software environment, it may still be a good idea: DFS is more secure, and easier to replicate and cache effectively than NFS; the security services are quite good and tested; and if RPC is to be used, DCE RPC has some important advantages over the traditional Sun ONC RPC.

The DFS features can be more useful with large campus-wide networks of workstations. DFS supports replicated servers for read-only data, which can be deployed following the network topology to improve performance, while also getting the DCE security benefits. For large conventional clusters, splitting the remote disk load across several servers can also be worthwhile; however, given the higher network speed and lower latencies, it is unlikely to improve performance at all unless the number of nodes is *really* large. DFS also provides the option of caching on the local filesystem, which is almost always a gain. Note that in order to use replication, some implementations require that the LFS filesystem must be used on the server. For networks using NFSv3 instead, some vendors provide local caching support with *cachefs*; although it is not so well suited for large networks, it is a clear performance improvement for big files, and does not impose restrictions on the supported local filesystems.

An additional DCE point are DFS administrative domains, or sets of machines configured for administration as a single unit as far as DCE is concerned.

In places where DCE is already in use outside the cluster, integrating the cluster into a cell is rather straightforward; however, it might be desirable to make the

[6]Note that this is an *active* solution, as the management workstation has to contact each node which from then on will have local information, instead of *passive* solutions like those based on directory services, which are consulted by the clients as needed. The performance and manageability differences can be large.

[7]Now The Open Group.

front-end a slave directory server so that the nodes can access the security services directly.

2.2.4 Global Clock Synchronization

For obvious reasons keeping an homogeneous notion of time in all the compute nodes is a need, and failing to do so tends to produce subtle and sometimes difficult to track errors. Whenever any kind of serialization is desired, a global time is needed; unfortunately, we do not always realize how many assumptions about serialization we make.

In order to implement a global time service, one possible choice is DTS (Distributed Time Service), part of DCE. However, whether DCE is used or not, it is probably better to use the Network Time Protocol (NTP) instead, which is widely employed on thousands of hosts across the Internet and provides support for a variety of time sources. Unless there are special needs for a strict UTC synchronization, using an external NTP host accessible through the net as a time source will be more than enough to get some external reference; this can then be used as a single source – or better duplicate, if some node has direct or tunneled access to other time servers – in the next stratum for synchronizing the cluster itself to a single reference. Ideally, a couple of nodes should act as time servers for redundancy and to compensate for possible clock skew; each should synchronize to several external time sources for similar reasons. Of course, a direct GPS receiver or other reliable source is also possible.

Provided that the room temperature is reasonably stable and the oscillators are reliable, getting a clock precision within a few milliseconds or better is normal. It should be enough for most tasks as long as one remembers that `gettimeofday()` and other calls can return higher accuracy in some architectures, and thus timestamps obtained that way cannot be trusted blindly. There is currently no way in a cluster of workstations to achieve a synchronization good enough to get a strict global timestamp ordering.[8]

2.2.5 Heterogeneous Clusters

Under the usual premise of keeping everything as homogeneous as possible among all nodes, an heterogeneous cluster might look undesirable. However, possible good reasons for this do exist, for example:

- Clusters deliberately heterogeneous in order to exploit the higher floating point performance of certain architectures and the low cost of other systems, or for research purposes. Nothing keeps you from including a vector supercomputer as a node.

[8]Clusters of high-end systems like the Origin2000 do get a reliable clock by providing support for an external "sync" input which is used by the hardware clock. In a simpler but related way, the NTP daemon in the clustered workstations could be set to receive these signals via serial or parallel ports, eliminating the variable latency of Ethernet.

- Networks of Workstations (NOWs). Existing workstations and other equipment can be part or the whole of a cluster, making use of otherwise idle hardware. Systems like *Condor* [13] or *Piranha* [12] use this approach.

An heterogeneous layout means automating administration work will obviously become more complex: filesystem layouts are converging but still far from coherent; software packaging is also different, and the POSIX attempt at standardizing has had little success; finally, administration commands are also different. For a medium to large heterogeneous cluster, a solution is to develop a per-architecture and per-OS set of wrappers with a common external view. In its simplest form, this can be just a system-dependent set of scripts accessible through `rsh` or `ssh` so the administrator can automate common tasks; in a more elaborate and efficient form, it can be a set of RPC exported procedures.

Ultimately, the greatest complexity is left up to the developers, who will face different APIs and conventions. While the endianness differences are the most typical example, in real life differences in word length are getting far more frequent and more difficult to solve; type-unsafe languages commonly used in these environments as C do not help much. On the other hand, it is surprising how such an environment helps cleaning the code.

2.2.6 Some Experiences with PoPC Clusters

As a simple example of cluster management, Figure 2.1 shows the *borg*,[9] a Linux cluster at the LFCIA laboratory (Department of Computer Science, University of A Coruña). The borg is currently composed of 24 nodes, one of which acts as a front-end. The nodes are based on the AMD K6 processor and have two Fast Ethernet interfaces, while the front-end is a dual processor PentiumII with an additional network interface attached to the departmental network. There is no conventional management workstation, and the front-end acts as a management gateway to external workstations.

The switches are 24-port 3Com SuperStack II 3300 units stacked in groups of two with a 1Gbit/s link. They are manageable directly from a serial console or, once they have an IP address assigned by SNMP, from a telnet session or from an HTML client with Java support. From a management point of view, the switches are crucial devices, especially with Ethernet, where they can be integrated with external networks. Switches are a suitable point for monitoring as only they can know the real status of physical links, and having them probe the nodes avoids extra traffic from a management workstation. In our case, switches implement RMON monitoring: Instead of directly managing the individual nodes from the front-end or an external workstation, most of the work is done by the switch itself, which is then queried by SNMP from the workstation, saving network traffic and complexity (Figure 2.2). Direct SNMP management of the nodes is also possible.

---

[9]Partially funded by Xunta de Galicia (`XUGA10504B96`) and the Secretaría Xeral de Investigación e Desenvolvemento (DOG 30.06.98).

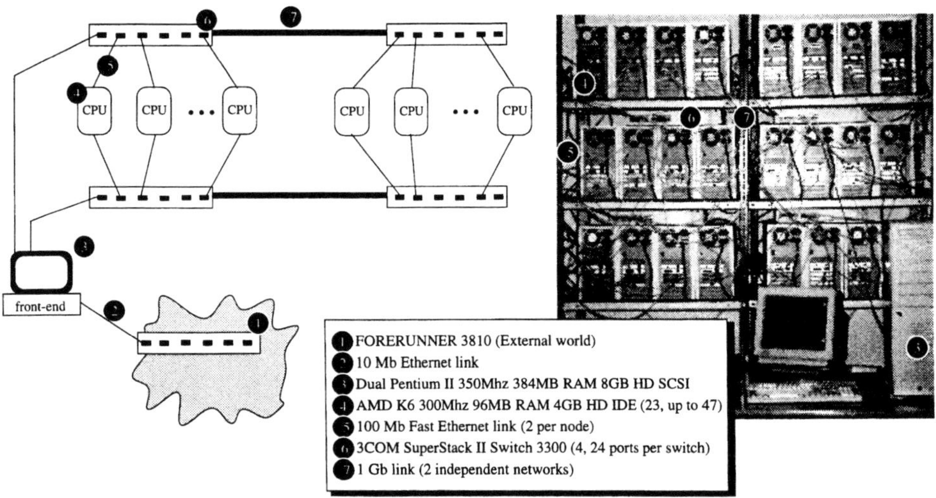

Figure 2.1 *borg*, the Linux cluster at LFCIA (University of A Coruña).

The front-end is monitoring the nodes with *mon*,[10] keeping track of anomalies and paging an operator if needed. Alerts are also forwarded to an Informix database in an external workstation running Solaris for later review or statistical analysis.

While simple and not expensive, this solution is giving good manageability, keeping the response times low and providing more than enough information when needed.

2.3 Security

2.3.1 Security Policies

No matter how secure a system is, either a security and use policy is agreed with the users and well established or they will subvert it. It is a fact that end users have to play an active role in keeping a secure environment; this means they must know the real need for security, the reasons behind the security measures taken, and the way to use them properly. Of course this means finding a suitable point where the system is reasonably secure but people do not get too annoyed; making them type half a dozen passwords at every login might improve security but is obviously not reasonable. There is a certain tradeoff between usability and security.

Getting the users motivated to embrace a common security idea and to understand that security is something good for them – not for an abstract entity as *the system* – means they will be a security guarantee instead of a risk.

[10] `http://www.kernel.org/software/mon`

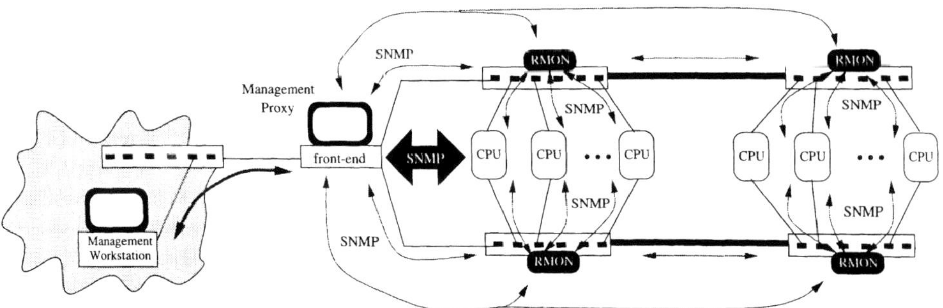

Figure 2.2 Monitoring the *borg*.

2.3.2 Finding the Weakest Point in NOWs and COWs

In an implicitly networked environment as is a cluster, and especially in somewhat heterogeneous ones, isolating services from each other is almost impossible. While we all realize how potentially dangerous some services are, it is sometimes difficult to track how these are related with other seemingly innocent ones. Obviously, allowing *rsh* access from the outside to each node just by matching usernames and hosts with each user's `.rhosts` file is a bad idea, as a security incident in a single node compromises the security of all the systems who share that user's home; this is clear. But a completely unrelated service, such as mail, can be abused in a similar way – just change that user's `.forward` file to do the mail delivery via a pipe to an "interesting" executable or script, and the same effect is reached. As the user's home might be exported from an external NFS server and shared by several workstations and the whole cluster, a single intrusion in any of those systems implies a security compromise for all of them, even if the server and the cluster were initially secure. This is probably not so obvious and illustrates the problem of services intersection (Figure 2.3). A service is not safe unless all of the services it depends on are at least equally safe, and finding these dependencies is not immediate.

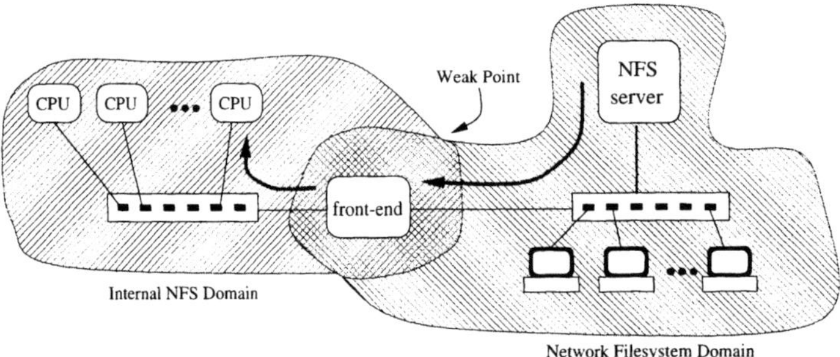

Figure 2.3 Weak point due to the intersection of services.

Additionally, for each individual service, its stack nature makes it more manageable and easier to implement and understand, but we have to consider how each layer may be doing insecure work on behalf of us.

2.3.3 A Little Help from a Front-end

Common sense says that keeping a single machine secure is easier than keeping dozens of them. However, in a homogeneous cluster where all the nodes are equally configured and keep a consistent image, should they all not be equally secure as well? If this were true, connecting all the nodes directly to the external network should mean no security problem at all. There are two main problems with this approach: first, the human factor; we tend to make temporary changes and forget to restore them, thus destroying the consistency. And secondly, there is a formal objection to that idea: systems tend to have "information leaks" and the sum of the leaks from all nodes is much higher than the leaks from a single front-end hiding the other nodes behind. These "leaks" are inherent to the heterogeneity of computer systems; interfaces are not as strict as they should be and sometimes have optional characteristics in which correct behaviour is weakly defined. Consequently, an outside observer can get a lot of information not intended to be public; and worse, if any system software happens to have any bug (like, for instance, the TCP stack) all the nodes could be attacked directly from the outside. The operating system and its version can often be easily guessed just with IP access, even with just harmless services running, and almost all operating systems have had serious security problems in their IP stack in the recent history.

These reasons are enough to justify a front-end from a security viewpoint in most cases. Also, clusters are often used from external workstations in other networks; this way a front-end can also serve as a simple firewall.

2.3.4 Security versus Performance Tradeoffs

Once again, security is a matter of tradeoffs: more usability versus more security, and better performance versus more security. The lack of security in certain cluster setups is often justified by a need for the highest possible performance. This is very seldom true. Most security measures have no impact on performance and proper planning can avoid that impact; very often, they are a sign of bad designing.

There are, however, certain cases where security does have an impact on performance; this is usually the case with strong ciphers. Secure channels are becoming common and the overhead of cryptography can severily damage performance. Table 2.1 shows the sustained bandwidth across an unencrypted TCP stream and encrypted *ssh* streams between AMD K6/300 nodes through a Fast Ethernet channel. Note that the unencrypted stream is limited by the Ethernet bandwidth. There are usually no barriers between nodes and the whole cluster is considered a single security domain, so these encrypted channels only make real sense from the outside network to the front-end. For the same reason, the authentication delay with secure channels is usually not worth it as long as it affects external connections only.

Table 2.1 Unencrypted Versus Encrypted Sustained Throughput

Unencrypted stream	>7.5MB/s
Blowfish encrypted stream	2.75 MB/s
Idea encrypted stream	1.8 MB/s
3DES encrypted stream	0.75 MB/s

2.3.5 Clusters of Clusters

Building clusters of clusters is common practice for large-scale testing. Special care must be taken on the security implications when this is done: usually, the applications being tested were designed and developed to run inside a safe cluster, and their security does not tend to be weak. As a result, the simplest approach for making these *metaclusters* secure is building secure tunnels between the clusters, usually from front-end to front-end (Figure 2.4). For remote systems where the cluster-to-cluster network performance is far slower than inside each individual cluster, this is unlikely to become a performance bottleneck; otherwise, it is just another security versus performance tradeoff.

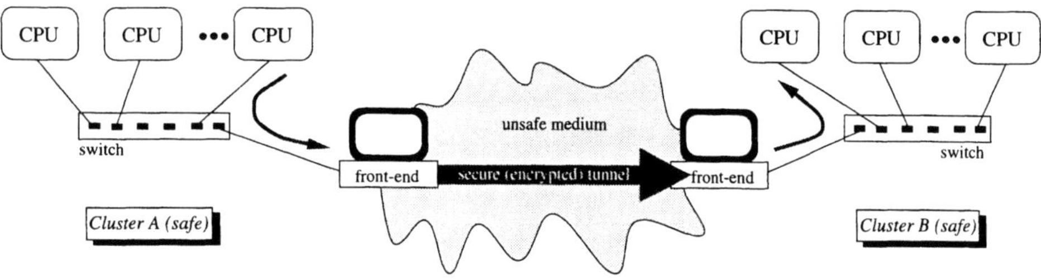

Figure 2.4 Intercluster communication using a secure tunnel.

When a network is assumed to be unsafe and the security requirements are high, a dedicated tunnel front-end or keeping the usual front-end free for just the tunneling may be desirable to minimize the throughput penalty. However, even then the latency will be higher due to an increased number of per-packet processing and the cryptography algorithms used. Another additional performance tradeoff: Stronger ciphers tend to mean slower ones.

On the other hand, for nearby clusters in the same backbone, letting the switches do the work is usually enough. As long as the intermediate backbone switches can be trusted (they often can) and have the necessary software and resources, they can setup a VLAN joining the clusters, achieving greater bandwidth and lower latency than routing at the IP level via the front-ends (Figure 2.5). Routing to the rest of the network is still done through the front-ends. The decrease in latency may be significant, as data flow avoids two complete trips through the IP stack of the front-ends, and less resources are used in them. Note, however, that adding resources to the routers (if needed for this setup) is usually far more expensive than to the front-ends, or even more costly than adding complete dedicated nodes for this task.

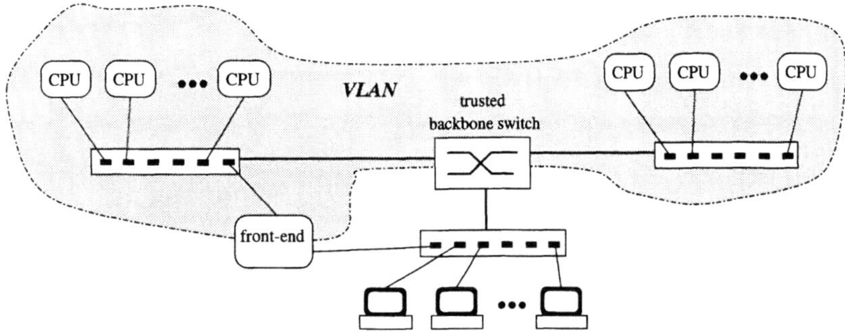

Figure 2.5 VLAN using a trusted backbone switch.

2.4 System Monitoring

Once the cluster is up and running in a production or stable development environment, it is vital to stay informed of any incidents that may cause unplanned downtime or intermittent problems. Given the distributed nature of clusters, some problems that are trivially found in a single system may be hidden for a long time before they are detected.

2.4.1 Unsuitability of General Purpose Monitoring Tools

Most available monitoring tools are designed for the management of middle or large networks and focused towards the needs of the corporations and institutions that are their main customers. However, no matter how powerful these tools are, their main purpose is *network* monitoring, as computer systems are generally too heterogeneous to be subject to nontrivial centralized monitoring. This obviously is not the case with clusters. The network is just a system component, even if a critical one, but not the sole subject of monitoring in itself.

Also, unlike in general purpose networks, in most cluster setups it is possible – and worthy – to install custom agents in the nodes. It is desirable to track their usage, load, network traffic statistics, and whatever other metrics are considered locally relevant in order to tune the operating system, find I/O bottlenecks, foresee possible problems, or balance future system purchases. As a result, clusters are usually monitored with somewhat custom systems, which evolve through time and eventually become established in-house solutions.

2.4.2 Subjects of Monitoring

Physical Environment

While at least some environmental monitoring facilities are assumed for server systems, most workstations and individual PCs do not have these capabilities yet. This poses a small problem for Beowulf-class clusters and similar systems, which play the role of servers but are made mostly of PCs or fast, cheap workstations. Most clusters are physically contiguous and thus monitoring most environmental variables at a single node is enough; there should be at least a measuring point in the cluster. Among all environmental variables, those more subject to change with time, when not tightly conditioned, are temperature and humidity, supply voltages, and the functional status of moving parts, namely fans. These are also the best candidates for monitoring for the same reasons. While temperature and humidity are easily kept within sane values in most climates (almost all equipment tolerates a 20–80 percent humidity range or more), correct power is sometimes not, and often produces elusive errors.[11]

The importance of monitoring the physical environment is often underestimated, as keeping some environmental variables stable within reasonable values greatly helps keeping the MTBF high. While the cost of replacing physical equipment is not outrageous and older components are not even worth repairing as prices keep falling, the consequent unplanned downtime does have a potentially high cost in human resources.

Logical Services

If physical monitoring is mostly preventive, the monitoring of logical services is aimed at finding current problems when they are already impacting the system. Thus, a low delay until the problem is detected and isolated must be a priority.

Logical services range from lower level, like raw network access and running processor, to higher level, like RPC and NFS services running, correct routing, etc. Each site ought to develop its own chart of desired services and, while doing so, other services can also be shut down to save resources and improve security.

All monitoring tools provide some way of defining customized scripts for testing individual services. While some basic services are simple (*ping* responding, *echo* server working), great care must be taken when automating these scripts. For instance, connecting to the telnet port of a server and receiving the "login" prompt is not enough to ensure that users can log in; bad NFS mounts could cause their login scripts to sleep forever. Connecting to the SMTP port and getting the MTA banner is not enough to know whether the mail service is working or not: an unwritable mail spool could prevent any mail from being delivered but the MTA would still accept connections.

[11]Even if the external supply is good, the power source in each system may output wrong values; an unstability problem with a local SMP PentiumPro machine was tracked to a marginal power supply, whose 3.3VDC output was maxed by the processors and cards in the system and could barely sustain 3V.

It is important to note that no monitoring system can find every possible error or misconfiguration, as it can be trivially demonstrated that it is impossible to do so. However, they can detect most problems, and usually they do find most before they impact users.

Performance Meters

Unlike other monitors, performance meters tend to be completely application-specific, for the simple reason that performance itself is not an absolute term and much less well defined.

Depending on the ultimate measure purpose [6], the optimal method of data aquisition will be different. For compute-intensive tasks running on a single node or when the effect of communications is not important, explicit instrumenting by code profiling is simple and effective, although cache pollution caused by the profiling code may distort the results if the time sample is not long enough.[12] When trying to profile network delays, implicit spying by a third in the network is the optimal solution if it is possible at all, as network topologies may avoid it. As a cheap and efficient solution for switched Ethernet systems, it is possible to plug each endpoint to a small hub together with a card in the measuring system, and then the hub to the switch; a "spy" node can then profile the traffic from each hub.

Finally, active or passive probing is commonly used by load-balancing systems as a low weight way of getting an approximation to the remote node load for job distributing purposes.

Performance monitors are commonly used as microbenchmarks in order to profile and optimize applications. Special care must be taken when tracing events that spawn several nodes, as it is very difficult to guarantee a good enough clusterwide synchronization (see *Global Clock Synchronization* earlier in this chapter).

2.4.3 Self Diagnosis and Automatic Corrective Procedures

All monitors try to address the need to know the state of a system in order to take corrective measures. The next logical step would be making the system take these decisions itself, and in some cases it is possible and even common use. While the system is obviously not going to do code analysis for us based on performance monitors, it is simple to make it take automatic preventive measures when the temperature is too high or a fan has stopped spinning. However, the system does not know facts, only symptoms, and lacks common sense. Cases where a simple symptom can be associated to a corrective action are rare in practice, so most actions end up being "page the administrator" which is far from optimal, both for the system uptime and for the administrator.

[12]This is a common problem in benchmarking. Many processors allow disabling its caches temporarily, but even then other caches and the TLB will be polluted. Even if they were not, for very short samples, the profiling code would alter the instruction sequence in the processor, possibly changing the delays between instructions because of different dependencies. In general, software-only solutions are not adequate for such a high resolution due to their intrusiveness.

In order to take some reasonable decisions, the system should know what sets of symptoms lead to suspect of what failures, and the appropriate corrective procedures to take. For any nontrivial service the graph of dependencies will be quite complex, and this kind of reasoning almost asks for an expert system. While it is questionable whether that kind of complexity is worth the human work and system downtime it saves, any monitor performing automatic corrections should be at least based on a rule-based system and not rely on direct alert-action relations.

2.5 System Tuning

2.5.1 Developing Custom Models for Bottleneck Detection

Obvious as it may seem, no tuning can be done without defined goals. Tuning a system can be seen as minimizing a cost function, so we must know precisely what this cost means for us. Higher throughput for a job may not be worthwhile if it increases network or server load in such a way that adversely impacts others. In general, no performance gain comes for free, and often that means losing or decreasing safety, generality, or interoperability.

2.5.2 Focusing on Throughput or Focusing on Latency

Traditionally, most UNIX systems have been tuned for high throughput rather than for low latency. Sometimes this is true even in the hardware design, as with Sun SBUS. While this may have been adequate for general timesharing systems, clusters are frequently used as a large, single user system, where the main bottleneck is latency. Very often each node runs a single active process or just a few. This drastically changes the way in which systems are balanced.

Network latency tends to be especially critical for most applications. However, once the hardware is chosen and bought, there is not too much that can be done to reduce it. Lightweight protocols do help somewhat, but with the current highly-optimized IP stacks there is no longer a huge difference in most hardware.

It is important to see this all from a higher level of abstraction. While on conventional systems the focus is on throughput, nodes in high performance clusters are usually best tuned for low latency; but this is just a way for achieving the same goal: high global throughput. Similarly, as modern processors need very low latency caches to keep its functional units busy and get a good overall speed, each node can be considered as just a component of the whole cluster, and its tuning aimed at global – not local – performance.

2.5.3 I/O Implications

Using the above approach, I/O subsystems as used in conventional servers are not always a good choice for cluster nodes. Although this will be very dependent on the exact job mix, for a typical setup where each node runs at most one disk I/O intensive process, sophisticated high-end I/O hardware is not worth installing.

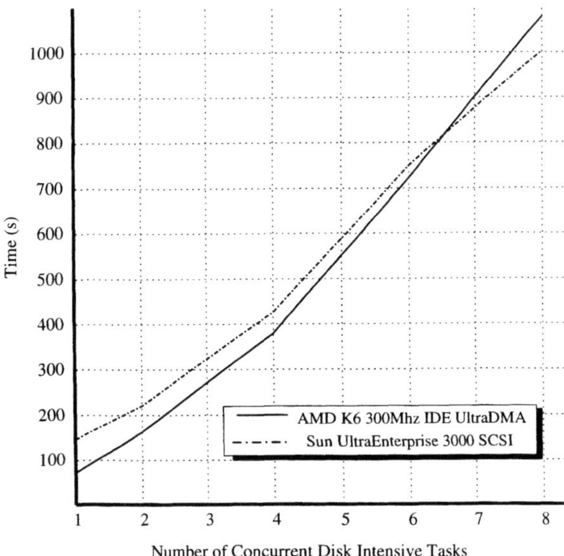

Figure 2.6 Behavior of two systems in a disk intensive setting.

Commodity off-the-shelf IDE disk drives are cheaper and faster and even have the advantage of a lower latency than most higher-end SCSI subsystems [2]. While they obviously do not behave as well under a high load, it is not always a problem, and the money saved may mean more additional nodes.

As there is usually a common shared space from a server, a robust, faster and probably more expensive disk subsystem will be better suited there for the large number of concurrent accesses. Figure 2.6 shows the elapsed time for varying numbers of concurrent instances of a certain disk-intensive job [13] on completely different I/O architectures and systems (a Sun UltraEnterprise 3000 with its internal striped disks and a single IDE UltraDMA drive on a clone AMD K6). Coincidentally, it also shows a $40000 machine from 1996 beaten by a $700 system from 1998 in filesystem throughput for a low number of concurrent processes, but the older system still wins under heavy load.

As usual, it is a good practice to consider the cluster as a system by itself. The same as many conventional servers implement software RAID across their disks, nothing keeps us from distributing data across nodes in a similar way in order to improve throughput; or even, at the expense of some write speed, perform distributed data replication, or parity. Note that the difference between raw disk and filesystem throughput becomes more evident as systems are scaled up.

[13]This job tried to closely resemble the behavior of certain workloads typical in the server used; it was I/O bound and limited both by raw throughput and by the filesystem. While it may or may not apply to other sites, it is still significant.

2.5.4 Caching Strategies

At a first glance, there is only one important difference between conventional multiprocessors and clusters: the availability of shared memory. However, it can be emulated and, with some hardware, even relatively efficiently (Figure 2.7). The only factor that cannot be hidden is the completely different memory hierarchy. This is very true of hardware evolution and is worth some thought. Conventional memory hierarchies also reflect more traditional software architectures. Nowadays, getting a data block from the network can provide both lower latency and higher throughput than from the local disk (Figure 2.8). The problem, then, is how to provide enough data flow from the other end to saturate the network; the obvious solution is to aggregate flow issued from several nodes.

The main point here is that the usual data caching strategies may often have to be inverted; the local disk is just a slower, persistent device for larger term storage, while faster rates can be obtained from concurrent access to other nodes. This concurrent access has a price: wasting other nodes resources. Globally, it is often a win, but each application is different and must be measured. In the extreme case of a purely sequential task, we are introducing some data parallelism just with this distributed access, improving global throughput; in the opposite, a saturated cluster with overloaded nodes may perform worse: each individual situation must be considered.

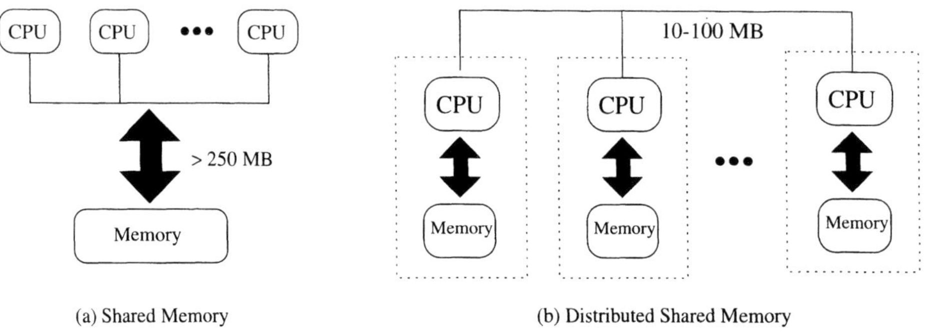

Figure 2.7 Shared versus distributed memory.

2.5.5 Fine-tuning the OS

It is very tempting to start tuning the operating system for some additional performance too soon. In practice, getting big improvements just by tuning the system is unrealistic most times, but certain changes do help, as outlined here.

- Virtual memory (VM) subsystem tuning. Optimizations depend on the application – some trivially parallel cryptography even fits in the caches – but

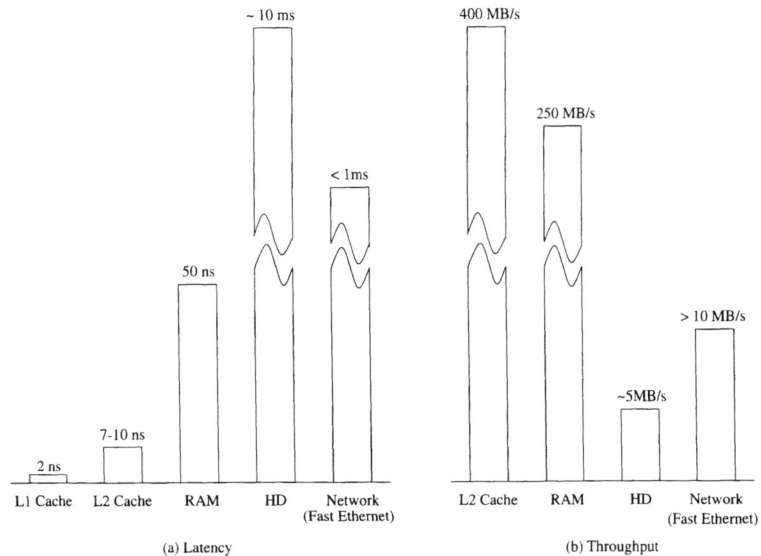

Figure 2.8 (a) Typical latency and (b) throughput for a memory hierarchy.

large jobs often benefit from some VM tuning. Highly tuned code will fit the available memory, so it will be wise to keep the system from paging until a very high watermark has been reached. Also, if the application behavior is well known, increasing page clustering when swapping in and out helps for processes working on large memory areas.

Sadly, tuning the VM subsystem has been traditional for large systems as traditional Fortran code uses to overcommit memory in a huge way. Performing tuning to overcome software limitations should be avoided, but is not always possible.

- Networking. When the application is communication-limited, sometimes big gains are possible. The IP suite is almost always used (directly, or as a layer under PVM or MPI) and allows for great customization; it is also quite fragile in the sense that wrong values can completely defeat the purpose of its algorithms and make performance far worse. For bulk data transfers, increasing the TCP and UDP receive buffers is almost a need in high speed networks; enabling large windows and window scaling is also helpful, especially when there is a tunneled access to another cluster. Large TCP window sizes and window scaling helps, although they are usually the default nowadays. Note that buggy implementations of the Nagle algorithm are fairly common, and disabling it sometimes does make a latency difference regardless of whether `TCP_NODELAY` is set or not.

In the very short range networks typical inside clusters, it is also desirable to limit the retransmission timeouts; switches tend to have large buffers and can generate important delays under heavy congestion, in general it is benefical to reduce the defaults. Systems like Solaris have raised the default initial and maximum timeouts in the latest versions, probably for better webserver performance on the Internet.

In any case, no matter how fine-tuned IP is, direct user-level protocols like U-Net [11] are likely to provide lower delay and less processor utilization.

Long timeslices have been traditionally stressed as important for high throughput. With current processors and relatively lightweight schedulers, it is rather unimportant nowadays and current tendency is for shorter quantums; the difference in throughput is usually negligible. However, for completely noninteractive systems like cluster nodes, long timeslices do not hurt, either.

Note that the front-end is a special case. Under most setups it serves NFS volumes to the cluster and will benefit from a somewhat different tuning, favoring large buffers.

Acknowledgments

This survey has been funded by *Xunta de Galicia* (`XUGA10504B96`) and the *Secretaría Xeral de Investigación e Desenvolvemento* (DOG 30.06.98).

2.6 Bibliography

[1] Donald J. Becker, Thomas Sterling, Daniel Savarese, John E. Dorband, Udaya A. Ranawak, and Charles V. Packer. Beowulf: A Parallel Workstation For Scientific Computation. In *Proceedings of the International Conference on Parallel Processing*, vol.1, pages 11-14, Boca Raton, FL, August 1996.

[2] Thomas Sterling, Donald J. Becker, Daniel Savarese, Michael R. Berry, and Chance Res. Achieving a Balanced Low-Cost Architecture for Mass Storage Management through Multiple Fast Ethernet Channels on the Beowulf Parallel Workstation. In *Proceedings of the 10th International Parallel Processing Symposium*, IEEE Computer Society Press, Honolulu, HI, April 1996.

[3] Samuel A. Fineberg and Kevin T. Pedretti. Analysis of 100Mb/s Ethernet for the Whitney Commodity Computing Testbed. *NAS Technical Report NAS-97-025*, October 1997.

[4] Allan Leinwand and Karen Fang. *Network Management – A Practical Perspective.* Addison Wesley, Reading, MA, 1993.

[5] William Stallings. *SNMP, SNMPv2 and RMON - Practical Network Management.* Addison Wesley, Reading, MA, 1996

[6] Raj Jain. *The Art of Computer Systems Performance Analysis.* John Wiley, NYC, 1991.

[7] Craig Partridge. *Gigabit Networking.* Addison Wesley, Reading, MA, 1994.

[8] David L. Mills. Measured performance of the Network Time Protocol in the Internet system. *Network Working Group Report RFC-1128.* University of Delaware, October 1989.

[9] David L. Mills. Network Time Protocol (Version 3) Specification, Implementation and Analysis. *Network Working Group Report RFC-1305.* University of Delaware, March 1992.

[10] Richard W. Stevens. *TCP/IP Illustrated.* Addison Wesley, Reading, MA, 1996.

[11] Thorsten von Eicken, Anindya Basu, Vineet Buch, and Werner Vogels. U-Net: A User-Level Network Interface for Parallel and Distributed Computing. In *Proceedings of the 15th ACM Symposium on Operating Systems Principles (SOSP)*, vol. 29(5), pages 303-316, Copper Mountain, CO, December 1995.

[12] David Gelernter and David Kaminsky. Supercomputing Out of Recycled Garbage: Preliminary Experience with Piranha. *Technical Report TR-883*, Yale University, Department of Computer Science, New Haven, CT, December 1991.

[13] Michael J. Litzkow, Miron Livny, and Matt W. Mutka. Condor : A Hunter of Idle Workstations. In *Proceedings of the 8th International Conference on Distributed Computing Systems*, pages 104-111, IEEE Computer Society Press, June 1988.

[14] Daniel A. Menasce, Virgilio A. F. Almeida, and Larry W. Dowdy. *Capacity Planning and Performance Modeling: From Mainframes to Client-Server Systems.* Prentice-Hall, Englewood Cliffs, NJ, 1994.

Chapter 3

Constructing Scalable Services

ORLY KREMIEN, MICHAEL KEMELMAKHER, IRIT ESHED AND MICHAEL KAPELEVICH

Department of Computer Sciences
Bar-Ilan University
Ramat-Gan, Israel

Email: *orly,kemelma,eshedi,kapelvch@macs.biu.ac.il*

3.1 Introduction

Complex systems provide access to a variety of resources. There are standard resources as well as nomadic ones. Local access suffices for some whereas others are far off, requiring distant access. Furthermore, there are multiple instances accessible for each resource type greatly differing in characteristics.

A complex network system may be viewed as a collection of services. There are workstations[1] which seek services and those available, which provide services. Much of the computing power is frequently idle. Resource sharing in complex network systems aims at achieving maximal system performance by utilizing the available system resources efficiently. The goal is to efficiently match workstations short of a service to those experiencing a surplus of the same service. The relationship between such a pair is termed mutual interest. This paradigm is used to propose a scalable and adaptive resource sharing service. Resource sharing is used as an illustrative example of the issues raised when building a scalable service.

There is a necessity to coordinate concurrent access to system resources. Without any mechanism for cooperation among nodes, it is likely that resources on one node will become congested while other nodes are idle, resulting in poor overall system performance. Resource sharing in complex network systems aims at achieving maximal system performance by efficiently utilizing the system resources available. This calls for cooperation and negotiation in order to better support resource sharing, i.e., whether to initiate processing of a resource request locally or locate a remote node from a large set of available ones and negotiate for its remote access.

[1]In this chapter the terms node, workstation, and processor are used interchangeably.

To complicate things even more, many algorithms developed for a distributed system environment should be scalable. A major benefit of a distributed system is that its size may flexibly grow as time passes [1], [2]. This growth is advantageous since it allows more users to benefit from more resources [12]. Ideally, as the system size grows, its performance deteriorates linearly [1]. No existing system has achieved this utopia, but a good design should approach it. In a well designed distributed system there should be no single point of failure. Thus, central control, which is simpler to design but creates a single point of failure and a potential risk of system congestion, should be avoided. In the absence of a central control the mechanism for orchestrating this matching of nodes sharing a common interest is nontrivial.

The remainder of this chapter is organized as follows. Section 3.2 describes the environment and defines the system model and the required properties of a resource sharing algorithm. Resource sharing in a complex network environment is discussed in Section 3.3, followed by methods for analyzing such algorithms. Section 3.4 describes the basic algorithm preserving mutual interests which is used in our study for resource sharing. It also shows how a symmetric algorithm is extended to account for resource proximity. The software development process is depicted by, first, describing algorithm assessment in simulation. We then consider, in Section 3.5, prototype design to complement simulation. PVM is used for prototype implementation followed by enhancements required to further improve locality in a complex network environment. Finally, conclusions derived from this study and directions recommended for future research are presented in Section 3.6.

3.2 Environment

Complex network systems consist of a collection of wide and local area networks differing in characteristics like speed, reliability and many others. All these networks are interconnected to form a single global complex network system. Nodes vary considerably in attributes, some of which are static (resources attached to nodes), whereas others are dynamic (processing loads). Similarly, communication channels connecting nodes vary greatly by static attributes like bandwidth and dynamic ones like channel load. There are wired connections as well as wireless ones. Some of the latter may use satellite communication and may also be mobile.

3.2.1 Faults, Delays, and Mobility

Mobility yields frequent changes in the environment of a nomadic host. Consequently, requests for resource access should respond to changes in system configuration caused by host movement. Network adaptation is crucial due to the high variability in connectivity conditions. A distinguishing feature of complex network systems is the inability to maintain consistent global state information at distributed points of control. A complex network system can thus be viewed as a collection of distributed decision makers taking decisions to achieve common goals under uncertain local and partial views of the system state. Network latencies further complicate these systems.

Scalable solutions are used to effectively utilize the aggregate processing power available and hide latencies. Scalability is discussed next.

3.2.2 Scalability Definition and Measurement

Scale is recognized as a primary scalability factor. Proximity, measured by communication delays, is also recognized as a dominant factor in algorithm design. In general, algorithms and techniques that work at small scale degenerate in non-obvious ways at large scale. This difficulty in scaling up is caused by the fact that many commonly used mechanisms, such as centralized servers, broadcast and multicast (which are system size dependent) lead to intolerable overheads or congestion when used in systems beyond a certain size. A topology dependent scheme or an algorithm which is system-size dependent are not scalable[1] .

The performance of a parallel algorithm is influenced by communications delays, system architecture, and system size. Thus, an algorithm may perform well given a certain number of processors and architecture, but its performance degrades as either changes. Ideally, the performance should increase linearly with the system size, but in reality performance degrades with the growth of the system.

Scalability may be defined as "the system's ability to increase speedup as the number of processors increase" [6]. The question which arises is what should the relation be between the rate of increase in the system size and the rate of increase in the problem size, in order for the performance to remain fixed?

In the following discussion, speedup measures the possible benefits of a parallel performance over a sequential performance. Efficiency is defined to be the speedup divided by the number of processors. A rigorous analysis of the scalability metric is required to identify its dominant factors and measure it in practice. A number of works propose different approaches to evaluate scalability. Some of these metrics measure the ability of the system to multiply resources (e.g., processing elements or memory) to solve problems of proportionally increasing size while preserving efficiency. Alternatively, the speedup gained when solving a problem of a certain size on a system which is scaled-up is measured. These works address the MPP parallel computing model environment. We review some of these works next.

Design Principles of Operating Systems for Large Scale Multicomputers

When designing a distributed system, one should aspire to allow for performance to grow linearly with the system size. No existing system has accomplished that goal, but well-designed systems approximate it[1]. What stands in the way of a real scalable system, is a use of resources that grows as more nodes are added to the system, while the resource itself remains with the same, constant, computational capability. An example of such a programming construct is message broadcast which interrupts more nodes as the system grows. The resource is bound to reach its maximal capacity, beyond which it is unable to satisfy the complete service demand. If the system indeed grows beyond this point, instability will result.

The demand for any resource should, then, be bounded by a constant which is independent of the system size (namely, the number of nodes composing the system). Distributed systems, in spite of their distributed nature, often contain centralized elements. Such elements, like file servers, should be avoided, thus assuring there are no bottlenecks, which might become congested as the system grows. This decentralization also assures that there is no single point of failure.

A relation of a server and a client (customer) is possible, and is commonly used in distributed systems. Yet, it is confined to a group of only two nodes, and is temporary and short-lived by nature. As soon as the specific request is fulfilled, the collaboration between the two nodes is broken, until another mutual interest causes them to reestablish sharing. In other words, "any interaction that involves more than one node is limited to the duration of a single system operation." Thus, a node may cooperate with all other nodes, but only with a few of them at once. The node is able to make decisions and create a client-server relationship without possessing global information about the state of the system as a whole. Rather, the single node makes use of nonlocal information about a bounded subset of the system. This nonlocal information might not only be partial but also inaccurate. This is due to the fact that there are communication and node delays and failures. The result is non-negligible delays. To reduce overhead we also try to minimize the amount of message exchange, thus reducing the rate at which information is updated.

In order to avoid system congestion, one should assure that service demand will be spread as evenly as possible throughout the system. Thus, a node should regularly select candidates for service providers at random, rather than filing requests to a fixed set of nodes.

Isoefficiency and Isospeed

It is easy to determine which of several sequential algorithms is the best. It is simply the algorithm yielding the fastest performance. Determining that one parallel algorithm is better than an alternative parallel algorithm is not that trivial. Measurements of scalability are developed in order to predict the behavior of large-scale systems when solving large size problems, based on analyzing the performance of smaller systems and problem sizes.

Isoefficiency [6] is defined to be the function which determines the extent at which the size of the problem can grow as the number of processors (that is, the system size) is increased, to keep the performance constant. A major disadvantage of the isoefficiency metric is its use of efficiency measurements and speedup. These measurements are indications for parallel processing improvement over sequential processing, rather than means for comparing the behavior of different parallel systems.

Scalability is an inherit property of algorithms, architectures, and their combination[15]. It can thus be stated that "an algorithm machine combination is scalable if the achieved average speed of the algorithm on a given machine can remain constant with increasing numbers of processors, provided the system (problem) size can be increased with the system size" [15]; this definition may be referred to as the isospeed constraint. If W is the amount of work for an algorithm when N processors are used, and W' is the amount of work corresponding to N' processors for the same average speed, for the same algorithm ($N \leq N'$), then the scalability from system size N to system size N' of the algorithm-machine combination is Ψ(N,N'). Assuming there are no communication delays, and that the work may be replicated on each processor, $W' = (N' \cdot W)/N$ and $\Psi(N, N') = 1$. That is, assuming no communication delays and a constant average speed, the ratio between the amount of work and the number of processors is constant. Under such ideal conditions the scalability is 1, meaning the system may grow without bound while performing efficiently. In reality, this assumption does not hold. When the system grows the cost of intercommunication may grow in a nonlinear manner. As a result, $W' > (N' \cdot W)/N$ and $\Psi(N, N') < 1$ [18].

In our study we adopt and customize the approach presented by isospeed[15] to suit the specifications of complex network systems composed of multiple interconnected smaller computer networks (i.e. Internet). Scalability (S) of a given system is measured as a continuous number in the range 0..1 indicating the extent the system manages to effectively utilize the aggregate processing power available and hide system characteristics.

Proximity abstracts resource latency (delay). A network system may experience periods of congested resources resulting in lengthy delays. Delays can also result from some resources of the system being enlarged while others remain unchanged. Whenever such changes take place, speed ratios (e.g., cpu versus communication) in the system change, directly affecting application performance. Our goal is to devise algorithms which exhibit minimum dependence on these physical characteristics and such speed ratio changes.

Assume a system comprises N hosts and E network connections. Let RT be the response time of the system for a problem of size W (W is the amount of execution code to be performed measured in the number of instructions). Let RT' be the system response time for the problem of an increased size W' being solved on the N'-sized system (N' ≥ N). We define:

$$W' = W \cdot \frac{N'}{N}$$

Scalability is given by :

$$S = \begin{cases} \frac{RT'}{RT} & if \quad \frac{RT'}{RT} < 1 \\ 1 & otherwise \end{cases}$$

A value close to 0 corresponds to a system that is unable to scale-up gracefully, i.e., its performance degrades as a result of the increased system size. A value close to 1 means the system adapts to changes in resource multiplicity and problem size and performs resource allocation efficiently. Parameters influencing system performance should be identified and precisely evaluated.

Response time is a function of L and T. L is the latency associated with network delays and synchronization in the system. T is the time consumed by the processing elements of the system to solve the problem.

3.2.3 Weak Consistency

The environment described so far is characterized by a high degree of multiplicity (scale), variable fault rates (reliability), resources with reduced capacity (mobility), and variable interconnections resulting in different sorts of latencies. These characteristics make the environment complex to handle. On the other side of the coin lies another attribute of weak consistency which is permissible for resource access. Weak consistency allows inaccuracy as well as partiality. State information regarding other workstations in the system is held locally in a cache. Cache members include a few other nodes equipped with the resource in question.[2] This data structure held locally is termed a cache in an analogy to the virtual memory cache. Cached data can be used as a hint for decision making, enabling local decisions to be made. A hint is a piece of information that substantially improves performance if correct but has no semantically negative consequence if erroneous[16]. Such state information is less expensive to maintain. The use of partial system views reduces message traffic, as less nodes are involved in any negotiation. For maximal performance benefit, a hint should nearly always be correct. When weak consistency is permissible, decisions can be based on a hint.

Resource Sharing hit-ratio is defined as the ratio of successful (positively acknowledged) resource access requests to the total number of such requests. This should be maximized. A request-reply negotiation is preferred to permit rejection by the remote node in the case of incorrect (out of date) cache data, thereby preventing an incorrect action from proceeding. However, our aim is to minimize such cases since they imply fruitless message exchanges. Furthermore, the algorithm must limit negotiation with other nodes in order to limit the subnet traffic and interruption to other nodes.

Complex network systems present serious difficulties in security, heterogeneity, operability, and performance. In this chapter special concern is devoted to the last two. Our aim is to first ensure that the algorithm for adaptive resource sharing is feasible. It then must continue to be effective and stable as the system grows. Scalable solutions are required in order to effectively utilize the aggregate processing power available and hide latencies. Such solutions strive to conceal physical characteristics such as system size, network topology, faults, and different sorts of latencies and resource capacity constraints.

---

[2]If such information is not available locally, a name service could be consulted to obtain other node identifiers. The latter relate to the local subnetwork and also neighboring ones.

3.2.4 Assumptions Summary

For simplicity, we limit our discussion to a single service. Node i requires Ti time units to provide the required service (resource access). When node i is unable to provide this service we set Ti to infinity. The following assumptions are made throughout this chapter:

- Full logical interconnection is assumed so that a message sent by a node can reach any other node in the system. Delays in the system are finite, and failed nodes are detected in finite time (fail-stop failure model).
- Connection maintenance while mobile is assumed to be transparent to the application and is provided by the network layer responsible for routing decisions. Nodes have unique identifiers numbered sequentially [1, 2, ..., system size]. These identifiers are kept intact as nodes move and cross wireless connection boundaries.
- Non negligible delays are assumed for any message exchange.

An algorithm providing scalable resource access must meet the requirements specified next.

3.2.5 Model Definition and Requirements

We assume the availability of a distributed system which supports distributed programming (i.e., PVM [5]), allowing the application components to perform location-transparent communication via message-passing. Our model of the physical distributed system assumes multiple independent processing nodes interconnected by a communication network. Our model of the logical distributed system is that of multiple independent applications, which may comprise single or multiple software component processes running on the same physical system. Resource access requests arrive randomly at any node of the system. The purpose of resource sharing is to achieve efficient allocation of resources to running applications; to map and remap the logical system to the physical system or the applications to the nodes. A resource sharing algorithm should meet the following requirements:

Adaptability - The algorithm should respond quickly to changes in the system state and adapt its operations to new evolving conditions.

Generality - The algorithm should be general to serve a wide range of applications and distributed environments. It should not assume prior knowledge of the system characteristics (e.g., load and delay).

Minimum Overhead - The algorithm should respond to requests quickly, incurring minimal overhead on the system, e.g., processing, memory usage, network I/O.

Stability - Stability is the ability of the algorithm to prevent poor resource allocation.

Scalability - An algorithm should be minimally dependent on the system's physical characteristics.

Transparency - Resource management should be transparent to the application, implying that programs should not be rewritten in order to use the scheduling service.

Fault-Tolerance - A failure of one or a few nodes should have a minimal impact on the entire system.

Heterogeneity - A complex network environment has to support heterogeneous hardware and software environments. To limit the scope of this chapter, heterogeneity is only partially covered.

The design and development of distributed algorithms is complex due to the non-deterministic behavior of the underlying distributed systems. To allow proper testing of the design, we use simulation as the first stage of software development. This is done to test whether functional and performance goals are likely to be met. Advances in simulation technology and workstation performance have made program development on top of simulators (debugging, testing, and some tuning) fast enough for real applications [17]. Simulation provides such valuable features such as repeatability, nonintrusive data collection and debugging. A subsequent smooth transition to prototype implementation is performed by using the source code produced by simulation [7]. This chapter advocates the simulation approach and suggests that it should be adopted as a method for development of distributed software. Before describing these extensions, we examine different published algorithms for resource sharing and show how the requirements can be met.

3.3 Resource Sharing

3.3.1 Introduction

The problem of resource sharing was extensively studied by DS (Distributed Systems) i.e., [13] and DAI (Distributed Artificial Intelligence) [14] researchers, particularly in relation to the load sharing problem in such systems. Distributed systems require some mechanism for cooperation among the processors, attempting to assure that no processor is idle while there are tasks waiting for service. Similarly, a solution to the resource access problem attempts to ensure that there are no such resources idling while requests are queued at other nodes.

Load sharing algorithms provide an example of the cooperation mechanism required when using the mutual interest relation. A location policy determines the approach used for locating a remote resource. Information propagation, request acceptance, and process transfer policies are other components of such algorithms.

When incorrect information can be detected and recovered, decisions can be based on weakly consistent information which may be inaccurate at times [4],[9],[16]. State information can be used as a hint for decision making enabling local decisions. Such state information is less expensive to maintain. The use of partial system view reduces message traffic, as less nodes are involved in any negotiation. For the benefit of maximal performance a hint should nearly always be correct.

Adaptive algorithms adjust their behavior to the dynamic state of the system. Thus, they are able to better approach the full computational power of the system. But, they also carry a lot of overhead. Their behavior might become unpredictable when faced with inaccurate information. Therefore, the complexity of the algorithms should be kept as low as possible while still allowing for a significant performance improvement. Few such algorithms are subsequently described.

3.3.2 Previous study

In an early study by [4] the performance of location policies with different complexity levels is compared. The research was performed on load sharing algorithms. Three location policies were studied: random policy (which is not adaptive), threshold policy, and shortest policy.

Random selection, which is the simplest, yields significant performance improvements in comparison with the no cooperation case. Still, a lot of excessive overhead is required for the remote execution attempts, many of which may prove to be fruitless.

Threshold policy probes a limited number of nodes. It terminates the probing as soon as it finds a node with a queue length shorter than the threshold. Threshold results in a substantial further performance improvement.

Shortest policy probes several nodes and then selects the one having the shortest queue, from among those having queue lengths shorter than the threshold. By probing nodes before actually sending a task for remote execution, the amount of data, carried by the communication network, is decreased. However, there is no added value to looking for the best solution but rather an adequate one.

It may thus be concluded that advanced algorithms do not necessarily entail a dramatic improvement in performance. Many approaches suggested later are based on [4], which illustrates a great advantage because of its simplicity. Its main drawback lies in having to initiate negotiation with remote nodes upon request. This may result in lengthy delays. To avoid such a remote message exchange state, information regarding other nodes in the system should be maintained locally.

In many algorithms state information is held locally and updated periodically. A node often deletes information regarding resource holders which are still of interest. In order to better support similar and repeated resource access requests, cache entries of mutual interest should be retained as long as they are of interest. Such an algorithm is described next.

3.3.3 Flexible Load Sharing Algorithm

In the flexible load sharing algorithm (FLS) [9] a location policy similar to Threshold is used. In contrast to Threshold, FLS bases its decisions on local information which is possibly replicated at multiple nodes. For scalability, FLS divides a system into small subsets which may overlap. Each of these subsets forms a cache held at a node. Cache members are nodes of mutual interest which are first discovered by (pure) random selection. Biased random selection is used from then on in order to retain entries of mutual interest and select others to replace discarded entries. The cache actually defines a subset of nodes, within which the node seeks a partner. That way the search scope is constrained, no matter how large the system is as a whole. The algorithm supports mutual inclusion and exclusion, and is further rendered fail-safe by treating cached data as hints. It can be compared to unbiased random selection where new nodes to be included in the cache of a node are selected periodically and randomly, even if nodes sharing mutual interests existed in the current cache. In order to minimize state transfer activity, the choice is biased and nodes sharing mutual interests are retained. In this manner premature deletion is avoided.

In addition, it is important to note that FLS does not attempt to produce the best possible solution, but like Threshold, it offers instead an adequate one, at a fraction of the cost. However, it presents an added value to the algorithms discussed in [4] research: the necessary information for matching partners, sharing a mutual interest, is maintained and updated locally on a regular basis, rather than waiting for the need to perform the matching to actually arise in order to start gathering the relevant information. Cache entries of mutual interest are retained as long as they are of interest. Premature deletion is thus avoided. This policy shortens the time period that passes between issuing the request for matching and actually finding a partner having a mutual interest. The FLS algorithm can be extended to other matching problems in distributed systems, as will be shortly demonstrated. In [10] the FLS algorithm, which proved to be an efficient algorithm for load sharing, was adapted as a skeleton for the mutual interest problem.

3.3.4 Resource Location Study

Another interesting approach for locating resources is described in [11]. A local data structure which is efficiently maintained is described where state information is held for all other nodes, not only those currently of mutual interest. Again this study was in the area of load sharing. The motivation is to improve the probability that remote requests would be directed towards nodes that share a mutual interest, thus lowering the cost of the search for a mutual partner. A disadvantage of this scheme is its dependency on system size which violates scalability. In the next section we describe how to analyze resource sharing algorithms. We then propose how to enhance locality considering proximity and also in line with [11]. These two extensions are done within the FLS framework.

3.3.5 Algorithm Analysis

The required properties listed above are interdependent. For example, lengthy delays in processing and communication can affect the algorithm overhead significantly, result in instability, and indicate that the algorithm is not scalable. How should a resource sharing algorithm be designed and evaluated, especially when design requires that some characteristics are sacrificed in favor of others? How can we aid the design and analysis process? This section presents a method which supports both qualitative and quantitative evaluation and aids the designer of an algorithm to make tradeoffs for a particular environment.

Qualitative Evaluation

The responsibility for resource sharing can be centralized or distributed. It can reside on a single node or be distributed among the nodes. To be fault tolerant, algorithms should avoid having a single point of failure. Furthermore, for low overhead, they should employ simple techniques for fault-tolerance such as periodic information exchange. Researchers generally agree that symmetrically distributed resource sharing algorithms are preferable for fault-tolerance and low overhead purposes.

Information Dissemination Information holding, exchange and update strategies play an important role in maintaining the local view of the system state at a node. Due to communication delays and state distribution, a complete and consistent view of the entire system, or even of a subset, may never be available at a node of the system.

Decisions made by a node are based on both local (such as local resource state, communication rates with other nodes) and non-local dynamic state information held in a state vector. A node may also choose to keep certain static information regarding other nodes in the system (e.g. node identifiers). For all types of information, we have to decide whether to hold state information regarding all nodes in the system, or only a subset of the system. If subsets are used, then criteria must be specified for selecting the nodes to be included in the subsets. Algorithms holding state information regarding all other nodes in the system are dependent on system size and therefore are not scalable. Answers to the questions raised above have a significant affect on performance in a complex network environment.

Decision Making A resource sharing policy tries to reduce the mean response time to resource access requests. A resource sharing policy should account for the fact that when the system is heavily congested, much higher delays than the average may be expected, which can severely degrade performance.

Who should initiate remote execution? It seems that a combination of negotiation initiated by the server when possible, and by the source when it is the only one aware of an event occurrence, can give the best results in terms of performance and stability but at a slightly higher cost than a single request.

When designing a resource sharing algorithm, there are numerous design choices and open issues left for the designer to resolve. These issues have to be examined carefully with respect to the required properties and applications environment. For a more quantitative evaluation, measures of performance and efficiency are necessary, as discussed next.

Quantitative Evaluation

For an objective evaluation of different approaches to resource sharing, one needs a quantitative analysis technique for these algorithms together with a set of characteristics which capture the essence of their behavior. To characterize the structure and behavior of distributed decision-making policies, with particular attention to resource sharing policies, the terms performance and efficiency are advocated. In a general sense, *performance* is an absolute measure which is described in terms of response-time (RT), utilization or any other objective function specified. A performance metric relevant to our study defines the distance of an improved algorithm from the original as a percentage:

$$distance(original, extended) = \frac{RT(original) - RT(extended)}{RT(original)} \tag{3.3.1}$$

where response time for a given application is evaluated by equation(3.3.2) as follows:

$$RT = \frac{\sum_{i=1}^{SystemSize} RT(HOST(i))}{SystemSize} \tag{3.3.2}$$

A positive distance indicates the improvement in performance. A negative distance signals a degradation in performance. Algorithms being compared must use the same models for hardware configuration and network and cpu delays. Algorithms being compared must operate under the same loads.

The *efficiency* of a particular solution is a relative term concerned with the cost or penalty paid for the level of performance attained. After using the performance measures to confirm that an approach to resource sharing will improve the overall performance of the system, efficiency measures can be used to check which of the specific requirements are satisfied. The following efficiency measures allow for tradeoffs to be made when comparing different resource sharing algorithms with comparable performance. Efficiency measures quantify the overhead or cost associated with the attainment of a specific level of performance in terms of the following:

- memory requirements for algorithm constructs
- state dissemination cost in terms of the rate of resource sharing state messages exchanged per node

- run-time cost (in terms of cpu time) measured as the fraction of time spent running the resource access software component
- percent of remote resources accesses out of all resource access requests

Finally, we use *stability* which can be defined as a system property measured by resource sharing hit-ratio. This measure provides guidance as to the quality of the decisions made. It should be maximized.

Stability is a precondition for scalability. If this precondition is met, minimization of sensitivity to scale is indicated for an algorithm if some parameters can be scaled up while others remain untouched. A *hit* is defined as a lookup request, which could be answered with the current contents of the cache. Hit measures the percent of successful decisions. We define a *miss* to be a lookup request which could not be answered with the current contents of the cache. Miss measures the percent of unsuccessful decisions.

Our main goal is to show the significance of certain design choices and their effect on the general behavior of an algorithm rather than the absolute performance results themselves. Additional performance and efficiency measures may be added for specific uses as will be subsequently demonstrated.

In the next section use of the evaluation method is demonstrated showing the combined effect of delays and the selection of specific design choices. Furthermore, the method is used to suggest improvements to an existing published algorithm for resource sharing [9]. The algorithm is subsequently further extended to exploit locality in line with [11].

3.4 Resource Sharing Enhanced Locality

In the previous section we described the flexible load sharing algorithm (FLS) [9] which supports scalable and adaptive initial allocation of processes to processors. In this section FLS is extended to enhance locality. To enable analysis of this complex environment, an idealized environment (basic case) is initially assumed characterized by the following:

- no message loss
- non-negligible (> 0) but constrained latencies for accessing any node from any other node
- availability of unlimited resource capacity, i.e., the number of nodes in a cache is not limited
- the selection of new resource providers to be included in the cache is not a costly operation and need not be constrained

A local cache is maintained at each node. The main cache parameter is:

- n, the number of nodes to try to include in the cache

A cache contains the identification of other nodes with mutual interest currently known to the node together with their current state. This is discussed in the following subsection.

3.4.1 State Metric

FLS defines three states for the nodes of the system: positive, negative, and neutral (Figure 3.1), with the following semantics. A negative node experiences resource shortage; a positive node has surplus resource capacity, i.e., it is capable of serving external resource access requests; a neutral node does not participate in resource sharing. A node is of interest to another node if and only if they are of "opposite states." This relation is symmetric and each is interested in having the other in its cache. A node resource state r is thus mapped into one of three possible states:

$$\textbf{state } r = \begin{cases} \textit{positive} & \textit{if} \quad R > T_+ \\ \textit{negative} & \textit{if} \quad R < T_- \\ \textit{neutral} & \textit{if} \quad T_- \leq R \leq T_+ \end{cases}$$

where R is the load measured. Note that even under the optimistic assumptions made, it is desired to constrain the scope of operation and resultant overhead. To achieve this goal, the algorithm takes advantage of weak consistency which permits both partiality and temporary inaccuracy. Partiality is dealt with first. By constraining the view a node has of the complex system to a small subset of it held locally in a cache, a node considerably constrains interaction with other nodes. Having such information available locally means that lengthy negotiation with the name server or other nodes before a resource location is found can be avoided.

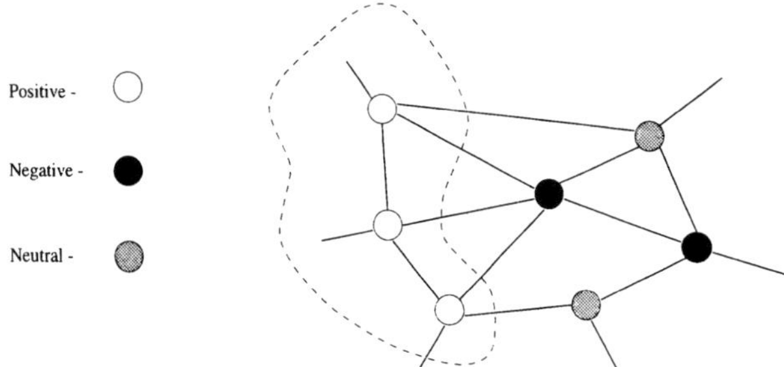

Figure 3.1 Resource states. A node's cache (view of the system).

A similar state definition is used in [11]. The main aim of FLS is hiding scale. We then extend the basic algorithm to enhance locality.

3.4.2 Basic Algorithm Preserving Mutual Interests

For preserving mutual interests the following location and acceptance policies are used by FLS. If the cache of a node is not empty, then a remote resource is randomly selected from it. A request to access the resource is sent with the command piggybacked to enable immediate access if the request is accepted. Otherwise, a negative acknowledgment is returned.

The remote resource holder employs the following acceptance policy. If the resource is available and capable of granting external requests, a positive acknowledgment is sent to the request originator; otherwise, a negative acknowledgment is sent. Note that as a cache usually holds information regarding several remote locations and as the hit-ratio is high, only a few requests are expected to be rejected. These locations are treated as a hint [16] for decision making and incorrect decisions will be terminated rapidly.

The information policy is performed upon a change in a node's local load state. This is in preference to a periodic update which can be hard to tune. All cache members are then notified. A remote resource access decision is thus applied within a node, independently of its application in other nodes. Caches may overlap. Cache membership is symmetric. This symmetry is a key property for ensuring that a node is kept informed of the states of the nodes in its cache.

In the following discussion:

- C_i denotes the current cache for resource r at node i
- $|C_i|$ is the size of the cache at i
- state_i denotes the current state of node i
- $\text{mutual}_{i,s}$ is true if nodes i and s are of 'opposite' states, false otherwise. i.e.:

$$mutual_{i,s} \equiv (state_i = positive and state_s = negative)$$

$$or (state_i = negative and state_s = positive)$$

$$\equiv not(state_i = neutral or state_s = neutral or state_i = state_s)$$

Obviously, this predicate on nodes i and s is symmetric and hence :

$$mutual_{i,s} = mutual_{s,i}$$

Parts of the algorithm are given as rules of the form "guard $\geq$ action" which form alternatives in a guarded command if...[]...[]... fi. Two events may cause a change to the cache contents: cache refresh and message receipt (described next).

Message Receipt - When a $state_s$ message arrives at i from node s, the following message receipt procedure is invoked :

```
if   ( s∉Ci and mutual_i,s) ⇒                      [mutual inclusion]
     insert s entry < s, state_s > into Ci;
     send a responding message state_i to node s;
  [] (s∈Ci and mutual_i,s) ⇒                        [retain candidate]
     update s entry < s, state_s > in Ci;
  [] ( s∈Ci and not mutual_i,s) ⇒                   [mutual exclusion]
     discard s entry from Ci;
  [] (s ∉Ci and not mutual_i,s) ⇒                   [mutual exclusion]
     skip (ignore);

fi
```

Thus, nodes with mutual interest are included and updated while others are discarded. Hence, C_i contains only nodes of mutual interest. The response in the first case, where s is a newly selected node of mutual interest for i, acts to confirm to s that i is of interest for s. The second case ensures that s is retained if it is still of interest, but terminates the state exchange between i and s by giving no further response. The other two cases ensure that nodes with no mutual interest are discarded and ignored, respectively.

Cache Refresh - The current cache is refreshed upon initialization (the cache is initially empty), and following a resource state change. Node i uses the following procedure:

```
{for all nodes k ∈ Ci}:
(disseminate state_i to node k;                    [disseminate new state to previous members]
        ;discard k)                                [discard non-members]
        if (state_i=positive or state_i=negative)⇒ [select new potential members]
randomly select n nodes {j1...jn} from the set
{1,2,...,system_size};
        {for all nodes k∈{j1...jn} :               [k's responding message will result in mutual]
        disseminate state_i to node k};            [inclusion if they are of mutual interest]
        [] (state_i=neutral)⇒ skip;                [No selection of new nodes as no node]
        fi                                         [is or can be of mutual interest]
```

Note that, since a cache only contains nodes of mutual interest, it will be empty immediately following a state change and consequent cache refresh. However, if the state of the node is not N, the responding messages will quickly re-establish cache membership. If the state is N, its cache will remain empty.

In FLS nodes are added to the cache of a node through message receipt operations. Information dissemination is performed on state change and in response to receipt of a state message from a new node. A state change results in a cache refresh which ensures dissemination of the new state to the previous members of its cache, which ensures its removal from their caches.

We study the performance of handling proximity in the framework of FLS. Extensions suggested are generally applicable to other distributed algorithms with the symmetry property. We start by defining parameters of the simulated distributed system (i.e., network of nodes), choose the performance measures of interest, and then discuss the goals of the experiment. We first describe an extension which gives preference to nodes in close proximity in the cache over distant ones (Figure 3.2). This is described next.

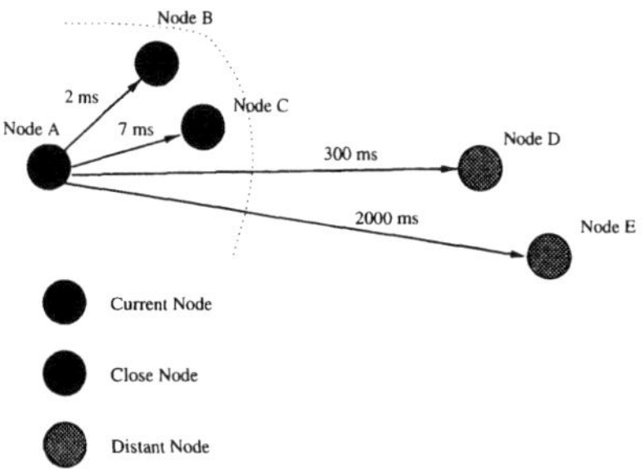

Figure 3.2 Network-aware resource allocation.

3.4.3 Considering Proximity for Improved Performance

Note that the algorithm was designed to minimize dependence on system size. The results obtained in simulation were calculated using equations (3.3.1) and (3.3.2). These results are presented in Figure 3.3. It can be seen that system size has a minimal affect on the performance of the algorithm, there are minor differences between the results for different system sizes.

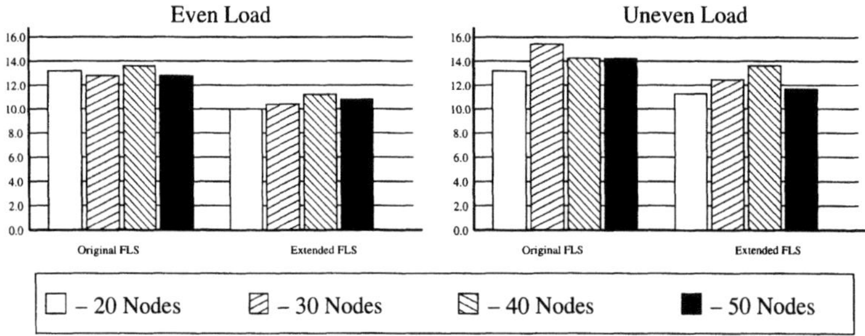

Figure 3.3 Response times of the original and extended algorithms (cache size 5).

This is also shown by the values of the scalability metric, presented in Table 3.6 below. The basic algorithm aiming at hiding scale is extended in this section to also cope with significant latencies and mobility. Extensions to achieve enhanced locality by considering proximity are described next.

In the following discussion it is assumed that communication connections are error free and there is no message loss. Our goal is to estimate the communication delay between two nodes. Communication delay comprises network transmission delay and the total time taken by the message to pass the protocol stacks of the source and the destination nodes. The latter depends on the load applied at the network interface of the node (the lower layers of the protocol stack) and the communication load on the particular application (higher protocol layers). The delay is measured by sending a round-trip message. Round-trip delay includes all the components mentioned above. Next, we describe the delay evaluation procedure performed by a node.

3.4.4 Estimating Proximity (Latency)

Assume that node A evaluates the delay of the communication connection with node B. The delay evaluation starts by sending a time-stamped message to the destination node. The destination node sends the message back. When the responding message is received at the source node, the round-trip delay is calculated and appended to the delay observation sequence. The delay between the two nodes is estimated as the mean of the sequence of observations. This delay evaluation is performed periodically.

The observation sequence is of a certain length and it contains the most recent observations (Figure 3.4). Thus, the sequence reflects recent behavior of communication delay. The sequence mean gives an estimate that approximates this behavior.

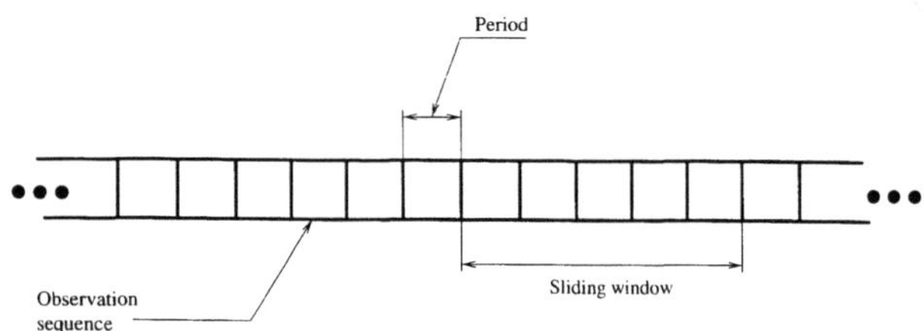

Figure 3.4 Proximity estimate evaluation.

The sequence length and the interval between two successive observations determine the precision of the calculated delay estimate. The longer the observation sequence, the more precise the delay estimate. The same holds for the interval between two successive observations: with a shorter interval the delay estimate is calculated more frequently; therefore, the description of the communication conditions is more precise. The two values should be controlled in order to maintain the required precision of the delay estimate [7].

Assume that the estimated error should fit the confidence level defined. While increasing the sequence length and decreasing the update interval enhances precision, it also causes additional computational and message traffic overhead. Thus, our goal is to maintain the minimal sequence length and maximal update interval that provide the required precision of the delay estimate.

3.4.5 Simulation Runs

The simulated distributed system consists of multiple nodes interconnected by a communication network. There is a communication link between each two nodes of the system. In our experiment we used systems comprising 15, 20, 30, 40 and 50 nodes. Our goal is to study the influence of system size on the performance of the algorithm and to verify feasibility of the extended FLS algorithm in large distributed systems. To study the performance of proximity handling we apply a heavy communication load to certain network connections. This load results in lengthy transmission delays.

The simulated model of interest is that of distributed systems comprising distant nodes. In our experiment each simulated network is assumed to be a WAN consisting of a number of interconnected LANs. Table 3.1 shows the partitioning of each simulated network.

Table 3.1 Sizes of Simulated Systems

System size	Number of LANs	Number of nodes in a LAN
15	2	7,8
20	2	10
30	2	15
40	2	20
50	2	25

Computation load and delay assumptions are drawn from exponential distributions which are not always realistic. Nevertheless, from this study we are able to draw some useful conclusions. The delay parameters for the exponent distribution were calculated from a large sample obtained by the ping utility.[3] For the LAN case exponential(0.002) was chosen and for the WAN exponential(6.000).

Each simulated node processes the arriving requests in first-come-first-served order. We define the arrival rate and resource-time required for six different node types. Performance is studied when even and uneven loads are applied to the system. Tables 3.2 and 3.3 define load conditions for both scenarios.

The description of the simulated system presented above is sufficient for reproduction of our simulation results. The simulation goals and performance measures

[3]Ping provides the statistics on the network conditions between a distant host and the current host. This information includes round-trip delay, the percentage of lost messages, message route, etc.

Table 3.2 Even Load

Type	#nodes of this type	Resource request (sec)	Arrival rate	Resulting intensity per node
1	1	Exponential(0.5)	Poisson(1.53)	76.5%
2	2	Exponential(0.7)	Poisson(1.25)	87.5%
3	1	Exponential(0.6)	Poisson(1.43)	85.8%
4	1	Exponential(0.5)	Poisson(1.43)	71.6%
Overall load				81.76%

Table 3.3 Uneven Load

Node type	#nodes of this type	Resource request (sec)	Arrival Rate	Resulting Intensity per Node
5	4	Exponential(0.695)	Poisson(1.43)	93.3%
6	1	Exponential(0.093)	Poisson(1.25)	11.6%
Overall load				81.76%

are discussed next.

The goal of this experiment is to measure the performance of the FLS algorithm and its extension for handling proximity under different simulated conditions. Performance is best measured by the average response-time of the system. The average system performance is calculated as the mean of the average performance estimates of all the nodes in the system.

As mentioned in the previous section, by comparing the performance of the original FLS algorithm with the performance of the extended one we evaluate the improvement as distance (original, extended). A positive estimate shows a performance improvement, a negative one signifies performance degradation.

In addition to performance improvement, the extent to which handling proximity improves the remote resource allocation decision should be measured. This is expressed by the percentage of close execution requests performed by the extended algorithm in comparison with the original algorithm. We proceed with the discussion of simulation results.

3.4.6 Simulation Results

Our aim is to measure scalability. For a scaling system size of 20 to 50 nodes, the results achieved were within a bound of less than 5 percent under these extreme conditions (Table 3.4). With a high scalability measure, evaluation of the scalability metric for a small system is sufficient to infer the performance of much larger configurations, as concluded in [18].

The results were produced by the NEST simulation environment. The absolute values of response time may be found in Table 3.5 and Figure 3.3.

The performance improvement is demonstrated better by presenting relative

Table 3.4 Percentage of Close Allocations

System Size	Original FLS(%)	Extended FLS(%)
15	38	49
20	40	53
30	37	51
40	39	52
50	34	49.66

improvement in response time, defined by the equation (3.3.2) (Table 3.5). Even and uneven load scenarios are studied. Cache size is set to 5. In most cases the improvement is approximately 20 percent, which is very promising. For a system comprising 20 nodes, for example, proximity handling resulted in reducing the average response time by 21.33 percent under the even load scenario and by 16 percent under the uneven (Table 3.5).

The number of close (in-LAN) remote allocations performed by the extended FLS is in average 13 percent higher than that of the original FLS algorithm, meaning that proximity handling minimizes the number of remote allocations to distant nodes. Table 3.4 compares the percentage of close allocation requests made by the original to that of the extended algorithm. The cache size in this case is set to 5. In a system comprising 20 nodes, for instance, the original algorithm addressed 40 percent of remote execution requests to nodes residing in the same LAN. The use of proximity handling increases it to 53 percent.

Table 3.5 Performance Improvement of Proximity Handling

System Size	Even Load(%)	Uneven Load (%)
15	17.99	12.36
20	21.33	16
30	19.76	21.67
40	19.15	21
50	19.45	18.55

Table 3.6 Scalability Metric for the Even Load case

	20	30	40	50
20	1	0.97	0.93	0.96
30		1	0.96	0.99
40			1	1
50				1

The results achieved are encouraging. Mutuality Preservation is shown to be adaptive, giving good performance results while incurring a small overhead on the system in terms of computation time, communication, and storage. It is also general, stable (exhibiting a high hit-ratio), scalable (high scalability measure), and can tolerate message loss. Dependence on system size and latencies is minimized. In addition to the improved performance of the extended algorithm, these features make us confident in respect to the suitability of the proposed algorithm. In addition, there are some design details that are not taken into account by simulation. For this, prototype implementation complements simulation.

PVM is used for prototype implementation. PVM together with the resource manager implemented for its extension [8] are described next.

3.5 Prototype Implementation and Extension

3.5.1 PVM Resource Manager

Parallel Virtual Machine (PVM) used worldwide enables a collection of heterogeneous computers connected by dissimilar networks to be used as a coherent and flexible concurrent computational resource. The concept of PVM plugability[4] describes a Resource Manager (RM) which can be transparently plugged into PVM offering improved process allocation. The default policy employed by PVM for resource allocation is round-robin. The main drawbacks of this policy are the fact that PVM ignores the load variations among the different nodes and also PVM is unable to distinguish between machines of different speeds. To redress this deficiency a tool that manipulates and administers system resources must replace round-robin allocation. Such a resource management system is described in this section. It provides a replacement for the round-robin policy with a scalable and adaptive algorithm for resource sharing [9].

Our RM implements the scalable and adaptive algorithm for initial allocation [9]. An RM interface was introduced in the version 3.3 of PVM. An RM is a PVM task. Once installed in the virtual machine, it is equivalent to a complete "takeover" of all scheduling policies. This includes host addition and deletion procedures, various event notifications, task information, and spawning placement.

We use RM to provide an alternative spawn service in PVM, which is completely transparent to the user. In our case when a PVM user uses pvm_spawn() function, the SM_SPAWN message is then sent to RM instead of the TM_SPAWN message which pvmlib sends to the pvmd by default. FLS code available from simulation is used for our RM. We extended PVM to provide an alternative spawn (execution) service which is scalable and adaptive [8].

[4]G. A. Geist, J. A. Kohl, P. M. Papadopoulos, S. L. Scott. "Beyond PVM 3.4: What We Have Learned, What's Next, and Why." Computer Science and Mathematics Division, Oak Ridge National Laboratory, Oak Ridge, URL http://www.epml.gov, 1997.

3.5.2 Resource Manager Extension to Further Enhance Locality

In [11] it is suggested to use information that is usually discarded. The motivation is to improve the probability that remote requests would be directed towards nodes that indeed share a mutual interest, thus lowering the cost of the search for a mutual partner. In line with this idea, we suggest that FLS keeps state information which is usually discarded. Our extension to FLS, however, will save information more selectively than is done by [11]. The underlying assumption is that while overly-simplified algorithms do not provide a significant performance improvement, as an algorithm becomes more and more complex its overhead grows and may overcome the benefits it tries to provide. Our work is concerned with finding that fine-line between an overly-simplified algorithm and an algorithm that is too complex and hence too expensive. Directing the probing towards nodes sharing a mutual interest may improve performance, compared to an entirely random probing, which is a total "shooting in the dark." While saving non-local information locally is plausible, it still needs to be saved selectively, otherwise managing the saved information becomes inefficient.

Hence, our improved FLS acts as follows: Two caches are used to save aside data that is no longer of interest to the local node: an old-positive-state-cache and an old-negative-state-cache. When a node changes its state from negative to some other state (neutral or positive), we clean the content of the old-negative-state, and insert in it the nodes of the current cache, before refreshing it. Likewise, when a node is in a positive state, and its state changes, the content of the current cache is copied to the old-positive-state-cache, to be saved until that information is needed once again. When a node state becomes positive (or negative), and a cache refresh is in order, the nodes in the old-positive-state-cache (or the old-negative-state-cache) are probed first. Once the old cache nodes are exhausted, probing is done at random, for a total of n probed nodes, similar to the way it is done in the original algorithm.

It was shown that a scalable and adaptive algorithm can improve PVM performance [8]. Initial performance measurement results are described next.

3.5.3 Initial Performance Measurement Results

We experimented on a system composed of six Pentium-based workstations that are connected by a Fast Ethernet LAN. Two are underloaded (on the average), two are overloaded, and two are medium-loaded. The average load imposed on the system was 80 percent.

The percentage of probing based on previous caches is defined to be the percentage of probed nodes which were chosen based on their appearance on previous caches, of all probed nodes. Notice that as this percentage increases, the percentage of successful probing, that is, probes that result in finding a node which indeed shares a common interest with the local node, is also increased. Hence, our first goal, to better direct the probing towards nodes that are more likely to share a common interest with the local node, assuming that this will increase the number of successful probes, was indeed realized.

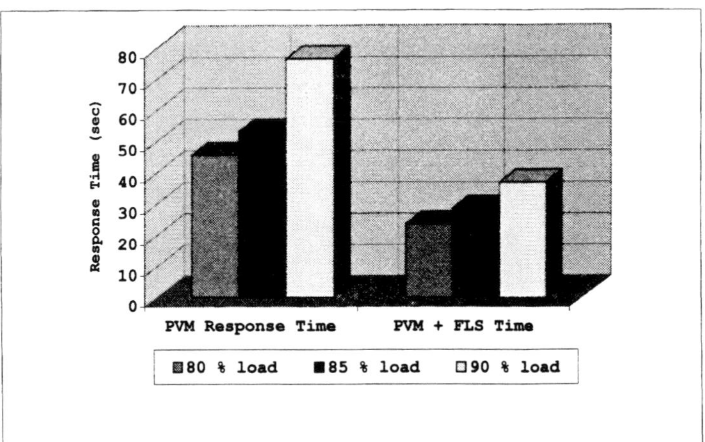

Figure 3.5 Basic benchmark on a system composed of 5 and 9 Pentium Pro 200 nodes. Each node produces 100 processes.

As the probing process becomes more efficient, the cache is updated within a shorter while, when a node changes its state. A faster update of the cache means it is empty for shorter periods of time. As a consequence the miss percentage decreases. Our results verify this phenomena: The percentage of misses when the extended FLS is used is lower than that percentage for the original FLS.

Our experiment showed that probing based on previous cache members yielded a more successful and efficient probing process. As a result caches are updated faster, and are empty less frequently. The miss ratio is thus decreased, and the number of remote execution possible to be carried out is increased. The percentage of remote executions was increased, from 19 percent for the basic FLS to 23.5 percent for the extended one. This influenced the overall average response time of the system.

3.6 Conclusions and Future Study

In complex network systems, decision makers must be able to make local decisions. This applies to resource sharing as well as to any other distributed application. In this chapter we described a cache based resource sharing algorithm. Its locality was enhanced in two respects:

1. Considering proximity

2. Reuse of state information

The algorithm is generally applicable to any system which can be represented as a network of communicating components. We have placed particular emphasis on the need for scalability. Aesthetically, scalable mechanisms can be more elegant and robust. Practically, scalable mechanisms imply less future work in adapting to new technologies. Techniques that are successful in dealing with small systems under normal conditions often break down in the face of the complexity of large systems or extreme conditions such as congestion and long delays.

This chapter presented a simulation and PVM-based implementation of an enhanced scalable and adaptive resource sharing facility. Our system is based on commodity hardware (PCs and networking) and software (PVM) offering a low cost solution as an alternative to mainframes and MPPs. Such a system adapts to state changes which are unpredictable in a complex network environment. Simulation [7] and prototype implementation [8] results demonstrate the utility of an algorithm preserving mutual interests to such environments. This was subsequently enhanced to optimize locality as described in this chapter. We are encouraged by the relative ease of implementation and its extension and the results it provides. An extensive performance measurement study of locality is planned. Our current implementation supports scalable and adaptive initial placement. It will be complemented by migration after start-up to support a general purpose PVM-based high performance computation server.

Finally, we believe that our adaptive algorithm preserving mutual interests is general and can be applied in other applications where scale is important and which have characteristics similar to load state which indicate symmetry and mutual interest. One example is the dynamic parking assignment problem. Initial results are already available for these problems encouraging further investigation.

Acknowledgments

We gratefully acknowledge the Ministry of Science Grant no. 8500 for its financial support. We extend our thanks to Peggy Weinreich for her valuable editorial work.

3.7 Bibliography

[1] A. Barak and Y. Kornatzky. Design Principles of Operating Systems for Large Scale Multicomputers. *In Proceedings of the International Workshop on Experience with Distributed Systems*, Springer-Verlag, September 1987.

[2] T.L. Casavant and J.G. Kuhl. Taxonomy of Scheduling in General-Purpose Distributed Computing Systems. *IEEE Transactions on Software Engineering*, vol.14(2), pages 141-150, February 1988.

[3] J. Schwartz, J. Dupuy. Nest: Network Simulation Tool. *Technical Report in Communications of the ACM*, vol. 33(10), October 1990.

[4] D. L. Eager, E. D. Lazowska and J. Zahorjan. Adaptive Load Sharing in Homogeneous Distributed Systems. *In IEEE Transactions on Software Engineering*, vol. 12(5), pages 662-675, May 1986.

[5] G. A. Geist, A. Beguelin, J. Dongarra, W. Jiang, R. Manchek and V. Sunderam. *PVM - Parallel Virtual Machine: A User Guide and Tutorial for Networked Parallel Computing.* MIT Press, Cambridge, MA, 1994.

[6] A. Gupta, A. Grama and V. Kumar. Isoefficiency: Measuring the Scalability of Parallel Algorithms and Architectures. *IEEE Parallel and Distributed Technology,* pages 12-20, August 1993.

[7] M. Kapelevich and O. Kremien. Scalable Resource Scheduling:Design, Assessment, Prototyping. *In Proceedings 8th Israeli Conf. on Computer Systems and Software Engineering,* IEEE Computer Society Press, 1997.

[8] M. Kemelmakher and O. Kremien. Scalable and Adaptive Resource Sharing in PVM. *Recent Advances in Parallel Virtual Machine and Message Passing Interface.* LNCS, Vol. 1479, pages 196-205, Springer-Verlag, 1998.

[9] O. Kremien, J. Kramer and J. Magee. Scalable, Adaptive Load Sharing Algorithms. *IEEE Parallel and Distributed Technology,* pages 62-70, August 1993.

[10] O. Kremien, M. Kemelmakher and I. Eshed. Preseving Mutual interests in High Performance Computing Clusters. *Informatica Journal* , vol. 23(1), 1999.

[11] P. Krueger and N. Shivaratri. Adaptive Location Policies for Global Scheduling. *IEEE Transactions on Software Engineering,* vol. 20(6), pages 432-444, June 1994.

[12] M. Satyanarayanan. Scale and Performance in Distributed File System. *IEEE Transactions on Software Engineering,* vol. 18(1), pages 1-8, January 1992.

[13] N. Shivaratri, P. Krueger and M. Singhal. Load Distributing for Locally Distributed Systems. *IEEE Computer,* pages 33-44, December 1992.

[14] R. G. Smith. The Contract Net Protocol: High-Level Communication and Control in a Distributed Problem Solver. *IEEE Transactions on Computers,* vol. C-29(12), pages 1104-1113, December 1980.

[15] X. H. Sun and D. T. Rover. Scalability for Parallel Algorithm-Machine Combinations. *IEEE Transaction on Parallel and Distributed Systems,* vol. 5, pages 599-613, June 1994.

[16] D. B. Terry. Caching Hints in Distributed Systems. *IEEE Transactions on Software Engineering,* vol. SE-13(1), pages 48-54, January 1987.

[17] W. E. Tichy. Should Computer Scientists Experiment More? *IEEE Computer,* pages 32-40, May 1998.

[18] X. Zhang, Yan and Q. Ma. Software Support for Multiprocessor Latency Measurement and Evaluation. *IEEE Transactions on Software Engineering,* 23(1), pages 4-16, January 1997.

Chapter 4

Dependable Clustered Computing

João Viegas Carreira[†] and João Gabriel Silva[‡]

[†]Critical Software Lda
Portugal

[‡]Dept. of Informatics Engineering
University of Coimbra, Coimbra, Portugal

Email: *jcar@criticalsoftware.com*, *jgabriel@dei.uc.pt*

4.1 Introduction

Clusters of computing systems have been built and used for more than a decade. The clustering model itself has emerged in two different areas of computing with slightly different motivations: High Performance (HP) and High Availability (HA) computing. Clusters may be generally defined as "a parallel or distributed system that consists of a collection of interconnected whole computers, that is utilized as a single, unified computing resource" [16]. While the parallel computing community sees clusters from the high performance and scalability perspective and refers to them as WSCs (Workstation Clusters) or NOWs (Network Of Workstations), business/mission critical computing sees clusters from a different perspective – high-availability, and refers to them as HA clusters.

In theory, the clustering model can provide both high-availability and high performance, and also manageability, and scalability, and affordability, i.e. almost the dream of Information Systems (IS) management departments. To accomplish the dream, however, cluster software technologies still have to evolve and mature.

In the parallel computing field, a cluster is primarily a mean to provide scalability and increasing processing power by enabling a parallel application to run across all the nodes of the cluster. The main advantage of a cluster as compared with traditional MPCs (Massively Parallel Computers) is its low cost. In fact, during the nineties, clusters appeared as the poor man's answer for the parallel high performance computing quest, in opposition to the expensive, proprietary, and massive parallel architectures of the eighties. This trend can be clearly observed in the well-known Gordon Bell prize. This contest has a special class of award for the best ratio Gflops per million dollars. This award usually goes to applications running on workstation clusters.

Clusters inherit much of the knowledge acquired from research in distributed systems. Of course, there are some typical differences between a cluster and a distributed system that make things less hard to the clusters. Clusters are typically homogeneous (a distributed system is a computer zoo, with lots of different kinds of computers), tightly coupled, and most important, nodes trust each other (distributed systems have to deal with untrusted nodes).

But using clusters is not a panacea: As the number of hardware components in a system rises, so does the probability of failure. A cluster can grow to hundreds or thousands of nodes, but the likelihood that a fault will occur while an application is running on the cluster increases proportionally. This fact is clearly illustrated by a statement by Leslie Lamport (one of the fathers of distributed computing systems): "A distributed system is one in which the failure of a computer you didn't even know existed can render your own computer unusable."

In clusters the increasing probability of fault occurrence can be particularly harmful for long-running applications, such as scientific number crunching. In these cases, the need for some kind of mechanism to guarantee the continuation of applications in the presence of faults becomes a must.

So much for the parallel computing perspective. From the mission and business critical system's perspective, a cluster is a configuration of a group of independent servers that can be managed as a single system, shares a common namespace, and is designed specifically to tolerate component failures and to support the addition or subtraction of components in a way that's transparent to users. The focus is not on performance, but rather on high availability.

Mission critical clusters were originally built, in most of the cases, with only two machines (the so-called primary and secondary nodes) and typically supported OLTP (Online Transaction Processing) applications for banking, and insurance, among other similar critical applications. The idea is simple in concept: In case of a failure of a component (hardware or software) in the primary system, the critical applications can be transferred to the secondary server, thus avoiding downtime and guaranteeing application's availability. This process is termed *failover*, and inevitably implies a temporary degradation of the service, but without total permanent loss. This is quite different from component level redundancy with voting which masks faults completely. The so-called Fault-Tolerant servers pioneered by Tandem [20] use component redundancy to provide continuous service in case of failures. Clusters also use redundancy but at the system level.

HA clusters have evolved from the two node configuration, and with the increasing performance needs, they came to support more than two nodes, and provide additional mechanisms to take advantage of the aggregate performance of the participating nodes through load-balancing. The two worlds became closer and closer.

The convergence between HA and HP is not a coincidence. In fact, high performance parallel computing and high-availability can be seen as enabling technologies of each other. Parallel processing uses the joint power of many processing units to achieve high performance. However, only fault tolerance can enable effective parallel computing because, as we have shown, fault tolerance allows application continuity. On the other hand, parallelism enables high-availability because parallelism intrinsically provides one of high-availability's most important architectural elements: redundancy.

4.1.1 Structure

Section 4.2 presents an historical perspective on the rising of clusters both in the high performance and high availability contexts, as well as the factors that drove their confluence. Section 4.3 provides the background for the remainder of the chapter: The attributes, impairments, and means of dependability are presented.

Section 4.4 focuses the discussion on HA clusters by presenting the most common architectures and configurations of these systems. In Section 4.5, hardware and software techniques for detecting errors are presented and discussed, while Section 4.6 discusses the mechanisms to recover from those errors.

Finally, Section 4.7 provides a practical overview of several commercial cluster solutions: MSCS (formerly Wolfpack) from Microsoft, Oracle Failover, and NCR LifeKeeper.

4.2 Two Worlds Converge

Clusters appeared both in the context of high performance and high availability. The motivation and factors for the confluence of both worlds are discussed in detail in this section.

4.2.1 Dependable Parallel Computing

Dependability arose as an issue as soon as clusters started to be used by the scientific HP community. There were two main reasons for this to happen: First, as systems scale up to hundreds of nodes, the likelihood of a node failure during the execution of a parallel application increases proportionally with the number of nodes.[1] The failure of a single node can crash the entire application and render all previous work useless. Problems may be caused not only by permanent faults (e.g., permanent damage of an hardware component) but mainly by transient ones (e.g., due to heating, electromagnetic interference, marginal design, transient software faults, and power supply disturbancies, among others).

[1] An interesting analogy with airplanes is that "A two engine plane has twice as many engine problems, and a thousand engine plane has thousands of engine problems."

A second and perhaps less obvious reason to consider dependability as an issue has to do with those faults that statistically don't cause node failures but have other insidious effects. Recent studies [2] based on fault-injection experiments [4] assessed the effect of faults on applications running in parallel systems (both in the processing nodes and communications). These studies have shown that a large percentage of faults do not cause nodes to crash, system panics, core dumps, or applications to hang.[2] In many cases, everything goes "apparently" fine, but in the end, parallel application generate incorrect results. In fact, transient faults do not necessarily have a clearly observable, catastrophic, and breathtaking effect. For instance, if a fault causes a bit flip in a block of data used by an application as input for a calculation, then the "only" visible effect may be a wrong calculation result. This can be catastrophic, though. Just imagine a simulation of air flow around airplane wings running for several days in a parallel system that produces an (maybe small) error in the wing model behavior. As strange as it may seem, when it comes to faults, it is preferable that faults just crash everything in the most noticeable manner. This guarantees at least that users are not deceived.

For those who are skeptic about the mentioned probability and impact of faults, the following example may help. Consider for this purpose the ASCI-Red machine (Accelerated Strategic Computing Initiative). The ASCI-Red is a 9000 Pentium Pro and 263 Gbytes memory machine of the U.S. Department of Energy (DOE) used primarily to enable "virtual" tests of nuclear weapons. Each Pentium of the ASCI-Red has around 21 million transistors which means around 190 GigaTransistors for the 9000 processors and some 300 GigaTransistors for the machine's main memory. If each processor memory pair has a MTFB (Mean Time Between Failures) of more than 10 years, let's say 100,000 hours, with 9,000 processors the overall MTBF will be around 10 hours. Not much.

Furthermore, if one remembers that the MTBF is calculated taking into account only permanent failures, and we correct it to consider also transient faults (from 4 to 10 times more frequent than permanent ones [17], [10] we go down to 1 to 2 hours MTBF.

Those who are still skeptic about these very low MTBF numbers may want to look at another example from the real world. The Oak Ridge National Laboratory (ORNL) web site[3] publishes the MTBF's measured from the Center's parallel machines. The average MTBF is somewhat below 20 hours. Of course, this is for the center's MPPs, not clusters, but clusters certainly aren't more reliable than a dedicated and tightly controlled parallel machine. In fact, Clusters used for parallel computing are sometimes built out of shared (and not dedicated) workstations which makes them much more prone to interferences from the environment (especially their users). For instance, a study from [12], which involved more than 400 machines at the Campus of Carnegie Mellon University, measured an overall MTBF

[2] A process is said to be crashed if its working image is not present in the system and hung if the process image is alive from the operating system standpoint, but it's not making any progress from the users perspective.

[3] http://www.ccs.ornl.gov/

of 14 hours.

Still another study [14] presents an extensive study about the reliability of heterogeneous workstations connected to the internet. About 1200 hosts were remotely monitored for a long period, using polling (with a few minutes interval) to check for availability. The results have shown that the measured aggregate time-to-failure of each machine was in the order of 311 hours (this value reflects the time between interruption of the machine's service). The availability was measured as 88 percent or about 46 unavailable days per year.

The scenario is not encouraging but, fortunately for parallel computing, there are a handful of mechanisms and techniques aimed at tolerating and recovering from faults in clustered systems. Some of them will be described throughout this chapter.

4.2.2 Mission/Business Critical Computing

Nowadays, as information systems become ubiquitous, and companies and organizations of all sectors become drastically dependent on their computing resources, the demand for HA applications increases. This class of sensitive programs include online transaction processing, electronic commerce, Internet/World Wide Web, data warehousing, decision support, telecommunication switches, Online Analytical Processing (OLAP), control systems, and server applications that generally run 24 hours a day. These servers must run perpetually, providing a service to its clients, and therefore demand high availability. In these environments, the cost of any outage can be substantial, either in terms of lost opportunities, loss of goodwill in the marketplace, or loss of customers to competitors. With the dependency of enterprises and organizations on critical applications rising dramatically, the TCO (Total Cost of Ownership) of special HA systems to protect against the disruption of service is often less than the costs associated with an outage. One effective way of providing high availability for these systems is using the cluster model.

Clusters are built upon the developments of dependable computing systems in the last decades. Historically, one of the first protection mechanisms for critical applications was the data offline backup, or *cold-backup*. Backups don't make systems more available, but at least at the end of the day data was stored in a safe place – it was a good start.

An evolution of the backup concept is the *hot-backup*. The hot-backup protects data, not just at a certain time of the day, but on a continuous basis using a mirrored storage system where all data is replicated. Also, redundant arrays of inexpensive disks, or RAID for short, were introduced to protect data integrity. Again, this protects data but doesn't increase availability. If the server fails, it has to be manually repaired before the system is launched again.

Environmental safeguards were also (and still are) employed with the purpose of protecting the system against environmental hazards. This includes protection against power surges and uninterruptible power supplies (UPSs) to provide operation during power outages. Of course this is effective only for transient faults.

Permanent faults in the power supply can only be tolerated though redundancy, i.e., using a hot dual-power supply system.

Until some years ago, after assembling a system from the best available components, including some of the options described above, businesses would simply wait and hope everything would go seamlessly. The alternative consisted in using advanced hardware redundant systems, as was the case with extremely highly available applications in telecommunications and banking. The redundancy in these systems is explored at all levels, including power supplies, I/O ports, CPUs, disks, network adapters, and physical networks, in order to eliminate any single point of failure within the platform. In the event of a failure in the hardware running a critical application, a duplicate component is always available to ensure that the application has resources to keep executing. These systems are also generally called fault tolerant, being capable of providing almost continuous availability – up to 99.999 percent availability or five minutes downtime per year. An example of these systems are the NonStop Himalaya servers from Tandem/Compaq [20].

But these levels of availability generally require the use of proprietary hardware and software, which kept users from taking advantage of off-the-shelf industry standard and cheap components. The holy grail is to combine highly reliable and highly scalable computing solutions with open and affordable components. This can be done with clusters. The first step in this direction was to employ two similar systems connected by a LAN (the primary and secondary nodes). The secondary node would then back up not only the data (through mirroring), but also the processes of the primary server so as to get into action in case of a failure. This marked the rise of mission/business critical clusters.

However, in parallel with the quest for high-availability, another trend slowly gained form. As a consequence of the increasing dissemination of information systems in general, it became vital for business critical systems such as electronic commerce, web sites, and corporate databases to handle increasingly high workloads. In addition to HA, the ability to scale to meet the demands of service growth also became a requirement. High performance joined high-availability as an additional requirement for mission/business critical systems.

The fact is that clusters intrinsically have the ability to provide HP and scalability. In contrast to pure failover schemes, a cluster node that can pick up from a failed node doesn't necessarily need to sit idle waiting for a failure to occur. It can use its full processing capabilities, so that with appropriate software, the load can be shared with other cluster members. This evolution marked the rise of high availability scalable clusters.

To summarize, today's mission/business critical cluster is, in a broad sense, seen as a combination of the following capabilities:

- **Availability:** Ability of one system to failover to another system.
- **Scalability:** Ability to increase the number of nodes to handle load increase.
- **Performance:** Ability to perform workload distribution.

- **Manageability:** Ability to be managed as a single system.

Manageability naturally derives from the others as a requirement for these systems, and is the current focus of corporate IS in controlling the TCO. The software that makes all this possible is generally termed *clusterware*.

In the remainder of this chapter, the discussion will focus on the first capability mentioned – availability – and the mechanisms, both in hardware and software, used to accomplish it.

4.3 Dependability Concepts

4.3.1 Faults, Errors, Failures

When a program running on a cluster produces incorrect results, a failure has happened. The same applies for any system – when the service delivered by that system deviates from the specified behavior, a failure has occured. Failures are what we want to prevent. To do it, we must have some kind of forewarning, so that we can take the necessary compensating steps for the failure not to occur. Fortunately, some time before the external behavior of a system is affected, a part of its internal state deviates from the correct value (the invalid system state is called the error). If we detect the error, which can be, for instance, an internal program variable with an invalid value, we may be able to compensate for it and prevent the system from failing. The time between the first occurrence of the error and the moment when it is detected, called the error detection latency, is particularly important, since the longer it takes to detect errors, the most affected the internal state of the system may become. Obviously, an error has some phenomenological cause, which we call fault. It can be an electromagnetic interference, a program bug, a wrong command given by an operator, or a defunct integrated circuit. It is important to notice that faults can have different durations. They can be transient, like an electromagnetic pulse, or permanent, like a defunct IC. While re-execution can compensate for a transient fault, permanent faults can be more complex to handle, requiring a different computer for the program's re-execution. Software faults (bugs) are apparently of the permanent kind – the program is either wrong or not, its straightforward re-execution would just produce the same wrong results again. But that is not always so. In concurrent programs, as is usually the case in clusters, many bugs are of some consequence only when the several parts of the program have a very particular relative timing. Since in a re-execution the timing will usually be slightly different, the bug does not happen again. These bugs are called Heisenbugs, as opposed to Bohrbugs (those that are always there again when the program is reexecuted) [6].

In clusters, another very important type of fault occurs during operation and maintenance tasks (e.g., software upgrades or utility operations). Experience shows that this kind of fault is responsible for a high percentage of the failures of HA clusters.

4.3.2 Dependability Attributes

Dependability can be seen from different perspectives, depending on the application. For instance, if you are building an airplane, you must assure that the critical flight control systems will operate correctly during the entire mission – the probability of that continuous correct operation is measured by the Reliability attribute. If your application is instead a phone switching center, you can tolerate some interruptions of service as long as calls are correctly processed most of the time – you are thus interested in the systems Availability – a measure of the probability that the system will be providing good service at a given point in time. Some other common figures of merit are MTBF – the Mean Time Between Failures, which is proportional to reliability, and MTTR – the Mean Time To Repair a failure and bring the system back to correct service. Availability can be expressed as MTBF/(MTBF+MTTR).

4.3.3 Dependability Means

There are essentially two ways of solving the dependability problem. One is preventing faults from occurring (Fault Prevention) and may be accomplished through conservative design, formal proofs, extensive testing, etc. The alternative is to prevent errors from becoming failures (Fault Tolerance). These two approaches are in fact complementary – a bad quality system cannot be turned into a HA system just by fault tolerance, and fault prevention is not able to deliver totally fault free systems. This chapter focuses on Fault Tolerance techniques for clusters.

A concept that is sometimes confused with Fault Tolerance is Disaster Tolerance. The latter concept refers to techniques aimed at handling a very particular type of faults, namely site failures caused by fire, floods, sabotages, etc, and usually implies having redundant hardware at a remote site [13].

4.4 Cluster Architectures

Clusters can be configured in a multitude of ways, depending on the interconnection systems used for storage, clients, and monitorization, the level of resource sharing, the maximum number of nodes, granularity of failover, the ability to use simultaneously all cluster resources, among others. However, one can classify them according to some general characteristics such as the failover, the interconnect, and the storage architectures.

4.4.1 Share-Nothing versus Shared-Storage

In the share-nothing cluster model, each node has its own memory and is also assigned its own storage resources (Figure 4.1). Share-nothing clusters may allow nodes to access common devices or resources, as long as these resources are owned and managed by a single system at a time. This avoids the complexity of cache coherency schemes and distributed lock managers[4] (DLM). One benefit of this model

[4]DLMs are used to serialize requests for access and negotiate contentions for shared resources.

may be the elimination of single-points of failure within the cluster storage. In fact, if a shared storage resource fails, all servers lose access to the data. Also, because of the lack of contention and overhead, this model can be quite scalable. There are also several strategies aimed at reducing bandwidth overhead when local disks are mirrored through the network. A special interconnect (perhaps a second Network Interface Card) can be used to support the mirroring and isolate its traffic from the clients interconnect, or mirroring can be made intelligent, e.g., transmitting deltas through the media instead of the whole data. The first approach, for example, is used in the Vinca Corp Standby Server [22].

In the shared-storage model, both servers share the same storage resource, with the consequent need for synchronization between disks accesses to keep data integrity. Distributed lock managers must be used in these cases and scalability becomes compromised.

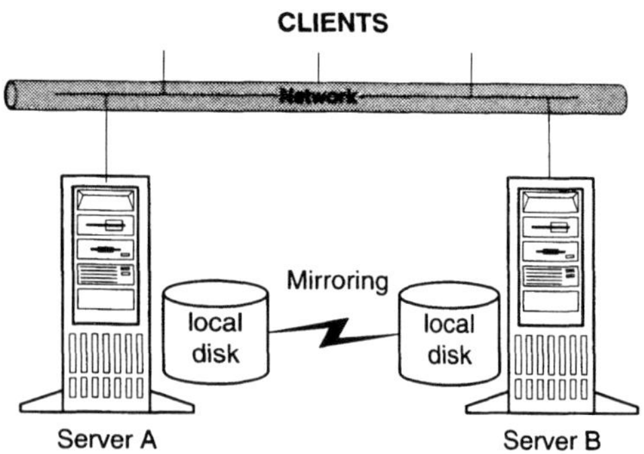

Figure 4.1 Share-nothing clusters.

4.4.2 Active/Standby versus Active/Active

The Active/Standby configuration is also called hot backup (Figure 4.2). In this scheme there is a primary server where the critical application runs, and a secondary server used as a backup or hot spare which is normally in standby mode. The two machines do not need to be absolutely identical: the backup machine just needs the necessary resources (disk, memory, connectivity, etc.) to support the application(s). It can be a lower performance machine as it only needs to keep the main application running while the main server is repaired (after a failure). In the Active/Active configuration all servers in the cluster are active and do not sit idle waiting for a fault to occur and take over. This solution is sometimes referred to as providing bidirectional-failover, as critical applications can run on servers that stand in for others. With all nodes productive, the price to performance ratio decreases.

Another configuration which is basically an extension of the Active/Active model is termed N-Way (Figure 4.3), and has several active servers that back up one another. For instance, server X can back up applications from servers Y and Z, while having applications that are backed up on servers Y and Z. When a failure occurs on any of the servers, protected application(s) are transferred from that server to the backup servers(s).

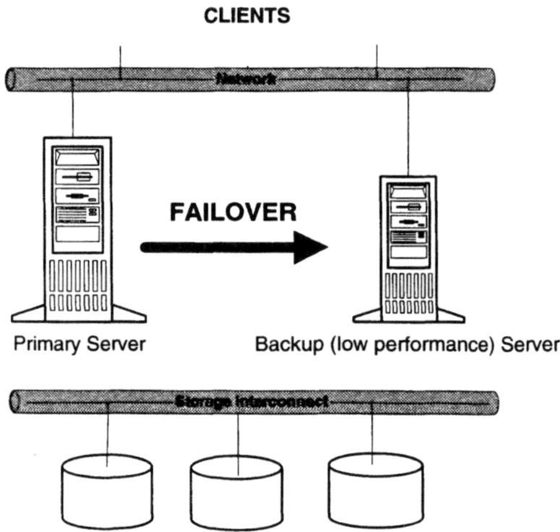

Figure 4.2 Active/Standby clusters.

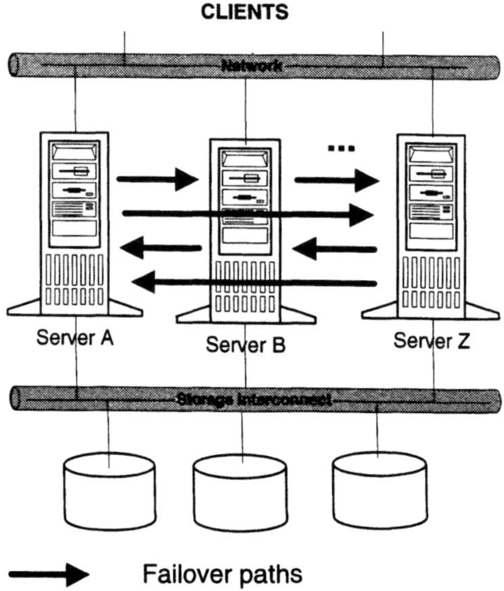

Figure 4.3 N-Way clusters.

4.4.3 Interconnects

There are three main kinds of interconnects to consider in a cluster: network, storage, and monitoring (Figure 4.4). Network interconnect refers to the communications channel that provides the network connection between the client systems and the cluster. It is generally ethernet or fast-ethernet. Storage Interconnect refers to the technology that provides the I/O connection between the cluster nodes and disk storage. Typical technologies are SCSI and Fiber Channel.

Concerning storage interconnects, Fiber Channel Arbitrated Loop (FCAL) permits fast connections – 100 Mb/s – and cable lengths up to 10 Km, but SCSI is still more popular. However, SCSI has an important drawback which is its limit in length that effectively also limits the distance between clustered servers. This can be overcome by using SCSI extender technologies, but Fiber Channel is definitely more appropriate, especially because the great distances supported enable the implementation of efficient disaster-recovery strategies [13]. Still, cluster solutions may use the LAN as the storage interconnect. This is the case of the Vinca Standby Server [22], which is a typical share-nothing system (where data is mirrored through the network in the disks of a backup machine).

Monitoring interconnects refer to additional communication media used for monitoring purposes such as heartbeats transfer. NCR LifeKeeper [15], for instance, can use both the network and storage interconnects for monitoring; it also has an additional serial link between the servers for that purpose.

Interconnecting technologies are vital for clusters. There are several recent advances in this area which are worth to discuss in detail. They are the VIA (Virtual Interface Architecture), SAN (Storage Area Network), and Fiber Channel (which is closely associated with SAN).

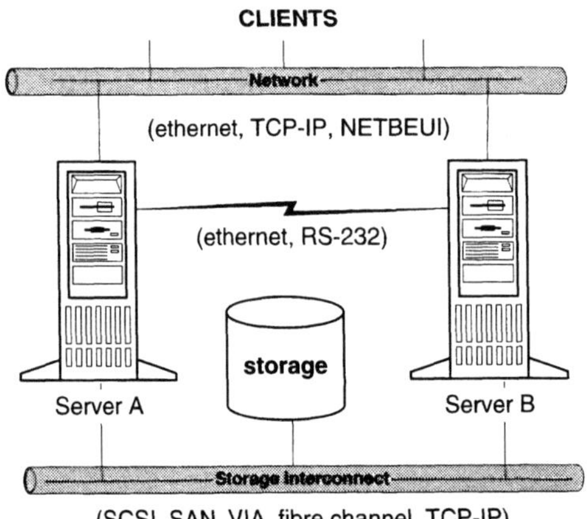

Figure 4.4 Cluster interconnects.

VIA: The Virtual Interface (VI) Architecture specification is an open industry specification promoted by Intel, Compaq, and Microsoft [21], aimed at defining the interface for high performance interconnection of servers and storage devices within a cluster. VIA is not a new network, it just defines the interface to the networking hardware in a media, processor, and operating system independent manner.

This special network that interconnects the servers and storage devices within a cluster is also termed SAN.[5] Moreover, this network does not connect the servers and storage within a cluster to the client nodes outside of the cluster. Standard LAN/WAN hardware is used for that purpose. VI proposes to standardize this network. Traditionally, this is typically not a high performance network as the communication between nodes in a cluster is done simply through the network infrastructure provided by the host operating system, with all the associated overhead. VI strategy goes through defining a thin, fast interface that connects software applications directly to the networking hardware while retaining the security and protection of the operating system.

A VI-SAN is specially optimized for high-bandwidth and low-latency communications not achieved by traditional LAN/WAN technologies. LANs/WANs are often too slow for cluster interconnects, and involve the overhead of a full protocol stack (which increases with faster LAN/WAN connections) causing the processing capacity to be consumed for communications (cpu drag). SAN promise is to allow any cluster component (server, disk, or I/O device) to communicate with any other component with minimum processor intervention.

VI seems to be a promising solution, and the fact that it is a open specification and supported by major companies can hasten its acceptance. Version 1 of the VI Architecture specification was released at the end of 1997. Tandem's ServerNet was soon announced as a VI compliant interconnect.

Storage Area Network and Fiber Channel: SAN is an emerging concept that appears as the counterpart of LAN and WAN for the storage world. The goal is to eliminate the bandwidth bottlenecks and scalability limitations imposed by previous storage (mainly SCSI bus-based) architectures. In fact, SCSI is based on the concept of a single host transferring data to a single LUN (logical unit, e.g., disk drive) in a serial manner.

A technology closely associated with SAN is Fiber-Channel. Over the past few years, Fiber Channel Arbitrated Loop (FC-AL) has emerged as the high-speed, serial technology of choice for server-storage connectivity. With wide industry acceptance, including industry leading disk drive, disk array, server and networking connectivity suppliers, it has become the most widely endorsed open standard for the SAN environment. This broad acceptance is attributed not only to FC-AL's high bandwidth and high scalability, but also to its unique ability to support multiple protocols, such as SCSI and IP, over a single physical connection.

[5] The terminology adopted by the VI consortia can cause some confusion to the reader. In fact, the SAN acronym has been used by the storage community as meaning Storage Area Network, while VI refers to SAN as System Area Network. These are different things though. In the remainder of this chapter we will refer to the latter as VI-SAN to avoid confusion.

One of the most important advantages of the SAN approach is its modular scalability. The scalability offered by the SAN environment is key to enabling an infrastructure for long term growth and manageability. The dissociation between server processing power and data storage capacity through a high speed interconnect enables the independent scaling of these two critical system attributes.

In addition to the flexibility in scaling server processing capacity and data storage capacity, the networking approach of FC-AL introduces other novel and interesting aspects of interconnect scalability. Through the use of networking devices such as hubs, switches, bridges, and routers, complex and advanced SAN topologies can be created in order to scale overall bandwidth in the most appropriate manner.

4.5 Detecting and Masking Faults

A dependable system is built upon several layers. These layers can comprise a handful of techniques based on either software or hardware, but the starting point for tolerating errors is always to detect them. Error detection mechanisms (EDM) can be implemented both in hardware and software at several levels of abstraction. EDMs can be classified according to two important characteristics: the error *coverage* and the detection *latency*. The first corresponds to the percentage of errors that are detected, while the second represents the time an error takes to be detected. The longer the detection latency, the higher the probability of extending the error to other parts of the system and contaminating relevant application/system data. After error detection, the diagnosis layer attempts to collect as much information as possible about the location, source, and affected parts of the system. Diagnosis is of utmost importance, specially in the cluster case. In fact, in traditional clusters, the detection of an error in one node generally causes the hosted application to be failed over to a backup machine. If the fault was, for example, a hardware transient, or a software bug, then the node can be brought back to the cluster (normally after a reset). On the other hand, if the fault is hardware permanent, the problem can only be corrected by substituting the failed component/system. The way to distinguish both cases precisely is to run a diagnosis over the "failed" system.

After diagnosis, recovery and reconfiguration actions can finally take place. In the following sections, a series of techniques to detect, mask, and recover from faults are presented, from the low-level hardware mechanisms to the software-only approaches. This does not intend to be an exhaustive presentation of all existing techniques. Many other important techniques have been left out of the discussion. The intention is to make the reader aware of the great diversity of approaches and open the way for further readings.

4.5.1 Self-Testing

Errors generated by permanent faults may be detected by *self-testing*. Usually this error detection mechanism consists of executing specific programs that exercise different parts of the system (e.g. processor, memory, I/O, communications, etc.) and validating the output to the expected known results. Such tests may be executed periodically, after power-up, or after the occurrence of an error to locate its source. Self-tests are not very effective in detecting transient faults since their effects in the system vanish with time.

4.5.2 Processor, Memory, and Buses

The modern workstations and PCs used as the cluster's building blocks have several built-in and advanced means of detecting and correcting errors. Primary memories have at least parity bits, which detect single bit-flips. System buses can also have parity checking circuitry, usually with special support from the microprocessor. Also, error detection and correction (EDAC) chips are becoming more and more common on workstations hardware. These chips monitor system buses looking for errors and have the capability of detecting double bit errors and correcting single bit ones.[6]

Microprocessors inside the cluster nodes also have several built-in error detection mechanisms, namely: detection of illegal instructions, illegal accesses, and privileged instructions, among many others.

These kind of mechanisms are good at detecting certain types of errors, such as control-flow errors, but fail when the problem occurs at a higher level or affects data in subtle ways. For instance, if an application hangs because, for some reason, it entered an endless loop, this built-in hardware error detection method won't be able to detect anything. Those are the kind of errors that can be detected using software techniques, as will be explained later.

4.5.3 Watchdog Hardware Timers

A watchdog timer provides a simple way of keeping track of proper process functions. A timing is maintained as a process separated from the one it checks. If the timer is not reset before it expires, the corresponding process has probably failed in some way; the assumption is that any failure or corruption of the checked process will cause it to miss resetting the watchdog. Of course, coverage is limited because data and results are not checked. All the timer provides is an indication of possible process failure. The process may be only partially failed and produce errors, yet still be able to reset its timer (this is specially true if the task of timer-reset is the responsibility of a dedicated thread in multithreaded applications). The watchdog timer concept can be implemented in software or hardware, and both the watchdog and the monitored process can be running on the same hardware. In the next subsection the software watchdog concept will be explored in more detail, as there are several enhancements which are quite useful in the context of clustering.

[6]Also called SECDED capability (Single Error Correction Double Error Detection).

4.5.4 Loosing the Software Watchdog

A software watchdog is simply a process that monitors other process(es) for errors. Monitoring is usually accomplished with different accuracy, depending on whether the monitored process is aware of the monitoring watchdog and cooperates on its task. The simplest watchdog only watches its application until it eventually crashes, and the only action it takes is to relaunch the application. If the monitored process is instrumented to cooperate with the watchdog, then the efficiency of the surveillance increases substantially. WinFT is a typical example of a software watchdog [3]. Cooperation with the watchdog can be accomplished through several mechanisms. Some will be explained in the following paragraphs:

Heartbeats: The heartbeat is a periodic notification sent by the application to the watchdog to assert its aliveness. It can consist of an application-initiated "I'm Alive" message, or a request-response scheme in which the watchdog requests the application to assert its aliveness through a "Are you Alive?" message and waits for acknowledgment. In both cases, when a specified timeout expires at the watchdog side, it assumes the application is hung or crashed, kills it, and restarts it all over again. Watchdogs can coexist in the same system as the protected application or on another system. In the first case, the watchdog is useless if the OS itself crashes, while if the watchdog is on another system, it will detect that problem. Some clustering solutions provide several alternate heartbeat paths, for example, LifeKeeper supports heartbeats through TCP-IP, RS-232, and a shared SCSI bus. Therefore, if the problem is on the network card, LifeKeeper will notice that and will be better informed when deciding to make a switchover or not.

Idle notifications: The idea behind this notification, initiated by the application is to inform the watchdog about periods when the application is idle, or is not doing any useful work (a server without client requests). The watchdog can then perform preventive actions such as simply restarting the application. The rationale for this approach, awkward at first glance, is found on the principle of Software Rejuvenation [9]. Software Rejuvenation builds on the recognition that software, like human beings, gets older, for instance, the probability of faults is higher if the software is running continuously for a long time. This is a well-known phenomenon for most programmers. Faults are caused by memory leaks, boundary checking, and other problems that only manifest themselves after the software is running for some time. In this context, periodic rejuvenation on idle periods (planned downtime) can effectively increase the unplanned downtime of the application.

Error notifications: The rationale for this notification is that an application that is encountering errors which it can't overcome can signal the problem to the watchdog and request recovery actions. A restart may be enough to correct the problem, but the watchdog can take other corrective actions, such as cleaning files, or even rebooting the whole system.

4.5.5 Assertions, Consistency Checking, and ABFT

Consistency checking is a simple fault detection technique that can be implemented both at the hardware and at the programming level. A consistency check is performed by verifying that the intermediate or final results of some operation are reasonable, either on an absolute basis, or as a simple function of the inputs or other data used to derive the result. At the hardware level there are built-in consistency checks for checking addresses, opcodes, and arithmetic operations. Checking addresses consists simply in verifying that the address being accessed exists.

Another simple form of consistency checking is the range check – confirming that a computed value is within a valid range. A simple example is that of a valve where the aperture can vary within the range of 0 to 100 percent.

At the algorithm level, a technique with some similarities is used instead, Algorithm Based Fault Tolerance, or ABFT for short [8]. In this approach, after executing an algorithm, the application runs a consistency check specific for that algorithm which permits quick and easy verification if the results are correct (of course, for the cases such consistency checks are feasible). In [8] for instance, checksums are used to detect errors in matrix operations. The basic idea is to extend the matrices with additional columns that represent weighted checksums of the matrix rows. When the matrix calculation ends, the extra columns can be used to assert the correctness of the results.

4.6 Recovering from Faults

After faults have been detected and diagnosed recovery and reconfiguration actions may take place. The following sub-sections deal with recovery and reconfiguration related techniques.

4.6.1 Checkpointing and Rollback

Checkpointing is a technique that generally allows a process to save its state at regular intervals during normal execution so that it can be restored later after a failure to reduce the amount of lost work. Using checkpoints, when a fault occurs, the affected process can simply be restarted form the last saved checkpoint (state) rather than from the beginning. This technique is especially interesting to protect long-running applications against transient faults. Long-running applications are generally number-crunching programs that run for several days or weeks and for which a restart from scratch due to a fault may be unacceptable. Furthermore, checkpointing may also be suitable to recover applications from software errors. Indeed, several studies, such as these [19] using AT&T production code, have shown that checkpointing and rollback-replay were able to bypass 90 percent of the exceptions raised by software errors.

Checkpointing techniques are generally classified according to the following characteristics: transparency, data to include in the checkpoint, and the checkpointing interval.

First, checkpoints can be transparently and automatically inserted at runtime or by the compiler, or inserted manually by the application programmer. In the transparent approaches, the checkpoint consists of a global snapshot of the processor address state, including all the dynamic data of the OS. Other transparent approaches include only the processor internal context, the stack, and the static and dynamic data segments. In either case, transparent checkpointing usually has to save large amounts of data, and some of them unnecessarily, since it is not possible to determine which data is really critical to the application. On the other hand, in the manual approach, it is the programmer's responsibility to define exactly which data is critical and should be checkpointed for the applications, which considerably reduces the size of the checkpoint.

The issue of what data to checkpoint is critical for the success of the transparent approaches both in terms of overhead and coverage. As we saw, since it is not possible to checkpoint everything that can affect the behavior of a program, it is usually decided to save certain information and disregard other. Of course, pure transparent checkpoint is very had to achieve and when it is implemented, it is always in a very software-version-dependent manner (kernel, OS, libraries, etc.)

Another important characteristic is the *checkpointing interval*. This is simply the time interval between consecutive checkpoints. The optimal checkpoint interval is not easy to predict as it depends on several factors, such as the frequency of failures, the workload of the system, the overall execution time, the checkpoint overhead, and, of course, the level of dependability required. Again, this problem is critical mainly for automatic checkpointing. When the checkpoints are inserted manually by the application's programmer, things become much easier. In this case, checkpoints can be inserted at key points of the internal algorithm in order to maximize its meaningfulness.

The place where the checkpoint data is stored is also critical for successful use of this technique. This medium is commonly designed as *stable-storage* and must be resilient to hardware crashes, software failures, and immune to the phenomenon of memory decay. Moreover, the write and read operations should be performed in an atomic way, for example, the operation is either made completely or not made at all. Stable storage is usually implemented using replication in disk, special memory cards, memory replication, or still archives such as tape devices (for very large checkpoints).

4.6.2 Transactions

A transaction is a group of operations which form a consistent transformation of the state [7]. The operations may be database updates, messages, or external actions of the computer. Transactions are generally characterized by the so-called ACID (see below) properties:

- **Atomicity:** Either all or none of the actions of the transaction should "happen." Either it commits or aborts.

- **Consistency:** Each transformation should see a correct picture of the state, even if concurrent transactions are updating the state.
- **Integrity:** The transaction should be a correct state transformation.
- **Durability:** Once a transaction commits, all its effects must be preserved, even if there is a failure.

Transactions usually have a simple interface to the application programmer. A transaction is started by using the "Begin Transaction" command and terminated using the "End Transaction" command (or equivalent keywords). Transactions free the programmer from the burden of dealing with many error conditions. If needed, the command "Abort Transaction" can be invoked and the transaction is cancelled, cleaning up the state by resetting everything to the beginning of the transaction.

4.6.3 Failover and Failback

The *failover* process is the core of the cluster recovery model. It is simply a situation in which the failure of one node causes a switch to an alternative or backup node. Failover should be totally automatic and transparent, without the need for administrator intervention or client manual reconnection. Note that failover is quite different from *takeover*, a term used in fault-tolerant systems such as the Tandem Himalaya Servers [20]. These systems are built with multiple components running in lock-step, so that in the event of a failure the remaining component will seamlessly takeover operations with little or no performance degradation.

The reverse process of failover is termed *failback* and consists basically of moving back the applications/clients to the original server once it is repaired. As the failover itself, this process should be automatic and transparent (to the clients). Moreover, the failover capability can also be used efficiently for another important purpose: maintenance.

Maintenance actions can be performed on a server simply by switching over protected applications to a second server. On-line maintenance reduces or even eliminates the need for scheduled (planned) downtimes for common maintenance tasks and upgrades on the OS or other software. This is quite important today, as several studies have shown that system unavailability typically results from maintenance actions.

4.6.4 Reconfiguration

The failover process requires a number of resources to be switched over to the new system. For servers, it is specially important to switch network identity. This involves TCP-IP to dynamically change the IP address associated with the primary network card to the network card of the secondary server. If servers support Netbeui or Ipx, network names must also be switched over. Depending on what kind of application is running on the server, additional procedures may be necessary. For instance, Lifekeeper provides recovery packs specially built for MS SQL server,

Oracle, Informix, Sybase, SAP R/3, MS Exchange and Lotus Notes. These recovery packs provide specific recovery procedures for each of the target applications.

4.7 The Practice of Dependable Clustered Computing

This section provides a practical overview of several commercial cluster solutions: MSCS (formerly Wolfpack) from Microsoft, Oracle Failover, and NCR LifeKeeper. These approaches to the clustering problem employ somewhat different mechanisms focused on different target systems, but also share others, and may even coexist in some cases.

4.7.1 Microsoft Cluster Server

Formerly codenamed Wolfpack, MSCS intends to provide high-availability over legacy windows applications, as well as providing tools and mechanisms to create cluster-aware applications. Cluster-aware applications take advantage of the fact that they know they will run in a clustered system in order to increase their availability. MSCS inherited much of the experience of Tandem in High Avalability. As a Microsoft technology partner, Tandem provided the NonStop software and the ServerNet technology [1] from its Himalaya Servers to the Microsoft Cluster Server.

MSCS was planned as a phased approach: Phase I simply supports two node clusters and failover of one node to another. Phase II is expected to be a multinode share-nothing architecture scalable up to 16 nodes, able to improve support for self-management of distributed applications and for the development of cluster-aware (parallel) applications.

Note that MSCS is not lock-step/fault-tolerant; that is, it does not support the "moving" of running applications. This means that applications within a Microsoft cluster are not 99.99999 percent available – usually defined as a maximum of three or four seconds of downtime per year. MSCS can go up to 20 to 30 seconds of downtime per year.

MSCS provides an interesting structured approach to the cluster paradigm using a set of abstractions [23]: *Resource*, *Resource Group*, and *Cluster*. A *Resource* is a program or device managed by a cluster (file service, database server, print service, etc...). A *Resource Group* is a collection of related resources. Finally, a *Cluster* is a collection of nodes, resources, and groups. Resources are the basic building block of the architecture. Resources can depend on other resources (e.g., the database resource depends upon the file service resource) and have a common interface to the outside world. When a resource is failed-over to other node, its dependent resources are also moved together. In the same way, a resource is only brought online after the resources it depends on are online.

Resources can be on one of the following states: *Offline* (exists but is not offering service); *Online* (exists and offers service); *Failed* (not able to offer service). Resource failures may cause either a local restart, other resources to go *offline*, or an entire resource group to move. Each Resource has set of properties which define its behavior in the cluster, for example, the restart policy (local restart N times, failover), the polling intervals for IsAlive messages, timeouts, and any other specific properties of the resource.

Resources can be built for every application using special developer tools. Built-in resource types are File Shares, TCP-IP address, network name, and Print Spooler, but there are also generic application and service resources. Application programmers can provide their own specific resources for their applications. Oracle, SAP R/3, and SQL server have specific resources to work under MSCS. An API is specially provided for this end. The starting point are generic application resources which just provide an interface to start/stop the application and make sure the associated process is alive. For more elaborate application resources, a wizard is provided to help build more complex features.

Cluster configuration information, such as directories of members, resources, and resource and group parameters are stored in a separate registry which is replicated in each node. An important component of this strategy is the Quorum resource. It is usually, but not necessarily, a SCSI disk which keeps the cluster registry and logs, tracking all changes so that that a missing cluster node can always get updated information when it gets back.

4.7.2 NCR LifeKeeper

Back in 1980 NCR began delivering failover products to the telecommunications industry. The NCR clustering solution is currently named LifeKeeper and was born in the Unix world in the beginning of the nineties, being recently ported to Windows NT. Lifekeeper has multiple fault detection mechanisms: heartbeat via SCSI, LAN, and RS 232, event monitoring, and Log monitoring. Lifekeeper supports three different configurations: active/active, active/standby, and N-Way (with N =3). Lifekeeper has recovery action software kits for core system components – TCP-IP, LAN manager, SQL Server, Lotus Notes, Oracle, MS Exchange, Informix, SAP R/3 and PeopleSoft.

In addition, Lifekeeper provides a single point of administration and remote administration capabilities.

4.7.3 Oracle Fail Safe and Parallel Server

Oracle Failsafe and Oracle Parallel Server [5] are Oracle Database options for clustered systems. They are the archetype of a cluster solution specially designed for database systems. Oracle FailSafe is based on MSCS, supports a maximum of two nodes (due to limitations of MSCS phase I), and is targeted for workgroup and departmental servers. On the other hand, Parallel databases such as Oracle Parallel Server can support a single database running across multiple nodes in a cluster. As opposite to Failsafe, Parallel Server does not requires MSCS, supports more than two nodes, and is targeted for enterprise level systems, seeking not only HA but also scalability. Parallel Server also supports Digital Clusters for Windows NT and IBM's "Phoenix" technology. As with other vendor products for enterprises, Oracle

Parallel Server dates back to 1989 on Unix and VMS. With both Parallel Server and Failsafe, Oracle servers become capable of supporting hot-backups, replication, and mirrored solutions.

The Oracle data server can be seen as a cluster-enabled application which takes advantage of the processing power of the entire system and can divide workload across the available nodes in the cluster to maximize system utilization. In addition, a cluster-enabled application provides data integrity by coordinating transactions across the cluster. For example, if two nodes are updating the same data file containing a customer's information, the cluster can synchronize any changes to provide that they are properly committed.

4.8 Bibliography

[1] W. Baker, R. Horst, D. Sonnier, and W. Watson. A Flexible ServerNet Based Fault-Tolerant Architecture. *Proceedings from the 25th Symposium on Fault Tolerant Computing, FTCS'95*. June 1995.

[2] J. Carreira, H. Madeira, and J. G. Silva. Assessing the Effects of Communication Faults on Parallel Applications. *Proceedings of the International Computer and Dependability Symposium*, pages 214-223, Erlangen, Germany, 24-26 April 1995.

[3] J. Carreira, D. Costa, and J. G. Silva. Fault Tolerance for Windows Applications. *BYTE magazine, Core Technology - Operating Systems Column*, February 1997.

[4] J. Carreira, H. Madeira, and J. G. Silva. Xception: A Technique for the Evaluation of Dependability in Modern Computers. *IEEE Transactions on Software Engineering*, vol. 24(2), February 1998.

[5] L. Clarke. Oracle Fail Safe Solutions for Windows NT Clusters. *Oracle White Paper*, Oracle New England Development Center, September 1998.

[6] J. Gray. Why do Computers Stop and What Can be Done About It? *5th Symposium on Reliability in Distributed Software and Database Systems*, pages 3-12, January 1986.

[7] J. Gray, and A. Reuter. Transaction Processing: Concepts and Techniques. *The Morgan Kaufmann Series in Data Management Systems*, San Mateo, CA, ISBN 1-55860-190-2, 1993.

[8] K. Huang, and J. Abraham. Algorithm-Based Fault Tolerance for Matrix Operations. *IEEE Trans. on Computers*, vol. C-33(6), pages 518-528, June 1984.

[9] Y. Huang, C. Kintala, N. Kolettis and N. Fulton. Software Rejuvenation: Analysis, Module and Applications. *Proceedings from the 25th Symposium on Fault Tolerant Computing, FTCS'95*, 1995.

[10] P. K. Lala. *Fault Tolerant and Fault Testable Hardware Design*. Prentice Hall, NJ 1985.

[11] J. C. Laprie (ed.). Dependability: Basic Concepts and Terminology. *Dependable Computing and Fault Tolerance*, Springer-Verlag, vol.5, 1992.

[12] J. Leon. Fail-Safe PVM. *PVM Users Group Meeting*, Oak Ridge, TN, May 1994.

[13] A. M. Levitt. *Disaster Planning and Recovery: A Guide for Facility Professionals*. John Wiley and Sons, NY 1997, ISBN 0-471-14205-0.

[14] D. Long, A. Muir, R. Golding. A Longitudinal Survey of Internet Reliability. *Proc. 14th Symposium on Reliable Distributed Systems*, pages 2-9, Germany, September 1995.

[15] NCR LifeKeeper. *Technical White Paper*, http://www.ncr.com, 1997.

[16] G. Pfister. *In Search of Clusters: The Coming Battle in Lowly Parallel Computing*. Prentice-Hall, NJ 1995, ISBN 0134376250.

[17] D. P. Siweiorek, and R. S. Swarz. *The Theory and Practice of Reliable System Design*. Digital Press, Digital Equipment Corporation, ISBN 0-932376-13-4, 1983.

[18] L. Silva. Checkpointing Mechanisms for Scientific Parallel Applications. *Phd Thesis*, University of Coimbra, Portugal, ISBN 972-97189-0-3, January 1997.

[19] G. Suri, Y. Huang, Y. Huang, W. K. Fuchs, and C. Kintala. An implementation and Performance measurement of the Progressive Retry Technique. *Proc. IEEE Int. Computer Performance and Dependability Symposium*, pages 41-48, 1995.

[20] NonStop Himalaya S70000SE Server. *Tandem White paper*, http://www.tandem.com, 1998.

[21] Virtual Interface Architecture Specification: Version 1.0. http://www.viarch.org, December 16, 1997.

[22] Co-Standby Server for NT. *Vinca Corporation Technical White Paper*, February 10, 1998, http://www.vinca.com.

[23] W. Vogels, D. Dumitriu, K. Birman, R. Gamache, M. Massa, R. Short, J. Vert, J. Barrera, J. Gray. The Design and Architecture of the Microsoft Cluster Service: A Practical Approach to High-Availability and Scalability. *FTCS'98*, Munich, Germany, June 23-25, 1998,

Chapter 5

Deploying a High Throughput Computing Cluster

Jim Basney and Miron Livny

Department of Computer Sciences
University of Wisconsin-Madison
Wisconsin, USA
Email: *jbasney@cs.wisc.edu*, *miron@cs.wisc.edu*

5.1 Introduction

A High Throughput Computing (HTC) environment strives to provide large amounts of processing capacity to customers over long periods of time by exploiting existing computing resources on the network. To maximize processing capacity, the HTC environment must utilize heterogeneous resources. This requires a portable solution, which includes a resource management framework that effectively encapsulates the differences between resources in the cluster. To provide capacity over long periods of time, the environment must be reliable and maintainable—surviving software and hardware failures, allowing resources to join and leave the cluster easily, and enabling system upgrade and reconfiguration without significant downtime.

Most importantly, the system must meet the needs of resource owners, customers, and system administrators, since without the support of any one of these groups the HTC environment will fail. Resource owners donate the use of their resources to the customers of the HTC environment. Before they are willing to do this, the owners must be satisfied that their rights will be respected and the policies they specify will be enforced. Customers will use the HTC environment to run their applications only if the benefit of additional processing capacity is not outweighed by the cost of learning the complexities of the HTC system. System administrators will install and maintain the system only if it provides a tangible benefit to its users which outweighs the cost of maintaining the system.

Resources in the HTC cluster may be distributively owned, meaning that the control over powerful computing resources in the cluster is distributed among many individuals and small groups. For example, many individuals in an organization may each have "ownership" of a powerful desktop workstation. The willingness to share a resource with the HTC environment may vary for each resource owner. The cluster may include some resources which are dedicated to HTC, others which are unavailable for HTC during certain hours or when the resource is otherwise in use, and still others which are available to only specific HTC customers and applications. Even when resources are available for HTC, the application may be allowed only limited access to the components of the resource and may be preempted at any time. Additionally, distributed ownership often results in decentralized maintenance, when resource owners maintain and configure each resource for a specific use. This adds an additional degree of resource heterogeneity to the cluster.

The deployment of an HTC cluster is both a technological and sociological process. The HTC software must be robust and feature-rich to meet the needs of resource owners, customers, and system administrators. However, even the best HTC system must have support within an organization before it can be deployed effectively. Often, developing this support is an evolutionary process. First, an HTC "evangelist" deploys a small cluster with his or her own resources and with resources donated by HTC "allies." The HTC evangelist then helps a few HTC customers effectively use the small cluster. By demonstrating the benefits of the HTC cluster to these customers, the evangelist creates demand for HTC within the organization. At this point, the customers may approach the system administrators and policy makers to request that the pool be expanded, or the customers may approach resource owners directly to ask for additional resource donations. The customers are also in the position to help more of their colleagues become customers of the cluster.

This chapter describes some of the challenges faced by software developers and system administrators when deploying an HTC cluster, and some of the approaches for meeting those challenges based on the experience of the developers and administrators of the Condor HTC environment, which has been deployed for over a decade at the University of Wisconsin-Madison Computer Sciences department [1]. We focus on those issues which become more important when the cluster grows large and is maintained for many years. In our experience, it is not exotic scheduling algorithms and mechanisms which make an HTC environment successful, but an emphasis on usability, flexibility, reliability, and maintainability.

5.2 Condor Overview

While a detailed description of Condor is outside the scope of this chapter, we give a short overview here to provide a concrete example of an HTC system architecture.

In Condor, each customer is represented by a customer agent, which manages a queue of application descriptions and sends resource requests to the matchmaker. Each resource is represented by a resource agent, which implements the policies of the resource owner and sends resource offers to the matchmaker. The matchmaker is responsible for finding matches between resource requests and resource offers and

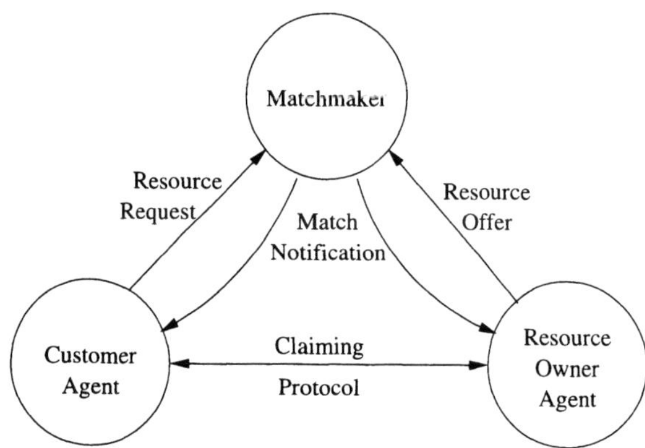

Figure 5.1 Condor resource management architecture.

notifying the agents when a match is found. Upon notification, the customer agent and the resource agent perform a claiming protocol to initiate the allocation. This architecture is illustrated in Figure 5.1.

Resource requests and offers contain constraints which specify if a match is acceptable. So, the customer agent includes a constraint in its resource request which specifies which resource offers are acceptable. For example, the customer agent may desire only resources running a specific operating system. The resource agent includes a constraint in the resource offer which specifies which requests it will service. For example, the resource agent may only be willing to service requests made by a specific customer. An offer matches a request when both constraints are satisfied.

The matchmaker implements systemwide policies by imposing its own set of constraints on matches. For example, the matchmaker implements a customer priority mechanism by matching resource requests in priority order, so resource requests from customers with better priorities have a better opportunity to find a match. The matchmaker may preempt allocations by matching a resource with a new request to maintain a fair distribution of allocations. The customer agent or the resource agent may also choose to break the allocation at any time.

5.3 Software Development

The developer of an HTC system must overcome four primary challenges: utilization of heterogeneous resources, evolution of network protocols, remote file access, and utilization of nondedicated resources. The utilization of heterogeneous resources requires system portability, which can be obtained most effectively through a layered system design. A smooth evolution of network protocols is required for a system where resources and customer needs are constantly changing, requiring the deployment of new features in the HTC system. A remote file access mechanism

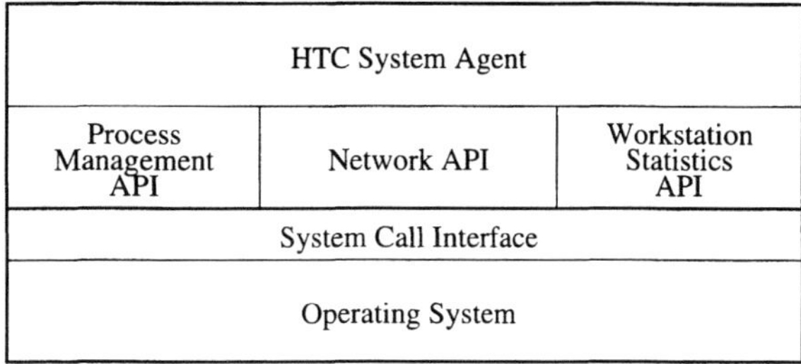

Figure 5.2 Layered software architecture.

guarantees that an application will be able to access its data files from any workstation in the cluster. Finally, the utilization of non-dedicated resources requires the ability to preempt and resume an application using a checkpoint mechanism.

5.3.1 Layered Software Architecture

The HTC system is a client of the workstation operating system. In particular, the HTC system relies on the host operating system to provide network communication, process management, and workstation statistics. Since the interface to these services differs on each operating system, the portability of the HTC system will benefit from a layered software architecture, as shown in Figure 5.2. The system is written to a system independent API, reducing the cost of porting to a new architecture, because the nonportable code is isolated in the API libraries.

The network API provides both connection-oriented and connectionless, reliable and unreliable interfaces, with many mechanisms for authentication and encryption. It performs all conversions between host and network integer byte order automatically, checks for overflows (when, for example, sending an integer from a 64-bit workstation to a 32-bit workstation), and provides standard host address lookup mechanisms.

The process management API provides the ability to create, suspend, unsuspend, and kill a process to enable the HTC system to control the execution of a customer's application. A parent process may pass state to new child processes, including network connections, open files, environment variables, and security attributes. Since the customer's application does not necessarily use any HTC libraries, the API implementation must not assume that the child process also runs an instance of the same API.

The workstation statistics API reports the information necessary to implement the resource owner policies and verify that the customer application requirements are met. The resource owner policy may refer to the CPU, network, and disk load, the time of day, the time since the last keyboard or mouse activity, the amount of available swap space, and other resource attributes. The customer application may, for example, require a specific operating system and CPU architecture, and a minimum amount of available physical memory, disk space, and network bandwidth.

Many libraries already exist to provide portable system services to applications. For example, the XDR (eXternal Data Representation) library provides translation services between data representations on different operating systems and processor architectures. There are obvious benefits to using standard libraries when developing the HTC system. Since the libraries are already written, the HTC developers save time by using the libraries in lieu of developing new libraries. The developers save time when porting the HTC system to new platforms if the existing libraries are already available for the new platform. Also, one can assume that a library which is already in wide use is better tested than a new library. However, these benefits are not always realized. General purpose libraries are often poor fits to the specific needs of an HTC environment, and so using such libraries adds unnecessary baggage to the system. Additionally, the library may not be available for all platforms or may work incorrectly on some platforms, resulting in porting and debugging work for the HTC developer.

5.3.2 Layered Resource Management Architecture

The resource management architecture of the HTC environment also benefits from a layered system design framework. Figure 5.3 shows such an architecture used in Condor. This approach yields a modular system design, where the interface to each system layer is defined in the resource management model, allowing the implementation of each layer to change so long as the interface continues to be supported. Customized customer agents may be developed with different scheduling algorithms optimized for specific classes of applications. Resource owner agents may be customized to implement desired access control mechanisms. The matchmaker (part of the System Layer) may be upgraded to utilize new resource management algorithms without requiring an upgrade of other agents in the cluster.

This architecture separates the advertising, matchmaking, and claiming protocols. The agents advertise resource offers and requests asynchronously to the matchmaker, and the matchmaker notifies the agents when a match is found. Since the matchmaker is not involved in the claiming protocol, the protocol may be customized for specific types of agents, and may be modified without affecting the negotiator. The matchmaker does not need to know the details of allocation establishment, and so many different allocation protocols may be easily supported by the same matchmaker [2].

5.3.3 Protocol Flexibility

As the distributed system evolves to provide new and improved services, the network protocols will be affected. Often, the protocols are augmented to transfer additional information. This often requires that all components of the distributed system be updated to recognize the additional information. In a large HTC system, it is often inconvenient to update all components at one time, and so new features are not deployed until a future major system upgrade.

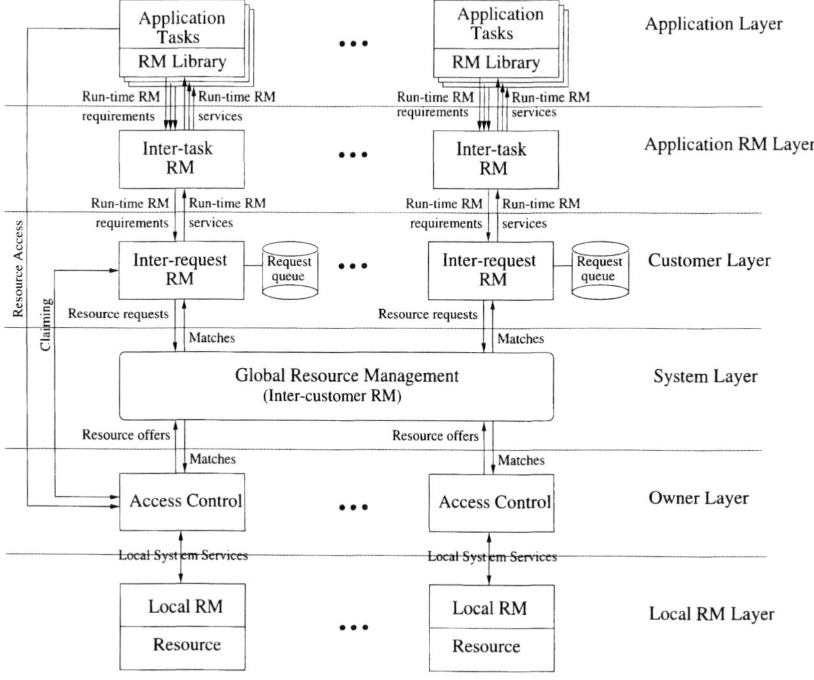

Figure 5.3 Layered resource management architecture.

To support this evolution, the HTC network protocols may utilize a general-purpose data format which allows more flexibility. For example, Figure 5.4 illustrates the protocol data format used throughout Condor. A leading integer specifies the protocol action to be performed, and the named parameter list which follows specifies the data associated with that protocol action. This is similar to an RPC protocol, where an integer first specifies the RPC being invoked and the parameters of the call follow. The parameters in the list[1] are named, so the receiver may iterate through the parameter list, or may simply look up the values for the named parameters of interest. To enhance the protocol, new parameters are simply added to the parameter list. Backward compatibility is ensured, since older agents will ignore the new parameters and new agents are written to accept packets with or without the new parameters.

5.3.4 Remote File Access

A remote file access mechanism guarantees that an HTC application will have access to its data files from any workstation in the cluster. This mechanism may use an

[1]The named parameter list is a use of the Condor ClassAd resource management language, which is described in more detail in [3].

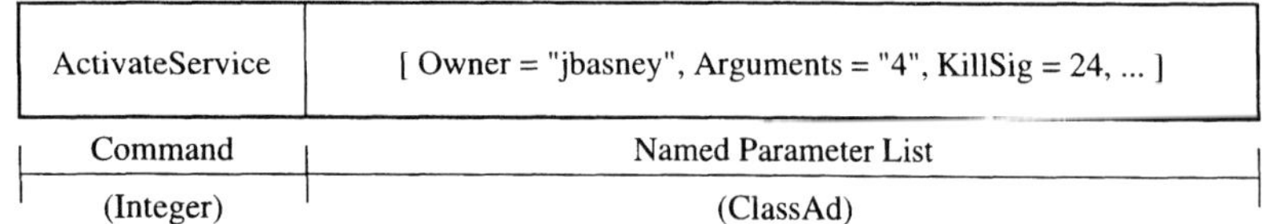

Figure 5.4 Example of protocol data format.

existing distributed file system, it may stage data files on the workstation's local disk, or it may redirect file I/O system calls to a remote file server via system call interposition.

To effectively use an existing distributed file system, the HTC environment must authenticate the customer's application to that file system. For example, NFS authenticates via user ID, while AFS and NTFS authenticate via Kerberos and NT server credentials. To run the customer's application with the appropriate distributed file system rights, the HTC environment may require administrator privileges on the remote workstation, the ability to transparently forward credentials, or the ability to obtain the customer's credentials (for example, using the customer's password). Alternatively, the customer may be required to grant file access permission to the HTC system before submitting the application for execution.

To implement data file staging, the HTC system requires a list of input files from the customer for each application. The system then transfers these input files to the local disk of the remote workstation before running the application. The system is responsible for gathering up the application's output files and transferring them to a destination specified by the customer when the application has completed. This requires free disk space on the remote workstation and the bandwidth to transfer the data files at the start and end of each allocation. For large data files, this results in high start-up and tear-down costs compared to a block file access mechanism provided by a distributed file system or redirected file I/O system calls.

To redirect file I/O system calls, the HTC environment must interpose itself between the application and the operating system and service file I/O system calls itself [4], [5], as illustrated in Figure 5.5. This may be accomplished by linking the application with an interposition library or by trapping system calls through an operating system interface. The HTC environment invokes an RPC to perform the file operation on a server with access to the customer's data files. Since the file operations are performed at the system call level, this may result in many high latency operations, reducing the performance of the application. Read-ahead and write-behind caching can effectively reduce this latency.

Redirecting file I/O system calls has the significant benefit that it places no file system requirement on the remote workstation. This enables the HTC environment to utilize a greater number of resources. The drawback is that developing and maintaining a portable interposition system can be very difficult, since different operating systems provide different interposition techniques and the system call

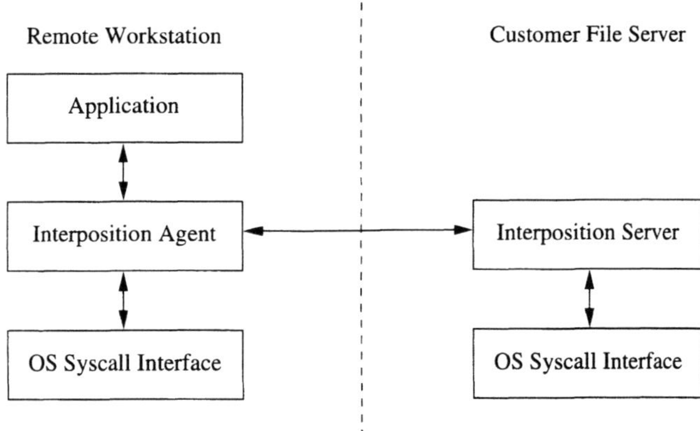

Figure 5.5 System call interposition.

interface differs on each operating system and often changes with each new operating system release. If an interposition library is used, then multiple compilers and linking techniques (static versus dynamic linking, 32-bit versus 64-bit executables, etc.) must often be supported. Thus, supporting the redirection of file I/O system calls can be a significant portion of the cost of deploying an HTC cluster.

5.3.5 Checkpointing

A checkpoint of an executing program is a snapshot of its state which can be used to restart the program from that state at a later time. Computing systems have traditionally employed checkpointing to provide reliability: when a compute node fails, the program running on that node can be restarted from its most recent checkpoint, either on that same node once it is restored or potentially on another available node. Checkpointing also enables preemptive-resume scheduling. All parties involved in an allocation can break the allocation at any time without losing the work already accomplished by simply checkpointing the application. Thus, a long running application can make progress even when allocations last for relatively short periods of time. Due to the opportunistic nature of non-dedicated resources in a cluster environment, any attempt to deliver HTC has to rely on a checkpointing mechanism.

Since most workstation operating systems do not provide kernel-level checkpointing services, an HTC environment must often rely on user-level checkpointing. Developing a portable, robust user-level checkpointing mechanism is a significant challenge for the developer of an HTC environment [6], [7], since operating system APIs for querying and setting process state vary and are often incomplete.

5.4 System Administration

The administrator of an HTC environment answers to resource owners, customers, and policy makers. It is the administrator's responsibility to guarantee that the HTC environment enforces the access policies of resource owners. Since resources in a cluster are often heterogeneous and distributively owned, these policies are often complicated and vary from resource to resource. The administrator is also responsible for ensuring that customers receive valuable service from the HTC environment. This involves working with customers to understand the needs of their applications and developing an approach for running each application in the HTC environment. It also often requires detecting application failures, investigating the causes of the failures, and developing solutions to avoid future failures. Finally, the system administrator often must demonstrate to policy makers that the HTC environment is meeting stated goals. This requires accounting of system usage and availability.

5.4.1 Access Policies

The resource access policy specifies who may use a resource, how they may use it, and when they may use it. The administrator determines an access policy in consultation with the resource owner and implements that policy through a configuration of the HTC environment. The configuration mechanism must be rich enough to express a wide variety of access policies.

One method for policy specification is to define a set of expressions which specify when an application may begin using a resource and when and how an application must stop using a resource. For example, consider the following set of expressions:

- The *Requirements* expression evaluates to *true* when an application may begin using the resource.
- The *Rank* expression evaluates to a larger numerical value for applications which the owner would prefer over others.
- The *Suspend* expression evaluates to *true* when the active application should be immediately suspended.
- The *Continue* expression evaluates to *true* when the active application should be immediately unsuspended.
- The *Vacate* expression evaluates to *true* when the active application should be notified to stop using the resource. The application may continue using the resource for a short time to save its intermediate results.
- The *Kill* expression evaluates to *true* when the active application should be immediately stopped.

These expressions may refer to both application attributes (such as the identity of the customer) and resource attributes (such as the time since the last keyboard event).

Consider the following example access policy. The owner of a desktop workstation will allow an application to use the workstation only when the owner has not been using it for fifteen minutes (i.e., the keyboard and mouse have been idle for that period of time, and the CPU load is low). Furthermore, the owner may prefer to run applications owned by "jbasney@cs.wisc.edu" over other applications. Finally, when the owner returns (i.e., the keyboard and mouse are no longer idle), the application should be immediately suspended. If the owner continues to use the workstation for five minutes, the application should be notified to stop using the resource. The application should be immediately stopped if it is still running five minutes later. This policy is implemented with the following expressions:

```
Requirements = (KeyboardIdle > 15*Minute) && (LoadAvg < 0.3)
Rank = (Customer == "jbasney@cs.wisc.edu") ? 1 : 0
Suspend = (KeyboardIdle < Minute)
Continue = (KeyboardIdle > 2*Minute)
Vacate = (SuspendTime > 5*Minute)
Kill = (VacateTime > 5*Minute)
```

Suspend, Vacate, and Kill provide three mechanisms for the owner to preempt a running application. Each mechanism results in different costs for the application and the resource owner. Suspend keeps the application state on the resource (i.e., in virtual memory) but suspends execution. This benefits the application when the owner reclaims the resource for only a short time, because it allows the application to immediately resume its execution (via Continue) when the resource is available again. Vacate allows the application to save any immediate results (i.e., checkpoint) before relinquishing the resource. Alternatively, Kill does not allow the application to save intermediate results, so the application's work is lost. Thus, by enabling Suspend and/or Vacate, the resource owner allows the application to better utilize the resource at the cost of a prolonged preemption.

The cost of application placement and preemption are significant factors in setting good access policies. Application placement requires transferring the executable, checkpoint, and data files to the remote host, and preemption requires transferring checkpoint and data files to a new remote host or to storage. Since the application checkpoint contains the memory state of the process, it may be very large (100MB+), and therefore transferring this data over the network may require a large amount of bandwidth. These costs motivate the use of Suspend, which avoids the cost of preemption and placement when the resource is reclaimed for only a short period of time.

In the example policy above, the application is allowed five minutes after the Vacate event to save its state before the Kill event occurs. On low-bandwidth networks, a large application will not be able to complete its checkpoint in this time period. To improve throughput in such an environment, the administrator will want to attempt to negotiate a longer Vacate interval with the resource owners.

In cases when the chance of successful checkpoint is very low, the administrator can configure the workstation to not attempt a Vacate, since it will only cause unnecessary network traffic. For example:

```
Vacate = (SuspendTime > 5*Minute) && (JobImageSize < 100*MB)
Kill = (JobImageSize < 100*MB) ? (VacateTime > 5*Minute) :
       (SuspendTime > 5*Minute)
```

The administrator may use a periodic checkpoint mechanism to reduce the amount of work lost as a result of failed preemption checkpoints and other system failures (network failure, workstation hardware failure, etc.). Applications are configured to perform checkpoints periodically so that they can rollback to the most recent checkpoint in the case of a failure. Since performing periodic checkpoints consumes CPU, network, and disk resources, the administrator must balance the periodic checkpoint frequency with the expected rate of failure.

The administrator may also steer matchmaking to utilize resources efficiently when network bandwidth is limited. Strategies include steering applications with greater network requirements to resources with greater available network bandwidth and longer expected allocation times. The administrator uses his or her knowledge of the networking infrastructure, network load, and application requirements to effectively configure the HTC environment.

5.4.2 Reliability

Reliability is a primary concern in an HTC environment because of the variety of risks of failure and the special needs of HTC customers. The HTC environment relies on the services provided by the network, hardware, and operating system of each node on the network. The system must strive to mask failures in these components and recover gracefully. The HTC environment must also handle failures in components of the HTC system itself, as such software failures are to be expected in such a complicated distributed system. HTC customers rely on the environment to manage the execution of their applications. Since these applications may have long execution times (weeks, months, or years), it is essential that applications survive these failures.

A distributed file system can be a frequent cause of system failures. The HTC environment may rely on a distributed file system to provide file access to applications, system configuration files, executables, and log files. A file system failure may appear to a long running as a failed system call. Many applications will simply abort when this occurs. The HTC environment can put this application "on hold" until the file system recovers and then restart the application from a previous checkpoint. If the HTC executables are accessed via a distributed file system, a file system failure may cause process crashes due to page faults which can not be serviced.[2] The HTC software must also react appropriately when configuration files

[2]This is caused by the operating system using the executable file as the backing store for the text pages of the process. When the executable file is inaccessible, the process fails once a page fault occurs in the text segment.

and log files are temporarily inaccessible.

Since the HTC system is responsible for enforcing the policies of the resource owner, it is essential that the system processes don't fail and leave running applications unattended. The HTC environment can provide functionality which enables the administrator to enhance the reliability of these processes. A Master process can be dedicated to monitoring the other HTC processes on a workstation to detect failures and invoke recovery mechanisms. This process can also cache executable files on the local disk of the workstation to avoid unserviceable page faults. Additionally, this process may serve as an administrative module of the HTC environment, to report which services are currently running, allow the administrator to start and stop services, and to detect and react to configuration changes and system upgrades. In a large cluster, a Master process can dramatically reduce the cost of system reconfiguration and upgrade by automatically retrieving new files from the distributed file system and gracefully restarting local services to take advantage of the upgrade.

There are a number of complications which arise when implementing a mechanism to allow applications to recover from system failures. The HTC software must be able to detect the difference between normal application termination, abnormal termination due to an environmental failure, and abnormal termination due to an unrecoverable application error. One approach is to monitor the system calls performed by the application to detect the source of failures. Alternatively, the system could defer to the customer, asking the customer to alert the system when an application terminates abnormally. The HTC software must also choose the correct checkpoint to use for restart. It is possible for an environmental failure to cause a failure in the application which results in an abnormal termination after a significant delay. During that delay, the application may have performed a checkpoint. The HTC system should ideally rollback to a checkpoint which was performed before the failure occurred. Finally, the HTC software must decide when it is safe to restart the application. If the source of the failure is known, the system could poll to determine when the failure has been resolved. Alternatively, the system could contact the customer or system administrator and request a response when the failure has been diagnosed and resolved.

An HTC environment is particularly susceptible to the "problem of one bad node." This problem occurs when one node in the cluster enters into a state which causes application failures (the node may run out of swap space, a memory module may go bad, network file services may fail, etc.). Thus, whenever an application begins running on this node, it terminates abnormally. The HTC environment must avoid naively running application after application on this workstation, or this single node will be able to quickly drain the system of applications (or put them all "on hold"). Thus, for an application failure, the system must determine if the application failed due to the specific environment of the current node, due to the current environment of the entire cluster, or due to an application error. This could be determined heuristically: if the application fails consistently on different nodes, then it is reasonable to conclude that the entire cluster environment is experiencing the problem for this application; if different applications fail on the same node, then it is reasonable to conclude that the particular node is to blame and should be disabled.

To summarize, the HTC environment must be prepared for failures and must automate failure recovery for common failures. This need grows significantly as the cluster grows in size. By successfully handling common failures, the HTC environment frees the administrator to investigate less common failures and to otherwise concentrate on managing the system for efficiency.

5.4.3 Problem Diagnosis via System Logs

Failures will occur in even the most reliable HTC environment—applications may terminate abnormally, resource owners may report that their resource is being used inappropriately, customers may report that they are not receiving a fair amount of service, etc. System log files are the primary tools for diagnosing system failures. Using good log files, the administrator should be able to reconstruct the events leading up to the failure, which in most cases will uncover the cause of the failure. Log files are also essential in determining if a failure actually occurred. For example, the resource owner who reports that the resource policy has been breached may be mistaken or may have a misunderstanding of the policy implementation. Knowing what occurred on the resource helps the administrator to decide if the customer's policy should be modified or if there is a system problem. Maintenance of good system logs requires the decision of what information to log and a mechanism for writing and accessing system logs.

Table 5.1 lists some of the useful information which can be logged by the HTC system. The information is categorized by HTC subsystem to show the importance of effective log file organization. For example, when investigating a reported scheduling problem, the administrator will first focus only on the scheduling logs, avoiding the distraction of unrelated log messages. There are a number of potentially useful organizations or views for system logs. For example, when investigating the failure of a specific application, it may be useful to trace the life of the application through the different subsystems to see when the application was scheduled, how long the allocation lasted, which system calls were performed by the application during the allocation, and which resource policy action (if any) coincided with the application failure. This example argues for an application-specific view of the system logs. Customer or resource specific views are also helpful. The administrator also needs to be able to view different levels of logging detail when diagnosing a problem. These views may be implemented by logging each view to a separate file or by tagging each log entry with a descriptive key which specifies the views to which it belongs.

System logs can grow to an unbounded size, so it is necessary to manage the amount of historical log information which is kept by the system. The logging facility can be configurable, so that detailed logs are kept for an administrator-specified period of time, and then only summaries are kept for older information. For example, when the administrator arrives on Monday morning to discover a

Table 5.1 HTC Environment Logs

application log:	system call trace checkpoint information and statistics remote I/O trace with statistics errors occurring during the allocation
customer log:	allocation information and statistics application arrival and termination matchmaking and claiming errors
resource log:	allocation information and statistics policy action trace
master log:	HTC agent (re-)starts administrative commands agent upgrades
scheduling log:	record of all matches allocation history (accounting)
security log:	record of all rejected requests record of all authenticated actions

problem report, it is useful to have detailed logs from the weekend to diagnose the problem. It is also useful to have a historical summary of system usage which goes back many years, to track changes in cluster capacity and customer demand, so the administrator may report the return received on the investment in the HTC system.

Managing distributed log files can be cumbersome, often requiring the administrator to remotely access workstation after workstation to follow the migration of an application or to examine many instances of a particular problem. One alternative is to store logs centrally on a file server or a customized log server. Another alternative is to provide a single interface to the distributed log files by installing logging agents on each workstation which will respond to log queries made by a client application.

5.4.4 Monitoring and Accounting

In addition to diagnostic logs, the HTC environment provides system monitoring and accounting facilities to the administrator. This allows the administrator to assess the current and historical state of the system and to track system usage.

For example, Figure 5.6 shows a stacked graph of the number of allocated ("Condor"), available ("Idle"), and unavailable ("Owner") resources in the UW-Madison Computer Sciences Condor cluster for the month of September 1998. From this visualization, the administrator can conclude that:

- Approximately 100 resources were added to the cluster during the month.
- Over 50 percent of the cluster capacity was harnessed by HTC applications

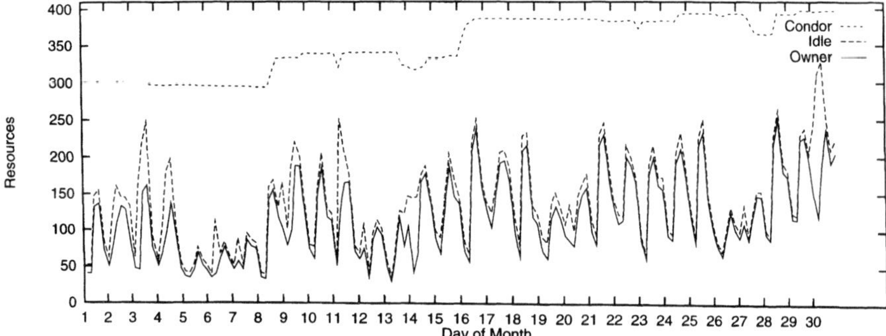

Figure 5.6 Monitoring resource usage.

during the month.

- Resource availability followed a daily cyclic pattern, where more resources were available for HTC during the night.
- On average, more resources were available to HTC applications on weekends compared to weekdays.
- Very few resources were left unutilized by either the owner or an HTC application, except on a few occasions (for example, September 14 and 30). A large number of unutilized resources is a sign of system inefficiency or a shortage of customer requests.

Figure 5.7 shows a stacked graph of the number of idle and running applications in the Condor cluster during September 1998. The daily cyclic pattern of available resources is seen again here in the number of running applications. Also, a shortage of customer requests is shown to be the cause of the unutilized resources on September 14.

Using the same accounting facilities which generated these graphs, the administrator can see that HTC applications were allocated approximately 155 thousand CPU hours during the month.[3]

5.4.5 Security

An HTC environment is potentially vulnerable to both resource and customer attacks. A resource attack occurs when an unauthorized user gains access to a resource via the HTC environment or when an authorized user violates the resource owner's access policy. A customer attack occurs when the customer's account or data files are compromised via the HTC environment.

[3]These statistics are available online at http://www.cs.wisc.edu/condor/.

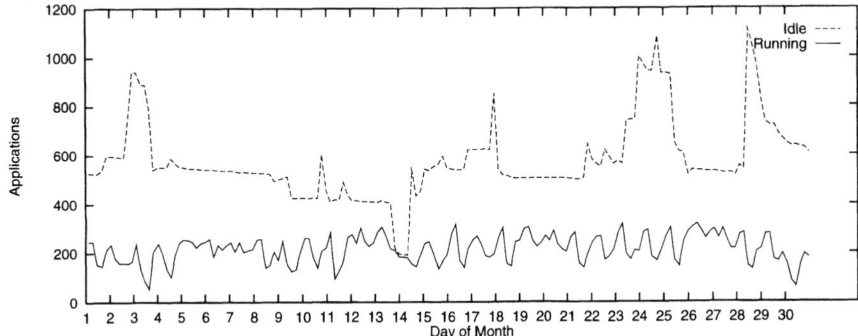

Figure 5.7 Monitoring HTC applications.

Protecting the resource from unauthorized access requires an effective user authentication mechanism. The resource owner may explicitly list authorized users in the access policy, using the Requirements expression. For example:

Requirements = (Customer == "jbasney@cs.wisc.edu" ||
Customer == "miron@cs.wisc.edu")

The HTC system must ensure the validity of the Customer attribute. The resource agent can verify the Customer attribute by requesting that the customer agent digitally sign the resource request with the customer's private key. The resource agent will then verify the signature and the fact that the *Requirements* expression is *true* for this resource request. Alternatively, the resource agent may establish a trust relationship with the customer agent, and rely on the customer agent to set the Customer attribute appropriately.

Protecting against violations of the resource owner's access policy requires that the resource agent maintain control over the application and monitor its activity. The resource agent may use the operating system API to set resource consumption limits for the application. It may also run the application under a "guest" account which provides only limited access to the workstation. To limit file system access, the agent may use operating system APIs to set the file system root directory to a "sandbox" directory. Perhaps the most effective approach, however, is to intercept the system calls performed by the application via the operating system interposition interface. This allows the resource agent to monitor all system access performed by the application and to enforce the owner's access policy by aborting any system calls which would violate it.

To submit an application to the HTC environment, the customer must grant the system access to the application executable and data files. This may be done by transferring the files to a directory or file system dedicated for HTC applications. In this case, the application may run with credentials specific to the HTC environment, without the need for the customer's credentials. When the application terminates, the customer retrieves the output files from the dedicated area. In this case, the customer's executable and data files are potentially vulnerable to snooping or modification. Alternatively, the HTC environment may run the application with the customer's file system credentials, allowing the customer's files to be accessed directly and conveniently. In this case, the customer's account is potentially vulnerable.

An untrustworthy resource agent can potentially mount a customer attack. To allow remote execution, the application must have access to its data files via a remote file access mechanism. The resource agent, therefore, has the opportunity to manipulate or replace the application to steal the customer's data or modify the customer's files. In the case when the application runs with the customer's file system credentials, the attacker has the opportunity to access all of the customer's files and install a trojan horse in the customer's file system. To protect against this attack, the HTC environment must ensure that all resource agents are trustworthy. Resource agents may be authenticated cryptographically or the cluster can be restricted to include only resource agents on trusted hosts (authenticated via IP-address,[4] for example).

Unencrypted network streams provide another potential vulnerability. Customer data and file system credentials sent unencrypted over the network are vulnerable to snooping. Unencrypted streams are also potentially vulnerable to hijacking, which would allow an attacker to modify executable and data files and gain unauthorized system access.

Finally, as with any network-enabled agent, HTC agents are potentially vulnerable to the common buffer-overflow attack. HTC developers and administrators should be aware of this potential attack and should assure themselves (using software quality assurance techniques) that the HTC system implementation is not vulnerable.

5.4.6 Remote Customers

Traditionally, customers were granted access to cluster computing environments via an account on one or more workstations in the cluster. The customer would transfer application data files to this workstation and compile the application for the cluster environment. However, it can be more convenient for both customers and administrators to provide remote access to the HTC cluster instead. The customer installs a customer agent on his or her workstation, and the administrator allows that agent access to the HTC cluster. The customer is no longer required to manually transfer data files, since an HTC remote file access mechanism is available from the customer's workstation. The administrator is no longer required to create a workstation account for the customer in the cluster, but instead must only create an HTC account.

Remote customers may require special consideration when configuring the HTC environment. These customer agents may not be considered as trustworthy as local customer agents, and so additional security precautions may be required. Addition-

[4]potentially vulnerable to IP-spoofing attacks

ally, these customer agents may connect to the cluster over a wide area network, which provides limited bandwidth, decreased reliability, and additional security concerns. Thus, there is a greater need for caching in the remote file access mechanism, local storage of intermediate files (including checkpoints) in the cluster, and encrypted network communication. The administrator may have limited access to the remote customer agents, since the agent runs on a remote workstation, so agent configuration and log file access may require assistance from the customer unless the HTC environment provides administration access mechanisms or the customer grants the administrator access to the remote workstation.

5.5 Summary

Deploying an HTC cluster presents many challenges for the developers and administrators of the HTC environment. The HTC software must be portable, reliable, and maintainable. A layered architecture with flexible network protocols provides such a framework. Remote file access and checkpointing mechanisms allow the HTC environment to utilize distributively owned, non-dedicated resources, but these mechanisms carry significant development and maintenance costs. The HTC system administrator must effectively balance the needs of resource owners and HTC customers, using an expressive policy configuration language. The HTC software must provide reliable, secure services with effective logging and accounting tools for monitoring resource usage and diagnosing problems. At its best, the HTC environment provides convenient access to cluster resources which are otherwise inaccessible, due to heterogeneity, distributed ownership, and other complexities. The HTC challenge is in effectively managing these complexities for the HTC customers, resource owners, and administrators.

5.6 Bibliography

[1] M. Litzkow and M. Livny. Experience with the Condor Distributed Batch System. *IEEE Workshop on Experimental Distributed Systems*, Huntsville, Alabama, October 1990.

[2] R. Raman, M. Livny, and M. Solomon. Matchmaking: Distributed Resource Management for High Throughput Computing. *Proceedings of the Seventh IEEE International Symposium on High Performance Distributed Computing*, Chicago, Illinois, July 1998.

[3] M. Livny, J. Basney, R. Raman, and T. Tannenbaum. Mechanisms for High Throughput Computing. *SPEEDUP Journal*, vol. 11(1), pages 36–40, June 1997.

[4] M. Litzkow. Remote UNIX - Turning Idle Workstations into Cycle Servers *Proceedings of the 1987 Usenix Summer Conference*, Phoenix, Arizona, 1987.

[5] M. Jones. Interposition Agents: Transparently Interposing User Code at the System Interface. *14th ACM Symposium on Operating Principles*, vol. 27(5), December 1993.

[6] M. Litzkow, T. Tannenbaum, J. Basney, and M. Livny. Checkpoint and Migration of UNIX Processes in the Condor Distributed Processing System. *University of Wisconsin-Madison Computer Sciences Technical Report 1346*, April 1997.

[7] J. Plank, M. Beck, G. Kingsley, and K. Li. Libckpt: Transparent Checkpointing under Unix. *Conference Proceedings, Usenix Winter 1995 Technical Conference*, New Orleans, Louisiana, pages 213–223, January 1995.

Chapter 6

Performance Models and Simulation

XING DU † AND XIAODONG ZHANG‡

†Department of Computer Science
University of Virginia
Charlottesville, VA 22903-2242

‡Department of Computer Science
P.O. Box 8795
College of William and Mary
Williamsburg, VA 23187-8795

Email: *xd2a@cs.virginia.edu, zhang@cs.wm.edu*

6.1 Introduction

With rapid development and advances of commodity processors and networking technology, parallel computing platforms are shifting from expensive customer-designed MPPs, such as CRAY and CM-5, to cheap and commodity-designed symmetric multiprocessors (SMPs) and clusters of workstations, personal computers (PCs), and even SMPs. Using off-the-shelf hardware and software to construct a parallel system provides a large range of scalability from "desktop-to-teraflop." Compared with simply buying an expensive MPP box, the cluster approach is highly flexible for users to construct, upgrade, and scale a parallel system. However, the flexibility also provides multiple system configuration options for a given budget and a given type of workload. The following new performance issues should be addressed in the performance evaluation of cluster computing:

- **New performance optimization objective.** Performance/cost ratio has been a commonly accepted metric for both customers and vendors to compare different parallel computer systems. However, the performance/cost metric may not correctly reflect the profit gained by a parallel computer system, which is becoming a major interest to both customers and vendors. More users are targeting this profit-oriented objective which should be addressed in the cluster computing performance metrics.

- **Heterogeneity and nondedication.** In practice, a cluster is heterogeneous and nondedicated, where computing power varies among the workstations, and multiple jobs may interact with each other in execution. The heterogeneity and nondedication of the cluster must be characterized for performance evaluation and for other system activities, such as task scheduling and resource management.

- **Job interactions of the cluster network.** Parallel and local jobs share a cluster network. The communication interactions should also be characterized for performance evaluation. The network interface below the TCP/IP protocol could form a major communication bottleneck during interactions, thus, small but important communication messages of a parallel job, such as a barrier synchronization, could be easily blocked by a communication request from a local job, which would degrade the performance of the parallel job significantly.

- **Cost effective cluster computing.** From a cost-effective point of view the following two questions are fundermental for cluster computing: First, what is an optimal or nearly optimal cluster platform for cost-effective parallel computing under a given budget and a given type of workload? Second, what is a cost-effective way to upgrade or scale an existing cluster platform for a given budget increase and a given type of workload? The cluster computing community demands optimization solutions to help users construct clusters in a cost-effective way.

In this chapter, we first overview some existing performance techniques to address the first three issues. We present a framework for constructing models and experiments to address the issue of the cost model. The framework is based on the prediction of the average execution time per instruction for an application. It is derived from the application's locality property and the memory hierarchy of a targeted parallel cluster platform. Using the framework, we can quickly determine a nearly optimal platform for a given budget and for a given application workload. It can also be used to guide how to upgrade an existing system in a cost-effective way for a given budget increase.

6.2 New Performance Issues

6.2.1 Profit-Effective Parallel Computing.

Academic research on parallel computing has been driven by high performance. Speedup, efficiency, and scalability are widely used by researchers to assess the performance of parallel computing. These performance metrics advocate researchers to concentrate on designing and/or improving a parallel system using any novel techniques, while paying less attention to the cost increase caused by the new techniques. As national defense-oriented applications are downsizing, commercial-oriented applications are becoming dominant in the usage of parallel systems. What customers and vendors are particularly concerned with is the issue on whether a parallel system could make a profit. Performance/cost ratio has been a commonly accepted metric for both customers and vendors to compare different systems. Yan and Zhang [12] extend the cost-effective model from the profit point of view, and evaluate the effectiveness of parallel computing by taking into consideration the performance, cost, and production of parallel computing. The goal is to study the issue of financially justified parallel computing, which is an important topic for using clusters.

The new performance model developed in [12] is called ***profitup*** metric which considers the profit as the major objective in using a parallel system. A computation on a parallel system is financially justifiable if and only if it makes more profit than the same computation on a sequential system. The profit is determined by the production of the system, which can be expressed as a function in dollars of the system performance. The paper also studies several commonly used production functions and their effects on the profits gained. Besides production function, two major cost components used in the model are software/hardware maintenance cost for a system, and the personal cost to develop efficient parallel programs. This study is useful for those companies to use cluster computing for profits.

6.2.2 Impact of Heterogeneity and Nondedication

A cluster of workstations/PCs introduces two new performance factors into parallel computing: a large variation of the computing power of the different workstations (heterogeneity), and interactions between local user jobs and parallel jobs (nondedications). These two unique factors make traditional performance models/metrics for homogeneous parallel computing measurement and evaluation unsuitable. Different heterogeneous systems serve different computing purposes. The types of heterogeneous systems have been classified by the "EM^3" model (Execution models/Machine Models) [7]. Four classes of computer systems are defined, where three classes belong to the heterogeneous systems:

- **SESM**: Single Execution model and Single Machine model. Examples of this class are uniprocessor systems and homogeneous parallel systems with single programming models.

- **SEMM**: Single Execution model and Multiple Machine model. A network of similar type of workstations with different computing powers belongs to this class.

- **MESM**: Multiple Execution model and Single Machine model. A homogeneous parallel system with multiple programming models, such as shared-memory, message-passing, and data-parallel, belongs to this class.

- **MEMM**: Multiple Execution model and Multiple Machine model. This type of heterogeneous system exploits different types of parallelisms from different types of multicomputers connected by a network.

The EM^3 classification indicates that there are two major heterogeneous system classes: the SEMM and the MEMM types. It would be highly difficult to model the MEMM class due to complex structures of each individual execution model and machine model. There are two other reasons why a MEMM heterogeneous system may not be highly demanding. First, with the downsizing of the MPP industries, there will be less and less MEMM type heterogeneous systems available. Second, it is reported that numerical software running on a MEMM type heterogeneous system may not be reliable due to different numerical representations and different execution models on different machines [3]. The problems can range from erroneous results to deadlock; [3] also shows that to make numerical software robust on MEMM type heterogeneous systems often requires additional communication.

On the other hand, with rapid networking software and hardware technology advances, clusters of workstations/PCs are becoming major computing infrastructure for data transactions and engineering—from low end interactive activities to large-scale sequential and parallel applications. Without considering multiprocessor workstations, these workstations/PCs usually have the same execution model and similar processor architecture and only differ in computing powers, such as Sun Sparc-5 versus Sun Sparc-20. The models in [14] focuses on performance issues of such a SEMM heterogeneous cluster, which quantify the heterogeneity of workstations and characterize the performance.

In order to avoid complicated measurements of the speed, we define a power weight $W_i(A)$ for running program A on workstation W_i, as follows:

$$W_i(A) = \frac{S_i(A)}{\max_{j=1}^{m}\{S_j(A)\}} \quad i = 1, ..., m \tag{6.2.1}$$

Formula (6.2.1) indicates that the power weight of a workstation refers to its computing speed relative to the fastest workstation in a system. The value of the power weight is less or equal to 1. Since the power weight is a relative ratio, it can also be represented by measured execution time. If we define the speed of the fastest workstation in the system as one basic operation per time unit, the power weight of each workstation denotes a relative speed. If $T(A, M_i)$ gives the execution time for executing program A on workstation M_i, the power weight can be calculated by the measured execution times as follows:

$$W_i(A) = \frac{\min_{i=1}^{m}\{T(A, M_i)\}}{T(A, M_i)} \tag{6.2.2}$$

The power weight of a workstation measured by running an application program is accurate as long as the memory demand of the program is limited by the available memory space in the workstation. In other words, the power weight is measured when no data swapping is conducted between the memory and the disk. This condition is fairly realistic. If a workstation does not have enough memory space for a parallel task, it should not be qualified for supporting a parallel job because the limited memory of a workstation node would significantly degrade execution performance of the parallel job.

Based on the power weight concept, speedup, efficiency, and scalability are defined. These models are general enough to cover performance evaluation of both homogeneous and heterogeneous computations in dedicated and nondedicated cluster systems. The models have also been used for a scheduling scheme to coordinate parallel processes on a cluster of workstations [4]. The measured power weight of each workstation is used to quantify the differences of computing capability in a cluster. The nondedication issue is addressed by making a computing power usage agreement between parallel jobs and local user jobs in each workstation. Using the quantified and deterministic system information, the scheduling scheme coordinates parallel processes independently in each workstation based on the coscheduling principle. The authors also discuss the implementation of the scheme on an Unix system.

6.2.3 Communication Interactions

Regarding the resource sharing in a cluster, parallel and local jobs will share not only the processors, but also the cluster networks. Most of local user jobs' communication involves using remote machines, file transfer, and WWW operations. Relatively, they are not very sensitive to response time and only involve two machines (local and remote ones). In contrast, a parallel job involves more machines in general and some short messages, such as a barrier synchronization, and should be sent as fast as possible. A local job could block the network for a long time and delay the execution of a parallel job significantly. In the worst case, the whole waiting time for each synchronized process in the parallel job could be as long as a local user network operation, such as to ftp a large file.

Dong, Du, and Zhang [6] examine the communication interactions on a cluster of workstations where TCP/IP protocol is used. They have also quantitatively modeled and measured the interaction process and related communication delays. In general, the network interface below the TCP/IP protocol forms a communication bottleneck during interactions because a standard network interface has a single input/output queue and is not able to distinguish communication requests from parallel and local jobs. Based on the models and experiments, the authors propose a double queue scheme in the network interface to distinguish and prioritize messages between both types of jobs. Their simulation shows that the double queue scheme significantly reduces the effects of communication interactions.

6.3 A Cost Model for Effective Parallel Computing

We present an analytical model for effective parallel computing on clusters. The model is developed by considering the memory hierarchy of a cluster. The memory access delays at different levels have become major bottlenecks in cluster computing. This model characterizes the computations and communications of parallel programs, and provides insights for performance improvement and cost-effectiveness.

6.3.1 The Memory Hierarchy

Our target cluster, which forms a standard parallel computing platform, consists of the following computing components:

- a single SMP
- multiple workstations or PCs, or
- multiple SMPs.

Because the capability and technology of workstations and high-end PCs are merging, we use the term "workstation" to refer to both types in the reminder of the paper.

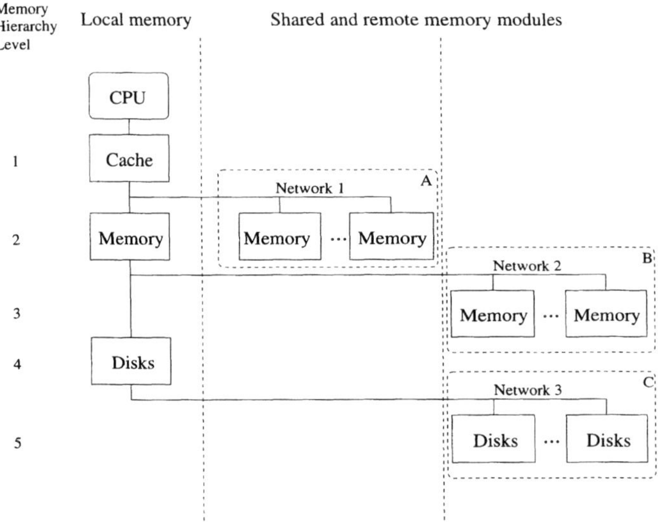

Figure 6.1 The memory hierarchy from the standpoint of one processor.

The memory hierarchy of a computing platform plays an important role in determining the performance of an application program running on it. From an architecture point of view, the way a parallel process accesses the memory hierarchy is shown in Figure 6.1. There are five memory access levels for a processor in the hierarchy of a cluster: 1) access to its own cache, 2) access to its own memory or the shared-memory associated with all the processors in an SMP, 3) access to a remote memory module associated with another machine in the cluster, 4) access to its own disk, and 5) access to a remote disk associated with another machine in the cluster. In general, access latencies to a lower level are smaller than the ones to a higher level. The access latency to any memory component at the same level is considered to be identical. Each machine in the cluster has its own cache, memory, and disks.[1]

The memory hierarchy in Figure 6.1 covers three targeted parallel computing platforms. For an SMP system, a processor may access the memory modules of other processors (at the same level) with the same latency through Network 1 (see the dotted line block A in Figure 6.1). These memory modules can also be viewed as a single shared-memory pool by all the processors in the SMP. Network 1 is usually a memory bus inside an SMP. For a cluster of workstations, the access to a remote memory module goes through Network 2 with a much higher latency than the access to the local memory (see the dotted line block B in Figure 6.1). Network 2 is the cluster network, an important part of off-the-shelf hardware. Two representative types are bus-based and switch-based networks. Remote disks can also be shared through Network 3, which in most cases uses the same physical networks used for Network 2 (see the dotted line block C in Figure 6.1). Their access latencies are higher than those to local disks which are performed through I/O buses. However, whether the access to a remote memory module has a lower latency than the one to the local disk or not is determined by the speed of Network 2. With the advances of low-latency, high bandwidth networks, it is more likely that the access to a remote memory has a relatively lower access latency. For a cluster of SMPs, uniform memory accesses are performed at level 2, and nonuniform memory accesses are performed at level 3. Remote disks may also be used. Table 6.1 classifies the three parallel systems by the cluster memory hierarchy of Figure 6.1.

Table 6.1 Classifying the Three Parallel Systems by the Cluster Memory Hierarchy

Parallel systems	Additional memory levels
a single SMP	dotted line block A
a cluster of workstations	dotted line blocks B and C
a cluster of SMPs	dotted line blocks A, B, and C

A single memory image of a system is provided either by hardware (SMPs) or by a software layer across Network 2 (Figure 6.1) to form a CC-NUMA shared-memory system. A small scale SMP usually consists of two to four processors connected by a bus (Network 1 in Figure 6.1). We consider such a case in this study. For a cluster

[1]We only consider these three types of storage media here. The models and approaches proposed in this paper may be extended to cover many other types.

of workstations or SMPs, Networks 2 and 3 in Figure 6.1 use the same physical network in most cases.

6.3.2 Parallel Program Structures

Parallel Programming Model

We consider the single-program multiple-data (SPMD) programming model, where a parallel application consists of one process per processor on a fixed number of processors throughout the execution. For each processor, it executes the same program but operates on different data sets. Each process is intended to run equal weight computation tasks for load balancing. The structure of many scientific applications is bulky-synchronous, where phases of purely local computation alternate with phases of interprocessor communications and synchronizations. Combining both SPMD and the bulk synchronous structure, here is the parallel programming model to be used in this study: each process independently executes a task defined as a loop, and it synchronizes with other parallel processes through the barrier at the end of the loop. The barrier may be implemented either by hardware or software locks.

```
Loop

   simultaneous tasks for local computation;
   data exchange or synchronization in critical sections;
   barrier;

end Loop
```

A shared-memory implementation has been shown to be a promising and most desirable paradigm for exploiting parallel execution. This is because a single image of memory is provided, which makes the parallel programming much easier. We adopt this implementation paradigm for the bulky synchronous structure. In the shared-memory paradigm, processes exchange data through reading/writing the shared data. No explicit communications occur. Synchronization is achieved through barriers only. The shared-memory is supported by hardware in SMPs. For clusters of workstations or clusters of SMPs, commercial product and research prototypes have been available for the emulation of shared-memory. We assume there is a software layer for programmers, which emulates the shared-memory in the cluster. Additional overhead caused by this layer is taken into account in our study as an increase of average access rates.

In addition to the wide use in practice, the combination of the bulky synchronous structure and the shared memory paradigm simplifies the characterization of parallel applications, thereby allowing us to build a consistent model for the prediction of parallel application execution time and for a cost estimation of its platform.

Application Program Characterizations

Our execution model of cluster computing is based mainly on the probabilities of references to different levels of the memory hierarchy in Figure 6.1. The probability is determined based on *stack distance curves* taken directly from an address stream [2].

The work in [9] uses the same approach for evaluating the performance of memory hierarchies of uniprocessor systems. In general, the stack distance of datum A at one position of the address stream is the number of unique data items between this reference and the next reference to A. The distribution of stack distances can be expressed as a cumulative probability function, denoted $P(x)$, which represents the probability of references within a given stack distance of x. This fits an LRU-managed and fully-associative cache hitting rate well if x is considered as the cache size. The probability density function, denoted $p(x)$, describes the frequency of references at stack distance x. Similar to [9], we model $P(x)$ in the form of

$$P(x) = 1 - \frac{1}{(x/\beta + 1)^{\alpha - 1}}, \tag{6.3.1}$$

thus, $p(x)$ in the form of

$$p(x) = \frac{\beta^{\alpha-1}(\alpha - 1)}{(x + \beta)^{\alpha}}, \tag{6.3.2}$$

where $\alpha > 1$ and $\beta > 1$ are workload parameters to characterize locality of a program. The program locality improves with the decrease of β or the increase of α. The memory modules at different levels in a hierarchy of the cluster can be viewed as caches of different sizes at different access speed. Thus, the stack distance model discussed above is suitable for our performance evaluation of the cluster memory hierarchy.

In addition to locality information expressed in terms of α and β, we use another parameter, γ, to represent the ratio between the number of instructions which incur any memory references (M) and the number of total instructions in an application ($m + M$), where m is the number of instructions which do not incur memory references. Parameter γ reflects the memory access variations of application programs. The larger γ is, the more significantly the memory accesses affect the application's performance. Parameters α, β, and γ may be obtained through address stream analysis and instruction counting in the execution of a program on a target cluster, or through a simulated execution of application programs.

6.3.3 The Cost Model and Memory Access Time Prediction

We assume that parallel tasks are evenly distributed among all processors. Based on Amdahl's Law, the average execution time of an application on a parallel system is modeled as the sum of the computation time without network communications (instructions without memory accesses) and the computation time with network communications (instructions with memory accesses):

$$E(App) = \frac{m}{nN}\frac{1}{S} + \frac{M}{nN}(\frac{1}{S} + T) = \frac{1}{nN}(\frac{m+M}{S} + MT), \qquad (6.3.3)$$

where *App* represents an application program, m is the number of instructions without memory accesses, M is the number of instructions with memory accesses, n is the number processors in a machine, N is the number of machines in the cluster, S is the processor speed as the number of instructions per second, and T is the average memory access time per reference in the cluster. The total number of instructions in the program is $m + M$. Consequently, we have the average execution time per instruction

$$E(Instr) = \frac{E(App)}{m+M} = \frac{1}{nN}(\frac{1}{S} + \gamma T), \qquad (6.3.4)$$

where $Instr$ represents a program instruction, and $\gamma = \frac{M}{m+M}$. The average memory access time per reference, T, is a key factor affecting the execution performance. We adopt the same model as the one used in [9] in computing the average memory access time:

$$T = \sum_{i}^{k} P_i t_i = t_1 + t_2 \int_{s_1}^{\infty} p(x)dx + t_3 \int_{s_2}^{\infty} p(x)dx + \ \dots \ + t_k \int_{s_{k-1}}^{\infty} p(x)dx, \qquad (6.3.5)$$

where P_i and t_i are the access probability and the average access time, respectively, to the memory hierarchy at the ith level, $i = 1, ..., k$. Simultaneous accesses to the same level of the memory hierarchy from several processors cause contention, and make the average access time to that level significantly higher than that without contention. The average access time varies due to variations of network architectures and of the number of simultaneous accesses.

Table 6.2 lists all notations used in the model and their descriptions in three different groups: cluster parameters, program parameters and budget/cost parameters. In the group of cluster parameters, except t_i, $(i = 1, ..., k)$ and T, all the other parameters are known for a given platform and architecture dependent. In the group of program parameters, λ_i and P_i, $(i = 1, ..., k)$ are modeled based on the program dependent parameters m, M, and γ. The budget/cost parameters are user-specified and case dependent.

For given cluster and program parameters, the execution performance in (6.3.3) and (6.3.4) can be determined if the average memory access time, T, is known. Therefore, T is the key variable to be modeled in this study.

The cost of a cluster is the sum of the cluster machine cost and the cluster network cost. It can be expressed as:

$$C_{cluster} = NC_{machine}(n) + NC_{net}, \qquad (6.3.6)$$

where N is the number of machines, $C_{machine}(n)$ is the cost of a machine with n processors, and C_{net} is the network cost to connect one machine in the cluster. We

Table 6.2 Notations for the Cost Model

Cluster	Parameter descriptions
N	The number of machines in a cluster.
n	The number of processors in a machine.
S	The CPU speed (the number of instructions per second).
k	The number of levels in the memory hierarchy.
s_i	The memory size in bytes at the ith level of the hierarchy.
τ_i	Access time per reference to the ith level without contention.
t_i	Access time per reference to the ith level with contention.
τ_{bus}	The service time per reference of a cluster bus network.
τ_{switch}	The service time per reference of a cluster switch network.
T	Average memory access time per reference in the cluster.
Program	Parameter descriptions
m	The total number of instructions without memory references.
M	The total number of instructions with memory references.
γ	$\gamma = \frac{M}{m+M}$.
λ_i	The access rate to the ith level of the memory hierarchy.
P_i	The probability of accessing to the ith level.
Budget/cost	Parameter descriptions
B	The budget in dollars for building a cluster.
B'	The budget increase in dollars for upgrading a cluster.
$C_{machine}(n)$	The cost in dollars of one machine with n processors.
C_{net}	The cost in dollars for connecting one machine in a cluster.
$C_{cluster}$	The total cost in dollars of a cluster.

assume that the cluster is a homogeneous platform consisting of identical machines, either SMPs or uniprocessor workstations.

One major goal in our study is to determine n, N and the types of networks of the cluster by minimizing the average execution time per instruction in (6.3.4), for a given budget B and the other given cluster, program and budget/cost parameters. This optimization problem forms our cost model, and is expressed as:

$$\begin{cases} minimize\ E(Instr) \\ subject\ to\ C_{cluster} \leq B. \end{cases} \tag{6.3.7}$$

Another goal in our study is a variation of the above optimization problem, which is to determine an optimal way to scale or upgrade an existing cluster system for a given budget increase. The problem can be defined as follows. For a given existing cluster with all the given cluster parameters, a budget increase B', and new cluster and cost parameters for upgrading, we determine a new cluster configuration by minimizing the execution time per instruction in (6.3.4).

Because our target solution variables are integer types in (6.3.6) and (6.3.7), this is a typical integer programming problem. Fortunately, in the real world, the problem domain is not very large, because n is a small number for an SMP, and N is also not a large number for a cluster, especially as the power of each machine has rapidly increased. We can determine these integer variables by enumerating solutions and choosing the best as the optimal solution. The quality of our predicted solutions are determined by the correctness and the accuracy of the model in predicting the average memory access time, T, for each of the three cluster platforms. The mathematical models of T's of different platforms are discussed in detail in [5].

For given architectural and application program parameters, the average memory access times, T, in the three types of cluster platforms can be modeled and predicted. Consequently, the average execution time per instruction, $E(Instr)$, is determined. By enumerating all practically possible n's, the numbers of processors in each machine, N's, the number of machines in the cluster, and types of networks with the aid of numerical calculations, we can determine an optimal cluster platform for a given budget, and for a given class of parallel applications.

The cost models can also be used for system upgrading purposes. The model revision can be done by including the budget increase, and parameters of an existing system, and architectural parameters to be changed with possible system upgrading. Similarly, using the models, we enumerate all practically possible changing parameters, such as the new switch networks, and additional numbers of workstations or SMPs. We then determine an optimal upgrading plan of an existing cluster system for a given budget increase.

Up to now, we have only discussed the modeling of homogeneous systems. The models can be extented to cover heterogeneous platforms as well.

6.3.4 Validation of the Framework and its Models

We verify the accuracy of the model in this section by comparing the model results with the simulation results. This section also introduces how a simulation and experiments are conducted.

Simulators

We used MINT [10] (Mips INTerpretor) as our simulation tool since our interest is primarily in the memory hierarchies of clusters. MINT provides a program-driven simulation environment that emulates multiprocessing execution environments and generates memory reference events which drive a memory system simulator, called the back-end. We developed five memory hierarchical system simulators, which correspond to the five parallel platforms, to serve as the back-ends of MINT. The simulators were run on an SGI workstation. By varying the configuration parameters such as the sizes of each level of memory hierarchy, we obtained the simulated execution time for a given application.

The simulated memory hierarchy of parallel systems is the one discussed in Section 2. For an SMP, we assume that a snooping-based protocol is used to maintain the cache coherence. In detail, the cache line size is 64 bytes, the cache is two-way set-associative, and the replacement policy is least-recently-used (LRU). The write invalidation protocol is used as the cache coherence protocol. Two- and four-processor SMPs are simulated because these configurations are used by most SMPs available in the market. Disks are employed as the backup storage.

For a cluster of workstations, a directory-based protocol is employed. The block size is 256 bytes. Each block of the memory has three states: shared, uncached, and exclusive. The states are identical to those in the snooping protocol. The state transition and the transactions are also similar to the snooping protocol, with explicit invalidate and write-back requests replacing the write misses that are formerly broadcast on the bus.

In a cluster of SMPs, the shared memory consists of two parts, the local memory shared by multiple processors of an SMP, and remote memory of other SMPs. To maintain the cache coherence in such a system, we applied a hybrid protocol. A directory-based protocol is used to maintain coherence between SMPs, and a snooping protocol is employed to keep the caches in an SMP coherent. We extend the directory in each node (SMP) to include the processor id. The directory entries are shared by the two protocols.

The principal cluster parameters we used in the simulators are given in Table 6.3. They are represented in the unit of cycles, and are consistent with the values given in [8].

Applications

We used three SPLASH-2 computational kernels [11] and one edge detection program as our applications. They are *FFT*, *LU*, *Radix*, and *EDGE*. We selected them as our benchmarks because the SPLASH-2's three kernels are representative components of a variety of computations in scientific and engineering computing, while EDGE is a real-world application which detects edges from an image map.

- The **FFT** kernel is a complex one-dimensional six step FFT algorithm. The data consist of some complex data points to be transformed, and another set of data points used as the roots of unity. Both sets of data are partitioned into submatrices so that each processor is assigned a contiguous subset of data which are allocated in its local memory.

- The **LU** kernel factors a dense matrix into the product of a lower triangular and an upper triangular matrix. The dense matrix is divided into blocks and the blocks are assigned to processors using a two-dimensional scatter decomposition to exploit temporal and spatial locality.

- The **Radix** sort kernel sorts integers based on a method proposed by [1]. The algorithm is iterative, performing one iteration for each radix r digit of the keys.

Table 6.3 Parameters and Their Values (in Processor Clock Cycles) in the Simulators

Parameter	Value		
Basic			
One instruction execution	1		
Cache hit	1		
Cache miss to local memory	50		
SMP			
Cache miss to remote cache	15		
Cluster of workstations			
	10M Ethernet	100M Ethernet	155M ATM
Cache miss to remote home	45075	4575	3275
Cache miss to remotely cached data	90150	9150	6550
Cluster of SMPs			
	10M Ethernet	100M Ethernet	155M ATM
Cache miss to local memory	23	23	23
Cache miss to remote cache in an SMP	18	18	18
Cache miss to remote home	45078	4578	3278
Cache miss to remotely cached data	90153	9153	6553

- **Edge detection** (EDGE): The edge detection program we used is a parallel version of *edge focusing* algorithm presented in [13]. This program combines high positional accuracy with good noise reduction. The algorithm iterates over four steps: 1) blurring, 2) registering, 3) matching, and 4) repeating or halting. A basic operation in the edge focusing algorithm is image blurring. Let $f(i,j)$ denote the gray level image and $g(i,j)$ the blurred image. Then the blurred image is computed from the discrete convolution:

$$g(i,j) = \frac{1}{2\pi\sigma^2} \sum_{x=-\lceil \frac{w}{2} \rceil}^{\lfloor \frac{w}{2} \rfloor} \sum_{y=-\lceil \frac{w}{2} \rceil}^{\lfloor \frac{w}{2} \rfloor} Gauss(i-x, j-y, \sigma) f(x,y),$$

  where

$$Gauss(i,j,\sigma) = e^{-(i^2+j^2)/2\sigma^2}$$

  is the Gaussian operator and w is the size of the convolution window. Usually, the size of a Gaussian window, w, is determined by the blurring scale: $w = \lceil 8\sigma \rceil$.

  We began the edge focusing process with an initial σ_0 of 3.8, and reduced σ by 0.5 at each iteration for a total of eight iterations. The algorithm is parallelized by partitioning the image in rows among multiple processors. A barrier is performed after each iteration.

Using the MINT-based simulator, we first collected the memory access traces on one processor for the four applications. The traces were analyzed to present each program's temporal locality, and to produce the stack distance curves. Using the standard least squares techniques, we fit (6.3.1) and (6.3.2) to the data, and determined the values of α and β for the applications.

We first collected the values of α and β of the four applications on a one-processor system. As we know from the discussion on parallel program structures in Section 3, when an application program is symmetrically distributed and run on n processors, its maximum stack distance reduces approximately by a factor of n, and the cumulative access probability at the corresponding reduced distance remains almost unchanged. Thus, if the cumulative probability function for an application running on a one-processor system is

$$P(x) = 1 - \frac{1}{(x/\beta + 1)^{\alpha-1}}$$

then the cumulative probability function for the same application running on a n-processor system can be approximated by

$$P(x) = 1 - \frac{1}{(nx/\beta + 1)^{\alpha-1}}.$$

We use the above revised formula as the approximation in the following model computation when there is more than one processor in the system. The parameter values of the four applications are listed in Table 6.4.

Table 6.4 Characteristics and Parameters of the Four Programs (the unit of the number of instructions is million).

Program	Problem size	Total Instr. $(m + M)$	Read/Write (M)	α	β	γ
FFT	64K points	34.79	6.95	1.21	103.26	0.20
LU	512 × 512 matrix	494.05	152.00	1.30	90.27	0.31
Radix	1M integers	50.99	19.09	1.14	120.84	0.37
EDGE	128 × 128 bitmap	88.75	39.84	1.71	85.03	0.45

Analysis of SMPs

Bus-based SMPs with two or four processors are most popular in the market. Due to the speed gap increase between the CPU and memory access, the maximal number of processors of SMPs is getting smaller. The cache sizes for them are usually 256 or 512 Kbytes, and the main memory sizes are 64 or 128 Mbytes. We selected these commonly used SMP configurations to verify the accuracy of the model. Table 6.5 lists these configurations.

Table 6.5 Selected SMP Configurations

Name	CPU MHz	n	s_1 (KB)	s_2 (MB)
C1	200	2	256	64
C2	200	2	512	64
C3	200	2	256	128
C4	200	2	512	128
C5	200	4	256	128
C6	200	4	512	128

Our simulation results show that the differences between the simulated results and modeled results are very small (less than 5 percent), which means that the model is sufficiently accurate when modeling the SMPs. The difference comes from the approximation of the probability function $P(x)$ in comparison with the actual reference probabilities.

The overhead of cache coherence is another factor. We do not take into account the effect of cache coherence activities in the modeling. Modeling this process accurately is very difficult and will make the model too complicated to use. In the simulation, we evaluated the memory bus traffic caused by the cache coherence protocol. It is 6.3, 4.7, 7.2, and 2.1 percents of the total traffic on the bus for applications FFT, LU, Radix, and EDGE, respectively. It indicates that it affects performance only slightly. That is the reason why the modeling results are still close to the simulated ones even though we do not model the memory bus traffic caused by the cache coherence activities.

Analysis of Clusters of Workstations

The cluster of workstations is constructed as a shared-memory system. The shared memory image is supported by a software layer. Compared with SMPs, the cluster of workstations has an additional memory level above the shared memory, the local memory. The local memory absorbs most of the references to the lower level (remote memory). So the overall memory traffic on the cluster bus/switch is relatively low. But since the shared memory is composed of the local memory of all workstations, the shared memory coherence overhead is not reduced. In addition, larger block sizes and longer shared memory access latencies incur additional cost. All make the coherence overhead effect on the performance more significant than those in SMPs. This overhead must be considered in the performance evaluation.

There are two general ways to address this problem by adjusting the model

Table 6.6 Selected Clusters of Workstations Configurations

Name	CPU MHz	N	s_1 (KB)	s_2 (MB)	Network (bits/s)
C7	200	2	256	32	10M bus
C8	200	4	256	64	100M bus
C9	200	4	512	64	100M bus
C10	200	4	256	64	155M switch
C11	200	8	512	64	155M switch

parameters: 1) adjusting the average access time to the remote memory, and 2) adjusting the average access rate to the remote memory. The second approach seems more reasonable in our scenario, and we used it.

We selected five cluster platforms (C7 to C11), as shown in Table 6.6; we then modeled, and simulated, the execution of the four applications on them. Through experiments, we find that by adjusting the average remote memory access rate by a factor of 12.4%, the differences between modeled results and simulated results for all applications are below 10 percent.

Analysis of Clusters of SMPs

We used SMPs with two CPUs and four CPUs to build the cluster. The network varies from a traditional 10M bus, through a 100M bus to a 155M ATM. Table 6.7 lists the platforms we used in the verification.

Table 6.7 Selected Clusters of SMPs Configurations

Name	CPU MHz	n	N	s_1 (KB)	s_2 (MB)	Network (bits/s)
C12	200	2	2	256	64	10M bus
C13	200	2	2	256	128	100M bus
C14	200	4	2	256	128	100M bus
C15	200	4	2	256	128	155M switch

In a way similar to the arrangement to the cluster of workstations, we adjusted the access rates to the remote memory in order to compensate for the overhead caused by coherence activities, which is not modeled in our formulas. We still adjusted the rate by a factor of 12.4 percent for each application. The difference between the simulation and the modeled results is within the range of 8 percent for all applications.

In summary, through verification, we find that the model system is sufficiently close to the simulated system. For the cluster of workstations and cluster of SMPs, an adjustment of 12.4 percent of the access rates to the remote memory makes the difference between the modeled results and simulated results reduce to less than 10 percent, which is acceptable in most application environments. However, comparing the computation time needed for simulation and modeling, the difference is extremely high. The modeling computation for each of almost all the above configurations took between 0.5 and 1 second, and required only a dozen bytes of memory. In contrast, it usually took more than 20 minutes to obtain one simulation result, let alone the time spent on developing the simulators.

6.4 Conclusions

We have overviewed new challenging issues of performance evaluation in cluster computing. We also presented a framework in order to find the most cost-effective or nearly optimal cluster computing platform for a given budget and for certain types of application workloads in a timely and cost-effective manner. Our framework quantitatively models the average execution time per instruction based on the locality parameter values obtained by program memory access pattern analysis. By comparing the average execution time per instruction for an application on different cluster computing platforms, we determine the optimal (or nearly optimal) configuration for that specific application. How to upgrade an existing cluster platform in a cost-effective way for a given budget increase can be addressed in the same model. We believe such a software modeling tool will provide a timely and effective vehicle to support the design of cost effective parallel cluster computing.

Acknowledgments

G. Li and Z. Zhu participated in technical discussions of this work and made constructive suggestions. This research has been supported in part by the National Science Foundation under grants CCR-9400719 and CCR-9812187, by the Air Force Office of Scientific Research under grant AFOSR-95-1-0215, and by the Office of Naval Research under grant ONR-95-1-1239.

6.5 Bibliography

[1] D. Bailey et al. The NAS Parallel Benchmarks. *International Journal on Supercomputing Applications*, vol. 5(3), pages 63-73, Fall 1991.

[2] E. G. Coffman and P. J. Denning. *Operating System Theory.* Prentice-Hall Inc., Englewood Cliffs, NJ, 1973.

[3] J. Demmel et al. The Dangers of Heterogeneous Network Computing: Heterogeneous Networks Considered Harmful. *Proceedings of the Heterogeneous Computing Workshop*, April, 1996, pages 64-71.

[4] X. Du and X. Zhang. Coordinating Parallel Processes on Networks of Workstations. *Journal of Parallel and Distributed Computing*, vol. 46(2) 1997, pages 125-135.

[5] X. Du and X. Zhang. An Analytical Model for Cost-Effective Cluster Computing. *Technical Report*, Department of Computer Science, College of William and Mary, September, 1998.

[6] Y. Dong, X. Du, and X. Zhang. Characterizing and Scheduling Communication Tasks of Parallel and Sequential Jobs on Networks of Workstations. *Computer Communications*, vol. 21(5), 1998, pages 470-484.

[7] I. Ekmecic, I. Tartalja, and V. Milutinovic. A Survey of Heterogeneous Computing: Concepts and Systems. *Proceedings of the IEEE*, vol. 84(8), 1996, pages 1127-1144.

[8] J. L. Hennessy and D. A. Patterson. *Computer Architecture: A Quantitative Approach.* 2nd Edition, Morgan Kaufmann, San Francisco, 1996.

[9] B. L. Jacob, P. M. Chen, S. R. Silverman, and T. N. Mudge. An Analytical Model for Designing Memory Hierarchies. *IEEE Transactions on Computers*, vol. 45(10), 1996, pages 1180-1194.

[10] J. E. Veenstra and R. J. Fowler. MINT: a Front End for Efficient Simulation of Shared-Memory Multiprocessors. *Proceedings of the Second International Workshop on Modeling, Analysis, and Simulation of Computer and Telecommunication Systems.* 1994, pages 201-207.

[11] S. C. Woo et al. The SPLASH-2 Programs: Characterization and Methodological Considerations. *Proceedings of the 22nd Annual International Symposium on Computer Architecture*, June 1995, pages 24-36.

[12] Y. Yan and X. Zhang. Profit-effective parallel computing. *IEEE Concurrency*, vol. 7(2), 1999.

[13] X. Zhang, S. G. Dykes, and H. Deng. Distributed Edge Detection: Issues and Implementations. *IEEE Computational Science & Engineering*, Spring Issue, 1997, pages 72-82.

[14] X. Zhang and Y. Yan. Modeling and Characterizing Parallel Computing Performance on Heterogeneous NOW. *Proceedings of the Seventh IEEE Symposium on Parallel and Distributed Processing*, (SPDP'95), IEEE Computer Society Press, October, 1995, pages 25-34.

Chapter 7

Metacomputing: Harnessing Informal Supercomputers

Mark Baker† and Geoffrey Fox‡

†Division of Computer Science
University of Portsmouth
Southsea, Hants, PO4 8JF

‡NPAC at Syracuse University
Syracuse, NY, 13244

Email: *Mark.Baker@port.ac.uk, gcf@npac.syr.edu*

7.1 General Introduction

The term metacomputing, when first encountered, seems a rather strange and typically "geek" word. Its origin is believed to have been the CASA project, one of several U.S. Gigabit testbeds around in 1989. Larry Smarr, the NCSA Director, is generally accredited with popularizing the term thereafter.

A search through an ordinary dictionary to try and decipher the term would, at the time of writing, be fruitless. So, what does metacomputing mean? There seems to be many, sometimes conflicting, interpretations. Perhaps one should refer back to the Greek word "meta" to help understand the full word. Among the many meanings of "meta," one will often find references to "sharing" and "action in common." These words are the key to understanding the concept of metacomputing. Using these terms one can interpret metacomputing and understand it to be computers sharing and acting together to solve some common problem.

At this point, to reduce potential confusion, it is worth distinguishing between a parallel computer and a metacomputer. The key difference is the behavior of individual computational nodes. A metacomputer is a dynamic environment that has some informal pool of nodes that can join or leave the environment whenever they desire. The nodes can be viewed as independent machines. So, in a slightly confusing sense, a parallel computer, such as an IBM SP2, can be viewed as a "metacomputer in a box." Whereas an SMP parallel computer, such as Tera MTA or Sun Enterprise 10000, cannot. The difference is that individual computational nodes in an SMP are not independent.

More recently Catlett and Smarr [1] have related the term metacomputing to "the use of powerful computing resources transparently available to the user via a networked environment." Their view is that a metacomputer is a networked virtual supercomputer. To an extent our usage of the term metacomputing still holds true to this definition apart from the need to explicitly refer to "powerful computing resources." Today's typical desktop computing resources can be viewed as powerful resources of yesterday.

The steps necessary to realize a metacomputer include:

- The integration of individual software and hardware resources into a combined networked resource.
- The implementation of middleware to provide a transparent view of the resources available.
- The development and optimization of distributed applications to take advantage of the resources.

7.1.1 Why Do We Need Metacomputing?

The short answer to this question is that our computational needs are infinite, whereas our financial resources are finite. As we are all well aware, the sophisticated applications that we run on our desktops today seem to require more and more computing resources with every new revision. This trend is likely to continue as users and developers demand, for example, additional functionality or more realistic simulations. The net result is that from desktops to parallel supercompters, users will always want more and more powerful computers. This is where metacomputing comes into its own. Why not try and utilize the potentially hundreds of thousands of computers that are interconnected in some unified way? The realization of this concept is the essence of metacomputing. It should be mentioned here that seamless access to remote resources is an uncontroversial topic. Whereas linking remote resources together to, say, execute a parallel application is more contentious as there are overheads involved. There are some situations where there is a strong case, for example, when linked resources must be geographically distributed, such as in filtering and visualization of scientific data. In general, it is fair to say that metacomputing comes with an efficiency penalty and it is usually better to run separate jobs on components of the metacomputer. However, linking of self contained applications is of growing importance in science (multidisciplinary applications) and industry (linking different components of an organization together).

It is not too bizarre to envision that at some stage in the not so distant future individuals – be they engineers, scientists, students, health-care workers, or business persons – will be able to access the computing resources that they need to run their particular application with the same ease that we switch on a light or turn on a kitchen appliance. Their application may be the simulation of the fluid flow around the after end of a ship, image processing of NMR scans, a Monte-Carlo financial simulation for a stockbroker, or a final year project for a student dissertation. It should be noted that these metacomputing resources can be accessed via a remote laptop or desktop [2].

7.1.2 What Is a Metacomputer?

The simplest analogy to help describe a metacomputer is the electricity grid. When you turned on the power to your computer or switched on your television, you probably did not think about the original source of the electricity to drive these appliances. It was not necessary for you to select a generator with adequate capacity or consider the gauge of wire used to connect the outlet or whether the power lines are underground or on pylons. Basically, you were using a national power grid sophisticated enough to route the electrons across hundreds of miles, yet easy enough for a child to use. In the same manner a metacomputer is a similarly easy-to-use assembly of networked computers that can work together to tackle a single task or set of problems.

It is not surprising, therefore, that the terms "The Grid" and "Computational Grids" are being used to describe a universal source of computing power [3]. A Grid can be viewed as the means to provide pervasive access to advanced computational resources, databases, sensors, and people. It is believed that it will allow a new class of applications to emerge and will have a major impact on our approach to computing in the twenty-first century. For our purposes, Computational Grids are equivalent to metacomputing environments.

Metacomputing encompasses the following broad categories:

- Seamless access to high performance resources.
- "Parameter" studies (embarrassingly parallel application, see FAFNER, Section 7.2.2).
- The linkage of scientific instruments, analysis system, archival storage, and visualization (so called four-way metacomputing, see I-WAY, Section 7.2.2).
- The general complex linkage of N distributed components.

7.1.3 The Parts of a Metacomputer

A metacomputer is a virtual computer architecture. Its constituent components are individually not important. The key concept is how these components work together as a unified resource. On an abstract level the metacomputer consists of the following components:

- *Processors and Memory*

  The most obvious component of any computer system is the microprocessor that provides its computational power. The metacomputer will consist of an array of processors. Associated with each processor will be some dynamic memory.

- *Networks and Communications Software*

  The physical connections between computers turn then from a collection of individual machines into an interconnected network. The link between machines could, for example, be via modems, ISDN, standard Ethernet, FDDI, ATM, or a myriad of other networking technologies. Networks with high bandwidth and low latency that provide rapid and reliable connections between the machines are the most favored. To actually communicate over these physical connections it is necessary to have some communications software running. This software bridges all of the gaps, between different computers, between computers and people, even between different people.

- *Virtual Environment*

  Given that we have an interconnected, communicating network of computers, processors with memory, and there needs to be something like an operating system that can be used to configure, manage, and maintain the metacomputing environment. This virtual environment needs to span the extent of the metacomputer and make it usable by both administrators and individual users. Such an environment will enable machines and/or instruments that may be located in the same building, or separated by thousands of miles, to appear as one system.

- *Remote Data Access and Retrieval*

  In a metacomputing environment there is the potential that multiple supercomputers performing at Gflop/s are interacting with each other across national or international networks streaming GBytes of data in and out of secondary storage. This is a major challenge for any metacomputing environment. The challenge will become ever greater as new data-intensive applications are designed and deployed.

7.2 The Evolution of Metacomputing

7.2.1 Introduction

In this section we describe two early metacomputing projects that were in the vanguard of this type of technology. The projects differ in many ways, but both had to overcome a number of similar hurdles, including communications, resource management, and the manipulation of remote data, to be able to work efficiently and effectively. The two projects also attempted to provide metacomputing resources from opposite ends of the computing spectrum. Whereas FAFNER [4] was capable of running on any workstation with more than 4 MBytes of memory, I-WAY [5], on the other hand, was a means of unifying the resources of large supercomputing centres.

7.2.2 Some Early Examples

FAFNER

Public key cryptographic systems use two keys: a public and private key. A user must keep their private key a secret, but the public key is publicly known. Public and private keys are mathematically related, so that a message encrypted with a recipient's public key can only be decrypted by their private key. The RSA algorithm [6] is an example of a public key algorithm. It is named after its developers Rivest, Shamir, and Adleman, who invented the algorithm at MIT in 1978.

The RSA keys are generated mathematically in part by combining prime numbers. The security of RSA is based on the premise that it is very difficult to factor extremely large numbers, in particular those with hundreds of digits. RSA keys use either 154 or 512-digit keys. The usage of this type of cryptographic technology has led to integer factorization becoming an active research area. To keep abreast of the state of the art in factoring, RSA Data Security Inc. initiated the RSA Factoring Challenge in March 1991. The Factoring Challenge provides a testbed for factoring implementations and provides one of the largest collections of factoring results from many different experts worldwide.

Factoring is computationally very expensive. For this reason parallel factoring algorithms have been developed so that factoring can be distributed over a network of computational resources. The algorithms used are trivially parallel and require no communications after the initial setup. With this setup, it is possible that many contributors can provide a small part of a larger factoring effort. Early efforts relied on Email to distribute and receive factoring code and information. More recently, in 1995, a consortium led by Bellcore Labs., Syracuse University and Co-Operating Systems started a project of factoring via the Web, know as FAFNER.

FAFNER was set up to factor RSA130 using a new numerical technique called the Number Field Sieve (NFS) factoring method using computational Web servers. The consortium produced a Web interface to NFS. A contributor then uses a Web-form to invoke server-side CGI scripts written in Perl. Contributors could, from one set of Web pages, access a wide range of support services for the sieving step of the factorization: NFS software distribution, project documentation, anonymous user registration, dissemination of sieving tasks, collection of relations, relation archival services, and real-time sieving status reports. The CGI scripts produced supported cluster management, directing individual sieving workstations through appropriate day/night sleep cycles to minimize the impact on their owners. Contributors downloaded and built a sieving software daemon. This then became their Web client that used HTTP protocol to GET values from and POST the resulting relations back to a CGI script on the Web server.

Three factors combined to make this approach succeed.

1. The NFS implementation allowed even single workstations with 4 Mbytes to perform useful work using small bounds and a small sieve.

2. FAFNER supported anonymous registration – users could contribute their hardware resources to the sieving effort without revealing their identity to anyone other than the local server administrator.

3. A consortium of sites was recruited to run the CGI script package locally, forming a hierarchical network of RSA130 Web servers which reduced the potential administration bottleneck and allowed sieving to proceed around the clock with minimal human intervention.

The FAFNER project won an award in TeraFlop challenge at SC95 in San Diego. It paved the way for a wave of Web-based metacomputing projects, some of which are described in Sections 7.4 and 7.5.

I-WAY

The Information Wide Area Year (I-WAY) was an experimental high performance network linking many high performance computers and advanced visualization environments. The I-WAY project was conceived in early 1995 with the idea not to build a network but to integrate existing high-bandwidth networks with telephone systems. The virtual environments, datasets, and computers used resided at 17 different U.S. sites and were connected by ten networks of varying bandwidths and protocols, using different routing and switching technologies.

The network was based on ATM technology, which at the time was an emerging standard. This network provided the wide-area backbone for various experimental networking activities at SC95, supporting both TCP/IP over ATM and direct ATM-oriented protocols.

To help standardize the I-WAY software interface and management, the key sites installed point-of-presence (I-POP) computers to serve as their gateways to the I-WAY. The I-POP machines were UNIX workstations configured uniformly and possessed a standard software environment called I-Soft. I-Soft helped overcome issues such as heterogeneity, scalability, performance, and security. The I-POP machines were the gateways into each site participating in the I-WAY project.

The I-POP machine provided uniform authentication, resource reservation, process creation, and communication functions across I-WAY resources. Each I-POP machine was accessible via the Internet and operated within its site's firewall. It also had an ATM interface that allowed monitoring and potential management of the site's ATM switch.

For the purpose of managing its resources efficiently and effectively, the I-WAY project developed a resource scheduler known as the Computational Resource Broker (CRB). The CRB basically consisted of user-to-CRB and CRB-to-local-scheduler protocols. The actual CRB implementation was structured in terms of a single central scheduler and multiple local scheduler daemons – one per I-POP machine. The central scheduler maintained queues of jobs and tables representing the state of local machines, allocating jobs to machine and maintaining state information on the AFS file system.

Security was a major feature of the I-WAY project. An emphasis was made on providing a uniform authentication environment. Authentication to I-POPs was handled by using a telnet client modified to use Kerberos authentication and encryption. In addition, the CRB acted as an authentication proxy, performing subsequent authentication to I-WAY resources on a user's behalf.

I-WAY used AFS to provide a shared file repository for software and scheduler information. An AFS cell was set up and made accessible from only I-POPs. To move data between machines where AFS was unavailable, a version of remote copy (`ircp`) was adapted for I-WAY.

To support user-level tools, a low-level communications library, Nexus, was adapted to execute in the I-WAY environment. Nexus supported automatic configuration mechanisms that enabled it to choose the appropriate configuration depending on the technology being used, for example, communications via TCP/IP or AAL5 when using the Internet or ATM. The MPICH and CAVEcomm libraries were also extended to use Nexus.

The I-WAY project was application driven and defined five types of applications:

- Supercomputer - Supercomputing
- Remote Resource - Virtual Reality
- Virtual Reality - Virtual Reality
- Multisupercomputer - Multivirtual Reality
- Video, Web, GII-Windows

The I-WAY project was successfully demonstrated at SC'95 in San Diego. The I-POP machine was shown to simplify the configuration, usage, and management of this type of wide-area computational testbed. I-Soft was a success in terms that most applications ran, most of the time. More importantly, the experiences and software developed as part of the I-WAY project have been fed into the Globus project described in Section 7.4.2.

A Summary of Early Experiences

The projects described in this section both attempted to produce metacomputing environments by integrating hardware from opposite ends of the computing spectrum. FAFNER was a ubiquitous system that would work on any platform where a

Web server could be run. Typically, its clients were at the low-end of the computing performance spectrum. Whereas I-WAY unified the resources at supercomputing sites. The two projects also differed in the types of applications that could utilize their environments. FAFNER was tailored to a particular factoring application that was in itself trivially parallel and was not dependent on a fast interconnect. I-WAY, on the other hand, was designed to cope with a range of diverse high performance applications that typically needed a fast interconnect. Both projects, in their way, lacked scalability. For example, FAFNER was dependent on quite a lot of human intervention to distribute and collect sieving results, and I-WAY was limited by the design of components that made up I-POP and I-Soft.

FAFNER lacked a number of features that would now be considered obvious. For example, every client had to compile, link, and run a FAFNER daemon in order to contribute to the factoring exercise. Today, one would probably download an already set up and configured Java applet. FAFNER was really a means of task-farming a large number of fine-grain computations. Individual computational tasks were unable to communicate with one another, or with their parent Web-server. Today perhaps, using technology such as Java RMI, tasks would register themselves, ask for work, coordinate their computation, deliver results, and so on, with even less human intervention or interaction.

Likewise, with I-WAY, a number of features would today seem inappropriate. The installation of an I-POP platform made it easier to set up I-WAY services in a uniform manner, but it meant that each site needed to be specially set up to participate in I-WAY. In addition, the I-POP platform created one, of many, single-points-of-failure in the design of the I-WAY. Even though this was not reported to be a problem, the failure of an I-POP would mean that a site would drop out of the I-WAY environment. Today, many of the services provided by the I-POP and I-Soft would be available on all the participating machines at a particular site.

Regardless of the aforementioned features of both FAFNER and I-WAY, both projects were highly successful. Each project was in the vanguard of metacomputing and has helped pave the way for many of the succeeding projects. In particular, FAFNER was the forerunner of projects such as WebFlow (described in Section 7.4.4), and the I-WAY software, I-Soft, was very influential on the approach used to design the components employed in the Globus Metacomputing Toolkit (described in Section 7.4.2).

7.3 Metacomputer Design Objectives and Issues

In this section we lay out and discuss the basic criteria required by all wide area distributed environments or a metacomputer. In the first part of this section we outline the underlying hardware and software technologies potentially being used. We then move on to discuss the necessary attributes of the middleware that creates the virtual environment we call a metacomputer.

7.3.1 General Principles

In attempting to facilitate the collaboration of multiple organizations running diverse autonomous heterogeneous resources, a number of basic principles should be followed so that the metacomputing environment:

- does not interfere with the existing site administration or autonomy
- does not compromise existing security of users or remote sites
- does not need to replace existing operating systems, network protocols, or services
- allows remote sites to join or leave the environment whenever they choose
- does not mandate the programming paradigms, languages, tools, or libraries that a user wants
- provides a reliable and fault tolerance infrastructure with no single point of failure
- provides support for heterogeneous components
- uses standards, and existing technologies, and is able to interact with legacy applications
- provides appropriate synchronization and component program linkage

7.3.2 Underlying Hardware and Software Infrastructure

As one would expect, a metacomputing environment must be able to operate on top of the whole spectrum of current and emerging hardware and software technologies. An obvious analogy is the Web. Users of the Web do not care if the server they are accessing is on a UNIX or NT platform. They are probably unaware that they are using HTTP on top of TCP/IP, and they certainly do not want to know that they are accessing a database supported by a parallel computer, such as an IBM SP2, or an SMP, such as the SGI Origin 2000. From the client browser's point-of-view, they "just" want their requests to Web services handled quickly and efficiently. In the same way, a user of a metacomputer does not want to be bothered with details of its underlying hardware and software infrastructure. A user is really only interested in submitting their application to the appropriate resources and getting correct results back in a timely fashion.

An ideal metacomputing environment will therefore provide access to the available resources in a seamless manner such that physical discontinuities such as differences between platforms, network protocols, and administrative boundaries become completely transparent. In essence, the metacomputing middleware turns a radically heterogeneous environment into a virtual homogeneous one.

7.3.3 Middleware – The Metacomputing Environment

In this section we outline and describe the idealized design features that are required by a metacomputing system to provide users with a seamless computing environment.

Administrative Hierarchy

An administrative hierarchy is the way that each metacomputing environment divides itself up to cope with a potentially global extent. For example, DCE uses cells and DNS has a hierarchical namespace. The reasons why this category is important stems from the administrative need to provide resources on autonomous systems on a global basis. The administrative hierarchy determines how administrative information flows through the metacomputer. For example, how does the resource manager find its resources? Does it interrogate one global database of resources or a hierarchy of servers, or perhaps servers configured in some peer-related manner?

Communication Services

The communication needs of applications using a metacomputing environment are diverse – ranging from reliable point-to-point to unreliable multicast communications. The communications infrastructure needs to support protocols that are used for bulk-data transport, streaming data, group communications, and those used by distributed objects.

These communication services provide the basic mechanisms needed by the metacomputing environment to transport administrative and user data. The network services used also provide the metacomputer with important Quality of Service parameters such as latency, bandwidth, reliability, fault-tolerance, and jitter control. Typically, the network services will be built from a relatively low-level communication API that can be used to support a wide range of high-level communication libraries and protocols. These mechanisms provide the means to implement a wide range of communications methodologies, including RPC, DSM, stream-based, and multicast.

Directory/Registration Services

A metacomputer is a dynamic environment where the location and type of services available are constantly changing. A major goal is to make all resources accessible to any process in the system, without regard to the relative location of the resource user. It is necessary to provide mechanisms to enable a rich environment in which information about metacomputing is reliably and easily obtained by those services requesting the information. The registration and directory services components provide the mechanisms for registering and obtaining information about the metacomputer structure, resources, services, and status.

Processes, Threads and Concurrency Control

The term process originates in the literature on the design of operating systems and is generally considered as a unit of resource allocation both for CPU and memory. The advent of shared memory multiprocessors brought about the provision of Light Weight Processes or Threads. The name thread comes from the expression "thread of control." Modern OSs, like NT, permit an OS process to have multiple threads of control. With regards to metacomputers, this category is related to the granularity of control provided by the environment to its applications. Of particular interest is the methodology used to share data and maintain its consistency when multiple processes or threads have concurrent access to it.

Time and Clocks

Time is an important concept in all systems. First, time is an entity that we wish to measure accurately, as it may be a record of when a particular transaction occurred. Or, if two or more computer clocks are synchronized it can be used to measure the interval when two or more events occurred. Second, algorithms have been developed that depend on clock synchronization. These algorithms may, for example, be used for maintaining the consistency of distributed data or as part of the Kerberos authentication protocol.

Naming Services

In any distributed system, names are used to refer to a wide variety of resources such as computers, services, or data objects. The naming service provides a uniform name space across the complete metacomputing environment. Typical naming services are provided by the international X.500 naming scheme or DNS, the Internet's scheme.

Distributed Filesystems and Caching

Distributed applications, more often than not, require access to files distributed among many servers. A distributed filesystem is therefore a key component in a distributed system. From an applications point of view it is important that a distributed filesystem can provide a uniform global namespace, support a range of file I/O protocols, require little or no program modification, and provide means that enable performance optimizations to be implemented, such as the usage of caches.

Security and Authorization

Any distributed system involves all four aspects of security: confidentiality – prevents disclosure of data; integrity – prevents tampering with data; authentication – verifies identity, and accountability – knowing whom to blame. Security within a metacomputing environment is a complex issue requiring diverse resources autonomously administered to interact in a manner that does not impact on the usability of the resources or introduce security holes in individual systems or the environments as a whole. A security infrastructure is key to the success or failure of a metacomputing environment.

System Status and Fault Tolerance

There is a very high likelihood that some component in a metacomputing environment will fail. To provide a reliable and robust environment it is important that a means of monitoring resources and applications is provided. For example, if a particular platform goes out-of-service, it is important that no further jobs are scheduled on it until it becomes in-service again. In addition, jobs that were running on the system when it crashed should be rerun when it is available again or rescheduled onto an alternative system. To accomplish this task, tools that monitor resources and application need to be deployed. So, when a platform is unavailable, information is passed to the directory services, or perhaps, when a job crashes, some part of the system reschedules that job to run again.

Resource Management and Scheduling

The management of processor time, memory, network, storage, and other components in a distributed system is clearly very important. The overall aim is to efficiently and effectively schedule the applications that need to utilize the available resources in the metacomputing environment. From a user's point of view, resource management and scheduling should be almost transparent; their interaction with it being confined to a manipulating mechanism for submitting their application. It is important in a metacomputing environment that a resource management and scheduling service can interact with those that may be installed locally. For example, it may be necessary to operate in conjunction with LSF, Codine, or Condor at different remote sites.

Programming Tools and Paradigms

Ideally, every user will want to use a diverse range of programming paradigms and tools with which to develop, debug, test, profile, run, and monitor their distributed application. A metacomputing environment should include interfaces, APIs, and conversion tools so as to provide a rich development environment. Common scientific languages such as C, C++, and Fortran should be available, as should message passing interfaces like MPI and PVM. A range of programming paradigms should be supported, such as message passing and distributed shared memory. In addition, a suite of numerical and other commonly used libraries should be available.

User and Administrative GUI

The interfaces to the services and resources available should be intuitive and easy to use. In addition, they should work on a range of different platforms and operating systems.

Availability

Earlicr in this section we mentioned the need to provide middleware that provided heterogeneous support. In particular, we are concerned about issues, such as if a particular resource management system works on a particular operating system, or will the communication services run on top of particular network architecture such as Novell or SNA. The issues that relate to this category are those that relate to the portability of the software services provided by the metacomputing environment. The metacomputing software should either be easily "ported" on to a range of commonly used platforms, or should use technologies that enable it to be platform neutral, in a manner similar to Java Byte-code.

7.4 Metacomputing Projects

7.4.1 Introduction

In this section we map the techniques and technologies that three representative current metacomputing environments use with the aid of the design objectives and issues laid out in the previous section. The main purpose of this template is to help the reader review the methodologies used by each project. The three projects reviewed in this section are: Globus from Argonne National Laboratory, Legion from the University of Virginia, and WebFlow from Syracuse University. The reasons why these three particular projects were chosen are:

- `Globus` - provides a toolkit based on a set of existing components with which to build a metacomputing environment.
- `Legion` - provides a high-level unified object model out of new and existing components to build a metasystem.
- `WebFlow` - provides a Web-based metacomputing environment.

7.4.2 Globus

Introduction

Globus [8], [9] provides a software infrastructure that enables applications to handle distributed, heterogeneous computing resources as a single virtual machine. The Globus project is a U.S. multiinstitutional research effort that seeks to enable the construction of computational grids. A computational grid, in this context, is a hardware and software infrastructure that provides dependable, consistent, and pervasive access to high-end computational capabilities, despite the geographical distribution of both resources and users. A central element of the Globus system is the Globus Metacomputing Toolkit (GMT), which defines the basic services and capabilities required to construct a computational grid. The toolkit consists of a set of components that implement basic services, such as security, resource location, resource management, and communications.

It is necessary for computational grids to support a wide variety of applications and programming paradigms. Consequently, rather than providing a uniform programming model, such as the object-oriented model, the GMT provides a bag of services from which developers of specific tools or applications can use to meet their own particular needs. This methodology is only possible when the services are distinct and have well-defined interfaces (API) that can be incorporated into applications or tools in an incremental fashion.

Globus is constructed as a layered architecture in which high-level global services are built upon essential low-level core local services. The Globus toolkit is modular, and an application can exploit Globus features, such as resource management or information infrastructure, without using the Globus communication libraries.

The GMT currently consists of the following:

- Resource allocation and process management (GRAM)
- Unicast and multicast communications services (Nexus)
- Authentication and related security services (GSI)
- Distributed access to structure and state information (MDS)
- Monitoring of health and status of system components (HBM)
- Remote access to data via sequential and parallel interfaces (GASS)
- Construction, caching, and location of executables (GEM)

Administrative Hierarchy

Globus has no obvious administrative hierarchy. Every Globus-enabled resource is a peer of every other enabled resource.

Communication Services

Communication services within Globus are provided by Nexus, a communication library that is designed specifically to operate in a grid environment. Nexus is distinguished by its support for multimethod communication, providing an application a single API to a wide range of communication protocols and characteristics. Nexus defines a relatively low-level communication API that can be used to support a wide range of high-level communication libraries and languages. Nexus communication services are used extensively in other parts of the Globus toolkit.

Directory/Registration Services

The Globus Metacomputing Directory Service (MDS) provides information about the status of Globus system components. MDS is part of the information infrastructure of the GMT and is capable of storing static and dynamic information about the status of a metacomputing environment. MDS uses a Lightweight Directory

Access Protocol [10] (LDAP) server that can store metacomputing-specific objects. LDAP is a streamlined version of the X.500 directory service. The MDS houses information pertaining to the potential computing resources, their specifications, and their current availability.

Processes, Threads, and Concurrency Control

Globus works at the process level. The Nexus API can be used to construct communication primitives between threads. There is no concurrency control in Globus.

Time and Clocks

Globus does not mandate the usage of a particular time service, it relies on those already used at each site.

Naming Services

Globus makes extensive usage of LDAP as well as DNS and X.500.

Distributed Filesystems and Caching

The Globus system currently provides three interfaces for remote access of user data:

- Global Access to Secondary Storage (GASS) – provides basic access to remote files. Operations supported include remote read, remote write, and append.
- Remote I/O – The RIO library implements a distributed implementation of the MPI-IO, parallel I/O API.
- Globus Executable Management (GEM) – enables loading and executing a remote file through GRAM using GASS caching calls.

The Remote I/O for Metasystems (RIO) library provides basic mechanisms for tools and applications that require high performance access to data located in remote, potentially parallel file systems. RIO implements the Abstract I/O (ADIO) device interface specification, which defines basic I/O functionality that can be used to implement a variety of higher-level I/O libraries. ROMIO has adopted the parallel I/O interface defined by the MPI forum in MPI-IO and hence allows any program already using MPI-IO to work without unchanged in a wide-area environment. The RIO library has been developed as part of the GMT, although it can also be used independently. ROMIO can be used with Nexus communications, GSI security, and MDS to provide configuration information.

The GMT data movement and access service, GASS, defines a global name space via URLs, allows access to remote files via standard I/O interfaces, and provides specialized support for data-movement in a wide-area environment. GASS addresses bandwidth management issues associated with repeated access to remote files by providing a file cache: where a "local" copy of a remote file can be stored. Files are moved in to and out of the cache when a file is opened or closed by an application. GASS uses a simple locking protocol for local concurrency control, but does not implement a wide-area cache coherency mechanism.

Security and Authorization

Globus employs an authentication system known as the Generic Security Service API (GSI) using an implementation of the Secure Sockets Layer. This system uses the RSA encryption algorithm and the associated public and private keys. The GSI authentication relies on an X509 certificate, provided by the user in their directory, that identifies them to the system. This certificate includes information about the duration of the permissions, the RSA public key, and the signature of the Certificate Authority (CA). With the certificate is the user's private key. The certificates can be created only by the CA, who reviews the X509 certificate request submitted by the user, and accepts or denies it according to an established policy.

System Status and Fault Tolerance

Globus provides a range of basic services designed to enable the construction of application specific fault recovery mechanisms. In Globus it is currently assumed detection of a fault is a necessary prerequisite to fault recovery or fault tolerance. The main fault detection service in Globus is the Heartbeat Monitor (GHM) that enables a process to be monitored and periodic heartbeats to be sent to one or more monitors. The Nexus communication library also provides support for fault detection.

Resource Management and Scheduling

The Globus Resource Allocation Manager (GRAM) is the lowest level of Globus architecture. GRAM allows jobs to run remotely and provides an API for submitting, monitoring, and terminating jobs. GRAM provides the local component for resource management and is responsible for the set of resources operating under the same site-specific allocation policy. Such a policy will often be implemented by a local resource management package, such as LSF, Codine, or Condor.

GRAM is responsible for:

- Parsing and processing the Resource Specification Language (RSL) specifications that outline job requests. The request specifies resource selection, job process creation, and job control. This is accomplished by either denying the request or creating one or more processes (jobs) to satisfy the request. The RSL is a structured language that can be used to define resource requirements and parameters by a user.

- Enabling remote monitoring and managing of jobs already created.

- Updating MDS with information regarding the availability of the resources it manages.

Programming Tools and Paradigms

Globus currently supports MPI, Java, Compositional C++, Simple RPC, and Perl. There are ongoing efforts to add a Sockets API, an IDL, Legion, and Netsolve.

User and Administrative GUI

Globus makes extensive usage of the Web and command line interfaces for administration. For example, LDAP can be browsed via the Web. There are also a growing number of Java components that can be used with Globus.

Availability

Globus is available on most versions of UNIX and is currently being developed for NT.

7.4.3 Legion

Introduction

Legion [11], [12] is an object-based metasystem developed at the University of Virginia. Legion provides the software infrastructure so that a system of heterogeneous, geographically distributed, high performance machines can interact seamlessly. Legion attempts to provide users, at their workstations, with a single, coherent, virtual machine. The Legion system is organized by classes and metaclasses (classes of classes).

In Legion:

- *Everything is an object* - Objects represent all hardware and software components. Each object is an active process that responds to method invocations from other objects within the system. Legion defines an API for object interaction, but not the programming language or communication protocol.
- *Classes manage their instances* - Every Legion object is defined and managed by its own active class object. Class objects are given system-level capabilities; they can create new instances, schedule them for execution, activate or deactivate an object, as well as provide state information to client objects.
- *Users can define their own classes* - As in other object-oriented systems users can override or redefine the functionality of a class. This feature allows functionality to be added or removed to meet a user's needs.
- *Core objects* - Legion defines the API to a set of core objects that support the basic services needed by the metasystem.

Legions has the following set of core object types:

- *Classes and Metaclasses* - Classes can be considered managers and policy makers. Metaclasses are classes of classes.
- *Host objects* - Host objects are abstractions of processing resources, they may represent a single processor or multiple hosts and processors.
- *Vault objects* - Vault objects represents persistent storage, but only for the purpose of maintaining the state of Object Persistent Representation (OPR).
- *Implementation Objects and Caches* - Implementation objects hide the storage details of object implementations and can be thought of as equivalent to executable files in UNIX. Implementation cache objects provide objects with a cache of frequently used data.
- *Binding Agents* - A binding agent maps object IDs to physical address. Binding agents can cache bindings and organize themselves in hierarchies and software combining trees.
- *Context objects and Context spaces* - Context objects map context names to Legion object IDs, allowing users to name objects with arbitrary-length string names. Context spaces consist of directed graphs of context objects that name and organize information.

A Legion object is an instance of its class. Objects are independent, active, and capable of communicating with each other via unordered nonblocking calls. Like other object-oriented systems, the set of methods of an object describes its interface. The Legion interfaces are described in an Interface Definition Language (IDL) .

A Legion object can be in one of two different states, active or inert. An active object runs as a process that is ready to accept function invocations. An inert object is represented by an OPR. An OPR is an image of the object which resides on some stable storage; this is analogous to a process that has been swapped-out to disk. In a similar manner, an OPR contains state information that enables the object to be reactivated. Legion implements a three-tiered naming system.

1. Users refer to objects using human-readable strings, called context names.
2. Context objects map context names to LOIDs (Legion object identifiers), which are location-independent identifiers that include an RSA public key.
3. A LOID is mapped to an LOA (Legion object address) for communication. A LOA is a physical address (or set of addresses in the case of a replicated object) that contains sufficient information to allow other objects to communicate with the object (e.g., an IP address and port number pair).

Administrative Hierarchy

Legion has no obvious administrative hierarchy. Objects distributed about the Legion environment are peers to one another.

Communication Services

Legion uses standard TCP/IP to support communications between objects. Every Legion object is linked with a UNIX sockets-based delivery layer, called the Modular Message Passing System (MMPS) .

Directory/Registration Services

A binding agent in Legion maps LOIDs to LOAs. A LOID/LOA pair is called a binding. Binding agents can cache bindings and organize themselves in hierarchies and software combining trees.

Processes, Threads and Concurrency Control

Currently Legion has one process per active object and objects communicate via MMPS. There is no concurrency control included in Legion.

Time and Clocks

Legion does not mandate the usage of a particular time service and relies on those already used at each site.

Naming Services

Legion Context objects map context names to LOIDs, allowing users to name objects with arbitrary-length string names. A LOID is mapped to an LOA for communication purposes. A LOA consists of an IP address and port number. It is assumed that Legion uses DNS to translate names to IP addresses.

The Context Manager is a Java GUI that can be used to manage context space. Context space is organized into a series of subcontexts (also called contexts) and each context contains context names of various Legion objects. In the Context Manager all context-related objects such as contexts, file objects, and objects are represented by icons that can be manipulated. Basic context manager commands are Move, Alias, Get Interface, Get Attributes, Destroy, Activate, and Deactivate.

Distributed Filesystems and Caching

Legion provides a virtual filesystem that spans all the machines in a Legion system. I/O support is provided via a set of library functions with UNIX-like file and stream operations to read, write, and seek. These functions provide location independent and secure access to context space and to "files" in the system. Different users can also employ the virtual filesystem to collaborate, sharing data files and even accessing the same running computations.

Legion has a special core object called a vault object. This represents persistent storage, but only for the purpose of maintaining the state of OPRs. The vault object may manage a portion of a UNIX filesystem, or a set of databases.

Security and Authorization

Legion does not require any special privileges from the host systems that run it. The Legion security model is oriented towards protecting objects and object communication. Objects are accessed and manipulated via method calls; an object's rights are centered in its capabilities to make those calls. The user determines the security policy for an object by defining the object's rights and the method calls they allow. Once this is done, Legion provides the basic mechanism for enforcing that policy.

Every object in Legion supports a special member function called `MayI`. An object with no security will have a null `MayI`. All method invocations to an object must first pass through `MayI` before the target member function is invoked. If the caller has the appropriate rights for the target method, `MayI` allows that method invocation to proceed.

To make rights available to a potential caller, the owner of an object gives it a certificate listing the rights granted. When the caller invokes a method on the object, it presents the appropriate certificate to `MayI`, which then checks the scope and authenticity of the certificate. Alternatively, the owner of an object can permanently assign a set of rights to a particular caller or group. `MayI` is responsible for confirming the identity of a caller and its membership of an authorized group, followed by comparing the rights authorized with the rights required for the method call.

To provide secure communication, every Legion object has a public key pair; the public key is part of the object's name. Objects can use the public key of a target object to encrypt their communications to it. Likewise, an object's private key can be used to sign messages. This ensures authentication and integrity. This integration of public keys into object names eliminates the need for a certification authority. If an intruder tries to tamper with the public key of a known object, the intruder will create a new and unknown name.

System Status and Fault Tolerance

Legion does not mandate any fault-tolerance policies; applications are responsible for selecting the level they need. Fault tolerance will be built into generic base classes and applications will be able to invoke methods that provide the functionality that they require. Legion will support object reflection, replication, and check pointing for the purposes of fault tolerance.

Resource Management and Scheduling

Host objects represent processors, and more than one may run on each computing resource. Host objects create and manage processes for active Legion objects. Classes invoke the member functions on host objects in order to activate instances on the computing resources that the hosts represent. Legion provides resource owners with the ability to initiate, manage and control, and kill their resources.

The Legion-scheduling module consists of three components:

- A resource state information database (*Collection*). The *Collection* interacts with resource objects to collect state information describing the system.

- A module which maps requests to resources (*Scheduler*). The *Scheduler* queries the *Collection* to determine a set of available resources that match the Scheduler's requirements. After computing a schedule, or set of desired schedules, the *Scheduler* passes a list of schedules to the *Enactor* for implementation.

- An agent responsible for implementing the schedules (*Enactor*). The *Enactor* then makes reservations with the individual resources and reports the results to the Scheduler. Upon approval by the *Scheduler*, the *Enactor* place objects on the hosts, and monitors their status.

Host objects can be adapted to different environments to suit user needs. For example, a host object may provide an interface to the underlying resource management system, such as LSF, Codine, or Condor.

Programming Tools and Paradigms

Legion supports MPL (Mentat Programming Language) and BFS (Basic Fortran Support). MPL is a parallel C++ language. Legion is written in MPL. BFS is a set of pseudo-comments for Fortran and a preprocessor that gives the Fortran programmer access to Legion objects.

Object Wrapping is used in Legion for encapsulating existing legacy codes into objects. It is possible to encapsulate a PVM, HPF, or shared memory threaded application in a Legion object. Legion also provides a complete emulation of both PVM and MPI with user libraries for C, C++, and Fortran. Legion also supports Java.

User and Administrative GUI

Legion has a command-line and graphical user interface. The Legion GUI, known as the Context Manager, is a Java application that runs context-related commands. The Context Manager uses icons to represent different parts of context space (file objects, subcontexts, etc.) and runs most context-related commands. The Context Manager can be run from the command-line of any platform compatible with the Java Development Kit (JDK) 1.1.3. In addition, there is a Windows 95 client application, called the Legion Server, that allows users to run the Context Manager from Windows 95.

Availability

Legion is available on: x86/Alpha (Linux), Solaris (SPARC), AIX (RS/6000), IRIX (SGI), DEC UNIX (Alpha), and Cray T90.

7.4.4 WebFlow

Introduction

WebFlow [13], [14] is a computational extension of the Web model that can act as a framework for the wide-area distributed computing and metacomputing. The main goal of the WebFlow design was to build a seamless framework for publishing and reusing computational modules on the Web so that end users, via a Web browser, can engage in composing distributed applications using WebFlow modules as visual components and editors as visual authoring tools. Webflow has a three-tier Java-based architecture that can be considered a visual dataflow system. The frontend uses applets for authoring, visualization, and control of the environment. WebFlow uses servlet-based middleware layer to manage and interact with backend modules such as legacy codes for databases or high performance simulations.

Webflow is analogous to the Web. Web pages can be compared to WebFlow modules and hyperlinks that connect Web pages to intermodular dataflow channels. WebFlow content developers build and publish modules by attaching them to Web servers. Application integrators use visual tools to link outputs of the source modules with inputs of the destination modules, thereby forming distributed computational graphs (or compute-webs) and publishing them as composite WebFlow modules. A user activates these compute-webs by clicking suitable hyperlinks, or customizing the computation either in terms of available parameters or by employing some high-level commodity tools for visual graph authoring.

The high performance backend tier is implemented using the Globus toolkit:

- The Metacomputing Directory Services (MDS) is used to map and identify resources.
- The Globus Resource Allocation Manager (GRAM) is used to allocate resources.
- The Global Access to Secondary Storage (GASS) is used for a high performance data transfer.

WebFlow can be regarded as a high level, visual user interface and job broker for Globus.

With WebFlow, new applications can be composed dynamically from reusable components just by clicking on visual module icons, dragging them into the active WebFlow editor area, and linking them by drawing the required connection lines. The modules are executed using Globus components combined with the pervasive commodity services where native high performance versions are not available.

The prototype WebFlow system is based on a mesh of Java-enhanced Web Servers (Apache), running servlets that manage and coordinate distributed computation. This management infrastructure is implemented by three servlets: Session Manager, Module Manager, and Connection Manager. These servlets use URL addresses and can offer dynamic information about their services and current state.

Each management servlet can communicate with others via sockets. The servlets are persistent and application-independent.

Future implementations of WebFlow will use emerging standards for distributed objects and take advantage of commercial technologies, such as the CORBA as the base distributed object model.

Administrative Hierarchy

WebFlow has no obvious administrative hierarchy. A WebFlow node is a Web server with a unique URL address, and it is a peer to other nodes.

Communication Services

WebFlow communication services are built on multiple protocols. Applet-Web Server communication uses HTTP; Server-to-Server communication is currently implemented using TCP/IP, soon to be replaced by IIOP. The module developer chooses communications between a backend module and its frontend control panel (Java applet) – typically it is either TCP/IP or IIOP. The modules exchange data (serialized Java objects) via input and output ports. Originally, the port-to-port connection was implemented using TCP/IP. This model is now being changed. The module is a Java Bean, and it interacts with other modules via Java events over IIOP. The data flow paradigm with port-to-port communication is the default that enables users to visually compose an application from independent modules. However, the user is not restricted to this model. A module can be a high performance application to be run on a multiprocessor machine with intramodule communications using any communication service (for example MPI) available on the target system. Also, the modules can interact with each other via remote methods invocation (Java events over IIOP).

Also, WebFlow supports multiple protocols for file transfer, ranging from HTTP to FTP to IIOP to Globus GASS. The user chooses the protocol to be used depending on the file, performance, and security requirements.

Directory/Registration Services

WebFlow does not define its own directory services. The usage of the CORBA naming services and interface repository is planned. It should be noted that WebFlow typically is used in conjunction with Globus and will coordinate with its directory services (MDS).

Processes, Threads, and Concurrency Control

Each module runs as separate Java threads, and all modules run concurrently. It is the user's responsibility to synchronize modules (for example, the user may want the module to block on receiving the input data).

Time and Clocks

WebFlow does not mandate the usage of a particular time service and relies on those already used at each site.

Naming Services

Currently, no specialized naming service other than DNS is used. CORBA services are planned.

Distributed Filesystems and Caching

WebFlow does not offer "a native" distributed filesystem or support caching. This is left to the user. As a part of WebFlow distribution there is a file browser module that allows the user to browse and select files accessible by the host Web server. The selected files can then be sent to a desired destination using HTTP, IIOP, FTP, or GASS. For example, a WebFlow module that serves as the Globus GRAM proxy takes the name of the input file and URL of the GRAM contact as input. This information is sufficient to stage the input file on the target machine and retrieve the output file using GASS over FTP.

Security and Authorization

WebFlow requires two security levels: secure Web transactions between client and the middle tier, and secure access to the backend resources. Secure Web transactions in WebFlow are based on TLS 1.0 and modeled after the AKENTI system; secure access to the backend resources is delegated to the backend service providers, such as Globus. The secure access to resources directly controlled by WebFlow has not yet been addressed.

System Status and Fault Tolerance

The original implementation of WebFlow did not address these issues. The new WebFlow middle-tier will use CORBA mechanisms to provide fault tolerance, including a heartbeat monitor. In the backend, WebFlow relies on services provided by the backend service provider.

Resource Management and Scheduling

WebFlow delegates the resource management and scheduling to the metacomputing toolkit (Globus) and/or a local resource management package such as PBS or CONDOR.

Programming Tools and Paradigms

WebFlow modules are Java objects. Object wrapping is used in WebFlow for encapsulating existing codes into objects. WebFlow test applications include modules

Table 7.1 Metacomputing Functionality Matrix

Design Objective	Globus	Legion	Webflow
Admin. Hierarchy	Peer	Peer	Peer
Comms Service	Nexus - Low-Level	MMPS - Sockets-based	Hierarchical - Sockets+MPI
Dir/Reg Services	MDS - LDAP	Via Binding agent	MDS - LDAP
Processes	Process-based	Object/process-based	Process-based
Clock	Not specified	Not specified	Not specified
Naming Services	LDAP + DNS/X.500	Context Manger + DNS	LDAP + DNS
Filesystems & caching	GASS + ROMIO	Custom Legion filesystem	GASS
Security	GSI (RSA + X.509 certs)	Object-based with RSA	SSL
Fault Tolerance	Heart-beat monitor	Not available yet	None
Resource Management	GRAM + RSL + Local	Host object + Local	GRAM-based
Prog. Paradigms	Many and varied	MPL, BFS + wrappers	MPI
User Interfaces	GUI + command-line	GUI + command-line	Applet-based GUI
Availability	Most UNIX	Most UNIX	Most UNIX and NT

with encapsulated Fortran, Fortran with MPI, HPF, C with MPI, Pascal, as well as Java.

User and Administrative GUI

WebFlow offers a visual-authoring tool, implemented as a Java applet that allows the user to compose a (meta-) application from preexisting modules. In addition, a developer can use a simple API to build a custom graphical user interface.

Availability

Since WebFlow is implemented in Java, it runs on all platforms that support JVM. So far it has been tested on Solaris, IRIX, and Windows NT.

Summary and Conclusions

In this section we have attempted to lay out the functionality and features of three representative metacomputer architectures with the design criteria we outlined in Section 7.3. This task in itself has been rather difficult as it has been necessary to map the developer's terminology for components within their environments to those used more commonly in distributed computing. In the final part of this section we summarize the functionality of each environment and conclude by making some observations about the approaches each environment uses.

Functionality Matrix

In the functionality matrix, shown in Table 7.1, we outline the components within each metacomputing environment that deals with our design criteria.

- *Administrative Hierarchy* - All three environments use a peer-based administrative hierarchy, which makes the services they provide globally scalable and reduces potential administrative bottlenecks and single-points of failure.

- *Communications Service* – Globus uses Nexus to provide its underlying communications services, whereas Legion and WebFlow use sockets-based protocol.
- *Directory/Registration Services* – Both Globus and Webflow use the commodity LDAP service, whereas Legion uses a custom binding agent.
- *Processes* – All three environments are process based - but each has the ability to encompass threads and enable consistency control.
- *Clock* – The three environments do not require special timing services.
- *Naming services* – Globus and WebFlow use LDAP in conjunction with DNS; Legion uses a custom context manager in conjunction with DNS.
- *Filesystems and caching* – Globus makes extensive use of the remote access tool GASS and the parallel I/O interface ROMIO. Legion has a custom global filesystem and the ability to interface with other I/O systems. WebFlow utilizes GASS to provide filesystem services.
- *Security* – All three environments use RSA in some form. Globus uses GSI to provide its security services. Legion uses an Object based system where every object has a security method `MayI`. WebFlow uses SSL for security purposes.
- *Fault Tolerance* – Of the three environments, only Globus provides tools, such as the heartbeat monitor.
- *Resource Management* – Globus implements an extensive resource management and scheduling system, GRAM. Legion has the concept of host object for local resource management. Both Globus and Legion have interfaces to other resource management system, such as Codine and LSF. WebFlow utilizes the services of GRAM.
- *Programming Paradigms* – All three environments provide a raft of tools and utilities to support various programming paradigms.
- *User Interfaces* – Globus and Legion provide both command-line and GUI interfaces. WebFlow uses just a GUI.
- *Availability* – All three environments are available on most UNIX platforms.

Some Observations

Globus is constructed as a layered architecture in which high-level global services are built upon essential low-level core local services. The Globus toolkit is modular. This means that an application can exploit an array of features without needing to implement all of them. Globus can be viewed as a metacomputing framework based on a set of APIs to the underlying services. Even though Globus provides the services needed to build a metacomputer, the Globus framework allows alternative local services to be used if desired. For example, the GRAM API allows alternative resource management systems to be utilized, such as Condor or NQE.

Abstracting the services into a set of standard APIs has a number of advantages. These include:

- the underlying services can be changed without affecting applications that use them

- this type of layered approach simplifies the design of a rather complicated system

- it encourages developers of tools and services; they need to support only one API, making their development and testing cycle shorter and cheaper.

Globus provides application developers with a pragmatic means of implementing a range of services to provide a wide-area application execution environment.

Legion takes a very different approach to provide a metacomputing environment, it encapsulates all its components as objects. The methodology used has all the normal advantages of an object-oriented approach, such as, data abstraction, encapsulation, inheritance, and polymorphism.

It can be argued that many aspects of this object-oriented approach potentially makes it ideal for designing and implementing a complex environment such as a metacomputer. For example, Legion's security mechanism, where each object uses RSA keys and a `MayI` method, seems straightforward and more natural than security mechanisms used in many other environments. In addition, the set of methods associated with each object naturally becomes its external interface and hence its API.

Using an object-oriented methodology in Legion does not come without a raft of problems. It is not obvious how best to encapsulate nonobject-oriented programming paradigms, such as message passing or distributed shared memory. In addition, the majority of real-world computing services have procedural interfaces and it is necessary to produce object-oriented wrappers to interface these services to Legion. For example, the APIs to DNS or resource management systems such as Condor or Codine are procedural.

WebFlow takes a different approach to both Globus and Legion. It is implemented in a hybrid manner using a three-tier architecture that encompasses both the Web and third party backend services. This approach has a number of advantages, including the ability to "plug-in" a diverse set of backend services. For example, currently many of these services are supplied by the Globus Matacomputing Toolkit, but they could be replaced with components from CORBA or Legion. WebFlow also has the advantage that it is more portable and can be installed anywhere a Web server supporting servlets is capable of running.

7.5 Emerging Metacomputing Environments

7.5.1 Introduction

There are a large number and diverse range of emerging distributed systems currently being developed. These systems range from metacomputing frameworks to application testbeds, and from collaborative environments to batch submission mechanisms.

In this section we briefly described and referenced a few of the better know systems (due to space considerations the full text for this section can be found elsewhere [15]). The aim of this section is to bring to the reader's attention not only some of the large number of diverse projects that exist, but also to detail the different approaches used to solve the inherent problems encountered.

7.5.2 Summary

The projects described in this section are a cross section of those currently undertaken. It is interesting to note that all are using Java and the Web as the communications infrastructure. It is also evident that Java has revolutionized the shape and characteristic of the software environments for heterogeneous distributed systems. It seems that the developers of distributed systems no longer have to focus on aspects such as portability and heterogeneity, by using Java they seem able to concentrate on designing and implementing functional distributed environments. It is not clear, among the raft of projects listed in this section, which environments will succeed. However, each project, in its own way, is contributing to our knowledge of how to design, build, and implement efficient and effective distributed virtual environments.

7.6 Summary and Conclusions

7.6.1 Introduction

In this chapter we have attempted to describe and discuss many aspects of metacomputers. We started off by discussing why there is a need for such environments. We then moved on to describe two early metacomputing projects. Here we also outlined some of the benefits and experiences learned. Having set the scene, we then laid out a design template to map out the critical services that a metacomputing environment needs to encompass. Then, using this template, we mapped the services of three differing environments onto it. This mapping made comparing and contrasting the services that each metacomputing environment provided clearer to understand. Having described three fairly mature environments, we then briefly described some 30-odd emerging distributed environments and tools. Finally, here, we summarize what we have discovered while researching this chapter and conclude by making a few predictions about metacomputing environments of the future.

7.6.2 Summary of the Reviewed Metacomputing Environments

Globus is constructed as a layered architecture in which high-level global services are built upon essential low-level core local services. The Globus toolkit is modular, and as such, an application can exploit an array of features without needing to implement all of them. Globus can be viewed as a metacomputing framework based on a set of APIs to the underlying services. Globus provides application developers with a pragmatic means of implementing a range of services to provide a wide-area application execution environment.

Legion takes a very different approach to provide a metacomputing environment; it encapsulates all its components as objects. The methodology used has all the normal advantages of an object-oriented approach, such as data abstraction, encapsulation, inheritance, and polymorphism. It can be argued that many aspects of this object-oriented approach potentially makes it ideal for designing and implementing a complex environment such as a metacomputer. However, using an object-oriented methodology does not come without a raft of problems, many of these are tied-up with the need for Legion to interact with legacy applications and services. In addition, as Legion is written in MPL, it is necessary to "port" MPL onto each platform before Legion can be installed.

WebFlow takes a different approach to both Globus and Legion. It is implemented in a hybrid manner using a three-tier architecture that encompasses both the Web and third party backend services. This approach has a number of advantages, including the ability to "plug-in" to a diverse set of backend services. For example, many of these services are currently supplied by the Globus toolkit, but they could be replaced with components from CORBA or Legion. WebFlow also has the advantage that it is more portable and can be installed anywhere a Web server supporting servlets is capable of running.

So, in summary, we believe that all three environments have their merits. Fundamentally, the Globus Metacomputing Toolkit is currently the most comprehensive attempt at providing a metacomputing environment. The Globus team has taken a very pragmatic approach to providing the services that are needed in a metacomputer. The design methodology they have used – abstracting the services of some underlying entity into a well thought out API – will give the project longevity, as the entities that provide the service can be updated without changing the fundamental service API. In addition, Globus uses existing standard commodity software components to provide many of its services, for example, LDAP, X.509, and RSA. This has a number of beneficial implications, including code reuse and avoiding the necessity to create all the services from scratch.

Alternatively, Legion is a very ambitious and impressive project. We believe the object-oriented approach they have taken has a lot of merit. A fundamental flaw with Legion currently is the reliance on MPL. If Legion were written in Java, which no doubt the University of Virginia is seriously contemplating, then we would have much more faith in Legion's longevity. Also, perhaps, we would question the use of this system as opposed to one based on the well-known standard CORBA.

WebFlow is still basically an experimental prototype system that is being used to explore a range of new and emerging technologies. It has much merit, particularly in its comprehensive GUI frontend and its ability to utilize standard backend components designed by other organizations.

7.6.3 Some Observations

The Java programming language successfully addresses several key issues that plague the development of distributed environments, such as heterogeneity and security. It also removes the need to install programs remotely; the minimum execution environment is a Java-enabled Web browser. Java has become a prime candidate for building distributed environments.

In a metacomputing environment it is not possible to mandate the types of services or programming paradigms that particular users or organizations must use. A metacomputer needs to provide extensible interfaces to any service desired.

Providing adequate security in a metacomputer is a complex issue. A careful balance needs to be maintained between the usability of an environment and security mechanisms utilized. The security methods must not inhibit the usage of an environment, but it must ensure that the resources are secure from malicious intruders.

7.6.4 Metacomputing Trends

It is very difficult to predict the future. In a field such as computing, the technological advances are moving very fast. Windows of opportunity for ideas and products seem to open and close in the seeming "blink of the eye." However, some trends are evident.

Java, with its related technologies and growing repository of tools and utilities, is having a huge impact on the growth and development of metacomputing environments. From a relatively slow start, the development of metacomputers is accelerating fast with the advent of these new and emerging technologies. It is very hard to ignore the presence of the sleepy giant CORBA in the background. We believe that frameworks incorporating CORBA services will be very influential on the design of metacomputing environments in the future.

Whatever technology or computing paradigm becomes influential or most popular, it can be guaranteed that at some stage in the future its star will wane. Historically, in the computing field, this fact can be repeatedly observed. The lesson from this observation must therefore be drawn that, in the long term, backing only one technology can be an expensive mistake. The framework that provides a metacomputing environment must be adaptable, malleable, and extensible. As technology and fashions change it is crucial that a metacomputing environment evolves with them.

7.6.5 The Impact of Metacomputing

Metacomputing is not only a computing paradigm for just providing computational resources for supercomputing-sized parallel applications. It is an infrastructure that can bond and unify globally remote and diverse resources ranging from meteorological sensors to data-vaults, from parallel supercomputers to personal digital organizers. As such, it will provide pervasive services to all users that need them.

Larry Smarr observes in "The GRID: Blueprint for a New Computing Infrastructure" [3] that metacomputing has serious social consequences and is going to have as revolutionary an effect as railroads did in the American mid-West in the early nineteenth century. Instead of a 30 to 40 year lead-time to see its effects, however, its impact is going to be much faster. He concludes that the effects of computational grids are going to change the world so quickly that mankind will struggle to react and change in the face of the challenges and issues they present.

So, at some stage in the future, our computing needs will be satisfied in the same pervasive and ubiquitous manner that we use the electricity power grid. The analogies with the generation and delivery of electricity are hard to ignore, and the implications are enormous.

Acknowledgments

The authors wish to thank Ian Foster (ANL) and Tom Haupt (Syracuse) for information and useful suggestions about their projects. We would also like to thank Wolfgang Gentzsch (Genias) for early access to a FGCS Special Issue on *Metacomputing* [16]. The authors would like to thank Kate Dingley, Tony Kalus, John Rosbottom, and Rose Rayner for proofreading the copy of this chapter.

7.7 Bibliography

[1] C. Catlett and L. Smarr. Metacomputing. *Communications of the ACM*, vol. 35(6), pages 44-52, 1992.

[2] Desktop Access to Remote Resources - `http://www-fp.mcs.anl.gov/~gregor/datorr/`

[3] I. Foster and C. Kesselman, eds. *The GRID: Blueprint for a New Computing Infrastructure*, Morgan Kaufmann Publishers, Inc., San Francisco, California, 1998. ISBN 1-55860-475-8.

[4] FAFNER - `http://www.npac.syr.edu/factoring.html`

[5] I-WAY - `http://146.137.96.14/`

[6] RSA - `http://www.rsa.com/`

[7] I. Foster, J. Geisler, W. Nickless, W. Smith, and S. Tuecke. Software Infrastructure for the I-WAY Metacomputing Experiment. *Concurrency: Practice and Experience*, vol. 10(7), pages 567-581, 1998.

[8] Globus - `http://www.globus.org/`

[9] I. Foster and C. Kesselman. The Globus Project: A Status Report. *Proceeding's IPPS/SPDP '98 Heterogeneous Computing Workshop*, pages 4-18, 1998.

[10] W. Yeong, T. Howes and S. Kille. Lightweight Directory Access Protocol. *RFC 1777*, 28/03/95. Draft Standard.

[11] Legion - `http://legion.virginia.edu/`

[12] A. Grimshaw, W. Wulf et al. The Legion Vision of a Worldwide Virtual Computer. *Communications of the ACM*, vol. 40(1), January 1997.

[13] WebFlow - `http://osprey7.npac.syr.edu:1998/iwt98/products/webflow/`

[14] T. Haupt, E. Akarsu, G. Fox and W. Furmanski. Web Based Metacomputing. Special Issue on Metacomputing, *Future Generation Computer Systems*, North Holland, to appear in early 1999.

[15] M. Baker and G. Fox. Metacomputing: Harnessing Informal Supercomputers. Portsmouth University preprint, December 1998. `http://www.dcs.port.ac.uk/~mab/Papers/Cluster-Book/`

[16] *Metacomputing*, Editor, Wolfgang Gentzsch, *Future Generation Computer Systems*, North Holland, due for publication in early 1999.

Chapter 8

Specifying Resources and Services in Metacomputing Systems

MATTHIAS BRUNE[†], JÖRN GEHRING[‡], AXEL KELLER[‡], ALEXANDER REINEFELD[†]

[†]Konrad-Zuse-Zentrum für Informationstechnik
Takustrasse 7, D-14195 Berlin

[‡]Paderborn Center for Parallel Computing
University of Paderborn, Fürstenallee 11, D-33102 Paderborn

Email: *brune@zib.de, joern@uni-paderborn.de, kel@uni-paderborn.de, ar@zib.de*

8.1 The Need for Resource Description Tools

With the metacomputing paradigm getting more and more accepted, an increasing number of network-based services is offered. Today, the available services range from traditional client-server applications over distributed Intra/Internet services, virtual organizations, teleworking, teleconferencing, up to autonomous agents for information gathering purposes. All these services are coordinated by a metacomputing 'middleware,' which is also geographically distributed. Clearly, this middleware must be generic and versatile to also serve newly emerging technologies.

In a much broader sense, a general tendency towards open, distributed computating environments is obvious: User interfaces have been improved from the early command line interfaces towards system-specific graphical user interfaces and furtheron to web-based job submission sheets that are executed under control of standard browsers. Resource management systems have mutated from a single-system view via a computing-center view towards fully distributed metacomputing environments. And, finally, the parallel programming models and execution environments have emerged from initial proprietary libraries (e.g., MPL, NX) via vendor-independent programming models (e.g., PVM, MPI) towards interconnected environments (e.g., PVMPI [8], PACX [5], and PLUS [6]).

In all these domains the representation of resources plays a major role. System services and resource requests can be represented by structured, attributed resource descriptions. Just like bids and offers at a public market place, the metacomputing market also deals with two sides: the user's resource requests and the system provider's resource offers. Assuming a set of compatible resource descriptions, the task is now to determine a suitable mapping between the two representations with respect to constraints such as node performance, connectivity, required software packages, etc.

In the following, we present a scheme for specifying resources and services in complex heterogeneous computing systems and metacomputing environments. The scheme is named RSD for Resource and Services Description. At the system administrator level, RSD is used to specify the available system components, such as the number of nodes, their interconnection topology, CPU speeds, and available software packages. At the user level, a GUI provides a comfortable, high-level interface for specifying system requests. A textual editor can be used for defining repetitive and recursive structures. This gives service providers the necessary flexibility for fine-grained specification of system topologies, interconnection networks, and system and software dependent properties. All these representations are mapped onto a single, coherent internal object-oriented resource representation.

Dynamic aspects, like network performance, availability of compute nodes or their load, are traced at runtime and included in the resource description to allow for optimal process mapping and dynamical task load balancing at runtime at the metacomputer level. This is done in a self-organizing way, with human system operators becoming involved only when new hardware/software components are installed.

8.2 Schemes for Specifying Hardware and Software Resources

8.2.1 Resource Specification in Local HPC Systems

For traditional high performance computers, there have been several initiatives to standardize resource descriptions and command line interfaces of the current batch queuing systems (POSIX standard 1003.2d). Still, the specific requirements of parallel and distributed computing systems of graphical interface technologies (e.g., JavaSwing) and the facilities of HPC management systems (e.g., CCS [11], or PBS [4]) are still not recognised. Further divergence is added by hardware vendors promoting proprietary interfaces. On an IBM SP2 with LoadLeveler [14], for example, the command `qsub -l nodes=2:hippi+mem+mem:disk+12` is used to allocate two processors with HIPPI connections, one processor with extra memory and diskspace, and 12 other processors. An alternative to the command line interface are batch script files, such as the one shown in Figure 8.1.

```
#@ min_processors = 6
#@ max_processors = 6
#@ cpu_limit = 14000
#@ requirements = (Adapter == "hps_ip")
#@ environment = MP_EUILIB=us
#@ requirements = (Memory >= 64)
#@ requirements = (Feature == "Thin")
...
```

Figure 8.1 Resource request with LoadLeveler.

8.2.2 Resource Specification in Distributed Client-Server Systems

The change from mainframe-based computing to a distributed client-server architecture raises the need for distributed system management software. Two popular representatives of this class are the Tivoli Management Environment TME10 [15] and the Athena project [1]. Tivoli was designed for the system management of enterprise-wide distributed computing environments. Supported platforms are MVS, UNIX, Windows NT, Windows 95, and OS/2. Tivoli aims at four disciplines: deployment (i.e., manage software configurations), availability (i.e., maximize network utilization), security (i.e., control the user access), and operations (i.e., perform routine tasks).

The Athena project started as early as 1983 with the goal to explore innovative uses of computing in the MIT curriculum. Athena provides access to computing resources for some one thousand users across the MIT campus through a system of computers connected to a campus-wide network. It follows a distributed client-server model for delivering services like fileservers scattered throughout the campus, print job spooling services, reservation of (sub) clusters, or specialized software for courses. Application servers provide services like electronic mail, access to the Internet (www, news, ftp, etc.), electronic databases, or programming tools (compiler, debugger, editor, etc.)

This kind of middleware is designed to simplify the management of large workstation clusters with distributed services. In contrast to our project, Tivoli and Athena do not consider the requirements of distributed high performance computing (e.g., system topology or interconnection networks). They focus on sequential applications and do not support multisite applications or linked parallel applications.

8.2.3 The Metacomputing Directory Service (MDS)

The Globus project [10] aims at building an adaptive wide area resource environment AWARE with a set of tools that enables applications to adapt to heterogeneous and dynamically changing metacomputing environments. In this environment, applications must be able to obtain answers to questions such as: "Which average bandwidth is available from 3pm until 7pm between host A and host B?" and

"Which PVM version is running on the MPP xy?" This information is obtained from multiple sources like the Network Information Service NIS, the Simple Network Management Protocol SNMP, or from system-specific configuration files.

The MDS [9] is a tool that addresses the need for efficient and scalable access to diverse, dynamic, and distributed information. Both static information (e.g., amount of memory, or CPU speed) and dynamic information (e.g., network latency, or CPU load) are handled by MDS. It has been built on the data representation and API defined by the lightweight directory access protocol LDAP [16], which in turn is based on the X.500 standard. This standard defines a directory service that provides access to general data about entities like people, institutions, or computers. The information base in MDS is therefore structured as a set of such entries. Each entry is an attribute/value pair which may be either mandatory or optional. The type of an entry defines which attributes are associated with that entry and what type of values those attributes may contain. All entries are organized in a hierarchical, tree-structured name space, the directory information tree DIT. Unique entry names are constructed by specifying the path from the root of the DIT to the entry being named. The DIT is used to organize and manage a collection of entries and to allow the distribution of these entries over multiple sites. MDS servers are responsible for complete DIT subtrees (e.g., for a single machine, or for all entries of a computing center).

To describe resources for a job request the Globus Resource Manager RM provides a Resource Specification Language, given by a string of parameter specifications and conditions on MDS entries. As an example, 32 nodes with at least 128 MB and three nodes with ATM interface are specified by:

```
+(&(count=32) (memory >=128M) )
 (&(count=3)  (network=ATM) )
```

The RM matches resource requests against the information obtained from the MDS.

8.2.4 The Resource Description Language (RDL)

The Resource Description Language RDL [3] is a language-based approach for specifying system resources in heterogeneous environments. At the administrator's level it is used for describing type and topology of the available resources, and at the user's level it is used for specifying the required system components for a given application. RDL originated in the "transputer world" with massively parallel systems of up to 1024 nodes and was later used for specifying PowerPC-based systems and workstation clusters.

In RDL, system resources consist of nodes that are interconnected by an arbitrary topology. A node may be either active or passive and the links between nodes may be static or dynamic. Active nodes are indicated by the keyword `PROC` while passive nodes are specified by `PORT`. Depending on whether RDL is used to describe hard- or software topologies, `PROC` may be read as "processor" or as "process." A port node may be a physical socket, a process that behaves passively within the parallel program, or a passive hardware entity like a crossbar. In addition to these built-in properties, new attributes can be introduced by the DEF Identifier [= (value,...)] statement, see Figure 8.2.

```
DECLARATION
BEGIN PROC MPP_with_frontend
   DYNAMIC;             -- system can be configured dynamically
   EXCLUSIVE;           -- allocate resources for exclusive use
   SYSTEM = (GC_Cluster_Size, 4, 4, 1); -- cluster size of MPP
   DECLARATION
   BEGIN PROC Parsytec_GCel
      DECLARATION
      { PROC; CPU=T8; MEMORY=4; SPEED=30; REPEAT=1024;}
      { PORT; REPEAT=4; }
   END PROC

   BEGIN PROC Unix_frontend
      DECLARATION
      { PORT; SBUS; OS=UNIX; REPEAT=4 }
   END PROC

   CONNECTION           -- of the MPP with the frontend
      FOR i=0 TO 3 DO
         Parsytec_GCel LINK i <=> Unix_frontend LINK i;
      OD
END PROC MPP_with_frontend
```

Figure 8.2 RDL specification of a 1024 node transputer system with a UNIX front end.

The hierarchical concept of RDL allows nodes to be grouped to build more complex nodes. Such a group is introduced by BEGIN [PROC|NODE] ComplexNodeName. A complex node definition consists of three parts. First, there is a definition section where attributes are assigned to the node. This is followed by the declaration section in which the subnodes are described. The final part defines connections between the various subnodes (node_a LINK n <=> node_b LINK m) and to the outside world (ASSIGN node_a LINK n <=> LINK m). Figure 8.2 depicts an example of a parallel machine that is connected to a UNIX front end via four external links.

8.3 Resource and Service Description (RSD)

8.3.1 Requirements

A versatile resource description facility should meet the following requirements:

- **Simple resource requirements should be easy to generate:** Users do not want to type in long and complex descriptions just for launching a small program. Therefore, a user-friendly graphical editor is needed.
- **Powerful tools for generating complex descriptions:** System administrators need adequate tools for describing complex systems made up of het-

erogeneous computing nodes and various kinds of interconnection networks. Although most of the system configuration is likely to remain constant over a long time, it might be quite difficult to specify all components, especially for large HPC centers. Furthermore, it is necessary to manage dynamic system data like network traffic and CPU load. Therefore, a simple graphical interface is insufficient; a combination of a text-based description language and a GUI is needed.

- **Application programming interface (API):** For automatical evaluation and mapping of resource descriptions an API is needed that allows access to the data by function calls and/or method invocations. Furthermore, the API encapsulates the internal structure of the resource description and allows future extensions without the need to update other software.

- **Portable representation:** Resource descriptions are sent across the network and they are exchanged between a vast variety of different hardware architectures and operating systems. The representation should be designed to be understood by each participating system.

- **Recursive structure:** Computing resources are usually organized in a hierarchical way: A metacomputer might comprise several HPC centers, which include several supercomputers that in turn consist of a number of processing elements. The resource description facility should reflect this general approach by recursive constructs.

- **Graph structured:** HPC hardware, software, and dynamic (time dependent) data flow are often described by graphs. Thus, the resource description facility should allow to define graph based structures.

- **Attributed components:** For describing properties of processors, network connections, jobs, and communication requirements, it should be possible to assign valued attributes to arbitrary nodes and edges of the resource description.

8.3.2 Architecture

Figure 8.3 depicts the general concept of the RSD framework. It was designed to fit the needs of both the user as well as the system administrator. This is achieved by providing three different representations: a graphical interface, a textual interface, and an application programming interface. Users and administrators are expected to use a graphical editor for specifying their resource descriptions (Section 8.3.3). While the GUI editor will usually suffice for the end user, system administrators may need to describe the more complex components by an additional text-based language. The editor combines the textual parts with the graphical input and creates an internal data representation (Section 8.3.5). The resulting data structure

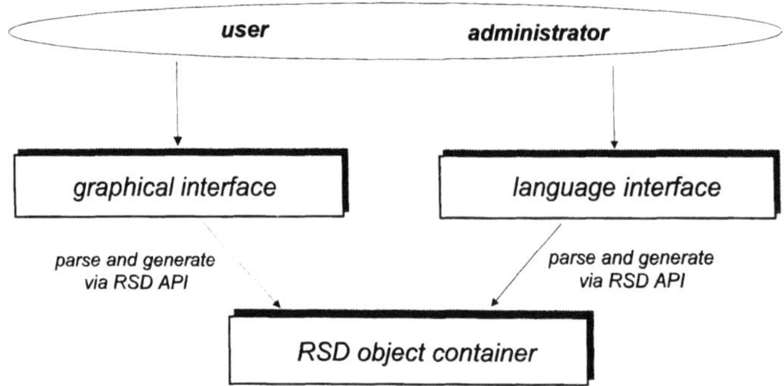

Figure 8.3 General concept of the RSD approach.

is bundled with the API access methods and sent as an attributed object to the target systems in order to be matched against other hard- or software descriptions.

The internal data description can only be accessed through the API. For later modifications it is retranslated into its original form of graphic primitives and textual components. This is possible because the internal data representation also contains a description of the component's graphical layout. In the following, we describe the core components of RSD in more detail.

8.3.3 Graphical Interface

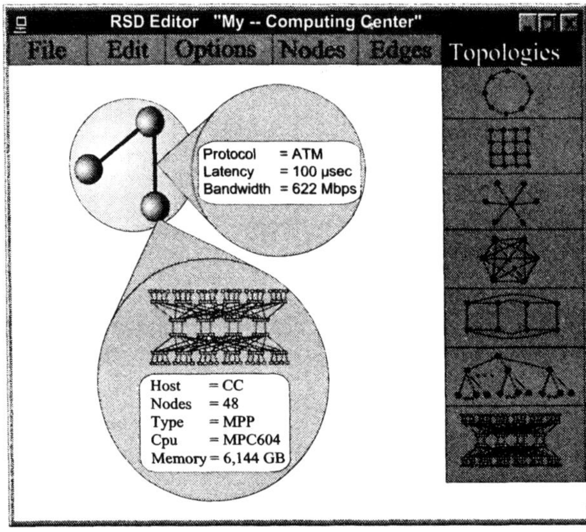

Figure 8.4 Graphical RSD editor.

In this section we present the general layout of a graphical RSD editor. It contains a toolbox of modules that can be edited and linked together to build a complex dependency graph or a system resource description.

At the administrator level, the graphical interface is used to describe the basic computing and networking components in a (meta-)center. Figure 8.4 illustrates a typical administrator session. In this example, the components of the center are specified in a top-down manner with the interconnection topology as a starting point. With drag-and-drop, the administrator specifies the available machines, their links, and the interconnection to the outside world. It is possible to specify new resources by using predefined objects and attributes via pull-down menus, radio buttons, and check boxes.

In the next step, the machines are specified in more detail. This is done by clicking on a node, whereby the editor opens a window showing detailed information on the machine (if available). The GUI offers a set of standard machine layouts like Cray T3E, IBM SP2, or Parsytec, and some generic topologies like grid or torus. The administrator defines the size of the machine and the general attributes of the whole machine. As described in Section 8.3.4, attributes can also be specified in a textual manner. When the machine has been specified, a window with a graphical representation of the machine opens, in which single nodes can be selected. Attributes like network interface cards, main memory, disk capacity, I/O throughput, CPU load, network traffic, disk space, or the automatic start of daemons, etc. can be assigned. At the user level, the interface can be customized. User generated configuration files contain the most common resource descriptions. Additionally, it is possible to connect to a remote site to load its RSD dialect (i.e., the attribute names and their valid values). This allows the user interface to perform online syntax checks, even if the user specifies remote resources. Likewise, it is possible to join multiple sites to a metasite, using a different RSD dialect without affecting the site-specific RSD dialects.

Similar to the wide-area metacomputer manager (WAMM) [2], the user may click on a center and the target machines. Interconnection topologies, node availability, and the current job schedule may be inspected. Partitions can be selected via drag and drop or in a textual manner. For multisite applications, the user may either specify the intended target machines or constraints in order to let the RMS choose a suitable set of systems.

8.3.4 Language Interface

For system administrators, graphical user interfaces may not be powerful enough for describing complex metacomputing environments with a large number of services and resources. Administrators need an additional tool for specifying irregularly interconnected, attributed structures. Hence, we devised a language interface that is used to specify arbitrary topologies. The hierarchical concept allows different dependency graphs to be grouped for building even more complex nodes, i.e., hypernodes.

Active nodes are indicated by the keyword NODE. Depending on whether RSD is used to describe hardware or software topologies, the keyword NODE is interpreted as a "processor" or a "process." Communication interfaces are declared by the keyword PORT. A PORT may be a socket, a passive hardware entity like a network interface card, a crossbar, or a process that behaves passively within the parallel program.

A NODE definition consists of three parts:

1. In the optional DEFINITION section, identifiers and attributes are introduced by Identifier [= (value,...)] .

2. The DECLARATION section declares all nodes with corresponding attributes. The notion of a node is recursive. They are described by NODE NodeName {PORT PortName; attribute 1, ...}.

3. The CONNECTION section is again optional. It is used to define attributed edges between the ports of the nodes declared above: EDGE NameOfEdge{NODE w PORT x <=> NODE y PORT z; attribute 1; ...}. In addition, the notion of a "virtual edge" is used to provide a link between different levels of the hierarchy in the graph. This allows us to establish a link from the described module to the "outside world" by "exporting" a physical port to the next higher level. These edges are defined by: ASSIGN NameOfVirtualEdge{NODE w PORT x <=> PORT a}. Note that NODE *w* and PORT *a* are the only entities known to the outside world.

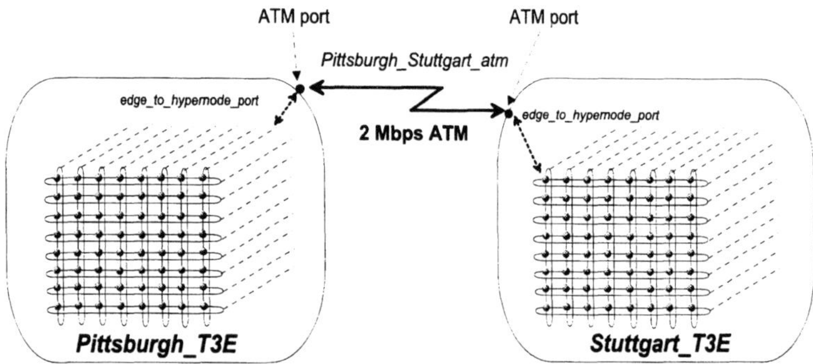

Figure 8.5 RSD example for multisite application G-WAAT.

Figure 8.5 illustrates a resource specification for the metacomputer application testbed G-WAAT (Global - Wide Area Application Testbed) presented at the Supercomputing conference in San Jose, 1997. In this project, a Cray T3E at Pittsburgh Supercomputing Center was connected via a trans-Atlantic ATM network to a Cray T3E at the High Performance Computing Center in Stuttgart, Germany. On this

```
NODE G-WAAT { // Global Wide Area Application Testbed
 // DEFINITION: define attributes, values and ranges
    BANDWIDTH = (1..1200); // valid range of bandwidth in Mbps

 // DECLARATION: include the two hyper nodes
    INCLUDE "Pittsburgh_Cray_T3E";
    INCLUDE "Stuttgart_Cray_T3E";

 // CONNECTION:
 // dedicated trans-Atlantic ATM net between Pittsburgh and Stuttgart
    EDGE Pittsburgh_Stuttgart_atm {
       NODE Pittsburgh_T3E PORT ATM <=> NODE Stuttgart_T3E PORT ATM;
       BANDWIDTH = 2 Mbps; LATENCY = 75 msecs;
       AVAILABLE_DAY = Thursday; FROM = 3pm UTC; UNTIL = 6pm UTC;};
};
```

Figure 8.6 RSD specification of Figure 8.5.

global metacomputer, the CFD code URANUS was run to simulate the re-entry of a space vehicle into the atmosphere.

The RSD definition of G-WAAT is straightforward (Figure 8.6). Figure 8.7 shows a more detailed specification of Stuttgarts' Cray T3E containing 512 nodes. For each node the following attributes are specified: CPU type, the CPU clock rate, memory per node, and the port to the Gigaring. All nodes are interconnected in a 3D-Torus topology by the 1.0 Gbps Gigaring. In the example, the first node acts as gateway between the Cray T3E system and the outside world. It presents its ATM port to the next higher node level (see ASSIGN statement in Figure 8.7) to allow for remote connections.

8.3.5 Internal Data Representation

In this section, we describe the abstract data type that establishes the link between graphical and text-based representations. This RSD data format is also used to store descriptions on disk and to exchange them across networks.

Abstract Data Types As stated in Sections 8.3.1, 8.3.3, and 8.3.4, the internal data representation must be capable of describing:

- arbitrary graph structures
- hierarchical systems or organizations
- nodes and edges with arbitrary sets of valued attributes

Furthermore, it should be possible to reconstruct the original representation, either graphical or text based. This facilitates the maintenance of large descriptions (e.g., a complex HPC center) and allows visualization at remote sites.

```
NODE Stuttgart_T3E {
  // DEFINITION:
  CONST N = 512;                          // number of nodes
  CONST DIMX = 8, DIMY = 8, DIMZ = 8;  // dimensions of machine in nodes
  // DECLARATION: // we have 512 nodes, node 000 is the gateway
  // the gateway provides one GIGARING port and one ATM port
  FOR x=0 TO DIMX-1 DO
     FOR y=0 TO DIMY-1 DO
        FOR z=0 TO DIMZ-1 DO
           NODE $x$y$z {
           PORT GIGARING; IF (x == 0 && y == 0 && z == 0) THEN PORT ATM;
           CPU=Alpha; CLOCKRATE=450 Mhz; MEMORY=128 MByte; OS=UNICOS};
        OD
     OD
  OD
  // CONNECTION: build the 1.0 Gbps 3D-Torus
  FOR x=0 TO DIMX-1 DO
     FOR y=0 TO DIMY-1 DO
        FOR z=0 TO DIMZ-1 DO
           neighborX = (x+1) MOD DIMX;
           neighborY = (y+1) MOD DIMY;
           neighborZ = (z+1) MOD DIMZ;
           EDGE edge_$x$y$z_to_$neighborX$y$z {
                    NODE $x$y$z PORT GIGARING =>
                    NODE $neighborX$y$z PORT GIGARING;
                    BANDWIDTH = 1.0 Gbps;};
           EDGE edge_$x$y$z_to_$x$neighborY$z {
                    NODE $x$y$z PORT GIGARING =>
                    NODE $x$neighborY$z PORT GIGARING;
                    BANDWIDTH = 1.0 Gbps;};
           EDGE edge_$x$y$z_to_$x$y$neighborZ {
                    NODE $x$y$z PORT GIGARING =>
                    NODE $x$y$neighborZ PORT GIGARING;
                    BANDWIDTH = 1.0 Gbps;};
        OD
     OD
  OD
  // establish a virtual edge from node 000 to the
  // port of the hyper node Stuttgart_T3E (=outside world)
  ASSIGN edge_to_hypernode_port {
     NODE 000 PORT ATM <=> PORT ATM;};
};
```

Figure 8.7 RSD specification of Stuttgarts' Cray T3E.

Following these considerations we define the data structure RSD_{Graph} as the fundamental concept of the internal data representation:

$$RSD_{Graph} := (V, E) \ \ with \ \left\{ \begin{array}{l} V \ being \ a \ set \ of \ RSD_{Node} \ and \\ E \subseteq (V \times V \times RSD_{Attribute}) \end{array} \right. \tag{8.3.1}$$

and

$$RSD_{Node} := RSD_{Attribute} \mid (RSD_{Graph}, RSD_{Attribute}) \tag{8.3.2}$$

Thus, an RSD_{Graph} is a graph which may have assigned attributes to its nodes and edges. Since a node may also represent a complete substructure, it is possible to represent hierarchies of any depth. For example, this may be used to describe a computing center that has its own set of attributes but whose internal hardware description needs further refinement.

For maximum flexibility, we define $RSD_{Attribute}$ to be either a (possibly empty) list of names and values or a single name for a more complex structure of attributes:

$$RSD_{Attribute} := \emptyset \mid (Name, Value), \ldots \mid (Name, RSD_{Attribute}) \qquad (8.3.3)$$

The name of an attribute follows the common naming conventions of programming languages while the value may have one of the following types: *boolean*, *integer*, *real*, *string*, *bytearray*, and *bitfield*.

Figure 8.8 depicts a small example of this concepture. There are two RSD_{Node} structures representing computing centers that are connected by a 34 Mbps ATM link. The substructure contained in Center A indicates that there are three machines within this center, one of them being an MPP system called "GCel-1024."

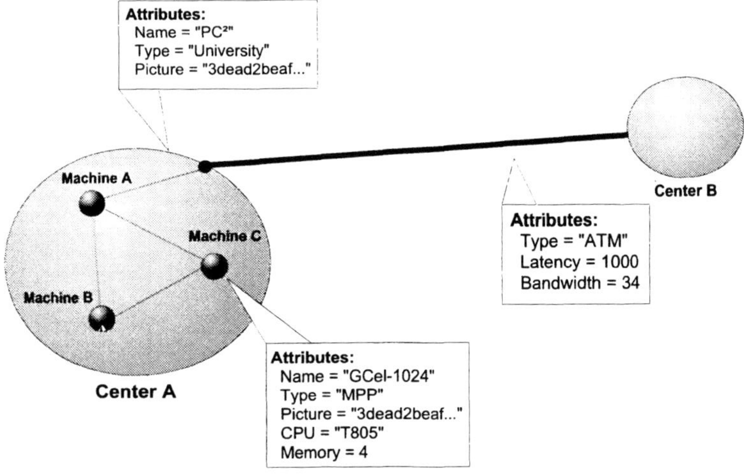

Figure 8.8 Example configuration for RSD.

Methods for Handling Abstract Data Types Having described the data structure, we now introduce the basic methods for dealing with the RSD abstract data type. Only those methods are provided that are absolutely necessary. All higher level functions build upon them.

- $Nodes(RSD_{Graph})$ – Returns a list of nodes in the highest level of the graph. Referring to Figure 8.8 these would be *Center A* and *Center B*.
- $Neighbors(RSD_{Node})$ – Gives a list of all nodes connected to RSD_{Node} in the same level. In Figure 8.8, *Center B* is a neighbor of *Center A* but not of *Machine A*.

- $SubNodes(RSD_{Node})$ – These are all nodes contained in RSD_{Node}. As an example the subnodes of *Center A* comprise *Machine A*, *Machine B*, and *Machine C*, but none of their processors.
- $Attributes(\ RSD_{Node} \mid (RSD_{Node}, RSD_{Node})\ )$ – Returns a list of all top level attributes of the specified node or edge.
- $Value(RSD_{Attribute})$ – Returns the value of an $RSD_{Attribute}$. This may also be a set of attributes in the case of hierarchically structured attributes.

In addition, there exists a number of auxiliary methods, e.g., for list handling, that build on the basic methods. These are not described in this chapter.

Note that the internal data types are also used for reconstructing the original graphical and/or text representation. As an example, a system administrator may have defined a large Fast Fourier Transformation (FFT) network by a few lines of the RSD language. The internal representation of such a node is much more complex and not easy to translate back into its original form. However, it is possible to keep the source code of this special node as one of its attributes. This can then be used by the editor whenever the FFT is to be modified. The same is possible with nodes that were created graphically and require a uniform layout of their components.

8.3.6 Implementation

In order to use RSD in a distributed environment a common format for exchanging RSD data structures is needed. The traditional approach to this would be to define a data stream format. However, this would involve two additional transformation steps whenever RSD data is to be exchanged (internal representation into data stream and back). Since the RSD internal representation has been defined in an object-oriented way, this overhead can be avoided, if the complete object is sent across the net.

Today there exists a variety of standards for transmitting objects over the Internet, e.g., *CORBA*, *Java*, or *COM+*. Unfortunately, it is currently impossible to tell which of them will survive in the future. Therefore, we only define the interfaces of the RSD object class but not its private implementation. This allows others to choose an implementation that best fits their own data structures. Interoperability between different implementations can be improved by defining translation constructors, i.e., constructors that take an RSD object as an argument and create a copy of it using another internal representation.

This concept is much more flexible than the traditional approach. It allows enhancements of the RSD definition and of the communication paradigm while still maintaining downward compatibility with older implementations.

8.4 Summary

Managing resources in metacomputing environments is much more complex than in local environments. This is not only because of the vast number of different resource types, but also because of their dynamic behavior: Resources and services may be added or withdrawn at any time.

With RSD, we presented a graph-oriented scheme for specifying and controlling resources and services in heterogeneous environments. Its graphical user interface allows the user to specify resource requests. Its textual interface gives a service provider enough flexibility for specifying computing nodes, network topology, system properties, and software attributes. Its internal object-oriented resource representation is used to link different resource management systems and service tools.

8.5 Bibliography

[1] *The Athena Project.* http://web.mit.edu/olh/Welcome/index.html.

[2] R. Baraglia, G. Faieta, M. Formica, and D. Laforenza. Experiences with a Wide Area Network Metacomputing Management Tool using IBM SP-2 Parallel Systems. *Concurrency: Practice and Experience.* John Wiley & Sons Ltd., NY, vol. 8, 1996.

[3] B. Bauer and F. Ramme. A General Purpose Resource Description Language. R. Grebe and M. Baumann (eds), *Parallel Datenverarbeitung mit dem Transputer.* Springer-Verlag, Berlin, pages 68–75, 1991.

[4] A. Bayucan, R. L. Henderson, T. Proett, D. Tweten, and B. Kelly. Portable Batch System: External Reference Specification. Release 1.1.7, NASA Ames Research Center, June 1996.

[5] T. Beisel, E. Gabriel, and M. Resch. An Extension to MPI for Distributed Computing on MPPs. In M. Bubak, J. Dongarra, J. Wasniewski (eds.), *Recent Advances in Parallel Virtual Machine and Message Passing Interface*, Springer LNCS, pages 25–33, 1997.

[6] M. Brune, J. Gehring, and A. Reinefeld. Heterogeneous Message Passing and a Link to Resource Management. *Journal of Supercomputing*, vol. 11, pages 355–369, 1997.

[7] M. Brune, J. Gehring, A. Keller, B. Monien, F. Ramme, and A. Reinefeld. Specifying Resources and Services in Metacomputing Environments. *Parallel Computing*, vol. 24, pages 1751–1776, 1998.

[8] G. E. Fagg, and J. Dongarra. PVMPI: An Integration of the PVM and MPI Systems. *Calculateurs Paralleles*, vol. 2, pages 151–166, 1996.

[9] S. Fitzgerald, I. Foster, C. Kesselman, G. von Laszewski, W. Smith, and S. Tuecke. *A Directory Service for Configuring High Performance Distributed Computations.* Preprint, Mathematics and Computer Science Division, Argonne National, Laboratory, Argonne, IL, 1997.

[10] I. Foster, and C. Kesselman. Globus: A Metacomputing Infrastructure Toolkit. *Journal of Supercomputer Applications*, vol. 11, pages 115–128, 1997.

[11] A. Keller, and A. Reinefeld. Resource Management in Networked HPC Systems. Heterogeneous Computing Workshop at IPPS'98, Orlando, March 1998.

[12] R. R. Lipman, and J. E. Devaney. WebSubmit: Running Supercomputer Applications Via the Web. *Supercomputing '96*, Pittsburgh, PA, pages 17–22, November 1996.

[13] L. Smarr, and C.E. Catlett. Metacomputing. *Communications of the ACM*, vol. 35(6), pages 45–52, 1992.

[14] *SP Parallel Programming Workshop: LoadLeveler.* http://www.mhpcc.edu/-training/workshop/html/loadleveler/LoadLeveler.html

[15] *The Tivoli Management Environment.* http://www.tivoli.com.

[16] W. Yeong, T. Howes, and S. Kille. *Lightweight Directory Access Protocol.* RFC 1777, 03/2895, Draft Standard.

Part II

Networking, Protocols, and I/O

Cluster systems are the supercomputers of tomorrow. However, the determining performance bottleneck of clusters compared to MPP systems lies in its interconnection network and the supporting software tools. Thus, the research is focusing on these areas, bringing with it scintillating new technologies on the network and the protocol layer.

For I/O intensive applications, clusters deliver a perfect platform by building large common storage pools using disks associated with their nodes. With appropriate and affordable hardware support the mentioned network bottleneck of cluster systems can be turned into the known disc bottleneck of high performance I/O problems. Hence, the already developed methods and techniques on MPP systems to overcome this I/O bottleneck can be equally applied to cluster systems. Thus, clusters present themselves as affordable and suitable I/O systems.

Part II starts in Chapter 9 with an overview of the state of the art of the network interconnection technology. After some general design issues for high speed networks are presented, several well-known cluster interconnects are described and evaluated based on their characteristics. The chapter discusses all important developments from Fast Ethernet, HiPPI, and ATM—to new promising approaches such as SCI, ServerNet, Myrinet, Memory Channel, and Synfinity.

In Chapter 10 a survey about communication systems in clusters is given. The focus is on message passing systems based on the distributed memory architecture of cluster systems nowadays. For the reader, the choice of a suitable communication system is eased by classifying the various approaches on their architecture and performance characteristics.

The Active Messages programming model represents a RISC approach to communication, providing simple primitives to realize libraries for higher-level communication. Chapter 11 motivates and justifies Active Messages as a notion of communication abstraction and describes the specific model and implementation of the University of California, Berkeley.

In Chapter 12 the Xpress Transport Protocol is presented as a new transport layer above IP. XTP represents an extension to TCP and UDP useful in cluster computing environment. Its versatility in providing reliable and unreliable transport multicast services and other services, allowing high-throughput computing, has made it part of the MIL-STD-2204, the American military standard mission-critical, networked computers.

Congestion control in networks is an important issue to guarantee a system's overall performance is acceptable. In Chapter 13 congestion management for ATM networks is discussed, a simulation model to study the traffic management is developed, and an algorithm for migration planning is provided.

Load Balancing is another way to ensure performance by distributing the workload or network traffic among the available nodes in the cluster. In Chapter 14 load balancing methods are examined, which exploit the contents information of the TCP/IP protocol packages independently from software applications using them. Common errors, which can destabilize efficient network clusters and practical implementations, are also described.

Besides the development of new network models, the exploitation of existing network resources is also a viable way to increase network throughput. In Chapter 15 the performance-based path determination technique, which utilizes the heterogeneity of multiple physical communication paths and protocols, is described to overcome bandwidth-limited situations.

Clusters accumulate huge resources on storage space in their nodes as main memory and disk space. One of the great challenges in cluster research is to exploit these resources in an efficient way and to put it at the application's disposal. In Chapter 16 the notion of network memory (network RAM) is introduced, and approaches for the efficient use of the cluster's combined available main memory are discussed.

The idea of network memory leads conclusively to the adaptation (from MPPs well known) of the distributed shared memory (DSM) programming paradigm to clusters systems. Distributed shared memory, compared to the message passing principle, provides on the one hand a much simpler programming paradigm, but pays for it on the other hand with slower implementations. In Chapter 17 DSM systems for clusters are discussed, the problem characteristics defined, and implementation issues tackled.

The last two chapters deal with the parallel Input/Output problem of high performance applications focusing on cluster systems. In Chapter 18 the parallel I/O problem is defined, and a motivation and justification for the use of cluster systems for I/O specific problems is given. The most common parallel I/O methods and techniques are described and an introduction to available architectures and systems is presented. The chapter finishes with a closer look at ViPIOS, an existing parallel I/O system of the University of Vienna.

The closing chapter of Part II, Chapter 19, concentrates on the filesystem issue for clusters. It discusses the specific characteristics of distributed and parallel filesystems as data placement, caching, and prefetching. Finally, it presents some commonly used interface models and example implementations.

Chapter 9

High Speed Networks

BHAVANA NAGENDRA[†] AND LARS RZYMIANOWICZ[‡]

[†]Lucent Technologies
Columbus, Ohio, USA

[‡]Dept. of Computer Architecture
University of Mannheim, Germany

Email: *bnagendra@lucent.com, lr@mufasa.informatik.uni-mannheim.de*

9.1 Introduction

The network is the most critical part of a cluster. Its capabilities and performance directly influences the applicability of the whole system for High Performance Computing (HPC). After describing some general design issues for high speed networks, several well-known cluster interconnects are presented in detail. Their architecture and main properties are described and evaluated in the order in which the networks have evolved over the years, starting from Local/Wide Area Networks (LAN/WAN) like Fast Ethernet and ATM, to System Area Networks (SAN) like Myrinet and Memory Channel.

9.1.1 Choice of High Speed Networks

In order to effectively work in a distributed environment, a fast network is of utmost importance. The growing importance of LANs today and the increasing complexity of desktop computing applications are fueling the need for high speed networks. The bandwidth provided by a 10 Mbit/s Ethernet connection is not adequate for a full fledged distributed system carrying the load of high speed computations for scientific studies or industry workload on a corporate network or even today's typical desktop computing applications. A more specialized networking approach and a low cost, high performance interconnect optimized specifically to enhance both the parallel performance and high availability aspects of a cluster is needed. There are a few technologies out there which could fit the bill; these are discussed in this chapter.

Fast Ethernet

Fast Ethernet is a generic term for a family of high speed LANs running at 100 Mbit/s over either UTP or fiber-optic cable. It uses the Carrier Sense Multiple Access with Collision Detection (CSMA/CD) protocol. Fast Ethernet is currently the upgrade path most users of 10 Mbit/s Ethernet systems are using to speed up their networks.

High Performance Parallel Interface (HiPPI)

High Performance Parallel Interface (HiPPI) is a copper-based data communications standard capable of transferring data at 800 Mbit/sec over 32 parallel lines or 1.6 Gbit/sec over 64 parallel lines. HiPPI is a point-to-point channel that does not support multidrop configurations.

Asynchronous Transfer Mode (ATM)

Asynchronous Transfer Mode (ATM) is a connection-oriented packet switching, fixed length (53 bytes) technology, highly suitable for wide area. It is the technology of choice for Broadband Integrated Services Digital Networks (BISDN). ATM can handle any kind of information, i.e., voice, data, image, text, and video in an integrated manner. ATM technology will play a central role in the evolution of clusters as ATM delivers important advantages over existing LAN and WAN technologies, including the promise of scalable bandwidths at unprecedented price and performance and Quality of Service (QoS) guarantees, which facilitate new classes of applications.

Scalable Coherent Interface (SCI)

Scalable Coherent Interface (SCI) is a recent communication standard for cluster interconnects. SCI addresses the need for more system resources and computing power by providing a cluster-wide shared memory, thus relieving the programmer of the task using explicit message passing techniques. This easy-to-use programming interface, and the fact that SCI is an IEEE standard, have made it quite popular as interconnect for recent PC clusters.

ServerNet

ServerNet is a SAN which clusters processors and other devices to provide the high bandwidth, scalability, and reliability required by HPC applications. The second generation of ServerNet provides 125 Mbyte/s bandwidth between two nodes in a clustered system.

Myrinet

Myrinet is a cost-effective, gigabit-per-second network based on the communication technology used in supercomputers. Due to the intracomputer environment the communication latencies between computing nodes are greatly reduced. One of the main reasons for its great acceptance is the onboard programmable microcontroller, which enables researchers to fit the interconnect to their specific needs.

Memory Channel

The Memory Channel network is a dedicated cluster interconnect that provides virtual shared memory among nodes by means of internodal address space mapping. The interconnect implements direct user-level messaging and guarantees strict message ordering under all conditions, including transmission errors. It provides a physical bandwidth of 100 Mbyte/s.

Synfinity

Synfinity supports Message Passing as well as Shared Memory computing at very high data rates (up to 1.6 Gbyte/s). Besides normal send/receive operations, remote memory transactions and hardware support for synchronization offer the ability to implement optimized protocol layers.

9.1.2 Evolution in Interconnect Trends

Historically, mainstream high performance UNIX server computational capacity has outpaced the ability of the network to meet the bandwidth required for large distributed data sets. High speed networking technology was restricted to Supercomputer Centers. The networking industry has undergone an exponential growth and is taking a leading role in making the technology usable for the masses.

Ethernet has been a popular networking technology due to its simplicity and the fact that existing networks need not be modified to accommodate a new technology. But Ethernet transmits a frame and waits for a response. As the distance between nodes increases, waiting for an acknowledge is not feasible. IEEE 802.5, which is the standard for token ring, holds the token while the frame goes around the network ring. FDDI holds the entire path while using only a part of it; spatial reuse is needed instead. These technologies are characteristic of the old generation where high speed was not a factor and the latencies they offered were very high (100 - 1000s of microseconds), together with relatively low bandwidth (1 - 10 Mbit/s). Out-of-order caching, selective retransmission, forward error correction, anticipation, prefetching, and implicit handshake are also characteristics required in the new generation of high speed networks. Another limitation of standard networking technologies is that there is a ceiling on the total bandwidth available to the network. This means that on a 100 Mbit/s network segment with eight systems, any system trying to communicate with the network might have only 12.5 Mbit/s of throughput available for its use.

For current interconnect needs, very high speed networks are required, and the high speed networking technology has now become an affordable interconnect solution for mainstream markets. Emerging networking technologies promise performance capabilities ranging from one to several Gbit/s. Additionally, many new network technologies provide enhanced distance capabilities over older copper networks through use of optical media. Older high performance network technologies were often proprietary, thereby limiting their connectivity. The recent transition to 100 Mbit/s Ethernet or switched LANs such as switched Ethernet or ATM increase the bandwidth somewhat while their latencies continue to be in the hundreds of microseconds range.

9.2 Design Issues

Before several cluster interconnects are presented in detail, this section gives an overview of the main design trade-offs for interconnect hardware. For each design topic, several possibilities are presented and evaluated. With this basic knowledge in mind, the reader should be able to rate concrete implementations according to their usability and performance for specific applications. The network adapter (I/O bus card, system chip) is referred to as network interface (NI), whereas the connection between two network nodes (adapters or switches) is referred to as the link.

9.2.1 Goals

Several decisions must be made when designing a cluster interconnect. The most important is undeniably the price/performance trade-off.

Price versus Performance

In the last few years clusters of PCs have gained huge popularity due to the extreme low prices of standard PCs. Traditional supercomputer technology is replaced more and more by tightly interconnected PCs. In the interconnect market, though, a huge gap exists between interconnects of moderate bandwidth like Fast Ethernet at a low price ($50-100 for a network adapter) and high performance networks like Myrinet or ServerNet ($1000 and more). Of course, this is also a consequence of low production volumes. But other factors, such as onboard RAM or expensive physical layers such as Fiber Channel, can raise costs significantly.

Scalability

Scalability is another crucial issue. It refers to the networks ability to grow almost linearly with the number of nodes. Interconnects in traditional supercomputers have a fixed network topology (mesh, hypercube) and hardware/software relies on the fixed topology. But clusters are more dynamic. Often a small system is set up to test, if the cluster fits to the application needs. With increasing demand for computing power, more and more nodes are added to the system. The network should tolerate the increased load and deliver nearly the same bandwidth and latency to small clusters (8-32 nodes) and to large ones (hundreds of nodes). A large mesh will show increased latency compared to a small one, since the average distance between nodes also increases. Large switches (16x16, 24x24) forming a cluster-of-clusters topology can help to compensate this effect. Similarly, a hypercube network cannot be upgraded from 64 to 96 nodes because it needs a power of two as node count. Therefore, modern cluster interconnects allow us to form an arbitrary network topology. Hardware/Software determines the topology at system start-up and initializes routing tables, etc.

Reliability

Applications for parallel computing can be roughly divided into two main classes, scientific and business computing. Especially in the business field, corrupted or lost message data cannot be tolerated. To guarantee data delivery, protocol software of traditional WAN/LAN networks computes CRCs, buffers data, acknowledges messages, and retransmits corrupted data. This protocol layer has been identified as one main reason for poor latency in current networks. For clusters with their needs for low latency and thin protocol layers, this overhead must be minimized. First, cluster interconnects with their short range physical layers have proven to be almost error-free. The computation of CRCs can be easily done on-the-fly by the NI itself. Possible errors can be signaled to software through interrupts or status registers. To relieve software from buffering message data, the NI could also temporary buffer the message data and initiate retransmissions in case of errors. Overall, the cluster interconnect should present itself to the user as a reliable network without additional software overhead for safe data transmission.

9.2.2 General Architecture

A general design decision must be made between a dumb NI, which is processor controlled, and an intelligent and autonomous NI performing most of the work by itself. The first solution has the advantage of low design effort resulting in short time-to-market and redesign costs. On the other hand, enabling the NI to do jobs, such as data transfer or matching receiver ID with its network address/path, can free the processor from this work and reduce start-up latency for message transfers. Advantages of both methods can be glued together by adding a dedicated communication processor to the system [21]. This node design has been chosen for some parallel architectures (Intel Paragon, MANNA [22]) and resulted in good performance values, especially for communication intensive applications. In the following, the two main trade-offs are presented.

Shared Memory versus Distributed Memory

The first decision of a designer of cluster interconnects is the memory (programming) model to be supported. The shared memory model makes the cluster network transparent to processes through a common global address space. Virtual memory management hardware and software (MMU, page tables) is used to map virtual addresses to local or remote physical addresses. Since the overhead of applying this model to the whole address space is quite large, interconnects supporting shared memory offer the ability to map remote memory pages into local applications address spaces, like DEC's Memory Channel [17]. Figure 9.1 shows an example of a write operation to remote memory, where the NI resides on the I/O bus.

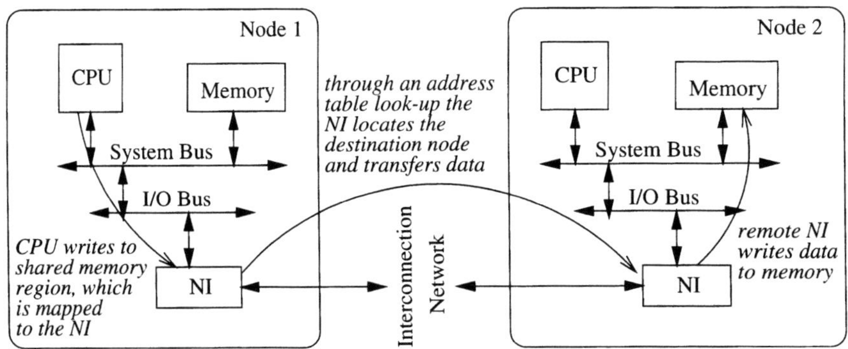

Figure 9.1 Write operation to remote memory.

A lot of work has to be done by the NI, if the virtual shared memory is intended to be cache-coherent across all cluster nodes, as known from SMP systems. A cache coherence protocol must observe the memory space on a cache line or page base. Writes must be propagated to all nodes owning a copy of the memory cell, or these copies must be invalidated. For short, the overhead of cluster-wide cache coherence can be manageable for small systems, but gets inefficient for large node numbers.

In the distributed memory model, message passing software makes the network visible to applications. Data can be sent to other nodes through send/receive API calls. Compared to the shared memory model, the user has to explicitly call communication routines to transfer data to or from the network.

Besides DEC's Memory Channel and SCI, which support the shared memory model, all remaining interconnects presented here are intended for message passing.

NI Location

The location of the NI inside a system has a great impact on its performance and usability. In general, the nearer it is to the processor, the more bandwidth is available. As depicted in Figure 9.2, there are three possible locations for the NI:

NI-1 An interesting solution is support for communication at the instruction set level inside a processor. By moving data into special communication registers, it is transferred into the network at a rate equal to the processor speed. This technique has been realized in the past in some architectures; its most famous representative is the Transputer from INMOS. Through four on-chip links at full processor clock speed, the Transputer was an ideal candidate as a building block for grid-interconnected massive parallel computers. Similar im-

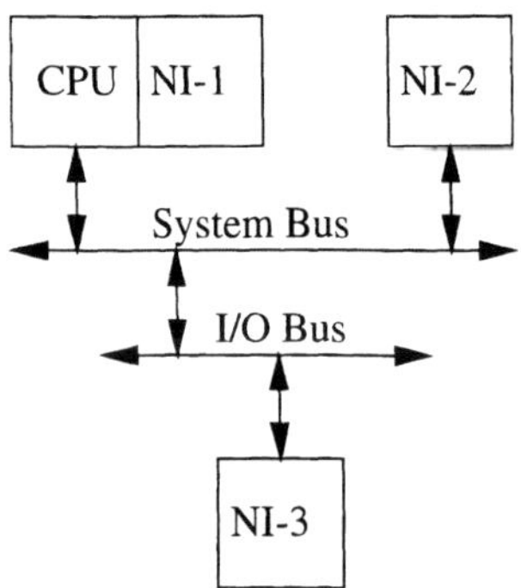

Figure 9.2 Possible NI locations.

plementations are the iWarp or related systolic architectures. Although these architectures are very interesting from the designers view, the market for this kind of processor was too small. Most implementations reached the prototype phase, but were commercially not successful. Some research projects also tried to include a network interface at the cache level, but this saw the same fate.

NI-2 Assuming a high performance system bus design, this location is an ideal place for a network interface. Today's system buses offer very high bandwidths in the range of several Gbytes/s. Common Cache-Coherence mechanisms can be used to efficiently observe NI status. The processor could poll on cache-coherent NI registers without consuming bus bandwidth. If the register changes its state (e.g., a status flag is set to indicate message arrival), the NI could invalidate the observed cache line. On the next load instruction, the new value is fetched from the NI. DMA controllers can read/write data from/to main memory using burst cycles at a very high bandwidth. Although there are several advantages to design the NI with a system bus interface, only a few NIs are implemented in this way. The reason for this is that each processor has its own bus architecture and thus ties an NI implementation to a specific processor. The market for interconnection networks is not yet large enough to justify such a specialization. Furthermore, commercial interests are likely to prevent the upcoming of standard bus architectures, even though more than just NIs would benefit from them.

NI-3 Most current interconnects have I/O bus interfaces, mainly PCI. The reason is the great acceptance of PCI as a standard I/O bus. PCI-based NIs can be plugged into any PC or workstation, even forming heterogeneous clusters. A 32 bit/33 MHz PCI device can deliver a peak data rate of 132 Mbyte/s, which can be nearly reached with long DMA bursts. To avoid that the PCI bus becomes the main bottleneck between system buses and physical layers with gigabytes per second bandwidth, it will be important that 64 bit/66

MHz PCI slots will be present in all computer systems in the near future. A disadvantage of the I/O bus location is the loss of some properties such as cache coherence.

Most interconnects presented in this chapter use the I/O bus as their interface to the host.

9.2.3 Design Details

In the next sections, a closer look is taken at some specific implementation details. Small modifications of the hardware can have a great impact on the NIs overall performance. This section can only present short and restricted descriptions of various mechanisms for interconnection networks; additional literature [20] is recommended for in-depth analysis.

A general rule of thumb could be: Keep the frequent case simple and fast. For example, mechanisms for error detection and correction should be implemented in a way that they do not add overhead to error-free transmissions. In the very rare case of a transmission error, some overhead can be accepted, since error rates of current physical layers are very low. The NI should also be able to pipeline data transfers. So the head of a message packet can be fed into the network, even if the tail is still fetched from memory. This enables low start-up latencies and good overall throughput.

Link Protocol

The term link protocol is used for the layout of messages, which are transmitted over the physical layer and the interaction between communicating link endpoints. Figure 9.3 shows two link endpoints (which could reside in a NI or a switch), connected by two unidirectional channels for sending and receiving data. Also, it depicts the general layout of a message. Typically, message data is enclosed by special control datawords, which can be used to detect start/end of message data and to signal link protocol events (receiver cannot accept more data, request for retransmission, etc.).

Physical Layer Choosing the right physical medium of a channel is a trade-off between raw data rate and cable costs. Serial mediums offer moderate bandwidth, but can rely on a standard link level transport layer such as Gigabit Ethernet or Fiber Channel. A 64 bit wide cable, as is used by the copper-based HIPPI network, enables very high data rates. But pin count is a limitation for the implementation of switches. To transmit signals at a very high clock rate (100 MHz and more) and a reasonable power consumption, the Low Voltage Data Signaling (LVDS) technique (two wires transmit complementary current levels of signals) can be used. So an 8x8 unidirectional Switch with 32 bit differential signal lines would result in 1024 pins only for the links, which is too much for today's ASIC fabrication. Bytewide links, as used by Myrinet and ServerNet, are a good compromise. Network switches of moderate sizes can be built, while raw data rate still exceeds the one of serial

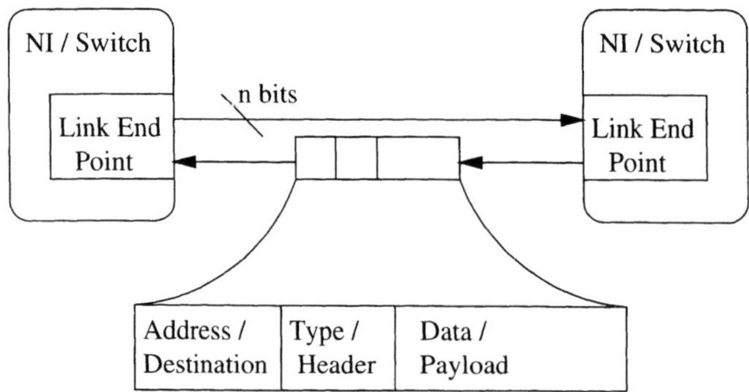

Figure 9.3 A bidirectional link and the general message format.

mediums. Since electrical transmit lengths are very restricted, optical layers could replace copper-based cables in the near future. But today high costs ($300 per optical serial interface) prevent the broad use of optical components.

Switching The connection between input and output ports and the transfer of data between them inside a network stage is called switching. Two main techniques (as depicted in Figure 9.4) are used in today's networks, packet and wormhole switching. The first stores a complete message packet in a network switch before the data is sent to the next stage. This store and forward mechanism needs an upper bound for the packet size (MTU, Maximum Transfer Unit) and some buffer space to store one or several packets temporary. On the left of Figure 9.4, packet p0 is just arriving at the switch through port 1 and is placed into the packet buffer pool. Packets p1 and p2 have been received in total and are now forwarded toward their destination through different ports. The more traditional LAN/WAN networks (Fast Ethernet and ATM) use packet switching.

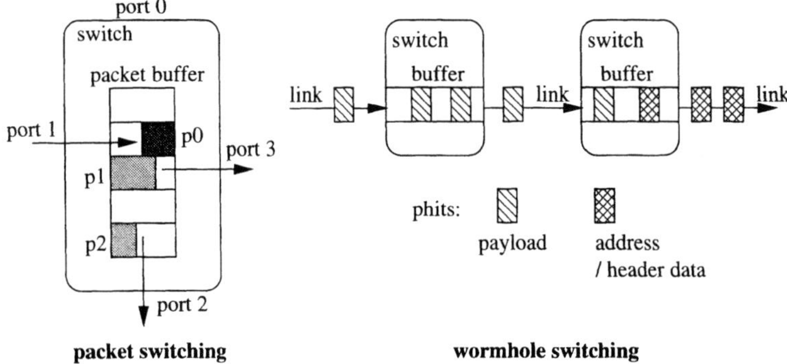

Figure 9.4 Switching techniques.

Newer SANs like Myrinet use wormhole switching (also referred to as cut-through switching), where the data is immediately forwarded to the next stage as soon as the address header is decoded. Low latency and the need for only a small amount of buffer space are the advantages of this technique. The right part of Figure 9.4 shows message data spread over several links and switches. Phits (Physical units) refer to single datawords, which can be transmitted in one cycle. The length of the message can be defined as variable, but the designer must keep in mind that long messages can block several stages at a time on their way to the destination. Also, the error correction is more difficult. Packet switching could first check a whole packet before it is forwarded to the next stage. Using the wormhole technique, corrupted data might be forwarded before it is recognized as erroneous.

Routing The address header of a message carries the information needed by routing hardware inside a switch to determine the right outgoing channel, which brings the data nearer to its destination. Although a lot of deterministic and adaptive routing algorithms have been proposed, the latter will not be studied here. Adaptive routing schemes try to find dynamically alternative paths through the network in case of overloaded network paths or even broken links. But adaptive routing has not found its way into real hardware yet. Two mechanisms are used in today's interconnects: source-path and table-based routing.

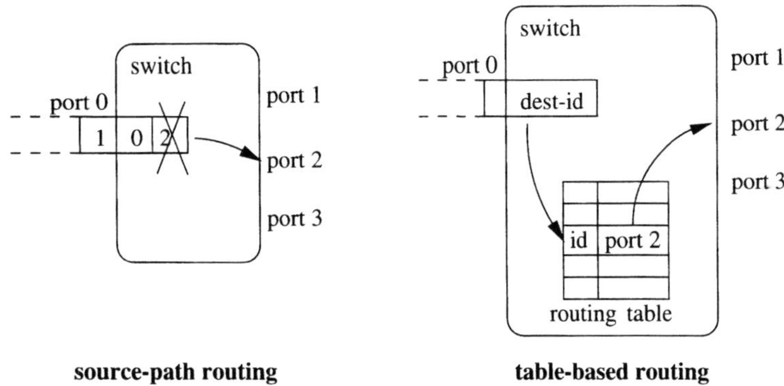

Figure 9.5 Routing mechanisms.

On the left side of Figure 9.5, a message enters a switch on port 0 and carries the routing information at the head of the message packet. As soon as the first dataword is received, routing hardware can determine the outgoing channel. Used routing data is stripped off, so the routing information for the next switch now leads the message. The entire path to the destination is attached to a message at its source location. On the right side of Figure 9.5, a switch containing a complete routing table is shown. For each destination node its corresponding port is stored. If messages enter the switch a table lookup determines the right outgoing channel. Routing table size is proportional to the number of nodes, which can be a limiting factor for large cluster configurations with hundreds or even thousands of nodes.

Flow Control Flow control is used to avoid buffer overruns inside switches, which can result in the loss of data. Before the sender can start the transmission, the receiver must signal the ability to accept the data. One possible solution is a credit-based scheme, where each sender gets a number of credits from the receiver. On each packet transmission, the sender consumes a credit point and stops when all credits are consumed. After freeing some buffer space, the receiver can restart the transmission through handing additional credits to the sender. Or, the receiver can simply signal the sender if he can accept data or not. In both cases, the flow control information travels in the opposite direction relative to the data (reverse flow control). For example, Myrinet inserts STOP and GO control bytes into the opposite channel of a link to stop or restart data transmission on the sender side.

Error Detection and Correction Though today's physical layers have very low error rates, the network must offer some mechanisms for error detection and possibly correction in hardware. In the era of user-level NI protocols, it is no longer acceptable that software has to compute a CRC. This task can easily be done in hardware. For example, the NI adapter can compute a CRC on the fly while data is transferred to it. This CRC is appended to the message data and can be checked at each network stage. If an error is detected, the message can be marked as corrupted. The receiver can then send a request for retransmission back to the sender. But, of course, this assumes that the complete data is buffered on the sender side.

Table 9.1 summarizes the different link parameters for several interconnects.

Table 9.1 Link Parameters

interconnect	unidirectional datarate	switching	routing
Fast Ethernet	100 Mbit/s	packet	table-based
Gigabit Ethernet	1 Gbit/s	packet	table-based
Myrinet	1.28 Gbit/s	wormhole	source-path
ServerNet II	125 Mbyte/s	wormhole	table-based
Memory Channel	100 Mbyte/s	packet	table-based
Synfinity	1.6 Gbyte/s	wormhole	source-path
SCI	400 Mbyte/s	packet	table-based
ATM(OC-12)	155(622) Mbit/s	packet	table-based
HiPPI	800 Mbit/s	packet	table-based

Data Transfer

Efficient transfer of message data between the nodes main memory and the NI is a critical factor in achieving nearly the physical bandwidth in real user applications. To reach this goal, modern NI protocol software involves only the OS, when the network device is opened or closed by user applications. Normal data transfer is completely done in user-level mode by library routines to avoid the costs of OS calls. The goal is a zero copy mechanism, where data is directly transferred between the user space in main memory and the network. Examples are shown for an NI located on the PCI bus, since this is the current (but not preferred, as earlier mentioned) location of today's network adapters. Also, the focus is more on interconnects for message passing because of the broader design space.

Programmed I/O versus Direct Memory Access Message data can be transferred in two ways: Programmed I/O (PIO), where the processor copies data between memory and the NI, and Direct Memory Access (DMA), where the network device itself initiates the transfer. Figure 9.6 depicts both mechanisms on the sender side.

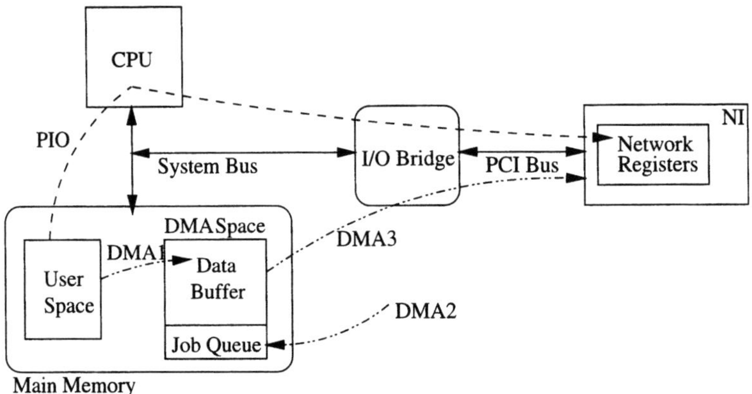

Figure 9.6 PIO versus DMA data transfer.

PIO only requires that some NI registers are mapped into the user space. The processor is then able to copy user data from any virtual address directly into the NI and vice versa. PIO offers very low start-up times, but gets inefficient with increasing message size, since processor time is consumed by simple data copy routines. DMA needs a bit more support, since the DMA controller inside the NI needs physical addresses to transfer the correct data. Most interconnects offering DMA transfer require that pages are pinned down in memory, so the OS cannot swap them out to disk. This makes it feasible to hand over physical addresses to the NI, but adds an additional copying step to transfer the user data into the DMA region (loss of zero copy property). After data is copied (step DMA1 in Figure 9.6), the processor starts the transfer by creating an entry in a job queue (DMA2), which can reside either in main memory or the NI. The NI sets up a DMA transfer to read the message data from memory (DMA3), which is then fed into the network. DMA is not suitable for small messages, but it relieves the processor so it can do useful work in case of large messages.

Several factors influence the performance of both mechanisms. The simplest PIO implementation writes message data sequentially into a single NI register, which resides in I/O space. This normally results in single bus cycles and poor bandwidth. To achieve an acceptable bandwidth, the processor must be enabled to issue burst cycles. This can be done by choosing a small address area as target, which is treated as memory. Writing on these consecutive addresses enables the processor or the bridge to apply techniques like write combining, where several consecutive write operations are assembled in a special write buffer and issued as burst transaction [19]. This mechanism can be found in processor architectures like DEC Alpha or Intel P6. Another solution would be an instruction set support for cache control (cache line flush, etc.), as implemented in the PowerPC architecture. Since the PCI bus implements variable-length burst transactions, a DMA controller inside the NI could try to read/write a large block of data in one burst cycle. Experiences have shown that it is possible to reach about 90 percent of the peak bandwidth with long bursts (110-120 Mbyte/s on a 32 bit/33 MHz PCI bus with 132 Mbyte/s peak bandwidth).

To sum it up, PIO is superior to DMA for small messages up to a certain size where the copy overhead stalls the processor too long from useful work. If one recalls that the majority of the typical network traffic is caused by small messages, it becomes clear that an NI designer should implement support for both mechanisms.

Polling versus Interrupts If DMA is used, another critical design choice is the mechanism to signal the processor of the complete reception of a whole message (also referred to as control transfer). In polling mode, the processor continuously reads an NI status register, where the NI sets a flag bit in case of a completed transaction. If the NI resides on the I/O bus, this could waste a lot of bandwidth. As an improvement, the NI could mirror its status into main memory. This would enable the processor to poll on cache-coherent memory, thus saving bandwidth. Another solution is to interrupt the processor. But this results in a context switch to kernel mode, which is an expensive operation. A hybrid solution could enable the NI to issue an interrupt when message data is present for a specific time value without data transfer. A programmable watchdog timer could be located inside the NI to do this job.

Collective Operations So far, we have only presented mechanisms to send or receive messages in a point-to-point manner. Software for cluster computing often needs collective communication techniques such as barrier synchronization or multicasts, especially networks for virtual shared memory, where updated data must be distributed to all other nodes. For example, supercomputers like Cray-X/MP or AlliantFX offered a dedicated synchronization network. Today's cluster networks leave this task to software, where tree-based algorithms map a broadcast to a hierarchical send/forward scheme. Only few interconnects have direct hardware support for collective operation; the barrier register of the Synfinity interconnect [23] is an example. Networks with a shared bus like Fast Ethernet can easily broadcast data, whereas the integration into point-to-point networks like Myrinet or ServerNet is more complicated. This issue is an area for further improvements of today's cluster networks.

9.3 Fast Ethernet

Fast Ethernet is a generic term for a family of high speed LANs running at 100 Mbit/s over either UTP or fiber-optic cable. Hewlett-Packard's 100VG-AnyLAN allows delay-sensitive continuous media traffic such as video and voice to be transmitted along with delay-insensitive data traffic. Fiber distributed data interface (FDDI) is another popular option available at this speed.

These networks use the Carrier Sense/Multiple Access with Collision Detection (CSMA/CD) protocol. Any device needing to transmit data to the network must first wait and listen to see if anyone else is transmitting. If the network is clear, then the device can transmit a packet to the network. On the other hand, if the network is not clear, then the device needing to transmit must wait until the transmission in progress ends before starting to send its data. The regular 10 Mbit/s Ethernet also uses CSMA/CD. In fact, the main difference between Fast Ethernet and the older 10 Mbit/s system is speed.

Fast Ethernet is currently the upgrade path most users of 10 Mbit/s Ethernet systems prefer to speed up their networks. There are several reasons for this popularity. The first is that it is fairly easy and inexpensive to convert to Fast Ethernet as opposed to FDDI. Fast Ethernet's support for all Ethernet frame types and software ensures that every upgraded machine does not need a lengthy reconfiguration to make it work after the upgrade. Normally, all that needs to be done to a PC to upgrade it to Fast Ethernet is to replace the Network Interface Card (NIC) with a new Fast Ethernet card and load the drivers for the new card. Fast Ethernet does not support coaxial cable and so needs to be replaced if an upgrade has to be performed.

In order for the CSMA/CD protocol to work properly, the worst-case round-trip signal delay between any two points on the network should not be so long that a device can finish transmitting before it can detect any collisions which may occur during the transmission. There is a small delay in the cabling, hubs, and NIC cards which could wreak havoc. This is called Propagation Delay and can cause a complete breakdown of the CSMA/CD protocol. This will result in a slow, unreliable network.

There are several interconnection devices used with Fast Ethernet, a repeater, a hub, a bridge, and a router, as depicted in Figure 9.7.

1. **Repeater:** Repeater is a physical device that restores data and collision signals. These devices are used at pre-determined intervals along a cable and are used to amplify and regenerate signals so that they can travel farther on the cable. When the signal is received at the destination, it will not be distorted and can be easily detectable.

2. **Hub:** Hub is a central connection point for wiring the network. A typical hub has multiple user ports to which computers and peripheral devices such as servers are attached. When an ethernet packet is transmitted to the hub by one station, it is repeated, or copied, over onto all of the other ports of

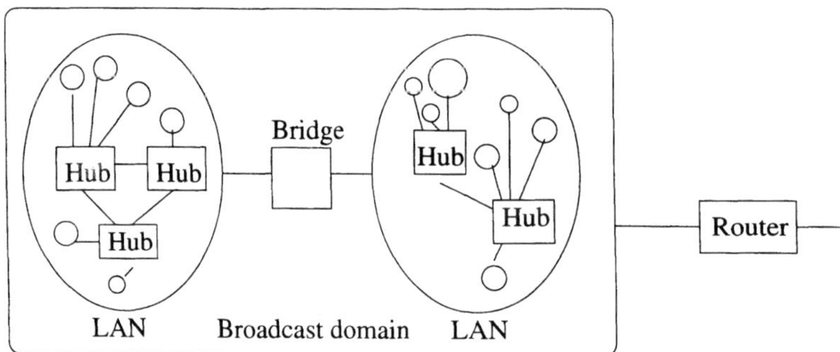

Figure 9.7 Ethernet interconnects with hub and router.

the hub. In this way, all of the stations "see" every packet just as they do on a bus network, so even though each station is connected to the hub with its own dedicated twisted pair cable, a hub-based network is still a shared media LAN. The hub can also be termed as a multiport repeater.

3. **Bridge:** Bridges are used to link adjacent LANs and are datalink layer devices connecting two or more collision domains. They are simpler, and often less expensive than the router (discussed below). Bridges filter packets between LANs by making a simple forward/don't forward decision on each packet they receive from any of the networks that they are connected to. Filtering is done based on the destination address of the packet. If a packets destination is a station on the same segment, it is not forwarded. If the destination is on a different segment, then it is forwarded to that segment.

4. **Router:** Routers are more complex internetworking devices which are used to link LANs together. They are network layer devices and they use network layer protocol information within each packet to route it from one LAN to another. This means that a router must be able to recognize all of the different network layer protocols that may be used on the networks linked together and such a router is termed multiprotocol router; can route several different protocols. Routers communicate with each other to determine which path is the shortest through the complex internetwork that links many LANs.

9.3.1 Fast Ethernet Migration

Most network managers would like to migrate from 10BASE-T or other Ethernet 10 Mbit/s variations to higher bandwidth networks. Typically, this starts at the workgroup with the replacement of hubs with Ethernet switches. These switches still operate at 10 Mbit/s speeds but help isolate and reduce overall traffic by localizing the bulk of the data flow to its own segment. From here, full- duplex connections can connect two Ethernet switches together, or connect the switch to a file server. Eventually, Fast Ethernet ports on these switches will be used to provide even greater bandwidth between the workgroups at 100 Mbit/s speeds. Equipment like the Fast Ethernet repeater will be used in common areas to group Ethernet switches together with server farms into large 100 Mbit pipes. This is the cost-effective method of growing most networks within the average enterprise. The Fast Ethernet repeater is the perfect complement to a LAN growth strategy.

9.4 High Performance Parallel Interface (HiPPI)

The High Performance Parallel Interface (HiPPI) protocol was designed to facilitate high speed communications between very high performance computers, and thereby to attempt to meet their I/O requirements. HiPPI was designed to be a rapid mover of data, as well as a very implementable standard.

HiPPI is an efficient simplex point-to-point link using copper twisted pair cable for distances of up to 25m. Simple signaling and control sequences allow average transfer rates for large size transfers to approach the peak transfer rate of 800 Mbit/s, with 32 bit data lines. Data is transferred in bursts of 1 to 256 words. One or more bursts make up a packet, while one or more packets make up a connection.

There are several HiPPI standards. The HiPPI-PH standard defines the mechanical, electrical, and signaling of the HiPPI physical layer; HiPPI-FP describes the format and content (including header) of each packet of user information, and HiPPI-SC allows for a switching mechanism to be built which could allow multiple simultaneous point-to-point connections to occur. HiPPI-SC does not specify any switching hardware or technology, but only provides functional mechanisms for these things to be used. The networking protocol details of these standards is beyond the scope of this chapter. Since HiPPI is a simplex protocol, a full-duplex link would be achieved by another HiPPI connection in the opposite direction.

HiPPI does not provide a complete, general purpose interconnection solution by itself and, hence, a collection of multiprocessors and management systems are needed without sacrificing HiPPIs data transfer speed or efficiency. There are two drawbacks to HiPPI, namely, the maximum distance between nodes and the number of connections.

9.4.1 HiPPI-SC (Switch Control)

HiPPI-PH supports only a single point-to-point connection. Though this is necessary to achieve the required data rates, it goes against the dominant paradigm of networking, which is to allow many computers to share data. HiPPI-SC was developed as one workable solution to this quandary. It allows for a switching mechanism to be built which could allow multiple simultaneous point-to-point connections to occur.

Although HiPPI-SC does help alleviate the number of connections limitation, it doesn't provide the final solution. The number of switches required for interconnecting devices grows by the square of the number of devices; the cost of such a device also grows in proportion as well. The size of HiPPIs 50-pair cable is large enough to cause switch banks to grow at least linearly with the number of connections, and all connected computers still have to be within the 25 m distance limitation.

9.4.2 Serial HiPPI

Serial HiPPI is an attempt to overcome the 25 m distance limitation by using devices that connect to HiPPI-PH, via the standard 50-pair connection on one side but which serialize the data and use another technology to transmit it longer distances to another complementary device, which converts it back to HiPPI-PH for transmission to the HiPPI destination. There are a couple of ways of extending the distance. One example includes Gigabit dark fiber optics devices, which could be ganged to achieve 1600 Mbit/s operation. If chipsets are developed, these could be brought onboard the source and destination devices, thus allowing the 50-pair cables to be eliminated completely. Copper coaxial cable devices can also be used.

These devices, though transparent to HiPPI-PH, inevitably increase the turn-around time of its signals. But due to the design of HiPPI-PH, latencies are well hidden, and only show up in making and breaking connections, which is reasonably infrequent.

9.4.3 High Speed SONET Extensions

High Speed SONET Extensions is a HiPPI extender device which will use SONETs STS-12c technology to transport HiPPI packets. Much like Serial HiPPI, they create a set of HiPPI terminating devices, which serialize the data, then place it into a STS-12c payload for transmission. The down-link device then converts it back to HiPPI for transmission into the destination HiPPI link. They lay out a physical layer convergence protocol (PLCP) which maps HiPPI bursts into STS-12c rows.

This device relies heavily on large RAM stores in the down-link extender (i.e., on the SONET receiving end). The rough estimate is that as much as 2x bandwidth x delaybytes storage is required in the down-link extender. For a 3,000-mile link, it is estimated that more than 1 Mbyte of data may be transmitted by the up-link extender before the HiPPI source can be stopped. This data must be buffered in the down-link extender.

The extenders have the following features:

- HiPPI to SONET Interface implemented completely in hardware.
- 4 Mbytes of RAM for data buffering (on the down-link side).
- 64 bit CRC transmitted with each STS-12c frame. Their devices carefully overlap error detection, generating the CRC before discarding the LLRC (and vice versa). Their message is clear: expect the SONET link to allow bit errors. (The CRC is generated in hardware, using a specialized, DEC-patented chip.)
- An i960 RISC-based microprocessor with diskette drive, LCD display, and RS-232 and Ethernet ports, is included for supervisory functions and mon-

itoring. Running the VxWorks realtime operating system, it monitors laser power consumption (to detect worn-out lasers), transmitted and received light levels, operating temperature, and SONET diagnostics. It has programmable thresholds for each monitored value and uses SNMP for network management.

9.4.4 HiPPI Connection Management

A HiPPI connection management policy is a method by which connections (a network resource) are shared. Three such policies are considered:

1. **Centralized:** One centralized, distinct management system, closely integrated with the switches, maintains all connection management information for the entire network. When a connection is established or broken, this system performs the next assignment which needs to be made.

2. **Broadcast:** A separate bus-type communications system allows nodes to broadcast information regarding the HiPPI links, and therefore manage connections by policies built upon this shared knowledge.

3. **Distributed:** Each HiPPI node works with no explicit knowledge of any others and hence distributed. Management policies are then built upon random waiting and retrying methods.

The broadcast and centralized policies are modeled identically with the main difference being broadcast incurs an overhead penalty on each node, for processing the broadcast information. The centralized system is the most efficient, maximizing overall system throughput, minimizing average connection delay, and requiring no overhead penalty on any node. But this system is also the least scalable since it requires hardware whose complexity grows nonlinearly with the number of connections. The broadcast and distributed systems are nearly equivalent, since each incurs an overhead penalty. In distributed systems, the overhead penalty is incurred when a retry must take place. For different sets of simulation parameters, the distributed systems could be tuned to closely match the broadcast systems performance. Since broadcast systems require additional hardware and distributed systems do not, the distributed approach is a reasonable solution.

9.4.5 HiPPI Interfaces

HiPPI interfaces are used primarily as a high speed networked data channel between computer systems and supercomputers. The combination of a source and a destination interface card can be used in a full duplex configuration to connect directly to another HiPPI interface pair, or in conjunction with a HiPPI switch that allows connections between many systems. There are various HiPPI Interfaces available currently, for example, VME-HiPPI Interface, SBUS interfaces, PC and workstation standard interfaces, and special interfaces used in CRAY computers.

Figure 9.8 shows an example of VME-HiPPI interface architecture. The host interface is implemented entirely with data structures residing in VME-addressable

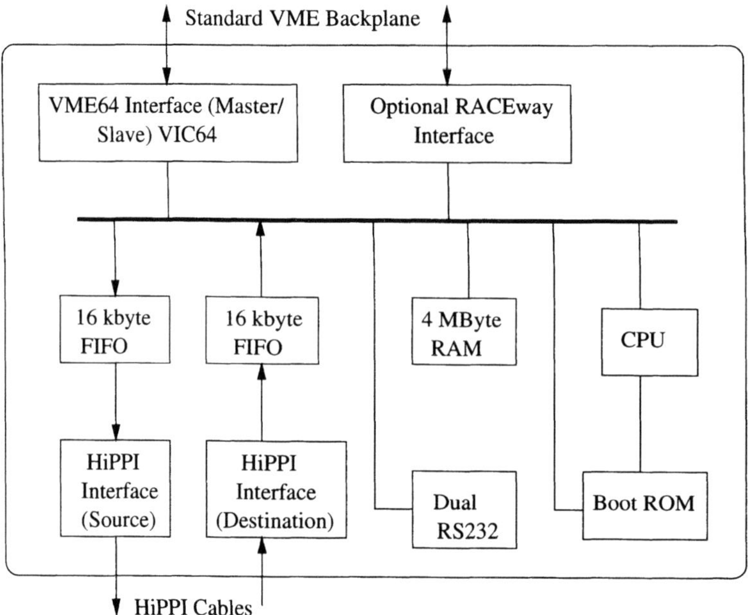

Figure 9.8 VME64 HiPPI interface block diagram.

memory. Separate command and response data structures are provided for both HIPPI Source and Destination channels. The VME host can chain up to 31 commands to autonomously transfer data between several areas in VME memory and the HIPPI channel. The data structures also allow the user to specify independent signaling mechanisms for normal and abnormal completion of each command. The interface can set up DMAs, control the HIPPI channel, and transfer data without direct involvement by the host CPU (with its inherent operating system overhead). Unique host-based drivers are not required as long as the host can access the data structures via VME addressing, it can control HiPPI data transfers.

The CRAY HiPPI provides high performance connectivity to HiPPI-based peripherals and for high speed network connectivity applications such as PVM. This high performance connectivity also greatly assists the transfer of large files to Cray Research's vector SMP and highly scalable systems. The CRAY J90 series can be configured with up to four 100 Mbyte/s HiPPI-to-memory channels.

9.4.6 Array System: The HiPPI Interconnect

An Array system is a distributed memory multiprocessor, scalable to 100 or more individual MIPS processors in as many as eight POWERnode computers, yielding a peak aggregate computing capacity in excess of 50 GFLOPS. The aggregation of SMP POWERnodes is interconnected by an industry standard 1.5 Gbit/s HiPPI network.

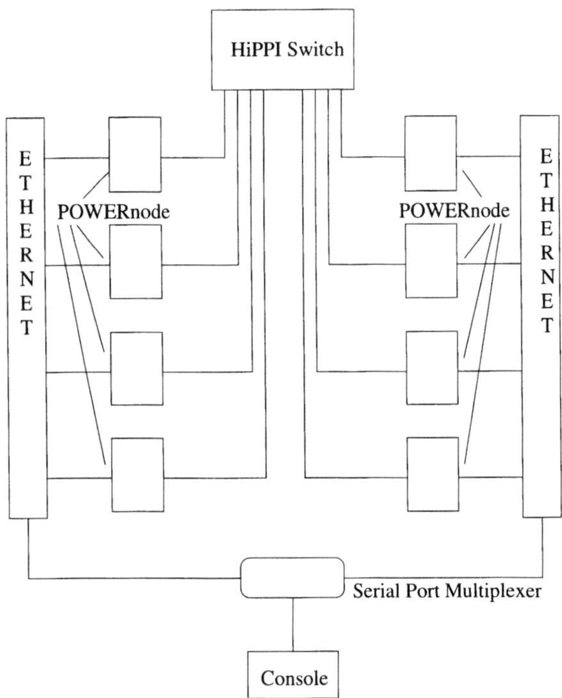

Figure 9.9 Array system schematic.

POWERnode servers are interconnected via a high performance, dual channel HiPPI network. Each POWERnode server is equipped with one or two bidirectional HiPPI interfaces. Each interface provides 100 Mbyte/s of data bandwidth in either direction. The HiPPI interfaces are connected via a high performance HiPPI crossbar switch (optional in a two-node array). The Array is shown in Figure 9.9. The POWERnodes are connected to the Serial Port Multiplexer. The HiPPI switch is nonblocking, with sub-microsecond connection delays. The network appears to be fully connected and contention occurs only when two sources send data to the same destination at the same time.

IRIX 6.2 and the Array 2.0 software provide protocol layers and APIs to access the HiPPI network, including direct physical layer, HiPPI framing protocol, and TCP/IP. The HiPPI support in Array 2.0 includes special bypass capabilities to expedite transmission of short messages. The bypass capability is transparent to the applications using it.

9.5 Asynchronous Transfer Mode (ATM)

Switched networks will offer significantly greater bandwidth, flexibility, and QoS service support than is possible on legacy Ethernet and token ring networks built with shared media hubs. They consist of a combination of ATM switches, ATM routers, and LAN switches, and are effective in supporting clusters over the wide area.

The huge bandwidth of ATM networks makes it cost-effective to transport large quantities of data. For clusters this means that large amounts of control information can be distributed, if it is done in large chunks, so that the overheads associated with message handling can be minimized. QoS attaches the required guarantee to the messages so that retransmissions are reduced to a minimum. The connection-oriented nature of ATM proves useful, as once the data virtual channel is set up, it need not be torn down until all the data is sent. Point to multipoint circuits can be easily set up to disseminate data to multiple hosts in the clusters.

9.5.1 Concepts

Here is a brief review of some ATM concepts covered in this section.

Virtual Circuit Identifier (VCI)

ATM is a virtual circuit technology meaning that information to be carried over the network is broken up into blocks (called cells) with an identifying label called Virtual Circuit Identifier (VCI) attached to each block. The VCI is used to forward information along a fixed path in the network. ATM networks can support virtual circuits that operate at any data rate, up to the capacity of the links that carry them. A collection of VCIs are grouped together and have a Virtual Path Identifier (VPI).

Multicast Virtual Circuit

A Multicast Virtual Circuit is used to transfer information from a single source to several recipients. In order to achieve this, the information from a single source is replicated and then distributed to all the destinations. The replication and forwarding is implemented in the switching system hardware. In the simplest case, a multicast virtual circuit has a single sender and multiple receivers. However, it can also be useful to have virtual circuits in which the participant can both send and receive.

Switched Virtual Circuit (SVC) vs Permanent Virtual Circuit (PVC)

A Switched Virtual Circuit (SVC) is a virtual circuit automatically set up by ATM signaling and is flexible. It has a fast connection setup time of 10 ms, whereas the Permanent Virtual Circuit (PVC) has to be manually set up and is used for leased lines applications.

ATM Adaptation Layer (AAL)

In order for the ATM to support many kinds of services with different traffic characteristics and system requirements, it is necessary to adapt the different classes of applications to the ATM layer. This function is performed by the ATM Adaptation Layer (AAL), which is service-dependent. Four types of AAL were originally recommended by CCITT, AAL1, AAL2, AAL3/4, and AAL5. AAL5 is most commonly used.

- **AAL1:** Supports connection-oriented services that require constant bit rates services like DS1 or DS3 and have specific timing and delay requirements.
- **AAL2:** Supports connection-oriented services that do not require constant bit rates, but service variable bit rate applications like some video schemes.
- **AAL3/4:** This AAL is intended for both connectionless and connection-oriented variable bit rate services.
- **AAL5:** Supports connection-oriented variable bit rate services. It is a substantially lean AAL compared with AAL 3/4 at the expense of error recovery and built-in re-transmission. This trade-off provides a smaller bandwidth overhead, simpler processing requirements, and reduced implementation complexity.

9.5.2 ATM Adapter

The of FORE Systems uses advanced cell processing architecture which utilizes a dedicated embedded Intel i960 RISC processor along with special purpose AAL5 and 3/4 Segmentation and Reassembly (SAR) hardware and scatter-gather DMA. The ATM networking capabilities can be added to the applications leaving the low level ATM cell processing, segmentation and reassembly, and signaling to the ATM adapter hardware and the device driver. The FORE ATM adapter is shown in Figure 9.10.

The user to network interface (UNI) signaling is supported in software and the API library offers applications access to the unique features of ATM such as guaranteed bandwidth reservation, per-connection selection of AAL5, 3/4, and multicasting with dynamic addition and deletion of recipients.

9.5.3 ATM API Basics

The Service Access point (SAP) address is composed of the ATM Address, ATM selector, Broadband low layer information (BLLI), and Broadband high layer information (BHLI). It is expressed as a vector of the form [ATM Address, ATM Selector, BLLI id2, BLLI id3, BHLI id]. BLLI id2 identifies layer 2 protocol; BHLI id identifies the application layer. Each SAP vector element (SVE) consists of a tag, length, and value field.

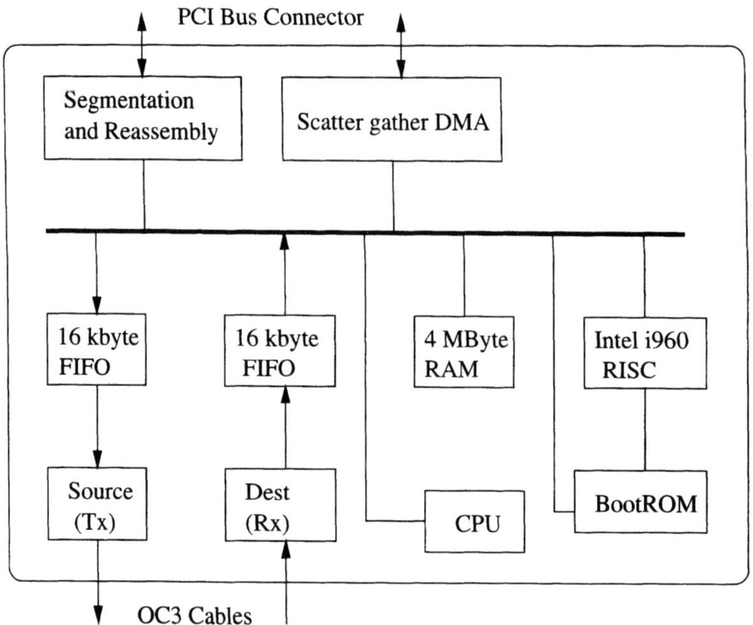

Figure 9.10 Block diagram of ATM adapter.

SAP is used to distinguish clients of a layer. Many clients can use a service to receive using the same SAP but have to have their individual SAPs for sending. On an outgoing call, destination SAP specifies the ATM address of the remote device and target software in the device. API services include data transfer, VC setup/release, traffic management, and network management.

The ATM library routines provide a connection-oriented server and client model. A Switched Virtual Circuit (SVC) or a Permanent Virtual Circuit (PVC) has to be established between the server and the client before data can be transmitted. After the connection is set up the network tries to deliver all the ATM cells to the destination, but some maybe dropped depending on the available resources. Retransmissions are left to each application, as is end-to-end flow control between hosts.

The ATM VCI and VPI allocated by the network during connection establishment is allocated with an application SAP, which is in turn associated with a file descriptor. Bandwidth resources are reserved for each connection, but if it isn't available, then the connection request will be refused.

9.5.4 Performance Evaluation of ATM

In order to evaluate the performance of ATM, two popular distributed programs are used. They are parallel partial differential equations (PDE) and parallel matrix multiplication, and they perform very differently over ATM LANs and Ethernet. Only the PDE results are discussed here.

The partial differential equations of integer, float, or double float, represent a typical type of communication and computation pattern. The parallel differential equations can be characterized as a communication intensive application. During execution each processing node repeatedly exchanges boundary values with its immediate neighbors and the messages are quite short. Parallel PDE can be used to compare the latency impact of different protocol combinations and networks.

Hardware The hardware equipment used for the experiment [12] was composed of four dedicated Sparc Sun workstations with a 10Mbit/s Ethernet adapter and a Fore Systems ATM adapter connected to a Fore Systems ASX-200 ATM switch. The parallel PDE was implemented in the master/slave programming model. In a master/slave model the master spawns and directs some number of slave processes to do the work. The master program, however, is responsible for collecting the computation results and recording the timing information.

Parallel Partial Differential Equations

Table 9.2 shows the time spent executing the parallel versions of PDE for different mesh sizes, protocol hierarchy, and networks. Since the PDE example is one of the most communication-intensive distributed applications, the overhead of the different APIs became more important. In the ATM LAN, Fore Systems' ATM API has the lowest protocol overhead when compared with the other APIs. A speedup of 2.49 was achieved. The BSD socket API provided good performance and a reliable communication interface in this scenario. The PVM message passing library had the worst performance in this scenario because PVM provides additional support for distributed programming, which results in additional overhead.

The experiment was conducted over Ethernet with two background traffic loads (silent and 30 percent load). The performance of both the PVM and BSD socket over a silent Ethernet is comparable to that over ATM. This is because chances of collision are less on silent Ethernet when transmitting messages. The Ethernet acts like an end-to-end channel for processing nodes when there is no collision.

In the Ethernet environment, the experiment was first run over silent Ethernet. The sniffer observed some consistent traffic due to each processing node needing to exchange data with its neighbors for every iteration. When a background load is offered on the Ethernet, the performance degrades.

When running distributed programs on ATM LAN the ATM switch was dedicated. The Ethernet being a shared media, a realistic scenario would be when the network is used by some other application as well. The network was 30 percent loaded to simulate a shared environment.

The reason why a loaded ATM network is not needed for an accurate result and the same is not true for an Ethernet network: A local ATM network is scalable, a traditional Ethernet is not. An ATM switch of N ports is capable of supporting N parallel channels. Therefore, in a mesh-connected distribution application, each

Table 9.2 Execution Time (sec) of Partial Differential Equation

Protocol hierarchy/			Mesh size			
Network	$16x16$		$64x64$		$256x256$	
Accuracy	10^{-6}	10^{-12}	10^{-6}	10^{-12}	10^{-6}	10^{-12}
Sequential	0.07	0.17	5.15	10.28	330.71	661.45
PVM						
ATM	0.30	0.58	3.09	6.13	137.28	273.83
Ethernet(Silent)	0.33	0.65	3.27	6.50	138.39	276.78
Ethernet(30% loaded)	0.35	0.68	3.41	6.70	140.24	279.18
BSD Socket						
ATM	0.11	0.26	2.47	4.91	133.69	266.84
Ethernet(Silent)	0.14	0.28	2.65	5.19	134.79	268.79
Ethernet(30% loaded)	0.19	0.37	2.69	5.44	135.96	271.75
FORE's API						
ATM	0.12	0.22	2.45	2.83	133.25	266.07

processor needs to communicate with four immediate neighbors. Four other processors share the channel connected to the processor. As long as the switch is capable of supporting N ports, as N increases, there are always only four processors sharing the same channel.

Usually, the distribution of work to individual processors is done statically. Performance degrades quickly if the work assigned to each node does not match the processor speed, or if the load changes during execution. Load balancing is needed to avoid degradation in performance. A central load balancer monitors the progress of each node, and if the difference in simulated time on the nodes becomes too large, it moves particles from the slow nodes to fast nodes. The task granularity when parallelizing the application has to be chosen with caution so that the load balancer works efficiently and reacts correctly when the environment changes.

The experimental results show that network computing is promising over local ATM networks, provided that the higher level protocols, device drivers, and network interfaces are improved. To improve performance, some type of hardware acceleration (depending on the platform) may be considered.

9.5.5 Issues in Distributed Networks for ATM Networks

Resource management: Data rates of individual virtual circuits could adapt to data traffic and available network availability, therefore, representing them with single numbers is an approximation. For some applications such as coded video, there is so much variation that representing them by the peak rate leads to significant inefficiency. If the link rate is larger than the peak rate of the virtual circuit, then it is possible to allocate more than the average data rate with high confidence that the aggregate traffic will not exceed the link capacity. However, determining if the given virtual circuit will fit on a given link needs considerable complex calculation and more information about the traffic currently flowing on the link than a simple aggregate value. In situations where the capacity of link groups is much larger than the capacity of a single virtual circuit (which is true in large scale systems) a simple representation for the state of the link group can suffice, since a representation that leads to conservative decisions will only have a small impact on the efficiency with which network resources are utilized in this case.

Multicast routing: For dynamically changing networks, the practical choices for calculating multicast routing are a variation of a greedy algorithm that adds new endpoints using a shortest path from the endpoint to the connection, and deletes endpoints by pruning the branch needed only by the endpoint being dropped. While the worst-case performance of this algorithm can be poor, simulations provide evidence that they should work well in practice.

Routing and network topology design is very interrelated. One cannot really understand how routing algorithms are likely to perform without understanding something about how networks are configured.

9.6 Scalable Coherent Interface (SCI)

The Scalable Coherent Interface (SCI, Local Area MultiProcessor) is effectively a processor memory and I/O bus, high performance switch, local area network, and optical network. It is an information sharing and information communication system that provides distributed directory based cache coherency for a global shared memory model and uses electrical or fiber optic point-to-point unidirectional cables of various widths. A single address space is used to specify data as well as its source and destination when being transported. Performance ranges from 200 Mbyte/s (CMOS) to 1000 Mbyte/s (BiCMOS) over distances of tens of meters for electrical cables and kilometers for serial fibers.

9.6.1 Data Transfer via SCI

SCI has been designed to be interfacable to common buses such as PCI, VME, Futurebus, Fastbus, etc., and to I/O connections such as ATM or Fiber Channel. It works in complex multivendor systems that grow incrementally, a harder problem than interconnecting processors inside a single product like MPP does. Its cache coherence scheme is comprehensive and robust, independent of the interconnect type or configuration, and can be handled entirely in hardware, providing distributed shared memory with transparent caching that improves performance by hiding the cost of remote data access, and eliminates the need for costly software cache management. The Dolphin PCI-SCI is shown in Figure 9.11.

The usual approach of moving data through I/O-channel or network-style paths, requires assembling an appropriate communication packet in software, pointing the interface hardware at it, and initiating the I/O operation, usually by calling a subroutine. When the data arrive at the destination, hardware stores them in a

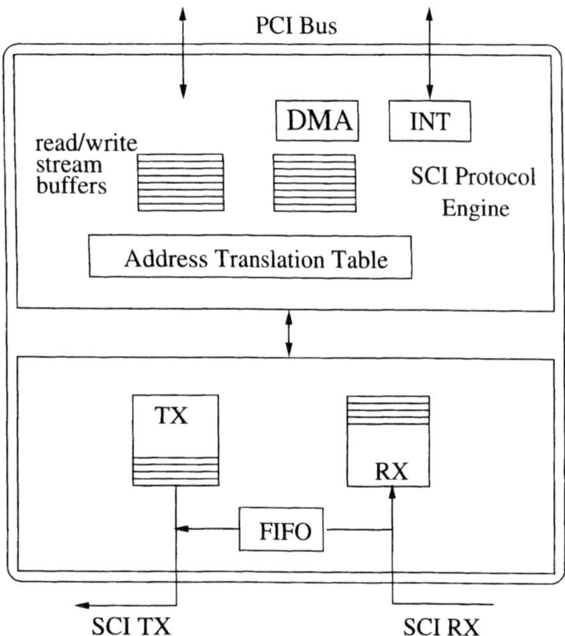

Figure 9.11 Block diagram of the Dolphin PCI-SCI bridge.

memory buffer and alerts the processor by an interrupt when a packet is complete or the buffers are full. Software then moves the data to a waiting user buffer and, finally, the user application examines the packet to find the desired data. Typically, this process results in latencies that are tens to thousands of times slower than SCI.

Bandwidth comparison with other common technologies: A single 1 Gbyte/s (8000 Mbit/s) SCI link has about the same bandwidth as 64 of today's 155 Mbit/s ATM links, or 32 of today's Fiber Channel 256 Mbit/s links, or 800 Ethernets, or 80 100baseT Ethernets. For applications that don't need SCI's full speed, the standard protocols also support a ring-style connection that shares the link bandwidth among some number of devices, avoiding the cost of a switch. Either an individual SCI device or an entire ring can be connected to an SCI switch port, giving a user the ability to trade off cost versus performance over a broad range. Rings can also be bridged to other rings to form meshes and higher dimensionality fabrics.

9.6.2 Advantages of SCI

Since SCI eliminates the need for runtime layers of software protocol-paradigm translation, it reduces the delay of interprocessor communication by an enormous factor compared to even the latest interconnect technologies that are based on the previous generation of networking and I/O channel protocols. A remote communication in SCI takes place as just a part of a simple load or store opcode execution in a processor. Typically, the remote address results in a cache miss, which causes the cache controller to address remote memory via SCI to get the data, and in a very short time, in the order of a hundreds of processor cycles, the remote data is fetched to cache and the processor continues execution.

When two tasks share data using SCI, the data remains stored in ordinary variables, with ordinary memory addresses, at all times. Thus, processor instructions like Load and Store suffice to access data for doing computation with it. Load and store are highly optimized in all processors, and the underlying SCI transport mechanism is transparent to the user, performing all the network protocol effectively as a fraction of one instruction.

SCI hides the latency of accessing remote data while other techniques we know of for hiding this latency involve using caches to keep copies of data near its users. Since cache entries are copies of data, they are duplicates and can become outdated when the data changes in value. Only SCI handles this problem, with SCI's distributed cache coherence mechanism. This mechanism adds only a bit or so to the command field in SCI's packets. This does not affect unshared cache entries, but when shared cache entries are modified, the coherence protocol quickly locates all the other copies so they can be discarded, and fresh copies can be fetched if those processors still want the data. The distributed protocol does not add to the traffic at main memory, and it so happens to increase the robustness of a system.

The RISC-style protocols SCI uses are simple in nature, which allow SCI links to deliver much higher performance for any given chip technology. SCI is very efficient with large blocks of data wherein hundreds of processors access data from a common shared memory space. Since a built-in DMA engine is used which has a high setup overhead, the interface is only appropriate for large chunks of data. Alternatively, each processor will have its own memory space, and 32 Kbyte block moves can be performed from the sender to a preallocated buffer in the receiver. This, however, results in a lot of handshaking and in lots of network traffic. Suppose smaller data transfers need to be performed (say 128 bytes), then the data from the sender can be deposited into the final destination and will result in a lot less handshaking traffic.

However, SCI is most useful for clustering over local area distances or less. It is least suitable over long distances. Each interface chip can only handle a certain number of concurrently active packets, which are in flight awaiting confirmed delivery to the destination or an intermediate bridge queue. When that number is less than the number of packets that can be in flight in the cables, efficiency drops. This could be compensated by using several SCI chips in series, to provide more queue storage, but for large distances it makes sense to use a wide area networking approach, such as ATM.

9.7 ServerNet

In 1995, Tandem introduced the first commercially available implementation of a SAN called ServerNet.[1] Since its introduction, ServerNet equipment has been sold by Tandem (now owned by Compaq) for more than one billion dollars. In 1998, Tandem announced the availability of ServerNet II [24], the follow-up to the first version, which raises the bandwidth and adds new features while preserving full compatibility with ServerNet I. With ServerNet, Tandem, a major computer manufacturer in the business area, addressed one of the main server problems: limited I/O bandwidth. Tandem's customers, mainly business companies running large database applications, needed more I/O bandwidth to keep up with the growing data volumes their servers should be able to handle. So ServerNet was intended as a high bandwidth interconnect between processors and I/O devices, but turned quickly into a general purpose SAN.

9.7.1 Scalability and Reliability as Main Goals

With scalable I/O bandwidth as the primary goal, ServerNet consists of two main components: endnodes with interfaces to the system bus or various I/O interfaces and routers to connect all endnodes to one clustered system. One main design goal was the ability to transfer data directly between two I/O devices, thus relieving processors of plain data copy jobs. By being able to serve multiple simultaneous I/O transfers, ServerNet removes the I/O bottleneck and offers the construction of scalable clustered servers. Figure 9.12 shows a sample system configuration. Most ServerNet configurations, besides the Himalaya series of Tandem itself, use an I/O (PCI) adapter instead of directly attaching to the system bus.

ServerNet Links ServerNet is a full duplex, wormhole switched network. The first implementation uses 9 bit parallel physical interfaces with LVDS/ECL signaling, running at 50 MHz. ServerNet II raises the physical bandwidth to 125 Mbyte/s, driving standard 8b/10b serializers/deserializers to connect to 1000BaseX (Gigabit Ethernet) standard cables. With the support of serial copper cables, ServerNet is able to span across significantly longer distances. For compatibility reasons, ServerNet II components also implement the interface of the first version. Together with additional converter logic, ServerNet I and II components can be mixed within one system, enabling the customer to easily upgrade an existent cluster with components of the new generation without the need to replace ServerNet I components.

Links operate asynchronously and avoid buffer overrun through periodic insertion of SKIP control symbols, which are dropped by the receiver. Special flow control symbols are exchanged between two link endnodes to ensure, that data does not have to be dropped due to lack of buffer space.

Data Transfer The basic data transfer mechanism supported is a DMA-based remote memory read/write. An endnode can be instructed to read/write a data

[1] www.servernet.com

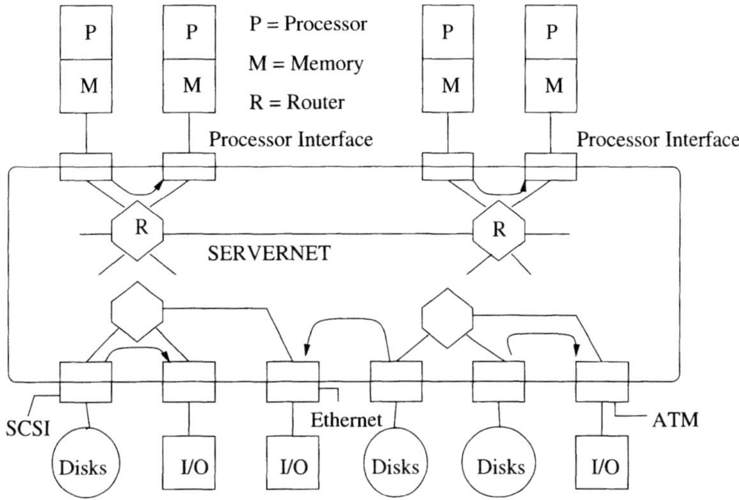

Figure 9.12 A sample ServerNet configuration.

packet of up to 64 byte (512 byte in ServerNet II) from/to a remote memory location. The address of a packet consists of a 20 bit ID and a 32/64 bit address field. The ServerNet ID uniquely identifies an endnode and the route towards the destination. The address can be viewed as a virtual ServerNet address. The lower 12 bits are the page offset, whereas the upper bits are an index into the Address Validation & Translation Table (AVT). Via this indirection, the receiver is able to check read/write permissions of the sender, as depicted in Figure 9.13. To support communication models, for which the destination of the message is not known in advance, the address can also specify one of several packet queues, to which data is then appended.

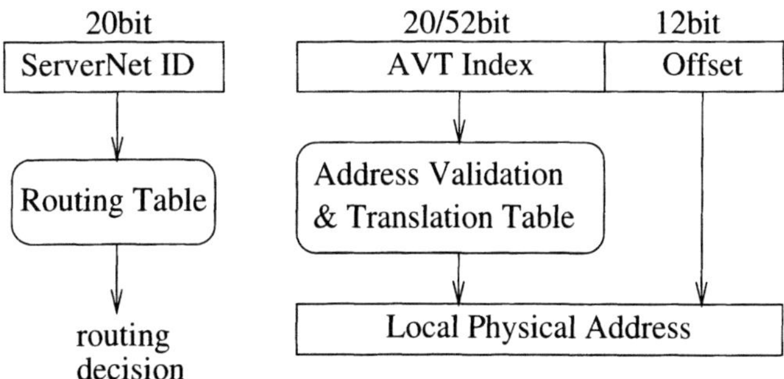

Figure 9.13 ServerNet address space.

Fault Tolerance A main feature of ServerNet is its support for guaranteed and error free in-order delivery of data on various levels. On the link layer, a CRC check is done in each network stage to validate the correct reception of the message. Each link is checked through the periodical exchange of heartbeat control symbols. Each endpoint assures correct transmission by sending acknowledges back to the sender. In case of errors, the hardware invokes driver routines for error handling.

Switches ServerNet I offers 6 port switches, which can be connected in an arbitrary topology. Router II, the next generation of ServerNet switches, raises the number of ports to 12. In- and Outports contain FIFOs to buffer a certain amount of data and are connected through a 13x13 crossbar. The additional port is used to inject or extract control packets. Each Router offers a JTAG and processor interface for debug or management services. One special feature of ServerNet switches is the ability to form so called Fat Pipes. Several physical links can be used to form one logical link, connecting two identical link endpoints. The switches can now be configured to dynamically choose one of the links, which leads to a better link utilization under heavy load.

9.7.2 Driver and Management Software

The good reliability of the ServerNet hardware makes it possible to implement low overhead protocol layers and driver software. Tandem clusters run the UNIX and WindowsNT operating systems. With its packet queues, the second generation of this SAN introduces a mechanism to efficiently support the message passing model of the Virtual Interface Architecture (VIA), a message layer specification for cluster networks.

To provide an easy way of managing the network, a special sort of packets is defined called In Band Control (IBC) packets. These packets use the same links as normal data packets, but are interpreted by an 8 bit microcontroller. The IBC protocol is responsible for initialization, faulty node isolation and several other management issues. IBC packets are used to gather status or scatter control data to all ServerNet components.

9.7.3 Remarks

Though it is hard to find detailed performance numbers, ServerNet technology seems to be a very reliable and, with its second generation, also high performance SAN. Price information for adapters and switches was not available. ServerNet focuses on the business/server market and has only poorly been accepted by researchers so far, though it would be interesting to see the performance of message layers such as AM and FM or message passing libraries such as MPI and PVM.

ServerNet implements a lot of properties, which are extremely useful for cluster computing: error handling on various levels, a kind of protection scheme (AVT), standard physical layers (1000BaseX cables) and support for network management (IBC). Several companies having agreed on cooperation with Compaq using Server-

Net as the interconnect technology of choice for their server systems and clusters, it will continue to be one of the leading SANs. Also, its considerable influence on the VIA specification (Compaq is one of the three founders of VIA) will raise the acceptance of ServerNet technology.

9.8 Myrinet

Myrinet is a SAN evolved from supercomputer technology and the main product of Myricom,[2] a start-up company founded in 1994. It has become quite popular in the research community, resulting in 150 installations of various sizes through June 1997. A major key to its success is the fact that all hardware and software specifications are open and public.

The Myrinet technology is based on two earlier research projects, namely Mosaic and Atomic LAN by Caltech and USC research groups. Mosaic was a fine grain supercomputer, which needed a truly scalable interconnection network with lots of bandwidth. The Atomic LAN project was based on Mosaic technology and can be regarded as a research prototype of Myrinet, implementing the major features such as network mapping and address-to-route translation; however, with some limitations (short distances (1 m) and a topology (1D chains) not very suitable for larger systems). Eventually, members of both groups founded Myricom to bring their SAN technology into commercial business.

9.8.1 Fitting Everybodys Needs

Regarding the link and packet layer, Myrinet is very similar to ServerNet (or vice versa). They differ considerably in the design of the host interface. A Myrinet host interface consists of two major components: the LANai chip and its associated SRAM memory. The LANai is a custom VLSI chip and controls the data transfer between the host and the network. Its main component is a programmable micro-controller, which controls DMA engines responsible for the data transfer directions host $\leftrightarrow$ onboard memory and memory $\leftrightarrow$ network. So message data must first be written to the NI SRAM, before it can be injected into the network. The SRAM also stores the MCP (Myrinet Control Program) and several job queues. The basic architecture is depicted in Figure 9.14.

Earlier versions of the host interface were based on Sun's SBus, but the latest versions use the 32/64 bit PCI interface. The LANai runs at frequencies from 33 MHz up to 66 MHz (33 MHz PCI clock multiplied by 1, 1.5 or 2). Besides controlling the data transfer, the LANai is also responsible for automatic network mapping and monitoring the networks status. The size of the onboard SRAM ranges from 512 Kbyte to 1 Mbyte. The LANai communicates with the hosts device drivers or user-level libraries through job queues residing in the SRAM.

---

[2] www.myri.com

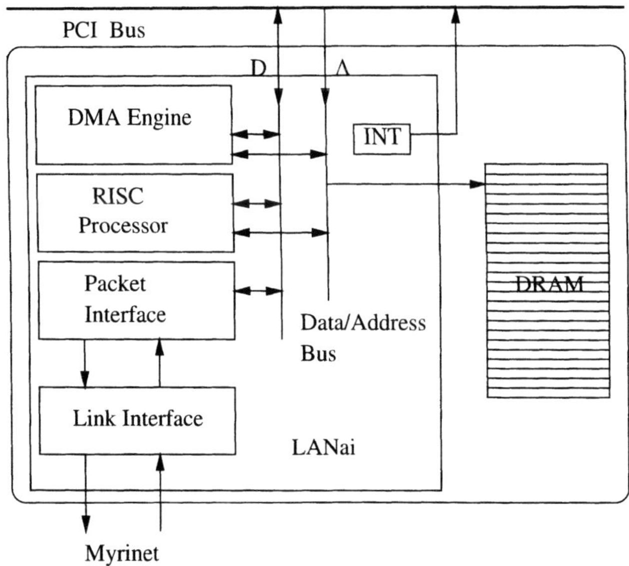

Figure 9.14 Myrinet host interface.

Link and Packet Layer Myrinet uses full-duplex links with 9 bit parallel channels in one direction running at 80 MHz. Since both clock edges are used for transmitting data, the network offers 160 Mbyte/s physical bandwidth over one channel. Two different cable types are used, so called SAN links up to 3 m (within a single cabinet) and LAN links, which can be used up to 10 m at full speed or up to 25 m at half speed. Optical links are also planned.

Data packets can be of any length and are routed using wormhole switching. They consist of a routing header, a type field, the payload and a trailing CRC. Myrinet uses source path routing. While entering a switch, the first header byte encodes the outgoing port. The switch strips off the leading byte and forwards the remaining part of the packet to the appropriate output port. When the packet enters its destination host interface, the routing header is completely eaten up and the type field leads the message. Special control symbols (STOP, GO) are used to implement reverse flow control.

Switches Myrinet cut-through switches are available with 4, 8 or 16 ports, also mixed with SAN and LAN links, so clusters of single cabinets can be connected. Any network topology can be created. Ports automatically detect the absence of a link. On start-up, the host interfaces automatically detect the network topology.

Error Handling On the link level, the trailing CRC is computed in each network stage and substituted for the previous one. A packet with a nonzero CRC entering a host interface then indicates transmission errors. MTBF (Mean Time Between

Failure) times of several million hours are reported for switches and interfaces. On detection of cable faults or node failure, alternative routes are computed by the LANai. To prevent deadlocks from long-time blocked messages, time-outs generate a forward reset (FRES) signal, which causes the blocking stage to reset itself.

9.8.2 Software and Performance

As mentioned before, all Myrinet specifications are open and public. The device driver code and the MCP are distributed as source code to serve as documentation and base for porting new protocol layers onto Myrinet. This has motivated many research groups to implement their own message layers and is one of the main reasons for the popularity of Myrinet. Device drivers are available for Linux, Solaris, WindowsNT, DEC Unix, Irix and VxWorks on Pentium (Pro), Sparc, Alpha, MIPS and PowerPC processors. A patched GNU C-compiler is available to develop MCP programs.

Table 9.3 Performance of Message Layers over Myrinet

Machine	API	Latency (μs)	Bandwidth (Mbit/s)	Ref.
200 MHz PPro	BIP	4.8	1009	LHPC
166 MHz Pentium	PM	7.2	941	RWCP
Ultra-1	AM	10	280	GAM
200 MHz PPro	TCP (Linux/BIP)		293	LHPC
200 MHz PPro	UDP (Linux/BIP)		324	LHPC
DEC Alpha 500/266	TCP (Digital Unix)		271	Duke
DEC Alpha 500/266	UDP (Digital Unix)		404	Duke

Table 9.3 summarizes some performance numbers (for unknown message sizes). BIP is a very simple protocol, thus achieving the best performance values. A new protocol layer called GM is developed by Myricom and replaces old device drivers and MCP programs. It provides reliable and ordered delivery of messages and supports protected kernel as well as user-level access routines to the Myrinet hardware. The raw bandwidth of the GM layer ranges from 50-75 Mbyte/s for message sizes above 4 Kbyte. Latency starts at 40 μs (4 byte) and scales up to 100 μs for 4 Kbyte messages (measured on Linux PCs). The performance of point-to-point MPICH calls with 200 byte payload is about 40 μs and 30 Mbyte/s.

9.8.3 Remarks

Myrinet offers a good price/performance ratio. Host interfaces vary in the range of \$1300-1800, whereas an 8-port SAN switch costs approximately \$2000. The great flexibility of the hardware due to a programmable microcontroller is one of the major advantages of Myrinet, but can also be a bottleneck with respect to performance, since the LANai runs only at moderate frequencies. The buffering of messages in the onboard SRAM prevents the implementation of true zero copy protocols since there is no direct interface to the network from the hosts view. This might be a reason for the moderate bandwidth of small/medium-sized messages.

Myrinet has shown its scalability in large cluster configurations (more than 256 nodes). Myrinet-on-VME has also become now an ANSI/VITA standard.

9.9 Memory Channel

Digital's Memory Channel [17] is a completely different approach towards SANs. It provides a portion of global virtual shared memory by mapping portions of remote physical memory as local virtual memory (also called reflective memory). The basis of Memory Channel were obtained from Encore and several other projects such as VMMC or SHRIMP. The first version has been shipping in production since April 1996. About one year later, Memory Channel 2 was introduced, which improves the overall performance and scalability of the Memory Channel architecture.

9.9.1 Bringing together Simplicity and Performance

Memory Channel consists of two components: a PCI adapter and an hub. The first version of Memory Channel implements the network as a shared medium, in which only one transmission can be active at any time. This was identified as one major bottleneck and the second implementation moved to a point-to-point, full-duplex switched 8x8 crossbar implementation. Adapters can also be connected directly to one another without using a hub.

Table 9.4 Comparison of Memory Channel 1 and 2

Characteristics	Memory Channel 1	Memory Channel 2
channel data width	37 bit (half-duplex)	16 bit (full-duplex)
link frequency	33 MHz	66 MHz
max. copper cable length	4 m	10 m
max. one way transfer rate	133 Mbyte/s	133 Mbyte/s
sustained pt2pt bandwidth	66 Mbyte/s	100 Mbyte/s
max. packet size	32 byte	256 byte
remote read	no	yes
supported page size	8 Kbyte	4/8 Kbyte
hub architecture	shared bus	crossbar

The host interfaces exchange heartbeat signals and implement flow control timeouts to detect node failure or blocked data transfers. The link layer provides error detection through a 32 bit CRC generated and checked in hardware. Table 9.4 lists the major hardware characteristics of first- and second-generation Memory Channel.

Data Transfer To enable communication over the Memory Channel network, applications map pages as read- or write-only into their virtual address space. Each host interface contains two page control tables (PCT), one for write and one for read mappings. For read-only pages, a page is pinned down in local physical memory. Several page attributes can be specified: receive enable, interrupt on receive, remote read etc. If a page is mapped as write-only, a page table entry is created for an appropriate page in the interface 128 Mbyte PCI address space. Page attributes can be used here to:

- store a local copy of each packet
- request acknowledgment messages from the receiver side for each packet
- define the packets as broadcast or point-to-point packets

Broadcasts are forwarded to each node attached to the network. If a broadcast packet enters a crossbar hub, the arbitration logic waits until all output ports are available. Nodes, which have mapped the addressed page as a readable area, store the data in their local pinned down memory region. All other nodes simply ignore the data. So once the data regions are mapped and set up, simple store instructions transfer data to remote nodes, without any OS intervention. This mechanism is shown in Figure 9.15.

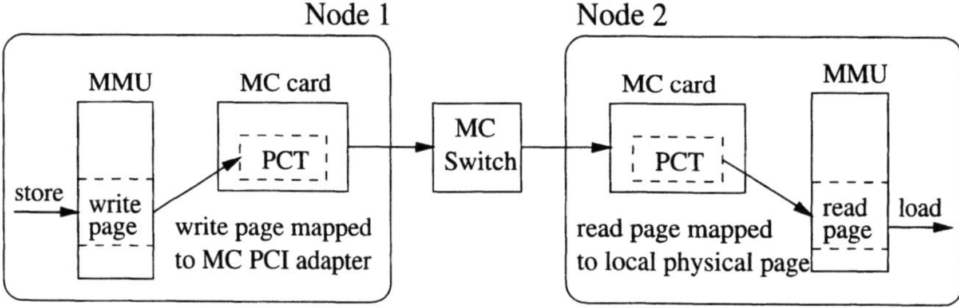

Figure 9.15 Data transfer over Memory Channel.

Besides this basic data transfer mechanism, Memory Channel supports a simple remote read primitive, a hardware-based barrier acknowledge and a fast lock primitive. To ensure correct behavior, Memory Channel implements a strict in-order delivery of written data. Also, a write invalidates cache entries on the reader side, thus providing clusterwide cache coherence.

9.9.2 Software and Performance

Digital provides two software layers for Memory Channel: the Memory Channel Services and UMP (Universal Message Passing). The first is responsible for allocating and mapping individual memory pages. UMP implements a user-level library of basic message passing mechanisms. It is mainly used as a target for higher software layers such as MPI, PVM or HPF. Both layers have been implemented for the Digital UNIX and the WindowsNT operating systems.

Performance measurements have been done for the low level layers as well as for MPI, PVM or HPF implementations. The following numbers were measured on Alpha 4100 nodes (300 MHz 21164 CPU) in a two node configuration without a hub and Memory Channel 2 adapters:

- one way latency for an 8 byte ping-pong test: 2.2 μs (raw), 5.1 μs (HPF) and 6.4 μs (MPI)
- 88 Mbyte/s bandwidth for 32 byte packets

9.9.3 Remarks

Memory Channel reduces communication to the minimum: simple store operations. As a consequence, latencies for single data transfers are very low. This also enables Memory Channel to reach the max. sustained datarate of 88 Mbyte/s with relative small data packets of 32 byte, which is a very remarkable fact, since most other SANs need far greater packets to get close to their physical limit.

The largest possible configuration consists out of 8 12-CPU Alpha server nodes, resulting in a 96-CPU cluster. This current limitation prevents Memory Channel from being used for clusters targeting today's Grand Challenges, which need hundreds of CPUs.

9.10 Synfinity

The Synfinity SAN [23] is developed and marketed by Fujitsu System Technologies (FJST),[3] a business unit of HAL Computer Systems and Fujitsu. Synfinity offers support for both parallel programming models: Message Passing and Shared Memory. Three components are available: Synfinity NUMA is an adapter to connect SMP nodes together to one ccNUMA cluster, Synfinity CLUSTER is a host adapter intended for Message Passing, and Synfinity NET is a six-port switch to connect several interfaces together to one cluster.

Synfinity is based on the technology of HAL's Mercury interconnect. Originally, this network was targeted at Shared Memory computing, but turned now into a full-featured SAN. Synfinity is also intended as a replacement for Fujitsu's APNet network in the AP3000 systems. The following description mainly focuses on the CLUSTER implementation.

9.10.1 Pushing Networking to the Technological Limits

Synfinity is an aggressive approach toward the highest possible physical bandwidth. Two sorts of 34 bit-wide link cables are used: 2 m cables running at 200 MHz and

[3] www.fjst.com

10 m cables at 100 MHz. With both clock edges used for transmitting data, this results in impressive 1.6/0.8 Gbyte/s raw data transfer rates.

Synfinity NUMA The NUMA adapter plugs into Intel's Slot-2 (Pentium II Xeon). It implements cache coherence across up to 4 connected nodes, thus forming a cc-NUMA style SMP cluster. Remote latencies of 1.1 μs were measured for an unloaded system and 1.3 μs for a system running a transaction processing benchmark.

CLUSTER interface Host interfaces are available as 32/64 bit, 33/66 MHz PCI adapters. The interface card consists of two chips: the PCI to Mercury Bridge (PMB) and the Mercury Interface Chip (MIC).

The MIC provides the electrical interface into the Mercury network and implements the end-to-end reliability services. It accepts data packets from the PMB, does the lookup on the routing table, generates EDC data and injects the packet into the network. PMB and MIC are clocked with the PCI clock at 66 MHz, the MIC converts the data stream to the 200/100 MHz clock domain of the Mercury interconnect. Furthermore, two packet buffers store incoming messages, one for plain data packets, the other one for special service packets. To provide end-to-end reliability, each outgoing packet is stored in a retransmission buffer, until the receiver has acknowledged it. Figure 9.16 shows the MIC block diagram.

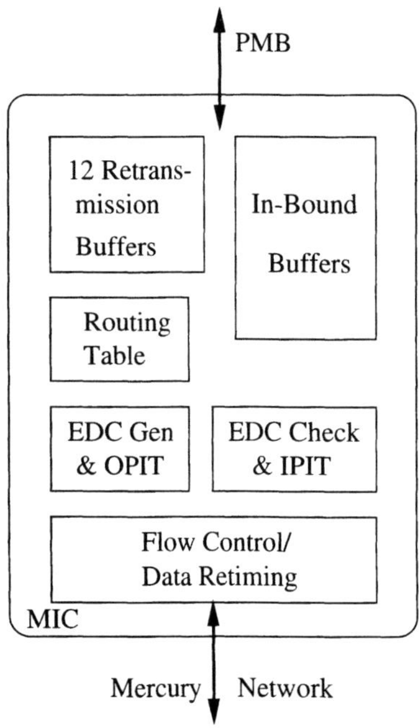

Figure 9.16 Synfinity Mercury Interface Chip (MIC).

The PMB chip, as seen in Figure 9.17, contains all necessary registers of the

DMA engines. Protocol machines fetch job entries from main memory, collect header and data and forward the packet to the MIC.

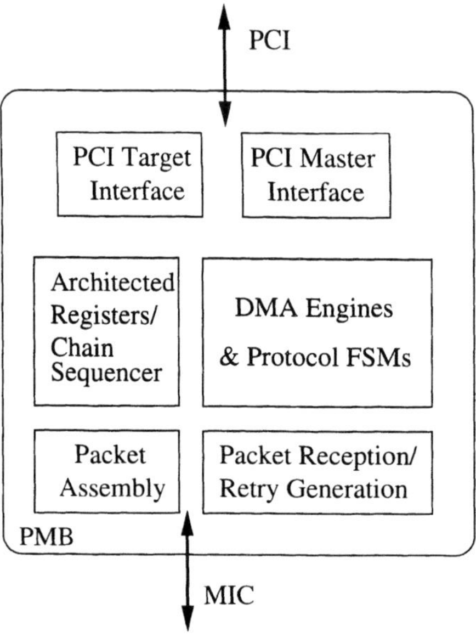

Figure 9.17 Synfinity PCI to Mercury Bridge (PMB).

Data Transfer Synfinity offers various data transfer and communication services. Plain Send/Receive transfers can be initiated to direct data toward other nodes. The receiving node stores the incoming data in message queues residing in main memory. Remote memory operations are supported through Put/Get calls. Here the sending/receiving node determines local and remote address of the data. Especially for fine grain parallel computations, Synfinity offers Remote Atomic Read-Modify-Write (RMW) operations. The user can choose between several operations such as Fetch and Add or Compare and Swap. This communication mode can be extremely useful for implementing system-wide locks. For collective operations, special barrier registers can be programmed to take part in a cluster-wide synchronization with an arbitrary number of nodes.

All communication mechanisms are initiated via chained descriptors residing in main memory. A communicating process simply builds a descriptor, enqueues it in one of several job queues and notifies the protocol engines inside the PMB. Completion of transactions can be signaled via interrupts or flag updates in local and/or remote memory.

To avoid network overloading (so called tree saturation), the Mercury interconnect uses a credit-based mechanism to prevent the sending of data in case of lacking buffer space. The PMB is also able to generate Busy/Retry acknowledgments, which instruct the sending side to retry the transaction at a later time.

Switches Synfinity NET implements a six-port, virtual cut-through switch running at 200 MHz. It can be used to connect up to 64 nodes in an arbitrary topology. Synfinity uses source-path routing, which results in a fall-through time of 42 ns. To prevent blocking of small, special-service packets (barrier, RMW), 3 arbitration priorities allow small messages to bypass large Put/Get packets.

9.10.2 Remarks

Software is currently available as a VIA implementation under WindowsNT. Detailed performance measurements are not available at this time, but FJST predicts about 220 Mbyte/s bandwidth on a 64 bit/66 MHz PCI Sun Ultra system. Synfinity looks like a good vehicle for message passing in clusters. Several communication mechanisms are directly supported in hardware (Put/Get, barrier), which enables the implementation of thin and fast protocol layers. Also, its advanced flow control mechanisms would make it very interesting to compare Synfinity with other interconnects under heavy load.

9.11 Bibliography

[1] Scott Pakin, Mario Lauria and Andrew Chien. *High Performance Messaging on Workstations: Illinois Fast Messages (FM) for Myrinet.* Association for Computing Machinery, 1995.

[2] Mario Lauria and Andrew Chien. MPI-FM: High Performance MPI on Workstation Clusters. *Technical Report*, University of Illinois at Urbana-Champaign, Available at http://www-csag.cs.uiuc.edu/papers/index.html.

[3] Maximilian Ibel, Klaus E. Schauser, Chris T. Scheiman and Manfred Weis. High Performance Cluster Computing Using SCI. *Tech Report*, University of California, Santa Barbara, Available at http://www.cs.ucsb.edu/research/sci.

[4] Hong Xu and Tom W. Fisher. Improving PVM Performance Using ATOMIC User-Level Protocol. *Tech Report*, University of Southern California, Available at http://www.isi.edu/isi-technical-reports.html.

[5] Robert Felderman, Annette DeSchon, Danny Cohen and Gregory Finn. A High-Speed Local Communication Architecture. *Journal of High Speed Networks*, pages 1-28, 1994.

[6] Dave Gustavson's Answers to Questions about SCI. http://www.SCIzzL.com.

[7] The HIPPI Protocol. http://www.cis.ohio-state.edu/~jain/cis788-95/hippi/

[8] Carolyn Curtis, updated by David Cortesi. *Getting Started with Array Systems.* Silicon Graphics, Document Number: 007-3058-002 and 008-3058-002.

[9] Craig Patridge. *Gigabit networking.* Addison-Wesley Publishing Company, 1993.

[10] Al Geist et al. *PVM Parallel Virtual Machine - A Users Guide and Tutorial for Networked Parallel Computing.* The MIT Press, 1994.

[11] Thomas E. Anderson, David E. Culler and David A.Patterson. Case for NOW (Networks of Workstations). *IEEE Micro*, pages 54-64, February 1995.

[12] Mengjou Lin and David H.C. Du. Distributed Network Computing over Local ATM Networks. *IEEE Journal on Selected Areas in Communications*, vol. 13(4), pages 733-748, May 1995.

[13] Jonathan S. Turner. Issues in Distributed Control for ATM Networks. *Tech Report WUCS-95-12*, Washington University, 1995.

[14] Nanette J. Boden et al. Myrinet: A Gigabit-per-second Local Area Network. *IEEE Micro*, pages 29-36, February 1995.

[15] Anthony Alles. *ATM Internetworking.* Cisco Systems, http://cell-relay.indiana.edu/cell-relay/docs/cisco.html.

[16] Shubhendu S. Mukherjee and Mark D. Hill. A Survey of User-Level Network Interfaces for System Area Networks. Computer Sciences Department, University of Wisconsin-Madison, *Technical Report 1340*, Available at http://www.cs.wisc.edu/ shubu/abstracts.html, February 1997.

[17] Marco Fillo and Richard B. Gillett. Architecture and Implementation of Memory Channel 2. *Digital Technical Journal*, vol. 9(1), 1997.

[18] Thomas Sterling, Donald J. Becker, Daniel Savarese, Michael R. Berry and Chance Res. Achieving a Balanced Low-Cost Architecture for Mass Storage Management through Multiple Fast Ethernet Channels on the Beowulf Parallel Workstation. *Proceedings, International Parallel Processing Symposium (IPPS)*, Available at http://cesdis.gsfc.nasa.gov/linux/beowulf/beowulf.html, 1996.

[19] Raoul Bhoedjang, Tim Rühl and Henri E. Bal. User-Level Network Interface Protocols. *IEEE Computer*, vol. 31(11), pages 53-60, November 1998.

[20] José Duato, Sudhakar Yalamanchili and Lionel Ni. Interconnection Networks, An Engineering Approach. *IEEE Computer Society Press*, 1997.

[21] Beng-Hong Lim et al. Message Proxies for Efficient, Protected Communication on SMP Clusters. *Proceedings High Performance Computer Architecture (HPCA)*, 1997.

[22] Wolfgang K. Giloi, Ulrich Brüning and Wolfgang Schröder-Preikschat. MANNA: Prototype of a Distributed Memory Architecture with Maximized Sustained Performance. *Proceedings Euromicro PDP Workshop*, 1996.

[23] Jeff Larson. The HAL Interconnect PCI Card. *Proceedings CANPC Workshop*, Lecture Notes in Computer Science 1362, 1998.

[24] David Garcia and William Watson. ServerNet II. *Proceedings CANPC Workshop*, Lecture Notes in Computer Science 1362, 1998.

Chapter 10

Lightweight Messaging Systems

GIOVANNI CHIOLA AND GIUSEPPE CIACCIO

DISI, Università di Genova
via Dodecaneso 35, 16146 Genova, Italy
Email: {*chiola,ciaccio*}*@disi.unige.it*

10.1 Introduction

As PCs and workstations become more and more powerful and fast network hardware more and more affordable, existing communication software needs to be revisited and possibly re-engineered in order not to become a severe bottleneck of cluster communications. Several research projects concerning efficient support to cluster-wide communications have been started so far, both from the hardware and the software standpoint. Many such research projects have a strong committment to implementation, therefore many new communication protocols, mechanisms, abstractions, and devices have been made available. New concepts have been developed, and some of them can now be found in commercial products.

In this chapter we provide a picture of the state-of-the-art in the field of cluster-wide communications. We claim that classifying existing prototypes based on a description of their architectural approaches and tradeoffs accompanied by a performance comparison facilitates the development of new ideas and may provide at least an insight, if not evidence, of the future trends of cluster computing.

Since NOWs and clusters are distributed-memory architectures the emphasis is deliberately put on message-passing communication systems. Distributed emulations of shared memory on clusters are always built on top of message-passing systems, so that our approach does not impact too much on generality.

All the communication systems and issues presented here have been developed as parts of research projects, and are based upon commodity off-the-shelf communication devices. Messaging systems running on specialized hardware are outside the scope of this chapter; although often quite interesting in many respects, they are not likely to spread in the user community, as custom interconnects are usually too expensive and do not enjoy the large R&D efforts that only commodity hardware vendors can sustain in the long term. Also industrial prototypes and commercial products whose source codes are not disclosed to the public (such as MicroSoft WinSock2, for instance) are not described in this chapter.

10.2 Latency/Bandwidth Evaluation of Communication Performance

Most performance measurements of communication systems are given in terms of two parameters, latency, L, and asymptotic bandwidth, B. The former deals with the synchronization semantics of a message exchange, while the latter deals with the (large, intensive) data transfer semantics.

Latency There is no general agreement about what "latency" is and how it should be measured. The purpose of latency evaluation is to characterize the speed of the underlying system to synchronize two cooperating processes by a message exchange. The faster the system is with such a task, the better the performance is for highly synchronous applications. From the standpoint of a message-passing application, a pure synchronization information can only be carried by a message exchange. However, the payload of such message carries no actual synchronization semantics, and as such it should be as small as possible, preferably empty. The most common definition of (one-way) latency is the time needed to send a minimal-size message from a sender to a receiver, from the instant the sender starts a send operation to the instant the receiver is notified about the message arrival. Normally, "sender" and "receiver" are application-level processes. The common technique to compute the latency parameter L is to use a ping-pong microbenchmark. Process "ping" sends a message then receives it back from "pong." Ping also measure the time needed to execute the send/receive pair; that is, the round-trip time. Process "pong" does the reverse. Actions are repeated a number of times to collect statistics, possibly discarding the first few measurements to exclude "warm-up" effects. L is computed as half the average round-trip time.

End-to-end and one-sided asymptotic bandwidth The asymptotic bandwidth B is intended to be a characterization of how fast a data transfer may occur from a sender to a receiver. In order to isolate the data transfer from any other overhead related to the synchronization semantics, the transfer speed is measured for a very large (ideally infinite, hence, "asymptotic") amount of data. If D is the time needed to send S bytes of data, measured from the instant the sender starts the "send" operation and the instant the receiver gets the complete message payload, then the asymptotic bandwidth B is computed as S/D when S is very large. At least three techniques have been reported so far to accomplish such large data transfers:

- *single-message*: send one single large message. This is feasible only if the underlying messaging system allows very large message sizes.
- *burst*: send a long rapid sequence of fixed-size messages. This is used when the maximum message size allowed by the underlying messaging system is

not large enough. Indeed, in a system which does not allow big messages, one should emulate one single large message by fragmenting it into a long sequence of fixed-size messages to be reassembled on the receiver side. A fair per-message bandwidth measurement should include the overhead of operations of fragmentation and reassembly.

- *stream*: send a long stream of bytes. This is feasible for stream-oriented communication systems like TCP/IP sockets.

Whatever the way a (large) data transfer is performed, there are in turn two techniques to perform the actual measurement:

- *End-to-end*: use a ping-pong microbenchmark to measure the average round-trip time. Actions are repeated a number of times to collect statistics, possibly discarding the first few measurements to exclude initial "warm-up" effects. Then D is computed as half the average round-trip time, and the asymptotic bandwidth is computed as S/D. This microbenchmark measures the transfer rate of the whole end-to-end communication path.

- *One-sided*: use a *ping* microbenchmark to measure the average send time. Process "pong" receives the data transfer then sends a short acknowledge message to process "ping" to inform it that data were successfully received. D is computed as the average data transfer time (differently from ping-pong, here the time is not divided by two), and the asymptotic bandwidth is computed as S/D. This microbenchmark measures the transfer rate as perceived by the sender side of the communication path, thus hiding the overhead at the receiver side. This implies that the measured throughput is greater than the one evaluated by an end-to-end technique. A similar technique could be used to measure the transfer rate at the receiver side.

An end-to-end latency/bandwidth characterization is usually supposed to correctly characterize the end-to-end delay $D(S)$ of the messaging system for any message size S through the following linear relation:

$$D(S) = L + (S - S_m)/B \tag{10.2.1}$$

where S_m is the minimal message size allowed by the system.

Equation 10.2.1 assumes that the per-byte delivery cost $1/B$ does not depend on the actual message size. However, this is not always the case. Especially with packet-oriented interconnects, which require data fragmentation and reassembly, such a linear model does not capture the behavior of the system when fragmentation starts to occur. Modeling performance of medium-size messages is important as they are frequently generated by medium-grained parallel applications.

Throughput We define the throughput curve as the graph of the throughput function $T(S) = S/D(S)$ where S is the message size in bytes and $D(S)$ is the (one-way) message delay defined as one of the following:

- Half the round-trip time for a message of S bytes as measured by the ping-pong microbenchmark, using either single-message or burst data transfers. In this case we obtain the end-to-end throughput.

- The data transfer time as measured by the ping (pong) microbenchmark, using either single-message or burst data transfers. In this case we obtain the sender-side (resp. receiver-side) throughput.

It is worth noting that the asymptotic bandwidth is nothing but the throughput for a very large (ideally infinite) message. A partial view of the entire throughput curve is given by the asymptotic bandwidth B together with the so-called "half-power point," defined as the message size S_h such that $T(S_h) = B/2$.

10.3 Traditional Communication Mechanisms for Clusters

Local Area Networks (LANs) happened to become crucial in systems operation at the very time when the focus in OS support was shifting from efficient use of hardware resources to convenience of interconnection of standard components. Inter-Process Communication (IPC) was only conceived as an event related to sporadic access to remote heterogeneous resources, and nobody was thinking about running parallel applications on clusters. Standardization for interoperation and portability was the key concern that led to the development of traditional LAN protocols, and their efficiency was not perceived as a relevant problem.

10.3.1 TCP, UDP, IP, and Sockets

Indeed, the most spread and accepted standard for communication at the network level is the Internet Protocol (IP), providing unreliable delivery of single packets to one-hop distant hosts. However, IP was developed far before LANs and clusters; this is a possible reason why nobody at that time could realize the potential advantage of exposing IP directly to application level. As a matter of fact, both the two basic kinds of communication Quality of Service (QoS), namely "connected" and "datagram," were implemented by two distinct additional layers atop IP, namely Transport Control Protocol (TCP) and User Datagram Protocol (UDP).

Both TCP/IP and UDP/IP were made available to the application level through the same kind of Application Programming Interface (API), namely Berkeley Sockets. Like IP, sockets were developed far before people could even realize the impact of the particular network abstraction on communication performance, scalability, and code optimization. Indeed sockets were designed with no goal other than to present a familiar Unix-flavored abstraction: The network is perceived as a character device, and sockets are file descriptors related to that device. Sockets and the IP protocol suite owe their success to the generality of purpose, similarity to other established abstractions, and initially favorable conditions (communications were perceived as sporadic events taking place on slow networks).

10.3.2 RPC

The socket interface is the current industry-standard, general-purpose abstraction for communication and interoperation. Unfortunately, its level of abstraction is quite low. Although all the standard communication services and higher-level specialized protocols (e.g., STMP for e-mail) were easily built atop sockets, there was a need for higher level but still general-purpose abstractions. Remote Procedure Call (RPC) by SUN is one such abstraction. Today RPC is the *de facto* standard for distributed client-server applications. Like with sockets and IP, the success of RPC is mainly due to familiarity and generality rather than efficiency:

- Services are requested by calling procedures with suitable parameters. The called service may also return a result. This semantical framework is perceived by programmers as very similar to sequential programming.

- In a heterogeneous environment, one major difficulty is to cope with different formats for representing the same data type across different systems connected to the network. RPC hides any format difference, therefore providing a transparent view of an heterogeneous distributed system.

10.3.3 MPI and PVM

RPC was established as a standard by the community of developers of distributed client-server applications. The large community of parallel programmers was not yet involved, as traditional parallel computers were uncomparably more powerful than distributed systems formed by networked uniprocessors at that time. However, networked computers could well serve as a low-cost parallel platform for educational as well as prototyping purposes. Therefore, general-purpose systems for message passing and parallel program management on distributed platforms started to be developed at the application level, based on available IPC mechanisms.

Parallel Virtual Machine (PVM) was the first of such message passing systems to establish a *de facto* standard for parallel programming. PVM provides an easy-to-use programming interface for process creation and interprocess communication, plus a run-time system for elementary application management. PVM runs nicely on the most general kind of distributed memory system, namely, a generic IP network, as well as on shared-memory systems and MPPs. This guarantees the widest portability of PVM programs across any range of parallel systems. Moreover, PVM processes may question the PVM run-time system about the computational power of their local processors. This greatly helps designing self-balancing parallel applications. PVM owes most of its popularity, and also its inefficiency, to its run-time management system.

The Message Passing Interface (MPI) is the other established standard for message passing parallel programming. MPI offers a larger and more versatile set of routines than PVM, but does not offer any run-time management system (at least in the currently implemented MPI-1 standard). Actually, MPI owes its popularity more to the greater efficiency of its existing implementations compared to PVM rather than to its rich programming interface (indeed, MPI users tend to exploit a small fraction of the huge MPI routine set).

10.3.4 Active Messages

Active Messages [19] is a slight departure from the classical send-receive model. It is a one-sided communication paradigm; that is, whenever the sender process transmits a message, the message exchange occurs regardless of the current activity of the receiver process. As an aside, there is no need of a receive operation.

The goal of Active Messages is to reduce the impact of communication overhead on application performance. The particular semantics of Active Messages may eliminate the need of many temporary storage for messages along the communication path, thus, remarkably speeding up communications. Moreover, with proper hardarware support it becomes easier to overlap communication with computation.

In traditional send-receive systems, messages delivered to a destination node may need to be temporarily buffered waiting for the destination process to invoke a "receive" operation which will consume them. The semantics of Active Messages is different: As soon as delivered, each message triggers a user-programmed function of the destination process, called receiver handler. The receiver handler acts as a separate thread which promptly consumes the message, therefore decoupling message management from the current activity of the main thread of the destination process. Here "consuming" means integrating the message information into the ongoing computation of the main thread, notifying the message arrival to the main thread, and possibly setting some data structures in order to promptly "consume" the next incoming message as soon as it arrives.

Many experimental high performance messaging systems described later on are Active Message-like systems. A well known commercial application is the Connection Machine Active Message Layer (CMAML) library by Thinking Machines Co., which runs on the CM-5 platform.

With most Active Messages-like systems, the receiver handler is sender-based. Each message is composed of two parts, namely the message body and an explicit pointer to the destination's receiver handler that will consume the message. Usually it is the receiver handler that extracts the message and stores it into a data structure in the receiver address space. Such a model requires the destination process to share its own code address space with the sender process, a condition which is easily fulfilled only with the Single Program Multiple Data (SPMD) paradigm.

10.4 Lightweight Communication Mechanisms

All the considerations that we summarized concerning the lack of efficiency of standard communication protocols for cluster computing led several research groups to investigate so-called lightweight protocols to cope with this crucial problem.

10.4.1 What We Need for Efficient Cluster Computing

The Linux OS is recognized to provide one of the most efficient implementations of the TCP/IP stack ever. We shall thus base our considerations on this state-of-the-art implementation for reference and comparison to lightweight protocols. TCP/IP sockets' one-way latency depends heavily on the specific network driver being used, which in turn depends on which NIC has been leveraged. Let us consider a basic cluster configuration comprising two Pentium II 300 MHz PCs, each running the Linux kernel 2.0.29 and equipped with a 3COM 3c905 Fast Ethernet NIC driven by one of the latest Linux drivers for this card. Consider two PCs connected by a UTP crossover cable and working in half-duplex mode (this provides an upper bound performance for the real case of a Fast Ethernet repeater hub) running a ping-pong test to evaluate one-way latency and asymptotic bandwidth (after disabling the Nagle "piggybacking" algorithm). Under such experimental conditions you should measure a one-way latency of about 77 μs and asymptotic bandwidth of about 10.8 MByte/s at socket level. The average half-power point is found at approximately 1750 bytes. Recalling that the maximum theoretical bandwidth of Fast Ethernet is 12.5 MByte/s, and assuming a reasonable lower bound for latency of 7 μs due to hardware characteristics:

- Latency is one order of magnitude worse than the hardware latency.
- Efficiency in the range of short (single packet, up to about 1500 bytes) messages is well below 50 percent.
- Efficiency is good (86 percent) only with very long data streams.

The overall impression is that Linux TCP/IP is very good for traditional networking but not very good for cluster computing, especially looking at performance numbers in terms of CPU cycles rather than microseconds.

Fig. 10.1 provides a comparison between throughput curves measured with slighly different system configurations. It is apparent that using the same hardware and OS but a different device driver leads to a substantial performance degradation. The reason is very simple: The 3c905 NIC can be programmed in two different ways, one called descriptor-based DMA (DBDMA) and another called CPU-driven DMA. When driven in DBDMA mode, the NIC itself performs DMA transfers between host memory and the network by simply scanning a precomputed list of so called "DMA descriptors" stored in host memory. The low-level memory-to-network and network-to-memory data transfers are operated by the NIC autonomously while the CPU is running the TCP/IP protocol and building the necessary DMA descriptors for subsequent data transfers. This pipelines the end-to-end communication path and yields high communication throughput. Previous drivers used the CPU-driven DMA mode, where the CPU triggers a DMA operation and then waits for the transfer to end before starting a subsequent DMA. This leads to a "store-and-forward" behavior and lower throughput. A very similar 3COM card operated in CPU-driven DMA mode on Pentium 133 CPUs yields even lower performance. This

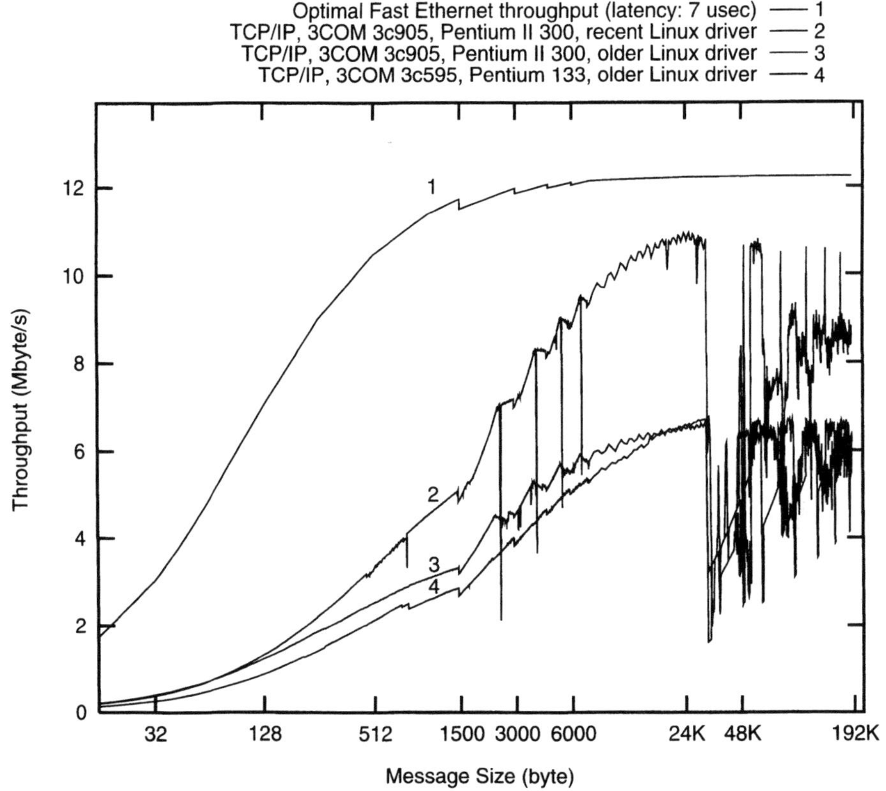

Figure 10.1 Linux 2.0.29 TCP/IP sockets: Half-duplex "ping-pong" throughput with various NICs and CPUs (Nagle Disabled).

provides an insight of the software overhead involved in running the TCP/IP stack: The larger this overhead, the larger degradation with slower CPUs.

Another drawback of TCP/IP that has often been pointed out is that its layered structure implies a certain number of memory-to-memory data movements. This is a time-consuming task and pollutes the working set of the user process upon communication, leading to a higher number of cache misses with additional performance degradation. Poor code locality is also implied by the layered software structure.

A consideration which does not emerge from Figure 10.1 is related to the communication performance on a congested LAN. It is well known that TCP uses a sliding-window flow control algorithm with "go-back-N" packet retransmission upon timeout. The flow control mechanism of TCP avoids packet overflow at the receiver side; however, it cannot prevent overflow to occur in a LAN switch in case of network congestion. When this occurs, some packets are discarded by the switch. Eventually the retransmission mechanisms of TCP on the sender hosts are triggered and start resending much more packets than needed, increasing network traffic and therefore making the LAN even more congested. Clearly LANs require more sophisticated retransmission policies, which should take into account that the only source of packet loss in a modern LAN is switch overflow.

From the above analysis we can draw some general conclusions about what we should do to implement an efficient messaging system on NOWs and clusters:

- Choose an appropriate LAN hardware. A NIC, which is "intelligent enough" to cooperate with the host CPU, may be of great help for higher performance.
- Tailor the protocols to the underlying LAN hardware. Knowledge about specific LAN's features, average error rate, etc., should be exploited.
- Target the protocols to the user needs. Different users and different application domains may need different tradeoffs between reliability and performance.
- Optimize the protocol code and the NIC driver as much as possible. The software overhead of protocol execution must be kept as low as possible.
- Minimize the use of memory-to-memory copy operations.

10.4.2 Typical Techniques to Optimize Communication

Various attempts to address the inefficiency of standard interprocess communication mechanisms on clusters have been carried out in the last few years. Most messaging systems are committed to efficiency, at least to a certain degree. Although following different architectural approaches, most of them share a number of common performance-oriented features which we briefly outline below.

Using multiple networks in parallel This is the most straighforward way to increase the aggregate communication bandwidth of the platform and reduce congestion. However, this cannot help reduce latency.

Simplifying LAN-wide host naming Indeed addressing conventions in a LAN might be much simpler than in a WAN.

Simplifying communication protocol Long protocol functions are time-consuming, and their poor locality in the access to huge data structures generates a large number of cache misses and pollutes the working sets of user processes, thus leading to even more cache misses. General-purpose networks with a high error rate (like WANs and highly congested LANs) may require complex protocols to recover from packet losses in an efficient way. However, when using low error rate LANs where congestion is unlikely or impossible and end-to-end communication performance is the main concern, the tradeoff between reliability and performance may change in favor of so-called optimistic protocols. A typical optimistic protocol is one which performs very well in the supposedly usual case of no communication errors and no congestion. In the unlikely event of a communication error, an optimistic protocol may either recover from the error in an inefficient way or regard the event as catastrophic and limit itself to raise an error condition to the upper layers. Other fast protocols base their "optimism" upon an *a priori* global knowledge of the communication patterns allowed on the network (see 10.5.2 for an example).

Avoiding temporary buffering of messages Making temporary copies of information along the communication path during the execution of complex protocols is a time-consuming task and pollutes the working sets of user processes. The ideal protocol would allow communications with no temporary message buffering. Protocols providing such a feature are called zero-copy protocols. A frequent answer to this challenge is remapping the kernel-level temporary buffers into user memory space. Such kernel-level buffers are usually directly accessed by the NIC when sending/receiving data, but remapping them into user space means that user processes also have direct access to them, so that the memory-to-memory transfers usually involved when crossing the user-kernel boundary are no longer needed. This however is often only a partial answer: Data must still be moved back and forth between user data structures and communication buffers, no matter whether they are mapped into user space or not. Another solution is to lock the user data structures into physical RAM and let the NIC access them directly upon communication via DMA. This is a partial answer also, as only those data structures spanning contiguous virtual memory regions fit this method. For noncontiguous data structures, data transfers between host memory and NIC must be done in chunks. This implies a proper structure of the communication system (it must provide so-called "gather/scatter" facilities).

Pipelining communication phases Some NICs may be programmed to start transmitting data over the physical medium while the host-to-NIC DMA or programmed I/O transfer is still in progress. This allows the NIC to transfer data in a pipelined way during transmission. A similar behavior can be programmed at the receiver side: The NIC-to-host data movement can be initiated while the data transfer from the physical medium to the NIC is still in progress. This way the end-to-end behaviour of the communication path is fully pipelined like in a wormhole routing. The performance improvements obtained by pipelining data transfers in this way may be impressive in terms of latency as well as throughput.

Avoid system calls for communication Invoking an OS system call is often considered too much of a time-consuming task. Therefore, one challenge is to minimize the need of system calls in the communication path. A frequent solution is to implement the communication system entirely at the user level: All buffers and registers of the NIC are remapped from kernel space into user memory space so that user processes no longer have to cross the user-kernel boundary to drive the device. This is the basic idea of the so-called user-level communication architectures (see Section 10.6). However, this poses protection challenges in a multitasking environment where more processes may share the same communication devices. Protection can be enforced only by leveraging programmable NICs which can run a code for protected device multiplexing, a feature currently offered only by expensive network devices.

Lightweight system calls for communication As an alternative to eliminate the need of system calls, so-called lightweight system calls are often implemented, which save only a subset of CPU registers and do not invoke the scheduler upon return.

Fast interrupt path The code path to the interrupt handler of the network device driver is optimized in order to reduce interrupt latency in interrupt-driven receives.

Polling the network device The usual method of notifying message arrivals by interrupts is time-consuming and sometimes unacceptable, especially in the case of short messages. The overheads of interrupt launch and service must always be paid, even if the incoming message processing overhead is low. Most high performance messaging systems provide the ability of explicitly inspecting or polling the network devices for incoming messages, besides interrupt-based arrival notification.

Providing very low-level mechanisms Following a kind of RISC approach, many high performance communication systems provide only very low-level primitives that can be combined in various ways to form higher level communication semantics (blocking or not, reliable or not, buffered or not, etc.) and APIs (standard, custom, etc.) in an "ad hoc" way. This solution can only be performance-effective if the calling overhead for the basic primitives is also minimized.

10.4.3 The Importance of Efficient Collective Communications

A crucial issue that must be addressed in order to turn the potential benefits of clusters into widespread use is the development of parallel applications exhibiting high enough performance and efficiency with a reasonable programming effort. High level standard communication libraries such as PVM or MPI have been introduced with the aim of facilitating parallel code development and porting. However, while an MPI code for instance is easily ported from one hardware platform to another, provided that both provide an implementation of MPI, performance and efficiency of the code execution is not "ported" across platforms because the same communication call implemented on different platforms according to different criteria may lead to quite different communication performance. Therefore, whenever an MPI programmer seeks best performance for a given parallel program on the parallel machine at hand, he/she is induced to restructure his/her program in order to avoid the use of all those communication calls and patterns that turn out not to be efficiently implemented on the local machine.

Of course, much lighter and effective porting effort would be required if parallel programs be written using high-level collective communications instead of *ad hoc* patterns of low-level point-to-point communications. Unluckily enough, collective routines often provide the most frequent and extreme instance of "lack of performance portability." In most cases, collective communications are implemented in terms of point-to-point communications arranged into standard patterns which do not take into account the potential benefits as well as the limitations of the underlying hardware interconnect. This is especially true with public-domain implementations of MPI and PVM for TCP networks. They assume nothing about the underlying interconnect, a LAN being treated the same way as a WAN. This implies very poor collective communication performance with clusters. As a result, parallel programs hardly ever rely on collective routines, even in cases where their exploitation would naturally lead to simpler or more modular code. The final consequence is that nobody gets trained with the usage of collective communications, and that message-passing parallel programming remains hard business.

A good tradeoff between the semantical expressiveness of a communication library and the efficiency of its actual implementation on clusters must be sought in order to turn clusters into really interesting environments for high performance parallel computing. Hence, the efficient implementation of standard collective communications such as barrier synchronization, gather-scatter, reduce, etc., is crucial.

10.4.4 A Classification of Lightweight Communication Systems

From a software-oriented standpoint, existing messaging systems for clusters fall into two main families, namely kernel-level systems and user-level systems.

In the kernel-level approach the messaging system is supported by the OS kernel with a set of low-level communication mechanisms embedding a communication protocol. Such mechanisms are made available to the user level through a number of OS system calls in order to ensure protected access to the devices in a multiuser, multitasking environment. Applications can either invoke these low-level mechanisms directly, or use higher level communication libraries built atop them. The former case is more typical for system applications (like the standard suite of Internet daemons and servers which make explicit use of BSD sockets), whereas the second case is typical for parallel and distributed high-level applications.

The kernel-level approach fits nicely into the architecture of modern OSs, providing protected access to the communication devices with no need to limit or modify its multiusers multitasking features, and even in the presence of commodity non-programmable devices. Although some minor additions to the OS kernel may be required, it is often possible to preserve both the standard OS interface and its functionality. For historical reasons, all the current industry-standard communication APIs are currently implemented following the kernel-level approach.

A drawback of the kernel-level approach is that traditional protection mechanisms may require quite a high software overhead, due to the standard system call mechanism (scheduling activity upon return), as well as the kernel-to-user data movement. This poses hard challenges to implementors of high performance messaging systems, forcing the exploitation of some optimization techniques (lightweight system calls, fast interrupt paths, see Section 10.4.2) while hampering other optimizations (e.g., the use of very low-level mechanisms).

The user-level approach aims at improving performance by minimizing the OS involvement in the communication path in order to obtain a closer integration between the application and the communication device. More precisely, access to the communication buffers of the network interface is granted without invoking any system calls. Any communication layer, as well as API, is implemented as a user-level programming library. In all the existing user-level systems, applications are provided with a nonstandard API. The choice of the API itself is often determined by performance considerations, and there is no *de facto* standard API for such systems, although the specification of the Virtual Interface Architecture (VIA) [2] promoted by CompaQ, Intel, and Microsoft can be regarded as a first attempt to standardize user-level communication architectures.

In order for such approach to allow protected access to the communication devices, either a single-user network access or strict gang scheduling are usually required. A third alternative is to leverage programmable communication devices which can run the necessary support for device multiplexing in place of the OS kernel. All three alternatives have their own drawbacks: Single-user network access appears to be an unreasonable restriction in a modern processing environment; gang scheduling appears inefficient and requires major interventions at the level of OS scheduler; moving multiplexing support from the OS kernel to the device is unfeasible with commodity, low-cost components, which are usually not programmable.

In the user-level approach, modifications to the OS kernel may range from simple addition of custom device drivers to deep interventions at the scheduler level, depending on the degree of protection to be preserved and the extent to which multiuser access to the communication device is to be allowed.

10.5 Kernel-Level Lightweight Communications

In the family of kernel-level systems running on commodity clusters we can identify two main subclasses, namely, industry-standard API systems and best-performance systems.

10.5.1 Industry-Standard API Systems

In the industry-standard API approach the main goal besides efficiency is to comply an industry-standard for the low-level communication API. Retaining an industry-standard communication interface allows portability and reuse of existing applications and libraries developed for that interface. Usually this approach does not force any major modifications to the existing OS; rather, the new communication system is simply added as an extension of the OS itself (e.g., a custom device driver, a Linux kernel module, or a user-level programming library). A drawback of this approach is that some optimizations in the underlying communication layer could be hampered by the choice of an industry standard, like Berkeley sockets, for instance, which was not originally conceived to address any performance issues.

Beowulf The Beowulf project [16] runs on a Linux-based cluster of PCs. It follows a very conservative way, namely retaining the standard Unix protocol suites. Improved communication performance is achieved by exploiting two or more LANs in parallel, a technique called "channel bonding" which Beowulf supports at the level of a Linux modified NIC driver. Of course much better results would have been obtained had the communication software been optimized, in addition to using more

LANs. However, this system is currently commercialized in the USA: The *Extreme Linux* software package by Red Hat is nothing but a commercial distribution of the Beowulf system. Besides the standard bus topology, a two-dimensional mesh topology has been investigated [8]. Each node in the mesh is connected to two distinct Ethernet LANs, namely the "horizontal" and the "vertical." Therefore, each node is adjacent to every node in the same row as well as in the same column. Moreover, each node acts as a software router in order to allow nonadjacent nodes to communicate. This way a node A can reach a nonadjacent node B by two distinct disjoint paths. The "channel bonding" technique is then applied to allow node A to communicate with node B using both such two independent network paths in parallel, with two intermediate nodes engaged in parallel for routing. However, a parallel disk I/O test conducted on such a two-dimensional meshxi topology has shown throughput improvement over bus topology only in case of small workloads.

Fast Sockets Fast Sockets [14] is an implementation of TCP sockets atop an Active Message communication layer. The underlying Active Message layer provides good performance, whereas the upper socket interface, implemented entirely as a user-level library, provides the messaging system with industry-standard characteristics. The protocol reverts to plain TCP/IP when the LAN boundary is crossed, e.g., through a router. In case of forking processes, Fast Sockets do not support the plain semantics of sockets, according to which socket descriptors which are open at fork time are shared with child processes. Fast Sockets have been reported not to have an efficient connection phase. Measurements carried out on a pair of UltraSPARC 1's interconnected by Myrinet and running the Solaris OS have shown poor performance (57.8 μs latency, 32.9 MByte/s asymptotyc bandwidth) compared to Myrinet raw communication performance. The relatively poor bandwidth is due to the UltraSPARC's SBus bottleneck, whereas the high latency is mainly due to the high (about 45 μs) latency of the underlying Active Messages layer.

PARMA^2 The PARMA^2 project [11] is aimed at reducing communication overhead in a cluster of PCs connected by Fast Ethernet and running the Linux OS by eliminating flow control and packet acknowledge from Linux TCP/IP and simplifying host addressing. The obtained protocol has "datagram" QoS. A distinctive goal of PARMA^2 is to retain a BSD socket interface in the standard multiuser Unix environment. This allows porting all the socket-based Unix applications and libraries to the new protocol suite with very limited effort. For instance, the MPICH implementation of MPI was able to run on PARMA^2 with only minor modifications. At the lowest level, the Linux interface to the NIC driver is preserved. No optimization was carried out at the level of a NIC driver. Very few data concerning PARMA^2 performance are available. At the time of publication (1997) PARMA^2 exhibited 74 μs one-way latency and 6.6 MByte/s asymptotic bandwidth at socket level, that is about half the Linux TCP/IP latency and 20 percent improvement over Linux TCP/IP maximum throughput on 3COM 3c595 NICs in that year. However, the latency improvement of over Linux UDP/IP sockets was not impressive (one-way latency of Linux UDP/IP sockets was about 100 μs on the same hardware platform), and the absolute communication performance of PARMA^2 appeared far from the raw Fast Ethernet performance. Porting the MPI library atop PARMA^2 resulted in a significant reduction of one-way latency at the MPI level (from 402 μs to 256 μs). A dedicated implementation of MPI called MPIPR, actually a simplified version of MPICH, has been developed and tested on PARMA^2. One-way latency has been furtherly reduced for synchronous point-to-point MPI communications (from 256 μs to 182 μs). A drawback of MPIPR is that it inherits the "datagram" QoS from the underlying PRP protocol, thus violating the semantics of MPI communications.

10.5.2 Best-Performance Systems

In the best-performance approach, the messaging system is supported by the OS kernel with a small set of flexible and efficient low-level communication mechanisms and by simplified protocols carefully designed according to a performance-oriented approach. Challenges like choosing the right mechanisms and degree of virtualization as well as implementing them efficiently are more important than the level at which the communication layer is placed in the overall OS architecture.

Genoa Active Message MAchine (GAMMA) In GAMMA [4], [3] the Linux kernel has been enhanced with a communication layer implemented as a small set of additional lightweight system calls and a custom NIC driver with a fast interrupt path. Most of the communication layer is thus embedded in the Linux kernel, the remaining part being placed in a user-level programming library. The adoption of an Active Message-like communication abstraction called Active Ports allowed a zero-copy optimistic protocol, with no need of either kernel-level or application-level temporary storage for incoming as well as outgoing messages. GAMMA implements pipelined communication paths among user processes. Multiuser protected access to the communication abstraction is granted. The GAMMA device driver is capable of managing both GAMMA and IP communication in the same 100base-T network. On 3COM 3c595 and 3c905 NICs, GAMMA yields very low one-way user-to-user latency (12.7 μs) and high asymptotic bandwidth (12.2 MByte/s, corresponding to 98% efficiency). It must be noticed that the communication protocol of GAMMA is unreliable: It detects communication errors (packet losses and corrupted packets), but then it simply raises an error condition without recovering. The GAMMA approach leaves to the user (application as well as library writer) the task of using the error detection mechanisms to build recovery policies of suitable complexity. However, the very low latency delivered by GAMMA potentially allows a wide range of error recovery and acknowledge policies to be implemented in a very efficient way.

Net* Net* [15] is a communication system for Fast Ethernet based upon a reliable protocol implemented at kernel level. A user process can be granted network access by initially allocating kernel-space buffers and queues for send and receive operations; such buffers and queues are remapped into user-space to allow direct access. Only one user process per node can be granted network access. To send a message, a process copies the message itself into the "user-level image" of a send buffer, then invokes the kernel-level transmission protocol function through a dedicated system call. Such a system call is not necessary if another send operation was submitted a short enough time before, since the interrupt launched at the end of each physical transmission is serviced by a routine which tests send queues for new messages to transmit. To receive a message, a process may perform either a busy or a sleeping waiting on the receive queue. Two levels of service are provided, namely a raw unreliable service for best performance, and a reliable service built atop the raw one. Net* appears to share architectural features from both user-level and kernel-level approaches. The main drawbacks of Net* are that no kernel-operated network multiplexing is performed despite the kernel being involved in the protocol execution, and that user processes have to explicitly fragment and reassemble messages longer than the Ethernet MTU. Very good performance is reported for Net*: the raw level exhibits 23.3 μs one-way latency and 12.2 MByte/s asymptotic bandwidth; the reliable level delivers 30.9 μs one-way latency with same bandwidth. However, the throughput performance of Net* has been evaluated with a one-sided technique, therefore, it does not model the end-to-end behavior of the communication system.

Oxford BSP Clusters A completely different approach to protocol optimization for LAN interconnects is to place some structural restriction on communication traffic by allowing only some well known patterns to occur. Such additional knowledge of the "shape of interaction" can be used to derive *a priori* assumptions to be exploited for optimized error detection and recovery strategies. This is the approach followed by the Oxford BSP Clusters [5]. A parallel program running on a BSP cluster is assumed to comply with the BSP computational model. In the BSP model each process is shaped as a sequence of supersteps. Each superstep is a computation phase followed by a global and synchronizing communication phase. The pattern of such a global communication phase is an any-to-any total exchange followed by a final barrier synchronization. We briefly report here the main features and assumptions of the optimized protocol of BSP clusters.

- In the total exchange phases, the destination scheduling is different from processor to processor. This avoids hot spots and greatly reduces the probability of network overflows resulting in very low packet loss rate.
- The interconnect is assumed to be a switched one, so that no network contention will ever occur.
- In a total exchange communication pattern some of the messages transmitted can be used to piggyback both positive and negative acknowledgements for other messages. This reduces the need of acknowledgement packets as well as timeouts for error detection and recovery.

The most efficient version of the BSP cluster protocol has been implemented as a device driver called BSPlib-NIC. The driver is placed at kernel level in the Linux OS, therefore, BSPlib-NIC should be regarded as a kernel-level messaging system. However, it shares some features and limitations with the user-level approach. For instance, the kernel-level transmit/receive FIFOs of the NIC are remapped into user memory space to allow user-level access to the FIFOs; such direct access occurs in a typically unprotected fashion forcing single-user mode. Moreover, the particular NIC leveraged, that is, the 3COM 3c905B Fast Ethernet adapter, has been programmed to automatically poll the transmit FIFO for packets to be sent; this makes it unnecessary to implement an explicit "start transmission" system call, thus, no system calls are required along the whole end-to-end communication path. BSPlib-NIC achieves a *minimum* (not average) one-way latency of 29 μs with 11.7 MByte/s asymptotic bandwidth. It is worth recalling that BSP cluster communications exhibit such performance while guaranteeing reliable delivery. Rather than trading reliability with performance, the BSPlib-NIC choice is to gain performance by placing restrictions on communication patterns and imposing single-user access.

U-Net on Fast Ethernet The basic principles of U-Net, described in Section 10.6.4, require a NIC's programmable onboard processor in order to implement device multiplexing without involving the host CPU. In the Fast Ethernet version of U-Net, called U-Net/FE [20], designed for a Fast Ethernet network of Pentium PCs running Linux, the low-cost commodity NIC has no programmable on-board processor. The host CPU itself multiplexes the NIC over user processes by means of proper OS kernel support. For instance, the send operation requires invoking a lightweight system call to warn the NIC driver about the presence of a fresh outgoing message in an output buffer. For this reason we do not consider U-Net/FE as a user-level system, but only as a kernel-level emulation of the original U-Net concept yielding still good communication performance (30 μs one-way latency, 12.1 MByte/s asymptotic bandwidth), but with the drawback of presenting the very raw U-Net programming interface. One of the key points of the original U-Net is that it exposes very low-level mechanisms to user level. Indeed, the U-Net programming interface is very similar to the programming interface of the NIC itself, and exhibits the same unreliability of communication as the NIC itself. In our opinion, implementing very low-level mechanisms at kernel level is a source of additional overhead for the upper communication layers, rather than an optimization technique.

10.6 User-Level Lightweight Communications

The user-level approach to fast communications is derived from the assumption that OS communications are inefficient by definition. Hence, the OS involvement in the communication path is minimized. System calls are avoided by allowing direct access to the NIC registers and storage areas, thus achieving a closer integration between applications and interconnection networks. This approach is rooted in the idea of F-Bufs [6], which was followed also in the Exokernel OS architecture [7]. Indeed, the user-level communication architecture shares the same fundamental idea of OS microkernels, that is, moving OS services away from the kernel.

Often (but not always) a primary challenge besides efficiency is to provide "direct access" to the communication device without violating the OS protection model.

Three solutions can be devised to guarentee protection, namely:

- Leverage programmable NICs which can run the necessary support for device multiplexing in place of the OS kernel. This implies higher hardware costs.
- Circumvent the problem by granting network access to one single trusted user. This is not always acceptable.
- Implement some form of "network gang scheduling:" A process has exclusive access to the network interface while it is running and cannot be descheduled while any communication partner is still exchanging data with it. This eliminates the need of the messaging system to operate a run-time device multiplexing. However, gang scheduling is inefficient and often unacceptable as a scheduling policy for many general-purpose environments.

10.6.1 BIP

A recent achievement in the field of user-level messaging systems is the Basic Interface for Parallelism (BIP) [13] implemented atop a Myrinet network of Pentium PCs running Linux. BIP offers both blocking and unblocking communication primitives following a send-receive paradigm implemented according to the rendezvous communication mode, with the exception of very short messages which are managed according to a buffered mode. The Myrinet hardware ensures in-order data delivery at a very low error rate, and controls the data flow through back-pressure. Under such conditions, Myrinet communication errors can be regarded as rare, catastrophic events. This is the reason why the BIP approach to communication errors is to offer a simple detection feature without implementing any recovery policy.

BIP pipelines the communication path by transparently fragmenting messages into packets whose size depends on the total message size. The Myrinet hardware does not require message fragmentation: The goal of BIP fragmentation is to allow the various DMA engines of the Myrinet adapters at both sides of a communication to work in a pipelined fashion. This is only possible if the message is fragmented into a stream of packets, where each packet traverses all the DMA engines in sequence. The fragmentation policy ensures best load balancing along such pipelines of DMA engines. Besides its many optimizations, BIP obtains best performance by getting rid of protected multiplexing of the NIC: The registers of the Myrinet adapter and the memory regions on which it operates are fully exposed to user-level access.

BIP is able to deliver more than 96 percent of the raw Myrinet bandwidth (that is 126 out of 132 MByte/s) with a very low (4.3 μs) one-way latency time. It must be said that published BIP performance is computed as the *median* value of a number of measurements rather than average values. Porting the TCP/IP stack atop BIP provides an impressive demonstration of the poor efficiency of industry-standard protocol layers on fast interconnects (one-way latency 70 μs, asymptotic bandwidth 35 MByte/s). However, porting of MPICH atop BIP [17] results in an acceptable degradation of communication performance at MPI level (median one-way latency is 12 μs and median asymptotic bandwidth is 113.7 MByte/s).

10.6.2 Fast Messages

Illinois Fast Messages (FM) [10] is an Active Message-like system running on Myrinet-connected clusters, and providing reliable in-order message delivery with flow control and packet retransmission. FM works only in single-user mode, despite the Myrinet adapter providing a co-processor (called LANai) which could have been programmed to multiplex the device among several processes. The earlier versions of FM, namely FM 1.0 and FM 1.1, were designed for Myrinet clusters of SPARC-Stations. FM 1.1 exhibited good one-way latency (12 μs) but quite poor efficiency in terms of asymptotic bandwidth (16.1 MByte/s out of a raw Myrinet bandwidth of 132 MByte/s), due to the particularly slow SBus.

Subsequent versions of FM, namely FM 2.x, have been implemented on Pentium Pro clusters, where it delivers much better performance (11 μs latency, 77 MByte/s asymptotic bandwidth) thanks to the much faster PCI bus. Clearly FM remains quite far from the communication performance of the raw Myrinet hardware. However, the main difference between FM 2.x and previous versions is in the programming interface. Porting MPICH atop FM [9] required a slight modification of the API in order to obtain a better match with the ADI layer of MPICH. Basically, FM has been enhanced with gather/scatter features in order to send/receive data from/to noncontiguous virtual memory regions without initiating a new send/receive operation for each region. With these enhancements to the programming interface, MPI atop FM could show a typical degradation of 6 μs in one-way latency at the MPI level with the same asymptotic bandwidth.

10.6.3 Hewlett-Packard Active Messages (HPAM)

Hewlett-Packard Active Messages (HPAM) [12] is one of the first user-level communication systems. It is an implementation of Active Messages on a FDDI-connected network of HP 9000/735 workstations. The FDDI interface is connected to the high-speed graphic bus of the HP workstation instead of the I/O bus. This leads to low (14.5 μs) latency and good (12 MByte/s) asymptotic bandwidth. Protected, direct access to the network is granted to a single process in mutual exclusion. An OS daemon schedules the processes to the network, and other major modifications to the OS allow the delivery of messages to nonscheduled processes. This way gang scheduling is avoided, but the OS plays a nonnegligible role in the communication path, at least in the general case of nonscheduled destination processes. HPAM provides reliable delivery with flow control and retransmission.

10.6.4 U-Net for ATM

Perhaps the most famous representative of the user-level approach is the ATM version of U-Net [18]. With U-Net, user processes are given direct protected access to the network device with no virtualization. The programming interface of U-Net is very similar to the one of the NIC itself. Any communication layer as well as standard programming interface for communication is implemented in user-level programming libraries. Support to protected device multiplexing runs on the Intel i960 processor located on the Fore Systems SBA-200 adapter.

The interconnect is virtualized as a set of "endpoints." An endpoint is a kernel memory buffer plus a send queue and a receive queue for host-to-adapter synchronization. Endpoint buffers are used as intermediate storage for the send/receive operations, and correspond direcly to portions of the NIC's send/receive FIFO queues. The role of the OS is limited to remapping one or more of such endpoints to the memory space of a user process by means of dedicated system calls. After endpoint remapping, the process is granted direct, memory-mapped, protected access to dedicated portions of the adapter's send/receive FIFOs with no further involvement of the OS kernel. If the number of endpoints required by user processes exceed the available endpoints directly supported by the NIC, additional endpoints can be emulated by the OS kernel, providing the same functionality at reduced performance.

U-Net achieves communication performance very close those of the raw 155 Mbps ATM hardware (one-way latency 44.5 μs, maximum throughput 15 MByte/s). The U-Net concept has also been implemented on Fast Ethernet LANs as a kernel-level emulation (see Section 10.5.2).

10.6.5 Virtual Interface Architecture (VIA)

The Virtual Interface Architecture (VIA) [2], a large effort promoted by CompaQ, Intel, and Microsoft, can be regarded as the first attempt to standardize user-level communication architectures. Basically, VIA specifies a communication architecture extending the basic U-Net interface with remote DMA (RDMA) services. It is oriented to SANs intended as high bandwidth, low latency, very low error rate, scalable, and highly available interconnects. The VIA specification requires error detection as a feature of communication services. Protected multiplexing among user processes is also explicitly required and recommended to be operated by the NIC itself for best performance. However, reliability of communications is not mandatory, although it is explicitly recognized as a plus; this means that VIA is also suitable for unreliable media, at least in principle.

The VIA promoters expect NIC designers and vendors to develop network adapters supporting VIA mechanisms in hardware. However, no VIA adapter seems to be available in the marketplace at the time of writing (that is, about one year after releasing the VIA 1.0 specification). Of course, emulating VIA at the level of the OS kernel would provide much less impressive improvement in communication performance. Nevertheless, an implementation of kernel-emulated VIA for Linux, called M-VIA [1], is in progress. Only the unreliable delivery service has been implemented yet. Both Fast Ethernet and Gigabit Ethernet NICs are supported. Performance figures on Fast Ethernet are very good (one-way latency is 23 μs and asymptotic bandwidth is 11.9 MByte/s on a cluster of Pentium II 400 MHz PCs), but the presented API is very low-level, as with U-Net.

10.7 A Comparison Among Message Passing Systems

Table 10.1 reports a latency-bandwidth characterization of messaging systems running on a number of NOW prototypes, including the standard TCP/IP stack implemented in Linux. A few communication layers running on commercial MPPs

Table 10.1 "Ping-Pong" Comparison of Message Passing Systems

Platform	Latency (μs)	Max. throughput (MByte/s)
Linux 2.0.29 TCP/IP sockets, half-duplex		
(3COM 3c595 100base-T, Pentium 133 MHz CPU-driven DMA)	113.8	6.6
(3COM 3c905 100base-T, Pentium II 300 MHz DBDMA)	77.4	10.8
Fast Sockets (Myrinet,UltraSPARC)	57.8	32.9
PARMA^2 sockets (3COM 3c595 100base-T, Pentium 133 MHz)	74.0	6.6
GAMMA [4] (3COM 3c905 100base-T, Pentium 133 MHz)	12.7	12.2
Net* (raw) (100base-T) [15]	23.3	12.2
Oxford BSP Clusters (100base-T) [5]	29.0	11.7
U-Net/FE (DEC DC21140 100base-T) [20]	30.0	12.1
M-VIA (DEC DC21140 100base-T) [1]	33.0	11.9
BIP (Myrinet,PPro) [13]	4.3	126.0
HPAM (FDDI) [12]	14.5	12.0
FM2.x (Myrinet,PPro) [10]	11.0	77.0
U-Net/ATM (FORE PCA-200 ATM) [20]	44.5	15.0
CM-5 CMAML ports	10 - 15	8.5
SP2 MPL [11, Table 2]	44.8	34.9
T3D PVMFAST [11, Table2]	30.0	25.1

are reported as well, in order to provide a rough comparison with more traditional expensive parallel computers. The table is divided into four sections, respectively, for industry-standard API, kernel-level systems, user-level systems, and traditional MPP messaging systems. It must be noted that the hardware platforms where measurements have been taken are often uncomparable with one another as for network devices and/or CPU speed. Especially for latency comparisons, measurements taken with CPUs of different speeds may lead to wrong conclusions. Also bandwidth comparisons may be misleading due to the different measurement techniques adopted: One-sided measurements give better numbers than end-to-end ones as they usually do not capture the effects of the protocol overhead at the receiver side.

10.7.1 Clusters Versus MPPs

The best performing messaging systems for NOWs and clusters appear to be competitive with respect to MPPs, although comparing nonstandard, low-level NOW programming interfaces with higher-level, standard message passing on MPPs is not completely fair. Of course NOW platforms cannot compete with MPPs for asymptotic and bisection bandwidth; and they lack one of the main MPP features, namely, scalability with respect to the number of processors. On the other hand, the current cost of the scalability characteristics of an MPP is hardly justified by a large number of applications where parallel processing would in principle make sense. Indeed, most of the MPP installations are "small" machines, equipped with only tenths of processors and thus exploiting only a limited fraction of their scalability characteristics. A "small" MPP configuration is clearly outperformed in terms of price/performance and even absolute performance by an efficient cluster.

10.7.2 Standard Interface Approach Versus Other Approaches

It is apparent from Table 10.1 that the standard interface architectural approach delivers quite a poor exploitation of the interconnection hardware. This is evident with low-cost 100base-T (PARMA^2, Linux TCP/IP sockets), as well as a much more expensive and performing interconnect like Myrinet (Fast Sockets). This seems to be the price to pay for retaining low-level industry-standard programming interfaces, which hamper many possible optimizations because of a bad match with the underlying LAN hardware.

10.7.3 User-Level Versus Kernel-Level

It is apparent that the user-level approach has been successfully adopted only with higher performance interconnects (Myrinet, FDDI, ATM). This is probably due to two reasons. First, higher-end network devices have onboard programmable processors that can run multiplexing/protection code. Second, a traditional OS kernel mediation between user processes and network hardware becomes a communication bottleneck only with fast LAN hardware. However, it could be argued that, in principle, user-level access to network devices should not be of primary concern for communication performance, given the loose integration allowed between high-speed commodity NICs and the host memory hierarchy. Porting efficient kernel-level communication systems on high-end LAN interconnects would provide more insight about the actual impact of kernel-mediated message multiplexing on communication performance with fast networks. To the best of our knowledge, no research project is currently engaged in such a task.

From the reported performance numbers it is clear that user-level systems range from very efficient (BIP) to quite poor (FM). The choice of a workstation equipped with a slow I/O bus (like the SUN SBus used in early prototypes of FM) is really a bad one in this respect. More and more NOW projects, although using high-speed interconnects, are leveraging high-end PCs instead of workstations due to unbeatable price/performance and sufficiently good capabilities of the PCI bus.

Kernel-level messaging systems exclusively run on low-cost commodity interconnected NOWs. This kind of platform, leveraging high-end PCs and Fast Ethernet LAN, is a low-cost alternative to fast NOWs, offering event better price/performance figures. The poorer network performance of low-cost interconnects poses harder efficiency challenges to the implementors of messaging systems. This could in principle induce implementors to follow the user-level approach. Nevertheless, no plain user-level messaging architecture (either with unprotected device multiplexing or no multiplexing at all) has been implemented on low-cost clusters so far. GAMMA shows that excellent results on low-cost clusters can be obtained even with the mediation of the OS kernel and even with a fairly high-level and flexible programming interface, provided that communication protocol and device multiplexing be carefully developed according to a performance-oriented approach.

10.8 Bibliography

[1] M-VIA Home Page. `http://www.nersc.gov/research/FTG/via/`, 1998.

[2] Virtual Interface Architecture Home Page. `http://www.viarch.org/`, 1998.

[3] G. Chiola and G. Ciaccio. GAMMA home page. `http://www.disi.unige.it/project/gamma/`

[4] G. Ciaccio. Optimal Communication Performance on Fast Ethernet with GAMMA. In *Proc. Workshop PC-NOW, IPPS/SPDP'98*, LNCS No.1388, Springer, pages 534–548, Orlando, FL, April 1998.

[5] S. Donaldson, J. M. D. Hill, and D. B. Skillicorn. BSP Clusters: High Performance, Reliable and Very Low Cost. *Tech. Rep. PRG-TR-5-98*, Oxford University Computing Laboratory, Programming Research Group, 1998.

[6] P. Druschel and L. Peterson. Fbufs: A High-Bandwidth Cross-Domain Transfer Facility. In *Proc. 14th ACM SOSP*, December 1993.

[7] D. Engler, M. Kaashoek, and J. O'Toole. Exokernel, an Operating System Architecture for Application-level Resorce Management. In *Proc. 15th ACM SOSP*, December 1995.

[8] C. Reschke et al. A Design Study of Alternative Topologies for the Beowulf Parallel Workstation. In *Proc. 5th IEEE Int'l Symp. HPDC*, August 1996.

[9] M. Lauria and A. Chien. MPI-FM: High Performance MPI on Workstation Clusters. *J. of Parallel and Distributed Computing*, vol. 40 no.1, pages 4–18, January 1997.

[10] M. Lauria, S. Pakin, and A. Chien. Efficient Layering for High Speed Communication: Fast Messages 2.x. In *Proc. 7th IEEE Int'l Symp. HPDC-7*, Chigago, IL, July 1998.

[11] P. Marenzoni, G. Rimassa, M. Vignali, M. Bertozzi, G. Conte, and P. Rossi. An Operating System Support to Low-Overhead Communications in NOW Clusters. In *Proc. of the 1st Int'l CANPC*, LNCS No.1199, Springer, pages 130–143, February 1997.

[12] R. P. Martin. HPAM: An Active Message layer for a Network of HP Workstations. In *Proc. of Hot Interconnect II*, August 1994.

[13] L. Prylli and B. Tourancheau. BIP: a New Protocol Designed for High Performance Networking on Myrinet. In *Proc. Workshop PC-NOW, IPPS/SPDP'98*, LNCS No.1388, Springer, pp. 472–485, Orlando, FL, April 1998.

[14] S. Rodrigues, T. Anderson, and D. Culler. High Performance Local-area Communication Using Fast Sockets. In *Proc. USENIX'97*, 1997.

[15] R. D. Russel and P. J. Hatcher. Efficient Kernel Support for Reliable Communication. In *Proc. 1998 ACM Symp. on Applied Computing*, Atlanta, GA, February 1998.

[16] T. Sterling, D.J. Becker, D. Savarese, J.E. Dorband, U.A. Ranawake, and C.V. Packer. BEOWULF: A Parallel Workstation for Scientific Computation. In *Proc. 24th Int'l Conf. on Parallel Processing*, Oconomowoc, WI, August 1995.

[17] The BIP Team. MPI-BIP: An Implementation of MPI over Myrinet. `http://lhpca.univ-lyon1.fr/mpibip.html`

[18] T. von Eicken, A. Basu, V. Buch, and W. Vogels. U-Net: A User-Level Network Interface for Parallel and Distributed Computing. In *Proc. 15th ACM SOSP*, Copper Mountain, CO, December 1995.

[19] T. von Eicken, D.E. Culler, S.C. Goldstein, and K.E. Schauser. Active Messages: A Mechanism for Integrated Communication and Computation. In *Proc. ISCA'92*, Gold Coast, Australia, May 1992.

[20] M. Welsh, A. Basu, and T. von Eicken. Low-latency Communication over Fast Ethernet. In *Proc. Euro-Par'96*, Lyon, France, August 1996.

Chapter 11

Active Messages[1]

NITIN PARAB AND M RAGHVENDRAN

Centre for Development of Advanced Computing
Bangalore, India

Email: {*nitin, mraghu*}*@cdacb.ernet.in*

11.1 Introduction

Active Messages (AM) is one of several lightweight protocols used in the specialized MPPs to couple the computing nodes (to leverage the coupling at the hardware level) so that computation can be done concurrently without incurring too much cost in communication for synchronization. AM is a popular interface because it reflects the basic network device abstraction whose flexibility enables a large number of programming models to run efficiently. Early work on AM on MPPs helped express the underlying philosophy of AM as a versatile set of primitives. With the networking technology of MPPs moving to SANs, the glue of clusters, lightweight protocols also moved into the realm of clusters. Implementation of AM on clusters not only brought out the issues involved in implementing high performance protocols, it also helped understand and characterize network interfaces [6], the impact of system architecture and network architecture [9], and helped analyze the support the system needs to give for a seamless integration of communication architecture with the host and the cluster architecture. Generic Active Messages (GAM) [5] was the first popular AM implementation on a cluster which demonstrated the capabilities of AM and also motivated an AM interface that could integrate general purpose computing requirements into the philosophy of AM. AM-II was proposed [8] as the new communication abstraction for the cluster with support for protected multiprogramming, MIMD style applications, and enable scalability. The big plus with AM-II interface was its smooth integration with the host-programming en-

[1]Active Message model and its implementation discussed in this chapter is heavily based on papers published by NOW team at the University of California Berkeley, the original developers.

vironment and the ability to map into the various host platforms and networks. AM-II interface will be from here on referred to as AM interface.

This chapter discusses the issue of communication abstraction which would seamlessly meet the programming needs of the cluster. This chapter identifies some of the motivating factors that make this issue one to be discussed in detail and lays down the requirements of lightweight protocols and cluster communication substrate. It discusses the Active Message programming model and implementation by University of California Berkeley and Centre for Development of Advanced Computing. It argues that Active Messages meets most of the requirements.

11.2 Requirements

The emerging clusters are being put to use in various applications like scientific computing, web servers, and databases that traditionally have been using different communication abstractions to communicate among the processors. At the same time a wide variety of NICs and SANs have been developed for integrating independent workstations into clusters. It could be said that the main issue is to decide the features and functionality a communication architecture should provide so that a varied number of abstractions could be supported (*top-down* requirement) on a variety of NICs and SANs (*bottom-up* requirement). The applications should be able to exploit the low latency and high bandwidth nature of the emerging high-speed networks. Apart from this approach towards the design of the communication abstraction, there are other requirements from the general purpose computing viewpoint to support features such as multiprogramming and scalability that concern the cluster as a whole.

11.2.1 Top-down Requirement

Each class of cluster application has its own requirement of communication abstraction that would suit its need. These applications expect a wide range of programming models like MPI, DSM (Distributed Shared Memory), DFS (Distributed File Systems), Distributed Object sharing, etc. This means that a variety of communication interfaces are desired with the common requirement being that the application should be able to exploit the hardware capabilities of the network, namely, low latency and high throughput. The communication architecture should thus export a low level communication substrate that would be generic enough to support efficient implementations of a variety of programming models.

It has been observed that the semantic gaps between the different software communication layers [17] contribute to substantial loss. The loss could be in terms of the computation needed to cross the semantic barrier or the multiple data copies required, making inefficient use of the resources. The design of the communication interface has often been influenced by the tendency to hide too many aspects and expose a simple generic interface that tends to solve general cases of a particular application class more effectively. Certain aspects of the application, like buffer management and flow control related to the communication over which the application has a better knowledge base, go wasted as the abstractions do not provide an effective interface to exploit them. An abstraction should then refrain from making too many guarantees and thus expose an overly simple, narrow and rigid abstraction that increases the chances of inducing semantic gaps. It should take care of providing just the right services and leave out the complex functionality to the upper layers if the upper levels of software have greater control and knowledge base over the implementation of the functionality at that level. Research indicates that exposing the communication architectures to runtime software can greatly improve the performance of parallel languages [4]. The communication abstraction should thus provide a common minimal interface so that abstraction could efficiently support common cases in the multiple application classes.

11.2.2 Bottom-up Requirement

Wide varieties of NICs are available that interface with the host at different levels of system hierarchy (memory bus or I/O peripheral bus) and typically exhibit different capabilities [10]. Systems also vary on the level of integration of the network interface with the rest of the system. Some of the NICs have full access to the main memory by virtue of its location (memory bus) or through system architecture support, while others have restricted access through DMA mechanisms. Still others exhibit no such features. The host processor does the data movement by generating either cycles on the memory bus or the I/O bus. Some NICs come with 'intelligence' in the form of an onboard processor so that some protocol processing could be offloaded onto the NIC itself and the host processor could fetch the message without much cost. These NICs have an added advantage: the NIC's personality could be modified to performance optimize the interface abstraction to suit the needs of the upper layers.

NICs provide the message arrival notification mechanism either through a status register update or by interrupting the host processor. Depending on the system architecture, the cost associated with each mechanism could vary. Some of the NICs provide support for multicasting and could effectively be mapped into a higher-level multicasting requirement. Some abstractions export the intelligence on the NIC by allowing some of the application code itself to be executed in the NIC [11]. The location of the NIC in the system could be exploited to improve the communication performance or give added functionality to the NIC. By exposing such features to the upper layers through the communication abstraction, the redundant computation could be avoided. For example, a NIC on a cache coherent bus removes the need to flush the I/O buffers and caches for each DMA transfer. Some such systems are able to support high level abstraction completely and efficiently [2].

So, from the NIC's point of view, the communication abstraction should not only expose the capabilities of the NIC to the upper layers but also map the hardware features efficiently into a flexible and versatile set of primitives that could support a wide range of protocols, high-level programming abstractions, or runtime environments. This implies that the communication abstraction should not export a functionality which is specific to a hardware feature, yet it should be versatile enough to efficiently use the feature if present.

11.2.3 Architecture and Implementation

Clusters are generally formed out of off-the-shelf components like PCs, workstations, and SMPs (CLUMPS) typically running multiuser operating systems that are utilized for different purposes. For effective utilization of system resources and leverage on the multiprocessing technologies, therefore, the communication abstraction should support protected multiprogramming. The API should not hinder scalability of the communication subsystems built on the communication abstraction with respect to the number of nodes in the cluster or the number of users, as the actual realization of scalable systems depends on the implementation techniques, system architecture support, and resources available in the different components that make up the communication subsystem.

The evolution of system and the bus technologies have made memory-based access semantics of the network interface quite possible. Traditional protocols treated network access like that of disk access. However, LWPs have helped express the network I/O with memory-based semantics. Further research has enabled the network interface to be integrated with the virtual memory architecture leveraging on the virtual memory hardware [3]. A related issue is that of scalability. Virtualization of network interface lends itself to supporting more users and applications and results in an effective utilization of system resources. The various other viewpoints to scalability are in terms of supporting multiple processors (though the architectural system facets like bus design play an equally important role), supporting multiple cards, and the ability to support a huge cluster with a large number of nodes.

The issue of scalability is affected by the following factors:

- Whether the communication abstraction itself allows scalability (by allowing multiple communication objects) or enables it (by allowing overlapping of communication and computation). The protocol guarantees (like connection-oriented or connectionless, ordered delivery) also affect the scalability by the complexity and the cost incurred by both the applications and the communication subsystem to implement or overcome a particular feature when the number of nodes increase.

- The cost incurred by the software architecture. Previous chapters have discussed a communication cost characterization model–Logp [6]. This characterization quantifies the overhead involved in the software architecture and raises the issues of layering (how much the software layers should be collapsed), data copies involved in the common case, network access mechanism, and protocol offloading at different levels that would determine the throughput of the messages through the host connected to the cluster. The implementation strategies for packet organization, flow control, reliability, and virtualization directly affect the performance and scalability of the cluster.

- Various aspects of the network like the switching mechanism (cut-through or store and forward), switch latency, routing mechanism, and link speed also play important roles in determining the scalability of the communication subsystem. These aspects should be very efficient because raw network performance places an upper bound on the performance that could be extracted from the machine.

11.2.4 Summary

The requirements of a high performance communication architecture are summarized below.

1. *Performance* The communication architecture should allow the application leverage faster processors and high speed networks.

2. *Scalability* The communication architecture should export a scalable interface and performance should not degrade with increasing nodes, radius of network, number of applications, etc.

3. *Efficiency* The communication architecture should utilize system resources efficiently and should be able to transparently optimize its implementations on special hardware.

4. *Versatility* The interface of the communication abstraction should not be tied to any particular system or network facet. It should be versatile enough to be easily implemented on a variety of systems. The interface should be generic and simple enough to support a wide range of application classes without any performance penalty.

5. *Multiprogramming and Multithreading Support* With the cluster of SMPs emerging as powerful computing platforms, the communication architectures should provide multiprogramming to enable applications to utilize the processors and multithreading to utilize the SMP paradigm.

6. *Multiple Device Support* The communication architecture should be able to accommodate multiple communication devices so that it unifies the communication across multiple devices. However, the AM implementation should optimize the primitives specific to the device.

7. *Network Management* The communication architecture should ingrain the concept of network management to provide a robust framework and incorporate the changes in the network topology and routes on the fly.

11.3 AM Programming Model

Active Messages provides an RPC styled request reply programming model. The basic communication port is called an endpoint. Applications can exchange two types of point-to-point messages: requests and replies. Associated with each message is a handler function which, upon arrival of the message, is executed on the receiving processor. Active messages differ from general RPC mechanisms in that the role of the active message handler is not to perform computation on the data, but to extract the data from the network and integrate it into the ongoing computation with a small amount of work. Thus, concurrent communication and computation is fundamental to the message layer. Active messages are not buffered except those required for network transport. Only primitive scheduling is provided: handlers interrupt the computation immediately upon message arrival and execute to completion. (See Figure 11.1)

A group of communication endpoints form a virtual network with unique protection domain. Traffic in one virtual network is never visible to a second virtual network, yet each virtual network retains direct user level network access necessary for high performance. When distinct virtual networks share the same physical resources, each continues to perceive private resources, albeit with potentially reduced performance. This communication multiplexing is critical to high performance message passing with CLUMPS, since many processes are expected to be communicating at once. Any two endpoints within a virtual network can communicate. This means that active messages can cross traditional protection domains and boundaries; it is no longer restricted to use among the members of individual user-level parallel process. Two examples show the interface's flexibility: a kernel filesystem endpoint can communicate with a user-level client endpoint, and an endpoint in sequential process can communicate with an endpoint in parallel process.

11.3.1 Endpoints and Bundles

An endpoint is the basic communication port exported by active messages. As shown in Figure 11.2, an endpoint has a send pool, receive pool, handler table, virtual memory segment, translation table, and a tag. The `AM_AllocateEndpoint()` returns an endpoint structure and the endpoint name. All endpoints have globally unique names within a system. Applications use the translation table to map small, integer indices to arbitrary endpoint names and tags in the system. Thus, using the `AM_Map()`, applications can have compact local names for remote endpoints. Applications can dynamically add and remove translation table mappings. An application can register a handler at a particular index by calling `AM_SetHandler()`. An endpoint tag is a 64-bit integer and can be set using `AM_SetTag()`. There are two special values for tags: a *never-match*, which, as the name suggests, never matches any tag, and a *wild card*, which matches all tags except the never-match one. An endpoint can send an active message to another endpoint if and only if the tag in the sender's translation table entry for that destination endpoint matches the

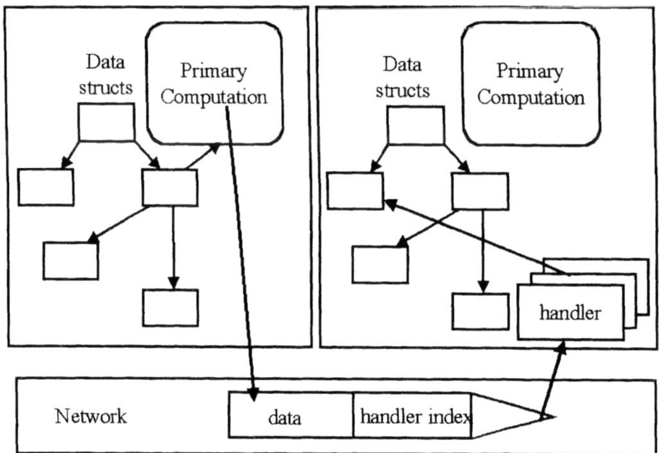

Figure 11.1 Active message communication model.

destination endpoint's tag at the time the message is delivered, or if the destination endpoint's tag is a wild card (a special value that matches all tags).

The management of an endpoint's translation table is local. However, multiple applications can coordinate and manage their translations to produce a convenient virtual network. For example, a SPMD parallel library or the system functions that initiate parallel programs can arrange that index i from every endpoint uniformly names *virtual processor i*. Managing translation tables and virtual networks require the application programs to exchange endpoint names and tags. The method of obtaining endpoint names and tags of remote endpoints is left open by the AM interface specification. Tags can be set to any value and, hence, applications can arrive at strategies of exchanging tags. However, endpoint names are dynamically allocated by the system, unlike in socket ports an application cannot request for a specific endpoint name and require a separate endpoint namespace management system.

An endpoint bundle is a set of endpoints created by one process (see Figure 11.3). These endpoints are treated as a single unit of communication, event management, and synchronization. Any process can create multiple endpoints and gather related ones into endpoint bundles and succinctly perform operations on the bundles. Each bundle has a unique event mask and synchronization variable, which is a binary semaphore. The bundle is the scope of the synchronization variable and the event mask. The endpoints in a bundle share common event mask and the synchronization variable. An application can set an event using `AM_SetEventMask()` and block for an event using `AM_Wait()`. Whenever the event is generated, the system auto-

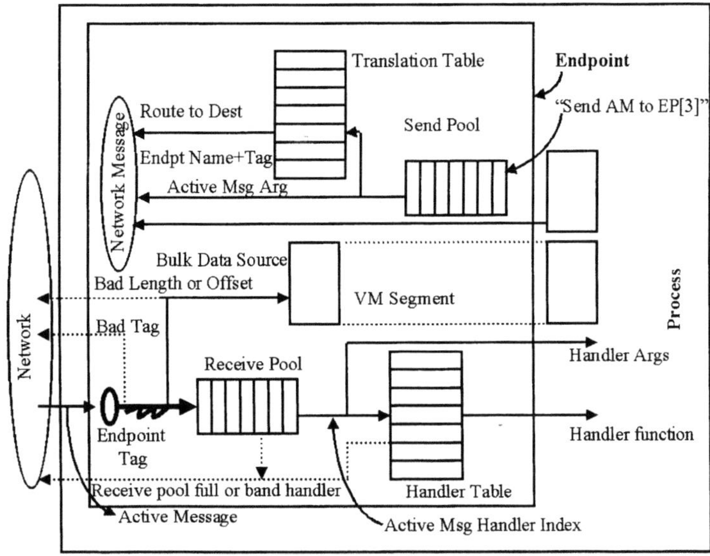

Figure 11.2 Anatomy of an endpoint. *Reproduced from [8] with permission.*

matically sets the bundle's binary semaphore to one and clears the corresponding event mask bit. If there are any threads blocked on the semaphore, one is unblocked. The identity of the endpoint producing an event is unavailable. The motivation of multiple endpoints is to avoid undesirable interactions that arise when independent software packages use a single shared port. The motivation for creating endpoint bundles is to support the need of single-threaded programs so that these can perform operations on aggregates of endpoints.

11.3.2 Transport Operations

The interface supports small messages, medium messages, and large memory-to-memory bulk transfers. An active message is sent from the source endpoint send pool to the receive endpoint receive pool. It carries an index into the handler table that selects the handler function for that message. Small messages can be sent using `AM_RequestM()`, which carries M integers as payload. Upon receipt of a message, the handler specified by the handler index in the message is invoked with the M integers as arguments to the function. The bulk data transfer functions copy memory from a sender's virtual address space to the receiving endpoint's receive pool (`AM_RequestIM()`, `AM_ReplyIM()`) or virtual memory segment (`AM_RequestXferM()`, `AM_ReplyXferM()`). The functions `AM_MaxMedium()` and `AM_MaxLong()` return the maximum transfer sizes for medium and bulk transfers, respectively.

The send operations implicitly poll the network for received messages. The application can explicitly poll for messages on a bundle using the `AM_Poll()` func-

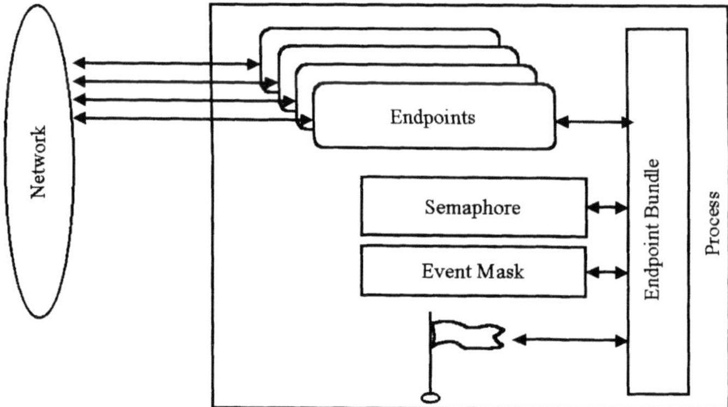

Figure 11.3 Anatomy of an endpoint bundle. *Reproduced from [8] with permission.*

tion. Request handlers reply exactly once to the source endpoint; it's an error to do otherwise. Reply handler should not send any message nor should it call any function that directly or indirectly polls the network. The system passes an opaque token as an argument to the request and reply handler functions. A token is an opaque pointer to data that identifies the source endpoint whose message caused the handler's invocation and the destination endpoint that handled the message. `AM_GetSourceEndpoint()` translates the token into the globally-unique endpoint name of the sending endpoint. `AM_GetDestinationEndpoint()` translates the token into the globally-unique endpoint name of the sending endpoint. `AM_GetMsgTag()` retrives the message tag from a token. Multiple threads may concurrently send requests and replies from an endpoint in a shared bundle. This allows multiple threads to poll concurrently a shared bundle and to handle individual incoming messages in parallel.

11.3.3 Error Model

An Active Message is considered to be sent when the source storage can be reused and a message is considered received when its handler function is invoked in the receiving process. The system delivers all messages exactly once, barring persistent error conditions. If such conditions occur, then the system may deem some messages to be undeliverable to their destinations and return the same to their senders. Requests are returned to the requesting endpoint, replies are returned to the replying endpoint; active messages are never dropped silently. Returned messages are received by the endpoints that sent them and are treated like ordinary active messages. By convention, the first entry in every handler table, denoted as handler0, is the undeliverable message handler, which notifies applications of undeliverable messages. Applications can register functions for handler0 that are tailored for their individual protocol requirements. The handler0 prototype is: *void handler(int status, opt_t opcode, void *argblock).* The status value describes why a message was undeliverable. The opcode argument identifies the type of the returned message, as well as the operation used to send it. For the request functions, the argblock points to a structure containing the original arguments to a request function. For the reply functions, the argblock points to a structure containing the token and the original arguments to a reply function.

11.3.4 Programming Examples

This section illustrates an implementation of a simple send-receive messaging protocol. These examples will highlight the features of AM and depict how AM enables the overlapping of communication and computation in the application.

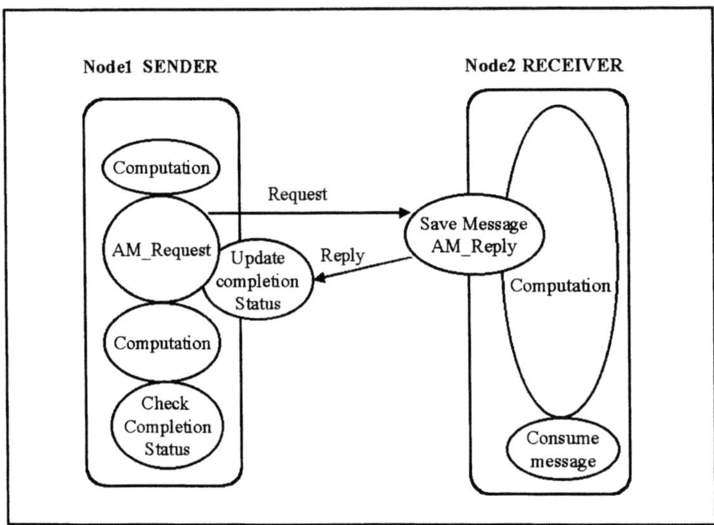

Figure 11.4 Conceptual depiction of send-receive protocol for small messages.

In Figures 11.4 and 11.5, the bubbles inside the shaded rectangular portion indicate the events that happen as a part of normal control flow of the program. The bubbles on the boundary of the shaded portion indicate the events that occur *concurrently* with the normal program control flow. In the above figures these bubbles indicate the AM handlers that essentially execute concurrent to the normal

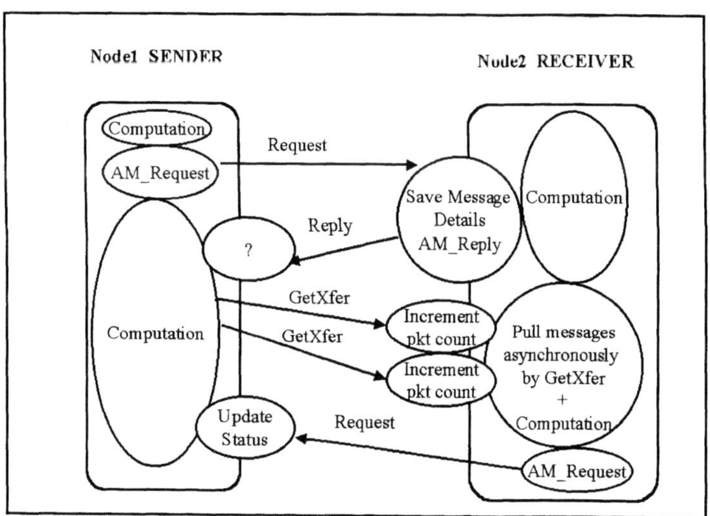

Figure 11.5 Conceptual depiction of send-receive protocol for large messages.

computation. In the small message protocol, as depicted in Figure 11.4, the sender just sends the message and continues with its computation; at the receiver side the message gets integrated to the application concurrently, as specified in the AM handler. This could either store the message for later consumption or perform some processing. This overlap of communication and computation enables high throughput for small messages. So also, this protocol, by making copies carefully, helps tolerate the skew in the communication which would affect the performance of the small messages the most. This protocol would perform the best for small messages.

On the other hand, Figure 11.5 depicts a typical protocol that would be used for a large message transfer and that would enable a zero-copy message transfer at the same time allowing for an overlap of communication and computation. Here, the sender sends a descriptor describing the send buffer and proceeds on computation. The handler on the receive side, which runs asynchronously to the main computation, saves the descriptor into a pending receive queue. The receiver, on reaching the recieve call, reads the descriptor and pulls the messages from the sender buffer. Ideally, during the pull, the remote (sender) processor would not be disturbed and the entire communication would be handled by the NIC (complete implementation requires system and NIC support as discussed in Section 11.7.6). The asynchronous nature of the GetXfer call also enables the computation on the receiver to proceed. This protocol is motivated by the observations that for large messages, transferring the messages on-the-fly is beneficial in reducing the buffer management and the cache pollution (during memory copies) on the receiver side. This also enables the computation to proceed at both ends while communication is occurring (assuming that I/O transfers do not go through processor cache).

11.4 AM Implementation

The Active Message System has four layers

1. an AM library that exports the programming interface to applications.
2. a virtual networks segment driver that abstracts network interfaces and communication resources.
3. firmware executing in the embedded processor on the NIC that does the protocol processing.
4. processor and interconnection hardware.

In this section we discuss the implementation of AM on Myrinet and Solaris 2.x operating system by the NOW team at the University of California at Berkeley and further enhancements to it at C-DAC.

The Lanai processor on the NIC processes the network protocol. The shared memory protocol is processed on the host using the *System V* shared memory system. Each endpoint structure thus resides on the NIC memory and the host memory. The "endpoint frame" on the NIC memory is mapped onto the application address space providing the application direct access to the NIC. Mapping only the endpoint frame onto the application address space enforces protection. The AM library requests services from the Lanai processor using the endpoint queues. The AM transport operations write/read the headers of the messages directly from the NIC memory without driver intervention [3] (see Figure 11.6).

Only a limited number of endpoint frames can reside on the NIC memory. However, the virtual network driver allows the applications to create more numbers of endpoints than the NIC memory can accommodate. The virtual network management is similar to that of virtual memory management. The implementation uses the existing segment driver framework of the Solaris VM layer. The endpoint frames on the NIC memory are viewed as the page frames and the host memory acts as the backing store. The active endpoints, i.e., the ones that are communicating, are cached onto the NIC memory and the less active ones are swapped off on the host memory, much like the VM system does with the memory pages and frames.

The firmware, i.e., the Lanai control program (LCP) implements the network protocol that provides reliable and unduplicated message delivery between NICs. The firmware and the segment driver communicate and request services from each other through an always pinned endpoint called system endpoint. A kernel thread created by the driver at the initialization time services the requests by the NIC firmware to the driver. The NIC firmware queues a request in the system endpoint's queue and interrupts the driver. The interrupt handler wakes up the kernel thread to service the request.

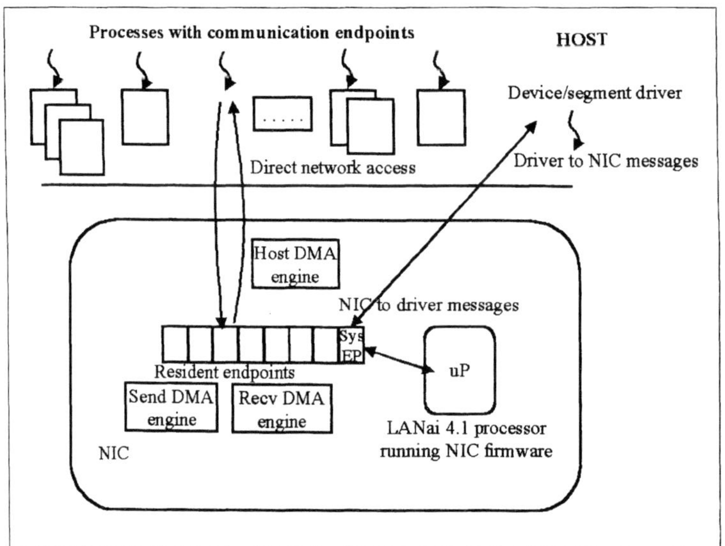

Figure 11.6 Processor NIC interaction (©1998 IEEE).

11.4.1 Endpoints and Bundles

The main components of an endpoint are the control block, shared memory queue block, network queue block, and the medium staging area (see Figure 11.2). The control block consists of such information as the translation table, handler table, tag, etc. The shared memory queue block is used for shared memory protocol (see Section 11.4.2). The network queue block resides on the NIC memory and the medium staging area is kernel memory (DMAble). These areas are added to the application address space as segments through the virtual network segment driver.

The AM system treats requests and replies as independent operations and has separate queues for each. The network queue resides in the NIC memory (resident endpoint) or host memory (nonresident endpoint). It consists of a send pool and receive pool. Each message pool has 16 descriptors. The descriptors hold all the information required by the firmware to correctly deliver the message. In the case of send pool (request/reply), because the host is a producer, it maintains the tail offset. The NIC firmware, being the consumer, maintains the head offset. In the receive pool the NIC firmware maintains the tail offset and the host maintains the head offset. Short messages use only one descriptor. Medium messages use a descriptor and an intermediate medium staging area (MSA) for the data.

The shared memory queue block is shown in Figure 11.8. It is placed in a *System V* shared memory segment to allow access by multiple processes within the SMP. It consists of only receive queues and no send queues. This is because, unlike in the network protocol, the shared memory transfer writes directly onto the

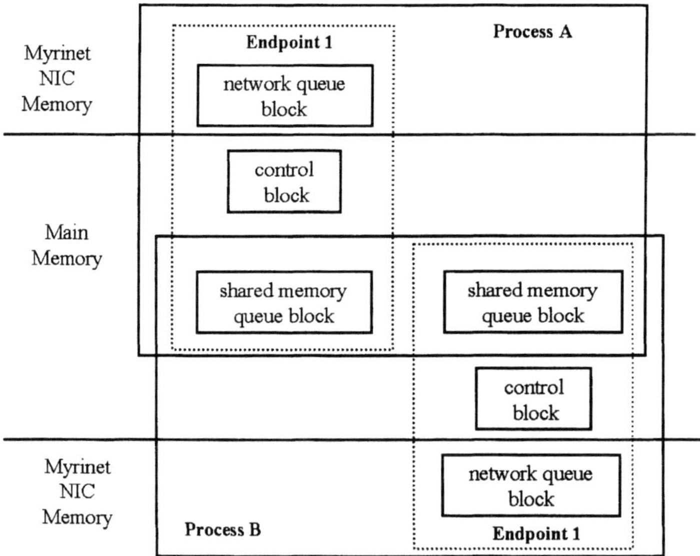

Figure 11.7 Endpoint data layout. *Reproduced from [7] ©1997 Association for Computing Machinery, Inc. Reprinted by permission.*

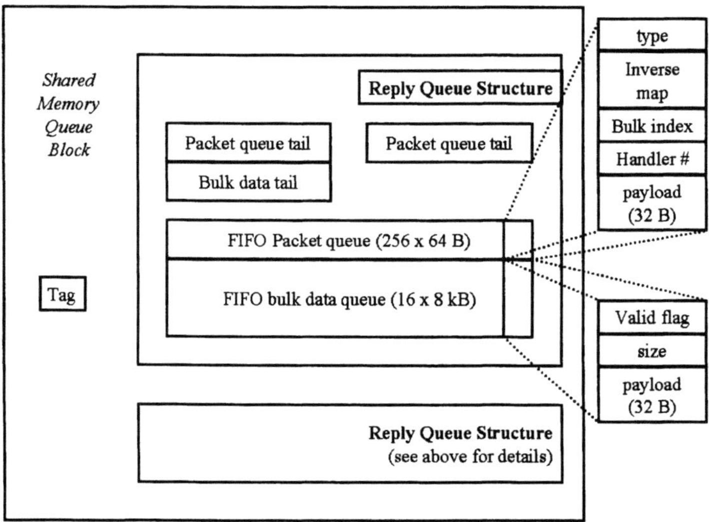

Figure 11.8 Shared memory queue block. *Reproduced from [7] ©1997 Association for Computing Machinery, Inc. Reprinted by permission.*

receive queue of the recipient through shared memory mappings (see Figure 11.7). A copy of the endpoint tag is used for access control, while two queue structures hold request and reply messages received by the endpoint. Each queue structure is further divided into three sections: queue tail information, accessed only by senders; queue head information, accessed only by recipients; and two FIFO data queues, accessed by both senders and recipients. The queues are the packet queue, containing the handler index and arguments, and the bulk data queue, holding data for bulk data transfers. Short messages use only the packet queue, while bulk data transfers use both queues.

AM is configured such that each NIC in the network is given a unique identifying number called *nic_number*. The NIC firmware maintains routes from itself to every other destination NIC in the network. In the network protocol, *nic number* and *endpoint number* within that NIC can uniquely address any endpoint. In addition to that, for the shared memory protocol, the source needs to map the receive pool of the destination endpoint and thus requires the shared memory key of that receive pool (see Section 11.4.2). Thus, given a Myrinet SAN, any endpoint within the cluster can be uniquely identified by the triplet *nic number, endpoint number, and shared memory key* which forms the endpoint name structure `en_t`.

11.4.2 Transport Operations

When sending a message, the AM layer first decides whether to use shared memory protocol or a network protocol. This is done by a simple comparison between the *nic_number* of the source endpoint and the destination endpoint names. Messages are received by polling at the receive pools. Network messages are queued onto the network send descriptor queue. The short messages, including the payload, fit entirely onto the packet descriptor in the network send queue. Thus, short messages are sent using programmed I/O only. In the case of medium messages and bulk messages, the library fills a descriptor in the network send queue and copies the data from the user buffer onto the medium staging area. The NIC uses DMA to fetch the data onto the NIC memory. The NIC firmware then sends the messages onto the network. On receiving a message, the NIC firmware fills the appropriate receive descriptor. In the case of medium messages, the NIC transfers the data in the receive MSA. (The firmware is discussed in more detail in Section 11.4.3.) The messages are received by polling at the head offset of the receive pool (request/reply). If the receive descriptor at the head offset contains a message, then the handler indicated by the descriptor is invoked. In the case of medium messages, the pointer to the received buffer in the MSA is passed as an argument to the handler. However, in the case of *Xfer* messages, the buffer is copied onto the indicated offset in the VM segment. The descriptor is freed after the completion of the handler.

The shared memory protocol directly deposits the message in the receiver's message receive queue (unlike in the network protocol, where the message is transferred from one address space to another across the network by the NICs). The shared memory protocol uses the System V IPC layer. The shared memory receive queue

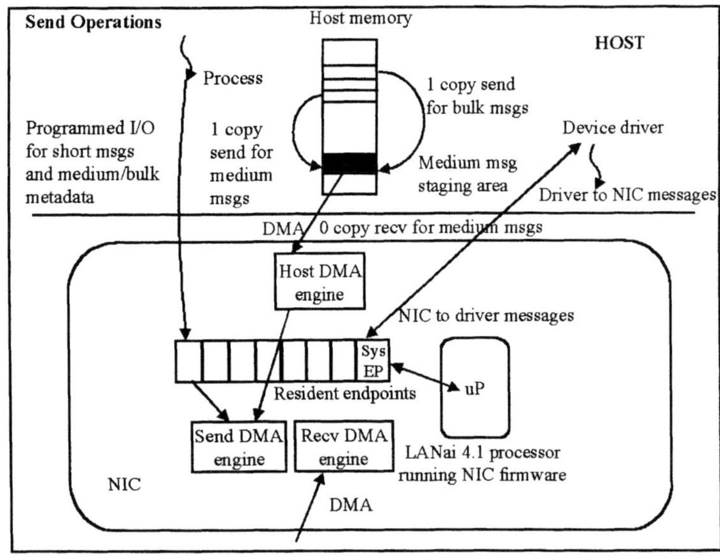

Figure 11.9 Network send (©1998 IEEE).

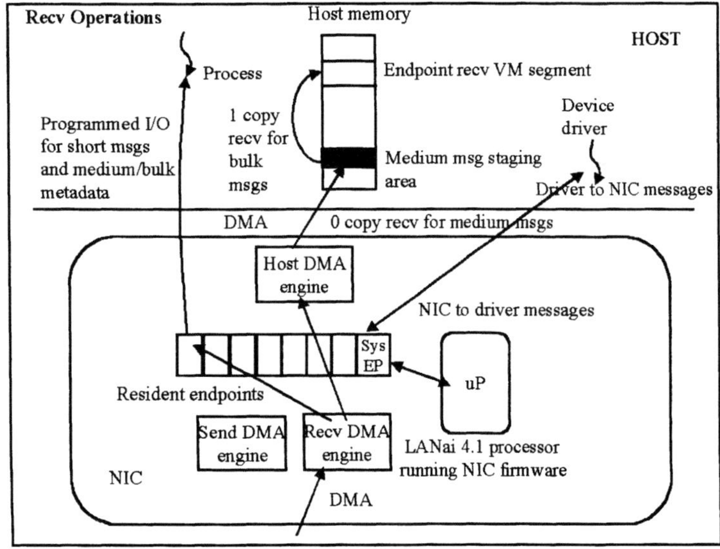

Figure 11.10 Network receive (©1998 IEEE).

block (see Section 11.4.1 and Figure 11.8) is actually a System V shared memory segment. The sender process maps the receive queue block of the destination endpoint onto its address space during the AM_Map call. The shared memory segment identifier required for mapping (or attaching to the shared memory segment) is made known to the sender process through the endpoint name (see Section 11.4.1). The inverse mapping (receiver mapping the sender's receive queue) is performed at the same time to guarantee that reply messages also travel through shared memory.

When sending a local message, the sender first checks for the tag in the destination queue block and returns any message that lacks access rights. After this check, the sender attempts to queue the message into the appropriate queue. To queue a short message, the sender first obtains a packet assignment by automatically incrementing the packet queue tail using the compare and swap (CAS) instruction, then claims the assigned packet by changing its type from **free** to **claimed**, again using CAS. If the claim fails, the queue is full, and the sender backs off exponentially and polls for messages to prevent possible deadlock. Once the claim succeeds, the sender writes the data onto the packets and completes the queue operation by changing the packet type to **ready**. For bulk data transfers, a sender claims a bulk data block before obtaining a packet assignment. After filling both packet and block, the sender marks the full packet with **ready-bulk**. When a message is available, the recipient advances the packet queue head and passes the arguments and, for bulk data transfers, the associated data block, to the appropriate handler routine. After the call returns, the packet is marked as **free** and the data block is marked invalid.

The AM specifications say that the send operations can also receive messages. This is implemented by introducing an implicit polling for messages in the send operations. The network queue resides in the NIC memory; hence, polling for network messages involves costly uncached reads across the system bus [3] (see Figures 11.9 and 11.10). The performance of the shared memory protocol can degrade due to network protocol polling. Performance impact is not from receiving messages from the NIC, but from the cost of checking for messages repeatedly when no messages are present. The empty packets in front of the shared memory queue are cache resident, whereas those of the network queue reside in uncacheable NIC memory. Thus, polling for network memory incurs an order of magnitude of extra cost. Obtaining high performance from multiprotocols for applications which have large shared memory communication or bursts of shared memory communication requires a sophisticated pooling strategy. The system should selectively avoid network polling depending on parameters like history, amount of shared memory and network communication, etc. Current implementation uses an adaptive polling strategy that adjusts polling rates dynamically in response to traffic pattern.

11.4.3 NIC Firmware

The firmware implements a protocol that provides reliable and unduplicated message delivery between NICs. The key issues in the design of LCP are: scheduling of outgoing traffic from a set of resident endpoints, NIC to NIC flow control mechanisms and policies, timer management to schedule and perform packet retransmissions, and detecting and recovering from errors [3]. One of the main responsibilities of the firmware is to schedule an endpoint frame for outgoing messages. The algorithm uses a weighted round-robin policy that focuses resources on active endpoints. Empty endpoints are skipped. For an endpoint with pending messages, the NIC makes 2^k attempts to send, for some parameter k (currently k=7). This holds even after the NIC empties a particular endpoint (it loiters should the host queue additional messages). Loitering also allows firmware to cache state, such as packet headers and constants, while sending messages from an endpoint, lowering per-packet overheads. The message transmission of both the requests and replies is the same except that they use different channels (see Section 11.4.4). Sending of a packet consists of three activities:

1. picking up the packet from the send pool and preprocessing the packet

2. starting the host to lanai DMA if required (medium / bulk messages)

3. starting the network DMA.

Each of these activities, though following a sequence, are quite independent of each other and are triggered by different events: scheduling of an endpoint frame; host DMA engine is free; and host DMA is completed and network send DMA engine is free, respectively.

The UCB implementation of the LCP processes only one packet at a time and receives messages while waiting for an event on the send processing. The only overlapping/parallelsm of activities it achieves this way is receiving messages while host DMA is busy. The same happens on the receive side. The LCP posts a buffer for receive and processes a previously received buffer. In the case of medium or bulk messages (where host DMA is required), it starts the DMA and shifts control to the sending of messages. The current algorithm does not exploit the possible pipelining/parallelism, which can be achieved within a send/receive operation.

The three activities in send (as mentioned earlier) can be pipelined. This requires that there should be a queue for each activity. The send pool is already a queue, we thus implemented a queue for host DMA engine and network DMA engines. The LCP now preprocesses a send packet and posts a host DMA (if required). Once the host DMA is done, the message is added to the network send queue. Similarly, the LCP has a queue of received messages. It picks up a received message, preprocesses it, and posts a host DMA (if required). Once the host DMA is done, the message is added to the receive pool. The outgoing messages thus move from host send queue (pool) to host DMA queue (medium / bulk messages only) and then to network send queue. The incoming messages move from network receive queue to host DMA queue (medium / bulk messages only) to host receive queue (pool). All these movements of messages from one queue to another are pipelined, and the processing of messages and the three DMA engines can run simultaneously. This implementation thus achieves near-optimal pipelining of the DMA transfers for successive outgoing packets.

11.4.4 Message Delivery and Flow Control

The NIC firmware maintains independent logical channels for each destination NIC. This is implemented by having a send table and a receive table. The row index in the send/receive table corresponds to the destination/source *nic number* and the column index corresponds to the channel. Each table entry thus formed maintains all the information of the packet sent to a particular destination (row index) on a particular channel (column index). This includes the sequence number, the pointer to the packet for potential retransmission, and the time the packet was sent. Each pair of source channel and destination channel maintains the sequence number of the next expected message. The packet is sent to the destination with sequence numbers from the send table. The firmware uses the stop and wait protocol, i.e., it sends a message on a channel and waits for a positive ACK before freeing the channel for another send on the same channel. On receiving a packet, the NIC matches the sequence number on the packet and the expected sequence number given in the appropriate receive table entry indexed with the sending NIC's id and channel on which the message was sent. If the sequencing information matches, the receiver sends an acknowledgment to the sender. On receiving an acknowledgment, the sender updates its sequencing information and frees the channel.

The system implements flow control at three levels:

1. user-level active message credits for each endpoints
2. NIC level stop and wait flow control over multiple independent logical channels
3. network back pressure

The user-level credits rely upon the request reply nature of the AM, allowing each endpoint to have at most n outstanding requests waiting for responses. The number of channels and requests credits (n) depends on the bandwidth delay product of bulk messages and short messages. Link-level back-pressure ensures that under heavy load, for example, all to one communication, the network does not drop packets. Credit based flow control in the library throttles individual senders but cannot prevent high contention for a common receiver. By also relying on link-level back-pressure, end-to-end flow control remains effective and its overheads remain small. Though this policy trades network utilization under heavy load for simplicity (by allowing packets to block and to consume link and switch resources), experience shows this hybrid scheme performs very well [3].

11.4.5 Events and Error handling

The NIC firmware ensures reliable delivery by a simple timeout and retransmission mechanism. Erroneous packets are simply dropped relying upon timeout and retransmissions. Sending a packet schedules a timer event, receiving an acknowledgment deletes the event, and all send table entries (i.e., all channels to all destinations) are periodically scanned for packets to retransmit. Timer event is scheduled by recording the time in the send table entry. On receiving the acknowledgment, the channel is freed and hence the timer event gets deleted. If no ACKs or NACKS are received for 255 retransmissions, the message is declared undeliverable (and the destination endpoint unreachable) and returned to the library. The application handles undeliverable messages as it would any other active message.

The driver and the NIC firmware coorporate to implement events. The NIC firmware maintains the event mask. The set and reset event mask requests are taken up by the driver (*ioctl()*) and given to the NIC firmware through the system endpoint request queue. When the application calls `AM_Wait()`, which in turn calls the driver *ioctl()*, the driver blocks on a condition. When the event takes place (i.e., a message arrives for an endpoint with an event mask as AM_NOTEMPTY), the NIC firmware interrupts the driver reporting the occurrence of the event. The kernel thread that picks up the NIC request sends a wake-up signal to the application thread that was blocked, since the driver call was waiting on the condition. In the case of shared memory messages, there is no third party (like the NIC in network protocol), to receive the events and interrupt the driver. Hence, the sender has to wake up the receiver. The receiver, before blocking into the driver, sets a flag in the shared memory queue block indicating that it is waiting on an event. When a sender tries to deposit a message onto the sleeping receiver's queue, it checks for the flag and wakes up the receiver. There are two ways the sender can wake up the receiver: by directly calling the driver *ioctl()* or by requesting the NIC to wake up. Since there is a copy of the event mask in the NIC, the sender uses the second method.

11.4.6 Virtual Networks

The segment driver also manages the endpoint (network queue) and the medium staging area (MSA) as its own segments. Though the MSA resides only on the host memory and does not move to the NIC memory or any other location, the DMA page mappings of MSA are set on and off depending on whether the owner endpoint is resident or nonresident. This is done to save the DVMA resources of the system.

At the endpoint create time two new segments are added to the process address space: the endpoint (network queue) and the MSA area. Even though memory resources are allocated for these segments, no mappings are established. The segment driver catches the first read page fault on these segments and establishes a read-only mapping. The first write fault on the page causes the segment driver to load the endpoint onto the NIC (by asking the NIC to do a DMA transfer), acquire DMA resources for the MSA, and establish read/write mapping for these objects. Thus, the host processor, i.e., the library, can request on demand the scheduling of an endpoint when it wants to send a message. Similarly, the NIC firmware can also demand for an endpoint to be scheduled if it receives a message. For the NIC firmware to schedule an endpoint it needs to generate a write fault on the endpoint to be scheduled. When a messages arrives for a nonresident endpoint, the receiver firmware NACKs the message, queues a request to the driver for the endpoint to

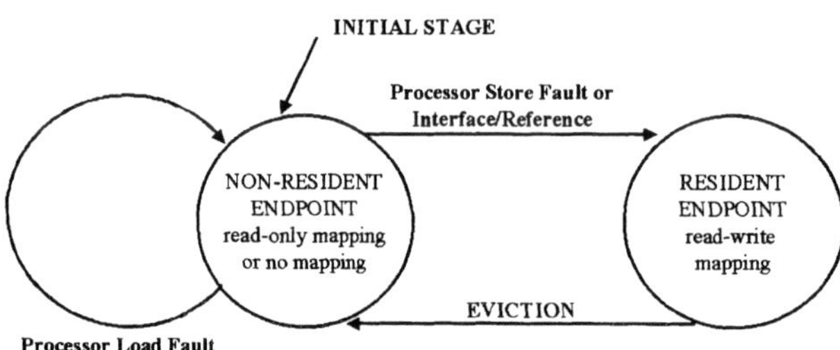

Figure 11.11 Endpoint state transition diagram showing processor and network initiated events and actions.

be swapped in, and interrupts the host, which in turn awakes the driver service thread. The service thread calls *as_fault()* to generate a pagefault, passing the base virtual address of the endpoint and a status encoding the action to take. The sender firmware retransmits the message after timeout and by then the receiver firmware completes loading of the endpoint. When the system wants to load an endpoint on demand (demanded either by host or NIC) and no free frame is available, then the system evicts a currently resident endpoint. Evicting a resident endpoint involves asking the NIC to DMA the endpoint frame onto the host memory and to change the application mappings to map onto the frame in the host memory with read-only access. Thus, when the endpoint is on the host memory, the application has read-only access and can only consume already received messages which are still in the receive pools and not consumed. However, for the endpoint to receive new messages over the network or send messages over the network, it needs to be resident and the application should have read/write mapping to the frame. Figure 11.11 shows the state transition diagram of endpoints.

The existing Solaris mechanisms and documented interfaces have necessary features for device context management. However, these facilities do not export interfaces to remap application virtual addresses from one backing store to another. Thus, an endpoint frame cannot be moved from the NIC memory to host memory and back to the NIC memory on demand. Applications can only read and write endpoints when they are resident on the NIC. Polling an endpoint requires it to occupy an endpoint frame even when no messages would be arriving anytime soon. Also, the existing interfaces have a processor centric management model and do not allow intelligent NICs to autonomously initiate device context switches. However, in the case of active message virtual networks, an endpoint can incur faults due to network events, such as receiving a message on a nonresident endpoint. Endpoints are cached in the NIC as result of processor references as well as NIC references. Thus, it is necessary to write a whole new segment driver and use a service thread that generates pseudo page faults on behalf of the NIC.

11.5 Analysis

Active Messages evolved out of the RISC approach to designing the communication subsystem which advocates doing 'the right thing at the right place.' A close observation of the AM abstraction would reveal that it exports the same interface a network device would export at a hardware level. Typically, the NIC, on receipt of a message from the network, interrupts the processor and the interrupt handler extracts the message from the network and buffers it in a suitable location for upper layers to process it. AM abstraction builds up on the similar philosophy and provides for invocation of a user-specified handler, which would integrate the message into the computation in the 'application-specified' way, on the receipt of the message. Here, the message handling code is *directly executed*, as opposed to, message being handled after interpretation [17]. This abstraction could be seen as bringing the raw network interface to the user-level where it could then be customized to provide higher level programming abstraction or runtime environments. Thus, the higher level abstractions implemented on top of Active Message should not incur any performance cost due to the semantic gap between AM and the higher-level programming model, as AM builds on the basic abstraction provided by the hardware.

The above argument establishes AM interface as providing a communication *substrate* rather than a full fledged communication subsystem. AM communication substrate strives to provide minimal but very flexible and versatile primitives to efficiently build the higher level protocols, which in turn could support a full-fledged communication subsystem. The communication substrate provided by AM could be tailored to build more complex protocols (like NFS, RPC, etc), communication models (like MPI and Fast Sockets [13]), or concurrent programming languages (like Split-C [4] and HPF).

11.5.1 Meeting the Requirements

Top-down requirement implies that the communication abstraction should support various programming models and concurrent runtime systems without any semantic gap. AM provides reliable message delivery and a connectionless model of communication with request-reply communication semantics that does not make any guarantee about ordering. A RISC approach would also point out that the issue of reliability should be decided at the lowest level possible to facilitate fast message recovery (by retransmission or other method). Considering the implication of supporting a wide class of high level abstractions to be supported, ordering does not seem to be a requirement to be met at the communication subsystem level. Given the AM message delivery model and the reliability of AM, it is straightforward to implement ordering (application specific, if desired).

Since AM is a connectionless communication model, it yields more easily to the implementation of many classes of higher level programming models and also enables scalability for a larger number of nodes. This connectionless model, coupled with the error model of AM, ensures a high degree of fault tolerance and reliability. Also, a connectionless model ensures that user applications have complete control over load balancing of communication traffic (in C-DAC, each node of the cluster supports multiple Myrinet cards and the application multiplexes the packets on the NICs to meet the bandwidth requirement dynamically). AM virtual networks facilitate multiplexing of limited physical network resources to a large number of applications.

AM ingrains the concept of overlapping computation and communication [17]. Interrupt, much like active message handler invocation, means that messages need not be *explicitly* waited for but computation could proceed and the messages could be consumed when the handler integrates it with the computation. This also implies that the communication subsystem needs to provide minimal buffering of messages and allow for application-specific buffer handling of messages. As the data is manipulated by the application, it is believed that the application has a better knowledge base to handle a message received and AM invokes the application-encoded action (the active message handler) which decides the state of the message. The buffering provided by the system and the NIC is efficiently used by the AM for network operations to pipeline the communication path so that the overhead in the communication path is tolerated. A minimal buffering in the communication subsystem also implies that a simple flow control mechanism is sufficient to avoid the overflow of the receive buffers. AM implements a minimal flow-control mechanism through the back pressure as is required to carry out its network operations efficiently. The request-reply kind of communication semantics of AM provides a framework through which an application can implement its own flow control mechanism. (A request handler depositing the message in the application area could control the message flow by replying to the sender on the receive buffer status.)

The performance of a communication subsystem depends on the performance attainable by the application. Synthetic benchmarks like latency and bandwidth convey only the upper bound on the performance attainable and, per se, convey very little about the application performance. Many interfaces strive to attain higher performance by severely restricting the interface features. Such interfaces often propose specialized extensions to overcome the weaknesess in the platforms. For example, some interfaces integrate buffer management along with the communication abstraction so that such buffers can be easily accessible to the NIC. But if any of the intermediate communication layer does not export this interface, then the purpose of such an extension is lost. In the above example, if MPI is layered over such a communication layer the buffer management would go to waste, as MPI does not export buffer management routines and data movement would still be required in the communication path. Such interfaces lack scalability and their integration with host programming environment is minimal; hence, they cannot keep track of developments in the host libraries. AM interface provides only communication-related features like communication from application buffer to application buffer, reliability, multiprogramming, multithread safety, etc., and, it integrates well with the host programming environment by not exporting any extensions relating to a general programming feature.

By providing a communication framework and mechanisms for applications to better control the aspects of the communication, AM provides enough flexibility for various classes programming models like MPI and runtime systems like Split-C to exploit the high speed networks and faster processors.

AM prevents a semantic gap from the *bottom-up* viewpoint and exports the capability that many of the SANs have–reliability. AM communication semantics resembles that of the message handling at the hardware level. The active message handler invocation is similar to the interrupt mechanism used at the low-level where the messages are received *concurrently* and integrated into ongoing computation. The actual method of handler invocation–upcall, user-level interrupt, or polling–however, depends on the particular implementation and the system support for it.

AM interface is not tied up to a particular system architecture or SAN architecture, though such features could be exploited by the implementation for better performance. AM uses a memory based interface to the network hardware that facilitates a fast access path avoiding the costly OS context switch (as discussed in earlier chapters), but refrains from exposing the exact data movement mechanisms (PIO or DMA) at the interface so that AM could be portable across platforms. The implementation could then optimize the data movement transparently depending on the support available from the system–NIC combination. Even though processor and SAN technologies are surging ahead, the memory subsystem continues to lag behind, proving to be a major bottleneck, the bad effects of frequent data movement have been often discussed [16]. Some of the NIC firmware, with the support of the system software, can handle some memory management tasks and move the data directly from the network buffer to the application buffer. Active Message facilitates a zero-copy message transfer by exporting a remote memory transfer like interface that exploits this feature.

11.6 Programming Models on AM

Traditional OS services still operate at the host level and are unaware of the cluster environment the host is part of. Thus, the cluster services have been looked upon as applications running on communication abstraction provided on networks of workstations. These include popular programming models like MPI and Fast Sockets, and the concurrent runtime systems like HPF and Split-C [4]. However, resources in the cluster can be shared and traditional OS calls can be serviced by a cluster OS rather than a host OS. This opens up a whole range of ideas/techniques such as network RAM, distributed filesystem, distributed lock manager, process migration, server fault tolerance, etc. In the current OS framework, this would require interaction between kernel modules in different nodes of the cluster and an efficient communication framework. The Trapeze [1] project has highlighted the need of an RPC style of communication framework at the kernel. With this motivation, the KSHIPRA communication architecture [12] exports the AM interface at the kernel level. Figure 11.12 shows the architecture of KSHIPRA.

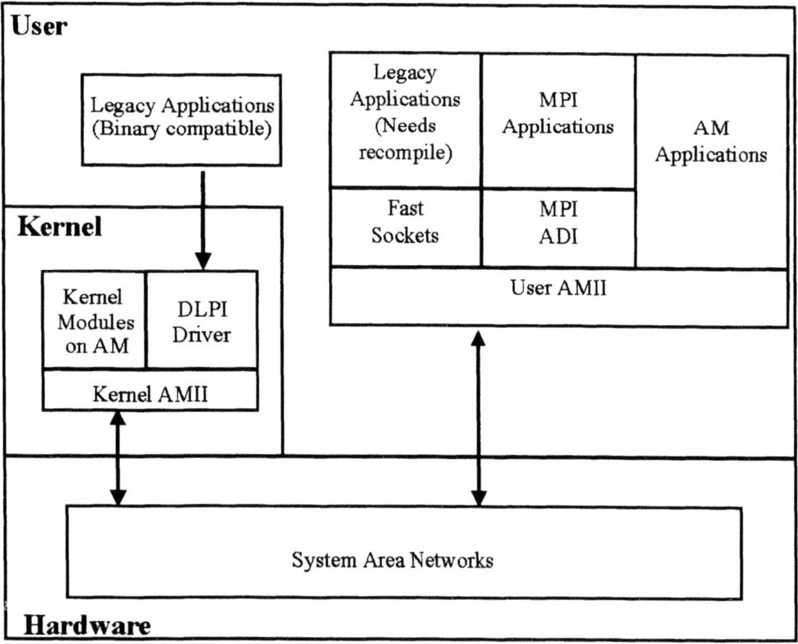

Figure 11.12 The KSHIPRA architecture.

The implementation of MPI, which exports the message passing programming model, and Fast Sockets, which exports the traditional sockets interface (stream-based model), have been discussed in this chapter to illustrate how different programming models can be easily implemented on top of AM. It can be seen that AM provides efficient and versatile primitives that serve as building blocks and enables the network capabilities to be exploited by the application using the personality interface of the machines provided by the MPI and FS. Because AM does not enforce any specific functionality to be placed at any level of the communication architecture, a variety of other novel concepts like Active Networking [15], which promises to be another cluster technology, and other higher level environments like CORBA, DSM, RPC, etc., can be easily integrated with AM.

11.6.1 Message Passing Interface (MPI)

MPI implementation is well structured and its API is supported by the MPI ADI (Abstract Device Interface) which actually provides the transport operations of the MPI. The ADI in turn can be implemented by the communication abstraction provided by the system such as sockets, AM, etc. This interface is flexible in that it can choose to provide the collective calls, application topologies, and support for MPI datatypes if it can map it efficiently to the underlying transport provider. In the general purpose machines, the collective operations are supported using the point-to-point calls.

KSHIPRA-MPI essentially provides MPI ADI on top of AM. The implementation philosophy is driven by the motivation to provide low latency and high bandwidth to the user application. Small messages are sent using the protocol, as shown in Figure 11.4. The receive side buffering is provided to buffer small messages to avoid synchronization. Application level flow control is provided by a credit based flow control mechanism exploiting the static nature of the MPI application. As the number of threads of control is fixed in MPI for a particular run, allocating credits during the startup becomes easy. The small messages get pipelined through the AM and the receive-side buffers, allowing the overlap of communication and computation.

For large messages, the protocol is motivated towards reducing the unnecessary data copies within the process (memory copies) and follows the protocol, as shown in the Figure 11.5. The sender notifies the receiver of the send buffer location and the communication actually starts when the receive buffer is also posted. The receiver *pulls* (using *GetXfer* call) the message from the send buffer and notifies the sender at the end of the transmission. From the abstraction point of view, the data transfer does not involve the host processor on the sender side at all due to the 'pull' nature of the data transfer and, hence, computation on the sender side could be overlapped with the communication. (Current implementations do not provide this facility and it is emulated, though this could be provided with memory management in the NIC as discussed in Section 11.7.6). This protocol facilitates a zero-copy data transfer by eliminating the data copies. Data copies tend to be costlier and incur a huge performance cost by polluting the cache and hogging the memory bandwidth [16].

MPI requires both nonovertaking (within the communicator) and overtaking (across the communicators) messages and as such, in a typical MPI implementation, ordering is not a basic guarantee required from the underlying transport provider. MPI implements a simple sequence number based mechanism to provide ordering wherever required and leverages on the reliability of AM to avoid retransmission of messages.

11.6.2 Fast Sockets

Fast Socket (FS) provides the familiar socket interface on top of AM so that typical client server application can take advantage of the fast communication path enabled by the new generation communication protocols. Unlike MPI, FS needs to support a connection-oriented and stream-based communication semantic on top of a connectionless and somewhat message-based communication semantic exported by AM. AM cannot be called a complete message passing system. There is no explicit receive primitive. Also, the abstraction supports 'remote memory transfer' communication primitive, resembling a shared memory interface that does not offer 'protection' of address spaces of communicating nodes that is inherent in the message passing systems. The issues involved in designing such an interface are:

1. *Buffer management and flow control* - To bridge the semantic gap between the AM and the FS interfaces and to implement the stream based interface efficiently, buffering of data is required. Sender-based buffer management of the receiver buffers on a per-connection basis simplifies the flow control and improves the small message latency, but it makes inefficient usage of buffers on the receiver side. Managing flow control on the receive side not only complicates the flow control but also requires sender side buffering to provide for retransmission of the data and may result in double buffering if not properly implemented. A related issue is zero-copy data transfer from the sender to the receive buffer if the receive buffer is posted earlier than the send. This requires complicated interaction between the sender and the receiver and may actually result in delays in skewed communication patterns and may be viable for large data transfers. The remote memory write (`AM_RequestXfer`) and the remote memory read (`AM_GetXfer`) primitives of AM enable such mechanisms so that such performance optimizations can be efficiently implemented. The connection-oriented nature of sockets require ordering AM messages, the exact mechanism depends on the flow control and buffer management techniques used.

2. *Connection management* - Mapping of the socket descriptors to the AM endpoints could affect the scalability of the FS application. A one-to-one mapping between a socket descriptor and an endpoint could exhaust the endpoints on an application with lots of connections, while multiplexing too many connections on an endpoint could make inefficient utilization of the endpoint resources. If multiple NICs are present then FS could leverage on the connectionless nature of AM to dynamically use both the links to improve bandwidth on a particular path in response to congestion.

11.7 Future Work

We have seen how AM, by exporting a simple interface coupled with the implementation techniques, enables high performance implementations of high level programming environments. Various novel implementation techniques proposed by other research projects have enabled the applications to achieve near hardware performance. With the perspective of the implementation discussed in Section 11.4, we now discuss further implementation optimizations that are possible in the current implementation of AM.

11.7.1 Bandwidth Performance

The current implementation pipelines the DMA transfers for successive outgoing packets by overlapping the network DMA and the host DMA and still incurs the cost of store-and-forward delay for the packet transmission time. This cost could be reduced by enabling intrapacket DMA pipelining, as in Trapeze [18], where the network DMA is overlapped with the host DMA for the same packet. The NIC is viewed as a cut-through device rather than a store-and-forward device, overlapping the transfer of a message across the send host I/O bus, the network, and the receive host I/O bus.

11.7.2 Flow Control and Error Recovery

The current AM implementation uses four channels (on per destination NIC basis) with stop and wait protocol to implement reliability and flow control. This implementation is optimistic; low latency of the links and the switch argue against more logical channels. Retransmissions of large messages, however, incur a huge cost because the messages are stored in the host buffers. Better implementation should concentrate on reducing the error rate and evolve some strategy to reduce the receiver buffer overflows. The acknowledgment packets could be piggybacked on the data packets to reduce network traffic.

11.7.3 Shared Memory Protocol

The straightforward implementation of the AM shared memory protocol by using standard UNIX shared memory [7] results in performance loss. This is because shared memory just becomes a medium for passing messages and does not exploit the shared nature of the memory. Experiences using MPI on CLUMPS indicate that collective calls perform badly owing to throttling of the memory. This is partly because of the lack of system support to allow arbitrary address space sharing and partly due to the message passing nature of AM. However, our experience using page re-mapping shows that message passing cost on shared memory could be alleviated by simple support. Similar techniques to implement AM (particularly AM calls with shared memory semantic) on shared memory would provide a unified interface without any performance loss for the shared memory.

11.7.4 Endpoint Scheduling

There are two levels of endpoint scheduling. One is scheduling of endpoints onto the NIC to make them actively sending/receiving endpoints (resident endpoints), and the second is scheduling active endpoints to service the message send on the NIC processor. The current policy of scheduling active endpoints for sends wastes the precious NIC processor cycles. It does not take into consideration the cycles utilized by a particular endpoint in receiving messages. An adaptive scheduling policy which reflects the usage of the endpoint in both sending and receiving may give better performance. Allocation of endpoints to the active endpoint frames in the NIC should also be adaptive.

11.7.5 Multidevice Support

UCB implementation supports multiple NICs, but one application can use only one NIC. The issues involved are whether to expose multiple NICs directly to the application (i.e., an application can specify the NIC for endpoint creation) or not (i.e., AM transparently handles allocation of endpoints on different NICs). Allowing AM to handle two NICs transparently would take away the flexibility of load-balancing that the application could do over the multiple NICs, and the application could utilize the resources more effectively. On the other hand, there are greater chances of a single threaded application deadlocking trying to multiplex packets on the NICs, given that the current implementation of AM does not allow spanning of an endpoint bundle across the NICs and also that message sends are blocking. Spanning the bundle across multiple cards is an ideal way out, but would require massive system support. The above problem could be circumvented, however, by having threads that the current implementation of KSHIPRA-MPI does. A related issue is that of utilizing multiple paths from a NIC to the other so that multiple packets could be in flight. But given the low latency and cut-through switches and the single physical channel for data reception, the idea would be appealing for a network of large radius and packets of small size. Also, the routes would have to be chosen carefully or else the packets would deadlock and could be lost.

11.7.6 Memory Management on NIC

Programmable NICs with full-fledged DMA engines and the development in system technologies have enabled memory management on the NIC. Integrating the network interface with the memory hierarchy of the operating system facilitates data transfer directly to the application buffers and avoids a stopover in the kernel pinned buffers. System support to pin application buffers and share page tables is required to implement this technique in a generalized way. Care should be taken, however, not to expose this feature as a special extension of communication abstraction by incorporating buffer management in the interface as in GM. This may result in a high performing interface, per se, but the higher level programming modules that use this abstraction may still incur performance penalty. More issues involved in memory management in NIC are discussed in [14].

Acknowledgments

We would like to thank Alan Mainwaring of UC Berkeley without whose enthusiastic support this chapter would not have seen the daylight. We are grateful to the

Berkeley NOW team whose original work has been the basis of this chapter. We are also grateful to IEEE, ACM, and various other authors for allowing us to reproduce some of the material and the diagrams. Our thanks also to the KSHIPRA team at C-DAC for their constant support and help.

11.8 Bibliography

[1] Darrell Anderson et al. Cheating the I/O Bottleneck: Network Storage with Trapeze/Myrinet. *Technical Report*, Department of Computer Science, Duke University, 1996.

[2] M Blumrich et al. Virtual Memory Mapped Network Interface for the SHRIMP Multicomputer. *Proceedings of 21st International Symposium on Computer Architecture*, pages 142-153, 1994.

[3] Brent N. Chun et al. Virtual Network Transport Protocols for Myrinet. *IEEE Micro*, pages 53-63, February 1998.

[4] David Culler et al. Parallel Programming in Split-C. *Proceedings of Super-Computing93*, 1993.

[5] David Culler et al. Generic Active Message Interface Specification. *Technical Report*, Department of Computer Science, University of California, Berkeley, 1995.

[6] David Culler et al. LogP Performance Assessment of Fast Network Interfaces. *IEEE Micro*, February 1996.

[7] Steve Lumetta et al. Multi-Protocol Active Messages on a Cluster of SMPs. *Proceedings of SuperComputing'97*, 1997.

[8] Alan Mainwaring. Active Message Application Programming Interface and Communication Subsystem Organization. *Technical Report*, Computer Science Division, University of California, Berkeley, 1995.

[9] Richard Martin et al. Effects of Communication Latency, Overhead, and Bandwidth in a Cluster Architecture. *Proceedings of International Symposium on Computer Architecture*, June 1997.

[10] Shubhendu Mukherjee et al. A Survey of User-Level Network Interfaces for System Area Networks. *Technical Report*, Computer Science Department, University of Wisconsin-Madison, 1997.

[11] D Oppenheimer et al. User Customization of Virtual Network Interfaces with U-Net/SLE. *Technical Report*, Computer Science Division, UC Berkeley, December 1997.

[12] N Mohan Ram et al. HPCC Software for Scalable UNIX Clusters. *Proceedings of ADCOMP'98*, 1998.

[13] Steve Rodrigues et al. High Performance Local-Area Communication Using Fast Sockets. *Proceedings of USENIX 97*, 1997.

[14] Ioannis Schoinas et al. Address Translation Mechanism in Network Interfaces. *Proceedings of 4th International Symposium on High Performance Computer Architecture*, 1997.

[15] David L. Tennenhouse et al. A Survey of Active Network Research. *IEEE Communications*, January 1997.

[16] Hiroshi Tezuka et al. Pin-down Cache: A Virtual Memory Management Technique for Zero-Copy Communication. *Technical Report*, Real World Computing Partnership, Japan, 1997.

[17] Thorsten von Eiken et al. Active Message: A Mechanism for Integrated Communication and Computation. *Proceedings of 19th Symposium on Computer Architecture*, IEEE CS Press, pages 256-266, Los Alamitos, California, 1992.

[18] Kenneth G. Yocum et al. Cut-through Delivery in Trapeze: An Exercise in Low-Latency Messaging. *Proceedings of the Sixth IEEE International Symposium on High Performance Distributed Computing (HPDC-6)*, pages 243-252, August 1997.

Chapter 12

Xpress Transport Protocol

ALFRED C. WEAVER

Department of Computer Science
University of Virginia
Charlottesville, VA 22903

Email: *weaver@cs.virginia.edu*

Cluster computing applications require low-latency communications, whether arranged in a shared-memory configuration or in a traditional LAN interconnect. In some cases, the application dataflow requires that duplicate data or even duplicate data streams flow from one processor (a data source) to a set of processors (a set of data sinks). In this case of point-to-multipoint distribution, TCP replicates the data stream, opening one connection with each recipient and treating each data stream independently even though they are identical; UDP can utilize multicast but it is an unreliable service. To overcome these obstacles, the Xpress Transport Protocol (XTP) was developed to support reliable and unreliable transport multicast services, multicast group management, fast connection setup and teardown, transactions, and other services that support high-throughput, low-latency computing. This paper describes XTP's development, characteristics, utility, and applications in a cluster computing environment.

12.1 Network Services for Cluster Computing

Cluster computing applications require low-latency communications, whether arranged in a shared-memory configuration or in a traditional LAN interconnect. In some cases, the application dataflow requires that duplicate data or even duplicate data streams flow from one processor (a data source) to a set of processors (a set of data sinks). If point-to-multipoint communications services are required, then there are two choices: (1) This service can be synthesized by using the Transmission Control Protocol (TCP) [3] in a serial unicast mode; the advantage is reliable delivery but the disadvantage is that data are duplicated for each receiver, thus consuming valuable bandwidth. (2) This service can be provided by the User Datagram Protocol (UDP) [1], but the delivery service is unreliable. In either case, both TCP and UDP require the services of the Internet Protocol (IP) [2] in the network layer below them to route messages to their destination.

In the ISO world, the Transport Protocol class 4 (TP4) [13] and the Connectionless Network Protocol (CLNP) [14] provide similar services. TCP, UDP, and IP are very important and very valuable protocols in the networking world; even though they are neither national nor international standards, they are defacto standards in the Internet. Having been designed years ago, however, TCP/UDP/TP4 did not anticipate cluster computing applications that now require fast interconnection across LANs (and, sometimes, clusters connected across Metropolitan Area Networks (MANs) and WANs). Thus, when these protocols are applied to some modern applications (e.g., interconnection of distributed applications, delivery of synchronized multimedia data streams, transmission of identical data to multiple destinations) they show some deficiencies. For example:

1. TCP supports only peer-to-peer connections (that is, one transmitter talking to one receiver) so a communication from, say, one transmitter to 10 receivers requires 10 connections and 10 independent transmissions. There is no concept of multicast. In cluster computing, it is increasingly common for many applications on different hosts to share a common data stream (e.g., sensor data, multimedia streams).

2. Since TCP and TP4 do not support multicast, they have no concept of multicast group management, i.e., there is no ability to define a group of transmitters and receivers, or for the application program to define the reliability requirements of the group members. Cluster multicast applications should have the option of knowing the identity and/or the status of the multicast receivers.

3. TCP provides little support for priority or latency control, both crucial for tightly-coupled or real-time systems. Cluster applications that source or sink real-time data profit from having the data on the network inherit the priority of the task that produced it.

4. TCP supports only fully reliable transmission (i.e., it repeats missing data until it finally arrives at the destination, no matter how long it takes) which is too strong for some applications. UDP supports only a "best-effort" service (i.e., the transmitter never knows if the receiver got the data) which is too weak for some applications. Data reliability is defined by the protocol, not by the application. Cluster applications should be able to define their own reliability paradigm on a connection-by-connection basis.

5. To send a single message reliably (as with transactions), TCP requires the exchange of six packets (two to set up and acknowledge the connection, two to send and acknowledge the data, and two to close the connection). This

slows the exchange of data for short-lived connections since connection setup and teardown are accomplished separately from data transfer. For cluster applications, transactions need to be fast and efficient.

6. When errors do occur, some TCP implementations recover using a go-back-n algorithm that retransmits all data beginning at the point of loss. That works well for LANs, where the round-trip time is short, but for those clusters interconnected via long-haul links or satellites this leads to inefficient use of the network when data previously sent and correctly received is nevertheless resent, only to be discarded at the destination as duplicate data. Instead of this scheme, clusters can use a selective retransmission algorithm that retransmits only the lost data. Recognizing this advantage, newer versions of TCP have implemented a similar scheme.

7. TCP, UDP, and TP4 all implement fixed policies defined by the protocol, not the application. For example, all connections are governed by flow control, which restricts the amount of data the transmitter can send. While this is usually correct, there are nevertheless some "streaming" applications within clusters that would benefit from unrestricted flow, but that option is simply not available. The point is that TCP and UDP embed policy with mechanism, and the two can not be untangled. For cluster computing, we think that the protocol should provide mechanisms, and the distributed applications should set policy.

12.2 A New Approach

In search of a better match between application requirements and transport protocol functionalities, an international group of protocol designers, composed of representatives from industry, academia, military, and government, has defined the Xpress Transport Protocol (XTP) [16], [4] which provides (all in one transport protocol) the traditional services found in previous transport protocols, plus important new functionality usable in cluster applications. XTP has been adopted as part of MIL-STD-2204, the U.S. military standard for mission-critical networked computers.

It is important to note that XTP is not intended as a replacement for TCP or UDP; these protocols have been so valuable to the networking community that they will never be replaced, only upgraded. XTP is simply another transport protocol with its own unique functionality which is available as an option for the system designer. Just as TCP and UDP operate side-by-side above IP, XTP operates simultaneously with other transport protocols, and utilizes the services of the network layer below it (if any). XTP operates over IP (which makes it usable in any Internet environment), over CLNP (which covers the ISO networks), directly over the LLC or MAC of any LAN (which covers Ethernet, token ring, FDDI, and ATM LAN emulation), and directly over the adaptation layer of an Asynchronous Transfer Mode (ATM) network. The possible interplay of transport protocols, network protocols, and networks is shown in Figure 12.1.

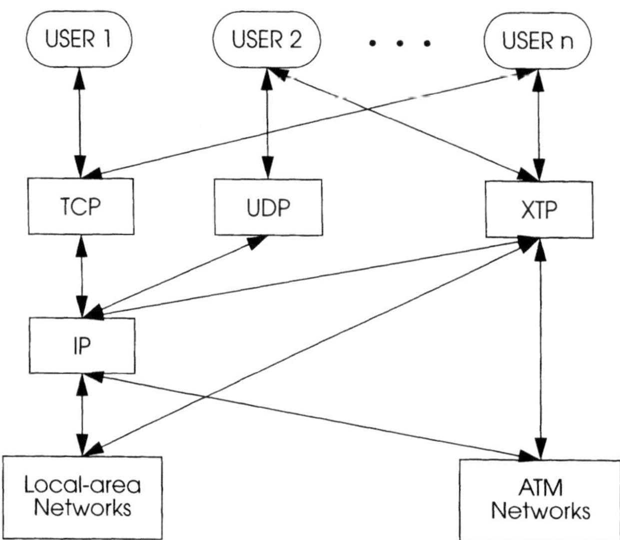

Figure 12.1 Interplay of protocols and networks.

12.3 XTP Functionality

If XTP has value to cluster computing, it is because it satisfies some need of the user's application. We examine these new functionalities and how they might be gainfully employed in a cluster application.

12.3.1 Multicast

Traditional transport protocols support only a unicast paradigm, that is, one transmitter talking to one receiver. As applications become more distributed, there is a need for network nodes to form groups that share certain types of data. For example, the cluster of computers on a ship's bridge share data among the navigation system, the autopilot, the collision-avoidance system, and the weapons systems. Rather than broadcasting this information to all computers (which requires each node to inspect and interpret it in software, and then discard it if it is not needed), the modern approach is to form a multicast group consisting of one transmitter and arbitrarily many receivers. Then every transmission to the multicast group goes only to those applications that have registered themselves as receivers of the data. Security algorithms can be employed here to monitor and/or enforce group membership. Receivers can join, leave, and rejoin an on-going multicast group as permitted by the multicast group manager (see the next section on Multicast Group Management). The reliability of data delivery is independent of whether the transmission is unicast or multicast and is controlled by the user's selection of the error control mechanism (see the section on Selectable Error Control).

In Figure 12.2, (a) represents a traditional unicast, (b) shows the basic one-to-

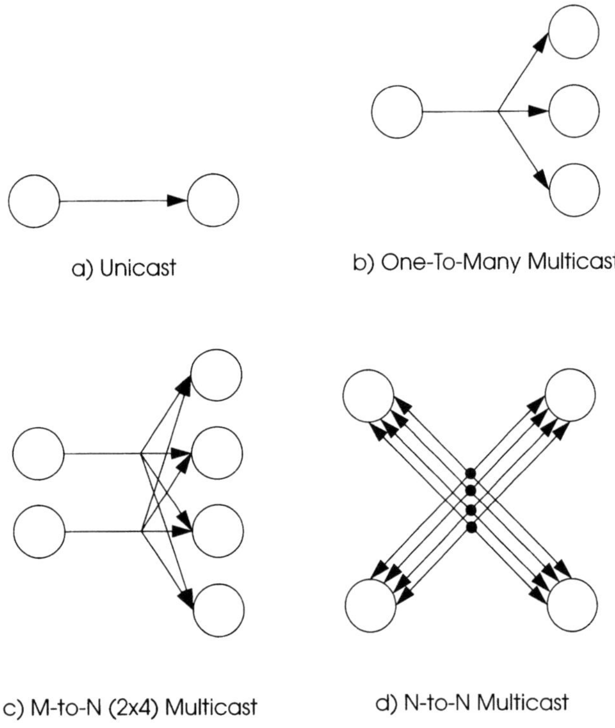

Figure 12.2 XTP multicast paradigms.

many approach of multicast, (c) shows an N-to-M multicast and groups that require more than a single transmitter can be synthesized by using N 1-to-N multicast groups to form a N-to-N multicast capability as shown in (d).

12.3.2 Multicast Group Management (MGM)

An application may form, or may join, any number of multicast groups. Membership in the group is controlled by the multicast group manager, and it in turn is controlled by the transmitting application. Using MGM, the user can selectively allow or deny the admission of any node to the multicast group; therefore, the resulting dynamic group membership can be known at all times (if desired). The user controls the reaction of the protocol when group members fail or voluntarily leave the group. If the members of a multicast group are required to be fully reliable, then the failure of any group member destroys the integrity of the multicast group, resulting in a failure report to the transmitting application. The application determines the consequences of group membership failure; it may choose to delete the failed member from the group and continue, or abandon transmission entirely, or take some other action that the application deems appropriate (see [9] and [7]).

Note how inappropriate it would be to have the protocol manage group membership via some predefined policy. Only the application can appreciate the side-effects of a change in group membership, so XTP reports group membership changes to the transmitting application and lets it decide what should be done. Since group membership is under program control, one could define a multicast group in which, say, three particular members must receive all data reliably and all other members may eavesdrop as they wish. Given that definition, XTP MGM would report failure of any of the three essential nodes, but would ignore the joining and leaving of other nonessential listeners. Also, we note that the reliability of group membership is orthogonal to the reliability of data transfer within a multicast group. As discussed in the section on selectable error control, XTP supports multiple paradigms for error control, but these are independent of the group membership issues.

12.3.3 Priority

A rich priority subsystem allows applications to define the importance of their data according to a system-wide scheme; XTP then operates on its most important data first. When XTP is coupled with a real-time operating system and a network that supports priorities, the system designer can then bound end-to-end delivery latencies for high-priority messages (see Figure 12.3). XTP puts a bit in the packet header that indicates whether or not each packet is participating in the overall priority scheme. If so, then an adjacent field indicates the relative priority of this packet compared to all other packets. XTP examines the priority bit and its associated numeric field and then processes that packet in accordance with its defined importance. One can say that, to a granularity of one packet's transmission time on the network, XTP is always operating on its most important packet. This is true not only in the end systems, but also in all interior routers if they support the necessary mechanisms to detect and respond to XTP priority (see the section on Applications).

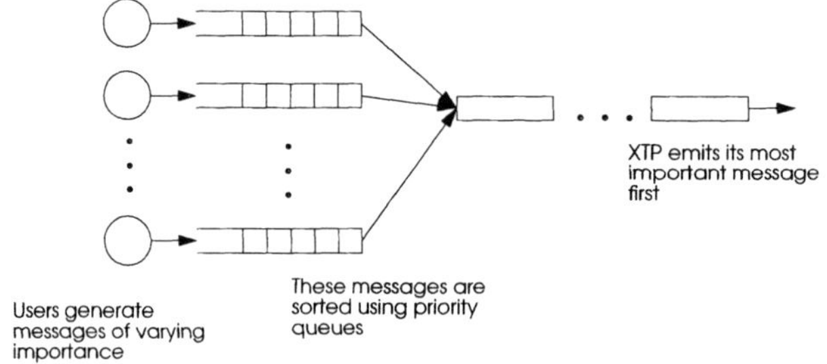

Figure 12.3 XTP priority mechanism.

The XTP priority scheme is based on a static priority encoded in a 16-bit numeric field; the lower the numerical value, the higher the importance. By defining the priority system this way, putting a delivery timestamp in the priority field automatically implements an earliest-deadline-first delivery policy with no additional work on the part of the user. Users generate messages of varying importance; XTP sorts those messages internally and emits them in the order of most important message first.

12.3.4 Rate and Burst Control

In a cluster environment interconnected via a modern fiber optic network, the usual source of errors is not bit errors on the medium but rather buffer overruns in the receiver or congestion in the routers. Recognizing this fundamental paradigm shift, XTP adds a mechanism for error prevention in addition to the classic mechanisms for error detection (e.g., CRCs) and correction (e.g., retransmission). When using XTP, a receiver can dynamically throttle a transmitter by using rate and burst control. The rate control parameter limits the amount of data that can be transmitted per unit time, while the burst parameter limits the size of data that can be sent (i.e., rate and burst control together control interpacket gaps). Figure 12.4 shows the effect of rate and burst control on the total amount of data transmitted over time.

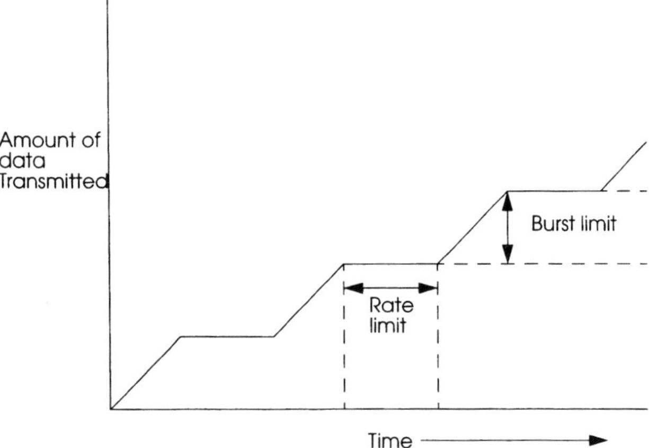

Figure 12.4 Rate and burst control.

When using TCP, a slow receiver's protection from a fast transmitter has to be synthesized by flow control; that is, the opening and closing of credit windows. This causes dynamic throughput fluctuation as transmission starts and stops in accordance with the demands of the flow control window. In contrast, rate control allows a steady stream of data to be emitted at a rate known to be acceptable to the receiver (and that rate can be dynamically adjusted to reflect changing conditions). Additionally, conventional flow control is only active end-to-end; that is, routers do not participate. Thus, a receiver with spare capacity can open a large flow control window to invite rapid transmission, but this might only result in further congestion of some intermediate router. XTP's rate and burst control algorithms allow the routers to participate; a congested router could temporarily reduce the rate control parameter of its incoming connections until the period of congestion has passed.

12.3.5 Connection Management

TCP and TP4 require the exchange of six data packets to transmit one data element reliably (two to set up and acknowledge the connection, two to send and acknowledge the data, and two to close the connection). XTP achieves the equivalent bidirectional reliability with only three packets because of XTP's powerful connection establishment mechanisms. In the XTP paradigm, host A sends its first packet which requests the connection with host B and sends its data, all in the same packet. Host B may then respond with packets flowing in the reverse direction. When the data transfer ends, the last packet from A to B is marked as such, which closes one side of the connection. Host B acknowledges having received the last data element from A and then closes the connection in the A-to-B direction. Traffic now flows in the reverse B-to-A direction until it ends, at which point the last packet is so marked. Host A acknowledges the receipt of the last packet from B and closes the connection in the B-to-A direction.

Thus, XTP needs only three packets to deliver one piece of data reliably: one to open the connection, send the data, and request the closure of the connection; one to acknowledge the data; and one to acknowledge connection closure. In the special case of a transaction, XTP requires only two packets. Host A sends its first packet to B that opens the connection and transfers the data (the transaction request); host B replies by sending its data (the transaction response) and closing the connection.

12.3.6 Selectable Error Control

XTP supports not one but three types of error control: a) a fully reliable mode like TCP and TP4, which would normally be used for applications such as file transfer; b) a UDP-like service, in which the receiver does not acknowledge transmission and thus the transmitter never knows whether the data was successfully delivered (i.e., a datagram); and c) a special mode called fast negative acknowledgment that can improve error repair in certain situations.

In a cluster environment with computers connected via a LAN, out-of-sequence data delivery is much more likely to mean that the missing data is truly lost, as opposed to delayed (as it might be by taking an alternate path in a WAN). Using the fastnak option, a receiver that identifies out-of-sequence delivery immediately (without waiting for any time-outs) sends a control packet that informs the transmitter about the missing data. The transmitter then immediately resends only the missing data.

Another independent option is noerror mode that suspends the normal retransmission scheme. Correctly received data is properly sequenced, but gaps, if any, are not retransmitted. This mode is useful for digitized voice. Not only does XTP provide a range of data reliability options, it does so in a single protocol. Each connection can support an independent choice of error control strategy, and the choice is entirely under the control of the application.

12.3.7 Selectable Flow Control

As with error control, three orthogonal options are provided. Traditional flow control based on credit windows is available for normal data. Reservation mode practices a conservative flow control policy whereby the receiver may only issue a credit for buffers dedicated to a particular connection; this assures that data will not be lost due to buffer starvation at the destination. The third mechanism is to disable flow control entirely by using the noflow option. Note that such a "free flow" or "streaming" mode of operation is not available in other protocols; this mode is useful for intracluster multimedia applications.

12.3.8 Selective Retransmission

Older TCP implementations respond to errors by using a go-back-n algorithm in which the transmission window is reset and begins again with the first byte which was lost or received in error. While this works well for local area networks with short delivery latencies, it is less efficient with networks that have either high capacity (fiber optic networks) or long delivery latencies (satellite networks) or both. On these networks, go-back-n may retransmit data that has already been received correctly. XTP can use either go-back-n or selective retransmission; in the latter, the receiver acknowledges spans of correctly received data and the sender retransmits only the gaps. The user selects which scheme to use, if any (recall that retransmission does not occur when using noerror mode).

Historically, retransmission has been regarded as either inappropriate or ineffective for jitter control in multimedia systems, and this may well be true if TCP-style retransmission is used. However, we have shown in [12], [11], [8], [10] that retransmission, layered on top of an efficient retransmission mechanism like that in XTP, can be very effective for controlling packet loss in delay-sensitive streams.

12.3.9 Selective Acknowledgment

Acknowledging every packet assumes that the network often loses packets, assumes that the transmitter wants acknowledgments, and embeds policy with mechanism. XTP allows the user to decide if and when acknowledgments are desirable. Acknowledgments are provided whenever the transmitter requests them, thereby allowing the user to select an acknowledgment frequency ranging from always to sometimes to never. Philosophically, acknowledgment generation from the receiver is decoupled from data arrivals or window sizes. Whenever the transmitter wants to know the status of the connection, it asks; when the receiver responds, it tells everything it knows about its current status.

12.3.10 Maximum Transmission Unit (MTU) Detection

A common problem with the independence of layers introduced by the OSI model is that the transport layer may segment a message into packets for the network layer, only to have the network layer fragment each of those packets into still smaller packets that are appropriate for a particular data link. XTP avoids this double effort by negotiating the proper MTU for the route in use. Both end systems and routers can declare their MTU for a particular link, and the transmitter will select the minimum of all MTUs encountered on any given path.

12.3.11 Out-of-band Data

It is sometimes useful to send information about the data stream without embedding it within the data stream itself. As an option, XTP can carry with each packet up to eight bytes of tagged data. Tagged data is passed from the transmitter to the receiver, and its presence is indicated to the receiver, but it is never interpreted by XTP. Tagged data can be used by the application for providing semantic information about the data. For cluster computing applications that handle real-time data, tagged data is an elegant way to associate a 64-bit timestamp with each packet transmitted.

12.3.12 Alignment

Although it is a simple notion, data alignment pays big dividends by avoiding excess data copies. The major fields of the XTP header are aligned on 4-byte boundaries; this minimizes the number of memory accesses needed to retrieve a field. The data segment begins and ends on 4-byte boundaries, and a length field identifies the last byte of the user data.

12.3.13 Traffic Descriptors

We anticipate that packet-switched networks like the Internet will eventually support quality-of-service requests from transmitters; the ATM Forum is already grappling with the problem of how to implement QoS in ATM networks. Since XTP is designed to work in both environments, it defines a traffic descriptor field that can be used to communicate QoS parameters among routers and end-systems. While XTP itself does not perform explicit resource reservation, it can supply the necessary information to other resource reservation protocols. Because resource reservation work is still a research topic, we expect the form and content of the traffic descriptor field to evolve over time.

12.4 Performance

Protocol performance measurement is a tricky subject; it is difficult to achieve a true "apples-to-apples" measurement unless the same person or group designed and implemented both protocols in the same environment. Since XTP has more functionality than TCP/UDP/TP4, one might predict that it would run slower, but that has not been our experience. In our experiments, XTP's unicast throughput was comparable to TCP; the big win is using XTP's reliable multicast mode versus serial unicast with TCP or unreliable multicast with UDP.

12.4.1 Throughput

For a particular real-time application running under pSOS+ on a cluster of 133 MHz Pentium-based PCs connected by FDDI interfaces, we measured the following when comparing TCP versus XTP versus UDP.

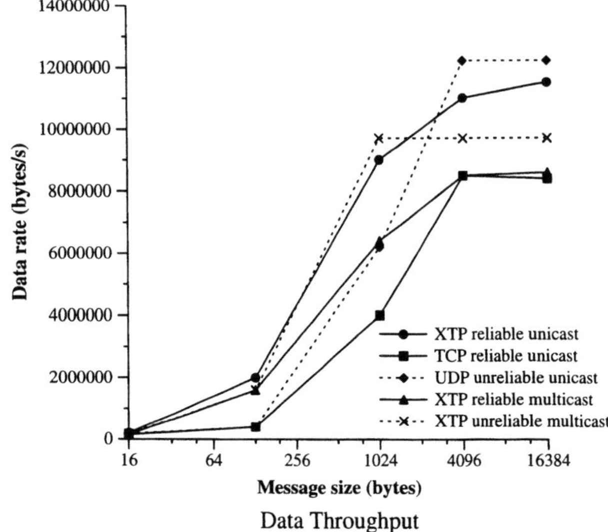

Figure 12.5 Throughput of XTP, TCP, and UDP.

As shown in Figure 12.5, throughput for all protocols is similar for small messages, for which throughput is governed by operating system overhead more than message size. For larger messages, protocol and network overhead do influence throughput, and in this particular measurement XTP's reliable delivery mode performed slightly better than TCP's.

12.4.2 Message Throughput

Figure 12.6 shows a comparison of how fast the various protocols can transmit messages of varying size. The need to transmit many small messages very quickly is very common for real-time control applications (e.g., a cluster computing fly-by-wire system that controls an airplane). For large messages, the performance of all protocols is similar because performance is dominated by getting the message transmitted on the network. For small messages, however, XTP shows a striking

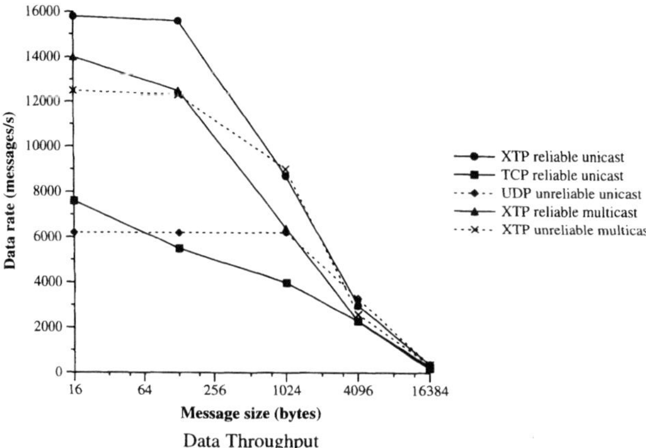

Figure 12.6 Message rate comparison.

performance advantage (here a factor of two) over TCP and UDP.

12.4.3 End-to-end Latency

The following table confirms that XTP can deliver messages quickly. In this measurement, the user-memory-to-user-memory one-way latency varies from an average of 228 microseconds for 16-byte messages to 1.7 ms for 16k-byte messages. TCP and UDP timings are comparable.

Table 12.1 XTP End-to-End Latency

User data message size (byte)	Minimum latency (microseconds)	Average latency (microseconds)	Maximum latency (microseconds)
16	201	228	325
128	216	241	322
1024	313	336	452
4096	636	657	815
16K	1638	1656	1780

In general, our experience has been that a skillful XTP implementation delivers to the application approximately 80 to 96 percent of the raw network bandwidth available at the level of the MAC device driver. Nevertheless, because it is difficult to separate the skill of the implementers from the inherent power of the protocol, XTP does not make the claim that it is faster than any particular protocol; the measured performance simply speaks for itself. XTP is a tool, just like TCP and UDP are tools, and all of them should be used wherever they are most appropriate. In my opinion, XTP's major contribution is not so much its performance but its functionality. The ability to utilize many different communications paradigms, all in the same protocol, and all under the user's control, is a major advantage for the system designer.

12.5 Applications

XTP has been utilized in a number of commercial and military applications. Its use is growing as application designers see its functional advantages (e.g., multicast, group management) in distributed systems. Here are some examples of how commercial companies and government agencies have used XTP's capabilities to achieve specific goals.

12.5.1 Multicast

A government contractor needed to interconnect a cluster of 22 CRAY supercomputers, all riding in the belly of a C-130 aircraft, to form a flying signal intelligence center. Since this environment required sending identical data streams to multiple processors, they chose XTP so that they could utilize its multicast capabilities. Each multicast transmission consumes only a fraction of the network bandwidth that would otherwise have been required by N serial reliable unicasts.

12.5.2 Gigabyte Files

A commercial company needed to transfer gigabyte files routinely across a satellite-based network that connected clusters of computers located on different continents. They chose XTP to utilize its selective retransmission capability. When errors corrupt the satellite channel, XTP retransmits only the data that was lost; it does not restart the data stream from the point of loss.

12.5.3 High Performance

A government agency needed a communications protocol that would support the real-time environment of weapons control. They chose XTP based on its low end-to-end latency characteristics. Being able to reliably send modest size messages with submillisecond latencies allowed them to write effective feedback control loops even in a packet-switched networking environment.

12.5.4 Image Distribution

One company faced the problem of having to send very high resolution medical images over an FDDI-based network. They needed to move multiple mammography images (40 MB each) to a workstation cluster for simultaneous review by a staff of radiologists. They chose XTP for its combination of high throughput and multicast distribution.

12.5.5 Digital Telephone

A government contractor wanted to operate a digital telephone/intercom system over an existing FDDI data network. The system had to support 120 simultaneous bidirectional conversations (64 Kbits/s each), and each conversation had to have the capability of being sent to any combination of destinations. They chose XTP because its multicast feature would allow any number of receivers to join a multicast group (under the supervision and control of the transmitter), thus making it simple to implement the cross-communications requirement.

12.5.6 Video File Server

A company needed the capability to send and receive "video mail" (synchronized audio/video) throughout their corporate network, in addition to their traditional text-based electronic mail. They chose XTP because it handled the multimedia requirements with ease. Personal computers were able to mount a remote disk drive (the file server) and retrieve a compressed multimedia stream in real time.

12.5.7 Priority Support

A government research lab required that its packet-switched network be able to support digital multimedia streams in addition to file transfer and electronic mail. They used XTP in combination with an XTP-aware IP router [6] to achieve this goal. This special IP router identifies XTP packets and handles them in accordance with the XTP priority option.

12.5.8 Real-time Systems

A government contractor needed to design a ship-board network, based on MIL-STD-2204, that would handle time-critical command and control messages, multimedia streams, background file transfer, and data distribution from one source to multiple destinations. The contractor chose XTP because it provided latency control, message-level priorities, multimedia support, high overall performance, and multicast capabilities to handle the distribution of identical data streams.

12.5.9 Interoperability

Desiring to preserve the connectedness and interoperability associated with the classic protocols, one government contractor built a MIL-STD-2204 network incorporating TCP and UDP and XTP, all operating over IP. Another vendor provided TP4 and XTP, both over CLNP. Yet another vendor, working with real-time data on a single-segment LAN, put XTP directly on top of the MAC of FDDI.

12.6 XTP's Future in Cluster Computing

XTP offers significant new functionality (especially the transport layer multicast, multicast group management, selective retransmission and transport layer priorities) that has already been shown to be of significant benefit to cluster computing applications. In an effort to speed the deployment of XTP, a public domain version has been developed at Sandia National Laboratories [17]; information is freely available from http://www.ca.sandia.gov/xtp/SandiaXTP. Commercial versions are available now from at least two sources [5], [15]. Commercial and military products developed from these XTP implementations are currently in everyday use.

12.7 Bibliography

[1] User datagram protocol. RFC 768, August 1980.

[2] Internet protocol–DARPA internet program protocol specification. RFC 791, September 1981.

[3] Transmission control protocol–DARPA internet program protocol specification. RFC 793, September 1981.

[4] Xpress transport protocol 4.0 specification. http://www.ca.sandia.gov/xtp/, 1995.

[5] Xpress transport protocol. http://www.cs.virginia.edu/ acw/netx/, 1998.

[6] R.W. Christie and A.C. Weaver. Design of an XTP-Aware IP Router. In *Distributed Technology Exchange*, San Diego, CA, March 13-17 1995. NCCOSC RDT&E Division (NRaD).

[7] B.J. Dempsey. An Analysis of Multicast and Multicast Group Management. *Master's Thesis.* Department of Computer Science, University of Virginia, January 1991.

[8] B.J. Dempsey. Retransmission-Based Error Control for Continuous Media Traffic in Packet-Switched Networks. *PhD Thesis.* Computer Networks Laboratory, Department of Computer Science, University of Virginia, May 1994.

[9] B.J. Dempsey, J.C. Fenton, and A.C. Weaver. The Multidriver: A Reliable Multicast Service for the Xpress Transfer Protocol. In *15th Local Computer Networks Conference,* Minneapolis, MN, October 1-3 1990.

[10] B.J. Dempsey, J. Liebeherr, and A.C. Weaver. A New Error Control Scheme for Packetized Voice over High-Speed Local Area Networks. In *18th IEEE Local Computer Networks Conference,* Minneapolis, MN, September 1993.

[11] B.J. Dempsey, M.T. Lucas, and A.C. Weaver. Design and Implementation of a High Quality Video Distribution System Using XTP Reliable Multicast. In *Second International Workshop on Advanced Communications and Applications for High-Speed Networks,* Heidelberg, Germany, September 1994.

[12] B.J. Dempsey, M.T. Lucas, and A.C. Weaver. An Empirical Study of Packet Voice Distribution Over a Campus-Wide Network. In *19th IEEE Local Computer Networks Conference,* Minneapolis, MN, October 1994.

[13] International Organization for Standardization. Information processing systems-open systems interconnection-transport protocol specifications. International Standard 8073, July 1986.

[14] International Organization for Standardization. Information processing systems-open systems interconnection-data communications protocol for providing the connectionless mode network service. International Standard 8473, March 1986.

[15] Mentat, Inc. http://www.mentat.com/, 1998.

[16] W.T. Strayer, B.J. Dempsey, and A.C. Weaver. *XTP: The Xpress Transfer Protocol.* Addison-Wesley, Reading, Massachusetts, 1992.

[17] W.T. Strayer, S. Gray, and R.E. Cline, Jr. An Object-Oriented Implementation of the Xpress Transfer Protocol. In *Proceedings of the Second International Workshop on Advanced Communications and Applications for High-Speed Networks (IWACA'94),* Heidelberg, Germany, September 26-28 1994.

Chapter 13

Congestion Management in ATM Clusters

SUNDARARAJAN VEDANTHAM[†], AMIT ANIL NANAVATI[‡], S.S. IYENGAR[†]

[†]Department of Computer Science,
Louisiana State University
Baton Rouge, LA 70803, U.S.A.

[‡]Netscape Communications Corporation,
Mountain View, CA 94043, U.S.A.

Email: *sundar@bit.csc.lsu.edu, amit@netscape.com, iyengar@bit.csc.lsu.edu*

13.1 Introduction to ATM Networking

The network fabric interconnecting the workstations forms the backbone of the Cluster Computing paradigm. While the CoW (Cluster of Workstations) model's performance degrades gracefully when individual workstations slowdown or crash, failure in the communication network can deteriorate the performance significantly in a short period of time. So the design, implementation and management of the network architecture gains added importance in this computing environment.

Present trends in computing indicate that the material that needs to be transported between machines in future is bound to become rich in multimdedia content. So network architectures are required to become increasingly efficient and reliable in transporting large volumes of audio and video information in addition to the traditional data types. The Asynchronous Transfer Mode (ATM) networking is designed ground-up trying to handle such considerations. There are several publications that provide a good introduction to the concept of ATM networking [11], [12], [16]. Chapter 9 of this volume also discusses ATM briefly. We will restrict our discussion to a few specific problems in congestion control and traffic management in ATM networking that are relevant to cluster computing.

In this chapter, this section describes a few basic concepts required to understand the rest of the chapter. Section 13.2 presents a brief discussion on existing procedures to control the congestion problem. Section 13.3 considers the simulation of ATM networks on legacy LANs in order to study the traffic management and performance characteristics of ATM for migration planning. Section 13.4 considers migration planning from a theoretical perspective and provides an algorithm to identify congestion causing network links for conversion from legacy LAN links to ATM links in order to increase overall throughput while ensuring maximum possible cost efficiency. Section 13.5 summarizes our contributions and presents the conclusions with direction for future research efforts.

13.1.1 Integrated Broadband Solution

ATM Network model is a Broadband ISDN (Integrated Services Digital Network) solution that is a compromise between the transmission requirements of audio, video, and traditional data. The basic idea behind ATM is to break down any data to be transported into fixed size cells of 53 bytes each (48 bytes of data and a 5 byte header) and transmit the information as a flow of cells regardless of the type of source generating the data. Therefore, the underlying switching fabric or the transmission medium need not be aware of the service being provided or the type of data being transmitted. This approach ensures that the new network will be well positioned to take advantage of any high speed transmission medium as well as improvements in digital data compression algorithms; it will also be capable of utilizing the available bandwidth effectively. In addition, ATM is expected to be implemented entirely on fiber optic networks that are capable of handling 155 to 650 Mbps data streams (compared to 2 to 10 Mbps speed of today's LANs and most of the internet) making it highly suitable for real time video. The protocol itself is capable of handling traffic rates of the order of 2.4 Gbps, thus making it fairly future proof. [13] Development of switches that can handle traffic of this magnitude is an area of enormous interest to the industry [7], [13]. The cell format is now stable and the technology to build ATM switches is currently available. But several fundamental issues concerning traffic control and connection usage enforcement remain unresolved.

The ATM network model does have a set of sources and destinations trying to communicate, as is the case of legacy networks. The system that is generating the traffic is expected to gauge the natural bit rate (data generation) of each device attached and should present a Source Traffic Description (STD) for the system while negotiating with the network for bandwidth allocation. A standard set of traffic parameters (Average connection holding time, Peak cell rate, Mean cell rate, Average burst duration, and Source type) are used in the negotiation to describe the traffic type. Once the negotiation is over, the network statistically guarantees the negotiated bandwidth between the source and the destination by setting up a virtual path (VP) between the two. Although the transmission medium may be multiplexed as in the case of packet switching networks, the existence of a virtual path makes the system resemble circuit switching, making it a viable option for on line video transmission and the like that require guaranteed QoS (services that have low tolerance for variations in transmission time delay).

Since the transmission rate is very high compared to X.25 type networks, addressing schemes are kept very simple with highly reduced header functionality so as to minimize the time spent in interpreting header information during transmission. Since the transmission medium is supposed to be fiber (as opposed to copper in case of present day LANs and WANs), the error rate introduced in transmission is expected to be very low. ATM takes advantage of this scenario by reducing the error detection and correction carried out during the transmission, thus increasing the rate of transmission. Since the network functions under the assumption that transmission will be error free and congestion free, if those assumptions fail even briefly, it results in significant deterioration of transmission quality.

13.1.2 Virtual Connection Setup

Figure 13.1 shows a schematic representation of an ATM switch. A switch has a set of input and output ports that are used to receive and send out the stream of cells constituting the ATM traffic. At the end of the initial call setup transaction, a series of switches are selected that bridge the distance between the source and the destination of the traffic to be generated. The switches agree on how the received cells will be directed from one switch to another (cells coming into port i of the switch P will be sent to output port j, which is in turn linked to input port k of switch Q, etc.). This information is stored in the *Switching Table* inside the switches at the end of call setup. The switching table is a lookup table that retains the information as to which stream of cells coming through which VC and VP should be routed to which outgoing Virtual Channel (VC) and Virtual Path (VP).

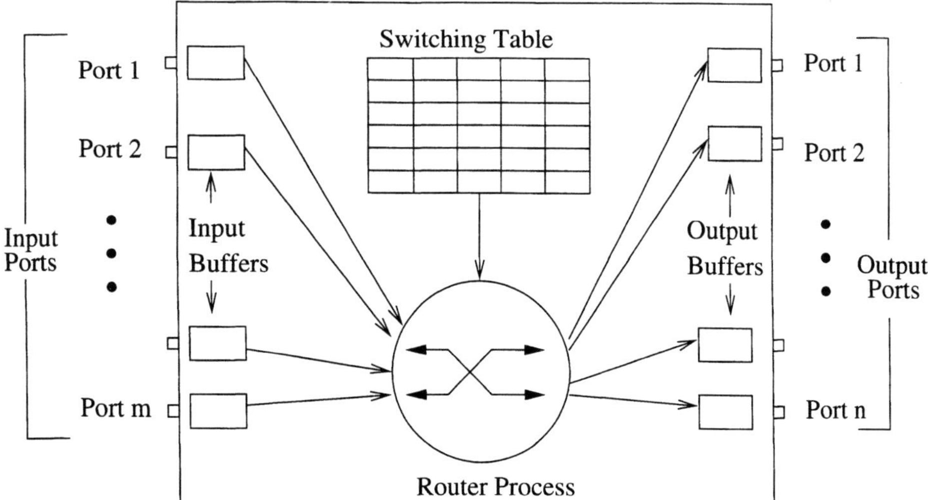

Figure 13.1 Schematic representation of an ATM switch.

Once the table entries are made, incoming cells need only contain a small VPI/VCI (Virtual Path Identifier/Virtual Channel Identifier) address field. The switch reads this information and determines the subsequent VPI/VCI information for the cell based on the table entries, changes the header entries to reflect the subsequent path information, and routes the cell through the correct output port. This system obviates the need for each cell carrying the complete destination address (that can be approximately 20 bytes long) in its header. Switches invariably have some buffer storage added to their input and output ports so that they can handle some amount of congestion in the flow without resorting to dropping the excess traffic from the stream. The physical medium (a fiber-optic cable, for example) can contain several virtual paths in it. Each virtual path in turn may contain several virtual channels. The combination of physical media, VPI, and VCI together define a given ATM link.

13.1.3 Quality of Service

The QoS factor, as the name indicates, is a measure of the quality of the connection from source to destination. It involves traffic characteristics such as peak and average cell rates, burstiness, Cell Loss Probability (CLP), end-to-end cell delay, ease of call acceptance and Cell Delay Variance (CDV). Depending upon the kind of information transmitted, one or more of the factors gain importance. To give an example, a packet oriented connection, like file transfer protocol, will be affected by peak and average cell rate; alternatively, a Constant Bit Rate (CBR) connection, like video transmission, will be affected more by the CDV factor. The ATM Forum has defined five numbered QoS classes 0 through 4, and sample applications that may require such levels of QoS. In the future, more QoS classes may be defined for a given service class. Services using the Class 0 will be handled as a *best-effort* service by the network operator. Such traffic contracts that can adapt well to the varying resource availability situations are still being defined under the names of Unspecified Bit Rate (UBR) or Available Bit Rate (ABR).

13.1.4 Traffic and Congestion Management

Congestion in an ATM network can be defined as the condition where the offered load (demand) from the user to the network is approaching or exceeds the network design limits for guaranteeing the QoS specified in the traffic contract [12]. Such a situation arises when the resources are overbooked or when a component in the network fails or when the source of traffic fails to abide by the agreed traffic contract. Thus, congestion may occur at different parts of the overall network such as switch ports, buffers, transmission links, ATM AAL processors, Connection Admission Control (CAC) processors, etc.

QoS is the factor that is studied against all the other characteristics of the system to verify congestion free flow. QoS may be measured at individual VPC or VCC or at higher levels for several VCCs or VPCs as a total aggregate. It is easy to understand that measurements at the individual VCC level are going to be resource-intensive to model, measure, and compute. But it may be justified where very high levels of QoS are mandatory on specific links.

Parameters like CLR and CDV are used as a measure of QoS. We have carried out such sample studies to understand traffic and switch performance characteristics. The results are discussed in Section 13.3. While carrying out simulations, it is important to remember the gains that may be realized when several traffic sources of varying characteristics are statistically multiplexed in real life situations, as the overall traffic will tend to be a lot smoother and so easier to handle than any of the individual traffic sources.

Congestion control can be broadly classified into three subcategories: congestion avoidance, management, and recovery. Congestion avoidance mechanisms are designed to prevent congestion during periods of peak network loads. Congestion management systems operate with the objective of ensuring that the congested network scenarios are never entered. Thus, allocation of resources, working under fully booked or bandwidth guaranteed systems, administering CAC, and using network engineering techniques, falls under the purview of congestion management. Congestion recovery procedures are used to ensure that any congestion that may be encountered will not result in severe degradation of user perceived QoS. Such procedures include cell discarding, modifying the UPC, and FECN and/or BECN notification procedures described in subsequent sections. Most of these procedures and techniques that may be found in network equipment today are ad hoc implementations by the vendors trying to use them as selling points without much regard for standardization and interoperability.

13.2 Existing Methodologies

Congestion control in B-ISDN networks has been an area of vigorous research during the past few years [6], [8], [14], [15]. Commonly found congestion handling procedures identify the cells that are in violation of the agreed contract and tag them for possible elimination (by simply discarding them) in the future. Algorithms used to identify the cells in violation are often not sophisticated enough to address all the concerns. This handicap is magnified by the limited time window available for such processes due to the high speed of the traffic. Guillemin and Dupuis [9] have shown how cell clusters of a given connection can pass transparently through pick-up policing mechanisms in multiplexed environments, resulting in bursty traffic causing severe degradation of transmission quality. There are a few techniques designed to handle bursty traffic conditions. Some of them emphasize controlling the source very strictly to prevent any unexpected traffic getting into the network [1]; others suggest improved bandwidth allocation algorithms that attempt handling bursty traffic more efficiently at the network level [3], [5]; there are some that attempt a mixed approach [18]. Since CCITT clearly states that the traffic sources may not always be obedient [4], control at the network level gains more importance. Solutions at the network level can be broadly classified into two groups: statistical approaches and operational approaches.

Statistical Approach: ATM traffic is measured in terms of parameters such as average cell rate, average burst duration, peak cell rate, etc. Statistical approaches use these parameters to regulate the flow. Whenever the set (or previously agreed upon) thresholds are exceeded, they trigger correction mechanisms like dropping excess packets. Unfortunately, for this approach to work properly, packet traffic should be monitored for prolonged periods of time making sure that the traffic codes have indeed been violated. If the corrective measures trigger too soon, they might choke the traffic frequently, unnecessarily. This inherently sluggish characteristic makes this approach unsuitable for real time applications and video transmissions, for example.

Operational Approach: Operational approaches, on the other hand, govern the traffic using preset rules. The algorithm clearly identifies a set of cells as nonconforming using set rules. Hence, they are called *parameterized conformance-testing algorithms.* CCITT Recommendation I.371 specifies these rules, referred to as Genetic Cell Rate Algorithm (GCRA). CCITT has defined two equivalent versions of the GCRA, Virtual Scheduling (VS) and Continuous-State Leaky Bucket (LB) Algorithm. Presented with the same sequence of cells, both algorithms mark the same set of cells as conforming or nonconforming [12].

Unlike the statistical approach, operational approaches are quick to react. But the correction procedure is, in general, simply dropping the packets that are found to be in violation. Traffic sources depend on the expiration of a timer, while waiting for an acknowledgement from the receiving end, to ascertain that the transmission was not completed.

Traffic Shaping and Congestion Notification: Traffic shaping is a process in which a gate is introduced at the point where a private cell stream is about to enter a public network to control the cell flow. The mechanism controlling the gate has the traffic contract that is agreed upon during the negotiation process. Using the bandwidth value allocated, the mechanism divides each second into n time slots and allows exactly one cell to pass through the gate during each time slot. Thus, the frequency with which cells enter public network becomes well streamlined eliminating the possibility of unexpected bursts of cells entering the network causing congestion. Although this technique helps eliminate congestion in the public network, if the cell generation process is erratic in the private network, congestion or buffer overflows may be encountered frequently in the private network domain. Since such a situation may be much more manageable than a congested public network, traffic shaping techniques are invariably used near the sources to streamline the cell flow.

In spite of shaping techniques that are employed, cells may encounter congestion due to various factors like the operational characteristics of the transmission medium, public networks, etc., or perhaps due to other private networks that may not be employing shaping techniques. When congested areas are encountered, the cells may be tagged for possible future deletion. If the cells are not discarded, then, when the cells reach the destination, the traffic receiver will be able to understand that the received cells passed through areas of the network that were congested. In certain implementations, when the cells are dropped, the device dropping the cells sends an explicit notification to the destination saying that the cells meant for that destination were discarded. This technique is called *Forward Explicit Congestion Notification* (FECN). If a message is sent to the source of the cells when they are discarded or marked for possible future discarding, the procedure is called *Backward Explicit Congestion Notification* (BECN). The source and destination thus notified may take appropriate corrective action. Unlike FECN, BECN is harder to implement as this requires the establishment of a return path from the destination to the source so that the notification can be sent to the source from any point in the circuit.

13.3 Simulation of ATM on LAN

In this section, we carry out a slow-motion study of ATM traffic, so that the problems associated with ATM traffic management and congestion control can be analyzed. By slow motion we mean simulating an ATM network using a 10base2 ethernet (alternatively called *ThinNet*, supporting just 10 Mbps bandwidth) and monitoring software. The focus of the simulation is to ignore the speed factor that dominates ATM congestion problems and concentrate on behavioral patterns of different traffic sources and destinations. In high speed ATM networks that carry traffic of the order of 655 Mbps, time available to analyze the flow in real time is so little that it precludes the possibility of using software-based traffic monitors. As a result network designers are forced to introduce hardware-based monitoring tools that can handle the traffic without disrupting the flow. Hence a slow-motion study of this kind is of enormous relevance when a switch to ATM from an existing 10base2, 10baseT (UTP) or slower network is being contemplated specifically for a small collection of workstations in a cluster computing environment. Such popular networks carry data using copper cable that does not support very high bandwidth. They are also error prone compared to fiber optic cable-based high speed networks. Implementing an ATM solution that is meant for high speed transmission media on such slow speed networks may not work very well due to some underlying assumptions of ATM networks (very low error rate in transmission, for example) not being satisfied. But a test bed of this kind helps us study the following issues:

1. Compatibility between the ATM protocol and existing hardware.
2. Possibility of multiplexing several slow traffic sources into one high speed ATM channel using a multiplexing switch as the bridge.
3. Congestion pattern formation due to the source of traffic alone, irrespective of the problems introduced by the speed of the network.

In order to carry out the study, we used an ATM Switch Simulator software modified to suit our requirements [10]. The simulation package consists of a Switch module, different types of traffic generators, a traffic sink, and a switch control program that is used to manipulate the Switch. The Switch module has a manually configurable routing table, a set of input ports and output ports, and a set of buffers each associated with individual ports or the entire switch. The module can be initiated with the required number of ports and the directions for channeling the traffic (i.e., traffic coming into the switch on port i should be pushed out through port j, etc.). A copy of the Switch can be located on different machines on the internet. Thus, we can interconnect port i on the switch (program) running on machine A to port k on the switch (program) running on machine B across the internet. Setting up several switches of this kind on different machines on the internet and interconnecting the ports to set up virtual channels for traffic flow allows us to set up and simulate as complicated a network as needed. There are three different types of traffic generators that generate constant bit rate, variable bit rate, and random bit rate traffic. We carried out a series of simulations. The results are discussed in the next section.

13.3.1 Different Types of Traffic

In these simulations, we studied the effect of buffer size (storage space where cells are stored in a switch while they are being processed for subsequent redirection) on the QoS. In order to understand the effect of buffer size on different kinds of traffic we generated CBR, ABR, and VBR traffic. The CBR or Constant Bit Rate traffic resembles ftp, e-mail, and http types of traffic where the traffic generation is easily maintained at a constant cell generation frequency level. ABR or Available Bit Rate model is used to handle traffic that is willing to accept and make use of any available bandwidth on the network. This kind of traffic will mostly be the type that is not affected by variation in the available bandwidth and time delays. The VBR or Variable Bit Rate traffic, on the other hand, resembles video traffic. This is due to the fact that depending upon the nature of the video that is being transmitted, the cell generation rate may go up or down.

The main thrust behind this series of simulations is to understand the effects of various traffic types (both homogenous as well as heterogenous) and switch characteristics on the QoS obtained. We used the CLR (Cell Loss Ratio) and the traffic processing delay at the switch as two factors used to represent the QoS. Processing delay is a good measure of CDV that is important for time sensitive traffic such as video transmission.

In one study, we used three different types of traffic sources, one at a time, to simulate CBR, VBR, and ABR traffic. Each traffic generator produced about 400 cells per minute. Since we wanted to have not just one but several traffic sources, we set up the switches with six input ports and six output ports. Each input port is dedicated to receiving cells from one specific traffic generator. This arrangement makes the simulation set up easier without any loss of accuracy (as several traffic sources feeding one nondedicated input port can be replaced by one super source providing the collective traffic feeding a dedicated input port). All the inputs received at the six input ports are directed to the seventh port in the switch. Port seven was connected to port eight so that all the traffic that reaches port seven is delivered to port eight. Incoming traffic at port eight is split again into six parts and delivered to six different output ports. The collection of traffic from six input ports to deliver into port seven and the splitting of traffic on port eight to several output ports is carried out through the routing table entries made when the switch is initialized for the simulation. Six traffic generator processes were started and linked to the input ports and six sink processes were attached to the output ports to simulate the destinations. The schematic of this set up is shown in Figure 13.2. Port seven of a switch process running on one machine is connected to port eight of the switch process running on another machine (using the DNS names across the internet) to direct traffic flow across switches in different machines with the flow directed to sink processes in the last switch.

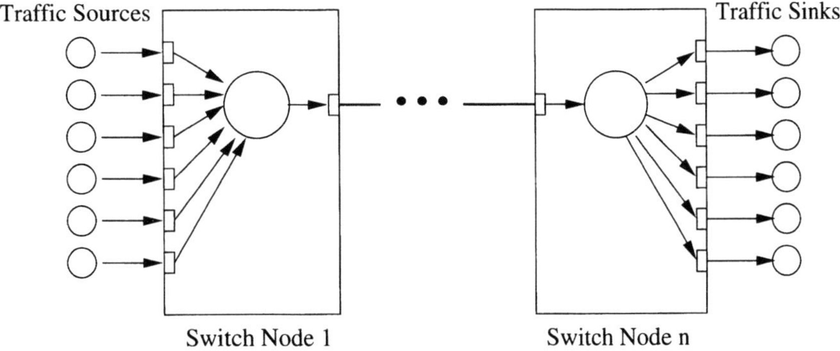

Figure 13.2 Schematic showing the simulation setup.

Once the processes are initiated, we waited for 30 seconds for the system to stabilize so that transient flow does not affect the observations made. Then we allowed the sustained flow to continue for five minutes, paused the switches, collected the required statistics, and shut the processes down. The total number of cells that came into a port as well as the entire switch, the total number of cells that went out of a port as well as the entire switch, the number of cells dropped due to congestion at the port level and at the switch level, the average delay encountered in the ports for the processed cells, and the number of simulated time units were the list of statistics collected. By trial, we found that the characteristics of the traffic flow was well captured in the observation once we ran the simulation for five minutes. Running the individual simulations for longer time periods increased the volume of total traffic handled in a linear scale without any difference in the QoS. This entire process was repeated for each buffer size and each traffic type.

13.3.2 Analysis of Results

During a series of simulations, we varied the buffer size on the port carrying this traffic from five cells to 15,000 cells. We used a total of 22 different buffer sizes listed. Since we wanted to study the effect of very small to very large buffer sizes, the sizes used are not evenly scaled across the entire range. Figure 13.3 shows a plot of CLR for the three traffic type for varying buffer sizes. As we can see from the plot, the cell loss ratio decreased overall as the buffer size of the handling port was increased. Since the CLR is more than 30 percent for very small buffer sizes, we understand that we may lose one-third the data transmitted if there is no buffer at the port level at all. This shows the importance of building buffers at the port levels in ATM switches. The increased loss experienced by the VBR traffic is explained by the burstiness normally found in the traffic of that kind that is more difficult for the switches to handle. The CLR of the CBR traffic is the easiest one to comprehend as it remains steady irrespective of the changes in the buffer size initially and declines almost linearly beyond a point. On the other end of the spectrum, ABR traffic provides the best QoS characteristics possible as its CLR remains lower than the other two all the time and reaches zero at the earliest, when the buffer size reaches 5000 cells. The plot indicates that the ABR traffic is the easiest one to handle (as one can expect) since the flow adjusts itself depending upon the available bandwidth. But in reality ABR mode is useful only for transmissions that are not hindered much by variations in CDV. This factor limits its use to regular data traffic. It does not work well with audio or video traffic.

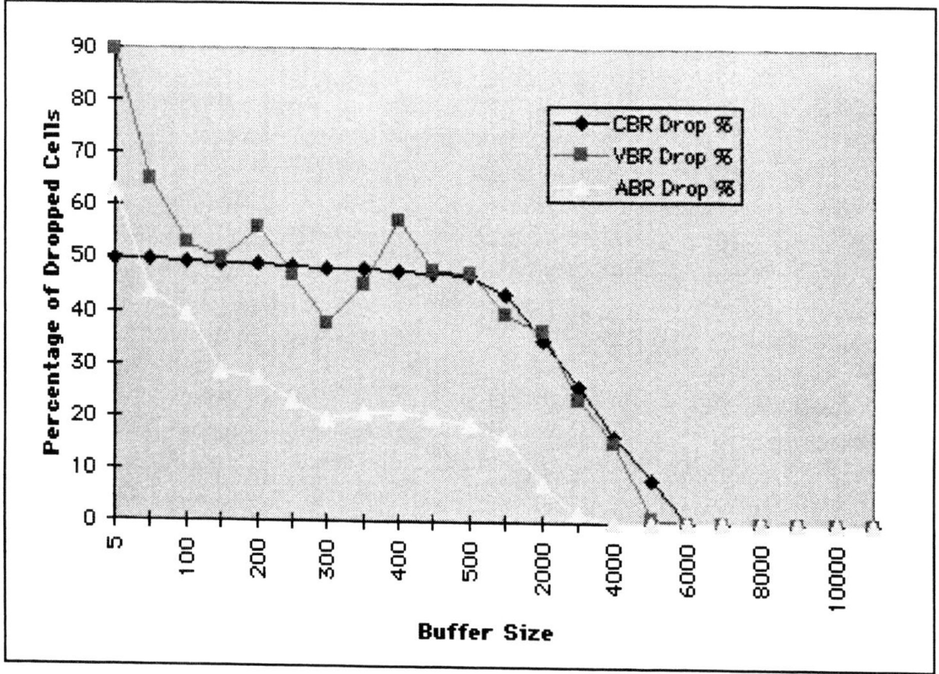

Figure 13.3 The effect of buffer size on cells dropped.

Figure 13.4 shows the CDV characteristics plot against varying buffer size for the

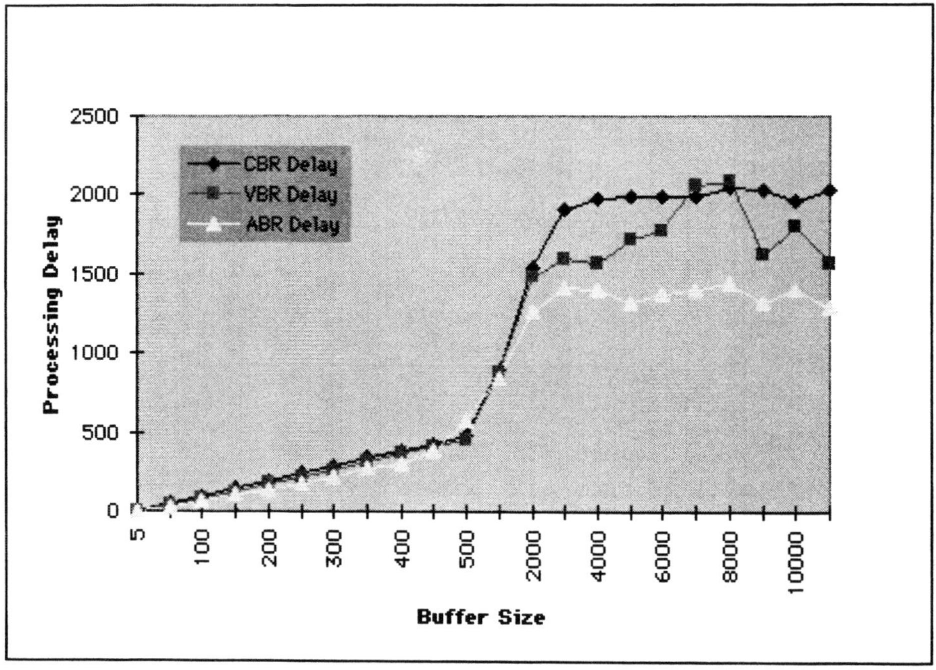

Figure 13.4 The Effect of buffer size on delay.

three different traffic types. As we can see, the VBR traffic is the one most affected by large processing delay, while ABR traffic is the least affected. Figures 13.5, 13.6 and 13.7 show both CLR and CDV together plotted against the size of the buffer for CBR, VBR, and ABR, respectively. We can see that the delay experienced is the maximum in the case of VBR. This indicates the difficulty involved in handling VBR traffic. On one hand, the burstiness in VBR traffic suggests maintaining large buffers in the switch ports handling such traffic so that the variation in the rate of cell generation by VBR sources can be accommodated without significant increase in the CLR. On the other hand, large buffer sizes increase the CDV experienced by the traffic which is unacceptable for video and (to a lesser extent) audio traffic that belong to the VBR category. The only good solution to handle this difficulty is to ensure that there is enough bandwidth readily available throughout the entire traffic route and the switches are fast enough in handling these cells so that there is no requirement for large buffer sizes to reduce CLR. This realization leads us to conclude that when migrations are planned from lower speed networks to ATM, it is important to identify the areas of network that may generate a lot of VBR traffic and give priority in increasing the bandwidth in those links first. ABR traffic sources can be brought on board towards the end of the upgrading process.

Alternatively, when we introduced a smoothing function called (traffic shaper) in between the VBR traffic source and the port receiving the flow, the burstiness

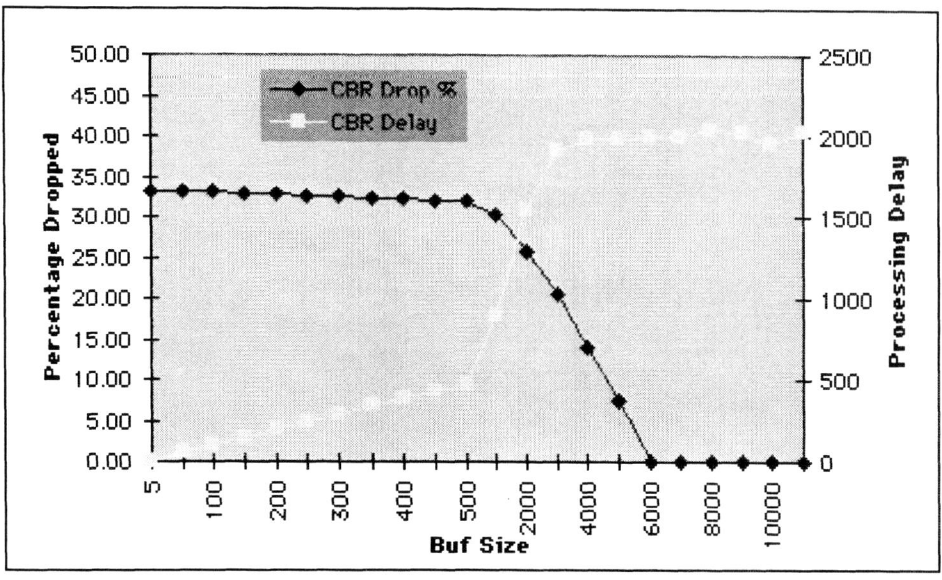

Figure 13.5 Cell loss and delay under CBR traffic.

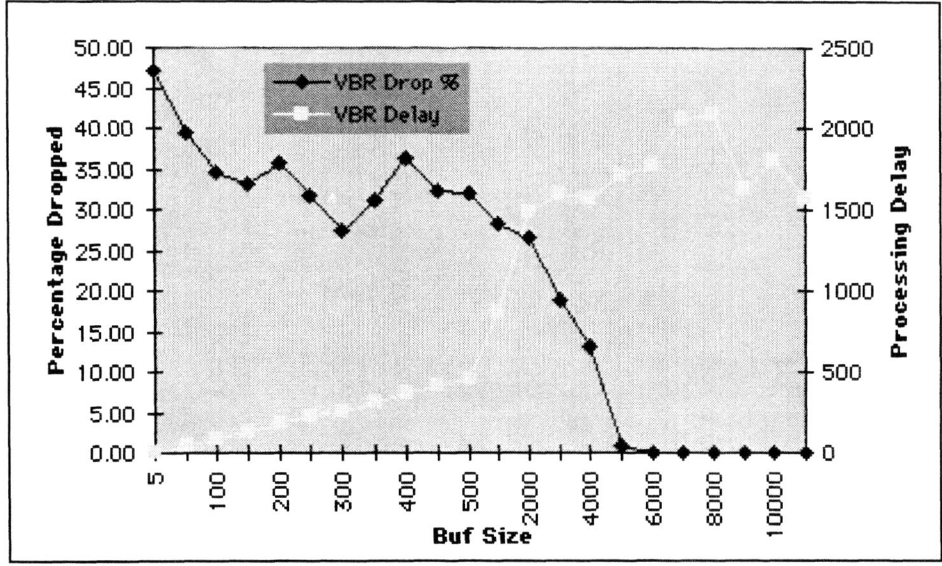

Figure 13.6 Cell loss and delay under VBR traffic.

in the flow got ironed out, making it CBR traffic. The extent to which a VBR flow is converted into CBR flow can be finetuned through the design factors in the traffic shaper. Thus, a good traffic shaper implemented at the VBR traffic source

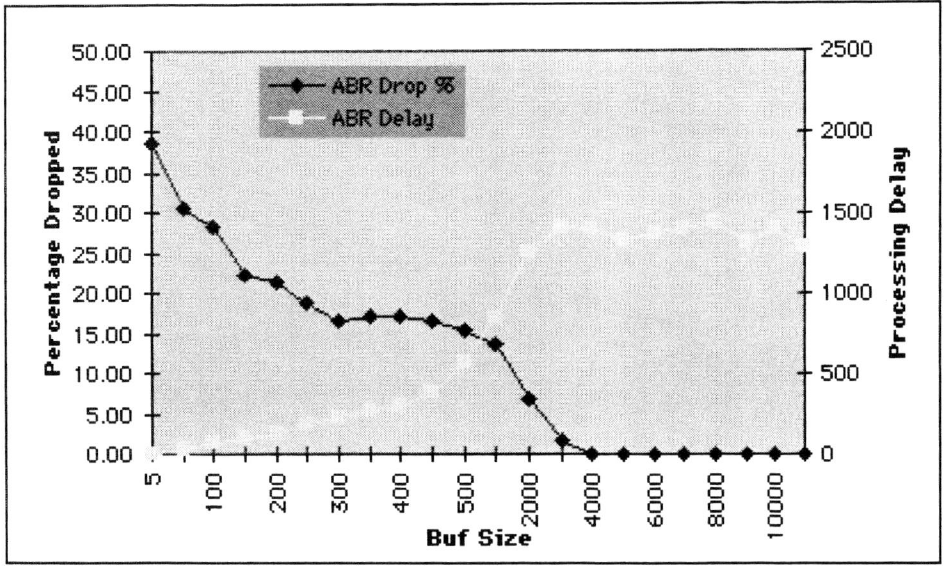

Figure 13.7 Cell loss and delay under ABR traffic.

itself will smoothen flow considerably, making it more suitable for slow speed ATM networks that may not be able to handle congestion well.

13.3.3 Heterogeneous Traffic Condition

In addition to the studies based on homogenous traffic generators, we also wanted to analyze the effect of mixed traffic types flowing into and out of a switch. So in another set of experiments, we mixed the traffic sources feeding into the six ports of the ATM switch. Instead of all six sources generating either CBR or VBR or ABR traffic during one run, we started two generators creating CBR traffic, another two generators creating VBR and a third set generating ABR traffic at the same time and fed all the generated flow into the six input ports of the switch. Results of this run are shown in Figure 13.8. Although approximately 12,000 cells were transmitted in each case (both under homogenous as well as heterogenous traffic conditions), the flow under mixed traffic conditions had much better QoS, resulting in lower CLR as well as delay. This is explained by the fact that the bursts introduced by the VBR traffic were compensated by the ABR traffic, resulting in a much more manageable total traffic flow. This shows that even slow speed networks switching to ATM networks may provide better overall QoS when the traffic sources are a good mix of different kinds.

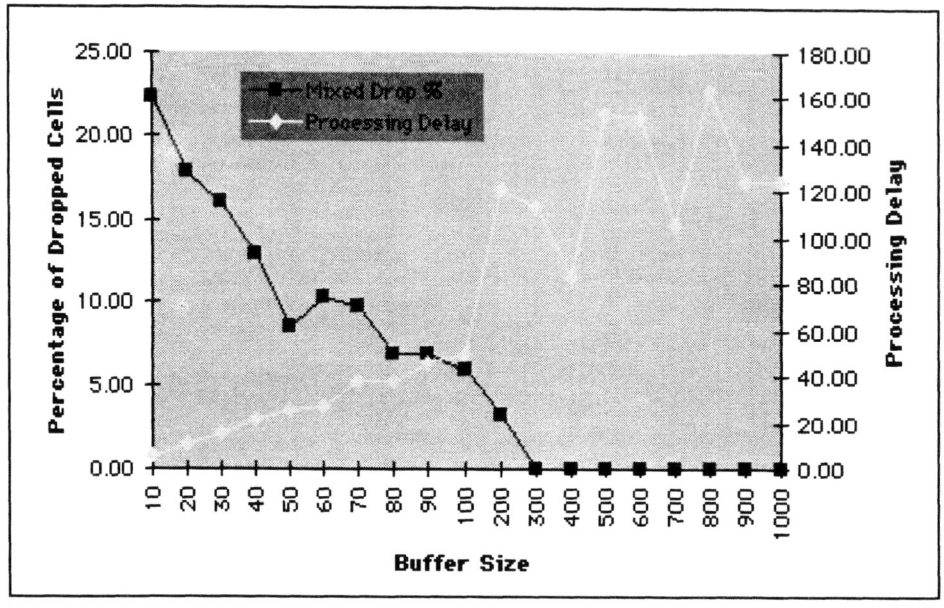

Figure 13.8 Cell loss and delay under mixed traffic.

13.3.4 Summary

An ATM network is a complex setup with several different parameters governing the traffic flow. What we tried to do in our simulations was to characterize the significant QoS factor variations with respect to different types of traffic. Our simulations can be modified taking into consideration factors that may be specific to one network so that the results obtained are more accurate and relevant to the network under analysis. These factors could be the mix of traffic sources, the burstiness found in the generated flow, the number of switches the traffic has to pass through, individual port and switch specifications, etc. Simulating every possible combination is simply impossible due to the large number of conceivable variations. We concluded our simulations after gaining an insight into some of the important characteristics. Interpretation of the results can be summarized as follows:

- The buffer size of the individual ports in ATM switches plays a significant role in traffic congestion management.
- It is desirable to keep a large buffer in switches handling CBR traffic.
- VBR traffic that may be sensitive to time delays in the transmission gets adversely affected by large buffer sizes.
- Although large buffer sizes may ensure that the cells are not dropped, they may introduce significant delay that may not be acceptable to certain types of traffic that are sensitive to time delay variation.

13.4 Migration Planning

The superiority of ATM technology is widely recognized today. But costs involved in migrating existing legacy LANs to ATM remains prohibitively high. So when there are budgetary constraints, network designers are quite often required to implement such migration in phases. The goal of such efforts will be to identify and enhance the capacity of a minimum number of edges to realize overall improvement in the traffic flow. In this section, we analyze this difficulty and provide an algorithm to identify and prioritize congested network links that deserve a switchover to ATM. Our algorithm is based on a graph theoretic approach that identifies flow congestion areas in a given network.

13.4.1 LAN to Directed Graph

Given an existing LAN, it can be represented in the form of a directed graph $G(V, E)$, where V is the set of vertices, each representing a node on the LAN, and E is the set of edges, each representing an existing link between two nodes on the network. Bandwidth available on each link can be defined as the edge capacity. The nodes in the LAN that generate traffic can be represented as the source nodes in the graph. Similarly, the traffic receivers (destinations) in the LAN can be the sinks of the digraph. Depending upon the actual usage of the bandwidth, each one of the edges in the graph can be either saturated or unsaturated. If we color the saturated edges red and unsaturated edges blue, existence of a blue path from the source to the sink reflects the presence of an unsaturated path from the source to the destination in the LAN. From a practical point of view, graphs where there are such paths are not of much interest to us as they indicate that the flow is not saturated and so none of the edges need capacity enhancement. But the algorithm we present still works on such graphs and identifies the bottlenecks, assuming that the network is pushing the maximum possible flow.

Graphs in which all the paths from the source to destination contain red edges contain paths that are already saturated by the traffic flow. What is of interest to us is developing a systematic way to identify specific red edges that, when converted into blue ones (i.e., made unsaturated by capacity enhancement), will increase the maximal flow of the graph significantly. In a flow graph with a maximal flow, not all edges may have flows equal to their capacity. The edges that have flows equal to their capacity are the bottlenecks, and are hence candidates for enhancement.

Given a directed graph with capacities on the edges, the problem of determining the maximal flow possible from the source to the destination has been well studied [2], [17]. We are interested in identifying the smallest set of edges such that increasing the capacity on each of these edges leads to a maximal increase in the flow of the modified graph. So, we pose the question formally as follows:

Problem: Given a network, i.e., a finite directed graph $G = (V, E)$ with source $S \in V$, destination $Q \in V$, and edge capacities $b : E \rightarrow R_0^+ \bigcup \{\infty\}$, $|b|$ denotes the value of a maximum flow from S to Q in the network. For every set $F \subseteq E$ define

$i(F) = |b_F| - |b|$ where $b_F(e) = b(e)$ if $e \in E \backslash F$ and $b_F(e) = \infty$ if $e \in F$. Now the problem is to identify a set $C \subseteq E$ such that $i(C) = max\{i(F) : |F| = m\}$ where $m = min\{|F| : i(F) > 0\}$.

We call this maximal flow of the modified graph the *enhanced flow* of the original graph. Before we present the algorithm to compute enhanced flow for a given digraph, we discuss the required preliminary details below.

Definition 1: An edge for which the flow equals the capacity is called a *saturated* edge.

Definition 2: A *saturated* graph is one in which all the edges are saturated. Otherwise, it is *unsaturated.*

Definition 3: The process of increasing the capacity of an edge is called *infinitizing.*

In reality, the term *infinitizing* might be a misnomer as upgrading a LAN link will increase the bandwidth of that particular link only by a finite amount and not to infinity. But the enhancement is expected to be substantial compared to the original bandwidth of the link. So in order to make the analysis of the graph easier, we consider this new bandwidth as infinity (as it is not expected to pose any bottleneck for the traffic flow until all the links of the LAN are upgraded to ATM).

Definition 4: The *enhancement set of the graph* is the smallest set of edges such that infinitizing the capacity on each of these edges leads to an increase in the maximal flow of the modified graph.

If there is more than one set with the same (minimum) number of edges, then the *enhancement set* is the one that provides maximum increase in flow. If the increase in maximal flow is also identical, then any one of those sets can be named the enhancement set.

Lemma 1: In a graph with a maximal flow, each path from the source to the destination has at least one saturated edge.

Proof: If not, then the flow can be increased along this path, and so the flow is not maximal. ∎

Lemma 2: If the graph is saturated, then the edges on the shortest path constitute the enhancement set for the graph.

Proof: By definition, enhancement set is the smallest set of edges that need to be infinitized to realize increase in overall flow. In a saturated graph, the shortest path from source to destination contains the least number of edges that form the bottleneck. ∎

Lemma 3: Enhanced flow of every saturated graph is the infinite flow.

Proof: Computation of the enhancement set in a saturated graph results in a list of all the edges found in the shortest path. When an entire path from source to destination is enhanced, the resulting flow is infinite. ■

Since we are interested in upgrading as few edges as possible to realize the maximum increase in the overall flow, shorter paths from source to destination are better candidates. In addition, paths with many unsaturated edges are desirable since they may require capacity enhancement for only a few edges in them. Keeping this perspective, we may use the words enhance or upgrade (an edge) to mean the same idea of increasing an edge's capacity. We consider graphs with only one source and one destination, since graphs with multiple sources and multiple destinations can be reduced to the single source and single destination case easily [2].

13.4.2 A Congestion Locator Algorithm

This section presents a new algorithm called wave front that identifies the areas of a network that present the most restrictive bottleneck for traffic flow. Once identified, if the capacities of these edges are enhanced, it will result in better overall traffic flow. It is loosely based on the Breadth First Search technique.

To explain the functioning of the algorithm intuitively, the search process exploring the edges can be considered as a wave front moving from the *source (S)* outward till either a saturated edge or the *destination (Q)* is reached. If a saturated edge is found along one of the paths, that path is not extended further until all the other paths also encounter a saturated edge. Thus, the paths are extended in synchrony, synchronized by the encounter of a saturated edge or Q. The purpose is to find all paths from S to Q with the smallest number of saturated edges. Therefore, the paths are progressively examined and extended in such a manner that all of them have almost the same number of saturated edges (they may differ by at most one at any time). Once the destination is found along any path, the number of saturated edges to be enhanced is determined.

- $\mathcal{C}$ - set of n-tuples of saturated candidate edges for enhancement. Each n-tuple corresponds to candidate edges in one path from S to Q.
- W - denotes the set of vertices forming the wave front
- $adj(W)$ - denotes the set of vertices adjacent to the set of vertices W in the direction of the wave front
- $head(e)$ - denotes the vertex at the head of the directed edge e
- $out(W)$ - denotes the set of outgoing edges from the set of vertices W

1. begin {**wave front**}
2. $W = \{ S \}$; $W' = \{ \}$; MAX=0; SET=1; $UNSET$=0; NUM_SAT=0; $DEST$=0;

3. Scan all $adj(W)$: /* BFS */

   - if ($Q \in adj(W)$), $DEST$=1;
   - if $e \in out(W)$ is saturated,
     $\mathcal{C}_i = \mathcal{C}_i \cup e$ /* add e to candidate list specific to this path i */
     if $MAX = UNSET, NUM\_SAT+ = 1$; $MAX = SET$;
     $W = adj(W) - head(e)$. /* do not extend this path */
     $W' = \{head(e)\}$ /* add this to the next wave front */

   else if $DEST$=0 then $W = adj(W)$. /* make next set of vertices the new front */
   else $W = \phi$

4. if $W \neq \phi$ /* is nonempty */
   go to step 3.
   else /* first wave front over, Q not found yet */
   $MAX = UNSET$
   $W = W'$
   $W' = \{\}$
   go to step 4.

5. Continue until Q is reached or no paths are left to explore. If there is no path from S to Q, exit with C = { }. /* As each iteration is completed, each $\mathcal{C}_i$ in $\mathcal{C}$ corresponding to path i gets one edge added */

6. If $DEST$ = 1, NUM_SAT indicates the smallest number of saturated edges in any path from S to Q. $\mathcal{C}$ is a set of n-tuples of edges that must be enhanced and the tuple that yields the maximum increase in flow must be selected.

   /* For example, $\mathcal{C}$ = {{e1,e3}, {e5,e9}} So, infinitize $e1, e3$. Compute flow. Then infinitize $e5, e9$. Compute flow. Select max of the two. */

7. end {**wave front**}

For the sake of brevity, we have left out the proof of correctness. It can be found in [16]. Figure 13.9 presents the algorithm in a flow chart form.

13.4.3 An Illustration

In this section, we consider a sample digraph, shown in Figure 13.10, and apply the algorithm discussed, to identify the minimum number of edges that need to be upgraded to realize an overall increase in the flow. The nodes S and Q represent the the source and the destination in the network, respectively.

1. Starting at the source node S, we search for the destination node Q in the next level of the tree. It is not found. We reach nodes a and c instead. So we proceed.

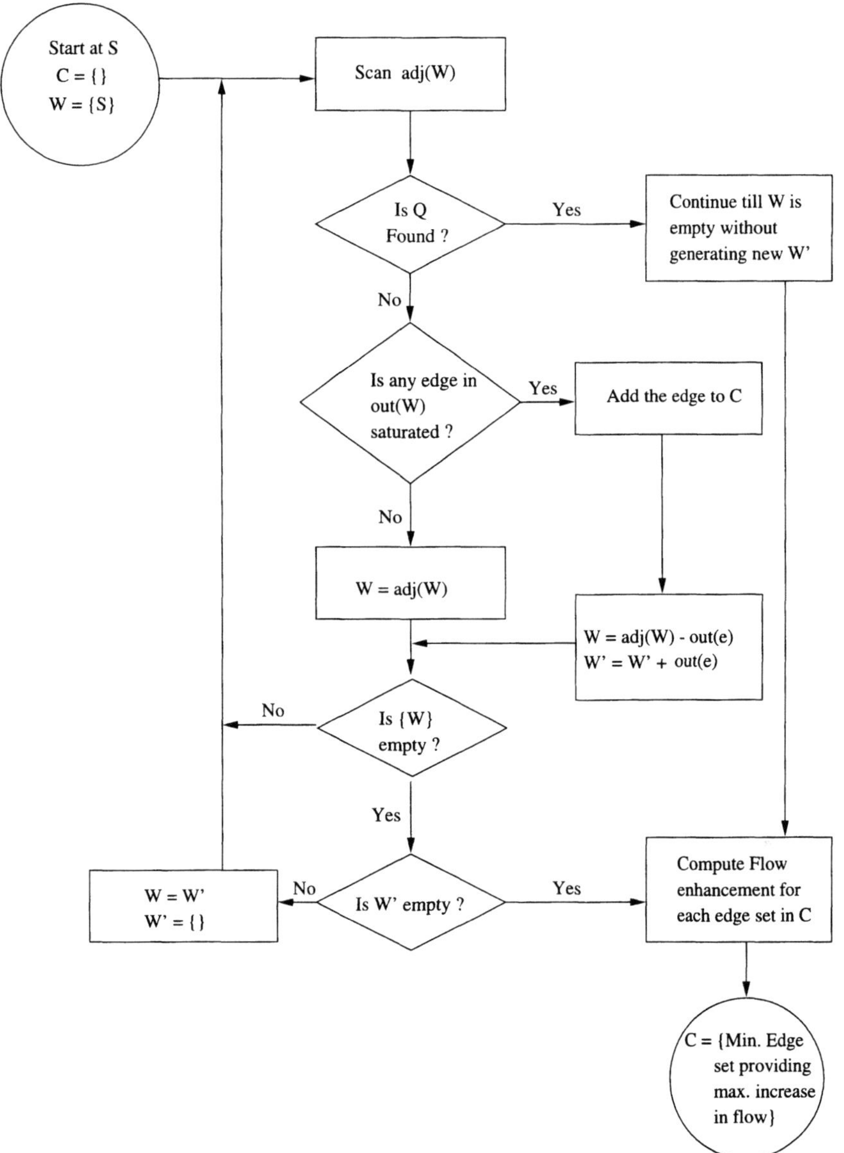

Figure 13.9 The Wave Front algorithm for flow enhancement.

2. We search the graph breadth first and look for paths leading from S to Q. On the third hop a path (*Scbe*) with two saturated edges is detected. Search on this path stops until all the other paths encounter two saturated edges each.

3. On the fourth hop another path (*Scefg*) with two saturated edges is found.

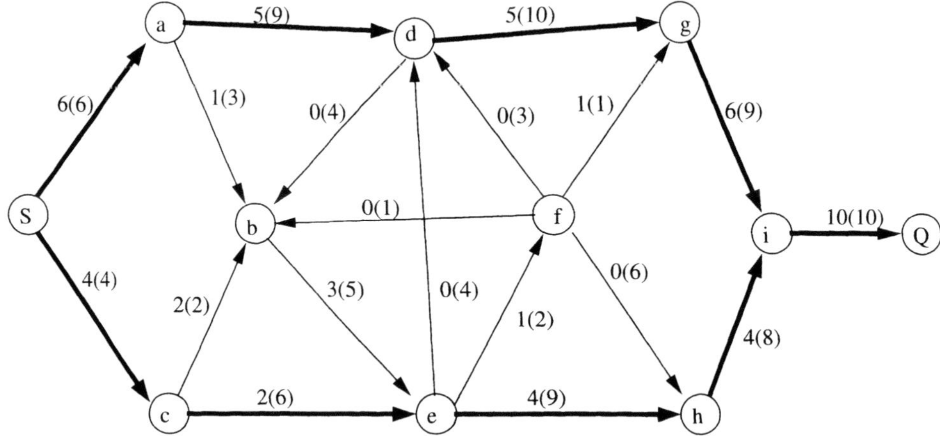

Figure 13.10 Chosen shortest paths.

Search continues on other paths for discovering two saturated edges each or to reach Q.

4. On the fifth hop, we have the following paths: *Sadbed, Sadbef, Sadbeh, SadgiQ, Sabedg, Sabedb, Sabefd, Sabefg, Sabefh, Sabehi,* and *ScehiQ*. Out of these, *SadgiQ* and *ScehiQ* are the two shortest paths (meaning paths with least number of saturated edges) from source S to destination Q. These two paths are shown in darker lines in Figure 13.10.

5. Both the paths have two saturated edges, i.e., Sa and iQ in case of *SadgiQ*; Sc and iQ in case of *ScehiQ*.

6. Since the number of saturated edges in each path is the same, we compute the enhancement in flow that will be achieved when all the saturated edges in one path are enhanced.

7. Sa and iQ enhancement results in a flow increase of six units. Sc and iQ enhancement results in a four unit increase.

8. So we choose $\{Sa, iQ\}$ as the enhancement set.

The algorithm we presented identifies the least number of saturated edges that need to be enhanced to realize an increase in the maximal flow. There can be budgetary constraints that may warrant a search for a specific number of edges that deserve an upgrade. So we pose the following interesting variants of the problem:

1. Given a directed graph, choose n edges for infinitizing, so that the resultant enhanced flow is maximal.

2. Given a directed graph with a maximal flow L, infinitize the smallest number of edges so that the enhanced flow is L_e.

If we are looking for just one edge for possible upgrade, we can use the concept of *minimum cutsets* defined in the *Max-flow Min-cut theorem* [2]. But, if we are trying to replace an arbitrary number of links, or if we are trying to increase the maximal flow by a specific value, the problem becomes compounded by the combinatorial nature of the solution space. Considering an efficiency factor η = *increase in flow/Number of links chosen for enhancement* may give a clearer image of the cost and benefit scenario. If we contrast a path where the successive links from source to destination have monotonically increasing capacities against another path of the same length where the successive links from source to destination have monotonically decreasing capacities, the need for such an efficiency factor becomes more apparent. The reader may try to work out the details or refer to [16] for a more elaborate discussion.

13.5 Conclusions

As we have been emphasizing all along, as of now ATM is the best suited technology to carry a wide array of data types as well as the burgeoning multimedia traffic at very high speeds across networks. Although there are very strong contenders in the form of Gigabit networks, fast ethernet, etc., for multimedia traffic hauling networks, such technologies do lag behind ATM in one or more areas. For example, gigabit networks do not possess the QoS guarantees found in ATM. Fast ethernet, though as of now more economical compared to ATM, does not work very well at very high speeds (600 Mbps and more). So the ATM technology has a lot of potential and is well set to become the dominant network technology in the nearby future.

Our research effort focused on ways and means to improve the traffic management and congestion control techniques in the ATM network model. Specifically, it focussed on two areas of paramount interest, simulation of ATM traffic on slower speed networks and migration planning. Work discussed in this chapter can be carried further in several areas. More realistic simulations than what we did for our study can be carried out with trace driven traffic of a specific network that may give better empirical understanding of the traffic characteristics of the network under consideration. There are several commercially available software/hardware packages that allow very detailed simulation of ATM operations on smaller LANs, yielding a better insight into the pros and cons of deploying ATM. This will allow network designers to justify the expense or make a decision to postpone the deployment to a later date. Similarly, development of better migration planning algorithms and improved negotiation techniques between the end terminals and the network will definitely improve the efficiency of resource utilization.

To quote from the book, *ATM: Theory and Application* [12], "The problem of achieving LAN-like flow and congestion control over ATM will take longer to solve, and is a critical issue for the success of ATM. ... The problem of determining Connection Admission Control (CAC) procedures to implement a network to provide multiple QoS classes will be a challenging one. The ability for a network provider to perform this balancing act will be a competitive differentiator." Our work, hopefully, contributes some positive ideas toward addressing these issues.

13.6 Bibliography

[1] M.E. Anagostou, M.E. Theologou and E.N. Protonotarios. Cell Insertion Ratio in Asynchronous Transfer Mode Networks. *Computer Networks and ISDN Systems,* vol. 24(4), pages 335–344, May 1992.

[2] J.A. Bondy and U.S.R. Murty. *Graph Theory with Applications.* Elsevier, North Holland, Inc., pages 191–211, 1976.

[3] P.E. Boyer and D.P. Tranchier. A Reservation Principle with Applications to the ATM Traffic Control. *Computer Networks and ISDN Systems,* vol. 24(4), pages 321–334, May 1992.

[4] CCITT Temporary Document 43, Com XVIII/8. On Networking and Resource Management. Matsuyama, Dec. 1990.

[5] S. Chowdhury and K. Sohraby. Bandwidth Allocation Algorithms for Packet Video in ATM Networks. *Computer Networks and ISDN Systems,* vol. 26, pages 1215–1223, 1994.

[6] A. Eckberg. B-ISDN/ATM Traffic and Congestion Control. *IEEE Network,* Sept. 1992.

[7] C. Fayet, A. Jacques and G. Pujolle. High Speed Switching for ATM: the BSS. *Computer Networks and ISDN Systems,* vol. 26, pages 1225–1234, 1994.

[8] A. Gersht and K. Lee. A Congestion Control Framework for ATM Networks. *IEEE J. on Selected Areas in Communications,* Sept. 1991.

[9] F. Guillemin and A. Dupuis. A Basic Requirement for the Policing Function in ATM Networks. *Computer Networks and ISDN Systems,* vol. 24(4), pages 311–320, May 1992.

[10] D.A. Junkins. ATM Switch Simulator. *Masters Thesis,* University of Washington, April 1996.

[11] J.-Y. Le Boudec. The Asynchronous Transfer Mode: A Tutorial. *Computer Networks and ISDN Systems,* vol. 24(4), pages 279–310, May 1992.

[12] D.E. McDysan and D.L. Spohn. *ATM Theory and Application.* McGraw-Hill, Inc., New York, 1994.

[13] S. Mehta. Network Monitoring and Testing. *Communications Week,* pages S4–S8, May 22, 1995.

[14] W. Roberts. Traffic Control in B-ISDN. *Computer Networks and ISDN System,* vol. 25, pages 1065–1064, 1993.

[15] W. Stallings. *ISDN and Broadband ISDN with Frame Relay and ATM,* 3rd Edition, Prentice Hall, NJ, 1995.

[16] S. Vedantham. Traffic Management and Congestion Control in the ATM Network Model. *Ph.D. Dissertation,* Louisiana State University, 1997.

[17] H. Walther. *Ten Applications of Graph Theory.* D. Reidel Publishing Company, Boston, MA, pages 31–68, 1984.

[18] J.L. Wang and L.T. Lee. Two-Level Congestion Control Schemes for ATM Networks. *ACM SIGICE Bulletin,* vol. 20(2), pages 13–32, October 1994.

Chapter 14

Load Balancing Over Networks

Rawn Shah

SunWorld Magazine
San Francisco, CA

Email: *rawn@rtd.com*

14.1 Introduction

Load balancing over a network is the use of devices external to the processing nodes in a cluster to distribute workload or network traffic load across the cluster. The decision to distribute the load to a particular node can be static preprogrammed settings or can dynamically change depending upon current network status. The nodes may be interconnected among themselves within the cluster, but more importantly, they must be connected directly or indirectly to the balancing device that performs the load distribution.

The processing nodes can further participate by providing various status information regarding their current processor load, the application system load, the number of active users, the availability of network protocol buffers, the availability of system memory, or other specific resources. This information is passed on to the balancing device that monitors the status of all the processing nodes within its domain and actively dictates where to direct the next processing job. The balancing device can be a single unit or a group of units working in parallel or under a tree hierarchy.

The balancing device uses one or more algorithms or methods together with static or dynamic settings to decide which node gets the next incoming connection request. These methods can be optimized for a particular application or be application-independent and depend solely upon network protocol and traffic.

These two ways of network load balancing, a network point of view and an application point of view, have different needs and involve different algorithms. With the network point of view, the load balancing system monitors incoming data to a cluster and distributes traffic based upon network protocol and traffic information. In an application-specific balancing system, the distribution algorithm is based upon particulars of the application. Application-specific balancing is at a higher level in the network communications model. It is possible to build an application-specific balancing system on top of an existing network-specific balancing system or combine the two into a more complex system.

The network protocol we will examine is TCP/IP, a packet-based system where network information is contained within each and every data packet. This allows every data packet to be considered as a key in a caching or balancing algorithm. However, the data packets by themselves are often segmented and usually do not contain an entire message and hence must be considered altogether as a stream of packets from a source to a destination. Furthermore, a session may often be established between the source and destination computers that may also affect the distribution algorithm.

TCP/IP, until recently, did not have any Quality of Service (QoS) guarantee system for reliable network delivery of information. In spite of the emergence of QoS protocols and compliant network hardware, a significant portion of the Internet and most intranet routers and servers do not implement them. Furthermore, most of the applications on the Internet do not yet use these QoS methods. Thus, various network load-balancing workarounds have been developed in lieu of QoS support. They have been implemented with success in commercial networks both for intranet and Internet use. In this chapter, we examine these methods and several commercially available implementations.

14.2 Methods

Load balancing over a network is achieved through the employment of several basic methods that can, in turn, be combined to create more advanced systems. The balancing device monitors incoming traffic and cluster status and uses these methods to determine how new traffic is to be distributed across the nodes of the cluster. The methods can be looked upon as mathematical functions that work on statistics of network traffic and node status to determine an appropriate target for receiving new load. Each of these functions are influenced by several factors that define behavior and role of the device.

14.2.1 Factors Affecting Balancing Methods

The factors affecting load balancing over a network define the capabilities and limits of the balancing device. These are influences of the environment that the device works in and have to support. The most basic factor, the structure of the TCP/IP protocol family, is a given. The four most important protocols in this family include the Internet Protocol (IP) and the Internet Control Message Protocol (ICMP) at the network layer; and the Transmission Control Protocol (TCP) and User Datagram Protocol (UDP) at the transport layer. For more details on how each of these protocols work, please read [9]. The following are details on other factors.

Network Address Translation

Network address translation is the process of converting internal or private network address and routing information into external or public addresses and routes. This is particularly significant due to the limited address space of the current version of the Internet Protocol, Version 4 (ipv4). Furthermore, many companies prefer an internal address space that is kept strictly within their computing environment, for security reasons; in such a case a *Network Address Translator* (NAT) is sometimes referred to as a Firewall.

Any balancing device required to perform network address translation must keep separate tables for internal and external representations of computer or host information. There is usually a check for addresses that are illegal or prohibited from access in the external space. NATs and Firewalls perform most checks based upon the host name of the destination computer.

The use of NATs is complementary to allowing a client to discover the address of a node. Security mechanisms, such as the Internet IPSec standard for encrypting transport layer activity between two nodes, cannot be used in such a situation. IPSec [2] is a required item in building *Virtual Private Networks* (VPNs). A VPN allows remote clients connected to the main network over public network links to participate as equal citizens on the main network by encrypting all packets between the client and the main network that travel over the public net. Products which rely on network address translation modify the address information which is used in generating a security key for encryption. Since the VPN relies on the address information of the destination node within the NAT's private network, this appears to the NAT as an access violation. In addition, the NAT's address translation process appears as an attempted violation to get to the VPN data.

Domain Names

Internet Domain names and host names form the basis of many balancing methods. The IP host name provides a recognizable and understandable tag for humans and can thus be used as a key or reference point by the balancing device. In many cases, host names and domain names form the primary element in deciding upon a distribution algorithm. In an intranet, the host name is the primary key; when distributing traffic across the Internet the domain part of the name is primary.

A *Fully Qualified Domain Name* (FQDN) is a combination of both the host name and the domain name to create a uniquely identifiable name for a system on the Internet. In some cases, there is also a subnet name between the host and domain parts to indicate another level of hierarchy. There can be as many multiple levels of subnets as a network manager likes but it is usually just kept to one or two. The subnet names belong to the domain part of an FQDN.

The mapping between an FQDN and an IP address is independent of the name or the level of hierarchy. For human readability, the IP address (in the current ipv4 version) is represented in four groups of 8-bit numbers; e.g., 198.102.68.2.

The *Domain Name System* (DNS) is the standard translation mechanism, mapping names to addresses and vice versa. Today, a domain name can map to multiple network addresses (a virtual domain) and an IP address can have multiple domain names associated with it (a virtual IP address). This translation step occurs in the DNS server system. As most computers are referenced by their FQDN and not their direct IP address, the DNS server becomes a crucial aid to the balancing device system to help determine load distribution.

With the ability to map multiple hosts or nodes to a single host name, you have the basis for creating an identifier for a whole cluster of nodes. Thus, the translation process from a host name to its corresponding IP address is where part of the balancing method is located.

Wire-speed Processing

Wire-speed processing is the ability to perform network traffic processing and redirection at the full speed of the incoming packets to prevent any traffic bottlenecks at the network device. Primarily, wire-speed processing affects the traffic at each node. Although the *Network Interface Card* (NIC) hardware at the node may be capable of receiving and transmitting data at the full speed of the network, the operating system may be limited in this capacity. This can result in a slower response, or an inability to accept new connections at individual nodes in a cluster.

Node Operating System Limitations

Some operating systems have limitations in the speed at which they can process packets, the number of connections they can support, and the type of traffic they can accept. High-speed networks can result in a large number of system interrupts as new packets arrive. Although, theoretically, the NIC and operating system should be able to handle the traffic, the OS may not be able to process large numbers of interrupts as quickly as needed. In addition, they may be limited by multiple layers of OS components each having to process incoming data at some level. This affects the cluster in much the same way as for wire-speed processing.

Balancing Device Limitations

All balancing devices have practical limitations incurred by memory and processing speed. Devices that keep tables of information on incoming connections and node status limit the size of the cluster and the traffic processing rate. Balancing methods which work well in small clusters may not be scaleable to large numbers of nodes. Furthermore, a balancing method used in one scenario (e.g., node load-based balancing, primarily on LAN clusters) may be inefficient in another (e.g., over the Internet).

Session- and nonsession-based Traffic

A TCP session usually consists of a set of IP packets with serialized numbers. Balancing devices often keep track of active TCP sessions in their connection tables to keep the proper traffic flowing to a node. Session-based traffic is now a common part of all balancing algorithms and thus do not affect them significantly.

When a TCP session begins, the source computer sends a packet with a TCP header containing the TCP Synchronize (TCP_SYN) flag bit set. This tells the destination to begin synchronizing TCP packet sequence numbers and send the starting number of the sequence back to the source so that it can begin sending data. When the session is complete and the connection is to be closed, either the source or destination computer sends a TCP Session Finished (TCP_FIN) message to its counterpart. The ports on both machines then close themselves and the session is closed [9]. Balancing devices look for IP packets with TCP_SYN and TCP_FIN messages as the start and end of a session and direct all traffic between the source and intended destination to a specific node in the cluster.

However, nonsession-based traffic, such as UDP datagrams, cannot be completely accounted for. UDP packets are independent of each other and there isn't necessarily a continuity between one packet and the next. However, at the application level, there may be a reliance upon receiving a packet from the same machine each time. A cluster that spreads UDP packets across its nodes may leave the application at an ambiguous state.

Some vendors have created a patchwork system for UDP by keeping track of incoming datagram from a source and establishing a time limit for a 'session.' When a new UDP packet is received, the device looks at the destination address and assigns it to a specific node. All incoming packets from that source IP address will continue to be directed at the same node. If no more packets from the source is received after a certain user-specified interval, the 'UDP session' is considered as closed and the device removes the source IP- destination node IP pair from its table in memory [1]. Although not 100 percent effective, it solves UDP load balancing.

Application Dependencies

Some applications require that once a source computer has accessed a particular node, they continue to connect to that same node every time in the future. This is usually evident in a shared-nothing cluster where each node is independent of the other. For example, a user logs in to a Web-based bulletin board and the node creates a Web-session along with profile information for that user. Although the TCP connection to the node is transient for each page access, the Web server needs to keep track of the user's activity until the user logs out.

These kinds of application dependencies can be fixed by changing the application code to build a more cluster-aware application, but this is not always possible. The balancing device must be made aware of the application level requirements for such cases and this affects the choice of balancing algorithms. This kind of session which requires a balancing device to continue to direct client requests to a specific server in spite of its existing load due to application-specific reasons is known as a sticky session.

A network load balancing system created specifically for the needs of a TCP/IP network application is often called a Layer 4 optimized system or a Layer 4 switched network to indicate that the optimization is performed at the ISO networking model Transport layer (number 4 from the lowest layer). Some vendors even label their products as Layer 5 (the Session layer) network systems to indicate the products focus on TCP session balancing. However, the TCP/IP protocol stack does not differentiate sessions from the transports and a TCP session is a feature of the TCP protocol and not an independent session management layer. Essentially, the products are the same as Layer 4 products.

14.2.2 Simple Balancing Methods

A simple balancing method is a single function that selects the node within a cluster to send a new request to. Some of these methods can be used by themselves, but others work properly only when used in conjunction with another simple or advanced method.

Weighting

The weighting method provides a simple way of conferring loads onto the nodes according to the priority value or weight of the node. Take, for example, four nodes in a cluster assigned the following weights: 2, 4, 8, 6. The sum total of weights is 20. When a new connection request arrives, the node with the highest weight is assigned the request. Weighting functions are only used in conjunction with other balancing methods such as Least Connections, Minimum Misses, Fastest Response, and Round-Robin assignment. The weights assigned to the nodes are based upon some assumption of each node's capacity.

Randomization

The randomization method assigns each node with a value generated by a pseudo-random algorithm. The node with the lowest or highest random number value is then given priority over others, following in sequence through the other nodes. Randomization is a automatic way of creating a weighting function without any specific bias towards a node. Since any machine is as likely to be the one with the highest priority over time, this system works best in identical node environments.

Round-Robin

The Round-Robin, Rotary, or Cyclic method is a simple moniker for rotating linearly through a list of nodes. The balancing device assigns the next incoming request to the next node in the list and rotates through the list continuously for further requests. Compared to the randomization system, the behavior of Round-Robin systems is predictable.

Round-Robin is still commonly used by itself in DNS name resolution as a balancing method, a system that has several limitations. The DNS server usually has no knowledge if a node is actually running since its only role is to resolve names.

Clients requesting a DNS name to address translation will cache the results locally which interferes with proper network load balancing since they will access only one node continuously. DNS servers do not keep track of server loads; this is not a function of the name resolution system. Simply implementing a Round-Robin DNS resolver creates an inefficient network balancing system.

Round-Robin is typically effective where all the nodes in the cluster are identical in capacity and performance. Although it does not provide equilibrium across the cluster, when used in combination with other simple balancing methods, it has proven quite effective in real-world cases.

Hashing

The Hashing method works similar to the simple weighting system with the added benefit that packets from the same source address will always get assigned to the same server. This allows higher level session-based transactions to work in proper fashion. As indicated in Section 14.2.1, some applications require that all packets from one source must interact with the same destination node for the duration of the application level session.

Least Connections

In the Least Connections method the balancing device keeps track of all currently active connections assigned to each node in the cluster and assigns the next new incoming connection request to the node which currently has the least connections. The problem with this method is that some application level sessions consume more system resources than others. Although the connections may be balanced across the cluster, the actual amount of processing may vary significantly. To alleviate this problem partially, an adaptation of this method sets a maximum limit on the number of connections assigned to each node.

Minimum Misses

With the Minimum Misses method, the balancing device keeps long-term track of all incoming requests assignments to the nodes, and assigns the next incoming request to the node which has processed the least number of incoming requests in its history. The differentiating factor between this and the Least Connections method is that it keeps track of the number of current and past connections.

Fastest Response

In this method, the balancing device keeps track of the network response time between the node and itself and assigns the next incoming connection request to the node with the fastest response. This method requires active monitoring of the individual nodes using techniques like sending ICMP packets with the *ping* command or a proprietary mechanism based upon UDP packets.

In most LAN clusters, Fastest Response makes little sense except when the servers are heavily loaded down. Most modern systems directly connected on an Ethernet respond in a millisecond or less even when partially loaded, making this method useless. However, in situations where the balancing device and the individual nodes are not on the same network segment, this can result in slightly different times. The further apart the balancing device and nodes are according to network topology, the greater the difference in latency and the more useful this method becomes. This is the primary method used in topology-based redirection, an advanced balancing method.

14.2.3 Advanced Balancing Methods

Advanced balancing methods use a combination of the simple systems described earlier. They may be application- or system-specific depending upon the method. They offer more useful or practical implementations of network load balancing by combining the simple methods and often other resources to build a cluster optimized in one vector. The primary optimization vectors are: network traffic optimization, fair load distribution, network route optimization, response latency minimization, administrative or network management optimization, and application-specific performance optimization. The advanced balancing methods and their associated optimization vectors are shown in Table 14.1.

Table 14.1 Primary Optimization Vectors of Advanced Balancing Methods

Advanced Balancing Method	Optimization vectors
Network Traffic-based Balancing	network traffic optimization, network route optimization, response latency minimization
Node Traffic-based Balancing	fair load distribution, response latency minimization
Node Load-based Balancing	fair load distribution, response latency minimization
Load-balancing DNS Resolution	network traffic optimization, fair load distribution
Topology-based Redirection	response latency minimization,network route optimization, network traffic optimization, application-specific performance
Policy-based Redirection	administrative management optimization, network management optimization
Application-specific Redirection	network management optimization, fair load distribution, application-specific performance

Network Traffic-based Balancing

This system requires active monitoring of incoming traffic from different sources and distributing them accordingly to the nodes. The focus is on predicting the volume of incoming traffic from a source on the network based upon past history. In simplest form, the balancing device keeps a counter of incoming traffic from a particular source in a lookup table. Based upon the value of the counter, the next incoming packet from that source may be directed to a particular node. The distribution to the node is based on a simple weighting function assigning traffic by load capacity (i.e., the higher the predicted incoming traffic is directed to a node with a higher weight.) The distribution algorithm is not specific to any of the simple methods we described earlier and can utilize any as necessary. Although this technique is mostly independent of the nodes within the cluster, it works best when the individual nodes are identical or provide near-identical function.

Node Traffic-based Balancing

Node traffic-based balancing is the converse of the network traffic balancing system. Here, the incoming traffic is distributed based upon the level of traffic and available network buffers at each node. The balancing device contacts a software agent on the node to keep track of the status of the network buffers. It then distributes incoming traffic to the system with the most available buffers. This is another prediction-based system measuring current and past network buffer availability to determine future needs. The primary method used in this system is Least Connections, although it can be combined with Minimum Misses and Fastest Response.

Node traffic balancing is strongly affected by the performance of the NICs. Many NICs intended for servers provide two functions, failover and trunking, and increase the effective bandwidth to or the availability of a node. A pair of NICs in a server can act as a redundant path for data; if one NIC fails, the second takes over the role. In trunking or aggregation, several NICs can be plugged into a server and provide symmetric or asymmetric aggregation of traffic between the network hub and the server. In *symmetric trunking*, both NICs can receive and send data using the same IP address but with two different Ethernet hardware or Media Access Control (MAC) addresses. *Asymmetric trunking* allows both NICs to send data out from the network using the same IP address but can only receive data on one of the NICs. Symmetric trunking may often require intelligence on the part of the network hub to identify the two controllers as separate devices sharing a single IP address. Trunking allows secondary NICs to add to the total bandwidth available to a node.

Node Load-based Balancing

An alternative distribution algorithm is to direct traffic to the node with the least loaded processor. Again, the balancing device maintains a software agent on the node which determines the current 'load' on the node. Determining the CPU or system load on any machine is quite subjective. On a UNIX system, the load average indicated by the system (usually available with the uptime or w command) is not indicative of the responsiveness of the disk or network status. On NT systems, you can determine the current system load through the Performance Monitor application. Thus, this method requires the nodes be running similar configurations and the same operating system.

Based upon the load information from each node, the balancing device can use any of the simpler balancing methods to assign incoming traffic. Since network bandwidth is not the primary concern, the Least Connections and Fastest Response methods are not as favored as the others.

Load-balancing Domain Name Resolution

This system primarily involves the Round-Robin method as applied to DNS servers often combined with a Weighting or Hashing function. The load-balancing occurs within the DNS server itself and is usually independent of the application that generates the traffic.

This is currently the most popular method in use because of its simplicity. By adding a few algorithms to a standard DNS server application, such as BIND for UNIX systems, you can create an effective load-balancing system for a network cluster. Like many of the other advanced methods described, it is best used in a cluster of like nodes with identical software applications. The restriction on identical operating systems is lifted as long as the applications on each node respond identically to each other. For example, a cluster with Web servers running on NT and others on UNIX serving basic HTML pages can work very well using this method.

Topology-based Redirection

Topology-based redirection is effective when there are several clusters deployed across a network. Within any network, this method redirects traffic to the cluster nearest to the user's computer in terms of network topology. There are two ways to measure the distance between the client and the cluster node: hop count and network latency.

Hop count is the number of routers the packets have to traverse to reach the destination. Each router that the packet traverses is counted as a hop. The higher the number of hops, the further apart the two devices. Network latency is the amount of time, measured in milliseconds, it takes for a network packet to travel between the client and the cluster balancing device. Hop counts are usually quite static in value unless there are multiple routes between the source and destination, as in a meshed network. Network latency, on the other hand, can vary significantly depending upon the current traffic on the network and loads on the various routers in between at any time. Latency makes for a better measure of the speed of the network since it takes into account current network bandwidth conditions as well as routes.

A quick way of determining network latency in TCP/IP is to use the Ping program that sends ICMP packets to test the response time of a node. Directly pinging a machine from a single node will give, on average, the same value each time, barring any changes in network routing and discounting sudden network traffic bottlenecks.

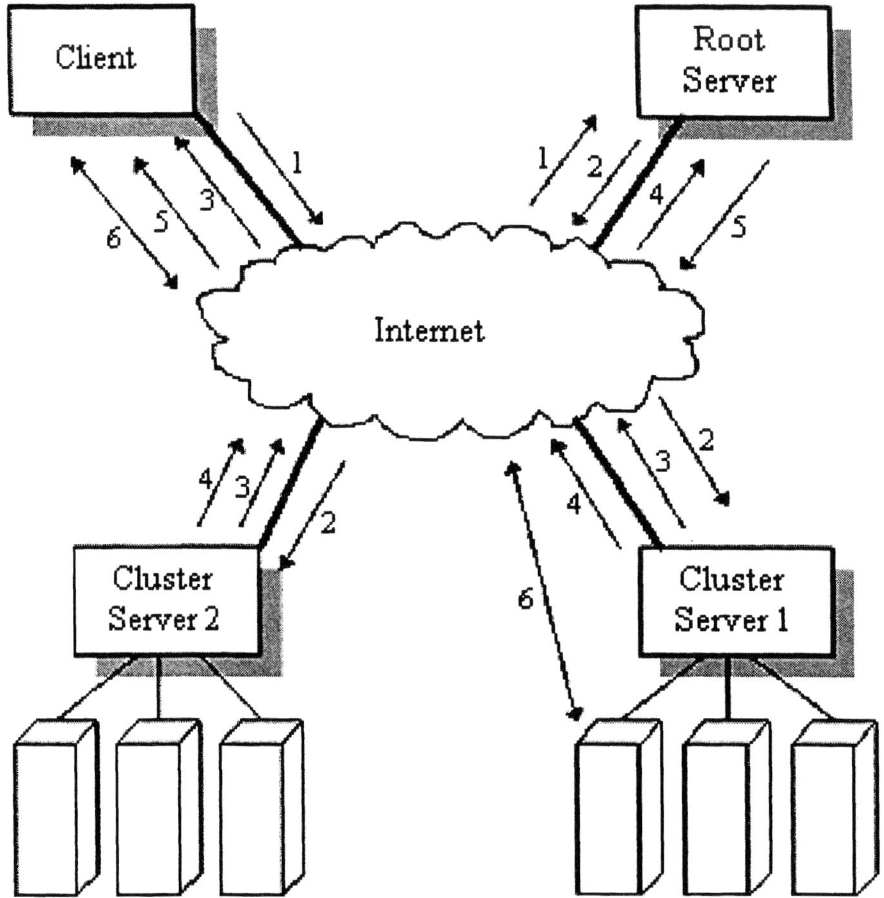

Figure 14.1 Ping triangulation in topology-based redirection.

For two nodes to determine which is closer to a third, a triangulation method is used. Steps 1 through 6 in Figure 14.1 describe how ping-triangulation works in a topology-based redirection system:

1. The client contacts the root server to establish a new connection to an Internet Web site.

2. The root server contacts all cluster servers and sends the client's IP address.

3. The cluster servers determine the distance between themselves and the client.

4. The cluster servers inform the root server of the distances between themselves and the remote client.

5. The root server updates its internal tables mapping that client's address to a specific cluster server and redirects the client to access a node in Cluster Server 1, in this example.

6. The client directly accesses the node in Cluster Server 1 by its IP address.

As you can see, this is the Fastest Response method taken to the WAN model sometimes with dynamic Weighting based upon the root node's preferences. Each time the client creates a new connection, he may be assigned to the same top level node. In a more generalized form, all clients from a particular domain may be assigned to a particular top level node. Since network topology can change with links going down and up, this assignment may also change. Furthermore, the root node maintains a global table of accessibility to each top level node and response times of various clients.

Some vendors, like Cisco and RND Networks, have implemented proprietary protocols that use a similar mechanism but may also pass along additional information such as server load, network traffic, etc. These additions may bring Node Load-based, Node Traffic-based, and Network Traffic-based methods into play.

Policy-based Redirection

Policy-based redirection is the application of a mathematical or functional set of rules that define the balancing behavior of the cluster. For example, all traffic from a remote office should be directed to a particular node or cluster. Policies can be based upon bandwidth allocation allowing some traffic higher priority and greater bandwidth; in administrative allocation, as in our example, all traffic from certain sources are directed towards a particular node or cluster; and in security policies access is permitted based upon the identity of a user or remote user.

Although the uses are different, most devices implement these rulesets in a similar fashion. The balancing device specifies a ruleset for each node and stores this in memory. Incoming traffic is tested against the rulesets and sent along to the appropriate node. Since rulesets may be complex, an identifier based upon the IP address or a user account can be used as a key to a hash table of rulesets. More complex operations that simply compare addresses may also be performed with custom software or specialized ASICs (Application-Specific Integrated Circuits); but in general, the simpler the rulesets, the faster the processing and traffic balancing.

Policy-based Redirection can be a overarching balancing system that uses a number of simpler and advanced balancing methods. Policies in effect create an automatic or semi-automatic weighting method on top of an existing balancing method. In almost all cases, policies require manual configuration. The network administrator can change policies, which in turn assigns higher weights to the priority items.

Bandwidth Allocation Policies

Bandwidth allocation policies establish priorities for incoming traffic to a cluster. For example, network administration and security control information usually need a higher priority than a Web access. Without true QoS features in IPv4, this serves as a filtering system and prioritization scheme based upon assignment of higher priority traffic to more nodes. In most cases, it will use Fastest Response and Least Connections to determine most available servers.

Administrative Policies

Administrative policies are based upon corporate workflow and business needs rather than on equal load-balancing for all requests. These may be assigned to give certain departments such as Finance or Sales higher priority access to the servers than Research. Administrative policies are specific to the needs of each network environment and administrative organization. Some of these policy subtypes include prioritization for single nodes or groups of computers, individual users or departments, specific application types, at specific times of day, and requests of specific resources.

Security Policies

Security policies are actually a subtype of administrative policies but are so prominently used in many networks that they deserve attention as a major policy type. A security policy requires that an incoming request has proper access rights before it can access the resource. In addition, security policies may be used to define time-prioritization to requests. There are several ways of establishing security policies, but most involve a database of access rights and a unique identifier or token within the request identifying its access rights. Private Key encryption based upon original work at RSA Datasystems is the most commonly used security policy system to date.

Application-specific Redirection

Application-specific redirection provides load-balancing features dependent upon the type application or resource the client is trying to access. Without a uniform independent session layer in the TCP/IP protocol architecture, some applications build their own session system. Balancing device vendors therefore have to build support for these types of sessions wherever possible into their product structure.

Database and Web load-balancing are the most popular of these. In databases, the content is spread across several nodes. When a query is made to the database server, it is split into multiple queries and sent along to the cluster for processing of the partial contents at each node. The root server then collates this into a complete response and sends it back to the client.

For the Web, HTTP is a simple TCP protocol to retrieve single files of data. Each Web document may contain a number of separate files and scripts as defined in the HTML code. When a client reads the main HTML source, it can send several separate requests to the server for each file. This kind of activity can easily be partitioned across multiple servers either by content type or area in a method known as URL partitioning, or simply by keeping identical information on each node.

A more complex type of Web access is for scripts. Some Web scripts need to be executed in sequence between the same client and server. If the sequential scripts were to be sent to different nodes each time, it may break the scripts since multiple copies may be spread across the cluster. One way to bypass this is to have all nodes access a separate database server to store the information, but this creates a bottleneck at the database and interferes with load-balancing. A better way would be to keep track of Web 'sessions' between a client and a specific node and maintain future traffic between the two rather than reassign the load, even if that node is already heavily used.

14.3 Common Errors

There are four common errors that can destabilize efficient network clustering: overflow, underflow, routing errors, and induced network errors. They affect the flow of traffic from the source and destination computers interfering with the distribution algorithm.

14.3.1 Overflow

Overflow occurs when there is too much network traffic to process, resulting in lost packets or throttling of packets intended for a destination node. It can occur at the balancing device or at individual nodes. It is possible to have an even flow of traffic at the balancing device and still overflow at a node, since the traffic processing capacity at the balancing device is usually much greater than that of individual cluster nodes. On the other hand, you can also have overflow at the balancing device resulting in throttling or deleting some of the data streams to the nodes, leaving an adequate level of traffic to the nodes.

In either case, overflow causes the loss of data and processing. With TCP connections, there is an idle timeout clock for receiving an acknowledgment reply to a series of transmitted packets. In an overflow situation, the acknowledgment may not be sent back by the receiver to the sender. This results in retries from the client (thus generating more traffic which in turn may be dropped) to deliver the same packets again until the timeout limit is reached and the connection dropped.

14.3.2 Underflow

Underflow is a problem within the cluster itself, where one node is not getting enough traffic as compared to the other member nodes. In effect, the node is underutilized or starved while others are getting loaded down, indicating an inefficient distribution of traffic. This is typically a problem with the algorithm itself or with the improper use of the system. In some cases it may also be a problem with non-symmetric nodes, where nodes in the cluster are not identical in power and one or more member nodes have far more computing resources than others.

It is very easy, for example, for nodes to become starved in a distribution system based solely upon a weighting function. The node with the highest weight value is assigned the job more often than others, which is why this method is used in conjunction with others. The Least Connections and Fastest Response methods can also result in node starvation if you have asymmetric clusters with the more powerful nodes being able to process requests more quickly, or simply respond faster than slower ones. Fastest Response is also affected by the network connection between the balancing device and the node. A node with a Gigabit Ethernet connection would respond more quickly than one with a standard 10 Megabit per second Ethernet.

14.3.3 Routing Errors

Routing errors can occur between a balancing device and the cluster nodes or between the source client and the cluster nodes. Typically, a routing error occurs from misconfiguration or a disconnected link. A misconfigured balancing device or node may insert the wrong destination IP address or specify an exit route which is illegal. A disconnected link should normally be detected by a router and identified as "No route to host." In such a situation, all load balancing methods fail until the route is restored. A cluster node may be up and running but there is no path to the node and thus it suffers from starvation.

Network balancing cluster designers should allow for disconnected or transactional operation if the application service absolutely requires a constant connection between the two systems. Such features must be built into both the balancing device and the node.

14.3.4 Induced Network Errors

Induced network errors differ from routing errors primarily in that the errors are generated by normal use of the network and not an incorrect or unstable network state. These are not really errors but results from delays in the propagation of packets along a network route. Sending packets over a network can increase the latency between two points as a portion of the path between the source and destination is used up by the traffic. Too much traffic can result in a bottleneck in the network route and appear as errors. Such induced errors are temporary but can last for hours. In particular, the Fastest Response method and Topology-based redirection are the most affected by these errors. Across the Internet, routes which are extremely slow temporarily due to unusual traffic load can timeout individual response test packets and show up as errors.

14.4 Practical Implementations

A number of vendors have approached network load balancing from different angles but arrived with similar solutions, independently. Most forms of the balancing methods described earlier can be readily identified within each implementation yet there are no commonly accepted standards or established protocols. In lieu of such standards, most vendor implementations are proprietary and work with only other products from the same vendor. The use of TCP/IP protocols is a saving grace, however. These clustering implementations described here can work independently of the application that runs over them, thus allowing them to be used in almost any network. An overview of the simple and advanced balancing methods used by these implementations is shown in Tables 14.2 and Table 14.3, respectively.

Table 14.2 Simple Balancing Methods in Vendor Implementations

Vendor	Product	Weighted	Random	Round-robin	Hashed	Least Connects	Minimum Misses	Fastest Response
Alteon	ACEdirector	Y	N	Y	N	Y	N	N
Check Point	FireWall-1	N	Y	Y	N	N	N	Y
Check Point	FloodGate-1	Y	N	Y	N	Y	N	Y
Check Point	VPN-1	N	N	N	N	N	N	N
Cisco	Distributed Director	Y	Y	Y	N	Y	N	Y
Cisco	Local Director	Y	N	Y	N	Y	N	Y
F5 Labs	3DNS & BIG/ip	Y	N	Y	N	Y	N	Y
HolonTech	HyperFlow	Y	N	Y	Y	N	N	N
HydraWEB	HYDRA	Y	N	Y	N	N	N	Y
Resonate	Central Dispatch	N	N	Y	N	Y	N	Y
Resonate	Global Dispatch	N	N	Y	N	Y	Y	Y
RND Networks	Web Server Director	Y	N	Y	N	Y	N	Y
RND Networks	WSD for Distrib. Sites	Y	N	Y	N	Y	N	Y
Sun	StorEdge	Y	N	N	N	N	N	Y

14.4.1 General Network Traffic Implementations

These products provide network load balancing at the network and transport layers and are independent of the software application using them. Some are focused on straight IP balancing as with the HolonTech HyperFlow unit. Others are made for TCP session load-balancing only, such as the Cisco LocalDirector and Distributed-Director, and the Resonate Central Dispatch and Global Dispatch. Still others can support UDP sessions as well as TCP, such as the Alteon ACEdirector and F5 Labs

Table 14.3 Advanced Balancing Methods in Vendor Implementations

Vendor	Product	Network Traffic	Node Traffic	Node Load	Load-Balanced DNS	Topology Redirect	Policy Redirect	Application Redirect
Alteon	ACEdirector	Y	N	N	N	N	N	Y
CheckPoint	FireWall-1	N	N	N	N	N	Y	Y
CheckPoint	FloodGate-1	Y	N	N	N	N	Y	Y
CheckPoint	VPN-1	N	N	N	N	N	Y	Y
Cisco	Distributed Director	Y	N	N	N	Y	Y	N
Cisco	LocalDirector	Y	N	N	N	N	Y	N
F5 Labs	3DNS & BIG/ip	Y	N	N	Y	N	N	Y
HolonTech	HyperFlow	Y	N	N	N	N	N	N
HydraWEB	HYDRA	N	N	Y	Y	N	N	Y
Resonate	Central Dispatch	N	Y	Y	Y	N	Y	Y
Resonate	Global Dispatch	N	Y	Y	Y	Y	Y	Y
RND Networks	Web Server Director	Y	N	N	Y	N	N	Y
RND Networks	WSD for Distributed Sites	Y	Y	Y	Y	N	N	Y
Sun	StorEdge	N	N	Y	N	N	N	Y

BIG/ip.

Balancing at the network or transport layer has different benefits. With the HolonTech product, you maintain complete independence of the TCP and UDP protocols. Since the IP protocol itself does not undergo changes very often (in the last two decades it has had one new generation, IP Version 6), any new developments to TCP and UDP do not affect these products. However, mapping IP packets may not be as functionally useful or as efficient as balancing TCP sessions. You do not have the finer control of separately balancing individual TCP sessions across multiple nodes. Traffic between a source and a destination can consist of many TCP sessions, and an IP-level balancing device will not be able to split these into separate streams and process these in parallel on several nodes.

Most major Internet software applications use TCP. Yet, there are still some major applications such as the File Transfer Protocol (FTP) which rely on UDP. FTP is still the second highest application protocol traffic on the Internet. This application is perfectly suited for balancing across a cluster; it involves a continuous stream between the two points, and multiple streams are better suited when served from several nodes. Thus, the ability to balance UDP traffic is a valuable feature of a network balancing device.

HolonTech HyperFlow

HyperFlow is a hardware Ethernet switch from HolonTech Corp. that performs network load balancing through multiple paths. It uses weighting in combination with round-robin DNS to provide a initial load balancing name resolution node assignment per client. It then uses hashing as the basic method for mapping source IP to destination IP addresses. It performs hashing on two levels, a single source-destination pair hash, and a many-sources-to-one- destination hash. The second hashing method is used when there are multiple balancing devices to transition an entire block to another balancing device. This multilevel scheme distributes the load more evenly across the multiple balancing device and allows for failover while still maintaining individual source-to-destination paths [11].

HyperFlow, in addition, works with IPSec. Since HyperFlow performs balancing at the IP network protocol level rather than the TCP session level, the IPSec data can pass through without change [12].

Cisco LocalDirector and DistributedDirector

Cisco is not the first but certainly it is one of the top vendors of network load balancing and routing systems. They offer two products which work in very different ways: LocalDirector and DistributedDirector. The LocalDirector product is a LAN-based system that primarily acts as a balancing device for a private network segment dedicated to the cluster. The product was originally based on a Network Address Translator and expanded to serve clusters of Web servers.

The products use a Channel Interface Processor (CIP), an ASIC optimized to handle TCP/IP connections. The CIP performs routing and address translation on incoming requests based upon assigned balancing algorithms.

LocalDirector allows the use of four methods: Least Connections (the default), Weighted percentage, Fastest Response, and Round-Robin. Cisco claims that their system can sustain 45Mbps throughput on all packet traffic for 64-byte packets (the smallest useful IP packet size) and 80Mbps throughput on 256-byte packets (a very common IP packet size). In total, a single system can monitor 700,000 simultaneous TCP connections. For address translation, the unit can map to 8,000 IP addresses to all the nodes in the cluster [6].

In spite of the name similarity, the DistributedDirector product is entirely different than LocalDirector. It is intended for Topology-based Redirection. Cisco has created a UDP-based Director Response Protocol (DRP) that queries Server agents on network routing metrics between the servers and between the client and a given set of servers. A DRP Server agent may be a router or a cluster node which responds to information about the distributed cluster. DRP relies on intermediate routers implementing the Interior Gateway Protocol (IGP) for network routing metrics information internal to the service providers intranet and the Border Gateway Protocol (BGP) for metrics between Internet service providers networks.

DRP collects three sets of metrics:

- The distance between the client and the border router of the service provider in terms of the number of between Autonomous Systems (AS) hops between the two. An AS is an administratively independent network; for the purpose of simplicity, consider each Internet service provider as an AS.
- The distance between the border router of the service provider and the DRP Service Agent within their network. If the DRP Service Agent is the border router, this distance is 0.
- The distance between the DRP Service Agent and the end-nodes of the cluster.

DistributedDirector takes all three into account as a set of distance vectors between the client and the various distributed nodes. It assigns the node with the shortest distance to service the request and records an entry in the global DRP Service Agent and the Service Agents on the path between the client and server node [7].

Cisco has made a theoretical calculation of the capacity of DistributedDirector clusters and arrived at the conclusion that each node should be created to handle

$$1 + 3\sqrt{averageexpectedload} \tag{14.4.1}$$

to minimize rejections of new connections. Furthermore, additional servers might be required for redundancy. For example, a system that is expected to handle 99,000 client connections, with each server handling 10,000 connections, should require a total of approximately 10,200. To handle this capacity, a total of 11 servers would be required. Add to this another server or two for redundancy, and you will have the appropriate number of servers to handle a given amount of load [8].

DistributedDirector uses a combination of several simple and complex methods: Fastest Response, Randomization, Weighting, and Policy-based redirection. Each of these can be applied to the entire system. Fastest Response and Randomization are automatic, whereas Weighting and Policy-based Redirection require manual parameters.

Resonate Central Dispatch and Global Dispatch

The Resonate Central Dispatch system uses software agents and the Resonate Exchange Protocol (RxP) to create a network cluster. Essentially, it promotes one node into a balancing device called the Primary Scheduler. Secondary Schedulers can also be set up as failover protection. The Scheduler communicates with the agents at each node to determine server and network traffic load. A software agent determines the CPU load while a specialized NIC driver monitor keeps track of the network traffic status at the node.

This system uses the simple methods of Round-Robin, Fastest Response, and Least Connections as well as the more advanced methods for Node Load-based Balancing, and Node Traffic-based Balancing. The products also support Sticky Sessions to maintain application-specific sessions over several separate TCP connections [14].

Although technically the Primary Scheduler is not entirely independent of the application of the cluster or its content (it is still a member node), you can limit content access activity at this device by throttling all activity other than load-balancing. The Global Dispatch system is an Topology-based Redirection server that works in concert with the Central Dispatch product. As in most systems using this advanced method, the primary simple method is Fastest Response. It can keep track of activity at nodes using the Minimum Misses and Least Connections methods as well. In addition, this product also uses the same agents of Central Dispatch to determine individual node load and node traffic load [15].

Alteon Networks ACEdirector

Alteon Networks sells the ACEdirector hardware traffic director. The products are essentially 10 or 100 Mbps Ethernet switches with added intelligence to perform balancing across the ports. ACEdirector can balance both TCP and UDP traffic.

ACEdirector supports the following distribution methods: Round-Robin, Least Connections with maximum threshold, and Node Weighting. ACEdirector 1 can handle up to 100,000 connections across the eight ports and map 256 virtual IP addresses to itself. The next model, ACEdirector 2, can handle up to 200,000 connections but still allows 256 virtual IP addresses across all eight ports; this new model can also apply the use of different balancing methods for up to 224 source IP address ranges per port. The products also support 'UDP sessions' as described earlier [1].

F5 Labs BIG/ip and 3DNS

F5 Labs has two products offering IP load-balancing and DNS services. The BIG/ip server provides node failover services for network link, network bandwidth, server hardware, protocol services, and application services failure. Together with their 3DNS product, they support both TCP and UDP session based load-balancing and implement several of the simple balancing methods: Round-Robin, Least Connecions, Fastest Response, and Weighting. BIG/ip can also act as a firewall to prevent unsecured direct access to the cluster nodes [10].

14.4.2 Web-specific Implementations

With much of the focus of the Internet aimed at the World Wide Web, it is not surprising that many vendors are focusing on a Web load-balancing solution only. Some of the products mentioned earlier which are non-specific to an application have optimizations for HTTP. These include products from Resonate, F5 Labs, and Alteon. We now consider other products which were designed for network load balancing for the Web, specifically.

HydraWEB Load Manager

HydraWEB Technologies has a product line directed at the Web clustering market. The Hydra product line consist of three models: the 5000, 2000, and 900. The three models can support 3 million, 140,000, and 40,000 active HTTP sessions, respectively. Additionally, they can support wire-speeds for 155Mbps, 80Mbps, and 45Mbps, respectively.

Since it is application-specific, the Hydra products offer Web content level clustering. Portions of the URL for a site may be distributed across several nodes for asymmetric balancing. This allows subsets of the site which get the most access to be spread across more servers, and those content subsets least used to be left on one or two nodes. WAN redirection is primarily for content distribution across multiple sites. Hydra also uses agents on nodes to monitor several factors (system load average, memory utilization, system operational status, and Web server load) to aid in Node Load-based Balancing. The product also uses the Fastest Response method in its load distribution algorithm [13].

RND Networks Web Server Director and Director Pro

RND Networks has products for LAN-based clusters called Web Server Director (WSD) and WSD Pro as well as a distributed system for multiple clusters named Web Server Director for Distributed Sites (WSD-DS). The WSD works with only one LAN while WSD Pro can provide failover between two cluster LANs. Additionally, WSD can support 100 virtual IP addresses compared to the 50,000 for the WSD Pro. The products are designed for LAN segments rather than building into the device a direct per-port switching system. They can handle any type of TCP or UDP traffic.

All the models support several basic balancing methods: Round-Robin, Least Connections, and Minimum Misses on a per-node basis. In addition, all nodes in the cluster can be weighted as well [16]. WSD-DS implements a Load Report Protocol (LRP) that each balancing device uses to communicate to others of its kind for multiple clusters and distributed clusters. These devices share current device loads so that a root global device is able to ascertain where to direct new incoming traffic.

The WSD family provides HTTP redirection based upon a distributed threshold for each cluster or node. This threshold is essentially a limit on individual client IP addresses that each cluster will support. It is an analogy to the number of users that can access the server. Rather than shutting down traffic to one fully loaded cluster, it dynamically reassigns nodes from other clusters to become part of the loaded system. The reassigned cluster is essentially expanded with new nodes in different locations but still serving a common Web site. LRP is used to determine overall throughput to the clusters; the same reassignment process can happen if one site is too slow even if the threshold has not been reached [17]. The WSD-DS product does not implement a Topology-based Redirection system.

14.4.3 Other Application Specific Implementations

Network load balancing has existed in other recognizable forms for years. In the disk storage area, the Redundant Array of Independent Disk (RAID) system is a precursor of network load-balancing systems, with the RAID controller acting as a balancing device and the individual disks acting as nodes. With the different RAID levels in particular mirroring (multiple copies of the same data) and striping (volumes partitioned across multiple disks), you can distribute incoming disk access requests across multiple drives.

Although SCSI-based RAID systems are not particularly thought of as a network, it has been used to create directly-connected two-node clusters for failover and some load balancing. With RAID expanded to Fiber-Channel (FC) networks, it becomes more plausible as a system of networking in itself. FC has support for a significant address space of separate nodes, can be routed, and can even support quality of service needs. FC even parallels Ethernet or ATM networks in some respects to the degree that there is an initiative to build a full TCP/IP stack and architecture on top of FC networks. Such network load-balancing is specific to one application (i.e., data storage).

Firewalls are not thought of as load-balancing devices but more as security monitors. At the application level, however, these can function to some degree as such by directing traffic to specific nodes. For example, you can create secure shell access through a firewall that can be spread across multiple login servers. The user has access to a shell, but may be placed on any number of separate nodes of identical type.

Sun Microsystems StorEdge

Sun Microsystems has a storage area network solution for a single network as well as supporting multiple sites. The Sun StorEdge systems support SCSI and Fiber-Channel based disks. For load-balancing and data consistency, they provide mirroring (RAID level 1), but more interestingly they can provide Remote Mirroring; that is, mirroring between two separate sites over a WAN link.

Creating a second copy of a drive across a WAN is normally called replication, where the process of making sure the multiple copies are identical occurs infrequently. The Sun system, however, can maintain synchronous mirroring of data between two controllers. Any change to the local disks is immediately reflected to the remote disks, and the drive system will wait for completion before reporting a successful disk operation.

The StorEdge products can also support asynchronous disk operations between the sites which falls in line with regular replication [18]. Since synchronous remote mirroring will create significant traffic between the node, it requires a high-bandwidth direct connection (100Mbps) between the two end-points such as a fiber-optic link. Sun provides such one system in their proprietary Fiber-Optic Reflective Memory System (FORMS) allowing disk systems to be up to 3 km apart. Another mechanism, using a dedicated circuit with Asynchronous Transfer Mode (ATM) technology, allows the disk systems to be extended to a near unlimited range.

Check Point FireWall-1, VPN-1, and FloodGate-1

Check Point Software Technologies' immensely popular FireWall-1 product is one of the leading network access security monitors or firewalls on the market. Version 3.0 includes the ConnectControl package and allows multiple remote users to be assigned to a cluster of login servers. The package can be used as a secured form of Web load balancing or for any number of different TCP or UDP based applications [4].

In essence, this product is a balancing device with a built-in secure authentication system and network address translation. The balancing methods used are Round-Robin, Randomization, and Fastest Response. With agent software on the server, it can also do Node load-based balancing and Intranet or Internet-based

Topology routing. To counter the deficiencies with NATs, a second product called VPN-1 acts as a secure IP gateway providing certificate-based authentication while still maintaining separate IP address spaces [3].

The FloodGate-1 product brings policy based redirection. Bandwidth can be assignment via domain names, IP addresses, or user information. Traffic is classified by the Network Administration staff, and based upon these, the system automatically assigns weights to the different traffic streams [5].

14.5 Summary

A network load balancing system involves the use of a separate balancing device which monitors traffic and executes a method of distributing this traffic to a cluster of nodes, either locally or distributed across other networks. A number of common methods of creating such systems have emerged in the past two years to solve problems associated with clustering TCP/IP nodes. These methods, although implemented independently, have very similar forms and uses. Several of these methods can be combined to create more complex abstractions of load-balancing. The Internet Domain Name System plays a very crucial part in many of these load-balancing methods. The TCP/IP protocol architecture can be effectively balanced primarily at two layers: the network layer (IP), and the transport layer (TCP and UDP). The lack of a separate session layer has led to alternative methods of multiplexing, some of which are effective as in the case of TCP, and others which work but suffer unpredictable behavior, as in UDP packets. The lack of appropriate Quality of Service guarantee systems in the TCP/IP architecture has led to best-guess and proprietary methods for determining the quickest way of processing an application request. Most product implementations of these distribution methods are proprietary, but will work with a number of different operating system platforms. The biggest focus has been on creating Web server load-balancing systems in local and distributed architectures.

Acknowledgment

This chapter is based upon the article "Network Balancing Act" originally published in the November 1998 issue of SunWorld Magazine, an online publication on Sun Microsystems computer systems and the UNIX industry. Please read: http://www.sunworld.com/swol-11-1998/swol-11-connectivity.html

14.6 Bibliography

[1] The Next Step in Server Load Balancing. Alteon Networks, Inc., 1998. http://www.alteon.com/products/white_papers/slbwp.html

[2] R. Atkinson. *RFC 1825: Security Architecture for the Internet Protocol.* IETF Network Working Group, 1995.

[3] The Check Point VPN-1 Product Family. Check Point Software Technologies Ltd. (CPSTL), 1998. http://www.checkpoint.com/products/vpn1/index.html

[4] ConnectControl Data Sheet: Enterprise Traffic Management. CPSTL, 1998. http://www.checkpoint.com/products/floodgate-1/ccdata.html

[5] Check Point FloodGate-1. Check Point Software Technologies Ltd., 1998. http://www.checkpoint.com/products/floodgate-1/index.html

[6] LocalDirector in the Data Center. Cisco Systems, Inc., 1997. http://www.cisco.com/warp/public/751/lodir/ldir_wp.htm

[7] Cisco DistributedDirector. Cisco Systems, Inc., 1998. http://www.cisco.com/warp/public/751/distdir/dd_wp.htm

[8] The Effects of Distributing Load Randomly to Servers. Cisco Systems, Inc., 1998. http://www.cisco.com/warp/public/751/distdir/ddran_wp.pdf

[9] D. Comer. *Internetworking with TCP/IP: Principles Protocols and Architecture, vol. 1.* Prentice-Hall, NJ, 1995.

[10] BIG/ip Product Data Sheet. F5 Labs, Inc., 1998. http://www.f5.com/index.phtml?page_id=03010000

[11] The HyperFlow Architecture for all/IP™Web Server Clustering. HolonTech Corp., 1998. http://www.holontech.com/pdf/WPHyperFlow.PDF

[12] The Advantages of all/IP™Flow Control for Web Server Load Balancing. HolonTech Corp., 1998. http://www.holontech.com/pdf/all_IPFlow.PDF

[13] HYDRA Features and Benefits. HydraWEB Technologies, Inc., 1998. http://www.hydraweb.com/z2_features_benefits.html

[14] A. Reback. *Resonate Central Dispatch: Powerful Internet Traffic Management.* Resonate, Inc., 1998. http://www.resonate.com/products/whitepapers/cdwp.html

[15] A. Reback. *Resonate Global Dispatch: Optimized Traffic Management Across Geographically-Dispersed Points-of-Presence.* Resonate, Inc., 1998. http://www.resonate.com/products/whitepapers/gdwp.html

[16] Technical Application Note 1025: Server Management in WSD. RND Networks, Inc., 1997. http://www.rndnetworks.com/appnotes/app1025.pdf

[17] Technical Application Note 1035: WSD for Distributed Sites (WSD-DS). RND Networks, Inc., 1997. http://www.rndnetworks.com/appnotes/app1035.pdf

[18] Remote Mirroring Technical White Paper. Sun Microsystems, Inc., 1998. http://www.sun.com/storage/white-papers/remote-mirroring.wp.html

Chapter 15

Multiple Path Communication

JUNSEONG KIM AND DAVID J. LILJA

Department of Electrical and Computer Engineering
University of Minnesota
200 Union St. SE
Minneapolis, MN 55455

Email: {*jskim, lilja*}*@ece.umn.edu*

15.1 Introduction

New high performance communication networks combined with the support of a machine-independent communication library, such as the Parallel Virtual Machine (PVM) and the Message Passing Interface (MPI), have made network-based computing a viable option for many large-scale applications. The Berkeley Network of Workstations (NOW) project [1], for instance, seeks to exploit the power of clustered machines connected via high-speed networks. Legion [5] is an example of an object-based, metasystem software project to support computing in wide-area environments. Nexus [4] is a portable run-time system for task-parallel programming languages specifically designed as a compiler target.

While communication in network-based computing is a very important factor in performance, little effort has been made to efficiently utilize all available network resources within a system. Although the AppLeS [2] and Nexus [4] projects utilize heterogeneous network types, there still exists only a single communication path between processors at any point in time. However, we have previously shown that there can be substantial benefits in simultaneously exploiting multiple independent communication paths between processors [7], [8].

This paper describes the *performance-based path determination (PBPD)* techniques [7], [8] for exploiting multiple physical communication paths and multiple communication protocols within a single parallel application program to reduce communication overhead. Applications typically use several different types of communication. Since the different physical networks and protocols have different performance characteristics, the different types of communication within an application might be best suited to one of several different communication paths. For instance, bulk data transfer, such as image data, requires high-bandwidth communication, while short control messages, such as synchronization and acknowledgments, require low-latency communication. The *performance-based path selection (PBPS)* strategy exploits this heterogeneity in communication paths and message types by dynamically selecting the best communication path among several in a given system that will minimize the communication time for each message sent. In addition to PBPS, we also investigate aggregating multiple communication paths into a single virtual path for sending an individual message in an application. Each independent path simultaneously carries a fraction of a single message. This *performance-based path aggregation (PBPA)* strategy is especially useful in bandwidth-limited situations.

We can use one of several different message or network characteristics to control the selection and aggregation in the PBPD schemes, such as the message size, the message type, or the network traffic load. In previous work [7], [8], we demonstrated the potential of the PBPD techniques using only the size of the message being transferred. In this paper, we examine the effect of the message type, such as point-to-point communication, broadcasting, or a synchronization message, as the controlling element in the PBPD techniques. The application-level performance improvement of this approach is demonstrated using a synthetic benchmark program running on a cluster of SGI Challenge systems.

In the remainder of this chapter, Section 15.2 provides additional background on heterogeneity in network-based computing. Section 15.3 then describes how the PBPD strategies are implemented and generalizes the basic ideas. Section 15.4 presents our experimental methodology and verifies the ideas by measuring the performance of a synthetic benchmark program that is based on the communication patterns of various parallel scientific application programs. Finally, Section 15.5 summarizes our results and conclusions.

15.2 Heterogeneity in Networks and Applications

There exists heterogeneity in computer architectures, including workstations, vector computers, massively parallel computers, and in the networks used to interconnect them, including Ethernet, ATM, and HiPPI. Applications that run in network-based computing environments can exploit this system-level heterogeneity to match the heterogeneous computational requirements and communication needs [7]. In this study we investigate how to exploit the heterogeneity inherent in interprocessor communication. In fact, several different types of messages are typically used in a single application program, some of which are latency-limited, while others are bandwidth-limited. Applications that run in a network-based computing environment may benefit from matching the heterogeneous communication requirements of each message with the characteristics of each network.

15.2.1 Varieties of Communication Networks

Computer networks provide the necessary means for communication between the components of a distributed system [3], [7], [11]. The first computer networks were wide area networks (WANs). They carried messages at low speeds, typically below 1 Mbps, between computers separated by large distances, often entire countries. Local area networks (LANs) in contrast, were designed to enable computer users to share resources within a single organization. They carry messages at relatively high speeds, on the order of several Mbps, and cover a single building or campus area. LANs are typically more reliable than WANs and thus can employ simpler and more efficient communication protocols.

The increasing demand for data communication beyond the local area has led to the introduction of metropolitan area networks (MANs). MANs can be considered as an evolution of the LAN falling between the LAN and WAN. It may cover an entire city with data transmission rates of 100 Mbps or more. System area networks (SANs) are emerging to support the demands of large-scale I/O. Unlike other networks that typically have high CPU overhead, SANs provide special-purpose hardware to guarantee message delivery and to avoid the need for time-consuming software checksums and protocols. SANs are intended for the moderate distances within a computer room, for instance, with data rates of 1 Gbps or more.

There now exists a wide variety of different network types, each developed to fill a specific need. For instance, Ethernet, which is based on a 10 Mbps contention bus, is still the most common LAN. Asynchronous Transfer Mode (ATM) has been proposed for wide area networks and can handle a wide variety of data, including multimedia, voice, and video. Fiber Distributed Data Interface (FDDI) is a ring network using an optical fiber for transmission with a data rate of 100 Mbps. The High Performance Parallel Interface (HiPPI) was originally developed to allow mainframes and supercomputers to communicate at very high speed using a point-to-point link at the rate of either 800 Mbps or 1.6 Gbps. All of these networks have been proposed to be used as the interprocessor communication network in a distributed parallel computing system. Since each of these networks were originally developed for a different application domain, they each have different performance characteristics. As a result, higher performance may be achieved by exploiting multiple heterogeneous networks simultaneously within a single application.

15.2.2 Exploiting Multiple Communication Paths

A typical network-based computing application has many different types of messages to be transferred among processors. Messages can be classified based on their size, communication groups, priority level, and so on. Different types of network services are provided to support different types of message communication. These network services can be classified as either connection-oriented or connectionless [11]. Either type of service is logically sufficient for the implementation of any desired communication pattern. However, each offers performance and programming benefits for some classes of applications. For instance, the Internet Protocol (IP) supports both the Transmission Control Protocol (TCP) and the User Datagram Protocol (UDP) services. UDP, which is a connectionless protocol, is capable of efficiently broadcasting messages when the underlying physical network supports broadcasting, while TCP, which is a connection-oriented protocol, can not. Supporting multiple communication paths in both physical networks and protocols provides a number of benefits.

- *Efficient network utilization.* Supporting multiple communication paths in a single application allows the most appropriate communication path to be used for each communication event.
- *Alternative network protocols.* Different network protocols also have different characteristics. For instance, connection-oriented communication is useful for network services, such as remote login and bulk file transfer, while a connectionless service is useful when small amounts of data are sent at sporadic intervals.
- *Robust communication.* Supporting multiple networks provides extra reliability to compensate for any single network failure. For example, the Fiber Distributed Data Interface (FDDI) [11] consists of two fiber rings which allows the system to continue work in case of a cable break or station failure.
- *Network load balancing.* When multiple networks are managed independently, one of them might be heavily used while the others are idle. By managing multiple networks as one resource, however, the network load can be spread evenly among all available networks.
- *Quality of service (QoS).* Each type of communication may have different QoS requirements [11]. While some interprocessor control information, such as synchronization or load balancing information, might require a low-latency, highly-reliable communication path, other types of communication, which may be able to tolerate higher-latency and intermittent errors, such as image or voice data, might use a high-bandwidth, unreliable path. Providing multiple paths for communication can support these diverse quality-of-service requirements.

15.3 Multiple Path Communication

A single application is likely to require several different types of messages for its interprocessor communication. Due to the differences in both network characteristics and application requirements, different types of messages may be better suited to a different type of communication mechanism. No single network or protocol can provide the best performance for all types of communication in an application program. Furthermore, many network-based computing systems are being assembled with several different types of communication links between the same processing nodes [3], [7], [8]. A common configuration, for instance, is a network of workstations interconnected with both Ethernet plus some higher-bandwidth network, such as Fibre Channel, ATM, or HiPPI.

In the following, we show that higher performance may be achieved by exploiting multiple communication networks or protocols within a single application. In particular, we summarize the basic ideas of using PBPD [7], [8] to support multiple path communication in an application using both multiple physical connections and multiple network protocols.

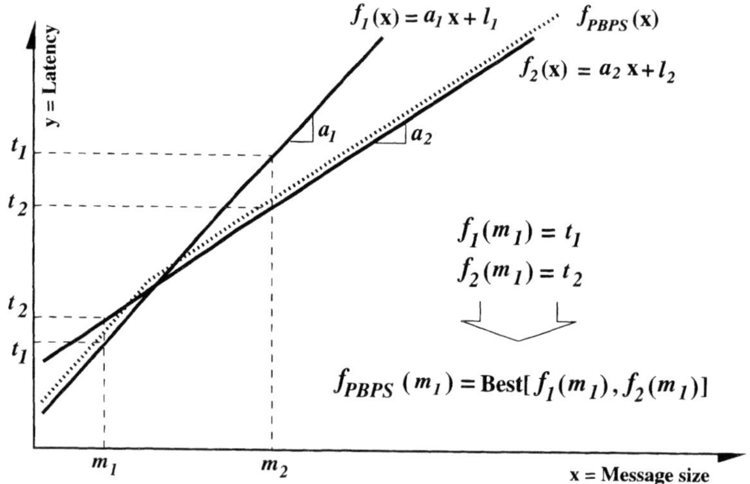

Figure 15.1 When sending a message of size m_i, performance-based path selection (PBPS) uses the lower latency curve among $f_1(m_i)$ and $f_2(m_i)$.

15.3.1 Performance-Based Path Selection

PBPS is useful when, among several different communication paths, one provides better performance in one situation while the other is better in another situation. It is then possible to dynamically select the appropriate communication path for a given communication event using some message parameters, such as message size, the type of communication, or the network traffic load, for instance. Figure 15.1 shows the concept of PBPS where, given the characteristics of two communication paths, $f_1(x)$ and $f_2(x)$, the new characteristic function of PBPS-enhanced virtual paths is

$$f_{PBPS}(x) = Best[f_1(x), f_2(x)].$$

If the characteristic is the message latency measured as function of message size, for instance, then $Best[f_1(x), f_2(x)]$ will be $Min[f_1(x), f_2(x)]$. By dynamically selecting the best network for each individual message sent by an application, we can achieve better communication performance than when using either network alone. To use these multiple networks, the message-passing library, or the application itself, can select the proper network. Compared to using only one network by itself, the additional overhead required for this PBPS is approximately the time required to execute one conditional statement to compare the message size to the selection threshold.

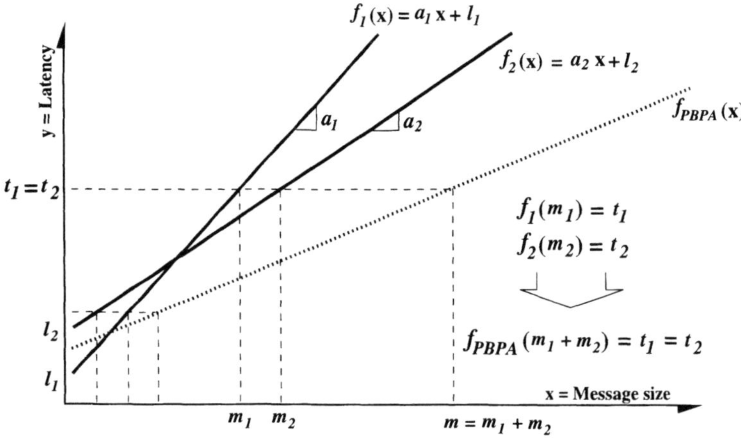

Figure 15.2 When using performance-based path aggregation (PBPA) with two networks, a message of size $m_1 + m_2$ is split into two submessages such that messages of size m_1 and m_2 are sent over networks $f_1(m_1)$ and $f_2(m_2)$ simultaneously.

15.3.2 Performance-Based Path Aggregation

While PBPS is applied when there is a clear tradeoff between communication paths, PBPA can be applied when different paths show similar characteristics. For instance, if we have two nearly identical networks, then we can aggregate the two networks into a single virtual network whose bandwidth will be nearly twice that of each network's individual bandwidth. With this approach, the original message is divided into several smaller submessages. Each of these submessages is then transferred over each available network simultaneously. This aggregated network appears to be a single higher-bandwidth virtual network to the application program.

One important consideration for this PBPA approach is determining the size of the submessages that should be sent over each of the networks. Figure 15.2 shows the basic PBPA concept when using two networks. The original message must be divided into two submessages with the goal of having the two submessages be completely received at the destination at the same time. More precisely, a message of m_1 bytes can be sent and received at the destination in time t with characteristic $f_1(x)$ on one network. Similarly, a message of m_2 bytes requires time t to be sent and received with characteristic $f_2(x)$ on the other network. Then the new characteristic of PBPA is

$$f_{PBPA}(x)|_{x=m} = f_1(x)|_{x=m_1} = f_2(x)|_{x=m_2}$$

and

$$m = m_1 + m_2$$

where m is the size of the original message. After solving these two equations the size of each of the submessages is determined to be

$$m_1 = \frac{a_2 m + l_2 - l_1}{a_1 + a_2} \qquad m_2 = \frac{a_1 m + l_1 - l_2}{a_1 + a_2}$$

This technique is particularly useful for bandwidth-limited applications.

15.3.3 PBPD Library

There are several interprocess communication libraries, such as PVM and MPI, that provide a machine independent communication layer. However, none of these libraries support multiple communication paths in a single application program. For instance, in PVM the interprocessor communication network to be used must be set at the beginning of a program's execution. Once one type of network is set, the application program cannot utilize other networks, if there are any, during its execution. To demonstrate the PBPD schemes, we developed a custom library whose main feature is the support of multiple communication paths in a single application program.

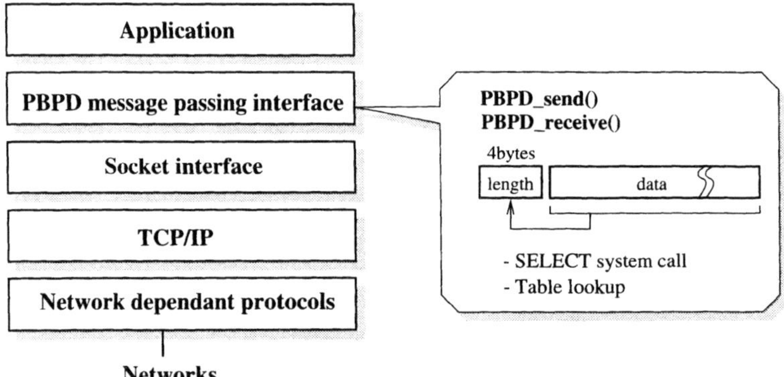

Figure 15.3 Implementation and protocol hierarchy of the PBPD communication routines.

This PBPD library is based on the common Transmission Control Protocol (TCP) layer. TCP is the most widely used and supported protocol throughout systems ranging from personal computers to the largest supercomputers. Since TCP provides reliable communication, no extra flow control mechanism is needed over the protocol layer. However, we add an integer field, *length*, that tells how many bytes are in the complete original message. This value is used to verify that the entire message is transferred between processors. This field is also used by the PBPA technique to determine if a message is too small to segment. Figure 15.3 shows the implementation and protocol hierarchy of our PBPD communication routines.

The PBPD technique must process send and receive primitives using multiple communication paths. To handle the multiplexing of different TCP connections, we use the Unix `select` system call with appropriate table lookups. The selection threshold table is preestablished based on the characteristics of the available networks. Given any message of size m, the network characteristic curves combined with the equations in Section 15.3.2 are used to determine appropriate values for the sizes of submessages to minimize the total communication latency. Since there exist multiple connections between processors, the submessages may not be delivered at precisely the same time. Also, depending on the size of the message, m, not all of the connections may be used. With a FCFS (First-Come First-Served) strategy, we use the `select` system call to detect a message arrival over any one of the multiple connections.

15.4 Case Study

In previous work [7], we demonstrated the PBPD techniques using the latency characteristics as a function of the message size for Ethernet, Fibre Channel, and HiPPI networks. There are clear tradeoffs between Ethernet and Fibre Channel in that Ethernet produces lower latency than Fiber Channel when sending small messages (a few hundreds of bytes) while Fibre Channel produces lower latency for larger messages. Using the PBPS technique with this network combination; that is, by sending the message on Ethernet when the message size is smaller than or equal to 768 bytes and on Fibre Channel otherwise, we demonstrated a speedup of as high as 2.11 for a Gauss [12] benchmark program compared to using Fibre Channel alone. Also, using the PBPA technique with a Fibre Channel and HiPPI network combination, a speedup of 1.51 for the TRFD [10] benchmark was shown compared to using HiPPI network alone. While this previous work based the aggregation and network selection on message size, in this section, we investigate the PBPD techniques when using the message type instead of size to make the appropriate path determination. We then estimate the application-level performance using a synthetic benchmark program.

15.4.1 Multiple Path Characteristics

Communication types in a parallel application program may be classified as either point-to-point, which involves only a single source and a single destination, or collective, which involves a group of processes in a communication such as broadcasting, selective multicasting, or barrier synchronization, for example. Collective communication is typically implemented in software unless there is direct support for broadcasting or multicasting in the network protocol and network hardware itself. For instance, Ethernet uses a shared medium among the processing nodes and is naturally suited for a broadcasting operation. Either TCP or UDP can be used as the message transport protocol over this network. UDP is a connectionless protocol that can directly exploit the broadcasting capability of Ethernet. TCP, on the other hand, is a connection-oriented protocol that transfers data only over preestablished point-to-point connections. As a result, it cannot exploit the broadcasting feature of the Ethernet. The simplest approach to broadcasting with the TCP protocol is to use a separate addressing method, in which an individual copy of the message is sent from the source to each destination [6]. While this approach may be efficient for small sets of processors, it obviously would introduce substantial overhead with large systems.

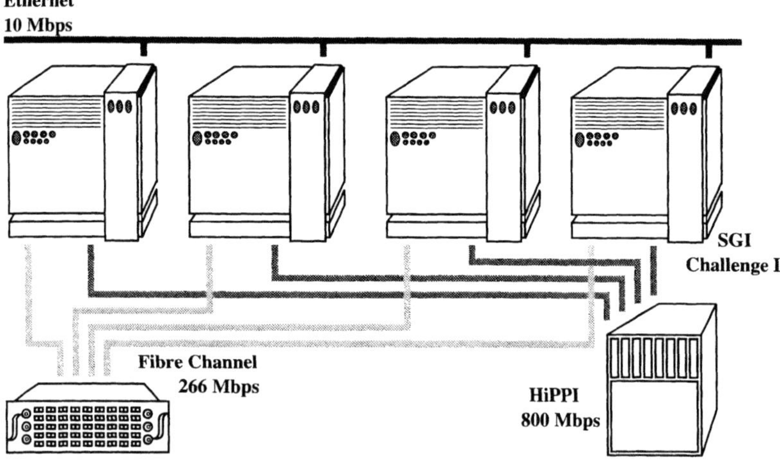

Figure 15.4 Multiple heterogeneous network configuration used in the experiments.

To demonstrate the characteristic differences in the various communication paths, we use a system consisting of four Silicon Graphics Challenge L shared-memory multiprocessors, as shown in Figure 15.4. Each of the nodes in this system contains four or eight R10000 processors running at 196 MHz on a shared bus. The nodes can communicate with each other via either an Ethernet running at a peak transfer rate of 10 Mbps, or a Fibre Channel network, using an Ancor CXT250 16 port switch, running at 266 Mbps. All nodes run version 6.2 of the IRIX operating system.

Figure 15.5 shows the measured latency characteristics of point-to-point and broadcast operations over the Ethernet using the TCP and UDP protocols. For TCP broadcasting we used the separate addressing method. Also, since UDP does not guarantee the same level of reliability as TCP, we added a simple flow control mechanism on top of the basic UDP datagram service. We also added a retransmission mechanism that uses a preset timeout to recover from messages that get

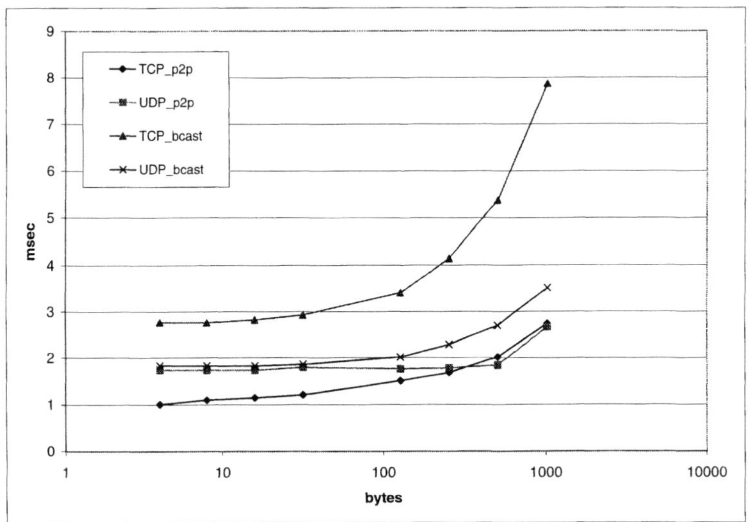

Figure 15.5 Point-to-point and broadcast characteristics of Ethernet using the TCP and UDP communication protocols.

lost or discarded somewhere in the network, and a sequence numbering mechanism that is used to detect duplicate and missing packets. It is clear from Figure 15.5 that UDP outperforms the TCP protocol when broadcasting, while there is little difference between them when sending large point-to-point messages. With small messages, the UDP protocol shows longer latency than TCP due to our added overhead to support reliable communication. Given these performance differences, it is feasible to use the PBPS technique to select the TCP communication path for point-to-point communication and the UDP path for broadcast operations in an application program running over the Ethernet.

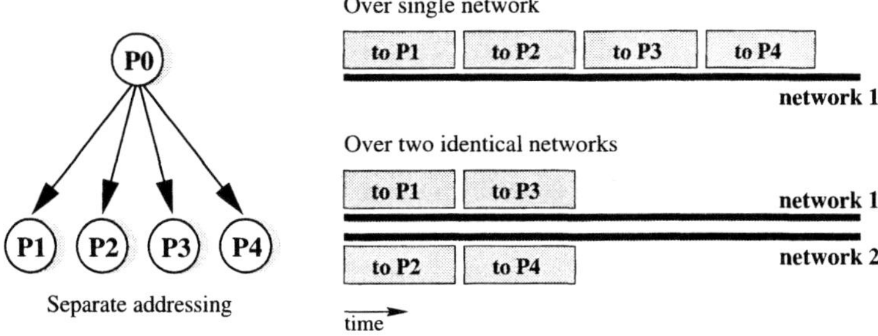

Figure 15.6 Example of a broadcast operation of a separate addressing method using the PBPA technique.

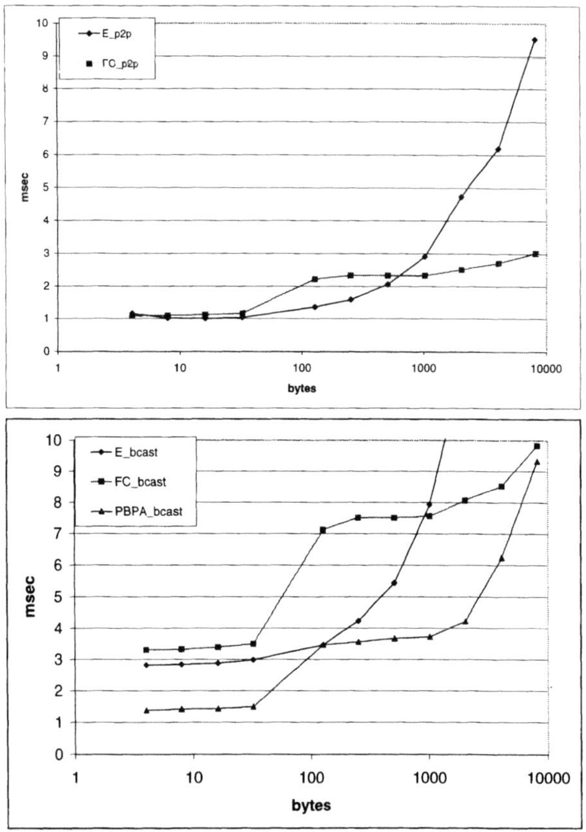

Figure 15.7 Point-to-point and broadcast characteristics of Ethernet and Fibre Channel using the TCP protocol.

When multiple networks are available at the same time we can send separately-addressed broadcast messages in parallel instead of sequentially. As shown in Figure 15.6, broadcasting a message over a single network will sequentially send the same message from processor 0 to processor 1, then processor 0 to processor 2, and so on. When there are two networks, however, we can simultaneously send a broadcast message from processor 0 to processor 1 over one network and from processor 0 to processor 2 over the other network.

Figure 15.7 shows the measured latency characteristics of point-to-point and broadcast operations over the Ethernet and the Fibre Channel networks both using TCP and the separate addressing method for broadcast operations. The PBPA curve in Figure 15.7 uses Ethernet and Fibre Channel at the same time for this type of broadcast operation. By aggregating the two networks, we see that we substantially lower the communication latency of broadcast operations than when using any single network alone.

Table 15.1 Parallel Benchmark Programs Tested

Programs	Description
CG	Conjugate gradient
MG	Multigrid
IS	Integer sort
Filter	Smoothing (averaging) filter
Gauss	Gaussian elimination
Hough	Line recognition algorithm
Kirsch	Image processing
TRFD	Two-electron integral transformation
Warp	Spatial domain image restoration
BT	Simulated CFD application using Block tridiagonal solver
LU	Simulated CFD application using LU solver
SP	Simulated CFD application using Pentadiagonal solver
MICOM	Miami isopycnic coordinate ocean model

15.4.2 Communication Patterns of Parallel Applications

The performance of the PBPD techniques at the application-level depends on the communication patterns of the specific application program being executed [7], [8]. This section summarizes the communication patterns of the parallel scientific application programs shown in Table 15.1. We use these characteristics to generate a synthetic benchmark program for evaluating the application-level performance of the PBPD techniques.

Computation Model

Network-based computing systems usually exploit medium and coarse-grained parallelism. A parallel application consists of several processes where each process is responsible for a portion of the application's computational workload. Oftentimes an application is parallelized in a data-parallel fashion so that many data items are subject to identical processing. That is, each processor executes the same program asynchronously, but each operates on only a fraction of the total data. Synchronization takes place in this execution model only when processors need to exchange data.

Figure 15.8 shows the occurrences in time of communication events for two of the test benchmarks shown in Table 15.1, IS and MG. The X axis represents elapsed time from the beginning of the program execution and the Y axis shows the message size of the corresponding communication event. Note that the Y axis is the base 10 logarithm of the actual message size. In both applications, all of the processors show similar communication patterns, except at the beginning of the execution. That is, each processor tends to alternate computation and communication at the same time so that they are all likely to communicate at the same time. As a result, communication congestion is likely to occur among the processors even when the

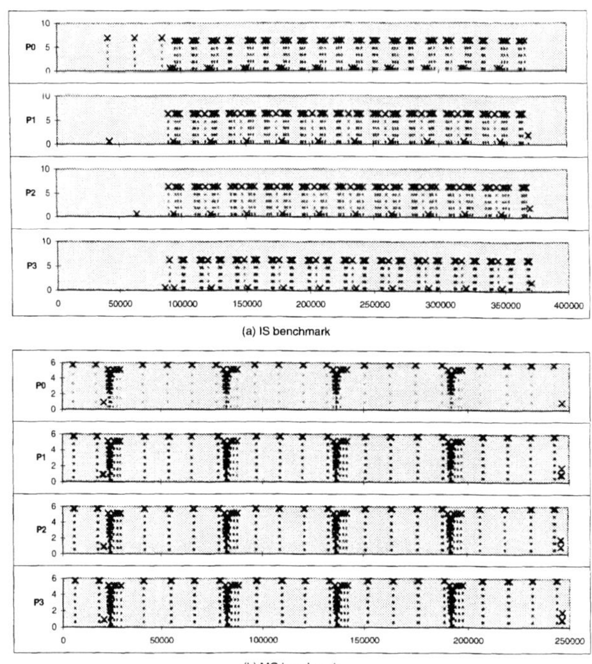

Figure 15.8 Relative times of communication events for the IS and MG benchmarks.

system is dedicated to a single application. We also saw similar results from the other benchmarks [9].

Message Size and Destination Distributions

The spatial behavior of an application's communication is characterized by the distribution of message destinations. The typical assumption is that the destinations of messages are evenly distributed among all of the processors. Figure 15.9 (a) appears to verify that assumption for our test programs since the overall destinations are uniformly distributed among all of the processors. However, destinations are not uniformly distributed from the viewpoint of the individual processors. Figure 15.9 (b) shows the message destinations of each individual processor for the *CG* benchmark with 16 processors. Except for P0, which is the favorite destination of all of the processors, each processor prefers one to five distinct processors out of the 15 available destinations as their communication partners. The other programs also show favored communication partners, except for the IS, TRFD, and Gauss programs, which communicate equally among all processors. We find that this pattern is consistent within an application when varying both the number of processors used to execute the application and the problem size [9].

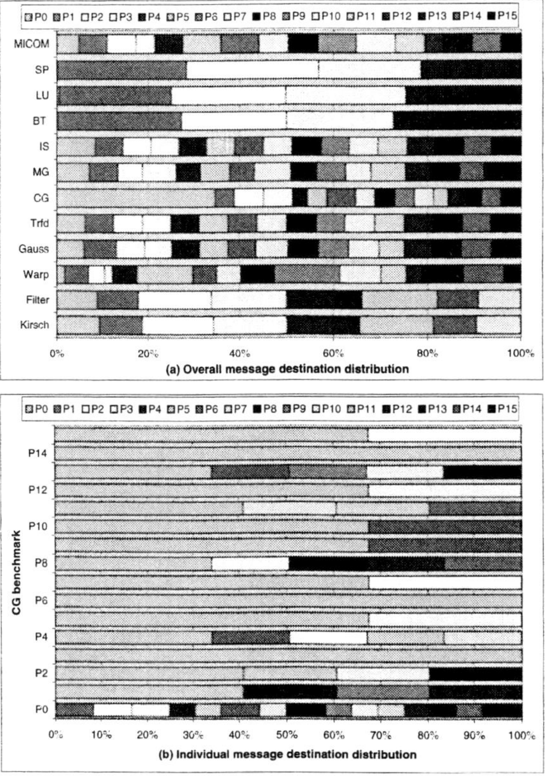

Figure 15.9 (a) Overall message destination distribution for all of the test programs, and (b) the message destination distribution for each processor in the CG benchmark.

The volume of data transferred is characterized by the distribution of message sizes which is shown in Figure 15.10. The horizontal axis in this figure represents the message size plotted on a logarithmic scale with the vertical axis showing the cumulative distribution of message sizes. Most benchmarks show two or three clear steps in the distribution indicating that all of the messages within an application have only two or three distinct sizes. Furthermore, some fraction of all the messages within an application tends to be very large while the remainder tends to be very small. For example, about 64 percent of the messages in the CG program are 8 bytes in length, whereas the remainder are around 28K bytes. Similarly, in the IS program, about 33 percent of the messages are 4 bytes and the remainder are around 130K bytes. Thus, the distribution of the sizes of the messages sent by these applications tend to be bimodal with two widely-separated peaks.

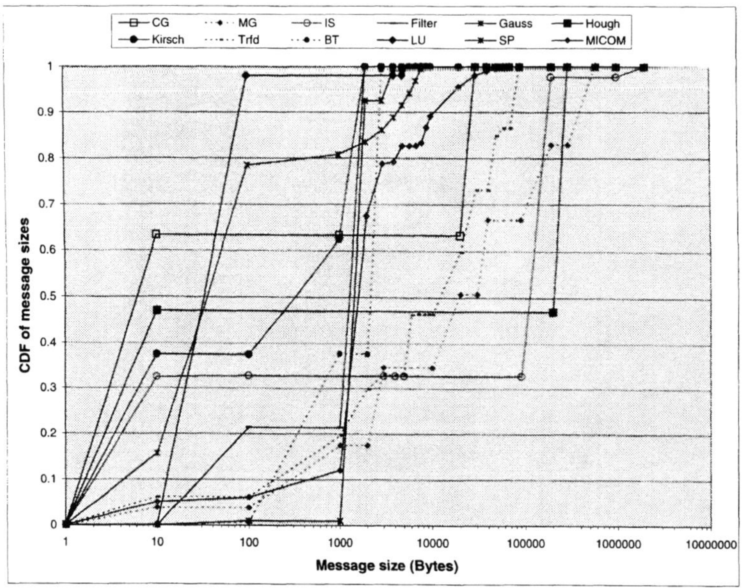

Figure 15.10 The cumulative distribution of message sizes in the test programs.

15.4.3 Experiments and Results

We developed a synthetic benchmark to estimate the improvement in communication performance that could be obtained at the application level when using the PBPD techniques. This synthetic benchmark is based on the communication patterns observed in Table 15.1 and is parameterized so that we may simulate the communication patterns of a variety of different application programs. The benchmark configures the system into one master processor and $p-1$ slave processors. For each communication event, the master processor generates several random numbers. The first of these numbers is a binary decision to determine the type of communication. Specifically, $(c*100)$ percent of the communication events will be broadcast operations with the remainder being point-to-point communication operations. In the case of point-to-point communication, the destination processor number is chosen to be uniformly distributed from 1 to $p-1$ so that each slave processor has an equal chance of becoming the destination of the current message. The message sizes for each communication follow a Poisson distribution with three different mean values, l_1, l_2, and l_3. Each of these mean values represents small, large, and broadcast message sizes, respectively. The final random number, g, which follows an exponential distribution, determines the computation time until the next communication event.

After generating these random values, an appropriate message is sent to the specified destination processor using the chosen communication strategy. The receiving processor responds to the sending processor with a 4-byte acknowledgment

Table 15.2 Parameter Values Used in the Synthetic Benchmark

Application Type	point-to-point message	small mean l_1	large mean l_2	broadcast message mean l_3
		b	$1-(b+c)$	c
A	90%	(45%	45%)	10%
B	50%	(25%	25%)	50%
C	10%	(5%	5%)	90%

message after it completely receives the message. The master (i.e., sending) processor then idles for the time g to simulate the processors' computation. Thus, when this synthetic benchmark is executed, the master processor will send an m-byte message to a randomly selected slave processor or will broadcast to all of the processors. The size of the message, m, follows a Poisson distribution such that $(c * 100)$ percent of the messages will be for broadcast communication with a mean size of l_3, $(b * 100)$ percent will be small messages for point-to-point communication with a mean size of l_1, and the remainder will be large messages for point-to-point communication with a mean size of l_2. These steps are repeated $N = 300$ times for each run of the benchmark program.

By appropriately choosing these parameters, we can approximate the communication patterns of several different types of benchmarks. Three different types of the synthetic benchmark were tested based on the ratio of point-to-point to broadcast operations, as shown in Table 15.2. The Type A parameters, for instance, simulate an application program in which 10 percent (i.e. $c = 0.1$) of its messages are Poisson distribution with a mean of l_3 bytes for broadcast, and the remaining 90 percent of the messages are evenly split between a Poisson distribution with a mean of l_1 bytes and a Poisson distributed with a mean of l_2 bytes for point-to-point communication.

Figure 15.11 shows the results of executing this synthetic benchmark using the PBPS scheme to dynamically select between the TCP and UDP protocols on the Ethernet of the SGI testbed. The parameters used in this figure are $l_1 = 8$ bytes, $l_2 = 1024$ bytes, and $l_3 = 32$ or 512 bytes. Each data point is the average of three different runs of the benchmark and represents the speedup over the execution time of the program when using the TCP protocol alone. In an application that has a small portion of its messages broadcast, i.e., the Type A program, using the UDP protocol is worse than using the TCP protocol due to the overhead of the flow control mechanism we implemented on top of the basic UDP datagram service. The PBPS scheme, however, can compensate for this overhead by taking advantage of the efficient broadcast operation in the UDP protocol. As the fraction of broadcast operations increases within an application, which is represented by the Type B and C programs, the benefit of the efficient UDP broadcast operation overwhelms the overhead of the added flow control operations. The results show a speedup of as high as 1.3 for the Type C benchmark with $l_3 = 512$ bytes.

Figure 15.12 shows the performance of the synthetic benchmark when using the

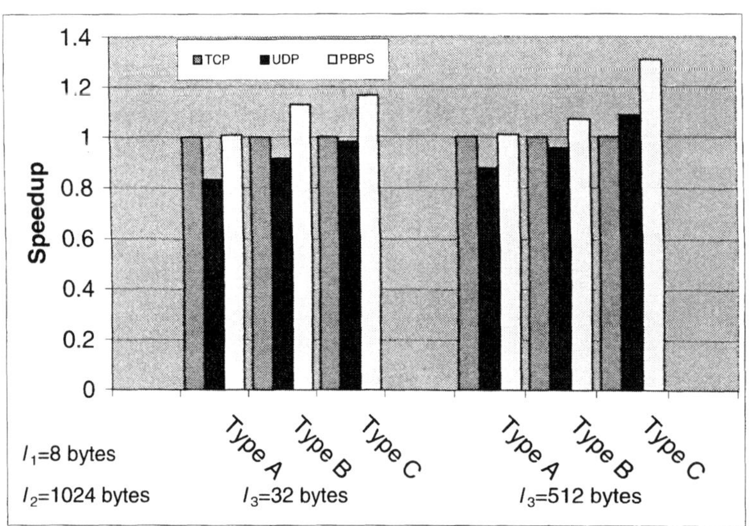

Figure 15.11 Speedup using PBPS with the TCP and UDP protocols over Ethernet. The speedups are normalized to the case when using the TCP protocol alone.

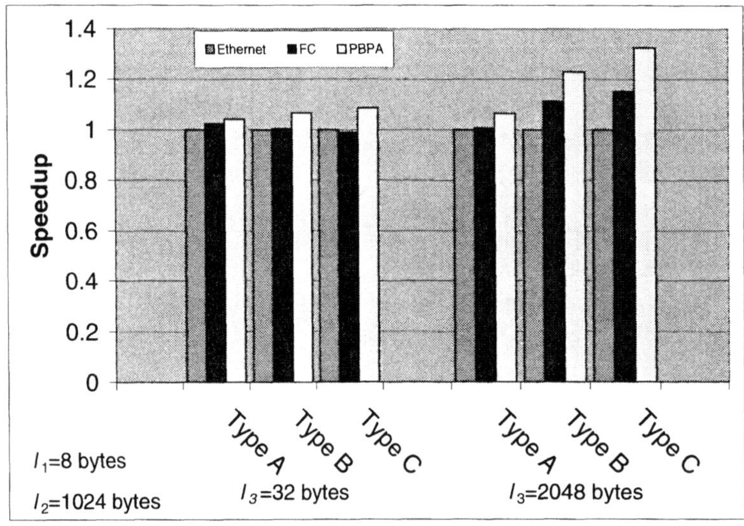

Figure 15.12 Speedup using the PBPA technique with Ethernet and Fiber Channel using the TCP protocol. The speedups are normalized to the case when using the Ethernet alone.

PBPA scheme to send broadcast messages simultaneously on both the Ethernet and Fibre Channel networks. As in Figure 15.11, each data point represents the speedup over the execution time of the benchmark when using only Ethernet alone. We chose the parameter values $l_1 = 8$ bytes, $l_2 = 1024$ bytes, and $l_3 = 32$ or 2048 bytes. Independent of the type of program (Type A, B, or C), the PBPA scheme shows the best overall performance demonstrating the potential improvement available at the application-level when aggregating these two networks into a single virtual network. The benefit of using PBPA increases as the percentage of broadcast operations increases. In the type C benchmark with $l_3 = 2048$ bytes, the PBPA scheme shows speedup of as high as 1.25, for example.

15.5 Summary and Conclusion

The importance of reducing communication overhead in network-based computing cannot be overemphasized since the communication delays in standardized interconnection networks can often become the performance bottleneck in parallel application programs. By exploiting heterogeneity in both communication paths and applications, communication overhead can be reduced since the different types of messages used in parallel application programs, such as short control information or bulk data transfers, have affinities for different types of communication paths.

In this study, we take advantage of communication path heterogeneity to reduce the overall communication delay experienced by parallel application programs. While our previous work [7], [8] exploited PBPD techniques based on message sizes, this paper demonstrates how PBPD can achieve performance improvement based on the message type, such as whether a particular message is a broadcast operation or point-to-point communication. That is, by selecting the best communication path based on its type (PBPS), and by aggregating multiple networks into a single virtual network (PBPA), the communication delays of parallel application programs can be reduced.

We used a synthetic benchmark to study the effectiveness of these approaches using a cluster of Silicon Graphics Challenge L multiprocessors interconnected with both Ethernet and Fibre Channel networks. We modeled the synthetic communication patterns after the communication patterns we measured in several scientific parallel benchmarks [9]. Our experimental measurements show that using these PBPD techniques produced the best communication performance for applications that have a mix of broadcast and point-to-point communication.

Acknowledgment

This work was supported in part by the National Science Foundation under grant no. CDA-9414015, and by the Minnesota Supercomputing Institute.

15.6 Bibliography

[1] T. E. Anderson, D. E. Culler, and D. A. Patterson. A Case for Networks of Workstations: NOW. *IEEE Micro*, vol. 15(1), pages 54–64, February 1995.

[2] F. Berman, R. Wolski, S. Figueira, J. Schopf, and G. Shao. Application-Level Scheduling on Distributed Heterogeneous Networks. In *Supercomputing*, 1996.

[3] R. Fatoohi and S. Weeratunga. Performance Evaluation of Three Distributed Computing Environments for Scientific Applications. In *Supercomputing*, pages 400–409, 1994.

[4] I. Foster, C. Kesselman, and S. Tuecke. The NEXUS Task-Parallel Runtime System. In *International Workshop on Parallel Processing*, pages 457–462, 1994.

[5] A. Grimshaw, W. Wulf, J. French, A. Weaver, and P. Reynolds. Legion: The Next Logical Step Toward a Nationwide Virtual Computer. *Technical Report CS-94-21*, Dept. of Computer Science, University of Virginia, 1994.

[6] C. Huang, E. P. Kasten, and P. K. McKinley. Design and Implementation of Multicast Operations for ATM-Based High Performance Computing. In *Supercomputing*, pages 164–173, August 1994.

[7] JunSeong Kim and David J. Lilja. Performance-Based Path Determination for Interprocessor Communication in Distributed Computing Systems. *IEEE Transactions on Parallel and Distributed Systems*, (in press).

[8] JunSeong Kim and David J. Lilja. Utilizing Heterogeneous Networks in Distributed Parallel Computing Systems. In *International Symposium on High Performance Distributed Computing*, pages 336–345, August 1997.

[9] JunSeong Kim and David J. Lilja. Characterization of Communication Patterns in Message-Passing Parallel Scientific Application Programs. In *Workshop on Communication, Architecture, and Applications for Network-based Parallel Computing, International Symposium on High Performance Computer Architecture*, pages 202–216, January 1998.

[10] David J. Lilja and J. Schmitt. A Data Parallel Implementation of the TRFD Program From the PERFECT Benchmarks. In *EUROSIM International Conference on Massively Parallel Processing Applications and Development*, pages 355–362, May 1994, Delft, the Netherlands.

[11] A. S. Tanenbaum. *Computer Networks.* Prentice Hall, Upper Saddle River, NJ, 3rd edition, 1996.

[12] S. VanderWiel, D. Nathanson, and D. J. Lilja. Complexity and Performance in Parallel Programming Languages. In *International Workshop on High-Level Parallel Programming Models and Supportive Environments, International Parallel Processing Symposium*, April 1997, Geneva, Switzerland.

Chapter 16

Network RAM

MICHAIL D. FLOURIS AND EVANGELOS P. MARKATOS

Foundation for Research & Technology - Hellas (FO.R.T.H.) and
Computer Science Department, University of Crete
Heraklion, Greece

Email: {*flouris, markatos*}*@ics.forth.gr*

16.1 Introduction

In this chapter, we discuss the efficient distribution and exploitation of main memory in a workstation cluster. We will use the term *Network RAM* or *Network memory* to denote the aggregate main memory of the workstations in the cluster. The term *Remote memory* will be used to denote the view each workstation in the cluster has of the other workstations' memory.

In order to view Network RAM in a real situation, consider a modern workstation cluster in a building consisting of 100 workstations spread on many floors, in various offices and laboratories, each with a modern mircroprocessor, a typical main memory of 64 or 128 MBytes, and a disk of 2 or 4 GBytes capacity. The workstations are connected with a 155 Mbps ATM network, which has a typical latency[1] of 20 μsec and a typical bandwidth[2] of 15 MB/s.

In this setting, there will be times when many workstations are loaded with each user's applications, and many of the cluster's resources (CPU, memory, disks, network) are in use. However, according to statistics [10], [18], [1], there is a significant amount of resources unused in the cluster *at any given time.* Even better, there will be times in the evening or late afternoon when 80% - 90% of the workstations will be idle. Reported measurements state that one third of the workstations are completely unused, even at the busiest times of the day, over one gigabyte of memory

[1]Latency of a network is the (compulsory) delay necessary for sending a message from one machine to another.

[2]Bandwidth or throughput of a network is the maximum rate at which data can be transferred from a user-level application running on one node to another running on another node through the network, and is measured in bits per second.

is sitting idle on a typical evening [10], and 30 machines in a 50-machine network are classified idle at any given time. Finally, a recent study concludes that 70% - 85% of the Network RAM in a cluster is idle [1]. These reported measurements provide evidence that in the majority of workstation clusters, there exist significant amounts of unused network memory.

The available unused memory in a workstation cluster can be used by several applications that have working sets larger than the physical memory of any single workstation. If such an application is executed on a workstation that does not have adequate memory, the application will suffer a significant performance degradation. Despite the fact that many other workstations and their memory are idle and accessible over the network, the application uses only the local physical memory on the machine it is running on, and the cost of page swapping dramatically prolongs its execution time. This is a typical example where memory resources in the cluster are not organized well and thus user time is wasted. Network RAM can also be used to speed up applications that frequently access large amounts of disk data (e.g., databases, filesystems).

Although Network RAM consists of volatile memory, it can offer good reliability because it is distributed across many independent workstations. If one workstation crashes, the data stored in the memory of the other workstations are still intact. Using some form of redundancy, such as replication of data or parity, one could reconstruct the data stored in the memory of the crashed workstation. Of course, there may be more than one crashed workstation, in which case other redundancy techniques could be used. Exploiting the Network RAM's reliability capabilities, using redundancy to provide data reliability in case of one or more workstation failures, is an issue explored further in Section 16.2.2 .

Under the above circumstances, Network RAM in the workstation cluster should be organized so that the applications running in the NOW can use it efficiently to speed up their tasks. Studying the status of modern NOWs, it can be argued that Network RAM has the ability to offer an excellent cost-effective alternative to magnetic disk storage in several circumstances, because current technological advances in network technology suggest that the access time of Network RAM is significantly better than the access time of traditional magnetic disks.

- *High performance networks.* Modern switched high performance local area networks allow bandwidth to scale with the number of workstations, and new low latency communication and messaging protocols [8] provide the means for very efficient communication in a NOW. In some implementations, an application-to-application latency of only $20\mu s$ was measured using Active Messages over ATM. As local memory performance is dependent on the memory bus, Network RAM performance is heavily dependent on the network, which in this case can be thought of as a memory bus. A low latency and high bandwidth network is a key requirement for the use of Network RAM. On the contrary, magnetic disk latency has been in the area of 10 ms for the last decade.

- *High performance workstations.* Modern workstations are becoming more powerful at an ever-increasing rate, driven by the power of mass production. Their components, one of which is main memory, have very low cost, so most workstations have large memories and high speed buses. This makes Network RAM even more attractive, because there is more remote memory out there for each workstation, and a larger amount of it should be idle.

- *The I/O - processor performance gap.* Microprocessors have been improving in performance at a rate of 50% to 100% per year, whereas disk performance increases very slowly. This well-known processor - I/O performance gap makes the use of Network RAM instead of disks much more attractive. Since the performance of Network RAM is dependent on the network performance, which is expected to improve with microprocessor speeds, the Network RAM - disk performance gap is expected to increase with time. More specifically, the performance improvement rate for disk latency is 10% per year and for disk bandwidth, 20% per year, whereas network latency improves at 20% per year and network bandwidth improves at 45% per year.

Apart from new techologies that make it appealing from the performance viewpoint, Network RAM has excellent cost/performance figures. Table 16.1 shows the memory hierarchy figures for a typical NOW with 100 workstations and a network of 20 μsec latency and 15 MB/s bandwidth. For the Network RAM capacity, we assume that at least 50% of the total Network RAM in the cluster is free. We can see that Network RAM offers much better performance than the disk, much larger capacity from local memory and even the disk, and costs practically nothing because it has already been purchased as local memory for each workstation. This cost-effectiveness makes Network RAM a big temptation.

Table 16.1 Memory Hierarchy Figures for a Typical Workstation Cluster

Memory Hierarchy	Latency (μsec)	Bandwidth (MB/s)	Capacity (MB)
Cache	0.002	500	2
DRAM	0.1	200	256
Network RAM	20	15	12800
Disk	10000	10	8000

Having discussed and accepted the hypothesis that network memory has the potential to effectively and inexpensively boost application's performance in a workstation cluster, we proceed in defining the network memory problem and discussing solutions for the issues it encompasses.

16.1.1 Issues in Using Network RAM

Using Network RAM consists essentially of locating and managing effectively unused memory resources in a workstation cluster. This is itself a complicated issue that requires the cooperation of several different systems.

Locating unused Network RAM requires an entity that keeps up-to-date information about unused memory in every workstation in a cluster. Once the idle memory is located, it should be exploited in a transparent way so that local users will not notice any performance degradation, which is a more complicated issue than it first appears. The context and setting in which Network RAM will be used, forms its location and management requirements, problems, and techniques.

The most common uses of Network RAM today are summarized below:

- *Remote Memory Paging.* Since the performance of Network RAM places it between the local DRAM and the disk, we can insert it in the memory hierarchy as an intermediate layer between local memory and the disk. All memory-intensive applications running in the workstation cluster could benefit from this additional memory layer, since swapping pages to the Network RAM would be faster than the disk and the overall memory access time would be much less. There are many ways to insert this Network RAM memory hierarchy layer, and each has its positive and negative sides. The issues in using Network RAM as a layer of memory hierarchy are presented in Section 16.2.

- *Network Memory Filesystems.* Network RAM can be used to store temporary data, which can be filesystem metadata, transaction metadata, web cache files, etc. This can be done by providing Network RAM with a filesystem abstraction, where applications would simply read and write files. This use of Network RAM and the issues related to it are presented in Section 16.3.

- *Network Memory Databases.* Network memory can be used as a large (distributed) database cache and/or as a fast non-volatile data buffer to store database sensitive data. The use of reliable Network RAM in transaction systems is explored in Section 16.4.

All the various systems that use network memory can be implemented in software using common off-the-shelf hardware components. Apart from these, there are hardware components, such as SCI [13], Telegraphos [17], and SHRIMP [6], which provide special primitive operations that can greatly enhance the performance of network memory systems.

16.2 Remote Memory Paging

Application's working sets have increased dramatically over the last few years. Software takes advantage of the 64-bit address spaces that most modern processors provide, resulting in heavy memory usage [18]. Programs with large working sets include sophisticated graphical user interfaces, multimedia applications, artificial intelligence applications, VLSI design tools, databases and transaction processing systems. Such applications usually need more memory than any single workstation can provide.

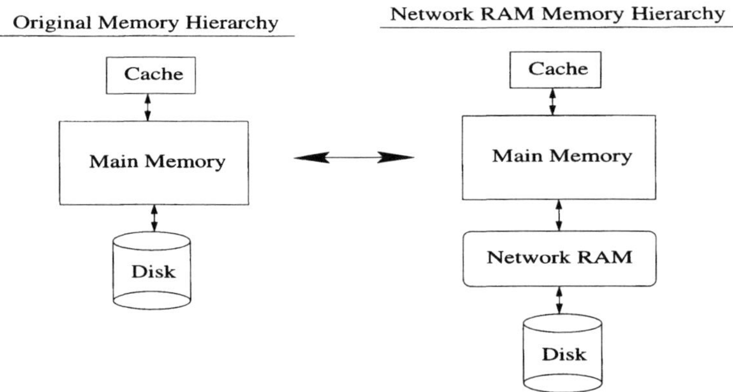

Figure 16.1 Changing the memory hierarchy.

One simple but expensive solution to memory shortage would be to add physical DRAM on all the workstations. On the other hand, one possible extension to the memory hierarchy, which does not increase the size of local main memory, but rather miminizes the overhead of memory paging, is the layer of Network RAM.

The use of Network RAM for memory address space of applications (i.e., to store memory pages) is so common that many people consider the term Network RAM equivalent to remote memory paging. This happens because we can easily think of Network RAM as a transparent intermediate layer between local memory and the disk, as shown in Figure 16.1. All memory-intensive applications running in the workstation cluster could benefit from this additional memory layer, because swapping pages to the Network RAM would be quite faster than the disk and the overall memory access time would be much less. Moreover, in mobile or portable computers where storage space is inherently limited, remote memory paging is not only desirable but necessary.

There are several ways we could exploit Network RAM as a level of memory hierarchy. Section 16.2.1 presents these implementation alternatives as well as their advantages and disadvantages.

16.2.1 Implementation Alternatives

The main idea of remote memory paging is to start memory server processes on workstations that are either idle or lightly loaded and have sufficient amounts of unused physical memory. When one workstation runs out of physical memory, it stores some of its pages in the main memory of another workstation, using the memory server process active on it. Naturally, this operation should be transparent to the user applications. When the server workstation is not idle, the server process is inactive and becomes operative only when the workstation becomes idle.

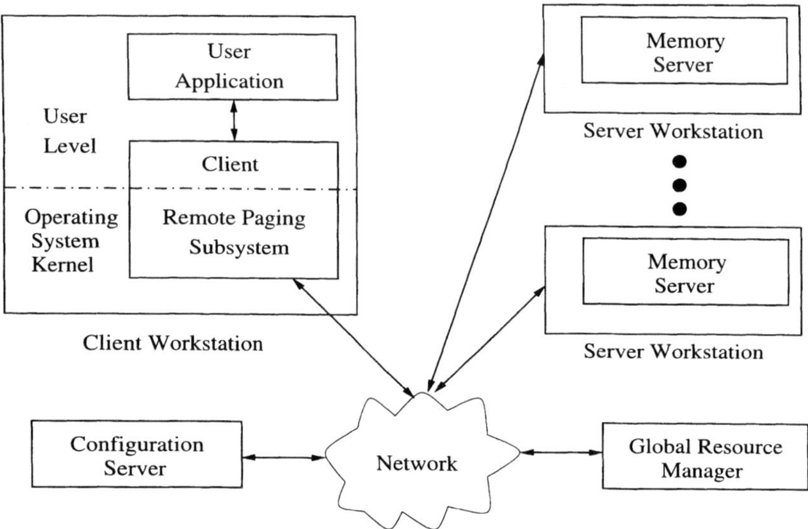

Figure 16.2 Remote paging system structure.

The structure of a generic remote memory paging facility is summarized in Figure 16.2. In this figure, apart from the memory server processes running on idle workstations, the client workstation has a remote paging subsystem which can be either user-level or in the operating system and which enables it to use network memory as backing store. There is also a global resource management process running on a workstation in the cluster, which holds information (which is updated periodically) about the memory resources and how they are being utilized in the cluster. The final component is a configuration server process which is responsible for the setup of the network memory cluster.

This configuration server (or registry server) is contacted when a machine wants to enter or leave the Network RAM cluster. When a workstation wants to enter the cluster of Network RAM-backed memory, it is authenticated according to the system administrator's rules, in case its participation is not desirable, because clearly we do not want to store memory pages to machines that are not trusted. Memory protection is provided by the virtual memory manager, network protection can be implemented using secure network protocols, and since the machines are checked on their entrance to the cluster, there should be no further security concerns.

The most important part of a transparent remote memory paging system, is the design and implementation of the client remote paging subsystem, which has two main components:

1. A mechanism for intercepting and handling page faults.[3]

2. A policy which, using this mechanism in an appropriate way, will implement the page management. This policy should keep track of which local pages are stored on which remote nodes, and should decide on which node to store newly allocated pages.

The policies used for page management depend on the mechanisms used for handling page faults. Generally, there are two main approaches to these mechanisms, which define respectively two alternative implementations of transparent remote paging subsystems on the client workstation:

1. Implementation of a transparent network memory subsystem, using the mechanisms provided by the existing client's operating system for handling page faults.

2. Implementation of a transparent network memory subsystem, by modifying the virtual memory manager and its mechanisms in the client's operating system kernel in such a way that it manages network memory along with local memory.

We discuss these two approaches, the mechanisms used in the design of remote memory paging systems, the policies that could be used for handling pages in each case, and the entire structure of the remote memory facility in each of them, in the next two paragraphs. Finally, in Section 16.2.1 we will discuss the usage of subpaging for transfering pages over the network and how this can enhance the performance of a remote memory paging system.

Transparent Network RAM Implementation Using Existing OS Mechanisms

There are two basic mechanisms in most existing operating systems which permit us to intercept page faults and handle them in our own way, one operating at the user level and the other at the operating system level.

User Level Memory Management In this approach, each program making use of Network RAM as a memory layer uses new memory allocation and management calls (i.e., a new `malloc`), which are usually contained in a library dynamically or statically linked to the user application. This solution also requires some program code modifications [2].

The mechanism used in this approach intercepts page faults through the use of segmentation faults. When the program tries to access a page that does not exist in the local main memory of the machine, it receives a segmentation fault signal (`SEGV`) from the operating system memory manager. This segmentation fault signal is intercepted by the user level signal handler routines, and the page management

[3]A page fault is generated by an access to a nonresident page (a page that does not reside in physical local memory).

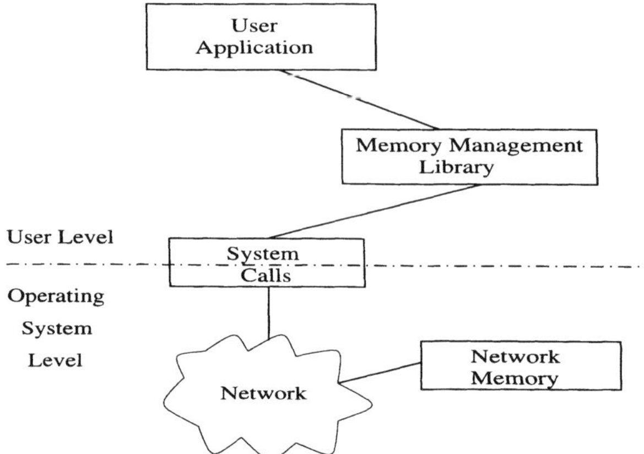

Figure 16.3 User level memory management solution's structure.

algorithm is called to locate and transfer a remote page into local memory, replacing a local page. A basic structure of such a system can be seen in Figure 16.3.

A user level pager prototype was developed by E. Anderson et al. [2] as a custom `malloc` library. The application initializes the library with specific calls, requests the amount of network memory it wants to use, and subsequently all calls to the `malloc` (memory allocation) will be serviced using network memory instead of local. Measurements reported by E. Anderson et al. show that by using TCP/IP, the user-level memory manager could perform a 4K page replacement in 1.5 - 8.0 ms, depending on the machine and the network, while the disk took 10 ms. This makes the user level pager prototype 1.3 - 6.6 times faster than the disk.

Swap Device Driver Another solution that operates at the operating system level using existing OS mechanisms is the implementation of a remote memory paging through a swap device driver. The key idea is to use one feature that all modern operating systems provide: the ability to define and use multiple block devices for virtual memory paging. All one must do is to create a custom block device and configure the virtual memory manager to use it for physical memory backing store before the usual magnetic disk [18].

When the machine runs out of physical memory, it will swap pages to the first device on the list of swap devices which will be the remote memory paging device driver. The device driver code will contain the page management algorithm, which will allocate new pages, send pages from the local to the remote memory, or locate and receive pages from the remote memory. Eventually, if and when this Network RAM device runs out of space, the virtual memory manager will swap pages to the next device, which could be the disk. An abstract architecture of such a device driver solution is shown in Figure 16.4.

The device driver solution is quite simple in concept and requires one minor

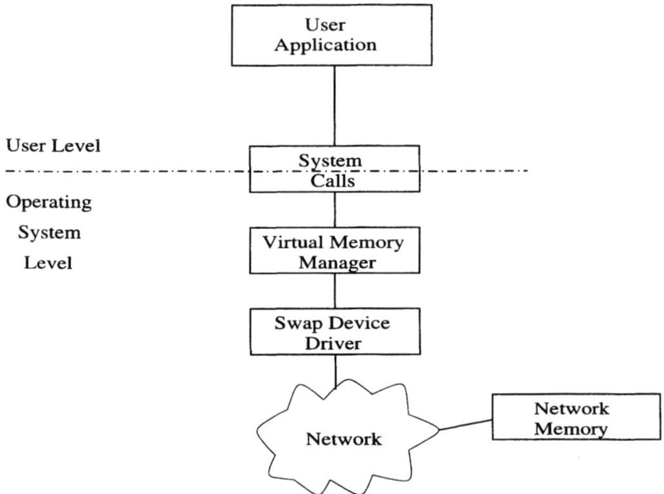

Figure 16.4 Swap device driver solution's structure.

modification to the operating system: the addition of a device driver. All modern operating systems provide a straightforward way of doing this, even though programming a device driver is coding at the system level, which is itself an intricate task.

Page Management Policies Two existing mechanisms that provide us with the means to intercept page faults have been discussed. The subsequent discussion deals with the scheme used by the remote paging system to handle the pages in a multi-client and multi-server network [10].

A first issue is which memory server should the client select each time to send pages. One possible solution is that the client periodically asks the global resource management process for memory statistics on the memory servers and also their network response times. Accordingly, the client would pick the most promising server and send the pages to it. Another possible solution is to distribute the pages equally among the servers. On the other hand, this may prove inefficient because load usually varies between servers. The above algorithms do not provide any fault-tolerance for the pages in case of a server crash. Later, in Section 16.2.2, we will discuss page placement policies which provide this necessary reliability.

Another scenario the page management policy should deal with is the handling of a server's pages when its workstation becomes loaded. One solution is to inform the client and the other servers of its loaded state, so that they will not send more pages, then migrate the pages to other idle servers and eventually become inactive until the machine is idle again. Another solution is, instead of migrating the pages, to transfer them to the server's disk and then deallocate them each time they are referenced. Lastly, there is the solution of transferring all the pages back to the client, which can store them on its disk. A final issue is what will happen when all servers are full. The solution for this problem is fairly simple: store the pages on disk. However, there is more to consider. When a server becomes loaded, page migration is no longer an option. The only available solution is storing pages to the disk, either the client's or the server's.

Transparent Network RAM Implementation Through OS Kernel Modification

The operating system modification is the software solution which offers the highest performance without modifying user programs, because Network RAM management is incorporated in the operating system kernel and no extra system calls, context switches or interrupts are required. However, OS kernel modifications are an arduous task and are not portable between architectures.

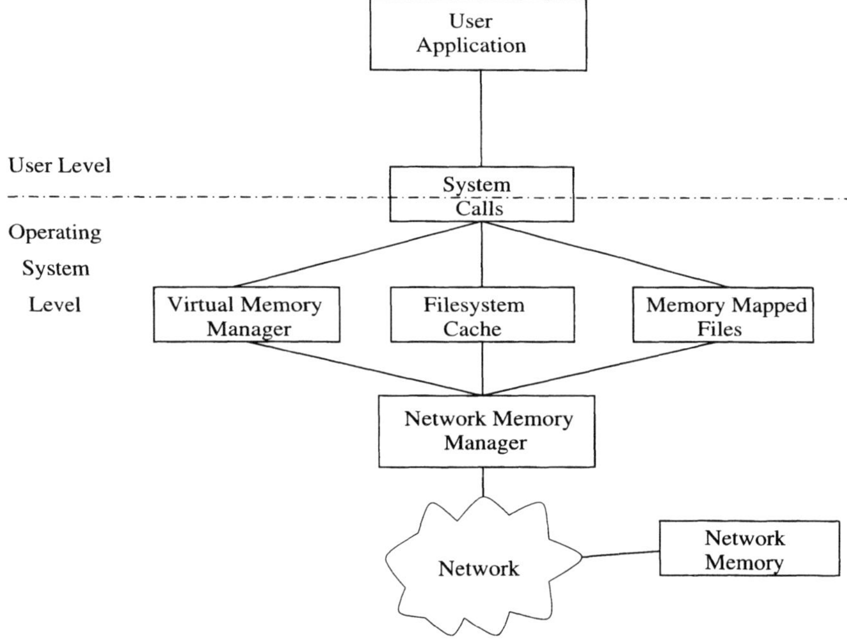

Figure 16.5 Operating system modification architecture.

The kernel modification solution can provide *global memory management* in a workstation cluster, using a single unified memory manager as a low-level component of the operating system that runs on each workstation [9]. Thus, it can integrate all the Network RAM in a NOW for use by all higher-level functions, including virtual memory paging, memory mapped files and filesystem caching. An abstract view of the kernel modification architecture can be seen in Figure 16.5. In the kernel modification approach, the crucial issues are the memory management and page replacement algorithms. We will address them and discuss some possible solutions.

All nodes participating in the remote memory paging cluster should run the same algorithm and attempt to make choices that are good in a global cluster sense, as well as for the node itself. In order to describe the algorithm used for this global/local memory management, we will define some useful concepts and terms.

We can classify the pages on a node P as being either *local pages*, which have been recently accessed on P, or *global/remote pages*, which are stored in P's memory on behalf of other nodes. Pages may also be *private* or *shared*. Shared pages may be found in the active local memories of more than one node, while a private page is stored on one node only. A page in global memory is always private, while shared pages occur, for example, when two or more nodes might access a common file exported by a file server.

The algorithm that is managing the pages changes the local/global memory balance as a result of a page fault. There are several page replacement algorithms. We will describe a simple replacement algorithm used in the GMS system [9]. Assume the case of a page fault on node P. There are four possible cases:

1. The faulted page is in the global memory of another node Q. We swap the desired page in Q's global memory with any global page in P's global memory. Once brought into P's memory, the faulted page becomes a local page, increasing the size of P's local memory by 1. Q's local/global memory balance is unchanged.

2. The faulted page is in the global memory of node Q, but P's memory contains only local pages. Exchange the LRU local page on P with the faulted page on Q. The size of the global memory on Q and the local memory on P are unchanged.

3. The page is on disk. Read the faulted page into node P's memory, where it becomes a local page. Choose the oldest page in the cluster (for example, on node Q) for replacement and write it to disk, if necessary. Send a global page from node P to node Q where it continues as a global page. If P has no global pages, choose P's LRU local page instead.

4. The faulted page is a shared page in the *local* memory of another node Q. Copy that page into a frame on node P, leaving the original in the local memory of Q. Choose the oldest page *in the cluster* (for example, on node R) for replacement and write it to disk, if necessary. Send a global page from node P to node R where it becomes a global page. (If P has no global pages, choose P's LRU local page).

This algorithm causes nodes that are actively computing and using memory to fill their memories, over time, and to start using remote memory in the cluster. Nodes that are idle for some time, and whose pages are old, will begin to fill their memories with global pages. The balance between global and local storage is thus dynamic and depends both on the node and the cluster workload.

The cost of page replacement depends on the state of the page in reference: in local memory, in global memory of another node, or on disk. Since a local hit is over three orders of magnitude faster than a global memory or disk access, and a global hit is only two to ten times faster than a disk access, using only LRU for page replacement would make wrong replacements. Thus, if the optimum performance is desirable, a special cost function based on both the age of the page (like LRU) and its state (local, global or on disk) should be used [9].

Boosting Performance with Subpages

Another issue that we should consider is the way each page is transferred over the network. Several studies [5], [16] suggest that using transfer units smaller than a single page, which are called subpages, across the network boosts remote memory paging performance. This happens for two reasons:

1. Subpages are transferred over the network much faster than whole pages. This is not the case with magnetic disk transfers, where transfers smaller than a page size do not result in significantly lower transfer times.

2. Using subpages allows a larger window for the overlap of computation with communication. This means that by transferring first the part of the page where the page fault occurred and the rest of the page later, the application that produced the fault can continue its execution as soon as the faulted subpage arrives, while the rest of the page is still transferred over the network.

The idea of subpaging can be incorporated into any remote paging system that transfers pages over the network, although its implementation is quite complex, because the size of the subpage is crucial for the performance of several applications. An equally important problem is to determine an effective access control mechanism to handle this subpage size. A third subpaging issue is to discover a suitable algorithm for fetching the fragments of a page (the subpages) from the remote memory, in the order which will ensure an application's optimum performance. The solutions to these issues should be flexible in order to accommodate the requirements of a diverse set of applications. The answers to the subpaging questions are beyond the scope of this book. For more information about subpaging, refer to [5], [16].

Reported measurements of a subpaging implementation in GMS [16] show that memory-intensive applications execute up to 1.8 times faster when executed with 1 KByte subpages than when compared to the same applications using full 8 KByte pages, and 4 times faster than when using the disk for paging.

16.2.2 Reliability

Researchers have noted that the main disadvantages of remote memory paging appear in the areas of security and fault-tolerance [10]. In Section 16.2.1 it has been noted that the security issue can be resolved through the use of a registry.

The issue that remains and is discussed in this section is the issue of reliability (mentioned also as fault-tolerance).

In a workstation cluster, workstation crashes and network failures are much more frequent than failures in the subsystems of a single machine. If we imagine each workstation being in the office of a typical user and not in a special room handled by trained personnel, the chances of failure become even more threatening: users turning their workstations on and off, accidentally unplugging the network cables, running software that causes the workstation to crash or the network to become unavailable, and so on.

Clearly, if one workstation that stores memory pages crashes, those pages will be lost. This would lead to important data loss for the client's processes, because the pages lost may belong to long running processes or system daemon processes, or even to the operating system code itself. The failure would cause these processes to crash, causing the user to lose valuable time, especially if these processes took a long time, or even causing the operating system to crash and all its processes to hang [2].

Obviously, such unstable behavior is neither desirable nor acceptable. To increase reliability of applications using Network RAM in a transparent way, several approaches have been proposed all based on using a form of redundancy to recover lost data. In the following paragraphs we will present the most popular policies for reliability as well as their pros and cons. Some of these policies have been used in RAIDs.

Using a Reliable Device

The simplest reliability policy is to use a reliable device such as the disk or other non-volatile memory systems. The pages stored on Network RAM are also written asynchronously to that fault-tolerant device. In case of a workstation or network failure, they can be safely recovered from the device. This is a very simple policy, and since the data is written asynchronously, it is satisfactory on the run-time overhead during normal operation, provided that we have enough bandwidth to the fault-tolerant device. It also provides maximum reliability, even in the case when all the servers fail. However, this level of reliability is not imperative in remote memory paging. Another advantage of this policy, is that when the servers become loaded they can simply discard their pages, since these pages can be retrieved from the reliable device.

On the other hand, there several drawbacks to this approach exist. One drawback concerns the performance of the system under failure, which is equal to the performance of the disk. Other policies reviewed in the following paragraphs perform better in that field. Another disadvantage of this policy is that it has much memory overhead, because it uses space on the device equal to the memory space used in Network RAM. This space overhead makes this method expensive. Finally, the performance of this policy is dictated by the write throughput of the magnetic disk which can eventually become the bottleneck [2].

To sum up, this policy offers a high degree of reliability, although it has merely adequate performance. As networks get faster, this method will suffer from poorer performance. In the next sections we will discuss policies which do not use a reliable device. On the contrary, they are trying to construct a mostly reliable system based on many independent unreliable ones.

Replication - Mirroring

A simple reliability policy that does not use the disk or another reliable device is page replication [2], [18]. The idea of this method is simple: In order to increase the reliability, the client replicates the pages one or more times and stores each copy on a different memory server. When there are two replicas of each page, the policy is called mirroring. If one server crashes, we still have a copy of the page in another server, which in turn can be replicated in another node to prevent a second failure. This policy is simple to understand and implement. On the other hand, the drawbacks of this policy are quite serious. First of all, it uses a lot of memory space to store the copies. Using mirroring, for example, wastes half of our network memory, because if the total number of pages stored is P, $2 \times P$ pages are stored on the memory servers. Another serious handicap is that the network overhead is very high, because for each page the client pages out, there are as many network transfers as the replicas, which can significantly degrade remote memory paging performance.

Variations of the basic replication algorithm try to address these issues. For example, in one implementation the page replication is performed by the memory server process in order to take the load off the client, while in another the pages are also remotely replicated on disk, which is a combination of replication and writing to disk policies. However, even if the replication takes place on the memory server, the network load is still high and if the replicas are written to disk, the disk will become a bottleneck under some workloads.

Simple Parity

A third reliability algorithm, called simple parity, is based on parity, a method extensively used in RAIDs. Parity reliability is based on the XOR (EXclusive OR) operation [4] and works as follows: Suppose that we have two blocks of data of the same size, A and B, for example. If we calculate C, where $C = A \oplus B$, then by XORing any two of the A, B, C blocks, we can reconstruct the third one. For example, if $A = 1$ and $B = 0$, then $C = A \oplus B = 1$ and we would reconstruct A as the result of $B \oplus C = 1 = A$. Of course, this holds for more than two blocks of data, e.g., if $E = A \oplus B \oplus C \oplus D$, then $B = A \oplus E \oplus C \oplus D$.

Since the memory pages are equal in size, there is an easy way of exploiting this parity theory to reduce the memory overhead of the page replication policy. Assume

[4]The XOR (EXclusive OR) operation is denoted by the symbol $\oplus$. The result of a binary XOR operation $A \oplus B$ is 1 if exactly one of the A, B is one. Thus, $1 \oplus 0 = 1$ and $0 \oplus 1 = 1$ but $1 \oplus 1 = 0$ and $0 \oplus 0 = 0$.

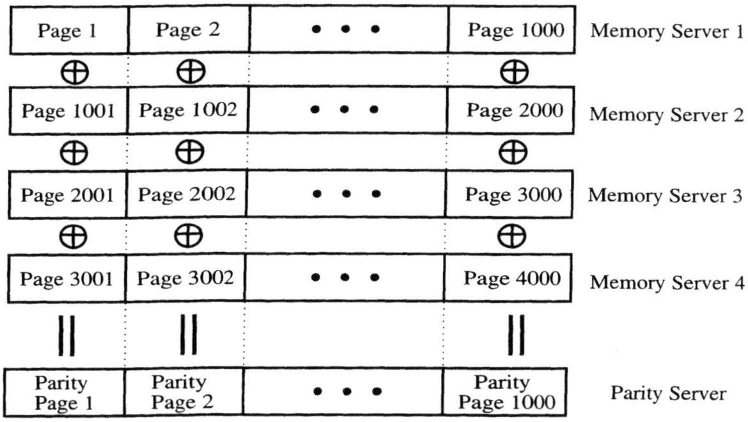

Page 1	Page 2	• • •	Page 1000	Memory Server 1
⊕	⊕		⊕	
Page 1001	Page 1002	• • •	Page 2000	Memory Server 2
⊕	⊕		⊕	
Page 2001	Page 2002	• • •	Page 3000	Memory Server 3
⊕	⊕		⊕	
Page 3001	Page 3002	• • •	Page 4000	Memory Server 4
||	||		||	
Parity Page 1	Parity Page 2	• • •	Parity Page 1000	Parity Server

Figure 16.6 An example of the simple parity policy. Each server in this example can store 1000 pages.

S memory servers, each capable of storing P pages. We will use the tuple *(i,j)* to denote page *j* on server *i*. One of the servers is used to store parity pages, which is accordingly called parity server. The j_{th} page on the parity server holds the XOR of all the j_{th} pages on all the other servers, as shown in Figure 16.6. If this condition is preserved, then in case of a server crash the lost pages can be reconstructed using the parity. For example, page *j* on the crashed server can be recovered by XORing all the j_{th} pages on the working servers, including the parity server. We say that all the j_{th} pages on all the servers belong to the same parity group because, as we have seen, every element of this group can be reconstructed from the rest of the elements.

Each client writes out a page to a server. It must update the parity page as well:

1. The client writes out the page to a regular server, which computes the XOR of the new and the old page. (If the page is completely new, the old page should be all zeros.)

2. The server sends the XOR computed to the parity server which XORs it with the old parity page, forming the new one.

This algorithm involves two page transfers, one from client to the server and one from the server to the parity server. Moreover, the client should not erase the swapped out page until the parity is updated, because in case of a crash data loss is inevitable.

The parity method increases the amount of memory storage only by a factor of (1+1/S), where S is the number of servers, thus significantly reducing the memory overhead. If, for example, the workstations have sent P total pages to the remote paging device, there are $(1 + 1/S) \times P$ pages stored on all the servers, where S is the number of servers. However, the network transfer overhead remains two network transfers per page, which is still very high. Moreover, this method provides fault-tolerance for only one server crash. If two or more servers fail at the same time, pages are lost [18].

Parity Logging

The main drawback of the simple parity algorithm is that the network transfer overhead still remains high. An enhanced parity policy called parity logging manages to reduce the network overhead to a factor close to (1+1/S), where S is the number of servers.

To accomplish this lower overhead, the parity logging method does not assign a fixed server for storing each page, but rather assigns a new server to each page it writes out. Let us describe the parity logging algorithm for S memory servers. For each set of S-1 pages written out in sequence, the client computes their parity page, which along with the S-1 pages forms a new parity group. The client then sends each of the pages to a different server and the parity page to the parity server. Of course, the client needs to keep bookkeeping information about the location of each page. This scheme is depicted in the left part of Figure 16.7 . In this example, the paging out sequence of the pages is 1, 2, 5, 4, 3, 9, 7, 10, etc. For this paging out sequence, memory server 1 will provide backing store for pages 1 and 3, memory server 2 for pages 2 and 9, etc. Thus, the parity groups are formed from this specific paging out sequence.

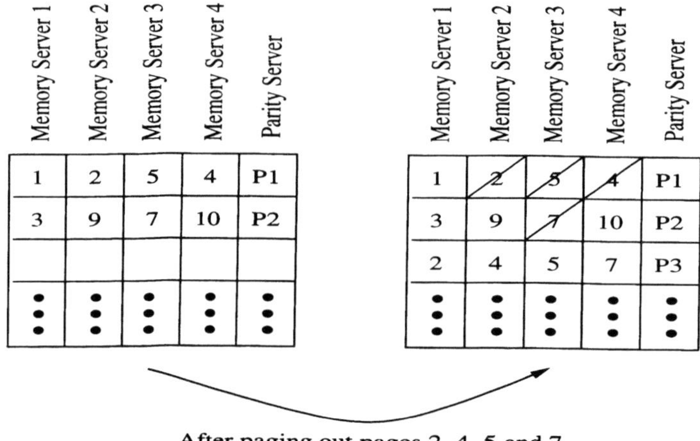

Figure 16.7 A parity logging example with four memory servers and one parity server.

The XOR computation on the client can be implemented easily in two ways. In the first implementation, the client keeps the pages locally until S-1 of them are present and then computes the parity page, while in the second the client keeps a buffer equal in size to a page which initially contains zeros. When a page is written out, it is XORed with the buffer and then sent to a server. When S-1 pages are sent out, the buffer contains the parity page which in turn is sent to the parity server [18]. The second implementation uses less local memory, while the first can, in some cases, gain performance from local caching of pages.

The parity logging algorithm appears simple at first. However, it hides difficult problems which arise mainly from page overwriting. When a page is written for a second time, it cannot be stored where the older version was stored, because then its parity page would need to be updated and consequently two network transfers would be made. Instead, the old page is invalidated and the new one is written to a different location. An example of such a situation appears in Figure 16.7. After pages 2, 4, 5, and 7 are written out for a second time, the old pages are invalidated. However, they cannot be deleted and free up memory space, because if one server fails all the pages in its parity group will be needed in order to recover the lost pages. If, for example, memory server 1 fails, the old versions of 2, 5, 4 and the parity page P1 will be needed to reconstruct page 1. To free space held by a parity group, all pages in that group must be invalid.

Obviously, the memory overhead in the parity logging algorithm rises more than a factor of (1+1/S) due to the redundant space needed for old pages. To free up this space one must implement cleaning algorithms, which in turn have a run-time overhead. This is the main drawback of parity logging, along with being complex and hard to implement. For details on this policy and its varations, refer to [18].

16.2.3 Remote Paging Prototypes

In this section, the two most important remote paging prototypes are presented, along with an overview of their performance results.

The Global Memory Service (GMS)

GMS, which stands for *Global Memory Service*, is a modified kernel solution for using Network RAM as a paging device [9]. It uses the algorithms described in Section 16.2.1. For page replacement, GMS uses a special cost function, which boosts the age of global pages to favor their replacement over local pages of the same age. For details on this cost function, refer to [9]. Reliability in GMS is provided by writing data asynchronously to disk, which is not the optimum solution.

The GMS prototype was implemented on the DEC OSF/1 (known also as Digital Unix) operating system, and was tested on a cluster of DEC Alpha workstations running DEC OSF/1 v3.2 and connected by a 155 Mb/s DEC AN2 ATM network. Feeley et al. report several performance results of the GMS prototype, the most important of which are summarized below:

- Under real application workloads (OO7, Render, Compilation, etc.), GMS shows speedups of 1.5 to 3.5, depending on the application.

- GMS responds effectivelly to load changes. It achieves a speedup of 1.9 even when load changes every second.

Table 16.2 Pros and Cons of GMS

+	+ Comprehensive exploitation of Network RAM in every level of the operating system (virtual memory paging, memory mapped files and filesystem buffering) + Global memory management in the NOW + Effective memory load balancing + Good performance
-	- Major changes to the operating system - Requires a homogeneous workstation cluster - Uses the disk for reliability

Table 16.2 summarizes the pros and cons of GMS. We conclude that GMS is generally a very efficient system for remote memory paging, at the cost of modifying the operating system.

The Remote Memory Pager

The Remote Memory Pager (RMP, in short) is another software solution for implementing remote memory paging, which uses the swap device driver approach described in Section 16.2.1 and was built in [18].

The Remote Memory Pager prototype was implemented on the DEC OSF/1 v3.2 operating system and was tested on a cluster of DEC-Alpha 3000 model 300 workstations, each with 32 MBytes of main memory connected with a 10 Mbit/s Ethernet network. The prototype consists of a swap device driver on the client machine and a user-level memory server program that runs on the servers. The RMP prototype implements and compares many reliability methods, including writing to disk, mirroring, and parity logging.

Table 16.3 Pros and Cons of the Remote Memory Pager

+	+ Good exploitation of Network RAM for paging + Does not modify the OS, thus it can be implemented in any commercial operating system + Good performance + Operates in a heterogeneous workstation cluster + Implements effective reliability policies without the disk
-	- No global memory management in the NOW - Uses Network RAM only for paging and not as a file cache or for memory mapped files.

The performance results for the Remote Memory Pager suggest:

- All applications measured ran faster than paging to disk, even when mirroring was used.
- Parity logging performs better than the other policies, as we have studied in theory earlier.
- Use of RMP resulted in up to 59% faster application execution time, using the parity logging reliability algorithm.
- For a kernel build, RMP without reliability performed 26.5% faster than disk, while RMP with parity logging reliability performed 24.6% faster than disk, which shows that the reliability overhead using parity logging is very low.

Table 16.3 summarizes the pros and cons of RMP. To sum up, the Remote Memory Pager is an effective remote paging system whose main advantage is that it does not modify the operating system, in contrast to GMS.

16.3 Network Memory File Systems

Disk I/O is a bottleneck in modern computer systems. Consequently, reading and writing files on a filesystem, which in turn writes them to the disk, often dominate the execution time of an application. The solution that Network RAM offers for this problem is simple. We can use Network RAM either as a filesystem cache [4], [7], or directly as a faster-than-disk storage device for file I/O [11]. These two directions have been extensively studied.

In this section we explore the use of network memory in filesystems. Section 16.3.1 presents the use of Network RAM as a file cache, while Section 16.3.2 discusses the direct use of reliable network memory for storing files. The former issue is presented more extensively in the next chapter which discusses filesystems in workstation clusters.

16.3.1 Using Network Memory as a File Cache

All filesystems which run on single workstations use a portion of the workstation's memory as a filesystem cache, trying to boost the filesystem performance by avoiding the disk access cost. Provided that the workstation has sufficient main memory and that the workload is not too heavy on file I/O, this solution performs well.

Considering this solution in a workstation cluster, there are several ways to improve the filesystem's caching performance. One problem with the workstations' local caches is that when many workstations can access the same files through a network filesystem like NFS, then a certain file can be cached in more than one clients, thus wasting valuable cache space. Naturally, the elimination of multiple cached copies is desirable. Consider another possible scenario, where one workstation has the file cached in its memory, and another one requests the file for reading. Since the latter workstation has no knowledge of the file's existence in another cache, it will read it from the disk, which could be a local disk or even a remote disk. In either case, asking the remote cache for the file would be much faster.

The above examples suggest that certain issues in the file caching scheme need improvement. The concept of the solution comes easily to one's mind. Since there is already a local filesystem cache in each workstation in the cluster, the way to create a global network memory filesystem cache is fairly obvious. One must unite these local cache into one global cache to enhance file caching performance. This technique is called cooperative caching, because all the local caches in the cluster cooperate by exchanging information, eliminating replicas of cached files and sharing their contents when needed. The concept of cooperative caching has been extensively studied and used in the xFS filesystem [4], [7].

16.3.2 Network RamDisks

File systems attempt to speed up file accesses by using a portion of the file server's main memory as a disk cache. However, there is another convenient way to attack the disk's I/O performance problem. We can use reliable network memory for directly storing temporary files. Many applications such as compilers, databases, document processing systems, Web servers, Web proxies, etc., use temporary files to process data and then delete them after writing the final results to the disk. If we used the file caching approach, we would cache the temporary files, write them to disk and then delete them. Avoiding the cost of writing and then deleting from the disk is naturally desirable. This direction has been studied extensively in [11], where a new device called the Network RamDisk (or NRD) is described.

A Network RamDisk is a block device that unifies all the idle main memories in a Network of Workstations (NOW) under a (virtual) disk interface. It behaves like any normal disk, allowing the creation of files and filesystems on top of it. However, since it is implemented in main memory (RAM), it provides lower latency and higher bandwidth than most traditional magnetic disks.

The theory and operation of the Network RamDisk is very similar to the theory of remote memory paging, where instead of memory pages we send disk blocks to remote memory. Of course, there are differences, because disk blocks are much smaller than memory pages (usually 512 or 1024 bytes) and on many operating systems variable in size (from 512 bytes to 8 KBytes). However, the main structure of a Network RamDisk is very similar to a remote paging system, with one client and many memory servers running on several workstations which communicate through an interconnection network.

The operation of a Network RamDisk is straightforward. The client workstation has the Network RamDisk device driver linked into its operating system which apprears as a disk. On this disk we can create any normal filesystem. When an application reads a file, the filesystem created on the Network RamDisk (e.g., NFS, UFS, LFS, ext2, NTFS) requests one or more disk blocks from the device driver of the Network RamDisk. The driver knows in which workstation's main memory the blocks reside, asks the memory server running on that workstation for these blocks, and returns the requested blocks to the filesystem. Write operations proceed in the same way, transfering the disk blocks' data to remote memories. Since disk block accesses involve only memory and interconnection network transfers, they proceed with low latency and high bandwidth. Thus, Network RamDisks may result in significant performance improvements over magnetic disks, especially when application performance depends on I/O latency.

The Network RamDisk, much like network memory filesystems [4], [14] exploits network memory to avoid magnetic disk I/O, but unlike these filesystems, the Network RamDisk, being a device driver, can be easily incorporated into any environment without modifying existing operating system sources or changing filesystems. Thus, by using a Network RamDisk, users will be able to exploit all network memory to store their files, without changing their operating system or their filesystem. For example, files created on a Network RamDisk can be accessed through any filesystem, e.g., NFS. NFS will not be aware of the fact that the files do not reside on magnetic disk.

The Network RamDisk device driver which resides on the client workstation has been implemented on two operating systems: Digital Unix and Linux [11]. The Digital Unix Client has been linked with the Digital Unix 4.0 kernel of a DEC-Alpha 3000 model 300 with 32 MB main memory, while the Linux Client was linked with the Linux 2.0.33 kernel of a Pentium II 233 MHz PC, with 64 MB of RAM. The prototypes have been tested using the standard TCP/IP protocol over an Ethernet and an ATM interconnection network. The experiments suggest that the performance of the Network RamDisk is usually four to eight times faster than the magnetic disk. In one benchmark, where many small synchronous writes were performed, the Network RamDisk was two orders of magnitude faster than the disk.

16.4 Applications of Network RAM in Databases

Transactions have been valued for their atomicity and recoverability properties that are useful to several applications ranging from CAD environments to large-scale databases and software development environments. Unfortunately, the performance of most transaction-based systems is limited by the magnetic disk(s) that is used to store the data. Decoupling the performance of a transaction-based system from the performance of the disk presents a major challenge [15], [20]. One direction for the performance enhancement of a transaction-based system is to use Network RAM.

16.4.1 Transaction-Based Systems

The basic concept is to substitute, to the higher possible extent, the disk accesses with Network RAM accesses, thus reducing the latency of a transaction. A transaction during its execution makes a number of disk accesses to read its data (or reads it from main memory), makes some designated calculations on that data, writes its results to the disk (via a log file) and, at the end, *commits*. The key property of transactions is that each commit point atomically enters a set of operations that transform the system from one consistent state to another. In case of a failure, some uncommitted transactions may be lost, but there is always a way to recover the last committed transaction and thus reach a consistent state [15].

There are two main areas where Network RAM can be used to boost a transaction-based system's performance. The first is at the initial phase of a transaction when read requests from the disk are performed. The use of Network RAM in this area can be exploited through the use of global filesystem caches, as we have studied in Section 16.3.1 and global memory databases [12]. The second area where we can use Network RAM is to speed up synchronous write operations to reliable storage at transaction commit time. Transaction-based systems make many small synchronous writes to stable storage, and thus they are going to receive a significant thrust from substituting the disk with Network RAM in this phase.

The steps performed in a transaction-based system that uses Network RAM are the following (in timely order):

1. At transaction commit time, the data are synchronously written to remote main memory.

2. Concurrently, the same data are asynchronously sent to the disk.

3. The data have been safely written to the disk.

In this modified transaction-based system, a transaction commits after the second step, without the delay of a synchronous write to the disk [15], [20]. It may seem that there exists a possibility of failure after the data have been written to network memory and before the write to disk has completed, but this does not hold. If the local system crashes through this interval, then the data are still safe in remote memory and can be recovered. To increase the reliability in the case of one remote workstation failure during data recovery, we can replicate the data in the main memories of two workstations. In case of more failures, data may be lost; however the probability of such an event is very small, unless it is a scheduled shutdown where the transaction processing system can be shut down. The conclusion is that this level of reliability is adequate for most transaction processing systems.

Experiments with implemented prototypes of such transaction processing systems [15], [19], using database benchmarks such as OO7 and TCP-A, show that the use of Network RAM can deliver up to two orders of magnitude higher performance. In one experiment, the normal RVM transaction processing system was able to sustain up to 40 transactions per second for small transactions, while the same system using Network RAM over the Memory Channel network can sustain close to 3000 transactions per second [15].

A different platform for main memory transaction processing systems, named PERSEAS [19], completely eliminates the log-file used in the Write-Ahead Logging Protocol, as well as synchronous disk accesses by storing replicated copies of data in network memory. PERSEAS was implemented and evaluated on two 133MHz Pentium PCs each with 96MB of main memory running Windows NT 4.0 and connected through the high performance SCI [13] network interface. Reported measurements of the TPC-B benchmark on the RVM system show that it barely achieves 100 transactions per second, while PERSEAS managed to execute more than 23000 transactions per second for the same benchmark. The TPC-C performance was also very high at 8500 transactions per second, while RVM achieved only 90 transactions per second [19].

16.5 Summary

The emergence of high performance interconnection networks added a new layer in the traditional memory hierarchy: Network RAM. This memory layer (which is placed between main memory and magnetic disk) consists of all main memories in a workstation cluster connected with a high-speed network. In this chapter we described how to use Network RAM to boost the performance of applications that have traditionally used the magnetic disk for the storage of their data.

One of the first applications of Network RAM is remote memory paging, which enables applications to store their working sets that do not fit in their computer's main memory in (unused) main memories of other computers, rather than on the magnetic disk. The existence of unused main memory coupled with fast interconnection networks resulted in very attractive performance for remote memory paging systems. Network RAM has also been used to speed up the performance of disk-bound databases. Network RAM can be used as a large database cache (larger than any single workstation can provide) and/or as a stable short-term storage that allows transactions to commit at high rates. Finally, Network RAM can be coupled with network filesystems to provide a large distributed (cooperative) cache, or a stable storage for filesystem metadata.

16.5.1 Conclusions

Several research prototypes that demonstrate the use of Network RAM have been built and evaluated. Based on the experiences and the performance results reported we conclude that:

- *Using Network RAM results in significant performance improvements.* Reported performance results suggest that the use of Network RAM offers application speedup ranging from 2-10 times for remote memory paging to 3 orders of magnitude in transaction processing systems.

- *Integrating Network RAM in existing systems is easy.* Several researchers report implementations that can be safely integrated within existing systems without changing the internals of the system. Some implementations are based on device-drivers, on loadable filesystems, or even on user-level code.

- *The benefits of Network RAM will probably increase with time.* Current computer architecture trends suggest that the gap between processor and disk speed continues to widen. Disks are not expected to provide the bandwidth needed by memory-limited applications unless a breakthrough in disk technology occurs. On the other hand, interconnection network bandwidth keeps increasing at a much higher rate than (single) disk bandwidth, thereby increasing the performance benefits of Network RAM.

16.5.2 Future Trends

Although research prototypes have proved the benefits of Network RAM, a significant amount of work remains to be done, especially in the following areas:

- *Reliability:* Network RAM is distributed in the main memories of several different workstations. If one (or more) of them crashes, applications that use Network RAM will not be able to access their data. The probability of a workstation's being down increases with the size of the cluster. Thus, the reliability of applications decreases with their use of Network RAM. To remedy the situation, Network RAM systems should be made reliable (much like RAID systems are), and they should provide transparent failover: If one workstation crashes, another one should (transparently) assume its responsibilities.

- *Filesystem Interfaces:* Traditional filesystems that usually manage magnetic disks are optimized for large block transfers since magnetic disks have high latency. However, Network RAM systems have significantly lower latency than the magnetic disks, which implies that they can be used to efficiently transfer even small units of data. Unfortunately, coupling Network RAM storage with traditional filesystems deprives Network RAM from short data transfers, and thus from its low-latency advantage. New filesystem interfaces need to be developed in order to fully exploit the advantages of Network RAM.

Acknowledgments

This work was supported in part by the USENIX Association and by PENED project, "Exploitation of Idle Memory in a Workstation Cluster" (2041 2270/1-2-95), funded by the General Secretariat for Research and Technology of the Hellenic Ministry of Development. We deeply appreciate this financial support.

We would also like to thank Manolis Katevenis, Dionisios Pnevmatikatos, Sotiris Ioanidis, George Dramitinos, Thanos Papathanasiou, Julia Sevaslidou, Gregory Maglis and all the people involved in the design and implementation of several Network RAM systems described in this chapter. Their contribution to this work has been invaluable.

16.6 Bibliography

[1] Anurag Acharya and Sanjeev Setia Using Idle Memory for Data-Intensive Computations. In *Proceedings of the 1998 ACM SIGMETRICS Conference on Measurement and Modeling of Computer Systems,* pages 278–279, June 1998.

[2] E. Anderson and J. Neefe. An Exploration of Network RAM. *Technical Report CSD-98-1000,* Computer Science Division, University of California, Berkeley, July 1998.

[3] T. E. Anderson, D. E. Culler, and D. A. Patterson. A Case for NOW (Networks of Workstations). *IEEE Micro*, vol.15(1), pages 54–64, February 1995.

[4] T. E. Anderson, M. D. Dahlin, J. M. Neefe, D. A. Patterson, D. S. Roselli, and R. Y. Wang. Serverless Network File Systems. *ACM Transactions on Computer Systems*, vol.14(1), pages 41–79, February 1996.

[5] M. Bangalore and A. Sivasubramaniam. Remote Subpaging Across a Fast Network. In *Proceedings of the Second International Workshop, CANPC '98,* pages 74–87, January 1998.

[6] M. A. Blumrich, Kai Li, R. Alpert, C. Dubnicki, E. Felten and J. Sandberg. Virtual Memory Mapped Network Interface for the SHRIMP Multicomputer. In *Proceedings of the 21st International Symposium on Computer Architecture,* pages 142–153, 1994.

[7] M. Dahlin. Serverless Network File Systems. *PhD thesis*, University of California, Berkeley, December 1995.

[8] Thorsten von Eicken, Anindya Basu, Vineet Buch and Werner Vogels. U-Net: A User-Level Network Interface for Parallel and Distributed Computing. In *Proceedings of the 15th ACM Symposium on Operating Systems Principles,* vol.29(5), pages 303–316, 1995.

[9] M. J. Feeley, W. E. Morgan, F. H. Pighin, A. R. Karlin, H. M. Levy, and C. A. Thekkath. Implementing Global Memory Management in a Workstation Cluster. In *Proceedings of the 15th Symposium on Operating Systems Principles,* pages 201–212, December 1995.

[10] E.W. Felten and J. Zahorjan. Issues in the Implementation of a Remote Memory Paging System. *Technical Report 91-03-09,* University of Washington, 1991.

[11] Michail D. Flouris and Evangelos P. Markatos. The Network RamDisk: Using Remote Memory on Heterogeneous NOWs. *Technical Report 226,* ICS - Foundation for Research & Technology Hellas (FO.R.T.H.), August 1998.

[12] M. Franklin, M. Carey and M. Livny. Global Memory Management in Client-Server DBMS Architectures. In *Proceedings of the 18th VLDB Conference,* pages 596 609, August 1992.

[13] David B. Gustavson and Qiang Li. Local-Area Multiprocessor: the Scalable Coherent Interface. In *Defining the Global Information Infrastructure: Infrastructure, Systems, and Services,* SPIE Press, vol.56, pages 131-160, 1994.

[14] J. Hartman and J. Ousterhout. The Zebra Striped Network File System. In *Proceedings of the 14th ACM Symposium on Operating Systems Principles,* pages 29-43, December 1993.

[15] Sotiris Ioanidis, Evangelos P. Markatos, and Julia Sevaslidou. On Using Network Memory to Improve the Performance of Transaction Based Systems. In *Proceedings of PDPTA '98,* Las Vegas, USA, July 1998.

[16] Herve A. Jamrozik, Michael J. Feeley, Geoffrey M. Voelker, James Evans II, Anna R. Karlin, Henry M. Levy, and Mary K. Vernon. Reducing Network Latency Using Subpages in a Global Memory Environment. In *Proceedings of the 7th ACM ASPLOS,* pages 258–267, October 1996.

[17] Manolis G.H. Katevenis, Evangelos P. Markatos, George Kalokerinos, and Apostolos Dollas. Telegraphos: A Subtrate for High-Performance Computing on Workstation Clusters. *Journal of Parallel and Distributed Computing,* vol.43, pages 94–108, 1997.

[18] E.P. Markatos and G. Dramitinos. Implementation of a Reliable Remote Memory Pager. In *Proceedings of the 1996 Usenix Technical Conference,* pages 177–190, January 1996.

[19] Athanasios E. Papathanasiou and Evangelos P. Markatos. Lightweight Transactions on Networks of Workstations. In *Proceedings of the 1998 International Conference on Distributed Computing Systems,* May 1998.

[20] Dionisios Pnevmatikatos, Evangelos P. Markatos, Gregory Maglis, and Sotiris Ioannidis. On Using Network RAM as a Non-volatile Buffer. *Technical Report 227,* Institute of Computer Science - Foundation for Research & Technology Hellas (FO.R.T.H.), September 1998.

Chapter 17

Distributed Shared Memory

Alan Judge, Paddy Nixon, Brendan Tangney,
Stefan Weber, and Vinny Cahill

Department of Computer Science
Trinity College, Dublin, Ireland

Email: *Paddy.Nixon@cs.tcd.ie*

17.1 Introduction

Loosely-coupled distributed systems have evolved using message passing as the main paradigm for sharing information. Other paradigms used in loosely-coupled distributed systems, such as RPC, are usually implemented on top of an underlying message-passing system. On the other hand, in tightly-coupled architectures, such as multi-processor machines, the paradigm is usually based on shared memory with its attractively simple programming model. The shared-memory paradigm has recently been extended for use in more loosely-coupled architectures and is known as "distributed" shared memory (DSM [43]) in this context. This chapter discusses some of the issues involved in the design and implementation of distributed shared memory systems in loosely-coupled distributed environments.

In DSM systems, processes share data transparently across node boundaries (Figure 17.1); data faulting, location, and movement are handled by the DSM system. Among other things, this allows parallel programs designed to use the shared-memory abstraction to execute without modification on a loosely-coupled distributed system. The advantages of the shared-memory programming model are well known. Shared memory gives transparent process-to-process communication, shared-memory programming is a well-understood problem (compared with message passing), shared-memory programs are usually shorter and easier to understand than equivalent message-passing programs, and large or complex data structures may easily be communicated without marshalling. This transparency and ease of use is associated with a cost, and DSM applications are sometimes slower than hand-coded message-passing implementations. In fact, it has traditionally been believed

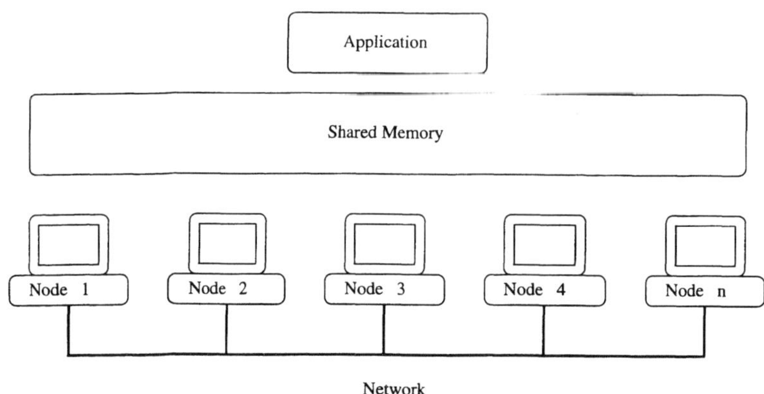

Figure 17.1 Distributed shared memory.

that a well-built, hand-tuned and optimized, message-passing implementation of a parallel program will out perform a shared-memory implementation. However, more recent work shows that this is not necessarily the case and that issues such as the relative costs of communication and computation are important factors. Moreover, in some cases, applications using DSM can execute faster than equivalent message-passing ones, even when the DSM system is implemented on top of a message-passing system.

DSM is not without its own complexities, and the simple model presented to the programmer is supported by a complex software or hardware structure. When a single piece of data is replicated in more than one place, consistency maintenance becomes a problem. In tightly-coupled architectures, the consistency problem is usually addressed in hardware, while in loosely-coupled architectures, consistency maintenance is usually addressed with a combination of software and hardware.

Chapter Road-map

The bulk of this chapter is divided as follows: in Section 17.2 we discuss consistency issues, concentrating particularly on the relationship with data location and synchronization issues; in Section 17.3 we discuss network latency and bandwidth as they relate to DSM systems; in Section 17.4 we discuss the other issues involved in implementing and using a DSM system. An extended version of this chapter, which gives a more detailed description of related work in this area, can be found in [27].

17.2 Data Consistency

Despite recent advances in both local and wide-area networking technologies, network latency is still a major factor in distributed systems and is likely to remain so. All the DSM systems studied in preparing this survey provide some sort of caching in an attempt to improve performance beyond that provided by doing a network access on every reference to a non-local data item. Each DSM system must decide whether or not to attempt to keep the data consistent, and, if so, what consistency strategy to use. Due to the network-latency problem, the choice of caching and consistency algorithms is of prime importance. This section discusses the issues involved in maintaining consistency.

The first choice that needs to be made is the type of semantics to be provided to the application programmer. There are several options that form part of a range of possible semantic models:

- provide "strict" consistency, where a read always returns the value written by the most recent write—this is effectively "sequential consistency" as defined by Lamport [35];
- provide a "loosely" consistent model where the system enforces some form of weaker consistency guarantees and the application (or compiler or user) can indicate synchronization points where consistency must be enforced; or
- enforce no fixed consistency mechanism, but provide the application programmer with the facilities necessary to implement user-level synchronization and consistency.

Many older DSM systems provide strict consistency using the single writer, multiple reader model, where at any one time only one of the following will be true:

- the data is located at exactly one node, and that node has read and, possibly, write access to the data; or
- the data is replicated on two or more nodes, each node only has read access to its copy of the data, and none of the nodes has write access.

DSM systems that do not enforce this model are becoming increasingly popular, due to the performance benefits of relaxing the consistency model, and will be discussed in more detail later, in Section 17.2.4). However, many of the issues discussed in this chapter apply to both strictly and loosely-consistent DSM systems.

Given the above readers/writer model, there are two problems that must be addressed. Firstly, we must locate a copy of the data when it is non-resident. Secondly, we must synchronize accesses to the data, so that no two sites are writing to separate copies at the same time. We discuss the data location problem in the next section and return to the access synchronization issue in Section 17.2.2.

17.2.1 Data Location

The most common solution to the data location problem is to assign an "owner" node to each item of data. The owner either has "the" writable copy of the data, or one of the read-only copies and a list of other nodes with read-only copies. The owner of the data is the "only" one allowed to write to the data. If other nodes have read-only copies at a time that the owner wants to write, then we have a write synchronization problem, which we will return to discuss in Section 17.2.2. Li and Hudak (authors of one of the first DSM systems, IVY [36]) provide a good survey of ownership algorithms and classify them as follows:

Fixed ownership Each piece of data is assigned a fixed owner; the owner can usually be calculated in an easy manner from the address of the data, for example, by hashing. Other processors are never given direct write access to the data and must negotiate with the owner every time they want to write to the data. The disadvantages of this scheme are obvious: There is a large overhead on every write access, and the data owner becomes a bottleneck in the DSM system. This is effectively a completely centralized algorithm.

Dynamic ownership The ownership of a data item moves around the DSM system, introducing the problem of locating the owner. In order to address this problem, we introduce the concept of a "manager" for an item of data. The manager need not "own" the data, but is responsible for tracking the current owner of the data. These algorithms can further be sub-divided into two classes.

Centralized A node is selected as the "manager" of all the shared data. This manager keeps track of the current owner of each item of data. Other processors negotiate with the manager for access to the data. The manager can also keep track of those who currently have read access to the data and can queue requests for read or write access. Since read access can be shared, access is usually granted to any readers waiting in the queue when a read request reaches the head of the queue.

Distributed Since a bottleneck can easily form at the manager, the next obvious step is to split the ownership information among the nodes. Here we have a similar location problem as for the owner above, i.e., how do we locate the manager for a given piece of data? As before, we can have a "fixed" or a "dynamic" scheme for locating the manager of a data item. The fixed scheme operates as before, with some simple scheme for finding the manager of a piece of data from its address. Li and Hudak propose several dynamic schemes:

Broadcast Each processor manages those data items that it currently owns and management information migrates around with the data. Faulting processors send a broadcast message to find the current owner of each data item. Although this algorithm is simple and appealing, performance is poor due to the number of network messages involved, especially when the underlying network does not provide hardware support for broadcasting.

Dynamic Each processor keeps track of the "probable" owner of each data item. This information is just a "hint" and may be incorrect. If incorrect, the hint at least provides the beginning of a sequence of processors through which the true owner may be located. Requests are forwarded until they reach the true owner. The probable-owner field is updated whenever more accurate information about the owner becomes available, such as when a data update is received. Such updates are always sent by the current owner of a data item.

Li and Hudak show that, in the worst case, the number of messages to locate a data item K times, if p processors are using the data item, is $O(p + K \log p)$, if all the contending processors are in the same set of p processors. This result is important as it shows that the DSM system does not degrade as processors are added, but only as more processors contend for the "same" data item.

Li and Hudak also investigated the possibility of further improving the algorithm by sending a broadcast message intermittently to announce the true owner of a data item. They concluded that it was a useful improvement, and show that, immediately after a broadcast, the number of messages required to find a data item for K faults on different processors is $2K - 1$.

Almost all of the DSM systems studied use either the centralized-manager scheme or a variant of the dynamic-distributed manager scheme.

Data-location Algorithm Extensions

Among the modifications and extensions to the IVY algorithms that have been proposed are the following:

- In Mirage [16], a writer or a set of readers gains access to the data for at least a minimum time interval Δ. The authors claim that this modification reduces thrashing and increases overall throughput. They added a `yield` system call so that a processor can release the data before Δ has expired. This call is used to avoid stalling waiting processors when the holder of the data is no longer using it. The `yield` call improved the worst-case performance considerably. Of course, the need for such a call reduces the transparency and simplicity of the system as a whole.

- Another modification implemented by the authors of Mirage allows upgrades and downgrades in the access mode of data items throughout the network. For example, when a site that has read access to a piece of data desires write access for the same data item, it just upgrades its read access to write access and then uses its local copy. Since Mirage implements multiple readers/single writer, the local readable copy is guaranteed to be up-to-date. Similarly, when a site loses write access to a piece of data, it keeps a read-only copy. These modifications save the cost of transferring a copy of the shared data when the local copy is known to be up-to-date.

  This extension does not work in conjunction with distributed management, as a page may be invalidated locally and updated remotely while a request for a read-to-write upgrade is outstanding and, as a result, the local copy of the data may become out of date while the request is outstanding. In this case, a page transfer must take place on every write fault, even if a read-only copy is held.

- Some of the DSM systems discussed allow read-only portions of the shared address space. This is a useful extension as it reduces or eliminates the bookkeeping overhead, and can be used for code and read-only data. Read-only sections of the shared address space can be replicated on demand and no write-access synchronization or management is needed.

- Time-stamps can be attached to the probable-owner fields, so that the age and reliability of hints can be assessed. Also, processors can piggyback some of their own hint information on other messages that they exchange. This is similar to the object identifiers and location time-stamps used in Emerald [29].

17.2.2 Write Synchronization

The other main issue in maintaining a strictly-consistent data set is synchronization of write accesses to the data. This section discusses the issues involved in controlling access to shared data. When there are multiple copies of the data spread around the DSM system, it must be ensured that no processor reads stale data once a write has been completed on some processor. There are two main approaches: A processor can broadcast writes, or it can invalidate all other copies before doing an update. These two approaches are variously known as "write-broadcast" or "write-update," and "write-invalidate." We discuss these two approaches in the next two sections.

Write Broadcast

One possible solution is to broadcast the effects of all writes to all nodes that have copies of the data, effectively replicating data. If a low-level broadcast primitive is not available, then there will be a problem locating all the sites with copies of the data set. This problem will be examined in more detail later when discussing invalidation.

Write broadcast is usually considered too expensive to be used as a general solution: Unless integrated with the language and the synchronization system, a broadcast may be needed on every write. As a result, only one of the DSM systems discussed uses it. The Orca shared data-object programming language [4] uses a reliable ordered-broadcast protocol to update all replicated copies of the data together. The use of write broadcast is more suitable in this case, as all updates to shared data are encapsulated in operations on objects, and can therefore be easily packaged up by the compiler and run-time system.

Some work has been done comparing algorithms that use broadcast-based replication with those using data migration. Due to the expense of write broadcast in unintegrated DSM systems, replication is not used by most general-purpose systems.

Ordering of broadcasts is a problem, and replication algorithms are usually implemented using a single "write sequencer" site that broadcasts writes to all involved sites. Stumm and Zhou [47] outline a number of methods for increasing the performance of replication systems, but conclude that performance is bad in large systems and in systems where there are many updates.

Invalidation

The other major solution to the problem of synchronizing write accesses is to "invalidate" all the other copies of the data item. The basic concept is to send a message to all processors holding a read copy of the data. Obviously, this can easily be done with broadcasts, but the expense of broadcasting can grow rapidly in large DSM systems and hosts may spend a lot of time handling broadcast messages.

If the DSM system is to use individual messages or multicasts instead, then we again have a problem of location: We need to locate the processors that currently have a copy of the data. The most common solution is for the manager site to maintain a "copy-set:" a list of processors with a copy of the data. Li and Hudak propose several methods for managing copy-sets, including schemes for compressing and representing very large copy-sets in large DSM systems.

They also propose a scheme for distributing the copy-set data: the copy-set data is represented as a tree of processors rooted at the owner node. Invalidations are passed down the tree. This modification also has the advantage that on a read fault a processor need only find "any" node with a read-only copy of the data. That node can add the new node to its copy-set data. In practice, the tree is bi-directional, with the links back towards the root formed by the probable-owner back reference.

If the write is allowed to proceed before the invalidation is complete, it is possible for non-current read-only copies of a page to exist for a short period of time. This factor can require invalidations to be acknowledged if strict consistency is required.

17.2.3 Double Faulting

"Double faulting" describes a form of behaviour common in many DSM algorithms. If a process first reads and then writes a page (such as to read and update a counter), many DSM algorithms will incur two network transactions: one to obtain a read-only copy of the page and a second to obtain write access to the page. This will usually result in the page itself being transmitted twice over the network.

The double-faulting problem is considered separately to the data-location problem. Several algorithms are discussed that attempt to solve this problem:

Hot Potato All faults are treated as write faults, and the ownership and data are transferred on every fault, resulting in one and only one copy of each page at any time. The performance disadvantages are obvious.

Li Li's most complex algorithm from IVY circumvents this problem by always transferring ownership on a read fault. A subsequent write fault may then be handled locally.

Shrewd This algorithm eliminates all unnecessary page transfers with the help of a sequence number per copy of a page, but does not eliminate the extra network transaction. The sequence numbers (or version numbers) are used to track whether a page has been updated since the read-only copy was obtained and therefore needs to be transferred when the request for write access is made. However, network transactions are still required to obtain access and check the sequence numbers.

An analysis of the algorithms with the help of simulations showed that neither the Li nor the Shrewd algorithm can be said to be superior in all cases. The crucial factor appears to be the read-to-write ratio of the application. A combination of the two algorithms is possible, but has not been examined.

17.2.4 Relaxing Consistency

Permitting temporary inconsistencies is a common method of increasing performance in a distributed system. This section examines the various approaches that have been taken in allowing inconsistencies in DSM systems.

The designers of the Munin DSM system [6] examined the issue of strict consistency (as defined in Section 17.2) very carefully and came to the following conclusion:

> A shared-memory parallel program specifies only a partial order on the events within the program, both through explicit synchronization between threads of the program, and through implicit knowledge within one thread of the order of events in another thread.

Based on this, they developed a more relaxed definition of memory consistency:

> Memory is "loosely consistent" if the value returned by a read operation is the value written by an update operation to the same object that "could" have immediately preceded the read operation in some legal schedule of the threads in execution.

This definition of loose consistency is somewhat related to the concept of "virtual synchrony" in the ISIS programming environment [8]. In ISIS, message operations appear to be synchronous, i.e., to happen everywhere at the same time. Messaging is implemented using standard asynchronous primitives, but complex protocols are used to prevent the application from seeing asynchronous behaviour. Loose consistency is also related to the concept of "serializability" in transaction systems.

By enforcing only the definition of loose consistency given above, Munin is able to delay sending updates until remote threads might see incorrectly ordered updates to shared data. This mechanism of "delayed updates" allows Munin to batch updates in a queue and send them out only when necessary. When the system being considered is not entirely based on DSM, detecting when objects need to be updated is not easy: There is no guarantee that programs will not exchange information outside the DSM system. This is a standard distributed systems problem when the system is not "complete" and is not considered further by most DSM implementors.

When combined with the type-specific semantics described in Section 17.2.5, the loose-consistency mechanism is quite powerful, as it can make use of some semantic knowledge about the objects involved. This semantic knowledge can be used to avoid performing updates to data that will not be accessed and to delay performing updates until actually needed. Of course, these approaches compromise the shared-memory concept somewhat and increase the complexity for the programmer.

Stumm and Zhou [47] describe a full-replication (write-broadcast) DSM system that uses delayed broadcasts to improve efficiency. They also describe an "optimistic" replication system where threads are permitted access to shared data before any checking is done. The system assigns version numbers to shared data updates and logs all accesses to shared data to a transactional system. If a thread has seen inconsistent data, it will be rolled back to a previous consistent state.

Release and Entry Consistency

Gharachorloo et al. [19] present another memory model for multi-processor cache consistency, known as "release consistency." In a release-consistent DSM, memory accesses are divided into ordinary and synchronization-related accesses. Synchronization accesses are further divided into "acquire" and "release" operations. The "acquire" operation signals that shared data is needed; a processor's updates after an "acquire" are not guaranteed to be performed at other nodes until a "release" is performed. The primary advantage of release consistency is that it allows updates to be tied to synchronization events and therefore delayed until actually needed by applications. The primary disadvantage is that most release-consistent DSMs require the programmer to make explicit use of "acquire" and "release" operations, and incorrect use of the operations can lead to nodes reading stale data or updates being lost. However, these types of operations, or similar synchronization operations, are required in any concurrent program in order to ensure correctness (see Section 17.4.1).

Release consistency is particularly well-suited to software DSM systems, and variants of this approach are used in several recent DSM systems. More recent versions of Munin [6] use release consistency combined with the type-specific support described in Section 17.2.5. A number of people from the Munin team at Rice have also been working on a variety of "lazy" release-consistent algorithms [31], where the transmission of updates are delayed as long as possible, and have compared these with "eager" algorithms that propagate updates rapidly. They have developed a hybrid algorithm that has good performance for a range of applications. They also examined available networking hardware and concluded that, while relaxed consistency, lazy algorithms, and multiple-writer protocols helped reduce the effects of "false sharing," latency (and specifically "synchronization latency") was still a serious problem. Keleher et al. [31] have implemented a lazily release-consistent DSM system called TreadMarks and have obtained good speedup results for a variety of applications running over ATM network hardware.

A number of other variants of release consistency have been suggested, each making the shared-memory abstraction more complex and less transparent in return for better performance. Feeley and Levy [14] present a modified release-consistent DSM system that supports object-based "version consistency" where applications are permitted to "acquire" specific versions of objects. Versions are immutable and an "acquire" for a specific version will block until a corresponding "release" has been performed. This approach permits multiple versions of data to co-exist in the DSM system and helps solve false sharing problems that occur in some types of parallel applications.

Bershad et al. [7] have implemented a DSM system called Midway that introduces another new consistency model, "entry consistency." Entry consistency is weaker than many of the other models suggested, including release consistency; entry consistency requires explicit annotations to associate synchronization objects with data. On an "acquire," only the data associated with the synchronization object is guaranteed to be consistent. This extra weakness permits higher performance implementations of the underlying consistency protocols to be written. Midway also supports stronger consistency models, so that the application programmer can trade off performance against the extra effort required to write entry-consistent programs. (The DiSOM DSM system [23] is also based on entry consistency.)

Kazimierczak and Andersen [30] propose a new model for DSM consistency maintenance. Their "object-consistent" system combines attributes of both entry consistency and version consistency as described above. Their system has yet to be implemented, but they hope to support the best attributes of both systems.

Iftode et al. [25] introduce scope consistency. Scope consistency associates synchronization mechanisms and data similar to entry consistency. The association, however, is not explicitly made by the developer. The developer declares the beginning and the end of a scope. The system dynamically detects the asssociation between data and scopes. The consistency of data is ensured in corresponding scopes.

Ananthanarayanan et al. [2] claim that neither release consistency nor type-specific consistency (as implemented by Munin) is sufficient to solve the consistency problem for some applications. For example, with algorithms such as the bounded buffer, both invalidation and write broadcast are inefficient since each new data item is read by only a single node before another update is done, and the synchronization system will know which node will be accessing and removing the object from the buffer. They suggest that the update mechanism needs to be linked to synchronization of access to shared variables and propose an extended set of primitives that support the implementation of an "Augmented Shared Memory" (ASM) system in the Clouds environment. The approach they propose is very similar to entry consistency and links synchronization variables to specific data items.

Slow Memory

Hutto and Ahamad [24] present a theoretical examination of "slow memories" (defined below) and other forms of weakly-consistent memory. They present several reasons in favour of weakly-consistent memory. Firstly, they claim that strictly-consistent memories must be "slow," quoting Lipton and Sandberg's Latency Theorem [37]:

> No matter how clever or complex a protocol is, if it implements a consistent shared memory, it must be "slow." A consistent shared memory cannot be both fast (memory access time independent of the message latency, τ) and scalable.

In a similar argument to that presented by Clouds, they also claim that access will always be controlled by a higher-level synchronization system, and therefore that strictly-consistent memory implicitly enforces unnecessary consistency.

In the cited papers, Hutto and Ahamad discuss various levels of consistency, categorized by various properties. They present two example memory types:

Slow memory: Reads must return "some" value that has previously been written to the location being read. Once a value has been read, no earlier writes to that location (by the processor that wrote the value read) can be returned. Local writes must be immediately visible.

Slow memory provides "very weak" consistency, as even writes by the same processor to different locations are not ordered. As a result, programming with slow memory is rather unusual. For example, traditional mutual exclusion algorithms do not work, though mutual exclusion can be achieved using modified algorithms and a working variant is presented.

Causal memory: All processors must agree on the order of causally-related effects. Events not related by potential causality (concurrent events) may be observed in different orders. In a later paper, Ahamad et al. [1] examine the issues involved in actual programming of causal memories. They conclude that most programs written for consistent memory work correctly in causal-memory systems as long as synchronization is done through shared-memory variables. They also note that for some algorithms, minor changes can be made to implement elegant solutions that make use of the properties of causal memory, particularly if the programmer is allowed to specify the procedure for merging concurrent writes.

Causal memory is closely related to the relaxed-consistency mechanisms discussed earlier, especially virtual synchrony in ISIS. In fact, Schmuck has proved that a large class of problems for which a "linearization function" can be found all have causal (ISIS cbcast) implementations [46] and, therefore, could also be implemented using causal memory.

In the next section, we move on to survey consistency systems that make use of some application-specific information in order to achieve higher performance.

17.2.5 Application/Type-specific Consistency

In the database arena, a fair amount of effort has been expended studying the effect of type and type-specific support on transactional systems. Research has shown that by adding some semantic-level knowledge of the application-level types in use and their inter-operation, performance gains can be realized. Issues addressed in this context include the theoretical aspects of performing transactions on typed objects and synchronization and recovery mechanisms when using type-specific concurrency control. Semantic-locking protocols for transaction management in an object-oriented database make use of semantic information. By doing so, these protocols can reorder transactions, cope with complex objects, nested transactions, and referentially-shared objects.

A similar application-specific approach has been proposed for use in DSM systems. The issue was first raised under the title, "Problem-oriented shared memory," by Cheriton [11]. Cheriton claims that there are three basic paradigms for handling shared state:

- Communication paradigm,
- (consistent) Shared-memory paradigm,
- Problem-oriented shared-memory paradigm.

To quote [11]:

> "Problem-oriented shared memory" is a shared memory that implements fetch and store operations specialized to the particular problem or application it is supporting. In particular, a problem-oriented shared memory commonly provides a specialized form of consistency and consistency maintenance that exploits application-specific semantics.

Cheriton goes on to propose that consistency constraints be relaxed and more use be made of problem semantics. He suggests that, in some cases, stale data may be detected upon use by the client, and the client may then recover. A example would be hint caching. In some applications, stale data may actually be sufficiently accurate, provided that the client can obtain up-to-date information when necessary. In other applications, some data may be optional in the sense that the client can continue without it. Other applications may tolerate having the results of store operations being lost or undone, for example, an application that regularly replaces the entire data set.

The first DSM system to implement application-specific support was Munin [5]. Munin supports multiple-consistency protocols and the run-time system accepts hints from the compiler or user to determine the consistency protocol to be used for each object. The default, in the absence of hints, is to use a general multiple-readers/single-writer consistency mechanism, much like that employed by IVY. Munin supports several different object types that are based on the results of a survey of shared-memory access characteristics. The main types of objects they identified are (from most specific to least specific):

Synchronization: Lock objects, which may be managed using the distributed lock system described in Section 17.4.1.

Private: Objects identified as private are not managed by the runtime at all. However, if the object is remotely referenced, the object is brought back under the control of the DSM system.

Write-once: Objects that are initialized once and then only read, and so may be efficiently replicated.

Result: Objects that are not read until fully updated. The DSM system knows that updates to different parts of the object will not conflict, so it can use the delayed-update mechanism to maximum benefit.

Producer consumer: Objects that are written by one thread, and read by a fixed set of threads. Munin performs "eager object movement" for this type of objects, where updates are transmitted to the readers before they request them.

Migratory: Objects that are accessed by a single thread at a time. These can be efficiently handled by integrating the movement of the object with the movement of the lock associated with the object, giving some of the benefits of the Clouds scheme.

Write-many: These are objects that are written by many different nodes at the same time, sometimes without being read in between. Write-many objects may be efficiently handled using delayed updates (see Section 17.2.4).

Read-mostly: These objects are updated rarely, so a broadcast scheme may be used for updating them.

General read-write: The default case, used when multiple threads are reading and writing the object, or when no hint of object type is given. The scheme used to handle this type of object is similar to the ownership scheme used in IVY that is itself a modification of a multi-processor caching algorithm called the Berkeley algorithm.

The results of the Munin survey showed that a very small percentage of all accesses to shared data fall under the general read-write type. They also note that a program moves through various stages of execution, and the types associated with objects change as time progresses. The authors suggest extending their run-time system to attempt to determine the type of an object dynamically, possibly using profiling information gathered by the DSM system.

In subsequent studies, the authors looked at a number of parallel applications using a simulation system. At small granularities, it would appear that many accesses do fall under the various categories outlined above. However, at larger granularities, almost all accesses seem to fall under the "WriteMany" and "WriteOnce" categories;

these are the classes of access most likely to be used in a page-based DSM system. The conclusion is that page-based access is at too large a granularity to allow fine type specific tagging to be used.

In more recent versions of Munin, the initial list of eight different access patterns is reduced to five: conventional, read-only, migratory, write-shared, and synchronization. The original set of access patterns contains some redundancy. As noted in Section 17.2.4, more recent versions of Munin also support release consistency, and in conjunction with this were extended with a new write-shared protocol based on page duplication and differencing. A study of performance benefits showed that for some application, a 30% performance improvement is obtained from using multiple protocols when compared with using their most flexible fixed protocol (write-shared with page differencing).

Another approach to application-specific support is to allow the programmer to control, at some level, the operation or implementation of the underlying DSM system. This approach draws on the open implementation (or meta-protocol) arguments presented by Kiczales et al. [33] proposing that the underlying implementations of an operating system service must be accessible and tunable by the application in order to maximize performance.

Kulkarni et al. describe the construction of a DSM system using the 'Π' architecture [34] that allows the DSM system to be tailored to suit the varying needs of applications and hardware configurations using a meta-protocol approach. Taking a more direct approach to supporting DSM specifically, Pérez-Cortés et al. [45] describe the Arias DSM service. Arias divides the shared address space into multiple zones; each zone may have its own synchronization and consistency protocol, built using generic primitives provided by the system.

Griffioen et al. [22] propose an novel application-specific alternative called "spatial consistency" for use in the Unify system. In a spatially-consistent system, the consistency algorithms can be linked to the application-level geometric meaning of the shared data. In this way, data that is "further away" from the node's workspace can be less consistently maintained than data that is nearby. This approach has application in many geometrically-based parallel applications.

In the next section, we discuss the effect that network performance has on the performance of a DSM system.

17.3 Network Performance Issues

Communications latency is generally much larger in a DSM system than it would be in a multi-processor, and bandwidth generally much lower. This leads to different design decisions in areas such as consistency and cache management where the increased latency increases the cost of operations, such as data invalidation, which is relatively cheap in a multi-processor. Latency also limits the rate at which threads on different nodes can communicate and synchronize.

It is interesting to note that recent advances in both local and wide-area networking technologies (such as ATM, SONET, switching technology) have had a significant effect on bandwidth and latency. In particular, bandwidths have climbed steeply and speeds of over 1Gbps are available even over wide-area networks. Meanwhile, end-to-end latencies have dropped, but not as steeply. This has narrowed the performance gap between hardware and software shared-memory systems somewhat, resulting in wider applicability of DSM technology and increased interest in research in the area.

However, latency is still an important issue and limits the speed that a DSM system can reach. In both local- and wide-area networks, latencies will remain much higher than in tightly-coupled architectures. This will remain the case even in the presence of increasing bandwidth and will continue to limit the degree of convergence of shared-memory systems for tightly- and loosely-coupled architectures. Work is being done to improve the latency of local-area systems in particular, since wide-area systems are limited by the speed of light in any case, and, using ATM networks in particular, local-area network latencies have dropped by several orders of magnitude.

As processor speeds climb, the relative importance of network latencies has also climbed. Where 10 years ago a processor might have been able to complete only a few thousand instructions during a network round-trip, newer processors can complete from one to several orders of magnitude more instructions in the round-trip time of newer networks. For applications running in parallel on such systems (including parallel applications running on DSM systems), a key factor is the computation-to-communication ratio. Applications with high computation-to-communication ratios generally perform well on loosely-coupled architectures, whereas applications with low ratios generally require the low latency of tightly-coupled architectures to achieve good speed-up ratios.

This is analogous to the "memory wall" that wories researchers such as Wulf and McKee [51] in traditional hardware design. As in the case of network latencies (and to a lesser extent bandwidths), processor speeds are climbing faster than memory speeds. Wulf and McKee speculate that the limit where memory speeds will dominate, and processor speed increases will no longer increase overall performance, is less than a decade away. A radical architectural rethink is needed.

In the next section, we will discuss a number of other issues that effect the design of DSM systems.

17.4 Other Design Issues

Aside from the primary issue of consistency, there are a number of other design issues that must be discussed.

17.4.1 Synchronization

Most parallel applications will use some sort of synchronization mechanism to order and control accesses to shared data. The most important thing to note in DSM systems is that just blindly using standard test-and-set operations on bytes in shared pages will produce a high fault rate; faults are usually expensive, making this approach unacceptable. The effect of any synchronization primitives on the fault behaviour must be carefully considered.

As previously mentioned, the designers of the Clouds DSM system [12] maintain that the synchronization primitives, such as semaphores, should be integrated with the data consistency protocol. Clouds merges locking with the cache consistency protocol, so that the user may obtain both a lock and the data in one network transaction. This approach has the advantage that no invalidation messages are required, since the granting of the lock guarantees that there are no conflicting copies; it has the disadvantage that an explicit unlock/discard operation is required to release access to the data. This is acceptable in Clouds, as the DSM system was designed specifically to support object invocation and the data can be discarded and unlocked when the invocation returns. In other DSM systems, the run-time, compiler, or application would need to be modified to discard data items at appropriate times.

IVY [36] provides "eventcounts" as the basic synchronization primitives. These are implemented outside of the DSM system, using RPC.

Mermaid [53] implements a separate distributed synchronization facility providing P and V operations and events.

Munin [6] provides a distributed lock mechanism using "proxy objects" to reduce network load. Proxy objects are maintained by a lock server on each node; when a thread wants to obtain a lock on an object, it attempts to lock the proxy instead. The server obtains the global lock if it is not already held locally. Global locking is done by negotiating with all the other lock servers in the system. Each lock may be migrated from server to server, and part of the Munin system allows objects to be migrated along with their locks: See Section 17.2.5 for more details.

Anderson et al. [3] suggest locking using an Ethernet-style back-off algorithm instead of spin or wait locks in a shared-memory environment. This approach reduces the amount of communication and contention in the shared memory area where the locks are held. Goodman et al. [21] propose a set of efficient primitives for software synchronization on a multi-processor that may be extendible to the DSM case. Their system uses busy waiting only on local memory (which is efficient) and uses broadcast and queuing operations to achieve global synchronization.

Another important issue, especially when relaxed consistency is used between synchronization points, is the granularity of synchronization used. A simulation study indicates that, for general parallel systems, synchronization at the loop-iteration level gives the best performance. An interesting alternative approach suggests implementing concurrently-accessible objects without using locking at all. Instead, update protocols are constructed using an atomic compare-and-swap operation to guarantee consistency.

In the next section, we discuss data-granularity issues.

17.4.2 Granularity

When caching objects in local memory, it is necessary to decide what level of granularity to use. Many of the DSM systems discussed use a fixed block size in the cache, rather than varying the granularity based on the size of the data item. Usually this is due to constraints imposed by the system hardware and memory management, as many DSM systems use virtual-memory hardware to trap accesses to shared data.

The choice of the block size in the cache depends on several issues. It depends on the cost of communication: for example, on many local area networks there is little difference between the time required to send a 1-byte message and that required to send a 1024-byte message. Transmitting bulk changes rather than single-byte modifications would therefore seem desirable. The choice of granularity also depends on the locality of reference in the application, as thrashing may occur when two machines are both accessing different parts of the same block (this is also known as "false sharing" or the "ping-pong effect"). This would seem to argue for a smaller block size. In practice, a compromise must be achieved, as with conventional virtual-memory systems.

There are good reasons for choosing a block size that is the same as that of the virtual-memory management unit on the system, or a multiple thereof. Among other things, it allows the hardware to be used to help in the maintenance of consistency. The choice is complicated somewhat when heterogeneous machines are being used, but in these cases, the lowest common multiple of hardware-supported page sizes can usually be used, e.g., in CMU's shared-memory server [17] built on top of Mach. Most of the DSM systems discussed use a page-based granularity with 1K-byte to 8K-byte pages. There is evidence that larger page sizes than this cause performance problems [36].

The only major DSM system that uses a fixed small granularity is Memnet [13], where a hardware based DSM system was implemented on a high speed token ring. Here they used a 32-byte block (or "chunk," as they call it). The choice of a small block size is appropriate since Memnet is much closer to a shared-memory multiprocessor than it is to a software DSM system, because the entire processor is blocked on a cache miss and a block size similar to cache line sizes in multi-processors is used; the processor is not actually aware of the distributed nature of its address space. Also, the ratio between remote and local memory-access times is much lower than in the software based DSM systems due to the dedicated token ring (200Mbps) and hardware assistance. In contrast, Mether [40], a software implementation of Memnet on top of SunOS, uses an 8K page size. However, the concept of a "short page" was later added to Mether, allowing access to the first 32 bytes of a full page.

A number of DSM systems avoid using hardware assistance to trap accesses to shared data and therefore are not constrained to use hardware page sizes to monitor access to shared data. Orca [4] and Object Consistency [30] (among others) use language-level objects as their fundamental granularity and therefore use a variable granularity. Zekauskas et al. [52] study the use of software write-detection at a lower level using compiler and run-time extensions, citing the cost of hardware faults as a significant issue in many systems. They conclude that software write-detection is faster, sometimes by a considerable margin, and that less data is transferred over the network, due to the finer granularity of access tracking. However, they concede that the handling of hardware faults is quite slow in the system that they study and that software write-detection is not always faster in systems with lower hardware overheads.

In the next section, we discuss address-space structuring issues in designing DSM systems.

17.4.3 Address-Space Structure

Another important issue is the structure of the address space supported by the DSM system. The single most important factor here is whether or not the user is presented with a single shared address space. A secondary issue is how the shared region itself is organized.

Single Shared Address-Space Systems

In a single shared address-space system (or single-level store), the system appears as a set of threads executing in a single shared distributed address space. Data items always appear at the same addresses on all nodes. This is the Amber model of computation [9]. In IVY [36], each address space is split into a private and a shared region; there is a single shared region for all processes. The Arias system [45] supports a single global address space made up of shared zones, each of which may be persistent.

Single address-space systems have had a resurgence in popularity with the arrival of 64-bit processors. A number of researchers believe that a 64-bit address space is large enough to act as a single global address space for all the memory (both primary and secondary) in a distributed system. Examples of such systems include Opal [10] and Angel [42]. Single address space systems are particularly popular in the object-oriented community as they allow secondary storage to be unified with primary storage and remove the need for pointer swizzling.

Security and protection are a major problem with single address-space systems, and current approaches rely on either hardware assistance (Opal), software capabilities (Arias) or probabilistic algorithms.

Separate Shared Address Spaces

Another approach is to divide each process's address space into different fixed regions, some of which are private and not shared, and some of which are shared with some other processes. Ra, the Clouds kernel [12], takes this approach using O, P, and K address regions, with the O region shared between all processes executing in a given object; the P and K regions are local to a process and kernel respectively. Here objects always appear at the same address but may not be visible from every address space.

By contrast, some DSM systems (including Mirage [16] and CMU's Mach server [17]) allow shared data to exist at differing addresses in different processes address spaces. However, neither system does transparent pointer translation, so the address changes are not entirely transparent to the application.

Shared-Region Organisation

The other important issue is the structuring of the shared region itself. Some of the DSM systems discussed—for example, IVY and Mether—use a single flat region: One continuous range of virtual addresses represents the shared address space and are managed by the DSM system. This single address space is usually sub-divided into pages.

Most of the other DSM systems (Choices [26], Clouds, Mach, Mirage, and Munin) use paged segmentation: The shared region consists of disjoint pieces that are usually managed separately and are not all mapped in any one process. Frequently, the segments (sometimes called memory objects, or windows) are related to the backing store. For example, in Clouds, the object address space consists of windows onto larger segments; these segments are usually maintained on secondary storage.

In the next section, we discuss how DSM systems interact with virtual-memory management and secondary-storage systems.

17.4.4 Replacement Policy and Secondary Storage

Since the memory of each machine in the DSM system is effectively a cache of part of the shared data set, there must be a policy to deal with cache overflow. The usual least-recently used (LRU) policy found in traditional virtual-memory systems does not work well without modification, as some pages that may have been referenced very recently should be replaced; for example, a page that has been invalidated since its last use should be replaced before any page that contains valid data. Also, pages that are read-only and replicated elsewhere should have a high replacement priority as they do not need to be saved to disk before being replaced. Pages that are writable, or do not have replicas on other machines, must be saved.

A related issue is the location at which to save pages that are being replaced. Traditional virtual-memory systems always save replaced pages on local disk, but, in a DSM system, we also have the option of saving pages into the main memory of other nodes. With the trend to have machines with larger and larger memory sizes and prospect of even faster networks, this option may become more attractive.

Markatos and Dramitinos [39] study the use of main memory in other nodes to store pages. They conclude that this is faster than disk storage and they also discuss an algorithm that allows this remote paging to be fault-tolerant in the presence of a single-node failure.

Malkawi et al. [38] examine the choice of pages to replace and present a number of algorithms that they evaluate using a trace-based simulator for both cube and mesh-based multi-processors. Their results suggest that when the cost of inter-node faults is low, it is best to pick replacement pages from the working set of the current process; when inter-node faults are costly, it is better to pick pages that belong to other local or remote processes. When memory contention is high, the best algorithm for selecting a node to send the page to is the least-active neighbor; round-robin and least-loaded neighbor algorithms have lower performance unless local memories are very large.

Memnet [13] is unique among the DSM systems discussed in that it actually reserves part of the main memory of each node as storage for chunks, so that each chunk is guaranteed a storage location on some node when it is pushed out of another machine's memory. The authors of IVY investigated the possibility of replacement to other nodes' memories and proposed piggybacking memory-state information (such as the amount of free memory) on other network messages.

In the database field, similar issues arise in client-server database-cache management. Franklin [18] discusses a wide range of algorithms, including algorithms that cache in other workstations' memory or cache on local disk. Some algorithms depend on transaction support and may not be suitable in every DSM system. When evaluated using a simulator and a wide range of workloads, no clear winner emerges, though local-disk caching proved to be worthwhile for scalability reasons. Franklin does not consider systems with multiple "servers," so it is not clear how his results would scale to such systems.

Feeley et al. [15] study the use of "global memory" (i.e., all the main memory in a workstation cluster) in the more general case, where global memory is used for everything in the OS: file buffer caching, VM for applications, and transactions. Their system runs on a cluster of machines connected via an ATM LAN. For memory intensive applications, performance improvements of a factor of 1.5 to 3.5 have been measured.

Of course, the underlying operating system may not allow control over the precise replacement policy used. This is an example of a general issue that must be considered in designing a DSM system: the relationship between the DSM system and the underlying operating system, if any. Most DSM systems have either been built into specialized operating systems or on top of operating systems such as Mach that allow considerable control over the memory management system. However, there can still be problems. For example, Mach allows control over what is done with a page only once the OS decides to page it out. In this case, however, a solution is available: Mach has been extended to allow user-level page-replacement policies.

In the next section, we discuss those DSM systems that support more than one hardware platform and those that support the automatic translation of data between hardware types.

17.4.5 Heterogeneity Support

A few of the DSM systems discussed make attempts to provide support for heterogeneous systems, including: the Mermaid system [53], CMU's Mach server [17], and DiSOM [23]. Mermaid is implemented between Sun workstations running SunOS and C, and DEC Firefly shared-memory multi-processor workstations running Topaz and Modula-2+. Mermaid is truly heterogeneous, while CMU's system assumes a homogeneous operating-system base. The Mermaid and CMU systems are page-based. DiSOM is an object-oriented DSM system that supports a number of different host systems. The first part of this section discusses heterogeneity issues for page-based systems; we return to language-level systems at the end of the section.

Page-based Heterogeneity

The first heterogeneity issue deals with support for different page sizes without considering the data contents of the pages; this is not strictly support for heterogeneous machines, as Mach permits the page size to be selected on a per-machine basis. The Mach page-size algorithm was as follows:

- for requests "smaller" than the scheduler[1] page size, the request is rounded up to the scheduler page size; and,
- for requests "larger" than the scheduler page size, the request is fulfilled by multiple scheduler pages (all shipped at once).

This problem is not as simple as it sounds, as difficulties arise when trying to avoid false contention between competing multi-page requests, and when trying to satisfy requests rapidly while maintaining fairness.

In Mermaid, Zhou et al. discuss two algorithms for handling the page size problem: the "smallest page-size" algorithm, and the "largest page-size" algorithm, i.e., use either the smallest or the largest page size that occurs in the DSM system. Using a large page size can increase thrashing and "false sharing," where non-overlapping accesses appear to overlap due to large page granularity. On the other hand, using a small page size can increase the overheads. The performance results they present show that the "larger" algorithm has better performance, but that the "smaller" algorithm has better stability in the presence of data interference problems.

The second issue is that of real heterogeneous-data support and goes beyond the byte-order and word-size problems faced by many network applications: Within pages of virtual memory, machines are free to assign any meaning they choose to a sequence of bits. The authors of the CMU DSM system divide the problem into two sub-problems: hardware data-types, such as integers and floating-point numbers, and software types, such as C structures. Their current system takes care of hardware-type translation and should be extensible to take care of software types. They do not address the issue of variable-size data and pointers.

The CMU DSM system works by attaching a type tag to each segment of the shared-memory object, and provides translated segments as required. At the application level, a typed memory allocator is used to place data in the appropriate regions. While this approach cannot deal with structures directly, it can handle

[1] In CMU's scheme, the manager node is known as the "fault scheduler," as it is responsible for scheduling a series of read and write requests.

them if an extra level of indirection is added: Each structure element is replaced by a pointer to storage allocated to store that data type. Another suggestion that they make is to pretranslate pages on (multi)processors with spare memory and CPU cycles.

A similar scheme is used in Mermaid, with each page containing only one data type. However, user level conversion routines are supported, so the types involved may be arbitrarily complex. The main limitations of page-translation systems are:

- the size of the data type must be the same on all involved DSM systems; and
- there is usually a loss of precision when converting floating-point data types.

Language-assisted Heterogeneity

In DiSOM, the entire system is object-oriented and operates at the language level. Heterogeneity is addressed by requiring the application programmer to provide customized packing and unpacking routines to marshal the data contained within a given object into host-independent form. (Though, for some uses, these routines could be generated by the compiler.)

Another approach is described by Gokhale and Minnich [20]. In their DSM system, they use a specialized compiler that supports IEEE 1596.5 machine-independent types. This allows most of the work to be done at compile time instead of run time. The main problem is with performance: for example, load/store is 2–6 times slower. Their system is implemented using CPP operator overloading. Pointers are not handled.

In the next section, we discuss fault tolerance as it impinges on DSM system design.

17.4.6 Fault Tolerance

Most of the DSM systems discussed so far ignore the fault-tolerance issue or maintain that it is an issue that should be handled by the underlying operating system. However, it would appear that in practice a DSM system would strongly effect the fault tolerance of a system. For example, in a DSM system where n systems are sharing access to a set of data, the failure of any one of them could lead to the failure of all the connected sites (or, at least, some of the processes on each site). We are also presented with an unusual failure-handling problem. It is fairly easy to see how to handle a failed message or RPC, but how do you handle a failed page-fault?

Interest in fault tolerance in DSM systems has increased in recent years as DSM has received more widespread use. Morin and Puaut [41] survey a number of fault-tolerant DSM systems in greater detail than this section presents.

The original Clouds DSM system [12] provided recoverability using shadowing of segments and a transactional system using commits. The recovery system was not really integrated with the DSM system and is merely implemented at the segment storage site. Recent work describes the implementation of a transactional system called "Invocation-Based Concurrency Control" (IBCC) above Clouds. The authors intended to implement IBCC as a separate layer, but found this to be impossible. In order to maintain a consistent view of data when one transaction is active at multiple nodes, they were forced to integrate the transaction system with the DSM support system.

Wu and Fuchs [50] describe a recoverable DSM system based on the IVY DSM model. Their DSM system consists of diskless workstations connected to disk servers over a LAN. A copy of a consistent shared-memory state is maintained on disk. Using an incremental checkpointing system based on a twin-page disk storage-management system, they provide rapid-rollback recovery. Two physically-contiguous disk pages are allocated for each writable page in the shared virtual-address space. When a page is fetched from disk, both are read and only one is retained, based on a simple time-stamp and state-based selection algorithm. Dirty memory pages can be written to disk at any time. They also describe a mechanism for reconstructing the "owner" and "copy-set"[2] data needed by the DSM system when there is a failure.

Ouyang and Heiser [44] discuss the addition of fault-tolerance using checkpointing and study in particular the effects of message loss on such systems. They present a variant of the two-phase commit protocol that has lower overhead and may be used in such systems. Kermarrec et al. [32] present an integrated DSM system for a tightly-coupled architecture (an Intel Paragon) where the management of the recovery information is integrated into the DSM consistency protocol. The DiSOM system [23] incorporates a checkpoint-based failure recovery system which has the interesting property that no extra messages are required during failure-free operations.

A different approach treats the DSM location and ownership ("token") information as a distributed database, and views page migrations as transactions on a global "token database." Transactions are committed using a unilateral-commit protocol that allows fast recovery of the token state with minimal run-time overhead. This approach can be based on one of Li's DSM algorithms. A checkpointing and logging scheme is used to store the actual pages; the token database just helps maintain a consistent view after a failure.

Vaughan et al. [49] describe a fault-tolerant persistent object system called Casper that provides a DSM service. Casper is implemented using shadow paging and concentrates primarily on maintaining a self-consistent view of the system that may be pushed to disk.

Markatos and Dramitinos [39] study the use of main memory in other nodes to store pages. They discuss an algorithm, based on duplicate copies of pages, that allows this remote paging to be fault-tolerant in the presence of a single-node failure.

Juul and Fleisch [16] discuss weakening of robustness in a DSM system. They argue that weakened robustness can be interesting in the same way that weakened consistency can. It is not always necessary to support complete and consistent recovery after a failure. Juul and Fleisch propose a model which distinguishes a

[2]The set of nodes holding a read-only copy of the data.

recoverable system, one that must be able to survive any single-site failure, from a reliable system that also ensures consistency after recovery.

Upfal and Wigderson [48] describe a formal model for distributing data in a distributed system that has very strong fault-tolerant properties. Where n is the number of processors in the system and $\epsilon \ll 1$, their scheme can sustain up to $O(\log n)$ "maliciously-chosen" faults and up to $(1 - \epsilon)n$ random ones, without any information or efficiency loss. The algorithm they present is effectively a majority-based replication system using time-stamps. Birman [8] presents a theoretical overview of the effects of virtual synchrony on fault tolerance in a DSM system. He discusses how to define consistency conditions for various DSM consistency models.

In the next section, we discuss how memory allocation effects the design of DSM systems.

17.4.7 Memory Allocation

In any shared-memory system where dynamic memory allocation is allowed, careful consideration must be given to the memory-allocation approach to be used: The same piece of shared memory must not be allocated more than once. A central memory-allocating node can be used, but the performance can be quite bad, due to networking overheads. Amber [9] allocates large chunks of the shared address space to each site at startup, and has an address-space server that hands out more memory on demand. This allows memory allocation to be done locally most of the time.

Another approach, taken by CMU in their Mach server [17], is to use a parallel memory-allocation algorithm. They implemented a parallel version of Knuth's FreeList algorithm and claim improved performance over the FirstFit scheme used in IVY. Other measurements used by CMU indicate that a two-level allocation scheme, such as that used by Amber, is effective in reducing shared-memory contention. They also suggest allocating and de-allocating memory in batches to reduce overheads.

17.4.8 Data Persistence

Many of the DSM systems surveyed support some form of secondary-storage persistence for data held in shared memory. It is in this area that the overlaps between DSM systems and database systems are most apparent. There are a number of design issues that a DSM providing persistency must address.

Due to the inherently distributed nature of the data in a DSM system, it is not easy to obtain a globally-consistent snapshot of the data on secondary storage. All of the fault-tolerant DSMs (see Section 17.4.6) address this issue in one way or another, and Casper [49] illustrates techniques that may be used to obtain a self-consistent view of the shared data to push to secondary storage. In a different approach, the application programmer is given explicit control over the migration of shared-data segments between memory and secondary store. The Arias system [45] divides the shared global address space into "zones"; each zone may be marked as persistent and Arias supplies stable storage and distributed logging to provide atomic updates on persistent zones.

Garbage collection can be a major problem in persistent DSM systems, as it is difficult to track references to shared data that may be simultaneously accessible on multiple nodes. A solution to this issue can be global garbage collection in a DSM-based distributed-object system.

Naming and location are also significant issues once data becomes persistent. If the entire system is persistent, based on shared memory, and all access is transparent, then naming may not be an issue as all data can be directly accessed through direct pointers. This is true for some single-level address-space systems such as Opal, see Section 17.4.3.

17.5 Conclusions

Overall, it appears that DSM is a useful extra service for a distributed system to provide. DSM provides a simple programming model that is suitable for a wide range of parallel-programming problems. With careful application of the DSM approach, good speedups may be achieved for many parallel programs [36]. It would also appear that DSM might be useful for distributed, as well as parallel, problems. DSM should not be viewed as a replacement for RPC or for a message-passing style of communications. In the DSM model of communication, data is moved to the user; in the RPC model, operations are moved to the data. Both models are useful and have their advantages and disadvantages. An advantage of DSM is that no explicit communication is necessary. Use may also be made of locality of reference. On the other hand, the handling of security and protection issues in DSM systems is unclear, and fault tolerance may be more difficult to achieve. Choosing between DSM and message passing for a given application is quite difficult, and the trade-offs must be considered carefully. Forin et al. [17] believe

> "...that the amount of data exchanged between synchronization points is the main indicator to consider when deciding between the use of distributed shared memory and message passing in a parallel application."

To achieve efficiency, synchronization issues must be explicitly handled by the DSM system itself, or by some integrated environment. The main reason for handling synchronization explicitly is the large performance problems introduced by using the ordinary synchronization primitives on distributed-memory locations.

Most of the recent DSM systems discussed no longer implement strict consistency in the way that IVY did. Most now use some form of consistency relaxation to increase performance. There doesn't appear to be consensus yet on the correct approach here, but the most promising avenue of research would appear to be in the area of release and entry-consistent DSM systems such as TreadMarks [31] and Midway [7]. There is much work to be done in the area of supporting the programming of release-consistent DSM systems so that the programmer is not required to explicitly annotate parallel programs. CMM described in [28] provides a mechanism where release consistency (and many other DSM protocols) may be implemented by inserting a few annotations in the functional code of the application.

Most of the DSM systems discussed use a paged segmented-memory model, where the address space is split into different sections, some of which are managed by the DSM system. However, the arrival of 64-bit processors has increased the popularity of single shared address-space systems, see Section 17.4.3.

As network latency dominates the performance timings of DSM systems, the choice of low-level network protocol is of prime importance. While there is no general consensus here, the most common choice is to use a reliable message-passing system rather than RPC or unreliable datagrams; however, end-to-end arguments would weigh against this choice. The ability to forward messages without having to reply to the original sender is important in several of the distributed algorithms.

Increased network speeds and enhanced switch-based network technology are becoming increasingly important in DSM systems. Newer technologies solve many of the bandwidth problems in DSM, but latency, and synchronization latency in particular, is still a major problem. Hybrid hardware and software DSM systems are also becoming common, particularly in the high performance multi-computer arena.

17.6 Bibliography

[1] Mustaque Ahamad, Phillip W. Hutto, and Ranjit John. Implementing and Programming Causal Distributed Shared Memory. In *Proceedings of the 11th International Conference on Distributed Computing Systems*, May 1991.

[2] R. Ananthanarayanan, Mustaque Ahamad, and Richard J. LeBlanc. Application Specific Coherence Control for High Performance Distributed Shared Memory. In *Symposium on Experiences with Distributed and Multiprocessor Systems*, pages 109–128, March 1992.

[3] Thomas E. Anderson, Edward D. Lazowska, and Henry M. Levy. The Performance Implications of Thread Management Alternatives for Shared-Memory Multiprocessors. In *Transactions on Computers*, vol. 38(12), Dec. 1989.

[4] H. E. Bal, R. Bhoedjang, R. Hofman, C. Jacobs, K. Langendoen, and T. Ruhl. Performance Evaluation of the Orca Shared-Object System. *ACM Transactions on Computer Systems*, vol. 16(1), pages 1–40, February 1998.

[5] John K. Bennett, John B. Carter, and Willy Zwaenepoel. Adaptive Software Cache Management for Distributed Shared Memory Architectures. In *Proceedings of the 17th Annual International Symposium on Computer Architecture*, pages 125–134, May 1990.

[6] John K. Bennett, John B. Carter, and Willy Zwaenepoel. Munin: Distributed Shared Memory Based on Type-Specific Memory Coherence. *Proceedings of*

the 2nd ACM SIGPLAN Symposium on Principles and Practice of Parallel Programming. SIGPLAN Notices, vol. 25(3), pages 168–176, March 1990.

[7] Brian N. Bershad, Matthew J. Zekauskas, and Wayne A. Sawdon. The Midway Distributed Shared Memory System. *Technical Report CMU-CS-93-119*, School of Computer Science, Carnegie Mellon University, 1993. A version of this paper appeared in COMPCON 1993.

[8] Kenneth P. Birman. The Process Group Approach to Reliable Distributed Computing. *Communications of the ACM*, vol. 36(12), Dec. 1993.

[9] Jeffery S. Chase, Franz G. Amador, Edward D. Lazowska, Henry M. Levy, and Richard J. Littlefield. The Amber System: Parallel Programming on a Network of Multiprocessors. In *Proceedings of the 12th ACM Symposium on Operating Systems Principles*, pages 147–158, December 1989.

[10] Jeffrey S. Chase, Henry M. Levy, Michael J. Feeley, and Edward D. Lazowska. Sharing and Protection in a Single-Address-Space Operating System. *ACM Transactions on Computer Systems*, vol. 12(4), pages 271–307, November 1994.

[11] David R. Cheriton. Problem-oriented Shared Memory: A Decentralized Approach to Distributed System Design. In *Proceedings of the 6th International Conference on Distributed Computing Systems*, pages 190–197, May 1986.

[12] Partha Dasgupta, Richard J. LeBlanc, Mustaque Ahamad, and Umakishore Ramachandran. The Clouds Distributed Operations System. In *IEEE Computer*, vol 24(11), pages 34–44, November 1991.

[13] Gary S. Delp and David J. Farber. MemNet: An Experiment on High-Speed Memory Mapped Network Interface. *Technical Report 85-11-IR*, Department of Electrical Engineering, University of Delaware, 1986.

[14] Michael J. Feeley and Henry M. Levy. Distributed Shared Memory with Versioned Objects. In *Proceedings of the OOPSLA '92 Conference on Object-oriented Programming Systems, Languages and Applications*, Oct. 1992.

[15] Michael J. Feeley, William E. Morgan, Frederic H. Pighin, Anna R. Karlin, Henry M. Levy, and Chandramohan A. Thekkath. Implementing Global Memory Management in a Workstation Cluster. In *Proceedings of the 15th ACM Symposium on Operating Systems Principles*, pages 201–212, December 1995.

[16] Brett D. Fleisch and Gerald J. Popek. Mirage: A Coherent Distributed Shared Memory Design. In *Proceedings of the 12th ACM Symposium on Operating Systems Principles*, pages 211–223, December 1989.

[17] Alessandro Forin, Joseph Barrera, and Richard Sanzi. The Shared Memory Server. In *USENIX Winter Conference*, pages 229–243, 1989.

[18] Michael J. Franklin, Michael J. Carey and Miron Livny. Global Memory Management in Client-Server Database Architectures. In *Proceedings of the 18th Conference on Very Large Databases*, pages 596–609, August 1992.

[19] Kourosh Gharachorloo, Daniel Lenoski, James Laudon, Phillip Gibbons, Anoop Gupta, and John Hennessy. Memory Consistency and Event Ordering in Scalable Shared-Memory Multiprocessors. In *Proceedings of the 17th Annual International Symposium on Computer Architecture*, pages 15–26, May 1990.

[20] Maya B. Gokhale and Ronald G. Minnich. An Implementation of the Shared Data Formats Standard for Distributed Shared Memories. In *Experiences with Distributed and Multiprocessor Systems Symposium*, Sept. 1993.

[21] James R. Goodman, Mary K. Vernon, and Philip J. Woest. Efficient Synchronization Primitives for Large-Scale Cache-Coherent Multiprocessors. In *Third International Conference on Architectural Support for Programming Languages and Operating Systems*, pages 64–75. *ACM*, April 1989.

[22] James Griffioen, Rajendra Yavatkar, and Raphael Finkel. Extending the Dimensions of Consistency: Spatial Consistency and Sequential Segments. *Technical Report CS248-94*, Department of Computer Science, University of Kentucky, April 1994.

[23] Paulo Guedes, Miguel Castro, and Nuno Neves. The DiSOM Distributed Shared Object Memory. In *Sixth SIGOPS European Workshop*, Sept. 1994.

[24] Phillip W. Hutto and Mustaque Ahamad. Slow Memory: Weakening Consistency to Enhance Concurrency in Distributed Shared Memories. In *Proceedings of the 10th International Conference on Distributed Computing Systems*, pages 302–309, May 1990.

[25] L. Iftode, J. P. Singh, and K. Li. Scope consistency: A Bridge between Release Consistency and Entry Consistency. In *Proceedings of the 8th ACM Annual Symp. on Parallel Algorithms and Architectures (SPAA'96)*, June 1996.

[26] Gary M. Johnson and Roy H. Campbell. An Object-Oriented Implementation of Distributed Shared Virtual Memory. In *Distributed and Multiprocessor Systems Workshop*, pages 39–58, October 1989.

[27] Alan Judge, Paddy Nixon, Vinny Cahill, Brendan Tangney and Stefan Weber. Overview of Distributed Shared Memory. *Technical Report TCD-CS-1998-24*, Department of Computer Science, Trinity College, Dublin, October 1998.

[28] Alan Judge. Supporting Application-Consistent Distributed Shared Objects. *Ph.D. Thesis*, Department of Computer Science, Trinity College, Dublin, October 1996.

[29] Eric Jul, Henry Levy, Norman Hutchinson, and Andrew Black. Fine-Grained Mobility in the Emerald System. *ACM Transactions on Computer Systems*, vol. 6(1), pages 109–133, February 1988.

[30] Czeslaw K. Kazimierczak and Birger Andersen. Object Consistency – A New Model for Distributed Memory Systems. In *Fourth International Workshop on Object-Orientation in Operating Systems (IWOOOS'95)*, August 1995.

[31] Pete Keleher, Alan L. Cox, Sandhya Dwarkadas, and Willy Zwaenepoel. TreadMarks: Shared Memory Computing on Networks of Workstations. In *IEEE Computer*, vol. 29(2), pages 18-28, February 1996.

[32] Anne-Marie Kermarrec, Gilbert Cabillic, Alain Gefflaut, Christine Morin, and Isabelle Puaut. A Recoverable Distributed Shared Memory Integrating Coherence and Recoverability. *Publication Interne 897*, IRISA, January 1995.

[33] Gregor Kiczales and John Lamping. Operating Systems: Why Object-Oriented? In *Proceedings of the 3rd International Workshop on Object-Orientation in Operating Systems*, pages 25–30, December 1993.

[34] Dinesh C. Kulkarni, Arindam Banerji, Michael R. Casey, and David L. Cohn. Structuring Distributed Shared Memory with the Π Architecture. In *Proceedings of the 13th International Conference on Distributed Computing Systems*, pages 93–100, May 1993.

[35] Leslie Lamport. How to Make a Multiprocessor Computer That Correctly Executes Multiprocess Programs. *IEEE Transactions on Computers*, vol. C-28(9), pages 690–691, September 1979.

[36] Kai Li and Paul Hudak. Memory Coherence in Shared Virtual Memory Systems. *ACM Transactions on Computer Systems*, vol. 7(4), November 1989.

[37] R. J. Lipton and J. S. Sandberg. PRAM: A Scalable Shared Memory. *Technical Report CS-TR-180-88*, Department of Computer Science, Princeton University, September 1988.

[38] Mohammad Malkawi, Deborah Knox, and Mahmoud Abaza. Page Replacement in Distributed Virtual Memory Systems. In *Proceedings of the 4th IEEE Symposium on Parallel and Distributed Processing*, December 1992.

[39] Evangelos P. Markatos and George Dramitinos. Implementation of a Reliable Remote Memory Pager. In *USENIX Technical Conference*, January 1996.

[40] Ronald G. Minnich and David J. Farber. The Mether System: Distributed Shared Memory for SunOS 4.0. In *USENIX Summer Conference*, 1989.

[41] Christine Morin and Isabelle Puaut. A Survey of Recoverable Distributed Shared Memory Systems. *Publication Interne 975*, IRISA, December 1995.

[42] Kevin Murray, Tim Wilkinson, Peter Osmon, Ashley Saulsbury, Tom Stiemerling, and Paul Kelly. Design and Implementation of an Object-Orientated 64-Bit Single Address Space Microkernel. In *Microkernels and Other Kernel Architectures Symposium*, pages 31–43, September 1993.

[43] Bill Nitzberg and Virginia Lo. Distributed Shared Memory: A Survey of Issues and Algorithms. *IEEE Computer*, pages 52–60, August 1991.

[44] Jinsong Ouyang and Gernot Heiser. Checkpointing and Recovery for Distributed Shared Memory Applications. In *Fourth International Workshop on Object-Orientation in Operating Systems (IWOOOS'95)*, August 1995.

[45] Elizabeth Pérez-Cortés, Pascal Dechamboux, and Jay Han. Generic Support for Synchronization and Consistency in Arias. In *Fifth Workshop on Hot Topics in Operating Systems*, pages 113–118. IEEE Computer Society Technical Committee on Operating Systems and Application Environments, May 1995.

[46] Frank Bernhard Schmuck. The Use of Efficient Broadcast Protocols in Asynchronous Distributed Systems. *Ph.D. Thesis*, Cornell University, August 1988.

[47] Michael Stumm and Songnian Zhou. Algorithms Implementing Distributed Shared Memory. *IEEE Computer*, vol. 23(5), pages 54–64, May 1990.

[48] Eli Upfal and Avi Wigderson. How to Share Memory in a Distributed System. *Technical Report STAN-CS-84-1024*, Deptartment of Computer Science, Stanford University, October 1984.

[49] Francis Vaughan, Tracy Lo Basso, Alan Dearle, Chris Marlin, and Chris Barter. Casper: a Cached Architecture Supporting Persistence. *Computing Systems*, vol. 5(3), USENIX Association / University of California Press, Summer 1992.

[50] Kun-Lung Wu and W. Kent Fuchs. Recoverable Distributed Shared Virtual Memory. *IEEE Transactions on Computers*, vol. 39(4), April 1990.

[51] Wm. A. Wulf and Sally A. McKee. Hitting the Memory Wall: Implications of the Obvious. *Computer Architecture News*, vol. 23(1), March 1995.

[52] Matthew J. Zekauskas, Wayne A. Sawdon, and Brian N. Bershad. Software Write Detection for a Distributed Shared Memory. In *Proceedings of the 1st USENIX Symposium on Operating System Design and Implementation*, pages 87–100, November 1994.

[53] Songnian Zhou, Michael Stumm, and Tim McInerney. Extending Distributed Shared Memory to Heterogenous Environments. In *Proceedings of the 10th International Conference on Distributed Computing Systems*, May 1990.

Chapter 18

Parallel I/O for Clusters: Methodologies and Systems

Erich Schikuta and Heinz Stockinger

Institute for Applied Computer Science and Information Systems
Department of Data Engineering, University of Vienna
Rathausstr. 19/4, A-1010 Vienna, Austria

Email: *schiki@ifs.univie.ac.at, heinz@vipios.pri.univie.ac.at*

18.1 Introduction

Today the dramatic improvements in processor technology often do not satisfy the needs and requirements of supercomputer applications, due to an apparent new bottleneck, the I/O subsystem. This is based on the fact that, on the one hand, microprocessors increase their performance by 50% to 100% per year, and on the other hand, disks mostly increase their capacity, hardly their performance [11]. This problem is even more exaggerated by a new type of problems, which have to process huge data sets. These scientific applications (e.g., weather forecast, physics or chemical applications, seismic processing, image analysis) require 100s of GBytes of data per run at data rates of 100s of MBytes per second. Obviously, such amounts of data do not fit into main memories, but have to be stored on disk and retrieved during program execution. However, sufficient performance can be gained only if the process can access the data on disk efficiently. This is the place where smart parallel I/O algorithms are required. Conventional parallel filesystems do not support special I/O features to ensure a sufficient performance. High performance languages such as High Performance FORTRAN (HPF) are not designed to provide good performance when it comes to disk I/O. Hence, in high performance computing the applications shifted from being CPU-bound to be I/O bound. Performance cannot be scaled up by increasing the number of CPUs any more, but by increasing the bandwidth of the I/O subsystem. This situation is commonly known as the I/O bottleneck in high performance computing. The result was a strong research stimulus on parallel I/O topics in high performance computing. However, the focus was on massive parallel processor (MPP) systems, mainly neglecting workstation clusters.

In this chapter, we present an overview of parallel Input/Output I/O research on cluster computers. We start with a feasibility study for cluster-based parallel I/O systems followed by an introduction to the parallel I/O problem. We give a comprehensive survey of the available techniques and methods and describe available systems and their unique properties. Further, a categorization scheme based on these characteristics is presented, which eases the process of choosing the right system for a specific task. This survey is followed by the presentation of an actual developed system based on the presented methodology, the Vienna Parallel Input Output System (ViPIOS), a novel approach to enhance the I/O performance of high performance applications. It is a client-server based tool combining capabilities found in parallel I/O runtime libraries and parallel filesystems. The main design principles of the approach presented are based on data engineering know-how. Finally, we point out future trends and areas of research in this highly promising and developing area.

18.2 A Case for Cluster I/O Systems

We claim that the world's largest supercomputer today is not placed in some hidden specialized lab costing millions and serving only a few scientists, but is at our disposal in the form of a world-spanning network connecting countless affordable personal workstations. Together, these single systems provide huge resources for processing power, main memory, and disk capacity.

Besides its cumulative processing power, a cluster system also provides a large data storage capacity. Usually each workstation has at least one attached disk, which is accessible from the system. Using the network interconnection of the cluster, these disks can build a huge common storage medium.

An architectural framework similar to a cluster of computers can be found in state-of-the-art MPP systems allowing scalable and affordable I/O systems. Generally two different types of I/O systems for MPPs can be distinguished (for a good overview see [10]):

- external attached I/O subsystems
- internal I/O nodes

These two approaches are depicted by Figure 18.1.[1]

In the external case the I/O subsystem is connected with the MPP by a (or a number of) separate interconnection bus(es) (denoted by the broken line in the figure). Even by using costly techniques, such as specialized high-speed bus systems, as

[1]In the course of this discussion, we do not distinguish between shared and distributed memory systems. For the issue of the I/O system this differentiation is insignificant. In the figure, we show a distributed memory architecture only.

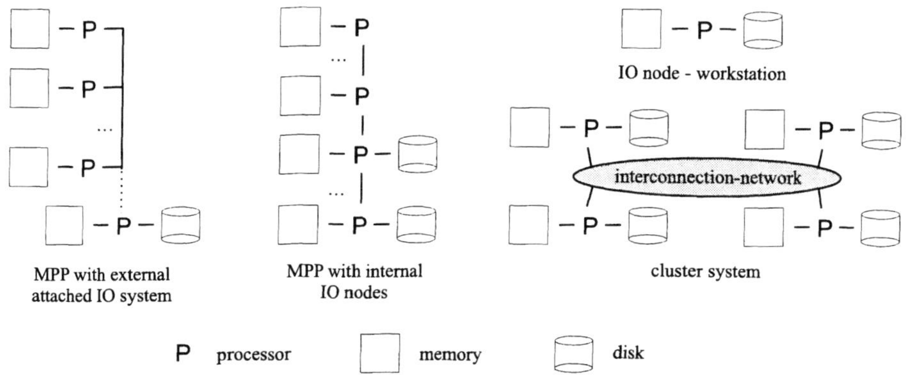

Figure 18.1 I/O architecture topologies.

HiPPI interfaces, this dedicated bus builds the I/O bottleneck of the system. However, the system administration and application development are relatively simple. Systems following this approach are the Intel hypercubes and the Cray C90.

Most of the modern MPP systems apply the approach using internal I/O nodes (e.g., Intel Paragon, Meiko CS-2, IBM SP2). An I/O node is generally a conventional processing node with a disk attached. Only the software (operating system, application program) distinguishes between I/O and computing node. In Figure 18.1, the workstation architecture is shown for comparison, consisting of a processor, memory and a disk. We also depict the situation of a cluster system, i.e., single workstations connected by an interconnection network. The similarity to the MPP I/O framework is apparent. We see that no architectural differences between a cluster and an MPP approach exist. Based on the workstation building block, it is straightforward to emulate any I/O architecture using a cluster. Basically, the describing components are the same as processors, memories and disks.

The differences to MPP I/O systems lie in the device characteristics. The most eminent drawback is the latency of the interconnection network. This is a severe problem for computational-bound applications on cluster systems. The bus is a major system bottleneck because of the increased load placed on it from network communication. However, research is on the way to overcome this problem by applying new bus technologies (Giganet, Myrinet) or by using multiple I/O buses in parallel.

For I/O intensive applications this problem is not as severe as it looks at first sight. It is shown [14] that with appropriate and affordable hardware support, the network bottleneck of cluster systems can be turned again into the known I/O bottleneck. Thus, the already developed methods and paradigms to overcome this I/O bottleneck on MPP systems can similarly be used on cluster systems. This leads to the conclusions that clusters are a suitable platform for I/O based applications.

Respectively, cluster systems for specific I/O tasks are in the development stage.

Examples are a serverless network filesystem based on NOW or a Bulk-Data Server to construct a secondary storage system using cheap EIDE disks applying Beowulf technology [14].

18.3 The Parallel I/O Problem

Galbreath et al. [6] grouped the I/O needs of typical supercomputing applications into 6 categories: input, debugging, scratch files, checkpoint/restart, output, and accessing out-of-core structures.

In the literature often only input, output and out-of-core (OOC) operations are handled as typical I/O issues. This derives from the scientific applications profile, where typically large data sets are read (e.g., weather forecast), written (e.g. CFD) or read/written (e.g., OOC handling of large matrices). This view is too limited because a number of I/O topics arise also in the area of pure calculation bound problems, as debugging, scratch files and checkpointing. Generally all tasks which transfer huge data sets between disk and main memory have to be targeted as a parallel I/O topic.

However, most of the parallel I/O needs of high performance computing are arising in Regular, Irregular and OOC problems.

18.3.1 Regular Problems

Most of the proposed parallel I/O approaches consider applications where data can be declustered at compile time of the application program, i.e., a kind of regular data in the form of a matrix is available. This approach is supported by the well-known Single-Program-Multiple-Data (SPMD) model, which is based on the following elements:

- Single threaded control - parallel execution: the statements to execute are defined by a single program, but executed simultaneously in parallel on (mainly) disjoint data sets.
- Global namespace: the programer must not care for the physical data distribution among the processor's physical memories.
- Loose synchronization: it is occasionally necessary for processors to synchronize, but they are not executing the same statement at the same time (no lockstep).

This model allows one to design a sequential program and to transfer it easily to parallel execution. This is supported by high performance programming languages, which basically extend the conventional language with data decomposition specifications providing a machine-independent data parallel programming model. The developed code is restructured into an SPMD program, basically consisting of a centralized host process and a number of identical node processes running on each node of the underlying hardware. This approach allows the programmer to develop the application within a sequential framework shifting the parallelization process to the parallelizing compiler. The compiler analyzes the source code, translating global data references as stated in the source program into local and non-local data references based on the data distributions specified by the user. The non-local references are resolved by inserting appropriate message-passing statements into the generated code. This approach is followed in HPF (High Performance FORTRAN), a machine-independent dialect of FORTRAN, which is established as the standard for high performance languages.

18.3.2 Irregular Problems

However, there also exist irregular problems where data access patterns cannot be predicted until runtime. This is an important consideration in parallel I/O research, since optimizations carried out occur in three different kinds:

- irregular control structures: These are conditional statements making it inefficient to run on synchronous programming models.
- irregular data structures: These are unbalanced trees or graphs.
- irregular communication patterns: These lead to non-determinism.

18.3.3 Out-of-Core Computation

In an Out-of-Core (OOC) computation, the primary data structures do not wholly fit into main memory and must, therefore, reside (partly) on disk. When OOC data is processed, it is loaded into main memory where the computation takes place, and afterwards it is stored back to disk (similar to demand paging in virtual memory systems). The computation is carried out in several phases, where in each phase part of the data is brought into main memory, processed and stored back onto secondary storage, if necessary.

18.4 File Abstraction

In a conventional system, the basic handle for accessing data on disk is sequential files. This model is equally applicable for parallel I/O operations. However, it must be adapted to support the notion of distributed stored information.

Conventionally, in most of the existing parallel I/O systems, this is realized by attributing a file with special access modes. Files can be accessed synchronized, which is supported by *collective* file operations, where all cooperating processes execute the operation at the same time. However, individual operations are supported as well. This leads to the following 4 execution modes for parallel file I/O [5], which can be found in one way or the other in most of the available systems:

- Broadcast - reduce: All processes access the same data collectively. For a read all processes get a copy of the read data; for a write the data (of one selected process) is written only once.
- Scatter - gather: All processes access collectively different parts of the file according to an underlying pattern. The parts can be of equal or different size.
- Shared offset: The processes share a common file handle but access the file individually. The access is therefore not synchronized and no pattern is defined for the order of processes' access operations.
- Independent: Each process has its own private file handle. The access pattern is totally the responsibility of the programmer.

Summing up, file pointers provide a data and problem independent view of the stored data.

In our opinion to allow full flexibility for the programmer and the administration methods, we must distinguish three independent layers in the file architecture, which can be realized in practice by different (types of) file handles:

- Problem layer. Defines the problem specific data distribution among the cooperating parallel processes.
- File layer. Provides a composed view of the persistently stored data in the system.
- Data layer. Defines the physical data distribution among the available disks.

These layers are separated conceptually from each other, providing mapping functions between these layers. *Logical data independence* exists between the problem and the file layer, and *physical data independence* exists between the file and data layer analogous to the notation in database systems.

This concept is depicted in Figure 18.2, showing a cyclic data distribution.

The data independent approach allows us to interpret commonly used programming paradigms used in high performance software development in terms of parallel I/O.

18.5 Methods and Techniques

Generally, all parallel I/O methods and techniques aim to accomplish the following:

- Maximize the use of available parallel I/O devices to increase the bandwidth.
- Minimize the number of disk read and write operations per device. It is advantageous to read the requested data in a few larger chunks instead of many small ones. This avoids disk specific latency time for moving the read/write arm and waiting for the positioning of the spinning disk.

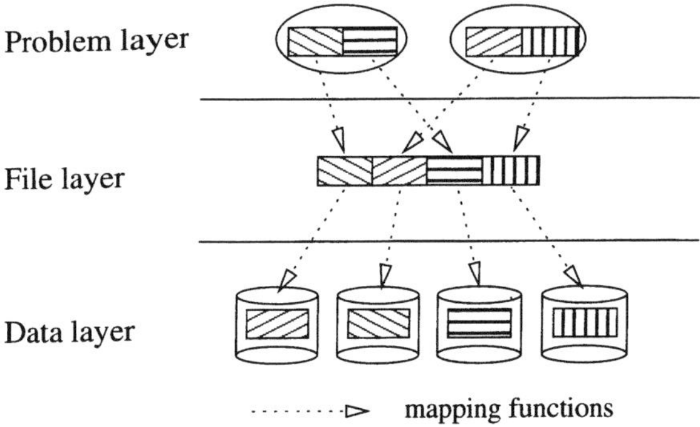

Figure 18.2 File abstraction.

- Minimize the number of I/O specific messages between processes to avoid unnecessary costly communication.
- Maximize the *hit ratio* (the ratio between accessed data to requested data), to avoid unnecessary data accesses. It is a common technique known as *data sieving* to read a large sequential block of the disk at once into main memory and then to extract smaller data blocks according to the application requests.

We distinguish three different groups of methods in the parallel I/O execution framework: application level, the I/O level, and access anticipation methods.

Application level methods try to organize the main memory objects mapping the disk space (e.g., buffer) to make disk accesses efficient. Therefore, these methods are also known as *buffering algorithms.* Commonly these methods are realized by runtime libraries, which are linked to the application programs. Thus, the application program performs the data accesses itself without the need for dedicated I/O server programs

Examples for this group are the Two-Phase method [2] (see Section 18.5.1), the Jovian framework [1], and the Extended Two-Phase method [16].

The *I/O level methods* try to reorganize the disk access requests of the application programs to achieve better performance. This is done by independent I/O node servers, which collect the requests and perform the accesses. Therefore, the disk requests (of the application) are separated from the disk accesses (of the I/O server). A typical representative of this group is the Disk-directed I/O method [8] (see Section 18.5.2).

Extending the I/O framework into the time dimension delivers a third group of parallel I/O methods: *access anticipation methods.* This group can be seen as an extension to data prefetching. These methods anticipate data access patterns which are drawn by hints from the code advance to its execution. Hints can be placed on purpose by the programmer into the code or can be delivered automatically by appropriate tools (e.g., compiler).

Examples for this group are informed prefetching [12], the PANDA project [3] or the Two-phase data administration (see Section 18.5.3), which is used by ViPIOS (see Section 18.7).

Now we will take a closer look at one representative of each group.

18.5.1 Two-Phase Method (TPM)

The Two-Phase Method [2] is a method for reading/writing in-core arrays from/to disk. The basic principle behind this method is based on the fact that I/O performance is better when processes make a small number of large (respective data size) requests instead of a large number of small ones. TPM splits the reading of an in-core array into main memory in two phases:

- In the first phase, the processes *read data* from disk.
- In the second phase, *data is redistributed among the processes* by using interprocess communication.

This results in high granularity data transfers and a use of the higher bandwidth of the interconnection network (for interprocess communication).

The simple TPM is suitable for in-core arrays, but it can be extended to the Extended Two-Phase Method (ETPM), where several I/O requests are combined into fewer larger requests in order to eliminate multiple disk accesses for the same data, thereby reducing contention for disks. Primarily, the ETPM assumes a collective I/O interface where all processes must call the ETPM read/write routine. Even if a process does not need any data, it has to participate in the collective operation. In such a case, it must request 0 bytes of data. The advantage of the collective operation is that the processes can cooperate to perform certain optimizations, especially when the same data is required by more processes. Note that collective I/O is a commonly used technique for increasing performance of a system (e.g., disk-directed I/O).

Thus, if each processor needs to read exactly the same section of the array, it will be read only once from the file and then broadcast to other processors over the interconnecting network. The algorithm for writing sections in OOC arrays is essentially the reverse of the algorithms described above.

18.5.2 Disk-Directed I/O

The disk-directed I/O technique [8] improves the performance of reading and writing large, regular data structures (see also irregular problems) such as a matrix distributed between memory and distributed disks.

In a traditional UNIX-like parallel filesystem, an individual processor makes a request to the filesystem for each piece of data, i.e., even if many processes request the same data, a file is read multiple times and the data is transmitted to each processor independently. Further, there exist interfaces that support collective I/O

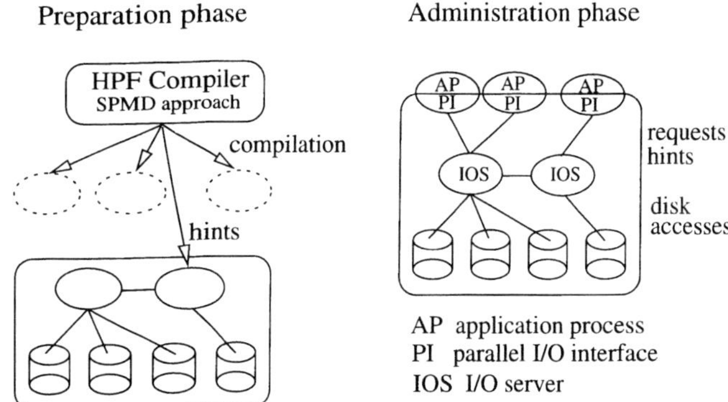

Figure 18.3 Two-phase data administration.

where all processes make a single joint request to the file system rather than many independent ones.

Disk-directed I/O is a technique for optimizing data transfer by a high-level interface. Here a high-level request is sent to an I/O node that examines the request, makes a list of disk blocks to be transferred, sorts the list and uses double-buffering and special remote-memory "get" and "put" messages to pipeline the transfer of data. The performance gain leads to a usage of less memory, less CPU and message passing overhead.

18.5.3 Two-Phase Data Administration

The Two-Phase Data Administration technique tries to anticipate data access patterns of the application program as early as possible in the program execution cycle and to use idle processor and disk time to adopt the data layout on disk accordingly.

Thus, the management of data is split into two distinct phases: the preparation phase and the administration phase (see Figure 18.3).

The *preparation phase* precedes the execution of the application processes (mostly during the startup time). This phase uses the information collected during the application program compilation process in the form of *hints* from the compiler. Based on this problem-specific knowledge, the physical data layout schemes are defined, and the actual server process for each application process and the disks for the stored data according to the locality principles are chosen. Further, the data storage areas are prepared, the necessary main memory buffers allocated, etc.

The following *administration phase* accomplishes the I/O requests of the application processes during their execution (i.e., the physical read/write operations) and performs necessary reorganization of the data layout.

The Two-Phase data administration method aims for putting all the data layout decisions, and data distribution operations into the preparation phase, in advance of the actual application execution. Thus, the administration phase performs the data accesses and possible data prefetching only.

Hints are the general tool to support the I/O subsystem with information for the data administration process. Hints are data and problem specific information from the "outside world" provided to the I/O subsystem, either by the application programmer or, in the context of a high performance language, by the compiler via the language interface.

Basically, three different types of hints can be distinguished: file administration, data prefetching, and administration hints.

The *file administration hints* provide information on the problem specific data distribution of the application processes (e.g., SPMD data distribution). These hints enforce the data locality principle. High parallelization can be reached if the problem specific data distribution of the application processes matches the physical data layout on disk.

Data prefetching hints yield better performance by pipelined parallelism (e.g., advance reads, delayed writes) and file alignment.

The *Administration hints* allow the configuration of the I/O subsystem according to the problem situation respective to the underlying hardware characteristics and their specific I/O needs (I/O nodes, disks, disk types, etc.)

18.6 Architectures and Systems

Now that we have stated the basic problem and sketched three basic techniques, we will discuss how different research teams address the I/O bottleneck problem.

In general, two different approaches can be distinguished: Parallel filesystems and runtime libraries for high performance languages.

Whereas parallel filesystems are a solution at a low level (the operating system is enhanced by special features that deal directly with I/O at the level of files), runtime libraries enhance conventional high performance languages such as Fortran or C/C++.

In the following section we will give a short survey of the characteristics of both approaches: runtime libraries and parallel filesystems. We will also present one specific example: MPI-IO.

The section concludes with a short statement on parallel database systems. Parallel database systems have a different focus from typical parallel I/O approaches, i.e., general purpose information systems versus specific problems in scientific computing. However, in order to cover all important topics of parallel I/O, we will give a short survey, at least.

18.6.1 Runtime Modules and Libraries

The aim of runtime libraries is to adapt graciously to the requirements of the problem characteristics specified in the application program. Moreover, they aim to be tools for the application programmer. The executing application can hardly react dynamically to changing system situations (e.g., number of available disks or processors) or problem characteristics (e.g., data reorganization) because the data decisions were made during the programming and not during the execution phase.

Another viewpoint that must be considered is the often-arising problem that the CPU of a node has to accomplish both the application processing and the I/O request of the application. Due to a missing I/O server, the application linked with the runtime library must perform the I/O requests as well. It is often very difficult for the programmer to exploit the inherent pipelined parallelism between pure processing and disk accesses by interleaving them.

All the problems can be limiting factors for the I/O bandwidth. Thus, optimal performance is nearly impossible to reach by the usage of runtime libraries.

More and more often the term *metacomputing* occurs, defining an aggregation of networked computing resources, in particular networks of workstations, to form a single logical parallel machine. It is supposed to offer a cost-effective alternative to massively parallel machines for many classes of parallel applications. I/O libraries in particular support this architecture and most libraries can either be implemented on massively parallel architectures or on clusters of workstations.

A detailed list of runtime libraries can be found in Table 18.1 (for a detailed comparison, see [15]).

Table 18.1 I/O Runtime Libraries

name	institution	sync/async	SPMD/SIMD/MIMD	strided access	data parallel	message passing	client-server	clustering	caching	prefetching	collective operations	shared file pointer	concurrency control	views	new ideas
ADIO	Dartmouth College	+ / +	+ / - / +	+	+	+	-	+	-	-	+	-	+	+	strategies for implementing APIs
CVL	Dartmouth College		/ + /												vector operations
DDLY	University of Malaga		/ + /			+					+				VDS, IDS
Jovian	University of Maryland	+ /	+ / /			+			+		+			+	global, distributed view
MPI-2	MPI Forum	+ / +	+ / + / +	+		+					+	+		+	I/O for MPI
MPI-IO	MPI-IO Committee	+ / +	+ / + / +			+					+	+		+	I/O for MPI
Multipol	University of California	+ / +								-					PD, distributed data structures
Panda	University of Illinois	+ / +	+ / - / -	+	-	+	+		+		+	-	+	-	server-directed I/O, chunking
PASSION	University of Syracuse	+ /	+ / /		+	+			+	+	+				TPM, irregular problems
ROMIO	Darmouth College	+/ +	+ / - / +	+	+	+	+	-	-	-	+	-	+	+	portable implementation of MPI-IO
TPIE	Duke Uni., Uni. of Delware														
ViPIOS	University of Vienna	+ / +	+ / + /	+	+	+	+	+	+	+	+	+		+	influence from DB technology

Annotation: + ... "is supported"

- ... "is not supported"

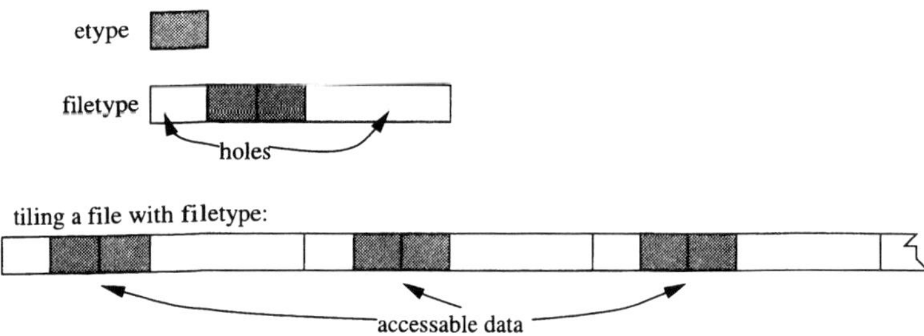

Figure 18.4 Tiling a file using a filetype.

18.6.2 MPI-IO

MPI-IO [9] was designed as a standard parallel I/O interface based on the MPI message passing framework. Despite the development of MPI as a form of interprocess communication, the I/O problem has not been solved there. (Note: MPI-2 already includes I/O features.) The main idea is that I/O can also be modeled as message passing. Writing to a file is like sending a message, while reading from a file corresponds to receiving a message. MPI-IO supports a high-level interface in order to support the partitioning of files among multiple processes, transfers of global data structures between process memories and files, and optimizations of physical file layout on storage devices.

The goal of MPI-IO is to provide a standard for describing parallel I/O operations within an MPI message passing application. MPI-IO provides three different access functions, including positioning, synchronization, and coordination. Positioning is accomplished by explicit offsets, individual file pointers, and shared file pointers. As for synchronization, MPI-IO provides both synchronous and asynchronous (blocking, nonblocking, respectively) versions. Moreover, MPI-IO supports collective as well as independent operations.

MPI-IO provides two different header files and, hence, can be used in the C and in the Fortran programming languages.

MPI-IO should be as MPI friendly as possible. As in MPI, a file access can be independent or collective. What is more, MPI derived data types are used for the data layout in files and for accessing shared files. The usage of derived data types can leave holes in the file, and a process can access only data that falls under holes (see Figure 18.4). Thus, files can be distributed among parallel processes in disjoint chunks.

Since MPI-IO is intended as an interface that maps between data stored in memory and a file, it basically specifies how the data should be laid out in a virtual file structure rather than how the file structure is stored on disk. Another feature is that MPI-IO is supposed to be interrupt and thread safe.

Implementations of MPI-IO exist as:

- PMPIO - Portable MPI I/O library developed by NASA Ames Research Center,

- ROMIO - A high performance, portable MPI-IO implementation developed by Argonne National Laboratory,
- MPI-IO/PIOFS - Developed by IBM Watson Research Center, and
- HPSS Implementation - Developed by Lawrence Livermore National Laboratory as part of its Parallel I/O Project.

Notable is the inclusion of ROMIO as MPI-IO extension into the widely distributed, portable MPI implementation MPICH.

18.6.3 Parallel File Systems

All important manufacturers of parallel high performance computer systems provide parallel disk access via a (mostly proprietary) parallel filesystem interface. They try to balance the parallel processing capabilities of their processor architectures with the I/O capabilities of a parallel I/O subsystem.

Compared to runtime libraries, parallel filesystems have the advantage that they execute independently from their application. Thus, the notation of dedicated I/O servers (I/O nodes) is directly supported, and the processing node can concentrate on the application program and is not burdened by the I/O requests.

There are also other fields where parallel filesystems appear to be advantageous:

- debugging
- tracing
- checkpointing

However, due to their proprietary status, parallel filesystems do not support the capabilities (expressive power) of the available high performance languages directly. They provide a limited disk access functionality to the application. In most cases, the application programmer is confronted with a black box sub-system. Many systems even disallow the programmer to coordinate the disk access according to the distribution profile of the problem specification. This makes the optimal mapping of logical problem distribution to the physical layout difficult or even impossible and prohibits an optimized disk access.

A detailed list of filesystems can be found in Table 18.2 (for a detailed comparison see [15]).

18.6.4 Parallel Database Systems

In the last few years, parallel database systems have gained an important role in database research. This was linked to the shift from the (actually failed) development of highly specialized database machines to the usage of conventional parallel hardware architectures. Most database research focused on specialized hardware,

Table 18.2 Parallel File Systems

name	institution	memory model	sync/async	SPMD/SIMD/MIMD	strided access	data parallel	message passing	client-server	clustering	caching	prefetching	collective operations	shared file pointer	concurrency control	views	new ideas
CCFS	University of Madrid	D	+/+	-/-/+		-	+	+	+	+	+	-	+	+	+	IBL, group operations, automatic preallocation of resources
CFS	Intel	D	+/												+	four I/O modes
ELFS	University of Virginia	D								+	+					OO, ease-of-use
Galley	Dartmouth College	D	+/+	+/-/+	+	-	+	+	+	+	-	-	-	-	-	3d structure of a file
HFS	University of Toronto	S							+							hierarchical clustering, ASF, storage objects
HiDIOS	Australian Nat. Uni.	S					+			+						disk level parallelism
OSF/1	Intel	D														
ParFiSys	University of Madrid	D	+/+	-/-/+	-	+	+	+	+	+	+	-	+	+	+	IBL, group operations, automatic preallocation of resources
PFS	Intel	D														I/O in parallel whereever possible
PFSLib	IBM	D		+/-/-	+		+	+	+	+		+	+	+		
PIOFS	Intel	D													+	
PIOUS	Emory University	D	+/+	+/+/+	-	+	+	+	+	-	+	+	+	+		I/O for metacomputing environment
PPFS	University of Illinois	D	+/+		+		+	+	+	+	+					
SPFS	Carnegie Mellon Uni.	S														
SPIFFI	Uni. of Wisconsin	D	+/								+	+	+			three types of threads
Vesta	IBM	D	+/+	/ / +			+	+			+	+	-	+	+	

Annotation: + ... "is implemented"
- ... "is not implemented"
D ... distributed memory
S ... shared memory

\+ + + + - + + + +

such as CCD, bubble memories, head-per-track disks or optical disks. None of these technologies fulfilled the expectations. Today the general opinion is that conventional CPU's, memory and disks will dominate the future of data-intensive parallel processing.

The development of parallel database systems was linked to the spread of the relational model as the common user interface. Relational queries are well-suited for parallel execution, since orthogonal operations are applied to uniform streams of data, resulting in a pipelined execution pattern. Generally, two different types of parallelism can be distinguished: inter-operator and intra-operator parallelism. Inter-operator parallelism is the type of parallelism resulting from the independent, but simultaneous, execution of different operators of the query execution tree. A special form is pipelined parallelism, produced by streaming the output of one operator into the input of another operator, so that both operators can work in series. Another form of parallelism can be achieved by partitioning the input data stream of one operator to a number of parallel query processes, all performing the same operation. Each process is executing the same operation on a different part of the data. This is called intra-operator parallelism.

Partitioning a data set involves distributing its records over several disks. Only simple partitioning strategies are applied in parallel database systems, such as round-robin, range, and hash partitioning. These are schemes independent of the problem distribution of the requested query execution plan. Redistribution of data sets is hardly supported, only temporarily for specialized operations, such as some forms of join operators.

18.7 The ViPIOS Approach

In the remainder of this chapter we will present the ViPIOS approach of the University of Vienna [13]. ViPIOS stands out from the other approaches because it represents a fully-fledged parallel I/O runtime system. It is available both as runtime library and as I/O server configuration; it can serve as I/O module for high performance languages (e.g., HPF) and supports the standardized MPI-IO interface. To make it even more appropriate in the context of this chapter, it was developed by focusing on workstation cluster systems.

In addressing parallel I/O for high performance languages, two issues must be addressed: *static fit property* and *dynamic fit property.*

The static fit property tries to adapt the disk access profile of the program according to the necessities of the problem specification or the programming paradigm (as the Single Program Multiple Data approach). This can be realized by the programmer or the compiler. For example, a specific SPMD distribution of the application resembles a corresponding data layout on disks.

The dynamic fit property denotes the adaptability of the I/O runtime subsystem to application's and/or environment's characteristics which could not be foreseen at compile time.

18.7.1 Design Principles

We see a solution to this problem in a combination of both approaches, which is a dedicated, smart, concurrent executing runtime system, gathering all available information on the application process both during the compilation process and the runtime execution. Initially, it can provide the optimal fitting data access profile for the application and may then react to the execution behavior dynamically, allowing optimal performance by aiming for maximum I/O bandwidth.

ViPIOS is an I/O runtime system which provides efficient access to persistent files by optimizing the data layout on the disks and allowing parallel read/write operations. ViPIOS is targeted as a supporting I/O module for high performance languages (e.g., HPF).

The design of ViPIOS followed a data engineering approach, characterized by the following design principles:

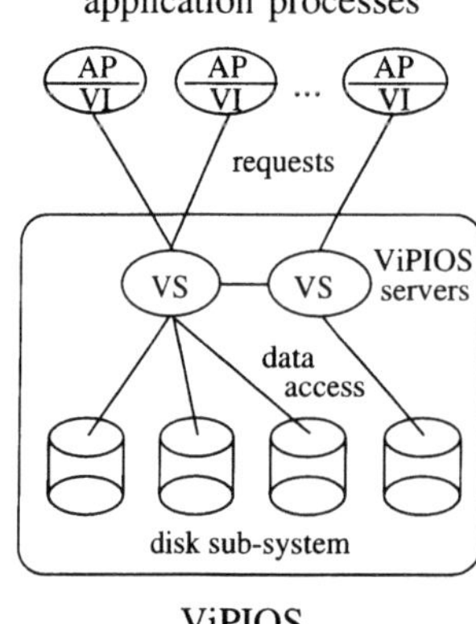

Figure 18.5 ViPIOS system architecture.

1. Scalability. The *system architecture* (Section 18.7.2) of ViPIOS is highly distributed and decentralized. This leads to the advantage that the provided I/O bandwidth of ViPIOS is mainly dependent on the available I/O nodes of the underlying architecture only.

2. Efficiency. The aim of compile time and runtime optimization is to minimize the number of disk accesses for file I/O. This is achieved by a suitable *data organization* (Section 18.7.3) by providing a transparent view of the stored data on disk to the "outside world" and by organizing the data layout on disks respective to the static application problem description and the dynamic runtime requirements.

3. Parallelism. All file data and meta-data (description of files) are stored in a distributed and parallel form across multiple I/O devices. The user and the compilation system have the ability to influence the distribution of the file data (in the form of hints). This allows the system to perform various forms of efficient and parallel *data access modes* (Section 18.7.3).

18.7.2 System Architecture

The basic idea to solve the I/O bottleneck in ViPIOS is *de-coupling*. The disk accesses operations are de-coupled from the application and performed by an independent I/O subsystem, ViPIOS, so that an application just sends disk requests to ViPIOS only, which performs the actual disk accesses in turn.

Thus, ViPIOS system architecture is built upon a set of cooperating server processes, which accomplish the requests of the application client processes. Each application process AP is linked by the ViPIOS interface VI to the ViPIOS servers VS (see Figure 18.5).

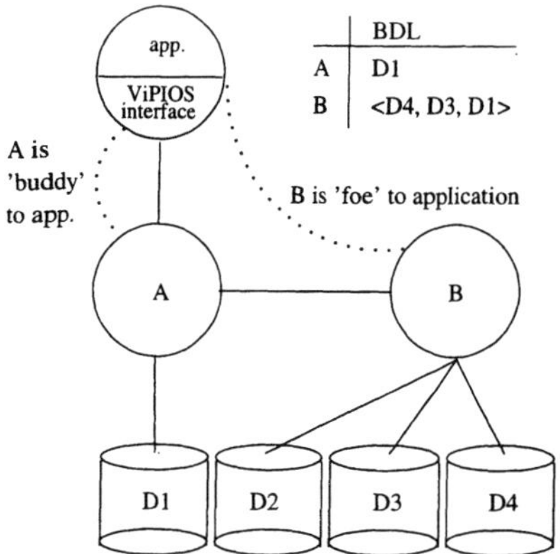

Figure 18.6 "Buddy" and "Foe" servers.

The server processes run independently on all or a number of dedicated processing nodes on the underlying MPP. It is also possible that an application client and a server share the same processor.

Generally, each application process is assigned exactly one ViPIOS server, but one ViPIOS server can serve a number of application processes, i.e., there exists a one-to-many relationship between the application and the servers.

Data Locality.

The main design principle of the ViPIOS to achieve high data access performance is *data locality*. This means that the data requested by an application process should be read/written from/to the best-suited disk.

We distinguish between logical and physical data locality as follows:

Logical data locality. This principle denotes to choose the best-suited ViPIOS server for an application process. This server is defined by the topological distance and/or the process characteristics.

Physical data locality. It aims to determine the disk set providing the best (mostly the fastest) data access.

ViPIOS Server.

A ViPIOS server process consists of several functional units as depicted by Figure 18.7.

Basically, we differentiate between 3 layers:

- interface layer
- kernel layer
- disk manager layer

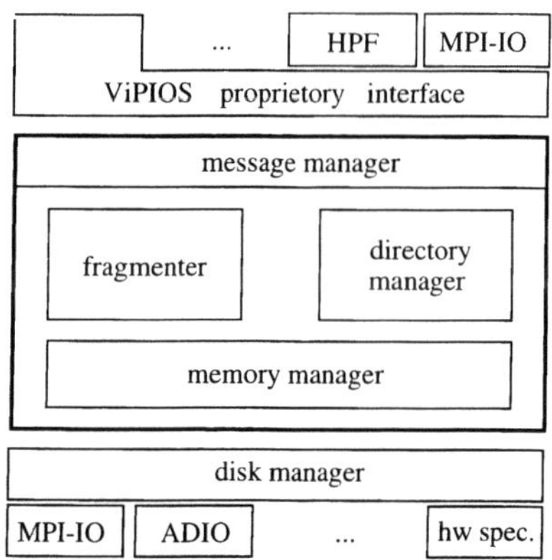

Figure 18.7 ViPIOS server architecture.

Interface Layer. The *interface layer* provides the connection to the outside world (i.e., applications, programmers, compilers, etc.). Different interfaces are supported by *interface modules* to allow flexibility and extendibility. Until now, we implemented an HPF interface module (aiming for the VFC, the HPF derivative of Vienna Fortran), a (basic) MPI-IO interface module, and the specific ViPIOS interface which is also the interface for the specialized modules.

Kernel Layer. The *kernel layer* is responsible for all server specific tasks. The ViPIOS kernel layer is built of four cooperating functional units:

- The *message manager* is responsible for communication externally (to the applications) and internally (to other ViPIOS servers). The message-passing module constitutes the interface to the application processes and to other ViPIOS servers. Currently, this module uses MPI calls for communication, but a PVM version is also available. Requests are issued by an application via a call to one of the functions of the ViPIOS interface, which in turn translates this call into a request message which is sent to the buddy server.

- The *fragmenter* can be seen as "ViPIOS' brain." It represents a smart data administration tool, which models different distribution strategies and makes decisions on the effective data layout, administration, and ViPIOS actions. The request fragmenter uses the directory information to split an external request (i.e., an I/O request issued by an application process via its ViPIOS interface) into several parts, which are to be processed by different servers. First, the part of the request which can be resolved locally (according to the local directory information[2]) is extracted and sent to the I/O subsystem. Secondly, if global directory information is available, the request parts for

[2]The *local directory* of the buddy server holds all the information necessary to map a client's request to the physical files on the disks.

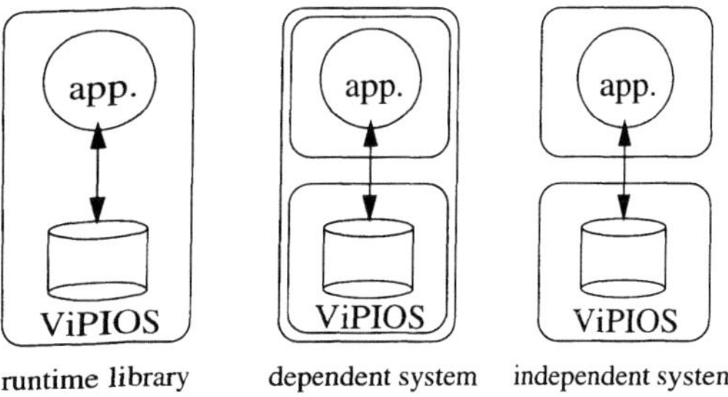

Figure 18.8 ViPIOS system modes.

specific servers are calculated and sent to them directly via an internal direct message. Thirdly, if parts of the request are still remaining, they are broadcast to all the ViPIOS servers by an internal broadcast.

- The *directory manager* stores the meta information of the data. We designed 3 different modes of operation: centralized (one dedicated ViPIOS directory server), replicated (all servers store the whole directory information), and localized (each server knows the directory information of the data it is storing only) management. Until now, only localized management is implemented. The local directory holds all the information of the files that are located on disks managed by this specific ViPIOS server. An optional global directory may be available to some or all of the servers. It can be used to directly send foe requests to the appropriate server process as described below. Clearly, a global directory imposes additional overhead to the system because it has to reflect all the updates on different servers. Nevertheless, on some systems this may well pay and improve the overall system throughput, especially when sending of messages is slow (e.g., via Internet connections) and/or write operations (and thus updates of the global dictionary) are rare.

- The *memory manager* is responsible for prefetching, caching and buffer management.

Disk Manager Layer. The *disk manager layer* provides the access to the available and supported disk sub-systems. Also, this layer is modularized to allow extensibility and to simplify the porting of the system. At the moment ADIO, MPI-IO, and Unix style filesystems are supported.

System Modes.

ViPIOS can be used in 3 different system modes, as runtime library, dependent system, or independent system. These modes are depicted by Figure 18.8.

Runtime Library. Application programs can be linked with a ViPIOS runtime module, which performs all disk I/O requests of the program. In this case, ViPIOS is not running on independent servers, but as part of the application. The ViPIOS interface is therefore not only calling the requested data action, but also performing it itself. This mode provides only restricted functionality due to the missing independent I/O system. Parallelism can be expressed only by the application (i.e., the programmer).

Dependent System. In this case, ViPIOS is running as an independent module in parallel to the application, but is started together with the application. This is inflicted by the MPI[3] specific characteristic that cooperating processes have to be started together in the same communication world. Processes of different worlds cannot communicate until now. This mode allows smart parallel data administration but objects the Two-Phase-Administration Phase by a missing preparation phase.

Independent System. This is the mode of choice to achieve highest possible I/O bandwidth by exploiting all available data administration possibilities. In this case, ViPIOS is running similar to a parallel filesystem or a database server waiting for application to connect via the ViPIOS interface. This connection is realized by a proprietary communication layer bypassing MPI. We implemented two different approaches, one by using PVM, the other by patching MPI. A third promising approach has just been evaluated by employing PVMPI, a possibly uprising standard under development for coupling MPI worlds by PVM layers.

18.7.3 Data Administration

The data administration in ViPIOS is guided by two principles:

- Two-phase data administration
- Data access modes

Data Access Modes.

One of the main design principles of the ViPIOS is the parallel execution of disk accesses. In the following we present the supported disk access types.

According to the SPMD programming paradigms, parallelism is expressed by the data distribution scheme of the HPF language in the application program. Basically, ViPIOS must therefore direct the application process's data access requests to independent ViPIOS servers only in order to provide parallel disk accesses. However, a single SPMD process is performing its accesses sequentially, sending its requests to just one server. Depending on the location of the requested data on the disks in the ViPIOS system, we differentiate two access modes:

- Local data access
- Remote data access

[3]The MPI standard is the underlying message-passing tool of ViPIOS to ensure portability.

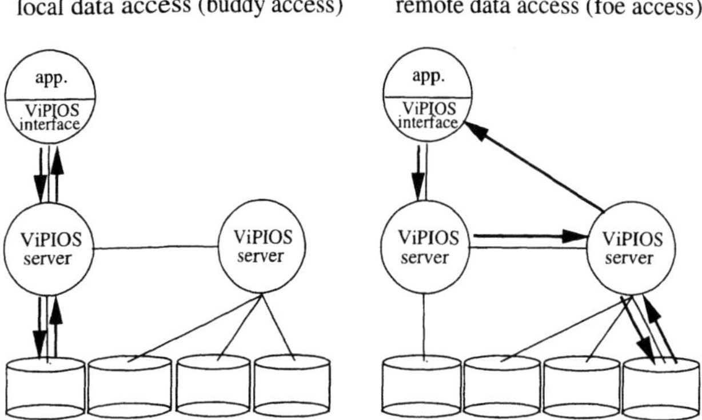

Figure 18.9 Local versus remote data access.

Local Data Access. Local data access describes the case where the buddy server can resolve the applications requests on its own disks (the disks of its BDL). We call it also *buddy access*.

Remote Data Access. Remote data access denotes the access scheme where the buddy server cannot resolve the request on its disks and must broadcast the request to the other ViPIOS servers to find the owner of the data. The respective server (foe server) accesses the requested data and sends it directly to the application via the network. We call this access also *foe access* (see Figure 18.9).

Intuitively, a remote access should be slower than a local access because of the additional broadcast message. Conclusively, for optimal performance, one should therefore aim to maximize the local accesses and to minimize the remote accesses. The performance analysis will clear up this assumption.

Based on these access types, three disk access modes can be distinguished in ViPIOS, which we call

- Sequential
- Parallel
- Coordinated mode

Sequential Mode. The sequential mode of operation allows a single application process to send a sequential read/write operation, which is processed by a single ViPIOS server in sequential manner. The read/write operation consists commonly of processing a number of data blocks, which are placed on one or a number of disks administered by the server itself (disks belonging to the best-disk-list of the server).

Parallel Mode. In the parallel mode the application process requests a single read/write operation. The ViPIOS processes the sequential process in parallel by

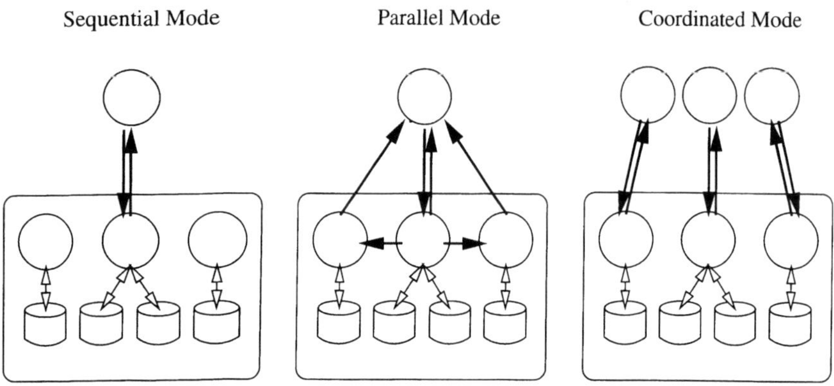

Figure 18.10 Disk access modes.

splitting the operation into independent sub-operations and distributing them onto available ViPIOS server processes.

This can both be the accessing of contiguous memory areas (sub-files) by independent servers in parallel and the distribution of a file onto a number of disks administered by the server itself and/or other servers.

Coordinated Mode. The coordinated mode is realized by the SPMD approach directly by the support of collective operations. A read/write operation is requested by a number of application processes collectively. In fact, each application process is requesting a single sub-operation of the original collective operation. These sub-operations are processed by ViPIOS servers sequentially, which in turn results in a parallel execution mode automatically.

It is also possible that the sequential server operations are processed in parallel by parallelization by the server itself (distributing it to other servers). The three modes are shown in Figure 18.10.

18.8 Conclusions and Future Trends

We presented an overview of parallel I/O focusing on cluster systems. We sketched the parallel I/O problem and gave a justification for the use of cluster systems, which provide a promising basis for a solution. We described the most common parallel I/O methods and techniques and gave an introduction of available architectures and systems. We finished the chapter with a closer look into one existing system, ViPIOS.

The needs for the storage of huge data sets is apparent, which is shown by the doubling in sales of storage systems each year. The need for support of fast and efficient access of this data is even more urgent, due to the ascendance of totally new application domains, as in the area of multimedia, knowledge engineering, and large-scale scientific computing.

We believe that cluster systems are the supercomputers of tomorrow. A workstation CPU can match the processing power of any single processor of a modern MPP. However, the weakness of a cluster system lies in its interconnection network and the software support for parallel computation. These are the two main areas for development in the near future.

Better interconnection networks are on the way (Giganet or its derivatives). The same is true for software support, as laid out in this chapter.

The final aim must be to free the application programmer from all parallel I/O specific considerations in his software development process. Programming of parallel I/O applications must be as simple as sequential ones. MPI-IO as a parallel I/O standard is too complex for the programmer. New techniques must be developed which will free the programmer from specifying parallel I/O specific calls. A solution lies in following a similar approach as in the SPMD programming by shifting the parallelization process to high performance compilers.

However, we showed only a few possibilities for future development. Further strategic directions in storage I/O issues can be found in [7] or [4].

In summary, it is easy to predict that the parallel I/O topic will remain an exciting and prospering area of research in the near future.

Acknowledgments

This work was carried out as part of the research project, "Language, Compiler, and Advanced Data Structure Support for Parallel I/O Operations," supported by the Austrian Science Foundation (FWF Grant P11006-MAT).

On this occasion we would like to thank Thomas Fuerle and Helmut Wanek, who have been the major contributors to the development of ViPIOS, and also Oliver Jorns, Christoph Loeffelhart, and Kurt Stockinger, who contributed their work on their theses, which resembled in various modules of ViPIOS, and Peter Brezany and Minh Dang, who always established a fruitful basis for cooperation with their research group headed by Prof. Hans Zima. Finally, we thank Toni Cortes for his valuable comments on our chapter.

18.9 Bibliography

[1] Robert Bennett, Kelvin Bryant, Alan Sussman, Raja Das, and Joel Saltz. Jovian: A Framework for Optimizing Parallel I/O. In *Scalable Parallel Libraries Conference*, IEEE Computer Society Press, MS, October 1994.

[2] Rajesh Bordawekar, Juan Miguel del Rosario, and Alok Choudhary. Design and Evaluation of Primitives for Parallel I/O. In *Supercomputing '93*, IEEE Computer Society Press, pages 452–461, Portland, OR, 1993.

[3] Y. Chen, M. Winslett, S. Kuo, Y. Cho, M. Subramaniam, and K. E. Seamons. Performance Modeling for the Panda Array I/O Library. In *Supercomputing '96*, ACM Press and IEEE Computer Society Press, November 1996.

[4] Alok Choudhary and David Kotz. Large-Scale File Systems with the Flexibility of Databases. *ACM Computing Surveys*, vol. 28A(4), December 1996.

[5] Dror G. Feitelson, Peter F. Corbett, Yarson Hsu, and Jean-Pierre Prost. Parallel I/O Systems and Interfaces for Parallel Computers. In *Topics in Modern Operating Systems*, IEEE Computer Society Press, 1997.

[6] N. Galbreath, W. Gropp, and D. Levine. Applications-Driven Parallel I/O. In *Supercomputing '93*, IEEE Computer Society Press, Portland, Oregon, 1993.

[7] G. A. Gibson, J. S. Vitter, and J. Wilkes. Strategic Directions in Storage I/O Issues in Large-Scale Computing. *ACM Computing Surveys*, vol. 28(4), December 1996.

[8] David Kotz. Disk-Directed I/O for MIMD Multiprocessors. *ACM Transactions on Computer Systems*, vol. 15(1), February 1997.

[9] MPI-IO: A Parallel File I/O Interface for MPI. The MPI-IO Committee, April 1996.

[10] Bill Nitzberg and Samuel A. Fineberg. Parallel I/O on Highly Parallel Systems—Supercomputing '95 Tutorial M6 Notes. *Technical Report NAS-95-022*, NASA Ames Research Center, December 1995.

[11] D. A. Patterson and K. L. Hennessy. *Computer Architecture: A Quantitative Approach.* Morgan Kaufmann Publishers Inc., 1990.

[12] R. H. Patterson, G. A. Gibson, E. Ginting, D. Stodolsky, and J. Zelenka. Informed Prefetching and Caching. In *Fifteenth ACM Symposium on Operating Systems Principles*, ACM Press, pages 79–95, CO, December 1995.

[13] Erich Schikuta, Thomas Fuerle, and Helmut Wanek. ViPIOS: The Vienna Parallel Input/Output System. In *Euro-Par'98*, Southampton, England, Springer-Verlag, September 1998.

[14] Thomas Sterling, Donald J. Becker, Daniel Savarese, Michael R. Berry, and Chance Res. Achieving a Balanced Low-cost Architecture for Mass Storage Management Through Multiple Fast Ethernet Channels on the Beowulf Parallel Workstation. In *International Parallel Processing Symposium*, 1996.

[15] Heinz Stockinger. Classification of Parallel Input/Output Products. In *Parallel And Distributed Processing Techniques and Applications Conference*, July 1998.

[16] R. Thakur and A. Choudhary. An Extended Two-Phase Method for Accessing Sections of Out-of-Core Arrays. *Scientific Programming*, vol. 5(4), 1996.

Chapter 19

Software RAID and Parallel Filesystems

TONI CORTES

Departament d'Arquitectura de Computadors
Universitat Politècnica de Catalunya
Barcelona, Spain

Email: *toni@ac.upc.es*

19.1 Introduction

19.1.1 I/O Problems

One of the main advantages of cluster of workstations is the great amount of resources available in the system (disks, memory, tape units, etc.). Traditionally, these large number of resources were not accessible from all the nodes in the network. Only the processes running on the node that had a given resource attached were able to use it. And, if there was a way to access those remote resources, the steps that had to be done were neither simple nor transparent. For example, the mechanism used to access files kept in a remote disk was to `ftp` the files needed into the local disk. In a cluster of workstations, these resources have to be accessible from any node in a friendly way. Actually, it would be ideal to be able to share all these resources in a transparent way to the applications. Users should have the feeling that a single system was built using the whole cluster of workstations and their resources, much as in a parallel machine. Following this approach, the ideal design of a filesystem for clusters of workstations should be able to use all the disks and caching memory in a transparent way to the user.

As these cluster of workstations end up being very similar to parallel machines, the same kind of applications can be run on them. The problem we find when executing these applications is that they usually need a high performance I/O system. These applications work with very large data sets, which cannot be kept in memory. They expect a fast filesystem that is able to write and read this data very rapidly.

Finally, when parallel applications are run on the cluster of workstations, the I/O system should allow cooperative operations. All running units in an application may want to access files in a coordinated way, and this coordination should be offered by the I/O system.

Summarizing, we need to design high performance filesystems that simplify the cooperation between processes. Furthermore, they should be able to use all the resources efficiently and in a transparent way.

19.1.2 Using Clusters to Increase the I/O Performance

If a high performance filesystem is to be achieved, we first need to examine the characteristics a cluster of workstations has and the way we should use them to build better filesystems.

The first advantage, and the most obvious one, is the great quantity of resources available in a cluster of workstations. These systems have many disks that can be used in parallel to increase the disk bandwidth. We can also use the large amounts of memory to build big filesystem caches to decouple the performance of the disks from the performance of the filesystem.

The second advantage found in this kind of environments is the high-speed interconnection network that connects all the nodes. Such fast networks allow the system to relay on remote nodes to perform many tasks. We can now use the memory of a remote node to keep the cache blocks that do not fit in the local cache. We can also request other nodes to gather all the I/O requests to build larger ones.

Finally, clusters of workstations are getting closer to parallel machines every day. This means that most of the lessons learned in the design of I/O systems for parallel machines can also be applied in this new environment.

In this chapter, we will present the way these characteristics have been used to increase the filesystem performance in clusters of workstations. We also present some examples designed for parallel machines, as we believe the assumptions made in their design can also be assumed in clusters of workstations.

19.2 Physical Placement of Data

As we have already seen, designing a filesystem for a cluster of workstations presents a couple of problems. The first one is the visibility problem. On one hand, we have many disks scattered among the nodes, and on the other hand, we want to be able to use them from any node in the cluster. In this section, we will present the mechanisms used to achieve this goal.

The second problem consists of achieving a high performance I/O system. In this section, we will also present solutions to the I/O performance problem from the disk point-of-view. The first thing of which we must be aware is that disks are mainly built of mechanical components that slow down the most common operations (head movement, disk rotation, etc.). Furthermore, the performance of these mechanical parts is not expected to keep pace with the rest of electronic components found in the system. For this reason, the only solution left to increase the disk performance at this level consists of placing the data in such a way that the mechanical parts have as little effect as possible on the global disk performance. In this section, we will address different ways of placing data on the disk (or disks) to increase the performance of the I/O subsystem. Some of the solutions presented here are especially targeted to parallel/distributed systems, while others were already used in traditional mono-processor systems but are frequently used in I/O subsystems for clusters of workstations.

19.2.1 Increasing the Visibility of the Filesystems

The first problem found in a cluster of workstations is that while many disks are available, only the ones attached to the node where a process is running are visible to that process. This small visibility of the filesystems should be solved if a good usage of the resources is to be achieved. To solve this problem, many distributed systems such as Sun NFS (Network File System), CODA (COnstant Data Availability), Sprite filesystem, etc., have used the mount concept of Unix to increase the visibility of the system.

Mounting Remote Filesystems

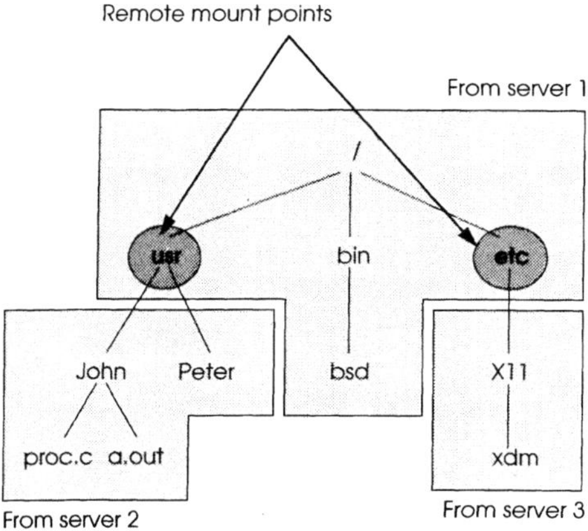

Figure 19.1 Directory tree build mixing remote and local filesystems.

The idea used in all these systems consists of managing remote filesystems as if they were local. The system administrator can mount a remote filesystem on any directory already accessible in the system structure (Figure 19.1). Whenever the requested data is stored in a remote node, the petition is forwarded to the node that owns the filesystem. This remote system performs the operation and sends the results to the requesting node. All these operations are done in a transparent way to the user, which has the impression of a single filesystem.

Two approaches can be used to maintain the remote-mount information. The first possibility consists of maintaining the mount information at clients, in which case each client has to individually mount every required filesystem. This approach is employed in the Sun NFS. Since each client can mount the filesystems in a different way, each client will not necessarily see an identical global filesystem structure. The second possibility is to maintain the mount information at servers. In this case, each client sees an identical global filesystem structure. A similar approach was used in the Sprite filesystem.

To improve the performance of this mechanism, caching is commonly used. However, caching optimizations will be described in Section 19.3.

Name Resolution

In any of the above-mentioned systems where a directory tree is built by combining local and remote filesystems, the name-resolution problem appears. This consists of locating a file or directory given its name. As it usually happens in computer science, there are two approaches to this problem: the centralized and the distributed one.

In a centralized name-resolution scheme, one node is responsible for maintaining the mapping table. Every time a file, or directory, is created, this server is informed and it records the physical location of this new object. Whenever a given application wants to access a file or directory, the system requests the location of the object to this centralized name server. Once the system knows the owner of the file, it contacts this node and accesses the requested data. The main problem with this approach is that a failure in the node that maintains the mapping information results in a failure of the whole filesystem. This happens because there is no way to find the physical location of any given object. It is also important to notice that this centralized server might become a bottleneck in large systems, thus decreasing the system performance.

In the distributed version, we also find two different ways to achieve this name resolution depending on whether each system builds its own name space (Sun NFS) or there is a unique global structure.

In the first case, each system knows the filesystems that have been mounted and the node that holds them. Each independent system has enough information to locate any given file or directory. The problem with this approach is that it is not very location-independent. If a disk is moved to a different node, all nodes have to re-mount this portion of their directory tree.

The second approach is used when there is a single name space for all the workstations. In this case, the directory tree is divided into domains and each name server is responsible for one of these domains. This does not mean that the node running the server responsible for a domain also has the data in that domain (although it could happen). It only means that this name server will know which node has the data in its disks. Let us see how this mechanism works by using an example. If a given application wants to access the file `/dir1/dir2/dir3/file2` in a system with the domains shown in Figure 19.2, a few steps will be done to locate the correct name server. The system will first contact the name server 1, as it is responsible for the `root` directory. This server will parse the name until it finds a file or directory that is not in its domain. In our case, it will parse `/dir1/dir2`. Once it gets to a portion that cannot resolve by itself, it forwards the rest of the request to the server responsible for the next step in the requested path (name server 2). This new server will know about `dir3` but not about the last part of the path, which means that it will forward the request once more. Finally, name server 3 knows the physical location of `file2` and returns this information to the client, which will contact the owner of the file to get the data. To increase the performance of this name resolution, the system may keep a cache of which nodes have the most popular files or directories. As we can see, this approach is more location-independent because only one name server has to be informed when a disk is moved to a different node.

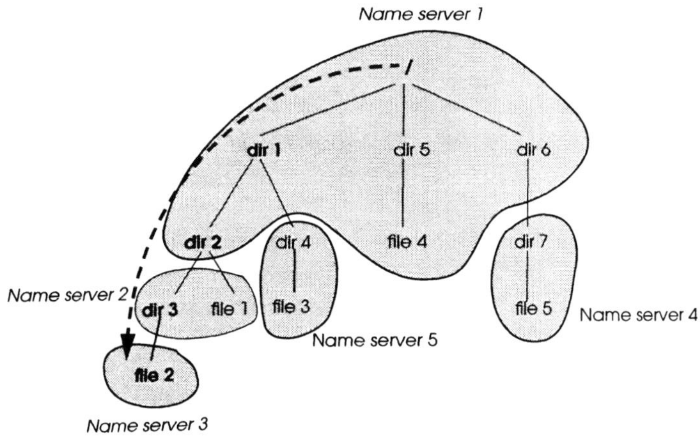

Figure 19.2 Example of dividing a directory tree into domains.

19.2.2 Data Striping

As we have already mentioned, clusters of workstations may have one or even several disks attached to each node. This property can be used to increase the bandwidth of the I/O system. The idea is to distribute the data among the disks so that it can be fetched from as many disks as possible in parallel. This will increase the data transfer bandwidth as many times as disks are used in parallel.

The first time this idea was used was not in a cluster of workstations but in building a high-bandwidth "single disk." The idea was to connect several disks to a single controller and give the impression that the disk had a higher data transfer bandwidth. This kind of disks is currently known as RAIDs (Redundant Arrays of

Inexpensive Disks) [3].

RAIDs

The high performance of a RAID is mainly due to three reasons. The first one is that data from each disk can be fetched at the same time, increasing the disk bandwidth. The second one is that all disks can perform the seek operation in parallel, decreasing its time, which is one of the most time-consuming disk operations. Finally, in some kinds of RAIDs, more than one request may be handled in parallel, which also increases the whole system performance.

As we want to be able to access as many disks in parallel as possible, the data must be distributed over the disks adequately. Interleaving the data among the disks seems to be the right way to do it. Using this distribution, if the request is big enough, each disk will keep at least one block of the request, and data from all disks will be fetched in parallel, achieving the highest possible bandwidth. This data interleaving can be characterized as either fine-grained or coarse-grained.

Fine-grained disk arrays conceptually interleave data in relatively small units so that all I/O requests, regardless of their size, access all the disks in the disk array. This results in very high data transfer rates for all I/O requests. On the other hand, it has the disadvantages that only one logical I/O request can be served at any given time and that all disks must waste time positioning for every request.

Coarse-grained disk arrays interleave data in relatively large units so that small I/O requests need only to access a small number of disks and large requests can access all disks. This allows multiple small requests to be serviced in parallel while still allowing large requests to achieve high transfer rates. Furthermore, if many small requests are served in parallel, all seek operations are also done in parallel, while on a fine-grained RAID they must be done consecutively.

Another important design issue is to achieve some degree of fault tolerance. As many disks are used, the probability of a failure in one of the disks is quite high. This means that a RAID needs a fault-tolerance mechanism to allow a disk failure without losing the information kept in the failed disk. This tolerance is achieved introducing redundancy. The way this redundancy is implemented along with the striping granularity is what distinguishes the five levels of RAIDs (Figure 19.3).

A RAID level 1 uses half of the disks in the array to keep a copy of the other half. Whenever data is written on a disk, it is also written to its redundant disk. When retrieving the data, the disks which need the smallest seek are used. The problem with this approach is that half of the disk space cannot be used to store useful data.

To solve this problem, new mechanisms to keep the redundant data have been proposed. For example, in a RAID level 2 the redundancy is implemented by Hamming codes. These codes contain parity information for distinct overlapping subsets of components. Since the number of redundant disks is proportional to the log of the total number of disks in the systems, storage efficiency increases as the number of data disks increases. If a single component fails, several of the parity

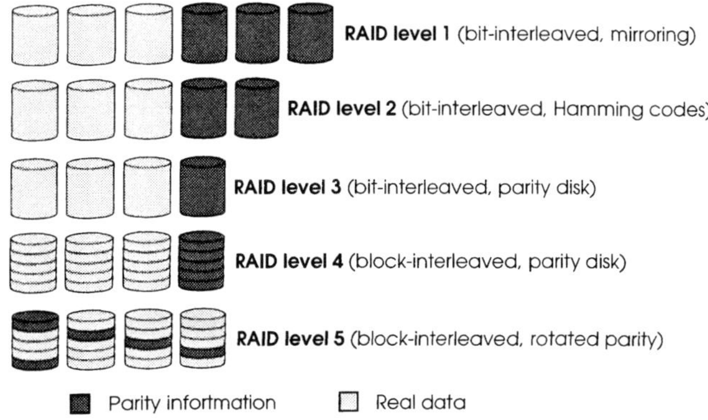

Figure 19.3 Graphic representation of the five levels of RAIDs.

components will have inconsistent values, and the failed component is the one held in common by each incorrect subset. The lost information is recovered by reading the other components in one of the subsets and setting the missing bit to 0 or 1 to create the proper parity value for that subset.

In a RAID level 3, a bit-interleaved parity is used. In this parity mechanism, data is conceptually interleaved bit-wise over data disks, and a single disk is added to tolerate any single-disk failure. Each read operation accesses all data disks while a write operation also accesses the parity one. This kind of RAIDs has a couple of problems. First, only one logical request can be handled at any given instant due to its fine-grain interleaving. The second problem is that the parity disk is never used in read operations, limiting the read performance.

RAID level 4 was designed to solve the first problem found in the previous level of RAID. In this version, the data is interleaved across disks in blocks of arbitrary size rather than in bits. The size of these blocks is called the striping unit. Using this solution, several read requests can be handled in parallel, but the problem of leaving one disk unused in read operations is still there. Write operations must be done sequentially as all of them have to access the parity disk.

Finally, a RAID level 5 is like the previous one but eliminates the parity-disk bottleneck by distributing the parity uniformly over all of the disks. With this modification, all disks can be used in read operations, increasing their performance. Write operations can also be done in parallel as the parity blocks are distributed among all disks. This version has the best small read, large read, and large write performance of any redundant disk array. On the other hand, small writes are somewhat inefficient compared with other redundancy schemes.

If the write operation is not large enough to use all the disks, the system will need more information to be able to update the parity. This small-write problem can be done using two different approaches: read-modify-write (Figure 19.4) or regenerate-write (Figure 19.5). The first one consists of reading the data to be modified and

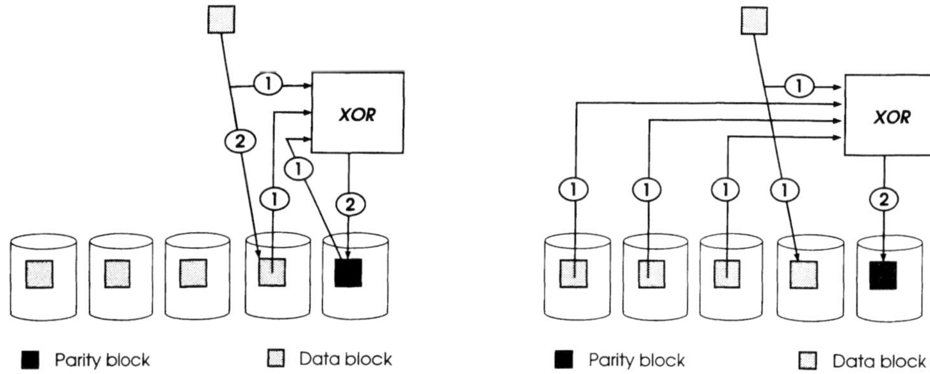

Figure 19.4 Read-write-modify solution to the small-write problem in a RAID level 5.

Figure 19.5 Regenerate-write solution to the small-write problem in a RAID level 5.

the parity-block before the write operation takes place. With this information, the system may rebuild the new parity block and update both parity and modified data to the disks. The second mechanism consists of reading the blocks from the disks not needed in the write operations. With these blocks and the ones to be written, the system has all the information needed to build the new parity block and can update both the parity information and the modified data. As we can see, both mechanisms add some overhead to the write operation. The read-modify-write is better suited if parallel writes can be done as only the disks with the blocks to be written plus the disk with the parity block are needed. This allows the system to perform more than one write in parallel. If the regenerate-write policy is used, all disks are used and only one write operation can be performed at a given instant.

Table 19.1 summarizes and compares the differences among the five levels of RAIDs.

Once the main RAID levels have been explained, we can describe some new levels that have come out as a mixture of the previous basic configurations. The first one is the RAID level 10, which is a combination between levels 0 and 1. This configuration is like a RAID level 0 (striping) where all its segments are arrays of level 1 RAIDs (mirroring). This kind of configuration has the same tolerance level as a RAID level 1, while achieving a much higher transfer rate.

The second important combination are the RAIDs level 53. This configuration combines the ideas of level 0 (striping) and level 3. The idea is to strip data among RAID-3 arrays. The performance is improved by the striping between multiple arrays. The fault-tolerance offered by the RAID-3 arrays is much more reliable than a single disk.

Table 19.1 Comparison Between RAID Levels

RAID Level	Data Reliability	Data Transfer Rate	I/O Request Rate	Application Strength	Fault-Tolerance Overhead
1	It can handle multiple disk failures in many cases.	Data transfer can be done in parallel, but only half of the disks can be used.	Read: two operations can always be performed in parallel (at least). Write: one operation at a time.	Any	Redundancy uses half the numbers of available disks.
2	It can handle multiple disk failures in many cases.	N - (log N) disks can be used in parallel. Codes have to be computed by hardware.	Similar to twice that of a single disk.	Any	Redundancy uses multiple disks (log n).
3	Higher than a single disk. It can handle the failure of one disk.	Highest of all types listed here for reading and writing.	All disks are always used in parallel (byte interleaved).	Multimedia (Video, imaging, sound, ...) Applications that use large files.	Only one disk is used for redundancy.
4	Higher than a single disk. It can handle the failure of one disk.	Reads use all disks but one in parallel. Writes may become slow for parity reasons.	Read: significantly high due to the transfer parallelism. Write: slow when small writes are needed.	Applications with many reads and few writes. Application with large writes.	Only one disk is used for redundancy.
5	Higher than a single disk. It can handle the failure of one disk.	Reads use all disks but one in parallel. Writes may become slow for parity reasons.	Read: significantly high due to the transfer parallelism. Write: slow when small writes are needed.	Transaction processing where many more reads than writes are done.	Only one disk is used for redundancy.

Logical RAIDs

The same idea has been used with disks that are not connected to a single controller. We may strip the data among the disks in the network. The only difference is that now the filesystem is responsible for both distributing the data and maintaining the desired tolerance level. This kind of data distribution among disks has been called Logical RAID or Software RAID. These logical RAIDs behave like RAIDs level 5 in most cases and have the same advantages and problems as in their hardware version. The most important difference is that the solutions to these problems can follow different approaches. Later in Section 19.2.4, we will present an example of how the small write problem can be addressed in a cluster of workstations.

Stripe Groups

When all the disks in a network are grouped together to build a logical RAID, we may end up with a very large number of disks. Having so many disks on a logical RAID has a few disadvantages.

First, as many disks are involved it becomes quite difficult to make a write operation that uses all the disks in the network. If no such large writes are possible, the system ends up performing many small-write operations. These operations are not very efficient in a RAID level 5 (the ones mostly used in logical RAIDs), as we have already discussed. For this reason, the system may not take full advantage of the write bandwidth of the disks. The second problem is that the node that is performing the operation may not have a network bandwidth large enough to read/write from/to all disks in parallel. Thus, only part of the theoretical disk performance is ever used. Finally, as the number of disks increases, the probability of a failure also increases. This means that the parity mechanism presented may not be sufficient, as more than one disks may fail at the same time.

The solution to all these problems consists of striping the data over a subset of all the disks [1]. Each one of these subsets is called a stripe group. Now, when performing a write operation, the system does not need to use all the disks to avoid a small-write problem, but only the disks that make the stripe group.

This modification solves all the above-mentioned problems. As we have already said, the number of times the system needs to perform a small-write decreases significantly. Second, the stripe groups match the aggregate bandwidth of the groups' disk to the network bandwidth of a client using both resources efficiently. While one client writes at its full network bandwidth to one stripe group, another client can do the same with a different group. Finally, the availability problem is also solved, as more than one disk can fail at the same time. The only restriction is that they cannot be from the same stripe group. This new restriction seems more reasonable in systems with a large number of disks.

The cost for this improvement is a marginal reduction in disk storage and effective bandwidth because the system dedicates one parity disk per stripe group rather than one for the entire system. It is clear that the advantages outweigh the disadvantages.

19.2.3 Log-Structured Filesystems

A second solution to increase the speed of the disks consists of organizing the filesystem using a log structure. This kind of filesystem was not especially designed for clusters of workstations but has been frequently used as it helps to reduce the small-write problem. We will discuss how this problem is solved in the next subsection (Section 19.2.4). Let us first describe how a log-structured filesystem works and how such structure can increase the disk performance.

This kind of filesystem is based on the assumption that caches obtain very high read ratios. As most reads are handled by the cache, the disk traffic is dominated by write operations. Thus, it seems reasonable to try to improve write operations even if read operations are slowed down a bit. It is also clear that if all writes could be performed sequentially, the system would avoid most seek and search operations that are the most time-consuming ones. This would increase the disk performance significantly. Summarizing, the idea is to build a filesystem where most write operations are done sequentially.

A log-structured filesystem behaves as log, where old information is never erased but superseded in a later page of the log. In filesystem terms, a modification of a block is not written where the original block was, but in the next sequential block after the last one written. This way of storing data not only increases the filesystem performance, but also simplifies the operation of recovering the filesystem to a consistent state, as blocks are not overwritten.

The best way to understand how this log works is to go through an example. In Figure 19.6, we present an example of the changes suffered in the structure of the filesystem when creating files `dir/file1` and `dir/file2`. These changes are presented for a traditional Unix filesystem and for a log-structured one. For each filesystem, we have drawn the evolution of the filesystem in three steps. The first one shows the portion of the filesystem in which we are interested before any modifications take place. The second step shows the modifications observed in the filesystem once the first file is created. In the Unix filesystem, a new i-node has been used and a new block for the file is allocated. On the other hand, in the log-structured filesystem, the data of `file1` is written and the i-node is sequentially written after the data. We should also notice that the directory has a new entry and thus it must be rewritten. This implies a modification on the i-node as the location of the block and the size of the directory have been modified. For this reason, the old directory block and i-node are also sequentially written after the file. This new version of the block and the i-node supersedes the old version existing before the file creation. The same steps can be observed in the creation of the second file.

Summarizing, we should notice that all writes are done sequentially in the log-structured filesystem, while no such thing happens on a traditional one. We can also see that neither the data blocks nor the meta-data ones change their location in a traditional system, while they are constantly moving in a log-structured one.

As all information (data and meta-data) is written sequentially, it is very important to have an efficient mechanism to access this information. Actually, once

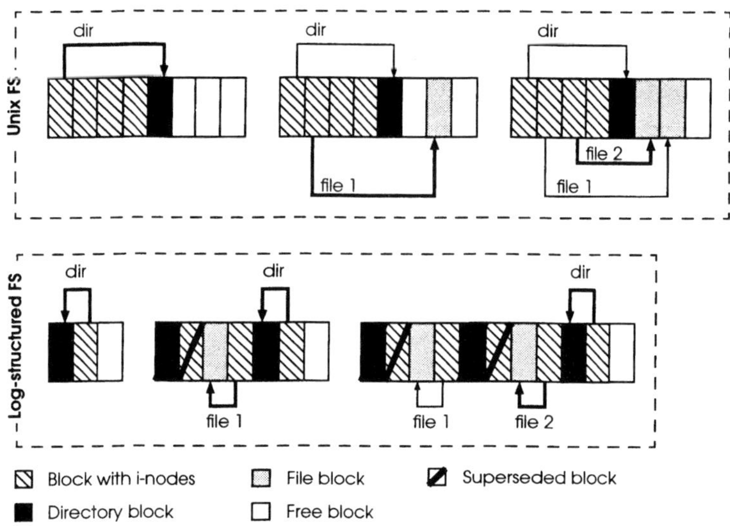

Figure 19.6 Differences between traditional Unix FS and log-structured ones.

we have the i-node of a file, the algorithm needed is the same as in a traditional Unix filesystem. Thus, we have to find an efficient way to locate a given i-node in the log. As we have already seen, the i-nodes are not placed in a fixed position that can be computed using the i-node number. To solve this problem, the i-node map is added to the system. This map is an array that contains all the information about which disk block contains the last copy of the i-node. As this data structure is compact enough, it can be kept in memory so that no disk accesses are needed to locate the block of an i-node.

To make this kind of filesystem work efficiently, it is necessary to keep large amounts of contiguous free blocks. These free areas are obtained by recovering the blocks that have been superseded by a new version of the information. Once these blocks have been freed, it is also necessary to compact the remaining filesystem information and to regroup these free blocks. The algorithms used to perform this task and the recovery are not needed to understand the rest of this chapter nor have been especially modified for clusters of workstations. For this reason, we will not go through them as it may interfere with the basic understanding of how such filesystems work.

19.2.4 Solving the Small-Write Problem

This problem has traditionally been addressed in many different ways. Using the cache to avoid writing until a large block is available, logging the parity, or building a two level RAID like the HP-AutoRAID are examples of how this problem has been minimized in the hardware version.

In this section, we will present a solution proposed in parallel/distributed filesystems that were designed to work on clusters of workstations. In this kind of environment, the small-write problem becomes even a bigger one. If information must be read from the disks to calculate the parity information, this information has to be requested from the remote nodes that have the disks. This is quite time-consuming and should be avoided whenever possible. The basic idea used to solve this problem consists of mixing the log-structured filesystem and the logical RAID so that small-writes never occur. In these systems, each client keeps a log of all the modifications done by its applications. This log is kept in memory (or in a small and fast local disk). Once the log is large enough to use all disks, the parity buffer is calculated. Then the client-log and the parity block are sent to the disks that are scattered among the nodes in the network. This update in the disks is also done in a log-structured fashion on the global log-structured filesystem. A graphic description of this mechanism is presented in Figure 19.7. In this figure, we present a cluster of workstations with two active clients and a logical RAID of four disks.

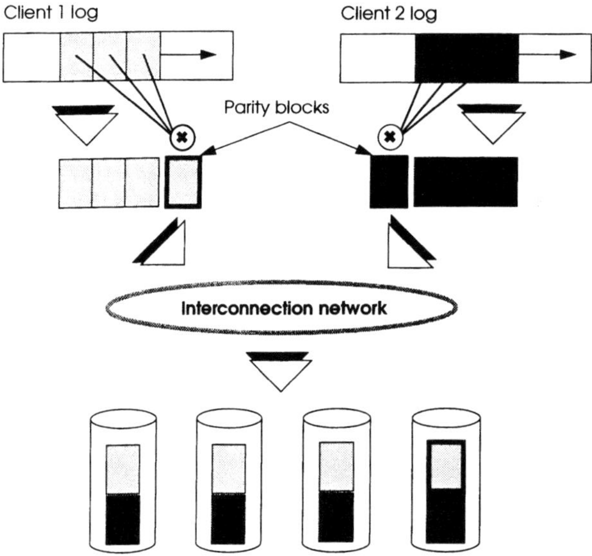

Figure 19.7 The log-structured filesystem as a solution to the small-write problem in a cluster of workstations.

19.2.5 Network-Attached Devices

One of the problems that may be found in a file server, or a node with a disk, is that the bandwidth of this disk is limited to the bandwidth of the memory in the server. The data requested from the disk must go through the server who is in charge of reading the information and forwarding it to the client that requested it. This means that the operations in the server may become the I/O bottleneck. To solve this problem, the network-attached devices have been designed.

The idea behind this proposal is that the I/O devices (i.e., very high-bandwidth RAIDs) should not only be connected to a host, but they should also be connected to a very high-bandwidth network. With this new approach, clients may request their I/O operations directly to the device using this high-bandwidth network. With this solution, the bandwidth limitation of the I/O operations comes from either the device or the I/O bandwidth of the client, but no limitation due an intermediate step appears.

Based on this idea, the RAID-II system was designed [6]. In this example of a network-attached device, we find three basic components: a high-bandwidth RAID, the high-bandwidth network and a host node (Figure 19.8). The XBUS is the high-bandwidth network designed to connect the clients with the disk. It is a synchronous, multiplexed (address/data) crossbar-based interconnect that uses centralized, priority-based arbitration scheme that can deliver around 100 Mbytes/s. Using this network, all clients may access to the disk to request high-bandwidth I/O operations. On the other hand, if the data-transfer bandwidth does not need to be a high one, or meta-data is requested, the traditional path through the host node is followed. This second path avoids transferring small requests through the high-speed network, as it would reduce its potential bandwidth.

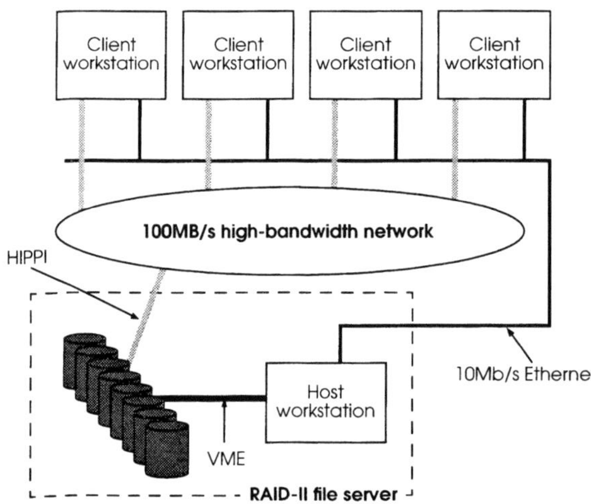

Figure 19.8 Example of a RAID-II file server and its clients.

Another interesting example can be found in the Global File System [13]. This is a prototype design for a distributed filesystem in which cluster nodes physically share storage devices connected via a network like Fiber Channel. The most important contribution of this work is the locking mechanism. As no node is responsible for the device, a way to lock the data must be implemented. In this project, a device lock is being prototyped in cooperation with some of the major disk manufacturers.

19.3 Caching

As we have already discussed, the most important performance limitation comes from the fact that disks are made of slow mechanical components. Solutions to this problem, such as RAIDs, have been proposed but are not sufficient to achieve the high performance needed by the applications running in a parallel/distributed environment. For this reason, the caching mechanism was proposed long ago.

A filesystem cache, or buffer cache, is a mechanism that tries to minimize the number of times the filesystem has to access the disks. This decouples the performance of the filesystem from the performance of the disks. The basic idea consists of keeping the file blocks used by the applications in memory buffers. If applications have temporal locality, the same set of blocks is used during a certain amount of time. In this case, the requested blocks only have to be fetched from disk the first time, as the next time they are requested they will be found in the cache. This simple mechanism increases the performance of read operations significantly. A filesystem cache also increases the write performance, as the modified blocks are not sent to the disks but kept in the cache. Whenever the system believes it appropriate, it sends these modifications to the disk. One of the most attractive characteristics of this approach is that the effectiveness of a cache is not limited by the mechanical parts of the disks.

19.3.1 Multilevel Caching

As one can easily imagine, this solution can be easily applied at many different levels. Among others, we may find a cache in the disk controller, in the operating system, in the I/O library and in the user code. Multilevel caching has been widely used as it increases the effectiveness of the caching system. On the other hand, on a multilevel caching system, the closer to the hardware the cache is, the less effective this cache is. This happens because most of the locality has already been profited by the higher-level caches. This means that, although some levels of cache may increase the system performance, if many levels are used, only the ones closer to the application will benefit from locality increasing the performance.

In a network of workstation, we may find even more levels where caching can take place. As the client application may be running in a node where no disks are attached, all their requests will go to a different node that has an I/O system which is running. This adds new possibilities for caching. We may now cache at the server side, at the client side, or even in both of them. Furthermore, if the client has a local disk, it may even decide to cache remote information in its own disk to reduce communication with the servers. In Figure 19.9, we present an example of a cluster of workstations and some of the many places where disk blocks may be cached.

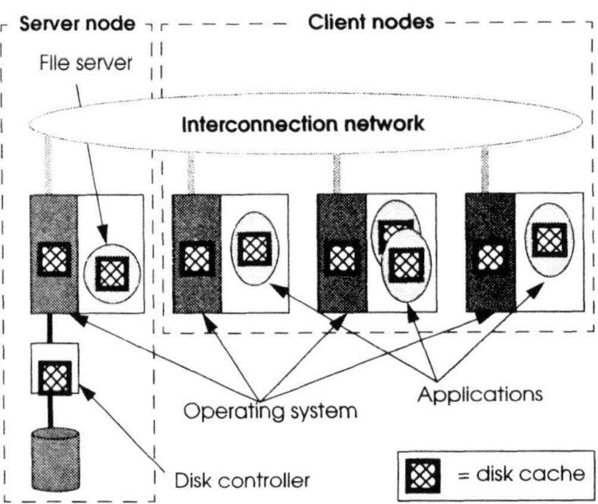

Figure 19.9 Possible locations of a disk cache in a cluster of workstations.

If we examine the situation where each client node caches the data its applications need, we discern one of the most important problems in any cluster of workstations: the cache-coherence problem. Each node may keep in its local cache a copy of a given block that is being used by all the applications. If one of these applications modifies its copy of the block, the rest of applications will not have an up-to-date copy. Solutions to this problem will be presented in Section 19.3.2. Until then, it is important to be aware of the problem.

As a good example of a multilevel file caching, we may present ParFiSys [2], a parallel filesystem for parallel machines. This system fully exploits data caching facilities at all levels. Both clients and servers have the following three caches: block, i-node, and name. Furthermore, disks may also have caches in their controllers and the user-libraries can also cache at their level. Data coherence is transparently ensured by a distributed coherence protocol. It is a token-based concurrent-readers exclusive-writers protocol. This kind of coherence mechanism will be described in detail in Section 19.3.2.

19.3.2 Cache-Coherence Problems

As we have already mentioned when talking about multilevel caching, using filesystem caches in client nodes may raise coherence problems. Two nodes may be caching the same file block and this one should be kept coherent when one of the nodes modifies it. To solve this problem, two basic approaches have been followed. The first one consists of relaxing the sharing semantics. This allows simpler and more efficient coherence algorithms. The second approach tries to find efficient algorithms that can fulfill the Unix semantic. In this semantic, a modified block is immediately seen by all applications in the system.

File-Sharing Semantics

The problem found with the Unix is that it is not easy to implement in a parallel/distributed system such a cluster of workstations. For this reason, some systems propose different semantics, easier to implement, that will allow achieving higher performance to the I/O systems. The problem with this approach is that application programmers will have to redesign their codes to consider these new semantics. In this section, we will present the semantic relaxations that have been most widely used in the design of parallel/distributed systems.

The first one is the session semantic. When the session semantic is used, all modifications done on a file are visible only, at the same time, to the processes running on that node. These modifications are not visible by any other process that has this file open and is running on a different node. Once the file is closed, all the modifications become visible to all the applications that open the modified file after it has been closed by the process that modified it. The Andrew File System is a classical example of where this kind of semantic is used.

For database-oriented filesystems, a transaction semantic has also been proposed. If a transaction semantic is used, all I/O operations are done between two control instructions: `begin-transaction` and `end-transaction`. All modifications done between these two instructions will be invisible to the rest of the nodes until the transaction is over. Once the transaction is finished, all the modifications done between the control instructions are propagated to the rest of the nodes in an atomic way. This kind of semantic has been used in parallel/distributed systems like Cambridge.

Finally, a semantic where files never change has also been proposed. When this semantic is used, once a file is created it can never be modified. Each modification in a file means that a new version of the file is created, but the old version is also available. Actually, all processes that have the file open, opened the old version and will never be aware that a modification has been done by another process.

Coherence Algorithms

As we have already seen, modifying the sharing semantic is a way to solve the coherence problem in an efficient way, but the load of keeping a more strict semantic is left to the programmer of the applications. As this solution is not always convenient, other systems have tried to solve the coherence problem maintaining the Unix semantic.

The first solution, and most drastic one, consists of not allowing the caching of write operations when a file is shared. This avoids all coherence problems allowing a Unix semantic. The main problem with this approach is that write operations are much slower than what they could be. This approach was followed in the design of the Sprite system.

The second option is based on the use of tokens. When a client wants to write on a file, it needs the write-token for that file in order to be able to modify the file. As long as a client keeps the token, it may do as many modifications to the file as needed without asking for any further permission. No other client will be allowed to use the file. On the other hand, while there are no clients holding the write-token, anybody may perform read operations on the file with no restrictions. Should one client decide to write on the file, the server invalidates all the data of this file kept in the client caches and gives the token to the client that requested it. This client will own the token and thus will be the only one allowed to work with the file until another client wants to perform a read or write operation. In such a case, the write permission is revoked and all the modifications made by the old owner become visible to the rest of the clients.

A problem found when protecting coherence with tokens is the revocation mechanism. In order to give the token to a new client, the current owner of the token must release it and stop making modifications on the file. If the node that holds the token fails, or it is disconnected from the network, there will be no way to revoke the token. Without the token, no other client will be able to modify the file. To solve this problem, a new mechanism was proposed: the lease. A lease is very similar to a token but has expiration time. This means that if a client has a lease to modify a file, this permission will last only for a predefined amount of time. In this way, if the client fails, or it is disconnected, the rest of the clients will only have to wait for the lease to expire to get their lease to modify the file. On the other hand, the disconnected client will stop modifying the file once the lease expires and will have to ask for a new one if it wants to keep modifying the file.

These two mechanisms, tokens and leases, may be used with different granularity. The first possibility, and the one assumed so far in the text, is to use the file as the basic sharing unit. This means that if a client wants to modify a block in a file, it must request the token or lease of the whole file and no other client may modify any other block. The second possibility is to use the file block as the basic sharing unit. With this granularity, many clients may be writing on the same file at the same time, but never on the same block. This block granularity is the one used in xFS [1] to maintain the coherence of the data kept in the client caches. Finally, a user-defined granularity has also been proposed. Clients define the region they are going to modify. A region is a set of bytes in a file that are not necessarily contiguous. Once this region is defined, the client may ask permission to modify it. The server will grant this permission whenever no overlapping appears between this region and all the other regions that have already been granted the write-permission. If there is any overlapping, it will behave as has already been explained. One such system has been implemented in ParFiSys [2], which is a parallel/distributed filesystem.

A different way to decrease the coherence problem has been proposed for write-only files: the ENWRICH scheme [12]. Although this scheme cannot work by itself and must be mixed with any of the previously mentioned solutions, it is a very intelligent solution for the write-only files case. An optimization of this kind of access is interesting, as it has been detected that write-only files are very frequent in parallel workloads. In this situation, each client writes all modifications to its cache and stamps them with the time when the modification was done. Once the client fills its cache, it discards these modified blocks and starts a flush operation. In this operation, the node that triggers it sends a message to all the other caches and tells them to flush all the blocks they have for that file. When the file-server gets all these blocks, it orders them, using the time-stamp of each block, and writes only the last version of the block. Using this scheme, no coherence mechanism is needed because nobody is going to read the modified information while the file is being accessed on write-only terms. This scheme also obtains a performance increase because only the last version of a many-times-modified block is sent to the disk. Furthermore, as the server receives a great number of blocks at the same time, it can reorder the write operations to minimize seek-and-search operation times, increasing the disk-access performance. The only drawback of this proposal is that the clock drift between all nodes should be less than the message-passing delay. Although this is a hard restriction in many systems, it is becoming more common that nodes have their clocks reasonably well-synchronized.

19.3.3 Cooperative Caching

So far, we have been assuming that there is no cooperation among the different caches. For instance, we assume that each client node keeps in its cache the most important blocks for their applications. This is the easy way and thus the way things have been done since a few years ago.

The problem with this greedy approach is that the cache space is not well managed. We may have nodes that are not using their cache space because the applications running on them are not performing I/O operations. On the other hand, we may have other nodes that do not have enough cache space to keep the blocks needed by their applications as they are I/O bounded. Another problem found in uncoordinated caches is that the file block needed by a node may already be cached in a different node. Instead of accessing the data from the disk, it could be forwarded from the node that already has the block, increasing the system performance.

It is also important to keep in mind that the speed of the interconnection network is currently quite high and that it is still being improved at a significant rate. This trend in technology encourages this kind of coordination among nodes, as sending information through the network is becoming affordable from the performance point-of-view.

Traditional Cooperative Caches

The first system that implemented such a cooperation was xFS [1]. This system was especially designed to work on clusters of workstations and tried to increase the cooperation among nodes. In this system, a cooperative cache was proposed that followed three design issues. First, the contents of all the client caches had to be accessible from any node in the network. Secondly, singlets (the last remaining cached copy of a block) were to be kept in the cache as long as possible. Finally, the physical locality was to be encouraged, which means that blocks should be cached in the node that will most probably need them.

In this system, the cache of each client is divided into two parts that are dynamically resized. The first one (or local part) is devoted to keep the blocks needed by this node's applications, while the second part (or global part) is used to keep blocks needed by other nodes but that cannot be kept in their caches. The replacement algorithm behaves as follows. Whenever a new file block enters the local cache of a node, the least-recently-used block of this local cache, that has a replica in any other local cache, is discarded. If no such block exists (all blocks are singlets), the least-recently-used block in this local cache is forwarded to a random pier that will be in charge of keeping it. This forwarded block is placed in the most-recently-used position of the new node's cache. It usually happens that the receiving node also must discard a block to keep this forwarded one. To make space for this new block, the same algorithm is used. The only difference is that if no replicated blocks are kept in the cache, the singlet that has been forwarded more times is discarded and not forwarded (we cannot afford an infinite number of forwardings). Finally, as blocks cannot be in the cache forever, once a block has been forwarded twice without being accessed by any application it is discarded from the cache. This mechanisms allows the system to keep file blocks in nodes that never requested them and also tries to keep singlets in the cache as long as possible. Getting back to the division of the cache in the local and global parts, we can understated now that all blocks kept in the local cache, because a local application requested them, form the local part. On the other hand, the blocks that have been sent by other nodes to this cache form the global portion of the cache.

Let us now see what happens when a block that is kept in a remote cache is requested (remote hit). When a remote hit occurs, the block kept in the remote node is copied into the local cache of the requesting node. This replication of the requested block increases the physical locality. As this block has been requested from this node, it is quite probable that it will be requested again from the same node. If a block from the local cache has to be replaced, the above-mentioned algorithm is used. This mechanism allows the system to be able to use the cache as a global one while still maintaining the advantages of physical locality.

New Generation in Cooperative Caching

Although traditional cooperative caches meant a great improvement in the system performance and cooperation, they had some drawbacks. As each local cache could have a copy of a given block, some kind of coherence mechanism had to be implemented, increasing the complexity of the system. As replication was allowed, the cache was under-utilized as a significant portion of the cache was used to keep replicas while it could have been used to keep more important blocks. Thus, the cache behaved as a smaller one. Finally, and most important, the performance benefits obtained by encouraging physical locality were outweighed by the overhead introduced when trying to increase this locality. To increase the physical locality, many blocks and messages were sent throughout the interconnection network while the applications was waiting for the block.

In PAFS, a new way to design cooperative caches is proposed [5]. The main idea is to build a big global cache, ignoring physical locality whenever increasing it adds some overhead. As no physical locality is encouraged, the need to keep replicated data disappears, which has two very interesting side effects. The first one is that because only one copy of any given file block is kept in the cache, there is no need to have a cache-coherence mechanism. The lack of such mechanism, besides simplifying the design, highly increases the performance of write operations. The second advantage is that the whole cache is used to keep different blocks, which allows the cache to be more effective as more different blocks can be kept in it.

In this kind of cache, when a block is requested and it is already located in a remote cache (most of the time), the bytes requested by the user are sent directly to the user address space. This is done without making any additional copy to increase the physical locality. This avoids much of the overhead detected in the traditional design, resulting in a higher performance cache.

Although this approach is not based on physical locality because achieving it has a high overhead, PAFS is not willing to ignore the advantages of physical locality when no overhead is present. There is a situation where increasing this locality will not have any undesired effects: when a new block is brought into the cache. For this reason, PG-LRU, a new replacement algorithm that increases the physical locality at no cost, is proposed. Whenever a new block has to be brought into the cache, instead of replacing the least-recently-used block in the whole cache, the system searches for a block that is in the same node that requested the block. If this block is among the 5% of the least-recently-used blocks in the system, this block is replaced. Otherwise, the least-recently-used block in the global cache is replaced regardless of in which node it is located.

19.4 Prefetching

After caching, prefetching is the next logical step to increase the performance of the I/O system. When caching, the system keeps in memory the blocks that have already been accessed in case they are requested again. This solution increases the system performance if blocks are used more than once, but no improvement is made the first time a block is needed. It has to be fetched from the disk. A solution to this problem is to prefetch these blocks before they are requested by the user. This new mechanism shares all the data structures already used for caching plus a block predictor that will be in charge of deciding which blocks are most likely to be accessed in the near future.

Although prefetching is a technique widely used in both commercial systems and research prototypes, most of the work has been devoted to mono-processor systems. These same unmodified algorithms are the ones used in clusters of workstations. In this section, we will describe how this technique has been used in parallel/distributed systems to increase their performance.

19.4.1 Parallel Prefetching

The simplest idea used to perform parallel prefetching is that each node prefetches its data in an isolated way. The parallelism offered by the multiple disks is used either to fulfill prefetching requests from each of the nodes or to prefetch large blocks for any of the nodes should a logical RAID be implemented.

We can see that this kind of parallel prefetching is a very simple way to use all the disks in the cluster. The reason behind this lack of coordination in the prefetching is that most caches implemented in clusters of workstations are not cooperative and thus behave as the ones found in a mono-processor system. With such kind of caches, it is difficult to build prefetching algorithms that take advantage of the inherent parallelism of a cluster of workstations.

The algorithm most-frequently used by each node is the One-Block-Ahead, which consists of prefetching the next sequential block after the last requested one. It is also quite frequent to find prefetching algorithms that deal in some manner with strided accesses.

Although not much work has been done on parallel prefetching, we believe that many new algorithms will appear in the near future to take advantage of the coordination offered by cooperative caches. These prefetching algorithms should take advantage of the great quantity of resources found in a cluster of workstations.

19.4.2 Transparent Informed Prefetching

It is well known that many of the applications that run on a cluster of workstations are not parallel but sequential. This kind of application cannot take advantage of the I/O parallelism offered by the system, as their requests are usually small ones. For this reason, it would be a good idea if the system could prefetch large portions of the file in parallel to increase the performance of those small requests. This is the idea used in the development of the Transparent Informed Prefetching [11].

In this proposal, the user is allowed to hint the I/O system. This gives the system a better knowledge of the way files are accessed, and it is able to perform a better prefetching. The user specifies the access pattern used in its files in a very high-level way. For instance, it tells the system that this file is accessed sequentially or that this other one is accessed using a strided pattern. With this information, the system may perform very aggressive prefetching. All the blocks that are prefetched are sure to be used by the applications and no miss predictions will occur. Because many blocks can be prefetched, they can be performed in parallel, taking advantage of the potential parallelism offered by the many disks available in the system. This mechanism allows sequential applications to take advantage of the parallelism found in a cluster of workstations that could not be used otherwise.

It is also important to notice that this mechanism can also be used, achieving the same performance benefits, in parallel applications.

A similar approach, without the hints, is also used in some filesystems to improve its performance. In these systems, a predictor decides which blocks have to be prefetched. The algorithm used may be any of the well-known ones used in mono-processor systems. The problem found in this approach is that the prefetching cannot be too aggressive because the predicted blocks may not be the ones the user application needs. If many miss-predicted blocks are brought into the cache, the system performance may decrease, which is exactly what the prefetching mechanism tries to avoid.

19.4.3 Scheduling Parallel Prefetching and Caching

When prefetching, we have to address the problem of constructing a good prefetching and caching schedule. If we prefetch blocks too early, they may replace blocks that are still needed in the cache. If we prefetch them too late, the applications will need to wait. In both situations, the application will not achieve the best performance. In a system with several disks, this problem becomes even more complicated as it has to take into account whether two blocks have to be fetched from the same disk or if they can be fetched in parallel.

This problem has been usually addressed in a theoretical way where the whole stream of accesses is known from the beginning [8]. Once good theoretical algorithms have been designed, the system designer may build an approximation for the case where the complete set of accesses is not known (very frequent in real systems).

Aggressive

The most intuitive way to do prefetching consists of what has been called the aggressive algorithm. It consists of initiating a prefetching whenever a disk is ready, and it replaces the block that will be referenced furthest in the future. However, this prefetch should be started only if this new block does not replace another block that will be used sooner.

Let us present an example of how this algorithm behaves. Suppose we have a system with two disks and a cache with three blocks. To fetch a block from a disk takes two units of time, and only one block per disk can be fetched in parallel. In Table 19.2, we present the scheduling of the disk accesses when accessing the following stream of blocks: F1, A1, B2, C1, D2, E1 and F1. The letter identifies the block in a disk and the number identifies the disk that keeps the block. To differentiate whether a cache buffer is being filled or its value can already be used, we have drawn the first ones in a darker color. As we can see, this algorithm needs 12 time units to fulfill the give stream of requests.

Table 19.2 Prefetching Scheduling Made by the Aggressive Algorithm

Time	t_1	t_2	t_3	t_4	t_5	t_6	t_7	t_8	t_9	t_{10}	t_{11}	t_{12}
Blocks Served			F1		A1	B2		C1	D2	E1		F1
Buffer 1	**F1**	**F1**	F1	**D2**	**D2**	D2	D2	D2	D2	**F1**	**F1**	F1
Buffer 2	**B2**	**B2**	B2	B2	B2	B2	B2	**E1**	**E1**	E1	E1	E1
Buffer 3			**A1**	**A1**	A1	**C1**	**C1**	C1	C1	C1	C1	C1

Reverse Aggressive

Although the aggressive algorithm has been shown to achieve very good performance results in systems with only one disk, it can be improved on a system with several disks. The problem with the aggressive algorithm is that it may achieve quite bad results for multiple disks when the load on the disks is unbalanced. For this reason, the aggressive prefetching algorithm was developed.

This algorithm exploits global knowledge in order to produce a prefetching schedule that achieves near-optimal elapsed time. It does this by balancing disk workload though carefully selected replacement decisions.

This algorithm is divided into 3 steps:

- Build the reversed sequence of requests.
- Build an aggressive scheduling but avoid the replacement in parallel of blocks that are in the same disk. This condition replaces the one that two blocks from the same disk cannot be fetched in parallel. In this step, more than one block from the same disk can be fetched in parallel.
- Transform this schedule back to a schedule for the original sequence by treating each fetch on the reverse sequence as an eviction on the forward sequence and vice versa.

Lets us now use this algorithm for the same sequence used in the previous example. Table 19.3 shows the aggressive scheduling for the reverse sequence (F1, E1, D2 C1, B2, A1 and F1). Finally, in Table 19.4, we present the scheduling obtained when transforming the reverse scheduling to the forward one. We can observe that this new algorithm has obtained a better scheduling, as only 11 units of time are needed to fulfill the sequence of requested blocks. The main difference is that the fetching of block D2 has been delayed so that the fetching of C1 can start one unit of time earlier.

There are two key properties of reverse aggressive that result in a better algorithm that the aggressive one. First, whereas aggressive chooses evictions without considering the relative loads on the disks, reverse aggressive greedily evicts as many disks as possible on the reverse sequence. In the forward direction, this translates to performing a maximal set of prefetches in parallel. The fact that these are fetches

Table 19.3 Scheduling of the Aggressive Algorithm on the Reversed Sequence

Blocks Served			F1	E1	D2	C1		B2	A1	F1
Buffer 1	**F1**	**F1**	F1	**C1**	**C1**	C1	C1	**F1**	**F1**	F1
Buffer 2	**E1**	**E1**	E1	E1	E1	**B2**	**B2**	B2	B2	B2
Buffer 3	**D2**	**D2**	D2	D2	D2	**A1**	**A1**	A1	A1	A1

Table 19.4 Prefetching Scheduling Obtained by the Reverse-Aggressive Algorithm

Time	t_1	t_2	t_3	t_4	t_5	t_6	t_7	t_8	t_9	t_{10}	t_{11}
Blocks Served			F1		A1	B2	C1		D2	E1	F1
Buffer 1	**F1**	**F1**	F1	F1	**C1**	**C1**	C1	C1	**F1**	**F1**	C1
Buffer 2	**B2**	**B2**	B2	B2	B2	B2	**E1**	**E1**	E1	E1	E1
Buffer 3			**A1**	**A1**	A1	A1	**D2**	**D2**	D2	D2	D2

in the forward direction means that at some point earlier in the sequence, corresponding blocks were evicted. Thus, the eviction decisions are based on the ability to prefetch the evicted blocks later in parallel. Secondly, whereas aggressive can wastefully prefetch ahead on some of its disks, reverse aggressive is greedy in the reverse direction. Consequently, it is fetching blocks in the forward direction just in time (to the extent possible) for them to be used. This results in performing close to the best evictions possible for those fetches.

19.5 Interfaces

The higher layer in an I/O system is the interface with the user. This layer is the one that allows the application to request the data from the I/O system. Furthermore, it may also allow the user (or compiler) to inform the system about what the application needs. We have already seen an example, in Transparent Informed Prefetching , where the user informed the system about how files were going to be used. The system used this information to fetch the data from disks before it was requested. In parallel environments such as clusters of workstations, the traditional interfaces have become inadequate because they cannot express concepts such as data parallelism, cooperative operations, etc. For this reason, plenty of work has been devoted to design new interfaces that can express this new semantic information.

In this kind of environment, there is a need to express the parallelism of the data kept in the filesystem. The application must be allowed to tell the system how the data will be used so that the system may place it to take full advantage of the potential parallelism offered by the hardware.

It also important to keep in mind that parallel applications have a special need to coordinate their I/O operations. A good interface for this kind of applications has to allow ways to share the data and to cooperate when requesting this data.

Finally, in many systems, regardless of whether they are parallel or not, the interfaces also offer ways to inform the kernel of how data should be used, which replacement algorithms are the best ones for a given application, etc. Although this idea can be exploited in sequential systems, it has much more power in parallel environments, such as a cluster of workstations, because more semantic information can be passed to the system.

In this section, we will present all these ideas in more detail along with some examples of systems that implement such interfaces. We have to keep in mind that no real standard parallel interface has been designed, as none has proved significantly better than the others.

19.5.1 Traditional Interface

Before getting into the details of how the interfaces have evolved to match the needs of a parallel/distributed environment, we will first describe briefly what we call the traditional interface. This interface is more or less the one proposed by Ritchie and Thompson in the early seventies. It was originally designed for Multics but was later developed as part as the Unix operating system.

In Unix, a file is nothing more than a linear sequence of bytes with no format at all. The format of the data kept in a file is not part of the file and must be interpreted by the application using it. The operations these applications can perform on a file are mainly `open ()`, `close ()`, `read ()`, `write ()` and `seek ()`.

Each time an open operation is performed, a new read/write pointer is created. This means that applications cannot have a shared read/write pointer to cooperate when accessing the file. The only way to have a shared pointer is to inherit it from the parent-process. This is quite restrictive, especially in a parallel/distributed environment where a process cannot create a child-process in a remote node. Thus, there is no way to coordinate the access to a file shared by more than one process.

Although this interface allows atomic read and write of sequential portions of the file, there is no way to perform an atomic operation to read or write a set of non-contiguous bytes. As only contiguous portions of bytes can be specified in a read/write operation, the previous access needs as many operations as non-contiguous regions. Besides placing a higher load on the programmer (more operations), this also forces the programmer to guarantee the atomicity at application level using complicated mechanisms.

Although this interface has achieved quite good results in mono-processor filesystems and sequential applications, it is not able to satisfy the needs of most parallel and distributed applications. This is due to its lack of flexibility to express the needs of such applications.

19.5.2 Shared File Pointers

A small improvement over the traditional interface is the introduction of the shared pointer. This mechanism allows several processes to work with the same file pointer. This gives these processes the possibility to coordinate themselves to access a shared file in a cooperative way. To allow this cooperation, many different kinds of shared pointers have been proposed. In this section, we will describe the ones that have been most widely used.

The first one, the global shared pointer, is the shared pointer that first comes to mind when thinking of shared pointers. It allows all the applications that share it to use it with no limitation. The read and write operations can be of any size and they can be performed in any order by the processes sharing it. After each read, write or seek operation, all the processes that share it see the new position of the pointer in the file.

As this kind of shared pointer is quite difficult to implement efficiently in a distributed system, another set of shared file pointers has been proposed. After studying the usage the applications give to these pointers, it was detected that it was very common to perform access operations in a round-robin order. For this reason, two special shared pointers were proposed. Both of them allow all the processes that share it to access the file in a round-robin order. This means that if process number 2 wants to access the file before process number 1, it must wait until process number 1 has finished its request. The difference between the two proposals is that one allows each process to request any number of bytes in each request, while in the second one all requests must be the same size. Both of these versions of a round-robin pointer are quite easy to implement. The last state of the pointer only has to be made visible to the next process that will use the file (next process in the round-robin order), and only the process with the pointer information can request data.

The last proposal is quite different from the previous ones. The idea of this distributed shared-pointer is to avoid, in a distributed manner, the overlap between the data accessed by any two processes. This new shared-pointer allows each process to access a different, and not overlapped, portion of the file. The control of this pointer has been designed to add as little overhead as possible because it is mostly handled locally by the processes. To achieve it, the filesystem assigns a disk to each process using a round-robin algorithm. Once a process knows which disk to access, it reads or writes all the blocks in the assigned disk that belong to this file. Once all blocks from the file that are located in this disk have been accessed, the filesystem assigns a new disk to the process. The process will use this new disk as before. This assignment of disks to processes is repeated until all disks where this file has blocks have been assigned to one process.

For example, MPI-IO is a library that offers the possibility to use a shared file pointer [10]. Whenever a file is opened by several processes, MPI-IO creates a set of pointers made of as many local ones as processes plus one global pointer. This last one behaves as the first one we described in this section; all processes can use it with no limitations. To distinguish between the two file pointers, the library offers two different read/write operations. When the programmer uses `MPI_File_Read` or `MPI_File_Write`, the traditional local pointer is used. If the functions used are `MPI_File_Read_shared` or `MPI_File_Write_shared`, the shared file pointer is used.

SPIFFI is an example of a filesystem that offers all the above-mentioned shared file pointers [7]. Each application decides, for each file, which of the proposed file pointers it wants to use.

19.5.3 Access Methods

Strides

The experience obtained from the CHARISMA project showed that a great number of the I/O operations done in a parallel environment use strided patterns. A strided operation is an operation that accesses several pieces of data that are not contiguous but separated by a certain number of bytes. As this kind of operation cannot be handled easily nor efficiently using the traditional interface, the Galley filesystem proposes three new interfaces to perform such operations [9]. A description of these three interfaces follows.

The first, named simple-strided, allows the user to access, in a single operation, to N blocks of M bytes placed P bytes apart from each other (Figure 19.10).

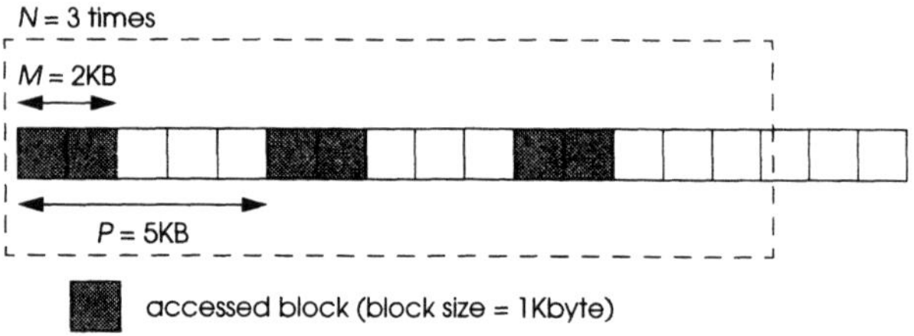

Figure 19.10 Example of a simple-strided operation.

The second proposal is the nested-strided operation. With this interface, the user can build a vector of strides that defines the different levels of stride. From these levels, only the last one represents the placement of data blocks. All other stride levels indicate in which positions does the next level of strides start. Figure 19.11 presents an example of this kind of operation. In this example, there are two levels of strides. The first one indicates that the next level has to be applied three times once every seven Kbytes. The second, and last, level indicates that the user wants to access three Kbytes leaving one unaccessed Kbyte after each accessed one. This last level is used three times, as indicated by the first level. The requested data is represented as the shaded blocks in the figure. To give an idea of how the strides are used, we present a portion of a program that specifies the previous operation in the Galley filesystem.

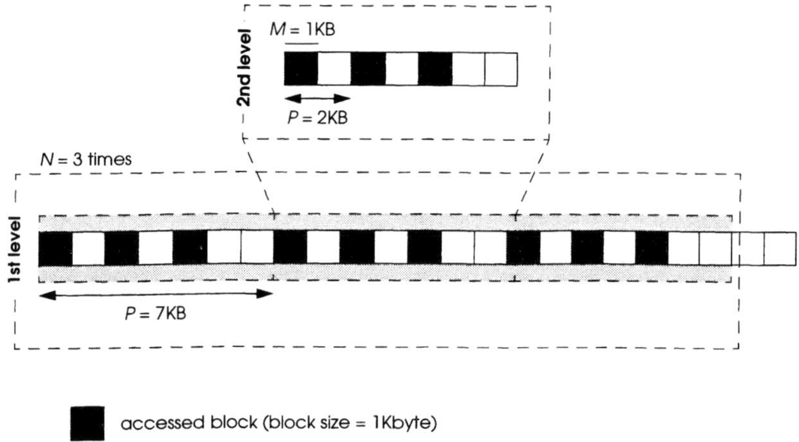

Figure 19.11 Example of a nested-strided operation with two levels of strides.

```
struct gfs_stride vec[2];
...
// Inner stride
vec[0].f_stride = 2048;    // File stride
vec[0].m_stride = 1024;    // Buffer stride
vec[0].quantity = 3;       // Applied 3 times
// Outer stride
vec[1].f_stride = 7168;
vec[1].m_stride = 3*1024;  // Space needed to keep the information read
                           // in one step in the previous level
vec[1].quantity = 3;
// Strided operation
b = gfs_read_nested(file_id, buffer, file_offset, size_to_read, vec, 2);
...
```

Finally, they also propose a nested-batched operation. This operation allows the user to make several simple and nested-strided operations as a single one. In order to do this, the user builds a list with the strided operations to be done. Afterwards, this list is used as one of the parameters in the read or write operation.

MPI-IO

MPI-IO was proposed as an I/O interface for the MPI message-passing library [10]. This interface allows the user to specify the distribution of the file blocks among the user space. The distribution of this data among the disks is left to the filesystem underneath.

This interface was designed with a very clear set of goals. It is targeted primarily for scientific applications. It favors common usage patterns over obscure ones. It tries to support 90% of parallel programs easily at the expense of making things more difficult in the other 10%. It also intends to correspond to real world requirements and new features are added only when they are proved necessary. Finally, the design favors performance over functionality.

In MPI-IO, the data partitioning is done in three steps. The first one consists of defining the size of the basic element or etype. This element is used to construct the patterns needed in the next two phases. The second step, done in the open operation, specifies which parts of the complete file will be used to construct the opened subfile. Finally, in the third step, the user defines how the accessed elements should be placed in the buffer. This third step can be done in each read/write operation. These two last steps, or mappings, are done building patterns from the basic element, or etype, defined in the first step. When a file is opened, the user specifies the filetype, which is a pattern of etypes. This pattern defines the subfile to access (Figure 19.12). Using this concept of subfile, the user may specify which blocks are going to be used by each process in the application. Once the subfiles have been specified, every read and write operation may specify a pattern telling the system where to place the elements accessed from the file. This new pattern is also built from etypes and is called bufftype (Figure 19.12). It is important to notice that there are no restrictions when building subfiles, and they may be overlapped.

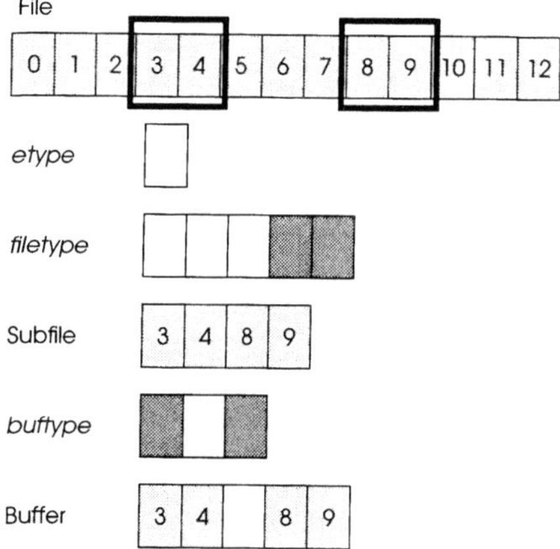

Figure 19.12 An example of data partitioning in MPI-IO.

Let us present an example of what an MPI-IO request looks like. In the following portion of a program, we can see the steps needed in MPI-IO to perform a read operation on a file of integers using a cyclic distribution.

```
...
// The basic type will be an integer
etype = MPI_INT;
// We create a filetype that will distribute the data in a cyclic way
MPI_Type_hpf_cyclic (...,&filetype);
// We create the views of the file for this process
```

```
MPI_File_set_view (fh, offset, etype, filetype,...);
// We create a bufftype to decide how will data be placed in my buffer
MPI_Type_vector (...,&buftype);
// Finally, we perform the read operation
MPI_File_Read (fh, buffer, count, buftype, &status);
...
```

Going back to the shared pointers issue, it is straightforward to see now that the global pointer will make sense only if all processes have the same subfile.

19.5.4 Data Distribution

So far, we have presented ways to tell the I/O system which data is to be accessed and where we want it on the user buffers. It is time now to explain the interfaces that allow the user to express the parallelism found in the data.

To allow the user to decide both (how data was distributed among the disks and how this data is to be accessed by the application), the Vesta filesystem proposed the concept of two-dimensional files [4]. In this system, a file is made of a set of cells, or partitions, where each of them is divided into Basic Striping Units (BSUs), or registers.

Cells are contiguous portions of a file. They are defined at creation time and their number remains constant during the whole life of the file. Each of these cells may be placed in a different I/O node (or disk). This means that the number of cells equals the maximum parallelism that can be obtained accessing a given file. This placement is made by the system with no interaction from the user. This means that the user can only hint the system on what parts of the file are best in the same disk, and which parts should be placed in different disks to increase the I/O bandwidth.

BSUs are sets of bytes that behave as the basic data units used by the repartition mechanism. The size of BSUs is also set at creation time and remains unmodified during the whole life of the file.

This division of a file into cells and BSUs allows us to see the file as a two-dimensional array. The cells behave as columns while the BSUs take the place of the rows (Figure 19.13). This interpretation of files as two-dimensional arrays allows the user to repartition the BSUs in the same way that array elements can be distributed using high performance Fortran. The same partition mechanisms are offered by the system.

As in MPI-IO, the user can specify which portion of the file is to be used. To do this, when the application opens the file, it actually opens a subfile. In the open operation, the user specifies the distribution parameters and only the bytes of the subfile built with these parameters are accessible to the application. In Figure 19.14, we present an example of an open function that divides a given file into 6 subfiles using a block-cyclic distribution.

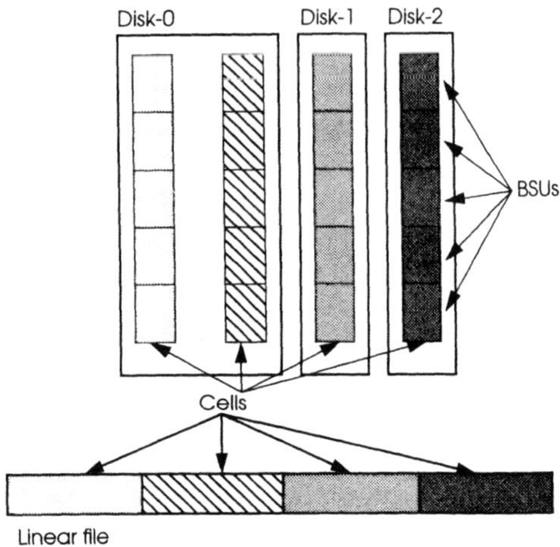

Figure 19.13 Schematic representation of a two-dimensional file in Vesta.

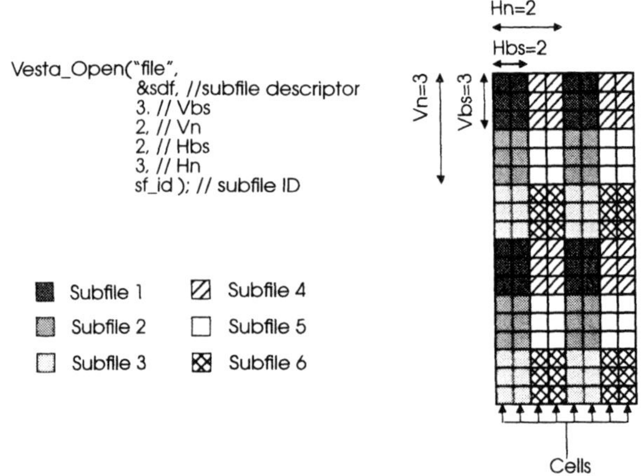

Figure 19.14 Example of an open operation in Vesta.

19.5.5 Collective I/O

As the degree of parallelism increases in an application, it is quite frequent that the I/O requests become very small. If each process requests very few bytes in each operation, the I/O system has problems in achieving high performance. As the data is so small, the system cannot take advantage of the parallelism. Furthermore, if requests are very small, the accesses to the disk are dominated by seek operation, which, as we already know, are the slowest ones. To solve this problem, the idea of collective I/O was proposed.

In collective I/O, all computing nodes cooperate to perform I/O operations from the disk in order to improve its efficiency. This allows the system to build a single big operation from all the small ones requested by each client. In this way, the system is able to obtain semantic information about the operations and may improve their efficiency. This cannot be done if many small operations are requested at different instants of time. A more detailed description of this mechanism and its alternatives is presented in the Parallel I/O chapter.

19.5.6 Extensible Systems

An idea that is becoming quite popular in the design of new operating systems is the extensibility. This consists of letting the users (or compiler) decide which algorithms are best suited for their applications, or at least, offering the user low-level operations so that they can affect these algorithms. In the I/O field, this idea has also been proposed especially for caching and prefetching strategies. Although this idea was not designed for parallel/distributed systems, it offers many possibilities for such a system.

The most simple way to allow the user to decide the prefetching policy consists of offering asynchronous read operations as it is done in the filesystem implemented in the Paragon. Using these asynchronous operations, the applications can decide what has to be prefetched and when it has to be done.

The next step of extensibility consists of choosing one of the predefined policies already implemented in the kernel. For instance, many systems allow the application to decide the caching policy and replacement algorithm to be used with each file among a set already defined in the kernel. This mechanism does not offer all the possibilities but, at least, the best algorithms in the kernel can be used. Furthermore, it takes the burden of deciding the policy away from the kernel.

Finally, some systems allow the user to implement their own policies that will be executed by the kernel. This is the most flexible option but it has the problem of maintaining the security of the system when an error occurs in the user code.

Acknowledgment

This survey has been supported by the Spanish Ministry of Education (CICYT) under the TIC-95-0429 contract.

19.6 Bibliography

[1] T. E. Anderson, M. D. Dahlin, J. M. Neefe, D. A. Patterson, D. S. Roselli, and R. Y. Wang. Server-less Network File Systems. In *Proceedings of the 15th Symposium on Operating Systems Principles*, December 1995.

[2] J. Carretero, F. Perez, P. de Miguel, and L. Alonso. ParFiSys: A Parallel File System for MPP. *Operating System Review*, vol. 30(2), pages 74–80, April 1996.

[3] P. M. Chen, E. K. Lee, G. A. Gibson, R. H. Katz, and D. A. Patterson. RAID: High Performance and Reliable Secondary Storage. *ACM Computing Surveys*, vol. 26(2), pages 145–185, 1994.

[4] P. F. Corbett and D. G. Feitelson. The Vesta Parallel File System. *ACM Transaction on Computer Systems*, vol. 14(3), pages 225–264, August 1996.

[5] T. Cortes. *Cooperative Caching and Prefetching in Parallel/Distributed File Systems.* Ph.D. Thesis, Universitat Politècnica de Catalunya, Departament d'Arquitectura de Computadors, December 1997. http://www.ac.upc.es/homes/toni/thesis.html.

[6] Ann L. Drapeau, Ken W. Shirrif, John H. Hartman, Ethan L. Miller, Srinivasan Seshan, Randy H. Katz, Ken Lutz, David A. Patterson, Edward K. Lee, Peter H. Chen, and Garth A. Gibson. RAID-II: A High-Bandwidth Network File Server. In *Proceedings of the 21st International Symposium on Computer Architecture*, pages 234–244, 1994.

[7] Craig S. Freedman, Josef Burger, and David J. Dewitt. SPIFFI – a Scalable Parallel File System for the Intel Paragon. *IEEE Transactions on Parallel and Distributed Systems*, vol. 7(11), pages 1185–1200, November 1996.

[8] T. Kimbrel et. al. A Trace-Driven Comparison of Algorithms for Parallel Prefetching and Caching. In *Proceedings of the 2nd International Symposium on Operating System Design and Implementation*, pages 19–34. USENIX Association, October 1996.

[9] D. Kotz and N. Nieuwejaar. Flexibility and Performance of Parallel File Systems. *ACM Operating Systems Review*, vol. 2(30), pages 63–73, April 1996.

[10] Message Passing Interface Forum. *MPI-2: Extensions to the Message-Passing Interface*, July 1997.

[11] R. H. Patterson, G. A. Gibson, E. Ginting, D. Stodolsky, and J. Zelenka. Informed Prefetching and Caching. In *Proceedings of the 15th Symposium on Operating Systems Principles*, pages 79–95. ACM Press, 1995.

[12] Apratim Purakayastha, Carla Schlatter Ellis, and David Kotz. ENWRICH: A Compute-Processor Write Caching Scheme for Parallel File Systems. In *Proceedings of the 4th Workshop on Input/Output in Parallel and Distributed Systems*, pages 55–68. ACM Press, May 1996.

[13] S. R. Soltis, T. M. Ruwart, and M. T. O'Keefe. The Global File System. In *Proceedings of the 5th Conference on Mass Storage Systems and Technologies.* NASA Goddard Space Flight Center, September 1996.

Part III

Process Scheduling, Load Sharing, and Balancing

Scheduling, load sharing, and load balancing are classic services provided by operating systems (OSs) of multiprocessor computers. To make a cluster of independent machines work transparently like a single system, these services (and others) must be supported. One way is to install a distributed operating system in the cluster, the other way is to build facilities on top of the individual OSs of the cluster machines. In the first case, process scheduling—the activity of deciding what process will run on what processor at what time—must become a part of the distributed OS. Process scheduling is built on top of the basic cluster operating systems in the second case.

Chapter 20 discusses the design and structure of the job and resource management systems (RMS) providing scheduling and load balancing services for clusters. The basic requirements for different types of usage, such as interactive work, batch jobs, parallel processing, and checkpointing applications, are derived. While several RMSs are used as examples, the discussion centers on the CODINE/GRD system. This system provides administrative controls over the cluster, and tools for the specification and enforcement of scheduling policies as chosen by the administrators.

Chapter 21 concentrates on the execution of parallel applications in clusters. Their specific requirements with respect to balanced load, as well as concurrent execution of interactive and other parallel work, are discussed. The chapter also raises the need to use admission controls to avoid flooding the system. These considerations are then used to identify four classes of systems that each place one consideration above the rest.

Chapter 22 focuses on a specific system, GATOSTAR, and shows how it combines the added features of load sharing and fault tolerance by using checkpointing. Load is estimated by a multicriteria method including response time, file affinity, communication needs, and memory needs, adjusted for processor speed. Checkpointing is done independently by each process in the application, to reduce synchronization costs. Consistency of the checkpoints is achieved by pessimistic message logging and replaying incoming messages upon restart.

The other three chapters deal with task scheduling within a parallel job. Chapter 23 discusses two classes of static scheduling algorithms: those that operate in a model where communication is not a problem but the number of processors is bounded, and those that operate in a model that takes the topology into account. In all cases the job is represented as a DAG (directed acyclic graph) of tasks, which are placed in a list and then scheduled in list order. The difference between the algorithms is in the way that the tasks are prioritized.

Chapter 24 discusses the dynamic task scheduling approach, where scheduling decisions are deferred to runtime because all the required information is not available for static compile-time scheduling. A major tool is load balancing, i.e., moving tasks at runtime if the benefit exceeds the cost. This can be done across a local subcluster or across the whole global cluster, with either centralized or distributed coordination. Finally, Chapter 25 discusses additional considerations and techniques which apply when the cluster being used is heterogeneous.

Chapter 20

Job and Resource Management Systems

FRITZ FERSTL

GENIAS Software GmbH
Neutraubling, Germany

Email: *ferstl@genias.de*

20.1 Motivation and Historical Evolution

20.1.1 A Need for Job Management

In principle, any operating system offers job and resource management services for a single computer. Nevertheless, the batch job control on multi-user mainframes was performed outside the operating system already in the early days of mainframe computing. The main advantages are:

- Allow for a structured resource utilization planning and control by the administration.
- Offer the resources of a compute center to a user in an abstract, transparent, easy-to-understand and easy-to-use fashion.
- Provide a vendor independent user interface.

The first popular Resource Management System (RMS) of this type was Network Queuing System (NQS) written by the Numerical Aerodynamic Simulation (NAS) Division of the NASA Ames Research Center in Moffet Field. Subsequently and particularly in connection with the proliferation of inexpensive, flexible and powerful computing equipment, such as modern networked workstations, several projects emerged to enhance NQS or to follow different approaches in order to manage workload distribution for computer networks also known as clusters. The following section will describe RMS for workstation clusters in more detail.

20.1.2 Job Management Systems on Workstation Clusters

Using workstation clusters imposes specific requirements on job management systems. According to [5], [1] a typical job management system used to control and balance the computational activity of a client/server environment usually offers a subset or all of the following features:

Heterogeneous Support: A heterogeneous job management system supports a computing environment consisting of a number of computers with dissimilar architectures and different operating systems.

Batch Support: A popular use of clusters is off-loading batch jobs from saturated supercomputers. Clusters can often provide better turn-around time than supercomputers for relatively small (in terms of memory and CPU requirement) batch jobs.

Parallel Support: A cluster can serve as a parallel machine because workstations are inexpensive and easier to upgrade because separate pieces may be purchased to replace older models. A number of packages, such as Parallel Virtual Machine (PVM) [14], [12] from Oak Ridge National Laboratories or Message Passing Interface (MPI) [6], add parallel support for computers distributed across a network.

Interactive Support: A cluster should provide users with the option to execute interactive jobs on the cluster. The input, output, and error messages should all be optionally returned to the user's interactive machine.

Check-pointing and Process Migration: Check-pointing is a common method used by cluster management software to save the current state of the job. In the event of a system crash, the only lost computation will be from the point at which the last checkpoint file was made. Process migration is the ability to move a process from one machine to another machine without restarting the program, thereby balancing the load over the cluster.

Load Balancing: Load balancing refers to the distribution of the computational workload across a cluster so that each workstation in the cluster is doing an equivalent amount of work.

Job Run-Time Limits: A run-time limit sets the amount of CPU time a job is allowed for execution. Providing a limit ensures that smaller jobs complete without a prolonged delay incurred by waiting behind a job that runs for an excessive period of time.

GUI: A well-designed Graphical User Interface (GUI) can aid in guiding users through the system.

20.1.3 Primary Application Fields

RMS were used first in high performance computing environments. The majority of the primary users were research centers; however, both research and production oriented industrial users investigated and employed RMS under real life conditions in an early stage. The typical environments at these sites either were characterized by an existing UNIX network infrastructure or by a recently purchased new cluster replacing/exonerating a mainframe/supercomputer or enhancing an existing cluster.

The jobs that were typically run in these environments are relatively long-lasting jobs with less sophisticated I/O requirements. Of course, they had to fit the memory and disk space resources that were offered in these clusters. With the increasing maturity of RMS, the sites were starting to look into the direction of more challenging applications, such as checkpointing and migrating jobs, parallel programs or I/O intensive jobs. There are still a number of open questions concerning these challenging applications (see Section 20.4).

20.2 Components and Architecture of Job- and Resource Management Systems

The following sections define a typical RMS as a set of standard components based upon several common prerequisites:

20.2.1 Prerequisites

RMS are in general suitable for any kind of computer network. Basic prerequisites are that the computers are interconnected by a network and that the computers provide multi-user as well as multitasking capabilities. Although homogeneous operating system architectures or particular operating systems are not a restriction, in practice the following situation occurs frequently:

- "Similar" operating systems run on all machines. If the operating systems are considerably different, they at least use the same standards for important operating system facilities such as machine-to-machine communication.
- UNIX (in all variants) is very customary in the context of using RMS (see the Section 20.1.3).
- Microsoft's Windows NT introduced the interest in the usage of relatively cheap PC hardware for clustered batch processing on top of this popular operating system. An attempt to port UNIX originated batch systems onto this platform has been made for some RMS, but such ports usually give NT servers the appearance of UNIX like batch servers with restricted functionality due to lack of operating system support.

Because of these reasons, the remainder of this chapter will be restricted to RMS basing upon UNIX operating systems.

20.2.2 User Interface

Any popular RMS at least provides a command line user interface. Typical commands are:

- A job submission command to register jobs for execution with the RMS.
- A status display command to monitor progress or failure of a job.
- A job deletion command to cancel jobs no longer needed.

Some of the popular RMS also offer a graphical user interface (GUI) for more ease of use, especially for the inexperienced user.

20.2.3 Administrative Environment

Administrative tasks in the context of a RMS, for example, are:

- Specify machine characteristics for the hosts in the RMS pool.
- Define feasible job classes and the appropriate hosts for the job classes.
- Define user access permissions.
- Specify resource limitations for users and jobs.
- Specify policies for the assignment of jobs according to load or other site specific preferences.
- Control and ensure proper operation of the RMS.
- Analyze accounting data to tune the system.

At least a command line interface needs to be available for those tasks being supported by a RMS, obviously. Again, some RMS offer an administrative GUI in addition.

20.2.4 Managed Objects: Queues, Hosts, Resources, Jobs, Policies

Queues

The concept of queues refers to the standard computer science first-in-first-out queue. Queues are defined by specifying a set of attributes such as the number of jobs being allowed to run concurrently in the queue or the CPU time and memory limitations to be imposed on the jobs started in the queue. All queues together build a profile for the job load that may be generated by the RMS on a cluster. A job is assigned to a queue and processed on a host bound to the queue. If all queues are busy with a job or suspended when a new job is submitted, the new job simply waits its turn in line until a queue becomes available. A job may be submitted by requesting its resource requirements. In this case, a suitable queue needs to be selected by the RMS allowing for the requested resources and being not busy.

Hosts

Two types of hosts can be distinguished in general in RMS: server nodes and submit/control hosts. Submit and control hosts provide the ability to pass jobs to the RMS for execution and to control jobs respectively. Some RMS also allow for configuration of special control hosts to administer the RMS.

On server nodes, two types of fundamentally different services are offered: compute services or RMS management services. The first type, in essence, consists of executing jobs, while the management service basically covers all types of tasks to guarantee the operability of the RMS including network communication, scheduling, RMS configuration, etc. There may be multiple hosts of each type in a RMS installation and each host may cover several functionalities as well.

Jobs

In general, a job in the context of a RMS is any agglomeration of computational tasks usually solving a complex problem. A job may consist of a single program, of several interacting programs, and a job may also utilize operating system commands. Commonly, a certain user is the initiator of all operations carried out in a job. Four different categories of jobs can be differentiated in the context of RMS as their handling differs considerably:

Batch Jobs: Jobs that require no manual interaction as soon as they are started.

Interactive Jobs: Jobs that do require interactive input during runtime.

Parallel Jobs: Jobs with subtasks spread across several hosts in a cluster.

Check-pointing Jobs: Jobs which periodically save their status to the file system and thus can be aborted anytime. Upon restart they resume execution from the last checkpoint. Under certain restrictions checkpointing jobs can also be migrated between different machines in a cluster.

Resources

Resources can be requested for jobs and are granted by queues via proper assignment of jobs to queues by the RMS. The term resources, often also called attributes, refers to the needed/available memory, CPU time, and peripheral devices. A job is accompanied by its resource requirements and queues are defined by specifying the resources they offer. Jobs once running on a system consume these resources. An RMS should ensure that resources offered by the cluster and individual machines therein are not oversubscribed by running jobs. This can be performed by internal bookkeeping and/or by comparing resource utilization information (e.g., current system load) with thresholds defined by the cluster administration.

Policies

Besides already described capabilities to manage the computational resources of a cluster, such as categorizing classes of jobs in terms of queues, a RMS may offer more abstract and advanced mechanisms to automate control of utilization of a compute server environment. Such mechanisms are often called policies. The cluster administration defines general rules of behavior for the system and the RMS is supposed to implement such policies automatically. We discuss the following important examples in more detail.

Resource Utilization Policies Ideally, such policies define long-term resource utilization goals for the entire computing environment, such as:

- Share based: Resource utilization entitlements with respect to the whole cluster are assigned to organizational entities such as users, departments or projects. Advanced RMS allow the definition of resource shares by means of a hierarchical share tree. This way utilization rights for the computing resources of an entire enterprise can be distributed starting from coarse grain department levels, for example, following down the organizational graph to the individual users. Likewise, a RMS may allow to distribute resource entitlements across a complex project organization.

  An important attribute of share based utilization policies is that they attempt to establish the defined resource entitlements within a (sliding) time window. Therefore, such policies take respect to past usage and compensate for low resource usage in an earlier time interval or punish for over-utilization. This way, over time, the entitlements of all parties utilizing a cluster can be met.

  Share based policies are typically required in cases where different organizations contribute to the funding of a cluster or where projects are aligned with a certain amount of computational cost or share of computational power in order to fairly distribute the resources among the participating parties.

- Functional: Such policies assign importance of various organizational entities based on their function. Like share based policies, they also define resource entitlements, but there are two important differences: The categories to which functional resource entitlements can be assigned are usually more versatile than in the case of share based policies. For example, they may include individual jobs and classes thereof. The other differentiator is that past usage is not taken into account in functional policies as the resource entitlements maintained by it are interpreted as fixed level of importance based on the function of the corresponding entity.

- Deadline: Time critical applications which are required to finish before a given dead-line represent a problem if they interfere with the day-to-day production utilization of a cluster. If resources are dedicated for dead-line applications, these resources may not be utilized while no dead-line application is executing. If no resources are dedicated for dead-line jobs, time critical applications may find not enough or no available resources at all and, therefore, may be endangered to exceed their dead-line.

An automated dead-line policy achieves a compromise between these two extremes. It may allocate only a certain (administrator-defined) percentage of all available resources to dead-line jobs and only if they require it (i.e., if at least one time critical application is close to its dead-line). If dead-line jobs are active, an automated dead-line policy will transfer resources from uncritical applications to the dead-line jobs dynamically on an as-required basis. Without time critical applications all resources are available for "normal" production.

- Manual override: Manual intervention into one of the policy schemes above or in a mix thereof may not be considered an automated policy, but in an advanced RMS it is as a matter of fact. Using a manual override, an administrator may raise the resource entitlement of a certain job or of all jobs of a user, department, project and job class by a certain and well-interpretable quantity (e.g., double the entitlement). The RMS is supposed to arbitrate the override against the other policies being active concurrently and to ensure that the administration goals are met.

Scheduling Policies While "Resource Utilization Policies" as described above influence both the resource consumption of jobs during runtime and the dispatching decision on when to start which job where, scheduling policies are meant to apply only to the process of dispatching jobs, also called static scheduling (as opposed to dynamic scheduling in the case of resource utilization policies).

A RMS may provide a variety of scheduling policies such as First-Come-First-Served, Select-Least-Loaded, Select-Fixed-Sequence and combinations thereof. In addition, important basic information for the scheduling process such as the formula used to compute a load weighting between hosts and the scaling of individual system information values (e.g., available memory) may be configurable. RMS supporting resource utilization policies will overload the static scheduling policies to implement administration goals such as certain resource share distribution automatically.

20.2.5 A Modern Architectural Approach

A structured design is vital for the quality of service that a RMS provides. If the design of a RMS and the distribution of its tasks to RMS components is not suitable for the requirements of a wide range of heterogeneous distributed environments, then the RMS will not be generally applicable. The RMS CODINE (Computing in Distributed Networked Environments) and the supplementary GRD (Global Resource Director) [4] both utilize a client/server approach integrating modern design concepts and offering a clear distribution of RMS management tasks. In the following the structure of both is described briefly: The central CODINE/GRD functionality is provided by three types of daemons:

cod_qmaster:

The CODINE/GRD master daemon. cod_qmaster is the center of the computational cluster's management and scheduling activities. cod_qmaster maintains tables about the recognized hosts, the configured queues, the load situation and the user permissions. Jobs are submitted to cod_qmaster which either forwards them to the cod_execd on another machine for execution or spools them if no suitable queue is available.

cod_schedd:

The CODINE/GRD scheduler is implemented in cod_schedd. Cod_schedd retrieves status information from cod_qmaster, computes a job assignment and sends its scheduling decision back to cod_qmaster using a well-defined interface.

cod_execd:

The CODINE/GRD execution daemon. cod_execd is responsible for the queues residing on its host and for the execution of jobs in these queues.

The three daemons communicate over a communication system based upon TCP and provided by the CODINE/GRD communication daemon cod_commd. Cod_qmaster manages CODINE/GRD objects such as queues, hosts, jobs, resources and policies and thus maintains a global view of the cluster. The other daemons and a variety of client programs building the user's and administrative interface use this database for operation.

By distributing the database management, scheduling, job execution and communication to the components cod_qmaster, cod_schedd, cod_execd and cod_commd the CODINE/GRD approach is flexible, straightforward to develop/maintain and scalable as it does not overload a single component with too many tasks. Together with the CODINE/GRD facility to partition large clusters into sub-clusters with their own cod_qmaster daemon, scalability is practically unlimited. In addition, reliability is ensured through a shadow master feature.

20.3 The State-of-the-Art in RMS

20.3.1 Automated Policy Based Resource Management

The definition of high-level resource utilization policies and their automated enforcement opens a new dimension of functionality for RMS and for their application in particular at shared resource centers. Shared resource centers provide services to and share resources among different organizational units, e.g., multiple projects accessing the center's hardware and software.

RMS offering such capabilities have become available just recently and GRD [4] is among the first and probably the most advanced. In the following sections, the goals and capabilities of automated policy management are outlined using GRD as a case study.

Requirements and Goals

Workload management is the process of controlling the use of shared computer resources to maximally achieve the performance goals of the enterprise (e.g., productivity, timeliness, level-of-service). This is accomplished through resource management polices and tools that strive to maximize utilization and throughput while being responsive to varying levels of timeliness and importance.

To accomplish these goals, management solutions must utilize the relative importance of competing jobs and correlate concurrent instances of the same users, jobs, projects, etc., in order to implement effective resource-sharing policies. Systems that lack this sophistication have inherent weaknesses in mediating the sharing of resources such as:

- Applications will rarely perform at the optimum performance because imbalanced load is the common situation in multiprocessing environments, not the exception.
- Important/urgent work may be deferred or starved for resources while other work is initiated and processed.
- Unauthorized users may inadvertently dominate shared resources (and decrease productivity) by simply submitting the largest amount of work.
- A user may grossly exceed her/his desired resource utilization level over time.

These limitations lower overall resource utilization, reduce throughput performance (especially when relative priority is considered), and increase the need for operational or administrative intervention.

Furthermore, initial job placement occurs at a single point in time and cannot take natural and unforeseen dynamics into account. Actual resource usage can diverge significantly from desired usage after dispatching. Therefore, dynamic reallocation of resources is a prerequisite to optimal workload management.

Quantifying Availability and Usage of Resources

To avoid improper dispatching of jobs, GRD performs resource tasking based upon the utilization and collective capabilities of an entire system of resources and with complete awareness of the total workload. Jobs executing anywhere in the pool of managed resources are correlated with users, projects, departments and job classes in determining how to allocate resources when new jobs are submitted or completed.

But GRD does not only take resource utilization policies into account when dispatching jobs. GRD continuously maintains alignment of resource utilization with policies, using a dynamic workload regulation scheme. GRD monitors and adjusts resource usage correlated to all processes of a job, the corresponding job classes, users, projects, and departments. Operational adjustments to resource entitlements are centralized and take effect globally because of workload correlation and workload regulation.

Policy Models

Section 20.2.4 introduces pivotal resource utilization policies for the management of shared resource centers. They can be summarized as:

- **Share based** – Supports hierarchical allocation of resources to users or projects during a configurable time period that typically exceeds the lifetime of individual jobs.
- **Functional** – Supports relative weighting among users, projects, departments, and job classes during execution.
- **Initiation deadline** – Automatically escalates a job's resource entitlement over time as it approaches its deadline.
- **Override** – Adjusts resource entitlements at the job, job class, user, project, or department levels.

These policies can be combined as depicted in Figure 20.1 using GRD's ticketing system. Each policy is assigned a total amount of tickets which defines the relative level of importance of this policy. Tickets can be compared with stock shares: The more shares a stock owner has, the more influence s/he has.

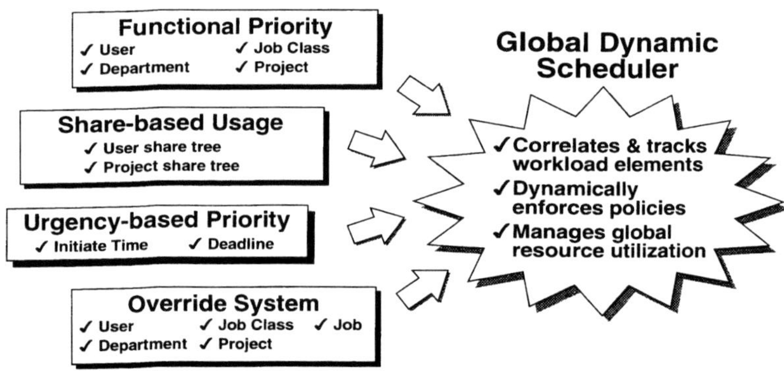

Figure 20.1 GRD policy integration.

While the relation between the different policies is defined at the top level, the policies internally collect resource usage for users, projects, departments and job classes and GRD arbitrates the usage against the policies as defined by the site management. Thus when a single user (or project or department) submits many jobs, other jobs that the user (or project or department) has in execution will receive fewer share allocation in order to keep associated resource usage at the appropriate level. Conversely, when a job completes, the resource entitlements of other executing jobs for the associated user are escalated.

Policy Enforcement

The policy scheme described in the last section is implemented in GRD by a *dynamic scheduling* facility. It uses multiple feed-back loops to adjust CPU shares of concurrently executing jobs towards the dynamically changing requirements defined in the policy configuration. This mechanism is very different from the static scheduling behavior of most other RMS (see Figure 20.2) and it is depicted in Figure 20.3.

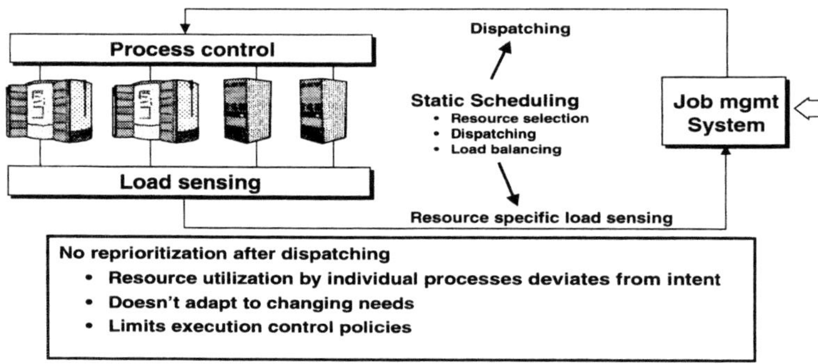

Figure 20.2 Static scheduling scheme.

20.3.2 The State-of-the-Art of Job Support

For the job types batch, interactive, parallel and checkpointing (refer to Section 20.2.4 for details), the most advanced RMS today offer the following services:

Serial Batch Jobs

As this is the simplest case, almost all RMS allow to submit batch jobs as defined in Section 20.2.4. In addition, advanced systems provide extensive accounting and

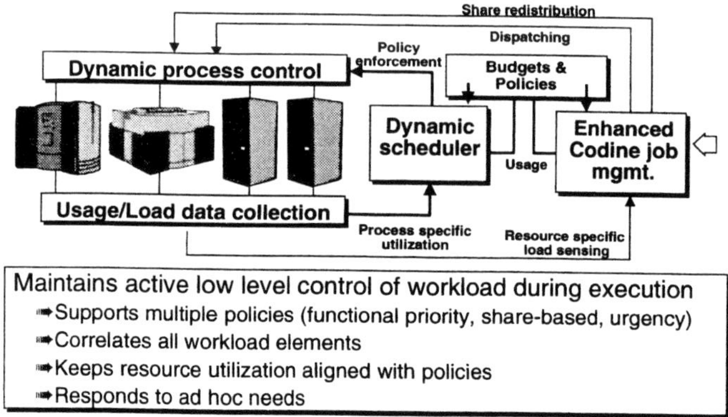

Figure 20.3 GRD's dynamic scheduling scheme.

monitoring facilities for this job class. The ability to suspend and resume execution of batch jobs and to restart batch jobs after system crashes also is a standard today.

Interactive Support

The difference between batch and interactive jobs and the problem in providing interactive job execution is the need to establish and maintain a terminal connection for the duration of the interactive session. Some RMS, among them CODINE/GRD [4], support interactive jobs by opening up a full interactive session on a lightly loaded and suitable host. Other RMS allow single programs to be run on remote hosts while providing a terminal connection (e.g., LSF [10]). It is also possible to modify public domain UNIX shells in a way that they automatically distribute certain commands via the RMS to suitable and lightly loaded hosts (e.g., LSF [10]).

Another aspect of providing interactive support is to take into account interactive usage of a machine while the RMS intends to put load on that system. Depending on the site's preferences whether RMS jobs have higher priority or interactive work is privileged, either the batch jobs do not get their full share of CPU access or the interactive users suffer from RMS jobs in the background.

A solution for the first case is provided by CODINE/GRD [4] and LSF [10], for example. Both systems allow for the configuration of load sensors for each host that detect interactive system usage. In CODINE/GRD the measured load information can be used for the definition of load thresholds (to avoid oversubscription) or as host selection criterion for jobs (i.e., a job may request a host that is utilized only to a limited extent by interactive usage). The case that the interactive user suffers from background RMS jobs is addressed by installing "watchdog" programs that detect when an user works interactively and that withdraw such machines from the RMS pool subsequently. This method is implemented, for example, by Condor [2].

Parallel Support

Not all RMS provide parallel support. Interfaces to parallel programming environments (PPEs) are offered for example by CODINE/GRD, Condor, DQS, LoadLeveler and LSF. However, the kind of support provided differs considerably. The following criteria can be used to differentiate between RMS concerning parallel support:

Support of Arbitrary or Particular PPEs A RMS may have integrated support for one or multiple PPEs, or those parts of the RMS which provide the interface to PPEs are configurable and allow for integration of arbitrary programming environments. A representative of those systems with fixed integrated parallel support is Condor [2] providing an interfaces to PVM [14], [12] only. As opposed to this CODINE/GRD [4], for example, offers freely configurable start-and-stop procedures for each PPE to be supported.

Level of Control for Parallel Processes A simple way to provide an interface between a RMS and PPEs consists of submitting a start-up procedure/script for the run-time environment of PPEs to the RMS instead of a simple job script. After the PPE run-time environment is active, the start-up procedure can then invoke the actual job script which has been specified in the submit command line as command line parameter. The only necessary enhancement in the RMS itself is to implement facilities to request and reserve multiple computers for a single parallel application. The choice of suitable machines as selected by the RMS needs only to be communicated (e.g., via environment variables) to the PPE start-up procedure/script. This approach has been implemented by LSF [10]. Besides its simplicity, this approach offers the advantage of being applicable for a variety of PPEs. A severe disadvantage, however, is that the generation of parallel processes occurs in the context of the PPE. Thus the RMS has neither the ability to grant any resource limitations to be imposed on the parallel application nor is it possible to retrieve reliable statistics about the application's resource usage.

A different approach has been proposed by the *psched* initiative [11]. Psched defines application programmer interfaces (APIs) linking a RMS and PPEs to exchange information such as resource allocations, resource limits and accounting records. This requires support of the psched APIs in both the RMS and the interoperating PPEs. The *Portable Batch System* PBS [9] is among the few RMS which currently implement the RMS part of the API. At the time of publishing this book, the two most important public domain implementations of PPEs, PVM and MPICH [14], [12], [7], do not seem to provide official support for the psched interface. Psched also has not been integrated into the recently released MPI-2 standard [6], hence little hope exists that the psched approach will become more widely used.

[13] describes an alternative solution (although more concerned with the integration of parallel checkpointing into a RMS). Here the PPE library function that generates the parallel processes is changed in such a way that the actual process generation occurs under responsibility of the RMS. This approach has the clear advantage that no PPE internal code has to be changed. The required modifications are rather wrappers to PPE process creation functions and hence can be applied easily on top of public releases of PPE packages. Subsequent versions of PPEs often do not change the process creation scheme, so that the wrappers remain valid across releases.

This approach is implemented by CODINE/GRD and PPE wrappers integrating standard versions of MPICH, PVM and Silicon Graphic's MPI implementation in the SGI Message Passing Toolkit (MPT) [8] are provided. Thus reliable process allocation, resource limitation and accounting can be provided for parallel jobs without the need to use an RMS vendor specific PPE implementation.

This "tight" PPE coupling is implemented on top of the standard CODINE/GRD Parallel Environment interface, which allows the integration of arbitrary PPEs in addition to the aforementioned MPI, PVM and MPT packages. The interface is freely configurable and allows the definition of PPE startup and shutdown routines, as well as the setting of process allocation rules (see [4]). Note, that this more "loose" coupling delivers less control than the "tight" interface described above.

Check-pointing

Mechanisms for dealing with the checkpointing of a job are provided, for instance, by the following RMS: CODINE/GRD [4], Condor [2], LoadLeveler [1], and LSF [10]. LSF and CODINE/GRD provide interfaces for so-called kernel level, application level and library based checkpointing. LoadLeveler and Condor provide checkpointing only for applications linked with operating specific libraries enabling the facility. The library based checkpointing scheme of LoadLeveler and LSF is derived from the Condor mechanism and thus all three are identical in principal. CODINE/GRD does not provide checkpoint libraries, but solutions available from the public domain can be integrated. It should be noted, that library based checkpointing is very restricted in its applicability. Third-party application codes usually cannot be re-linked and applications performing specific file operations or using inter process communication (in particular, any form of application spawning a process hierarchy) are excluded in principal.

CODINE/GRD is the only package which uses regular job scripts with invocations of a potentially arbitrary number of applications being prepared for checkpointing; the other packages support only the handling of single programs. In particular, it is not possible for the other packages to embed checkpointing programs with standard UNIX commands. The referenced systems use checkpointing to offer dynamic load balancing. Dynamic load balancing means to interrupt checkpointing programs in case of an overloaded host machine, to migrate the jobs to other lightly loaded systems and to restart the applications from the last checkpoint. CODINE/GRD also provide this facility, but GRD offers a far superior approach for most cases in which dynamic load balancing is needed. Refer to Section 20.3.1 for details.

20.4 Challenges for the Present and the Future

The following sections contain a description of future requirements that are already important or are foreseen to be become important in the near future. Yet, most of the current RMS do not provide suitable solutions for these problems.

20.4.1 Open Interfaces

Although RMS are usually applied in cases where the environment is relatively homogeneous (see Section 20.2.1), the requirements that must be satisfied for each site differ considerably. The usage policies for the cluster are different, the users behave different, the applications have different needs, the hardware/operating systems are different and the machines are differently equipped. In addition, RMS on UNIX clusters need to integrate into an open environment of third-party applications with their own user interfaces and into open system management software.

Application Programmers Interface (API)

Advanced APIs for RMS are needed for the following reasons:

- Developers of complex applications might want to use a RMS's load balancing and load distribution capabilities to distribute computational subtasks across a network of compute hosts. From inside their application they should be able to identify independent subtasks and to submit and control them as RMS jobs.
- For various reasons it is necessary to retrieve the following kind of information from inside RMS related applications:
  - The overall load situation.
  - The status of jobs.
  - The status of queues.
- A software developer might want to pass information such as what kind of data is needed for an application or on what hosts the required software is available to a RMS system, e.g., to support the scheduler.
- Especially for the purpose of low-level integration of RMS with other software systems (e.g., network management systems like HP-OpenView), the software

engineers integrating the software packages could want to directly influence RMS behavior driven by events from outside the RMS.

- An RMS's graphical user's and administrator's interface should use the API to configure the RMS objects or to submit and monitor batch requests. An alternative user's/administrator's interface (e.g., integrated into an application related GUI) might wish to perform similar tasks.
- RMS administrators might wish to write special-purpose RMS commands in case the site's users expect a very special behavior.

In order to be usable for the purposes outlined above, an advance RMS API must satisfy the following requests:

- The API must be easy to use. In this context, this means straightforward tasks should be trivial to implement, while more sophisticated tasks may become complicated to a certain extent.
- The API needs to be usable from any programming language.
- The API must hide RMS implementation details from the application developer.
- Internal RMS changes (e.g., an API function is extended in functionality) should not necessarily require software built upon the API to be changed.

The CODINE/GRD API already meets these requirements and serves the needs outlined above. The CODINE/GRD API

- is applicable for any client/server in CODINE/GRD.
- is extensible without requiring recompilation for every API-based program.
- has a SQL inspired interface.

20.4.2 Resource Control and Mainframe-Like Batch Processing

Ideally, a RMS controls the following resources:

- Compute cycles.
- Main memory.
- Disk space.
- Peripheral devices such as printers, tape drives, etc.
- Different operating system and hardware architectures.
- Licenses for the installed base and application software.

- The network interconnect and its bandwidth.

Administrators of mainframes are used to RMS showing a strong relation and interdependence to the proprietary operating systems of these machines. Via this relation between RMS and operating systems, mainframe RMS can almost fully control running applications. As an example, such a RMS is able to retrieve the resource usage of an application any time and any violation of a resource limitation can be punished immediately. Also, the ways of responding to such violations can be manifold and may often be specifically adjusted to important application cases. Furthermore, it can be possible to book and control peripheral devices directly from mainframe RMS.

With the trend to more flexible, less vendor-dependent and more powerful structures based on heterogeneous clusters of workstation type machines, lots of the functionalities got lost, which heavily depend upon direct operating system support. The operating systems of the different vendors in current environments offer standard interfaces, but these interfaces satisfy only restricted requirements. Already the implementation of job-related resource limits, such as memory usage or CPU time consumption, turns out to become problematic. Almost no popular UNIX operating system provides the means to control resources in relation to a whole job. Most UNICES just offer limitations for single processes. The RMS, which depends upon such operating system interfaces (memory allocation, for instance, cannot be controlled outside the operating system), actually becomes unable to offer reliable resource control.

The absence of such mechanisms in some cases endangers the secure and reliable operation of a cluster and thus reduces the usefulness of a RMS. Therefore, offering mainframe-like control mechanisms together with the RMS for compute clusters is an important requirement for the future.

CODINE, and in particular GRD, improves its ability to provide mainframe-like resource control by exploiting vendor-specific (although not portable) control techniques (see 20.3.1). In cases in which even no vendor-specific control facilities are available, a feature called *Consumable Resources* offers an efficient means to manage limited resources such as available memory, file space, network bandwidth or floating software licenses. Total available capacities for such resources can be defined by CODINE/GRD administrators and the consumption of the corresponding resources by jobs is monitored by CODINE/GRD internal bookkeeping.

20.4.3 Heterogeneous Parallel Environments

Compute centers utilizing dedicated machines demand better integration of the parallel machines into their customary environment. Embedding parallel machines into a RMS framework is an ideal way to provide transparent access to these machines and thus to further enhance their acceptance in the compute center's user community.

Shared Memory Parallel Machines

Processor affinity is one of the common requirements that are demanded by users of shared memory parallel machines. Processor affinity is defined as partitioning the CPUs of a shared memory parallel machine and assign them to different user groups being allowed to access the assigned CPUs only. Some of the shared memory parallel machine operating systems support space sharing in a way that a privileged administrative user can assign processes belonging to a user session to a set of CPUs. Thus, there must be explicit support of this feature by the RMS in order to have it available for RMS jobs also.

CODINE/GRD already supports processor affinity by allowing for an assignment of a processor group to a CODINE/GRD queue. Naturally, a RMS on a shared memory parallel machine also must recognize shared memory parallel jobs and has to make sure that such a job does not allocate more CPUs than are available to prevent from overloading the machine. CODINE/GRD uses the processor affinity feature to ensure this. A user must request the number of CPUs to be used for parallel jobs. If not explicitly requested, CODINE/GRD assumes that the job needs only one CPU and will bind the job to a single CPU. Otherwise, the requested number of CPUs will be allocated, if available.

Dedicated Distributed Memory Parallel Machines

The problem in providing RMS support for dedicated distributed memory machines is that there are several types of machines available from several vendors showing strongly different characteristics. Many of these machines do not have a full service operating system on their compute nodes but a small kernel optimized for compute intensive work only. Very often, the local memory of the single nodes of such machines is also restricted. Therefore, it is usually not possible to directly port a RMS with execution agents for each compute unit. For porting to such systems, the node allocation and control mechanisms provided by the hardware vendor have to be used. However, they rarely provide interfaces for easy integration into RMS.

The CODINE/GRD Parallel Environment (PE) interface (see Section 20.3.2 for details) has been ported successfully to dedicated parallel machines such as IBM's SP2 or Parsytecs GC systems.

Cluster Based Distributed Memory Parallel Machines

Using clusters as distributed memory parallel machines brings in several complications. The most important are difficulties in interfacing parallel programming environments (see Section 20.3.2 for details) and problems caused by the multi-user and multitasking nature of cluster computers. Such machines are not only used by the RMS and by parallel applications but also by users being logged in interactively and imposing non-negligible load on the systems. As a consequence, parallel applications may perform insufficiently because interactive load may cause imbalanced response from the parallel processes and thus slow down the parallel application at each synchronization step.

A possible solution is to re-balance load dynamically during the runtime of the parallel application via checkpointing and migration as described in [16], [5]. The integration of CODINE with parallel checkpointing schemes has proven to be successful in the research project SEMPA (see the chapter on "Portable Parallel CFD Simulation" by Peter Luksch in Volume 2 of this book) in which CODINE is used as RMS.

An alternative approach is being addressed via the dynamic scheduling facilities of GRD (see 20.3.1). Rather than redistributing parallel tasks, dynamic scheduling can ensure that each task receives adequate CPU shares to allow balanced progress of the computation. *Coarse grain gang scheduling* is a feature being developed for GRD implementing this solution.

20.4.4 RMS in a WAN Environment

Many large industrial and research organizations operate with several branches being separated by long distances. The personnel of such organizations frequently uses compute resource from other branches over a wide area network (WAN). Using a RMS to integrate clusters from separate localities offers the ability to provide a transparent method of access for the whole compute environment and to hide the administrative details of each cluster from the user. However, applying a RMS to a WAN yields a number of problems related to security, remote file access, accounting and network bandwidth. The UNICORE project [15], in which CODINE is used as basic RMS infrastructure, is addressing these problems.

20.5 Summary

Today's RMS offer good utilization of compute resources for a wide variety of applications. They have proven their usefulness in production environments and still extend their application area. However, to satisfy the challenging requirements of the expanding client/server market, they need to evolve and integrate with other client/server software to build an environment that is comparable with the up-to-now unmet administrative comfort of the mainframe RMS of the past. CODINE/GRD is well recognized as one of the leading RMS for clusters today and is well-equipped for the challenges of the future.

20.6 Bibliography

[1] Mark A. Baker, Geoffrey C. Fox and Hon W. Yau. *Cluster Computing Review.* `http://www.npac.syr.edu/techreports/hypertext/sccs-748/cluster-review.html`, 1996.

[2] D. Wright. Condor Version 6.0 Manual. `http://www.pds.twi.tudelft.nl/ condor/condor-V6-Manual/`, 1998.

[3] C. Durka. Anwendungsintegration am Beispiel einer Managementanwendung für ein verteiltes Batch-System. *Diploma thesis*, Technical University Munich, 1995.

[4] GENIAS Software GmbH. CODINE & GRD Manual Set. 1998.

[5] J.A. Kaplan and M.L. Nelson. A Comparison of Queueing, Cluster and Distributed Computing Systems. *NASA TM 109025 (Revision 1)*, 1994.

[6] The MPI Forum Home Page. `http://www-c.mcs.anl.gov/mpi/`, 1998.

[7] Argonne National Laboratory. MPICH – A Portable Implementation of MPI. `http://www.mcs.anl.gov/Projects/mpi/mpich/index.html`, 1998.

[8] Silicon Graphics Inc. Message-Passing Toolkit (MPT). `http://www.sgi.com/Products/software/mpt.html`, 1998.

[9] MRJ. PBS Documentation. `http://pbs.mrj.com/docs.html`, 1998.

[10] Platform Computing Inc. LSF Suite 3.2 Documentation. 1998.

[11] Psched, API Standards for Parallel Job/Resource Scheduling. `http://parallel.nas.nasa.gov/Psched/index.html`, 1998.

[12] Oak Ridge National Laboratory. PVM - Parallel Virtual Machine. `http://www.epm.ornl.gov/pvm/pvm_home.html`, 1998.

[13] G. Stellner. Consistent Check-points of PVM Applications. *PhD thesis*, Technical University Munich, 1994.

[14] V.S. Sunderam. PVM: A Framework for Parallel and Distributed Computing. *Concurrency: Practice and Experience*, vol. 2(4), pages 315-339, 1990.

[15] UNICORE, Uniform Interface to Computing Resources. `http://www.kfa-juelich.de/zam/RD/coop/unicore/unicore.html`, 1998.

[16] J.J.J. Vesseur, R.N. Heedrik, B.J. Overeinder and P.M.A. Sloot. Experiments in Dynamic Load Balancing for Parallel Cluster Computing. 1995.

Chapter 21

Scheduling Parallel Jobs on Clusters

DROR G. FEITELSON

Institute of Computer Science
The Hebrew University of Jerusalem
91904 Jerusalem, Israel

Email: *feit@cs.huji.ac.il*

21.1 Introduction

Clusters are increasingly being used for high performance computing (HPC) applications, due to the high cost of MPPs on one hand and the wide availability of networked workstations and PCs on the other hand. The question is how to add the HPC workload to the original general-purpose workload on the cluster, providing the required high performance for the HPC applications, but not degrading the service of the original workload. This chapter surveys several approaches.

The issues that need to be addressed in order to integrate support for HPC application are

- The acquisition of resources, i.e., how to distinguish between workstations that are in active use and those that have available spare resources.
- The requirement to give priority to workstation owners, and not cause noticeable degradation to their work.
- The requirement to support different styles of parallel programs that may place different constraints on the scheduling of their processes.
- The possible use of admission control and scheduling policies to regulate the additional HPC workload.

These issues are interdependent, and the choice regarding one of them affects the choices regarding the others. For example, if only idle workstations are used for the

HPC workload, this implies an infinitely higher priority for workstation owners over the guest HPC workload. Another example is that parallel applications in which the different processes communicate and synchronize frequently require them all to execute at about the same rate, so they cannot make efficient use of workstations with widely disparate capabilities and loads.

21.2 Background

Before commencing a detailed discussion of scheduling parallel jobs on clusters, we need to define the scope of this chapter and describe possible parallel application structures.

21.2.1 Cluster Usage Modes

Clusters are typically used in either of two main modes of operation:

- NOW (network of workstations).

  This mode is based on tapping the idle cycles of existing resources, specifically networked workstations and PCs. Each such machine has an owner, who gets priority in using his machine, but when the owner is inactive the resources become available for general use. Basically this is a general-purpose (typically Unix) environment, with additions for supporting HPC applications in the background. Examples include the NOW project from Berkeley, Condor, and MOSIX.

- PMMPP ("poor man's" MPP).

  This mode involves a dedicated cluster acquired for running high-performance parallel applications. As such, there are less constraints regarding the interplay between the regular workload and the HPC workload, because there is no regular workload. Examples include the Beowulf project, RWC PC cluster, and ParPar.

Scheduling on PMMPPs is essentially the same as on commercial MPP systems and has been surveyed elsewhere [9], [12]. Here we concentrate on scheduling in a NOW environment.

21.2.2 Job Types and Requirements

Parallel jobs include multiple interacting processes. The structure of the job and the types of interactions place various requirements on the scheduling system. The three most common types are:

- Rigid[1] jobs with tight coupling.

[1]Rigid jobs are comprised of a predefined number of processes that does not change during execution [13].

Such jobs are typical of MPP environments. They contain a fixed number of processes, which communicate and synchronize at a high rate. Therefore, the processes are required to execute simultaneously on distinct processors in order to make good progress [11]. In MPPs this is handled in either of two ways. One is giving each job a dedicated partition of the machine, that is, a dedicated set of processors for its own use. The other is using gang scheduling, whereby time slicing is used (so processors are not dedicated), but all the processes of a given job are scheduled *simultaneously* on their respective processors. In clusters, nodes cannot, in general, be dedicated, so some sort of gang scheduling is needed.

- Rigid jobs with balanced processes and loose interactions.

  Such jobs do not require that the processes execute simultaneously, because they do not interact frequently. However, there remains the requirement that the processes progress at about the same rate, because the completion of the job as a whole depends on the slowest one. Therefore, the processes need to be mapped to processors with commensurate capabilities.

- Jobs structured as a workpile of independent tasks.

  Such jobs are executed by a number of worker processes that take tasks from the workpile and execute them, possibly creating new tasks in the process. This is a very flexible model that allows the number of workers to change at runtime, leading to malleable[2] jobs that are very suitable for a NOW environment. In particular, additional workers can be added as resources become available, and deleted when the resources are reclaimed by their owners.

21.3 Rigid Jobs with Process Migration

We start our discussion by considering support for rigid jobs and the possible use of process migration.

21.3.1 Process Migration

In a dynamic environment such as a NOW, as opposed to an MPP, the subsystem responsible for the HPC applications does not have full control over the system. Therefore, it needs to be able to respond to changes in the environment. An important tool is process migration.

Migration involves the remapping of processes to processors during execution. Reasons for migration include the need to relinquish a workstation and return it to its owner, and the desire to achieve a balanced load on all workstations. Metrics for the quality of migration are the overheads involved in it, and the degree to which the process is indeed detached from its previous location (in some implementations, it might have to leave some of its state behind).

[2]Malleable jobs are able to adapt to dynamic changes in their degree of parallelism as dictated by the system at runtime [13].

Algorithmic aspects of migration include the choice of which process to migrate and where to migrate it. These decisions, in turn, depend on the data that is available about the workload on the local node and on other nodes. Thus, the issues of load measurement and information dissemination are also important.

21.3.2 Case Study: PVM with Migration

PVM (Parallel Virtual Machine) is a software package for writing and executing parallel applications on a LAN. It includes support for communication and synchronization operations, configuration control, and dynamic spawning of processes.

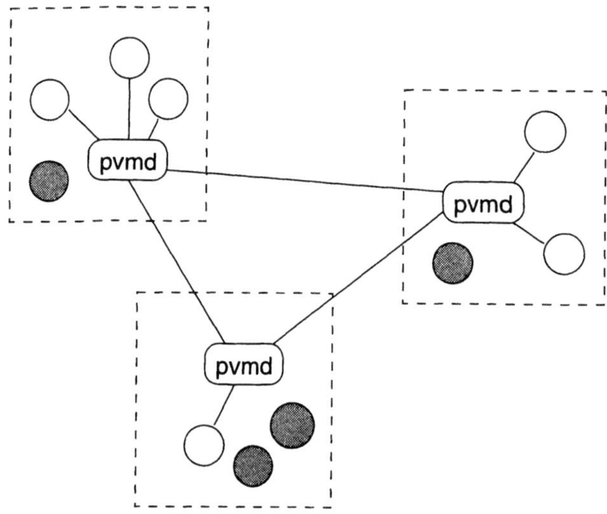

Figure 21.1 Communication in PVM is mediated by a daemon (pvmd) on each node. Circles represent processes; shaded ones are local processes unrelated to PVM.

To create a virtual parallel machine, a user spawns PVM daemon processes on a set of workstations. These daemons establish communication links among themselves, thus creating the infrastructure of the parallel machine. Processes in the parallel application connect to the local PVM daemon, which forwards their communications to other PVM daemons, and through them, to other application processes (Figure 21.1).

The original version of PVM distributes its processes in an oblivious round-robin manner among the workstations being used. This may create unbalanced loads and may lead to unacceptable degradation in the service provided to the workstation owners. Therefore, several experimental versions of PVM, such as migratable PVM [7] and dynamic PVM [19], include migration in order to move processes to more suitable locations. PVM has also been coupled with MOSIX and Condor to achieve similar benefits.

The design and functionality of migratable PVM and dynamic PVM are very similar, so we will describe only migratable PVM [7]. In this system, migration decisions are made by a global scheduler, based on information regarding load and owner activity. This is done in four steps. First, the global scheduler notifies the responsible PVM daemon that one of its processes should be migrated. The daemon then notifies all of the other PVM daemons about the pending migration, and requests that they refrain from sending it any more messages. After all the daemons acknowledge this request, the process state is transferred to the new location, and a new process is created. Finally, the new process connects to the local PVM daemon in the new location, which notifies all the other PVM daemons so that they will know how to communicate with it. Note that migration in this system is asynchronous: It can happen at any time, and affects only the migrating process and other processes that may try to communicate with it while it is migrating.

21.3.3 Case Study: MOSIX

MOSIX is a Multicomputer Operating System for unIX [4]. It is based on a Unix kernel augmented with a process migration mechanism and a scalable facility to distribute load information. The system is symmetric and distributed, with no central control facility, in the interest of scalability.

MOSIX does not include admission controls, nor does it actively track the activity of workstation owners. Instead, it maintains a balanced load on all the workstations in the cluster [5]. In addition, an attempt is made not to exceed the memory capacity of any machine. Thus, all processes (both sequential jobs and components of parallel jobs) enjoy about the same level of service. Indeed, the notion of ownership is somewhat vague, because the owner's (sequential) work may also migrate to other less-loaded machines.

The load information is distributed using a randomized algorithm. Each workstation maintains a short load vector with data about its own load and the load of a few other machines. At certain intervals (e.g., once every minute) it sends this information to another, randomly selected machine. With high probability, it will also be selected by some other machine, and receive such a load vector. The incoming information is integrated with the information available earlier, and only the most up-to-date part is stored. If it is found that some other machine has a significantly different load, a migration operation is initiated.

Migration is based on the home-node concept. Each process has a home node: its owner's workstation. When it is migrated, it is actually split into two parts. The *body* of the process, containing all the user-level context and some site-independent kernel context, is migrated to another node. The *deputy*, containing the site-dependent kernel context, is left on the home node. A communication link is established between the two parts, so that the process can access its local environment via the deputy, and so that other processes can access it (Figure 21.2).

Experiments show that running PVM over MOSIX leads to considerable improvements in performance relative to the original oblivious PVM.

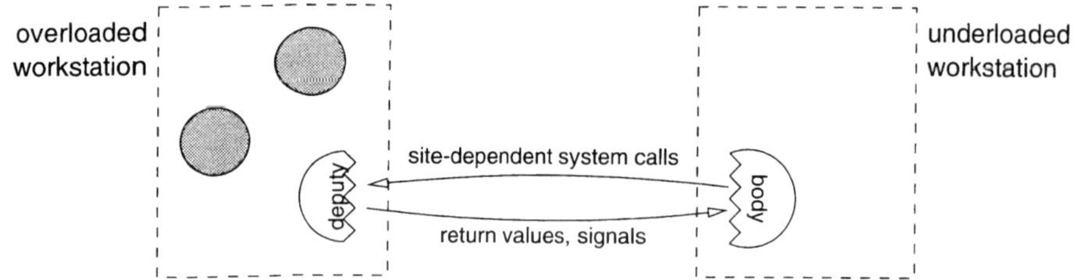

Figure 21.2 Process migration in MOSIX divides the process into a migratable body and a site-dependent deputy, which remains in the home node.

21.4 Malleable Jobs with Dynamic Parallelism

Another approach emphasizes the dynamics of workstation clusters: Workstations become available and are then reclaimed by their owners at unpredictable times, and parallel jobs, therefore, should adjust to such varying resources.

21.4.1 Identifying Idle Workstations

Executing parallel jobs on a workstation cluster is often thought of in terms of a background activity. Each workstation is primarily intended to support the work of its owner, and only spare cycles are available to the parallel jobs. The owners give access to such spare cycles provided it does not interfere with their normal work.

The best way to ensure that workstation owners are not alienated is to use only idle workstations, rather than also trying to harvest the spare capacity of workstations that are not being fully utilized. While this is a rather conservative approach, it still provides the parallel workload with plenty of computing resources. Depending on the exact definition of "idle," studies have shown that 60–90% may be idle at any given moment, even at the busiest times of the day [16], [18], [1]. At night and on weekends this may approach 100%.

Using idle workstations to run parallel jobs requires two things:

- The ability to identify idle workstations. This is relatively easy based on monitoring keyboard and mouse activity. Typically, workstations that show no such activity for a few minutes are considered idle.
- The ability to retreat from workstations that are reclaimed by their owners. This is possible if the application is structured as a set of independent tasks, executed by worker processes. When a workstation has to be evicted, the worker is killed and its tasks re-assigned to other workers.

21.4.2 Case Study: Condor and WoDi

Condor is a system for running batch jobs in the background on a LAN, using idle workstations [17]. When a workstation is reclaimed by its owner, the batch process is first suspended, and if the owner continues to work, it is killed and restarted from a checkpoint on another node. Condor is the basis for the LoadLeveler product used on IBM workstations.

In order to provide good support for parallel applications, Condor was augmented with a resource management interface (called CARMI, for Condor Application Resource Management Interface). This interface allows jobs to request additional resources and to be notified if resources are taken away [20]. When requesting resources, it is possible to specify required attributes, such as architecture, operating system, and available memory. Requests are asynchronous, meaning that when the function call making the request returns, the request has been registered but not necessarily serviced. The application later receives notification about the servicing of requests, as well as notifications about resources that have been reclaimed, using the same mechanism as it uses for interprocess communication — e.g., PVM messages. This allows the application to use a single mechanism for all types of communication, whether internal or from the external resource manager.

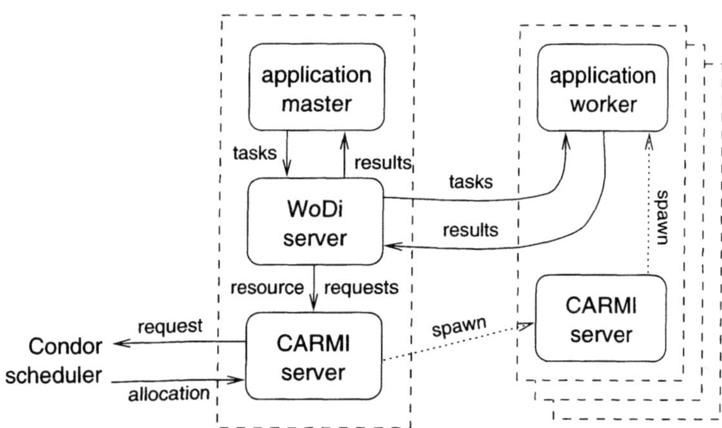

Figure 21.3 Master-worker applications use the WoDi server to coordinate task execution regardless of the fate of workers. WoDi, in turn, uses CARMI servers to acquire resources and create workers. The CARMI server interacts with the Condor scheduler for the actual allocation, using Condor's pool of idle workstations. Condor daemons used to monitor machines and start processes remotely are not shown.

Using the CARMI interface, the WoDi (Work Distributor) package was written to support simple programming of master-worker applications (Figure 21.3). The master process sends work requests (tasks) to the WoDi server. The WoDi server uses CARMI to obtain the required resources, starts worker processes on them, and sends them the tasks for execution. It also monitors the dynamics of the system in order to guarantee that each task will be executed exactly once, regardless of what happens to the workers during execution. As tasks are completed, the results are returned to the master process.

21.4.3 Case Study: Piranha and Linda

Linda is a parallel programming language, or rather, a coordination language that can be added to conventional programming languages such as Fortran or C. It is based on an associative tuple space that acts as a distributed data repository [2]. Parallel computations are created by injecting unevaluated tuples into the tuple space. Thus, the tuple space can also be viewed as a workpile of independent tuples that need to be evaluated.

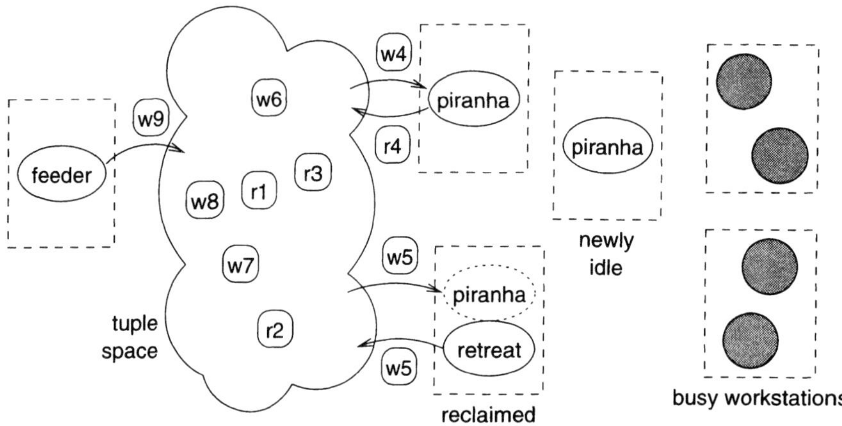

Figure 21.4 Piranha programs include a feeder function that generates work tuples (w), and piranha functions that are executed automatically on idle workstation and transform the work tuples into result tuples (r). If a workstation is reclaimed, the retreat function is called to return the unfinished work to tuple space.

Piranha is a system for executing Linda applications on a NOW [6]. Programs that run under Piranha must include three special user-defined functions called `feeder`, `piranha`, and `retreat`. The `feeder` function is run continuously on the first node allocated to the program. Its job is to create tuples describing work to be done (see Figure 21.4). The `piranha` function is called automatically on each node that becomes available during the execution (in other words, the program does not have to create new processes explicitly). Its job is to retrieve work tuples created by the `feeder`, to perform the required computation, and to create result tuples that can subsequently be collected in order to generate the output of the program. The `retreat` function is called in case the `piranha` function has to be interrupted, as may happen if the workstation on which it is running is reclaimed by its owner. Its job is to perform the required cleanup so that the computation will not be affected by the removal of the running `piranha`. For example, this can be achieved by re-injecting the work tuple into the tuple space, so that another `piranha` will be able to pick it up.

21.5 Communication-Based Coscheduling

If the processes of a parallel application communicate and synchronize frequently, it may be beneficial for them to actually execute simultaneously on different processors [11]: This saves the overhead of frequent context switches, and reduces the need for buffering during communication. Such simultaneous execution, combined with time slicing, is provided by gang scheduling, which is quite popular in MPP environments. However, gang scheduling implies that the participating processes are known in advance. The alternative is to identify them during execution [10]. Thus, only a sub-set of the processes are scheduled together, leading to coscheduling rather than gang scheduling.

21.5.1 Demand-Based Coscheduling

Demand-based coscheduling bases the decision about what processes should be scheduled together on actual observations of the communication patterns. This approach requires the cooperation of the communication subsystem, so that it will notify the scheduler of communication events. In practice, the communication subsystem monitors the destinations of incoming messages, and raises the priority of the destination processes [22], [21]. Thus, a process that sends a message may cause the recipient to be coscheduled with it.

An obvious problem with naively raising the priority of any process that receives a message is that it is unfair. Indeed, users can artificially raise the priority of their programs by sending spurious messages among their processes. Therefore, the communication subsystem raises only the priority of processes that receive messages if this does not violate fairness considerations.

Another problem occurs when multiple parallel jobs co-exist in the system. Consider two nodes, each hosting two processes from two competing parallel jobs. Assume that process A_1, the process belonging to job A running on node 1, sends a message to process A_2, that job's process running on node 2. However, at the same time process B_2 is actually running on node 2, and it sends a message to process B_1 on node 1. Again, a naive implementation will fail to resolve this conflict, and might just switch the processes on both nodes without coscheduling either job.

The proposed solution is to use epoch numbers (Figure 21.5). The epoch number on each node is incremented when a spontaneous context switch is made (that is, when the context switch is *not* the result of an incoming message). This epoch number is appended to all outgoing messages. When a node receives a message, it then compares its local epoch number with the one included in the incoming message, and switches to the destination process only if the incoming epoch number is greater. When such a switch is performed, the node also updates its local epoch number and adopts the incoming value. As a result, it will not switch back to the previous process if a message arrives for it, thus enabling the new job to spread its influence and be coscheduled across all the nodes.

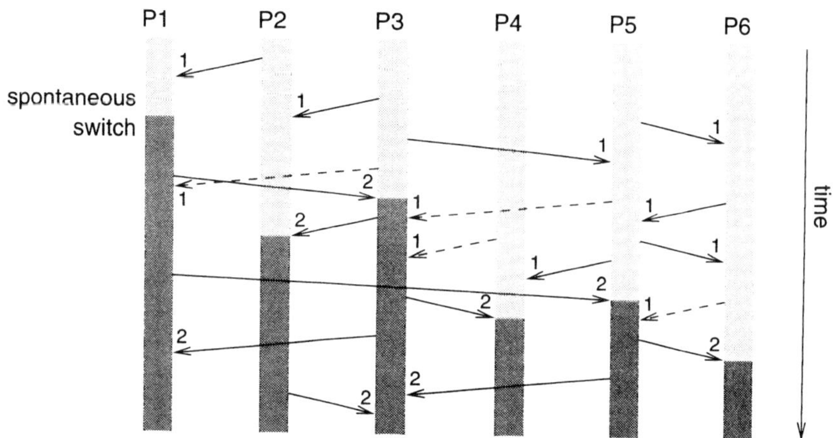

Figure 21.5 Epoch numbers allow a parallel job to take over the whole cluster, in the face of another active job. The first process is scheduled spontaneously, and increments the epoch number from 1 to 2. Thereafter, processors switch from the light-gray job to the dark-gray one based on incoming messages with higher epoch numbers, and reject those with lower epoch numbers (dashed arrows).

21.5.2 Implicit Coscheduling

In a LAN environment, explicit control over the scheduling based on communication may be difficult. However, it may be unnecessary, if the communication is done using Unix facilities (sockets), and applications are coarse-grained (long phases of computation interspersed by phases of intensive communication, as in bulk-synchronous application). The reason is that in Unix processes that perform I/O (including communication) get a higher priority. Therefore, those processes participating in a communication phase will get high priority on their respective nodes, and will be coscheduled for the duration of the communication phase [8], [3]. This raises the intriguing possibility of completely implicit coscheduling, where the required coscheduling behavior emerges without any explicit measures being taken.

While explicit measures for scheduling are not required, one does have to make sure that a communicating process is not *de*-scheduled while it is waiting for a reply from another process. This is done by using two-phase blocking, also known as spin-blocking. The idea is that a waiting process will initially busy wait (spin) for some time, waiting for the anticipated response. But if the response does not arrive within the pre-specified time, the process blocks and relinquishes its processor in favor of another ready process. It is easy to see that spinning for a duration that is equal to the context switch overhead leads to a 2-competitive on-line algorithm [15]. However, practical considerations indicate that the spinning time should be 5 times the context switch overhead [3]. This provides enough time to wake up the peer process if it is blocked.

Note that implicit coscheduling keeps processes in step only when they are communicating. During the computation phase the processes may fall out of step with each other. However, this is not important because they are not interacting at this time, and do not need to be coscheduled.

21.6 Batch Scheduling

An observation that is sometimes made is that there is a qualitative difference between the work done by workstation owners and the parallel jobs that try to use spare cycles: Workstation owners do interactive work, and require immediate response from their workstations, whereas the parallel jobs are intrinsically compute-intensive, run for long periods, and therefore do not require immediate response. In particular, it is possible to queue them until suitable resources become available.

21.6.1 Admission Controls

HPC applications require high performance, but also place a heavy load on the system. Therefore, consideration for interactive users implies that these HPC applications be curbed if they "hog" the system. In particular, one can refuse to admit them into the system in the first place.

A general solution is to use a batch scheduling system, such as DQS or PBS [14]. Such systems define a set of queues to which batch jobs are submitted. Each queue contains jobs that are characterized by a certain combination of attributes, such as expected run-time and memory requirements. The batch scheduler then chooses jobs for execution based on their attributes and on the available resources, guided by the local scheduling policy. Other jobs are queued so as not to overload the system.

The question remains as to which workstations are used by the batch scheduling system. One approach is to use only idle workstations. However, this is problematic because the pool of idle workstations keeps changing. An alternative is, therefore, to use all workstations, with preference for those that are lightly loaded. This seems to work because the *average* utilization required by the owner's interactive workload is usually rather stable, even when it has large momentary fluctuations. In addition, each workstation hosts only a single parallel job at a time, allowing for fast preemption in favor of the interactive workload.

21.6.2 Case Study: Utopia/LSF

Utopia is an environment for load sharing on large scale heterogeneous clusters. It includes three main components: a mechanism for collecting load information in order to make process placement decisions, a mechanism for transparent remote execution, and a library to use them from applications [23]. Upon this base are built components for workload control and analysis, batch scheduling, and support for parallel applications. LSF (Load Sharing Facility) is a commercial offspring of Utopia.

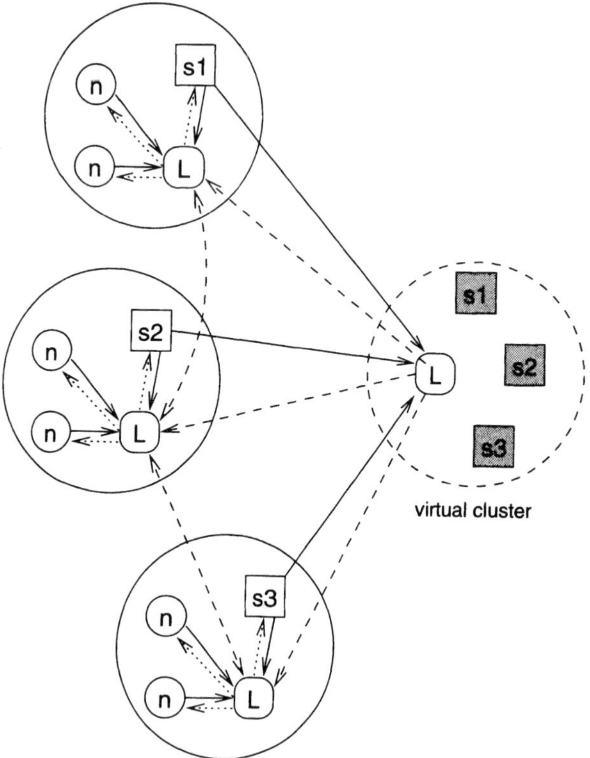

Figure 21.6 Utopia uses a two-level design to spread load information in large systems: nodes (n) send their local status to their local LIM (L, solid arrows), who broadcasts it to all nodes (dotted arrows); LIMs also communicate among themselves (dashed arrows). Virtual clusters are used to collect information about desirable machines (such as strong servers, s) that are not physically co-located.

The collection of load information is done by a set of daemons, one on each node. The daemons elect the one with the lowest host ID to be the master Load Information Manager (LIM). The master collects load vectors (including information such as recent CPU queue length, memory usage, and the number of users) from all the nodes in the cluster, and distributes this information to all slave nodes. The slaves can then use this information to make placement decisions for new processes.

As using a centralized master does not scale to large systems, this mechanism is used only within confined physical clusters. Support for load sharing across clusters is provided by communication among the master LIMs of the different clusters. In addition, it is possible to create *virtual* clusters that group together powerful servers that are physically dispersed across the system (Figure 21.6). Thus a single communication with the LIM of the virtual cluster provides information about all the most desirable servers in the system.

Utopia's batch scheduling system uses this infrastructure to obtain information about the availability of resources for queued parallel applications. However, due to the typical long running time of batch applications, it uses long-term CPU usage averages, rather than the more recent averages used for other purposes. Queueing and allocation decisions are done by a master batch daemon, which is co-located with the master LIM. The actual execution and control over the batch processes is done by slave batch daemons on the various nodes.

21.7 Summary

Many different approaches to the issue of scheduling parallel jobs on a NOW have been proposed and implemented. Regrettably, it is hard to compare them to each other, because they are typically based on different assumptions and strive to achieve different goals. The systems described in Sections 21.3 through 21.6 are based on the following orthogonal assumptions:

- It is most important to balance the loads on the different machines, so that all processes get equal service.
- It is most important not to interfere with workstation owners, so only idle workstation may be used, and they must be relinquished once the owner returns.
- It is most important to provide parallel programs with a suitable environment, such as simultaneous execution of interacting processes.
- It is most important not to flood the system with low-priority (non-interactive) compute intensive jobs, so admission controls and batch scheduling are necessary.

While each of these assumptions is valid, none captures the full picture. Therefore, there is room for improvement by considering how to combine multiple assumptions, and merge the approaches used in different systems. For example, the following combination is possible:

- Have a tunable parameter that selects whether workstations are in general shared, or used only if idle. Intermediate values guarantee a certain percentage of the resources for the owner, and share the rest. This parameter modulates the measured load values.
- Provide migration to enable jobs to evacuate workstations that become overloaded, are reclaimed by their owners, or become too slow relative to others participating in the same parallel job.
- Provide communication-based coscheduling for jobs that seem to need it. While this is an attribute of the job, it is better not to require the user to specify it.
- Provide batch queueing with a check-point facility so that heavy jobs will run only when they do not degrade performance for others.

The technology for such a system exists, and its different components have been demonstrated in isolation. Now we are faced with the challenge of integrating them together to provide the best service for users.

21.8 Bibliography

[1] A. Acharya, G. Edjlali, and J. Saltz. The Utility of Exploiting Idle Workstations for Parallel Computation. In *SIGMETRICS Conference on Measurement & Modeling of Computer Systems*, pages 225–236, June 1997.

[2] S. Ahuja, N. Carriero, and D. Gelernter. Linda and Friends. *Computer*, vol. 19(8), pages 26–34, August 1986.

[3] A. C. Arpaci-Dusseau, D. E. Culler, and A. M. Mainwaring. Scheduling with Implicit Information in Distributed Systems. In *SIGMETRICS Conference on Measurement & Modeling of Computer Systems*, pages 233–243, June 1998.

[4] A. Barak, S. Guday, and R. G. Wheeler. The MOSIX Distributed Operating System: Load Balancing for UNIX. Springer-Verlag, 1993. Lecture Notes in Computer Science, vol. 672.

[5] A. Barak and A. Shiloh. A Distributed Load-Balancing Policy for a Multicomputer. *Software — Practice & Experience*, vol. 15(9), pages 901–913, September 1985.

[6] N. Carriero, E. Freedman, D. Gelernter, and D. Kaminsky. Adaptive Parallelism and Piranha. *Computer*, vol. 28(1), pages 40–49, January 1995.

[7] J. Casas, R. Konuru, S. W. Otto, R. Prouty, and J. Walpole. Adaptive Load Migration Systems for PVM. In *Supercomputing '94*, pages 390–399, November 1994.

[8] A. Dusseau, R. H. Arpaci, and D. E. Culler. Effective Distributed Scheduling of Parallel Workloads. In *SIGMETRICS Conference on Measurement & Modeling of Computer Systems*, pages 25–36, May 1996.

[9] D. G. Feitelson. A Survey of Scheduling in Multiprogrammed Parallel Systems. *Research Report RC 19790 (87657)*, IBM T. J. Watson Research Center, October 1994. URL http://www.cs.huji.ac.il/~feit/survey.ps.gz.

[10] D. G. Feitelson and L. Rudolph. Coscheduling Based on Runtime Identification of Activity Working Sets. *International Journal of Parallel Programming*, vol. 23(2), pages 135–160, April 1995.

[11] D. G. Feitelson and L. Rudolph. Gang Scheduling Performance Benefits for Fine-Grain Synchronization. *Journal of Parallel & Distributed Computing*, vol. 16(4), pages 306–318, December 1992.

[12] D. G. Feitelson and L. Rudolph. Parallel Job Scheduling: Issues and Approaches. In *Job Scheduling Strategies for Parallel Processing*, D. G. Feitelson and L. Rudolph (eds.), pages 1–18, Springer-Verlag, 1995. Lecture Notes in Computer Science, vol. 949.

[13] D. G. Feitelson and L. Rudolph. Toward Convergence in Job Schedulers for Parallel Supercomputers. In *Job Scheduling Strategies for Parallel Processing*, D. G. Feitelson and L. Rudolph (eds.), pages 1–26, Springer-Verlag, 1996. Lecture Notes in Computer Science, vol. 1162.

[14] R. L. Henderson. Job Scheduling Under the Portable Batch System. In *Job Scheduling Strategies for Parallel Processing*, D. G. Feitelson and L. Rudolph (eds.), pages 279–294, Springer-Verlag, 1995. Lecture Notes in Computer Science, vol. 949.

[15] A. R. Karlin, K. Li, M. S. Manasse, and S. Owicki. Empirical Studies of Competitive Spinning for a Shared-Memory Multiprocessor. In 13th *Symposium on Operating Systems Principles*, pages 41–55, October 1991.

[16] P. Krueger and R. Chawla. The Stealth Distributed Scheduler. In 11th *International Conference on Distributed Computing Systems*, pages 336–343, May 1991.

[17] M. J. Litzkow, M. Livny, and M. W. Mutka. Condor - a Hunter of Idle Workstations. In 8th *International Conference on Distributed Computing Systems*, pages 104–111, June 1988.

[18] M. Mutka and M. Livny. The Available Capacity of a Privately Owned Workstation Environment. *Performance Evaluation*, vol. 12(4), pages 269–284, July 1991.

[19] B. J. Overeinder, P. M. A. Sloot, R. N. Heederik, and L. O. Hertzberger. A Dynamic Load Balancing System for Parallel Cluster Computing. *Future Generation Computer Systems*, vol. 12(1), pages 101–115, May 1996.

[20] J. Pruyne and M. Livny. Parallel Processing on Dynamic Resources with CARMI. In *Job Scheduling Strategies for Parallel Processing*, D. G. Feitelson and L. Rudolph (eds.), pages 259–278, Springer-Verlag, 1995. Lecture Notes in Computer Science, vol. 949.

[21] P. G. Sobalvarro, S. Pakin, W. E. Weihl, and A. A. Chien. Dynamic Coscheduling on Workstation Clusters. In *Job Scheduling Strategies for Parallel Processing*, D. G. Feitelson and L. Rudolph (eds.), pages 231–256, Springer Verlag, 1998. Lecture Notes in Computer Science, vol. 1459.

[22] P. G. Sobalvarro and W. E. Weihl. Demand-Based Coscheduling of Parallel Jobs on Multiprogrammed Multiprocessors. In *Job Scheduling Strategies for Parallel Processing*, D. G. Feitelson and L. Rudolph (eds.), pages 106–126, Springer-Verlag, 1995. Lecture Notes in Computer Science, vol. 949.

[23] S. Zhou, X. Zheng, J. Wang, and P. Delisle. Utopia: A Load Sharing Facility for Large, Heterogeneous Distributed Computer Systems. *Software — Practice & Experience*, vol. 23(12), pages 1305–1336, December 1993.

Chapter 22

Load Sharing and Fault Tolerance Manager

BERTIL FOLLIOT AND PIERRE SENS

Laboratoire d'Informatique de Paris 6 / CNRS
University of Paris VI, Paris, France

Email: *folliot@src.lip6.fr, sens@src.lip6.fr*

22.1 Introduction

The increasing need for processing power for scientific calculations combined with the large development of distributed information systems makes the computation distribution over workstation networks very attractive. A large range of studies has shown that the workstations are idle from 33% to 78% of the time. A similar study in one of our campus facility (18 workstations) over a six-month period shows that the workstations were free 69% of the time and the processors were free 93% of the time. Consequently, to achieve high performance the system has to provide an efficient mechanism for program allocation. Two load sharing policies may be applied to react to dynamic system change: dynamic placement, that allocates programs according to the current system state, and migration, that moves processes according to system and application evolution.

In spite of the advantage of process allocation, only a few systems have implemented load balancing strategies [3] and most of the proposed algorithms use only simulation results indicating their efficiency. In such systems, processes are initially allocated on a set of workstations according to multi-criteria placement algorithms taking into account the host loads and the user activities. These algorithms use mechanisms for system state monitoring and application executions supervising. Based on this knowledge, the allocation policies allow the improvement of application response time as well as the effective use of the distributed system resources. A migration facility that moves processes from one workstation to another one usually copes with three main cases: a user comes back to his/her workstation after an initial placement decision has been done, a host becomes overloaded and there exists an underloaded host in the system, a fast host is underloaded and a slow one is loaded.

Load sharing is dedicated to long-lived application. For this kind of application, fault tolerance becomes an essential component. Many hours of computation can be lost not only if a hardware failure occurs, but also if one of the processors is rebooted, turned off or disconnected from the network. As a consequence, developing parallel programs also requires expertise in fault tolerance. To release application designers from this task, systems must include fault tolerant facility where processes affected by a crash are automatically recovered on a new set of workstations.

The main scope of this chapter is to describe the interaction between load balancing and fault tolerance in a cluster of workstations and to show that the combination of the two facilities can outperform reliable parallel applications.

This chapter is organized as follows: Sections 22.2 and 22.3 describe usual techniques to balance load between hosts and to tolerate host failures. Then, Section 22.4 presents results of an experimental platform which integrates both facilities. Finally, Section 22.5 outlines some related works in fault tolerant and load sharing management.

22.2 Load Sharing in Cluster Computing

Supports for parallel programming over workstations network often ignore programs' needs, real load conditions and users' activities (as PVM [9]). Some degree of load sharing has been adapted in existing packages such as lsPVM [14] or Dynamic PVM [5]. For better usage of unused hosts, several different policies and systems have been realized to balance the load [3], [11], [14]. However, there are few published methods that allow programmers to specify parallel application in a load sharing perspective. Indeed, optimum load sharing strategies are very hard to implement and are well-known as NP-complete, even in simple cases. The main reasons are:

1. It is impossible to get an exact knowledge of the global state of the system at a given instant.
2. The execution of complex allocation algorithms may represent a heavy burden.
3. The instability behavior of allocation algorithms is due to inaccurate information.

Parallel program placement has been widely studied. A number of works concentrated on static allocation, adapted for multiprocessor systems (dedicated environment) without interference between users or concurrent applications. A well-known parallel application environment is the PVM system. It uses a user-managed host file indicating a list of hosts to run an application. This scheme is adequate for a dedicated environment, but may lead to over-utilization of resources in a local area networks of workstations, if different PVM users use overlapping sets of hosts. It may also lead to unacceptable interference with hosts supporting interactive users.

Concerning dynamic load sharing in a local area network of workstations, most of the works deal only with the processor load and are not adapted for the allocation of entire parallel applications. Some other works, such as Utopia [14] or Mosix [3], consider the program needs other than CPU, but do not offer a parallel programming environment: naming, communication, attraction/repulsion between components. These works are divided in two groups:

- dynamic placement (as Rem [13], Utopia [14]) where processes are allocated at start-up and stay on the same location, and

- process migration (as Condor [11], Mosix [3], Sprite [6]) where processes can move according to overload conditions or the reactivation of workstations by their owners.

22.3 Fault Tolerance by Means of Checkpointing

Checkpointing and rollback recovery are well-known to provide fault tolerance in distributed systems. This section reviews the common techniques.

22.3.1 Checkpointing a Single Process

The checkpoint of a single process is a snapshot of the process's address space at a given time. To reduce the cost of checkpointing, two complementary techniques can be applied: incremental and non-blocking checkpointing [8].

Incremental methods reduce the amount of data that must be written. Only those pages of the address space modified since the last checkpoint are written to stable storage.

Non-blocking methods allow the process to continue executing while its checkpoint is written to stable storage. However, if the process modifies any of its pages during the checkpoint, the resulting checkpoint may not represent the real state of the process. The internal copy-on-write memory protection may be used to protect pages during the checkpoint. At the start of the checkpoint, the pages to be written are write-protected. After writing each page to stable storage, the checkpoint manager removes the protection from the page. If a process attempts to modify a protected page, the page is copied to a newly allocated page, and the protection of the original page is removed. The newly allocated page is not accessible to the process. Only the checkpoint manager uses it to finish the checkpoint.

These complementary techniques improve significantly the response time: between 3.4 times and 4.7 times faster checkpointing, according to experimental results presented by [8].

22.3.2 Checkpointing of Communicating Processes

When processes exchange messages, the simple approach to recovery for independent processes is no longer adequate. To recover from a fault, the execution must be rolled back to a consistent global state The rolling back of one process could result in an avalanche of rollbacks of other processes before a consistent state is found. For example, when the sender of a message m is rolled back, m is recorded as "received but not yet sent." Message m becomes an *orphan message* and the system is inconsistent. To discard this orphan message, the corresponding receiver must also be rolled back. This domino effect is illustrated in Figure 22.1.

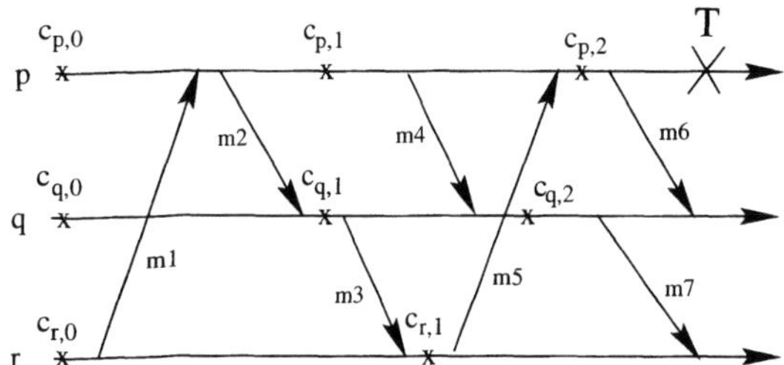

Figure 22.1 Domino effect.

The Xs indicate checkpoints and the arrows represent the messages. If p fails at time T, it would be rolled back to $Cp, 2$. Since message $m6$ becomes an orphan, q must be rolled back to $Cq, 2$. Then $m7$ becomes an orphan and r must be rolled back to $Cr, 1$ and so on. Finally, to recover from the failure of p, all processes must be rolled back to their initial checkpoints.

A substantial body of work has been published regarding fault tolerance by means of checkpointing. The main issues that have been covered are limiting the number of hosts that have to participate in taking the checkpoint or in rolling back [10], reducing the number of messages required to synchronize a checkpoint, or using message logging [8]. Checkpointing techniques can be classified into two categories: coordinated and independent checkpointing.

Coordinated checkpointing. With coordinated checkpointing, processes coordinate their checkpointing actions such that the collection of checkpoints represents a consistent state of the whole system. When a failure occurs, the system restarts from these checkpoints. Looking at the results of [8], the main drawback of this approach is that the messages used for synchronizing a checkpoint are an important source of overhead. Moreover, after a failure, surviving processes may have to rollback to their latest checkpoint in order to remain consistent with recovering processes. Alternatively, analyzing the interactions between processes can reduce the number of processes to rollback [10].

Independent checkpointing. In independent checkpointing, each process independently saves its state without any synchronization with the others. Message logging was introduced to avoid the domino effect [8]. Logging methods fall into two classes: pessimistic and optimistic. In pessimistic message logging, the system writes incoming messages to stable storage before delivering them to the application [12]. To restart, the failing process is rolled back to the last checkpoint and replies to outgoing messages are returned immediately from the log. The receiver is blocked until the message is logged on stable storage. Alternatively, the system delivers the message to the application immediately but disallows the sending of further messages until the message has been logged. In optimistic message logging, messages are tagged with information that allows the system to keep track of inter-process dependencies [8]. Inter-process dependency information is used to determine which processes need to be rolled back on restart. This approach reduces the logging overhead, but processes that survive a failure may still be rolled back. Alternatively, messages are gathered in the main memory of the sending host and are asynchronously saved to stable storage. The benefits listed above are obtained at the expense of the space and time required for logging messages. The space overhead is reasonable, given the current large disk capacities. Furthermore, at each new checkpoint all messages are deleted from the associated backup (a log is completely deleted after each checkpoint). The main drawback is the input/output overhead (i.e., the latency in accessing the stable storage).

22.4 Integration of Load Sharing and Fault Tolerance

This section presents and discusses a realization of a fault tolerant load sharing facility, GATOSTAR, that we developed at University of Paris 6. It is based on the implementation of two applications: GATOS and STAR. GATOS is a load sharing manager which automatically distributes parallel applications among hosts according to multicriteria algorithms. STAR is a software fault manager which automatically recovers processes affected by host failures.

22.4.1 Environment and Architecture

Unix is becoming a standard in networked environments. Granted, applications developed above an unmodified Unix version are portable at very low cost and can easily be distributed. These reasons led us to build GATOSTAR on top of Unix without any kernel modification.

System Environment

GATOSTAR relies on a BSD Unix operating system (SunOS). It works on a set of heterogeneous workstations connected by a local area network. We define migration domains of compatible hosts, where processes can freely move. In this environment, failures are uncommon events. Clark and McMillin measured the average crash time in a local area network to be once every 2.7 days [4] for a local area network of 10 workstations. Therefore, we favor solutions with a low overhead under normal operation, possibly to the detriment of an increase in recovery time. We consider that the system is composed of fail-silent processors, where the faulty nodes simply stop and the remote nodes are not notified. We do not consider the network partition problem.

Application Model

We have adopted the classic application model where an application is a set of communicating processes connected by a precedence graph. The graph contains all qualitative information needed to execute the application and helpful for the load sharing manager: precedences and communications between processes, and files in use. The application programmer can provide this information both by an execution graph (a file containing the graph description using a parallel application grammar), and/or by dynamic operations that allow, while running, to modify the execution graph. We are interested in applications running for extended periods of time, such as high number factoring, VLSI applications, image processing. This kind of application may be executing for hours, days or weeks. In that case, the failure probability becomes significant, and load sharing and the need for reliability are important concerns.

GATOSTAR Architecture

GATOSTAR architecture consists of a ring of hosts which exchange information about hosts' functioning and processes' execution. Having this type of information available on-line allows us to automatically recover the system and quickly return it to operation, thus increasing the availability of the distributed system resources. Each host maintains a load vector which contains a view of all host loads. Periodically, each host sends its vector to its immediate successor. Load messages are also used to detect host failure.

The current prototype is composed of four daemons running on each host (Figure 22.2): (1) a load sharing manager (LSM) in charge of allocation and migration strategies, (2) a fault tolerance manager (FTM) responsible of checkpointing and message redirection, (3) a ring manager (RM) in charge of load transmission and failure detection, and (4) a replicated file manager (RFM) that implements the reliable storage.

22.4.2 Process Allocation

Process Placement

To be executed, application processes need resources that vary from one process to another. To evaluate the need of each process, we transparently keep track of previous executions and/or we allow application designers to give appropriate indications. Dynamic process allocation can be operated according to the following criteria: hosts load, process execution time, required memory, and communication between processes. In the application description, the programmer can specify appropriate allocation criteria for each program according to its execution needs.

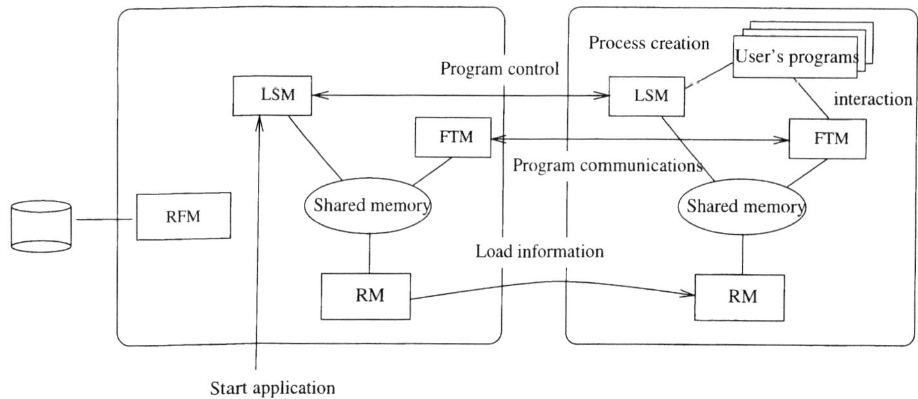

Figure 22.2 GatoStar architecture.

He/she specifies the set of hosts involved in the load distribution and provides different binary code versions for each program in order to deal with system heterogeneity.

Selecting the less loaded host. Allocating processes according to load allows us to benefit from idle workstations power. To take into account the heterogeneous character of hosts, the load of a host is defined as directly proportional to CPU utilization and inversely proportional to its CPU speed [14]. On each host, the load sharing manager locally computes an average load and uses failure detection messages to exchange load information. Thus, no extra communication is needed when allocating programs. The program is allocated to the most lightly loaded host, if the load of this host is below the overload threshold. Otherwise, the program is started on the originating host as all hosts in the system are heavily loaded, or used by interactive users. The main difficulty is to find a good value for the overload threshold. A number of simulation studies on load sharing have been performed. Eager et al. [7] show that the overload threshold depends on the average load of the system and is between 1 and 2. These results and our experience with the GATOSTAR system lead us to set the overload threshold value to 1. Another problem is to get global state information. Indeed, every host cannot have exact knowledge about the load of the other hosts: first, because of network transmission time, and secondly there is a delay between the instant when a host receives the information and the instant it uses the information to decide where to allocate a process. Large load fluctuations can occur unexpectedly. If the delays mentioned above are significant, a program can be allocated to a host, which becomes heavily loaded. This problem is solved by re-directing the program allocation request, if the load of the selected host is higher than the overload threshold. We add to every remote execution request the expected load and a list of alternative hosts. Thus, re-allocating a program consists only in re-directing the execution request to one of these hosts. The load fluctuations coming after the initial placement can be solved only by migrating a sub-set of processes (see the next section).

Multicriteria load sharing algorithm. Encouraged by the fact that an application programmer has a good knowledge of his application execution needs, we specified program placement policies that take into account several criteria related to the applications execution needs. Indeed, application programs need resources (processor, memory, file, communication) which vary from one program to another. In the application description, the programmer may specify appropriate performance criteria for each program. In GATOSTAR, we propose the following ones:

1. Response time: The allocation policy corresponding to the response time criterion aims at minimizing the total execution time of the whole application. Reducing the response time of each program individually is not enough. Indeed, the application is run by batches of parallel programs that should be allocated at the same time. These considerations suggest that the longest running programs would be placed first. The selected hosts are allocated to programs in the order of their decreasing execution time values. Thus, the longest programs are allocated on the less loaded and fastest hosts (similar to the Longest Job First algorithm for a mono-processor machine).

2. File accesses: The policy for the file access criterion consists of finding the host where a program should be allocated so that the total cost of file accesses is minimized. The allocation decision is based on a number of parameters such as number of accesses, size of file accesses, disks and network speed. Once a host is selected to execute the program, a complementary policy allows us to decide whether to migrate one or more of the remaining files or to access them remotely (according to the previous parameters and the files size). The file access algorithm has not been implemented.

3. Communication between programs: The usage of this criterion aims to minimize the total cost of communications between programs. This is equivalent, in practice, to reduce the number of remote communications. To make this possible, we keep information of the location of all the application's programs already allocated in the system. Given this information, the most communicating programs are clustered on the same host.

4. Memory needs: In this case, the host on which a program will be allocated must have enough memory to run it. This is done by determining the memory needs of the program to be allocated and the available memory on every host. In contrary to the other criterion, which resources may be shared, the memory criterion provides an exclusive allocation. Program allocation on one host must not exceed the maximum physical memory of this host. The memory allocation criterion in GATOSTAR is conservative: Programs using this criterion are managed by a batch queue system, waiting for the appropriate memory space to be available. This ensures the correct execution of the application but may increase its response time.

5. Performance criteria combination: The previous performance criteria may be combined to ensure program placement according to several policies at the same time. We take at the beginning the set of available hosts, then, this set is reduced according to the first criterion on the given list of criteria. This mechanism is repeated with the remaining criteria until only one host remains or all the refinements have been done. The obtained host is the best compromise between the intervening criteria in the order in which the programmer specifies them.

Other recent works have shown that the multicriteria approach is very efficient for a general-purpose load sharing system, as in Isatys [2], as it can adapt the allocation to a wide spectrum of applications and programs behaviors.

Process Migration

Process migration is complex and difficult to realize. The GATOSTAR system immediately incorporates a migration mechanism by means of the checkpoint/restart already developed for STAR.

The load sharing algorithms, described in the previous section, has been extended to process migration according to applications and environment evolution. Environment evolution results from foreign activities: A user logs in or sends a remote job to an already loaded host. Application evolution stems from variations in resource usage (processor occupation, communication between processes, and memory demands). Since mechanisms to monitor such variations were already integrated, the adaptation of the multi-criteria load sharing algorithms has been straightforward.

The three main questions that must be answered when migrating processes are: when to migrate a process, which process to choose, and where to move the chosen process. Our proposed answer to the first and the third questions is based on two opposite load thresholds: a migration and a reception threshold. In the symmetrical scheme, the load sharing server periodically computes two conditions: (1) a faster workstation load is under the reception threshold, (2) the local host load is above the migration threshold and at least one workstation load is under the reception threshold. The former condition allows the potential use of fast available hosts, and the latter one allows us to decrease the overload of the local station. If one or both conditions are true, the server starts the process selection step. In the process selection step, the local server chooses a process that has been executed locally for at least a given local execution time. It prevents short-lived process to be migrated and it also prevents a process from spending all its time in migration from one host to another.

If there is more than one process that can be migrated, execution graph information (containing program description) is used. This graph indicates the estimated running time of each process, and the longest remaining process is selected. If such information is not available, we use a combination of the age of the process and its size. A logarithm function with the age of the process in input returns a number between 0 and 100. 0 means the process has not be running locally during the local execution time. 100 means the process has been running for more than 30 minutes. If several processes have a 100 value, then the smallest program in size is selected.

As with the overload threshold (the one used when a host is initially chosen), it is difficult to choose good values for the migration and reception thresholds. This threshold seems to depend on the behavior of the migrated processes, on the load ratio (available processing power / mean number of processes), and on users' behavior. There are few studies on the reception threshold. Most of the time, it is assimilated with the overload threshold. Again, our experiments lead us to set the migration threshold to 2 and the reception threshold to 0.5. These values depend on the overload threshold (1.0), and the three values cannot be changed independently. A future work will attempt to model the execution presented in the next section, and to simulate the change in the three thresholds.

22.4.3 Failure Management

In order to get an efficient failure detection mechanism, we operate a structuring of hosts in a logical ring. Each host independently checks its immediate successor in the ring. The checking process is straightforward and the cost in messages is relatively low.

Our recovery method uses a checkpoint/rollback management. By checkpointing, user processes save their states to prevent their local host failures. We adopt an independent checkpointing with a pessimistic message logging (see Section 22.3). This technique is particularly adapted for application composed of processes exchanging small streams of data. Otherwise, the cost of the logging is proportional to the number of messages. This method has the following advantages:

- the domino-effect is eliminated,
- checkpoint operation can be performed unilaterally by each process and any checkpointing policy may be used,
- only one checkpoint is associated to each process,
- checkpoint cost is lower than in a consistent checkpointing and recovery is implemented efficiently because all interprocess communications do not take place during a replay.

To reduce the cost of checkpointing, GATOSTAR implementes incremental and non-blocking checkpointing. We will see in the performance section that these techniques highly reduce the cost of checkpointing.

22.4.4 Performance Study

We present performance measurements of the process allocation and the migration strategies. These measurements were done in a real system within our laboratory. The supporting environment is composed of a set of Sun workstations connected by a LAN (Ethernet 10 Mbit/s). The environment has not been modified (usual daemons were running). All results presented are averages over a number of trials.

Cost of initial placement. The time to compute an initial placement for an application is rather low. Indeed, hosts selection is done locally when starting the application, and the only exchange of message is the request from the local load sharing manager to the remote one to execute a given program. The maximum size of such a request is 2 kilobytes (program name, options, global identification and some of the shell environment variables). In the presented measurements the request length is about 500 bytes, and the time for an initial placement is 100 milliseconds. Compared to other systems, the mean time for a placement request is 5 seconds in REM [13], and 12 seconds in DAWGS [4]. These allocation times are essentially due to highly communicating algorithms, while GATOSTAR does not perform any extra communication when allocating hosts.

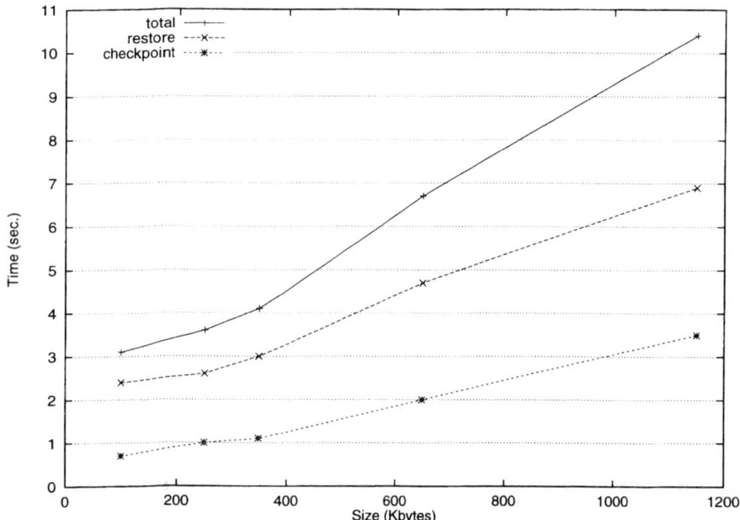

Figure 22.3 Migration time according to process size.

Cost of process migration. The time for a process migration is proportional to the amount of data to be transferred from the source host to the selected one. Figure 22.3 shows the time to migrate a process (that is, the sum of the checkpoint time and restore context time) according to the process size.

In the following, the size of each test process is less than 100 kilobytes. Thus, migration time of these processes is less than 3 seconds.

Process allocation. Figure 22.4 presents the execution time of six parallel programs running on six hosts. We compare the non-preemptive placement strategy with the migration. Each program is computing a given number of iterations, from

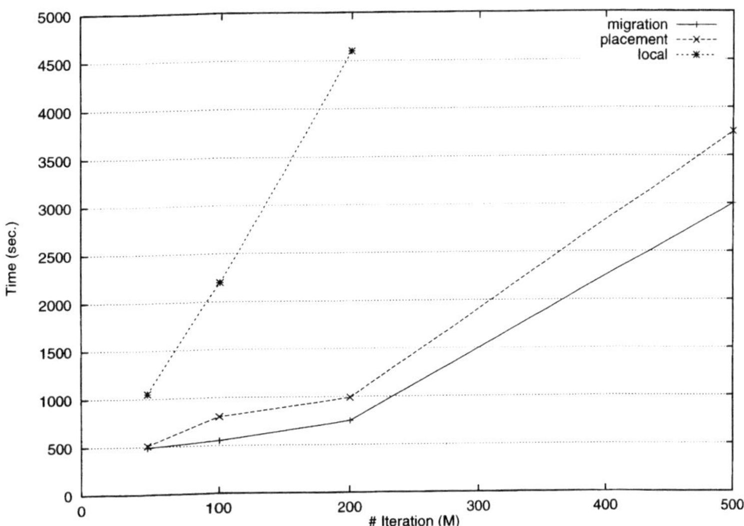

Figure 22.4 Execution time of six programs according to the number of iterations.

50 million to 500 million. There is no communication between programs. The local execution time (i.e., without any distribution) is from 1080 seconds for 50 million iterations to 11,160 seconds for 500 million iterations (not shown in the figure).

When there is a small number of iterations, less than 30 million, the execution time of the application is too short for the migration strategy to provide significant improvements. When the number of iterations increases, we obtain a difference of 28% between execution with and without migration. This difference is due mostly to the correction of the initial placement. Indeed, when this application is launched, all the six hosts are possibly not unused. Then, when they become unused, migration allows us to share the work with them, while in case of non-preemptive allocation the hosts stay unused. On the other hand, when a station becomes overloaded because of some users' activities, migration allows us to select a more suitable host.

Figure 22.5 presents the speed-up obtained by migration compared to non-preemptive placement. There are six parallel programs, each program running for 1800 seconds, and the number of hosts varies from one to five. With one host we obtain the degradation of the migration strategy, because no migration is possible. Then, we observe that even with a limited number of hosts, migration reduces the execution time by adapting the number of programs on each host according to the users' activity. This good improvement is due mostly to migrations occurring when a program ends. For instance, with four hosts, a typical placement will be one program on each of the two first hosts and two programs on each of the two others. Consequently, the two first hosts will finish two times faster than the other ones. At this time migration allows us to move two programs in order to have one program on each host that reduces remaining execution time. The decrease of speed-up for three hosts is due to the initial optimal placement: two programs on each host. In that case, migration is used only to react to user activities.

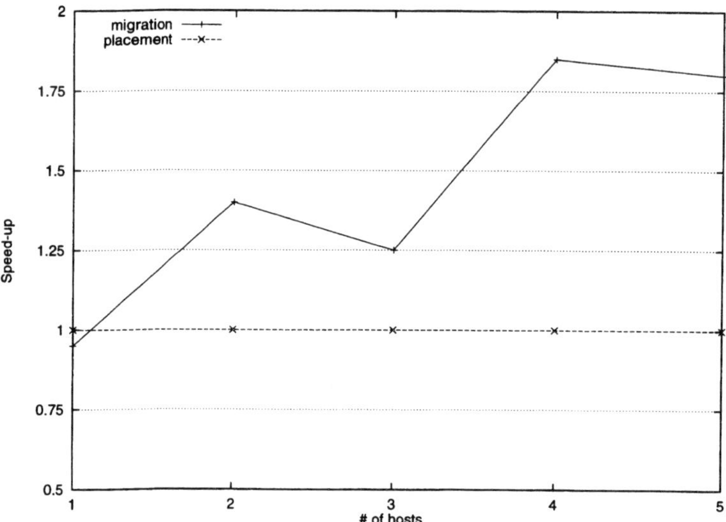

Figure 22.5 Speed-up according to the number of hosts.

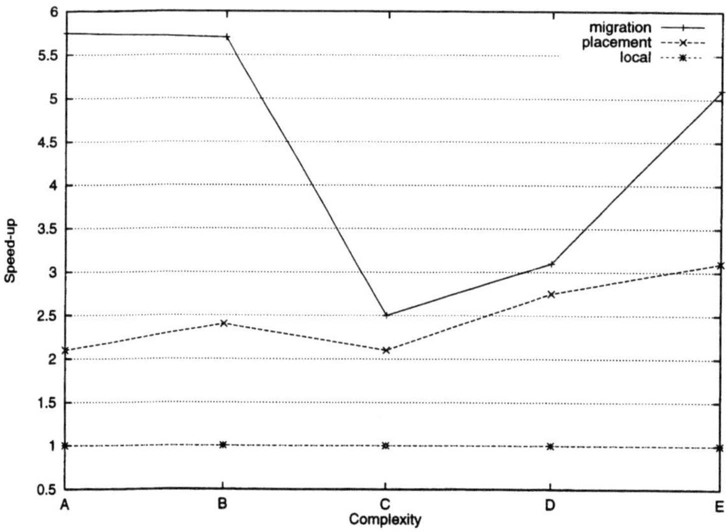

Figure 22.6 Speed-up according to application complexity.

Response time. Figure 22.6 compares the speed-up obtained by placement and migration when the complexity of an application evolves. These measures are related to the response time algorithm, where placement and migration policies know in advance the running time of each program. The various applications are given below:

A: 1.50M 1.100M 1.200M 1.500M (4 programs, 850M)
B: 3.50M 4.100M 2.200M 1.500M (10 programs, 1250M)
C: 5.50M 5.100M 2.200M 1.500M (13 programs, 1650M)
D: 10.100M 2.200M 2.500M (14 programs, 2400M)
E: 10.100M 5.200M 5.500M (20 programs, 4500M)

For instance, application A is composed of 4 parallel programs with a total number of 850 million iterations, the first one with 50 million iterations, the second one with 100 million, the third one with 200 million and the last with 500 million. Tests have been done with six hosts.

The single process of 500 million iterations bound the response time of the two first applications. In that case, migration improves greatly the speed-up. The other programs needing less execution time are kept on different hosts of the 500 million iterations program, and this last always profits from the better unloaded host. There is no such bound in applications C and D, which implies little difference between placement and migration. For the last application, the migration is beneficial for the five 500 million iterations programs.

Extrapolation by simulation. We present some results from a simulation study that show the impact of threshold values. We have simulated two strategies. In the classical one, which is implemented in GATOSTAR, allocation and migration decisions are based on fixed threshold. In the adaptive one, thresholds depend on the global load of the network. Figure 22.7 presents a performance evaluation of these two policies according to the number of hosts. We have simulated two applications: Application A is composed of 48 parallel CPU intensive processes with different execution times, application B is composed of 40 parallel processes with the same execution time. In all cases, the adaptive strategy improves the response time. We see that speed-up also depends on the application behavior.

In Figure 22.8, we vary the overload threshold value to optimize the response time of three different application configurations : 30 identical CPU intensive processes allocated on 10 hosts, 50 processes allocated on 10 or 20 hosts.

We can conclude, from these two simulation studies, that an allocation manager should adapt the threshold values not only according to the global load but also to the behavior of the current applications.

Performance of checkpointing. Finally, we evaluate the cost of checkpointing (used for process migration and to tolerate host failure). We chose three long-running, compute-intensive applications exhibiting different memory usage and communications patterns:

1. The *Gauss* application performs Gaussian elimination with partial pivoting

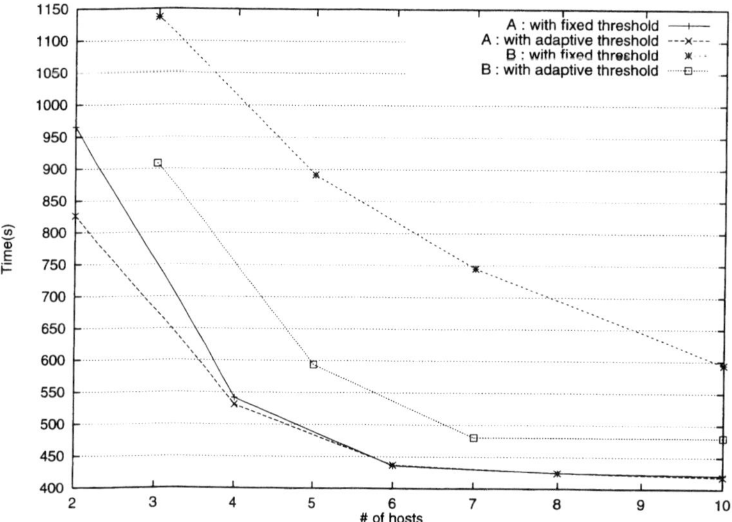

Figure 22.7 Simulation of response time according to the threshold policy.

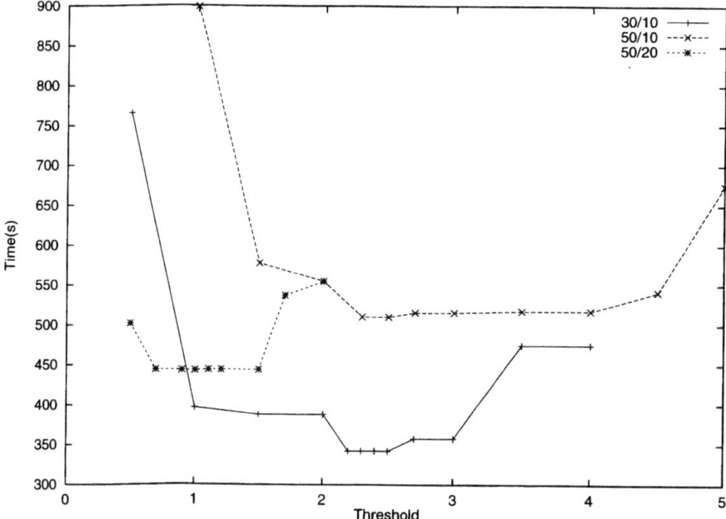

Figure 22.8 Simulation of response time according the overload threshold value.

on a 1024 x 1024 matrix. The matrix is distributed among several processes. At each iteration of the reduction, the process that holds the pivot sends the pivot column to all other processes.

2. The multiplication application, called *matmul*, multiplies two square matrixes

of size 1024 x 1024. The computation is distributed among several processes. No communication is required other than reporting the final solution.

3. The *fft* application computes the Fast Fourier Transform of 32768 data points. The problem is distributed by assigning each process an equal range of data points. Like the previous application, no communication is required other than reporting the final solution. Table 22.1 presents the overall running time and per process communication and memory requirements for the three applications when run without fault tolerance management (i.e., without checkpointing and message logging). Each application is distributed on five hosts: One host executes a master process and the four other hosts execute the computational processes.

Table 22.1 Applications Requirements

Applications	Time (sec.)	Memory (Kbytes)	Sending data (Kbytes)
Gauss	344	1704	2700
matmul	723	2688	0.06
fft	1177	1200	0.06

Gauss and *matmul* require a sizeable amount of data, stressing the checkpoint and state restoration mechanisms. Moreover, the *Gauss* application exhibits a large amount of communication especially stressing the message logging. The *fft* application is long-running and requires a medium amount of data.

Table 22.2 presents the running times of the applications programs when run with independent checkpointing and pessimistic message logging. Applications run with a 2- minute checkpointing interval. Checkpoints and logs are duplicated.

Table 22.2 Parallel Applications Evaluation

Appli.	Full checkpoint		Non-blocking		Incremental	
	Time (sec.)	%	Time (sec.)	%	Time (sec.)	%
Gauss	567	64.82	505	46.80	457	32.85
matmul	844	16.79	768	6.34	748	3.57
fft	1244	5.75	1228	4.36	1194	1.50

In spite of checkpoint optimizations, we observe a high overhead for the *Gauss* application. In fact, this application is not a good candidate for message logging approaches, specifically because of its communication rate. The overhead due to message logging for this application is 14.53%. The cost of message logging represents half of the global overhead when we apply incremental checkpointing.

For all three applications, incremental checkpointing provides a sizeable reduction of the overhead. Comparing to the full non-blocking checkpointing, we obtain reduction in overheads of between 24% and 63%. This difference is partly due to different communication rates. Moreover, applications can be divided into two categories: applications with an address space that is modified with high locality (matrix multiplication and *fft* applications) and applications with an address space that is modified almost entirely between any two checkpoints (*Gauss* application). For applications of the first category, incremental checkpointing is very successful (79% of reduction for matrix multiplication and 75% of reduction for *fft*). For the applications in the second category, incremental checkpointing is less effective (about 49% of reduction for the *Gauss* application).

22.5 Related Works

Few experiences have been reported with load sharing systems with a fault tolerance mechanism. The major ones are the systems REM (Remote Execution Manager) [13], Paralex [1], Condor [11], and DAWGS (Distributed Automated Workload sharing System) [4]. These four systems have been developed essentially as load sharing manager, since fault tolerance is a limited extension. To our knowledge, no work has compared and unified the two concepts.

REM and Paralex are load sharing managers that support cooperative applications. REM provides a mechanism by which processes may create, communicate with, and terminate child processes on remote workstations. Active process replication is used to ensure the fault tolerant execution of the child processes. Thus, the fault tolerant property is gained at the expense of computing power. Moreover, failure of the local user's machine implies a failure of the whole computation. As the failure rate in a local area network is low, the process replication mechanism is not adapted to a load sharing scheme. Furthermore, the target applications of software fault tolerance are long-lived ones, and users are not supposed to be always connected with the same local machine. Paralex provides a package for distributing cooperative computation across a network. It uses passive process replication to achieve both fault tolerance and load balancing. Since process migration can be done only between replicas, the load sharing capability is strongly limited.

Condor and DAWGS rely on the same principle as GATOSTAR. Processes are initially allocated to an idle host, and a checkpoint/rollback mechanism allows the migration of processes and the restarting of processes after a host failure. In both systems, migration is essentially used to respect the privacy of workstation owners. The main drawback of Condor is that it deals only with independent processes, since Condor processes cannot communicate or synchronize. Some extensions, as Dynamic PVM [5], have adapted Condor to communicating processes. DAWGS is a complete load sharing fault tolerant facility, including I/O redirection. The two main differences between DAWGS and GATOSTAR are that (1) DAWGS relies on kernel modification and (2) DAWGS' fault tolerant part is not configurable and a process running on a faulty host must wait for the host to restart (there is no easy way to replicate a checkpoint file). The kernel modifications allow full user-transparency without the need to link with a special library, but it highly limits the portability of such a system (and thus, of the supported applications).

22.6 Conclusion

This chapter has described the advantages of load sharing and fault tolerance unification. Such unification may improve parallel applications' response time and decrease the overhead of the software fault management.

We presented GATOSTAR, a unified load sharing and fault tolerance facility. This system takes advantage of the overall system resources and allows the distribution of the applications processes on the most appropriate hosts. Process allocation policy takes into account both information about the system state and resource needs for the execution of applications. A checkpoint mechanism allows the recovery of processes after hosts' failures and is used to move processes in case of load fluctuations. Measures of GATOSTAR show the benefit of the load sharing and of the multi-criteria allocation algorithms in a local area network of workstations and indicate that the combination of dynamic placement and process migration outperforms dynamic placement only. Dynamic placement allows us to use the available machine at launch time at very low cost (one request). Then, for long-lived applications, process migration allows to correct this initial placement according to failures or changes of the program behaviors, in the hosts load, or in interactive users activities.

22.7 Bibliography

[1] O. Babaoglu, L. Alvisi, A. Amoroso, and R. Davoli. Paralex: An Environment for Parallel Programming in Distributed Systems. *Proceedings of the International Conference on Supercomputing*, pages 178–187, July 1992.

[2] M. Banâtre, Y. Belhamissi, V. Issarny, I. Puaut, and J-P. Routeau. Adaptive Placement of Method Executions Within a Customizable Distributed Object-Based Runtime System. *Proceedings of the 15th IEEE International Conference on Distributed Computing Systems*, pages 279–286, June 1995.

[3] A. Barak, O. Laden, and Y. Yarom. The NOW MOSIX and Its Preemptive Process. *Bulletin of the IEEE Technical Committee on Operating Systems*, vol. 7(2), pages 5–11, 1995.

[4] H. Clark and B. McMillin. DAWGS - a Distributed Compute Server Utilizing Idle Workstations. *Journal of Parallel and Distributed Computing*, vol. 14, pages 175–186, February 1992.

[5] L. Dikken, F. Van der Linden, J. Vesseur, and P. Sloot. Dynamic Load Balancing on Parallel Systems. *High Performance Computer Network*, pages 273–277, 1994. Lecture Notes in Computer Science 797.

[6] F. Douglis and J. Ousterhout. Transparent Process Migration: Design Alternatives and the Sprite Implementation. *Software - Practice and Experience*, vol. 21(8), pages 757 785, 1991.

[7] D. L. Eager, E. D. Lazoska, and J. Zahorjan. Adaptive Load Sharing in Homogeneous Distributed Systems. *IEEE Transactions on Software Engineering*, vol. SE-12(5), pages 662–675, May 1986.

[8] E. N. Elnozahy and W. Zwaenepoel. On the Use and Implementation of Message Logging. *Proceedings of the 24th International Symposium on Fault-Tolerant Computing Systems*, pages 298–307, June 1994.

[9] G. A. Geist and V. S. Sunderam. Network Based Concurrent Computing on the PVM System. *Concurrency: Practice and Experience*, vol. 4(4), pages 293–311, June 1992.

[10] J. M. Hélary, A. Mostefaoui, R. H. B. Netzer, and M. Raynal. Preventing Useless Checkpoints in Distributed Computation. *Proceedings of the 27th International Symposium on Fault-Tolerant Computing Systems*, pages 68–77, June 1997.

[11] M. J. Litzkow, M. Livny, and M. W. Mutka. Condor - a Hunter of Idle Workstations. *Proceedings of the 8th International Conference on Distributed Computing Systems*, pages 104–111, January 1988.

[12] P. Sens and B. Folliot. The STAR Fault-Tolerant Manager for Distributed Operating Environments. *Software Practice and Experience*, vol. 28(10), pages 1079–1099, August 1998.

[13] G. C. Shoja, G. Clarke, and T. Taylor. REM: a Distributed Facility for Utilizing Idle Processing Power of Workstations. *Proceedings of the IFIP Conference on Distributed Processing*, October 1987.

[14] S. Zhou, J. Wang, X. Zheng, and P. Delisle. Utopia: a Load-Sharing Facility for Large Heterogeneous Distributed Computing Systems. *Software - Practice and Experience*, vol. 23(2), pages 1305–1336, December 1993.

Chapter 23

Parallel Program Scheduling Techniques

YU-KWONG KWOK[†] AND ISHFAQ AHMAD[‡]

[†]Department of Electrical and Electronic Engineering
The University of Hong Kong
Pokfulam Road, Hong Kong

[‡]Department of Computer Science
The Hong Kong University of Science and Technology
Clear Water Bay, Hong Kong

Email: *ykwok@eee.hku.hk*, *iahmad@cs.ust.hk*

23.1 Introduction

Parallel processing using a cluster of workstations or personal computers is a promising approach to meet the computational requirements of a large number of current and emerging applications at a low cost. However, the concept of cluster computing entails tackling a number of difficult problems, including designing a parallel algorithm for the application, partitioning of the application into tasks, coordinating communication and synchronization, scheduling of the tasks onto the machine, and routing and scheduling of messages on the communication links. If these problems are not properly handled, parallelization of an application may not be beneficial. A large body of research efforts addressing these problems has been reported in the literature [14], [18]. Scheduling and allocation are very important issues, since an inappropriate scheduling of tasks cannot exploit the true potential of the system and can offset the gain from parallelization. In this chapter, we focus on the scheduling aspect.

The objective of scheduling is to minimize the completion time of a parallel application by properly allocating the tasks to the processors and sequencing the execution of the tasks. In a broad sense, the scheduling problem exists in two forms:

static and *dynamic*. In static scheduling, which is usually done at compile time, the characteristics of a parallel program (such as task processing times, communication, data dependencies, and synchronization requirements) are known before program execution [4], [18]. A parallel program, therefore, can be represented by a node- and edge-weighted *directed acyclic graph* (DAG), in which the node weights represent task processing times and the edge weights represent data dependencies as well as the communication times between tasks. In dynamic scheduling, few assumptions about the parallel program can be made before execution, and thus, scheduling decisions have to be made *on-the-fly* [7]. The goal of a dynamic scheduling algorithm as such includes not only the minimization of the program completion time but also the minimization of scheduling overhead, which represents a significant portion of the cost paid for running the scheduler. In a cluster of workstations, such dynamic scheduling algorithms usually employ the so-called "idle-cycle-stealing" approach which attempts to dynamically balance the work load evenly across all the machines. However, when the objective of scheduling is to minimize the execution time of a given application, such scheduling algorithms are not suitable. On the other hand, the approach of using static scheduling algorithms is particularly effective for many scientific applications such as the adaptive simulation of N-body problem, object recognition using iterative image processing algorithms, and some other numerical applications. In this chapter, we focus on employing efficient static scheduling techniques to generate off-line schedules for irregular and arbitrarily structured applications. Thus, hereafter, we refer to static scheduling as simply *scheduling*.

The scheduling problem is NP-complete for most of its variants except for a few highly simplified cases [7], [9], and, therefore, many heuristics with polynomial-time complexity have been suggested [3], [7], [14]. However, these heuristics are highly diverse in terms of their assumptions about the structure of the parallel program and the target parallel architecture, and thus need to be categorized.

Common simplifying assumptions include uniform task execution times, zero inter-task communication times, contention-free communication, full connectivity of parallel processors, and availability of unlimited number of processors. These assumptions may not hold in practical situations for a number of reasons. For instance, it is not always realistic to assume that the task execution times of an application are uniform because the amount of computations encapsulated in tasks are usually varied. Furthermore, parallel and distributed architectures have evolved into various types such as distributed-memory multicomputers (DMMs) shared-memory multiprocessors (SMMs), clusters of symmetric multiprocessors (SMPs), and networks of workstations(NOWs). The latter two types of parallel processing platforms are becoming promising environments for tackling high performance computational problems at a very low cost. Therefore, their more detailed architectural characteristics must be taken into account. For example, inter-task communication in the form of message-passing or shared-memory access inevitably incurs a non-negligible amount of latency. Furthermore, a contention-free communication and full connectivity of processors cannot be assumed for a DMM, a SMP or a NOW. Thus, scheduling algorithms relying on such assumptions are apt to have restricted applicability in real environments.

From a system point of view, there are two classes of scheduling algorithms suitable for allocating tasks to clustered machines statically. The first category, called the BNP (Bounded Number of Processors) scheduling algorithms, is suitable for scheduling applications in a cluster environment when the network is fast enough to ignore the contention of messages on the communication medium. In such an environment, the processors are effectively fully connected and the only major system constraint is that the number of processors is limited. Examples of such relatively tightly-coupled networks can be constructed by using fast Ethernet, giga-bit ATM switches, or Myrinet adaptors. Scheduling tasks to such platforms is relatively simple because the scheduler needs only to optimize the allocation of tasks and, thus, scheduling can be done very efficiently. For networks in which such an assumption does not hold, the second category of algorithms, called the APN (Arbitrary Processor Network) scheduling algorithms, is useful since they schedule communication messages in addition to computational tasks. In such an environment, the topology of the network must also be taken into account. Compared to BNP scheduling, APN scheduling is a much more difficult problem because the scheduler has to schedule tasks and messages simultaneously.

To apply the scheduling algorithms in practical problems, many experimental software tools have been suggested and implemented. To use these tools, the user provides an annotated sequential application which is statically analyzed and partitioned into a set of interacting tasks. The tasks are then scheduled and mapped onto the clustered machines. Finally, the tool generates parallel code in which some message-passing primitives of standard package like PVM or MPI are inserted. In this chapter, we also describe one such tool called CASCH (Computer-Aided SCHeduling).

This chapter is organized as follows. Section 23.2 defines the scheduling problem and describes some more background about the problem in the aspects of NP-completeness and basic techniques used. Section 23.3 contains a qualitative discussion of several representative BNP scheduling algorithms. Illustrative scheduling examples are used to highlight the different characteristics of the algorithms. Some theoretical results are also described. Section 23.4 describes the algorithms for the relatively less explored APN scheduling problem. Section 23.5 introduces the CASCH tool for automatic parallelization and scheduling of applications to computer networks. The final section concludes the chapter.

23.2 The Scheduling Problem for Network Computing Environments

In this section, we first describe the models used for representing a parallel application and the target cluster system. This is followed by a discussion of the NP-completeness of the scheduling problem. Finally, we introduce some basic techniques used in scheduling tasks to multiprocessors systems.

23.2.1 The DAG Model

A parallel program can be represented by a directed acyclic graph (DAG) $G = (V, E)$, where V is a set of v nodes and E is a set of e directed edges. A node in the DAG represents a task, which in turn is a set of instructions which must be executed sequentially without pre-emption in the same processor. The weight of a node n_i is called the *computation cost* and is denoted by $w(n_i)$. The edges in the DAG, each of which is denoted by (n_i, n_j), correspond to the communication messages and precedence constraints among the nodes. The weight of an edge is called the *communication cost* of the edge and is denoted by $c(n_i, n_j)$. The source node of an edge is called the *parent* node while the sink node is called the *child* node. A node with no parent is called an *entry* node and a node with no child is called an *exit* node. The *communication-to-computation-ratio* (CCR) of a parallel program is defined as its average edge weight divided by its average node weight. Hereafter we use the terms *node* and *task* interchangeably. We summarize in Table 23.1 the notations used throughout the chapter.

The precedence constraints of a DAG dictate that a node cannot start execution before it gathers all of the messages from its parent nodes. The communication cost between two tasks assigned to the same processor is assumed to be zero. If node n_i is scheduled to some processor P, then $ST(n_i, P)$ and $FT(n_i, P)$ denote the start time and finish time of n_i, respectively. After all the nodes have been scheduled, the *schedule length* (or *makespan*) *SL* is defined as $max_i\{FT(n_i, P)\}$ across all processor P. The objective of scheduling is to minimize *SL* by proper allocation of the tasks to the processors and arrangement of execution sequencing of the tasks. Scheduling is done in such a manner that the precedence constraints among the program tasks are preserved.

23.2.2 Generation of a DAG

A parallel program is commonly modeled by a DAG. Although program loops cannot be explicitly represented by the DAG model, data-flow computations parallelism in loops can be exploited to subdivide the loops into a number of tasks by the *loop-unraveling* technique [1], [4]. The idea is that all iterations of the loop are started or *fired* together, and operations in various iterations can execute when their input data are ready for access. In addition, for a large class of data-flow computation problems and most of the numerical algorithms (such as matrix multiplication), there are very few, if any, conditional branches or indeterminism in the program. Thus, the DAG model can be used to accurately represent these applications so that the scheduling techniques can be applied. Furthermore, in many numerical applications, such as Gaussian elimination or fast Fourier transform (FFT), the loop bounds are known during compile time. As such, one or more iterations of a loop can be deterministically encapsulated in a task and, consequently, be represented by a node in a DAG. The node- and edge-weights are usually obtained by estimation, using profiling information of operations such as numerical operations, memory access operations, and message-passing primitives [1], [4], [18].

Table 23.1 Definitions of Notations

Symbol	Meaning
n_i	the node number of a node in the parallel program task graph
$w(n_i)$	the computation cost of node n_i
(n_i, n_j)	an edge from node n_i to n_j
$c(n_i, n_j)$	the communication cost of the directed edge from node n_i to n_j
v	number of nodes in the task graph
e	number of edges in the task graph
p	the number of processors in the target system
CP	a critical path of the task graph
CPN	Critical Path Node
IBN	In-Branch Node
OBN	Out-Branch Node
b-level	bottom level of a node
t-level	top level of a node
sl	static level of a node
dl	dynamic level of a node
ASAP	as soon as possible start time of a node
ALAP	as late as possible start time of a node
$T_s(n_i)$	the actual start time of a node n_i
$DAT(n_i, P)$	the possible data available time of n_i on target processor P
$ST(n_i, P)$	the start time of node n_i on target processor P
$FT(n_i, P)$	the finish time of node n_i on target processor P
$VIP(n_i)$	the parent node of n_i that sends the latest data
PE	a processing element (processor plus memory) in the system
PivotPE	the target processor from which nodes are migrated
Proc(n_i)	the processor accommodating n_i
CCR	communication-to-computation Ratio
SL	schedule length
BNP	Bounded Number of Processors
APN	Arbitrary Processor Network

23.2.3 The Cluster Model

In DAG scheduling, the target cluster system is assumed to be a network of *processing elements* (PEs), each of which is composed of a processor and a local memory unit so that the PEs do not share memory and communication relies solely on message-passing. Such PEs may be workstations or even personal computers. The processors may be heterogeneous or homogeneous. Heterogeneity of processors means that the processors have different speeds or processing capabilities. However, we assume that every module of a parallel program can be executed on any processor, even though the completion times on different processors may be different. The PEs are connected by an interconnection network with a certain topology. The topology may be fully connected or composed of a particular structure such as a hypercube.

23.2.4 NP-Completeness of the DAG Scheduling Problem

The DAG scheduling problem is, in general, an NP-complete problem [7], [9], and algorithms for optimally scheduling a DAG in polynomial-time are known only for three simple cases [7]. The first case is to schedule a uniform node-weight free-tree to an arbitrary number of processors. Hu [7] proposed a linear-time algorithm to solve the problem. The second case is to schedule an arbitrarily structured DAG with uniform node-weights to two processors. Coffman and Graham [7] devised a quadratic-time algorithm to solve this problem. Both Hu's algorithm and Coffman's algorithm are based on node-labeling methods that produce optimal scheduling lists leading to optimal schedules. Sethi [7] then improved the time complexity of Coffman's algorithm to almost linear-time by suggesting a more efficient node-labeling process. The third case is to schedule an *interval-ordered* DAG with uniform node weights to an arbitrary number of processors. Papadimitriou and Yannakakis [7] designed a linear-time algorithm to tackle the problem. A DAG is called interval-ordered if every two precedence-related nodes can be mapped to two non-overlapping intervals on the real number line. In all of the above three cases, communication between tasks is ignored. Ali and El-Rewini [7] showed that interval-ordered DAG with uniform edge weights, which are equal to the node weights, can also be optimally scheduled in polynomial time.

23.2.5 Basic Techniques in DAG Scheduling

Most scheduling algorithms are based on the classic *list scheduling* technique [3], [7], [14]. The basic idea of list scheduling is to make a scheduling list (a sequence of nodes for scheduling) by assigning them some priorities, and then repeatedly execute the following two steps until all the nodes in the graph are scheduled: (1) Remove the first node from the scheduling list; (2) Allocate the node to a processor which allows the earliest start time.

In a traditional scheduling algorithm, the scheduling list is statically constructed before node allocation begins, and, most importantly, the sequencing in the list is not modified. Recently a number of scheduling algorithms based on a *dynamic* list scheduling approach have been suggested [13], [16], [19]. In contrast to the traditional approach, after each allocation, these algorithms recompute the priorities of all unscheduled nodes, which are then used to rearrange the sequencing of the nodes in the list. Thus, these algorithms essentially employ the following three-step approach: (1) Determine new priorities of all unscheduled nodes; (2) Select the node with the highest priority for scheduling; (3) Allocate the node to the processor which allows the earliest start time.

Scheduling algorithms which employ this three-step approach can potentially generate better schedules. However, a dynamic approach can increase the time complexity of the scheduling algorithm.

There are various ways to determine the priorities of nodes [7], [14], such as HLF (Highest Level First), LP (Longest Path), LPT (Longest Processing Time) and CP (Critical Path).

Two frequently used attributes for assigning priority are the *t-level* (top level) and *b-level* (bottom level) [14], [19]. The *t-level* of a node n_i is the length of a longest path (there can be more than one longest path) from an entry node to n_i (excluding n_i). Here, the length of a path is the sum of all the node and edge weights along the path. The *t-level* of n_i highly correlates with n_i's *earliest start time*, denoted by $T_s(n_i)$, which is determined after n_i is scheduled to a processor. The *b-level* of a node n_i is the length of a longest path from n_i to an exit node. The *b-level* of a node is bounded from above by the length of a *critical path* (CP), which is an important structure in the DAG, is a longest path in the DAG. Clearly, a DAG can have more than one CP. Consider the task graph shown in Figure 23.1. In this task graph, the lower label in each node is the computation cost of the node and the label of each edge is the communication cost of the edge. Notice that nodes n_1, n_7, n_9 are the nodes of the only CP and are called CPNs (Critical Path Nodes).

The values of the priorities discussed above are shown in Table 23.2. Below is a procedure for computing the *t-level*:

Computation of t-level:

```
Construct a list of nodes in topological order.
Call it TopList.
for each node n_i in TopList do
    max = 0
    for each parent n_x of n_i do
        if t-level(n_x) + w(n_x) + c(n_x, n_i) > max then
            max = t-level(n_x) + w(n_x) + c(n_x, n_i)
        endif
    endfor
    t-level(n_i) = max
endfor
```

The time complexity of the above procedure is $O(e + v)$. A similar procedure, which also has time complexity $O(e + v)$, for computing the *b-level*, is shown below:

Computation of b-level:

```
Construct a list of nodes in reversed topological order.
Call it RevTopList.
for each node n_i in RevTopList do
    max = 0
    for each child n_y of n_i do
        if c(n_i, n_y) + b-level(n_y) > max then
            max = c(n_i, n_y) + b-level(n_y)
        endif
    endfor
    b-level = w(n_i) + max
endfor
```

In the scheduling process, the *t-level* of a node varies while the *b-level* is usually a constant, until the node has been scheduled. The *t-level* varies because the weight of an edge may become zero when the two incident nodes are scheduled to the same

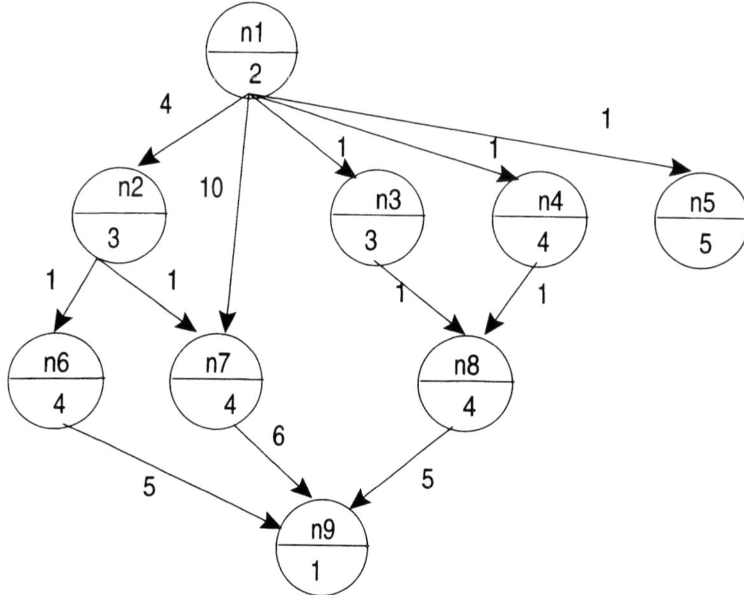

Figure 23.1 A simple task graph.

processor. Thus, the path reaching a node, whose length determines the *t-level* of the node, may cease to be the longest one. On the other hand, there are some variations in the computation of the *b-level* of a node. Most algorithms examine a node for scheduling only after all the parents of the node have been scheduled. In this case, the *b-level* of a node is a constant until after it is scheduled to a processor. Some scheduling algorithms allow the scheduling of a child before its parents, however, in which case the *b-level* of a node is also a dynamic attribute. It should be noted that some scheduling algorithms do not take into account the edge weights in computing the *b-level*. In such a case, the *b-level* does not change throughout the scheduling process. To distinguish such a definition of *b-level* from the one we described above, we call it the *static b-level* or simply *static level* (*sl*).

Note that the procedure for computing the *t-level* can also be used to compute the start times of nodes on processors during the scheduling process. Indeed, some researchers call the *t-level* of a node the ASAP (As-Soon-As-Possible) start time because the *t-level* is the earliest possible start time.

Some of the DAG scheduling algorithms employ an attribute called ALAP (As-Late-As-Possible) start time [13], [18]. The ALAP start time of a node is a measure of how far the node's start time can be delayed without increasing the schedule length. An $O(e+v)$ time procedure for computing the ALAP time is shown below:

```
Computation of ALAP:
(1)  Construct a list of nodes in reversed topological order.
     Call it RevTopList.
(2)  for each node n_i in RevTopList do
(3)      minft = CPLength
(4)      for each child n_y of n_i do
(5)          if alap(n_y) - c(n_i, n_y) < minft then
(6)              minft = alap(n_y) - c(n_i, n_y)
(7)          endif
(8)      endfor
(9)      alap(n_i) = minft - w(n_i)
(10) endfor
```

Table 23.2 The Static Level, *t-level*, *b-level*, and ALAP of Each Node of the Graph

node	*sl*	*t-level*	*b-level*	ALAP
n_1	11	0	23	0
n_2	8	6	15	8
n_3	8	3	14	9
n_4	9	3	15	8
n_5	5	3	5	18
n_6	5	10	10	13
n_7	5	12	11	12
n_8	5	8	10	13
n_9	1	22	1	22

After the scheduling list is constructed by using the node priorities, the nodes are then scheduled to suitable processors. Usually a processor is considered suitable if it allows the earliest start time for the node. However, in some sophisticated scheduling heuristics, a suitable processor may not be the one that allows the earliest start time. These variations are described in detail in Section 23.3.

23.3 Scheduling Tasks to Machines Connected via Fast Networks

In this section, we illustrate the techniques used in the BNP class of scheduling algorithms. In particular, we discuss in detail three BNP scheduling algorithms: the ISH, MCP, and ETF algorithms. The DAG shown in Figure 23.1 is used to illustrate the scheduling process of these algorithms. The analytical performance bounds of BNP scheduling are also discussed in the last subsection.

23.3.1 The ISH Algorithm

The ISH (Insertion Scheduling Heuristic) algorithm [7] uses the "scheduling holes"—the idle time slots—in the partial schedules. The algorithm tries to fill the holes by scheduling other nodes into them and uses static *b-level* as the priority of a node. The algorithm is briefly described below:

```
(1) Calculate the static b-level of each node.
(2) Make a ready list in descending order of static b-level.
    Initially, the ready list contains only the entry nodes.
    Ties are broken randomly.
Repeat
(3) Schedule the first node in the ready list to the processor
    that allows the earliest execution, using the non-insertion method.
(4) If scheduling of this node causes an idle time slot, then
    find as many nodes as possible from the ready list that
    can be scheduled to the idle time slot but cannot be
    scheduled earlier on other processors.
(5) Update the ready list by inserting the nodes that are now ready.
Until all nodes are scheduled.
```

The time complexity of the ISH algorithm is $O(v^2)$. For the DAG shown in Figure 23.1, the ISH algorithm generates a schedule shown in Figure 23.2. In the schedule, the message-passing between tasks is not explicitly shown because the underlying network is modeled as fully connected and contention-free such that multiple messages can be simultaneously transmitted in the link between any two PEs. The ISH algorithm schedules the nodes in the following order: n_1, n_4, n_3, n_2, n_5, n_8, n_7, n_6, n_9.

23.3.2 The MCP Algorithm

The MCP (Modified Critical Path) algorithm [18] uses the ALAP of a node as the scheduling priority. The MCP algorithm first computes the ALAPs of all the nodes, then constructs a list of nodes in ascending order of ALAP times. Ties are broken by considering the ALAP times of the children of a node. The MCP algorithm then schedules the nodes on the list one by one so that a node is scheduled to a processor that allows the earliest start time using the insertion approach. The MCP algorithm and the ISH algorithm have different philosophies in utilizing the idle time slot: MCP looks for an idle time slot for a given node, while ISH looks for a hole node to fit in a given idle time slot. The algorithm is briefly described below:

```
(1) Compute the ALAP time of each node.
(2) For each node, create a list which consists of the ALAP
    times of the node itself and all its children in descending order.
(3) Sort these lists in ascending lexicographical order.
    Create a node list according to this order.
Repeat
(4) Schedule the first node in the node list to a processor that
    allows the earliest execution, using the insertion approach.
(5) Remove the node from the node list.
Until the node list is empty.
```

The time complexity of the MCP algorithm is $O(v^2 \log v)$. For the DAG shown in Figure 23.1, the MCP algorithm generates a schedule shown in Figure 23.3. The MCP algorithm schedules the nodes in the following order: $n_1, n_4, n_2, n_3, n_7, n_6, n_8, n_5, n_9$.

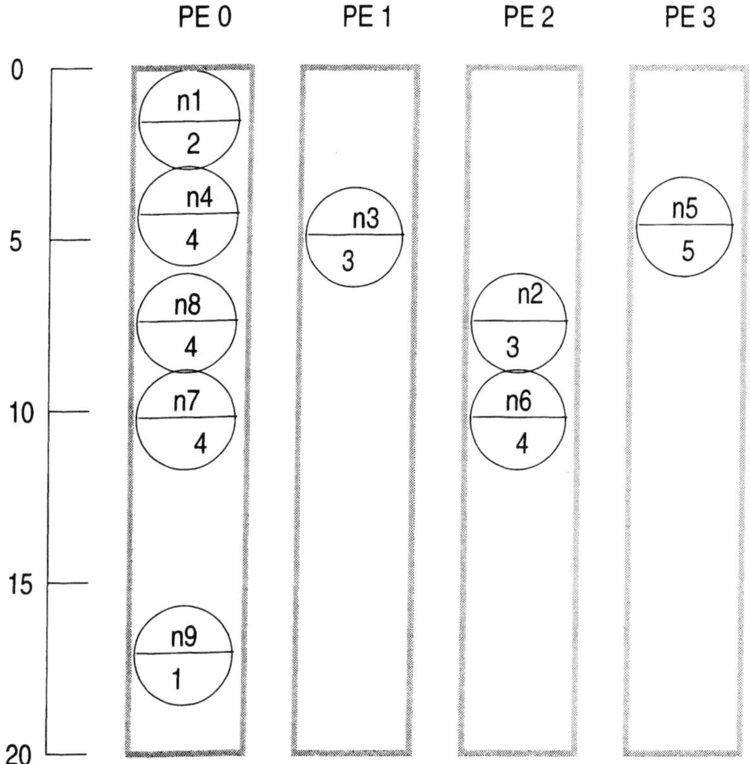

Figure 23.2 The schedule generated by the ISH algorithm (schedule length = 19).

23.3.3 The ETF Algorithm

The ETF (Earliest Time First) algorithm [10] computes, at each step, the earliest start times for all ready nodes and then selects the one with the smallest start time. Here, the earliest start time of a node is computed by examining the start time of the node on all processors exhaustively. When two nodes have the same value in their earliest start times, the ETF algorithm breaks the tie by scheduling the one with the higher static level. The algorithm is described below:

(1) Compute the static *b-level* of each node.
(2) Initially, the pool of ready nodes includes only the entry nodes.
Repeat
(3) Calculate the earliest start time on each processor for each node in the ready pool. Pick the node-processor pair that gives the earliest time using the non-insertion approach. Ties are broken by selecting the node with a higher static *b-level*. Schedule the node to the corresponding processor.
(4) Add the newly ready nodes to the ready node pool.
Until all nodes are scheduled.

The time complexity of the ETF algorithm is $O(pv^2)$. For the DAG shown in

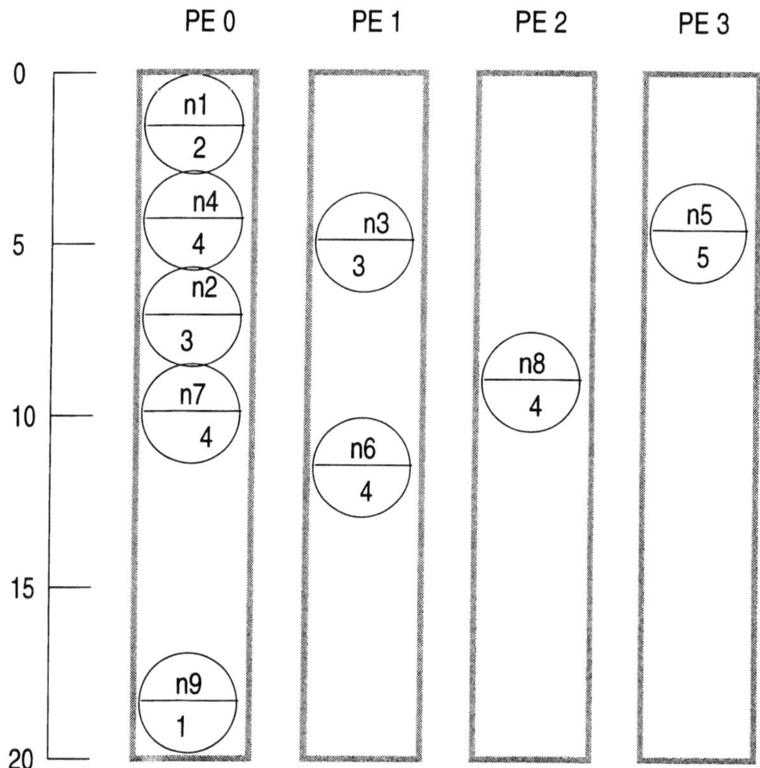

Figure 23.3 The schedule generated by the MCP algorithm (schedule length = 20).

Figure 23.1, the ETF algorithm generates a schedule shown in Figure 23.4. The ETF algorithm schedules the nodes in the following order: $n_1, n_4, n_3, n_5, n_2, n_8, n_6, n_7, n_9$.

Hwang et al. also analyzed the performance bound of the ETF algorithm [10]. They showed that the schedule length produced by the ETF algorithm SL_{ETF} satisfies the following relation: $SL_{ETF} \leq (2 - 1/p)SL_{opt}{}^{nc} + C$ where $SL_{opt}{}^{nc}$ is the optimal schedule length without considering communication delays and C is the communication requirements over some parent-parent pairs along a path. An algorithm is also provided to compute C.

23.3.4 Analytical Performance Bounds

For the BNP class of scheduling algorithms, Al-Mouhamed [2] extended the work by Fernandez et al. [8] on the case of no communication and devised a bound on the minimum number of processors for optimal schedule length and a bound on the minimum increase in schedule length if only a certain smaller number of processor is available. This algorithm extends the techniques of Fernandez et al. for arbitrary

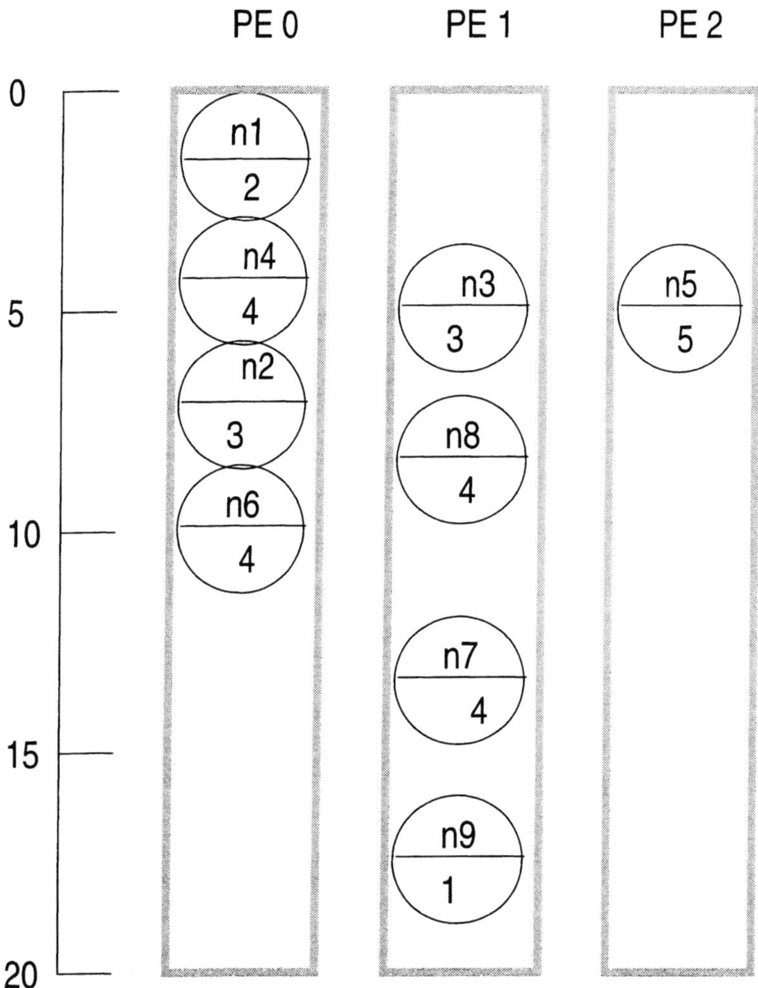

Figure 23.4 The schedule generated by the ETF algorithm (schedule length = 19).

DAGs with communication. The expressions for the bounds are similar to the ones reported by Fernandez et al. except that Al-Mouhamed conjectured that the bounds need not be computed across all possible integer intervals within the earliest completion time of the DAG. However, Jain and Rajaraman [11] in a subsequent study found that the computation of these bounds in fact needs to consider all the integer intervals within the earliest completion time of the DAG. They also reported a technique to partition the DAGs into nodes with non-overlapping intervals so that a tighter bound is obtained. In addition, the new bounds can take lesser time to compute. Jain and Rajaraman also found that using such a partitioning scheme facilitates all possible integer intervals to be considered in order to compute a tighter bound.

23.4 Scheduling Tasks to Arbitrary Processors Networks

In this section, we describe the APN class of DAG scheduling algorithms. In particular, we describe in detail three APN algorithms: the MH (Mapping Heuristic) algorithm [6], the DLS (Dynamic Level Scheduling) algorithm [16], and the BSA (Bubble Scheduling and Allocation) algorithm [12].

In APN scheduling, a processor network is not necessarily fully connected, and the contention for communication channels need to be addressed. This, in turn, implies that message routing and scheduling must also be considered.

23.4.1 The Message Routing Issue

Wang [17] suggested two adaptive routing schemes suitable for use in APN scheduling algorithms. The first scheme is a greedy algorithm which seeks a locally optimal route for each message to be sent between tasks. Instead of searching for a path with the least waiting time, the message is sent through a link which yields the least waiting time among the links that the processor can choose from for sending a message. Thus, the route is only locally optimal. Using this algorithm, Wang observed that there are two types of possible blockings: (1) a later message blocks an earlier message (called LBE blocking), and (2) an earlier message blocks a later message (called EBL blocking). LBE blocking is always more costly than EBL blocking. In the case that several messages are competing for a link and blocking becomes unavoidable, LBE blockings should be avoided as much as possible. Given this observation, Wang proposed the second algorithm, called the least blocking algorithm, which works by trying to avoid LBE blocking. The basic idea of the algorithm is to use Dijkstra's shortest path algorithm to arrange optimized routes for messages so as to avoid LBE blockings.

Having determined routes for messages, the scheduling of different messages on the links is also an important aspect. Dixit-Radiya and Panda [5] proposed a scheme for ordering messages in a link so as to further minimize the extent of link contention. Their scheme is based on the *temporal communication graph* (TCG) which, in addition to task precedence, captures the temporal relationship of the communication messages. Using the TCG model, the objective of which is to minimize the contention on the link, the earliest start times and latest start times of messages can be computed. These values are then used to heuristically schedule the messages in the links.

23.4.2 The MH Algorithm

The MH (Mapping Heuristic) algorithm [6] first assigns priorities by computing the *sl* of all nodes. A ready node list is then initialized to contain all entry nodes ordered in decreasing priorities. Each node is scheduled to a processor that gives the smallest start time. In calculating the start time of node, a routing table is maintained for each processor. The table contains information as to which path to route messages from the parent nodes to the node under consideration. After a node is scheduled, all of its ready successor nodes are appended to the ready node list. The MH algorithm is briefly described below.

(1) Compute the *sl* of each node n_i in the task graph.
(2) Initialize a ready node list by inserting all entry nodes in the task graph. The list is ordered according to node priorities, with the highest priority node first.
Repeat
(3) $n_i \leftarrow$ the first node in the list
(4) Schedule n_i to the processor which gives the smallest start time. In determining the start time on a processor, all messages from the parent nodes are scheduled and routed by consulting the routing tables associated with each processor.
(5) Append all ready successor nodes of ni, according to their priorities, to the ready node list.
Until the ready node list is empty.

The time complexity of the MH algorithm is $O(v(p^3v+e)$. For the DAG shown in Figure 23.1, the schedule generated by the MH algorithm for a 4-processor ring is shown in Figure 23.5. Here, in contrast to the schedules generated by the BNP algorithms shown earlier, the messages between tasks are explicitly scheduled and routed. In particular, it should be noted that since the network is assumed to be a ring, there is no communication channel directly linking PE 0 and PE 2, and thus, the message from n_2 to n_6 has to traverse links L01 and L12. The MH algorithm schedules the nodes in the following order: $n_1, n_4, n_3, n_5, n_2, n_8, n_7, n_6, n_9$. Note that the MH algorithm does not strictly schedule nodes according to descending order of *sl* in that it uses the *sl* order to break ties. As can be seen from the schedule shown in Figure 23.5, the MH algorithm schedules n_4 first before n_2 and n_7, which are, in fact, more important nodes. This is because the MH algorithm ranks nodes according to the descending order of their static levels. The nodes n_2 and n_7 are more important because n_7 is a CPN and n_2 critically affects the start time of n_7. As n_4 has a larger static level, the MH algorithm examines n_4 first and schedules it to an early time slot on the same processor as n_1. As a result, n_2 cannot start at the earliest possible time—the time just after n_1 finishes.

23.4.3 The DLS Algorithm

The DLS (Dynamic Level Scheduling) algorithm [16] uses an attribute called *dynamic level* (*dl*), which is the difference between the static level of a node and its earliest start time on a processor. At each scheduling step, the algorithm computes the *dl* for every node in the ready pool on all processors. The node-processor pair which gives the largest value of *dl* is selected for scheduling. This mechanism is similar to the one used by the ETF algorithm (a BNP algorithm). However, there is one subtle difference between the ETF algorithm and the DLS algorithm: The ETF algorithm always schedules the node with the minimum earliest start time and uses static *b-level* merely to break ties. In contrast, the DLS algorithm tends to

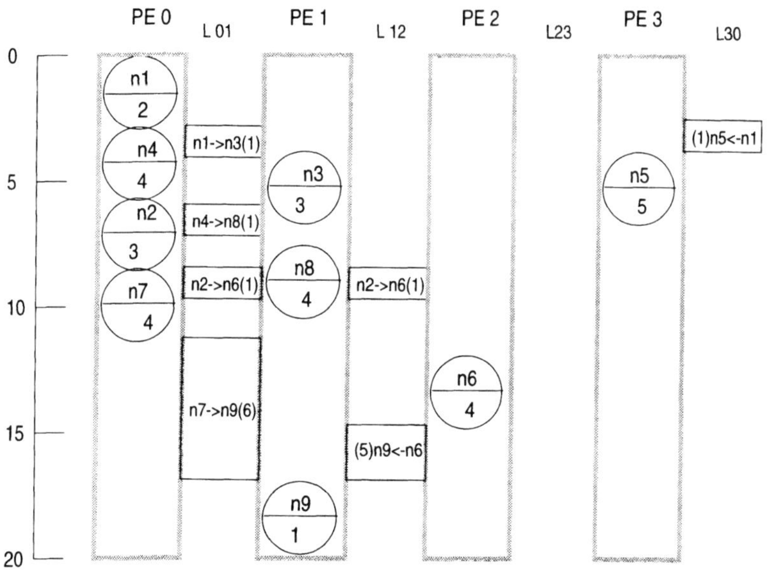

Figure 23.5 The schedule generated by the MH and DLS algorithms (schedule length = 20, total communication costs incurred = 16).

schedule nodes in descending order of static *b-level* at the beginning of scheduling process but tends to schedule nodes in ascending order of *t-level* (i.e., the earliest start times) near the end of the scheduling process. As to scheduling of messages, the DLS algorithm also requires the user to supply a routing table. The algorithm is briefly described below:

(1) Calculate the *b-level* of each node.
(2) Initially, the ready node pool includes only the entry nodes.
Repeat
(3) Calculate the earliest start time for every ready node on each processor. Hence, compute the *dl* of every node-processor pair by subtracting the earliest start time from the node's static *b-level*
(4) Select the node-processor pair that gives the largest *dl*. Schedule the node to the corresponding processor.
(5) Add the newly ready nodes to the ready pool.
Until all nodes are scheduled.

The time complexity of the DLS algorithm is $O(v^3pf(p))$, where $f(p)$ is the time complexity of the message routing algorithm based on the given routing table. For the DAG shown in Figure 23.1, the schedule generated by the DLS algorithm for a 4-processor ring is the same as that generated by the MH algorithm shown in Figure 23.5. The DLS algorithm also schedules the nodes in the following order: $n_1, n_4, n_3, n_5, n_2, n_8, n_7, n_6, n_9$.

23.4.4 The BSA Algorithm

The BSA (Bubble Scheduling and Allocation) algorithm [12] is proposed by us and is based on an incremental technique which works by improving the schedule through migration of tasks from one processor to a neighboring processor. The algorithm first allocates all the tasks to a single processor which has the highest connectivity in the processor network and is called the pivot processor. In the first phase of the algorithm, the tasks are arranged in the processor according to the CPN-Dominant sequence (discussed in detail below). In the second phase of the algorithm, the tasks migrate from the pivot processor to the neighboring processors if the start times improve. This task migration process proceeds in a breadth-first order of the processor network in that after the migration process is complete for the first pivot processor, one of the neighboring processors becomes the next pivot processor and the start time minimization process repeats.

The crucial step of the BSA algorithm is based on partitioning the DAG into three categories: critical path nodes (CPN), in-branch nodes (IBN) and out-branch nodes (OBN). An IBN is a node from which there is a path reaching a CPN. An OBN is a node which is neither a CPN nor an IBN. In a DAG, the CPNs are the most important nodes since their finish times effectively determine the final schedule length. Thus, the CPNs in a task graph should be considered as early as possible for scheduling in the scheduling process. However, we cannot consider all the CPNs without first considering other nodes because the start times of the CPNs are determined by their parent nodes. Therefore, before we can consider a CPN for scheduling, we must first consider all its parent nodes—the IBNs—because their timely scheduling can help reduce the start times of the CPNs. The OBNs are relatively less important because they usually do not affect the schedule length. Based on this reasoning, we make a sequence of nodes called the CPN-Dominant sequence which can be constructed by the following procedure:

Construction of CPN-Dominant Sequence:
(1) Make the entry CPN to be the first node in the sequence.
    Set *position* to 2. Let n_x be the next CPN.
Repeat
(2) If n_x has all its parent nodes in the sequence then
(3)   Put n_x at *position* in the sequence and increment *position*.
(4) else
(5)   Suppose n_y is a parent node of n_x which is not in the sequence and
      has the largest *b-level*. Ties are broken by choosing the parent with
      a smaller *t-level*. If n_y has all its parent nodes in the sequence,
      put n_y at *position* in the sequence and increment *position*.
      Otherwise, recursively include all the ancestor nodes of n_y in the sequence
      so that the nodes with a larger communication are considered first.
(6)   Repeat the above step until all the parent nodes of n_x
      are in the sequence. Put n_x in the sequence at *position*.
(7) endif
(8) Make n_x to be the next CPN.
Until all CPNs are in the sequence.
(9) Append all the OBNs to the sequence in descending order of *b-level*.

The CPN-Dominant sequence preserves the precedence constraints among nodes as the IBNs reaching a CPN are always inserted before the CPN in the CPN-Dominant sequence. In addition, the OBNs are appended to the sequence in a topological order so that a parent OBN is always in front of a child OBN.

The CPN-Dominant sequence of the DAG shown in Figure 23.1 is constructed as follows. Since n_1 is the entry CPN, it is placed in the first position in the CPN-Dominant sequence. The second node is n_2 because it has only one parent node. After n_2 is appended to the CPN-Dominant sequence, all parent nodes of n_7 have been considered and, therefore, n_7 can also be added to the sequence. Now the last CPN, n_9, is considered. It cannot be appended to the sequence because some of its parent nodes (i.e., the IBNs) have not been examined yet. Since both n_6 and n_8 have the same *b-level* but n_8 has a smaller *t-level*, n_8 is considered first. However, both parent nodes of n_8 have not been examined, thus, its two parent nodes, n_3 and n_4 are appended to the CPN-Dominant sequence first. Next, n_8 is appended followed by n_6. The only OBN, n_5, is the last node in the CPN-Dominant sequence. The final CPN-Dominant sequence is as follows: $n_1, n_2, n_7, n_4, n_3, n_8, n_6, n_9, n_5$. Note that using static level as a priority measure will generate a different ordering of nodes: $n_1, n_4, n_2, n_3, n_5, n_6, n_7, n_8, n_9$.

In the following outline of the BSA algorithm, the *BuildProcessorList* procedure constructs a list of processors in a breadth-first order from the first pivot processor. The *SerialInjection* procedure constructs the CPN-Dominant sequence of the nodes and injects this sequence to the first pivot processor.

The BSA Algorithm:

```
(1) Load processor topology and input task graph
(2) PivotPE ← the processor with the highest degree
(3) BuildProcessorList(PivotPE)
(4) SerialInjection(PivotPE)
(5) while ProcessorList is not empty do
(6)   PivotPE ← first processor of ProcessorList
(7)   for each n_i on PivotPE do
(8)     if ST(n_i, PivotPE) > DAT(n_i, PivotPE) or
        Proc(VIP(n_i)) ≠ PivotPE then
(9)       Determine DAT and ST of n_i on each adjacent processor PE'
(10)      if there exists a PE' such that
          ST(n_i, PE') < ST(n_i, PivotPE) then
(11)        Make n_i migrate from PivotPE to PE'
(12)        Update start times of nodes and messages
(13)      else if ST(n_i, PE') = ST(n_i, PivotPE) and
          Proc(VIP(n_i)) = PE' then
(14)        Make n_i migrate from PivotPE to PE'
(15)        Update start times of nodes and messages
(16)      end if
(17)    end if
(18)  end for
(19) end while
```

The time complexity of the BSA algorithm is $O(p^2ev)$. The BSA algorithm, as shown in Figure 23.1, injects the CPN-Dominant sequence to the first pivot processor PE 0. In the first phase, nodes n_1, n_2, and n_7 do not migrate because they are already scheduled to start at the earliest possible times. However, node n_4 migrates to PE 1 because its start time improves. Similarly, node n_3 also migrates to a neighboring processor PE 3. In the next phase, n_8 migrates to PE 1 following its VIP n_4. Similarly, n_6 also migrates to PE 3 following its VIP n_3. The last CPN, n_9, migrates to PE 1 to which its VIP n_8 is scheduled. Such migration allows the only OBN n_5 to bubble up. The resulting schedule is shown in Figure 23.6. This is the final schedule as no more nodes can improve the start time through migration.

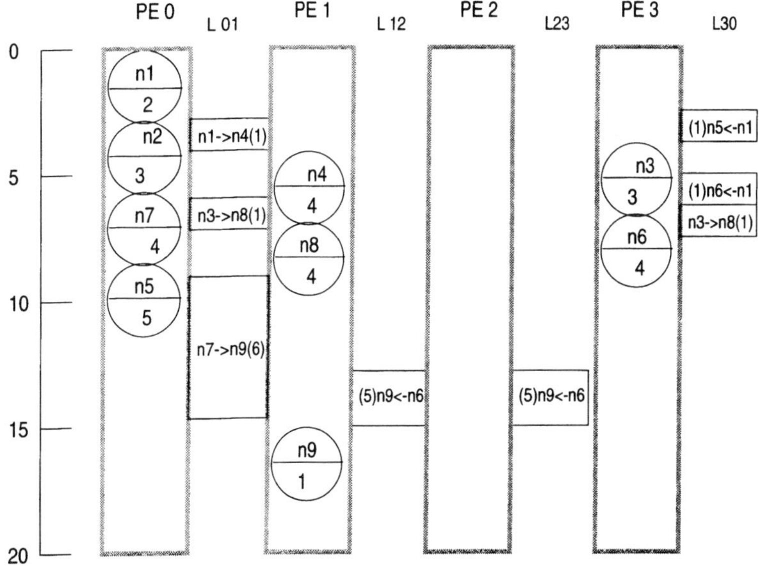

Figure 23.6 The final schedule produced by the BSA algorithm (schedule length = 16, total communication cost = 21).

23.5 CASCH: A Parallelization and Scheduling Tool

In this section, we introduce a software tool called CASCH (Computer-Aided SCHeduling) [1] for automatic parallelization and scheduling of tasks to parallel machines or clustered workstations. CASCH is a unique tool in that it provides many important facilities for developing parallel programs. It frees the user from carrying out the tedious chores and can significantly improve the performance of a parallel program. CASCH provides an extensive library of state-of-the-art scheduling algorithms from the recent literature. The library of scheduling algorithms is organized into different categories that are suitable for different architectural environments. These scheduling and mapping algorithms are used for scheduling the task graph generated from the user program. The weights on the nodes and edges of the task graph are inserted using a database that contains the timing of various computation, communication, and I/O operations for different machines. These timings have been obtained through benchmarking and analytical code profiling [1].

An attractive feature of CASCH is its graphical facility that provides a flexible and easy-to-use interactive environment for analyzing various scheduling and mapping algorithms, using task graphs generated randomly, interactively, or directly from real programs. Multiple windows can be opened to show the schedules of task graphs generated by different scheduling algorithms for a given machine. The best schedule generated by an algorithm can be used by the code generator to generate a parallel code for a particular platform and the same process can be repeated for another platform.

CASCH can also be used as a teaching aid for learning scheduling and mapping algorithms since it allows an interactive creation of task graphs and machine topologies, and provides traces of a schedule to determine the order in which tasks are scheduled by a particular algorithm.

The overall organization of CASCH is shown in Figure 23.7. The main components of CASCH are briefly described below. For more detailed information about CASCH, the reader is referred to [1].

23.5.1 User Programs

Using the CASCH tool, the user first writes a sequential program from which a DAG is generated. To facilitate the automation of program development, we use a programming style in which a program is composed of a set of procedures called from the main program. A procedure is an indivisible unit of computation to be scheduled on one processor. The grain sizes of procedures are determined by the programmer and can be modified with CASCH. Data dependencies are defined by the single assignment of parameters in procedure calls. Communications are invoked only at the beginning and the end of procedures. In other words, a procedure receives messages before it begins execution, and it sends messages after it has finished the computation.

23.5.2 Lexical Analyzer and Parser

The lexical analyzer and parser examine the data dependencies and user defined partitions. For a static program, the number of procedures are known before program execution. Such a program can be executed sequentially or in parallel. It is system independent since communication primitives are not specified in the program. Data dependencies among the procedural parameters define a macro dataflow graph, i.e., the task graph or the DAG.

23.5.3 Weight Estimator

The weights on the nodes and edges of the DAG are inserted with the help of an estimator that provides timings of various instructions as well as the cost of communication on a given machine. The estimator uses actual timings of various

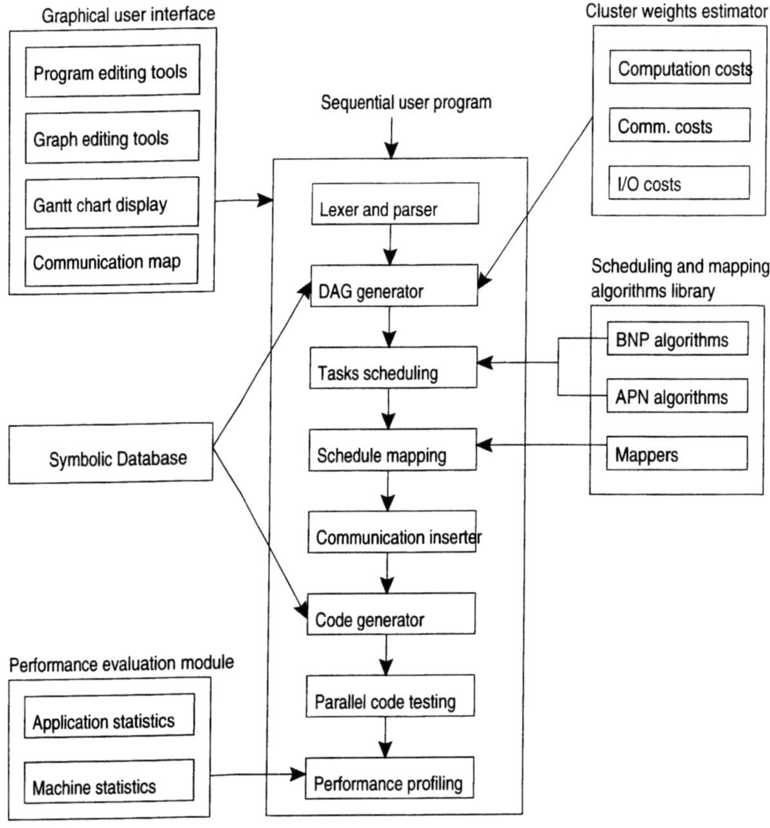

Figure 23.7 The various components and functionalities of CASCH.

computation, communication, and I/O operations on various machines. These timings have been obtained through benchmarking using an approach similar to [1], [4], [18]. The current version of the computation estimator is a symbolic estimator. The estimation is based on reading through the code without running the code. Its symbolic output is in the form of a function of input parameters of a code. Communication cost estimation, which is also obtained experimentally, is based on the cost for each communication primitive, such as *send*, *receive*, and *broadcast*.

With a symbolic estimator, the code does not need re-estimation for different problem sizes. This estimator estimates a restricted class of C codes. The code may include functions and procedures, and the estimator generates performance for each of them. The code may have *for* loops. The boundaries of a loop can be either constants or input parameters. The cost of each operation or built-in function is specified in the cost files. The cost can be measured from experiments. Then, the total amount of computation can be obtained by summing all costs of operations and functions for a segment of code.

23.5.4 DAG Generation

A macro dataflow graph, which is generated directly from the main program, is a DAG with a start and an end point. Each node in the DAG corresponds to a procedure, and the node weight is represented by the procedure execution time. Each edge corresponds to a message transferred from one procedure to another procedure, and the weight of the edge is equal to the transmission time of the message. When two nodes are scheduled to a single PE, the weight of the edge connecting them becomes zero. In static scheduling, the number of nodes is known before program execution. The execution time of a node is obtained by using the estimator. The transmission time of a message is estimated by using the message start-up time, message length, and communication channel bandwidth.

23.5.5 Scheduling/Mapping Tool

A common approach to distribute workload to processors is partitioning a problem into p tasks and performing a one-to-one mapping among the tasks and the processors. Partitioning can be done with the "block," "cyclic," or "block-cyclic" pattern [1], [18]. Such partitioning schemes are suitable for problems with regular structures. Simple scheduling heuristics such as the "owners compute" rule work for certain problems but could fail for many others, especially for irregular problems, as it is difficult to balance load and minimize dependencies simultaneously. The way to solve irregular problems is to partition the problem into many tasks which are scheduled for a balanced load and minimized communication. In CASCH, a DAG generated based on this partitioning is scheduled using a scheduling algorithm. However, one scheduling algorithm may not be suitable for a certain problem on a given architecture. Thus, CASCH includes various algorithms which are suitable to various environments. The advantages of having a wide variety of algorithms in CASCH are:

- The diversity of these algorithms allows the user to select a type of algorithm that is suitable to a particular architectural configuration;
- The common platform provided by CASCH allows simultaneous comparisons among various algorithms, with a number of performance objectives such as schedule length, number of processors used, algorithm's running time, etc.;
- The comparison among the algorithms can be done using manually generated graphs as well as real data from a number of applications;
- For a given application program, the user can optimize the code by running various scheduling algorithms and then choose the best schedule;
- CASCH provides an interactive graphical interface which includes a trace of the schedule generated by an algorithm. Using this trace, an algorithm's operation can be observed to determine why it performs better or worse for a given task graph.

23.5.6 Communication Inserter

Synchronization among the tasks running on multiple processors is carried out by communication primitives. The basic communication primitives for exchanging messages between processors are *send* and *receive*. They must be used properly to ensure a correct sequence of computation. These primitives are inserted automatically, reducing a programmer's burden and eliminating insertion errors. The procedure for inserting a communication primitive is as follows. After scheduling and mapping, each node in a macro dataflow graph has been allocated to a PE. If an edge leaves from a node to another node which belongs to a different PE, the *send* primitive is inserted after the node. Similarly, if an edge comes from another node in a different PE, the *receive* primitive is inserted before the node. However, if a message has already been sent to a particular PE, the same message does not need to be sent to the same PE again. If a message is to be sent to many PEs, *broadcasting* or *multicasting* can be applied instead of sending separate messages. The insertion method described above does not ensure a correct communication sequence. Thus, we use a send-first strategy for a reordering of communication primitives. That is, we reorder receives according to the order of sends. Reordering of *sends* and *receives* may not be necessary for a system supporting typed messages. However, even for such systems, message transmission reordering may reduce the message waiting time and the demand for communication buffers.

23.5.7 Code Generation

With the symbolic schedule generated by a scheduling algorithm, the code generation module is then invoked to produce the target parallel code. Code generation is a relatively straightforward process because the generator just needs to translate the source statements of the serial program into corresponding statements in the target language, and inserts the primitives according to the communication inserter's instructions. Such a cross-compilation approach is particularly effective if the source and target language are similar. In the current version of CASCH, the source language is C and the target language for most platforms supported is also C (with MPI or PVM communication libraries).

23.5.8 Graphical User Interface

The graphical capabilities of CASCH provide the user with an easy-to-use window-based interactive interface. With the GUI, the user can create, edit, or browse through sequential programs. There are also facilities on the windows for generating a DAG from the user program. In addition, CASCH provides a DAG editor which includes facilities to display a DAG generated from the user program. Other options include displaying a randomly generated DAG or creating a DAG interactively. The editing facilities include node and edge insertion. Also, node IDs as well as weights on the node and edges can be labeled with numbers interactively. Multiple windows of various task graphs can be opened simultaneously. Zooming facilities (horizontally or vertically or both) are included for proper viewing. An interactive help function is included as well.

The graph editing facility also allows the user to display a processor architecture (including the processors and the network topology). The editing facilities, similar to DAGs, allow the user to interactively create various network topologies. The schedule generated as the results of invoking a scheduling algorithm can be displayed using this facility. The schedule is displayed using a Gantt chart showing the start and finish times of tasks on various processors. Clicking on any task in the Gantt chart displays its start and finish times; the total schedule length is also shown on the window. A schedule also includes communication messages on the network (displayed through another window which is invoked by clicking on any two processors). The scale of the display can be changed to zoom the Gantt chart. An important features of this facility is the trace option which shows a step-by-step scheduling of each task. This is very useful for understanding the operation of a scheduling algorithm by observing the order in which tasks are scheduled by the algorithm. Multiple such charts can be opened, allowing a comparison among the schedules generated by various algorithms.

23.6 Summary and Concluding Remarks

In this chapter, we have presented algorithms for the static scheduling problem encountered in a network environment such as a cluster of workstations. We first introduced the DAG model and the multiprocessor model, followed by the problem statement of scheduling. In the DAG model, a node denotes an atomic program task and an edge denotes the communication and data dependency between two program tasks. Each node is labeled a weight denoting the amount of computational time required by the task. Each edge is also labeled a weight denoting the amount of communication time required. The target multiprocessor systems is modeled as a network of processing elements (PEs), each of which comprises a processor and a local memory unit, so that communication is achieved solely by message-passing. The objective of scheduling is to minimize the schedule length by properly allocating the nodes to the PEs and sequencing their start times so that the precedence constraints are preserved.

We have also presented a scrutiny of the NP-completeness results of various simplified variants of the problem, thereby illustrating that static scheduling is a difficult optimization problem. As the problem is intractable even for moderately general cases, heuristic approaches are commonly sought. To better understand the design of the heuristic scheduling schemes, we have also described and explained a set of basic techniques used in most algorithms. With these techniques, the task graph structure is carefully exploited to determine the relative importance of the nodes in the graph. More important nodes get a higher consideration priority for scheduling first. An important structure in a task graph is the critical path (CP), a longest path in the graph. The nodes of the CP can be identified by the nodes' *b-level* and *t-level*.

Depending upon the speed of the underlying communication network, we have classified the scheduling algorithms into two categories: the BNP (bounded number of processors) scheduling and the APN (arbitrary processor network) scheduling. Analytical results as well as scheduling examples have been shown to illustrate the functionality and characteristics of the surveyed algorithms. Finally, an experimental software tool for scheduling and mapping is also described.

Acknowledgment

This work was supported by the Hong Kong Research Grants Council under contract numbers HKUST734/96E and HKUST6076/97E.

23.7 Bibliography

[1] I. Ahmad, Y.-K. Kwok, M.-Y. Wu, and W. Shu. Automatic Parallelization and Scheduling of Programs on Multiprocessors using CASCH. *Proceedings of the 1997 International Conference on Parallel Processing*, pages 288-291, August 1997.

[2] M.A. Al-Mouhamed. Lower Bound on the Number of Processors and Time for Scheduling Precedence Graphs with Communication Costs. *IEEE Transactions on Software Engineering*, vol. 16(12), pages 1390-1401, December 1990.

[3] T.L. Casavant and J.G. Kuhl. A Taxonomy of Scheduling in General-Purpose Distributed Computing Systems. *IEEE Transactions on Software Engineering*, vol. 14(2), pages 141-154, February 1988.

[4] M. Cosnard and M. Loi. Automatic Task Graph Generation Techniques. *Parallel Processing Letters*, vol. 5(4), pages 527-538, December 1995.

[5] V.A. Dixit-Radiya and D.K. Panda. Task Assignment on Distributed-Memory Systems with Adaptive Wormhole Routing. *Proceedings of the International Symposium of Parallel and Distributed Systems*, pages 674-681, December 1993.

[6] H. El-Rewini and T.G. Lewis. Scheduling Parallel Programs onto Arbitrary Target Machines. *Journal of Parallel and Distributed Computing*, vol. 9(2), pages 138-153, June 1990.

[7] H. El-Rewini, T.G. Lewis, and H.H. Ali. *Task Scheduling in Parallel and Distributed Systems*, Englewood Cliffs, New Jersey:Prentice Hall, 1994.

[8] E.B. Fernandez and B. Bussell. Bounds on the Number of Processors and Time for Multiprocessor Optimal Schedules. *IEEE Transactions on Computers*, vol. C-22(8), pages 745-751, August 1973.

[9] M.R. Garey and D.S. Johnson. *Computers and Intractability: A Guide to the Theory of NP-Completeness*, W.H. Freeman and Company, 1979.

[10] J.J. Hwang, Y.C. Chow, F.D. Anger, and C.Y. Lee. Scheduling Precedence Graphs in Systems with Interprocessor Communication Times. *SIAM Journal on Computing*, vol. 18(2), pages 244-257, April. 1989.

[11] K.K. Jain and V. Rajaraman. Lower and Upper Bounds on Time for Multiprocessor Optimal Schedules. *IEEE Transactions on Parallel and Distributed Systems*, vol. 5(8), pages 879-886, August 1994.

[12] Y.-K. Kwok and I. Ahmad. Bubble Scheduling: A Quasi-Dynamic Algorithm for Static Allocation of Tasks to Parallel Architectures. *Proceedings of the 7th IEEE Symposium on Parallel and Distributed Processing*, pages 36-43, October 1995.

[13] Y.-K. Kwok and I. Ahmad. Dynamic Critical-Path Scheduling: An Effective Technique for Allocating Task Graphs onto Multiprocessors. *IEEE Transactions on Parallel and Distributed Systems*, vol. 7(5), pages 506-621, May 1996.

[14] Y.-K. Kwok and I. Ahmad. Benchmarking the Task Graph Scheduling Algorithms. *Proceedings of IPPS'98*, pages 531-537, March 1998.

[15] C.H. Papadimitriou and K. Steiglitz. *Combinatorial Optimization: Algorithms and Complexity*, Englewood Cliffs, New Jersey:Prentice-Hall, 1982.

[16] G.C. Sih and E.A. Lee. A Compile-Time Scheduling Heuristic for Interconnection-Constrained Heterogeneous Processor Architectures. *IEEE Transactions on Parallel and Distributed Systems*, vol. 4(2), pages 75-87, February 1993.

[17] M.-F. Wang. Message Routing Algorithms for Static Task Scheduling. *Proceedings of the Symposium on Applied Computing*, pages 276-281, 1990.

[18] M.-Y. Wu and D.D. Gajski. Hypertool: A Programming Aid for Message-Passing Systems. *IEEE Transactions on Parallel and Distributed Systems*, vol. 1(3), pages 330-343, July 1990.

[19] T. Yang and A. Gerasoulis. DSC: Scheduling Parallel Tasks on an Unbounded Number of Processors. *IEEE Transactions on Parallel and Distributed Systems*, vol. 5(9), pages 951-967, September 1994.

Chapter 24

Customized Dynamic Load Balancing

MOHAMMED J. ZAKI[†], SRINIVASAN PARTHASARATHY[‡], WEI LI[§]

[†]Computer Science Department
Rensselaer Polytechnic Institute, Troy, NY 12180, USA

[‡]Computer Science Department
University of Rochester, Rochester, NY 14627, USA

[§]Intel Corporation
2200 Mission College Blvd., Santa Clara, CA 95052, USA

Email: *zaki@cs.rpi.edu, srini@cs.rochester.edu, wei.li@intel.com*

24.1 Introduction

Efficient scheduling of loops on a NOW requires finding the appropriate granularity of tasks and partitioning them so that each processor is assigned work in proportion to its performance. This load balancing assignment can be *static* – done at compile-time, or it may be *dynamic* – done at runtime. The distribution of tasks is further complicated if processors have differing speeds and memory resources, or due to transient external load and non-uniform iteration execution times. While static scheduling avoids the runtime scheduling overhead, in a multi-user environment with load changes on the nodes, a more dynamic approach is warranted. Moreover, different schemes are best for different applications under varying program and system parameters. Application-driven customized load balancing thus becomes essential for good performance. This chapter addresses the above problem. In particular we make the following contributions: 1) We compare different strategies for dynamic load balancing in the presence of transient external load. We examine both global vs. local, and centralized vs. distributed schemes. 2) We present a hybrid compile and runtime system that automatically selects the best load balancing scheme for a given loop/task from the repertoire of different strategies. We also automatically transform an annotated sequential program to a parallel program with appropriate calls to our runtime load balancing library. 3) We present experimental results to substantiate our approach. The evaluation indicates that different strategies are best depending on the parameters. Different phases of the same application may also require different strategies. Our modeling is able to capture these variations quite accurately, and thus our analysis can be used to select an appropriate load balancing scheme for an application.

24.1.1 Related Work

We begin by looking at some existing load balancing schemes.

Static Scheduling

Compile-time *static* loop scheduling is efficient and introduces no additional runtime overhead. For UMA (Uniform Memory Access) parallel machines, usually loop iterations can be scheduled in *block* or *cyclic* fashion. For NUMA (Non-Uniform Memory Access) parallel machines, loop scheduling must take data distribution into account [5]. The simplest approach is the *static block* scheduling scheme, which assigns equal block of iterations to each of the available processors. *Static interleaved* scheme assigns iterations in a cyclic fashion.

There has been relatively little work in static scheduling for heterogeneous clusters. Static scheduling algorithms for heterogeneous programs, processors, memory, and network were proposed in [4].

Dynamic Scheduling

When the execution time of loop iterations is not predictable at compile-time, runtime *dynamic* scheduling can be used at the additional runtime cost of managing task allocation. The dynamic scheduling strategies fall under different models, which include schemes based on predicting the future from past loads, the *task queue model*, and the *diffusion model*.

Predicting the Future A common approach taken for load balancing on a workstation network is to predict future performance based on past information. For example, in data parallel C [8], loop iterations are mapped to virtual processors, and these virtual processors are assigned to the physical processors based on past load behavior. The approach is global distributed, where the processor's load is given as the average computation time per virtual processor, and load balancing involves periodic information exchanges. Dome [1] implements a global central scheme and a local distributed scheme. The performance metric used is the rate at which the processors execute the dome program, and load balancing involves periodic exchanges. Siegell [12] also presented a global centralized scheme, with periodic information exchanges, and where the performance metric is the iterations done per second.

The main contribution of this paper is the methodology for automatic generation of parallel programs with dynamic load balancing. In Phish [2], a local distributed receiver-initiated scheme is described, where the processor requesting more tasks, called the *thief*, chooses a *victim* at random from which to steal more work. If the current victim cannot satisfy the request, another victim is selected. CHARM [11] implements a two-phased scheme. Initially, in the static phase, work is assigned to the processors proportional to their speed, and inversely proportional to the load on the processor. The dynamic phase implements a local distributed receiver-initiated scheme. The information exchanged is the *Forecasted Finish Time* (FFT), i.e., the time for the processor to finish the remaining work. If the FFT falls below a threshold, the node requests a neighbor with higher FFT for more work. If the request cannot be satisfied, another neighbor is selected.

Our approach also falls under this model. Instead of periodic exchanges of information, we have a interrupt-based receiver-initiated scheme. Moreover, we look at both central vs. distributed, and local vs. global approaches. In the local schemes, instead of random selection of a processor from which to request more work, work is exchanged among all the neighbors (the number of neighbors is selected statically). These strategies are explained in more detail in Section 24.2. [3] presents an application-specific approach to schedule individual parallel applications. [9] presented an approach, where a user specifies homogeneous load balancers for different tasks within a heterogeneous application. They also present a global load balancer that handles the interactions among the different homogeneous load balancers. However, our goal is to provide compile and runtime support to automatically select the best load balancing scheme for a given loop from a repertoire of different strategies.

Task Queue Model A host of approaches have been proposed in the literature targeting shared memory machines. These fall under the *task queue model*, where there is a logically central task queue of loop iterations. Once the processors have finished their assigned portion, more work is obtained from this queue. The simplest approach in this model is *self-scheduling* [13], where each processor is allocated only one iteration at a time, which leads to high synchronization cost. In *guided self-scheduling* [10], the chunk size is changed at runtime. Each processor is assigned $1/P$-th of the remaining loop iterations, where P denotes the number of processors. Although the large chunk sizes in the beginning reduce synchronization, they can cause serious imbalances in non-uniform loops. Moreover, this scheme degenerates to the case of self-scheduling towards the end due to small chunk sizes. A number of more elaborate schemes based on this idea are extant. For example, *affinity scheduling* [7] also takes processor affinity into account while scheduling, i.e., iterations using the same data are scheduled on the same processor, unless they must be moved to balance load.

Diffusion Model Other approaches include *diffusion models* with all the work initially distributed, and with work movement between adjacent processors if an imbalance is detected between their load and their neighbor's load. An example is the *gradient model* [6] approach.

24.2 Dynamic Load Balancing (DLB)

The goal of load balancing is to assign to each processing node work proportional to its performance, thereby minimizing the execution time of the application. In this section we describe our dynamic load balancing approach, and the different strategies we chose to study our concepts.

After the initial assignment of work (the iterations of the loop) to each processor, dynamic load balancing is done in four basic steps: monitoring processor performance, exchanging this information between processors, calculating new distributions and making the work movement decision, and actually moving the data. The data is moved directly between the slaves, and the load balancing decisions are made by the *load balancer*.

Synchronization In our approach, a synchronization is triggered by the first processor to finish its portion of the work. This processor then sends an interrupt to all other active slaves, who then send their performance profiles to the load balancer.

Performance Metric We try to predict the future performance based on past information, which depends on the past load function. We can use the whole past history or a portion of it. Usually, the most recent window is used as an indication of the future. The metric we use is the number of iterations done per second, since the last synchronization point.

Work Movement Once the load balancer has all the profile information, it calculates a new distribution. If the amount of work to be moved is below a threshold, then work is not moved, since this may indicate that the system is almost balanced, or that only a small portion of the work remains to be done. If there is a sufficient amount of work that needs to be moved, we invoke a ***profitability analysis*** routine. We redistribute work as long as the potential benefit of the new assignment results in an improvement. If it is profitable to move work, then the load balancer broadcasts the new distribution information to the processors. The work is then redistributed among the slaves.

Data Movement and Profitability Analysis Work redistribution also entails the movement of the data arrays which will be accessed in the iterations. There is a trade-off between the benefits of moving work to balance load, and the cost of data movement. Accounting for this cost/benefit is a subtle matter. The reason is that inaccuracies in data movement cost estimation may predict a higher cost for the work redistribution, thereby nullifying the potential benefits of moving work.

In our scheme, since we synchronize only when a processor needs more work, cancelling work redistribution would lead to an idle processor, lowering the overall utilization, and degrading the execution-time. We thus redistribute work as long as the potential benefit (predicted execution time, excluding the cost of actual data movement) of the new assignment results in at least a 10% improvement (empirically, this number worked well).

24.2.1 Load Balancing Strategies

We chose four different strategies differing along two axes. The techniques are either *global* or *local*, based on the information they use to make load balancing decisions, and they are either *centralized* or *distributed*, depending on whether the load balancer is located at one master processor (which also takes part in computation), or if the load balancer is distributed among the processors, respectively. For all the strategies, the compiler initially distributes the iterations of the loop equally among all the processors.

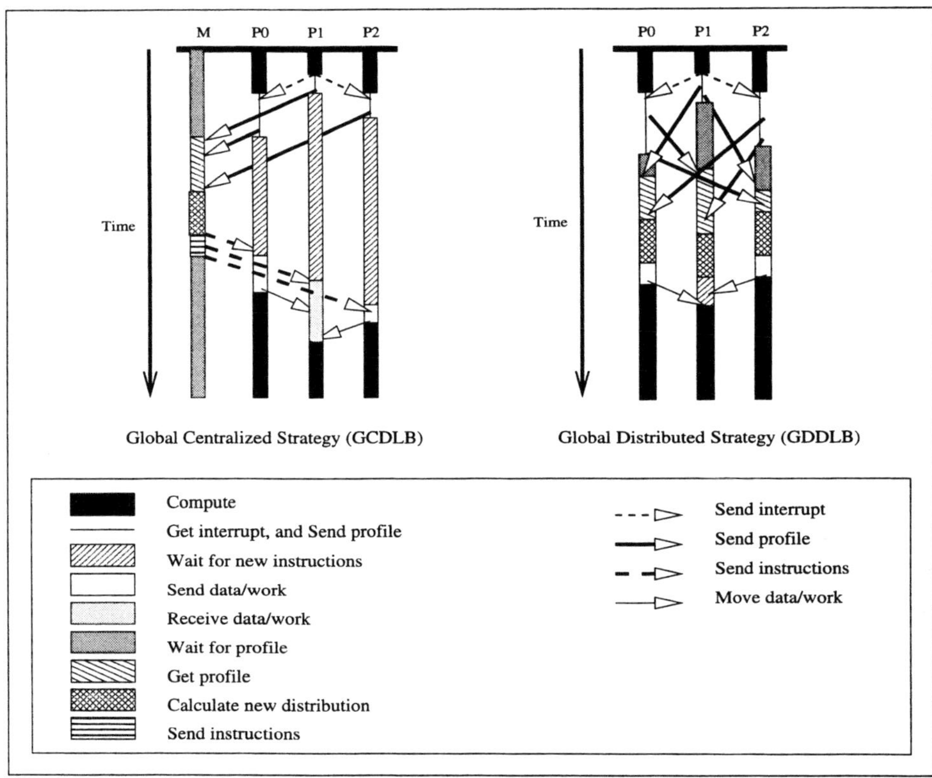

Figure 24.1 Centralized vs. distributed strategies.

Global Strategies

In the global schemes, the load balancing decision is made using global knowledge, i.e., all the processors take part in the synchronization, and send their performance profiles to the load balancer. The global schemes we consider are given below.

Global Centralized DLB (GCDLB) In this scheme the load balancer is located on a master processor (centralized). After calculating the new distribution, and profitability of work movement, the load balancer sends instructions to the processors who have to send work to others, indicating the recipient and the amount of work to be moved. The receiving processors just wait till they have collected the amount of work they need.

Global Distributed DLB (GDDLB) In this scheme the load balancer is replicated on all the processors. So, unlike GCDLB, where profile information is sent to only the master, in GDDLB, the profile information is broadcast to every other processor. This also eliminates the need for the load balancer to send out instructions, as that information is available to all the processors. The receiving processors wait for work, while the sending processors ship the data. Figure 24.1 highlights the differences between the two strategies pictorially.

Local Strategies

In the local schemes, the processors are partitioned into different groups of size K. This partition can be done by considering the physical proximity of the machines, as in *K-nearest neighbors* scheme. The groups can also be formed in a *K-block* fashion, or the group members can be selected randomly. Furthermore, the groups can remain fixed for the duration of execution, or the membership can be changed dynamically. We use the K-block fixed-group approach in our implementation, where the load balancing decisions are made only within a group. If the processors have different speeds, we can perform a static partitioning so that each group has nearly equal aggregate computational power. The global strategies are essentially an instance of the respective local strategies, where the group size, K, equals the number of processors. The two local strategies we look at are:

Local Centralized DLB (LCDLB) This scheme is similar to GCDLB. The fastest processor in a group interrupts only the other processors in that group. There is one centralized load balancer, which asynchronously handles all the different groups. Once it receives the profile information from one group, it send instructions for redistribution for that group before proceeding to the other groups.

Local Distributed DLB (LDDLB) Here the load balancer is replicated on all the processors, but profile information is broadcast only to members of the group.

24.2.2 Discussion

These four strategies lie at the four extreme points on the two axes. For example, in the local approach, there is no exchange of work between different groups. In the local centralized (LCDLB) version, we have only one master load balancer, instead of having one master per group. Furthermore, in the distributed strategies we have full replication of the load balancer. There are many conceivable points in between, and many other hybrid strategies possible. Exploring the behavior of these strategies is part of future work. At the present time, we believe that the extreme points will serve to highlight the differences, and help to gain a basic understanding of these schemes.

Global vs. Local The advantage of the global schemes is that the work redistribution is optimal, based on information known until that point (the future is unpredictable, so it's not optimal for the whole duration). However, synchronization is more expensive. On the other hand, in the local schemes, the work redistribution is not optimal, resulting in slower convergence. However, the amount of communication or synchronization cost is lower. Another factor affecting the local strategies is the difference in performance among the different groups. For example, if one group has processors with poor performance (high load), and the other group has very fast processors (little or no load), the latter will finish quite early and remain idle, while the former group is overloaded. This could be remedied by providing a mechanism for exchange of data between groups. It could also be fixed by having dynamic group memberships, instead of having static partitions. In this chapter we restrict our attention to the static group partition scheme only.

Centralized vs. Distributed In the centralized schemes, the central point of control could prevent the scalability of the strategy to a large number of machines. The distributed schemes help solve this problem. However, in these schemes the synchronization involves an all-to-all broadcast. The centralized schemes require an all-to-one profile send, which is followed by a one-to-all instruction send. There is also a trade-off between sequential load balancing decision making in the centralized approach and the parallel (replicated) decision making in the distributed schemes.

24.3 DLB Modeling and Decision Process

We now present a compile and runtime modeling and decision process for choosing among the different load balancing strategies. We begin with a discussion of the different parameters that may influence the performance of these schemes. This is followed by the derivation of the total cost function for each of these approaches in terms of the different parameters. Finally, we show how this modeling is used.

24.3.1 Modeling Parameters

The various parameters which affect the modeling are presented below. These include processor parameters such as the number of processors, processor speeds and number of neighbors; program parameters such as the data size, number of loop iterations, work and time per iteration and communication; network parameters such as latency, bandwidth and topology; and finally, modeled external load parameters such as the maximum load and duration of persistence.

Processor Parameters

These give information about the different processors available to the application.

Number of Processors We assume a fixed number of processors available for the computation. This number is specified by the user, and is denoted as P.

Number of Neighbors This is used for the local strategies and may be dictated by the physical proximity of the machines, or it may be user specified. It is denoted as K.

Processor Speeds There are a number of ways to calculate the speed of the processor. For example, we could use the MIPS (*million instructions per second*), MFLOPS (*million floating-point operations per second*), Whetstone, or the Dhrystone ratings. In modern processors different operations have different cost, and we would need to consider the speed of a processor in terms of the number of floating-point operations per second, and the number of integer operations per second. We also need to consider memory access time, and the interaction of these with different cache and memory sizes. Multiple instruction issue and instruction pipelining would further complicate the performance model. Therefore, while these figures may give an indication of the processor capabilities, reliable and consistent performance measure can be found only by using the execution time of different real applications on the machines in consideration.

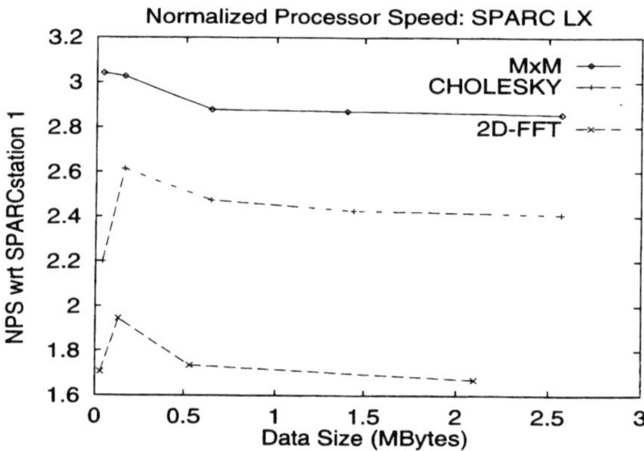

Figure 24.2 NPS: Sun SPARC LX vs. SPARC 1.

Based on our study of heterogeneous loop scheduling [4], we summarize the processor speeds via the notion of *normalized processor speed* (NPS), defined as the ratio of the time taken to execute on the processor in consideration, with respect to the time taken on a base processor. The speed for processor i is denoted as S_i. Consider Figure 24.2, which show the processor performance of a SUN SPARCstation LX on some common scientific kernels – Matrix Multiplication, Cholesky Factorization, and two-dimensional Fast Fourier Transformation. The execution time is normalized against the performance of a SUN SPARCstation 1. Our experiments indicate that machine performance varies for different applications. Since the processor speeds vary from one application to another, we approximate the speed based on small trial application runs. On the other hand, we may obtain these by compile-time performance prediction.

Program Parameters

These parameters give information about the application.

Data Size This could be different for different arrays (it could also be different for the different dimensions of the same array). This is denoted as N_{ad}, where d specifies the dimension, and a specifies the array name.

Number of Loop Iterations This is usually some function of the data size, and is denoted as $\mathcal{I}_i(N_{ad})$, where i specifies the loop.

Work per Iteration The amount of work is measured in terms of the number of basic operations per iteration, and is a function of the data size. This is denoted as $\mathcal{W}_{ij}(N_{ad})$, where i specifies the loop, and j specifies the iteration number.

Data Communication This specifies the communication cost due to data movement caused by the load balancing process. This is a per array cost, which indicates the number of bytes that need to be communicated per iteration. In a row or a column distribution of the data arrays, this is simply the number of the columns and number of rows, respectively. This is denoted as $\mathcal{D}_{aij}(N_{ad})$, where a is the array name, i is the loop, and j is the iteration. There is another source of communication, called *intrinsic communication*, which specifies the amount of communication per iteration, which is inherent to the program, for example, communication caused due to data dependencies. In this chapter, we consider only parallel loops, which by definition do not have any intrinsic communication.

Time per Iteration This specifies the time it takes to execute an iteration of a loop on the base processor. It is denoted as $\mathcal{T}_{ij}(\mathcal{W})$, where i is the loop, and j is the iteration. Since this time is with respect to the base processor, the time to execute an iteration on processor k is simply $\mathcal{T}_{ij}/S_k$. This time could be obtained by profiling, static analysis, or with the help of the programmer.

Network Parameters

These specify the properties of the interconnection network.

Network Latency This is the time it takes to send a single byte message between processors. Although the communication latency could be different for the various processor pairs, we assume it to be uniform, and denote it as $\mathcal{L}$.

Network Bandwidth This is the number of bytes that can be transferred per second over the network. It includes the cost of packing, receiving, and the "real" communication time in the physical medium. We denote this as $\mathcal{B}$.

Network Topology This influences the latency and bandwidth between pairs of processors. It also has an impact on the number of neighbors (for local strategies), and may help in reducing expensive communication while redistribution. In this chapter, however, we assume full connectivity among the processors, with uniform latency and bandwidth.

External Load Modeling

To evaluate our schemes, we had to model the external load. In our approach, each processor has an independent load function, denoted as ℓ_i. The two parameters for generating the load function are:

Maximum Load This specifies the maximum amount of load per processor, and is denoted as $m\ell$. In our experiments, we set $m\ell = 5$.

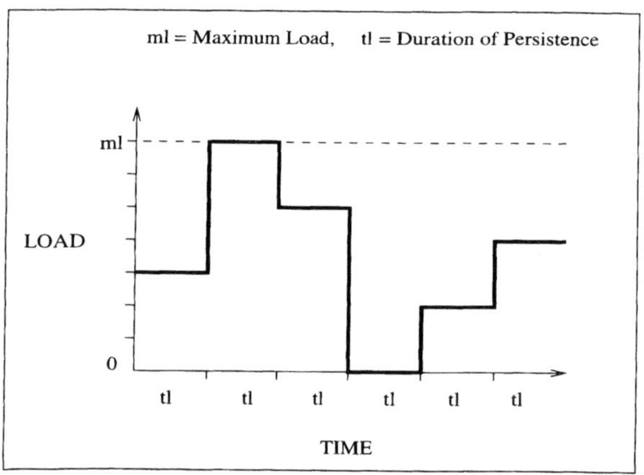

Figure 24.3 Load function.

Duration of Persistence The load value for a processor is obtained by using a random number generator to get a value between zero and the maximum load. The duration of persistence, denoted as $t\ell$, indicates the amount of time before next load change, i.e., we simulate a discrete random load function, with a maximum amplitude given by $m\ell$, and the discrete block size given by $t\ell$. A small value for $t\ell$ implies a rapidly changing load, while a large value indicates a relatively stable load. We use $\ell_i(k)$ to denote the load on processor i during the k-th duration of persistence. Figure 24.3 shows the load function for a processor.

24.3.2 Modeling the Strategies – Total Cost Derivation

We now present the cost model for the various strategies. The cost of a scheme can be broken into the following categories: cost of synchronization, cost of calculating new distribution, cost of sending instructions, and cost of data movement.

Cost of Synchronization

The synchronization involves the sending of interrupt from the fastest processor to the other processors, who then send their performance profile to the load balancer. This cost is specified in terms of the kind of communication required for the synchronization. The cost for the different strategies is given below:

- GCDLB : ξ = one-to-all(P) + all-to-one(P)
- GDDLB : ξ = one-to-all(P) + all-to-all(P^2)
- LCDLB (per group) : ξ = one-to-all(K) + all-to-one(K)
- LDDLB (per group) : ξ = one-to-all(K) + all-to-all(K^2)

Cost of Distribution Calculation

This cost, denoted δ, is usually quite small. It is replicated in the distributed strategies. The cost for the local schemes would be slightly cheaper, since each group has only K instead of P processors. However, we ignore this effect.

Cost of Data Movement

We now present our analysis to calculate the amount of data movement and the number of messages required to redistribute work.

Notation Let $\chi_i(j)$ denote the iteration distribution, and $\gamma_i(j)$ the number of iterations left to be done by processor i after the j-th synchronization point. Let $\Gamma(j) = \sum_{i=1}^{P} \gamma_i(j)$, and let t_j denote the time of the j-th synchronization.

Effect of Discrete Load The *effective speed* of processor is inversely proportional to the amount of load on it, which is given as $S_i/(\ell_i(k)+1)$, where $\ell_i(k) \in \{0, \cdots, m\ell\}$. Since the performance metric used by the different schemes is the processor performance since the last synchronization point, the processor's performance is given as the average effective speed over that duration. Let the $(j-1)$-th synchronization be during the a-th duration of persistence, i.e., $a = \lceil t_{j-1}/t\ell \rceil$. Similarly, let $b = \lceil t_j/t\ell \rceil$. Let $\lambda_i(j)$ denotes the *effective load* on processor i between the j-th and the previous synchronization. Then the *average effective speed* of processor i between two these synchronizations is given as

$$\sigma_i(j) = \frac{\sum_{k=a}^{b} S_i/(\ell_i(k)+1)}{b-a+1} = S_i/\left(\frac{b-a+1}{\sum_{k=a}^{b} 1/(\ell_i(k)+1)}\right) = S_i/\lambda_i(j)$$

Total Iterations Done We now analyze the effect of the j-th synchronization. We will first look at the case of uniform loops, i.e., where each iteration of the loop takes the same time.

Uniform Loops We will use $\mathcal{T}$ for the time per iteration. At the end of the $(j-1)$-th synchronization, each processor had $\chi_i(j-1)$ iterations assigned to it. Let f denote the first processor to finish its portion of the work. Then the time taken by processor f is given as

$$t = t_j - t_{j-1} = \frac{\chi_f(j-1) \cdot \mathcal{T}}{\sigma_f(j)}$$

The iterations left to be done on processor i is simply the old distribution minus the iterations done in time t

$$\gamma_i(j) = \chi_i(j-1) - \left\lceil \frac{t \cdot \sigma_i(j)}{\mathcal{T}} \right\rceil$$

Using the value of t from above, we get

$$\gamma_i(j) = \chi_i(j-1) - \chi_f(j-1)\left(\frac{\sigma_i(j)}{\sigma_f(j)}\right) \tag{24.3.1}$$

Non-Uniform Loops We now extend the analysis for non-uniform loops. The time taken by processor f to finish its portion of the work is given as

$$t = t_j - t_{j-1} = \sum_{k=1}^{\chi_f(j-1)} \frac{\mathcal{T}_k}{\sigma_f(j)}$$

where k is in set of iterations assigned to processor f. The iterations done by processor i in time t, denoted by $\aleph \leq \chi_i(j-1)$, is now given by the expression

$$\sum_{k'=1}^{\aleph} \frac{\mathcal{T}_{k'}}{\sigma_i(j)} \geq t$$

Substituting the value of t from above and moving $\sigma_i(j)$ to the other side, we get

$$\sum_{k'=1}^{\aleph} \mathcal{T}_{k'} \geq \left(\frac{\sigma_i(j)}{\sigma_f(j)}\right) \sum_{k=1}^{\chi_f(j-1)} \mathcal{T}_k$$

The iterations left to be done on processor i are then given as

$$\gamma_i(j) = \chi_i(j-1) - \aleph \tag{24.3.2}$$

New Distribution The total amount of work left among all the processors is given as $\Gamma(j) = \sum \gamma_i(j)$. We now distribute this work proportional to the average effective speed of the processors, i.e.,

$$\chi_i(j) = \left(\frac{\sigma_i(j)}{\sum_{k=1}^{P} \sigma_k(j)}\right) \cdot \Gamma(j) \tag{24.3.3}$$

Recall that initially we start out with equal work distribution among all the processors, therefore, we have

$$\lambda_i(0) = 1, \;\; \chi_i(0) = \mathcal{I}(N_{ad})/P, \text{ and } \gamma_i(0) = \chi_i(0), \;\; \forall i \in 1, \cdots, P$$

Note that $\lambda_i(0)$ could be proportional to initial processor speed for heterogeneous processors or to the initial processor loads, if known beforehand. These equations, together with equations (24.3.1), (24.3.2), and (24.3.3), give us recurrence functions which can be solved to obtain the total iterations left to be done, and the new distribution at each synchronization point. The termination condition occurs when there is no more work left to be done, i.e.,

$$\Gamma(\eta) = 0 \tag{24.3.4}$$

where η is the number of synchronization points required.

Amount of Work Moved The amount of basic units of work (usually iterations) moved during a synchronization is given as

$$\alpha(j) = \frac{1}{2}\left(\sum_{i=1}^{P} |\gamma_i(j) - \chi_i(j)|\right)$$

Data Movement Cost The movement of iterations entails movement of data arrays. The number of messages required to move the work and data arrays, denoted by $\beta(j)$, can be calculated from the old and new distribution values. The total cost of data movement is now given by the expression

$$\kappa(j) = \beta(j) \cdot \mathcal{L} + \alpha(j) \cdot \sum_{a} [\mathcal{D}_a/\mathcal{B}] \tag{24.3.5}$$

where a belongs to the set of arrays that need to be redistributed.

Cost of Sending Instructions

This cost is incurred only by the centralized schemes, since the load balancer has to send the work and data movement instructions to the processors. The number of instructions is the same as $\beta(j)$, which is the number of messages required to move data, since instructions are sent only to the processors which have to send data. The cost of sending instructions is, therefore, $\psi(j) = \beta(j)\mathcal{L}$ for the centralized schemes, and $\psi(j) = 0$ for the distributed schemes.

Total Cost

Global Strategies The above set of recurrence relations can be solved to obtain the cost of data movement (see equation 24.3.5), and to calculate the number of synchronization points (see equation 24.3.4), thereby getting the total cost of the global strategies as

$$\mathcal{TC} = \eta(\xi + \delta) + \sum_{j=1}^{\eta} [\kappa(j) + \psi(j)]$$

where ξ is the synchronization cost, η is the number of synchronizations, δ is the redistribution calculation cost, $\kappa(j)$ is the data movement cost, and $\psi(j)$ the cost of sending instructions for the j-th synchronization.

Local Strategies In the local centralized (LCDLB) strategy, even though the load balancer is asynchronous, the assumption that groups can be treated independently from the others may not be true. This is because the central load balancer goes to another group only once it has finished calculating the redistribution and sending instructions for the current group.

Delay Factor This effect is modeled as a delay factor for each group, which depends on the time for the synchronization of the different groups, and is given as

$$\Delta_g(j) = \sum_{k=1}^{\nu(j)} [\delta + \psi_k(j)]$$

where $\nu(j)$ is the number of groups already waiting in the queue for the central load balancer. Note that in the local distributed scheme, the absence of a central load balancer eliminates this effect (i.e.,$\Delta_g(j) = 0$). There may still be some effect due to overlapped synchronization communication, but we do not model this.

For the local schemes, the analyses in the previous subsections still hold, but we have a different cost per group for each of the different categories. The total cost per group is given as

$$\mathcal{C}_g = \eta_g(\xi + \delta) + \sum_{j=1}^{\eta_g} [\kappa_g(j) + \psi_g(j) + \Delta_g(j)]$$

The total cost of the local strategy is simply the time taken by the last group to finish its computation

$$\mathcal{C} = \mathrm{MAX}_{g=1}^{\lceil P/K \rceil} \{\mathcal{C}_g\}$$

24.3.3 Decision Process – Using the Model

Since all the information used by the modeling process, such as the number of processors, processor speeds, data size, number of iterations, iteration cost, etc., and particularly the load function, may not be known at compile time, we propose a hybrid compile and runtime modeling and decision process. The compiler collects all necessary information, and may also help to generate symbolic cost functions for the iteration cost and communication cost. The actual decision making for committing to a scheme is deferred until runtime when we have complete information about the system.

Initially at runtime, no strategy is chosen for the application. Work is partitioned equally among all the processors, and the program is run until the first synchronization point. During this time, a significant amount of work has been accomplished, namely, at least $1/P$ of the work has been done. This can be seen by using equation 24.3.1 above, and plugging $j = 1$, i.e., at the first synchronization point we have

$$\chi_f(0) = \mathcal{I}(N_{ad})/P$$

Summing over all processors, we obtain the total iterations done at the first synchronization point as

$$\sum_{i=1}^{P}\left(\frac{\mathcal{I}(N_{ad})}{P}\cdot\frac{\sigma_i(1)}{\sigma_f(1)}\right) > \frac{\mathcal{I}(N_{ad})}{P}$$

At this time, we also know the load function seen on all the processors so far, and the average effective speed of the processors. This load function, combined with all the other parameters, can be plugged into the model to obtain quantitative information on the behavior of the different schemes. This information is then used to commit to the best strategy after this stage. This also suggests a more adaptive method for selecting the scheme, where we refine our decision as more information on the load is obtained at later points. We plan to study the adaptive load balancing strategy selection approach as part of future work.

24.4 Compiler and Runtime Systems

In this section, we describe how our compiler automatically transforms annotated sequential code into code that can execute in parallel, and that calls routines from the runtime system, using the dynamic load balancing library where appropriate.

24.4.1 Runtime System

The runtime system consists of a uniform interface to the DLB library for all the strategies, the actual decision process for choosing among the schemes using the above model, and it consists of data movement routines to handle redistribution. Load balancing is achieved by placing appropriate calls to the DLB library to exchange information and redistribute work. The compiler, however, generates code to handle this at runtime. The compiler can also help to generate symbolic cost functions for the iteration and communication cost.

24.4.2 Code Generation

For the source-to-source code translation from a sequential program to a parallel program using PVM (from Oak Ridge National Labs.) for message passing, with DLB library calls, we use the SUIF compiler from Stanford University. The input to the compiler consists of the sequential version of the code, with annotations to indicate the data decomposition for the shared arrays, and to indicate the loops which have to be load balanced.

The compiler generates code for setting up the master processor (pseudo-master in the distributed schemes, which is responsible only for the first synchronization, initial scattering, and final gathering of arrays). This involves broadcasting initial configuration information parameters such as the number of processors, the size of arrays and task IDs, calls to the DLB library for the initial partitioning of shared

SEQUENTIAL CODE

```
for i = 1, n
    for j = 1, m
        for k = 1, r
            Z[i][j] += X[i][k] * Y[k][j]
```

TRANSFORMED CODE

```
DLB_init(DLB, P, K, DLB_arrayZ, DLB_arrayX, DLB_arrayY)
DLB_scatter_data(DLB)
if (master) DLB_master_sync(DLB)
else while (DLB.more_work)
        for (i = DLB.start; i < DLB.end && DLB.more_work; i++)
            for j = 1, m
                for k = 1, r
                    Z[i][j] += X[i][k] * Y[k][j]
            if (DLB_slave_sync(DLB) && DLB.interrupt)
                DLB_profile_send_move_work(DLB)
        if (DLB.more_work)
            DLB_send_interrupt(DLB);
            DLB_profile_send_move_work(DLB)
DLB_gather_data(DLB);
```

Figure 24.4 Code generation.

arrays, final collection of results and DLB statistics (such as number of redistributions, number of synchronizations, amount of work moved, etc.), and a call to the *DLB_master_sync()* routine which handles the first synchronization, along with the modeling and strategy selection. It also handles subsequent synchronizations for the centralized schemes. The arrays are initially partitioned equally based on the data distribution specification (BLOCK, CYCLIC, or WHOLE). We currently support *do-all* loops only, with data distribution along one dimension (row or column).

The compiler must also generate code for the slave processors, which perform the actual computation. This step includes changing the loop bounds to iterate over the local assignment, and inserting calls to the DLB library checking for interrupts, for sending profile information to the load balancer (protocol dependent), for data redistribution, and, if local work stack has run out, for issuing an interrupt to synchronize. The sequential matrix multiplication code and the code generated by the compiler with appropriate calls to the DLB library, are highlighted in Figure 24.4. In the figure *dlb.more_work* is a flag which indicates whether this processor is active. It becomes false when there are no more iterations assigned to the processor. This may happen if there is no more work left, or if the processor is extremely slow, and all the work migrates to the other processors. For each shared array we also have an *DLB_array* structure, which holds information about the arrays, such as the number of dimensions, array size, element type, and distribution type. This structure is also filled by the compiler, and is used by the runtime library to scatter, gather, and redistribute data.

24.5 Experimental Results

In this section, we first present experimental evidence showing that different strategies are better for different applications under varying parameters. We then present our modeling results for the applications.

MXM(Matrix Multiplication)

```
for i = 1, n /*parallel*/
    for j = 1, m
        for k = 1, r
            Z[i][j] += X[i][k] * Y[k][j]
```

AC (Adjoint Convolution)

```
for i = 1, n 2 /*parallel*/
    for j = i, n 2
        A[i] += X * B[j] * C[j-1]
```

TRFD

```
for i = 1, n(n+1)/2 /*parallel, L1 */
    for j = 1, n /*uniform*/
        for k = 1, j
            A[j(j+1)/2 + k][i] = B[k]

for i = 1, n(n+1)/2 /*parallel, L1 */
    for j = i, n /*triangular*/
        for k = 1, j
            A[j(j+1)/2 + k][i] = B[k]
```

Figure 24.5 Main computation loop(s): MXM, TRFD, and AC.

All the experiments were performed on a network of homogeneous SUN (Sparc LX) workstations, interconnected via an Ethernet LAN (however, our model can easily handle processor heterogeneity). Applications used C as the source code language, and were run on dedicated machines, i.e., there were no other users on the machines. External load was simulated within our programs as described in section 24.3. PVM (from Oak Ridge National Labs.) was used to parallelize the applications. PVM (Parallel Virtual Machine), is a message passing software system mainly intended for network-based distributed computing on heterogeneous serial and parallel computers. PVM supports heterogeneity at the application, machine and network level, and supports coarse grain parallelism in the application. The applications we consider are given below (pseudocode is shown in Figure 24.5):

- **Matrix Multiply (MXM)**: Multiplication of a $n * m$ with a $m * r$ matrix.
- **TRFD**: It is part of the Perfect Benchmark suite (from University of Illinois, Urbana-Champaign). It simulates the computational aspects of two-electron integral transformations. We used a modified version of TRFD, in the C programming language, which was enhanced to exploit the parallelism.
- **Adjoint Convolution (AC)**: Convolution of two n^2 length vectors.

The overhead of the DLB schemes is almost negligible, since they are receiver-initiated, and in the absence of external load, all processors will finish work at roughly the same time, requiring only one synchronization.

24.5.1 Network Characterization

The network characterization is done off-line. We measure the latency and bandwidth for the network, and we obtain models for the different types of communica-

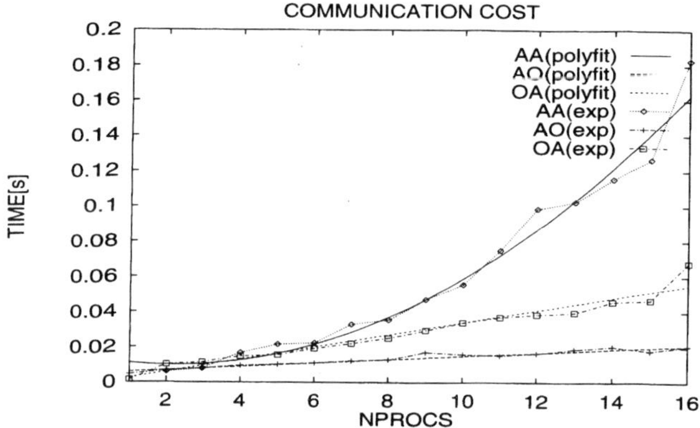

Figure 24.6 Communication cost.

tion patterns. The latency obtained with PVM is 2414.5 μs, and bandwidth is 0.96 Mbytes/s. Figure 24.6 shows the experimental values (exp), and the cost function obtained from the experimental values by simple polynomial fitting (polyfit), for the all-to-all (AA), all-to-one (AO), and one-to-all (OA) communication patterns.

24.5.2 MXM: Matrix Multiplication

Matrix multiplication has only one computation loop nest, as shown in Figure 24.5. We have $Z = X \cdot Y$, where X is a $n \times r$ matrix, Y is a $r \times m$ matrix, and Z is a $n \times m$ matrix. We parallelize the outermost loop i, by distributing the rows of Z and X, and replicating Y on the processors. Only the rows of array X need to be communicated when we redistribute work. The data communication is, therefore, given as $\mathcal{C} = N_{X2} = r$. The work per iteration is uniform, and is given as $O(n * m)$, i.e., it is quadratic. We ran the matrix multiplication program over 4 and 16 processors. The local strategies used two groups, i.e., with 2 neighbors on 4 processors, and 8 neighbors on 16 processors. Two sets of experiments were run with $m = 400$ and different values of n and r. In the first set, we used 100 rows per processor, with $n = 400$ on 4 processors, and $n = 1600$ on 16 processors. In the second set, we used 200 rows per processor, with $n = 800$ on 4 processors, and $n = 3200$ on 16 processors.

Experimental Results

Figure 24.7 shows the experimental results for MXM for different data sizes on 4 and 16 processors, respectively. In the figure, the legend "(no DLB)" stands for a run of the program in the presence of external discrete random load, but with no attempt to balance the work, i.e., we partition the iterations in equal blocks among all the processors, and let the program run to completion. The other bars correspond to running the program under each of the dynamic load balancing schemes, with time normalized against the case with no dynamic load balancing. Table 24.1 shows the total execution time for the run without load balancing.

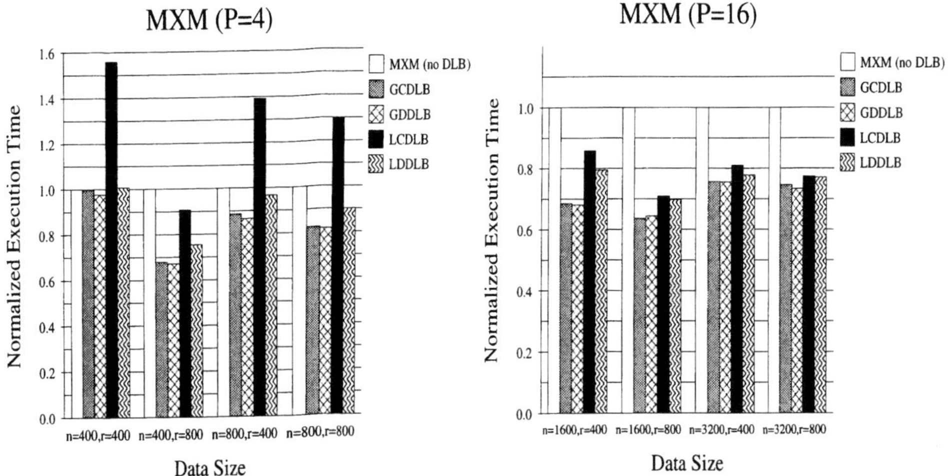

Figure 24.7 Matrix multiplication (P=4, 16).

Table 24.1 MXM: Total Execution Time Without DLB

#Processors	Data Size	Time (s)
4	n=400, r=400, m=400	143.7
4	n=400, r=800, m=400	428.6
4	n=800, r=400, m=400	351.0
4	n=800, r=800, m=400	722.3
16	n=1600, r=400, m=400	266.1
16	n=1600, r=800, m=400	535.9
16	n=3200, r=400, m=400	532.1
16	n=3200, r=800, m=400	1057.3

We observe that the global distributed (GDDLB) strategy is the best, which is followed closely by the global centralized (GCDLB) scheme. Among the local strategies, local distributed (LDDLB) does better than local centralized (LCDLB). Moreover, the global schemes are better than the local schemes. We also notice that on 16 processors the gap between the globals and locals becomes smaller. From our earlier discussion in Section 24.2.2, local strategies incur less communication overhead than global strategies.

However, the redistribution is not optimal. From the results, it can be observed that if the computation cost (work per iteration) versus the communication cost (synchronization cost, redistribution cost) ratio is large, global strategies are favored. This tilts towards the local strategies as this ratio decreases. The factors that influence this ratio are the work per iteration, number of iterations, and the number of processors. More processors increase the synchronization cost and should favor the local schemes. However, in the above experiment there is sufficient work to outweigh this trend, and globals are still better for 16 processors. Comparing across distributed and central schemes, the centralized master, and sequential redistribution and instruction send, add sufficient overhead to the centralized schemes to make the distributed schemes better. LCDLB incurs additional overhead due to the delay factor (see Section 24.3.2), and also due to the context switching between the load balancer and the computation slave (since the processor housing the load balancer also takes part in computation).

24.5.3 TRFD

TRFD has two main computation loops, shown in Figure 24.5, with an intervening transpose. The two loops are load balanced independently, while the transpose is sequentialized, i.e., after the first loop nest, all the processors send their portion of data to the master, who then performs the transpose. This is followed by the second loop nest. We parallelized the outermost loop of both the loop nests. There is only one major array used in both the loops. Its size is given as $[n(n+1)/2]\cdot[n(n+1)/2]$, where n is an input parameter. The loop iterations operate on different columns of the array, which is distributed in a column block fashion among all the processors. The data communication, $\mathcal{D}$, is simply the row size. The first loop nest is uniform with $n(n+1)/2$ iterations and work per iteration given as $O(n^3+3n^2+n)$, which is linear in the array size ($\frac{n^3+3n^2+n}{(n^2+n)/2} \approx 2n+4$). The second loop nest has triangular work per iteration, given as $O(n^3+(3-r/2)n^2+(2-r-r^2/2)n+(r-r^2)/2)$, where $r=(1+sqrt(-7+8*i))/2$, and i is the outermost loop index. We transform this triangular loop into a uniform loop using the *bitonic scheduling* technique [4].

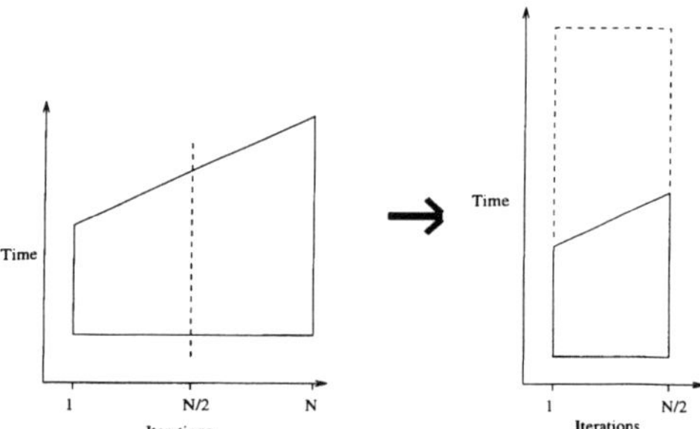

Figure 24.8 Transforming a heterogeneous loop into a homogeneous loop.

Bitonic Scheduling In a triangular loop, the work in iteration i is given as $x_i = ai+b$, for $i=1,\ldots,n$, where a and b are some constants. Let's assume the n is even (see [4] for the more general case). We can transform this triangular loop with n iterations into a uniform loop with $n/2$ iterations. Note that the sum of the work in iterations i and $(n - i + 1)$ is a constant:

$$x_i + x_{n-i+1} = ai + b + a(n - i + 1) + b = a(n + 1) + 2b$$

We can therefore combine iterations i and $(n - i + 1)$ into one iteration of a new parallel loop. This new loop is homogeneous with $a(n + 1) + 2b$ operations in every iteration. Figure 24.8 illustrates this transformation.

For TRFD, we combine iterations i and $n(n + 1)/2 - i + 1$ into one iteration, to get loops with uniform iterations. The number of iterations for loop 2 is now given as $n(n + 1)/4$. The work is also linear in the array size. We experimented with input parameter value of 30, 40, and 50, which correspond to the array size of 465, 820, 1275, respectively, and we used 4 and 16 processors, with the local strategies using 2 groups (2 and 8 processors per group, respectively).

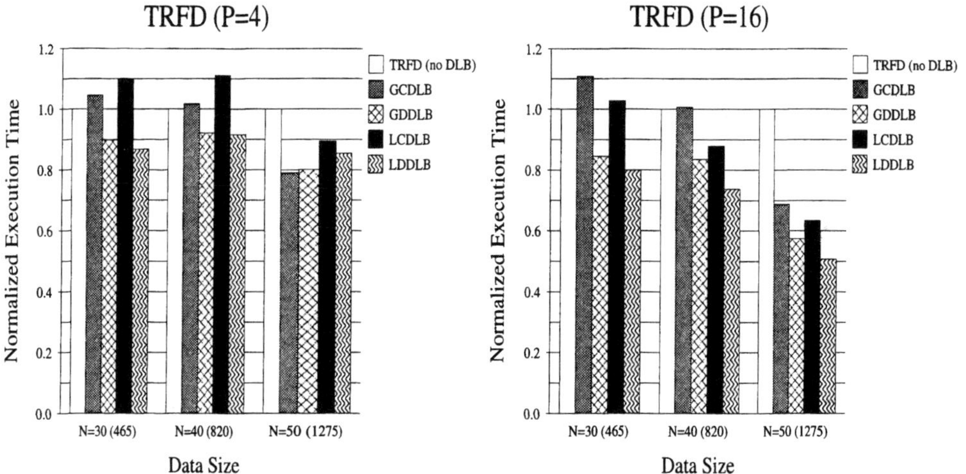

Figure 24.9 TRFD (P=4, 16)

Table 24.2 TRFD: Total Execution Time Without DLB

#Processors	Data Size	Time (s)	#Processors	Data Size	Time (s)
4	n=30(465)	31.4	16	n=30(465)	23.0
4	n=40(820)	111.6	16	n=40(820)	70.0
4	n=50(1275)	417.4	16	n=50(1275)	246.9

Experimental Results

Figure 24.9 shows the results for TRFD with different data sizes for 4 and 16 processors, respectively. Table 24.2 shows the total execution time of a run of TRFD without load balancing.

We observe that on four processors, as the data size increases we tend to shift from local distributed (LDDLB) to global distributed (GDDLB). Since the amount of work per iteration is small, the computation vs. communication ratio is small, thus favoring the local distributed scheme on small data sizes. With increasing data size, this ratio increases, and GDDLB does better. Among the centralized schemes, the global (GCDLB) is better then the local (LCDLB). On 16 processors, however, we find that the local distributed (LDDLB) strategy is the best, which is followed by the global distributed (GDDLB) scheme. Among the centralized strategies also, the local (LCDLB) does better than the global (GCDLB), since the computation vs. communication ratio is small. Furthermore, the distributed schemes are better than the centralized ones.

The results shown above are for total execution time of TRFD. It is also instructive to consider the loops individually, as shown in Table 24.4 under the *Actual* column. Loop 2 (L2) has almost double the work per iteration than in loop 1 (L1). We see that for L1 on 4 processors, LDDLB is the best. For L2, however, since the work per iteration is more, GDDLB tends to do better with increasing data size. On 16 processors, LDDLB remains the best throughout for both L1 and L2.

24.5.4 AC: Adjoint Convolution

Adjoint Convolution has only one computation loop nest, shown in Figure 24.5. We parallelize the outermost loop. All the arrays are replicated, and there is no communication of data when we redistribute work. Therefore, $\mathcal{D} = 0$. The loop nest has triangular work per iteration, given as $O(n^2 - i)$. Using the *bitonic scheduling* technique described above, we transform this into a uniform loop by combining iteration i and $n^2 - i + 1$ into one iteration. The resulting work per iteration is given as $O(n^2 - i + n^2 - (n^2 - i + 1)) = O(n^2 - 1)$. We experimented with input values of $n = 100, 150, 200, 250$, on 4 and 16 processors (2 groups were used for the local strategies).

Table 24.3 AC: Total Execution Time Without DLB

#Processors	Data Size	Time (s)	#Processors	Data Size	Time (s)
4	n=100	58.1	16	n=100	16.0
4	n=150	290.3	16	n=150	82.8
4	n=200	879.8	16	n=200	224.2
4	n=250	2163.4	16	n=250	549.7

Experimental Results

Figure 24.10 shows the results for AC with different data sizes for 4 and 16 processors, respectively. Table 24.3 shows the total execution time for a run of the AC program in the presence of external load, but without dynamic load balancing. An mentioned above, this application has no communication due to movement of data arrays when we redistribute work. However, communication is still required

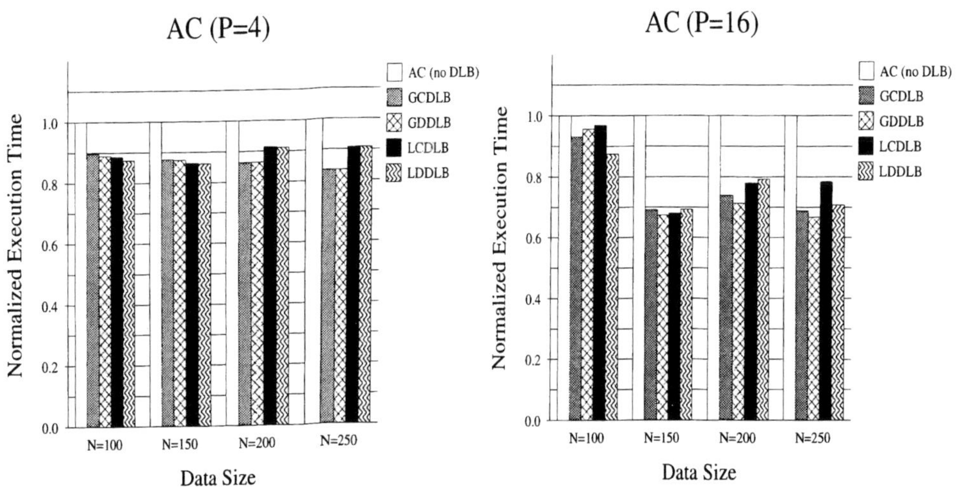

Figure 24.10 Adjoint convolution (P=4, 16).

for profile and instruction exchanges.

On four processors, at small data sizes, the local strategies are better than the globals. This trend reverses as we increase the data size. Similar results were obtained for 16 processors. Moreover, the distributed schemes have a slight edge over the centralized ones.

24.5.5 Modeling Results: MXM, TRFD, and AC

Table 24.4 shows the actual order and the predicted order of performance of the different strategies under varying parameters for the MXM, TRFD and AC programs. We observe that the actual experimental best and the predicted best strategy match in most of the cases. For the cases where our prediction differs from the actual run, the predicted scheme is usually the second best in the actual experiments. For these cases the table shows the difference in the actual execution between the actual and predicted best schemes in terms of the time and as a percentage. For example, consider the row for TRFD, with $P = 4$ and data size $n = 40(820), L2$. The actual best scheme was GDDLB, and the predicted best was LDDLB. Looking at the actual runs, we found that the total execution time of GDDLB and LDDLB was 24.2s and 25.7s, respectively. The difference between these two schemes is thus 1.5s, or about 6.2%. Similarly, we can observe that whenever there is a mismatch between the actual and predicted best schemes, the actual differences in execution time is very small, with an average difference of 2.7% and a maximum of 8.2%. Another factor to keep in mind is that the table presents the actual best scheme averaged over several runs. Since the differences are really small, in practice, one or the other scheme may do better from one run to another, which makes the prediction task extremely difficult. Moreover, the modeling discrepancy usually occurs at the crossover points along the two axes under consideration, i.e., when a best scheme starts to shift from a local to a global strategy (and vice versa), or from a centralized to a distributed strategy (and vice versa). This can be seen, for example, for L2 of TRFD with $P = 4$. As the data size increases, the actual best scheme starts to shift from a LDDLB to a GDDLB. It is well nigh impossible to predict the best scheme with such fine-grained accuracy. As the table shows, even for these difficult points, while our modeling doesn't predict the best scheme, the scheme it predicts is only slightly worse than the actual best.

Table 24.4 MXM & TRFD: Actual vs. Predicted Best DLB Scheme

Program	Parameters		Actual	Predicted	Difference	
	P	Data Size	Best	Best	Time(s)	% Diff
	4	n=400, r=400	GDDLB	GDDLB		
	4	n=400, r=800	GDDLB	GDDLB		
	4	n=800, r=400	GDDLB	GDDLB		
MXM	4	n=800, r=800	GDDLB	GDDLB		
	16	n=1600, r=400	GDDLB	GCDLB	1.2s	0.7%
	16	n=1600, r=800	GCDLB	GDDLB	3.7s	1.1%
	16	n=3200, r=400	GDDLB	GDDLB		
	16	n=3200, r=800	GDDLB	GDDLB		
	4	n=30(465), L1	LDDLB	GDDLB	0.9s	8.2%
	4	n=40(820), L1	LDDLB	LDDLB		
	4	n=50(1275), L1	LDDLB	LDDLB		
	4	n=30(465), L2	LDDLB	GDDLB	0.2s	3.5%
	4	n=40(820), L2	GDDLB	LDDLB	1.5s	6.2%
TRFD	4	n=50(1275), L2	GDDLB	GDDLB		
	16	n=30(465), L1	LDDLB	LDDLB		
	16	n=40(820), L1	LDDLB	LDDLB		
	16	n=50(1275), L1	LDDLB	LDDLB		
	16	n=30(465), L2	LDDLB	LDDLB		
	16	n=40(820), L2	LDDLB	LDDLB		
	16	n=50(1275), L2	LDDLB	LDDLB		
	4	n=100	LDDLB	LDDLB		
	4	n=150	LDDLB	GDDLB	3.6s	1.43%
	4	n=200	GCDLB	GDDLB	0.8s	0.1%
AC	4	n=250	GCDLB	GDDLB	0.5s	0.03%
	16	n=100	LDDLB	LDDLB		
	16	n=150	GDDLB	LDDLB	1.6s	2.9%
	16	n=200	GDDLB	GDDLB		
	16	n=250	GDDLB	GDDLB		

24.6 Summary

In this chapter, we analyzed both *global* and *local*, and *centralized* and *distributed*, interrupt-based receiver-initiated dynamic load balancing strategies, on a network of workstations with transient external load per processor. We showed that different strategies are best for different applications under varying parameters such as the number of processors, data size, iteration cost, communication cost, etc. We then presented a modeling process to evaluate the behavior of these schemes. We showed that our model is reasonably accurate in its predictions and can guide the decision process effectively.

Presenting a hybrid compile and runtime process, we showed that it is possible to customize the dynamic load balancing scheme for a program under differing parameters. Given the host of dynamic scheduling strategies proposed in the literature, such analysis would be useful to a parallelizing compiler. To take the complexity away from the programmer, we also automatically transform an annotated sequential program to a parallel program with the appropriate calls to the runtime dynamic load balancing library.

24.7 Bibliography

[1] J. Arabe et al. Dome: Parallel Programming in a Heterogeneous Multi-User Environment. *Tech. Report 95-137*, Carnegie Mellon University, April 1995.

[2] R. Blumofe and D. Park. Scheduling Large-Scale Parallel Computations on Network of Workstations. *3rd IEEE International Symposium on High Performance Distributed Computing*, August 1994.

[3] F. Berman et al. Application-Level Scheduling on Distributed Heterogeneous Networks. *Supercomputing*, November 1996.

[4] M. Cierniak, M. J. Zaki, and W. Li. Compile-time Scheduling Algorithms for a Heterogeneous NOW. *The Computer Journal*, vol. 40(6), pages 356–372, December 1997.

[5] W. Li and K. Pingali. Access normalization: Loop Restructuring for NUMA Compilers. *ACM Transactions on Computer Systems*, vol. 11(4), pages 353–375, November 1993.

[6] F. Lin and R. Keller. Gradient Model Load Balancing Method. *IEEE Transactions on Software Engineering*, vol. 13, pages 32–38, January 1987.

[7] E.P. Markatos and T.J. LeBlanc. Using Processor Affinity in Loop Scheduling on Shared-Memory Multiprocessors. *IEEE Transactions on Parallel and Distributed Systems*, vol. 5(4), April 1994.

[8] N. Nedeljkovic and M. Quinn. Data-Parallel Programming on a Heterogeneous NOW. *1st IEEE International Symposium on High Performance Distributed Computing*, September 1992.

[9] H. Nishikawa and P. Steenkiste. General Architecture for Load Balancing in Distributed-Memory Environment. *13th IEEE International Conference on Distributed Computing*, May 1993.

[10] C. Polychronopoulos and D. Kuck. Guided Self-Scheduling: Practical Scheduling Scheme for Supercomputers. *IEEE Transactions on Computers*, vol. 36(12), December 1987.

[11] V. A. Saletore, J. Jacob, and M. Padala. Parallel Computing on CHARM Heterogeneous COW. *3rd IEEE International Symposium on High Performance Distributed Computing*, August 1994.

[12] B.S. Siegell. Automatic Generation of Parallel Programs with Dynamic Load Balancing for a NOW. *Ph.D. Thesis*, Carnegie Mellon University, May 1995.

[13] P. Tang and P.-C. Yew. Processor Self-Scheduling for Multiple Nested Parallel Loops. *International Conference on Parallel Processing*, August 1986.

[14] M. J. Zaki, W. Li, and S. Parthasarathy. Customized Dynamic Load Balancing for a NOW. *Journal of Parallel and Distributed Computing*, vol. 43(2), pages 156–162, June 1997.

Chapter 25

Mapping and Scheduling on Heterogeneous Systems

WEILAI YANG AND PIYUSH MAHESHWARI

[†]School of Computer Science and Engineering
University of New South Wales, Sydney NSW 2052, Australia

Email: *weilaiy, piyush@cse.unsw.edu.au*

25.1 Introduction

With the development of efficient network technology, now it is popular to use a set of computers to deal with distributed applications. As the performance of stand-alone computers is beginning to saturate, using multi-computers is a practical and cost-effective choice. The emergence of parallel computers opens up new frontiers in the application of high performance computing. Homogeneous computing uses one or more machines of the same type to provide high performance for many applications [4]. A homogeneous system can meet the requirements of only one type of embedded parallelism. However, a given application may have various types of parallelism. This may lead to little parallelism in applications, which cannot offer desired speedups. So the quest for higher computational power suitable for a wide range of applications at a reasonable cost continues. Heterogeneous Computing (HC) is a cost-effective approach that makes up for the disadvantages of homogenous computing. Khokhar et al. [4] define heterogeneous computing as "the well-orchestrated and coordinated effective use of a suite of diverse high performance machines to provide superspeed processing for computationally demanding tasks with diverse computing needs." An HC system includes heterogeneous machines, high-speed networks, interfaces, operating systems, communication protocols and programming environments, all combining to produce a positive impact on ease of use and performance. A simple heterogeneous computing environment could be a departmental network with 5 Solaris machines, 10 SUN workstations, and 2 or 3 VAX machines. In distributed heterogeneous computing, dissimilar computing machines are spread around a network geographically. An integrated heterogeneous computing system consists of dissimilar machines used in one system, linked by a bus or back plane, which gives the user great flexibility in matching the capabilities of the system to the particular needs of a special application.

Parallel programs for such heterogeneous computers are partitioned into concurrently executable communication tasks (or processes). Before tasks are executed on processors, each task must be assigned to a specific processor. One of the obvious problems is how to allocate tasks to processors in a way that minimizes the overall execution time of the parallel program. The assignment of tasks to processors is called a mapping. In a homogeneous environment, a mapping problem is a simple task assignment problem. Only the execution time and communication time between tasks should be considered. However, for heterogeneous systems, other costs such as code type matching, interference costs, etc, need to be considered. From another perspective, we can say mapping in heterogeneous systems includes that in homogeneous ones since all the machines can be divided into different homogeneous pools according to their performances. So, mapping in a heterogeneous environment is definitely much more complicated. After mapping is done, the process of determining the best time for tasks execution (that is, the scheduling strategy) should be employed. Scheduling problem is one of the most challenging problems in parallel computing and known to be NP-complete in its general form. An optimal schedule determines both the allocation and the execution order of each task such that the tasks should complete in the shortest time. Similar to the mapping problem, scheduling in heterogeneous systems can be divided into two levels: one is at the system (macro) level, while the other is at the micro level of homogeneous machines. Obviously, much more research is needed to study mapping and scheduling in heterogeneous computing environments.

In this chapter, we discuss different views, ideas and approaches presented by researchers in the area of mapping and scheduling. The rest of the chapter is organized as follows. Section 25.2 elaborates on the mapping and scheduling problems and gives several examples. In Section 25.3, we focus on the factors on which efficient scheduling depends – the effective partitioning of the program into modules or partitions. Section 25.4 discusses static and dynamic scheduling approaches in detail. We also present some survey work in this section. In Section 25.5, we emphasize some load balancing issues in HC. Finally, we present the summary of the chapter.

25.2 Mapping and Scheduling

In this section, we introduce some typical mapping and scheduling problems with-examples. General comparisons of some techniques are also presented.

25.2.1 The Mapping Problem

Developing efficient software which can extract performance from parallel computers is more difficult than for traditional uniprocessor sequential computers because of the unique problem of organizing computation among multiple processors. Executing a parallel program on a parallel computer requires allocation of the tasks to different processors in the computer. A critical problem is how to allocate tasks to processors in the way that minimizes the overall execution time of the parallel program. An assignment of tasks to processors is called a mapping and the problem of finding a mapping that minimizes execution time, commonly referred to as the process-to-processor mapping problem, has been widely known as one of the most significant problems in parallel processing.

Process-to-Processor Mapping Problem

The process-to-processor mapping is to assign processes to processors in an effective manner so that each process run on a processor to achieve the minimum execution time for the overall program. If the number of processors is more than the processes, it is easy to assign. But, in general, processes greatly outnumber processors. In such cases, to fully utilize all the processors, tasks should be spread as evenly as possible to achieve maximum parallelism. However, as processes are assigned across the parallel machine, the communication between them goes up accordingly. This forces us to assign tasks having high communication to the same or nearby processors. These two objectives pose conflicting requirements as the quality of mapping is determined by a combination of computation and communication load. Process-to-processor mapping can be theoretically formulated as a graph embedding problem where parallel programs are modeled by weighted graphs whose vertices represent tasks in the programs and whose edges represent communication between tasks.

An example of a task graph and a mesh processor graph are shown in Figure 25.1. Let $G_t(V_t,E_t)$ be a task graph with V_t denoting the set of vertices of the nodes and E_t denoting the set of edges between nodes, and let $G_p(V_p,E_p)$ be a processor graph.

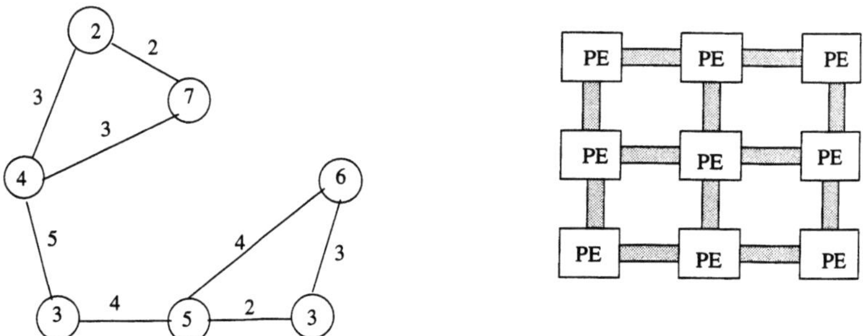

Figure 25.1 Task and processor graph.

When given a task graph and a processor graph, the aim of mapping is to achieve an assignment M: $V_t \rightarrow V_p$. The simplest way to mapping m tasks on n processors presents an unmanageably large space of m^n possible assignments. In the past, most of the algorithms generated are suboptimal since, in general, optimal mapping is NP-hard.

The assumption has been widely adopted by many researchers that the underlying machine architecture must provide some indirect communication mechanism like message routing and multiplexing to enable communication between tasks assigned to indirectly connected processors. This, in general, has been realized by using measures such as the number of communication links in the shortest path between indirectly connected processors to minimize interprocessor communication.

With parallel computers employing circuit-switching or wormhole routing [9], communication time depends heavily on link contention. Previously, communication time depended mostly on the number of communication links between communication processors, but now it depends largely on link contention. So it is important to take such issues into account.

The Contention-Free Mapping Problem

It is obvious that we should have a number of interprocessor connections, while it is not normally available to have direct communication links between every pair of processors. So the applications should be embedded onto processors in a way that the communication requirements are met by the available communication links.

The contention-free problem does not assume that the parallel computer must provide indirect communication. Also, it does not need to estimate the cost of indirect communication as dedicated communication routes are set up between communicating processors. Communication routes are not shared, so all messages can be passed through them in parallel without any hidden communication cost due to multiplexing.

25.2.2 The Scheduling Problem

The scheduling problem is to solve a set of tasks serviced by a set of processors to get the best result according to a certain policy, which can be described in a number of different ways in different fields. According to the objectives which scheduling policy works for, scheduling techniques can be classified as local and global. Local scheduling is used in scheduling concurrent processes to the time slices of a single processor. The operating system normally handles local scheduling. What the most researchers are concerned about is global scheduling, which deals with finding the best possible way to organize a given work load to let the execution time be minimum.

In a broad sense, scheduling problems can be classified in many ways. One of the possible classifications is static and dynamic scheduling. Static scheduling deals with all the information known beforehand such as precedence-constrained task graph and overhead due to data exchange. Typically, the goal of static scheduling methods is to minimize the overall execution time of a concurrent program which cannot meet our needs when the task graph is not known before execution of the application. For example, conditional branch is one of the program constructs that may cause nondeterminism. Only when a program is midway in execution is the direction of it known, which cannot be handled using static policy. At that time, using dynamic scheduling is essential. When the whole information cannot be obtained before the program executes, the parallel system must attempt to schedule tasks on the fly. The disadvantage of dynamic scheduling is its inadequacy in finding global optimums and the corresponding overhead which occurs because the schedule must be determined while the program is running.

All the scheduling problems described above may be either preemptive or non-preemptive. For preemptive scheduling, interruption and subsequent resumption of execution of a load, either in the same processor or elsewhere, is permitted. In nonpreemptive scheduling the currently executing load is allowed to run until completion without any interruption.

Job scheduling or task scheduling can also be used as two categories of scheduling. Job scheduling means the job containing a number of tasks assigned to one processor, while task scheduling indicates different tasks allocated to different processors, used in parallel processing systems.

Scheduling in Distributed Homogeneous and Heterogeneous Systems

In the past, researchers have done a lot of work on scheduling in homogeneous systems. It is an important part of processing an application. In such environments, a scheduler assigns each program module to a processor to achieve the desired performance in terms of processor utilization and throughput. Khokhar et al. [4] present three scheduling levels. High-level scheduling, also called job scheduling, selects a subset of all submitted jobs competing for the available resources. Intermediate-level scheduling responds to short-term fluctuations in the system load by temporarily suspending and activating processes to achieve smooth system operation. Low-level scheduling determines the next ready process to be assigned to a processor for a certain duration. Different scheduling policies, such as FIFO, round robin, shortest-job-first, and shortest-remaining-time, can be employed at each level of scheduling.

As in homogeneous parallel systems, scheduling is also one of the important phases of heterogeneous processing. Improper load balancing caused by differences in processor capability can lead to reduced performance. In heterogeneous computing, apart from the usual scheduling methods, a different level of scheduling is needed at the system level. The scheduler has to maintain a balanced system-wide workload by monitoring the progress of all the tasks in the system communication bottlenecks; queuing delays are more prominent due to the heterogeneity of different hardware architectures, which add different constraints on the scheduling policies. The scheduler also needs to know the different types of tasks and available machine types. Hence the issues related to scheduling become more complicated in heterogeneous computing machines, which definitely require further research.

25.3 The Issues of Task Granularity and Partitioning

As we have known, the efficient execution of parallel programs largely depends on the effective partitioning of the programs into modules and scheduling those modules for execution on a set of processors. There are many factors that affect exploiting parallelism in programs. The main ones include partitioning of programs, balancing of computational load among processors, and overheads created by data communication. Given a parallel program, the partitioning of the program specifies the sequential units of the program, called clusters, that can be executed concurrently by processors so that the total parallel computation time of the program is minimized when inter-processor communication costs are included. In this chapter, the terms *clusters* and *clustering* refer to "group/grouping of task nodes" and should not be confused with their use in other chapters as clusters of PCs/workstations.

25.3.1 Two Strategies of Scheduling in Clustering

Clustering is a mapping of the tasks of a DAG (directed acyclic graph) onto m clusters. We can use two strategies of scheduling in clustering:

- mapping independent tasks in one cluster
- mapping tasks which are in a precedence path of the DAG in one cluster

The former is called *nonlinear clustering*, which reduces the parallelism by serializing independent tasks to avoid high communication. The latter one is named *linear clustering*, which fully exploits the parallelism in the DAG. To maximize parallelism, tasks should be spread as evenly as possible over the processors to balance the computation. From this point of view, linear clustering should be used. However, communicating tasks should be allocated to the same or nearby processors to maintain the locality of data and minimize communication load. Then nonlinear clustering need to be applied. Figure 25.2 gives an example of the two clusterings. If the grain of computation is too large, parallelism is limited; if the grain is too small, communication delays reduce performance. A trade-off analysis is required using a factor called task granularity. The granularity of a task is defined as the ratio between task computation and communication. Suppose R represents execution time and C represents communication delay generated by the task, then R/C is the granularity of the task. When the communication cost becomes high, then the granularity is too fine and parallelization should not be suggested.

It is well-known that finding the optimal ordering is NP-complete, but for linear clustering, the problem of computing the parallel time is tractable in a polynomial time complexity. It is crucial to know when to use linear clustering strategy.

The granularity of a task graph is sensitive to both architecture parameters and program partitioning. It is obvious that nonlinear clustering should be used for fine-grain tasks, and the size of local granularity and its effect on global parallel time should be considered when a heuristic algorithm selects an appropriate strategy. For example, the DSC algorithm is such a clustering algorithm [15].

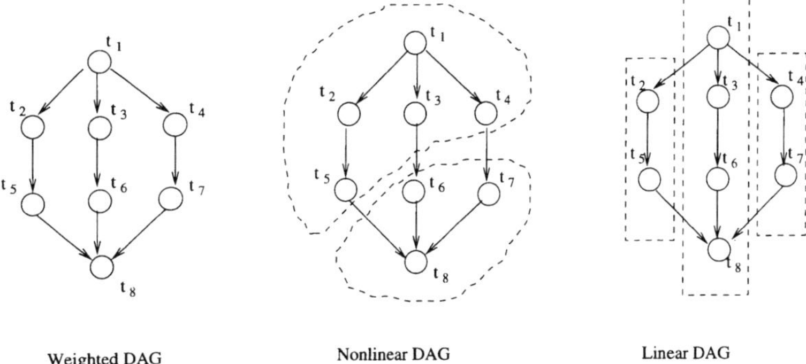

Figure 25.2 Different DAGs.

In addition, for a fixed-size problem, the number of processors is also related to the granularity, since by increasing N, the grain size of subproblems executed on each processor decreases. It has been proposed that for algorithms where the communication overhead can be fully decomposed among N processors, the speedup grows as the number of processors N increases for all values of bandwidth except the worst case value; and for algorithms where the communication overhead cannot be decomposed, the speedup approaches its maximum for a value of N which is determined by the ratio of processing to communication, and then it decreases approaching zero.

So it is essential to balance the amount of parallelism among the program modules and the associated overhead. After clustering tasks, the partitions are then scheduled on the PEs. Therefore, partitioning is a preprocess step to scheduling. Now we introduce some partitioning algorithms.

25.3.2 Some Effective Partitioning Algorithms

Critical Path Partitioning

It should be clear that the fine-grain tasks that rely on a critical path of a program graph must be executed sequentially. Thus, once the nodes on a critical path are identified, they should be clustered into one partition so that they can be assigned to one processor for execution.

An example is shown in Figure 25.3. Each time the critical path of the graph is searched, clustered to one partition and removed from the path. It is iteratively carried out until there are no nodes left.

Eliminating Communication Delay Partitioning

As the name says, the key point of this method is to eliminate the communication overhead, then cluster the task into partitions. The general approach is to cluster the successors of a node, along with the node itself, into a partition, provided that

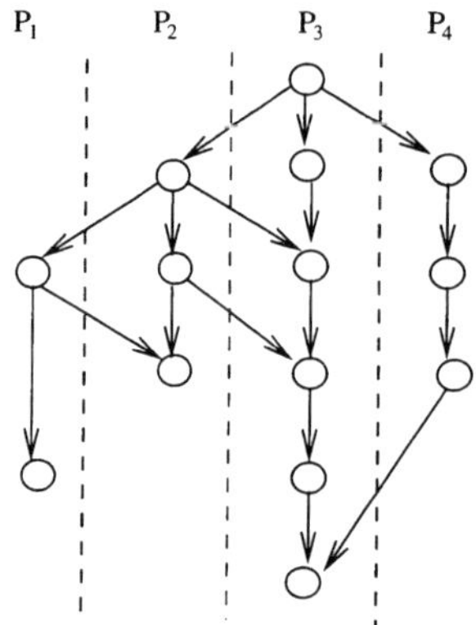

Figure 25.3 One type of partition.

the overall completion time of these nodes is not prolonged. We know that if tasks are put into a cluster, their communication cost will be zero, and the parallelism will be reduced. So these algorithms try to find the balancing of benefits of zeroing the communication and concurrency.

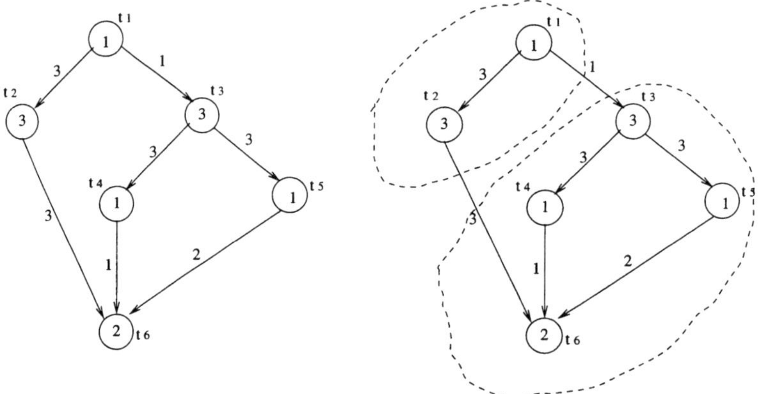

Figure 25.4 A task graph and a good partition.

Figure 25.4 is a DAG. We can start from task 1. First we decide whether or not t_1 should be put in the same cluster as t_2. If t_2 is not put in the same partition as t_1, it will take 7 time units to finish t_1 and t_2. But if we put them together, only 4 time units is needed. By iterating the similar process for t_3 and other remaining tasks, we can get the final partition as shown in the figure.

Task Duplication

Sometimes in order to eliminate the communication cost among tasks, duplicating the tasks among the PEs is the most effective way. It is an alternative method of partitioning process, and it can also preserve the original program parallelism as well as reduce the communication cost. This approach is not practical when the PEs have limited space because to duplicate tasks will occupy a lot of space.

Let's see a simple example. The input and result is shown in Figure 25.5.

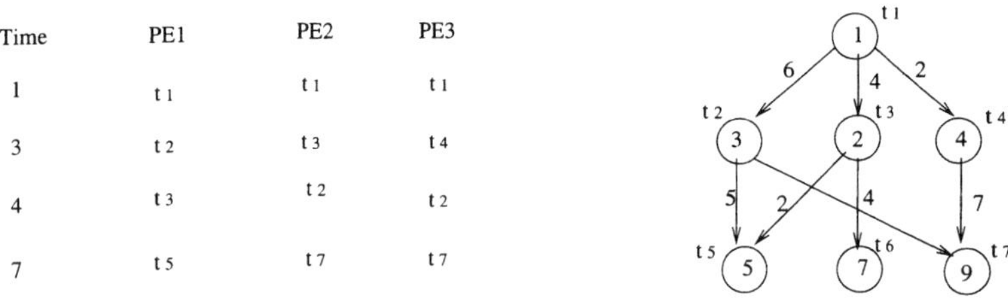

Time	PE1	PE2	PE3
1	t1	t1	t1
3	t2	t3	t4
4	t3	t2	t2
7	t5	t7	t7

Figure 25.5 Input and result of an assignment using task duplication.

It is quite clear that duplicating t_1 on every processor effectively eliminates the communication cost between t_1 and t_2, t_3, t_4.

Other Techniques

The above three methods are the general ways to partition. There are also some other techniques dealing with the partitioning problem. Let us take a glance at them.

Kim and Browne [5] proposed a linear clustering technique which repeatedly applies a critical path algorithm to transform an APG into a set of linear clusters connected by edges showing data dependencies. A linear cluster is a structure in which every node has at most one immediate predecessor and one immediate successor. At each step, the most expensive directed path in computation and communication is grouped into a single linear cluster and the clustered nodes are removed from the graph. This process is iteratively applied to the remaining graph until the entire graph has been partitioned into clusters. The internalization clustering method, suggested by Sarkar [11], divides the APG nodes into clusters by initially placing each node in a separate cluster and considering the APG arcs in a descending order according to the communication costs over the arcs. The algorithm repeatedly tries to merge two clusters to form a larger one. If the larger cluster generated in this merge process does not increase the estimate of the parallel execution of this clustered graph, the merge process will be accepted. This process continues until no more action is required.

25.4 Static Scheduling and Dynamic Scheduling

In a word, static scheduling is done before program executes, while dynamic is based on the redistribution of processors during execution time. Both of them have their own advantages and disadvantages due to the way they are performing. A detailed comparison of some scheduling algorithms is presented in earlier chapters. Here we discuss the different method in homogeneous and heterogeneous systems.

25.4.1 Related Work in Homogeneous Systems

In the past, numerous algorithms about scheduling have been presented in homogeneous systems. The theory and methodology are relatively more mature than the same work in heterogeneous systems. We now introduce some methods of homogeneous environment.

We distinguish between cases where an optimal solution can be achieved and other cases in which the problem becomes computationally infeasible. The most general form of this problem is known to be NP-complete. Optimal solutions are required in many situations where performance is the primary goal, but they exist only for restricted cases or small problem size. There are few known polynomial-time scheduling algorithms even when severe restrictions are placed on the task graph representing the program and the parallel processor model.

A polynomial algorithm can be obtained in the following two cases: (1) when the task graph is a tree and (2) when there are only two processors available. If the task graph is a tree, a linear algorithm introduced by Hu uses a level number equal to the length of the longest path from the node to the ending node as a priority number. Coffman and Graham [2] give an $O(n^2)$ scheduling algorithm similar to Hu's except that the task scheduling priorities are assigned in such a way that nodes at the same level have different priorities. The algorithm gives an optimal length schedule for an arbitrary graph containing unit-time delay tasks on a 2-processor system.

In [12], we see an example of an optimal, enumerative approach to scheduling problems. The criterion function is defined in terms of optimizing the amount of time a task will require for all interprocess communication and execution, where the tasks submitted by users are assumed to be broken into suitable modules before execution. The cost function is a minimax criterion, which means it is intended to minimize the maximum execution and communication time required by any single processor involved in the assignment. The solution also achieves a certain degree of processor load balancing as well.

The above is an optimal algorithm using static scheduling. Now let us see some optimal dynamic algorithms.

Stone [13] proposes another rare example existing in the form of a physically distributed, cooperative, optimal solution in a dynamic environment. The solution is given for the two-processor case in which critical load factors are calculated prior to program execution. The method employed is to use a graph theoretical approach to solving for load factors for each process on each processor. These load factors are then used at runtime to determine when a task could run better if placed on the other processor.

When an optimal solution is computationally infeasible, suboptimal solutions can be reached using approximations by restricting the model representing the parallel program, or the machine, or both. Also, fast heuristics are another way to obtain suboptimal solutions. A heuristic produces an answer in less than exponential time, but does not guarantee an optimal solution. Therefore, the term *near-optimal* means the solutions obtained by a heuristic fall near the optimal solution. Here, we briefly introduce two heuristic methods:

- List scheduling. In list scheduling, each task is assigned a priority, then a list of tasks is constructed in decreasing priority order. Whenever a processor is available, a ready task with the highest priority is selected from the list and assigned to the processor.

- Task duplication. Task duplication heuristics use duplication of tasks to offset communication. The duplication solves the maximum problem by duplicating the tasks that influence the communication delay.

25.4.2 Further Work Relating to Heterogeneous Systems

Heterogeneous computing is the use of different types of processors, processing components, or connectivity paradigms to maximize performance, cost-effectiveness, and development effort. One of the fundamental challenges in HC is to provide a schedule of tasks on a set of hosts that will result in minimum overall execution time. Compounding the problem is the need for data to be moved to different hosts in the HC system as needed by executing tasks. HC scheduling constraints are the sequential and concurrency dependencies between tasks requiring transfer of data between them. A key obstacle to achieving performance improvement is the determination of schedules for the execution of these tasks so that overall completion time is minimized and scheduling constraints between the task to be executed are observed, so it is easy to see that more work need to be done because of the complicated environment. As we have mentioned earlier (in Section 25.1), there are, in general, three levels for scheduling in homogeneous systems plus one more system level in heterogeneous computing [4]. The information on the different module types and available machine types should be collected to this level and then maintain the load balancing.

Optimal Selection Theory (OST) is based on the mathematical programming formulation for selecting the most appropriate suite of heterogeneous machines for a given code type. In OST, it is assumed that the computational task consists of heterogeneous code segments serially, and in each segment there are blocks in which code can be executed in homogeneous environment. Different parts of code segments of an application may require different types of machines, and OST makes the optimal selection for these codes. After this phase, within a special machine group, mapping those codes is, in fact, in homogeneous systems. That means we reduce the complexity from heterogeneity to homogeneity, which is our main concern about the algorithm.

Later, OST was augmented to Augmented Optimal Selection Theory (AOST), Heterogeneous Optimal Selection Theory (HOST) and Genetial Optimal Selection Theory (GOST). GOST builds on network heterogeneity as well as machine heterogeneity, compared with the former ones, which is the trend of development of parallel computing. Using this module, Narahari et al [8] get polynomial time algorithms for optimal matching in the case of series-parallel dependency graphs. Another extension of the AOST is heterogeneous processing greedy mapping. The processor starts the assignment with the heaviest task and proceeds by mapping the top level of the independent subgraphs to the bottom. Actually, for the scheduling problem, there are various methods such as A* algorithm from the area of artificial intelligence, genetic algorithm and neural network.

25.5 Load Balancing Issues

In this section, we give the clear comparison of load balancing in homogeneous and heterogeneous systems. First, definition and general descriptions are discussed and then some typical algorithms that cover different types of load balancing are presented. And finally, we point out the future trends in this area.

25.5.1 Load Balancing in Homogeneous Environment

The quality of mapping and scheduling is decided by both the computation and the communication load of processors. Keeping the load on each processor well-balanced leads to an efficient program execution. Within a load balancing agent, the process should go through three stages: calculation of load, transfer and placement. In the first stage, the load information is collected at a central or distributed processor. Then, according to the calculation, including estimated execution time, communication time and overhead, the decision of whether to transfer or not is made in the second stage. Finally which processor is the destination of transfer is determined. The calculation of load needs load indices. Generally, it is the size of the ready queue of a processor. The size of a queue means the length (the number of tasks) and execution time of each and the communication time with each other. Since all of these are done during runtime, we cannot get the exact estimation of computation time. This is one problem of load balancing issues which need to be studied more. As for the transfer problem, a critical question is whether an executing task should be suspended and migrated to another processor and resume its execution on the target machine. Krueger [6] proposed, in order to avoid thrashing, that the process needs to ensure that an eligible task is larger than a threshold value, has been executed on the source machine for longer than a threshold value, and belongs to the set of processes that have been transferred least often among those residing on the source machine. Some survey work about this is presented later.

Next, we focus on the work which has been done in recent years and show the general trends. Since parallel computing uses several computers running subtasks and exchanging data with each other, the topology of connection network should be seriously considered while designing the scheduling strategy. Based on connection networks, several typical algorithms, such as mesh, hypercube and BUS architecture, are introduced below. Mickle and Paul [7] are concerned with load balancing mapped onto a mesh with an equal distribution of computational load. Under this condition, it is hard to take advantage of wraparound communication links due to computational work instead of communication links. In a mesh, because not all nodes have the same number of links, it may cause communication imbalance. Assume there is one processor with maximum links and that any other ones with less than it is expected to do less communication with a latency. The simple measure proposed by Mickle and Paul is the percentage of unused communication as measured by links unused out of the total possible links. They intend to reduce latency for any processor. In a homogeneous processor array, balance can be achieved by an uneven or unequal load distribution. Then the matrix-based analysis, which is a natural representation, is used for determining communication and execution balance.

As for hypercube structure, in the late of 1980s, Ranka et al. [10] presented a fully load balancing algorithm for the hypercube: Dimension Exchange Method (DEM). It balances the load for independent tasks on distributed memory machines. The principle is very simple: Load balancing is performed iteratively in each of the logN dimensions (N is the number of nodes). In a particular dimension, only node pairs exchange their load information with each other and each one tries to get the average of the number of tasks. Thus after logN steps iteration, the load is balanced. Xu and Lau [14] extend it to a new level, but they still cannot reach the balanced state in one sweep. Besides mesh and hypercube type of static network structures, dynamic networks are also used in homogeneous systems. Dasgupta et al. [3] present a new adaptive algorithm for dynamic load balancing on a shared BUS architecture. Their algorithm (V_Thr) adapts itself to the limited bandwidth of the BUS by dynamically monitoring the *threshold*. Threshold is one of the most important parameters used by most dynamic load balancing schemes. If a task arrives at a processor whose load is greater than or equal to threshold, then it becomes eligible for transfer. In general, threshold is good when it holds low value. Because processors are connected by BUS, the high contention may occur if many tasks transferred and lead to poor performance. Therefore, in view of the limited bandwidth of the BUS, some amount of load imbalance should be tolerated. Under such condition, threshold is chosen not to make the task and message traffic saturating and its own value as small as possible. According to this principle, the strategy of load balancing can be met.

25.5.2 Heterogeneous Computing Environment (HCE)

The processing capacity of a heterogeneous computing system cannot be effectively exploited unless the resources are properly scheduled. In homogeneous systems, a scheduler typically consists of two components: load distributor and local scheduler. The former one corrects anomalies arising in distribution of the load among nodes by process transfer to improve performance. The latter allocates local resources among the resident processes. Load sharing algorithms improve performance by supervising so that no processor lies idle. For heterogeneous computing environment (HCE), we can assume that it consists of pools of machines with each pool being a homogeneous system. There are three steps to scheduling in such a system: task assignment, load balancing and local scheduling. Task assignment is the process of matching tasks to machines that are best suited for their execution. Local scheduling acts within each pool of machines, following some distributed scheduling policy. Local balancing acts at a higher level and tries to reduce the idle time of machines. It should be noted that, in HCE, a machine can be idle if there are no tasks that matches with its architecture. Due to this reason, load sharing algorithms are not applicable in HCE. In the context of heterogeneous computing, the distributed components of the load balancing algorithm should cooperate with each other in decision-making and work towards a common system-wide goal.

Cermele et al. [1] contribute an important step to the load balancing strategies designed to heterogeneous distributed environment referred to SPMD algorithms. The dynamic load balancing model proposed is based on activation mechanism, load monitoring, decision, and reconfiguration (data migration) phases. In a heterogeneous system with different types of machines, each node has a nominal power and a duty cycle, which is the fraction of mode processing capacity consumed by local tasks. So they, firstly, use a passive method in which the load parameter was induced by the time difference through executing a significant portion of code without communications or synchronizations among the processes. Then they adopt two active methods for load monitoring, which can give an immediate estimate about the available capacity for executing scientific-based programs. Two decisions, whether to re-distribute and how to re-distribute, are employed for decisiön policies. Based on a centralized approach, they propose four decision policies, which all have the linear complexity.

The activation and reconfiguration phases are the interface between the load balancing support and the application. Two protocols are used with explicit activation. In the first case (Synchronous activation Synchronous reconfiguration), each time it is necessary to check load, all the execution should stop and restart after the evaluation is sent to the reconfiguration master. For the second policy (Asynchronous activation Synchronous reconfiguration), when the information on individual load is sent to the reconfiguration master, the internal processes continue their operations. At the second checking load call, each node waits for the message about the reconfiguration. The synchronous reconfiguration augments the simplicity and correctness of the reconfiguration strategy and data migration will be easy since all processes are blocked in the same execution point.

Observe again the algorithm we referred to earlier. Mickle [7] proposed an algorithm for heterogeneous processors after introducing a homogeneous one. Assume a 16-processor heterogeneous mesh containing three different types of processors A, B, C, and heterogeneous numbers of tasks assigned to A, B, C as K_A, K_B, K_C. Communications balance requires a balance among $f(K_A)$, $f(K_B)$, $f(K_C)$ (f is some function relating communication to computation load). Mickle and Paul present a model of execution time incorporating communication which takes into account the latency of execution. The zero latency balance can be achieved by heterogeneous processing or with an unequal distribution of the computational load. If the computation load must be evenly distributed, less powerful processors can be used for certain nodes. The point of their work is the balancing of load by adjusting the relative amounts of computation and communication. Heterogeneous in this case implies the combination of communication and computation at each node, giving the same completion time for every node. More computation is offset by less communication. However, communications balance does not improve net processing speed unless heterogeneous computation potential is utilized for the three types of regions. Then a matrix_case analysis is used for computational requirements of processors in each of the regions A, B, C.

25.6 Summary

Heterogeneous computing is a promising cost-effective approach to the design of high performance computers, which generally incorporates proven technology and existing designs and reduces new design risk from scratch. For both homogeneous or heterogeneous systems, the mapping process is very crucial, which basically involves allocation of tasks to processors to get the minimum execution time. This process is one of the most important phases of parallel computing as improper assignment could lead to reduced performance. The mapping problem becomes more complex in heterogeneous systems due to the overhead associated with the code and data-format conversions. In this chapter, we have presented an overview of mapping and scheduling on heterogeneous systems by addressing a few theories and techniques proposed by researchers. In the future, the applications of parallel computing will become larger and larger, so the overhead due to job transfer will increase accordingly. Up until now, the emphasis of research has focused on the identification and evaluation of efficient policies on information distribution and placement decision. Maybe it will be a better way to extract the advantages of both static and dynamic scheduling methods, overcome their disadvantages, and design hybrid schemes.

25.7 Bibliography

[1] M. Cermele, M. Colajanni, and F. Necci. Dynamic Load Balancing of Distributed SPMD Computations with Explicit Message-Passing. *Proceedings IEEE Workshop on Heterogeneous Computing*, pages 2-16, 1997.

[2] E. Coffman. *Computer and Job-Shop Scheduling Theory,* New York: Wiley, 1976.

[3] P. Dasgupta, A. K. Majumder, and P. Bhattacharya. V_THR: An Adaptive Load Balancing Algorithm. *Journal of Parallel and Distributed Computing,* vol. 42, pages 101-108, 1997.

[4] A. A. Khokhar, V. K. Prasanna, M. E. Shaaban, and C. Wang. Heterogeneous Computing: Challenges and Opportunities. Proceedings *IEEE Heterogeneous Computing Workshop,* pages 18-27, June 1993.

[5] S. J. Kim and J. C Browne. A General Approach to Mapping of Parallel Computation upon Multiprocessor Architectures. *Proceedings of the International Conference on Parallel Processing,* vol. 3, pages 1-8, 1988.

[6] P. Krueger and M. Livny. A Comparison of Preemptive and Non-Preemptive Load Distributing. *Technical Report,* Department of Computer Science, University of Wisconsin, Madison, WI, 1988.

[7] M. H. Mickle and J. M. Paul. Load Balancing Using Heterogeneous Processors for Continuum Problems on a Mesh. *Journal of Parallel and Distributed Computing,* vol. 39, pages 66-73, 1996.

[8] B. Narahari, A. Youssef and H. Choi. Matching and Scheduling in a Generalized Optimal Selection Theory. *Proceedings of the IEEE Heterogeneous Processing Workshop,* pages 3-8, 1994

[9] L. M. Ni and P. K. McKinley. A Survey of Wormhole Routing Techniques in Direct Networks. *IEEE Computer,* vol. 26(2), pages 62-76, February 1993.

[10] S. Ranka, Y. Won and S. Sahni. Programming a Hypercube Multicomputer. *IEEE Software,* pages 69-77, September, 1988.

[11] V. Sarkar. *Partitioning and Scheduling Parallel Programs for Multiprocessors.* Cambridge, MA: M.I.T. Press, 1989.

[12] C. Shen and W. Tsai. A Graph Matching Approach to Optimal Task Assignment in Distributed Computing Systems Using a Minimax Criterion. *IEEE Transactions on Computers,* vol. C-34(3), pages 197-203, March 1985.

[13] H.S. Stone. Critical Load Factors in Two-Processor Distributed Systems. *IEEE Transactions on Software Engineering,* vol. SE-4(3), pages 254-258, May 1978.

[14] C. Z. Xu and F. C. M. Lau. Analysis of the Generalized Dimension Exchange Method for Dynamic Load Balancing. *Journal of Parallel Distributed Computing,* vol. 16(4), pages 385-393, 1992.

[15] T. Yang and A. Gerasoulis. A Fast Static Scheduling Algorithm for DAG's on an Unbounded Number of Processors. *Proceedings of IEEE Supercomputing'91,* pages 633-642. Albuquerque, NM, November 1991.

Part IV

Representative Cluster Systems

Cluster computing systems come in many shapes and sizes. At one extreme, a group of business executives sharing data between their palm computers constitutes a cluster. At another extreme, a computational grid of supercomputers stretched around the world is also a form of cluster. However, a computing cluster is more commonly classified as a collection of interconnected workstations or PC processors. Even within this apparently limited scope, it is possible to introduce many variations in system design, software architecture, and application execution models. The remaining chapters present examples of clusters and associated software systems built and used by research and commercial organizations around the world to perform real work.

You will find that two general classes of clusters are popularly employed: dedicated and nondedicated. Dedicated clusters are systems built specifically to run parallel applications all of the time, day in and day out. These machines often have only one monitor and keyboard that are shared by all system nodes for installation, diagnostic, and bootstrapping purposes. Nondedicated clusters do not exclusively serve as parallel compute engines. They are typically formed from collections of individual workstations sitting on user desktops across a departmental LAN. When these workstations are idle, sequential or parallel programs are scheduled to run on the machines. This approach is often called "cycle harvesting," because it makes use of processor cycles that would otherwise go unused. Both classes of clusters share the same programming models, but require different resource management and scheduling support.

Chapter 26 introduces Beowulf-class computing systems, which were first built by NASA to cost effectively meet the computational needs of research scientists. Beowulf clusters leverage open source software, including the Linux operating system, and purely off-the-shelf hardware to create dedicated parallel computing systems, programmed primarily through message passing APIs. The chapter provides an overview of the history of the Beowulf project and the evolution of Beowulf systems into increasingly powerful computational resources. A summary of the basic system architecture, application domains, and design challenges are discussed before describing future directions that will be taken in the next generation of Beowulf systems.

Chapter 27 presents the Real World Computing PC cluster, developed as a dedicated parallel computer by the Real World Computing Partnership in Japan. The RWC cluster is distinguished by its SCore software environment, which includes scheduling facilities, an optimized implementation of MPI, and a unique multithreaded programming language called MPC++. The chapter describes the RWC system design, including the construction of custom packaging and the use of Myrinet. The development of a zero-copy message protocol, its use in optimizing MPI, and the derived performance benefits are explained.

Chapter 28 describes a particular design point in clustered PC systems represented by the COMPaS cluster, another system developed by Japan's Real World Computing Partnership. The COMPaS cluster utilizes quad-processor Pentium Pro

SMPs connected by both Myrinet and Fast Ethernet. SMP clusters present unique challenges because processors on the same SMP must share bus bandwidth, reducing the effective per-processor bandwidth. A detailed analysis of the performance of shared memory, distributed memory, and hybrid programming models is discussed along with application performance results.

Chapter 29 introduces a software architecture, named NanOS, for managing cluster systems. A detailed description of this CORBA-based distributed operating system is included. The microkernel architecture, HIDRA high availability extensions, reliable object invocations, and group membership protocols are all discussed in a context that highlights how object-oriented technology can be applied to cluster resource management.

Chapter 30 demonstrates how a nondedicated cluster of workstations can be programmed using the Bulk-Synchronous Parallel (BSP) model. The authors of this chapter have extended BSP to adapt to changes in the degree of available parallelism in nondedicated workstation clusters. The BSP model is explained along with the adaptive extensions. Application performance results using this alternative programming model provide insight into its benefits.

Another take on cycle harvesting is portrayed in Chapter 31, which describes the MARS scheduling system. MARS is based on the popular PVM programming library and provides adaptive scheduling mechanisms. MARS reallocates tasks as the availability of idle workstations changes. Experimental results are presented, including efficiency and fault-tolerance analyses.

The Gardens programming language and run-time environment, discussed in Chapter 32, further exemplifies the variety of approaches that can be taken in order to harness unused computing power in nondedicated computing cluster. Gardens attempts to provide adaptive execution support, programming safety guarantees, and efficient communication performance. By developing a new programming language, the authors are able to perform compile-time checks that ensure the safe use of Active Messages as well as optimize communication. A comprehensive treatment of the entire Gardens environment is described, including the programming language, run-time support, and features such as task migration.

Chapter 33 revisits dedicated computing clusters, but focuses on software support that enables clusters to execute general-purpose multiuser workloads in the style of MPPs. It describes the ParPar job management software infrastructure and experimental results on a 17 PC cluster running the BSDI OS. Remote job control and scheduling are highlighted.

Chapter 34 introduces the Pitt Parallel Computer (PPC), a type of cluster quite different from the rest. The PPC is an application specific computer, dedicated to the solving of one particular problem at a time. The cluster is reconfigurable, but both the application program and operating system must be burned into an EPROM that replaces the original BIOS of each CPU board. The authors explain the design of the system and the performance of several applications.

Chapter 35 presents an overview of the IBM RS/6000 SP computer. This is a commercially available scalable cluster system that is used both as a parallel supercomputer as well as a flexible cluster for mainstream business applications that require performance, scalability, and high availability beyond what can be achieved by a single SMP server. The chapter introduces the reader to the architecture and structure of the system and the primary system components. Wherever relevant, the rationale for major system design decisions is discussed.

The final chapter, Chapter 36, uses the example of building a web server to examine the requirements placed on a cluster computer used for Internet commerce and dynamic web page generation. It first uses the growth of the Internet and availability and scalability requirements to introduce the IBM SP architecture for use as a web server. It then discusses alternatives for dynamic web page creation, load balancing across clusters of web servers, shared filesystems and parallel I/O, and high availability.

Together, these chapters survey the spectrum of research activities being conducted in the field. They should give you a feeling for some of the possible design points and the reasons for choosing such designs. While not a comprehensive treatment, the presented material illustrates how some real systems are being used and also discusses ongoing research issues.

Chapter 26

Beowulf

DANIEL F. SAVARESE AND THOMAS STERLING

Center for Advanced Computing Research
California Institute of Technology
Pasadena, California

Email: *dfs@cacr.caltech.edu, tron@cacr.caltech.edu*

Beowulf is an epic poem first put in writing in the eighth century, although the earliest surviving text is an 11th century Old English manuscript, which comprises the first known piece of English literature. It recounts the tale of the Geat warrior, Beowulf, who saves the Lord of the Danes and his court from the ravages of the evil monster, Grendel. Although the poem contains no references to parallel computing, having been written over a thousand years before computers as we know them were invented, it has inspired the development of Beowulf-class computing systems during the final years of the second millennium.

The hero Beowulf liberated the Danes from the monster Grendel, who would visit the hall Heorot each night and terrorize its people. In much the same way, Beowulf systems have liberated scientists from the recurring oppressive tasks of porting their codes to new architectures every year, sharing computing resources with hundreds of other users, and paying millions of dollars for these dubious pleasures.

26.1 Searching for Beowulf

Today, on the World Wide Web, in USENET news groups and Internet mailing lists, at both academic and industry conferences, as well as in research papers, the name Beowulf is often used without definition to describe a particular class of parallel computing. In spite of, or perhaps because of, the common usage of the term, heated debates often arise centering around the central question, "What is a Beowulf?" Rather than provide a well-defined answer to this question, we will give you a brief history of Beowulf machines: who uses them, how they use them, and where you can learn more about them, leaving you to answer the question for yourself.

26.1.1 The Beowulf Model: Satisfying a Critical Need

Although you have by now become well-acquainted with the motivations and concepts behind clustered computing, it bears explaining that clustered computing is not always synonymous with low-cost computing. Clusters can be built with anything from desktop PCs (or even palm computers) to high-end SMP servers for processing, and anything from Ethernet to ATM or Myrinet for an interconnect. The operating systems and software used on clusters can fall anywhere in the range of licensed proprietary products to no-cost open source software. Beowulf systems define a class of clustered computing that focuses on maximizing the price-to-performance ratio of the overall system without compromising its ability to perform the computational work for which it is being built. This design model typically results in machines that are an order of magnitude less expensive than an MPP of comparable performance. In this respect, the Beowulf model has almost come to define low-cost supercomputing.

While cost-optimization is the most notable aspect of the Beowulf model, price is not the sole component. By tracking the evolution of commodity hardware, Beowulfs are able to incorporate the very latest technology advancements well before proprietary parallel machines. This rapid pace of change would be a curse if not for the consistent software environment and programming model. Moving from one generation of an MPP to the next often requires learning a new set of development tools and even changes in the programming model to best exploit the performance of the machine. In constrast, when you move from one Beowulf generation to the next, all your software stays the same and the programming model doesn't change. That is not to say that the software does not improve through time. Most Beowulf systems employ some version of the Linux operating system, the GNU development environment, and the PVM and MPI libraries as the foundations of parallel programming. All of these software components are constantly being improved and refined, but not in ways that conflict with existing programming practices. A first generation Beowulf program will compile and run on a fourth generation system, only faster.

26.1.2 A Short History of Large Achievements

Sometimes a number of conditions come to a confluence and allow the emergence of a new way of doing things. In the past, scientifc applications have been run on special purpose supercomputing hardware because they required not only fast processing, but also large memories and secondary storage capacities. Beowulf computing relies on cheap, yet powerful, hardware and software. These were traditionally conflicting characteristics. But in 1994, PC processor performance had reached a point where it could handle the lower end of scientific computation. Memory densities and prices had also come down to a level where it was affordable to equip a cluster of PCs with sufficient DRAM to run science applications. Likewise, disk storage and bandwidth had increased to the point where large data set manipulation and out-of-core computation could be cost-effectively accommodated by off-the-shelf PC hard drives. All the pieces of hardware necessary to build a parallel scientific workstation could now be satisfied with PC components. The only missing component was a low-cost operating system and software environment suitable for scientific computing. This last piece of the puzzle fell into place when the 1.0 release of the Linux operating system neared its final beta-testing with release 0.99-pl14.

At the same time as these events, the Earth and Space Sciences Project at NASA's Goddard Space Flight Center, part of NASA's broader HPCC program, had a need for a single user workstation that could generate and process large data sets from grand challenge applications that typically ran on MPPs. The cost of the system could not exceed the price of high-end scientific workstations at the time (on the order of $50,000), but at the same time it required at least 10 GBytes of storage and 1 GFLOPS peak performance. All commercially available systems satisfying those requirements at the time cost at least 10 times as much as desired. Scientists at Goddard recognized that the the time was ripe to build such a machine, using mass market components. All of the parameters could be met, except for the 1 GFLOPS peak performance. At the time, Intel processors were the only cost-effective option for building such a system, but their floating point performance was lacking. It was decided to build an initial prototype with 1 GOPS peak, which could be attained using 100 MHz Intel DX4 processors, and use the experience gained to build a follow-on machine incorporating Pentium processors, with enhanced floating point, when available. As part of the process of developing the first machine, the necessary networking software that was identified as missing would be developed. This led to the development of many of the Linux Ethernet drivers by Donald Becker. Other commodity cluster projects were also underway at academic institutions around the country, but most of them relied on academically licensed versions of commercial operating systems. Beowulf was one of the first projects to rely completely on no-cost open source software as the foundation of the system. This was essential to meeting NASA's price requirements.

The first Beowulf contained 16 Intel 66 MHz 486 processors that were quickly upgraded to 100 MHz DX4 processors [5]. Even with its non-optimal poor floating point perfomance, this system delivered comparable performance to an equal number of processors on MPPs of the time such as the Paragon and CM-5. In real applications, up to 4.6 MFLOPS per node was achieved, or 42 FLOPS total. This was a far cry from the desired 1 GFLOPS objective, but that would soon change as the demand for high-end graphics on PCs would drive the Intel architecture to incorporate more powerful floating point performance. The second Beowulf, built in 1995, traded in the 486 processors for 100 MHz Pentium processors. The 10 Mbps Ethernet networks employed in the first machine were also replaced with 100 Mbps Ethernet. These changes alone yielded a performance increase to a sustained 17.5 FLOPS per node, or 280 MFLOPS. This was very close to the 1 GFLOPS peak, given that most applications are lucky to achieve 30% of peak performance on an MPP.

The third generation of Beowulfs were built both at NASA and other national research laboratories. JPL and Los Alamos National Laboratory each built 16 processor machines incorporating Pentium Pro processors. These machines were combined to run a large N-body problem, which won the 1997 Gordon Bell Prize for price performance. Without any custom modifications, the system delivered a sustained performance of over 2 GFLOPS. By 1997 much larger systems, incorporating between one and two hundred processors, were being built at Caltech, Los Alamos, and Goddard. These machines all demonstrated sustained performance in the 10 GFLOPS range, and the very latest machines in 1998 exceed 20 GFLOPS. In just four short years, the performance gap was closed and Beowulf systems routinely appear on the list of the 500 top-performing supercomputers in the world.

26.1.3 Application Domains

The potential application of Beowulf-class systems is broad and ranges from high-end floating point intensive scientific and engineering problems to commercial data intensive tasks such as Web servers and data bases. While the area of applications for clustered computing is covered in detail in other sections of this book, it is valuable to summarize some of the key observations that have accrued from experience with a large number of large programs performed on Beowulfs. Examples of applications for real-world computation include finite element and finite difference algorithm, conjugate gradient solvers, tree codes, ray tracing problems, and numerous other algorithms. These range from highly uniform, sometimes embarrassingly parallel or at least with modest communications, and processing regular data to heterogeneous computations managing irregular time-varying data structures with substantial communication demands. Performing many of these problems on loosely coupled clustered systems, including Beowulf-class systems, can be a challenge. However, with careful data partitioning and the development of latency tolerant algorithms, the domain of effective application of these systems has proven to be broad.

A number of applications, originally programmed for tightly coupled MPPs, have been ported to Beowulf-class systems and empirical comparative studies conducted by the authors and their collaborators. From this base of experience have emerged some general observations that give a good sense of the general utility of Beowulfs. Where same generation MPP and Beowulf systems of comparable number of nodes and memory capacity are compared, behavior can be most readily divided into the time to perform the computational work, and the time required to carry out the necessary communications. In the majority of cases observed, Beowulf-class systems perform the computational component of applications at a level equal to or better than the MPP counterpart. This is because even if the two systems are contemporaries, the microprocessor in the Beowulf is generally newer due to the ability to adopt the latest technology for that time frame. With the MPP's longer development lead time, older parts are usually used. The time for communication on the Beowulf is substantially worse than on the highest bi-section bandwidth MPP, sometimes by as much as an order of magnitude.

Programming of Beowulf-class systems requires attention to detail. Interestingly, optimizing the code with Beowulf in mind usually dramatically improves the communications aspect of the Beowulf execution. For example, much of the communication can often be avoided by reorganizing the computation. Bunching of data between nodes greatly improves communication efficiency. Increasing coarseness of synchronization granularity can have a significant effect on program execution. Organizing computation so that it overlaps the communication is another way to improve performance on Beowulf systems. When these techniques are brought to play, Beowulfs have been seen to outperform their MPP contemporaries by as much as 15% for some problems, while poorer performance of about 40% of that of the control MPPs has been seen on unfavorable problems. But even then, Beowulf exhibits an overall price-performance advantage of a factor of six or more.

26.1.4 Other Sources of Information

Although this chapter provides a good introduction to Beowulf-class computing, there are other perspectives and sources of information, many of which are available online. We list a few of the more helpful resources that provide more information for readers interested in delving further into Beowulf.

Avalon - http://swift.lanl.gov/avalon/ Avalon is a 140 processor Beowulf system that uses DEC Alpha 21164A processors and has 36 GBytes of memory. A 70 processor version of Avalon was a finalist for the 1998 Gordon Bell Prize for best price/performance.

Beowulf Project - http://www.beowulf.org/ The Beowulf Project Web site, currently hosted by NASA's Goddard Space Flight Center, contains a collection of software and information related to Beowulf systems around the world.

Extreme Linux - http://www.extremelinux.org/ The purpose of Extreme Linux project is to improve Linux and its associated software for high performance computing tasks.

Grendel - http://www.cacr.caltech.edu/beowulf/ Grendel is a part of the Beowulf Project at the Center for Advanced Computing Research at Caltech. It is an initiative to organize and develop a coherent system software infrastructure for Beowulf systems.

How to Build a Beowulf - http://www-mitpress.mit.edu/book-home.tcl?isbn=026269218X This book describes how to build your own Beowulf, what software you need, how to program the machine, and how to avoid common pitfalls. See [6].

Linux Documentation Project - http://sunsite.unc.edu/LDP/ The Linux Documentation Project organizes reliable documentation about Linux in several different on-line and printable formats.

Linux Information Headquarters - http://www.linuxhq.com/
The LinuxHQ Web site is a resource for Linux kernel users and hackers, including the latest official and unofficial kernel patches.

26.2 System Architecture Evolution

Beowulfs distinguish themselves from other clustered systems in that they do not impose a fixed system architecture. It is not much of a stretch to say that no two Beowulfs are built the same. The price/performance parameters of commodity hardware can change from one month to the next. But the constant factor remains that the hardware is readily available, with a broad selection of models and manufacturers for any specific component, eliminating any constraints that would be imposed by a single-vendor solution. As a consequence, it is possible to configure and optimize an installation at the last minute, or whenever it might be advantageous to restructure the system to optimally run a particular application. Vendor-supplied parallel machines do not provide this level of flexibility, called "just in place" configuration.

Given their sensitivity to the rapid change of mass market technology, Beowulf architectures have constantly evolved since their inception in 1994. Although on the most general level the architecture has remained the same, following the canonical cluster model, the specific roles of the system components, their impact on performance, and their influence on design decisions, have all changed. The primary system components that drive the architecture can be decomposed into the processor, memory, network, and secondary storage systems. But the processor and network have had the most visible impact on the changes in Beowulf architecture.

26.2.1 The Processor

The very first Beowulf system was built using Intel DX4 processors, the 100 Mhz version of the 80486 chip, in 1994. At the time, the DX4 delivered the best price for aggregate operations per second. Even though the total system of 16 processors could deliver over a GigaOPS peak performance, the floating point performance did not approach an equivalent level. DX4 chips were designed to run business applications efficiently, which did not necessitate optimizing the floating point unit. Given the initial performance parameters, this first system was intended as a single-user parallel workstation for NASA scientists.

Clearly, one of the restrictions of Beowulf design is that your system must contend with the limitations of prevailing business-oriented hardware. The scientific computing market is too small to have a significant influence on hardware design. Beowulfs must make do with what commodity hardware is available, and adapt to the prevailing circumstances.

Responding to new competition from the PowerPC and DEC Alpha chips, Intel made significant strides in improving its processors with the release of the Pentium and Pentium Pro. The Pentium Pro featured more advanced floating point performance, and a dedicated bus for the second-level cache, contained on the same multi-chip module. The Pentium Pro could also be paired with a second processor on an SMP motherboard. That made it a favorite choice for use in certain Beowulf configurations, which could drive down the per-FLOPS cost by using dual-processor boards. However, the Pentium Pro line was not evolved further, and its cost did not fall at the same rate as its Pentium brethren, eventually making it a poor choice for building Beowulfs if you did not need SMP capabilities. In addition, as we will discuss later, the use of SMP nodes degrades the performance of memory intensive applications, because both processors share the same bus, effectively halving the per-processor memory bandwidth.

The increasing importance of computer graphics led to the development of the MMX instruction set (multimedia extensions), introduced in the Pentium MMX chips. A byproduct of this focus on graphics resulted in floating point performance competitive with that of some RISC chips. Here computer games and multimedia software were responsible for driving processor design, but scientific computing reaped the benefits as well. The next generation Intel processor was dubbed the Pentium II, and incorporated both Pentium Pro and Pentium MMX technology. At the time of this writing, the highest clock rate available for this processor is 450 MHz, but faster versions will soon be in production. The optimal price/performance choice for an Intel-based Beowulf right now is the 400 MHz Pentium II, but that will soon change.

In 1994 you could purchase a DX4 processor for about $550 [1], or roughly five and a half dollars a MegaOPS. Two years later, Pentium and Pentium Pro price/performance had improved by a factor of two, at two and a quarter dollars a MegaOPS. At the time of this writing, 400 MHz Pentium II processors are available for about one dollar a MegaOPS, and floating point performance has improved to the point where the price per MFLOPS is about one dollar as well. The latest DEC Alpha processor delivers an even better cost-to-performance ratio, and GigaHertz clock speeds are on the horizon. Whereas in 1994 the processor performance was a primary constraining factor in the design of a Beowulf, this is no longer the case. Increases in processor speeds have far outstripped increases in memory access times and bus bandwidth. The limiting factor on the performance of a Beowulf has now become the memory bandwidth, which has barely changed.

26.2.2 The Network

Even though the DX4 processors used in the first Beowulf lacked the horsepower to challenge the higher end of the MPP spectrum, they were too fast for the 10 Mbps Ethernet network used at the time. To avoid saturating the network, a scheme was devised whereby multiple networks could be connected to distribute the communication traffic. This channel bonding technique was able to increase the sustained network throughput by 75% when dual networks were used. Three networks did not provide as great an improvement, but nonetheless did increase overall throughput. But despite these increases in network throughput, certain communication intensive applications could still saturate the network. Higher bandwidth networking technology was needed.

Fortunately, within a year 100 Mbps Ethernet was standardized and the price of the hardware started to fall. The second generation Beowulf system incorporated 100 Mbps Ethernet, and even included two networks in order to evaluate the need for channel bonding with the technology. It was discovered that the second network would also yield approximately a 75% gain in throughput over a single network. But the total utilization of the network as a percentage of theoretical peak was lower, measured at 65% for 100 Mbps Ethernet as compared to 80% for 10 Mbps.

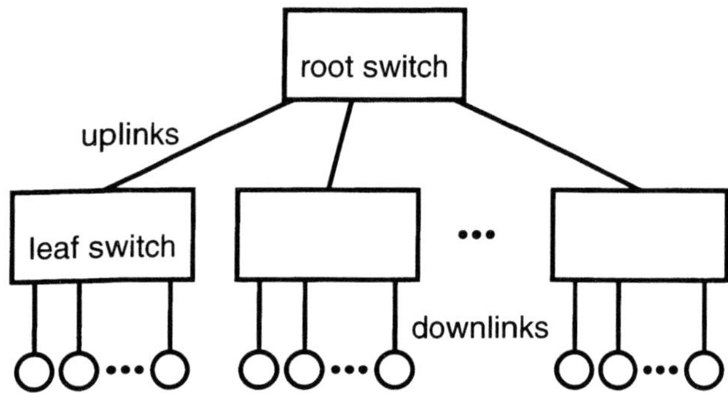

Figure 26.1 Tree of switches showing a root switch connecting leaf switches which, in turn, connect 16 processing nodes. Per processor bi-section bandwidth through the root switch decreases as the number of switches increases.

An important aspect of the overall network performance is the switching technology employed. Initially, only 8 port switches were available for 100 Mpbs Ethernet, but today switches with over 48 ports can be purchased, and by the time this book is published, certainly more will available. The number of available switch ports has affected the network topologies employed by Beowulfs, as well as their scalability. When only 8 ports were available, it was practical to build only small systems. These would typically consist of groups of eight nodes connected to a switch, which would then be connected to each other through uplink ports, creating a hierachical tree. Figure 26.1 shows such a tree, but using the 16 port switches commonly used in late 1997. As the number of ports per switch increased, it became possible to assemble larger numbers of nodes in the same manner. However, not just any switch is suitable for building a Beowulf. You need a high backplane speed, full-duplex ports, and cut-through routing. These have all become standard features on most equipment, but in the early days of 100 Mbps Ethernet, that was not the case.

Even though the bandwidth of commodity networks has increased dramatically, with 1 Gbps technology on the verge of becoming affordable, the latency of the networks remains rather high. This makes Beowulfs unsuitable for running applications that depend on low network latencies, especially those that transmit many small messages. Applications deployed on Beowulf systems must be restructured for latency tolerance. Fortunately, many applications implemented using MPI and PVM are already latency tolerant as a byproduct of the message passing programming model's influence on their algorithms. However, not all applications can be structred to tolerate high latencies. These applications can still be run on Beowulf-type systems, but such systems require expensive interconnection technology that delivers low-latencies, such as Myrinet [2]. In some sense such machines can be considered not to be Beowulfs. But even though their price increases significantly as a result of using specialty networks, it is still lower than that of equivalent MPPs.

26.2.3 Putting It All Together

Processing power was a dominant limiting factor on the performance of initial Beowulf systems. But as successive generations of hardware appeared, the processor decreased its impact on the overall performance of the system. Memory bandwidth has now replaced the role of the processor as a performance bottleneck. The network has always been a performance limiting factor since the early days, but is not quite such a limitation with 100 Mbps Ethernet. However, the network still imposes a strict limit on the scaling of Beowulf systems. Once you move to between 100 and 200 nodes, the network can easily become saturated. The availability of affordable 1 Gbps Ethernet will mostly eliminate this problem, and allow scaling to even larger numbers of nodes for applications that can incorporate that much parallelism. As you create larger systems, to extract a reasonable percentage of peak performance, it is necessary to run even larger problem sets. Otherwise, the level of parallelism becomes too fine-grained, making inefficient use of the available computational resources. You can see the way larger problems can make better use of larger systems by looking at Figure 26.2 in the next section. In this performance graph, smaller problem sets were not able to deliver the same level of performance as larger problems. However, keep in mind that this will not necessarily be true of all applications.

Secondary storage capacity is no longer a limiting factor on the size of data sets that can be processed by Beowulf systems. Whereas the first Beowulf contained a total of 10 GBytes of disk, a modern Beowulf might have that much storage on a single node, or even more if multiple disks are assigned to a node. The total disk capacity of a 100 node Beowulf now exceeds the 1 TeraByte mark. But while processor performance, network performance, and secondary storage capacity have all made order of magnitude improvements, memory access times and bandwidth have remained largely unchanged. Beowulf systems will become victims of their dependence on PC hardware and hit a performance wall unless memory subsystems see large performance improvements.

26.3 Prevailing Software Practices

Vendor-developed high performance computing platforms are typically delivered with an integrated set of development and system software. Assessments of the quality and utility of the integrated packages will vary, depending on the user, but it is, at the very least, a fair statement to say that there is a cogent order to the provided software. Custom performance monitoring libraries, tailored to work with the special hardware, are often provided along with specialized compilers, communication libraries, system management tools and other software. Unfortunately, the amount of testing and general quality assurance that vendors are able to perform on these software packages is not overly great. So even though the tools are well-integrated, the software is often unreliable and generally buggy.

In the realm of do-it-yourself supercomputing, the situation is a little different. The degree of software integration is almost nonexistent. The operating system, compilers, debugging libraries, and related system software are not designed for use on clustered machines. The parallel programming libraries, including PVM and MPI, are not optimized for a special interconnect that might be present on an MPP, but rather rely on TCP/IP sockets, incurring an associated overhead. Only the most minimal system management tools are available, and are, in almost all cases, designed for single workstations. Despite these shortcomings, the software enjoys a high level of reliability. Hundreds of thousands of people use the software every day, which accelerates bug detection and susbsequent bug fixing. The result is that Beowulfs lack certain types of software, such as parallel debuggers, and a lot of the software is not designed for a parallel machine. But the software they do have is extremely robust, and a large part of the LAN oriented services, such as NFS and NIS, can be applied to building a coherent and administerable environment.

26.3.1 Small Scale Software Provides Big Scale Performance

All Beowulf machines rely heavily on open source software to provide program development and system resource management services. It is often a shock to some that freely available workstation software can be used to build applications on a pile of PCs that surpass the performance of the same applications on many commercial supercomputers. The core development environment for Beowulf machines is typically a GNU compiler, of which C, C++, and Fortran are the most commonly used. Commercial compilers are also available, and many Beowulf installations actually invest in a commercial Fortran compiler to extract more performance from their code. But the GNU compilers alone are capable of delivering most of the performance that can be extracted through compile-time analysis and code generation.

Figure 26.2 shows the scaling properties of an N-body simulation, written by John Salmon [3], running on between 1 and 64 processors on a Pentium Pro based Beowulf. The code was written in C, using the MPI message passing library and compiled with the GNU C compiler. With just the GNU programming environment and the Linux OS, this N-body problem was able to achieve over 4 GFLOPS

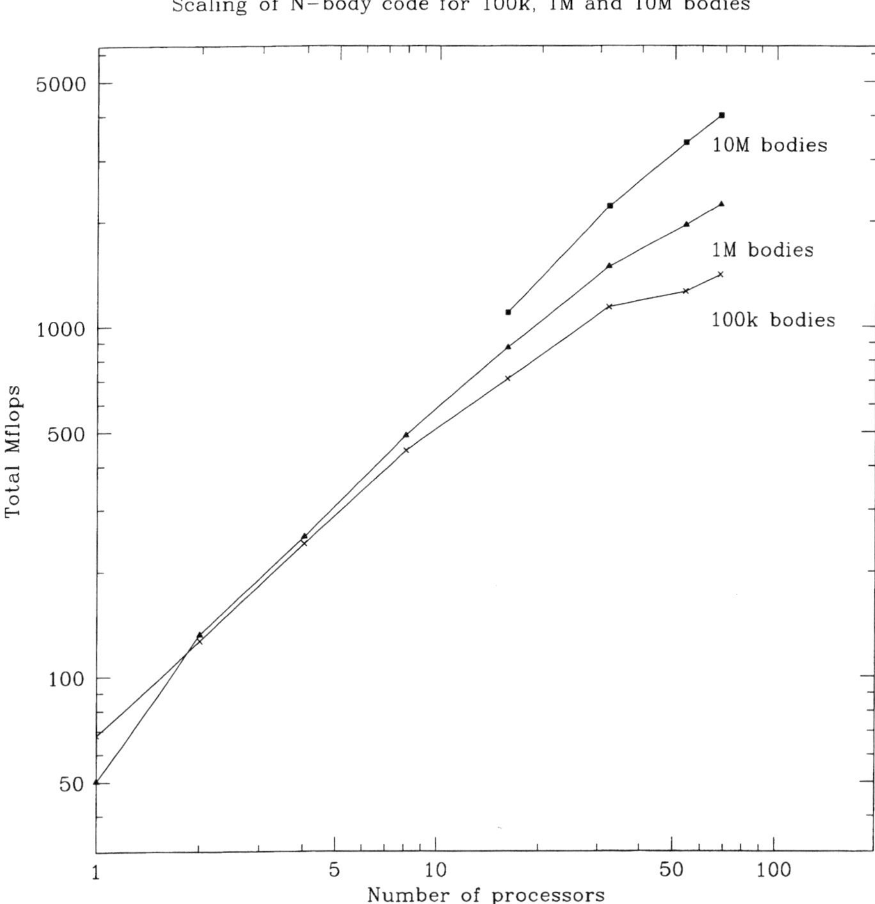

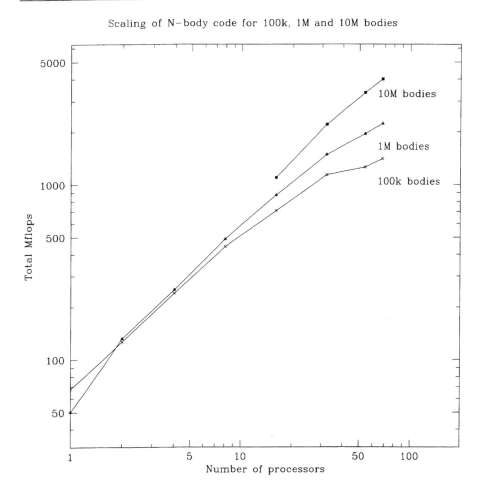

Figure 26.2 Scaling of N-body code for 100k, 1M, and 10M bodies.

sustained performance on 64 processors (62.5 MFLOPS per processor), simulating the interactions of 10 million gravitational bodies. It was also able to scale close to linearly across the range of processors. The scaling of the smaller problem runs degraded more quickly than the larger problem runs as the number of processors increased. This is a classic example of how communication latency can start to dominate the execution time of an application as the computation required of each processor decreases. If you spread a small problem too thinly across a large number of processors, each processor becomes starved for computation, and communication latency begins to dominate execution time, adversely impacting scaling. But scaling is not always an important metric to programmers. The bottom line is often wall clock time. If a program will execute faster by running it on a larger number of processors, then it is worth doing so. Scaling gives you a measure of when it is no longer worth adding more processors to a system because they will never be utilized effectively. Not all problems are well-suited for execution on Beowulf-class clusters, but this N-body problem is only one example of how the software environment is more than adequate to compile and execute problems that are suited to this class of machine.

26.3.2 The Linux Operating System

Linux is a no-cost open source operating system which is very well supported by its users and developers. Several successful companies have built a lucrative business from packaging Linux software into organized distributions and selling them on CD-ROM. In 1998, Intel Corp. felt that Linux was of sufficient importance that it bought a minority stake in privately held RedHat Software, Inc., based in Raleigh, NC.

Despite the fact that Linux is one of only two operating systems that are currently gaining a market share, a misperception persists among a portion of the computer industry that Linux is a toy operating system. If you have never used the Linux operating system, rest assured that it delivers all the features associated with commercial POSIX compliant Unix systems. In fact, Linux has been found to exceed the performance of several commercial Unix flavors in several areas. Up until recently, one of its weak points was the lack of kernel scheduled threads, but the most recent Linux distributions, including RedHat 5.x, fully support this feature. However, Linux threads are heavyweight, containing all the overheads associated with processes and therefore should not be used for tasks requiring lightweight parallelism. Linux does support SMP motherboards along with multiprocessor scheduling of threads, but most Linux distributions require that you custom compile the kernel to add this support.

The main attraction of the Linux operating system is its publicly available source code. Early Beowulf development work could not have been done without it. To overcome the limitations of 10 Mbps Ethernet, Don Becker wrote special network drivers that allowed multiple physical networks to be used as one logical network [5]. Others have made similar modifications to Linux by taking advantage of the accessible source code. I/O performance monitoring, dynamically loadable scheduling policies, and global process id spaces are just a few such modifications. But the most important advantage to using Linux when building a Beowulf is that it is simply very efficient. Network and disk I/O performance has been benchmarked at much higher levels than the leading commercial operating systems for desktop computers and servers. Combine that high performance with low or no cost, and you've got an ideal operating system for low-cost commodity cluster computing.

26.4 Next Steps in Beowulf-Class Computing

Beowulf clusters were motivated by the needs of the scientific community. The initial requirements of that community have been met, but some challenges still remain. Clusters are not particularly easy to use, nor is it clear how to scale them to very large sizes. In addition, new classes of data-intensive applications outside of scientific computation are being explored as we start to take the next steps in Beowulf-class computing.

26.4.1 Grendel - Towards Uniform System Software

The two characters that spring to mind when we think of the Beowulf legend are its hero, Beowulf, and its villain, Grendel. They form two parts of one whole. When we think of Beowulf clusters, there lies a similar parallel. The Beowulf hardware is the hero, delivering a high performance, cost-effective system architecture that tracks technology through time. But the software is something of a villain. Even though Beowulf systems leverage an enormous amount of quality open source software, the level of integration of the software is almost nonexistent, and a great deal of software is missing, especially system management tools. Therefore, a new systems software initiative for Beowulf machines has been started at Caltech to solve that problem. This initiative has been named Grendel because after the software is coupled with the hardware, the Beowulf story will be complete.

There is no standard distribution of software that you can install to create a Beowulf and perform all the tasks you might conceive for a parallel machine. The software that is available must be gathered up from individual academic and government research institutions. Sometimes the software is well-maintained, but often the potential user community for a given package is completely unaware of its existence, leading the authors to stop maintaining the software. In addition, the software is usually independently created, without regard for the existence of some other work that might be leveraged to create a better-integrated product. As a result, the level of inter-operability can be quite low. The root cause of the aforementioned situation is that the parallel computing community is rather small, and also does not cooperate closely. The small size of the community prevents the creation of the critical mass of users that will drive the improvement of existing software and the development of new programs that fill in the gaps in functionality.

The Grendel initiative will attempt to remedy the lingering software problem by addressing three main issues. The first issue is that of assembling a standard distribution of software for Beowulf systems. There already exists a large array of software, sometimes redundant, that is applied to Beowulf systems around the world. However, many Beowulf installations incorporate only a fraction of that software, and are largely unaware of the rest. When a need arises that could be well-satisfied by an existing software package, such as a particular parallel filesystem, Beowulf users often cannot find the right tool for the job. For example, we know of more than one Beowulf installation that went through several process schedulers and finally gave up and stopped using schedulers. To address this, Grendel will assemble a collection of most known software deployed on Beowulf systems. It will solicit users to evaluate the suitability of individual packages for various tasks, and any special errata necessary to make the best use of it on a Beowulf. In a sense, the objective is to turn the Beowulf user community into its own vendor. As a community, we will then be able to organize standard Beowulf software distributions for specific applications. For example, if you want to use a Beowulf for parallel Web serving, your requirements are significantly different from someone who just wants to run CFD codes using MPI. But there will also be a common substrate of software that every Beowulf needs to use. The Grendel repository will identify what those essential software configurations are, and simplify the process of configuring Beowulfs in the same way that standard Linux distributions and packages have streamlined the configuration of single processor workstations and servers.

A byproduct of providing a repository for Beowulf software and information on how to use it addresses the second issue tackled by Grendel, which is how to jump-start active development and maintenance of Beowulf software. In addition to helping solidify the Beowulf community, Grendel seeks to encourage the large open source community, primarily Linux users, to involve themselves with clustered computing software. This recognizes the fact that most Beowulfs run some version of the Linux operating system on each of their nodes. Some incorporate custom modifications to the kernel or standard Linux tools. Rather than keeping such developments fragmented, it behooves us to work within the Linux community to help address the needs of Beowulf users. Before the open source phenomenon gained widespread acceptance, you would have to lobby with your vendor to have changes incorporated into the operating system or system libraries. But if you use a Linux-based Beowulf, you can simply make the changes to the source code yourself. However, it is a difficult process to keep those changes up-to-date with subsequent Linux software releases, which is why it is extremely desirable to inject Beowulf needs into the mainstream Linux effort.

In its second phase, Grendel will move on to a third issue that plagues Beowulf system software development: the lack of standard APIs for cluster aware system software development. This is not to be confused with applications software that relies on messaging libraries such as MPI and PVM which are used to write user programs. There are currently no industry standards for writing cluster software. While some distributed object technologies such as CORBA and DCOM can be applied to the task, they constitute only a means of implementation. What is really needed is a set of interfaces (in the object-oriented sense) that define the operations and services that can be applied and requested on a cluster. Once these functional abstractions are identified and implemented, new system software can be written without reinventing the wheel. Existing software, such as schedulers, can be ported to utilize these new APIs, simplifying the code structure and enhancing functionality. For example, a standard service commonly requested by Beowulf system software developers is the ability to partition the system, restricting various classes of users and processes to be able to access a subset of a machine's processors.

This is a standard function, available on several MPP systems, that is used by several system management applications. But there is no standard way of achieving this end on a Beowulf, and any software that requires it tends to implement some ad hoc method.

Another example is a set of system monitoring APIs. More than just system monitoring tools need to be able to discover the number of processors on a system and their respective IP addresses. Often user applications would also like this information. However, it is essential to any system monitoring tool. How can you monitor the system if you don't know how big it is and what its components are? Following this most basic system query would be an extensible set of information gathering calls that could identify the status and health of every node in a system. Even though LAN-based protocols such as SNMP can be applied to some of these tasks, they do not always scale well, given their reliance on a single monitoring station. Also, any development APIs they possess do not integrate well with an overall clustered computing API framework. These existing APIs might be used to implement a higher level cluster API when appropriate, to avoid reinventing fundamental protocols that already perform a task well. This cluster aware systems programming API would form a basis for future development of new functionality, such as process migration and load balancing. These features have been invented several times in different research projects, and the time is right to finally integrate their functionality into a standard system. Many open source projects have produced de facto standard APIs for single workstation development, such as graphics and compression libraries. Grendel seeks to extend that model to cluster systems programming and involve the Beowulf community at large in the process.

26.4.2 Large System Scaling

A significant challenge faced by Beowulf architectures is how to scale effectively to over 100 processors. Tree structures such as that shown in Figure 26.1 are suitable for building small Beowulf systems. But as you add more switches and processors, the per-processor bi-section bandwidth across the root switch falls to extremely low levels. This is tolerable if you structure your applications to mostly communicate across the local switches and infrequently communicate across the root switch. But this requires an intimate familiarity with the network topology of the machine on which you are running. Many scientific programmers are used to tailoring their codes to the pecularities of specific machines, so this is not something unusual. But only a subset of applications can be structured to meet the requirements of this particular topology. When using 100 Mbps switches, it is possible to sidestep the problem by using switches with a 1 Gbps uplink port, and connecting them to a root Gigabit Ethernet switch. The cost of Gigabit Ethernet hardware is prohibitive today, but the cost of a single Gigabit switch is still only a fraction of the cost of a 100-200 node Beowulf cluster. In addition, once Gigabit Ethernet hardware prices come down to the level of 100 Mbps prices and Gigabit switches can replace 100baseT switches, the same bi-section bandwidth problem remains, albeit at higher bandwidth levels.

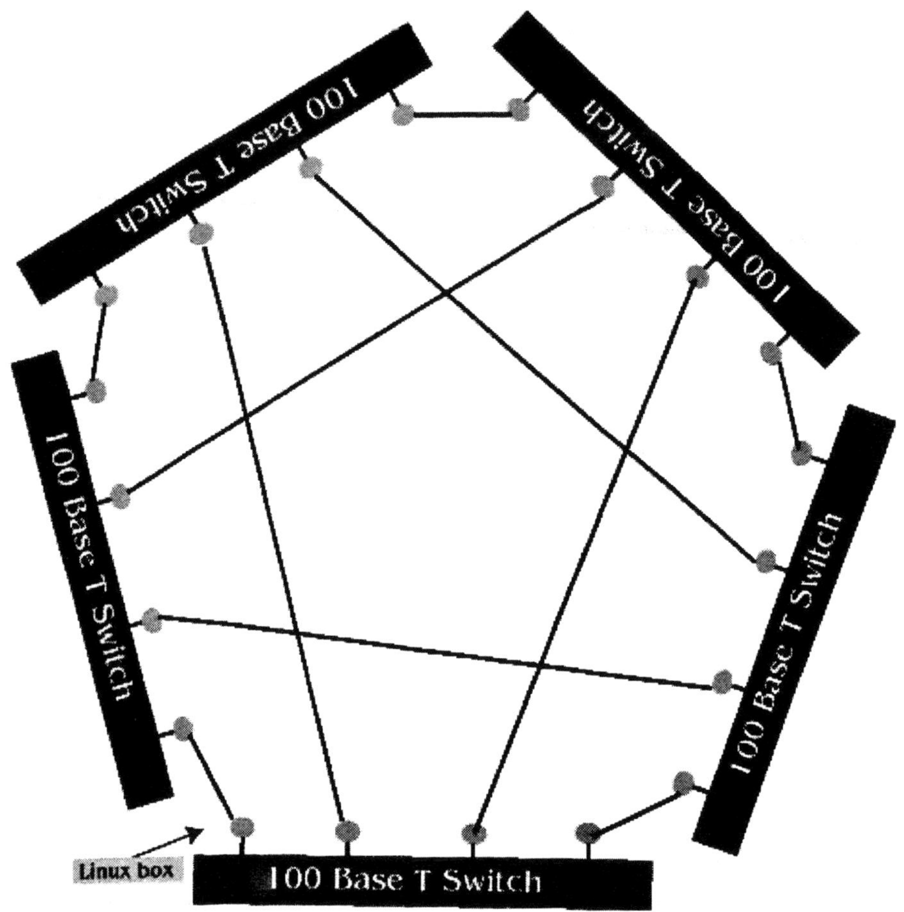

Figure 26.3 A routed topology combining 100baseT switches and routing nodes.

To allow general scaling of applications on Beowulfs incorporating over 100 processors, alternative network topologies may be necessary. Figure 26.3 shows a topology that has been successfully applied to scale raw communication bandwidth [4]. Each switch connects some subgroup of nodes. And each node connects to a second node via a point-to-point connection using a second network card. Rather than directing all inter-switch traffic through a master root switch, software routing on the processing nodes themselves is used to redirect traffic. The bi-section bandwidth of such configurations can approach 75% of the peak point-to-point bandwidth, a marked improvement over equivalent tree-based networks. The price that must be paid for this bandwidth improvement is an extra variable latency introduced by the software routing. Not only does it take more time to route a packet through a processing node, but that packet may require more than one hop to reach its destination. Most applications will have unpredictable communication patterns when mapped to this routed topology, and will suffer if they are latency sensitive. It is highly probable that the commoditization of high-end networking hardware will solve the scaling problems of current systems in much the same way that 100baseT allowed much larger systems to be built than those that used 10baseT. But then the next question becomes, how do we put together ensembles of 1000 processors without compromising network communication?

26.4.3 Data-Intensive Computation

Up to now, most Beowulf-class machines have been used for scientific computing. Scientists have simulated everything from nuclear explosions to weather patterns and galaxy cluster formation using Beowulf computers. All of these problems can generate enormous amounts of data as output, and also require similar amounts as input. It has been well-demonstrated that Beowulfs are up to the task of running data-intensive programs. In light of these successes with scientific computation, a growing number of individuals have realized that they can apply these systems to more mundane tasks that are equally demanding in terms of data processing. Already, Beowulfs have been used as high-volume Web servers, and several corporations have expressed an interest in applying them as data-warehouse and transaction processing engines. These applications have become all the more plausible with the commitment by every major database vendor to port their databases to Linux. The year 1999 will see the availability of Oracle, Informix, Sybase, DB2, and Ingres for the Linux operating system, and therefore also the vast majority of Beowulf systems.

With the availability of high performance commercial databases, the next generation of data-intensive Beowulf applications will want to leverage their capabilities. The challenge will be to develop the middleware that harnessess the databases in an application-friendly manner without sacrificing parallelism. Astronomical research organizations are evaluating the use of one or more Beowulf systems to perform data reductions on the large volumes of data that will be generated by their telescopes. Medical institutions are also studying the use of Beowulfs for processing large amounts of medical images. These applications have traditionally been implemented in a three-tier client-server model, where large amounts of data are retrieved from a database server and transferred to a compute server, which processes the data before shipping off results to a client. By storing the database on a Beowulf, these applications will be able to combine the data retrieval and processing operations, performing accelerated parallel data processing to satisfy client requests. If these specialized applications can demonstrate a high level of reliability when deployed on a Beowulf cluster, then more traditional transaction processing applications will likely follow. One day, all of your bank and credit card transactions may be processed by Beowulf clusters.

26.5 Beowulf in the 21st Century

The timing of thc emergence of Beowulf was not arbitrary. It hinged on the concurrent advances in hardware and software technologies that made low-cost high-end computing feasible for the first time. A year earlier, the opportunity simply did not exist. Critical to this emergence were the mass market 66 MHz Intel 80486 microprocessor, low-cost 10 Mbps Ethernet, beta-test version of the Linux operating system with source code, and PVM providing cross platform message passing parallel programming. Today's Beowulfs, while far more capable in every dimension, owe their heritage to this first generation of system technologies and those computational scientists who first applied them to real-world problems. As the horizon of the next decade, century, and millennium comes in to sharper focus, it is possible to project the emerging technologies that will enable and define the next generation of Beowulf-class computers. In this section, the future of Beowulf is briefly considered in terms of innovative enabling technologies and software requirements.

26.5.1 Processing Nodes

The performance gap between PC and workstation microprocessors has been closed, and the term, "desktop," is rapidly replacing those two, now archaic, terms. Clock rates between 333 MHz and 533 MHz are now commonplace with one or two floating point operations issued per cycle, putting one-time supercomputer performance in the hands of everyday workers. Processing nodes for future Beowulf systems will benefit from favorable trends along several dimensions: clock rate, density, and size. By the beginning of the 21st century, clock rates will have approached or slightly exceeded 1 GHz. Each processor will be capable of up to 4-way floating point instruction issue per cycle. And more than one processor (probably 2) will be incorporated on a single die or MCM, sharing secondary cache of many MBytes. The combination of these factors will be processing nodes capable of 10 GFLOPS peak performance before 2004 for Beowulf-class computing.

26.5.2 Storage

Memory capacities of 128 MBytes are typical today with 512 MBytes possible in some more expensive configurations. By the beginning of the next century, 1 GByte memory modules will be available in mass market systems with system capacities of 4 GBytes or more frequently found. Secondary storage has become so inexpensive that new systems are often provided with an installed capacity of 10 GBytes or more. The most dramatic trend in disk storage is in its size, driven by the needs of laptop and handheld computing systems. Disks will migrate from separate units to those mounted directly on motherboards, reducing the size and costs of systems.

26.5.3 System Area Networks

The most significant factors limiting generality and usability of Beowulf-class computers today are the network technology's bandwidth and latency. Sustained throughput of 10 MBytes per second with latency of approximately 100 microseconds is observed using low-cost Fast Ethernet technology. While this is sufficient for many applications, it imposes a serious barrier to effective execution of some problems. Both Myrinet and Gigabit Ethernet offer peak throughput of 1 Gbps, but at costs comparable to the rest of the system. These prices are likely to drop significantly over the next three years to levels commensurate with the economics of Beowulf-class systems.

The total latency experienced by an application is at least as much a consequence of the intervening software as of the hardware technology employed. VIA and other schemes for eliminating much of the overhead of communicating between program modules will reduce apparent latency to below 10 microseconds by the turn of the century. The next generation PCI bus will also improve bandwidth performance between the system and the network. Laboratory experiments are demonstrating that wire off-chip bandwidths of 4 Gbps or more may be feasible in the near future and made available as part of mass market systems.

Optical communications networks, driven by the needs and resources of the long-haul telecommunications industry, will provide 10 Gbps bandwidth per channel. Wave division multiplexing, allowing multiple colored signals to traverse a single fiber simultaneously, will support anywhere from 8 to 256 separate signals per channel. With optical communications, 100 Gbps fiber optics networks will be incorporated within Beowulfs within the first decade of the next century.

26.5.4 The $1M TFLOPS Beowulf

The first sustained rates of 1 TeraFLOPS are being reported on the world's fastest computers costing on the order of 100 million dollars. Today a Beowulf-class computer employing a thousand processors and capable of 1 TeraFLOPS peak performance can be assembled for approximately 3 million dollars. By 2001, the 1-million-dollar TeraFLOPS Beowulf should be possible. Price-performance of less than $10 per sustained MFLOPS on favorable but non-trivial problems is being reported on Beowulf-class computers. By 2004, Beowulf systems will be reporting sustained price-performance of $1 per MFLOPS or better, at least for some applications, thus providing a real TFLOPS for a million dollars.

The importance of this is far greater than simply the scale or price of the systems. It is the wealth of applications that will become feasible because of the dramatic shift in price. The medical field, design optimization, air traffic control, and real time computer visualization will all be enabled through the wide availability of TFLOPS scale Beowulfs. Few, if any, industries will go unaffected by this powerful new tool in data processing.

26.5.5 The Software Barrier

The earliest Beowulf-class systems were employed as single-user systems dedicated to one application at a time, usually in a scientific/engineering computing environment. But the future of Beowulf will be severely limited if it is constrained to this tiny niche. At the same time, the structure of the nodes that will make possible $1/MFLOPS price-performance and the million dollar TeraFLOPS Beowulf will also complicate applications programming. The nodes themselves will be hierarchical systems with between 2 and 8 processors per symmetric multiprocessor (SMP). To add to the challenge will be the increasingly heterogeneous nature of the Beowulf systems. The need to enhance Beowulf system usability while incorporating more complicated node structures will call for a new generation of software technology to manage Beowulf resources and facilitate system programming.

Adequate system management may depend on the virtualization of all its resources. This will separate the user application processes from the physical nodes upon which the tasks are executed. The result is a system that dynamically adapts to workload demand, and applications that can be performed on a wide range of system configurations trading time for space. Therefore, a new class of workload scheduler will be required, developed, and incorporated in most Beowulf systems. It will support multiple jobs simultaneously, allocating resources on a to-be-defined priority basis. It will also distribute the parallel tasks of a given job across the allocated resources for performance through parallel execution. Such schedulers are not widely available on Beowulfs now and will be essential in the future. They will incorporate advanced checkpoint and restarting capabilities for greater reliability and job swapping in the presence of higher priority workloads. Compilers to use the more complicated structures of the SMP nodes will be required as well to exploit thread level parallelism across the local shared memory processors. The software used on these systems will have to be generally available and achieve the status of de facto standard for portability of codes among Beowulf-class systems.

26.5.6 Not the Final Word

It is impossible to predict what computing technologies will be developed in the future and how they will change parallel computing. It is reasonable, however, to expect, whatever the fundamental unit of program execution is, that you will always be able to connect many of these units with a network and perform some type of clustered computing. Whether the commodity units are 8 processor SMPs, exotic nano-computers, or biological computers, one would think that the Beowulf model could be applied, and that in some sense, Beowulfs are forever. But we should do our best not to convince ourselves that clustered computing is the final word in parallel computing. Clustered computing and the Beowulf model were solutions to an immediate problem. If we start to think of them as answers to all of our problems, we will inadvertently stifle the advancement of the field by not looking for new solutions and approaches to parallel computer architecture. It might help to remember that at the end of that Dark Ages legend, Beowulf was ultimately killed in his old age by a dragon.

Acknowledgments

We thank John Salmon, a senior scientist and our colleague at the Center for Advanced Computing Research, for providing the N-body data shown in Figure 26.2. We also extend our appreciation and thanks to the entire Beowulf user community for its enthusiastic adoption and evolution of the Beowulf model beyond its original scope.

26.6 Bibliography

[1] *Byte Magazine*, vol. 19(12), December 1994.

[2] N. J. Boden, D. Cohen, et al. Myrinet – A Gigabit-per-Second Local-Area Network. *IEEE Micro*, vol. 15(1), pages. 29-36, February 1995.

[3] J. Salmon, G. Winckelmans, and M. Warren. Fast Parallel Treecodes for Gravitational and Dynamical N-Body Problems. *International Journal on Supercomputer Applications*, vol. 8(2), 1994.

[4] J. Salmon, C. Stein, and T. Sterling. Scaling of Beowulf-Class Distributed Systems. *Proceedings of Supercomputing98*, November 1998.

[5] T. Sterling, D. Becker, D. F. Savarese, et al. BEOWULF: A Parallel Workstation for Scientific Computation. *Proceedings of the International Conference on Parallel Processing*, 1995.

[6] T. Sterling, J. Salmon, D. Becker, and D. F. Savarese. *How To Build a Beowulf*. MIT Press, March 1999.

Chapter 27

RWC PC Cluster II and SCore Cluster System Software

YUTAKA ISHIKAWA, ATSUSHI HORI, HIROSHI TEZUKA, FRANCIS O'CARROLL, SHINJI SUMIMOTO, HIROSHI HARADA, AND TOSHIYUKI TAKAHASHI

Parallel and Distributed System Software Laboratory
Real World Computing Partnership, Japan

Email: {*ishikawa, hori, tezuka, ocarroll, s-sumi, h-harada, tosiyuki*}*@rwcp.or.jp*

27.1 Introduction

Many high performance clustering research projects, using commodity hardware with high-speed networks, have been widely investigated. Our distinguished approach to realizing such a cluster system is to design and develop (1) a compact and well-maintainable PC-based cluster and (2) a total system software architecture on top of a commodity operating system without any kernel modifications.

The RWC PC Cluster II is the second generation of our PC cluster, which consists of 128 Intel Pentium Pro 200 MHz microprocessors connected by a Myricom Myrinet giga-bit network. To make the system compact and well-maintainable, we employ the PICMG PCI-ISA passive backplane standard[8]. The SCore system is our cluster system software running on top of several Unix kernels, i.e., Linux, NetBSD, and Sun OS. Key software technologies realized in the SCore are:

- User-level zero-copy message transfer as well as message passing mechanisms realized using a high performance low-level communication library called PM,
- A high performance MPI implementation called MPICH-PM that integrates both zero-copy message transfer and message passing facilities in order to maximize performance,
- A multi-user environment using gang scheduling without degrading the communication performance realized by an operating system daemon called SCore-D, and

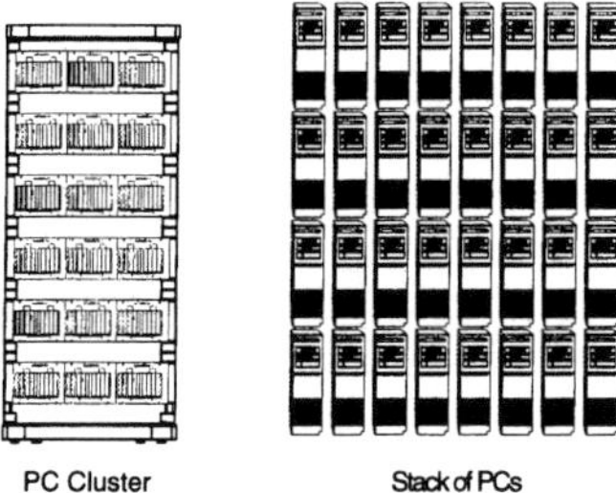

Figure 27.1 PC cluster and a stack of PCs.

- Parallel description primitives called Multi-Thread Template Library (MTTL) realized by C++ template features to describe a parallel system software easily.

We achieve 15 μ second round trip communication latency and 113 MB/sec bandwidth on the RWC PC Cluster II. The gang scheduler overhead is less than 4% of the total application execution time.

27.2 Building a Compact PC Cluster Using Commodity Hardware

27.2.1 Overview

The easiest way to build a PC cluster is to stack off-the-shelf PCs into a rack and connect them. This method makes possible a cheap parallel machine composed of commodity hardware components. However, it has some disadvantages, for instance, it requires a lot of space and suffers from maintenance problems.

The RWC PC Cluster II was designed to make the system compact and easily maintainable, unlike the example above. We use the PCI-ISA passive backplane standard specified by the PICMG [1] (PCI Industrial Computer Manufacturers Group).

The PCI-ISA passive backplane does not include any active devices which are normally located on a motherboard in a PC. Instead, a PICMG processor board contains all active devices. The advantages of the passive backplane are, (1) it is more maintainable than a motherboard system and has a much lower mean time to repair, and (2) it is easy to upgrade to the latest processor technology. Those advantages are very useful in constructing a cluster of PCs. Figure 27.1 depicts comparison with our system and a stack of PCs.

As shown in Figure 27.2, each node consists of a PICMG Pentium Pro 200 MHz processor card, a local disk, a 100 Base-T network card, and a Myrinet[7] giga-bit network card. Those cards are plugged into the PCI-ISA passive backplane. Two

[1]PICMG is a consortium of over 350 industrial computer product vendors who collaboratively develop specifications for PCI-based systems and boards for use in industrial and telecommunications computing applications[8].

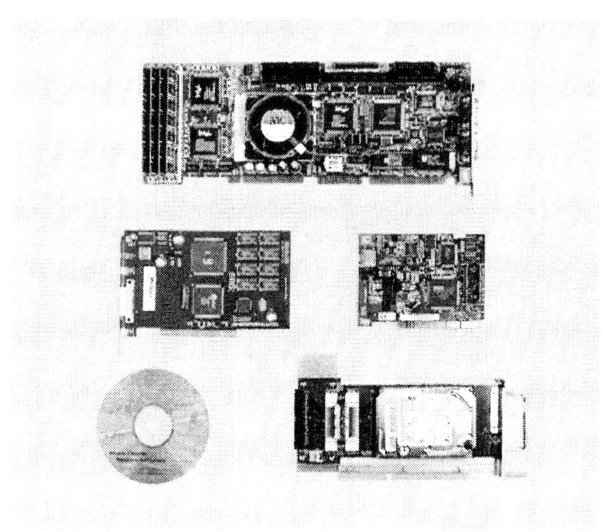

Figure 27.2 Components of each node.

Figure 27.3 The RWC PC Cluster II.

Table 27.1 RWC PC Cluster II Specification

Number of Processors	128
Processor	Pentium Pro
Clock [MHz]	200
Cache [KB]	512
Memory [MB]	256
I/O Bus	PCI
Local Disk	4GB IDE
Network	Myrinet

nodes are packed into one module. As shown in Figure 27.3, the RWC PC Cluster II has four cabinets, each of which contains 16 modules and one monitor PC. The 32 processor's serial lines are connected to one monitor PC. Thus, the system has 128 Intel Pentium Pro processors. In addition to 128 processors and two monitor PCs, some server PCs are also installed to perform a file system function and provide other services. Table 27.1 summarizes the system specifications.

In the rest of this chapter, we describe the design of the RWC PC Cluster II.

27.2.2 Networks

The RWC PC Cluster II has three types of networks: serial, Ethernet, and a high-speed network. The serial line is used for system maintenance. Thirty-two PCs' serial lines are connected with a monitor PC so that kernel messages can be monitored. The monitor PC is never involved with any user computation.

We had been seeking a good high-speed network. In Table 27.2, some available PCI compatible network interface cards are compared. We paid attention not only to bandwidth, but also to packet loss. If network hardware does not guarantee reliable transmission, an extra software overhead is added, which results in larger latency and lower bandwidth.

We found that Myrinet was the best network for inter-processor communication in terms of its availability and openness. By openness, we mean that the Myrinet hardware specification and firmware developer's kit are freely obtained so that we can develop our own network protocol, using the Myrinet network interface card. Thus, we implemented the PM high performance low-level communication library using the Myrinet network.

Figure 27.4 is a connection diagram of the RWC PC Cluster II. Two types of Myrinet switches are used to connect 128 Processors and server PCs: One, called M2M-OCT-SW8, is 16 x 16 ports and the other, called M2FM-SW8, is an eight-port switch. Eight M2M-OCT-SW8 switches connect 128 processors using Myrinet SAN cables. The topology follows that of the Myrinet White Paper[7]. Four M2FM-SW switches connect those processors with the server PCs.

Table 27.2 Comparison of Various Networks

Network	Bandwidth (Mbps)	Reliability
FastEthernet	100 Mbps	unreliable
ATM	155 Mbps	unreliable
Myrinet	1280 Mbps	reliable

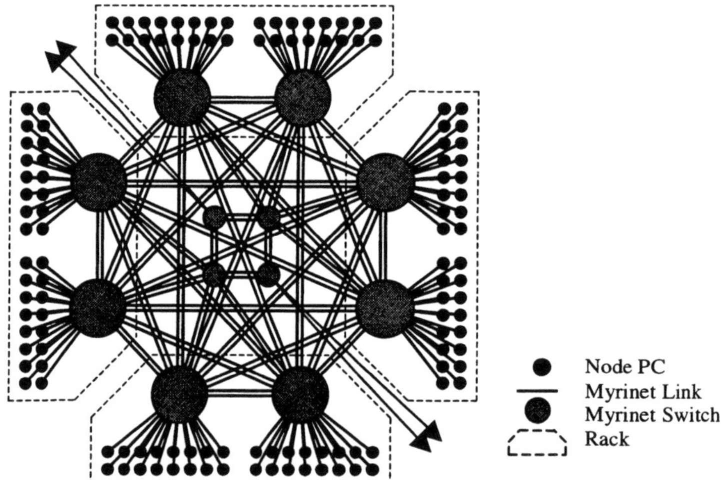

Figure 27.4 Network in PC cluster.

27.2.3 Processor Card

We chose the PICMG PCI/ISA processor board, which is electronically identical to the PC/AT. The PICMG PCI/ISA processor board and I/O cards mount on the PICMG PCI/ISA passive backplane, allowing a more compact PC to be built. This is preferable to the standard PC motherboard, which is larger than the PICMG processor board. We also looked at single board computers, which are much smaller than the PICMG processor card. Most, however, are neither fully compatible with the PC/AT, nor have the PCI I/O bus.

The other possible alternative is the CompactPCI, which is another standard from PICMG. It has some advantages over the PICMG PCI/ISA standard, which include smaller size and higher reliability. At the time we made our choice, however, the CompactPCI was not fully matured, but may be a strong alternative to PC clusters now.

The other advantage of using the PICMG standard is its availability from many manufacturers all over the world. Many Pentium and Pentium Pro boards are already available. DEC has Alpha boards, and some manufacturers offer dual Pentium and dual Pentium Pro boards. With this availability, we are able to choose a processor board that meets any specific requirement.

The PICMG standard also has some disadvantages: (1) The processor card is more expensive, and (2) its technology is usually two or three months behind off-the-shelf PC boards. Nevertheless, we chose the PICMG standard.

27.2.4 Chassis Design

Production cycles of processor boards, Myrinet and other peripheral cards are fast, so we cannot expect that the same board or card will be available a year from now. Also, because our PC cluster is used for research, the hardware configuration will change more often than a system in normal use. Therefore, maintainability is very important.

To make access easier, we designed an aluminum box, called a module, which contains two PICMG backplanes, each of which can hold one processor board, two ISA, and two PCI slots. The module can also hold a +5V power supply and a cooling fan (Figure 27.5). This configuration puts two PCs in a module, and each can operate and be tested as a stand-alone unit. Although it would have been possible to use a central power supply system to feed all PCs, power cables thick enough to conduct hundreds of Amperes would have made assembly difficult.

The rack for the PC cluster holds 18 modules, 3 modules to a row, 6 rows to the rack. A monitor PC and circuit breakers are located on two modules. The monitor PC on each rack includes four 8-serial line ISA cards to connect 32 processors.

Various cables (Myrinet, Ethernet, serial and power) are harnessed on the rack frame. This modular design makes the PC cluster easy to maintain. When a PC fails, the cluster can be restored merely by replacing the module. Removing a module is as simple as disconnecting the cables and pulling out the module.

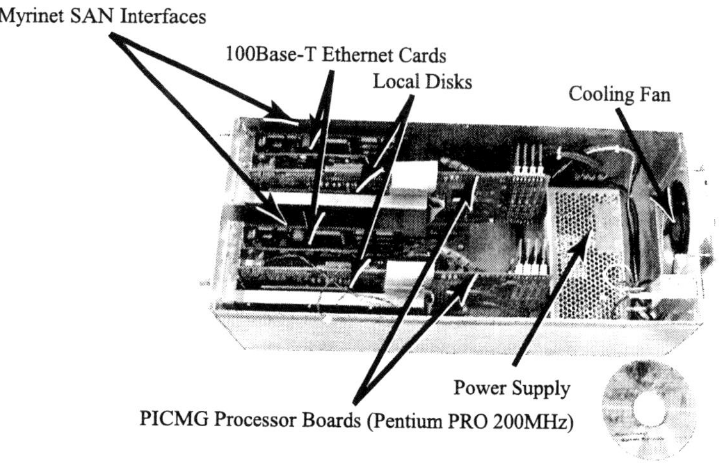

Figure 27.5 A PC cluster module.

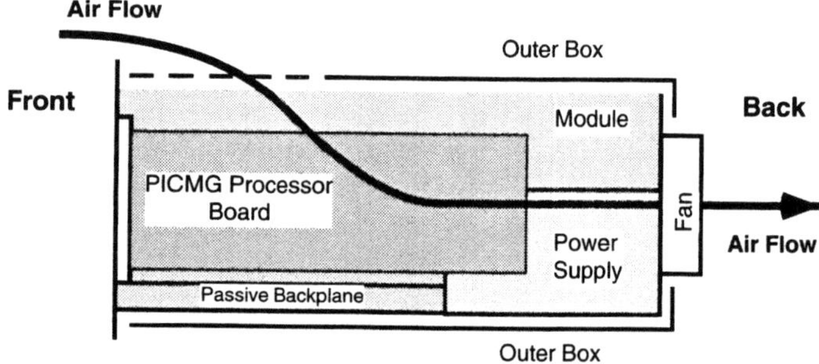

Figure 27.6 Cooling air flow (side view).

27.2.5 Cooling System

We designed an aluminum outer box to hold three modules. The height of the outer box is 4U (7 inches). A 1 U (1.75 inches) space is left between any two boxes. There are a number of open slots on the ceiling panel of the box. Since the top of a module box is open, a cooling fan on the back pulls incoming air from the slots (Figure 27.6). This cooling system works well. The frontal side of the space is used for air intake and cabling, and the back side allows space for a Myrinet switch and a Fast Ethernet hub. Placing Myrinet switches at each gap of the rows shortens the length of the Myrinet cables.

27.3 SCore Parallel Operating System Environment on Top of Unix

27.3.1 Software Overview

Our software environment, called the SCore Cluster System Software, is realized on top of Unix kernels including Linux and NetBSD. As shown in Figure 27.7, it consists of a global operating system called SCore-D, a communication driver and handler called PM, MPI implemented on PM called MPICH-PM, and a multi-threaded programming language called MPC++.

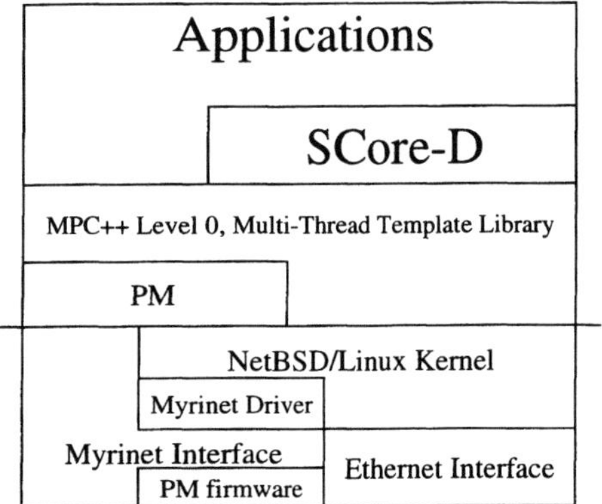

Figure 27.7 SCore architecture.

27.3.2 PM High Performance Communication Driver and Library

We have been designing and developing a high performance network driver called PM on a Myricom Myrinet network which has a dedicated processor consisting of DMA engines that can transfer data between the host memory and network. In order to eliminate the data copy between user and kernel memory spaces and to eliminate issuing operating system primitives, a user memory mapped communication facility has been realized[1]. In user memory mapped communication, the communication buffer area, handled by the network hardware, is mapped to the user virtual address space. The network hardware is controlled by the user program instead of by the operating system.

PM achieves not only high performance communication but also enables multi-user access in a time-sharing manner using gang-scheduling[5], [4], if the SCore-D is running with the PM. PM may be used without the SCore-D if the user does not need to have a multi-user environment.

In PM 1.0, the communication buffer area is reserved as a special virtual address area, whose physical area is never paged out, so that the network hardware can trigger DMA. This area is called the *pinned-down* area. PM 1.0 does not allow the user program to pin a user virtual memory area to physical memory because malicious user requests can exhaust physical memory. An application program will benefit from high performance communication if the program directly accesses the buffer area. However, an application program usually does not access the buffer directly. For example, a high-level communication library such as MPI may be implemented in such a way that a memory area specified in the user program must be copied to the PM buffer area. Though the PM 1.0 low-level communication library avoids data copy, the high-level communication library does not. Our experiments show that the MPI data transfer bandwidth is 50 MBytes/sec. while the PM data transfer bandwidth is 113 MBytes/sec. on our PC cluster.

We designed a zero copy message transfer mechanism incorporated with the pinned-down area in order to avoid memory copies between the user specified memory area and a communication buffer area. The API provides the pin-down and release operations for the application specified memory area and zero copy message transfer operations. Though the user is required to issue pin-down and release operations, pinned-down areas are controlled by the system. A pinned-down area is not freed until the total area pinned-down exceeds the maximum size. If the total size of pinned-down areas exceeds the maximum size, some pinned-down areas are freed in the LRU fashion. Thus we call it the *pin-down cache*. The proposed mechanisms have been implemented in PM 1.2. PM 1.2 is realized by a user-level library, a kernel driver, and a communication handler sitting on the Myrinet interface. No operating system kernel modifications have been done to implement the system.

27.3.3 MPI on PM

When a message passing library such as MPI is implemented on top of a lower level communication library that supports the zero copy message transfer primitive, the message passing library must handle pinned-down memory area, which is a restricted quantity resource under a paging memory system. Allocation of pinned-down memory by multiple simultaneous requests for sending and receiving without any control can cause deadlock. MPICH-PM, based on the MPICH implementation, overcomes this issue and achieves good performance[3]. An overview of our design to avoid deadlock due to starvation of the pin-down area is: (1) separate control of send/receive pin-down memory areas to ensure that at least one send and receive may be processed concurrently, and (2) when the message area can not be pinned down to the physical area, the request is postponed.

Using the PM zero copy message transfer primitive, the sender must know the address of both user buffers before data can be sent. This implies that both the send and receive must have first been posted, and that the receiver can inform the sender of the address of its buffer. This negotiation protocol is implemented using the PM message passing primitives. Though this overhead is added, long message bandwidth improves greatly due to the much higher bandwidth of the remote memory write primitive. On the other hand, small message bandwidth is worse than using the PM message passing primitives. Thus, two implementation mechanisms must be utilized.

In the current implementation on the RWC PC Cluster II, a message of less than 8 Kbytes uses the message passing protocol while a message greater than 8 Kbytes uses the zero copy protocol determined by our MPI experimentation.

27.3.4 SCore-D Parallel Operating System

First, let us define a set of processes, which are execution entities derived from an SPMD program, a parallel process. Each process in a parallel process is called an element process of the parallel process.

The SCore-D global operating system is implemented as a parallel process on top of a Unix operating system without any kernel modification. All user parallel processes are created by the SCore-D. Issuing the SIGSTOP and SIGCONT signal kernel primitive to stop/resume a process, the user parallel processes are scheduled by the SCore-D. To utilize processor resources and to enable an interactive programming environment, user parallel processes are multiplexed in the processors' space and time domains simultaneously. Parallel processes are gang-scheduled when multiplexed in the time domain.

To realize gang scheduling under a communication layer which accesses the network hardware directly, the network hardware status and messages in-flight on the network must be saved and restored when switching to another parallel process. This mechanism is called *network preemption.* The network preemption technique has been developed co-designing PM and SCore-D.

27.3.5 MPC++ Multi-Thread Template Library

MPC++ Version 2 is designed in two levels: level 0 and level 1. Level 0, called Multi-Thread Template Library (MTTL), specifies parallel description primitives, realized by the C++ template feature without any language extensions, that define the MPC++ basic parallel execution model[10]. The MTTL contains (1) `invoke` and `ainvoke` function templates for synchronous and asynchronous local/remote thread invocation, (2) `Sync` class template for synchronization and communication among threads, (3) `GlobalPtr` class template for pointer to remote memory, (4) `Reduction` class template for reduction, (5) `Barrier` class for barrier synchronization, and (6) `yield` function to suspend the thread execution and yield another thread execution.

The SCore-D is written in MTTL. Communication among element processes of the SCore-D parallel process is implemented using the synchronous and asynchronous thread invocation. This reduces the protocol design and implementation, e.g., construction of a message header, marshaling/unmarshaling parameters, and dispatching. A control structure is distributed over processors. Pointers to the structure are implemented using the `GlobalPtr` class.

Level 1 specifies the MPC++ meta-level architecture which enables library designers to provide an optimizer specific to their class/template library in the library header file[6]. The library user may use such a high performance library by including the header file. The meta-level architecture also enables a language designer to realize higher parallel/distributed constructs, such as data parallel statements and distributed active objects[9].

27.4 Performance Evaluation

27.4.1 PM Basic Performance

As shown in Figure 27.8, the maximum bandwidth is 113.5 MBytes/sec. for 256 KBytes in the case of 100% pin-down cache hit ratio. In the case where the pin-down cache is always miss, the maximum bandwidth is still 78.7 MBytes/sec., which is higher than the bandwidth of data transfer with data copy, i.e., using the PM message buffer. PM also achieves a low latency, 7.5 μ second one-way latency.

27.4.2 MPI Basic Performance

Figure 27.9 shows the MPICH-PM basic performance. The performance results show that 13.16 μ second latency and 104 MBytes/sec. maximum bandwidth is achieved.

27.4.3 NAS Parallel Benchmarks Result

Figure 27.10 shows a performance comparison with other machines using NAS parallel benchmark programs. The EP benchmark program reflects the floating point performance. Although the EP shows that the floating point performance is 2.5 to 4.5 times slower than UCB NOW and Cray T3E-900, the performance of other benchmark programs is about half of those machines. The notable result is that our cluster achieves better performance than other machines in the IS (integer sort) pro-

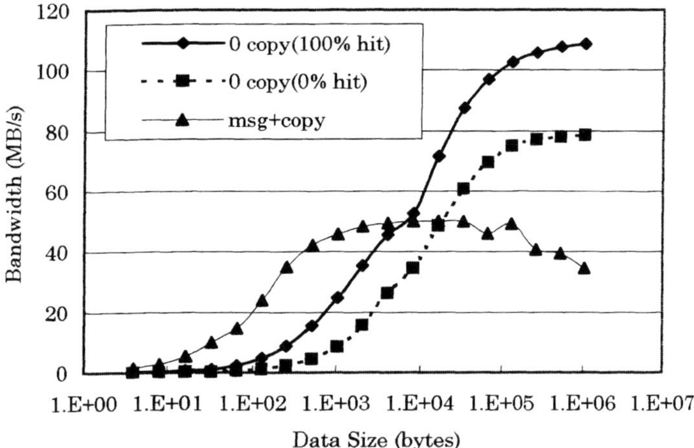

Figure 27.8 PM data bandwidth.

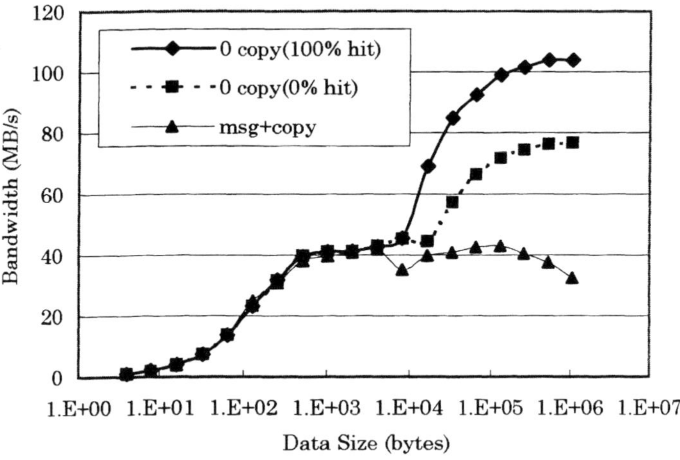

Figure 27.9 MPICH-PM bandwidth.

gram, which is a communication intensive program. According to this benchmark program, we conclude that our software environment supports a better communication environment than other commercial machines.

For more results, visit our Web page: http://www.rwcp.or.jp/lab/pdslab/

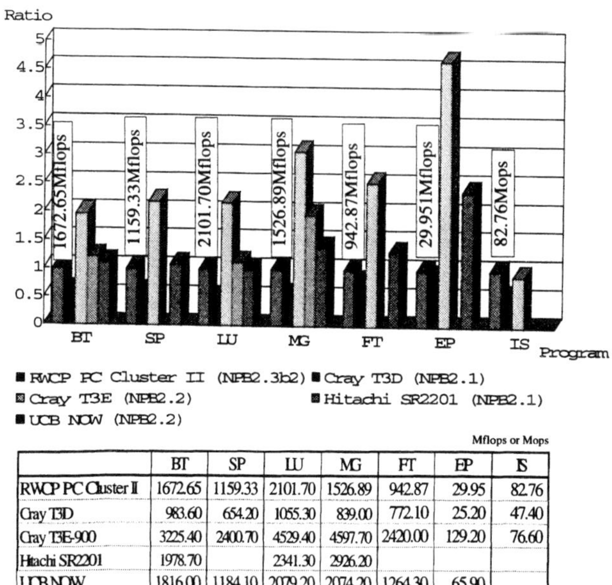

Mflops or Mops

	BT	SP	LU	MG	FT	EP	IS
RWCP PC Cluster II	1672.65	1159.33	2101.70	1526.89	942.87	29.95	82.76
Cray T3D	983.60	654.20	1055.30	839.00	772.10	25.20	47.40
Cray T3E-900	3225.40	2400.70	4529.40	4597.70	2420.00	129.20	76.60
Hitachi SR2201	1978.70		2341.30	2926.20			
UCB NOW	1816.00	1184.10	2079.20	2074.20	1264.30	65.90	

Figure 27.10 NAS parallel benchmarks result(64 nodes, class A).

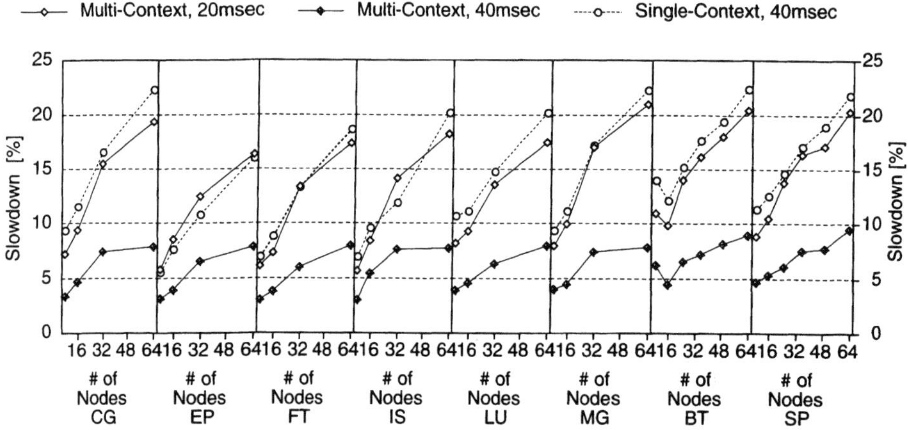

Figure 27.11 Gang scheduling overhead.

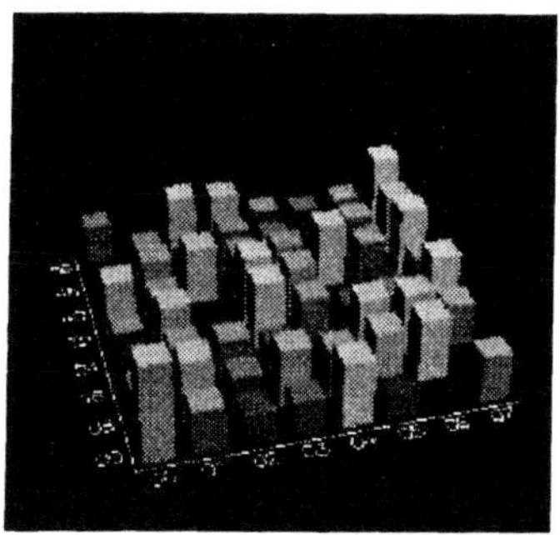

Figure 27.12 Load Monitor

27.4.4 SCore-D Gang Scheduling Overhead

The overhead of the gang scheduler was measured. NAS parallel benchmark programs were used for the evaluation. The message flushing time and network preemption time depends on the communication patterns of the application programs. We found that the time of saving and restoring network context occupies more than two-thirds of the gang scheduling overhead on applications with 64 processors. Evaluation shows that the slowdown of user program execution due to the gang scheduling is less than 9% when the time slice is 100 milliseconds.

Basically, saving and restoring network context is just copying between the network context save area on the host machine and memory on the network interface card. To reduce this overhead, we have designed and implemented the multi-context mechanism on the network interface card so that contexts are kept on the network interface card. Figure 27.11 shows the effects of the multi-context mechanism. Introducing the multi-context mechanism, the gang scheduling overhead becomes less than 4% of the total application execution time in the case of a 100-millisecond time slice.

It should be noted that network preemption and the gang scheduler enable detection of a global state of a parallel process by investigating a process on each processor and network context at the context switch time. An application using this feature is the parallel process load monitor shown in Figure 27.12.

27.5 Concluding Remarks

We have described our unique approach to building a high performance cluster of PCs. The hardware was built using the PICMG PCI-ISA passive backplane standard to realize a compact and easily maintained PC-based cluster. To achieve a high performance multi-user environment on the cluster, we have designed and implemented the SCore system software realized on top of Unix kernels. The system includes the PM low-level communication library, the MPICH-PM, MPI implementation on top of PM, the SCore-D global operating system, and the Multi-Thread Template Library. We achieve 15 μ second round trip communication latency and 113 MBytes/sec. bandwidth on the RWC PC Cluster II. The gang scheduling overhead is less than 4% of the total application execution time.

We are further developing cluster system technologies, including a high performance communication facility using a Gigabit Ethernet, a software distributed shared memory system on top of PM, a cluster of SMPs, and a heterogeneous cluster environment. The SCore System is currently available from the following URL: http://www.rwcp.or.jp/lab/pdslab/dist/

27.6 Bibliography

[1] H. Tezuka, A. Hori, Y. Ishikawa, and M. Sato. PM: An Operating System Coordinated High Performance Communication Library. *High Performance Computing and Networking*, vol. 1225, LNCS, Springer-Verlag, April 1997.

[2] H. Tezuka, F. O'Carroll, A. Hori, and Y. Ishikawa. Pin-Down Cache: A Virtual Memory Management Technique for Zero-Copy Communication. *Proceedings of the First Merged IPPS/SPDP*, pages 308 – 314, April 1998.

[3] F. O'Carroll, H. Tezuka, A. Hori, and Y. Ishikawa. The Design and Implementation of Zero Copy MPI Using Commodity Hardware with a High Performance Network. In *Proceedings of ACM SIGARCH ICS'98*, pages 243–250, July 1998.

[4] A. Hori, H. Tezuka, and Y. Ishikawa. Highly Efficient Gang Scheduling Implementation. *SC'98*, November 1998.

[5] A. Hori, H. Tezuka, F. O'Carroll, and Y. Ishikawa. Overhead Analysis of Preemptive Gang Scheduling. In *Proceedings of IPPS'98 Workshop on Job Scheduling Strategies for Parallel Processing*, pages 217 – 230, April 1998.

[6] T. Takahashi, Y. Ishikawa, M. Sato, and A. Yonezawa. Class Specific Optimization Environment Using Compile-Time Metalevel Architecture. In *Lecture Notes in Computer Science*, vol. 1343, Springer-Verlag, December 1997.

[7] N. J. Boden, D. Cohen, R. E. Felderman, A. E. Kulawik, C. L. Seitz, J N. Seizovic and Wen-King Su. Myrinet – A Gigabit-per-Second Local-Area Network. In *IEEE MICRO*, vol. 15(1), pages 29–36, February 1995.

[8] PCI Industrial Computer Manufactures Group. http://www.picmg.com/

[9] Y. Ishikawa, A. Hori, M. Sato, M. Matsuda, J. Nolte, H. Tezuka, H. Konaka, M. Maeda, and K. Kubota. Design and Implementation of Metalevel Architecture in C++ – MPC++ Approach –. *Reflection '96*, pages 141–154, 1996.

[10] Y. Ishikawa. Multi Thread Template Library – MPC++ Version 2.0 Level 0 Document –. *RWC Technical Report, TR–96012*, 1996. http://www.rwcp.or.jp/lab/pdslab/mpc++/mpc++.html

Chapter 28

COMPaS: A Pentium Pro PC-Based SMP Cluster

YOSHIO TANAKA, MOTOHIKO MATSUDA, KAZUTO KUBOTA AND MITSUHISA SATO

Parallel and Distributed System Performance Tsukuba Laboratory
Real World Computing Partnership
Ibaraki, Japan

Email: {*yoshio, matu, kazuto, msato*}*@trc.rwcp.or.jp*

28.1 COMPaS: A Pentium Pro PC-Based SMP Cluster

SMPs are becoming popular, both as compute servers and as platforms for high performance parallel computing. SMPs provide parallel computing environment on a single system. Inter-processor communications are done by writing/reading to/from shared memory, and no explicit message sending/receiving procedure is necessary. Furthermore, communication through shared memory may provide higher bandwidth than through network cables such as Ethernet and Myrinet[6]. Since each processor on an SMP node has its own cache memory and cache-bus bandwidth is considerably higher than memory-bus bandwidth, SMPs have the potential of high performance parallel systems for parallel computing.

We have built a cluster of SMPs, COMPaS (Cluster Of Multiprocessor Systems)[10], [11]. Figure 28.1 illustrates the configuration of COMPaS. COMPaS consists of eight quad-processor Pentium Pro PC servers (Toshiba GS700, 450GX chip-set, 200MHz, 16KB L1 cache, 512KB L2 cache, 384MB Main Memory) connected by both Myrinet high-speed network and 100Base-T Ethernet.

The operating system on each node is Solaris 2.5.1. Solaris provides multi-threaded programming environment for shared memory parallel systems. For communications between nodes, Message Passing Interface(MPICH 1.1.0 for tcp/ip) is available for 100Base-T Ethernet. The combination of Ethernet and MPICH is a standard programming environment for cluster systems. For inter-node communications through Myrinet, we have designed and implemented a remote-memory

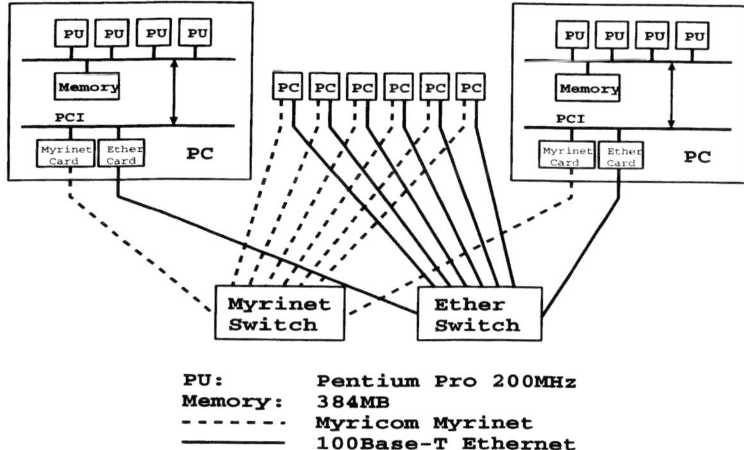

Figure 28.1 Configuration of COMPaS.

based communication layer, NICAM (Network Interface Communication layer using Active Messages). NICAM provides considerably higher performance than MPICH on 100Base-T Ethernet. The details of NICAM is described in Section 28.2.3.

An SMP cluster may be a good choice for building cluster systems, but there are many unknown programming factors and performance characteristics. This chapter describes the following topics:

- Overview of COMPaS.
- Remote memory based inter-node communication layer for COMPaS.
- Programming schemes for SMP clusters.
- Performance characteristics of COMPaS.
- Guidelines for building Pentium Pro PC-Based SMP clusters.

28.2 Building PC-Based SMP Cluster

This section describes the basic performance of COMPaS and overview of NICAM.

28.2.1 Pentium Pro PC-Based SMP Node

Memory-Bus Bandwidth

Table 28.1 shows the memory-bus bandwidth for memory read, memory write, memory copy, and *memcpy* when multiple threads execute the operations simultaneously.

Note: The total bandwidth of all threads does not depend on the number of threads, i.e., the memory-bus bandwidth per thread is limited by the total bandwidth.

Table 28.1 Memory-Bus Bandwidth

threads	read(MB/s)	write(MB/s)	copy(MB/s)	*memcpy*(MB/s)
1	360.0	91.1	66.5	85.6
2	258.2	106.6	70.6	88.9
3	251.7	106.6	70.1	87.7
4	250.3	99.7	70.7	88.3

Synchronization Time Between Threads

Table 28.2 shows the synchronization time between threads. Figure 28.2 shows our barrier synchronization algorithm.

Table 28.2 Synchronization Time Between Threads

Number of Threads	2	3	4
Synchronization Time (μsec)	1.222	1.761	1.960

```
procedure barrier(my_id, num_threads)
  begin
    if my_id = 0 then
      for i := 1 to num_threads do
        while barrier_slot[i] ≠ 1
        end
      end
      wakeup_flag := 1
    else
      barrier_slot[my_id] := 1;
      while wakeup_flag ≠ 1
      end
    end
  end;
```

Figure 28.2 Barrier synchronization algorithm.

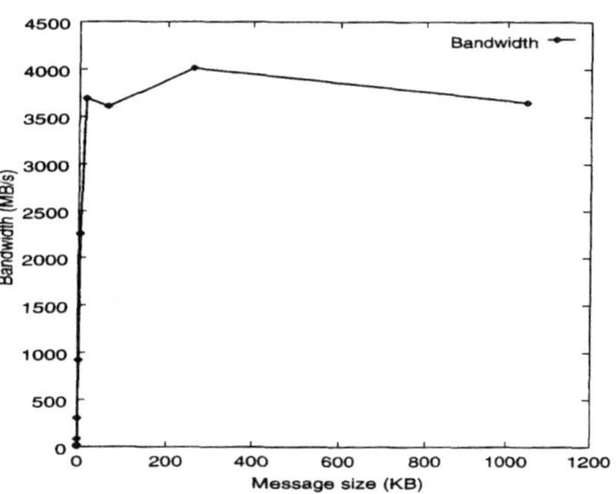

Figure 28.3 Bandwidth of MPICH.

Our algorithm uses a spin lock, and does not use any mutex or condition variables provided by the operating system. Our algorithm provides very fast barrier synchronization, and takes less than 2 microseconds for four threads. The synchronization using Solaris operating system mutex variables takes about 180 microseconds for four threads.

28.2.2 Inter-Node Communication on 100Base-T Ethernet

Figure 28.3 shows the bandwidth of inter-node communication on MPICH. The maximum bandwidth is approximately 4MB/sec., which is considerably lower than memory-bus bandwidth and may be a bottleneck when running applications on COMPaS.

28.2.3 NICAM: User-Level Communication Layer of Myrinet for SMP Cluster

For communication between nodes, we consider remote memory operations to be more suitable than message passing on SMP clusters, because message passing suffers from the handling of incoming messages. Message passing operations need mutual exclusions on buffers and message copying burdens the limited bus bandwidth. To overcome these problems, we designed and implemented a user-level communication layer for Myrinet, NICAM. NICAM provides high-bandwidth and low-overhead remote memory transfers and synchronization primitives.

NICAM Design

From the observation of the bus bandwidth performance, reduction of overhead is important. The term, "overhead," taken from the LogP model [7], means the involvement of processor in data transfer. Remote memory operations are preferable to message passing for their lower overhead. Generally, message passing incurs overhead of coordination between processors in an SMP node as well as a need for flow-control of messages. The overhead includes management of message buffers and mutual exclusion of accesses to the NI. Moreover, message passing sometimes needs copying of messages, which sacrifices the bandwidth of memory which is shared and limited. So we designed a user-level communication layer based on remote memory operations for Myrinet.

A communication system based on remote memory operations requires synchronization primitives, because each node writes remote memory asynchronously. This is contrasted to message passing, where sender and receiver synchronize implicitly when they send/receive messages.

NICAM utilizes the micro-processor equipped on the NI of the Myrinet host interface to reduce overhead in implementing remote memory operations and synchronization primitives. Since all the operations are performed solely on the NI, they do not involve main processors at all and the overhead of main processors is reduced just to start the micro-processor on the NI. Also, all communications necessary to implement a barrier synchronization are performed between the NIs. While the barrier uses a multi-stage algorithm (which requires log(P) steps), there is no need to poll incoming messages by a main processor. This design makes barriers faster, in addition to reducing overhead. It is because it reduces the costly interaction between the main processor and the NI.

NICAM extensively uses the cache coherence mechanism for synchronization primitives. Events to the host processors are notified via a memory location. NICAM synchronization primitives assert a flag when a condition is met. Processors waiting for a memory location do not generate bus traffic at all on the cache coherent bus, since checking an event is done in the cache.

NICAM makes exclusive use of the NI and other resources for communication. This design is practically not a problem because our target environment is the single user and the single job. Our research objective is to investigate the utilization of the resources in an SMP cluster and is naturally a single job.

NICAM Primitives

Initialization
`nicam_init()`
Initialize NICAM environments.
`nicam_lock_memory(addr, range)`
Pin-downs a region of memory.

Simple data transfer
`nicam_bcopy(src_node, src_addr, dst_node, dst_addr, size)`
Invokes remote memory copy.
`nicam_sync(flag_addr)`
Know the completion of currently issued copies.

Data transfer combined with synchronization
`nicam_bcopy_notify(src_node, src_addr, dst_node, dst_addr, size, flag_addr, onoff)`
Remote memory copy operation combined with a point-to-point synchronization.
`nicam_set_counter(flag_addr, count)`
Specifies count and flag address used to signal completion of remote copying.
`nicam_bcopy_countup(src_node, src_addr, dst_node, dst_addr, size)`
Remote memory copy operation which provides a counted completion.

Barrier `nicam_barrier(flag_addr)` Barrier synchronization operation between nodes.
Broadcast `nicam_bcast(src_node, src_addr, dst_addr, size)` Broadcast operation.

Figure 28.4 Main operations of NICAM. `nicam_lock_memory` are used to pin down a region of memory. `nicam_bcopy` invokes remote memory copy. A variant with `notify` is a combined operation with a point-to-point synchronization. `nicam_sync` is used by the invoking node to know the completion of currently issued copies.

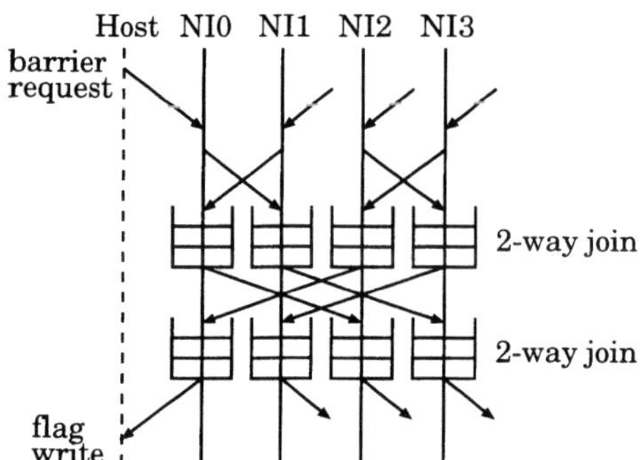

Figure 28.5 Steps of the multi-stage barrier performed between NIs. Each 2-way join has a small queue to accommodate multiply issued barrier.

Remote Memory Operations

Figure 28.4 lists the set of primitive operations currently supported in NICAM. Remote memory operations of NICAM have a similar interface as the local `bcopy` operation. It has additional arguments to specify source and destination nodes. If the source is specified as a node other than local node, it acts as remote read. The Active Messages mechanism forwards the request to the specified source node. `nicam_sync` is used by the invoking node to know the completion of currently issued copies. The region of memory may not be touched during data transfer, unless you are sure the data is corrupt.

A variant of copy operation `nicam_bcopy_notify` provides a primitive of data transfer combined with point-to-point synchronization. It notifies the destination node about completion of a copy by setting a flag. In some cases, implicit synchronization of message passing is desirable, where the data flow controls execution. The combination of data transfer with synchronization makes the grain size of computation finer than in a bulk synchronous model where the only synchronization is a barrier. We expect that the finer grain size increases the chance of overlapping of communication and computation.

Another variant of copy operation `nicam_bcopy_countup` provides a counted completion. Sometimes a synchronization point is known by the messages exchanged. For example, in all-to-all communication, the synchronization point is reached when the count becomes equal to the number of nodes involved. This avoids explicit barriers completely. `nicam_set_counter` specifies the count and the flag address used to signal completion.

Relaxed Barrier Operations

NICAM also provides a relaxed barrier as a primitive for synchronization. This barrier works as a fuzzy barrier because the completion is signaled by setting a flag in memory. In addition, this is relaxed to allow multiple barriers in concurrent progress. That is, barrier operation can be invoked multiple times before a completion of a previously issued barrier. This does not mean to perform a matching on the flag addresses, because it is not necessary in an SPMD operation environment.

Since the barrier is implemented using multi-stage Log(P) step algorithm, it is beneficial to avoid the involvement of the host processors. It would be worthless in relaxing barriers if the execution of barriers required polling of the host processors. Our implementation of the barrier runs solely on the NI and does not involve the host processors at all. Figure 28.5 shows how barriers are performed.

Implementation

NICAM runs Active Messages mechanism [3] on the micro-processor on the NI. That is, all the message handlers for incoming messages are executed on the NI. Since remote memory operations are singled-sided, Active Messages are suitable for implementing them. Requests for remote operations are exchanged between NIs, and they directly invoke DMA on a remote node without involving the processors in the host PC. Similarly, synchronization primitives are well-suited to Active Messages. Each stage of barrier performs a 2-way join and forwards a message to the next stage. This is straightforwardly implemented by handlers of Active Messages. Figure 28.5 shows how barriers are performed.

Also, Active Messages are used for local requests from main processors to the NI. The micro-processor on the NI polls requests from main processors as well as requests from remote nodes. This makes the implementation very simplified, because the local requests and remote requests are handled in the same way.

While Active Messages imposes some cost to the relatively slow micro-processor on the NI, it allows experiments of new primitives. Since the handlers of Active Messages are almost independent, extending NICAM by adding new handlers are relatively easy. The combined operation `nicam_bcopy_notify` is an outcome of such experiments.

For efficiency and simplicity of implementation, NICAM requires that all regions of memory accessed remotely should be pinned down in advance to remote memory operations. The pin-down operation protects the region of memory from the paging system in a virtual memory environment. It makes mapping from virtual address to physical address fixed and DMA using physical addresses safe. Active Messages in NICAM pass only virtual addresses between nodes. NICAM maintains its own copy of the address translation table in the memory of the NI. The Myrinet board has a large enough memory to hold the table for the entire physical memory in the current system. Some other systems take alternative approaches to use only the limited areas pinned down [9].

Handling of incoming requests of Active Messages is also very simple. NICAM does not utilize the interrupt capability of the Myrinet board, but uses polling to check requests. It is found that interruption has no gain in our system.

The Active Message packet consists of a tag, a handler address, packet length and 6 word of arguments (32bit word). The minimal packet size is 10 words (one word reserved). The packets for data transfer have extra data payload of the data size. Every packet has a CRC word in its tail.

Since the Myrinet links are highly reliable, error situations, such as CRC errors, are detected, but not corrected. In addition, dead lock condition does not exist in our system, because all messages are drained from the network and written into the memory.

Basic Performance

Figures 28.6 and 28.7 show the bandwidth (throughput) and the latency. The maximum bandwidth is about 105MB/s in copying over 64K bytes, and the $N_{\frac{1}{2}}$ is about a little below 2K bytes. The minimum latency for small messages is about 20.7μsec (one way).

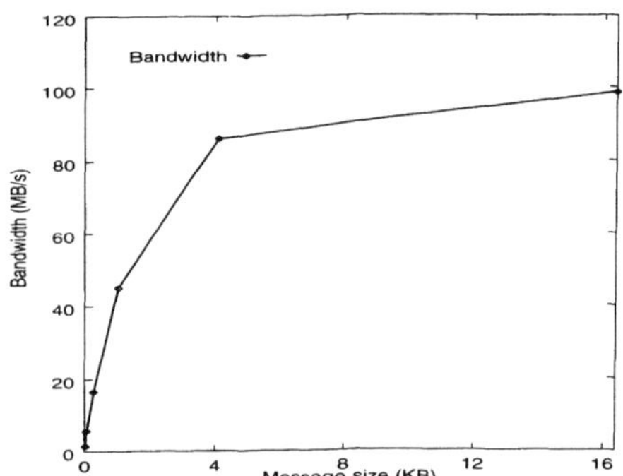

Figure 28.6 Bandwidth (throughput) of NICAM.

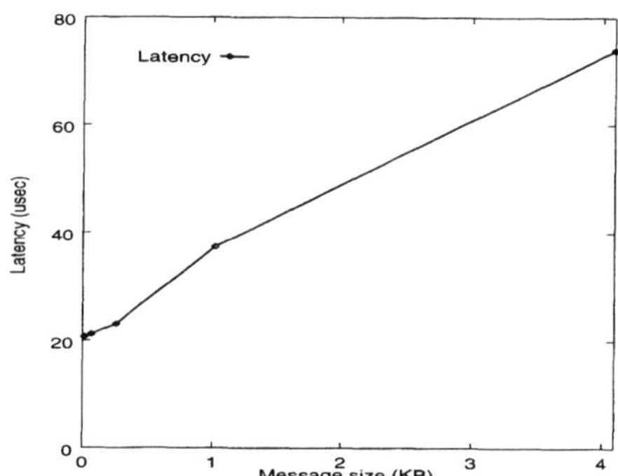

Figure 28.7 Latency of NICAM.

Figure 28.8 compares the synchronization time between nodes using NICAM and PM. PM is a very fast message passing library for Myrinet [8]. To compare the synchronization time, we implemented a barrier on top of PM. The barrier synchronization in PM is performed by main processors using point-to-point communication. It uses essentially the same algorithm as the one used in NICAM. Synchronization between two nodes by NICAM is slower than PM, because the cost of interaction is large between a main processor and the NI. However, since the communication time taken for each step on NICAM is about the half of the time of PM, NICAM gets faster than PM when the number of nodes increases.

The call overhead of `nicam_bcopy` is about 5.7μsec. The breakdown of the overhead is: (1) simple argument checks, (2) copy the handler address and arguments into SRAM on the NI, and (3) a word write to set a flag in SRAM to start processing of the handler. Serializing instructions (CPUID instruction) are inserted after writing SRAM to flush the write buffer. The serializing instruction has a large cost, but it is necessary because the write buffer of Pentium Pro reorders write requests.

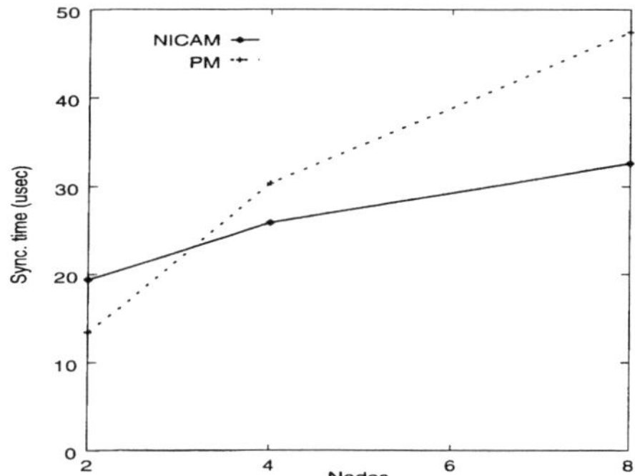

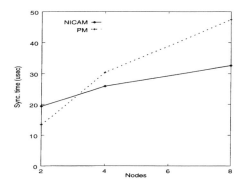

Figure 28.8 Barrier synchronization time between nodes using NICAM and a message passing library PM.

28.3 Programming for SMP Cluster

Architectures of parallel systems are broadly divided into two categories: shared memory and distributed memory. While multi-threaded programming is used for parallelism on shared memory systems, the typical programming model on distributed memory systems is message passing. A comparison of the programming and performance of each architecture reveals the following:

- Shared memory architecture

    1. Threads need to synchronize at some points explicitly because each thread reads and writes memory asynchronously.
    2. Mutual exclusion is necessary for access to critical regions.
    3. Communication overhead is very low.
    4. Communication performance is limited by the shared memory bus bandwidth.
    5. If the working set is small, each thread can efficiently process local data on the processor's cache.

- Distributed memory architecture

    1. Sender and receiver synchronize implicitly when they send/receive messages.
    2. Communication overhead is high.
    3. Communication performance is limited by the network bandwidth.

SMP clusters are considered to be a mixed configuration of shared memory and distributed memory. To achieve high performance on SMP clusters, we need to take advantage of both architectures. There are several programming schemes on SMP clusters[4], [5]. We proposed a hybrid shared memory/distributed memory programming on SMP clusters. This section introduces programming schemes on SMP clusters including *all message passing programming*, *all shared memory programming*, and *hybrid shared memory/distributed memory programming*.

28.3.1 All Message Passing Programming

The first choice of programming on SMP clusters is based on message passing programming. Message passing programming is a standard parallel programming on cluster systems. In message passing programming, inter-processor communications are done by sending/receiving messages. When using message passing programming on SMP clusters, each processor communicates with other processors by using the message passing facilities even if the communication partner is on the same node, which means that this programming gives up one of the advantages of SMPs.

28.3.2 All Shared Memory Programming

The second choice of programming on SMP clusters is a combination of shared memory programming and the function of a distributed shared memory (DSM) system. Although each node has its own local address space, a DSM system manages their local address spaces as the global address space. In this programming, programmers can write programs using the global address in the same manner on a shared memory system. A DSM system translates the global address to the local address and invokes inter-node communication, if necessary. Although programmers do not need to be conscious of inter-node communications, they cannot estimate the inter-node communication costs which affect the execution performance of applications.

28.3.3 Hybrid Shared Memory/Distributed Memory Programming

We designed a hybrid programming model in order to take advantage of locality in each SMP node. Intra-node computations utilize a multi-threaded programming style (Solaris threads), and inter-node programming is based on message passing and remote memory operations. In data parallel programs, we can phase the partitioning of target data such as matrices and vectors easily. First, we partition and distribute the data between nodes and then partition and assign the distributed data to the threads in each node. Therefore, it is easy to implement data parallel programs based on the hybrid programming model for COMPaS. The hybrid programming model is based on the SPMD programming style. The following steps show the outline of our implementation using Solaris threads and NICAM as examples:

Step 1:

Initialize and partition the data according to the number of nodes and distribute them to corresponding nodes. Users must pin down the regions to transfer by calling *nicam_lock_memory()* in advance. To distribute the data, users use *nicam_bcopy()* or *nicam_bcopy_notify()*. Figure 28.9 is a sample C code fragment for data distribution.

```
if (NODENO == 0) {
  nicam_lock_memory(data, NNODES * LOCALSIZE);
  nicam_barrier();
  for (i = 1; i < NNODES; i++)
    nicam_bcopy(NODENO, data[i * LOCALSIZE], i, data, LOCALSIZE);
  nicam_sync();
  nicam_barrier();
}
else {
  nicam_lock_memory(data, LOCALSIZE);
  nicam_barrier();
  nicam_barrier();
}
```

Figure 28.9 A sample C code fragment for data distribution.

NNODES is the total number of nodes and *NODENO* is the node ID. They are automatically set by *nicam_init()*. We assume that *data* is an array of characters. *LOCALSIZE* is the size of data in each node.

At first, every node pins down the region for data to transfer. The first call of *nicam_barrier()* guarantees the completion of the pin-down. Next, the parent node starts remote copying by calling *nicam_bcopy()*. The second argument specifies the source address and the fourth argument specifies the remote address. By calling the function, NICAM copies LOCALSIZE bytes from my node to the target node. The destination address is automatically translated to the physical address by NICAM. The parent node waits for the completion of data transfers by calling *nicam_sync()*. The second call of *nicam_barrier()* guarantees that the distribution of data is completed.

Step 2:
Invoke multiple child threads in each node and assign data to them.

Step 3:
Each thread refers to its assigned area and processes local computations.

Step 4:
When all nodes complete **Step 3**, exchange data between nodes. Only the parent thread communicates with threads on other nodes. Figure 28.10 is a sample C code fragment for inter-node communication using Solaris threads and NICAM as examples.

id is the thread ID and the ID of the parent thread is 0. *thread_barrier()* is a barrier synchronization primitive between threads. *nthreads* is the number of threads in each node. All the child threads wait until the inter-node communication complete.

Step 5:
Repeat **Step 3** and **Step 4** as needed.

```
if (id == 0) {
  nicam_bcopy(NODENO, data[target], target, data, 1);
  nicam_sync();
  nicam_barrier();
}
thread_barrier(id, nthreads);
```

Figure 28.10 A sample C code fragment for inter-node communication using Solaris threads and NICAM.

The data decomposition and distribution methods between nodes at **Step 1** and inter-node communications at **Step 4** are the same as the distributed programming technique. Data allocation to threads at **Step 2** and local computation at **Step 3** are the same as a multi-threaded programming on shared memory systems. Hybrid programming is considered as one of distributed programming such that multiple threads are used for the computation in each node. Although some operations such as *reduction* and *scan* need more complicated steps for hybrid programming, we can easily implement hybrid programming.

28.4 Case Studies – Benchmarks Results on COMPaS

We implemented some workloads, including a Laplace equation solver, matrix-matrix multiplication, Conjugate Gradient Kernel from the NAS Parallel Benchmarks, and a Radix Sort. We measured the execution time of the four benchmarks on COMPaS. The matrix size of the Laplace equation solver is 640 × 640. The matrix size of the matrix-matrix multiplication is 1800 × 1800. The size of the CG Kernel is class A. In Radix Sort, we sorted 4M 32 bit integers. We varied the number of nodes by using 1, 2, 4, or 8. In each case, we also varied the number of threads by using 1, 2, or 4 threads. The results for one node represent that of the multi-threaded programming version on shared memory systems. The results for one thread indicate the results of the message passing/remote memory based programming version of the benchmarks on distributed memory systems. This section describes the algorithm of both distributed and shared memory programming of each workload and its experimental results. The hybrid schemes of those are described above.

28.4.1 Explicit Laplace Equation Solver

The Laplace equation solver is an iterative matrix solver. In our experiments, we used the Jacobi method to solve the Laplace equation. In each iteration, a new matrix U' is computed from the old matrix U according to the following formulation:

$$u'_{i,j} = \frac{u_{i-1,j} + u_{i+1,j} + u_{i,j-1} + u_{i,j+1}}{4}. \tag{28.4.1}$$

A parallel Laplace equation solver requires only short-range communication, that is, communication with neighbor processors. It also has high data locality suitable for multi-threaded programming.

Shared memory programming

The matrix is partitioned by rows according to the number of threads and each area is assigned to an individual thread. Each thread updates its own area. To phase the update, every thread synchronizes when the update is completed. No data copying is necessary for data exchange between threads.

Distributed memory programming

The matrix is partitioned by rows according to the number of nodes and each area is distributed to the nodes. Each node updates its own area. In each iteration, each node exchanges its border row with its neighbors.

Figures 28.11 and 28.12 show the execution time of the Explicit Laplace equation solver. Figure 28.11 shows the results done through Myrinet, using NICAM. Figure 28.12 shows the results done through Ethernet, using MPICH.

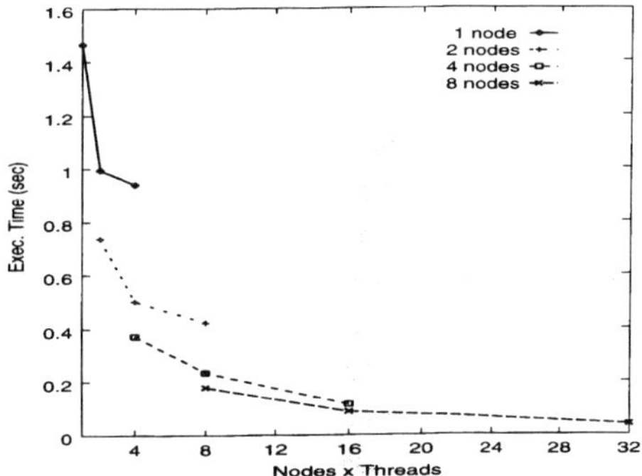

Figure 28.11 Execution time of Laplace equation solver (N=640, NICAM/Myrinet).

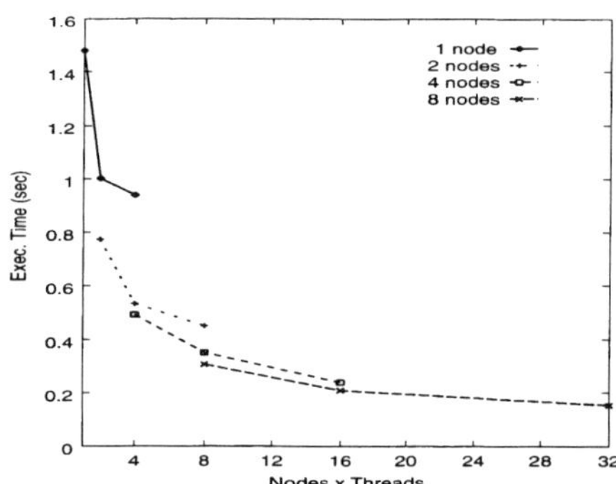

Figure 28.12 Execution time of Laplace equation solver (N=640, MPICH/Ethernet).

Each line represents the execution time for 1 node, 2 nodes, 4 nodes, and 8 nodes, respectively. Horizontal coordinates are the product of the number of nodes and the number of threads in each node, that is, the total number of threads.

The results for one node (meaning an ordinary multi-threaded version) cannot provide high performance because the data size is so large that access to main memory occurs frequently and the performance of the memory bus becomes bottlenecked. As the number of nodes increases, the amount of local computation decreases, but the message size of inter-node communication does not depend on the number of nodes. Although all inter-node communications on the Explicit Laplace equation solver are between neighbor processors, the experimental results reflect the performance of inter-node communications clearly. The performance done through Myrinet, using NICAM, has twice or more the speed as one done through Ethernet, using MPICH. Figures 28.13 and 28.14 show the speedup of the Explicit Laplace equation solver done through Myrinet, using NICAM. *ideal* shows the ideal speedup.

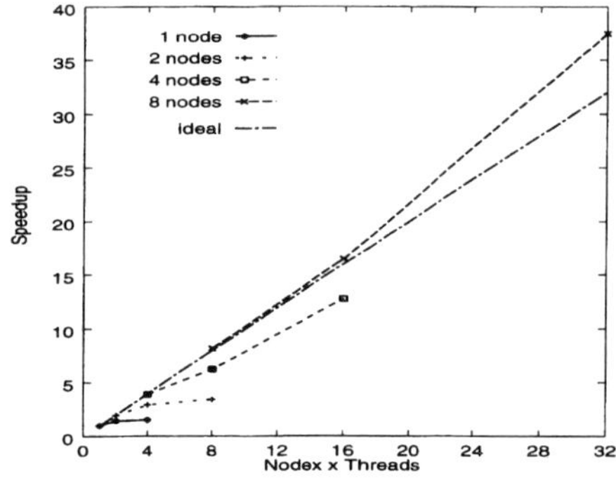

Figure 28.13 Speedup of Laplace equation solver (N=640, NICAM/Myrinet).

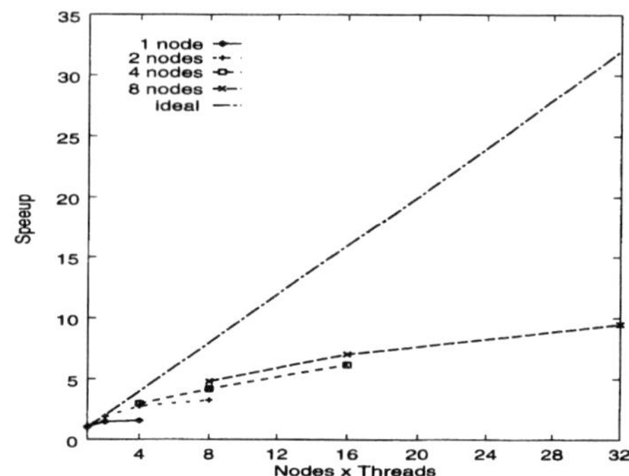

Figure 28.14 Speedup of Laplace equation solver (N=640, MPICH/Ethernet).

The speedup for the eight node case exceeds the ideal speedup because the working set becomes small enough to fit into the cache and NICAM provides fast inter-node communications.

28.4.2 Matrix-Matrix Multiplication

There are many algorithms of parallel matrix-matrix multiplication because there are various data decomposition schemes and computing orders such as *ijk, jki*. In our implementation, we chose the algorithm which provides high data locality.

Shared memory programming

We used a block-decomposition scheme and a tiling *jik* algorithm to get high data locality.

Distributed memory programming

Our implementation is based on the Cannon's algorithm. If the matrix size if N, the order of inter-node communication is $O(N^2)$ and the order of multiplication is $O(N^3)$. Therefore as N increases, the performance of multiplication becomes more significant.

Figures 28.15 and 28.16 show the speedup of the matrix-matrix multiplication done through Myrinet, using NICAM, and Ethernet, using MPICH, respectively.

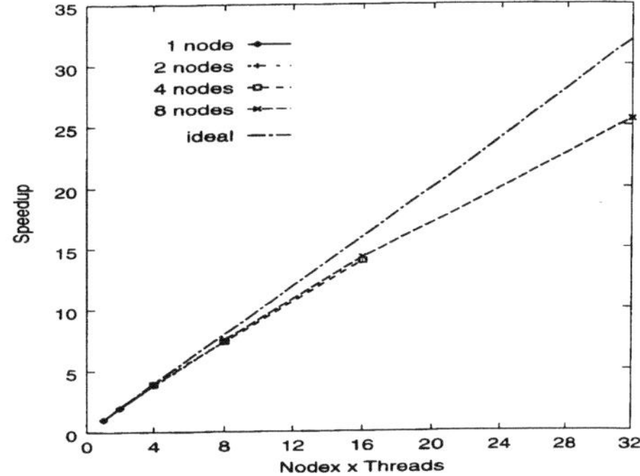

Figure 28.15 Speedup of matrix-matrix multiplication (N=1800, NICAM/Myrinet).

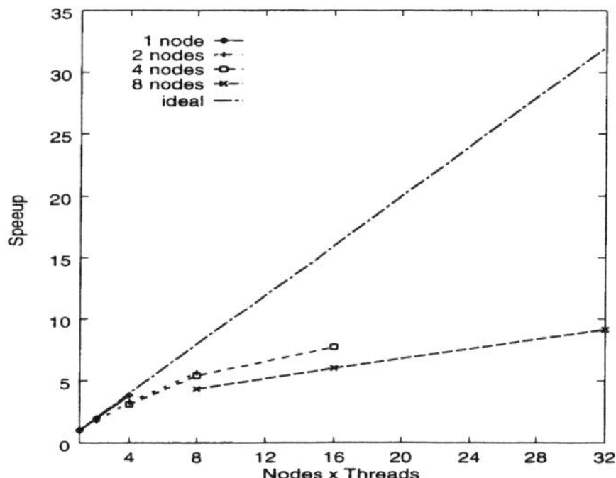

Figure 28.16 Speedup of matrix-matrix multiplication (N=1800, MPICH/Ethernet).

Although the matrix size is too large to fit into the cache, our blocking and tiling algorithm, which uses the cache effectively, can provide high performance for the single node case. When using NICAM on Myrinet, the efficiency for the 8 node and 4 thread case is about 80%. The combination of high data locality by using cache effectively and high performance inter-node communications enables high performance with hybrid programming.

28.4.3 Sparse Matrix Conjugate Gradient Kernel

The Conjugate Gradient (CG) Kernel is used to compute an approximation to the smallest eigenvalue of a large sparse symmetric positive definite matrix. This kernel is typical of unstructured grid computations in that it tests irregular, long-range communication, employing unstructured matrix-vector multiplication. Our implementation of the CG Kernel is based on the NAS Parallel Benchmarks, version 1.

Shared memory programming

- Initialize the data such as matrices and vectors and invoke multiple threads.
- Partition the data and assigned them to threads.
- Each thread refers to its assigned area and does local computations such as matrix-vector multiplication.
- The only communication between threads is a *reduction* operation for the production of vectors.

Distributed memory programming

- Initialize and partition the data such as matrices and vectors and distribute them to the corresponding nodes.

- Each node processes local computations such as matrix-vector multiplication.
- The communications between nodes are *reduction* for the production of vectors and *complete exchange* of vectors.

The *reduction* operation needs more complicated steps for hybrid programming. At first, reduce the values between threads, then reduce the values between nodes, and finally the parent thread broadcasts the value between child threads.

Figures 28.17 and 28.18 show the speedup of the CG Kernel done through Myrinet, using NICAM, and Ethernet, using MPICH.

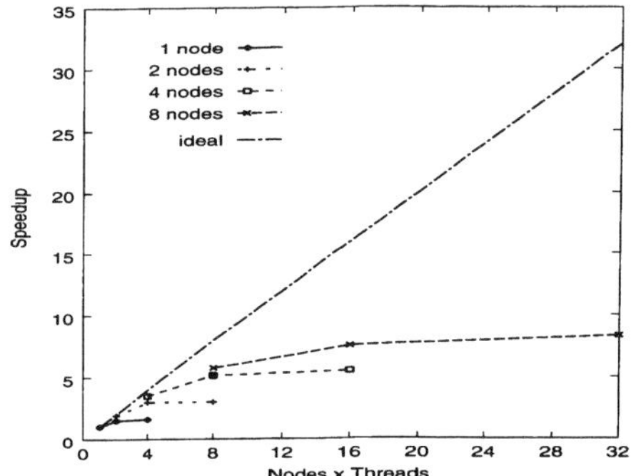

Figure 28.17 Speedup of CG Kernel (Class A, NICAM/Myrinet).

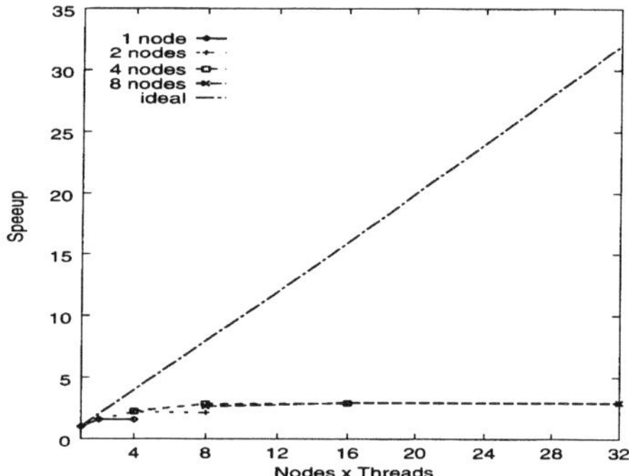

Figure 28.18 Speedup of CG Kernel (Class A, MPICH/Ethernet).

The performance for one node is very low. The execution time with four threads is almost the same as the time for two threads. Because the data size of CG Kernel (class A) is very large and accessing the main memory occurs frequently, the performance of the memory bus becomes a bottleneck.

28.4.4 Radix Sort

A serial Radix Sort is a distribution sorting algorithm which can be carried out as follows: Start with a distribution sort based on the least significant digit of the keys (in radix M notation), moving records from the input area to an auxiliary area. Then do another distribution sort, on the next least significant digit, moving the records back into the original input area, etc., until the final pass (on the most significant digit) puts all records into the desired order. If the maximal data can be represented in K bits and we choose radix as R bits, we complete the sorting in K/R passes. If the data size is very large, Radix Sort is an efficient sorting algorithm and we can expect high performance for parallel Radix Sort. Figure 28.19 shows how a parallel Radix Sort can be applied to example numbers.

In the example, the number of processors is 4, the number of data is 32, and the radix is 4, and the figure illustrates sorting on the unit digits. The following is the sorting method:

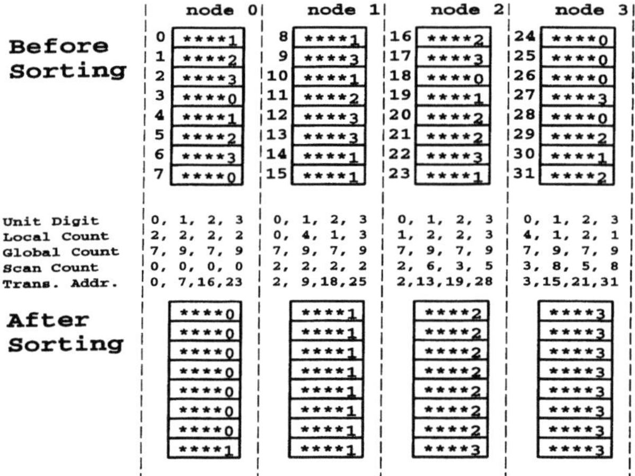

Figure 28.19 Radix Sort.

1. Each node counts for units digit distribution (*local count*).
2. Get the sum of the results of (1) of all nodes (*global count*).
3. Get the sum of the results of (1) of some nodes whose number is less than my node number (*scan count*).
4. Get the transfer address from the *global count* and the *scan count* (*transfer address*).
5. Transfer data according to the *transfer address* (*transfer*).

Shared memory programming

- Initialize the data and invoke multiple threads.
- Partition the data and assign them to threads.
- Each thread refers to its assigned area and does local computations such as *local count* and *transfer address.*
- Each thread refers to the areas of the other threads for *scan count* and *global count.*
- Each thread writes into the areas of the other threads for *transfer.*
- All threads need to synchronize for *scan count*, *global count* and *transfer.*

Distributed memory programming

- Initialize and partition the data and distribute them to the corresponding nodes.

- Each node processes local computations such as *local count* and *transfer address.*
- The communications between nodes are *vector scan* for *scan count*, *broadcast* for *global count*, and *complete exchange* for *transfer.*

Figures 28.20 and 28.21 show the speedup of Radix Sort done through Myrinet, using NICAM, and Ethernet, using MPICH.

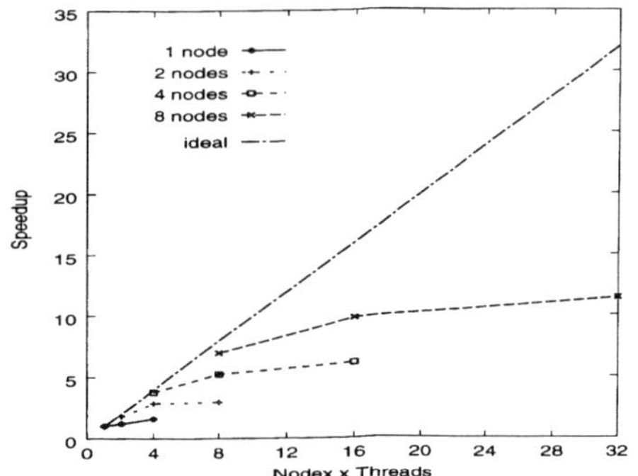

Figure 28.20 Speedup of Radix Sort (N=4M int, NICAM/Myrinet).

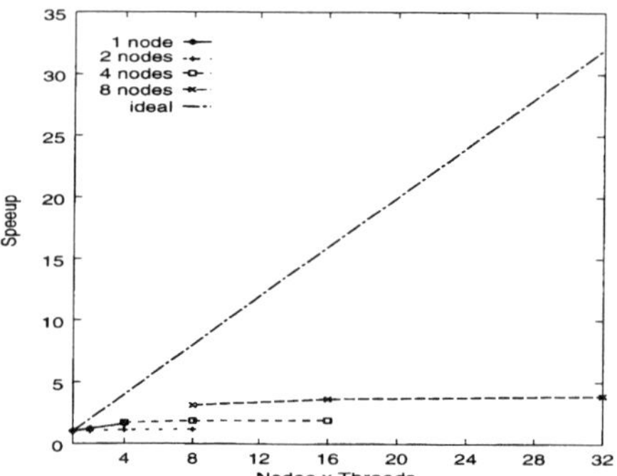

Figure 28.21 Speedup of Radix Sort (N=4M int, MPICH/Ethernet).

The results for one thread (meaning an ordinary distributed programming version) is scalable for the number of nodes. But the performance of multi-threaded version is very low. The results for CG Kernel and Radix Sort are not satisfactory when compared to the results for Laplace equation solver because their data exceeds cache capacity and they run into the memory-bus bottleneck.

28.5 Guidelines for Programming in PC-Based SMP Cluster

We obtain high performance for the Laplace equation solver and Matrix Multiply; however, the performance of the CG Kernel is not satisfactory because of the memory-bus bottleneck and the global communications bottleneck. We broke down the execution of the CG Kernel. Figure 28.22 shows the time for matrix-vector multiplication, vector operations such as addition and production, and *all-to-all* communication between nodes for one and eight node cases. In each case, we varied the number of threads by using 1, 2, or 4.

In one node case, most of the execution time is spent for matrix-vector multiplication. In the eight node case, the *all-to-all* communication time does not depend on the number of threads because only one thread per node attends to inter-node communications in our implementation, and the matrix-vector multiplication is not scalable as in one node case. We can find that in-scalability of the multiplication

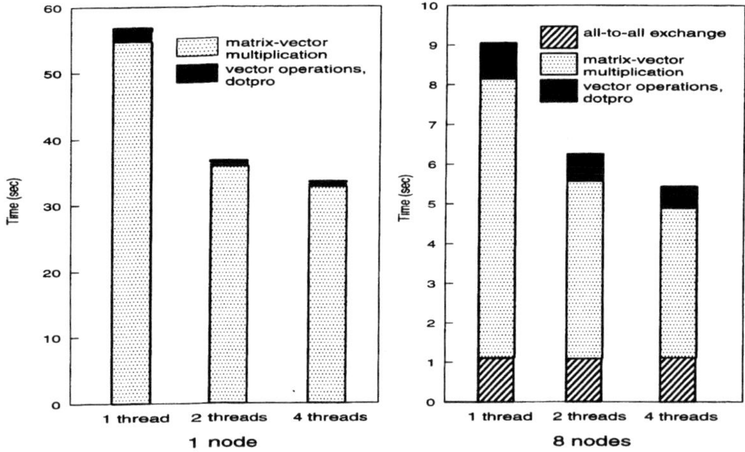

Figure 28.22 Breakdown of the CG Kernel.

reduces the execution performance of the CG Kernel. We analyzed the code of the matrix-vector multiplication of the CG Kernel and made a rough estimate of the peak performance memory-bus bandwidth required by each thread to read the matrix. It is approximately 120MB/s. As shown in Table 28.1, the memory-bus bandwidth for memory read is 208MB/s and when multiple threads are invoked, the bandwidth for each thread is limited by that value. If we invoke four threads for the CG Kernel, each thread requires 120MB/s bandwidth for matrix-vector multiplication; however, all threads actually acquire 50MB/s of bandwidth on average. The results for CG Kernel and Radix Sort show that for any number of nodes, the execution time for 2 threads and 4 threads is almost the same. This is because the memory-bus bandwidth becomes a bottleneck.

Here are some guidelines when programming PC-Based SMP clusters:

- If multiple threads are invoked on each node and the data size for each thread is very large, memory-bus performance may limit the performance of the SMP cluster system.
- If the data size is small enough to fit into the cache, we can take full advantage of multiple threads in each SMP node. The Laplace solver with 32 processors achieves good scalability because the data size is reduced and all fits into the cache.
- To achieve high performance on a Pentium Pro PC-Based SMP cluster, it is important to exploit locality, which means reducing the ratio of the memory accesses to the number of operations on the data in the cache. If this ratio is low, then PC-Based SMP clusters can provide high performance even if the data size is large. For example, in matrix-matrix multiplication, if a good blocking algorithm can be applied and the data on the cache are frequently

accessed by processors, we can get high performance.

- In SMP clusters, a multi-thread safe implementation of message passing libraries such as MPI is necessary. To circumvent the bottleneck caused by the bus system, communication primitives which allow direct access to remote memory are desirable. We implemented such primitives by using Active Message and DMA mechanisms on the Myrinet NI.

Fast communication is also important for scalability as the number of processors in SMP node is increased. For example, in case of matrix multiply with 8 nodes, the local computation (sub-matrix multiplication done by threads) takes 17.09 seconds, 8.59 seconds, and 4.46 seconds for 1, 2, 4 threads, respectively. While the the local computation is scalable in a SMP node, the time for inter-node communications is 0.83 seconds, which does not depend on the number of threads. As the number of threads increases, the inter-node communication time is revealed more clearly even if a fast communication layer, NICAM, is used.

28.6 Summary

We have built the COMPaS cluster of SMPs, which consists of eight quad-processor Pentium Pros. We reported the basic performance of COMPaS and a hybrid shared memory/distributed memory programming model and its preliminary evaluation. Our user-level communication layer NICAM is based on Active Messages and on the Myrinet Network Interface(NI) and provides low-overhead and high-bandwidth. We found that the performance is limited by the low memory-bus bandwidth of immature PC-Based SMP nodes for some memory intensive workloads.

In order to tolerate inter-node communication, we are now investigating a programming scheme which overlaps communication and computation. Our experimental results show that the inter-node communication time is hidden when many threads are running in some workloads. In such cases, the overlapping technique is expected to provide high performance. The blocking algorithms such as in level 3 BLAS are also promising for the SMP cluster.

In this chapter, we applied hybrid shared memory/distributed memory programming for data parallel applications to achieve high performance. In general, however, a SMP cluster makes programming complicated because the programmer must take care of both programming models. This complication should be hidden by a high-level programming language such as OpenMP and HPF in the future.

28.7 Bibliography

[1] Pentium Pro Cluster Workshop. http://www.scl.ameslab.gov/workshops/.

[2] The Jazznet Project. http://math.nist.gov/jazznet/index.html.

[3] T. von Eicken, D. E. Culler, S. C. Goldstein and K. E. Schauser. Active Messages: A Mechanism for Integrated Communication and Computation. In

Proceedings of the 19th International Symposium on Computer Architecture, pages 256–266, 1992.

[4] D. A. Bader and Joseph JaJa. SIMPLE: A Methodology for Programming High Performance Algorithms on Clusters of Symmetric Multiprocessors (SMPs). *UMIACS Technical Report 97-48*, May 1997.

[5] Stephen J. Fink and Scott B. Baden. Non-Uniform Partitioning for Finite Difference Methods Running on SMP Clusters. http://now.cs.berkeley.edu/clumps/.

[6] N. J. Boden, D. Cohen, R. E. Felderman, A. E. Kulawik, C. L. Seitz, J. N. Seizovic and S. Wen-King. Myrinet – A Gigabit-per-Second Local-Area Network. *IEEE MICRO*, vol. 15(1), pages 29–36, 1996.

[7] D. E. Culler, R. M. Karp, D. A. Patterson, A. Sahay, K. E. Schauser, E. Santos, R. Subramonian, and T. von Eicken. LogP: Towards a Realistic Model of Parallel Computation. In *Proceedings of the 4th ACM SIGPLAN Symposium on Principles and Practice of Parallel Programming*, 1993.

[8] H. Tezuka, A. Hori, Y. Ishikawa and M. Sato. PM: An Operating System Coordinated High Performance Communication Library. *Lecture Notes in Computer Science*, vol. 1225, pages 708–717, Springer-Verlag, 1997.

[9] H. Tezuka, F. O'Carroll, A. Hori, and Y. Ishikawa. Pin-down Cache: A Virtual Memory Management Technique for Zero-Copy Communication. In *Proceedings of the 12th International Parallel Processing Symposium (IPPS/SPDP'98)*, pages 308–314, 1998.

[10] Y. Tanaka, M. Matsuda, M. Ando, K. Kubota and M. Sato. COMPaS: A Pentium Pro PC-Based SMP Cluster and its Experience. *Lecture Notes in Computer Science*, vol. 1388, pages 486–497, Springer-Verlag, 1998.

[11] Y. Tanaka, M. Matsuda, M. Ando, K. Kubota and M. Sato. Programming Strategy and the Performance of COMPaS with Overlap of Communication and Computation. In *Proceedings of the International Conference on Parallel and Distributed Processing Techniques and Applications (PDPTA'98)*, vol. 1, pages 275–282, 1998.

Chapter 29

The NanOS Cluster Operating System

F. D. Muñoz-Escoí, P. Galdámez and J. M. Bernabéu-Aubán

Institut Tecnològic d'Informàtica
Universitat Politècnica de València
València, Spain

Email: *{fmunyoz,pgaldam,josep}@iti.upv.es*

29.1 Introduction

Traditionally, some support for highly available applications has been achieved using group communication protocols [1], [4], [8], [16], which are provided in form of libraries that these applications may use. However, this approach may be costly if the majority of the applications being run in a system must use replicated components, since there will be a big number of groups and each group usually requires a given message delivery order for all of its members. Also, when failures arise each group needs a membership service [10] to report which group members have failed, removing them from their groups. Finally, the implementation of this group support at user level does not allow the addition of fault tolerance properties to some critical components of the operating system.

To solve these problems, another approach can be taken. It is based on the integration of the components needed to provide fault tolerance in the operating system. This objective can be achieved if these services are included in the lower levels of a microkernel-based architecture, enabling other basic services—as the memory manager or the file system server—to use their functions.

This approach is being followed in our system. We have taken the NanOS microkernel [9] as the basis to develop a distributed object-oriented system. This microkernel provides only a reduced set of abstractions, mainly *objects* as the pieces of software that are managed by this kernel, *agents* as protection domains which are associated to different virtual address spaces and *tasks* as threads of execution.

Additionally, a local object invocation service is provided to enable the invocation of objects placed in other agents.

NanOS also provides a minimal set of memory management operations and allows the installation of new objects at kernel level, mainly device drivers. To provide an appropriate base to develop a distributed operating system on top of this microkernel, the next element to be included in our architecture is a group membership monitor [13] which will check periodically which machines constitute the system and will report any change in the group view to other system objects as soon as possible. This group membership monitor enables the development of a reliable transport protocol that intercommunicates the nodes of the resulting system, and it also reduces the cost of the protocols needed to provide replication services. These replication services provide the basis to develop highly available system components and applications.

29.1.1 Design Objectives

Our system architecture has to provide the appropriate support to build an object-oriented distributed operating system for a cluster of machines, offering a single-system image. Additionally, support to develop highly available operating system components and applications is considered.

To provide this support, some objectives were defined:

- **Object orientation**

  Object orientation provides a programming model which is easy to understand and produces programs that can be easily maintained. The encapsulation provided by this model makes possible that the implementation of an object could be changed transparently to the rest of objects, which know only its interface of public operations. Thus, the improvements in a piece of code do not introduce the risk of altering the behavior of other code which uses the modified part.

- **Efficiency**

  The bottom layers of our architecture have to provide their services in an efficient manner, since other critical operating system services may rely on them. For instance, the invocation service provided by our microkernel has to be extremely fast to allow the development of other efficient operating system services on top of it.

- **Minimal set of services**

  The services provided by our basis have to be minimal, to guarantee that they can be easily provided in any hardware architecture. The object abstraction and the management of memory, domains of protection and threads of execution constitute this minimal basis, which is complemented by a group membership service as the support needed to build reliable distributed components.

- **Extensibility**

  The use of a microkernel guarantees this extensibility, allowing the inclusion of new objects that provide the new required services.

- **Modularity**

  The proposed basis has to accept the inclusion of a variety of modules to extend the range of operating system services. These modules have to depend only on the services provided by the bottom layers of our architecture. For instance, the layer being used for distributed communication —the ORB, as we will see below— may be replaced by another service with similar functionality. However, the microkernel and the group membership service cannot be eliminated from the architecture, since they are its basic building blocks.

The resulting architecture is based on a set of components, which are a microkernel, a group membership service, an ORB and some additional components for high availability support. These components of the architecture are described in detail in the following sections, outlining their main advantages and comparing them with other alternatives. In Section 29.2, the overall architecture of our system is outlined and its main components are described. Section 29.3 gives some details on the NanOS microkernel. Its main abstractions and its architecture are presented focusing on its portability to other hardware platforms. Section 29.4 explains the MCMM cluster membership protocol. Section 29.5 presents the replication models supported by HIDRA, the ORB taken as its basis, and the additional support required by the coordinator-cohort replication model. Section 29.6 provides a final summary.

29.2 Architecture Overview

Our system architecture is depicted in Figure 29.1. The bottom layer of the architecture is the NanOS microkernel. On top of it, there is an unreliable communication protocol that uses the network device driver placed in the microkernel. Its services are used by the Multi-Computer Membership Monitor that controls which is the current set of active machines. This information is needed by the reliable communication protocol and by the object request broker. The MCMM provides a notification service that is used by some components of the ORB to rebuild the reference counts and to reconfigure the state of the replicated objects in case of failures.

Some components of the ORB are also merged with the microkernel support for object invocation. Thus, local invocations need only some ORB support in the caller and invoked agents to do the marshaling and unmarshaling tasks, but the reference management is integrated into the microkernel, enabling a fast local interagent invocation mechanism.

The extensibility provided by a microkernel ensures that once all these layers are carefully tested, they can be integrated into the kernel. This is possible for all components except for some parts of the ORB that have to be present in the protection domains of the objects being intercommunicated. So, the stubs needed in the client domains, the skeletons of the server domains, and the marshaling and unmarshaling components have to be left at user level.

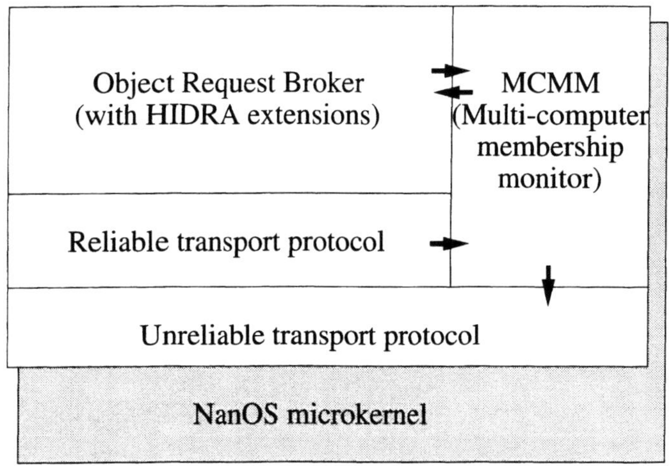

Figure 29.1 System architecture.

The inclusion of an ORB into our architecture gives the basis needed to manage all system components in a uniform way. So, all the components that have to be managed to provide the single-system image for our multicomputer cluster will be available and usable through the invocation service given by this ORB. Since some high availability support is also introduced in the ORB management by our HIDRA extensions, we will be able to implement some highly available system components on top of this ORB.

29.2.1 NanOS Microkernel

The NanOS microkernel has been taken as the basis for our cluster operating system architecture. A microkernel design offers support for multiple operating system personalities. To implement a given personality, some server objects are needed at user level, and they service all system calls of the operating system that is being emulated.

NanOS also allows the inclusion of additional objects in the kernel domain. Thus, the functionality of the microkernel can be improved if the new objects have been thoroughly tested at user level before they are included. In our case, this possibility is attractive since we plan to include group membership services into the kernel to assist the reconfiguration requirements of the object request broker.

A careful microkernel design also enhances the portability of the system code. In NanOS there is a group of machine-dependent objects which encapsulate all hardware dependencies. So, a port of the NanOS microkernel to several machine architectures requires only the reimplementation of those objects. We have already ported the original NanOS implementation to the PC architecture, and the changes needed to do this task were minimal.

Extending this microkernel with a membership service and a distributed object request broker, we have a good basis to develop all the services that must be present in a cluster operating system.

29.2.2 Membership Service

The next component in our architecture is the multicomputer membership monitor (MCMM) [13]. Each node in our system has a monitor of this kind to find out which machines compose the current membership set. This set of active machines must be known by each one of the system objects that share part of their state or functionality among their instances placed on different machines of the cluster. For instance, it has to be known by the objects that cooperate to model the file system server.

Our membership monitors need the services provided by an unreliable communication protocol. This protocol is being implemented on top of a network device driver that can be included in the proper microkernel. Besides the network device driver, the membership monitor needs support only for memory allocation, memory mapping, thread synchronization and the use of multiple threads of execution to deal with the sending and reception of messages and with timer control. All these services can be found in the NanOS microkernel. So, the membership monitor can be placed in a dedicated protection domain or directly into the microkernel.

Several objects in the system may be interested in the services provided by the membership monitor. These objects must request to the MCMM the notification about any change related to the current membership set. When any change arises, the MCMM notifies all these objects in the order specified. To this end, a sequence of lock steps is followed. In each lock step, all MCMM's notify their locally registered objects about the change and later all of them have to agree on the step termination before the next step is initiated. So, the MCMM provides the mechanisms needed to manage appropriately the reconfiguration of the whole system in case of failure of some machines or when some machines have been added to it.

Besides the notification steps, each time the membership changes, the group sequence number is also increased. This sequence number is included in the messages and it can be used to discard all messages that have not been sent in the current cluster configuration.

Comparing our solution with traditional group communication protocols developed for a general network of computers, several considerations apply. Our target system is a known cluster of machines which constitute our distributed system, and multiple upper level services need to know which set of live machines compose the current cluster. So, a machine-based membership service is used. In group communication protocols, the objects to be managed are processes which form the different instances of a group. Thus, these protocols provide, among other things, a mechanism for process replication. Obviously, their focus is a process-based membership service. However, the process-based membership service has several disadvantages because:

- The number of processes to be managed is usually much greater than the number of machines managed by our protocol. This occurs because a big number of groups may be needed in a distributed system and each one consists of multiple members.
- The number of messages needed to check the membership stability will be extremely high or, if it is maintained at a moderate level, the time needed to detect a failure could be large.
- The users of these services have to be processes. Usually, the operating system components, which are our target users, cannot employ them.

As a result, a machine-based membership service is more convenient than a process-based one. Moreover, the machine-based service can also be used to develop a process-based membership service on top of it, reducing the number of messages needed to do so.

29.2.3 Object Request Broker

The object invocation mechanism provided by the basic microkernel can be improved if a system-level ORB [14] is included. This ORB has to provide the base needed to unify the image of the system, providing location transparency for the clients which invoke objects placed in different parts of the cluster system being considered.

In our case, the ORB core will be implemented using the reliable transport protocol built on top of the MCMM membership service. On top of this reliable transport, two layers are distinguished. The bottom layer deals with reference management that will be included in the microkernel with the reliable transport and MCMM components. The top layer deals with marshaling and unmarshaling procedures, and the code needed to develop these tasks will be placed on the agents where the objects to be communicated reside. Note that the microkernel is also an agent, so it can also maintain objects of this kind.

29.2.4 HIDRA Support for High Availability

Currently, the OMG specification of the CORBA architecture does not include any support for replicated objects. High availability can be easily introduced in a distributed system if replicated objects are supported. So, we have extended our ORB machinery to include this kind of support.

To this end, it is necessary to insert new types of object references which must be used to represent and invoke replicated objects. These new types of object references require a different management. Also, some reconfiguration tasks are needed when new replicas are added or a node failure occurs.

As a result, our HIDRA architecture for high availability extends the ORB with several components, such as a replication manager and a concurrency control service, and it also needs to extend the internal ORB machinery to add support for the newly required object reference types. All these extensions give, as a result, a very efficient support for highly available objects.

29.3 NanOS

The basis of our distributed operating system is the NanOS microkernel, which provides a minimal set of abstractions that can be used by the user level code to develop applications. These abstractions are objects, agents and tasks. To work with them, only one service is provided: the inter-agent object invocation service.

29.3.1 An Object-Oriented Microkernel

In NanOS, an *object* is any piece of software that publicly offers a set of operations that can be invoked by the tasks running in any agent if these tasks have the appropriate references to access them. To become publicly accessible, an object has to be registered into the kernel. Once the object has been registered, its server agent receives an *object descriptor* or reference that can be transmitted to other agents, giving them the capability to invoke it.

An *agent* is a protection domain. The agents are also the owners of the object descriptors, which are used when an external object is invoked. Object descriptors are obtained by the server agent when it registers an object and they can be transferred to other agents as input or output arguments of an object invocation.

There are two types of agents: the *kernel agent* and the *user agent*. There is only one instance of the kernel agent class. It holds the microkernel objects and it is always mapped in supervisor mode in the top addresses of all virtual address spaces. Each user agent has the rest of a virtual address space, so only a user agent can be installed at a given time. Figure 29.2 depicts the organization of a group of objects into a set of agents.

The last abstraction provided by NanOS is the *task*. A task is a thread of execution. It can traverse multiple agents as a result of an object invocation; i.e., when an external object is invoked, the microkernel allows the task to be moved to the target agent. Each agent has a pool of allocated stacks that are assigned to the incoming tasks as soon as they start the execution of the code placed in the unique agent's entry point. These stacks are returned to the pool when their owning tasks leave the agent. As a result, no context switch is needed when a task invokes an object placed in another agent.

Finally, let us take a look to the objects invocation service. This is the basic service provided by the microkernel. Other complementary services are available when some of the microkernel objects which have registered their interfaces are invoked

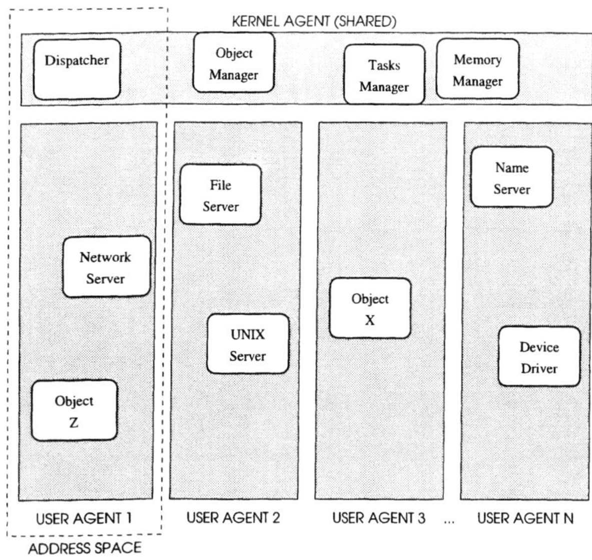

Figure 29.2 Objects, agents and virtual address spaces in a system node.

by user-level tasks, but to use them, the invocation service is needed, too. To start an invocation, the invoker task must have a valid reference or object descriptor to the object it wants to call.

If the invoker task's agent has the appropriate descriptor, a call to the microkernel is initiated. When the microkernel serves the invocation request, it checks the validity of the object reference and, if it is correct, translates the object descriptor to an object identifier that is known only by the server agent for this object and by the microkernel. Then the server agent is located and installed. Later, the task returns to user-level at the entry point of the server agent, where it gets a new stack and executes the skeleton code that drives it to the invoked method. When the task terminates the execution of the invoked method, it releases its stack and calls the microkernel again. The microkernel finds out the state of the task in its previous agent, and returns the task to that agent. Note that all these changes are made avoiding any task switch. As a result, this invocation mechanism is fast.

29.3.2 Microkernel Architecture

The microkernel has been designed as a set of related objects which serve the invocation service and provide different interfaces that user-level tasks may invoke at any time.

This set of objects is decomposed in two layers. The bottom one consists of a reduced amount of machine-dependent objects (the CPU, CPUContext, MMU, TableMgr and IntrMgr, which have machine-dependent code but offer machine-independent interfaces). On top of this bottom layer, and using its interfaces, exists a collection of machine-independent objects which manage the abstractions and services provided by the microkernel. Having a small number of machine-dependent objects, the migration of the microkernel to other hardware architectures is easy. In fact, we developed the initial version of NanOS on Sun SPARC machines and later we have ported this kernel to PCs.

Machine-Dependent Objects

The machine-dependent objects do the following tasks. The CPU is used to enable and disable interrupts. Also, if a multiprocessor implementation is considered, there are multiple CPU, MMU and TableMgr objects to model each one of the processors being considered.

A CPUContext models the set of registers of the CPU and allows the change of any of their contents. So, an object of this kind is used to model the state of a task when it has to release the CPU when the Scheduler requests this action. In the Intel x86 release of NanOS, a CPUContext maintains the general CPU registers in the format of a TSS segment. As a result, the task switching capability of the x86 processors is used.

The MMU provides methods to change the current virtual address space and to update the mappings placed in the page tables of each processor. The TableMgr uses its services to provide a higher-level interface which hides the physical representation of the page tables and the number of page table levels maintained by the MMU, offering the image of a unique and large page table for each address space. At this level it is possible to associate physical pages to any virtual address space.

Finally, the IntrMgr is used to install different interrupt handlers for each interrupt level of the CPU, routing the incoming interrupts to the appropriate interrupt handler. At this level there are multiple semi-active tasks, each one associated to a different interrupt level. When an interrupt arrives, the processor automatically does a task switch, blocking the current task and activating the one associated to the incoming interrupt level. Support is also provided to undo this task switching when the interrupt handling is terminated, and to report the task change to the Scheduler. This second alternative allows the interrupt task to be scheduled and to invoke objects placed outside the kernel agent. Thus, if an interrupt task is made schedulable, the device driver attached to its interrupt handler may be placed in a user-level agent.

Machine-Independent Objects

The set of machine-independent objects is a little bigger. We describe only the most important objects of this type. The ObjectMgr maintains all the registrations of objects that have been made, holding the identifier of the agent which serves the new object and its private identifier in that server. This information is needed to locate the agent where an object is placed when this object is being invoked. It also deals with object descriptor management, maintaining a reference count for each registered object.

The TasksMgr is used to create new tasks and to register the interdomain calls made by any of them, allowing in this way their return to their home agents. To achieve this, each time a task calls an external object, the TasksMgr saves the place where the invocation was made (to this end, the instruction and stack pointers plus the client agent identifier are saved), and this information is chained to the current list of invocations made by that task. When a task returns from the called object, the kernel restores its previous state, returning it to the agent and routine where the call was initiated.

The Scheduler manages the state of all system tasks, arranging them in any of the 32 available priority classes. It provides methods to prepare and suspend tasks, so its services are required by the synchronizing objects. It uses a Dispatcher object to do the task switching in each one of the available processors. All these Dispatchers have access to a global pool of CPUContext objects, which maintain the states that had all local tasks when they released the CPU.

Also related to tasks are the Semaphore, Lock and EventVar objects, which are three different classes of synchronization objects, each one with their own semantics:

- A Semaphore object provides the `P()` and `V()` methods. They follow the behavior of the original semaphore primitive.
- Locks constitute a variant of the semaphore object that does not block the owner of the lock if it requests its suspending method several times. However, to release a lock, its owner has to call its `Release()` method as many times as it called the `Request()` one.
- In an EventVar object, many tasks may be blocked waiting for the signaling of an event. When its `Signal()` method is requested, all the blocked tasks are immediately restarted. Later, the EventVar remains signaled. As a result, if a new task calls its `Wait()` method again, it is not suspended unless its `Reset()` method was previously called.

Each type of synchronization object accepts in its suspending method an additional argument which may be used to provide a timeout value or to request the test of the blocking state of the object; i.e., if the current state of the synchronization object will block the requesting task or not.

The CallMgr serves the kernel entry point, distinguishing between user-level targets, which receive the generic invocation service, and the kernel-level ones, whose routing is optimized.

There is also an AgentMgr which allows the creation and destruction of agents in the local node.

Device drivers are not included as a collection of objects placed in the kernel. However, the IntrMgr object described in the previous section provides support to install the interrupt handlers associated to these drivers, either in the kernel or in user agents. Drivers can be also placed in the kernel or in user agents, but they do not belong to the set of objects that build the microkernel essential services. They have to be registered and installed in the agent chosen by its programmer.

Finally, the memory management is provided by a collection of objects, based on a MemObj object which represents some piece of memory and a VirSpc object that models a virtual address space. Intermediate objects are Regions, Caches and external Pagers. A detailed description of these objects can be found in [9].

29.4 MCMM

The group membership protocol used in our system is the MCMM [13]. It deals with the set of machines that constitute the current cluster configuration, accepting the joining of new machines and the voluntary departure of some current members, and checking periodically the state of the current components to detect the failure of any of them. These are the common functions of all group membership protocols, but the MCMM also provides some other operations that are needed to assure a good reconfiguration of the system state. These additional operations are needed to synchronize the reconfiguration steps.

29.4.1 MCMM Protocol

To provide its services, the MCMM has three different modes of operation. These modes are: agreement, notification and checking.

The *agreement mode* is needed to find out which is the current membership set, and it is started when some machine failure is being suspected. In this mode, all nodes interchange their knowledge about the current state of the rest of machines. Eventually, all machines agree on the current membership set and all discarded machines are not considered until they apply to join the group again. When a machine has been removed from the membership set, all its messages are discarded until it rejoins the group.

The *notification mode* is needed to control the adequate order in the reconfiguration of all the objects that have requested to be notified when the membership set changes. This mode is initiated each time the agreement mode has finished giving a membership set different from the previous one. Since multiple objects may have requested to be notified, they have to report to the MCMM in which order they have to be informed about the changes. To do so, these objects request a given reconfiguration step number and they must have a well-known operation in its interface which will be used by the MCMM to notify the change. As a result, the notification mode consists of a sequence of steps whose completion is coordinated among all the system MCMM's. Thus, the first reconfiguration step starts when the agreement mode has finished. At this time, the MCMM checks its data structures to find out if any object has requested this step. If so, a timer is set to avoid infinite waits and the registered object is invoked. When the timer expires or the invocation returns, the MCMM reports the completion to one of the MCMM's that was elected at the end of the agreement mode as the coordinator. If no object was registered at this step, its completion is immediately notified to the coordinator. When the coordinator gets all the completion messages, it replies to all other MCMM's and the following step is initiated. The number of steps in each MCMM is variable. The notification mode terminates when all the MCMM's have reported to the coordinator that they do not have any other objects to be notified.

This notification mode is convenient because it guarantees that all machines in the cluster execute the same reconfiguration steps in the same order and at the same time. This is important for some protocols needed by the ORB (in particular for the reference recovery protocol and for the additional protocols needed to deal with replicated objects). To achieve this, the internal objects of the ORB which will carry the recovery protocols have to be registered in the same steps of each one of the MCMM's present in the different nodes that compose the system.

The *checking mode* is also executed when the agreement mode has produced an stable membership set. So, the MCMM's execute in notification and checking mode until the notification procedures have ended or the checking operations detect a new failure of any cluster machine. In the checking mode, the MCMM's are logically organized in a ring and each monitor checks only the state of its neighbors. To this end, the monitor periodically sends a message to its neighbors and expects the messages sent by them. If a monitor does not receive any heart-beat message for a given time, it suspects its neighbor is faulty and proceeds to drive all other monitors to the agreement mode.

The implementation of the MCMM is based on a local automaton, whose states are depicted in Figure 29.3. The BEGIN state corresponds to the agreement mode described above. In the STEP(i) states, the automaton follows the notification and checking modes. The last step state marks the end of the notification mode in the current membership view. The END state is dedicated only to the checking mode until a failure or joining is detected and the automaton goes to the RETURN state.

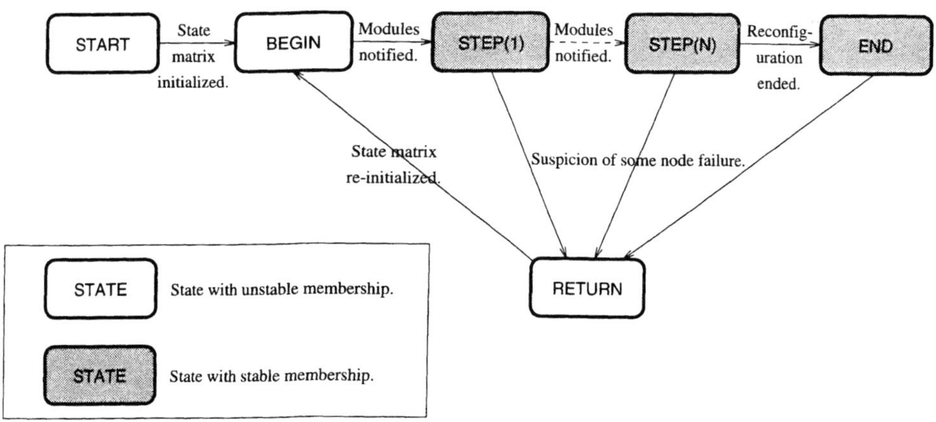

Figure 29.3 MCMM automaton.

To manage the agreement in the BEGIN state, a local state matrix is needed which has as many rows and columns as pre-configured machines are in the cluster.

Each row of the matrix represents the knowledge which its associated node has about the states of all other cluster machines. The information transferred in each message consists in the state matrix row associated to its sender. When a monitor receives a message, it updates accordingly its state matrix. The agreement on the current membership set is achieved when all the live nodes have the same values in the matrix cells associated to all of them.

The state matrix is also used in the rest of the states to maintain the current configuration of the cluster and to reflect the current state of all the system monitors. For instance, Figure 29.4 shows two matrices in a cluster pre-configured for three machines. The first of these matrices shows a stable state built by nodes 2 and 3, and the second matrix shows how the contents are updated in node 2 when it has received a message from node 3 which has detected the joining of node 1 and is returning to initiate a new agreement phase. In these matrices, the UNK state represents that the state of that node is unknown —possibly because its row represents a crashed node— while the DOWN state represents that a live node knows that another one has crashed.

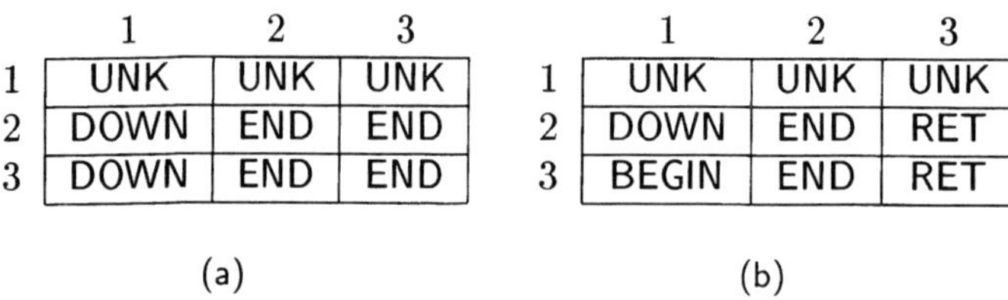

	1	2	3
1	UNK	UNK	UNK
2	DOWN	END	END
3	DOWN	END	END

(a)

	1	2	3
1	UNK	UNK	UNK
2	DOWN	END	RET
3	BEGIN	END	RET

(b)

Figure 29.4 State matrices of node 2 before (a) and after (b) receiving a message from node 3.

Finally, let us remark that the most appealing characteristics of this group membership protocol are its capability to drive the reconfiguration of the distributed system and its low dependence on other services, which allows its inclusion in the microkernel agent.

29.5 HIDRA

HIDRA [6] is a set of extensions for high availability support in distributed object-oriented environments where an ORB is needed to manage all object invocations. This set of extensions includes some support for replicated object references, a distributed reference counting protocol, and several other components that depend on the replication model being used.

Since our ORB is partially included into the microkernel layer of NanOS, the HIDRA services may be used to develop other operating system components such as the file system, some upper-level communication protocols, etc. This support at this low level is difficult to integrate in monolithic operating system architectures, because it requires a lot of modifications and the inclusion of several additional components into the kernel. In our microkernel approach, each component may be developed and tested progressively, making these tasks easy.

29.5.1 Overview of HIDRA

HIDRA is an architecture for highly available object oriented systems that need a kernel level ORB to be developed. NanOS provides the basis needed to include the ORB at the lowest level, enabling the use of this ORB to develop some other operating system components that will provide a single-system image. The inclusion of the HIDRA support in this ORB gives high availability support for all operating system components that need ORB services.

Besides having an ORB, the development of HIDRA needs the cluster membership services provided by MCMM. The notification phase of this membership service guarantees that all the reconfiguration protocols of the HIDRA support are correctly run in all cluster nodes. As a result, in case of a node failure the state of the replicated object references is updated accordingly and some maintenance protocols are executed to change the role of some object replicas. Without the help of the MCMM these reconfiguration tasks had required protocols that would have been more complicated.

The ORB that has been taken as the basis to develop HIDRA provides support for extension, allowing the inclusion of new types of object references associated with object handlers that are needed for the marshaling and unmarshaling tasks. Its design is similar to the one used in [2]. As an extension to the CORBA specification, this ORB manages object reference counts. Each object registered in the ORB maintains a count of the number of external client references that exist in the system. Thus, when an object loses all its client references, the ORB machinery generates an *unreferenced notification* that is delivered to it. When this notification is received, an object knows that it can release all its state.

This ORB has been extended to support different replication models. To this end, some *replication managers* are included into the ORB machinery to deal with the replicated object references that are needed. The use of these replication managers reduces the number of components that have to be notified when a replica failure or a replica addition arises.

29.5.2 Replication Models

Several different replication models exist. Each one has different advantages and inconveniences that may condition the choice of the model, depending on the guarantees needed by the highly available object. HIDRA provides some support for three different replication models, although the coordinator-cohort approach is its preferred solution. These models are:

- **Passive replication** [5]. In the passive replication model, all requests are received by a primary replica which updates its state and makes a checkpoint to the secondary replicas before replying to the client.

Several variants of this model exist, depending on when the checkpoint is made, how many secondaries are used, and who replies to the client.

The main advantage of this replication model is its simplicity and that it only requires an active replica. However, its disadvantage is its long recovery time, because a secondary has to be promoted to the primary role and has to match the state of the crashed primary.

- **Active replication** [15]. In the active replication model, all object replicas receive and process all client requests. So, all object replicas are active. To ensure the consistency of the replicas state, an atomic ordered multicast protocol is needed to guarantee that all object replicas receive all requests in the same order. A multicast protocol of this kind requires additional messages and delivery delays to guarantee the delivery order. So, this replication model is quite expensive. Additionally, since all object replicas are active, all the system nodes where an object replica is placed have to serve all the requests. This leads to some waste of computing power, at least when this model is compared to the passive one.

  However, in case of failure the recovery time is very short and this has led all group communication protocols to adopt this replication model and to include this support in some ORB's [7].

- **Coordinator-cohort replication** [3]. The coordinator-cohort replication model is a variation of the passive model where the primary replica may be different for each client request. So, all replicas have to be able to directly process a client request and to receive the checkpoints made by another replica. When a replica behaves as a primary for a given request, it is the coordinator for that request. When it receives the checkpoints for a request, it is the cohort.

  The main advantages of this model are its need of only one active replica for each request, its short recovery time (because all replicas are able to behave as coordinator or as cohort and no promotion nor degradation of roles is needed), and the possibility of concurrent service of multiple requests in different machines. Moreover, no atomic ordered multicast protocol is needed in this replication model.

  However, its disadvantage is the need of a distributed concurrency control mechanism to ensure that all concurrent requests that are being served do not update the same part of the object state. Additional support to ensure the atomicity of the checkpoint updates is also needed.

29.5.3 Object Request Broker

Since NanOS provides the object abstraction and an object invocation service, an ORB is the natural extension to this basic service, allowing the invocation of objects placed in any node of the distributed system.

As it has been described above, NanOS gives object descriptors to the agents as references to objects placed in other agents. Some internal objects of the kernel have to cooperate when an invocation request is received to find out the agent where the object being invoked resides, translate any object descriptor being transferred in the arguments, install the object's agent and, finally, place the task in the skeleton code which serves the invoked object. Similar steps occur if an ORB is used, but some changes are needed, too. These changes are:

- The format of the object references being used must be extended. The data associated to an object reference at the microkernel level has to express in which node is the target object placed, in which agent and which marshaling requirements has its object class.
- Multiple types of object references must be supported by the ORB. Thus, objects with special requirements might be managed by our ORB; for instance, replicated objects. Some of these types of object references may require distributed reference counting protocols to find out when the object being represented does not have any reference in the system. The ORB may deliver an *unreferenced* notification to the object, which may perform the appropriate actions before being released.
- The marshaling and unmarshaling procedures must be done in the client and server agents. However, the objects used to do so have to be extended to be able to deal with the new types of object references managed in the kernel.

As a result, the most practical implementation of the ORB core will consist in the extension of the microkernel services to include the management of new types of object references. Also, since the ORB needs communication support, the reliable transport protocol server and the MCMM must be also included at this level to improve efficiency. Therefore, NanOS will provide the reference management layer of the resulting ORB.

Additional ORB components that deal with marshaling and unmarshaling procedures have to be placed into the agents which hold objects that will use the ORB. This forms the top layer of the ORB core.

Thus, the HIDRA support in the ORB is decomposed. The reference management tasks are integrated in the microkernel while all other components are placed in the agents, as shared libraries.

29.5.4 Coordinator-Cohort Replication Model

Besides the management of replicated object references, either for choosing the appropriate coordinator replica for a given client and to make the checkpoints from the coordinator to the cohorts, or for reference counting purposes, our support for the coordinator-cohort replication model also needs a mechanism to ensure the atomicity of an invocation and a distributed concurrency control mechanism.

Although the coordinator-cohort is the replication model that offers the best characteristics, its implementation is a bit difficult and some care must be taken to ensure that the state of a replicated object is consistent. Since multiple requests may proceed concurrently on different coordinator replicas, a concurrency control mechanism is needed to ensure that there is no conflict among the parts of the state that are being read or modified by these requests. Also, this concurrency control mechanism has to be complemented by some invocation mechanism that ensures the atomicity of the updates and the request termination in all object replicas, allowing other conflicting invocations to proceed when this happens.

In HIDRA, these two mechanisms are the *reliable object invocation* (or ROI, for short) mechanism [12] for ensuring atomicity and consistency and the *HIDRA concurrency control* (HCC) mechanism [11].

Reliable Object Invocations

The ROI mechanism uses some additional objects managed by our ORB support to identify each invocation and to control when all replicas of the invoked object have updated their state according to the information given in the coordinator checkpoints.

Previous implementations of the coordinator-cohort replication model [3] had the problem that the cohorts had to maintain a copy of the results provided by the coordinator to avoid the replay of an invocation service when the coordinator crashed. In those implementations, there were no means to find out when these retained results could be released. The ROI mechanism also provides a solution to this problem.

The ROI mechanism is used for the following purposes:

- To identify retries of a given invocation in case of failure of the coordinator or the client. To this end, it uses a RoiID auxiliary object.

  When a retry is made, the results of the previous invocation attempt are collected and they are returned immediately. It is not necessary to repeat the whole service process for this new retry.

- To detect the completion of the invocation in all replicas of the server side. To this end, it uses a TObj auxiliary object. When this happens, other conflicting invocations are allowed to proceed. So, the TObj objects are also used by the HCC mechanism.

- To detect the reception of the results in all replicas of the client. To this end, it uses a CObj auxiliary object. When all client replicas have gotten the results, the retained copy maintained on the server replicas may be safely discarded.

The protocol also behaves correctly in case of multiple failures on the client or server sides. It aborts an invocation only when all replicas of the invoked object have crashed, otherwise it enforces the forward progress property and the remaining replicas complete the invocation. The HCC mechanism is helpful in this purpose because its services and the layered structure of the HIDRA replicated services enforce that no deadlock will occur.

A detailed description of the ROI protocol, its auxiliary objects and its behavior in case of failures may be found in [12].

HIDRA Concurrency Control

The HIDRA concurrency control mechanism uses the information provided by the programmer about the incompatibilities between each pair of the operations present in the object interface. Two operations are considered in conflict when they have to access the same part of the object state and at least one of them modifies that part.

The information about the compatibility or conflicts between these operations is specified in an extended version of the IDL language. When this specification is compiled, a *concurrency control specification* object is generated and this object is registered into the *service serializer* object of the HIDRA support for this replication model.

Each time a request arrives to the coordinator node, our HIDRA support gets the ROI context information and invokes its local service serializer agent to make the concurrency control checks. The serializer maintains a list of the invocations that are currently in progress and another list with the blocked invocations. The arriving invocation is checked against the running and blocked invocations and a list of invocations in conflict with it is built (this is the precedent list). If the list is empty, the invocation is allowed to proceed and is inserted in the list of active invocations. It the list has at least one precedent invocation, the invocation is blocked and it will not be allowed to proceed until all its precedent invocations have finished. To detect the termination of these invocations, the serializer uses the auxiliary TObj object that was provided by the HIDRA support.

The HCC is able to provide concurrency control only at the operation granularity. On the other hand, the checks needed to find out the list of precedent invocations need an invocation only to the service serializer object, so the concurrency control mechanism does not introduce excessive delays in an invocation that is allowed to proceed. The state of the service serializer can be rebuilt in case of failure. To this end, the state maintained by its distributed agents has to be merged. Additional details on the HCC may be found in [11].

29.6 Summary

We have presented the architecture of an object-oriented distributed operating system based on the NanOS microkernel and the MCMM membership protocol. The use of membership protocols in the lower layers of a distributed operating system is an appropriate choice, since it provides support to reconfigure the entire system in case of failure of some of its machines and notifies these failure events promptly.

So, the membership service is the component that provides the basis to deal with a distributed environment where the machines and the network may fail.

Having this support in the basis of the architecture, other components such as the ORB are added easily. The ORB offers location transparency on object invocations and, if the CORBA specification is entirely implemented, it also provides interoperability with other ORB-based systems. Additionally, the HIDRA extensions for the ORB also rely on the underlying membership services and provide different models of object replication and support for highly available components.

The resulting architecture allows the development of a distributed operating system which supports multiple personalities (due to the extensibility of the microkernel), offers a single-system image to the upper level applications (since the location transparency provided by the ORB is enforced by the rest of objects that implement the operating system functionality), and allows the development of highly available operating system components and applications (because the services provided by the membership protocol are used by the HIDRA extensions as the basis to build a replication service).

29.7 Bibliography

[1] Ö. Babaoğlu and A. Schiper. On Group Communication in Large-Scale Distributed Systems. In *Proceedings of ACM SIGOPS European Workshop, Dagstuhl, Germany, ACM Operating Systems Review*, vol. 29(1), pages 62–67, 1995.

[2] J. M. Bernabéu-Aubán, V. Matena and Y. Khalidi. Extending a Traditional OS Using Object-Oriented Techniques. In *Proceedings of the 2nd Conference on Object-Oriented Technologies & Systems (COOTS)*, pages 53–63, June 1996.

[3] K. P. Birman, T. Joseph, T. Räuchle and A. El Abbadi. Implementing Fault-Tolerant Distributed Objects. *IEEE Transactions on Software Engineering*, vol. 11(6), pages 502–508, June 1985.

[4] K. P. Birman and R. van Renesse. *Reliable Distributed Computing with the Isis Toolkit.* Los Alamitos, CA: IEEE Computer Society Press, 1994.

[5] N. Budhiraja, K. Marzullo, F. B. Schneider and S. Toueg. The Primary-Backup Approach. In S. J. Mullender, editor, *Distributed Systems (2nd edition)*, pages 199–216, Wokingham, England: Addison-Wesley, 1993.

[6] P. Galdámez, F. D. Muñoz-Escoí and J. M. Bernabéu-Aubán. High Availability Support in CORBA Environments. In F. Plášil and K. G. Jeffery, editors, *24th Seminar on Current Trends in Theory and Practice of Informatics, Milovy, Czech Republic*, vol. 1338 of LNCS, pages 407–414. Springer Verlag, November 1997.

[7] S. Maffeis. *Run-Time Support for Object-Oriented Distributed Programming.* Ph.D. Thesis, Department of Computer Science, University of Zurich, February 1995.

[8] C. Malloth, P. Felber, A. Schiper and U. Wilhelm. Phoenix: A Toolkit for Building Fault-Tolerant Distributed Applications in Large Scale. *Technical Report.* Dépt. d'Informatique, École Polytechnique Fédérale de Lausanne, Lausanne, Switzerland, July 1995.

[9] F. D. Muñoz-Escoí and J. M. Bernabéu-Aubán. The NanOS Microkernel: A Basis for a Multicomputer Cluster Operating System. In *Proceedings of the International Conference on Parallel and Distributed Processing Techniques and Applications, Las Vegas, Nevada, USA*, pages 127–135, July 1997.

[10] F. D. Muñoz-Escoí, J. M. Bernabéu-Aubán and P. Galdámez. Fault Handling in Distributed Systems with Group Membership Services. *Technical report, DSIC-II/8/97*, Universitat Politècnica de València, Spain, May 1997.

[11] F. D. Muñoz-Escoí, P. Galdámez and J. M. Bernabéu-Aubán. HCC: A Concurrency Control Mechanism for Replicated Objects. In *Proceedings of the VI Jornadas de Concurrencia, Pamplona, Spain*, pages 189–204, July 1998.

[12] F. D. Muñoz-Escoí, P. Galdámez and J. M. Bernabéu-Aubán. ROI: An Invocation Mechanism for Replicated Objects. In *Proceedings of the 17th IEEE Symposium on Reliable Distributed Systems, West Lafayette, IN, USA*, October 1998.

[13] F. D. Muñoz-Escoí, V. Matena, J. M. Bernabéu-Aubán and P. Galdámez. A Membership Protocol for Multi-Computer Clusters. *Technical report, DSIC-II/20/97*, Universitat Politècnica de València, Spain, May 1997.

[14] OMG. *The Common Object Request Broker: Architecture and Specification. Revision 2.2.* Object Management Group, February 1998.

[15] F. B. Schneider. Replication Management Using the State-Machine Approach. In S. J. Mullender, editor, *Distributed Systems (2nd edition)*, pages 166–197, Wokingham, England: Addison-Wesley, 1993.

[16] R. van Renesse, K. P. Birman and S. Maffeis. Horus: A Flexible Group Communication System. *Communications of the ACM*, vol. 39(4), pages 76–83, April 1996.

Chapter 30

BSP-Based Adaptive Parallel Processing

MOHAN NIBHANUPUDI AND BOLESLAW SZYMANSKI

Department of Computer Science
Rensselaer Polytechnic Institute,
Troy, New York

Email: {*nibhanum, szymansk*}*@cs.rpi.edu*

30.1 Introduction

In this chapter, we focus on clusters consisting of a group of workstations connected through a local area network, often run under a single administration. In particular, we target clusters with fast communication network achieved thanks to low-overhead protocols and use of switched networks that allow bandwidth to scale with the number of processors. Message passing libraries such as PVM [17], MPI [10] and BSP Oxford Library [9] allow for portable parallel programs. The SPMD (Single Program Multiple Data) paradigm lends the programmer flexibility in structuring parallel applications with varying degrees of granularity. Accordingly, we explore parallel processing on clusters of nondedicated workstations using the Bulk-Synchronous Parallel model. We extend the BSP model to enable the BSP computation to adapt to the changing degree of parallelism available on clusters of nondedicated workstations and demonstrate its use for efficient parallel programming.

30.2 The Bulk-Synchronous Parallel Model

The Bulk-Synchronous Parallel model [18] defines an abstract parallel computer in terms of the following primitives:

- *components* (processors) which execute programs

- a *router* that provides point-to-point communication between pairs of components, and
- a *synchronization mechanism* to synchronize all or a subset of the components at regular intervals. The *periodicity* parameter L represents the minimum time between synchronizations.

A computation consists of a sequence of *supersteps*. In each superstep, a component performs some local computation and/or communicates with other components. The data communicated is not guaranteed to be available at the destination until the end of the superstep in which the communication was initiated.

In analyzing the performance of a BSP computer, a *time step* is defined as the time required for a component to perform an operation on data available in the local memory. The performance of a BSP computer is characterized by the following parameters: number of processors (p), processor speed (s), synchronization periodicity (L), and a parameter to indicate the global computation to communication balance (g). The processor speed is measured in the number of time steps executed per second. L is the minimal number of time steps between successive synchronization operations. g is the ratio of the total number of local operations performed by all processors in one second to the total number of words delivered by the communication network in one second. It should be noted that the parameters L and g are dependent on the number of processors p. This dependency is defined by the network architecture and the implementation of the communication and synchronization primitives.

For example, consider a cluster of workstations interconnected by a fixed bandwidth communication medium such as an Ethernet. Communicating large amounts of data using a fixed bandwidth communication medium will cause the interconnection network to sequentialize message flow from/to the active processors. Under this assumption, the parameter g can be expressed as follows: $g(p) = g_0 p$, where g_0 is a constant. If we assume that the synchronization mechanism is implemented in software using a tree structure for the participating processors, the parameter L is defined as $L = L_0 \log(p)$, where L_0 is a constant.

BSP parameters allow the user to analyze the complexity of a BSP algorithm in a simple and convenient way. The complexity of a superstep, S in a BSP algorithm is determined as follows. Let w be the maximum number of local computation steps executed by any processor during the superstep. Let h_s be the maximum number of messages sent by any processor and let h_r be the maximum number of messages received by any processor during the superstep. In the original BSP model, the cost of S is given by $\max\{l, w, gh_s, gh_r\}$ time steps. An alternative formula for the complexity of a superstep [5] is to charge $\max\{l, w + gh_s, w + gh_r\}$ time steps for the superstep. Yet another definition [2] charges $l + w + g\max\{g_s, g_r\}$. Different cost definitions reflect different assumptions about the implementation of the supersteps, in particular about which operations can be done in parallel and which ones must be done in sequence. The last formula assumes that the local computation, communication and synchronization are done in sequence. The difference is not crucial, since the asymptotic costs of a BSP superstep computed according to the above formulae are of the same complexity. The cost of the entire BSP algorithm is just the sum of the costs of its supersteps.

By designing algorithms that are characterized by the size of the problem (n), the number of processors (p) and the two parameters that characterize the performance of the communication network (l and g), we can ensure that the algorithms can be efficiently implemented on a range of BSP architectures. Such a design leads to architecture independent BSP algorithms [2].

30.2.1 Cluster of Workstations as a BSP Computer

In terms of the BSP parameters, parallel computers are often characterized by large values of s (fast processors) and low values of L and g (a communication network with low latency and large bandwidth). A general-purpose cluster of workstations, on the other hand, is characterized by values of s that are somewhat lower and values of L and g that are much larger than the corresponding values for the parallel machines (high latency and low bandwidth of local area networks in comparison with the custom-design switching networks of parallel architectures). As a result clusters of workstations may not efficiently execute algorithms designed for parallel computers. For example, to mask high value of g, every non-local memory access should perform approximately g operations per local data.

As an example, consider the task of broadcasting data from a single processor to all other processors using the point-to-point communication primitives. In a parallel computer, broadcasting of data is often performed by organizing the participating processors into a (binary) tree with the processor initiating the broadcast at the root of the tree and the other processors occupying the other nodes. In the first superstep, the processor at the root communicates the data to the processors at its child nodes. In each subsequent step, processors at nodes in the currently active level communicate the data to processors at their child nodes in the next higher level. The communication is increasingly parallel as data move from the root of this tree to the leaves. We refer to this scheme as *logarithmic broadcast*. The communication in the opposite direction (from the leaves to the root) implements data gathering. Both operations take a number of steps proportional to the logarithm of the number of processors involved. The cost of logarithmic broadcast of h units of data on a cluster is

$$L\log(p) + g(p-1)h = L_0\log^2(p) + g_0(p-1)h \tag{30.2.1}$$

In the *linear broadcast*, the broadcasting node simply communicates the data to all other nodes in a single superstep. Hence, the cost of the linear broadcast of h units of data is

$$L + g(p-1)h = L_0\log(p) + g_0(p-1)h \tag{30.2.2}$$

Comparing 30.2.1 and 30.2.2 shows that, unlike in a parallel computer environment, linear broadcast is always faster in a cluster environment. However, when logarithmic gather is used, computations can be performed on the data being broadcast in parallel at the nodes of the tree, whereas linear gather forces computations to be delayed until all of the data arrives at a processor. This feature may make logarithmic gather more attractive than linear gather under some circumstances. For example, using logarithmic gather, summation can be performed on the data being gathered.

30.2.2 Program Reorganization for Parallel Computing on Dedicated Clusters: Plasma Simulation

The Particle-in-Cell (PIC) method simulates the trajectories of millions of particles in their self-induced fields. The interactions between the particles are modeled indirectly through the fields induced by the particles at the fixed points of a grid. The General Concurrent Particle-in-Cell (GCPIC) algorithm partitions the particles and grid points uniformly among the processors of a distributed memory machine. This allows for efficient computation of positions and velocities of the particles. As particles move among partitioned regions, they are passed to the processor responsible for the new region. To enable efficient solution of the field equations on the grid, a secondary temporary decomposition is used to partition the simulation space evenly among the processors. After computing charge deposition by the particles, grid point data is exchanged among the processors to allow processors to solve field equations in their secondary partitions. For computational efficiency, field/grid data on the border of partitions is replicated on the neighboring processor to avoid frequent off-processor references.

The distributed grid described above require a parallel machine with fast interconnection because interactions between particles and grid points belonging to different processors gives rise to frequent communication. To improve performance of plasma simulation on a cluster, we use a replicated grid that eliminates communication associated with interactions of particles on one processor with grid points on another. It also eliminates communication associated with solving the field equations on a distributed grid. In addition, a replicated grid allows particles to remain on the same processor for the entire duration of the simulation eliminating communication associated with particle redistribution.

As a result, the replicated grid version of plasma simulation performs well on clusters of workstations [12]. This application demonstrates that it is possible to execute computation intensive parallel applications on a cluster of workstations. However, the application may need to be restructured by changing the data distribution to avoid frequent communication.

30.3 Parallel Computing on Nondedicated Workstations

Workstations in a cluster are often under-utilized [11], [3]. Arpaci et al. [1] report that, although the set of idle machines changes over time, the total number of idle machines stays relatively constant. Our objective is to use the idle workstations in a cluster to run additional parallel jobs.

30.3.1 Nondedicated Workstations as Transient Processors

There have been several systems that attempt to make use of idle workstations to execute sequential programs [8]. Such additional computation is suspended when primary user activity is detected to avoid performance degradation for primary users. It is resumed when primary user activity ends and the workstation becomes idle. The workstations that are available for use only when they are idle are referred to as *transient processors* [7]. A transition of the host processor from an available to a non-available state is referred to as a *transient failure.* When using a network of transient processors for parallel computation, each component process of the parallel application is assigned to a processor; the component process is scheduled when the host processor is idle and suspended when the processor is busy.

The impact of transient failures on sequential programs and long-duration parallel programs with many independent tasks is analyzed by Kleinrock et al. [7] who showed that the rate of progress is proportional to the fraction of time the processor is idle. The impact of transient failures on frequently synchronizing parallel programs with relatively small amounts of computation between synchronizations is much more severe; if a single participating processor becomes unavailable, the entire parallel computation is delayed for the duration of the non-available period, making use of parallelism inefficient. In some cases synchronous parallel programs may take longer to execute on nondedicated clusters of workstations than on a single workstation sequentially. To deliver acceptable performance, parallel applications executing in such environments must be able to adapt to the changing computing environment; we refer to such ability as *adaptive parallelism.*

30.3.2 Approaches to Adaptive Parallelism

Recall that a transition of the host processor from an available to a non-available state is referred to as a *transient failure* of the component process. The effect of a transient failure is to delay the parallel application. Conversely, a transition of the host processor from a non-available to an available state is treated as *recovery* of this process. In the following discussion, we assume that transient failures of processors are independent events.

In general, there are two ways to deal with failures in a system: prevent (or avoid) occurrence of failures or recover from them. Prevention or avoidance of failures is usually achieved through redundancy, i.e., use of multiple instances of certain critical resources. In case of parallel computations, we can use multiple instances of either data or computations to prevent or avoid failures. Alternatively, we can try to recover after a failure has occurred by re-executing the failed (delayed) computations.

Based on these general principles, we identify three schemes to deal with transient failures. The schemes try to mask or reduce the impact of processor state transitions by replicating processes, computations and/or data to varying degrees. They can be classified based on the eagerness with which the replication takes place, as in Table 30.1. The straightforward execution simply delays the completion of the computation step until all participating processes finish their computation, even if some of the processors participating in the computation change their state from available to non-available. This scheme requires the least effort, but is also susceptible to the full impact of the unavailability of participating processors.

Table 30.1 Classification of Schemes to Deal with Transient Processor Failures Using Replication of Data and Computations as well as Migration of Processes

Scheme	Replication of Computations	Replication of Data	Migration of Processes
Straightforward execution	No	No	No
Full process replication	Eager	Lazy	Not needed
Standard failure recovery	Lazy	Lazy	Needed
Adaptive replication	Lazy	Eager	Needed

The first approach to reduce the impact of transient failures is based on eager (preventive) replication of component processes which increases the probability that at least one replica finishes the computation step without transient failure. Such replication can be justified by the argument that the idle time on a processor is free for use and, therefore, costs nothing. This approach is called the *full replication scheme.* This scheme uses (lazy) data replication to enable replicas that have fallen behind to catch up with the leading process that has finished its computation. The problem with this solution is that it is often too costly to update replicas with the status of the fastest processor in each group.

Another approach is based on *recovery from failures* by another component process executing on a different processor than the failing one. We further assume that at least one of the component processes is immune to transient failures due to processor unavailability. This assumption is easily satisfied, since it is possible to place at least one component of the parallel computation on a workstation owned by the user. We refer to this process as the *master process.* The computations of the failed component process can be recovered by sending the computation state of the failed process to the master process. The master process can use this data to recreate the computation state of the failed process and execute its computations. This approach requires the services of the master process for each process that failed. Consequently, the master process can become a bottleneck in case of multiple transient failures.

Yet another approach is to deal with transient failures preventively. In the *adaptive replication scheme*, the computation state is eagerly replicated on a neighbor process at the beginning of a computation step. In the event of a failure of the sender process, the receiver process uses the state data it received to replicate the computations of the failed process. Recovery of computations in this approach is distributed among the components and hence this scheme has the potential to be scalable. Due to the advantages this scheme offers, we choose this scheme to implement adaptive parallelism in the Bulk-Synchronous Parallel model.

30.4 Adaptive Parallelism in the Bulk-Synchronous Parallel Model

As explained above, the adaptive replication scheme relies on executing (replicating) the computations of a failed process on another participating processor to allow the parallel computation to proceed. Note that in the Bulk-Synchronous Parallel computation, the computation states of the participating processes are consistent with each other at the point of synchronization. By starting with the state of a failed process at the most recent synchronization point and executing its computations on another available participating workstation, we are able to recover the computations of the failed process. This allows the parallel computation to proceed without waiting for the failed process. Thus, our approach uses *eager replication of computation state and lazy replication of computations.*

30.4.1 Protocol for Replication and Recovery

The master process coordinates recovery from transient failures without replicating for any of the failed processes. Figure 30.1 illustrates the protocol. The participating processes, other than the master process, are organized into a logical ring topology in which each process has a predecessor and a successor. At the beginning of each computation step, each process in the ring communicates its computation state C_s to one or more of its successors, called *backup processes*, before starting its own computations. Each process also receives the computation state from one or more of its predecessors.

When a process finishes with its computations, it sends a message indicating successful completion to each of its backup processes. The process then checks to see if it has received a message of completion from each of its predecessors whose computation state is replicated at this process. Not receiving a message in a short timeout period is interpreted as the failure of the predecessor. The process then creates new processes — one for each of the failed predecessors — and restores the computation state of each new process to that of the corresponding failed predecessor at the beginning of the computation step, using the computation state received from that predecessor. Each of the newly-created processes performs the computations on behalf of a failed predecessor and performs synchronization on its behalf to complete the computation step. In general, such a newly created process assumes the identity of the predecessor and can continue participating in the parallel computation as a legitimate member. However, for the sake of better performance, this new process is migrated to a new host if one is available. For more details on the protocol, refer to [13]. It should be noted that the assumption of existence of a master process is not necessary for the correctness of the protocol. Using the standard techniques from distributed algorithms, synchronization can be achieved over the virtual ring, regardless of transient failures. However, the master

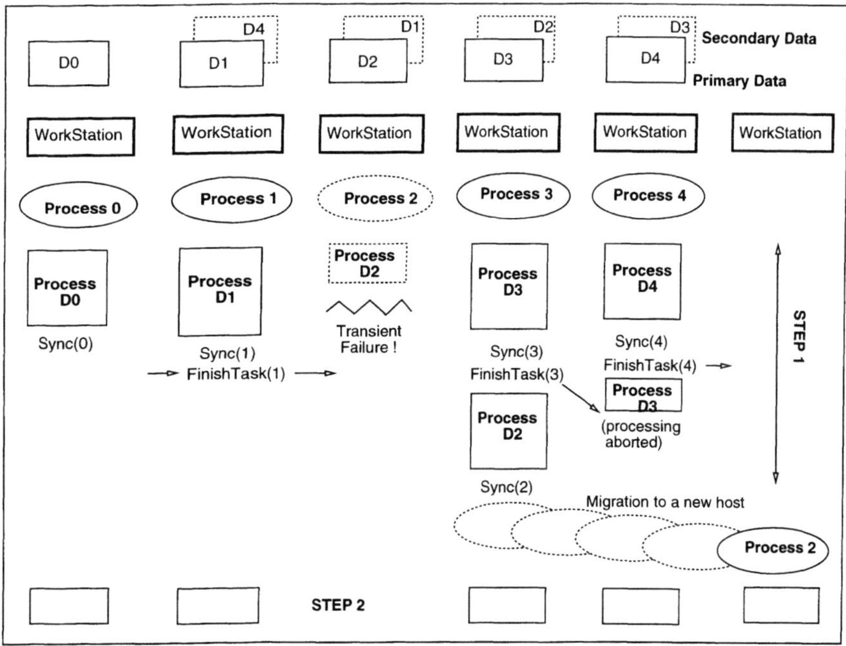

Figure 30.1 Protocol for replication and recovery illustrated for a replication level of one.

process is a convenient solution for a majority of applications, so we used it in this prototypical implementation of the system.

In our approach, the recovery of the failed computations and subsequent migration to a new available host are performed on an available host, which is much less intrusive than migrating from the failed (i.e., non-available) process.

The number of successors at which the computation state of a process is replicated is referred to as the *replication level*, denoted by R. R is also the number of predecessors from which a process will receive the computation state. A process can therefore act as a backup to any of the R predecessors from which it receives the computation state. It is easy to see that the replication level defines the maximum number of consecutive process failures in the logical ring topology that the system can tolerate. Failure of more than R consecutive processes within the same computation step will force the processes to wait until one of the host processors recovers. A higher level of replication increases the probability of recovery from failures, but it also increases the overhead during normal (failure-free) execution. The probability of transient failure of R consecutive processes is P_f^R, where P_f is the probability of transient failure of a single workstation. Assuming the duration of the computation step is small compared to the mean available and non-available periods, the probability of failure is small ($P_f \ll 1$). This assumption is justified because we are interested in the small total parallel computation time, so the larger the computation, the more processors we are willing to use. Hence, the computation step on each processor is relatively small, regardless of the size of the application. Under this assumption, the probability of irrecoverable failures decreases exponentially with the replication level R. The optimal for scalability level of replication growths as a logarithm of the number of processors and for sufficiently large degrees of parallelism (that are most important for practical applications) is very small.

30.4.2 Performance of Adaptive Replication

The cost of data replication includes the additional memory required for the replicated data and the cost of transferring the computation state to the successors. The additional memory needed for data replication is proportional to the level of replication, R, and the size of the computation state, C_s. The cost of communicating the computation state depends on the replication level, R, the size of the computation state, C_s, and the underlying communication network. A communication network that scales with the number of processors allows for a higher level of replication and a higher degree of tolerance to transient failures without incurring overhead during normal execution.

To minimize overhead during normal execution, our approach overlaps the computation with communication associated with data replication. For those applications in which the cost of data replication is smaller than the cost of computation in the superstep, replication of the computation state can be done without any overhead during normal execution. We refer to such applications as *computation dominant applications*. Under these assumptions, the scheme is scalable with high efficiency. Applications for which the cost of data replication is larger than the computation have an overhead associated with data replication, and therefore they are referred to as *data replication dominant applications*. A more detailed discussion of the performance of the adaptive replication scheme, along with the analysis, can be found in [15]. It should be noted that for scalability, it is sufficient that the cost of data replication will be of the same order (when expressed as a function of the problem size and the number of processors) as the cost of computation in a superstep.

30.5 A Programming Environment for Adaptive Bulk-Synchronous Parallelism

A programming environment developed at Rensselaer known as Adaptive BSP (A-BSP) library, is designed within the framework of the BSP model [18] and developed using the Oxford BSP Library [9]. A-BSP consists of dynamic extensions to the Oxford BSP library and the adaptive replication scheme designed in two levels of abstraction: *replication layer* and *user layer*. The replication layer implements the functionality of the adaptive replication scheme, including the protocol for recovery and replication, as a set of primitives. These primitives are accessible only through the user layer. By designing the run-time support in two layers, we intend to insulate the applications from changes in the implementation. By implementing the replication layer for other architectures, we can maintain the portability of applications using our library.

30.5.1 Dynamic Extensions to the Oxford BSP Library

The Oxford BSP Library implements a simplified version of the Bulk-Synchronous Parallel model. It is simple, yet robust, and was successfully used by us for implementing plasma simulation on a cluster of workstations [12]. We extended the Oxford BSP Library to provide dynamic process management and virtual synchronization as described in [13]. The extensions include the following features: the component processes can be terminated at any time, new processes can be created to join the computation, and component processes can perform synchronization for one another.

The A-BSP prototype implementation was based on the following assumptions. The supersteps that make use of adaptive replication contain computation only. This is not overly-restrictive, since a superstep containing computation and communication can always be expressed as a sequence of computation and communication supersteps. This assumption greatly simplifies the design of the protocol for the recovery of failed processes. We assume a reliable network, so a message that is sent by a process will always be received at the destination.

In A-BSP, restoring the computation state of the failed process involves

- restoring specific system state from the backup copy received from that process,
- restoring common system state from local checkpoint, and
- executing the user supplied recovery function.

Each of the newly-created processes performs the computations on behalf of a failed process and performs synchronization on its behalf to complete the computation step. In general, such a newly created process assumes the identity of the corresponding failed process and can continue participating in the parallel computation as a legitimate member. However, for the sake of better performance, this restored process is migrated to a new host if one is available.

30.5.2 The Replication Layer

The replication layer implements the functionality of the adaptive replication scheme, including the protocol for replication and recovery. It provides the following functionality for a component process:

- Replicate the specific system state on the backup process as determined by the replication protocol.
- Checkpoint the common system state locally on the same process.

- Detect the failure of the process whose computation state is replicated on this process.

- Create a new process to execute the computations of a failed process. The new process is created as a child of the process performing the recovery.

- Restore the computation state of the newly created process from the backup copies of the specific and common system states.

- Execute the recovery function supplied by the user.

- Perform synchronization on behalf of a failed process.

- Terminate lagging processes whose computations have been successfully replicated.

- Migrate the process to another available host.

The replication layer allows a process to detect and replicate for failed processes. However, functionality of this layer is not directly accessible to the user.

30.5.3 The User Layer

The user layer provides the application programming interface (API) for the A-BSP library. It includes the following primitives that transparently allow access to the functionality of the replication layer:

- Constructs to specify data to be replicated and to specify memory management for the replication data.

  The construct `bsp_replication_data` (see Figure 30.2 for the full syntax) allows the user to specify data to be replicated. The user can specify static storage for replication data by defining a valid location for the `store` parameter. Otherwise, automatic memory management is assumed and the system allocates dynamic storage for the replication data. It keeps track of the dynamic storage across process replications.

- Constructs to specify computation state.

  A predefined structure `BspSystemState` can be used to declare variables that hold specific or common system state. The function `bsp_init_system_state` can be used to initialize a `BspSystemState` variable. Using the function `bsp_set_system_state`, the state variable can be made to hold variables that comprise the computation state (specific or common system state). The specific system state can be specified for a computation superstep using the construct `bsp_specific_system_state` and the common system state using the construct `bsp_common_system_state`.

```
/* Constructs to specify a computation superstep */
bsp_comp_sstep(int sstepid);
bsp_comp_sstep_end(int sstepid);
/* Constructs to specify replication data and allocate storage */
bsp_replication_data(void* data, long nbytes, void* store,
                     char* tag, int subscript);
bsp_setup_replication_environment();
/* Constructs to specify Computation State */
struct BspSystemState;
bsp_init_system_state(BspSystemState* bss);
bsp_reset_system_state(BspSystemState* bss);
bsp_set_system_state(BspSystemState* bss);
bsp_specific_system_state(BspSystemState* bss);
bsp_common_system_state(BspSystemState* bss);
RecoveryFunction();
```

Figure 30.2 Adaptive parallel extensions to the Oxford BSP Library (User Layer).

- Constructs to specify a computation superstep.

  The constructs `bsp_comp_sstep` and `bsp_comp_sstep_end` are used to delimit a computation superstep. The replication and recovery mechanism is embedded into these constructs; the process of data replication, detection of failures and recovery is transparent to the user.

- Recovery Function.

  The predefined function `RecoveryFunction` is executed after restoring the computation state of a failed process from the backup. The user must supply the code required for any operations required for recovering the computation state of a failed process. Specification of the recovery function is optional.

Figures 30.2 - 30.5 illustrate the use of BSP constructs for adaptive parallelism. These examples were taken from a C++ implementation of a plasma simulation using the adaptive replication system. Figure 30.2 shows the constructs provided by the user layer described above. Figure 30.3 illustrates the use of these constructs to specify replication data. Figure 30.4 illustrates the use of the constructs to specify the computation state of a component process. Figure 30.5 illustrates the use of the A-BSP construct for the computation superstep. The specific and local system states must be specified for each computation superstep. The computation superstep requires no additional constructs; adaptive replication and recovery of failed computations are done transparently to the user.

```
/* case (a): (static) storage available for replication data */
bsp_replication_data((void*) &plasma_region, sizeof(plasma_region),
                     (void*) &plasma_region_backup,
                     "PLASMA_REGION", -1);
/* case (b): storage to be allocated by the BSP library */
bsp_replication_data((void*) elec_pos,
                     PTMAXNP * sizeof(ChargedParticle),
                     0,"PLASMA_POS", -1);
/* case (c): A 2 dimensional array, with no static storage available
         for replication data */
for(i=0; i < SYSLEN_MX; i++)
  bsp_replication_data((void*) ForceFieldX[i],
                       SYSLEN_Y*sizeof(Scalar),
                       0,"FORCE_FIELD_X", i);
```

Figure 30.3 Use of A-BSP constructs to specify replication data.

30.6 Application of A-BSP to Parallel Computations

We applied the A-BSP library to two different applications that illustrate the performance of the scheme for *computation dominant* applications and *data replication dominant* applications described in Section 30.4.2.

```
BspSystemState* plasmaState = new BspSystemState;
bsp_init_system_state( plasmaState );
/* Specify the data for the state variable, using symbolic names */
bsp_set_system_state(specific, "PLASMA_REGION", -1);
bsp_set_system_state(specific, "PLASMA_POS", -1);
for(i=0; i < SYSLEN_MX; i++)
  bsp_set_system_state(specific, "FORCE_FIELD_X", i);
```

Figure 30.4 Use of A-BSP constructs to specify computation state.

30.6.1 Maximum Independent Set

A set of vertices in a graph is said to be an *independent set* if no two vertices in the set are adjacent [4]. A *maximal independent set* is an independent set which is not a subset of any other independent set. A graph, in general, has many maximal independent sets. In the maximum independent set problem, we want to find a maximal independent set with the largest number of vertices. Given a graph G, we start with a vertex v of G in the set. We add more vertices to this set, selecting at each stage a vertex that is not adjacent to any of the vertices already in the set. This procedure will ultimately produce a maximal independent set. In order to find a maximal independent set with the largest number of vertices, we find all the

```
bsp_specific_system_state( plasmaState );
bsp_local_system_state( localCharge );

bsp_comp_sstep( bsp_step );
CalcEField( vpm, energy );
InitChargeDensity();
energy.ke( 0.0 );
Advance( elec_pos, elec_vel );
bsp_comp_sstep_end( bsp_step );
```

Figure 30.5 An A-BSP computation superstep.

maximal independent sets using a recursive depth first search with backtracking [6]. To conserve memory, no explicit representation of the graph is maintained. Instead, the connectivity information is used to search through a virtual graph. To reduce the search space, heuristics are used to prune the search space. Each processor searches a subgraph and the processors exchange information on the maximal independent set found on each processor. Since the adjacency matrix is replicated on each processor, the computation state that needs to be communicated to a successor to deal with transient failures is nil. That is, the computation state of a failed process can be recreated based on the knowledge of its identity alone. This application can therefore be categorized as a computation dominant application.

30.6.2 Plasma Simulation

The plasma Particle-in-Cell simulation model was described in Section 30.2.2. In the replicated grid version of this model [12], the particles are evenly distributed among the processors sharing work load; the simulation space (field grid) is replicated on each of the processors to avoid frequent communication between processors. The computations modify the positions and velocities of the particles, forces at the grid points, and the charge distribution on the grid. Hence, the computation state data that needs to be replicated includes the positions and velocities of the particles, the forces at the grid points and the grid charge. However, at the beginning of each superstep, all processors have the same global charge distribution and hence the charge data does not need to be replicated on a remote host. Instead, each process can save this data locally, which it can use to restore a failed predecessor. Checkpointing data locally when possible reduces the amount of data communicated for data replication. Due to the overhead associated with the communication of computation state, this application can be categorized as a replication dominant application (also see discussion in Section 30.6.3). It is still scalable, as long as the interconnection network of an executing cluster is scalable.

30.6.3 Results

Figure 30.6(a) shows a plot of the execution times of maximum independent set problem on transient processors using the A-BSP library with $t_a = 40$ minutes and $t_n = 20$ minutes respectively. These values for t_a and t_n are within the range of values reported in earlier works [11]. The measurements were taken on a cluster of Sun Sparc 5 workstations connected by a 10 Mbps Ethernet. The number of processors available is much larger than the degree of parallelism used in the simulations and, therefore, migration to an available processor was always possible. The execution times of the runs on transient processors using the A-BSP library were compared with the execution time on dedicated processors and with execution time on transient processors without using the adaptive replication scheme. Runs on transient processors that do not use A-BSP simply suspend the execution of the parallel computation when the host processor is busy. The execution time on a single processor is also shown for reference. As can be seen from these timings, the runs on transient processors using the A-BSP library compare favorably with runs on dedicated processors. Our measurements indicate that a significant amount of computation was performed using idle workstations. Since a dedicated workstation is used to execute the main process, when using a parallelism of p, a fraction of $\frac{p-1}{p}$ of the total computation is performed by the idle machines.

Figure 30.6(b) shows the results of application of A-BSP library to plasma simulation with $N = 3,500,000$ particles. As mentioned in Section 30.6.2, the computation state data that needs to be replicated includes the positions and velocities of particles in the local partition and the forces at the grid points in the local partition. The replicated data includes four floating point numbers for each particle. As a result, for runs with four processors, the size of data replicated for particles is about 14 MBytes. On a 10 Mbps cluster, replicating the computation state of three processors takes up to about 40 seconds while the computation step, t_s, is half as long. In addition, the network is shared with other users, so heavy network traffic may increase the time needed for replication. Figure 30.6(b) shows a plot of execution times on transient processors with and without adaptive replication for degrees of parallelism of 4, 8 and 12. These measurements were obtained using $t_a = 30$ minutes and $t_n = 20$ minutes, respectively. For plasma simulation, due to the overhead associated with communication of computation state in each step, simulation runs on transient processors using the adaptive replication scheme take longer to execute, compared to the runs on dedicated processors. The execution time on transient processors with adaptive replication is also longer than the sequential execution time, as estimated from the execution times on dedicated processors. However, even in this case, the adaptive replication scheme is relevant for the following reasons. The execution time on transient processors with adaptive replication is still much smaller than the execution time without adaptive replication. Further, the simulation used for our measurements was too large to fit on a single workstation and hence single processor runs were not even possible. For simulations that are too large to fit on a single workstation, parallel runs are mandatory. When dedicated machines are

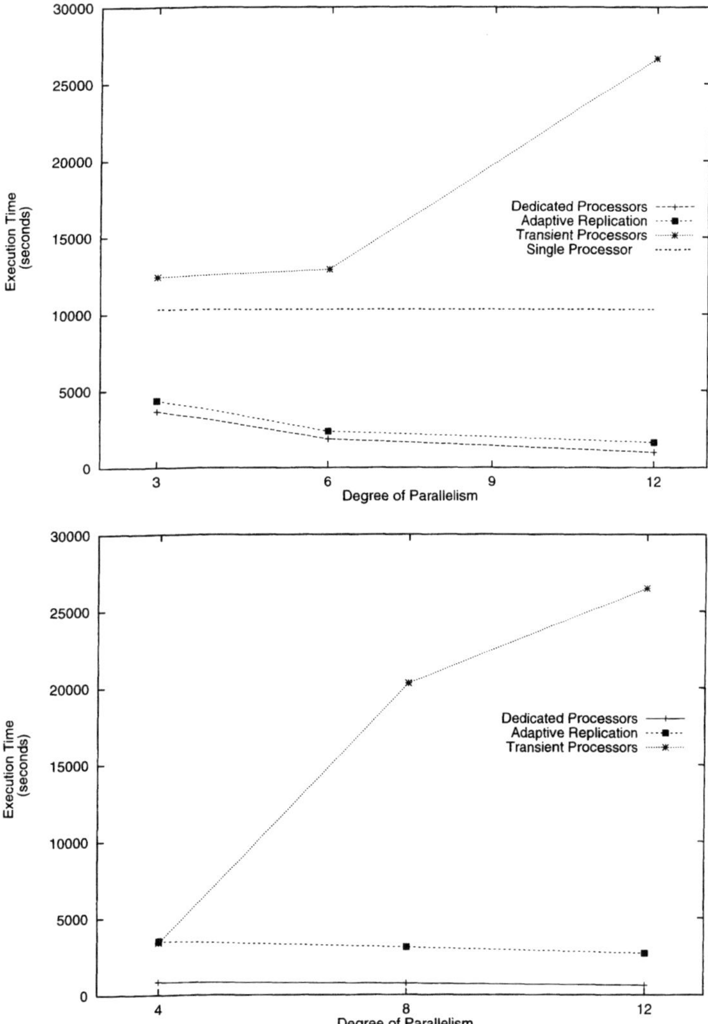

Figure 30.6 Plot showing execution times of (a) maximum independent set and (b) plasma simulation on dedicated processors, on transient processors using adaptive replication and on transient processors without adaptive replication. Execution time on a single processor is shown for comparison purposes.

not available for parallel computation, application of A-BSP library ensures that parallel runs using idle workstations complete in a reasonable time.

Any approach intended to tolerate transient failures will necessarily incur some overhead to checkpoint the computation state of the processes. Overhead incurred by replication of computation state as done in the adaptive replication scheme (which can be considered a form of diskless checkpointing) is no larger than the overhead caused by checkpointing to disk. The network used to obtain the measurements is a 10 Mbps Ethernet, which is quickly becoming obsolete. With a faster network such as an ATM network or a 100 Mbps Ethernet, the overhead due to data replication should be much smaller.

30.7 Application of A-BSP to Clusters of Nondedicated Workstations

The results shown in Section 30.6 are obtained with simulated transient processors with exponentially distributed available and non-available periods. In this section, we present the results of executing a graph search algorithm using the adaptive replication on a cluster of nondedicated workstations in the Department of Computer Science at Rensselaer.

In the graph search algorithm described above, the connectivity information (the adjacency matrix) is replicated on all the processors. Replication of the adjacency information improves the efficiency of the parallel graph search by reducing the amount of data communicated. Replication of the adjacency information also reduces the state information that is required for recovering from transient failures. However, replication of the adjacency matrix on all participating processors limits the maximum size of the problem that can be solved. It is desirable to find a parallel graph search algorithm that allows for solution of problems of size larger than that can be solved on a single processor. In this section, we describe an improved graph search algorithm with these characteristics.

In the improved graph search algorithm, the adjacency matrix is partitioned among the participating processes in the following manner. The rows of the adjacency matrix are partitioned among the participating processes such that each process contains the complete connectivity information for a subset of the vertices. We refer to this subset of vertices as *belonging* to the corresponding processor. At each level of the recursive depth first search, a new vertex is added to the independent set being constructed and all vertices in the current graph that are adjacent to this vertex are deleted to form the vertex list for the new graph to be searched. Since each processor contains only a portion of the adjacency matrix, each processor needs to obtain adjacency information for vertices that *belong* to other processors. When the subgraphs generated are of sufficient granularity, they are searched locally on one of the participating processors. To avoid communication during the local search, each participating process needs to have adjacency information for all pairs of vertices in its subgraph. For this purpose, before starting local search on its subgraph, each processor obtains adjacency information for vertices in the subgraph that belong to other processes. Once the adjacency matrix is constructed for the subgraph to be searched, the processors do not need to communicate during the local search.

The adaptive performance of the graph search algorithm depends on the amount of data to be replicated. Since the adjacency matrix is partitioned among the processes, the adjacency matrix partition of each process needs to be replicated on a backup process. The replicated adjacency information is used to recover the predecessor in case of a failure. Replication of the adjacency matrix partition can be done at the beginning of the search. When a process performs the recovery for its failed predecessor and assumes its identity, the adjacency matrix information is no longer valid since the process now has a different predecessor. The new process needs to update the adjacency information from its predecessor. Updating the adjacency information of the predecessor needs to be done once per recovery. The cost of refetching the adjacency matrix partition can therefore be included in the cost of recovering a failed process.

In addition to the adjacency matrix partition, the adjacency matrix of the subgraph that is searched locally also needs to be replicated. However, since the subgraphs searched locally on the participating processors differ only slightly, we can avoid replicating the adjacency matrix of the local subgraphs if we construct the adjacency matrix for the largest of these subgraphs. This is the approach followed in our implementation. Since the subgraphs differ slightly from each other, a mapping that identifies these vertices needs to be replicated on the backup process. This cost is proportional to the number of vertices in the original graph. Thus the amount of communication required for replication during normal execution is smaller than the communication inherent to the algorithm.

The processor pool used for these runs consisted of about 20 machines that included Sparc 5 (Models 110 and 70) and Sparc 20 processors. A host monitor [14] is used to determine the status of the workstations based on the cpu load and the activity of the console user. The runs used a degree of parallelism of 6, with 5 of them using nondedicated machines. For 10,000 vertices with a mean probability of connectivity of 0.54, the execution time on nondedicated processors is about 12 hours, compared to about 10.5 hours on dedicated processors.

The maximum size problem that can be solved on a single processor is a graph of 10,000 vertices. Using the scalable graph search algorithm, we are able to solve graphs of size 15,000 vertices. The execution time for a graph with 15,000 vertices and a probability of connectivity of 0.56 is about 7.5 hours when using a degree of parallelism of 12. The corresponding execution time on nondedicated processors is about 10 hours. Parallel run on dedicated processors used the faster processors (Model 110) while the run on nondedicated processors used a mixture of fast and slow processors (both Model 110 and Model 70), so part of the execution is on the slower processors. Scalable parallel algorithms are essential to solve problems that are too large to fit in the memory of a single processor. Adaptive replication scheme allows efficient execution of parallel runs on nondedicated processors.

30.8 Conclusions

In this chapter, we described a programming environment for clusters of nondedicated workstations to facilitate efficient parallel computations. Our approach to adaptive parallelism is based on the Bulk-Synchronous Parallel model. It enables parallel computations executing on nondedicated workstations to tolerate frequent unavailability of the workstations in a nondedicated cluster and thereby adapt to the changing computing environment. Our approach offers a general framework for adaptive parallelism and is application independent. We described a protocol for the replication of computation state and replication of computations. We extended the Oxford BSP library [9] with dynamic process management and virtual synchronization and implemented the protocol on top of the extended library. The adaptive parallel extensions to the library include primitives for specification of replication data, memory management for replication data and specification of computation state. We integrated the adaptive parallel extensions into the Oxford BSP library. The A-BSP library performs data replication and recovery of failed computations transparently to the user. We have demonstrated the adaptive capabilities of the library by applying it to two applications: a graph search problem and plasma simulation. Our results demonstrate that the A-BSP library can be used to execute parallel computations efficiently using idle machines in a cluster of nondedicated workstations.

30.9 Bibliography

[1] Remzi H. Arpaci, Andrea C. Dusseau, Amin M. Vahdat, Lok T. Liu, Thomas E. Anderson, and David A. Patterson. The Interaction of Parallel and Sequential Workloads on a Network of Workstations. In *Proceedings of SIGMETRICS/Performance '95*, pages 267–277, 1995.

[2] R. H. Bisseling and W. F. McColl. Scientific Computing on Bulk Synchronous Parallel Architectures (Short Version). In B. Pehrson and I. Simon, editors, *Proceedings of the 13th IFIP World Computer Congress*, vol. 1, Elsevier, 1994.

[3] Clemens H. Cap and Volker Strumpen. Efficient Parallel Computing in Distributed Workstation Environments. *Parallel Computing*, vol. 23, pages 1221–1234, 1993.

[4] Narsingh Deo. *Graph Theory with Applications to Engineering and Computer Science.* Englewood Cliffs, N.J.: Prentice-Hall, Inc., 1974.

[5] A. V. Gerbessiotis and L. G. Valiant. Direct Bulk-Synchronous Parallel Algorithms. In O. Nurmi and E.Ukkonen, editors, *Proceedings of the Third Scandinavian Workshop on Algorithmic Theory,* Lecture Notes in Computer Science, pages 1–18, Berlin: Springer Verlag, 1992.

[6] Mark K. Goldberg and David L. Hollinger. Database Learning: a Method for Empirical Algorithm Design. In *Proceedings of the Workshop on Algorithm Engineering*, September 1997.

[7] L. Kleinrock and W. Korfhage. Collecting Unused Processing Capacity: An Analysis of Transient Distributed Systems. *IEEE Transactions on Parallel and Distributed Systems*, vol. 4(5), May 1993.

[8] Michael J. Litzkow, Miron Livny, and Matt W. Mutka. Condor - A Hunter of Idle Workstations. In *Proceedings of the 8th International Conference on Distributed Computing Systems*, San Jose, California, June 13-17, 1988.

[9] Richard Miller. A Library for Bulk-Synchronous Parallel Programming. In *British Computer Society Workshop on General Purpose Parallel Computing*, December 1993.

[10] MPI: A Message Passing Interface Standard. *Technical Report*, Message Passing Interface Forum, May 5, 1994.

[11] M. W. Mutka and M. Livny. Profiling Workstations' Available Capacity for Remote Execution. In *Proceedings of the 12th Symposium on Computer Performance*, Brussels, Belgium, December 7-9, 1987.

[12] M. V. Nibhanupudi, C. D. Norton, and B. K. Szymanski. Plasma Simulation on Networks of Workstations Using the Bulk-Synchronous Parallel Model. In *Proceedings of the International Conference on Parallel and Distributed Processing Techniques and Applications (PDPTA'95)*, Athens, Georgia, November 1995.

[13] M. V. Nibhanupudi and B. K. Szymanski. Adaptive Parallelism in the Bulk-Synchronous Parallel Model. In *Proceedings of the 2nd International Euro-Par Conference*, Lyon, France, August 1996.

[14] M. V. Nibhanupudi and B. K. Szymanski. Adaptive Parallel Computing on Nondedicated Networks of Workstations Using the Bulk Synchronous Parallel Model. *Technical report*, Department of Computer Science, Rensselaer Polytechnic Institute, Troy, NY, April 1998.

[15] Mohan V. Nibhanupudi. Adaptive Parallel Computations on Networks of Workstations. *Ph.D. Thesis*, Computer Sciences Department, Rensselaer Polytechnic Institute, 1998.

[16] D. A. Nichols. Using Idle Workstations In A Shared Computing Environment. In *Proceedings of the 11th ACM Symposium on Operating System Principles*, ACM, November 1987.

[17] V. S. Sunderam. PVM: A Framework for Parallel Distributed Computing. *Concurrency: Practice and Experience*, vol. 2(4), pages 315–339, 1990.

[18] Leslie G. Valiant. A Bridging Model for Parallel Computation. *Communications of the ACM*, vol. 33(8), pages 103–111, August 1990.

Chapter 31

MARS: An Adaptive Parallel Programming Environment

E-G. TALBI, J-M. GEIB, Z. HAFIDI AND D. KEBBAL

LIFL / Université de Lille 1
Bâtiment M3, Cité Scientifique
59655 Villeneuve d'Ascq, France

Email: {*talbi, geib, hafidi, kebbal*}*@lifl.fr*

31.1 Motivation and Goals

The proliferation of powerful workstations and fast communication networks (ATM, Myrinet, etc.) with constantly decreasing cost/performance ratio has shown the emergence of networks of workstations (NOWs) and clusters of workstations (COWs) as parallel platforms for high performance computing. These parallel platforms have become increasingly available in companies and research institutions. They are generally composed of an important part of heterogeneous machines shared by many users. Load analysis of NOWs during long periods of time showed that only a small percentage of the available power was used. The machines are mainly used for editing files, reading e-mail and similar non-CPU consuming tasks (Web, etc.). There is a substantial amount of idle time. In addition, a workstation belongs to an "owner" who will not tolerate external applications degrading the performance of his machine. Therefore, dynamic scheduling of parallel applications exploiting the aggregate idle time and avoiding noticeable interference with "owner" activities is essential.

Parallel programming environments such as PVM, MPI and Linda provide different programming paradigms (message passing, virtual shared memory). In addition, several programming styles are often used on these paradigms (master/worker, bag-of-tasks, pipelining). However, they do not provide advanced programming tools (such as load balancing, application and system reconfiguration, and fault tolerance) to efficiently use NOWs. In a large system, it is certain that at any given instant, several machines or communication links will fail. Thus, dealing with fault tolerance and dynamic reconfiguration is a necessity for both the scheduling system and for applications.

Many scheduling systems have been proposed in the literature. They differ from each other in the way scheduling of applications over nodes is done. They fall into three main categories depending on whether *the number and/or the location* of tasks depend or not on the load state of NOWs (Table 31.1). The first category represents systems for which both the number and location of tasks are static. We call these systems *non-adaptive* because the allocation of nodes to tasks remains unchanged during the execution of the application regardless of the current state of the NOW (PVM, MPI, etc.). The second category represents systems for which the number of tasks is fixed but the locations are determined and changed at runtime. All dynamic load balancing and process migration systems fall into this class (MPVM [4], Sprite [3], LSF [7], etc.). We call this class *semi-adaptive* since the parallelism degree is not related to load variation in the computing environment: When the number of tasks exceeds the number of idle nodes, multiple tasks are assigned to the same node. Moreover, when there are more idle nodes than tasks, some of them will not be used. In the third category, scheduling systems support applications which dynamically change the set of tasks in number and location with respect to the number of available idle nodes. These systems are called *adaptive* because the locations and the increasing/decreasing of the number of tasks are related to load variation in the computing environment. The user is totally preserved from managing the availability of nodes and the dynamics of NOWs. Piranha under Linda [5] and CARMI/Wodi under PVM [12] are examples of such scheduling systems.

Table 31.1 Scheduling Systems Classification

	tasks		
	number	**location**	**examples**
non-adaptive	static	static	PVM, MPI, Linda
semi-adaptive	static	dynamic	MPVM, Amber, Sprite, LSF, PRM
adaptive	dynamic	dynamic	Piranha, CARMI/Wodi

Our aim is to develop an adaptive parallel scheduling system (MARS) to harness idle cycles of time (keeping in mind the ownership of workstations) and to support adaptive parallelism to dynamically reconfigure the set of tasks composing a parallel application. Parallel applications can benefit greatly from a platform having combined computing resources of massively parallel machines (MPPs), COWs and NOWs.

Throughout this chapter, we use the term *node* to denote a workstation in a NOW and COW, or a processor of an MPP. The remainder of the chapter is organized as follows. In the next section we describe some of the related work in this area. Section 31.3 analyses the available capacity of NOWs. Section 31.4 gives a brief overview of the MARS runtime system and the associated program development methodology. The performance of our system on some parallel applications is presented in Section 31.5. Finally, Section 31.6 presents concluding remarks and future work.

31.2 Related Work

This section presents an overview of the diverse body of related work.

31.2.1 Exploiting Idle Time

Among the first systems which use idle time are systems that identify idle workstations and schedule sequential jobs on them. Systems such as *Condor* [7], *Butler* [11], *Stealth* [9], *Process Servers* [6] and *DAWGS* [2] are representative. When a node becomes busy, different strategies are used to schedule the jobs:

- Condor and DAWGS migrates jobs: First, implementing a migration mechanism is a complex task, and the resource overhead used is relatively high. Second, actual migration mechanisms don't allow migration of tasks between heterogeneous nodes.

- Butler kills jobs and restarts them on another nodes: The drawback of this approach is that we lose the time already used by the job.

- Process Server and Stealth change the priority of the jobs: In this class of systems, the concept of "ownership" is loosely interpreted. The "owner" receives poorer services (CPU time, memory usage, etc.) than would be provided by an autonomous workstation.

One key aspect of our approach is its support for parallel applications; this is an aspect which is absent in most of the above systems. We assume that there are users with compute-intensive parallel applications capable of using all available CPU time.

The *Charlotte* [1] and *NOW* projects [14] attempt to combine a large number of workstations and MPPs for parallel computing. Many of the objectives of our project are similar to those projects. Our approach differs from these systems in its capabilities, mechanisms and assumptions:

- The programming model in Charlotte is based on shared memory and employs the Java language enhanced with classes for expressing parallelism. The decision to involve a node in a computation is made explicitly by the owner of the machine. An eager scheduling approach has been adopted, where a single process is assigned to available idle machines until it is executed to completion by at least one machine.

- The *NOW* project is an attempt to combine a large number of workstations over ATM/Myrinet for parallel computing. They are building a new operating system GLUnix (Global Layer Unix) to perform global resource allocation in a NOW. Their system glues together individual Unix operating systems to provide a single system image of the machines in a network.

31.2.2 Adaptive Schedulers

One of the earliest experiments in designing an adaptive scheduler was the *Worm* project [13]. A worm is a computation composed of multiple segments. A segment continually searches for idle machines on the network on which it could replicate itself. *Spawn* is another adaptive system which uses a microeconomic approach for resource management [15]. Spawn is constrained to be used on the NFS shared file system.

There are a few systems where mechanisms used for resource management and control are more sophisticated and flexible. The most important are *Piranha* [5] and *CARMI/WoDi* [12].

- *Piranha* is designed for master/workers applications like MARS, but it is restricted to the Linda (tuple-space) model. Worker processes look for the tuple-space for tasks to be performed. When a task is found, it is retracted from tuple-space, executed, and the result is written back into tuple-space. The shared memory management is the principle bottleneck of the Piranha approach. Fault-tolerance mechanisms are not provided. This makes the Piranha system very sensitive to node failures, which are frequent in networks of workstations.

- *CARMI/WoDi* is designed on top of PVM and Condor. It supports SPMD applications, but it is not a multi-user system. This can generate conflicts between applications of different users which want to allocate the same resources. In addition, when a node becomes busy, the allocated task is killed and the work done is then wasted, as in Piranha. Load balancing and fault tolerance is based on process migration, which could not be used in heterogeneous platforms.

31.3 The Available Capacity of NOWs

It is very important for a scheduling system to quantify node idleness or node availability. Idleness criteria define the conditions under which each node is idle, and thus determine the aggregate amount of idle time available.

31.3.1 Node Idleness

Node idleness in scheduling systems is highly related to both load indicators and owner behavior. The Sprite system declares a node idle if the CPU utilization is below 1% and the keyboard is idle for 30 seconds [3]. Piranha requires 5 minutes of inactivity for the keyboard, mouse and remote logins, and the one-minute, five-minutc, and ten-minute load average must be below 0.4, 0.3 and 0.1, respectively [5]. Condor detected idle nodes if the CPU utilization was below one-quarter of one percent [7].

Several load indicators are provided by the MARS monitoring system such as: CPU utilization, load average, number of users logged in, user memory, swap space, paging rate, disk transfer rate, /tmp space, and NFS performance. In the experiments presented, owner activity is detected by controlling keyboard and mouse idle times. Node's idleness criteria must be selected to be non-intrusive and relatively stable over the time. A node is IDLE if the 1, 5 and 10 minutes load average are below 2.0, 1.5 and 1.0 respectively and the keyboard/mouse are inactive for more than 5 minutes. A node is OWNED if the keyboard/mouse are active regardless of the load average i.e we consider it as a node in a maximum load state.

Figure 31.1 shows a state transition diagram for MARS nodes. Nodes not hosting MARS applications toggle between IDLE, OWNED and BUSY based, respectively, on node underload, owner claim or node overload due to non-MARS applications. If a node is IDLE when a MARS application is submitted, the node becomes a RUNNING node and will host "worker threads." In this mode, other "worker threads" can be created for other MARS applications (time sharing between different applications allowed) while the load of the node does not exceed a certain threshold, in which case the node becomes LOADED and MARS proceeds to load balancing. If all "worker threads" complete on a MARS node, the node becomes IDLE.

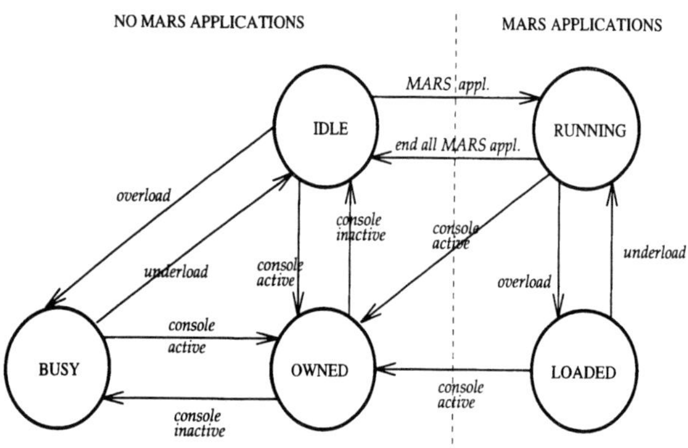

Figure 31.1 Transition states of a MARS node.

31.3.2 Aggregate Idle Time

Once idleness criteria are in place, we can measure aggregate idle time. In the Sprite system, 66 – 78% of node idle time was reported. In Condor, they found that 70 – 80% of nodes were idle on week-ends and 50% were idle at peak times (2 to 4 p.m. on week-days). In the Piranha system, it was reported that 86% of workstation time was idle, and idle time peaked at 96% on week-end nights.

For our experiment study, we collected results from a network of heterogeneous workstations. The network is composed of 51 workstations owned by research workers of our laboratory and graduate students (Figure 36.3).

To illustrate node use in a week-day over a 24-hour period that begins at 0:00 a.m., we draw in Figure 36.3, the curves representing the number of IDLE, BUSY and OWNED nodes with a scan period of one minute. Nodes toggle between idle, busy and owned state. According to load indicators chosen, we observed 82.9% IDLE nodes against 8.5% of BUSY nodes and 8.6% of OWNED ones. The same results have been obtained for other week-days, which shows that the amount of unused capacity is periodic. The aggregate idle time available represents a large amount of computer time. This supports our assertion that a tool based on recycling lost resources is essential.

Our idle-time measurements are consistent with those of the literature. There is a substantial amount of idle time at off-peak times and, even at times of peak use, a significant fraction of workstations are idle. The idle time observed is, on the average, 83%. The standard deviation of our observations is 2.5%, indicating that the amount of idle time is rather constant.

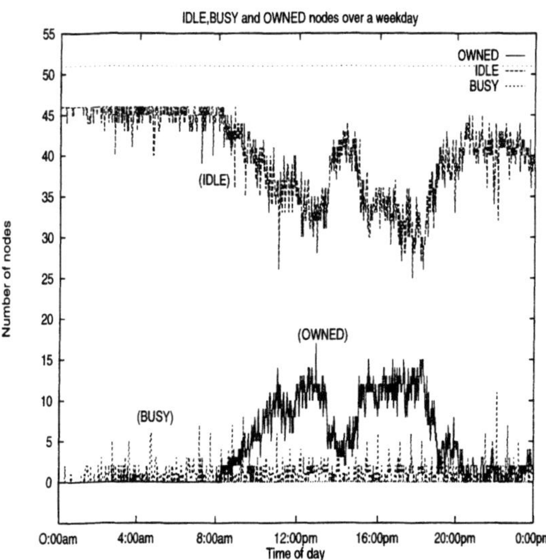

Figure 31.2 Load analysis of the network of workstations (51 workstations).

31.4 The MARS Approach

We present in this section, respectively, the main components of the MARS infrastructure, the programming methodology for developing parallel adaptive applications, and the MARS scheduler.

31.4.1 MARS Infrastructure

The MARS system is implemented on top of the UNIX operating system (Figure 31.3). We use an existing communication library which preserves the ordering of messages: PVM (Parallel Virtual Machine). Data representations using XDR are hidden for the programmer. The execution model is based on a preemptive multi-threaded runtime system: PM^2 (Parallel Multi-threaded Machine) [10]. The basic functionality of PM^2 is the LRPC (Lightweight Remote Procedure Call), which consists in forking a remote thread to execute a specified service.

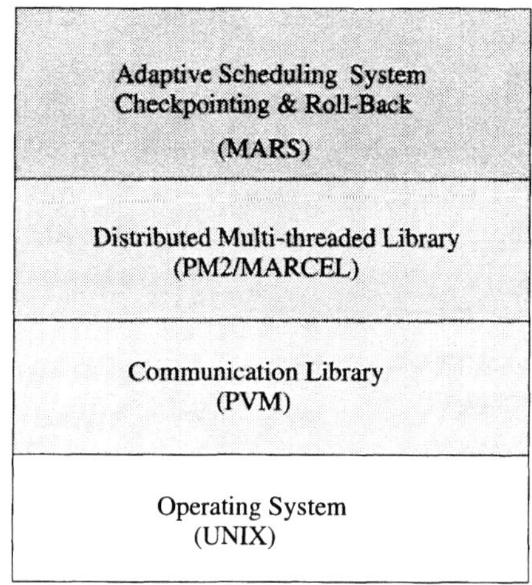

Figure 31.3 Layered structure of the platform.

MARS is designed to be a multi-application and multi-user system. Other features of MARS are:

- **portability**: It is entirely implemented at user-level, using facilities available through standard Unix system calls and libraries. The advantage of such an implementation is that there is no need for kernel modification, making it portable to various Unix flavors (SunOS, OSF, Solaris, Linux, etc.).
- **heterogeneity in load balancing**: Worker processes running in slow machines ask for tasks less frequently, and thus do less work. This results in load balancing that takes into account implicitly the heterogeneous aspect of

NOWs.

- **protection**: There is no need for superuser privileges to run applications of different users which do not raise any security or administrative concerns. We don't require that MARS run as "root."
- **Scalability**: MARS has a hierarchical structure which makes it scalable for large NOWs.
- **dynamic reconfiguration**: Any machine can join or leave the MARS virtual machine at any moment, according to changes in NOWs.
- **fault tolerance**: Detecting and removing failed machines are transparently provided by the runtime system. A checkpointing/rollback mechanism which periodically saves the state of the application tasks has been developed [8].
- **utilisability** : We have developed a GUI that allows observation and control of the MARS system by the administrator, and a GUI for the user to control his parallel application.

31.4.2 Parallel Programming Methodology

The programming style used is the master/workers paradigm (Single Program Multiple Data model). The master task generates work to be computed by the workers. Each worker task receives a work from the master, computes a result, and sends it back to the master. MARS will best support relatively coarse-grain applications. The master/workers paradigm works well in an adaptive dynamic environment because:

- when a new node becomes available, a worker task can be started there,
- when a node becomes busy, the master task gets back the pending work, which was being computed on this node, to be computed by the next available node.

The number of workers created initially by the master is equal to the number of idle nodes in the parallel platform. A parallel adaptive algorithm reacts to two events (Figure 31.4):

- **Transition of the load state of a node from idle to busy/owned**: If a node hosting a worker becomes loaded or owned, the master *folds up* the application by withdrawing the worker. The concerned worker puts back all pending work to the master and dies.
- **Transition of the load state of a node from busy/owned to idle**: When a node becomes idle, the master starts a new worker on it. In this case, we *unfold* the application. A worker is then created, and receives from the master the work to be done.

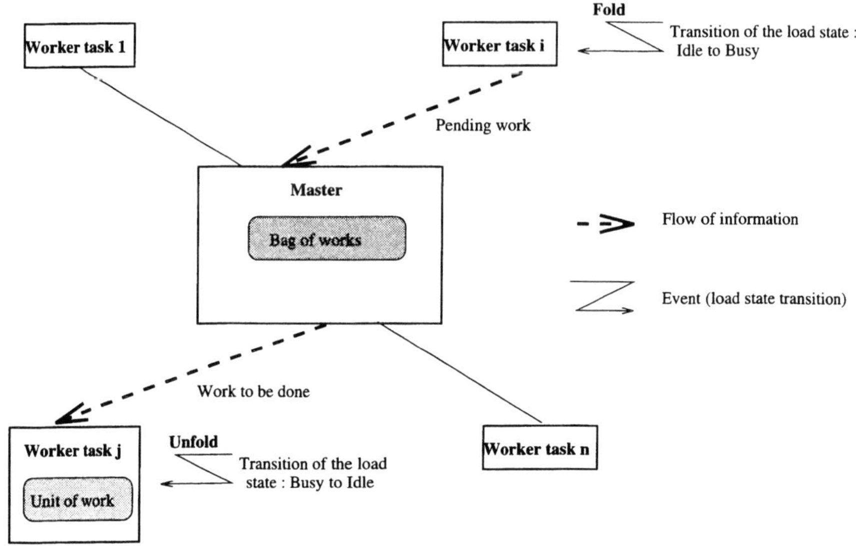

Figure 31.4 Architecture of a parallel adaptive application.

Developing a parallel adaptive application consists of the following steps:

- Specify two modules: The *application manager module* (AMM) for the master and the *worker module* (WM) for the workers. The AMM is composed mainly of the *work server thread* (Figure 31.5). The WM acts essentially as a template for the *worker threads* (Figure 31.6).
- Define two coordination services in the master module (Figure 31.5): They are *mars_get_work* and *mars_put_back_work*. The first coordination service specifies the function to execute when an unfolding operation occurs and the second one specifies the folding operation.
- Define a termination function (*mars_stestterm_func* primitive) which is called automatically when the number of workers falls to zero (Figure 31.5).

When a MARS application is submitted, the master is executed on the home node and the MARS runtime system knows about it just after enrolling. The "work server thread" is responsible for providing work descriptors (which define the work to be done) for the "worker threads." The number of "worker threads" is a function of the available idle nodes. When all work descriptors have been consumed, the computation is completed. The MARS runtime scheduling system handles transparently the adaptive execution of the application on behalf of the user.

The master task begins by enrolling in the MARS system (*mars_init* primitive) and makes a call to the *mars_spawn* primitive to create the worker tasks. The main parameters are the minimal number *min* and the maximal number *max* of tasks to be created (parallelism degree control). The user may also use the wild card -1 to specify no limits on the number of tasks.

```
/* coordination services */
LRPC_SERVICE(LRPC_GET_WORK)
if (!any initial solution available)
    /* Generate a random initial solution and send it */
else
    /* Send one of the pending solutions (FIFO strategy) */
END_SERVICE(LRPC_GET_WORK)

LRPC_SERVICE(LRPC_PUT_BACK_WORK)
 /* Keep the current best solution and
 the tabu list of the worker */
END_SERVICE(LRPC_PUT_BACK_WORK)

/* Termination detection when the number of workers falls */
/* to zero. Function automatically called by MARS */
void term()
{
if (no pending work) {
    tfprintf(stderr, "The application is completed");
    mars_exit();
   }
/* Don't exit. Wait for resources to be available */
}

int main(int argc, char **argv)
{
/* Enroll into the MARS run-time system */
mars_init(MASTER, ...);
mars_stestterm_func(term);

/* Create a number of workers in the range of min..max */
NbWorkers = mars_spawn("tabu", ..., min, max);

mars_waitexit();
}
```

Figure 31.5 The master program skeleton.

The worker task begins by enrolling in the MARS system (*mars_init* primitive), and makes a lightweight remote procedural call (LRPC) to the *get_back_work* service to get the values of the initial data. Then the worker creates a thread which executes a sequential task. The worker task has to define a *cleanup* function which is called automatically when the folding operation was initiated (Figure 31.6). Mainly, this function makes a lightweight remote procedural call (LRPC) to the *put_back_work* primitive.

```
/* This function is used when folding the worker thread */
void cleanup(any_t arg)
{
/* Send the pending work to the master */
ASYNC_LRPC(Master_tid, LRPC_PUT_BACK_WORK, ...);

/* The worker exits here */
}

/* This is the "Worker Thread" */
any_t tabu(any_t arg)
{
mars_sputbackwork_func(cleanup, NULL);
/* execute a sequential tabu search */
mars_exit();
}

int main(int argc, char **argv)
{
/* Enroll into the MARS run-time scheduling system */
mars_init(WORKER, ...);

/* Get initial work from the master */
LRPC(Master_tid, LRPC_GET_WORK, ...);

/* Start the worker thread tabu */
mars_startworkerthread(wt, NULL);

mars_waitexit();
}
```

Figure 31.6 The worker template.

Such a programming methodology can be used for certain classes of applications, but may be too complex for other applications with strong dependencies between tasks. The necessary software engineering effort will therefore quickly pay off by providing runs of large-scale problems.

31.4.3 The MARS Scheduler

The MARS scheduler makes hierarchical clustering of nodes with two levels where a *global MARS scheduler* (GMS) controls a set of *group servers* (GSs) and ensures a link between them. Each GS maintains a pool of nodes (Figure 31.7), which may be heterogeneous, selected on criteria such as geographical location and administrative usage, among others. A daemon called a *node manager* (NM) runs on each node and keeps its peer GS informed about state changes of the node with a period of 5 seconds. GSs schedule MARS applications on the nodes they control and on nodes managed by other GSs via the GMS.

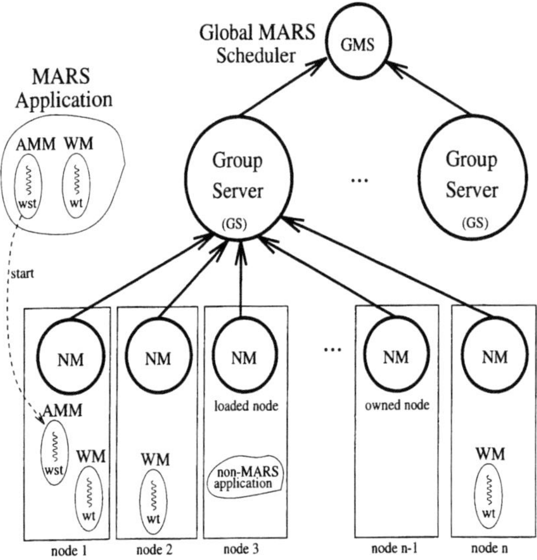

Figure 31.7 The architecture of the MARS scheduler.

The MARS scheduler handles transparently the adaptive execution of the application on behalf of the user: When a node becomes idle, the MARS runtime system automatically starts new "worker threads" on it, getting work descriptors from the "work server thread." In this case, we say that MARS *unfolds* the application. In contrast, if a node hosting "worker threads" is reclaimed or becomes loaded, the MARS runtime system *folds up* the application by withdrawing the "worker threads." In this case, concerned "worker threads" put back all pending work to the "work server thread" and die.

When a processor becomes idle, the node manager communicates the state transition to the GS, which in turn communicates the information to the application through the master using the RPC mechanism. Then the master creates a worker task. Once the worker is created, it makes a lightweight remote procedure call (LRPC) to the *get_work* service to get the work to be done. Then the worker creates a thread to carry out the work (Figure 31.8).

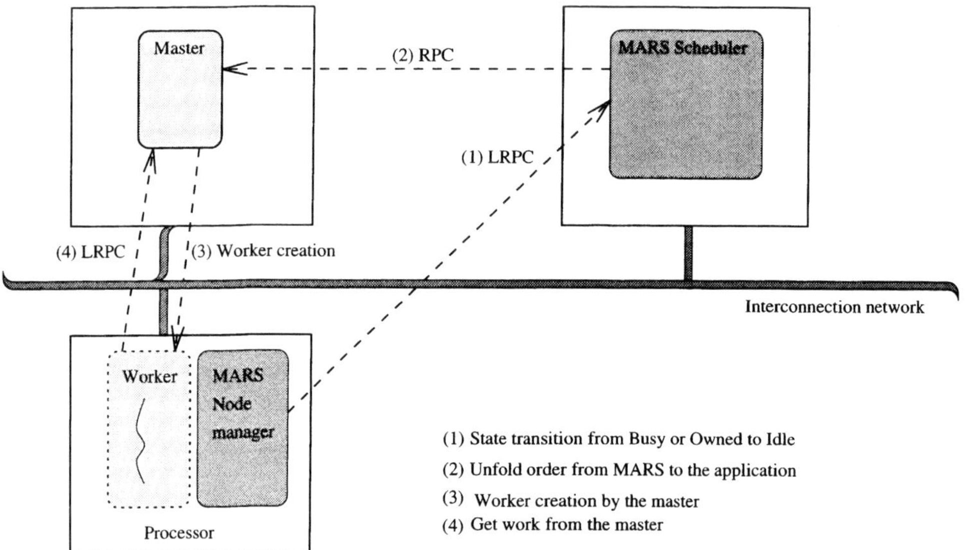

Figure 31.8 Operations carried out when a processor becomes idle.

When a processor becomes busy or owned, the same process is initiated by the MARS scheduler. In this case, the worker makes a lightweight remote procedure call (LRPC) to the *put_back_work* service to return the pending work and dies (Figure 31.9).

31.5 Experimental Results

We have conducted a number of experiments to quantify the ability of the MARS scheduling system to make use of idle machines (efficiency), respond to a changing environment (adaptability), and minimize the intrusion to owners of workstations.

The platform used for our experiments consists on a COW combined with NOWs. The COW is an Alpha-farm, which is composed of 16 Alpha-processors having a peak performance of 500 MIPS and connected by a 200Mb/s high-speed interconnection network with a crossbar based topology. The NOW is composed of 126 heterogeneous workstations (PC/Linux, Sparc/Sunos, Alpha/OSF, Sparc/Solaris)

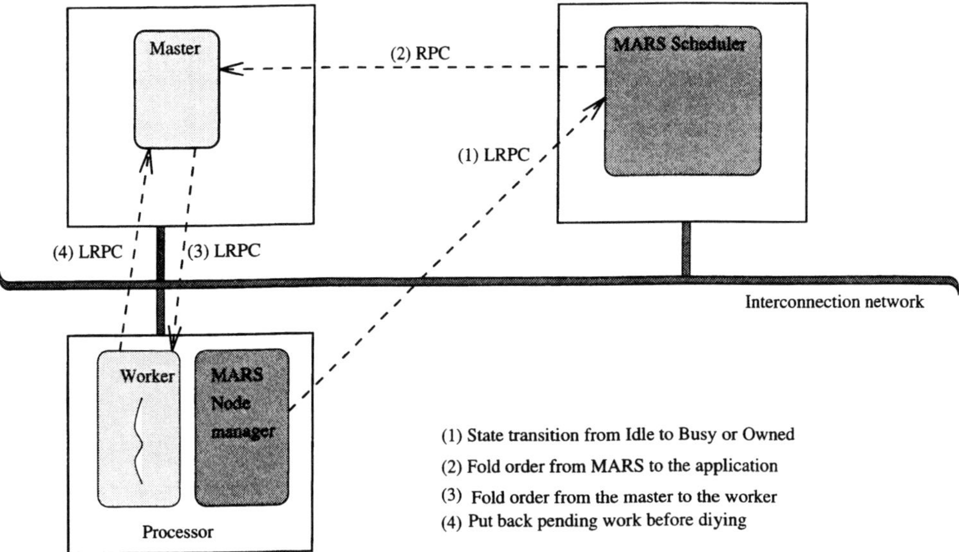

Figure 31.9 Operations carried out when a processor becomes busy or owned.

owned by researchers and students of our University. The workstations are connected by a 10Mb/s Ethernet.

Many applications have been developed in the following domains:

- numeric applications: block-based Gauss-Jordan, and fuzzy clustering on magnetic resonance image segmentation.
- combinatorial optimization applications: IDA*, branch and bound, genetic algorithms, tabu search and simulated annealing.

In this section we present the results of the parallel tabu search optimization algorithm. The parallel adaptive heuristic has been used to solve a NP-hard combinatorial optimization problem: the quadratic assignment problem (QAP). The QAP represents an important class of combinatorial optimization problems with many applications in different domains (such as facility location, data analysis, task scheduling and image synthesis).

The performance results were obtained by the execution of the parallel application under normal conditions in a multi-user environment. The parallel adaptive application competes with other users (sequential and parallel jobs) and owners of the workstations.

31.5.1 Efficiency and Adaptability

The performance measures we use when evaluating the efficiency and the adaptability of the parallel TS algorithm are execution time, overhead, the number of nodes allocated to the application, and the number of fold and unfold operations. The overhead is the total amount of CPU time required for scheduling operations. Table 31.2 summarizes the results obtained for 10 runs.

Table 31.2 Experiment Results Obtained for 10 Runs of a Large Problem (Sko100a) on 100 Processors (16 processors of the Alpha-farm, 54 Sparc/Solaris, 25 Sparc/SunOs, 5 PC/Linux)

	Mean	Deviation	Min	Max
Execution time (mn)	145.75	23.75	124	182
Overhead (sec)	8.36	0.24	8.18	8.75
Number of nodes allocated	71	15.73	50	92
Number of fold operations	79	49.75	24	149
Number of unfold operations	179	45.55	120	248

The average number of nodes allocated to the application does not vary significantly and represents 71% of the total number of processors. However, the high number of fold and unfold operations shows a significant load fluctuation of the different processors. During an average execution time of 2h25mn, 79 fold operations and 179 unfold operations are performed. This corresponds to one new node every 0.8mn and one node loss every 2mn. These results demonstrate the significance of the adaptability concept in parallel applications.

The parallel algorithm is efficient in terms of the scheduling overhead due to the adaptability. The overhead is low comparing to the total execution time (0.09% of the total execution time). We see also that the deviation of the overhead is very low (0.24% for 10 runs). The classical speedup measure cannot be applied to our application, which executes on a heterogeneous multi-user nondedicated parallel platform. Unfortunately, quantitative analysis of heterogeneous dynamic parallel systems is still in its infancy.

31.5.2 Fault Tolerance and Intrusion

Table 31.3 presents the running times on a network of 13 SUN4 workstations of the parallel algorithm without checkpointing, and the overhead induced by the mechanism with a 5 *mn* checkpointing period over all its checkpoints represented in the *Checkp number* column. The results show that the overhead induced by the checkpointing mechanism for the master is not important (under 1% of the running time of the application).

Table 31.3 Running Times and Checkpointing Overhead

Without Ckpt (sec)	Checkp number	Checkp Overh (sec)	%
18821	63	127	0.67

Table 31.4 Checkpointing Overhead Measurements at the Worker Level

Mean Number Workers/Ckpt	Min Ckeckp Overhead (s)	Max Ckeckp Overhead (s)	Mean Ckeckp Overhead (s)	Standard deviation	Average %
10.96	0.39	1.56	1.05	0.18	0.32

In fact, the master plays the role of the coordinator and the effective work is done by the workers. Table 31.4 shows the percentage of the time the computation is suspended for a checkpointing operation. The *Mean number of Workers per Checkpoint* column represents the mean number of workers which participate in each checkpoint. This gives us an idea about the parallelism degree which is significant. The *min checkpointing overhead*, which represents the best circumstances for which a worker takes its checkpoint, is equal to 0.39 *sec.* In opposite to this measurement, the max checkpointing overhead represents the worst circumstances in which a worker takes its checkpoint. We have registered a checkpoint in which the overhead of all workers is about 1.56 *sec.* The *mean checkpointing overhead* of all checkpoints gives us an idea about the average of time spent by the application in each checkpointing operation. Finally, the average percentage of time used by the checkpointing mechanism is under 0.5%, which is insignificant.

Beside these enhancements, the checkpointing mechanism tries to reduce the amount of data stored in the checkpoint file by checkpointing only the master task and the data structures handled by workers without their address spaces. The results in Table 31.5 present the storage space required by the checkpointing mechanism.

Let's present our experience with user reactions. There are psychological obstacles to stealing performance from the owner of a workstation. In general, users don't detect any effect on their nodes. From time to time we were suspected of effects, which turned out to come from a totally different source.

Only one incident is generated by the MARS system: For low performance workstations, the fold operation makes an effect (limited in time) on the local machine. We have therefore designed a priority local scheduling system, which assigns lower priority to the folded MARS process. After installing this mechanism, no problems have been reported.

Table 31.5 Checkpoint Files Size

Mean checkp file size (Kbytes)	Standard Deviation
1713	76

31.6 Conclusion and Future Work

The goal of our work is to exploit the unused computing capacity of large NOWs. We found that the unused capacity of a NOW is considerable, averaging 83% and always exceeding 75% of the total capacity. The MARS scheduler efficiently harnesses wasted idle time, without undermining the quality of service the NOW provides to workstation owners.

The dynamic and fault nature associated with the load of a multi-user NOW system makes essential the existence of a fault-tolerant adaptive scheduling tool for parallel applications. In addition to exploiting idle time, the main feature of our MARS runtime system is to adjust transparently the number of tasks of a parallel application with respect to available nodes. The "owner" of the workstation does not notice any other activities on his workstation in addition to his own.

Parallel applications can be efficiently managed with acceptable overhead. This allows certain classes of parallel applications that are commonly run on massively parallel computers to execute on existing underutilized NOWs. Applications that will perform well will be latency tolerant and relatively large-grain. Preliminary applications with MARS include parallel tree search (IDA*, Branch-and-Bound) and parallel meta-heuristics (genetic algorithms, tabu search, simulated annealing).

The major bottleneck for parallel applications is the high latency and low bandwidth of the Ethernet interconnection network. We believe that with NOWs over ATM/Myrinet networks, the performance gains can be very significant at low cost for applications that have significant amount of communications. Incorporation of ATM technology into wide area networks will help eliminate the seams between LANs and WANs. We want to emphasize that the MARS approach will be useful in wide area networks (WANs) for certain important application problems.

31.7 Bibliography

[1] A. Baratloo, M. Karaul, Z. Kedem, and P. Wyckoff. Charlotte: Metacomputing on the Web. In *IEEE International Conference on Distributed Systems*, pages 181–188, 1994.

[2] H. Clark and B. McMillin. DAWGS–a Distributed Compute Server Utilizing Idle Workstations. *Journal of Parallel and Distributed Computing*, vol.14, pages 175–186, 1992.

[3] F. Douglis and J. Ousterhout. Transparent Process Migration: Design Alternatives and the Sprite Implementation. *Software Practice and Experience*, vol.21, pages 757–785, August 1991.

[4] J. Casas et al. MPVM: A Migration Transparent Version of PVM. *Technical Report*, Oregon Graduate Institute of Science and Technology, 1995.

[5] D. Gelernter and D. L. Kaminsky. Supercomputing Out of Recycled Garbage:

Preliminary Experience with Piranha. In *6th ACM International Conference on Supercomputing*, July 1991.

[6] R. Hagmann. Process Servers: Sharing Processing Power in a Workstation Environment. In *IEEE International Conference on Distributed Computing Systems, Cambridge*, pages 260–267, May 1986.

[7] J. A. Kaplan and M. L. Nelson. A Comparison of Queueing, Cluster and Distributed Computing Systems. *Technical Report TM 109025*, NASA Langely Research Center, June 1994.

[8] D. Kebbal, E. G. Talbi, and J-M. Geib. A New Approach for Checkpointing Parallel Applications. In *International Conference on Parallel and Distributed Processing Techniques and Applications PDPTA'97*, pages 1643–1651, Las Vegas, USA, June 1997.

[9] P. Krueger and R. Chawla. The Stealth Distributed Scheduler. In *International Conference on Distributed Computing Systems*, 1991.

[10] R. Namyst and J. F. Mehaut. PM^2: Parallel Multithreaded Machine, A Computing Environment for Distributed Architectures. *Parco'95 Proceedings, Gent*, 1995.

[11] D. A. Nichols. Using Idle Workstations in a Shared Computing Environment. *ACM Operating System Review*, vol.21(5), pages 5–12, November 1987.

[12] J. Pruyne and M. Livny. Parallel Processing on Dynamic Resources with CARMI. In *Proceedings of the Workshop on Job Scheduling for Parallel Processing IPPS'95, LNCS No.949*, pages 259–278. Springer Verlag, April 1995.

[13] J. F. Shoch and J. A. Hupp. The Worm Programs - Early Experience with a Distributed Computation. *Communications of the ACM*, vol.25(3), pages 172–180, 1982.

[14] A. Vahdat, D. Ghormley, and T. Anderson. Efficient, Portable, and Robust Extension of Operating System Functionality. *Technical Report CS-94-842*, UC Berkeley, 1994.

[15] C. A. Waldspurger, T. Hogg, B. A. Hubermann, J. O. Kephart, and W. S. Stornetta. Spawn: A Distributed Computational Economy. *IEEE Transactions on Software Engineering*, vol.18(2), pages 103–117, February 1992.

Chapter 32

The Gardens Approach to Adaptive Parallel Computing

PAUL ROE AND CLEMENS SZYPERSKI

School of Computing Science
Queensland University of Technology
Brisbane, Australia.

Email: {*p.roe, c.szyperski*} *@qut.edu.au*

32.1 Introduction

Idle workstations represent a considerable computational resource—as yet untapped. Gardens is an integrated programming language and system designed to utilize such resources; it supports parallel computation across networks of otherwise idle workstations. Gardens is targeted at workstation networks which utilize state-of-the-art communications networks such as Myrinet and ATM. Such systems have the potential to provide supercomputer levels of performance. Thus Gardens enables a virtual supercomputer to be dynamically constructed from idle workstations.

Why is yet another new programming language and system required? It is because no existing system meets all the requirements of Gardens (see next section). Gardens' requirements are: *adaptation*, *safety*, *abstraction* and *performance* (*ASAP*).

Performance: The whole point of creating a virtual supercomputer is performance. To achieve overall performance of a parallel system, in terms of latency and throughput, it is crucial to have high performance communications. State-of-the-art communications networks offer the required performance; however, this can be lost in the software layers of high-level communications libraries. (This rules out many distributed systems approaches to the requirements.) For this reason, special lightweight communications libraries have been developed, e.g., Active Messages (AM) [16]. These communications libraries are very efficient, but rather low-level in nature. In order to perform well, Gardens has been heavily influenced by AM.

We achieve a performance comparable to using C and Active Messages, and meet the other requirements.

Safety: This is the prevention of untrapped program errors, e.g., dereferencing an uninitialized pointer. Static safety checking prevents a large class of subtle runtime errors from occurring. The current trend is towards programming languages which statically guarantee safety, e.g., Java. Unfortunately, high performance communication libraries, such as AM, have safety requirements exceeding the capabilities of traditional programming languages. Currently, the use of such libraries entails either runtime checking to ensure that communications libraries are used safely (negating performance), or the following of unchecked programming conventions. The Gardens programming language statically enforces the safe use of AM, or similar high performance messaging libraries.

Adaptation: Idle workstations come and go over time. Thus a parallel computation must adapt to a changing set of idle workstations: adaptive parallelism. Such adaptation must be transparent to the workstation user, and, ideally, also to the application programmer; Gardens achieves both goals. A modified screen saver, together with user configurable parameters, is used to determine when a workstation is idle and when a machine should be returned to the user. Lightweight tasks and fast task migration are used to map the parallel computation across the set of available workstations, as it changes over time. In particular, seed tasks (new tasks which have never been run) can be very efficiently migrated.

Abstraction: The final requirement of Gardens is to support the programming of abstractions, necessary for large-scale software development. Unfortunately, the low-level nature of AM does not support the programming of abstractions. For this reason, Gardens has elevated the level of AM to *global objects*. Global objects (GOs) map directly to AM with virtually no performance penalty, and support abstraction. GOs also support the addressing of mobile tasks, necessary for adaptive parallelism.

These four facets of Gardens are orthogonal; for example, it is possible to use global objects without task migration. However, what makes Gardens unique is addressing all these requirements.

The Gardens programming language, Mianjin [15], is based on Oberon, the latest in the Pascal line. Like Java, Oberon is safe and supports abstraction via objects. Unlike Java, Oberon is a very efficient language and has been used for systems programming; in performance terms it is similar to C. (Nevertheless, the Mianjin extensions could be adapted to Java.) Mianjin extends Oberon with support for global objects and their safe use.

The remainder of this chapter is organized as follows. The next section covers related work. Sections 32.3 and 32.4 describe the communications and tasking model of Gardens. Section 32.5 presents some performance figures. Section 32.6 summarizes the approach.

32.2 Related Work

There are three main fields contributing work that is related to Gardens: traditional parallel computing, parallel computing on clusters, and distributed computing. Traditional parallel computing and, in many cases, cluster computing assume a fixed number of processors for any given run of a parallel program. In other words, such systems do not adapt dynamically to a changing set of available processors. Distributed computing does consider such dynamics, but emphasizes availability, transparency and fault tolerance over performance.

Table 32.1 summarizes some of the key differences between the various approaches. While Gardens is efficient and safe, and supports abstraction and adaptation without restricting the model of computation, all the other approaches are deficient in one or more of these dimensions.

Table 32.1 Comparison of Approaches

	efficient	safe	abstractions	adaptive	unrestricted model
Java RMI	N	Y	Y	N[3]	Y
MPI 2.0	Y	n/a[1]	Y	N	Y
UPVM	Y	n/a[1]	N	Y	Y
Split-C	Y	N	N	N	Y
Orca	Y	Y	Y[2]	N	N
Piranha	Y	n/a[1]	N	Y	N
Cilk v2	Y	Y	Y	Y	N
Charm(++)	Y	N	Y	N	N
Millipede[4]	n/a	n/a	n/a	Y	Y
Gardens	Y	Y	Y	Y	Y

Remarks: [1]not inherently unsafe, but depends on language binding; [2]limited abstraction since Orca objects cannot refer to each other; [3]adaptation is not part of the current Java specifications; [4]Millipede is a system, not a language.

Java Remote Method Invocations (RMI) [11] is an approach for traditional distributed computing, but, like Gardens, advocates communication via remote method invocation. Java RMI is synchronous and parameter passing uses a costly serialisation protocol, ensuring platform independence. The overall model, and definitely its current implementations, are far too costly for most parallel applications. Unlike current Java, a number of attempts have been documented to integrate general process migration facilities into operating systems, e.g., MOSIX [2]. All these systems aim at distributed computing with much coarser granularities than those required for high performance parallel computing.

The Message Passing Interface (MPI) and the Parallel Virtual Machine (PVM) are both libraries supporting parallel computing based on message passing and abstracting from the specific platform. Both support dynamic process creation (MPI v2.0), but not process migration. MPI, but not PVM, provides a (crude) means to support abstraction ("communicators"). An extension to PVM, UPVM [13], supports lightweight user-level processes and their migration. A more recent project, Mist [7], considers migration of full OS processes, rather than lightweight tasks; however, this is very expensive compared with lightweight task migration. Unlike Gardens, Mist addresses fault tolerance.

Active Messages (AM) is a low-level message passing library particularly designed to support parallel computing across clusters. Since Gardens builds on AM, a detailed description follows in Section 32.3.1. Split-C [9] is a parallel extension of ANSI C and was originally designed to map efficiently to AM. Split-C is efficient but unsafe and supports neither abstraction nor adaptation. This is the language used by the NOW project [1].

Orca [3] is an integrated language and system that is safe and supports partial abstraction. Orca separates active processes from passive shared objects. Shared objects cannot have mutual references, thus limiting both the model of computation and the degree of abstraction. All communication between processes is via atomic (indivisible) side-effecting operations on such objects. Shared objects can be transparently replicated or sliced across available machines, but overall efficiency relies heavily on compiler optimizations. Adaptation/process migration is not supported.

Charm [12] is another integrated language and system. The key concept is message-driven execution where context switching is used to hide communication latencies. Charm uses sophisticated load balancing strategies and works well for irregular problems. Task migration is possible only for new, never-activated tasks (seed tasks); once a task is running, it cannot be migrated, ruling out true adaptation. A particularly interesting concept is that of *branch office chares*. These are replicated exactly once per processor and support the programming of processor-local functionality (a similar facility is being considered for Gardens).

Piranha [6] is one of the few adaptive parallel programming systems. It is based on the tuple space abstraction introduced by Linda to which it adds a few run time hooks to support adaptive parallelism. It relies on a restrictive flat master worker model and requires programmers to explicitly code the actions required to release a machine. Cilk(v2) [5] is an integrated language and system that supports only a very limited functional style of parallel computing. However, Cilk supports transparent adaptation and fault tolerance on the basis of automatic cancellation and restart of subtasks that have yet to report their result.

Millipede [10] is a virtual parallel machine supporting adaptive computation. It is based on distributed shared memory, and is designed to support different languages. It is similar to Gardens in supporting adaptive computation based on migration of computation. Unlike Gardens, it cannot leverage efficiency from tight language system integration.

32.3 Communication

Our system is predicated upon high performance communication networks, characterized as being: reliable, low latency, high throughput, connection-less and switched. Efficient utilization of such hardware requires a very lightweight and efficient messaging software layer, such as Active Messages (AM). Our programming language, Mianjin, supports global objects and type annotations. Together these provide a safe interface to AM which supports abstraction, and this is achieved without incurring any significant performance overheads. The whole of Gardens has been heavily influenced by AM; however, similar systems, such as Fast Messages, U-Net, GM, etc, could equally well be utilized as a base.

32.3.1 Active Messages

In essence, AM [16] is a lightweight form of asynchronous remote procedure call, with a synchronous poll (accept) mechanism. The AM design assumes a few strong invariants that guarantee the following properties:

1. Non-preemptive semantics.
2. Local AM calls almost as efficient as local procedure calls.
3. No self-inflicted deadlock despite non-preemptive semantics.
4. No distributed network deadlock caused by buffer overflow.

Our programming language, Mianjin, statically guarantees these important safety properties.

In AM, request operations may be issued which asynchronously send a message to a remote processor, consisting of a handler (function pointer) and some data. On receipt, messages are queued until a poll operation is performed. `Poll` processes messages by invoking handlers on associated data; this gives the recipient control over when handlers are invoked (Property 1). Note that `Poll` may process any message; it is not possible to filter particular messages. `Poll` does guarantee that messages are processed atomically and in order if from the same sender. A request handler may invoke a reply operation (similar to a request) to return a message to the original sender; however, reply handlers may perform no communication. Thus communication operations cannot be nested via handlers.

If the destination of a request (or reply) is the local processor, the addressed handler will be called immediately, approaching the efficiency of a local procedure call (Properties 2 and 3). Thus all request operations also perform a poll on completion; this ensures that the semantics of local requests is consistent with that of non-local requests.

A credit counting scheme is used to control network deadlock (Property 4), as opposed to application deadlock. Each host maintains a credit count that represents current buffer usage per destination. Credits are lost by sending messages to a host, and gained by receiving reply or acknowledgment messages from hosts. Therefore, no protocol is needed to handle buffer overflow at the receiving end; in general, AM's performance is largely a result of trimming back traditional network and transport protocol overheads. If a request is issued when the credit count is zero, the request operation will poll until credit is available, after which the request will be performed. Thus, a request operation may cause a poll before and after its operation.

32.3.2 Global Objects

Active messages is very efficient but difficult to use. Typical programs use global variables for communication, which do not support abstraction—violating one of our goals. Also, AM does not support the addressing of mobile tasks (see Section 32.4.3). The key goal of our global objects is to support abstraction of communications, and to do so without sacrificing the performance which AM provides.

In Gardens, tasks may perform point-to-point communication with other tasks via global objects (GOs). In general, a task will manage several GOs, which act as communication "ports" for that task. Global objects support asynchronous remote dynamic dispatch; that is, a task may invoke a method on an object which is located on a different processor. This is implemented by AM's request operation. GOs are ordinary objects created within the heap of the creating task, and are managed by that task. Thus GOs have the same visibility as ordinary programming language values: no name space issues arise, cf. distributed systems. The only difference between ordinary local objects and GOs is that GOs are globally contactable. Any object can be made globally contactable by handing out a global reference to it. The task owning a GO may access it as a normal object (a record), and, for it, the GO is indistinguishable from any other heap allocated record. Global references cannot be dereferenced, and they support only a subset of the original object's methods, in particular those methods labelled `GLOBAL`. Global methods are required to have a restricted interface. In particular, VAR parameters, and return values are disallowed, and local pointers are coerced (demoted) to global ones. These restrictions prevent local (i.e., non-GO) references escaping from tasks, including implicit ones created by VAR parameters. A simple example is shown below:

```
TYPE Accumulator = POINTER TO RECORD count: INTEGER; sum: REAL END;

GLOBAL PROCEDURE (self: Accumulator) Add (s: REAL);   (* a global method *)
BEGIN
  self.sum := self.sum + s; self.count := self.count - 1
END Add;

POLL PROCEDURE Worker (gsum: GLOBAL Accumulator);
  VAR localsum: REAL;
BEGIN
  ...                  (* expensive calculation of localsum *)
  gsum.Add(localsum)   (* global method invocation *)
END Worker;
```

```
POLL PROCEDURE Master;
  VAR acc: Accumulator;
BEGIN
  NEW(acc); acc.sum := 0; acc.count := NTasks;
  ...    (* create NTasks worker tasks performing Worker(acc) *)
  WHILE acc.count>0 DO Poll END;    (* wait for all results *)
  ...
END Master;
```

The example shows how a global object (`acc`), managed by a master task, may accumulate the sum of several local sums, each calculated by worker tasks. Some code has been elided; this will be revealed in subsequent sections, as will the significance of the `POLL` annotations. The only way worker tasks can access `acc` is via its global methods, in this case `Add`. When a worker task invokes the global method `Add`, actual parameters and the method index are communicated via an AM request operation to the task owning the object. After communication, the method is invoked locally on the object. The master task owning and managing the global object (`acc`) waits for all local sums to be contributed to the object. It busy waits, polling to receive GO method invocations; this will be improved upon in a subsequent section.

Global object reading, corresponding to AM reply operations, is not described here; for information see [15]. Also, our system supports the efficient streaming of large data structures using user-programmable packers [17].

32.3.3 Poll Procedure Annotations

Global objects support abstraction and the addressing of mobile tasks. However, there remain the safety restrictions on message handlers (global object methods). In particular, a global method may not directly or indirectly poll or invoke a global object method. These safety restrictions cannot be enforced by traditional programming languages such as C.

An important characteristic of program code is whether it may perform a poll operation or definitely will not. Polling may be performed explicitly via `Poll` or implicitly, e.g., via global method invocation; in either case, such code is termed *polling*. Code which is not polling is termed *atomic*. Mianjin captures the notion of polling in its type system. Atomic code is the default; all polling methods and procedures must be labelled `POLL`. The compiler is able to statically check that:

- Polling code is invoked only by other polling code.
- Global methods are invoked only on GOs by polling code, since such invocations are polling.
- Global method implementations (bodies) are atomic (i.e., cannot poll). Thus a global method may not invoke other global methods or call `Poll`.

These POLL annotations are also useful for the programmer. In particular, if a library routine is labelled POLL the programmer knows that poll operations may occur, and hence any GOs under his control must be prepared for global method invocations. If a routine is not labelled POLL, the default, no poll operations (implicit or explicit) will be performed by the library. Thus GOs need not be in a consistent state when the library is called.

Note that, unlike other parallel object-based systems, there is no possibility of deadlock as the result of recursive or cyclic invocations, since nested invocations are statically prohibited. (The restrictions required by AM are automatically and naturally met.) Furthermore, a task may invoke a global method on one of its own objects with no possibility of deadlock.

32.4 Adaptation and Tasking

Tasks are our unit of work, they are used for adaptation:, that is, for dynamically mapping a parallel computation across a changing set of idle workstations. This is accomplished by over-decomposing a problem into more tasks than there are workstations. To adapt to a changing set of workstations, tasks are migrated. The task migration machinery is described in detail in [4]. Task migration is primarily targeted at supporting the release and acquisition of workstations; however, it may also be used for some coarse-grained load balancing of tasks across a stable processor set. The key goal of our tasking system is to efficiently support adaptive parallelism without sacrificing performance.

A Gardens computation consists of a network of communicating tasks, dynamically mapped onto a network of processors. Tasks are created dynamically and there may be multiple tasks per processor. Each task consists of a stack and a collection of heap segments in which dynamic data structures are stored [4]. Heap segments are not shared between tasks; they are partitions of a global virtual address space, which is partitioned across processors. Thus tasks occupy disjoint regions of an address space partitioned across processors, see Figure 32.1.

Tasks communicate with other tasks, using GOs, independent of which processor they occupy. Note that there is no concept of task identifiers, since such values tend to break abstraction. Instead, we rely on GOs to support communication between tasks.

We allow only a single Gardens application per workstation; this avoids problems associated with parallel multitasking – in particular, co-scheduling (gang scheduling).

Due to the dynamic nature of tasks and the arbitrary references to GOs they can maintain, system-wide garbage collection and task termination detection are important issues in Gardens. A task in Gardens is said to have terminated totally if its thread of control terminated and all of its GOs became unreachable from all other non-terminating tasks. Currently, a global mark scan collector is used to both collect objects (including GOs) and to detect task termination [8]. Other garbage collection strategies could be investigated.

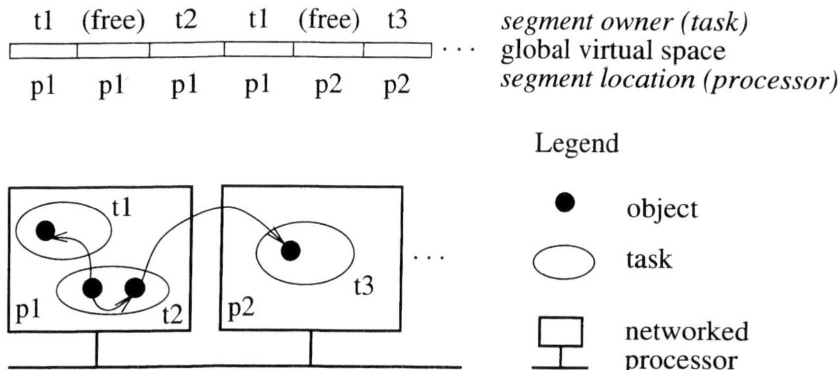

Figure 32.1 Heap segments, tasks and processors

It is desirable to control the number of tasks in the system; prevention of task generation can be simply programmed. Deleting seed tasks and task coalescing are more complex ideas that are the subjects of ongoing work.

32.4.1 Multitasking

How can multitasking and AM/GOs coexist? They can coexist by allowing a context switch to occur only while a task is at a poll point [14]. A poll point is any point in a program where a poll operations may occur directly or indirectly, e.g., when invoking a global method.

The Gardens system supports lightweight non-preemptive tasks which typically inhabit a relatively heavyweight OS process (e.g., Unix or NT process). Each task has its own stack and heap. Non-preemption simplifies programming, is compatible with our AM/GO programming model and is more efficient than preemptive multitasking. Furthermore no protection or isolation is enforced at runtime; this is enforced statically by our programming language. Thus when a task executes a purely sequential (atomic) portion of code performing no communication or blocking (see next section), that code will be run at maximum speed, incurring no overheads due to parallel execution.

Tasks are created using Fork, a Gardens' library procedure similar to the Unix fork operation. The fork operation is atomic, but the new task is not:

```
PROCEDURE Fork (p: POLL PROCEDURE (go: GLOBAL ANYPTR); go: GLOBAL ANYPTR);
```

For example, the worker tasks of the previous example may be created thus:

```
FOR i:= 1 TO NTasks DO Fork (Worker,acc) END
```

Fork is asymmetric: there is no implicit synchronization between child and parent tasks. A single global object is passed to the child task; this is sufficient to bootstrap communication. Notice that no task may communicate with the child task until the child task has initiated some communication. This allows simple migration of new tasks which have not yet been activated, see Section 32.4.3.

32.4.2 Blocking

Blocking has two roles: it causes a context switch, and eliminates unnecessary context switches to tasks still waiting to synchronize.

Gardens prides itself on its unfairness! Unless a task explicitly gives up control by voluntarily blocking, or is migrated (see next section), it will run top speed to completion at the exclusion of all other tasks on that processor. Only blocking guarantees to perform a context switch; thus blocking must be used to guarantee progress of a program. If a program is running on a single processor, only `Block` will force the current task to be descheduled, and hence permit other tasks to be scheduled. The poll operation *may* perform a context switch (e.g., due to migration); however, blocking *will* perform a context switch.

Efficient tasking requires support for blocking: even with asynchronous communication, tasks will eventually need to synchronize. Blocking eliminates unnecessary context switches to tasks waiting to synchronize.

The `Block` and `Unblock` routines implement blocking; they take no arguments. `Block` blocks the currently running task by removing it from the runnable queue and putting it in the blocked pool. Semantically, `Block` is equivalent to a poll and context switch; hence `Block` is declared as polling.

Blocking blocks a task but does not prevent global method invocations on that task's GOs, which may unblock it. `Unblock`, usually performed by a GO's method, unblocks the associated task. `Unblock` is atomic and hence is not labelled `POLL`. (Where no unblocked tasks remain, the kernel continues polling for incoming messages.) `Block`/`Unblock` operations have direct effect regardless of their nesting level. In a non-preemptive system such as Gardens, the sophistication of semaphores and equivalent mechanisms is not required.

We may add blocking to our previous example thus:

```
GLOBAL PROCEDURE (self: Accumulator) Add (s: REAL);
BEGIN
  self.sum := self.sum + s; self.count := self.count - 1;
  IF self.count=0 THEN Unblock END  (* if last result unblock master task *)
END Add;

POLL PROCEDURE Master;
  VAR acc: Accumulator;
BEGIN
  NEW(acc); acc.sum := 0; acc.count := NTasks;
  FOR i:= 1 TO NTasks DO Fork (Worker,acc) END;
  WHILE acc.count#0 DO Block END;
  ...
END Master;
```

It is necessary to wrap a while loop around `Block` since other abstractions may also perform `Block` and `Unblock` operations. Note that, in general, we expect such detailed coding to be encapsulated in abstractions. Our blocking and unblocking is general and efficient. For example, there is no need for a kernel task to repeatedly test a flag to see whether a task should be unblocked. Blocking can also occur implicitly; a special kind of blocking occurs when a task tries to communicate but is out of credits.

32.4.3 Task Migration

To support the acquisition and release of workstations, work must be dynamically reallocated to workstations. Tasks are our unit of work, hence reallocation implies migration of tasks. Currently, task migration is supported only across homogeneous platforms, although we are researching heterogeneous task migration. The tasking implementation partitions the virtual memory address space of a Gardens application across processors. Tasks occupy disjoint regions of virtual memory. Thus task migration can be achieved by copying a task's heap and stack from one processor to the same regions on another processor.

Migration is non-preemptive, and can occur only when all tasks are at poll points, i.e., in `Poll`, performing a global method invocation, or in `Block`. At each poll point the *release workstation* flag is tested, and, if set (see next section), migration is initiated. Migration requires global synchronization; this enables all messages in transit to be flushed before migration, hence no message forwarding mechanism is needed. It also means that our model invariants are preserved (see Section 32.6). Thus the programmer must ensure that programs poll frequently enough to enable workstation release within a reasonable time. Programs failing to voluntarily release workstations within a specified time are killed.

New tasks, which have never been run, support a much more efficient form of migration. Until a task is run, no other task can communicate with it and all the state that needs to be kept in such a *seed task* are the arguments to `Fork` (two addresses). Seed tasks can be migrated without requiring global synchronization. In fact, one AM request/reply communication can be used for migration of seed tasks. Such tasks do not even need a heap or stack until they are first run. In Gardens, general load balancing is thus performed using seed tasks, while migration of activated tasks is usually used only for adaptation to a changing processor set.

32.4.4 Gardens Screen Saver

A modified screen saver, together with user configurable parameters, is used to determine when a workstation becomes idle and when a machine should be returned to the user. A simple signal mechanism is used to communicate between the screen saver and the Gardens application. The signal sets a flag in the Gardens application indicating that the workstation should be released (returned to the user). Task migration, and hence workstation release, is non-preemptive. However, if voluntary release does not occur before some time limit expires, the Gardens application is killed. Issues of user acceptance, screen saver behaviour and parameters are not considered here.

32.5 Performance Results

We have a prototype system implemented and are currently working on optimizing its performance. (Note: our GOs require distributed garbage collection, which has been implemented.) The test platform consists of four 32MByte 120MHz Sun SparcStation-4s connected via a Myrinet.

The first set of measurements shows the overhead of using global objects versus raw active messages (times are for one-way communication).

data size (bytes)	AM (μs)	GO (μs)
16 (short message)	20	23
1024 (long message)	137	139

The following figures demonstrate the efficiency of our current tasking system:

fork (seed task creation)	$4\mu s$
fork (eager task creation)	$26\mu s$
block (block task, poll and context switch)	$18\mu s$
unblock task	$3\mu s$

The time taken for task migration depends on the task size and the time required to synchronize processors, which is application dependent. The figures below give times for synchronizing all processors and migrating a single task:

Task size (Kbyte)	8	16	32	64	128
Migration time (ms)	1.6	2.1	3.7	6.8	13.5

The time to create (via fork) and migrate a seed task, which consequently has no stack or heap data and requires no global synchronization, is just $24\mu s$! A typical time to release a workstation, including synchronization and task migration, is of the order of one second (given several megabytes of task state to migrate).

32.6 Summary

In this chapter, we have described the approach to parallel computing on networks of workstations that underlies the Gardens language and system. In particular, Gardens allows parallel applications to be safe, efficient, adaptive, and composed using programmable abstractions, without severely restricting the model of computation.

As demonstrated by some experimental applications, the current implementation on Sparc/Solaris and Myrinet fulfills all these requirements. The system runs entirely in one user-level process per participating machine and does not require any special permissions to execute, thus not interfering with workstation users' safety requirements. Nor does the system interfere with the needs of workstation users; workstations are quickly acquired and released.

The model of tasking, task migration and communications can be summarized using the following invariants, which guarantee safe use of AM:

- Tasks can be in one of three states: seed, runnable, or blocked.
- On each host, at most one runnable task is not at a poll point; all blocked tasks are at poll points.
- Message handlers are called only if all local (non-seed) tasks are at poll points.
- Migration can occur only if all (non-seed) tasks on all processors are at poll points (i.e., calling `Poll`, a global method, or `Block`), and there are no outstanding messages.
- No "network deadlock" can occur, as is the case with AM.
- Messages are causally ordered, even across migration.
- Seed tasks are not involved in any communications.
- Tasks occupy disjoint regions of a single global virtual address space.

Acknowledgments

Our thanks for their efforts in discussing and implementing Gardens go to: Ashley Beitz, S-Y Chan, Geoff Elgey, Wayne Kelly, Nik Kwiatkowski and all other members of the team. This work has been supported by the Programming Languages and Systems group at QUT and partially by Australian Research Council grants.

32.7 Bibliography

[1] Th. E. Anderson, D. E. Culler, D. A. Patterson et al. A Case for NOW (Networks of Workstations). *IEEE Micro*, February, 1995.

[2] A. Barak, A. Braverman, I. Gilderman and O. La'adan. The MOSIX Multicomputer Operating System for Scalable NOW and its Dynamic Resource Sharing Algorithms. *Technical Report 96-11*, The Hebrew University, 1996.

[3] H. E. Bal, M. F. Kaashoek and A. S. Tanenbaum. Orca: A Language for Parallel Programming of Distributed Systems. *IEEE Software Engineering*, vol. 18(3): pages 190–205, March, 1992.

[4] A. Beitz, S-Y. Chan and N. Kwiatkowski. A Migration-Friendly Tasking Environment for Gardens. In *Fourth Australasian Conference on Parallel and Real-Time Systems (PART'97)*, Newcastle, Australia, Springer, 1997.

[5] R. D. Blumofe and P. A. Lisiecki. Adaptive and Reliable Parallel Computing on Networks of Workstations. In *Proceedings of USENIX 1997 Annual Technical Conference on UNIX and Advanced Computing Systems*, California, 1997.

[6] N. Carriero, E. Freeman D. Gelernter and D. Kraminsky. Adaptive parallelism and Piranha. *IEEE Computer*, pages 40–49, January, 1995.

[7] J. Casas et al. MPVM: A Migration Transparent Version of PVM. *Computing Systems*, vol. 8(2), pages 171–216, 1995.

[8] S-Y. Chan, P. Roe, C. Szyperski. Recycling in Gardens: Efficient Memory Management for a Parallel System. In *Fifth Australasian Conference on Parallel and Real-Time Systems (PART'98)*, Adelaide, Australia, Springer, 1998.

[9] D. E. Culler et al. Parallel Programming in Split-C. In *Proceedings of Supercomputing '93 Conference*, 1993

[10] A. Itzkovitz, A. Schuster, L. Wolfovich. Supporting Multiple Parallel Programming Paradigms On Top Of The Millipede Virtual Parallel Machine, In *Proceedings of the Second International Workshop on High Level Programming Models and Supportive Environments*, Geneve, 1997.

[11] JavaSoft. Java RMI. *Technical report*, Sun Microsystems, Inc. http://java.sun.com/products/rmi/.

[12] L. V. Kale and S. Krishnan. CHARM++: A Portable Concurrent Object Oriented System Based on C++. In *Proceedings of Conference on OOPSLA'93*, 1993.

[13] R. Konuru, J. Casas, S. Otto, R. Prouty and J. Walpole. A User-Level Process Package for PVM. In *Proceedings of the Scalable High Performance Computing Conference*, pages 48–55, 1994.

[14] P. Roe and C. Szyperski. Integrating Tasking and Active Message Style Communication in Gardens. In *Online Proceedings, 2nd NOW/Cluster Workshop: Building Systems of Systems at ASPLOS 7*, Boston, http://www-csag.cs.uiuc.edu/individual/achien/asplos/now-cluster.html, 1996.

[15] P. Roe and C. Szyperski. Mianjin is Gardens Point: A Parallel Language Taming Asynchronous Communication. In *PART'97 Conference*, Australia, Springer, 1997.

[16] T. von Eicken, D. Culler, S. C. Goldstein, and K. E. Schauser. Active Messages: A Mechanism for Integrated Communication and Computation. In *Proceedings 19th International Symposium on Computer Architecture*, 1992.

[17] C. Szyperski et al. Gardens Autobahn: Efficient and Safe Streaming of Data Structures for High Performance Communication Architectures. In *Proceedings 3rd Australasian Computer Architecture Conference*, Perth, Australia, Springer, 1998.

Chapter 33

The ParPar System: A Software MPP

DROR G. FEITELSON, ANAT BATAT, GABRIEL BENHANOKH, DAVID ER-EL, YOAV ETSION, AVI KAVAS, TOMER KLAINER, URI LUBLIN, AND MARC A. VOLOVIC

Institute of Computer Science
The Hebrew University of Jerusalem
91904 Jerusalem, Israel

Email: *feit@cs.huji.ac.il*

33.1 Introduction

To place ParPar[1] in context, we must first review the different modes of operation common on clusters. Probably the most common approach is to view the cluster as a Network Of Workstations (NOW). With this approach, each node is owned by a certain individual and is usually also physically located in his work area. The owner uses his workstation for administrative work, such as e-mail, and also for processing, e.g., text processing or engineering applications. But such work typically consumes only a fraction of the workstation's resources. The remaining resources are therefore available for general use by others, who need more resources than their local workstations can provide. Examples of projects based on this approach are the Berkeley NOW, Condor, and MOSIX [2].

At the other extreme are clusters dedicated to a single user at a time, with the explicit goal of executing parallel programs. The motivation is to provide resources for the solution of very demanding problems, and use them as efficiently as possible. Clusters, due to their use of commodity components, are cheap enough to make this possible. The best-known system of this type is the Beowulf project. ParPar is related to this approach, but attempts to provide an inexpensive approximation of a

[1] "Parpar" means "butterfly" in Hebrew, which is irrelevant; the name was chosen for its sound, because "par" is short for "parallel," and because two is better than one.

complete MPP system, capable of servicing a general-purpose multi-user workload of parallel programs. This enables the creation of a workload mix where different jobs complement each other, and together make better use of the resources.

While clusters usually emphasize the use of off-the-shelf technology, some do in fact use special components, especially for the network interface. For example, PAPERS (Purdue's Adapter for Parallel Execution and Rapid Synchronization) implements barrier synchronization in hardware, and is competitive with MPP systems [5]. The price is, of course, added cost for both the components and their design, and more important, the need to support them through successive generations of the commodity components. We do not use any such special hardware.

In summary, the ParPar project aims to create a general-purpose, multi-user, MPP-like system, using only off-the-shelf components. The emphasis is on operating system functionality, such as job control and parallel I/O, as opposed to communication which has been handled by multiple other projects (e.g., Active Messages [13], Fast Messages [11], or U-Net [12]). The environment is created entirely in software. The next section presents an overview of the system structure; subsequent sections describe various system functions in some detail.

33.2 The ParPar System

In this section, we describe the components of the ParPar system and their interrelations.

33.2.1 Hardware Base

The ParPar prototype cluster comprises 17 high performance PCs: A host, called "parpar," and 16 nodes, called "par1" through "par16" (Figure 33.1). The PCs have an Intel Providence motherboard with a Pentium Pro 200 processor, 128 MB DRAM with parity checking, and a 2.1 GB SCSI disk. Any other configuration could be used instead.

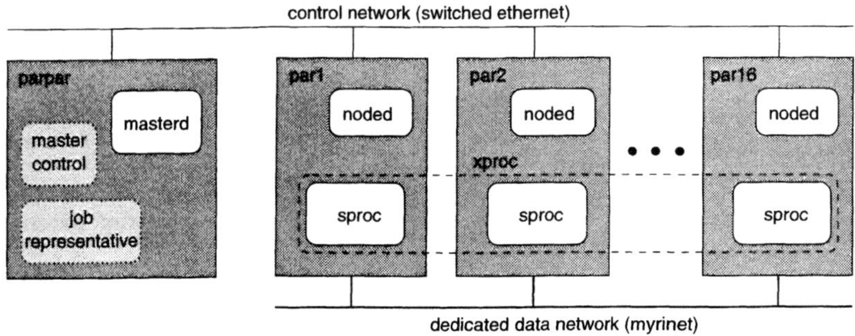

Figure 33.1 Hardware components of the ParPar system, and software components that run on each one.

The nodes are connected by two independent networks. One is a switched Ethernet that serves as the control network. All the system-oriented communication required to implement the functions described below passes on this network, using a combination of conventional TCP/IP and a reliable multicast protocol that we implemented. The other is a 1.28 Gb/s Myrinet [3], which is dedicated to the communication needs of user applications (this is called the data network). Communication is done using MPI over FM [11]. As user processes do not run on the host, the data network connects only the 16 nodes.

Future plans call for the inclusion of 4 I/O nodes in the system that will also be connected to both networks. These nodes will also be high performance PCs, and will have several larger disks. They will run a parallel file system that will support parallel access to files that are spread across all their disks (see Section 33.6.2). The currently available disks are used only for swap space and a local /tmp file system.

33.2.2 Software Structure

The ParPar software is based on the Unix BSDI system and runs at user level. The software components that make up the ParPar system are shown in Figure 33.1. These include daemons that run on the host and on the nodes, and graphical user interfaces that run either on the host or on each user's workstation. In addition, there are the user processes that make up the parallel applications executed by the system. The interactions among the different components are summarized in Figure 33.2.

The master daemon (masterd) is the heart of the ParPar system. It is responsible for tracking system configuration (which nodes are up and part of the system) and for job management and resource allocation. There is one masterd in the system, and it runs on the host.

The node daemons (noded) provide local control over the processes running on the system's nodes. As such, they are agents acting for the masterd. There is a single noded on each node.

The job representative (JR) is a GUI that provides an interface to the system and terminal I/O facilities (see Figure 33.9). Users use the JR to launch jobs, by specifying the executable, its arguments, etc. The system displays status messages on the JR. Normally, there is a separate JR for each job running on the system. The JR can run on the host or on the user's workstation. A non-graphical job representative is also available for use in batch scripts.

The master control (MC) is a GUI that provides an interface for obtaining configuration and load information, and for controlling the system (e.g., shutdown). Normally, each user may invoke one MC interface, but this is not necessary in order to use the system.

Parallel jobs are known as extended processes (xproc), but this abstraction exists only on the masterd and the JRs. Xprocs are composed of sub-processes (sproc) running on nodes. Sprocs connect directly to the job's JR to support terminal I/O activity.

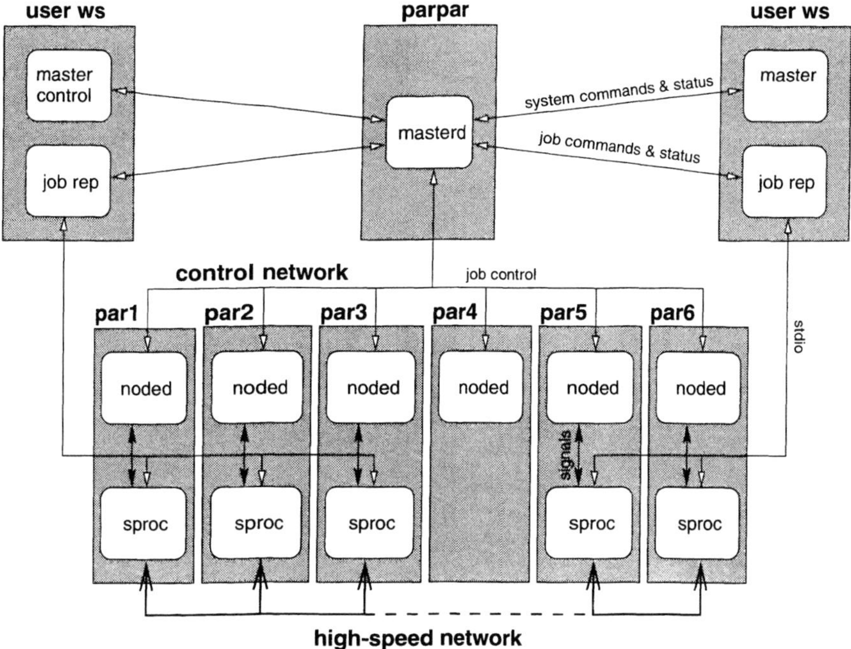

Figure 33.2 Interactions among the system components.

33.2.3 Design Principles

The system's software components described above are all reactive: Most of the time they just wait for some input, be it user input to one of the GUIs or an incoming message to one of the daemons. The behavior and interactions among the different components are governed by the following two design principles, which are actually two facets of the same idea:

1. *Operations are atomic.* This means that when a system component receives some input, it reacts, and then returns to the wait-for-input state. Each message stands for itself. The daemons don't have any states in which they wait for a specific follow-up message from some other system component.
2. *Synchronism is minimized.* The system components, especially the daemons, operate in an asynchronous manner as much as possible. They do not block and wait for each other.

33.2.4 Control Protocols

The flow of control and information among the system components is outlined in Figure 33.2. Obviously, the masterd is the hub of the system: All the GUIs and nodeds communicate with it. In addition, there are some direct communications from JRs to sprocs.

However, the topology does not give the whole picture. Focusing on the most important interactions, those between the masterd and the nodeds, we find that the following scenarios are common:

- The masterd notifies a set of nodeds about a new job that they should spawn.
- The masterd sends a (meta)signal to a set of nodeds, who forward it to the sprocs on their respective nodes.
- Nodeds notify the masterd about termination of sprocs.

Generalizing these interactions, we see that they always follow the same pattern: The masterd multicasts the same message to a set of nodeds, whereas the nodeds respond individually.

The naive way to implement such a communication pattern is to establish a TCP/IP connection from the masterd to each noded. The multicasts are then implemented as a loop in which the masterd sends the message to all the relevant nodeds. However, this suffers from increasing overhead as the system size increases, and does not utilize the broadcast capability of the underlying Ethernet medium. We therefore implemented a reliable multicast protocol based on UDP/IP.

The resulting communication structure is asymmetric: The masterd sends messages to nodeds using reliable multicast over UDP, and the nodeds send acks and other messages to the masterd using TCP. The multicast is in fact a broadcast with a destination bitmap. Thus the communication layer on all nodes receives all messages, but passes them to the noded only if the bit for this node is set. This allows a single numbering scheme to be used for all multicast packets.

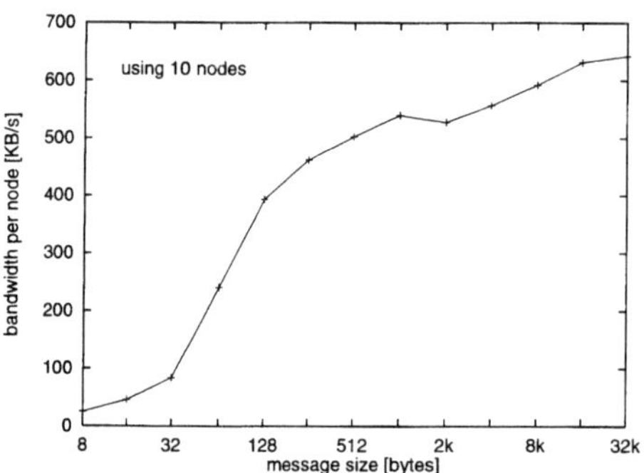

Figure 33.3 Bandwidth achieved by the multicast protocol.

Reliability is achieved by a sliding window protocol. The masterd may send a number of messages without waiting for immediate acks; instead, the messages are stored until acks are received from all the nodes. An ack for package i indicates that all packets up to and including i have been received. A nack on packet j indicates that all packets from $i+1$ (one after the last ack'd packet) to $j-1$ are missing, but j itself was received. This allows masterd to re-transmit only those packets that are indeed missing, instead of re-transmitting everything after any loss of a single packet.

If neither an ack nor a nack arrive, the masterd re-transmits after a timeout period. The timeout period is calculated dynamically based on measurements of previous ack times, so as to avoid premature re-transmissions. A weighted average of ack times is used, in order to adjust to changing network conditions. This is similar to the calculations used in TCP [4].

The bandwidth achieved by the multicast protocol is shown in Figure 33.3. It peaks at just under 650 KB/s for 32 KB messages. This result is not sensitive to the number of nodes participating in the multicast.

33.2.5 Data Network

The data network provides user-level communication for application processes. This allows the crucial communication operations to circumvent the operating system, thus improving the bandwidth delivered to the application and reducing the latency. The interface used is the popular MPI standard. The implementation is a port of MPI-FM, the Illinois Fast Messages software [11]. Myrinet is currently the best commercially available LAN for this purpose [1].

A sufficient condition for Myrinet operation is that the network be connected, that is, that there be a path between any two nodes. However, such a topology may imply a much lower bandwidth between clusters of nodes connected to different Myrinet switches than within such clusters. In particular, the bisection bandwidth of the network may be as low as that of a single link. It is therefore advisable to use a richer topology.

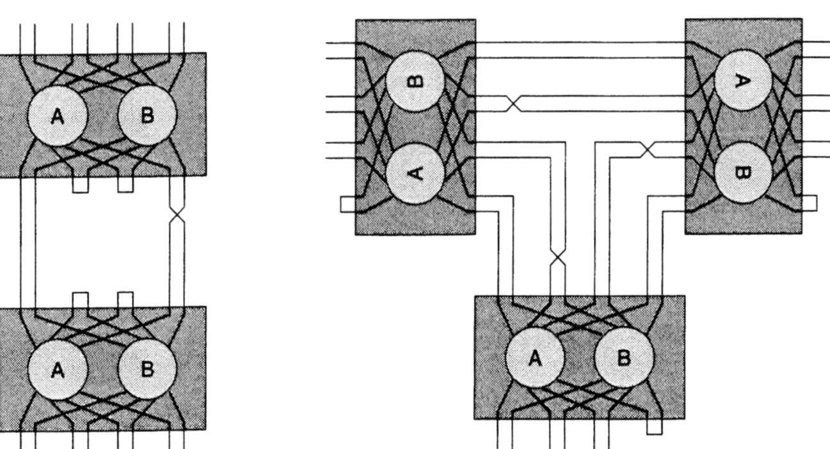

Figure 33.4 Possible topologies for 16-node Myrinet networks (the 3-switch topology actually supports up to 18 nodes).

Due to the specific switch configurations sold by Myricom, two dual switches are required in order to connect 16 nodes (a dual switch contains two eight-port switches referred to as A and B, but at least one port is needed to connect the switches to each other, so at most 14 nodes can be connected to a single dual switch). It is therefore possible to construct a topology with a bisection bandwidth of 4 links (Figure 33.4, left). With three dual switches, a topology supporting 18 nodes with bisection bandwidth of 9 links is possible (Figure 33.4, right).

33.3 System Configuration and Control

The previous section described the components of the full system. This section explains how the components recognize each other when the system is booted, and how they react to fault conditions.

33.3.1 Dynamic Reconfiguration

As far as the software daemons are concerned, the configuration of the ParPar system is completely dynamic.

Upon startup, the masterd creates three sockets, binds them to well-known ports, and starts to listen on them. These ports are used for connections from nodeds, JRs, and MCs, respectively. In principle, the masterd does not have to know about these entities in advance in order to accept connections. In practice, we require the nodes to be listed in a configuration file, so that the full configuration can be loaded on each node when it connects. This is used to set up routing tables for the data network.

When a noded comes up, it enters a loop in which it tries to establish a connection with the masterd. As the noded is useless unless it is connected, it stays in the loop until a connection is made. Thereafter it serves as one of the nodes in the configuration maintained by the masterd. As part of the initial handshake, the node's serial number in the system is determined, and information about its capabilities and resources is registered with the masterd.

Node failures are identified by the masterd by the termination of the TCP connection with the noded. When this happens, the masterd updates its configuration information to reflect the fact that the node in question can no longer be used. This affects jobs running on this node, as described below, but does not affect the rest of the system.

33.3.2 Reliability and Availability

ParPar provides fault containment in the sense that the failure of any single node affects only jobs with sprocs running on that node, and even these jobs are not necessarily killed. In fact, node failure is simply regarded as the abnormal termination of the sprocs running on it. The details of handling abnormal termination are described below.

The masterd, on the other hand, is a single point of failure. This can be rectified by duplication or logging of all activities. However, we intend to perform measurements regarding the severity of this problem before complicating the system in order to solve it.

33.3.3 The Master Control

The MC GUI allows users to obtain information about the system configuration and load, and to perform certain operations on the system.

The basic items of information provided are a list of the connected nodes with their capabilities, and a list of the current jobs with their requirements and current status (e.g., running or queued). The items in each list are decorated with check-buttons, allowing selected nodes or jobs to be marked. Then an operation can be applied to the marked nodes or jobs.

For normal users, the only operations are to kill or stop their own jobs. System operators can also kill or stop jobs owned by others, shut down the whole system, or shut down a specific set of nodes. Stopping jobs is useful to enable performance measurements in a controlled environment. Shutdowns include a grace period in which jobs are allowed to terminate.

33.4 Job Control

A major objective of parallel systems is to run parallel jobs. This includes not only the initiation of jobs, but also control over jobs (e.g., being able to kill them) and debugging.

33.4.1 Job Initiation

Jobs are launched by users via the JR interface (Figure 33.9). The minimal information required is the executable file name and the number of nodes to be used. It is also possible to provide arguments and specify what parts of the environment should be passed as well.

When the user hits the "load" button, the JR sends all this information to the masterd. The masterd is responsible for scheduling the new job, as described in Section 33.5. When the job is first scheduled, the masterd instructs the relevant nodeds to fork the required sprocs. Between the fork and the exec of the user's executable, the noded sets up the correct environment, redirects stdin, stdout, and stderr to sockets connected to the JR, and sets the user ID to that of the invoking user. Thus the job will have the correct permissions for accessing files.

Verification of the user ID claimed by the JR is based on a simple authentication protocol conducted when the JR first connects to the masterd. The masterd creates a file that is readable only by its owner, writes a random string into this file, and changes the owner to be the user claimed by the JR. It then challenges the JR to read the contents of the file. If the JR succeeds, the identity of the user is accepted.

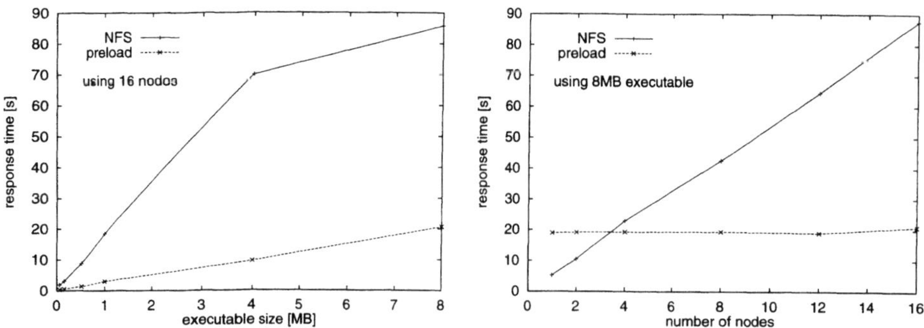

Figure 33.5 Performance of executable file copying vs. NFS.

The sproc can exec the user's executable in either of two ways. One is to use demand paging via NFS. The other is to first copy the executable to the local disk. In order to reduce the pressure on NFS, the copying is done through the masterd, which broadcasts the file to all the nodes. The performance implications are shown in Figure 33.5. As the executable file size increases, the advantage of copying to the local disk becomes greater (left). Likewise, as more nodes are used, the advantage of local copying is increased (right). As the file is always copied to *all* the nodes, whereas NFS brings pages only to the nodes that are actually used, NFS is better for jobs that use only 1–3 nodes.

The masterd keeps a table of executables that have been copied. Thus if a user runs the same job again, the executable does not have to be copied again, but rather the existing copy is used. Verification that the executable has not changed is based on recording its last modification time. When the disk space to keep executables runs low, the ones that have been used the least number of times and the least recently are evicted. This is calculated as the sum of two terms that are both in the range [0, 1]. The first term is the fractional age of the executable: The time since it was last used, divided by the maximum over all executables of the time since the last use. The second term is the reciprocal of the number of times it was used. The executable with the highest score is evicted. Thus jobs that were run repeatedly are allowed to stay longer, out of anticipation that they will be used again.

33.4.2 Job Termination

Upon termination of a sproc, the noded that had forked it receives a SIGCHLD signal. It then uses the wait4 system call to obtain information about the cause of termination and the resources consumed.

If the sproc terminated normally, the noded simply forwards the information to the masterd, using a message we call a metaSIGCHLD. The masterd collects the information about all the sprocs, and when all of them terminate, it declares the whole xproc terminated and informs the JR.

If the sproc terminated abnormally, the noded forwards the termination infor-

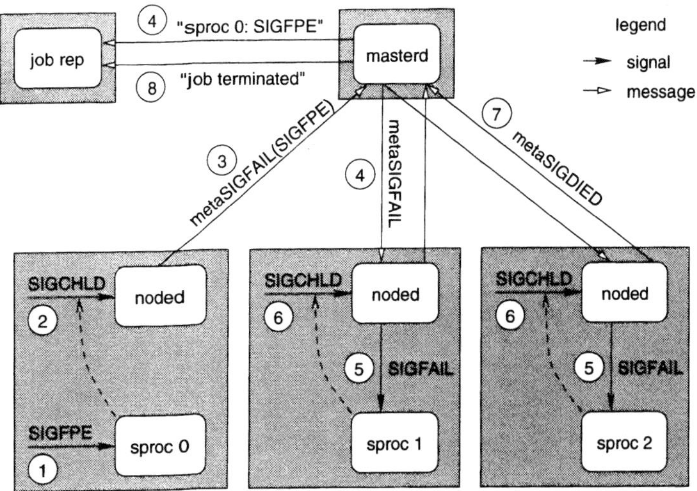

Figure 33.6 Handling abnormal termination of sprocs.

mation to the masterd in the form of a metaSIGFAIL (an example is given in Figure 33.6, where sproc 0 has a floating point exception). The masterd forwards this message to other nodeds that have sprocs of the same job. The nodeds then send a Unix SIGFAIL (implemented by SIGUSR1) to these sprocs. If the application was so coded, the sprocs can catch this signal and regroup to continue the computation. If not, the sprocs are killed, and the nodeds are notified by a SIGCHLD. The termination information is then forwarded to the masterd in the form of a metaSIGDIED, indicating that this is an expected abnormal termination, and need not be forwarded to other nodes.

Signals can also be sent by the user to all sprocs via and JR interface. In particular, SIGKILL is sent when the "kill" button is pressed. Such signals are sent in the form of a metaSIGSIG message from the JR to the masterd, which forwards them to the relevant nodeds, which then send the requested Unix signal to the sprocs.

33.4.3 Debugging

Debugging parallel jobs is difficult due to their concurrent nature. A debugger for parallel jobs must provide control over all the sprocs, and also be able to present concise status information.

The control structure used by the ParPar debugger is shown in Figure 33.7. The debugger's graphical front-end is created by the JR when the job is loaded. Each noded forks a debugger back-end to control its local sproc. The back ends establish connections with the front end, and control the sprocs per the instructions they receive.

A key feature of the front end is the notion of "focus." The focus is the set

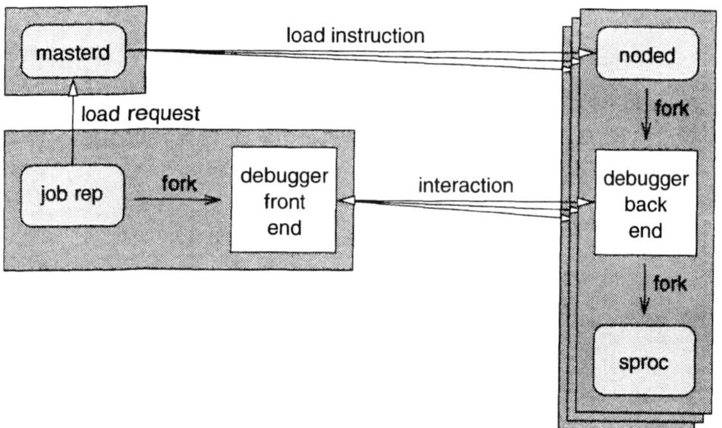

Figure 33.7 Debugger control structure.

of sprocs being targeted at a given time. Debugger commands issued by the user, such as setting a breakpoint or stepping through the execution, are sent only to the sprocs in this set. Likewise, only information relating to these sprocs is displayed to the user. This mechanism allows the user to control single sprocs, the whole job, or any subset, using the same interface.

33.5 Scheduling

If the combined requirements of submitted jobs exceed the system resources, scheduling decisions have to be made. Two schemes have been implemented in ParPar: One based on space slicing, and the other adding a dimension of time slicing.

33.5.1 Adaptive Partitioning

Adaptive partitioning gives each job a dedicated partition of the machine, where the partition size is a compromise between the scheduler and the job that takes both the job's requirements and the current load into account.

Users can specify a set of possible partition sizes when a job is submitted, rather than demanding a single size. For example, in Figure 33.9, the sizes 2, 4, 6, or 8 have been requested. The scheduler then allocates the largest size that is available. This has the desired outcome: The system automatically allocates the largest size that is available that is suitable for the job, thus allowing it to start running as soon as possible.

If none of the desired sizes is available, the job is queued and awaits the termination of some running jobs. When more processors become available, jobs are started in FIFO order from the queue. But if the first job in the queue requires more nodes than are available, subsequent smaller jobs may skip over it. This is limited to a predefined number of times, e.g., 5, so as not to starve the large jobs.

33.5.2 Gang Scheduling

Gang scheduling provides coordinated time slicing among multiple jobs. At any given time, either all the sprocs in a job are running on distinct processors, or none is running.

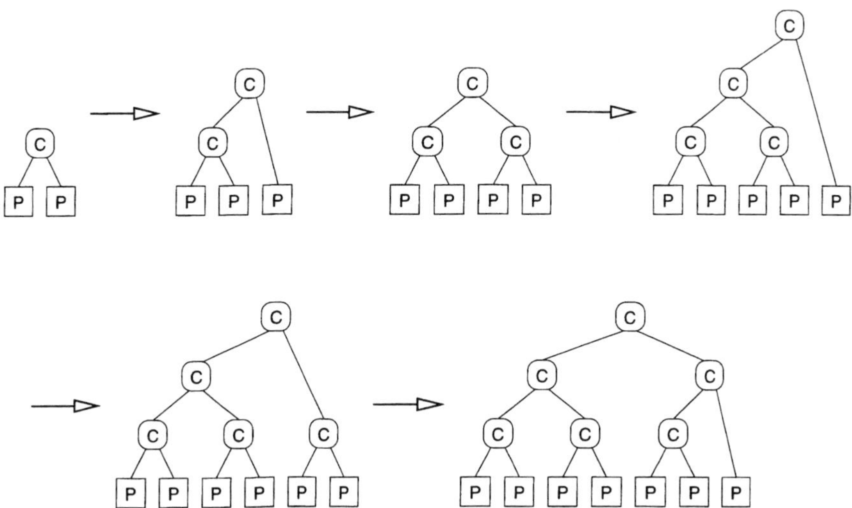

Figure 33.8 Growing the Distributed Hierarchical Control structure incrementally from 2 to 7 nodes.

The first issue in the implementation of gang scheduling is how to map sprocs to nodes. We use an extension of the Distributed Hierarchical Control framework, which defines a binary tree of control points [9]. The extension supports non-power-of-two systems, and builds the control tree incrementally as additional nodeds join the system (Figure 33.8). This scheme nevertheless tends to pack jobs using groups of processors that are powers of two, which improves the ability to perform alternative scheduling. This is crucial in order to achieve high utilization and reduce fragmentation [6].

The second issue is the implementation of the coordinated context switching across multiple nodes. This is done by metaSIGSWITCH messages that are broadcast from the masterd to the nodeds. Upon receipt of such a message, the nodeds send a SIGSTOP to the currently running sproc on their node, and a SIGCONT to the designated sproc that should run next. As all the nodeds do this at about the same time, the effect is that of descheduling the current xproc and scheduling another in its place.

A potential problem with gang scheduling is memory pressure, because multiple jobs have to be memory resident at the same time. If the sum of the working sets of the sprocs mapped to the same node exceeds the available memory, thrashing will ensue. We have therefore implemented a version of the gang scheduler that includes such memory considerations. This version is able to queue or swap additional jobs rather than running them all at the same time, so as to reduce the danger of excessive paging.

A major problem in dealing with memory requirements is to assess how much memory is needed. Our scheduler bases this assessment on two inputs: An analysis of the executable file, and historical data from previous runs of the same executable. While not perfect, this provides estimates that are within a few percentage points of actual usage more than 90% of the time.

Given an estimate of how much memory is needed, the scheduler searches for the least-loaded set of processors that can run the submitted job. The load function is the sum of two terms: The number of jobs already scheduled on this set of processors, and the memory load function. If enough free memory is available, the memory load is 0. If it is exhausted, the memory load increases so as to represent the extra delays expected due to paging.

33.6 Parallel I/O

I/O falls into two categories: Terminal I/O and file I/O. Both have special requirements and characteristics in a parallel system.

33.6.1 Terminal I/O

Terminal I/O is a much-neglected issue in many parallel systems. However, it is a useful device, especially during program development. ParPar includes extensive support for efficient control and use of terminal I/O.

The most common form of terminal I/O is text: The user types text at the keyboard, and views text on the screen. In a parallel system, this is complicated by the fact that a single keyboard and screen must connect to multiple sprocs running on distinct nodes. It is therefore necessary to be able to control exactly which sprocs should be involved. In ParPar, this is done by input and output menus that are located just above the standard I/O window in the JR (Figure 33.9). By default, all nodes are included. However, any subset may be selected instead. Input typed at the keyboard is sent only to nodes indicated in the input set. Output from the sprocs is only displayed if they are in the output set. In addition, the node's serial number is indicated at the beginning of each line of output.

An innovative form of output supported on ParPar is a so-called LED array [7]. Part of the JR's panel is partitioned into a set of small squares. The number of such squares per node is setable by the application. The application can also color these squares in different colors, causing an effect similar to flashing LEDs on the front panel of a machine. This is convenient for displaying the status of the program. For example, instead of printing a string to the terminal from each node to indicate that "initialization complete; starting computation," one can change the color of a LED from red to blue. The user sitting at the terminal will immediately see if all nodes perform the transition correctly at the beginning of the execution, or if some

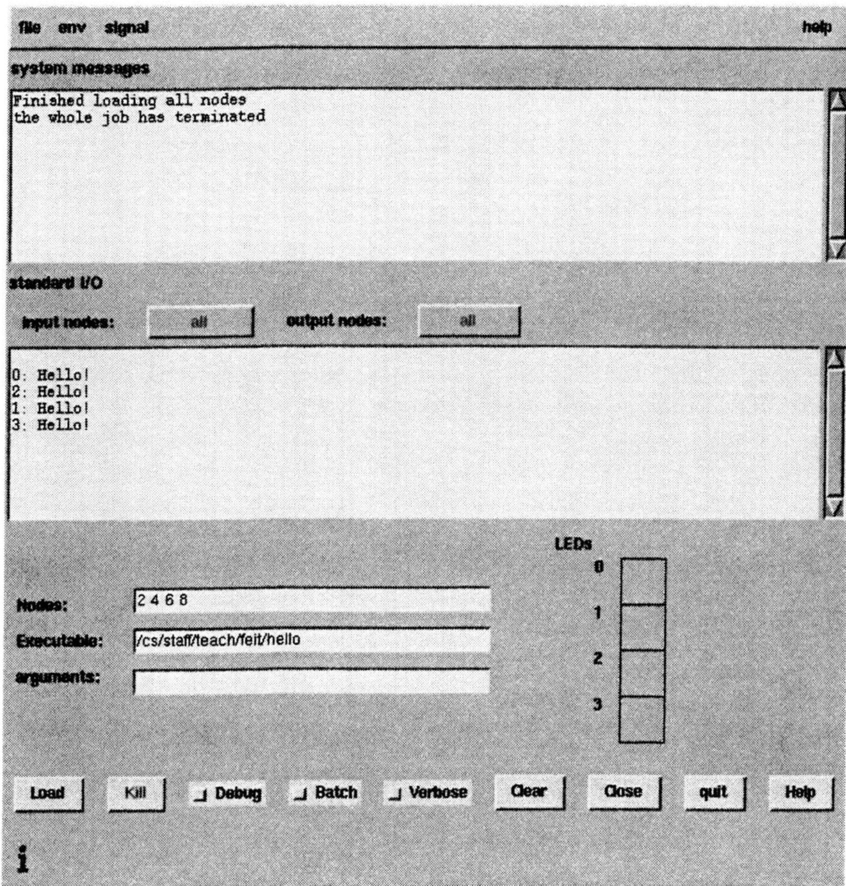

Figure 33.9 The Job Representative GUI, after running a "hello world" program on 4 nodes.

remain stuck in the initialization phase. This is easier than having to locate and count the printed outputs which may be interleaved with other printouts and with inputs.

33.6.2 Parallel Files

The initial prototype of the ParPar system circumvents the issue of parallel file I/O by relying on two mechanisms. First, user files are accessed using NFS services. As each node runs a full Unix system, it is simple to mount the user's file systems on all the nodes. It is up to the application programmer to ensure that different processes don't interfere with each other, for example, by writing to the same file. The second is a large /tmp space (about 1GB) that is provided locally on each node. This is useful for the implementation of out-of-core algorithms.

While NFS provides convenient support for remote file access, it has many drawbacks when used by a parallel program. In parallel programs, concurrent access to the same file by numerous processes is the rule rather than the exception. The NFS design assumes the opposite. As a result, various NFS design decisions complicate the use of NFS files by parallel programs. In particular, NFS's caching policy implies that if multiple processes write *disjoint* parts of the same file, they might still corrupt each other's data. Moreover, NFS might also become a performance bottleneck, as each file is ultimately handled by a single server.

The solution is to use a parallel file system within the parallel machine [8]. We plan to add 4 dedicated I/O nodes to ParPar for this purpose. These nodes will run a parallel file system that provides efficient support for file partitioning.

Studies of parallel file access patterns have revealed that in many cases processes make multidimensional strided access patterns [10]. For example, a process may access contiguous spans of 16 bytes that are separated by strides of 1024 bytes. These access patterns correspond to rectilinear partitions of multidimensional data structures, such as rows or blocks of a matrix. Typically, all the processes taken together access the whole data structure, but each one accesses only its partition.

Partitioned access, by its nature, involves multiple requests for small parts of the file. Performing such requests explicitly leads to inefficient use of the disks, which are optimized for large sequential access. It is therefore imperative to inform the file system about the global access pattern, so as to optimize disk access. The file system is then responsible for reorganizing the data and distributing it to the different processes as needed. In order to do so, the programmer must specify the access pattern in advance. Several interfaces for this purpose have been proposed, including the MPI-IO interface that is part of MPI-2.

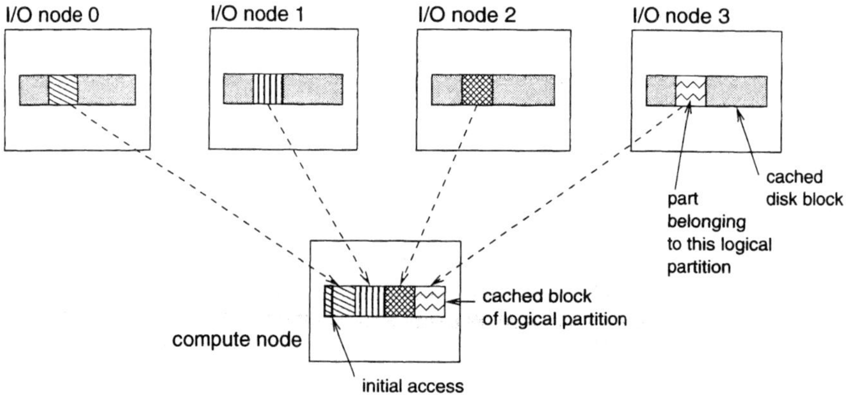

Figure 33.10 Caching logical partitions on compute nodes.

We intend to integrate the idea of file partitioning with the mechanisms of caching and prefetching in the file system. Caching and prefetching are well-known techniques to improve performance, but they suffer from problems of coherence and false sharing when applied to parallel files. Our solution is to apply these mechanisms at the logical level of file partitions rather than at the physical level of disk blocks. In other words, blocks of logical partitions will be cached at compute nodes, rather than disk blocks (Figure 33.10). This will have profound implications: It will simplify the implementation of these mechanisms, will improve their performance due to the increased possibility of caching and the reduced communication, and might even eliminate the need for additional more complicated and costly performance optimizations.

33.7 Project Status

At the time of writing (October 1998), a cluster of 17 Pentium-Pro 200 machines connected by both Ethernet and Myrinet networks has been acquired, and a first prototype of the system is essentially operational. Of all the features described above, only the debugger and MC GUIs and the parallel file system are not finished yet. This cluster is being used for two purposes: First, we are conducting research on additional enhancements to the system software. Initial examples of such research are the use of reliable multicast for control functions, and memory-cognizant gang scheduling, as described above. Ongoing and future projects include logical caching in the parallel file system, and improved integration of the user-level communication library. Second, we are nurturing a budding collaboration with users from the Physics department who intend to use the system to run large-scale numerical computations. This will both help in exposing the strengths and weaknesses of the system design, and allow us to observe real usage patterns. Such observations will then be used to guide future developments.

For updates and the ParPar design document, see URL

http://www.cs.huji.ac.il/labs/parallel/parpar.html.

Acknowledgments

This research was supported in part by The Israel Science Foundation, founded by the Israel Academy of Sciences & Humanities, and by the Ministry of Science.

33.8 Bibliography

[1] H. Bal, R. Hofman, and K. Verstoep. A Comparison of Three High Speed Networks for Parallel Cluster Computing. In *Communication and Architectural Support for Network-Based Parallel Computing*, D. K. Panda and C. B. Stunkel (eds.), pages 184–197, Springer-Verlag, February 1997. Lecture Notes in Computer Science, vol. 1199.

[2] A. Barak, S. Guday, and R. G. Wheeler, *The MOSIX Distributed Operating System: Load Balancing for UNIX*. Springer-Verlag, 1993. Lecture Notes in Computer Science, vol. 672.

[3] N. J. Boden, D. Cohen, R. E. Felderman, A. E. Kulawik, C. L. Seitz, J. N. Seizovic, and W-K. Su. Myrinet: A Gigabit-per-Second Local Area Network. *IEEE Micro*, vol. 15(1), pages 29–36, February 1995.

[4] D. E. Comer, *Internetworking with TCP/IP, Vol. I: Principles, Protocols, and Architecture.* Prentice-Hall, 3rd ed., 1995.

[5] H. G. Dietz, R. Hoare, and T. Mattox. A Fine-Grain Parallel Architecture Based on Barrier Synchronization. In *International Conference on Parallel Processing*, vol. I, pages 247–250, August 1996.

[6] D. G. Feitelson. Packing Schemes for Gang Scheduling. In *Job Scheduling Strategies for Parallel Processing*, D. G. Feitelson and L. Rudolph (eds.), pages 89–110, Springer-Verlag, 1996. Lecture Notes in Computer Science, vol. 1162.

[7] D. G. Feitelson. Terminal I/O for Massively Parallel Systems. In *Scalable High Performance Computing Conference*, pages 263–270, May 1994.

[8] D. G. Feitelson, P. F. Corbett, S. J. Baylor, and Y. Hsu. Parallel I/O Subsystems in Massively Parallel Supercomputers. *IEEE Parallel & Distributed Technology*, vol. 3(3), pages 33–47, Fall 1995.

[9] D. G. Feitelson and L. Rudolph. Distributed Hierarchical Control for Parallel Processing. *Computer*, vol. 23(5), pages 65–77, May 1990.

[10] N. Nieuwejaar, D. Kotz, A. Purakayastha, C. S. Ellis, and M. L. Best. File-Access Characteristics of Parallel Scientific Workloads. *IEEE Transactions on Parallel & Distributed Systems*, vol. 7(10), pages 1075–1089, October 1996.

[11] S. Pakin, V. Karamcheti, and A. A. Chien. Fast Messages: Efficient, Portable Communication for Workstation Clusters and MPPs. *IEEE Concurrency*, vol. 5(2), pages 60–73, April-June 1997.

[12] T. von Eicken, A. Basu, V. Buch, and W. Vogels. U-Net: A User-Level Network Interface for Parallel and Distributed Computing. In 15th *Symposium on Operating Systems Principles*, pages 40–53, December 1995.

[13] T. von Eiken, D. E. Culler, S. C. Goldstein, and K. E. Schauser. Active Messages: A Mechanism for Integrated Communication and Computation. In 19th *Annual International Symposium on Computer Architecture Conference Proceedings*, pages 256–266, May 1992.

Chapter 34

Pitt Parallel Computer[1]

ROLF H. KNUTSEN, MARLIN H. MICKLE, AND RONALD G. HOELZEMAN

Department of Electrical Engineering
348 Benedum Hall
University of Pittsburgh
Pittsburgh, PA 15261

Email: *rolf.knutsen@ericsson.no, {mickle, hoelzema}@ee.pitt.edu*

34.1 Introduction

The Pitt Parallel Computer (PPC) is a reconfigurable parallel computer that can be configured with a variety of nodes and topologies. It is used to evaluate performance models for parallel computation, especially those that recognize the importance of the ratio of communication time to computation time, i.e., t_{comm}/t_{calc}. The PPC is a part of the Parallel Computing and Networks Laboratory in the Department of Electrical Engineering at the University of Pittsburgh.

In addition, the PPC is an experimental test platform for teaching and evaluation of parallel computers and networks using off-the-shelf hardware technologies and state-of-the-art concepts. The rationale is to exploit topology, communication, synchronization, algorithms, etc., for parallel computation without being locked into a particular technology for processors, interconnections, fabrication or interfacing. The version primarily discussed in this chapter is realized with 4 nodes connected in a 2 by 2 mesh. Other versions of the PPC will be presented at a later stage.

One of the objectives of the parallel computer research is the ability to test theories concerning performance, mapping, load balancing, etc., on actual hardware under controlled conditions of computational speed and communication. By using nodes that are off-the-shelf motherboards, it is possible to actually test different software packages for communication and synchronization.

The PPC is designed without an operating system in the traditional sense. It is to be used to test alternatives in communications, synchronization, etc. As such, it

[1]This work was supported by the National Science Foundation under Grant No. DUE 9703079.

is important to be able to reduce system overhead to a minimum. Therefore, a set of utility routines has been made available to be incorporated into a problem specific piece of software that can be used to evaluate and time the various parameter choices.

The IEEE floating-point standard (IEEE 754) is the standard format used in most computers when storing floating-point numbers. This is also the format the PPC programs use in displays presenting floating-point computational results to show the full precision of all results.

There are currently two fully operational programs available for the four node PPC: (1) The Laplace grid continuum problem, and (2) The linear simultaneous equation problem (LSE). A third program currently under development solves (3) The N-body problem.

The PPC is constructed from off-the-shelf motherboards with simple hardware assembly components. Communication is through cards using the Industry Standard Architecture (ISA) bus. The communication can be accomplished using a number of standard cards such as Ethernet or RS232. While the RS232 may be somewhat slower, it provides a method of evaluating, t_{comm}/t_{calc}, under a variety of circumstances where, for example, t_{calc} can be held constant and the t_{comm} can be varied over a wide range of BAUD rates. In a typical system, the RS232 cables are designed to connect a PC (DTE) to a modem (DCE). In the PPC all nodes are PC boards giving a DTE-DTE connection. No modem is connected and therefore a null modem cable is used. The connection scheme is shown below in Figure 34.1.

For a 2 x 2 node mesh, the connections are: (a) COM 2 of node (1,1) to COM 1 of node (1,2); (b) COM 2 of node (1,2) to COM 1 of node (2,2); (c) COM 2 of node (2,2) to COM 1 of node (2,1); and (d) COM 2 of node (2,1) to COM 1 of node (1,1).

34.2 The Operating System

The operating system is distributed among all of the nodes with node (1,1) connected as the server providing the user interface. Control among the processors is accomplished using message passing where all messages are one byte in length. Data frames vary in length. The PPC concept is one in which each configuration of processors is dedicated to solving a particular problem. Thus, the program and operating system are burned into an EPROM that is substituted for the original BIOS EPROM.

Included with the operating system is a hardware-testing program that enables the user to test the hardware connections for the particular PPC configuration. The PPC test-program will test all the communications connections in the PPC by sending test-data and control signals through all the connections needed to successfully use the PPC. If a bad connection is found, the test-program will stop with diagnostic information. By observing where the program stopped, the user can identify which connection is bad.

In most configurations, each node has a connection to a dumb terminal for the

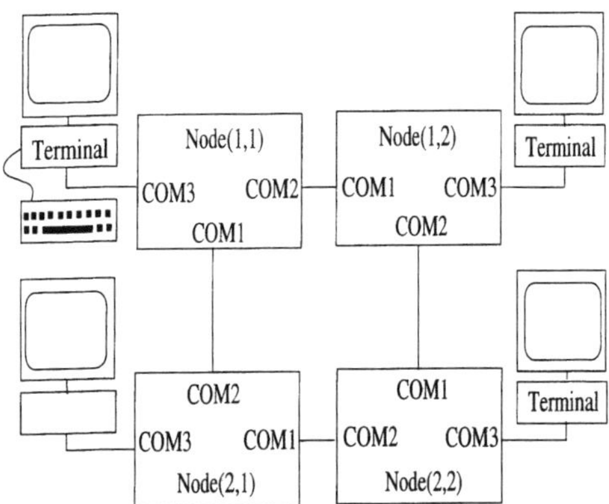

Figure 34.1 A schematic view of the PPC 4 node setup.

Figure 34.2 A 4 Node PPC Example.

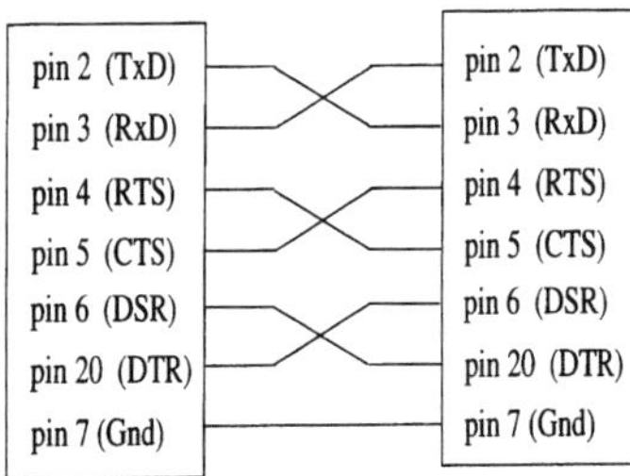

Figure 34.3 Configuration of serial cables used between the nodes.

display of user information and presentation of results. Other configuration include an option on the server to allow the user to display the results for all nodes on a single terminal, thus reducing the need for a CRT to be connected to each node. This type of operation is typical of PPCs consisting of larger numbers of nodes.

34.2.1 Internode Communication

Consider the PPC configuration consisting of four nodes. Each node is connected to two neighboring nodes and a terminal. We therefore have a total of three communication connections for each node (serial communication ports 1, 2 and 3). Communication ports 1 and 2 are connected to neighboring nodes. The connections are made so that COM 2 from one node is connected to COM 1 of the neighboring node. Communication port 3 of each node is connected to a terminal. Each port is capable of full duplex serial communication with handshaking in the PPC configuration.

Since the PPC programs use full duplex communication, the use of the signals between the nodes is non-standard. (Full duplex is not standard for a DTE-DTE RS232 connection. However, the standard is capable of this by using a null modem and a few tricks.) Note that all the connections, except ground, are flipped so that each output is connected to an input.

When the connections are tested, each node will first send an output signal and then wait to receive the corresponding input signal. For example, the first connection this program will test is the RTS output from COM 1. All the nodes will first send a RTS signal out COM 1. We know that RTS from COM 1 is connected to CTS (COM 2) of a neighboring node. So if all the nodes send out a RTS on COM 1, all the nodes should also receive a CTS on COM 2. If each node can read the CTS-signal from COM 2, then we know that this connection is good. This procedure is done for all the output/input pairs for both communication ports set as the transmitter.

The program will also test the communication with the terminals. Of course, if the messages given from the program have appeared on the screen, the communication from the PPC to the terminals is good. After the communication between the nodes is tested, the program will prompt the user for an input through the keyboard connected to the terminal of node (1,1). This will test the communication from the terminal back to node (1,1). This test is done only for node (1,1) because the user gives commands to the PPC programs only through this terminal.

The last test the program will do is to test if the nodes are connected together in the right order according to the specified topology. If the order is found to be right, no messages will prompt the user for an input through the keyboard connected to the terminal of node (1,1). This will test the communication from the terminal back to node (1,1). This test is done only for node (1,1) because the user gives commands to the PPC programs only through this terminal.

When the message, "THIS NODE IS PROPERLY CONNECTED," appears on all the terminal screens, the nodes of the PPC are correctly connected together. If one or more screens do not display this message, there is at least one error somewhere. The possible conditions are discussed in the PPC User's Manual [1].

34.2.2 Typical Usage

The PPC is used as a pedagogical as well as a research tool. In both cases, concepts such as granularity, scalability, performance measures, etc., are extremely important. It was initially decided not to develop an operating system to accommodate all possible modes of usage. Instead, a common operating system and communication kernel allow software to be developed to support a particular problem or configuration test. In order to measure performance under varying computation and communication speeds, it is necessary to vary both to perform validation tests. Such a variation is easily accomplished with the PPC. Processors can be simply changed, and the clock speeds of the motherboards forming the nodes can be varied. These two alternatives provide variation in computation speed from 25MHz to 99MHz.

Communication is the second parameter to be changed. The RS232 type cards make it possible to use BAUD rates from 2400 to 230.4K BAUD. While 115.2K BAUD is typically the maximum with the crystal and divide configuration of most cards, newer cards provide a higher-frequency crystal that can be implemented typically with a shorting jumper.

Given a particular type of problem such as Laplace or LSEs, and a particular mapping, the multiprocessor performance can be compared with a single processor (or other topology) by holding either calculation speed or communication speed constant while varying the other. The experiments can then be rerun with another granularity to demonstrate the effects of the different parameters.

The thorough analyses on the basis of t_{comm} and t_{calc} make it possible to analyze performance on the basis of much higher clock and communication rates when the architectures (topologies) are extensible. In particular, it is possible to analyze the complete communication scenario where TOF is communication channel time-of-flight and OH is the overhead:

$$\text{SENDER OH} + \text{TOF} + \text{MESSAGE LENGTH/BANDWIDTH} + \text{RECEIVER OH} \tag{34.2.1}$$

Using the variable communication rates and variable granularity, it is possible to separate the software overhead of the sender and receiver into those components that are a function of problem size and message length. This analysis allows accurate prediction of communication times as well as an evaluation of the software protocols used at both ends of the communication channel.

Timing can be done using the options with a typical chip set. However, in order to demonstrate the timing with a minimum of complication, the problems run are sufficiently large to use an off-the-shelf interval timer with the user pressing the START/STOP button. These tests can be made sufficiently accurate by appropriate choice of problem size or iterations and have been shown to be accurate.

34.2.3 A Problem Suite for Research

The Laplace problem produces a solution based on a "cookie cutter" mapping where computation and communication are balanced (equal). The linear simultaneous equation (LSE) problem is more interesting due to the unbalanced situation between computation and communication in addition to different possible array sizes.

The LSE example on the PPC uses a mapping formed by choosing an element along the diagonal of the matrix, and the identified row and column mark the four quadrants mapped onto the four processors. The system allows the direct choice of any diagonal element from (2,2) to (n-1,n-1), thus giving a means to simply test each mapping against theoretical results. Alternate row/column options are under development.

34.3 The Laplace Problem

The Laplace grid continuum solution is a numerical method of calculating a value anywhere in a discrete region, given a boundary value at the edges of that region. This section will describe how this method is used. The requirement for using the Laplace grid continuum method to solve the problem is a uniform distribution in the given continuous region. The region in examples is usually two-dimensional, but, as the next section will show, the method can be applied to other regions as well.

The procedure of the method is that for each of the discrete cells, we will replace the value with the average value of the neighboring cells [1]. By repeating this operation, and keeping the boundary value constant, the value of each cell will converge. We repeat the process until the results have the required accuracy.

34.3.1 A One-Dimensional Example

The first example considers an electrical conducting wire. The region to be investigated is then a straight line (one-dimensional). Assuming that the wire has a uniformly distributed electrical resistance per meter, we can calculate the total resistance of the wire. Let us say that we have 10 meters of wire, with an electrical resistance of 1Ω/meter. The total resistance of the wire is then 10Ω. If we ground one end of the wire, and apply a voltage of 5 volts to the other end, we have an electrical circuit. Figure 34.4, shows a schematic of the circuit.

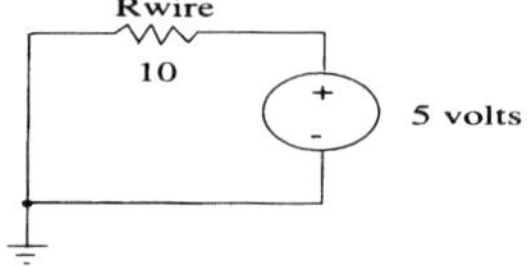

Figure 34.4 The electrical circuit example.

Now let us examine the wire in detail. Figure 34.5 shows the resistive wire. It is obvious that the voltage on one side of the wire is 0 volts, since this is grounded. Let this be the side where the wire is labeled "0 m." By the same reasoning, it should also be obvious that the voltage at the other end (labeled "10 m") is 5 volts. Given that the resistance of the wire is uniformly distributed, we can easily use Ohms Law to prove that so is the voltage across the wire. The voltage at any point on the wire can be expressed by the following formula:

$$V_d = (l_d/l_{tot}) \cdot V_{tot} \tag{34.3.1}$$

where V_d is the voltage on the wire a distance l_d from the grounded side of the wire. The total length of the wire is l_{tot}, and the total voltage across the wire is V_{tot}. For example, the voltage 7 meters from where the wire is grounded will then be 3.5 volts.

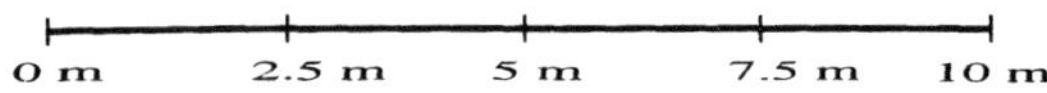

Figure 34.5 The resistive wire (10 meters).

So far we have solved this problem with continuous values. Let us now make the problem discrete. We divide the wire into 9 different sections (cells). We then assume that the voltage on the wire is the same in each section. The boundary values are still 0 and 5 volts. We can use the formula above to calculate the voltage at the middle of each section, and use this value as an approximate voltage for the entire section. Table 34.1 shows the results when doing this (with the boundary values included). Note that the section number and the distance l_d in meters is the same value for this problem.

Table 34.1 Results when Using Formula

Section number:	-	1	2	3	4	5	6	7	8	9	-
Voltage:	0	0.5	1	1.5	2	2.5	3	3.5	4	4.5	5

This is a straightforward way of solving an easy one-dimensional problem. For more complicated problems, we might not have an equation to use as we had here. Let us now solve the same problem by using the Laplace grid continuum method. First, take Table 34.1 and fill it with zeros in all cells. These zeros are simply our first guesses in order to initialize the table.

We will now take the value of each cell of the table, add the values from the adjacent cells, and divide by two. In other words, we will replace the value in each cell with the average of the neighboring cells. If we repeat this process many times we will see that the values converge to the values given in Table 34.1. Table 34.2 shows the initial values, the result after three iterations, after the 20th iteration and after the 150th iteration for each of the 9 cells. After 20 iterations, we can see that the values are distributing through the sections. After 150 iterations, we get very close to the initial table we calculated. The more iterations we execute, the closer the values will get to the first table. We can confirm this by taking any cell in Table 34.1, adding the value of the two adjacent cells and dividing by two. We will then get the original value we had in that section. This should convince the reader that Table 34.1 in this sense is stable. The process described here is a linear version of the Laplace grid continuum problem.

Table 34.2 Results after 100 Iterations

Iteration #:	-	1	2	3	4	5	6	7	8	9	-
0	0	0	0	0	0	0	0	0	0	0	5
1	0	0	0	0	0	0	0	0	0	2.5	5
2	0	0	0	0	0	0	0	0	1.25	2.5	5
3	0	0	0	0	0	0	0	0.625	1.25	3.125	5
20	0	0.148	0.356	0.564	0.939	1.314	1.915	2.517	3.318	4.119	5
150	0	0.499	0.999	1.499	1.998	2.498	2.998	3.499	3.999	4.499	5

34.3.2 A Two-Dimensional Example

In this next example, we will look at a two-dimensional problem. Figure 34.6 shows a sketch of this new problem, with four lines defining a square. The value on each boundary (line) is constant. Note that the value is not defined at the corners between the lines. The value at any point (x_i, y_j) in the square has a value that will depend on the values at the lines (boundary values) and the distance to the lines.

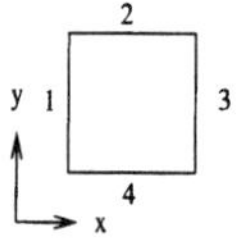

Figure 34.6 The two-dimensional Laplace problem.

This problem can now be discretized in the same way as the first example. Define a 5 by 5 matrix, and define the initial and boundary values. For this example, choose boundary values of 3, 24, 12 and 8 for the four sides. Initially, all of the values within the square will be set equal to zero.

Table 34.3 shows this problem with the initial values. The solution algorithm is to calculate the new value for each cell by taking the average of the four neighboring cells. Neighboring cells are the two cells on each side, the cell above and the cell below. Repeated calculation gives a result that converges as in the first example. The solution after 100 iterations is shown in Table 34.4.

Table 34.3 Initial Values

	24	24	24	24	24	
3	0	0	0	0	0	12
3	0	0	0	0	0	12
3	0	0	0	0	0	12
3	0	0	0	0	0	12
3	0	0	0	0	0	12
	8	8	8	8	8	

Table 34.4 Results after 100 Iterations

	24	24	24	24	24	
3	13.28 1	17.12 7	18.57 6	18.69 1	17.21 7	12
3	8.996 1	12.65 2	14.48 7	14.97	14.17 8	12
3	7.052 1	9.996	11.75	12.52 3	12.52 5	12
3	6.216 3	8.530 3	9.993 9	10.84 8	11.39 8	12
3	6.282 8	7.915	8.846 9	9.478 6	10.21 9	12
	8	8	8	8	8	

34.4 Technical Description of the Laplace Program

The problem is decomposed into 4 square grids of equal dimensions (N * N). Each grid is mapped onto one of the four processors (quadrants). The total grid computed by the system will then have the dimensions (2N * 2N). How this mapping is done is shown in Figure 34.7. Sub-grid A is calculated by processor (1,1), sub-grid B is calculated by processor (1,2), and so forth. Since the calculation of each point requires all the newest neighboring values, the boundary data between the different nodes need to be exchanged following each iteration. Each processor will wait until the completion of all the processors before the next computation iteration is initiated. This is the synchronization required for the solution.

Every unit in the array will need all four neighboring values in order to calculate the new value for this unit. This means that each processor needs the values of the neighboring processor along the boundary between the two nodes. This is why it is necessary to communicate between the nodes after every single iteration. The updated boundary values need to be transmitted to the neighboring processor. In other words, each processor will have a copy of the values on the boundary from a neighboring node. Figure 34.8 shows the algorithm for solution.

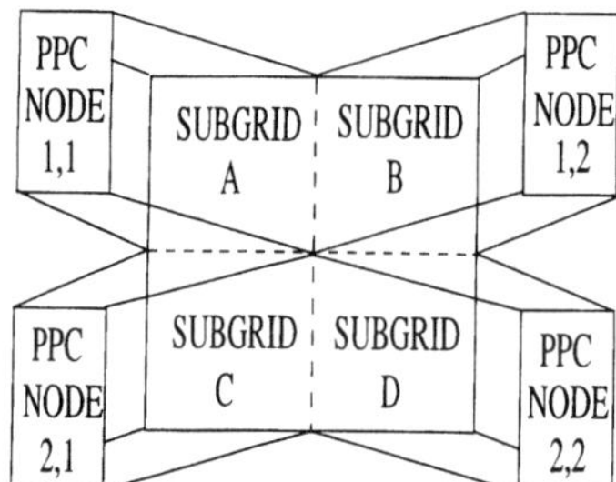

Figure 34.7 The mapping of processor to the Laplace grid.

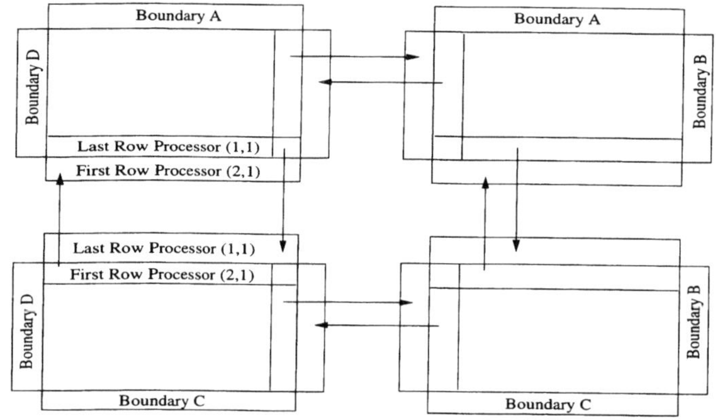

Figure 34.8 Each processor needs to have a copy of the boundary values of neighboring nodes.

34.5 User Description of the Laplace Operating System

A communication utility presents the user with a menu displayed on the server (node 1,1) when the PPC is turned on. The menu for node (1,1) is shown in Table 34.5. Note that the node is identified at the upper left corner. Each of the three other nodes will also display this menu, but with a different node identifier in the upper left corner. When selecting a menu option, this is done only for node (1,1). After receiving a command from the user, this node will pass the command on to the other nodes. All the selections can be made in either upper or lower case. When running this program, the menu will eventually scroll out of the screen area, or other menus will be displayed. However, all the commands presented in the menus are available from anywhere in the program. This means that it is not necessary to display a menu before using the selections in that menu.

The menu choices are as follows:

(i) Initiate System - Typing "i" will initialize the PPC system. The array in each of the nodes will be set to the initial values. These initial values are predetermined by the program and cannot be changed by the user. When the PPC is turned on, each of the processors will be initialized, as a part of the start-up, so there is no need to initialize the system when powering on the system.

(o) Display the Matrix - This choice will display the buffered array at the different processors. When the problem is solved, it is necessary to use this command to observe the results.

(z) One Computation Step - When this command is given, each of the processors will perform the calculations associated with one iteration. However, the processors will not do any communication between each other. Use the x-command if communication between the nodes is desired.

(x) Interchange of Data - This selection will make the processors exchange the data at the boundaries.

(t) Ten Iterations - This command will make the system run through ten complete iterations. That means that both the computation and the communication are done for each of the iterations. This command will give the same result if the user types "z" and then "x" ten times. To observe the calculated results, use the 0-command.

(h) Hundred Iterations - This command is similar to the t-command, except that this will perform one hundred iterations.

(y) Solve the Matrix - This selection will cause the PPC to run through the entire computation and completely solve the Laplace problem. The results are not presented, and in order to do so, the 0-command must be used.

(s) Communication Speed Menu - Note that this setting does not affect the communication speed with the terminals. This speed is fixed at a rate of 19,200 *bps*. The links to the terminals are not used when solving the matrix, so the fixed speed will not affect the calculation time.

(m) Display the Main Menu - This menu is similar to the menu given in Table 34.5. All the menu choices are the same, but the heading is different.

34.6 Linear Simultaneous Equations

The following is a description of a numerical method for solving linear simultaneous equations. The method described is termed Crout elimination and is the method used by the PPC to solve linear simultaneous equations.

Numerical techniques are widely used in computations in most engineering fields. A considerable number of these numerical methods require solving simultaneous linear equations as a key step. Solving differential equations is one good example. Effective solution of the linear simultaneous equations is therefore very important in order to reduce computation time. Historically, this has been one of the most important driving forces in the development of computers.

Table 34.5 The Menu Presented at Node (1,1) After Start-Up of PPC

```
Node (1,1)==================================
                PITT PARALLEL COMPUTER
        Operating Software for the Laplace Problem
Copyright 1998, University of Pittsburgh (Dept. of EE) All Rights Reserved
============================================
      Welcome to the Pitt Parallel Computer (PPC) System
          This menu can be displayed later by pressing m
 Note that all commands are available independent of displayed menu
      (i) Initiate System
      (0) Display the Matrix
      (z) One Computation Step
      (x) Interchange of Data
      (t) Ten Iterations
      (h) Hundred Iterations
      (y) Solve the Matrix
      (s) Communication Speed Menu
      (m) Display the Main Menu
PPC\Laplace(Press (m) for Menu)>
```

There are several methods that could be used in order to solve linear simultaneous equations. Some of these are the Gaussian elimination, Crout elimination, Jordan elimination, Cramer's rule, iterative methods like Jacobi or Gauss-Seidel and more. Each of these methods has its advantages and disadvantages. Factors such as the order of the system, number of calculations, complexity and so forth, are important when choosing which method to use. For the calculation of linear simultaneous equations on the PPC, the Crout elimination method is used. This method will be briefly described in the following. The Crout elimination method will not be proved. If the reader needs a more thorough description, or a description of other methods, there are many books available on this subject.

The general form of linear simultaneous equations, with n different equations and n unknowns, is given in Equation (34.6.1). This system can also be written in the form of an augmented matrix, shown in (34.6.2).

$$
\begin{aligned}
a_{11} \cdot x_1 + a_{12} \cdot x_2 + \cdots + a_{ln} \cdot x_n &= b_1 \\
a_{21} \cdot x_1 + a_{22} \cdot x_2 + \cdots + a_{2n} \cdot x_n &= b_2 \\
&\cdots \\
a_{n1} \cdot x_1 + a_{n2} \cdot x_2 + \cdots + a_{nn} \cdot x_n &= b_n
\end{aligned}
\qquad (34.6.1)
$$

$$\begin{bmatrix} a_{11} & a_{12} & \cdots & a_{1n} & | & b_1 \\ a_{21} & a_{22} & \cdots & a_{2n} & | & b_2 \\ \cdots & & & & & \\ a_{n1} & a_{n2} & \cdots & a_{nn} & | & b_n \end{bmatrix} \qquad (34.6.2)$$

In the Crout elimination method, the object is to convert the matrix to a form where all the elements on the diagonal are 1, and all of the elements below the diagonal are zero. From this form it is easy to perform back substitution to find all the unknowns. But first, we will calculate a new matrix from the original. This new matrix is necessary to derive the final matrix before the back substitution.

The order in which the different elements are calculated in the new matrix is very important because each of the calculations will use the results from previous calculated elements. The order is as follows: (1) Column 1, (2) Row 1, (3) Column 2, and (4) Row 2, etc.

X	X	X	X	X	2
X	X	X	X	X	4
X	X	X	X	X	6
X	X	X	X	X	8
1	3	5	7		

Figure 34.9 The order of calculation for an augmented 4 x 4 matrix.

This process is repeated until all the elements are calculated. Note that each positional element of the new matrix is calculated only once. That means that when calculating row 1, do not calculate the element on this row that also is a part of column 1 and so on. The order of calculation is shown for a (4 * 5) matrix in Figure 34.9. This matrix will be similar to the case with four equations and four unknowns. The right hand side of the equations is augmented as a fifth column in the matrix.

There are two different formulae for the calculations of the different elements. The first formula is for the elements on and below the diagonal and is given in Equation (34.6.3). This formula will be used for the elements in sections 1,3,5 and 7 of Figure 34.9. These new elements are denoted "s_{ij}."

$$s_{ij} = a_{ij} - \sum_{k=1}^{j-1} s_{ik} \cdot t_{kj}, \quad i \geq j \qquad (34.6.3)$$

The second formula, for the elements above the diagonal, is given in Equation (34.6.4). This formula will be used for the elements in sections 2,4,6 and 8 of Figure 34.9. These new elements are denoted "t_{ij}." Note that in the case where j = 1 in (34.6.3), the new elements will equal the original elements. We therefore do not have to do any calculations for the first column.

$$t_{ij} = \frac{a_{ij} - \sum_{k=1}^{j-1} s_{ik} \cdot t_{kj}}{s_{ij}}, \quad i < j \qquad (34.6.4)$$

The new matrix calculated will be of the form shown in (34.6.5).

$$\begin{bmatrix} s_{11} & t_{12} & t_{13} & t_{14} & | & t_{15} \\ s_{21} & s_{22} & t_{23} & t_{24} & | & t_{25} \\ s_{31} & s_{32} & s_{33} & t_{34} & | & t_{35} \\ s_{41} & s_{42} & s_{43} & s_{44} & | & t_{45} \end{bmatrix} \tag{34.6.5}$$

When all the new elements are calculated, we will have a new matrix consisting of the "s" and "t" elements. We now need to do a back substitution in order to find the solutions. When doing this, we will use only the elements "t" of this matrix. All the "s" elements are discarded. We needed only these elements in order to calculate the "t" elements

Make a new matrix based on the "t" values. Fill all the diagonal elements with the value 1, and fill all the elements below the diagonal with zeros. The matrix (34.6.6), shows the format of this matrix. From here it is easy to find each of the unknowns by doing back substitution. For this example, first use the bottom row to find the value of x_4. This value should simply be equal to t_{45}. Then substitute this value in the row above to find x_3, and so on.

$$\begin{bmatrix} 1 & t_{12} & t_{13} & t_{14} & | & t_{15} \\ 0 & 1 & t_{23} & t_{24} & | & t_{25} \\ 0 & 0 & 1 & t_{34} & | & t_{35} \\ 0 & 0 & 0 & 1 & | & t_{45} \end{bmatrix} \tag{34.6.6}$$

34.6.1 A Calculation Example

The following is an example of this method to solve linear simultaneous equations. Given the equations of (34.6.7),

$$\begin{aligned} 2 \cdot x_1 + 2 \cdot x_2 + x_3 &= 7 \\ x_1 + 2 \cdot x_2 + 2 \cdot x_3 &= 6 \\ 3 \cdot x_1 + 2 \cdot x_2 + 2 \cdot x_3 &= 10 \end{aligned} \tag{34.6.7}$$

the matrix form of these equations is given in (34.6.8):

$$\begin{bmatrix} 2 & 2 & 1 & | & 7 \\ 1 & 2 & 2 & | & 6 \\ 3 & 2 & 2 & | & 10 \end{bmatrix} \tag{34.6.8}$$

As mentioned above, it is not necessary to calculate the first column since these elements will equal the values from the original matrix. The first step of calculations will therefore be to use (34.6.3) to calculate all the elements of row 1 that is not a part of column 1. After following the procedure described above, we end up with the results shown in (34.6.9).

$$\left[\begin{array}{ccc|c} 1 & 1 & 1/2 & 7/2 \\ 0 & 1 & 3/2 & 5/2 \\ 0 & 0 & 1 & 1 \end{array}\right] \qquad (34.6.9)$$

We can write this matrix in the form of three different equations, as shown in (34.6.10).

$$\begin{aligned} x_1 + x_2 + 1/2 \cdot x_3 &= 7/2 \\ x_2 + 3/2 \cdot x_3 &= 5/2 \\ x_3 &= 1 \end{aligned} \qquad (34.6.10)$$

From these equations it is easy to perform a back substitution. First, we can see directly that $x_3 = 1$. Substitute this value into the middle equation, and we get that $x_2 = 1$. When substituting these values into the first equation, we should get that $x_1 = 2$. We have solved the given linear simultaneous equations using the Crout elimination method.

34.6.2 Technical Description

As explained in the previous section, this program uses the Crout elimination method to solve the problem. The method will calculate the equations in the form of a matrix. The elements of this matrix are distributed among the different nodes. This is shown in Figure 34.10. In this program, the user can partition the matrix in any desired way among the nodes. However, the matrix must be divided along the diagonal of the matrix going from the upper left corner to the lower right corner.

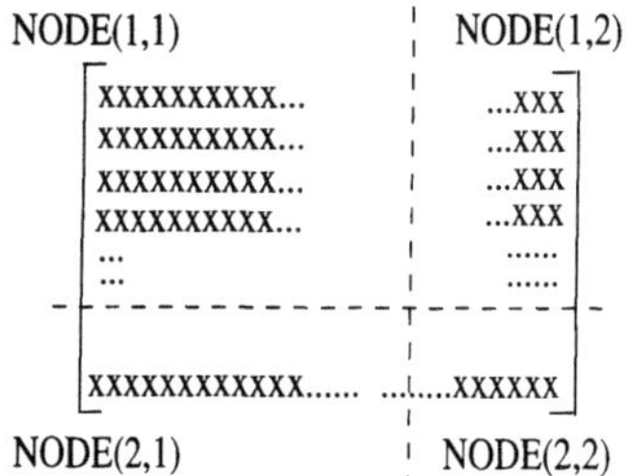

Figure 34.10 The Layout of the nodes in a matrix.

Because of the order in which the linear simultaneous equations are solved with the Crout method, all nodes will not be active all the time. First, the values for column 1 is calculated, then row 1, then column 2, row 2, and so on. Apparently, node (2,2) will therefore not be active in the beginning of the program execution. However, we can calculate partial solutions in order to activate more nodes simultaneously. We will, in the following, use an example to illustrate this method. Note from this example that as we get to the end of the program, we will be calculating elements in the bottom right portion of the matrix, and only node (2,2) will be active.

34.6.3 User Description

When the program is turned on, the user will be presented with a menu. Table 34.6 shows this initial menu. This is done only for node (1,1). After receiving a command from the user, this node will pass the command on to the other nodes. When running this program, the menu will eventually scroll out of the screen area, or other menus will be displayed. However, all the commands presented in the menus are available from anywhere in the program. This means that it is not necessary to display a menu before using the selections in that menu.

Table 34.6 The Menu Presenting the Command Options

```
==========================================
PITT PARALLEL COMPUTER
Operating Software for the Linear simultaneous equations Problem
Copyright 1998, University of Pittsburgh (Dept. of EE). All Rights Reserved
==========================================
Welcome to the Pitt Parallel Computer (PPC) System.
This menu can be displayed later by pressing m.
Note that all commands are available independent of displayed menu
(i) Initiate System
(t) Initiate Trivial Matrix
(n) Initiate Non-trivial Matrix
(s) Change Communication Speed
(+) Increase Size of Matrix
(-) Decrease Size of Matrix
(l) Move Diagonal to the Left
(r) Move Diagonal to the Right
(d) Show Matrix Division
(c) Change Corner to Display
(0) Display the Matrix
(y) Solve the Matrix
(m) Display the Main Menu
PPC\LSE(Press (m) for menu)>
```

The following is an explanation of each option:

(i) Initiate System - This function must be selected first to load all of the variables for the linear simultaneous equations execution. The matrix will be reset to 17 by 16, with the matrix division placed in the middle. The initial values of the matrix will not be set.

(t) Initialize the Trivial Matrix - This function will load the positions along the diagonal to a value of 100 and all of the other positions to a value of 1. This initialization is included mainly for debugging reasons. Note that it is necessary to initialize the matrix if the size of the matrix is changed.

(n) Initialize the Non-Trivial Matrix - This function initializes the non-trivial linear simultaneous equation. The values in this matrix are determined by a semi-random scheme. This initialization illustrates how a real life problem could look. The solution method is the same for the two matrix initializations and the execution time should therefore not be affected by which initialization is selected. (The execution time should not change even if no initialization of the values in the matrix is done. However, a system initialization (i) is necessary.) It is not possible for the user to define other sets of values to the matrix. Note that it is necessary to initialize the matrix if the size of the matrix is changed.

(s) Change Communication Speed - This command will display the different communication speeds available. No communication speed is set or changed by pressing "s." In order to change the communication speed, select from this menu. Note that all the communication speed options are available without pressing "s" first.

(+) Increase the Size of the Matrix - This function will increase the size of the matrix. When this function is selected, the elements of the matrix will be divided equally among the four nodes, no matter what the previous division was. Note that it might be necessary to initialize the matrix after the size of the matrix has been changed. The maximum matrix size is limited to 85×84 elements. This is a software limitation.

(-) Decrease the Size of the Matrix - This function will decrease the size of the matrix by decreasing the length of the diagonal by one. When this function is selected, the elements of the matrix will be divided equally among the four nodes, no matter what the previous division was. Note that it might be necessary to initialize the matrix after the size of the matrix has been changed. The minimum matrix size is limited to 4×5 elements. This is a software limitation.

(l) Move Diagonal to the Left - This function will change the distribution of the matrix elements among the nodes. The elements must be divided along the diagonal going from the upper left corner to the lower right corner of the matrix.

This command will move the division point among the nodes one step to the left. This means that the number of elements will increase in the lower right node and decrease in the upper left node. The two other nodes will change accordingly.

After completing the shift of the diagonal, the new division of the matrix elements among the nodes will be displayed on the screens.

(r) Move Diagonal to the Right - This function will change the distribution of the matrix elements among the nodes. The elements must be divided along the diagonal going from the upper left corner to the lower right corner of the matrix.

This command will move the division point among the nodes one step to the right. This means that the number of elements will increase in the upper left node and decrease in the lower right node. The two other nodes will change accordingly.

After completing the shift of the diagonal, the new division of the matrix elements among the nodes will be displayed on the screens.

(D) Show Matrix Division - This command will display the number of elements of the matrix at each of the four nodes. The matrix will initially be divided equally among the nodes. This command does not change any settings.

(c) Change What Corner of the Node to Display - When the size of the matrix exceeds the size of the screens, only a portion of the matrix can be displayed. However, it is possible to choose which part of the elements at each of the nodes to display. The user can display the elements of one of the four corners of the node. For large matrices, a number of elements would still not be displayed.

This function will change which corner to display for each of the nodes. All the nodes will display the same corner. The default setting is to show the upper left corner. When this command is given, the new setting will be displayed on the screens

(0) Display the Matrix - This function will display the matrix. Each of the screens has the capability (because of limited screen sizes) to display a maximum of 8×8 elements. If the matrix is larger, the user can use the "Change Corner to Display" function above to make more elements visible.

(y) Start Solving the Matrix - This function will start the calculations for the matrix. The message, "The PPC is executing," will appear as the calculations begin. When each node is done, the message, "The PPC has completed execution," will be displayed. Note that all the nodes must display this message before the problem is solved.

(m) Display Main Menu - This function will display the main menu. This menu is similar to the menu given in Table 34.6. The only difference is the heading.

34.7 An Example Application

One question that must always be asked when a parallel computer is being considered is, "Does it run faster than a single processor of the same type?" The situations under which the answer is yes are important to understanding many of the limitations of parallel hardware. In this example, a system of LSEs is to be solved with a four (4) node mesh with variable communication (BAUD) rate and variable problem size (granularity). The question posed is the break-even point, i.e., at what value is the parallel configuration equivalent to a single processor.

The situation is depicted in Figure 34.11, for variable BAUD rate and granularity. From the figure, at a BAUD rate of 115.2K, a problem size of 80 LSEs is required to achieve the break-even point. At a BAUD rate of 230.4K, a problem size of 69 LSEs is required. The granularity is determined from the point on the diagonal at which the row/column mapping is determined. The point is chosen as 0.70*n, where n equations are to be solved. The point 0.70 is an optimal mapping point determined by other evaluations.

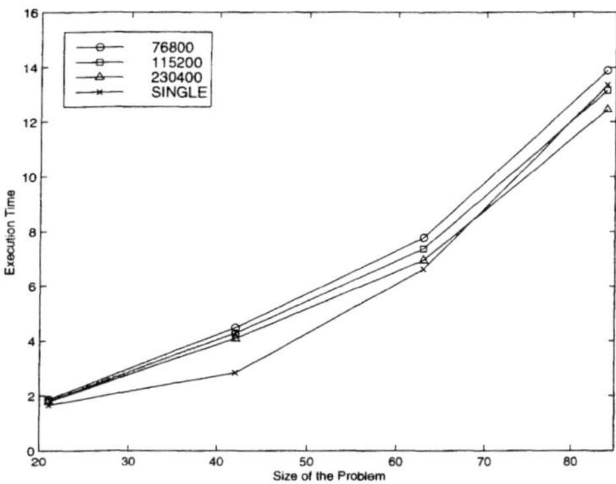

Figure 34.11 Execution time as a function of problem size under varying communication rates.

34.8 Summary

A parallel computer composed of off-the-shelf components can be a useful research tool to evaluate theoretical parallel concepts. The same parallel computer can be used as a pedagogical tool.

Classical problems such as the solution of the Laplace equation and Linear Simultaneous Equations serve as excellent examples for parallel computing concepts.

34.9 Bibliography

[1] *Pitt Parallel Computer User's Manual,* Parallel Computing and Networks Laboratory, Department of Electrical Engineering, University of Pittsburgh, 1998.

[2] *Pitt Parallel Computer Homepage,* `http://whopper.ee.pitt.edu/~ppc/`

Chapter 35

The RS/6000 SP System: A Scalable Parallel Cluster

JAMSHED H. MIRZA

Server Group Architecture,
IBM Corporation
Poughkeepsie, New York

Email: *mirza@us.ibm.com*

35.1 Dual Personalities

The IBM RS/6000 SP system is a general-purpose scalable parallel computer designed to address a wide range of application areas in high-end UNIX technical and commercial computing. SP systems range from two to 512 nodes, where a node is an RS/6000 uniprocessor or symmetric multiprocessor (SMP) enterprise server, each with its own copy of the AIX operating system. The nodes are interconnected via a high performance multistage packet-switched network for internode communications. Built on top of the individual AIX operating systems is a set of cluster-aware services for system management and administration, job management, high availability, and application development and execution for the cluster and parallel environment. The system is designed with scalability, flexibility, usability, and high availability in mind.

The SP system has a split personality—and intentionally so. On the one hand, it is a scalable parallel supercomputer; on the other, it is a flexible cluster. Often, SP systems are configured to exhibit both of these personalities in the same system.

As a scalable parallel platform, the SP system is designed to be a capability machine, allowing the combined power of hundreds or thousands of processors to be applied to the solution of complex problems—problems that either cannot be run at all, cannot be run cost-effectively, or cannot be run in reasonable time, on even the largest SMP servers. Researchers use SP systems to discover the secrets of life within the DNA molecule, simulate the earth's environment using global climate models, and probe the depths of the universe. Corporations employ these systems as a way to gain competitive advantage; for example, by simulating product designs in order to shorten their time to market, or by predicting the purchasing patterns of buyers. Governments use their computational power for national security purposes, such as cryptography and nuclear weapons simulation, and for projects of national importance, such as mapping the human genome.

On the other hand, the SP system is also a capacity machine, designed to function as a flexible, scalable, high-availability cluster. Small- to modest-sized systems (from two to a few dozen nodes) are used to address the capacity or throughput requirements beyond a single SMP server for applications such as Enterprise Resource Planning (ERP), transaction processing, business intelligence, file serving, web serving, or data management. They are being configured with hardware and software failover capability to provide high availability solutions in business critical situations. And they are being used for server consolidation where the workload of multiple SMP servers is moved to the SP platform for ease of management and administration.

The genesis of this dual personality is rooted in the recognition of some basic realities (Figure 35.1):

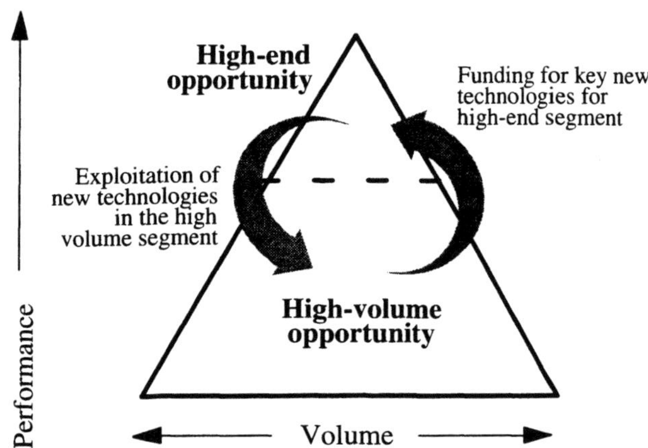

Figure 35.1 The RS/6000 SP system development philosophy.

- Very large capability systems (two or more orders of magnitude more powerful than typical servers of the day) do not have a viable business model. Few systems of that class will ever be required at any time. The high-volume opportunity for scalable systems is in the few to a few tens of nodes—the region addressed by clusters.
- However, ultralarge capability systems often drive the development of key system technologies; these technologies, if driven down to the high-volume segment, can provide product differentiation and competitive advantages in

the cluster environment. So one can justify development of ultralarge systems if smaller clones of these systems can be used effectively for mainstream applications. In effect, ultralarge systems become the proving ground for new technologies that will later find application in the mainstream computing environment; and the use of these technologies in mainstream applications, in turn, can provide the eventual high volume exploitation of these technologies.

- So, if designed well, there is a synergy between ultralarge and mainstream systems—between the high-end and the high-volume. If the high-end system can be designed to also address the high-volume opportunity, that will generate the revenue required to develop new technologies necessary to address the requirements of high-end systems such as ASCI [ASCI] [6]; the new technologies developed for the high-end in turn, will be the technology required for mainstream applications a few years later.

In recognition these realities, the SP system was designed from the beginning for this dual personality. Fundamental architectural decisions were guided by the goal to avoid any compromises on scalability and availability so that ultralarge capability systems can be configured. At the same time, it was also clear that the cluster personality is extremely important for the long-term success of the SP system. This collectively has guided the design of the system.

This dual personality has resulted in a systems structure and architecture that has enjoyed broad-based success in both commercial and technical computing environment. Over 5000 systems have been installed in the five years since the SP system first became generally available. The ASCI Blue Pacific system installed at Lawrence Liveremore National Laboratory is arguably the fastest supercomputer available as of the publication of this book. SP systems enjoy a strong presence in the list of Top 500 supercomputer sites [7]. At the same time, the vast majority of SP systems are being used as cluster systems for server consolidation, and to run mainstream business applications that require performance, scalability, and high availability beyond what can be achieved by a single SMP server.

The rest of this chapter will give an overview of the architecture and structure of the system and the primary system components. Wherever relevant, the rationale for major system design decisions will be discussed.

35.2 SP System Architecture

Right from the beginning, the goal was to design a system that could be used across a wide variety of applications and environments—from small enterprise servers used for mainstream technical and commercial applications, to ultralarge parallel systems used to solve complex, long-running problems of national importance. Hence, system scalability was extremely important. At the same time, system reliability and availability were also critical to ensure commercial success; customers should be able to use SP systems for their production work, and not merely as a research machine. This defined the fundamental guiding principle used in designing SP systems:

- Select an architecture that avoids compromises on system scalability and availability.
- Provide for maximum configuration and operational flexibility in the system so that users can tailor the system to their specific requirements.
- Leverage standard hardware and software technology as much as possible.
- Judiciously add custom technology in key areas only where standard technology cannot meet requirements.

There are three dominant parallel system architectures in use today: SMP, Non-Uniform Memory Access (NUMA), and cluster. Both SMP and NUMA make fundamental compromises on system scalability and availability. In SMPs, the tight coupling at the hardware level required to maintain a coherent global shared memory, the symmetric sharing of all resources, and the single operating system are all fundamental limiters to scalability. NUMA systems improve scalability beyond what is achievable with conventional SMPs by distributing and limiting the sharing of some of the hardware resources—namely the memory and I/O subsystems.[1] But other scalability limiters in the system still remain. For example, the single system-wide coherent global real address space still requires hardware that must keep track of an ever-increasing number of concurrent memory requests; the ability to cost-effectively scale this capability and yet maintain acceptable performance levels is ultimately the limiter to how large these systems can grow. Similarly, with the larger number of processors, the single operating system becomes even more of a critical performance bottleneck in NUMA, especially in applications that rely on many operating system services.

Both SMP and NUMA systems also have inherent system availability limitations resulting from the single global real address space and the single operating system. The loss of one processor results in a system outage for both hardware and software reasons. In hardware, loss of a processor's cache will leave memory with corrupt, stale data in random locations in the single shared address space. In software, the existence of a single set of operating system data structures forms a single point of failure. For example, if a processor crashes while holding a system lock, it won't be long before the whole system grinds to a halt. So even if the scalability limitations inherent in SMP and NUMA systems can be magically removed, the single points of failure inherent in these structures will limit them to relatively small system sizes.

Today, SMPs with a few tens of processors, and NUMA systems with several tens of processors, are commercially available. However, unless the applications are finely tuned and are written to avoid stressing the inherent system bottlenecks discussed above, these structures typically hit a scalability limit much earlier than their largest available configurations.

[1]This increased scalability of NUMA architecture comes at a cost. The performance of a NUMA system is very sensitive to the degree to which data can be partitioned and located close to the processor that will access it. Thus, the advantage of data location transparency that SMPs provide is lost.

These considerations led to the cluster-like architecture of the SP system. Like a cluster, it consists of a set of nodes (each with its own CPUs, memory, and IO), each managed by its own copy of the operating system; the nodes are connected together via a custom designed SP switch or a standard LAN; and there is a set of software that makes this all appear as one system in key areas such as system management and control, job management, and programming environment.

The nodes of the SP system are essentially repackaged RS/6000 workstations and servers, and the operating system is the standard AIX operating system; no fundamental changes were made to them. Furthermore, the standard, open, distributed UNIX programming and execution environment was preserved. As a result, hardware or software options available on the base RS/6000 workstation or server can be installed on an SP node. Similarly, all of the several thousand RS/6000 applications are available to an SP user. This greatly improves the applicability of the system in diverse environments and application areas.

Particular attention was also paid to avoiding undue restrictions on how an SP system can be configured and operated (Figure 35.2):

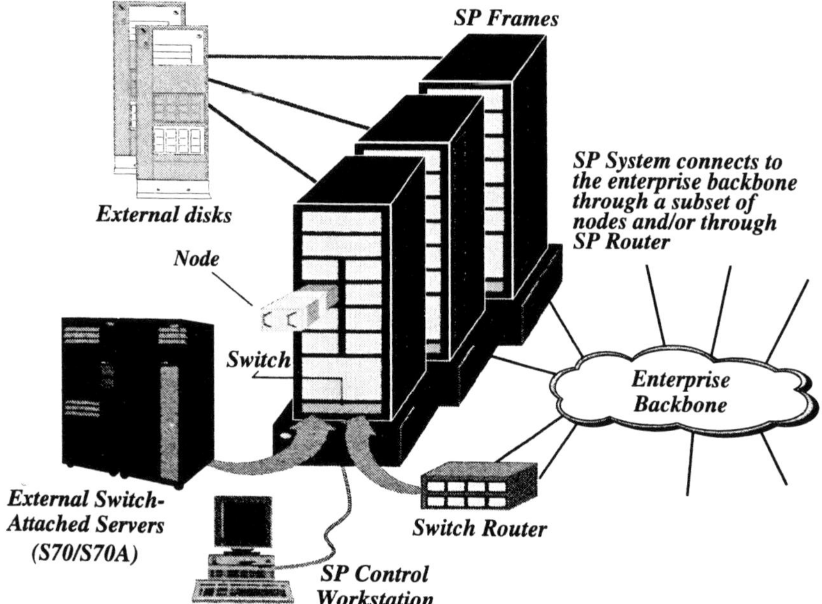

Figure 35.2 The RS/6000 SP system components.

- The system can scale up over a very wide range (from two to 512 nodes) in increments of a single node. All hardware and software system components that impact application performance scale up as nodes are added.

- Several different node types with different performance and configuration options are available; they provide a variety of price/performance points and configuration capabilities for different environments. The nodes can be POWER3 SMP, PowerPC 604 SMP, or POWER2 Super Chip (P2SC) uniprocessor. The nodes are packaged up to 16 to a frame, depending on the node type, and different node types can be intermixed within a frame.

- Selected RS/6000 servers can be directly attached to the SP switch. Such external servers appear as logical SP nodes and can be managed, administered, and used in the same manner as a node that is physically within an SP frame. This capability provides a wider choice to the user without requiring each and every RS/6000 server to be repackaged to fit within the SP frame. Today, large RS/6000 S70 and S70A SMP enterprise servers can be switch-connected to the SP system.

- At one extreme, like in any cluster, each node can be separately configured for memory, I/O, network adapters, and software to match its function. Each node runs a standard full function AIX operating system, and different nodes may run different releases of AIX. This makes the SP system very attractive for server consolidation, with each node replacing a different server in the network. At the other extreme, all (or majority) of the nodes can be symmetrically configured so a particular job may be executed anywhere, or a large parallel application can be run across multiple nodes.

- The SP architecture is designed to allow functionally specialized units to be attached to the SP switch. These are special purpose attachments, optimized for narrow, targeted services. Currently, SP Router units are available for cost-effective, high performance connectivity to the enterprise network. Over time, other specialized attachments (such as switch-attached storage subsystems, that provide shared storage across all the nodes) may be provided.

This architecture provides several key advantages:

- It allows the use of standard hardware and software building blocks, thereby leveraging advances in conventional server technology. This improves price or performance and time-to-market.

- There is considerable flexibility in the choice of the components of the cluster and in the configuration and operation of the cluster.

- There are no inherent scalability limitations in the architecture. Key hardware and software components (processors, memory, devices, bandwidth, interconnect interfaces, operating system, and other software subsystems) of the SP system scale globally in capacity and performance; as more processors are added to the system by adding a node, all of the other complementary components are also added to maintain system balance. Additionally, different components interact at the hardware or software level only as and when required. This avoids unnecessary overheads.

- There are no inherent system availability limitations in the architecture. The system has redundant hardware and software component components. Further, the components are not tightly coupled so that there is good fault isolation; a failing node need not impact other nodes in the system since each is managed by its own copy of the operating system. A node may be added or removed, the hardware or software in a node may be upgraded, or a node may be serviced without impacting the availability of existing services and applications in the rest of the system.
- Finally, keeping the different nodes relatively loosely-coupled results in a system with an erector-set-like approach to building systems. One or more hardware or software components (processors, memory, devices, interconnection network, operating system, middleware, etc.) in the system can be replaced with newer versions without having to change the whole system. This provides an important advantage of easier migration and investment protection as new technology is introduced.

35.3 SP System Structure

Settling on the cluster architecture for the SP system was relatively straightforward; settling on the exact nature of that cluster was a more difficult task. The definition of clusters is very broad and encompasses systems that vary greatly in the degree to which the different component systems are coupled, the communications and programming model they support, and the key system characteristics of scalability, manageability, and high availability they present. In other words, different cluster implementations differ in the degree to which they present a single system view.

At one extreme, a cluster in its simplest and most typical form is a set of standard LAN connected workstations with minimal focus on tying them together into a single system. The set of nodes may constitute one IP domain, they may share the same filesystem, the same password file, the same name server, etc. A network management tool may be used to manage and monitor these nodes from one control point. Such a distributed system, built of commodity-off-the-shelf components (COTS), fits the basic definition of clusters.

In such basic cluster systems there are no shared resources between nodes, so applications cannot share any state across nodes and typically share data through replication. Applications are written assuming that there is no trust between nodes and that the communications mechanism between nodes is not secure. The advantage of this is that the cluster has improved fault isolation and system availability. However, this improvement comes at the cost of reduced efficiency and limited scalability because of the additional overheads. No special software or hardware support is provided to facilitate system scalability to a very large number of nodes—either in the area of managing and administering them, using them effectively for solving large parallel applications, or providing high availability and recoverability from hardware and software faults. As such, they lack the scalability, manageability, availability, and usability characteristics that were necessary to make the SP system more generally applicable across a wide spectrum of applications and user environments.

At the other extreme is a cluster comprised of nodes that are very tightly-coupled in hardware, and implementing a layer of software to present a single system image (SSI). All resources, including operating system resources such as memory and processes, are global. This makes the system appear logically (almost) like an SMP from a programming model perspective.

While SSI is attractive for some environments, it has many disadvantages for others. For example, key database vendors prefer not to have SSI for multicomputer systems. Their database subsystems have been written for distributed environments and expect to see the totally distributed view; these subsystems explicitly manage the different operating system images for performance, load balancing, and recovery, and provide a single system image at the database subsystem level. With SSI, they lose control over where their processes run and what overheads they have to accept. This impacts their scalability, load balancing, and recovery processing.

There are other costs associated with SSI. First, it is expensive to implement, requiring a significant investment in cluster software to present the single system image. It requires fundamental restructuring of key performance-sensitive parts of the base operating system, and software to make all the operating system services work across multiple machines. Second, the additional overhead of SSI limits system scalability. Third, the scaling and availability of a single application that was written for an SMP will not be much improved over an SMP without significant modifications to it. This is because most SMP applications do not partition their state and data, and do not run multiple instances of themselves. Without these modifications (which are similar to those required in a system without full SSI), scaling will be limited because of resource contention. Resource contention is further exacerbated by the fact that accesses to non-local resources are much slower than on an SMP. Further, the entire application will likely fail if there is a fault in the application software or in the memory holding the shared state. Thus, by tying the multiple operating systems together tightly, SSI reduces scalability, fault isolation and system availability compared to a less tightly-coupled cluster.

Neither of the above two extreme design points satisfy the objectives for the SP system completely. Instead, a more pragmatic approach is required—an approach that can be viewed as partial SSI, in which a judiciously selected set of resources and services are globalized. The SP system provides multicomputer-aware subsystems on top of the base operating system that unify the multiple machine images in key areas, and provide various services to applications, other subsystems, and administrators. These subsystems enhance the system capabilities in internode connectivity, programming models, system availability, usability and manageability (Figure 35.3). For these globalized resources and services, the API is the same as for the single system equivalent, unless overloading the standard interface creates complexity or unacceptable overhead.

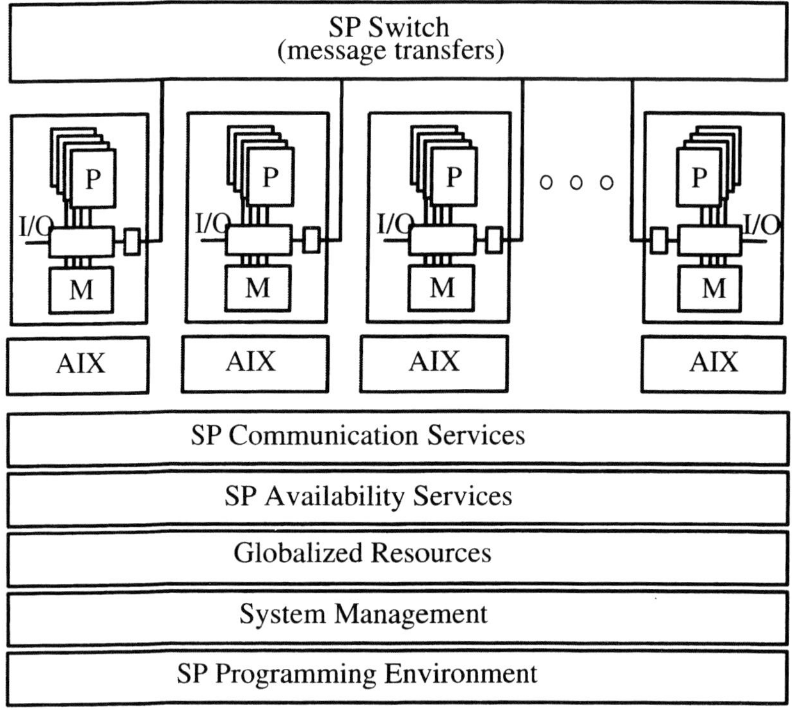

Figure 35.3 The RS/6000 SP system structure.

The key SP global subsystems are described below. Over time, globalization of additional resources and services may be provided as required.

35.3.1 SP Communications Services

One of the major design decisions for a scalable system such as the SP system is selection of the right interconnect. The interconnect options and communications services that are supported have a direct defining effect on the characteristics of the system in the area of scalability and usability.

For supercomputing applications where an application runs in parallel across multiple nodes, a key determinant of performance is the process-to-process communication latency and bandwidth, and the corresponding overhead at the node for executing the communications protocol. The closer the internode latency and bandwidth are to local memory accesses, the easier it is to efficiently support communications-intensive parallel applications, and the easier it is to facilitate resource sharing and load balancing across the cluster. For large scalable parallel systems to be properly balanced, the general rule of thumb is that the internode bandwidth and latency should be within a small multiple of the bandwidth and latency to local memory.

While several interesting "commodity" network technologies (such as Gigabit Ethernet, Fiber Channel Standard (FCS), and Asynchronous Transfer Mode (ATM)) have emerged recently, these alternatives are optimized for a very different environment and do not provide the right system balance for high-end, supercomputing applications; this is especially true when the nodes are powerful RISC-based SMPs. These networks connect to the cluster nodes via a standard I/O bus (such as PCI), which is optimized to support bulk transfers to devices that are orders of magnitude slower than memory. These networks are designed for long-distance, bulk communication rather than for short messages across short distances. They provide no guaranteed delivery or flow control in the low level protocols, and there may be no protection implemented at low levels. Typically, higher level protocols provide these functions, and this implies higher effective latencies and overhead and lower effective bandwidths. Networks for scalable parallel supercomputing systems must optimize for these functions at the lowest levels. Further, the high bandwidth, low latency and low overhead can be achieved only by attaching the interconnection fabric directly to a system interface that provides direct access to the memory subsystem. This implies the use of a nonstandard, proprietary attachment, which cannot be achieved with standard COTS networks.

Given the dual personality of the SP system, it was necessary to allow for both options. The cluster system software is designed to function correctly over TCP/IP protocol over any medium that is supported by the nodes of the cluster. In environments where high interconnect performance is not critical, a customer may choose to use any standard LAN technology as the cluster interconnect. But the SP system also offers a high performance, high availability proprietary interconnect network that addresses the requirements of communications-intensive or availability-critical environments. In fact, of the more than 5000 systems to date, a vast majority have the SP switch installed because of its performance and availability advantages.

The SP Switch [3] (Figure 35.4) is designed for scalability, low latency, high bandwidth, low processor overhead, and reliable and flexible communications between the nodes. The switch is modular in design, with additional switchboards being added as the system scales up. Topologically, the switch is an any-to-any packet-switched multistage (or indirect) network similar to an Omega network. Such network topologies allow configurations where the bisection bandwidth can scale linearly with the size of the system, which is critical for system scalability.

The SP nodes connect to the switchboard through an intelligent switch adapter. Depending on the node type, the adapter is attached to the I/O bus or an internal system bus. The adapter has an onboard microprocessor that offloads part of the work associated with moving messages between nodes. The switch adapter provides multiple protected communications channels that allow multiple user processes on an SMP node to communicate with processes on other nodes without requiring system calls. This allows implementation of message passing libraries

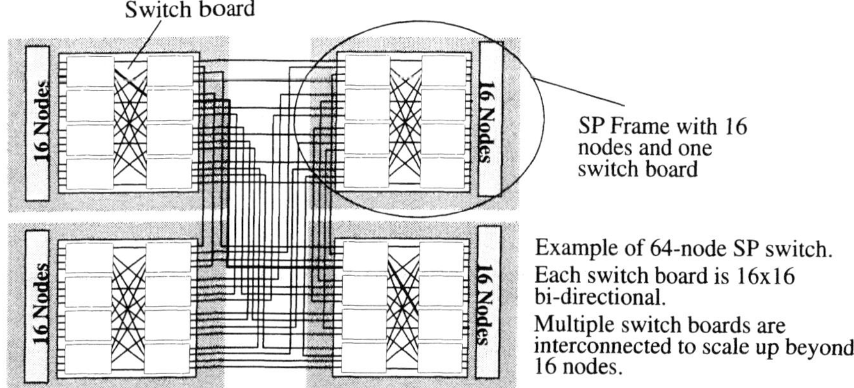

Figure 35.4 The RS/6000 SP switch.

with lower application-to-application message latency by bypassing the operating system. Communications over the switch using standard IP protocol is also supported for applications and kernel services that rely on that. In this case, multiple communications channels (e.g., sockets) are multiplexed across a single channel in the adapter by a trusted kernel code.

The SP Communications Services hardware and software are designed for reliability and transparent recovery from hard and soft failures. The switch hardware is designed to detect most hard and soft errors. The switch topology provides multiple paths between a pair of nodes; in the presence of hard errors in the switch, the switch can be reinitialized with new routes to bypass failing components. The message protocol supports end-to-end packet acknowledgment, so the loss of a packet is detected by the source node. The communication software automatically retransmits packets if an acknowledgment is not received within a preset interval of time.

35.3.2 SP System Management

The RS/6000 SP system provides a full suite of system management applications to mitigate the complexity of managing multiple operating systems. These applications are built upon the system management tools and commands of the AIX operating system, and enable easier administration of system installation, configuration, device management, user management, security administration, performance monitoring, error logging, problem determination, system recovery, and resource accounting in the SP environment. These services make managing SP systems considerably simpler than managing an equivalent cluster of servers.

The SP system management software provides the administrator with a single point of control for managing and monitoring all resources within the system. A Control Workstation (CWS), an RS/6000 workstation, is the system console and allows the administrator/operator to perform all local and remote administrative functions.

Common system management commands and tools have been enabled for parallel execution; a given command can be applied to a single node, or in parallel to a defined group of nodes or the entire system. This maintains the flexibility of multiple operating systems, but at the same time makes common administrative tasks simpler to perform on logical partitions of the system.

Since inconsistency of key management data on different nodes is a major problem in a cluster environment, the SP system management tools use a common System Data Repository (SDR) for storing management data that can be retrieved from any node in the system. Also file collection support is provided for managing files and directories that are replicated on multiple SP nodes. By grouping these files into file collections and using the provided tools, the consistency and accuracy of these files are maintained across the SP system.

The SDR is the result of an important design decision to require that critical system data be externalized from the servers that implement the functions using that data; instead, this data is maintained externally in a system-wide repository. The rationale for this is twofold. First, it eliminates redundancies and inconsistencies between servers using the same data. But more importantly, it is the first step toward solving the server availability problem in large scalable parallel systems. The goal is that critical global servers (such as the resource manager and filesystems) should be restartable. If a primary system server fails, then it should be possible to restart the server without affecting other servers and user jobs in the system in any catastrophic manner. The way that a failing server gets restarted is by inspecting the SDR objects which contain all the necessary information for it to bring itself back to its state prior to the failure. The SDR is maintained on the CWS.

A consolidated system graphical user interface is provided as a common launch pad for SP system management applications through direct manipulation of system objects represented by icons. This interface is tightly integrated with the problem management infrastructure. It allows users to easily create and monitor system events and provide notification when events occur. The interface is highly scalable for large systems, and can be easily customized to accommodate varying environments.

The SP system management software provides several capabilities and functions to reduce unplanned outages, minimize the impact of outages that do occur, and thus improve system availability. For example, the system partitioning capability allows an administrator to create a separate logical system partition to test software changes in a nondisruptive manner. The system management software can support coexistence of up to three different releases of that software within an SP partition, thus allowing easier migration to new software levels. The node isolation capability allows individual SP nodes to be removed from an active partition and to be later reintegrated without disrupting the rest of the partition. This isolation is useful for correcting an error condition or installing new hardware and software without impacting production work. High Availability Control Workstation (HACWS) capability allows a customer to configure two CWSs with IBM's high availability software called HACMP/6000 [10]; one is configured as the backup CWS in the event the primary one becomes unavailable. A twin-tailed disk configuration, along with the IP address takeover support of HACMP/6000, enables rapid switchover to the backup CWS, with little or no impact on operational access to the SP system or to the data in the System Data Repository. Users access the SP system through an external network, either in batch mode or interactively. Several options are available for workload management.

LoadLeveler [15] is a scalable distributed network-wide job management program for dynamically scheduling serial and parallel batch jobs on the SP nodes (and on other IBM and non-IBM systems). It matches the application's processing needs to available resources to select the node(s) on which the application is run. LoadLeveler offers the option of using its own scheduler or an API to use alternative customer supplied schedulers.

The IBM eNetwork Dispatcher [14] is a software router of TCP connections that supports load-balancing across multiple TCP servers. Its main goal is to enable scalable TCP/IP server clusters that can handle millions of TCP connections per hour. This goal is achieved by routing incoming TCP connections to a set of servers so that they share load efficiently. It supports fast IP packet forwarding, using a dynamic load sharing algorithm for allocation of TCP connections among servers according to their real-time load and responsiveness. In effect, many individual servers can be linked into what appears to be a single, virtual server with a single IP address. eNetwork Dispatcher has been used to scale up several high-load Internet sites such as the Olympic Games, Wimbledon Tennis Tournament, and other sports sites. This is described in more detail in the next chapter.

Both LoadLeveler and eNetwork Dispatcher can be configured for high availability so that there is failover support for all key components used to provide the workload balancing function. They can be informed of failed servers so that they can avoid forwarding work to an unavailable server.

Alternatively, given that the SP system is an open, UNIX-based cluster, the user has the option of using any third party workload management package that may be available.

35.3.3 SP Globalized Resources

As discussed earlier, providing a full single system image was not a design goal for the SP system. Much of the benefit associated with a single system image can be derived from providing elements of this functionality as global services. Global access to specific resources such as disk, tape, files, and communication networks are the primary requirement. Further, as different types of resources are globalized, the SP availability infrastructure is utilized to provide recoverability from faults, and the system management infrastructure is extended to make the resource easier to configure and maintain.

Global Device Access

Commercial applications in the UNIX environment are largely based on a few key subsystems—primarily database management systems and transaction monitors; and it is these subsystems that need to be enabled for parallel execution or throughput on the SP system. Other applications, such as ERP, BI, and e-commerce, rely on these subsystems for database and transaction services, and generally the bulk of CPU time is spent in these subsystems. So a host of other applications can be enabled by enabling these essential subsystems on the SP system.

Many of these key database and transaction monitoring subsystems have been enabled for cluster environments. Separate instances of the single server code is run on each node of the cluster, with a layer of software that ties these instances together to provide a single system image to higher level application software. To do this, one of two principal programming models are used. These models are described briefly here, and in greater detail in the next chapter.

In the function shipping model [11] the database is physically partitioned among the multiple subsystem instances running on the different cluster nodes, and remote function calls are made to operate on remote data. This matches the shared nothing architecture of a cluster. In the data sharing model [12], [13] the database is shared among the multiple subsystem instances on the different nodes. This requires shared access to disks on which the database is configured. On small clusters, a direct physical connection can be provided from all nodes to all devices storing the database (for example, with multitailed devices). But this is not a viable option on large scalable platforms such as the SP system; instead, global access to disks must be provided such that the database appears to be logically shared among the nodes even though in reality it is physically partitioned across devices attached to multiple nodes.

This global access to disks on the SP system is provided by the Virtual Shared Disk support. Using VSD, an application running at any SP node can transparently access a disk that may be physically located on any other node. This is done by trapping a request for a remote shared disk at the disk driver level and shipping the request to the corresponding node. In effect, VSD is a device driver layer that sits on top of the AIX Logical Volume Manager (LVM) and exports a raw device interface. If an access is to a shared disk that is locally connected, the VSD layer passes the request directly on to the LVM on that node. If, however, the access is to a shared disk attached to a remote node, the VSD layer sends the request to the VSD on that remote node, which in turn passes it on to the remote LVM for access. The response is returned to the VSD on the originating node and on to the requesting application. Currently, VSD is primarily used by GPFS (General Parallel FileSystem, the SP cluster-wide filesystem) and by database subsystems based on the data sharing model. A recoverable form of VSD (called RVSD) can also be configured for transparent failover capability. The following chapter discusses this in greater detail.

Global File Access

Global access to files can be provided by standard networked file solutions such as NFS, DFS, and AFS. These filesystems provide for concurrent shared access to file data and their capability may be sufficient for some customers. However, these filesystems today are limited in one or more of the following capabilities that are important to many SP customers. They are not designed for high performance parallel access to a file by a parallel application. Instead, they are designed for a single-server environment, so adding additional file servers doesn't necessarily improve the file access performance. Also, they do not support efficient fine-grained sharing with write at the file level. They are not designed for scalability to the extent required for the SP system, and they have limited recoverability from failures. To mitigate these limitations, an SP customer may choose to use GPFS [9] for global file access.

GPFS is a POSIX standard-based, parallel cluster filesystem that is designed for high performance, high availability, and high scalability, while preserving the application interfaces used in standard filesystems. GPFS allows access to files within an SP system from any node, and can be exploited by serial as well as parallel jobs running on multiple nodes. GPFS supports the filesystem standards of X/Open 4.0, with minor exceptions, allowing most AIX and UNIX applications to use GPFS without requiring any modifications.

A GPFS filesystem is configured across multiple nodes; large files are striped across these nodes for high bandwidth parallel access, while small files may be replicated on multiple server nodes for concurrent access. The filesystem is based on a shared disk model rather than a client-server model, so the filesystem code runs on the nodes where the applications run. It uses VSD to access file data that may be located on a different node. Other features such as VSD client-side data caching, large file block support, and the ability to perform read-ahead and write-behind functions help optimize performance.

GPFS can be configured to survive many system and I/O failures. Through its use of the SP availability services RVSD, it is able to automatically recover from node, disk connection and disk adapter failures. GPFS will transparently failover lock servers and other GPFS central services. With RVSD, GPFS continues to operate in the event of connection failures. GPFS allows data replication to further reduce the chances of losing data if storage media fail. Since GPFS is a logging file system, it allows the recreation of consistent structures for quicker recovery after node failures.

GPFS provides functions that simplify multinode administration and can be performed from any node in the SP configuration. These functions are based on, and are in addition to, the AIX administrative commands. A single GPFS multinode command can perform a filesystem function across the entire SP system. In addition, most existing UNIX utilities will also run unchanged. All of these capabilities allow GPFS to be used as a replacement for existing UNIX filesystems where parallel optimization is desired.

Global Network Access

Global network access on the SP system is provided via normal network routing functions and TCP/IP and UDP/IP support over the switch. In this way, SP nodes which are not physically attached to an external network still have the ability to communicate through nodes which are physically attached (i.e., a node configured as a gateway node).

Alternatively, for better performance and price/performance, the SP Router can be used. This is a functionally specialized node designed for IP gateway function, and provides a high performance, efficient, and cost-effective means of communication between an SP system and the outside world. The router is based on the GRF 400 and 1600 IP Switches from Ascend Communications, Inc. It accommodates special SP switch adapters to allow direct attachment to the SP switch. Multiple SP switch adapters within an SP Router can be used to get scalable IP performance in and out of an SP system, allow alternate paths into an SP system, or provide communication between separate SP systems or SP partitions.

35.3.4 SP Availability Services

In ultralarge systems probability of failure in a component increases because of the sheer number of hardware and software components involved. As discussed earlier, the architecture provides inherent redundancy and failure isolation so that failing components need not bring down the whole system. However, a failing node would result in the failure of the application running on that node or the disruption of services provided by that node. In certain environments this may be acceptable, especially if the applications are checkpointed and can be restarted. But there are also customer applications (such as a business-critical transaction processing application) or key system services (such as the enterprise filesystem) whose failure may not be tolerable. For such applications, a mechanism is required for graceful degradation rather than complete disruption of service when a system component fails.

The SP system recognizes the importance of such capabilities and today provide's an open and well-documented set of availability services. These services form a scalable infrastructure that can be used by software developers to build recoverable subsystems and applications for the SP system. The infrastructure consists of three principal elements:

- *Event Management* provides services for monitoring hardware and software resources in the SP system and notifying applications and subsystems that have registered for certain events associated with resource state changes.

- *Topology Services* maintains up-to-date information about availability of key resources such as nodes and network adapters in a cluster, and the connectivity between them. It uses a scalable heartbeat mechanism to keep track of the current state of these resources.

- *Group Services* provides a set of interfaces which enables distributed subsystems (such as GPFS) to orchestrate coordinated and synchronized recovery actions among the processes making up the subsystem.

Applications use the API provided by these services to monitor critical resources (such as a key process), detect events (such as the failure or imminent failure of a key resource), notify other related processes (such as peer processes capable of taking over for the failing process), and initiate coordinated recovery action so that the critical service can continue without disruption. These services can also be used to monitor and collect data that can be used for planning and performance management, as well as to undertake preventive action to avoid imminent failures.

Several SP subsystems already exploit various aspects of the availability services. For example, Virtual Shared Disk provides transparent failover capability. To do that, each VSD server is logically paired with an alternate secondary server. Twin-tailed disks are configured to have a physical path from both the primary and secondary server nodes; however only the primary connection to a disk is normally active. The resource monitoring service is used by the primary and secondary nodes to monitor each other. If the secondary node detects a primary node failure, the secondary node invokes the specified recovery actions so that control of the disks attached to the failing node is transparently switched over to the secondary server; from then on, requests to those disks continue to be serviced by the secondary server node transparently to the application, until the failing node is brought back into service.

Another example of the use of the SP availability services is in providing automatic recovery for the GPFS filesystem; suitably configured, this filesystem will be able to recover from failing components without disruption of service or loss of data. This benefits all users of SP systems because central enterprise-wide services such as file serving are very critical, and even minor disruptions may not be tolerable. Similarly, a key software vendor today uses these services to provide failover support for its subsystem on the SP platform. Over time, a growing number of the internal SP subsystems, as well as other third-party subsystems and middleware can be expected to exploit the SP availability services.

The SP system also supports HACMP/ES, an alternative software product that allows up to 32 SP nodes to be configured in a highly available cluster. HACMP/6000 [10] software has been available for several years for small clusters of RS/6000 servers, and is widely used. Its scalability has been enhanced by using elements of the SP high availability infrastructure and services, thus allowing HACMP/6000 users to continue to use that software as they consolidate their clusters on an SP system.

35.3.5 SP Programming Model and Environment

The programmer can view the SP system in several ways. When writing applications that run on a single server, programmers see the standard SMP model. Any software that runs on a stand-alone uniprocessor or SMP server will run unmodified on an

SP node. Similarly, the programmer can use the standard distributed UNIX model; all applications written for a distributed environment will execute on the SP system unmodified. In both of these cases, the application does not exploit any of the SP cluster services directly.

For improved availability and scalability, an application may choose to exploit the availability services and parallel capabilities of the SP system. Applications can be developed that spread their workload across multiple nodes and to recover from failures. Such an application is written with the view of a cluster of homogeneous nodes (processor architecture and operating system) where a single binary can execute on any node in the cluster. The application can be implemented using a shared nothing or a shared storage model for achieving parallelism across the nodes of a cluster.

The SP services/capabilities that allow the programmer to write such an application include:

- Communication services, specifically standard Sockets and MPI.
- Trusted communications between the nodes in a cluster over the SP switch. This results in lower overhead than using distributed protocols, especially in a secure environment.
- GPFS, a cluster filesystem for sharing files across all nodes in the cluster.
- Globalized devices. Disks and tapes can be configured to be accessible from all nodes in the cluster.
- Load balancing services to assist in distributing a workload across the nodes in a cluster.
- Group Services for coordinating actions between nodes and between subsystems.
- Event Management services for performing in-order, reliable notification between nodes and components. This is used for failure notification and events related to performance or resource levels.

The SP system also supports the MPI [2] standard-based message passing programming model for the parallel supercomputing environment. The model is supported by the SP Parallel Environment (PE) [4] which provides an integrated set of tools and environments for developing, debugging, analyzing, tuning, and executing parallel FORTRAN, C, and C++ programs on the SP system. It consists of the following components:

- The *MPI Library* provides parallel message passing APIs for communication between parallel tasks. It is a full multithreaded implementation of the MPI 1.2 standard, and exploits lightweight user-space communication over the SP switch. Alternatively, a user can elect to have the MPI library run using the IP protocol over the switch or over a LAN in the absence of a switch.

- The *Parallel Operating Environment* (POE) provides the environment for developing and executing parallel applications. It can be used to compile and link parallel code with message passing libraries, to create a parallel partition with the required nodes, to load the parallel job on the nodes in the parallel partition, and to communicate with and monitor the job while it is executing.
- The *Visualization Tool* (VT) provides performance monitoring and traces visualization for a parallel application. VT can be used to debug an application by identifying deadlock situations and analyzing interprocess communications; it can also be used to analyze and tune a parallel application by identifying performance bottlenecks and load imbalances.
- The *Parallel Debugger* is a source level debugger with both a command line and Motif-based graphical interface. It extends traditional AIX capabilities and provides features for parallel application task debugging.

The SP system also provides the Low-level Application Programming Interface (LAPI) [5] which extends the standard send/receive message passing programming model with a flexible, active message and get/put style programming model.

35.4 Concluding Remarks

Scalable clusters can be designed to address a wide spectrum of applications and customer environments. The philosophy used to architect and design the SP system has resulted in a very flexible scalable cluster design that spans three orders of magnitude in performance. The decision to exploit standard technology as much as possible has improved time-to-market and allowed cost-effective solutions to be introduced quickly. Consistent focus on scalability, flexibility, high availability, manageability, and investment protection has largely been responsible for its broad-based success today.

In the area of supercomputers, a 1464-node SP system at the Department of Energy's Lawrence Livermore National Laboratory is used to simulate complex multiphysics models of nuclear weapons to evaluate the health of the nation's nuclear stockpile. A 512-node SP system at DOE's Pacific Northwest National Laboratory is used for research on critical environmental problems such as cleaning up polluted sites and safely treating and storing hazardous wastes. Weather forecasters at the National Weather Service will use a large SP system for complex high-resolution numerical weather models with improved physics to produce forecasts farther out in the future with better resolution. Smaller clones of these same systems are used for all types of engineering, design, and simulation applications in automotive, aeronautics, pharmaceutical, and petroleum industries. All of these require much greater computational power than what a single SMP server is capable of, and a scalable cluster is the only viable cost-effective solution for these problems.

The majority of SP systems today are used for traditional and emerging commercial applications. A state health agency in Australia uses an SP system to run

Enterprise Resource Planning (ERP) software and to manage statewide health services. A European automotive company uses an SP system both for ERP to manage the manufacturing processes, as well as to run its engineering design workload. A major fast food chain uses Business Intelligence (BI) applications on an SP system to achieve substantial growth in restaurant sales, reduction in restaurant operating costs, highly targeted promotional campaigns, and improved supply management and restaurant development. The coach of a National Basketball Association team has used prototype BI software running on an SP system to organize, analyze, and interpret the mountains of data amassed at games and use that to make decisions on plays, match-ups, substitutes, and myriad other calls. RS/6000 SP systems have hosted the official web sites for major sports events such as the '96 Summer and '98 Winter Olympics, the PGA golf tour, and Wimbledon, and U.S. Open tennis tournaments. One of the largest financial services firms in the U.S. uses SPs to offer trading via the Internet, allowing a customer to trade stocks and mutual funds, get real-time quotes, and access their account information.

In the future, we can expect increasing use of cluster solutions as the demand for higher performance and high availability increases. Most computer system vendors see clusters as a key strategic direction, and many are beginning to roll out cluster support software. Integrated clusters will become more commonplace, built by partitioning the resources of large SMP and NUMA systems and allowing each partition to be managed by its own copy of the operating system. Application and middleware providers recognize this trend and are enabling their products for clusters.

The SP system will continue to evolve in the future and build upon the strengths of the current SP cluster offering. Major focus will continue to be on making the system easier to use and manage so that the cluster appears as close to a single server as possible. Over time, additional system resources will be globalized as required. And as these additional resources are globalized, the goal is to use the SP Availability Services to provide recoverability from faults, and to provide services that use cluster performance information to balance the load across these resources.

35.5 Bibliography

[1] T. Agerwala, D. M. Dias, J. Martin, J. H. Mirza, D. Sadler, and M. Snir. The SP2 System Architecture. In *IBM Systems Journal,* vol. 34 (2), May 1995.

[2] MPI Forum. Document for a Message Passing Interface. *Technical Report CS-93-214*, University of Tennessee, November 1993.

[3] C. B. Stunkel et al. The SP2 Communication Subsystem. In *IBM Systems Journal*, vol. 34 (2), May 1995.

[4] M. Snir, P. Hochschild, D. Frye, and K. Gildea. The SP2 Communication Software and Parallel Environment of IBM SP2. In *IBM Systems Journal*, vol. 34 (2), May 1995.

[5] G. Shah, J. Nieplocha, J. H Mirza, C. Kim, R. Harrison, R. Govindaraju, K. Gildea, P. DiNicola, and C. Bender. A High Performance Communication Library for the IBM RS/6000 SP. In *Proceedings of the First Merged International Parallel Processing Symposium & Symposium on Parallel and Distributed Processing*, Orlando, Florida, March 1998.

[6] Accelerated Strategic Computing Initiative (ASCI). http://www.llnl.gov/asci/

[7] Top500 Supercomputer Sites. http://www.top500.org/

[8] Transaction Processing Performance Council. http://www.tpc.org/

[9] An Introduction to GPFS 1.2. http://www.rs6000.ibm.com/resource/technology/paper1.html

[10] RS/6000 HACMP for AIX. http://www.rs6000.ibm.com/resource/technology/ha42ov.html

[11] D. W. Cornell, D. M. Dias, and P. S. Yu. On Multisystem Coupling Through Function Request Shipping. In *IEEE Transactions on Software Engineering*, SE-12(1):1006-1016, October 1986.

[12] A. Sekino, K. Moritani, T. Masai, and K. Goto. DCS - A New Approach to Multi-System Data-Sharing. In *Proceedings of National Computing Conference*, Las Vegas, NV, July 1984.

[13] P. S. Yu, D. M. Dias, D. W. Cornell, and A. Thomasian. Performance Comparison of I/O Shipping and Database Call Shipping: Schemes in Multisystem Partitioned Databases. In *Performance Evaluation*, pages 15–33, vol. 10 (1), 1989.

[14] The IBM eNetwork Dispatcher. http://www.software.ibm.com/network/dispatcher/library/

[15] IBM Corporation. Overview of LoadLeveler. In LoadLeveler V2.1 Documentation - Using and Administering. http://www.rs6000.ibm.com/resource/aix_resource/sp_books/loadleveler/index.html

Chapter 36

A Scalable and Highly Available Clustered Web Server

Rajat Mukherjee

IBM Almaden Research Center
San Jose, California

Email: *rajat@almaden.ibm.com*

36.1 Introduction

The Internet has seen a tremendous surge with the growing popularity of the World Wide Web (WWW), improved ease of use, increased web presence of organizations, and now, significant enablement of on-line commerce on the wire. The total number of Internet addresses and the number of web sites have both grown exponentially over the last few years.

There are two trends that are now being observed: first, more sites will enable Internet commerce, requiring some degree of computation and database processing on the web server; second, a growing fraction of web pages are nonstatic, being created dynamically from component filesystem objects, server-side programs, and database content. Both these trends point towards higher server-side computing resources and the resulting mandatory software requirements—management, scalability, and availability. Information technology is moving to filling these requirements in terms of products, solutions, and technologies.

This chapter presents the issues that are key to building a web server that scales with increased computing requirements, makes efficient use of clustering technology, and allows on-line maintenance while providing high availability of web services. We examine the technologies that make web server processing more efficient, allowing increased concurrency and faster response. We also discuss database access from the web, a key element in determining the success of electronic business, a potential paradigm shift in global commerce. While the specific technical solutions presented in this chapter may be superseded by new technologies in the future, the principles developed in the chapter are, no doubt, critical to the success and deployment of scalable web services in the future.

36.1.1 The Internet and the Need for Clustered Web Servers

A business that depends on server performance for successful operations, such as an on-line airline reservation system, or an on-line store, must pay attention to the programs used on the server, the programming approach used to access back-end databases, the configuration of the server machines, and the clustering technology adopted.

With the growth in maturity of the Internet, and with on-line business becoming commonplace, more organizations are going to have to resort to some mode of clustering to solve their capacity problems. Not only will more consumers become web enabled, increasing the number of accesses, but increasing amounts of business logic will be executed on web servers as on-line services diversify and become more secure and robust. Another requirement for clustering will be the increase in the richness of data to traverse the Internet, as more bandwidth is made available. As technologies such as faster modem bit rates, cable modems, asymmetric digital subscriber line (ADSL), satellite communications, etc., get deployed, on-line organizations will be quick to fill the pipe with increasingly large data chunks, such as video and other multimedia objects.

Keeping these pipes going and satisfying increased numbers of subscribers will cause Internet Service Providers (ISPs), entertainment service providers, as well as large on-line businesses, to resort to increasingly powerful clustered machines. Adoption of the right clustering and other Internet technologies will significantly affect the operating costs and customer satisfaction, and hence, the viability of these businesses.

36.1.2 Availability

Availability is, in several cases, more important than scalability. No business likes to miss a transaction that can potentially lead to a purchase. Customer service is of tremendous significance, and mind share is critical in industries where competition is high. Businesses, such as on-line trading houses, banking services, etc., will differentiate themselves on the basis of transaction latency and availability. Clustering is often required purely on an availability basis, even if scalability is not an issue.

Availability is often confused with fault-tolerance; fault-tolerance may require higher investments in terms of duplicate networks, redundant hardware, and fail-safe software. Fault tolerance is often a requirement in business-critical operations, while, in many cases, high availability may suffice. In this chapter, we present a solution for high availability, not fault tolerance.

High availability also has implications on system maintenance. On the Internet, a global business is working twenty-four hours a day. To bring the system down for maintenance, even for a few hours during the night, can cause loss of business in several parts of the world. System maintenance, therefore, should be as unobtrusive as possible, with high availability characteristics.

36.1.3 Scalability

Most successful sites need to scale to some degree. For a search engine, or a site for a worldwide sporting event, such as the Olympic games or the Soccer World Cup, scalability is one of the highest priorities.

A site that sees a few hundred or a few thousand hits to static pages can be successfully constructed out of a single web server machine, with little heed to clustering technology. On the other hand, sites that record millions of hits in a day, those that serve several thousand dynamic pages constructed out of the results of complex relational database queries, or those that serve hundreds of video or audio objects, must provide sufficient computing power to handle these capacities. Often, while the average throughput required may be small, peak throughput requirements may be significantly higher, requiring a different design point. For such servers, scalability is mandatory.

Scalability is not just the number of machines that are configured to serve documents; memory and network capacity are critical in fail-safe operations of a web site. Often, insufficient scalability can cause a system to halt, as in the case of sufficient processing power, but insufficient memory to handle thousands of concurrent connections to a web site being made over slow modems. The ability of the underlying storage system to serve documents, the degree of load-balancing achieved, and the avoidance of bottlenecks in the system, are all critical in determining the scalability of a large system.

A scalable clustered web server can be built from machines of several types. Service providers use machines of different categories, ranging from low-end Intel machines to high-end Unix workstations. These systems have different capacities.

The subsystems described in this chapter have been prototyped and implemented on the IBM Scalable Parallel (SP) system. There are many features of the SP machine described in the previous chapter that are conducive to scalability, high performance, manageability, and availability. However, it should be noted that the principles developed in this chapter are general and will apply to systems constructed of any other specific clustering hardware.

The remainder of the chapter is organized as follows: In Section 36.2, we discuss the alternatives for dynamic web page construction. In Section 36.3, we outline solutions for fine-grained load balancing across a cluster of web servers. Section 36.4 discusses shared filesystems and parallel I/O. Access to data in relational databases is presented in Section 36.5. Finally, we discuss high availability in Section 36.6 and summarize the coverage of this chapter in Section 36.7.

36.2 Web Servers and Dynamic Content

36.2.1 Introduction

Web servers are now ubiquitous [1]. The paradigm on the Internet is evolving from web presence to web business. A direct consequence of this is the migration of web content from static files and data to dynamically generated web content. There is a business need to publish data that resides in database systems and other legacy storage.

In this section, we discuss some of the methods available to create dynamic web content, and specifically, some approaches to access data that resides in relational database systems. We see that some options, while being less general, may afford better performance than others. The numbers presented here are estimates based on real measurements performed with WebStone [2], a web benchmark.[1] Section 36.5.3 presents an architecture that enables efficient dynamic access to data in relational databases using any of the dynamic web server approaches described in this section.

36.2.2 Static Files on the Web

The first web servers developed were quite primitive in that they only allowed file content to be made available to the browsers. Thus, all content was published as files in a filesystem. The portion of the filesystem that is publishable is mapped to the document root of the web server. Even today, a huge portion of all web content uses static files. Although many pages are created dynamically today, via the methods described below, these are usually constructed out of components, such as images, that typically reside in the filesystem. Therefore, the performance of a web server in serving static files is key in determining overall performance, even if a significant portion of the web server content is created dynamically by server-side programs.

The performance of web servers in serving files out of filesystems has increased dramatically over the last couple of years. Servers typically served about 100 small files (few bytes per file) a second in 1995, but most servers today, well tuned, can comfortably serve 500 to 600 small files per second at 100 percent CPU utilization. This number varies, of course, with the file content and average file size, and the percentage of time the file is cached in memory (most filesystems provide caches, and several web servers also allow the configuration of an in-memory cache for commonly accessed documents).

36.2.3 Common Gateway Interface

The first approach presented to web programmers to generate dynamic web pages is the Common Gateway Interface (CGI). CGI specifies a protocol by which a web server can propagate information to a program that it invokes. This is done by

[1] Other benchmarks, such as SPECweb96 [3], are available. SPECweb99, being developed, plans to include dynamic content, multiple workloads, and persistent connections.

means of environment variables that are set by the web server before the program is invoked, and which the program can access.

The CGI variables are uniformly accessible by programs executing in different computing environments. CGI programs can, therefore, be written in any language, including interpreted languages such as PERL, as long as there is a way to access these variables. All web servers support CGI, making CGI programs portable across servers. The way in which a web server invokes a CGI program is by forking a separate process that executes the program. Communication between the server and the CGI program is via the environment variables that the server sets.

Since CGI programs are very simple to develop, can be prototyped very quickly, and have few restrictions, CGI is a commonly accepted way to generate dynamic web content, including access to traditional databases. As long as performance is not a criterion, the CGI model is acceptable. It is also the most convenient prototyping tool for developing new web applications.

Since a CGI program executes in a different address space from the web server, as shown in Figure 36.1, it is not possible for a faulty CGI program to crash a web server. However, this fact also causes CGI to have significant performance penalties in cases where there are many concurrent invocations of the programs. Since forking a process (creating a separate address space) is an expensive operation on most operating systems, CGI programs tend to use more resources and involve interprocess communication. Typical web servers, executing on Unix workstations, can serve about 20 to 40 simple CGI (dummy CGI programs that perform no computations) requests per second at 100 percent CPU utilization, more than an order of magnitude lower than simple file requests.

Another inherent limitation of CGIs is that a CGI process is a short-lived process and cannot maintain state across multiple invocations of the same program in a simple way. The web server application programming interfaces described in the next section address these issues.

36.2.4 Web Server Application Programming Interfaces

The performance drawbacks of CGI became apparent soon after it was adopted. Although CGI continues to be a very powerful way in which a web server can access arbitrary programs to generate dynamic web content, including database information, the important web servers, including Netscape, Apache, Microsoft, and IBM, defined and implemented application programming interfaces (APIs) that allow programs to be directly linked into and invoked from these web servers. Thus, NSAPI (Netscape), ISAPI (Microsoft) and GWAPI (IBM) were created, and programs written to use these APIs could be directly invoked from the appropriate web server, providing tight coupling and high performance, as shown in Figure 36.2.

Invocation of these programs is effectively a function call from within the web server, and web application programs are bundled as dynamically loadable libraries that can be accessed directly by the web servers. With these high performance APIs, simple content (few bytes) can be generated as fast (sometimes faster, if

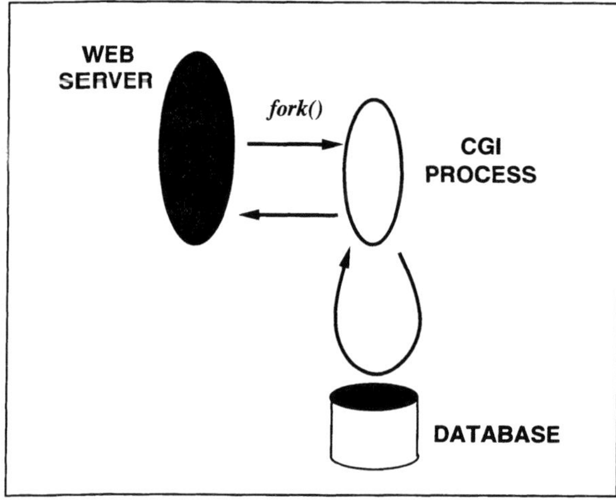

Figure 36.1 CGI architecture.

a filesystem is not accessed) as corresponding filesystem documents (400 or more connections per second at 100 percent CPU utilization)

Another advantage is that program state can now be saved within the web server process, which is a long-running entity as opposed to a CGI program that forks, executes, and dies. This is critical in accessing databases, as database connections may be opened, pooled, and shared across requests; opening a new connection to a relational database can be prohibitively expensive.

A problem with this approach is that an erroneous program/library can cause the web server to crash, which can be highly disruptive to normal operations; thus, these programs have to be tested thoroughly before deployment.

The major concern about the web server APIs is that there is no one standard, and use of these APIs leads to vendor-lock, as web servers are usually not compatible with other vendors' APIs. To this end, the Domino Go Webserver's API (GWAPI) is a superset of Netscape's NSAPI, and allows NSAPI programs to be invoked as well. Most major web servers now also support the increasingly popular Java Servlet API (Section 36.2.6) developed by Javasoft [4], which is portable across multiple platforms as well.

36.2.5 FastCGI

A middle ground between the CGI approach and the API approach is adopted by FastCGI [5], a technology from Open Market. FastCGI extends the CGI model with long-lived CGI processes that can maintain state, and the number of which can be controlled. Since FastCGI processes are separate entities, there is still interprocess communication between the web server process and the FastCGI processes. This is likely to cause slightly higher overheads than the server API's such as NSAPI,

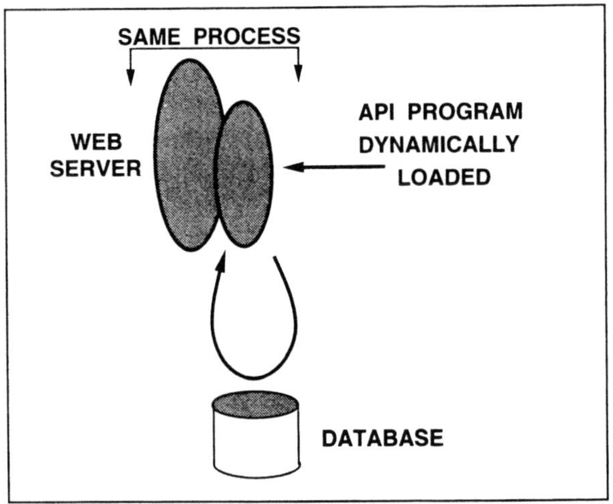

Figure 36.2 Web server APIs.

ISAPI, and GWAPI, which do not require interprocess communication.

FastCGI, shown in Figure 36.3, provides the additional protection boundary between the web server process and the server-side application, and an errant FastCGI program cannot crash the web server, as is possible in the case of the APIs. Another advantage is that existing CGI applications can be converted to FastCGI versions with minor changes, FastCGI applications can be written in any language, and applications are not tied to a given web server (no vendor-lock). FastCGI also supports distributed computing, i.e., applications can execute remotely, allowing for load to be distributed across machines distinct from the web server.

After weak initial acceptance, FastCGI support is now available for web servers from Netscape, Zeus, Apache, Lotus, Microsoft, etc., which could contribute to its popularity.

36.2.6 Servlets

Javasoft introduced the Java Servlet API (Figure 36.4) to dynamically execute server-side functions in a portable way across any web server that supports the API. Server variables are passed as parameters to the servlet objects. Javasoft's Java web server is written to use the servlet API. A feature is that server-side functionality can be dynamically updated by loading new servlets across the network, and administration can be performed without bringing down the server.

Modules have been made available for web servers such as Netscape, Microsoft, and Apache, that allow servlets to execute on them; some non-Java web servers, such as Lotus' Go Webserver, also support the servlet API. Specialized servlet engines, such as IBM WebSphere [23], allow ease of configuring and managing servlets with many web servers. It is also possible to configure tested servlets to execute in the

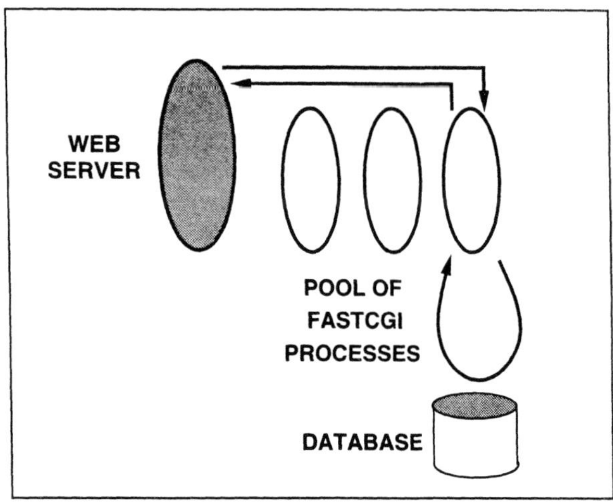

Figure 36.3 FastCGI: Predefined, long-running, high performance.

same process context as the web server, thereby improving performance.

Servlet performance has been compared to that of FastCGI. Servlets allow an attractive alternative to server-side development, and this approach is quickly becoming popular. Java servlets also allow simple firewall-friendly access to independent Java servers that provide other services, such as collaboration, etc.

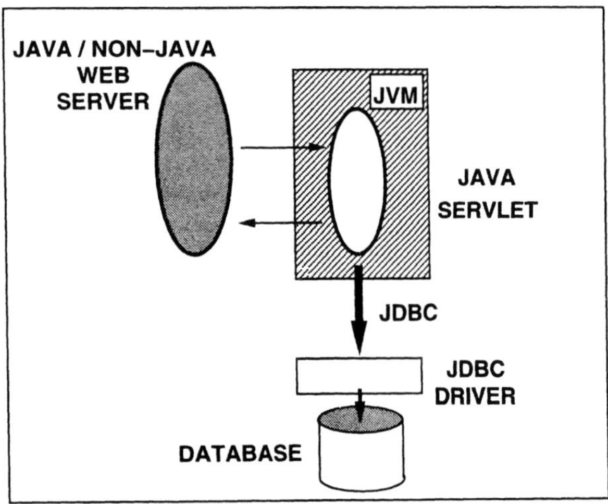

Figure 36.4 Java servlet architecture.

36.2.7 Summary

Web servers have become faster and more complex and now support several different means to create dynamic content. Creation of content from databases is becoming critical, requiring the use of standard APIs and architectures that enable publishing content from various legacy data stores.

Since web server processing per request has become more complex, clustering is mandatory to handle even a small number of concurrent requests to a web site. Enabling business processes, applications, and transactions on-line and causing complex database queries to be issued to databases more frequently makes scalability and clustering critical to performance. Availability and nondisruptive management of such clustered systems become the factors that differentiate businesses from each other.

36.3 Fine-Grain Load Balancing

36.3.1 Introduction

The traditional way to serve a single web site with a cluster of workstations is to use the Round-Robin Domain Name System, where a single name is mapped to different IP addresses. However, this technique can lead to severe load imbalances across nodes and is a bottleneck for scalability. In this section, we outline a technique that achieves much finer grain load-balancing across a set of nodes that serve the same resources. This approach also helps in incremental maintenance and improves the availability characteristics of a clustered web server, as described in Section 36.6.

36.3.2 Domain Name System (DNS)

Although computer hosts on the Internet are known by their IP addresses, humans work best using the *names* of the hosts. The Domain Name System (DNS) [6] is a distributed database that provides a mapping between IP addresses and hosts. There are standard library functions that allow lookups for both names and IP addresses.

Each site on the Internet maintains its own database of information that external clients on the Internet can query. Thus, programs such as a web browser, can contact a *name server* to determine the IP address of a web site. Each domain *zone* is responsible for providing multiple name servers (primary and one or more secondary name servers) for the zone. A name server does not need to know how to contact all other name servers if it does not have mapping information for a given host; it must be able to contact the *root* name servers, which, in turn, can forward the requests to other name servers. This is shown in Figure 36.5, which depicts a browser client accessing a remotely located web server.

To reduce DNS traffic on the Internet, name servers cache mapping information that can then be used by multiple client programs on multiple hosts. Thus, in Figure 36.5, the local name server at the client's site, as well as any intermediate

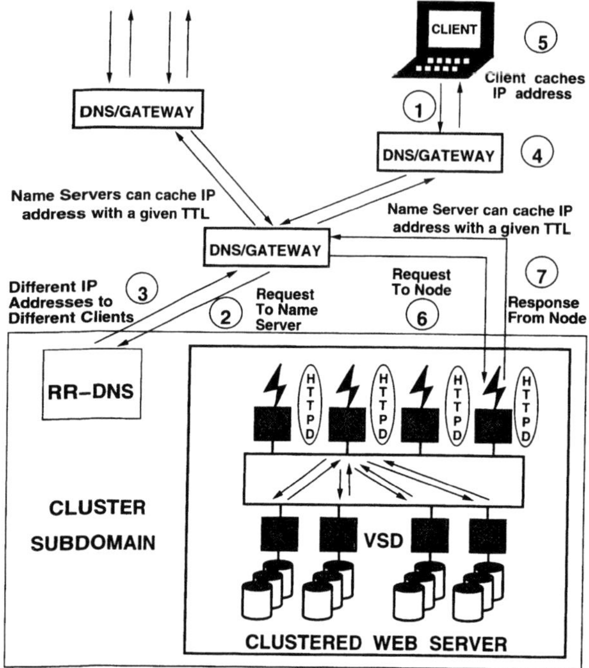

Figure 36.5 Domain name server: Flow.

name servers queried, may choose to cache the IP address returned from the name server at the web server's domain.

36.3.3 Round-Robin DNS

Typically, name servers map a host name to a single IP address. For improved load balancing, a scheme called Round-Robin DNS (RR-DNS), which maps a single host name to a set of IP addresses, allowing different clients to connect to one node of a cluster serving the given name, was proposed [7]. In web terms, this allows a simple way of mapping a single URL to a clustered set of servers, providing a way to scale the server site. Initial scalable web servers, such as the NCSA prototype [8], [9], used RR-DNS to achieve load balancing. Some high throughput sites, e.g., Yahoo, continue to use this simple approach.

Thus, in Figure 36.5, different browsers connecting to the web site and querying the site's name server can be provided the IP addresses of different nodes in the clustered web server.

Several modifications to the round-robin scheme have been suggested, such as adding weights and being able to dynamically change them. However, these are all affected by the fact that caching in intermediate name servers, and in the browser clients themselves, can lead to significant load imbalances in these clusters.

36.3.4 Load Imbalances with Round-Robin DNS

As illustrated in Figure 36.5, there are typically several name servers between clients and the site RR-DNS that cache the resolved name-to-IP address mapping. In order to force a mapping to different server IP addresses, the RR-DNS can specify a time-to-live (TTL) for a resolved name, such that requests made after the specified TTL are not resolved locally, but are forwarded to the authoritative RR-DNS to be remapped to a different IP address. Multiple name requests made during the TTL period will be mapped to the same address. Thus, bursts of requests from new clients will appear at the same server machine, leading to significant load imbalance. If the TTL is made very small, there is a significant increase in network traffic for name resolution. Therefore, name servers often impose their own minimum TTL, and ignore very small TTLs (e.g., 0) given by the RR-DNS.

A related problem is that clients (such as browsers) cache the resolved name-to-IP address mapping. Since the clients may make future requests at any time, the load on the servers cannot be controlled and will subsequently vary due to statistical variations in client access patterns. Further, clients typically make requests in bursts as each web page involves fetching several objects, including text and images, and this burst is directed to a single server node, increasing the skew. With dynamic workloads increasing server computation, these effects can lead to significant dynamic load imbalance, requiring that the cluster be operated at lower mean loads in order to be able to handle peak loads. A study of scalability problems using RR-DNS can be found in [10].

36.3.5 Packet Forwarding for Fine-Grain Load Balancing

TCP Routing is a fine-grained solution to load balancing where the above problems are eliminated. In this scheme, a router node, which could be a hardware router box or one of the nodes of the clustered server configured with special software, receives all requests for the web site and forwards the requests to the nodes of the cluster using an internal load-balancing algorithm.

Only the router node's IP address is publicly known as the address of the site. Thus, caching of IP addresses becomes a non-issue. Section 36.6 presents the availability aspects of this approach. Multiple objects within a single web page, such as images, can be served from different nodes in the cluster, providing a much finer level of control than the RR-DNS scheme. To prevent the router node itself from becoming a bottleneck, the return path for the data (from server to client) does not include the router node.

IBM's eNetwork Dispatcher product and the routing method is described in detail in [11]. eNetwork Dispatcher intercepts packets destined for a given address between the TCP and IP software layers in the communications stack, as shown in Figure 36.6, and forwards them to one of the server nodes using a simple weighted allocation strategy. Packets belonging to an existing connection are forwarded to the right node. Embedding the routing logic in the operating system improves performance significantly by eliminating expensive communications with user-level

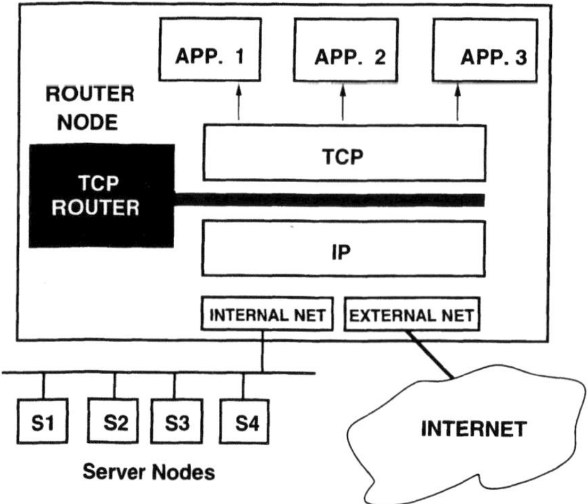

Figure 36.6 eNetwork Dispatcher architecture.

daemon processes. It is possible to change these weights dynamically, based on server load or other parameters, as well as select a preferred server node, as in the case when processing state is saved on the server.

Measurements on early prototype versions of eNetwork Dispatcher (several improvements have been made since then) indicated that a single SP class node can handle more than 2200 connections per second (close to 200 million in 24 hours). This means that a single router node can serve a large number of underlying web server nodes. This number increases as the workload becomes more complex (as each web server handles fewer requests per second). Since the router only sees incoming packets, the complexity of the connection, and the amount of data returned per request, have little bearing on router scalability.

The software that executes in eNetwork Dispatcher can be executed on one of the nodes that is also a web server. This allows multiple router nodes to be configured, if required. RR-DNS can be used to perform an additional level of coarse-grained load balancing, if required, as depicted in Figure 36.7. This can be useful for high availability, as described in Section 36.6.

36.3.6 Summary

In large and scalable clustered web server configurations, simple strategies such as RR-DNS will not work effectively. eNetwork Dispatcher represents a solution for fine-grained load balancing in web servers using the concept of packet forwarding. This solution avoids the problems of name service caching, and scales to a large number of web server nodes per router node. eNetwork Dispatcher has been effectively used in a number of large-scale web server deployments, including the 1996 Summer Olympics in Atlanta, the 1998 Nagano Winter Games, and the Deep Blue-

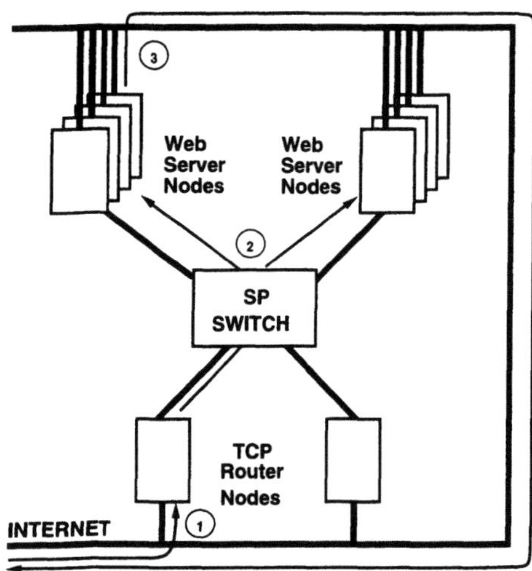

Figure 36.7 eNetwork Dispatcher nodes in a clustered web server.

Kasparov chess games, which have been large scale configurations involving large numbers of SP-class server nodes.

Configuration of the routing logic in software on general purpose machines gives a lot of flexibility to solutions, allowing dynamic configuration of router function in a cluster. This is different from related solutions, where routing functionality is placed in a hardware router box that takes part in both incoming and outgoing network communications, as in the solutions adopted by CISCO [12] and the IBM hardware routers.

36.4 Shared Filesystems and Scalable I/O

36.4.1 Introduction

Thus far we have assumed that scalability can be achieved if we can replicate our servers on clusters and load-balance across the nodes of these clusters effectively. The implicit assumption we have made is that all nodes of the cluster can access the same content to serve. This means replication, or sharing of the data store.

Replication may be effective for a small cluster, when data does not change frequently, and for locality and performance. However, replication is *not* a solution for scalability. Managing a large number of replicated server nodes can be a nightmare, not to mention a major risk for data inconsistency. This becomes highlighted if the data is being updated constantly, as is likely to be the case in most active web sites. Section 36.5 refers to the issues of maintaining constantly changing data in databases. In this section, we will investigate options for data stored in files, and outline means for providing *real* scalability and high performance.

36.4.2 Shared Fileservers

One way to scale storage is to provide shared filesystems across multiple nodes. There are several distributed filesystems, such as AFS, DFS, etc., which allow for multiple client nodes to access a set of server nodes where the data is partitioned. Such systems are often plagued by hot spots and server bottlenecks, and depend on efficient caching at the client machines to provide scalability. Figure 36.8 illustrates this model, with multiple nodes (web servers) accessing a set of shared fileservers.

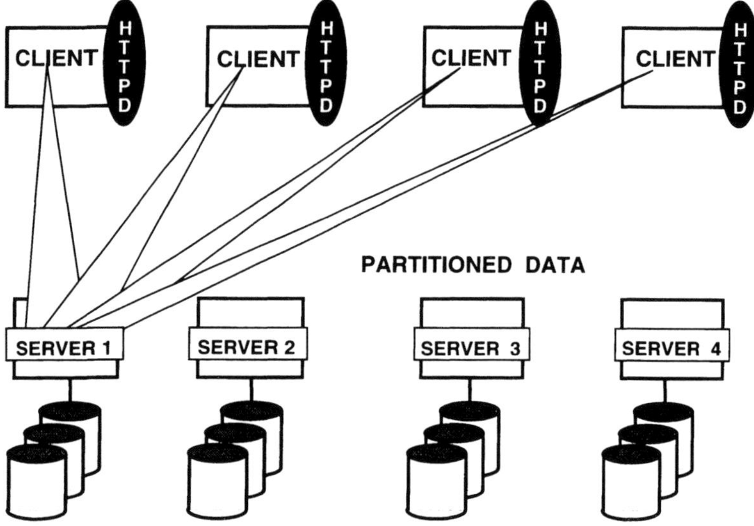

Figure 36.8 Shared fileserver architecture.

If workloads are significantly skewed, with some data being accessed more frequently, the fileservers serving the popular data can become hot spots. Replication of such data may alleviate this problem while introducing the problems of consistency across multiple data copies. This problem is exacerbated if the data that is replicated changes frequently.

Single fileservers can also be single points of failure in the system, forcing replication. Replication is also wasteful of resources, and can cause worse performance after failure if using existing fileserver resources.

Such systems are easily configurable, however, and have been used frequently in large systems [8], [9]. In special cases, such as web-based mailservers, Usenet newsgroups, etc., where load to certain data can be predicted with reasonable accuracy, such filesystems can be very useful.

36.4.3 Wide Striping

For general purpose clustered services, it is essential to have a way to scale storage and filesystems. Creating partitioned data can cause hot spots and contention, causing bottlenecks in the system. Wide striping can alleviate some of these problems and provide high bandwidth. With wide striping, blocks belonging to a single file are allocated across a large number of shared disks in the cluster, allowing parallel access to these blocks and eliminating bottlenecks.

The SP systems support a scalable, high-performance, parallel filesystem called GPFS (General Parallel File System) [13]. The architecture of GPFS on the SP is presented in Figure 36.9. GPFS allows files to be striped across clusters of disks that could reside on different nodes of the cluster. Wide striping of every file allows for files to be accessed with uniformity and very high bandwidth since the blocks residing on different disks can be accessed in parallel. GPFS also allows for tuning the size of the individual blocks, which enables high bandwidth for multimedia objects, such as images and video. Disks can be shared physically (via multiple connections to server nodes) or virtually. On the SP, GPFS uses software called Virtual Shared Disk (VSD), described in the next section, to support large numbers of shared disks.

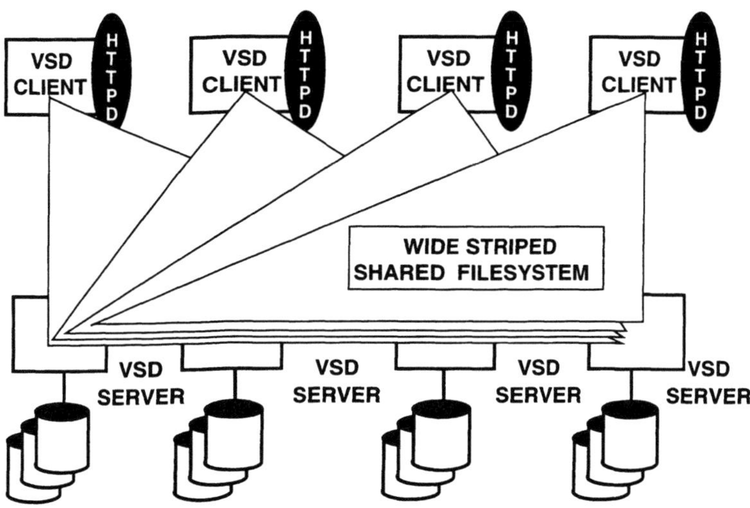

Figure 36.9 GPFS architecture

The performance and availability issues related to wide striping and real-time behavior in multimedia servers have been investigated in detail [14], [15].

GPFS is an announced IBM product to be supported on the SP platform. It supports multiple data sizes and wide striping, which enables high bandwidth shared filesystem access. GPFS filesystems can also be mounted on other nodes in the network via NFS. VSD is also shipped on SP machines. See Section 36.6 for a discussion on availability.

36.4.4 Scalable I/O - Virtual Shared Disk Architecture

Shared disks are used by several software subsystems such as GPFS and the Oracle Parallel Database server. Conceptually, sharing disks may not be complex, and hardware architectures, including SCSI and SSA, support shared disk devices to some extent. However, in practical situations involving large numbers of nodes and disks in a cluster, wiring the disks to the nodes in a reliable way poses a major practical problem.

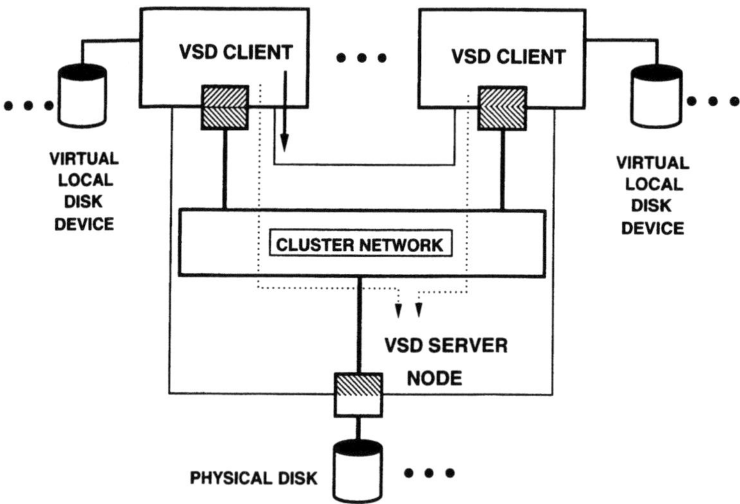

Figure 36.10 VSD architecture.

VSD [16] is a software solution, configuring a virtual disk device at each node in a cluster and allowing all nodes to have a uniform view of all the disks in the system as though they were local devices. The VSD software intercepts calls to remote disks and uses a standard ubiquitous protocol (IP) over the cluster network to forward requests to the node on which the physical device is attached. VSD, implemented in AIX, IBM's flavor of UNIX, executes a device driver as part of the operating system at interrupt level; since it does not involve a separate daemon process, the performance is within a small percentage of local disk access. Figure 36.10 depicts the VSD architecture. Because VSD supports disk sharing across clusters via software, there is no physical wiring between all the nodes and the disks, which would be a management and maintenance nightmare.

The next section describes a related technology called Real-Time Virtual Shared Disk that enables real-time applications on the SP, making it an ideal choice for scalable high-bandwidth multimedia service.

36.4.5 Real-Time Support for Multimedia Content

A research version of GPFS, called Tiger Shark, is being used in a high-bandwidth video server trial in Tokyo, Japan. For further real-time support of high bandwidth video streams (hundreds of concurrent MPEG streams at about 6 Mb/sec), the filesystem uses a research prototype version of VSD, called Real-Time VSD (RTVSD) [17], that provides support for deadline scheduling for guaranteed real-time performance of the system. Figure 36.11 shows the architecture of RTVSD.

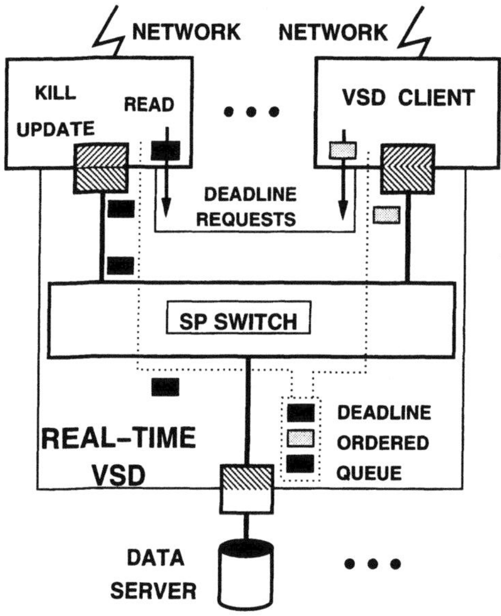

Figure 36.11 Architecture of RTVSD.

Multiple requests can be issued from different nodes (filesystem nodes) in the cluster to the same disk on one of many VSD server nodes. Individual requests are tagged by the filesystem with deadlines that are computed based on the playback rate of the related file. These requests are propagated by RTVSD to the server nodes, where the RTVSD software assures that disk requests are satisfied based on deadlines, so that the filesystem's quality of service guarantees are satisfied. While tested in Tokyo in a high-bandwidth interactive TV environment, RTVSD and real-time enabled GPFS are not, at this time, supported IBM products.

36.4.6 Summary

Real scalability in filesystem storage cannot be achieved via data partitioning and replication, which is a simple and commonly used approach in building scalable servers today. For high bandwidth, and real-time performance, wide striping is a favorable choice, since it also provides very good load balancing properties. The main drawback of wide striping is that support for high availability must be provided since loss of a disk can affect potentially all web assets. Remote disks also depend on network availability.

Virtual sharing of disks across a cluster (in software) can offer scalability without an interconnection nightmare. As the number of nodes on the network increases, software systems, such as VSD, present the only viable alternative for large-scale shared I/O. For small files, or specific workloads where load can be predicted, multiple shared fileservers can be used effectively.

36.5 Scalable Database Access on the Web

36.5.1 Introduction

With more enterprises becoming web-enabled, increasing proportions of web data are being generated from traditional database systems. Not only does this enable the webification of legacy data and existing business processes, but it also allows the management of new data using traditional transaction semantics.

This section explores effective access of dynamic data from relational databases, enhancements that can improve performance, and models that enable these database products to scale.

36.5.2 On-Line Commerce and Databases

Shopping on the web is now commonplace. With further deployment of authorization schemes and data authentication and encryption on networks, more businesses will offer on-line commerce. Implicit in an on-line business service is the availability of certain databases on the web. For manageability, legacy data, and transaction semantics, the solution of choice has been relational databases (RDBMS); it is thus mandatory to provide efficient access to databases. On-line trading, airline reservations, on-line catalogs and stores, all require access to a relational database as a basis for business. Receiving and storing user profile and credit card information is now commonplace, and is a prerequisite to setting up e-commerce capability.

Both e-business as well as web publishing have the requirements of being able to access relational databases efficiently: to publish data that resides in traditional databases; to be able to manage the large amounts of data that are being published, updated, and archived; and to provide the transactional semantics that are required for business-critical applications.

36.5.3 Connection Management for Scalability

Each of the web access techniques described in Section 36.2 can be used to access data from a traditional database engine associated with the web server. For best performance, we assume that the database engine is colocated on the same machine/node on which the web server process executes, although the choice may be different if multiple web server nodes are sharing database resources, or if the database node is separate for security reasons. These methods present different trade-offs with respect to performance and transaction state, as outlined in Section 36.2. For real scalability in a large site, a parallel database (Section 36.5.6) will likely be the best choice. With multiple servers sharing a single database resource that is inherently nonscalable, a bottleneck is soon reached when the database transaction rate increases beyond a certain threshold.

Since opening a new database connection is typically a very expensive operation in most commercially available RDBMS systems, it is mandatory to maintain a pool of open database connections for scalability; this is independent of the web application programming paradigm used (CGI/API/Servlet). Figure 36.12 depicts a system where CGI or API programs can use a pool of *cliette* processes [18] (like FastCGI) to maintain open database connections. This system has high performance and allows a maintenance of connection state, allowing a user-transaction to span more than a single web request.

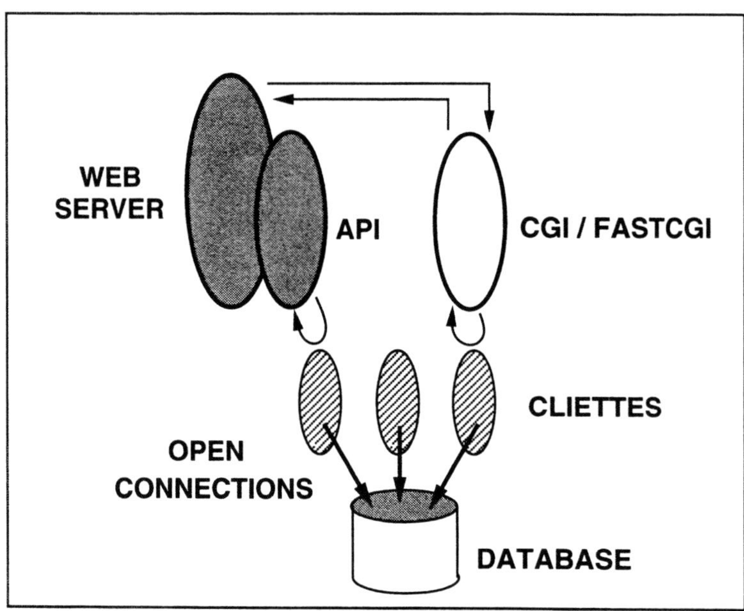

Figure 36.12 Connection management for database connections.

Even if database connections can be reused, the execution of database queries can be complex enough to limit the web server to a few connections per second. As the computation required per connection increases, more server nodes are required to handle the same number of completed web connections. Thus, while a small number of web server machines can handle thousands of connections per second to static files, or simple API programs, the same set of server nodes may only be able to scale to less than 100 connections per second for queries to database.

36.5.4 Java Database Connectivity (JDBC)

JDBC [19] is a low-level Java API for accessing databases from Java environments. JDBC is becoming a very commonly adopted standard for accessing database resources; it allows both applications as well as Java applets to uniformly access RDBMS resources. All major database vendors currently ship JDBC drivers with their database products.

JDBC is portable across hardware platforms, as well as across multiple database engines and operating systems. JDBC can be used by servlets running within Java servers, and is therefore an excellent choice for database connectivity in a web environment with Java servlets.

Javasoft has also proposed other object layers on top of JDBC, such as Java Blend [20] (a software product from Sun), so that object environments can map tables and other schema onto objects. The JDBC specification is a low-level database access layer; for greater abstraction, other layers, such as Java Blend, are likely to be built on top of JDBC by different organizations. JDBC Servers can also use connection pools for better performance.

36.5.5 Caching

Executing a query, especially a complex one, can chew up processing cycles. This is also the case when complex server-side programs are executed to generate web content. Server-side performance can be significantly improved if these heavyweight operations are avoided as far as possible. It is in these cases that content caching can play a very important role in web server performance and scalability.

The caching concept is simple and is depicted in Figure 36.13. The web server initially queries the cache to retrieve a document or the formatted results of a database query. It is more efficient to cache the final document, as no processing is required on a cache hit. On a miss, the server can recreate (and subsequently cache) the data. The cache may actually be a separate process, for management and portability, or be built into the web server for performance.

An important issue in caching dynamic pages is the validity and lifetime of the cached data [21]. In many cases, data in the underlying store (database/filesystem) does not change frequently (e.g., merchandise catalogs may be updated weekly), causing cache entries to live longer. There are several ways in which caches can manage data. Dynamic content can be tagged to expire after a certain period if this information is available at creation time. In the case of dynamic data extracted from relational tables, where the data can change frequently (as in the case of prices and inventory information), this information is not always available, and sophisticated techniques, such as using database triggers to invalidate cached entries, must be used.

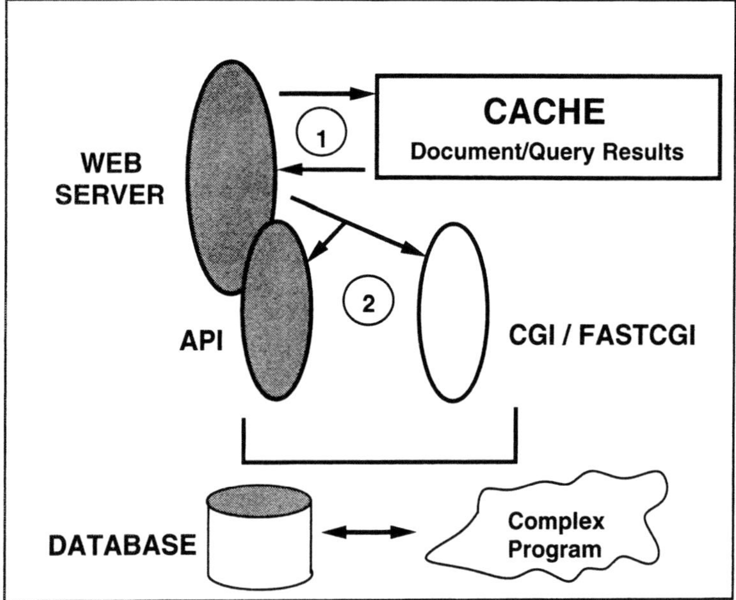

Figure 36.13 Caching dynamically generated content.

36.5.6 Parallel Databases

Local (sequential) databases, while likely to have higher performance, require multiple replicas, since a single database node, or a small set of database machines, can be a potential bottleneck. Replication presents a significant management problem, as all replicas must be consistent at all times. This problem is more severe in the case where the database data is frequently updated.

For the long term database scalability, parallel database products such as UDB's Extended Enterprise Edition (previously called DB2 Parallel Edition), or Oracle's Parallel Server can be used. While UDBEEE has a function shipping model (data is partitioned, and queries are executed where the data resides), Oracle provides a data shipping model (data is shared and shipped to the node where the query is executed). Each model has its advantages and disadvantages. Both these can often run on the same hardware platform, such as the SP cluster.

36.5.7 Advanced Metadata Management

Metadata, and in many cases, data, will benefit from residing in databases. Databases provide referential integrity of data, allow flexible queries, and support transactions, backup, and recovery. However, while buying additional functionality, database access usually has poorer performance than standard filesystem performance on the

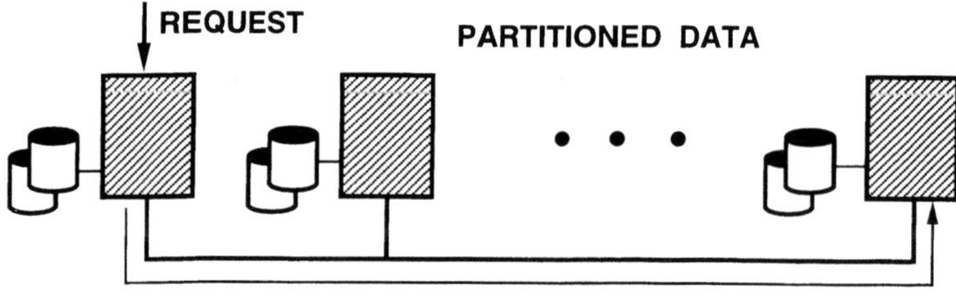

Figure 36.14 Parallel databases: Function shipping.

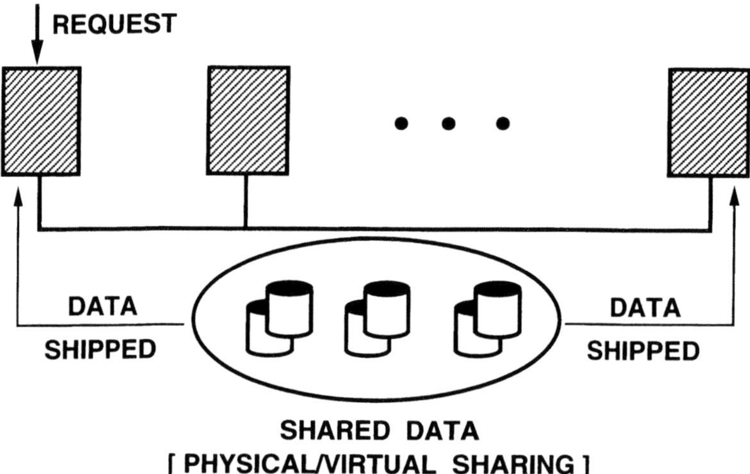

Figure 36.15 Parallel databases: Data sharing.

web. To address this issue, new IBM technology, called DataLinks [22], has been integrated into the DB2 UDB product. The SQL DATALINK datatype is in the process of being adopted as an ISO and ANSI standard.

DataLinks allows data to reside in filesystems or object servers, where applications expect them to be, but provides links within the database that enforces referential integrity and database access control. While DataLinks ensures that a file/object that has been linked cannot be removed without database permission, it does not affect the normal access path of the object. This is extremely important, since this does not affect the performance of normal file access operations, such as read and write. Only operations that can compromise integrity, such as rename and delete, are affected. Oracle has recently announced support for a filesystem interface on top of its database (iFS in Oracle 8i), but filesystem accesses may involve higher overheads, and require movement of files into the database as Binary Large Objects (BLOBS).

With DataLinks, files in the filesystem can be accessed directly and independently, or access may be controlled by the database as desired. When controlled by the database, integrity is guaranteed, and coordinated backup and recovery of files is provided along with the rest of the database. Thus, the file assets are managed as though they are within the database, while in actuality they are not.

36.5.8 Summary

A business must provide scalable and efficient access to data residing in relational databases. For performance to database, connection management is extremely important. Caching data can significantly alleviate the processing requirements of generating dynamic content, although maintaining data legitimacy of data generated from a database is a hard problem.

For a system to really scale with business needs, parallel databases should be used. Replication is not a long-term scalable option, for it does not evolve and results in a massive data management nightmare. There are several flavors of parallel database products available commercially, with different characteristics for different workloads. Based on other enterprise needs, a scalable database is required to feed web servers via efficient web-based interfaces, such as web server APIs or JDBC.

For management of external data repositories, including file systems, database products are now providing functions that translate robustness, integrity, access control, backup, and recovery, from the traditional database environment to other environments as well, including the Internet.

36.6 High Availability

36.6.1 Introduction

There are many resources in any clustered system whose failure can cause disruption in services. It is important to ensure that in the case of failure, the disruption is detected soon, contained as far as possible, and recovery initiated swiftly.

Making subsystems fault-tolerant is usually very expensive, since this typically involves redundancy in hardware and software. High availability can, however, cover several common failure scenarios and provide significant returns on investment. In this section, we will discuss technology that provides high availability in clustered systems, and also study specific functions that need to be incorporated to provide high availability in the critical subsystems that constitute a clustered, scalable web server.

36.6.2 High Availability Infrastructure

Detecting failures and recovering from them requires clusterwide infrastructure, such as the one described in [24]. As shown in Figure 36.16, the infrastructure consists of distributed components running on all cluster machines, and maintaining a consistent, uniform view of the cluster state that all the nodes agree on.

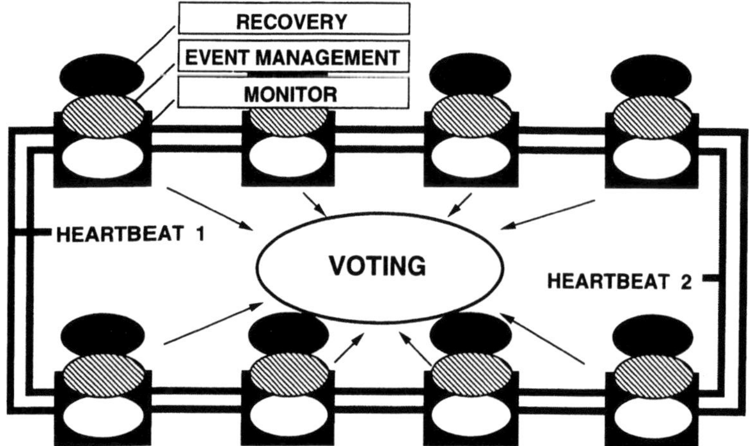

Figure 36.16 High availability infrastructure.

By using *heartbeats* between the distributed components, nodes can effectively monitor the state of their neighbors, and collectively, via two-phased voting algorithms [25], determine the current membership of the group. Using multiple heartbeats (on the SP, for example, using the Ethernet as well as the high bandwidth switch) can give more reliable information about whether a failure is in the network or in the processor, i.e., a processor is declared as having failed only if it fails to communicate over both networks.

Using duplicate (multiple) networks also offers a communications path between two nodes as long as they are both alive, i.e., a hardened, communications channel, which can become a medium for producing and subscribing to an open class of events. An infrastructure built using these concepts is available on the SP as a product (HACMP-ES), enabling subsystems to subscribe to, and recover from, failures in the system.

Once an event is registered using these reliable channels, each node can have a high degree of confidence on cluster status and independently take recovery actions. These recovery actions may include either invocations of low-level API calls to the underlying high availability infrastructure, or high-level recovery programs and scripts written in a variety of languages (that typically mimic what a system administrator may do manually). HACMP-ES allows subsystems to use either approach, as appropriate. HACMP-ES also allows the system to detect and recover from both hardware and software failures.

Systemwide availability is only possible if such an infrastructure is itself recoverable. Subsystem recovery can then be implemented over the infrastructure and can provide varying degrees of coverage, e.g., such an approach will likely not support multiple simultaneous subsystem failures. A well designed infrastructure and well-designed programs can provide recovery in a large number of practical scenarios. Systemwide availability depends on the robustness provided by the component subsystems.

Figure 36.17 depicts the different subsystems that need to be made highly available in a clustered web server. These include redundant communications (heartbeat) for a reliable infrastructure; the front-end load balancing subsystem, which handles router and web server failures; maintenance and reconfiguration; the filesystem, which handles redundant allocation of blocks for disk and server node failure, recoverable VSD, which handles VSD server failure with twin-tailed disks; and finally, database logging and recovery. These subsystems are discussed in the following sections.

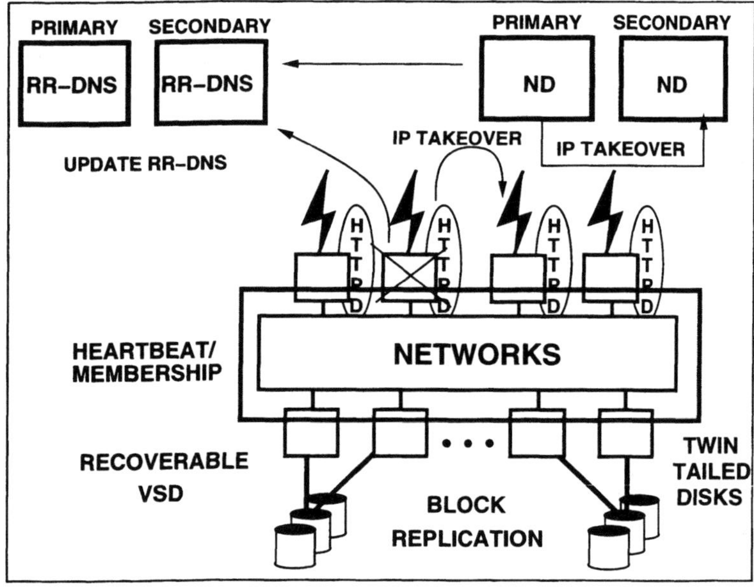

Figure 36.17 High availability in a clustered web server.

36.6.3 Web Server and Router Recovery

The most important failure in a clustered web server is that of the web server nodes themselves, and, in the case of a fine-grained load balancing scheme using routers (eNetwork Dispatchers), the failures of router nodes.

Failure of a server node in a system without routers is simpler: when a server node goes down, the Round-Robin Name Server tables are updated to not give out the IP address of the failed node to new clients. Note that this does not address the problem of IP addresses cached in name servers and clients, which was discussed in Section 36.3. To address this requires takeover of the IP address of the failed node by a secondary or backup. Failure of the name server itself is separately handled by a statically configured secondary (requirement of the Domain Name System). This solution is simple, but can lead to significant load imbalances, especially during recovery.

Figure 36.18 shows such a system with multiple routers and server nodes. Note that the routers are shown as external entities for simplicity, but can be colocated with web server nodes. Server failure is very gracefully handled by reconfiguration of the routers; the routers just don't send any new connections to the failed server node. When the server comes back up, the routers are reconfigured to resume forwarding connections to the server node. This availability mechanism can also be used for incrementally adding server nodes to the system, or for taking a server node down gracefully for maintenance.

Failure of a router involves IP address takeover and possible reconfiguration of the other routers if the failed node was also a server (this is possible with the software router solution). For load smoothing purposes, RR-DNS may require to be updated to not give out the failed router's address to new clients, as the IP address may be taken over onto an existing server (which now acts as a router as well) for clients that have cached the failed IP address. Note that RR-DNS is involved only if there were multiple router nodes in the system, which allows continuous availability, at least via one path.

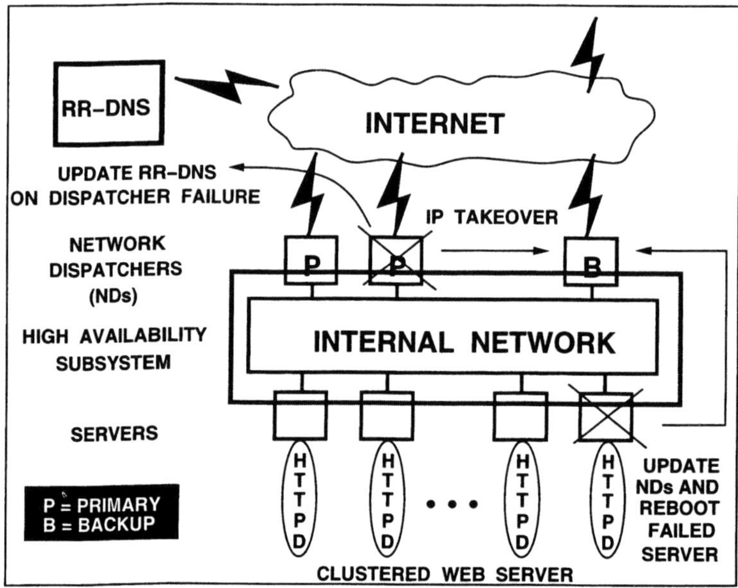

Figure 36.18 Load balancing, incremental scalability, and maintenance

Existing connections on the failed router are lost. Clients can reconnect (using the same IP address) after IP address takeover has completed. The hardware router solution from IBM supports multiple routers that synchronize snapshots of connection state, which allows long-lived sessions, such as *ftp, telnet* to be preserved on router failure, a highly desirable behavior.

36.6.4 Filesystem and I/O System Recovery

The GPFS filesystem, which performs wide striping of files on disks, also supports maintaining multiple copies of each block. When a block request is not satisfied within a given time period (critical for multimedia applications such as audio/video), the filesystem, which has buffers to smooth out variations in I/O access times, can choose to make a new request to the replica. Real-time VSD supports requests with deadlines, as well as requests for the same block with updated deadlines [17]. Thus, upon disk failure and after flagging the I/O error, the filesystem replaces requests for blocks on the failed disk device with requests to the replica blocks, which are located on all the other disks for load-balance. A software RAID solution that uses parity blocks to cut down on the disk space requirements of full replication can also be used [14]. It has also been shown that the computation of the block from other blocks in the parity group can be performed in real-time.

For back-end node failure, Recoverable VSD (RVSD), available as a product, can provide takeover of VSD server functionality on a backup node that also has a path to the physical disk device (via twin-tailed disks). Recoverable VSD, on the SP cluster, is driven directly by the high-availability infrastructure (HACMP-ES), as it is a core component in the system. No specific recover scripts or programs are required.

36.6.5 Database Recovery

Databases have their own recovery mechanisms to maintain consistent data, mostly via logging and transactional semantics. The high availability (HA) infrastructure does not interfere with subsystem recovery mechanisms.

However, the HA infrastructure can be extremely useful in preventing certain failures from occurring in the first place. Often, failures as simple as filesystems filling up, or problems with paging space, etc., can cause subsystems to crash. Special software events can be flagged by the infrastructure before these events take place, and corrective action can automatically be taken by recovery programs, preventing the occurrence of the failure. The HA subsystem can also initiate automatic restart of software components, such as the database engine, on the same node or a backup, based on policy.

36.6.6 Summary

HACMP-ES represents a high availability infrastructure that is scalable across a large set of nodes, is extensible in that it supports open-ended events (hardware, software, and user-defined), and provides a *recovery driver* that can drive appropriate subsystem recovery.

It is required that the HA infrastructure is itself robust and recoverable and affords a reliable way that nodes can communicate with each other in the presence of failures.

While comprehensive fault tolerance is usually extremely expensive, high availability often suffices in practical situations, and has been shown to offer recovery in several subsystems on the SP. The SP system has hardware support to enable node reboot even when the standard communications to the node have failed. In combination with the HA infrastructure, hardened mission-critical subsystems such as VSD, and extensive administration and management tools, the SP is an open-systems platform that offers high-end performance and high availability.

36.7 Conclusions

This chapter has presented an overview of how a scalable and highly available web server can be built using a cluster of workstations, and what subsystem components are key. Successful approaches to scaling database access and filesystem storage, with high performance across the board, have been outlined.

All the subsystems described in this chapter have been built; some are available as products. The SP platform has been used effectively at several high-profile Internet events, such as the 1996 Atlanta Olympics, Deep-Blue's historic Kasparov defeat and the 1998 Nagano games. Some of the subsystems described in this chapter, such as the fine-grained load balancing, have been tested in these high-throughput situations, offering a unique opportunity for validation.

Now, you should know what to consider when building a *real* web site.

Acknowledgments

Much of the work described in this chapter was done by several individuals and teams at IBM's Watson and Almaden Research labs, and specific development teams. I'd like to thank Daniel Dias, Christos Polyzois, William Kish, Renu Tewari, Richard King, Arun Iyengar, Avraham Leff, Jim Challenger, Paul Dantzig, Roger Haskin, Daniel McNabb, Jim Wiley, Frank Schmuck, Jim Thoensen, Jehan Sanmugaraja and Guerney Hunt.

36.8 Bibliography

[1] T. Berners-Lee et al. The World-Wide Web. *Communications of the ACM*, vol. 37(8), pages 76–82, August 1994.

[2] Gene Trent and Mark Sake. WebSTONE: The First Generation in HTTP Server Benchmarking. http://www.sgi.com/Products/WebFORCE/WebStone/paper.html, February 1995.

[3] Jason Levitt. Measuring Web-Server Capacity. http://www.specbench.org/osg/web96/infoweek/, January 1997.

[4] Phil Inje Chang. Inside the Java Web Server. http://www.javasoft.com/features/1997/aug/jws1.html, October 1997.

[5] Open Market Inc. FastCGI: A High Performance Web Server Interface. http://www.fastcgi.com/kit/doc/fastcgi-whitepaper/fastcgi.htm, April 1996.

[6] P. Mockapetris. Domain Names - Implementation and Specification. RFC 1035, USC Information Sciences Institute, November 1987.

[7] T. Brisco. DNS Support for Load Balancing. RFC 1794, Rutgers University, April 1995.

[8] Eric Dean Katz, Michelle Butler, and Robert McGrath. A Scalable HTTP Server: The NCSA Prototype. *Computer Networks and ISDN Systems*, vol. 27, pages 155–163, 1994.

[9] Thomas T. Kwan, Robert E. McGrath, and Daniel A. Reed. NCSA's World Wide Web Server: Design and Performance. *IEEE Computer*, pages 68–74, November 1995.

[10] Daniel M. Dias, William Kish, Rajat Mukherjee, and Renu Tewari. A Scalable and Highly Available Web Server. In *COMPCON 96*. IEEE, March 1996.

[11] Guerney Hunt, German Goldszmidt, Richard P. King, and Rajat Mukherjee. Network Dispatcher: A Connection Router for Scalable Internet Services. In *Seventh International World Wide Web Conference (WWW7)*, World Wide Web Consortium, Brisbane, Australia, April 1998. Also in *Computer Networks and ISDN Systems*, vol. 30, pages 347–357, 1998.

[12] CISCO Systems. Local Director. http://www.cisco.com, October 1996.

[13] Roger Haskin and Frank L. Stein. A System for Delivery of Interactive Television Programming. In *COMPCON 95*. IEEE, March 1995.

[14] Renu Tewari, Rajat Mukherjee, Daniel Dias, and Harrick Vin. High Availability in Clustered Multimedia Servers. In *International Conference on Data Engineering*, IEEE, New Orleans, February 1996.

[15] Renu Tewari, Rajat Mukherjee, Daniel Dias, and Harrick Vin. Design and Performance Tradeoffs in Clustered Multimedia Servers. In *International Conference on Multimedia Computing and Systems*, IEEE, Hiroshima, Japan, June 1996.

[16] C.R. Attanasio, M. Butrico, C.A. Polyzois, S.E. Smith, and J.L. Peterson. Design and Implementation of a Recoverable Virtual Shared Disk. IBM Research Report RC 19843, NY 10598, 1994.

[17] Rajat Mukherjee. Real-Time Virtual Shared Disk: Enabling Multimedia on Clusters. In *Proceedings of the PDPTA-98 Conference*, July 1998.

[18] Yew-Huey Liu, Paul Dantzig, Eric C. Wu, and Lionel M. Ni. A Distributed Connection Manager Interface for Web Services on IBM SP Systems. In *International Conference on PDCS*, IEEE, Tokyo, Japan, September 1996.

[19] Javasoft. The JDBC Database Access API. http://www.javasoft.com/products/jdbc/index.html, April 1998.

[20] Javasoft. Java Blend: Integrating Java Objects with Enterprise Data. http://www.javasoft.com/marketing/collateral/java-blend.html, April 1998.

[21] Arun Iyengar and Jim Challenger. Improving Web Server Performance by Caching Dynamic Data. In *Proceedings of the Usenix Symposium on Internet Technologies and Systems*, December 1997.

[22] IBM Corporation. DataLinks: Managing External Data with DB2 Universal Database. White Paper. http://www.software.ibm.com/data/pubs/papers, February 1999.

[23] IBM Corporation. WebSphere. http://www.software.ibm.com/webservers/index.html, 1998.

[24] Richard P. King, Avraham Leff, Daniel M. Dias, and Rajat Mukherjee. HAV: Providing High Availability for Clustered Systems. In *International Conference on PDCS*, ISCA, New Orleans, September 1997.

[25] F. Jahanian, S. Fakhouri, and R. Rajkumar. Processor Group Membership Protocols: Specification, Design and Implementation. In *Proceedings of the 12th Symposium on Reliable Distributed Systems*, IEEE Computer Society, pages 2–11, Princeton, NJ, October 1993.

Index